Executive Editor, Psychology:	Carolyn O. Merrill
Development Editor:	Lisa McLellan and Susan Messer
Series Editorial Assistant:	Kate Edwards
Senior Marketing Manager:	Wendy Gordon
Editorial Production Administrator:	Joe Sweeney
Editorial Production Service:	Heckman & Pinette
Composition and Prepress Buyer:	Linda Cox
Manufacturing Buyer:	Megan Cochran
Cover Administrator:	Linda Knowles
Interior Design:	The Davis Group, Inc.
Photo Research:	Sarah Evertson, ImageQuest
Electronic Composition:	Publishers' Design and Production Services, Inc.

Library of Congress Cataloging-in-Publication Data
Zimbardo, Philip G.
    Psychology / Philip G. Zimbardo, Ann L. Weber, Robert L. Johnson.—4th ed.
      p.   cm.
    Includes bibliographical references and index.
    ISBN 0-205-35660-5 (alk. paper)
   1. Psychology. I. Weber, Ann L. II. Johnson, Robert L. III. Title.
BF121.Z53 2003
150—dc21   2002018550

Printed in the United States of America

10 9 8 7 6 5 4 3 2 1 VHP 07 06 05 04 03 02

PSYCHOLOGY
CORE CONCEPTS

FOURTH EDITION

Philip G. Zimbardo
Stanford University

Ann L. Weber
University of North Carolina at Asheville

Robert L. Johnson
Umpqua Community College

Allyn and Bacon

Boston   New York   San Francisco
Mexico City   Montreal   Toronto   London   Madrid   Munich   Paris
Hong Kong   Singapore   Tokyo   Cape Town   Sydney

BRIEF CONTENTS

CONTENTS

2   Biopsychology   38

3   States of Mind   80

4 Psychological Development   114

5 Sensation and Perception   160

6   Learning   204

7   Memory 244

8 Thinking and Intelligence 284

9   **Emotion and Motivation   336**

14 Social Psychology   544

TO THE STUDENT...

T here is one big "secret" to academic success, and a simple demonstration will show you what it is. Study the following array of letters for a few seconds.

IBMUFOFBICIA

Now, without peeking, write down as many of the letters as you can (in the correct order).

Most people remember about five to seven letters correctly. A few people get them all. How do they do it? They find a pattern. (You may have noticed some familiar initials in the array above: IBM, UFO, FBI, CIA.) Finding the pattern greatly eases the task because the learner can draw on material that is already stored in memory. In this case, all that needs to be remembered are four "chunks" of information.

The same principle applies to material you study for your psychology class. If you try to remember each piece of information as a separate item, you will have a difficult time. But if you instead look for patterns, you will find your task greatly simplified—and much more enjoyable. So, how can you identify the patterns? We, the authors of your text, have developed several learning features that will make meaningful patterns in the material stand out:

Connection

Chapter 7
Learn more about making your memory work more efficiently for you by reading Chapter 7.

▶ **Core Concepts** We have organized each major section of every chapter around a single, clear idea called a Core Concept. For example, one of the four Core Concepts in the "Memory" chapter says:

> **Human memory is a cognitive system composed of three stages that work together constructively to encode, store, and retrieve information.**

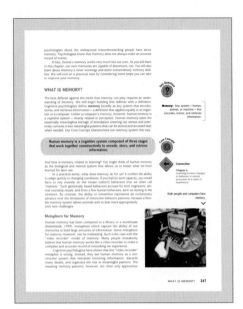

The Core Concept, then, becomes the central idea around which about 10 pages of material—including several new terms — are organized. As you read the chapter, then, keeping the Core Concept in mind will help you encode the new terms and ideas related to that concept, store them in your memory, and later, retrieve them.

▶ **Key Questions**   Each Core Concept is introduced by a Key Question that also serves as a main heading in the chapter. Here, for example, is a Key Question from the Memory chapter:

WHY DOES MEMORY SOMETIMES FAIL US?

Key Questions such as this will help you anticipate the most important point, or the Core Concept, in the section. In fact, the Core Concept always provides a brief answer to the Key Question. Think of the Key Question as the high beams on your car, helping you focus on what lies ahead.

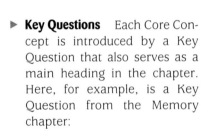

▶ **Psychology in Your Life**   Psychology has many connections with events in the news and in everyday life, and we have explored one of these connections at the end of each major section in every chapter. To illustrate, here are some examples from the "Memory" chapter:

Would You Want a Photographic Memory?
"Flashbulb" Memories: Where Were You When...?
On the Tip of Your Tongue
Improving Your Memory with Mnemonics

Such connections—practical, down to earth, and interesting—link your reading about psychology with your real-life experiences. They also help you critically evaluate many of the psychological ideas you encounter in the popular press.

▶ **Do It Yourself!** We have scattered active-learning demonstrations (such as the one at the beginning of this student preface) throughout the book. Besides being fun, these activities have the serious purpose of illustrating principles discussed in the text. In the Memory chapter, for example, one Do It Yourself! box helps you find the capacity of your short-term memory; another lets you test your "photographic memory" ability.

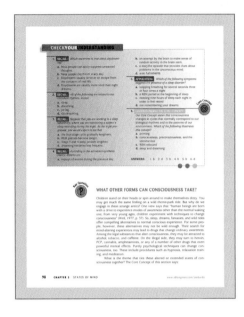

▶ **Check Your Understanding** and **Review Tests** Whether you're learning psychology, soccer, or the saxophone, you need feedback on your progress, and that's exactly what you will get from the Check Your Understanding quizzes and the Review Tests. These will let you gauge how well you have mastered the material.

▶ **Using Psychology to Learn Psychology** In a section near the end of every chapter, we explain how you can apply your new knowledge of psychology to make your studying more effective. For example, in Chapter 2, "Biopsychology," we tell you how to put your understanding of the brain to work for more efficient learning. Similarly, at the end of the chapter on "Emotion and Motivation," we explain how to use the concept of "flow" to boost your own academic motivation. Thus, Using Psychology to Learn Psychology not only reinforces points that you have studied, it brings the material home with immediate and practical applications to your life in college.

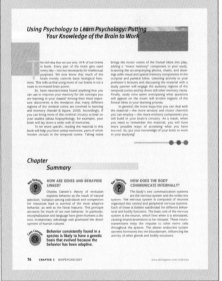

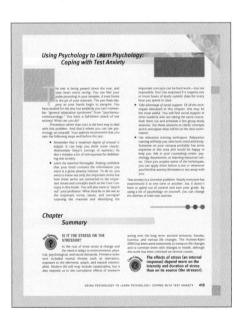

▶ **Chapter Summaries** Our summaries are deliberately brief—intended to provide you with an overview of each chapter, showing the patterns instead of the details. One caution: They are *not* a substitute for reading the chapters! In fact, we recommend that you read the summary both *before* and *after* you read the rest of the chapter. Reading the summary before will help you organize the material so that it can be more easily encoded and stored in your memory. And, a perusal of the summary after reading the chapter will reinforce what you have just learned—easing future retrieval.

▶ **If You're Interested**   Your authors hope that your interest in psychology will give you new eyes with which to look at the world beyond this book. There, you will discover something related to behavior and mental processes nearly everywhere. To pique this interest, every chapter offers a list of relevant, stimulating books and videos that will extend the scope of your learning.

We have built into this text many other learning features, such as the **connections arrows, marginal glossary,** and the extensive **references** list (which can be a good resource for term papers). You will learn more about these as you use the book; but if you want more information on the psychological basis of these features, please read the *Preface*.

We have one final suggestion to help you succeed in psychology: While this book is filled with examples to illustrate the most important ideas, you will remember these ideas longer if you generate your own examples as you study. This habit will make the information yours, as well as ours. And so, we wish you a memorable journey through the field we love.

Phil Zimbardo
Ann Weber
Bob Johnson

SUPPLEMENTS FOR STUDENTS

Grade Aid Workbook with Practice Tests   This robust study guide, written by Nancy Mellucci of the Los Angeles Community College District, includes chapter summaries, chapter learning objectives, a collection of activities and exercises, practice tests, and essay questions.

iSearch: Psychology   Updated to reflect the most current URLs related to the study of psychology, this easy-to-read guide helps point you in the right direction when looking at the tremendous array of information on the Internet as it relates to psychology. The iSearch also contains your access code to ContentSelect.

Zimbardo/Weber/Johnson Companion Web Site   This helpful site contains a wide variety of valuable study tools for each chapter of the textbook, including learning objectives, chapter summaries, interactive online quizzes, learning activities, and Web links to relevant psychology sites to reinforce learning.

ContentSelect   Available to instructors and students using the textbook, ContentSelect Research Database is an online collection of leading scholarly and peer-reviewed journals grouped by discipline. The titles were chosen to reflect as many of the major subject areas in the psychology curriculum as possible. Instructors and students alike have instant access to thousands of full-text articles anywhere and anytime they have an Internet connection.

Evaluating Psychological Information   This workbook, *Sharpening Your Critical Thinking Skills,* 3rd edition, developed by James Bell, focuses on helping students evaluate psychological research systematically and improving critical thinking skills.

How to Write Psychology Papers, 2nd edition   Les Parrot provides a brief overview for writing APA-style psychology papers, including information on overcoming paper panic, using the Internet, preparing a working reference list, avoiding plagiarism, and using inclusive language.

PREFACE

he expansion of knowledge in psychology shows no signs of abating. Since the last edition of this text, neuroscience has revealed brain mechanisms underlying development, thinking, learning, perception—in fact, having an impact on the whole field of psychology. At the same time, gender and culture issues have increased in prominence, as psychologists have realized that the field has too long neglected these important variables. Likewise, genetic variables have moved into the spotlight, as biologists deciphered the human genome, forcing psychologists to consider anew the old questions about nature and nurture.

Cognitive psychologists, too, have been busy expanding the frontiers of knowledge about, for example, implicit memory, concept learning, and cognitive development. But they have been pressured by their colleagues working on "hot" cognition to recognize the role of emotion in memory and thinking. Meanwhile, on the clinical front, psychologists have been accumulating evidence for psychological therapies of demonstrable effectiveness—some of which challenge the hegemony of Prozac and Valium.

And, of course, the terrorist attacks of September 11, 2001, have refocused our attention on the origins of aggression and violence.

The problem for writers of psychology texts is this: How can we include the exciting new developments in the field and still acquaint students with the classic studies, historical trends, and multiple perspectives of the field—and, at the same time, keep the size of the book within manageable proportions? For this 4th edition of *Psychology: Core Concepts,* your authors have had to make difficult choices. We hope you will agree with our selections and deletions—although please remember that you may introduce additional material to students and emphasize favorite topics if you feel we have slighted them.

But as teachers, we realize that the problem for students is not just one of sheer volume and information overload; it is also a problem of meaningfulness. With this in mind, we have again found inspiration in a classic study of chess players. As you may recall, Adrian de Groot (1965) and his colleagues

(Chase & Simon, 1973) showed that experts did no better than novices at remembering the locations of pieces on a chess board when the pieces were placed at random. Only when the patterns made sense—because they represented positions that would be found in real games—did the experts show an advantage. Clearly, meaningful patterns are easier to remember than random arrangements.

In applying this finding to *Psychology: Core Concepts,* 4th edition, our goal has been to help students take the first steps toward expertise by showing them meaningful patterns that occur throughout the field of psychology. The pedagogical features of this text help us achieve this goal:

▶ **Core Concepts** We have organized the major sections of every chapter around a single, clear idea that we call a Core Concept. Here is an example from the chapter on "Sensation and Perception":

The brain senses the world indirectly because the sense organs selectively convert stimulation into the language of the nervous system: neural impulses.

To borrow an old saying, the Core Concepts become the "forest," while the details of the chapter become the "trees."

▶ **Key Questions** The main headings in each chapter appear in question form, as in this example, which introduces the Core Concept shown above:

HOW DOES STIMULATION BECOME SENSATION?

This question helps students anticipate and focus on the most important point: the Core Concept, which is the brief answer to the Key Question. Both the Key Questions and the Core Concepts later reappear as organizing features of the **Chapter Summary.**

▶ **Psychology in Your Life** Psychology has many connections with everyday life and students' interests. We explore one of these connections at the end of each main division of every chapter. Here are some examples:

Emotional Differences between Men and Women Depend on Culture
The Origins of Sexual Orientation
A Critical Look at "Learning Styles"
Side Effects of Psychoactive Drugs

These connections make psychology come alive. They also promote critical thinking by helping students evaluate some of the pop psychology they encounter in the media.

▶ **Do It Yourself!** These active-learning boxes offer simple and effective demonstrations of principles discussed in the text. Many are borrowed from demonstrations we use in our own classrooms. They include, among other topics, locating the blind spot, demonstrating mental set, finding the capacity of working memory, checking one's locus of control, wrestling with IQ test items, and second-guessing a surprising social psychology experiment.

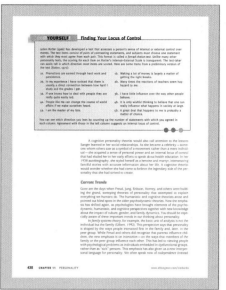

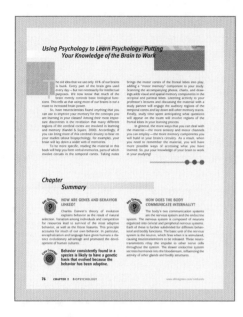

▶ **Using Psychology to Learn Psychology** In a special section of every chapter, we explain how some aspect of the chapter applies to studying and learning. For example, in the context of biopsychology, we show students how to put their knowledge of the brain to work for more efficient learning. And in the discussion of thinking, students learn how the psychology of expertise (as in de Groot's studies of chess masters) applies to their mastery of the concepts in psychology. Thus, Using Psychology to Learn Psychology not only reinforces points that students have studied, it brings the material home with immediate and practical applications to their college lives.

▶ **Connection arrows** As you saw in the previous paragraph, important topics in other chapters are often cross-referenced with an arrow in the margin, used in place of the phrase, "as we will see in Chapter X." An explanatory note accompanies these icons, to give the reader a quick preview of the discussion to be found in the referenced chapter. We intend this feature to convey the sense of psychology as a "web" of interconnecting ideas.

Connection

Chapter 8
Expert knowledge is organized into elaborate schemas.

Along with the unique features of this book, discussed above, the new edition of *Psychology: Core Concepts* offers the content and pedagogy you would expect from any outstanding introductory psychology text:

▶ **Marginal glossaries** In this 4th edition of *Psychology: Core Concepts,* the most important terms again appear in **bold face,** with glossary definitions in the margin. Then, at the end of the book, a comprehensive **Glossary** section gathers the terms and definitions from each chapter.

▶ **Check Your Understanding** and **Chapter Review Tests** Reviewers have told us that they want a book that promotes active reader involvement. The 4th edition of *Psychology: Core Concepts* does this in many ways. One of the most important for student learning is the Check Your Understanding feature, which offers a brief quiz at the end of each main chapter section. We have written these quizzes so that they reinforce specific information from

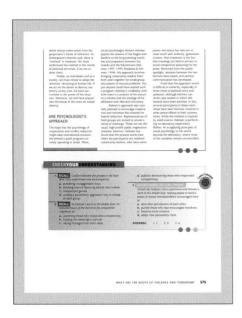

the chapters as well as the more abstract concepts. Accordingly, some questions call for simple *recall,* while others call for deeper *analysis* or *application* of material. In addition, at least one question in each Check Your Understanding quiz is aimed squarely at the Core Concept of the section. Similarly, the Review Test at the end of each chapter helps students assess their overall retention and understanding of the material.

▶ **Chapter Summaries** The goal of our Chapter Summaries, organized around the Key Questions and Core Concepts of the chapters, is to provide students with a brief overview of the chapter—rather than a précis that can be read as a substitute. We hope that professors will advise students to peruse the chapter summary both *before* and *after* reading the chapter.

▶ **Culture and Gender** Nearly every chapter brings in a culture- or gender-related concept. We have not trivialized this material by setting it aside in special boxes. Rather, culture and gender have been fully integrated with psychology in the running text.

Finally, this edition of *Psychology: Core Concepts* addresses the timely problems of aggression, violence, and terrorism from multiple perspectives, including biopsychology, social learning, and cognitive psychology. Then, in the social psychology chapter, we bring this material together. There we suggest that psychology can offer valuable insights into the problem of terrorism and the issues that surround it.

We think you will like the introduction to psychology presented in this book—both the content and the pedagogical features. After all, it's a text that uses well-grounded principles of psychology to teach psychology.

Instructor's Supplementals

The following supplements will also enhance teaching and learning for you and your students:

Instructor's Manual Written by Anita Rosenfield of Yavapai Community College, this helpful teaching companion includes chapter outlines, summaries, experiments and demonstrations, lecture launchers, class activities, and plenty of teaching tips and course organization material.

Test Bank David Baskind of Delta College has provided a new, updated question test bank available in both print and computerized formats. The Test Bank for the 4th edition of *Psychology: Core Concepts* offers a new article by Kay Burke, as well as 150 questions per chapter, including multiple choice, true-false, short answer, and essay questions.

Allyn & Bacon Test Manager—Computerized Test Bank (Available for Windows and Macintosh; DOS disk available on request): Allyn & Bacon Test Manager is an integrated suite of testing and assessment tools for Windows and Macintosh. You can use Test Manager to create professional-looking exams in just minutes by building tests from the existing database of questions, editing questions, or adding your own. Course management features include a class roster, gradebook, and item analysis. Test Manager also has everything you need to create and administer online tests. For first-time users, there is a guided tour of the entire Test Manager system and screen wizards to walk you through each area.

Allyn & Bacon Transparencies for Introductory Psychology, 2001 (0–205–32168–2) A full set of color acetate transparencies is available to enhance classroom lectures and discussions.

PowerPoint Presentation (CD-ROM) This book-specific presentation provides detailed outlines of key points for each chapter supported by charts, graphs, diagrams, and other visuals from the textbook. Resources from the

Zimbardo/Weber/Johnson Companion Web site are also integrated for easy access to the Web site from your classroom.

Allyn & Bacon Digital Media Archive CD-ROM for Psychology, 3.0 Version (0-205-34963-3) Allyn & Bacon provides an array of media products to help liven up your classroom presentations. The Digital Media Archive provides charts, graphs, tables, and figures electronically on one cross-platform CD-ROM. The Digital Media Archive also provides video and audio clips along with the electronic images that can be easily integrated into your lectures. This helpful resource extends the coverage found on the Zimbardo/Weber/Johnson PowerPoint Presentation CD-ROM.

Allyn & Bacon Mind Matters CD-ROM (0-205-32179-8) This student CD-ROM features in-depth units on the history of psychology, research methodology, biopsychology, learning, memory, sensation and perception, social psychology, and development. Each unit includes self-contained modules that cover core psychological concepts through a combination of text, graphics, humor, activities, and extensive assessment.

Allyn & Bacon Mind Matters Faculty Guide (0-205-38141-3) This helpful instructor resource offers detailed overviews of each unit of the CD-ROM supplemented by additional test questions and chapter-by-chapter references correlating content from the CD-ROM with Allyn & Bacon introductory psychology textbooks. This in-depth guide makes it easy to integrate the Allyn & Bacon Mind Matters CD-ROM into your syllabus.

Pearson Course Management System The PearsonCMS enables professors to easily create password-protected online courses and empowers professors to manage their courses in many ways. Each course Web site contains the content of the highly popular and successful Allyn & Bacon Companion Web site along with an integrated syllabus. Each site is PIN activated and password protected. PearsonCMS has been created in collaboration with the higher education community at every stage of its development. Please contact your Allyn & Bacon publisher's representative for more details.

Allyn & Bacon Video Library A wide variety of videos are available upon adoption of Zimbardo/Weber/Johnson *Psychology: Core Concepts,* 4th edition. Please contact your local Allyn & Bacon publisher's representative for more details.

A NOTE OF THANKS

Nobody ever realizes the magnitude of the task when taking on a textbook-writing project. Rebecca Pascal, our Acquisitions Editor, deftly guided us through this Byzantine process.

The vision confronted reality under the guidance of Susan Messer, our Developmental Editor, whose instincts were (we have said before, and will say again) always right. Susan did the difficult job of making our prose smooth and clear. She always let us know when it was good, and she was masterful at giving helpful and tactful suggestions when it was not.

The job of making the manuscript into a book fell to Joe Sweeney, Senior Editorial-Production Administrator, and Margaret Pinette, our Puckish copyeditor, in whom we met a stickler for style with a great sense of humor. We think they did an outstanding job— as did our tireless photo researcher, the tenacious Sarah Evertson, who had the class and brass to get photos from even the most reluctant of sources.

We are sure that none of the above would be offended if we reserve our deepest thanks for our spouses and closest colleagues. Phil thanks his wonderful wife, Christina Maslach, for her endless inspiration and for modeling what is best in academic psychology. He also acknowledges his appreciation to John Boyd for his constant research and teaching support, as well as to Jackie Wagner, whose passion for life is infectious, and whose dedication to always getting it "right" is so admirable.

Ann thanks her long-suffering spouse, John Quigley, for always and readily encouraging her efforts and assuring her that she's "the best." It will surprise no one who knows her that Ann also thanks her six cats and one perfect dog for their abiding, accepting love and for providing perspective and acceptance, no matter what. She also would like to thank her students and colleagues in the Department of Psychology at UNC Asheville for providing feedback, input, and inspiration of the teaching profession as well as the minutia of composing a book—lessons, examples, gimmicks, and especially ideas and images that don't work and so have to be deleted before the manuscript ever sees the light of publication!

Bob is grateful to his spouse and friend, Michelle, who put up with long conversations on topics psychological, Bob's undone household chores, and much gratification delayed—mostly without complaint. She has been a wellspring of understanding and loving support. His thanks, too, go to Rebecca, their daughter, who has taught him the practical side of developmental psychology—and now, much to her own astonishment, possesses a graduate degree in psychology.

Many experts and teachers of introductory psychology also shared their constructive criticism with us on every chapter and feature of this text. We thank the reviewers of previous editions of this text:

Gordon Allen, Miami University

Beth Barton, Coastal Carolina Community College

Linda Bastone, Purchase College, SUNY

Michael Bloch, University of San Francisco

Susan Beck, Wallace State College

John H. Brennecke, Mount San Antonio College

T. L. Brink, Crafton Hills College

Sally S. Carr, Lakeland Community College

Saundra Ciccarelli, Gulf Coast Community College

Authur Gonchar, University of LaVerne

Peter Gram, Pensacola Junior College

Mary Elizabeth Hannah, University of Detroit

Carol Hayes, Delta State University

Peter Hornby, SUNY Plattsburgh

Laurel Krautwurst, Blue Ridge Community College

Judith Levine, SUNY Farmingdale

Margaret Lynch, San Francisco State University

Marc Martin, Palm Beach Community College

Steven Meier, University of Idaho

Yozan Dirk Mosig, University of Nebraska

Melinda Myers-Johnson, Humbolt State University

Michael Nikolakis, Faulkner State College

Faye Plascak-Craig, Marian College

Chris Robin, Madisonville Community College

Christina Sinisi, Charleston Southern University

Mario Sussman, Indiana University of Pennsylvania

John Teske, Elizabethtown College

Robert Wellman, Fitchburg State University

We also thank the reviewers of the 4th edition of *Psychology: Core Concepts* and hope that they will recognize their valued input in all that is good in this text:

Lynn Haller, Morehead State University

Carol Hayes, Delta State

Richard Mascolo, El Camino College

Nancy Mellucci, Los Angeles Community College District

Ginger Osborne, Santa Ana State

Vernon Padgett, Rio Hondo College

Mark Shellhammer, Fairmont State College

If you're interested in learning more about psychology as you do your course work and read *Psychology: Core Concepts,* try to have some confidence and consult your own observations of human behavior. But if you're short on time or want to focus your search, let us recommend some worthwhile reading and viewing. At the end of each chapter in the 4th edition, you'll find a short section titled "If You're Interested," in which we list our top picks of worthwhile books and rentable videos, both classics and more contemporary works.

If you have any recommendations of your own that we should not overlook for the next edition, please write to us! Address your comments to:

Dr. Ann Weber
Department of Psychology, CPO #1960
UNC at Asheville
Asheville, NC 28804-8508

or send e-mail to:

weber@unca.edu

Thanks for your help—and enjoy pursuing your continuing interest in *Psychology!*

KEY QUESTION	CORE CONCEPT	PSYCHOLOGY IN
CHAPTER OUTLINE		**YOUR LIFE**

WHAT IS PSYCHOLOGY, AND WHAT ARE ITS ROOTS? The Long Past and Short History of Psychology The Structuralist Tradition and the Beginnings of Scientific Psychology The Functionalist Tradition	Psychology is the science of behavior and mental processes, and it has grown out of many, often conflicting, traditions.	**PSYCHOLOGICAL SCIENCE OR PSYCHOBABBLE?** Try this test of your psychological common sense. 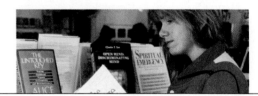
WHAT ARE THE PERSPECTIVES PSYCHOLOGISTS USE TODAY? The Biological View The Evolutionary View The Cognitive View The Psychodynamic View The Humanistic View The Behavioral View The Sociocultural View The Changing Face of Psychology	Seven perspectives dominate modern psychology: the biological, evolutionary, cognitive, behavioral, psychodynamic, humanistic, and sociocultural views.	**THE EFFECTS OF YOUR OWN CULTURE:** Like a fish that doesn't notice the water, you may not notice how your own culture affects you. 
WHAT DO PSYCHOLOGISTS DO? Two Main Kinds of Psychology Psychology's Relation to Other Disciplines	Psychology is a broad field with many specialities, grouped in two major categories: experimental psychology and applied psychology.	**PSYCHOLOGY AS A MAJOR:** To call yourself a psychologist, you'll need graduate training. 
HOW DO PSYCHOLOGISTS DEVELOP NEW KNOWLEDGE? The Five Steps of the Scientific Method Types of Psychological Research Sources of Bias Ethical Issues in Psychological Research	Psychologists, like researchers in all other sciences, use the scientific method to test their ideas empirically.	**GETTING IN DEEPER:** Whatever your major, consider getting a student membership in a professional organization and starting to read some of the journals. 

USING PSYCHOLOGY TO LEARN PSYCHOLOGY: Studying with the Key Questions and Core Concepts

MIND, BEHAVIOR, AND SCIENCE

an a fourth grader be a psychological scientist? Meet Emily Rosa of Loveland, Colorado, whose experimental results not only challenged the widely held belief in the power of therapeutic touch (TT) but made her the youngest author of a published article in the prestigious *Journal of the American Medical Association.*

Emily describes her project this way: "I became interested in testing therapeutic touch because I really didn't know if nurses who do therapeutic touch were telling the truth about their ability to feel the 'human energy field.' One day my mother, who is a nurse, was watching a video on nurses who practice therapeutic touch, and I wanted to find out for myself if they could really do it. . . . I also needed to think of an experiment for my science fair at school, and that was it" (Web site: *Scientific American Frontiers, Ask the Scientists*). Emily suspected that the nurses were really detecting their own beliefs and expectations, rather than the "human energy field."

Tens of thousands of TT practitioners claim that by moving their hands over a person's body without directly touching it, they can detect and manipulate an energy field that radiates from it. These health-care professionals claim that they can use TT to treat a wide range of medical and psychological problems from colic to cancer and arthritis to depression (Gorman, 1999). The technique is taught

(continued)

in more than 100 colleges and universities in 75 countries and used by nurses in at least 80 U.S. hospitals.

What Emily did was put their claims to a simple experimental test: Could TT practitioners accurately detect the presence of her hand when it was placed above one of their hands but out of sight? She predicted that they could not. To test her prediction, Emily invited each of 21 TT practitioners (varying in experience from 1 to 27 years) to determine which of their two hands (stuck through a screen palms up) was closest to one of hers (palm down a few inches from either of their hands). By a coin flip, Emily randomized the order of presenting her hand above either of the practitioners' hands. The task set for the TT practitioners was to say whether they felt energy from her hand above their left or right hand. Emily knew that, just by guessing, nurses could be right 50 percent of the time. So, the participants would have to perform significantly above the chance level to validate the claim that they can detect the "energy field." But they did not; they were correct only 44% of the time (123 of 280 trials). Length of experience slightly improved their score, but the effect was not significant (Rosa et al., 1998).[1]

Some critics remain unconvinced by Emily Rosa's results. They claim that TT depends on the transfer of emotional energy during a medical crisis, and because Emily was not sick she did not have disturbances in her energy field that could be detected by TT practitioners. However, Emily's curiosity and her use of the scientific method to disprove the most basic claim of TT practitioners — that they can detect a person's energy field — surely raises doubt about their more elaborate treatment claims.

Emily's research earned her a check of $1,000 from the Skeptics Society and a plaque from *The Guinness Book of Records* editors for being the youngest researcher to have a paper published in a major medical journal. We, too, applaud her achievement, and we use her experiment to introduce you to psychological science for several reasons. First, we want to illustrate that some firmly entrenched beliefs and practices, such as TT, may be wrong or ineffective and thus cost people who blindly follow them money, time, and better treatment. Second, we want to reveal how open-minded skepticism and curiosity are at the core of the scientific enterprise in the social sciences as well as the physical sciences. Finally, we want to inspire you to think critically when you encounter a seductive claim about how people think, feel, and act. Don't accept without question anything you hear, see, or read — even in this book!

E mily Rosa has the mind-set of a good psychologist: curious, interested in human behavior and mental processes — and just a bit skeptical. "Show me," her experiment says. This is exactly the motto that will guide us on the journey through psychology that we begin in this chapter.

In a broad sense, everyone is a psychologist. That is, everyone studies people, analyzes their behavior, tries to understand what they are thinking and

---

[1]Throughout this book you will find that we use brief citations, such as this one, to call your attention to a complete bibliographic reference found in the References section, beginning on p. R-1, near the end of this book. The brief in-text citations appear in parentheses, giving the authors' last names and the publication date. (The "et al." in the citation for Rosa's study tells you that the source has several authors.) With the complete reference in hand, your library can help you find the original source.

feeling, and attempts to predict what they will do next. But the difference between the casual, commonsense psychology of everyday life and the psychology you will learn about in this book lies in the "show me" approach—the method of *science*. Let's see where this brand of psychology comes from.

WHAT IS PSYCHOLOGY, AND WHAT ARE ITS ROOTS?

Tracing the word **psychology** to its ancient Greek roots reveals that *psyche* means "mind"—which the Greeks believed to be separate and distinct from the physical body. The suffix *ology* means "a field of study." Therefore, the literal meaning of *psychology* is "the study of the mind." Modern day psychologists, however, use a broader definition, found in our Core Concept for this section:

> **Psychology is the science of behavior and mental processes, and it has grown out of many, often conflicting, traditions.**

But psychology has not always been a science, as we will see from a brief sketch of its history.

The Long Past and Short History of Psychology

Some of the earliest speculations on the nature of consciousness and the origins of madness were recorded in the 5th and 4th centuries B.C. by the Greek philosophers Socrates, Plato, and Aristotle. Among their contributions were the observations that emotions can distort thinking and that our perceptions are merely interpretations of the external world. Most people today would probably agree with these ideas—and so would modern psychology.

But the Greeks also came up with some bizarre psychological notions. They believed, for example, that emotions flow from the heart, the liver, and the spleen and that mental disorder could be caused by excessive bile. (Following their lead, we still speak metaphorically of *heart*felt emotions.)

It never occurred to these ancient thinkers to put their speculations to the test in the same way that Emily Rosa tested her suspicions about therapeutic touch. To them, "truth" came from logic, casual observation, and the authority of experts. And so, human understanding of behavior and mental processes remained a combination of speculation, opinion, and folklore for two more millennia.

When the medieval Roman Catholic Church gained control of Europe, it added its own ideas to the Greeks' philosophy of the mind. With little interest in the physical world, the Church taught that the mind and soul operate completely outside the natural laws that govern worldly objects and events. The human mind—like the mind of God—was an unsolvable mystery.

This view prevailed until the 17th century, when French philosopher René Descartes (Day-CART) dared to assert that human sensations and responses are based on activity in the nervous sys-

Psychology: The science of individual behavior and mental processes.

The ancient Greeks believed that anger comes from the spleen, but it never occurred to them to put their theories to a controlled test.

tem. The idea fit well with new discoveries being made concerning the biology of nerve circuits in animals, and soon the mysteries of the mind and behavior began to make more sense. Research showing how the sense organs convert stimulation into the nerve impulses and muscular responses allowed scientists, for the first time, to glimpse the biological processes behind sensation and simple reflexive behaviors.

In spite of these revolutionary advances, however, psychology would still not become a distinct scientific discipline in its own right for another two centuries after Descartes. Oddly enough, it was a breakthrough in the field of chemistry that led to the world's first psychology laboratory.

The Structuralist Tradition and the Beginnings of Scientific Psychology

Structuralism: A historical school of psychology devoted to uncovering the basic structures that make up mind and thought. Structuralists sought the "elements" of conscious experience.

Introspection: The process of reporting on one's own inner conscious experience.

In the mid-1800s, scientists noticed patterns in the characteristics of the chemical elements, suggesting that all the elements could be arranged into a "periodic table." At one stroke, this discovery brought order to the previously chaotic field of chemistry and captured the attention of the entire scientific community. Perhaps a similar insight could bring order to the emerging field of psychology, thought Wilhelm Wundt, a German scientist who was probably the first person ever to refer to himself as a "psychologist." The new discipline of psychology would, he declared, search for "the elements of conscious experience." This declaration established **structuralism,** a "school" (or viewpoint) in psychology devoted to uncovering the basic "structures of the mind."

To pursue this dream, Wundt built, in 1879, the first laboratory devoted to experimental psychology. There he presented trained volunteers with a variety of simple stimuli and asked to respond with the press of a lever or a description of their sensations—a technique called **introspection.** Psychologists still rely on this introspective method for obtaining dream reports and evidence of perceptual changes, such as you can experience in the accompanying *Do It Yourself!* box.

Connection

Chapter 3:
The technique of introspection has been criticized for its subjectivity.

In 1879, Wilhelm Wundt (1832–1920) founded the first formal laboratory devoted to experimental psychology. He's shown here (center) in his laboratory in Leipzig in 1912.

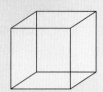

If you look at the Necker cube for a few moments it will seem to change perspectives. For a time you may see it as a cube viewed from the upper right, and then it will suddenly shift and appear as though you were seeing it from the lower left, something like this:

Once you see the cube change, you won't be able to prevent it shifting back and forth, seemingly at random.

When you have seen how the perspective shifts, show the cube to a friend and explain what will happen. Your description will be an introspective report of your mental experience — much like the introspective reports that Wundt trained his volunteers to give.

In 1892, structuralism emigrated to America when Edward Titchener, who had studied with Wundt in Germany, returned to the United States. There it encountered its harshest critics, who considered the goals of structuralism too simplistic: to reduce complex experiences to basic components of consciousness. The critics also considered structuralism too subjective and "mentalistic" because it relied on unverifiable introspective reports.

The Functionalist Tradition

Among the critics of structuralism was a group of psychologists who had no interest in a search for the "elements" of consciousness. Instead, their **functionalism** focused on how consciousness could help us deal with the problems of everyday living. Consistent with this approach, one of functionalism's founders, John Dewey, was a driving force in the "progressive education" movement, which emphasized learning by doing, rather than by sheer memorization of facts.

Such ideas made a lot of sense to William James (1842–1910), a giant figure in American psychology, who tried to bridge both the structuralist and functionalist camps. James agreed with the functionalist idea that behavior must be adaptive. He also agreed with the structuralist contention that consciousness must be central to psychology. He disagreed, however, with the structuralist search for mental "elements." Instead, in a famous metaphor, James pictured consciousness as an ongoing "stream," a process of mind continually flowing, changing, and interacting with the environment.

The legacies of structuralism and functionalism can still be found in modern psychology — although people don't call themselves by these labels any more. And, to complicate the picture, 20th century psychology assimilated new ideas from several external sources, such as medicine, literature, linguistics, and anthropology — and in the process, became further divided. We will look at these modern factions right after we find out whether your knowledge of behavior and mental processes is more closely associated with psychological science or with "psychobabble."

Connection

Chapter 9
William James taught that physical responses are the source of our emotions.

Functionalism: A historical school of psychology that believed mental processes could best be understood in terms of their adaptive purpose and function.

Psychology

In Your Life

Psychological Science or Psychobabble?

Structuralism and functionalism did agree on one thing: Psychology should be based on scientific evidence. This rule has not penetrated our popular culture, where books tell us that men are from Mars and women are from Venus and that some people think with their "left brain" and others with their "right brain." In fact, much that is called "psychology" by the popular press and on TV is not based on science at all. Accordingly, most of the volumes in the "Psychology and Self-Help" section of your local bookstore are likely to be speculation, exaggeration, or misunderstanding — what Carol Tavris (2000) calls "psychobabble." Your authors hope that this book will help you spot psychobabble for what it is.

In the spirit of inquiry, then, let's see how you do at distinguishing a few popular, but unfounded, ideas about behavior and mental processes from others that do have a scientific foundation. Some of the following statements are true, and some are false. Don't worry if you get some — or all — of the items wrong: You will have lots of company, and you will have the opportunity to learn some important psychological concepts that many people don't know. The point is that what common sense teaches us about psychological processes may not withstand the rigorous scrutiny of a scientific test.

Directions: Mark each of the following statements as "true" or "false." (The answers are given at the end.)

_____ 1. Your brain makes a painkiller similar to heroin.

_____ 2. Some merchants persuade their customers to buy merchandise by means of subliminal messages embedded in background music.

_____ 3. Many things that happen to us leave no record in memory.

_____ 4. You were born with all the brain cells that you will ever have.

_____ 5. Nearly everyone has several dreams every night.

_____ 6. Intelligence is a pure genetic trait that is fixed at the same level throughout a person's life.

_____ 7. Damage to certain parts of your brain could prevent you from remembering new events, even though you could still retrieve old memories.

_____ 8. A majority of American people would refuse to give a dangerous electric shock to a stranger in the course of a scientific experiment.

_____ 9. The most common form of mental disorder occurs in about 30% of the population.

_____ 10. Polygraph ("lie detector") devices are remarkably accurate in detecting physical responses that indicate when a suspect is lying.

Answers: All the odd-numbered items are true; the even-numbered items are false. Below are some brief explanations for each item; you can find more detail in the chapters indicated in parentheses.

1. True: These chemicals are called *endorphins.* (See Chapter 2, Biopsychology.)

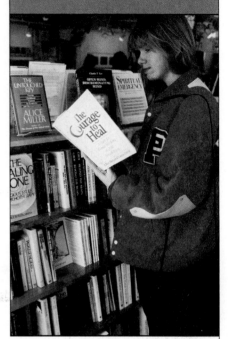

Most of the books in the psychology section of your local bookstore are based on speculation rather than on psychological science.

2. False: There is no evidence that stimuli you cannot consciously detect can influence how you shop. (See Chapter 5, Sensation and Perception.)

3. True: Although many details of our lives are remembered, there is no evidence that memory records all the details of our lives. In fact, there is good reason to believe that most of the information around us never reaches memory and that what does reach memory becomes distorted. (See Chapter 7, Memory.)

4. False: We used to think this was true, but recent research shows that some parts of the brain continue to create new cells throughout life. (See Chapter 2, Biopsychology.)

5. True: People dream on the average of four to six times a night, although they often do

not remember their dreams. (See Chapter 3, States of Mind.)

6. False: Intelligence is the result of both heredity and environment. Because it depends, in part, on environment, your level of intelligence (as measured by an IQ test) can change throughout your life. (See Chapter 8, Thinking and Intelligence.)

7. True: This happened in the famous case of H. M., whom brain surgery has forced to live in the present moment. He has recollections only of events that occurred prior to his surgery, some 50 years ago. (See Chapter 7, Memory.)

8. False: In a dramatic series of studies involving hundreds of volunteers, most were willing, when ordered by the experimenter, to flip a switch that they thought would give a dangerous shock to another person. (See Chapter 14, Social Psychology.)

9. True: The single most common disorder is depression, which may affect up to a third of all people at some time during their lives. (See Chapter 12, Psychopathology.)

10. False: Even the most expert polygrapher can incorrectly classify a truth-teller as a liar or fail to identify someone who is lying. Objective evidence supporting the accuracy of lie detectors is conspicuously lacking. (See Chapter 9, Emotion and Motivation.)

CHECK**YOUR**UNDERSTANDING

1. **RECALL:** *One of the roots of cognitive psychology sought to identify the "elements of conscious experience." Adherents to this viewpoint were called*
   a. structuralists.
   b. functionalists.
   c. mentalists.
   d. behaviorists.

2. **RECALL:** *The ancient Greeks' approach to psychology was not scientific because they:*
   a. failed to check their opinions against controlled observations.
   b. were more interested in art and music than in truth.
   c. believed that all truth was revealed in sacred texts given by their gods.
   d. lived in an age before precise measuring instruments had been developed.

3. **RECALL:** *René Descartes made a science of psychology possible when he suggested that:*
   a. science should be based entirely on common sense, rather than on religion.
   b. sensations and perceptions are the result of activity in the nervous system.

c. the elements of conscious experience could be arranged into a periodic table.
   d. psychology should be a branch of philosophy.

4. **APPLICATION:** *Which of the following methods would you use to tell whether a friend had experienced a perceptual shift while viewing the Necker cube?*
   a. functionalism
   b. introspection
   c. structuralism
   d. sensation

5. **UNDERSTANDING THE CORE CONCEPT:** *Modern psychology has strong roots in all of the following traditions EXCEPT:*
   a. Greek philosophy.
   b. biology.
   c. astrology.
   d. functionalism.
   e. structuralism.

ANSWERS: 1. a   2. a   3. b   4. b   5. c

WHAT ARE THE PERSPECTIVES PSYCHOLOGISTS USE TODAY?

In the past century the picture of psychology has been both enriched and complicated by ideas borrowed from many sources. The result is a field that resembles a slightly dysfunctional family, with a few common interests and lots of family squabbles. In our Core Concept we simplify this "family portrait" by focusing on seven especially important members of the psychological family.

 Core Concept

> **Seven perspectives dominate modern psychology: the biological, evolutionary, cognitive, behavioral, psychodynamic, humanistic, and sociocultural views**

The proponents of each view see behavior and mental processes in a different way — much like seven painters portraying the same scene from different vantage points.

The Biological View

The **biological view** suggests that you may inherit some of your behaviors from your parents. More generally, psychologists taking this approach search for the causes of behavior in heredity and in the function of the nervous system and the endocrine (hormone) system. As you might imagine, the biological view has strong roots in medicine and biological science.

Biological psychologists have begun to unravel the mystery of how our eyes and brain convert light waves into vision. They have also learned how damage to certain parts of the brain can destroy specific abilities, such as speech, social skills, or memory. And they have discovered brain wave patterns associated with the hidden world of dreams.

The Evolutionary View

The **evolutionary view** suggests that you have acquired mental and behavioral traits from your remote ancestral past. In this view, your genetic makeup — including your most deeply ingrained behaviors — were shaped by the conditions those in your genetic lineage faced thousands of years ago.

Through the history of our species, environmental forces have "pruned" the human family tree, favoring the survival and reproduction of those individuals with the most adaptive mental and physical characteristics. The famous British scholar and naturalist Charles Darwin called this "natural selection." Through this process, the physical characteristics of a species *evolve* (change) in the direction of characteristics that give the fittest organisms a competitive advantage.

Obviously, the evolutionary perspective is related to the biological view, but it has become a force of its own in psychology only recently. The evolutionary view says that all human behavior — even the most destructive behavior, such as warfare, homicide, and racial discrimination — has grown out of tendencies that once may have helped humans adapt and survive. This has also helped us understand certain gender differences — why, for instance, men typically have more sexual partners than do women. And, coming back to sleep (which we will use as a point of comparison for all seven perspectives), evolutionary psychology has helped us understand sleep as a protective mechanism. It probably evolved to help animals preserve their energy at times of the day when activity is not necessary for survival and reproduction.

The Cognitive View

The next of psychology's seven perspectives suggests that our thoughts and actions derive from the way we *interpret* our experiences. From this perspec-

Biological view: The psychological perspective that searches for the causes of behavior in the functioning of genes, the brain and nervous system, and the endocrine (hormone) system.

Evolutionary view: A relatively new perspective in psychology that views behavior and mental processes in terms of genetic adaptations for survival and reproduction.

The biological view led to the discovery that certain patterns of brain waves are associated with the hidden world of dreams.

tive, understanding ourselves requires that we look in our *minds,* as well as our biology.

In this **cognitive view,** our actions are profoundly influenced by the way we process information coming in from our environment. Cognitive psychologists study mental processes, or **cognitions**—thoughts, expectations, perceptions, and memories, as well as states of consciousness. Accordingly, their interest in sleep involves the mental processes that are altered during "quiet" sleep and while we dream.

Modern cognitive psychologists have borrowed from linguistics the idea that our most basic language abilities are wired into our brains at birth. From computer science they have borrowed the metaphor of the brain as a biological computer —designed as a processor of information (Gardner, 1985; Gazzaniga, 1998b; Sperry, 1988). And from medicine they have borrowed the technology that now allows visualizing the activity of the brain and connecting it to mental processes.

The Psychodynamic View

The term *psychodynamic* comes from the notion that the mind *(psyche)* is a reservoir of energy *(dynamics).* Accordingly, the **psychodynamic view** says that we are motivated largely by the energy of irrational desires, arising from the dark side of human nature that harbors our unconscious aggressive and sexual impulses and mental conflicts (Murray et al., 2000). This approach has been especially attractive to many practitioners who specialize in psychotherapy. As a result, the psychodynamic perspective has emphasized the treatment of mental disorders over doing scientific research.

Sigmund Freud founded psychoanalysis, by far the most influential and well-known of the psychodynamic theories. Originally a medical technique devised to treat mental disorders, psychoanalysis portrays the mind as a sort of mental boiler that holds the rising pressure of unconscious sexual and destructive desires, along with memories of traumatic events.

While psychodynamic theorists have been especially interested in personality and mental disorder, they have also been interested in sleep and dreaming. From this viewpoint, dreams represent unconscious urges inserting themselves in disguised forms into the restricted consciousness of the sleeping mind. Thus, dream interpretation as the "royal road to the unconscious" is an important technique in psychodynamic therapy.

The Humanistic View

According to the **humanistic view,** your actions are strongly influenced by your self-concept and by a need for personal growth and fulfillment. In contrast with the psychodynamic perspective, the humanistic outlook emphasizes the positive side of our nature: human ability, growth, and potential. It has been critical of those who are preoccupied with the threatening unconscious forces and mental disorders that figure so prominently in the psychodynamic theories. Humanistic psychologists, as believers in free will, assume that people make unhealthy choices when they perceive only unhealthy alternatives.

Led by the likes of Abraham Maslow (1968, 1970, 1971) and Carl Rogers (1951, 1961, 1977), humanistic psychologists have also rejected what they saw as the cold, mechanical approach of scientific psychology. In its place they have offered a model that portrays people as having the free will to make choices that affect their lives. They have also pressed psychology to take a greater interest in feelings and self-concepts (Cushman, 1990).

Humanistic psychologists have not produced much scientific research, although they have had a major impact on the practice of counseling and psy-

Connection

Chapter 3
Some psychologists question the existence of a "dynamic" unconscious.

Connection

Chapter 11
Freud's psychoanalytic theory was the first comprehensive explanation of personality.

Connection

Chapter 8
Cognitive psychologists have done most of the research on thinking.

Cognitive view: The psychological perspective that emphasizes mental processing and interpretation of experience.

Cognitions: Mental processes, such as thinking, memory, sensation, and perception.

Psychodynamic view: A viewpoint that emphasizes the understanding of mental disorders in terms of unconscious needs, desires, memories, and conflicts.

Humanistic view: A viewpoint that emphasizes human ability, growth, potential, and free will.

Connection

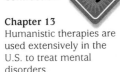

Chapter 13
Humanistic therapies are used extensively in the U.S. to treat mental disorders.

Behavioral view or **behaviorism:**
A psychological perspective that finds the source of our actions in environmental stimuli, rather than in inner mental processes.

Sociocultural view: A psychological perspective that emphasizes the importance of social interaction, social learning, and a cultural perspective.

Culture: A term referring to a complex blend of language, beliefs, customs, values, and traditions developed by a group of people and shared with others in the same environment.

Humanistic psychologists are interested in discovering how self-actualizing individuals, such as Martin Luther King, are able to unleash their potential for leadership and creativity.

chotherapy. Their interest in sleep and dreaming would most likely involve the contribution of dreams to creativity. They would also be interested in comparing the dream contents of people who are "fully functioning" with those with unmet psychological needs (for love or safety, for example).

The Behavioral View

Life is filled with rewards and punishments that shape how we act. That's the emphasis of a wholly different approach to psychology that says we should look for the causes of behavior in our environment rather than in our biology or our minds (Murray et al., 2000).

This **behavioral view** first emerged as a reaction against the subjective methods used by Wundt, Titchener, James, and others in the structuralist and functionalist traditions. In brief, the behaviorists rejected a science of inner experience. Instead, they chose to study the person entirely from the outside, emphasizing what they could observe directly: the effects of people, objects, and events on behavior.

B. F. Skinner, arguably the most influential of American behaviorists, claimed that the concept of "mind" has led psychology in circles, chasing something that cannot even be proved to exist (Skinner, 1987, 1989, 1990). (Think about it. Can you *prove* that you have a mind?) As Skinner noted wryly: "The crucial age-old mistake is the belief that . . . what we feel as we behave is the cause of our behaving" (Skinner, 1989, p. 17).

Behaviorism has made its greatest contribution to the psychology of learning. Nevertheless, a behavioral perspective can be applied in many areas of psychology. For example, a behavioral approach to understanding sleep would focus on observable behaviors of the sleeper. This tactic has helped researchers understand *sleep apnea,* a disorder involving the cessation of breathing during certain phases of sleep.

The Sociocultural View

People are social animals, and the presence of others exerts a powerful influence on our behavior, according to the **sociocultural view.** Accordingly, social psychologists have probed the mysteries of liking, loving, prejudice, aggression, obedience, and conformity.

Until quite recently, most of psychology overlooked the effects of the larger social context called **culture,** a complex blend of human language, beliefs, customs, values, and traditions. This oversight was due, in part, to the origins of scientific psychology in Europe and North America, where most psychologists lived and worked under similar cultural conditions (Cole, 1984; Sexton & Misiak, 1984).

Now the climate has begun to change. Although nearly half the world's half million psychologists still live and work in the United States, it is encouraging to note that interest in psychology is also growing in countries outside of Europe and North America (Pawlik & d'Ydewalle, 1996; Rosenzweig, 1992a, 1999). Even so, most of our psychological knowledge still has a North American/European flavor (Cushman, 1990). Recognizing this bias, *cross-cultural psychologists* have begun the long task of reexamining the "laws" of psychology across cultural and ethnic boundaries (Fowers & Richardson, 1996; Gergen et al., 1996; Segall et al., 1998; Triandis, 1994, 1995).

In order to compare the sociocultural approach with the other perspectives we have been examining, let us return briefly to the problem of sleep. A psychologist employing the sociocultural perspective might look for distinctive sleep patterns in different cultures. Why, for example, do many people in Latin countries take *siestas,* while the practice of napping is much less common in the

United States, Canada, and Northern Europe? Cross-cultural psychologists have also been interested in comparing the content of dreams in different parts of the world.

Now, to summarize the seven perspectives we have just covered, please study Table 1.1. There you will find an overview of the main viewpoints that make up the spectrum of modern psychology. Taking a few moments to fix the seven perspectives in your mind will pay big dividends in your understanding of the chapters that follow.

The Changing Face of Psychology

Psychology is a field in flux. Over the last several decades the biological and cognitive perspectives have become dominant, but only recently have the evolutionary and cross-cultural perspectives gained prominence. At the same time, the psychodynamic perspective seems to be losing ground.

Cross-cultural psychologists, such as this researcher in Kenya, furnish important data for checking the validity of psychological knowledge.

APPLIED PSYCHOLOGISTS IN THE MAJORITY   Another big change can be seen in a shift in the proportion of psychologists from experimental and academic psychology to the application of psychology (American Psychological Association, 1996; Howard et al., 1986). In the past 40 years the number of psychologists trained in clinical, counseling, and school psychology has increased markedly. As a result, the proportion of new doctorates in these *applied* fields now comprises a majority, whereas applied psychologists were a distinct minority in the first half of the 20th century. Meanwhile, since the mid-1970s, the total number of psychologists engaged primarily in research has actually declined.

WOMEN AND MINORITIES BECOME A MAJORITY   Perhaps the biggest change of all involves the increasing numbers of women and members of minority groups in the field. The result of these trends can be seen in growing concern among psychologists about issues of gender and culture.

The majority status of women in psychology is especially striking when seen in a historical perspective. In 1906, only 12 % of American psychologists listed were women (according to a listing in *American Men of Science*). By 1921 the proportion had risen above 20 %. Women now receive approximately two-thirds of the new doctorates awarded in psychology each year (Kohout, 2001). Although psychology has always included a higher proportion of women than any of the other sciences, women have typically found their psychological career path strewn with gender-related biases (Furumoto & Scarborough, 1986). For example, G. Stanley Hall, one of the pioneers of American psychology, maintained that academic work would ruin a woman's health and cause deterioration of her reproductive organs. Yet, as early as 1905 the American Psychological Association elected its first female president, Mary Whiton Calkins (Furumoto, 1991). (Even though she had completed all the requirements, Calkins had earlier been denied a doctorate by Harvard University because of her gender.)

In the early days of psychology, as in all fields of science, women were pressured to choose between marriage and career. Even those who managed a career were usually limited to teaching at the less prestigious women's colleges. Still, they made important contributions to their developing field, as you can see in Table 1.2.

TABLE 1.1

Six Major Perspectives in Modern Psychology

PERSPECTIVE	VIEW OF HUMAN NATURE	WHAT DETERMINES BEHAVIOR	FOCUS OF STUDY
Biological	We are complex biological systems that respond to both hereditary and environmental influences.	Neural structures, biochemistry, and innate responses to external cues for survival and procreation	The nervous system, endocrine system, and biological/genetic disorders that cause abnormal behavior
Evolutionary	We are adapted to dealing with the problems of ancient human environments.	Hereditary mechanisms that were acquired by natural selection	Evolved behaviors that have conferred a survival or reproductive advantage
Cognitive	We are information-processing systems.	Interpretation of experience by means of mental processing	Mental processes, including sensation, perception, learning memory, and language
Psychodynamic	We are essentially irrational creatures, driven by unconscious motives that must be controlled.	Unconscious needs, conflicts, repressed memories of early experiences, and unfinished business from earlier stages of development	Abnormal behavior as a reflection of unconscious motives; applications of psychodynamic theory to psychotherapy
Humanistic	We have free will and unlimited potential, but we act in accordance with our self-concept.	The self-concept, perceptions, interpersonal relationships, and the need for personal growth	Life patterns, values, goals, self-actualizing individuals; applications of humanistic theory to counseling and psychotherapy
Behavioral	We respond to our surroundings, according to the principles of behavioral learning.	Stimulus cues and the organism's history of rewards and punishments	The "laws" connecting our responses to stimulus conditions in the environment
Sociocultural	People are social animals; human behavior must be interpreted in its social context.	Culture, social norms and expectations, and social learning	Social interaction, socialization, and cross-cultural differences

TABLE 1.2	Early Contributions Made by Women in Psychology, Taken from the 1906 Edition of American Men of Science	
	RESEARCH AREA	INSTITUTIONAL AFFILIATION
Christine Ladd Franklin	logic and color vision	Johns Hopkins University
Kate Gordon	memory and attention	Mt. Holyoke, Carnegie Tech.
Julia Gulliver	dreams and the subconscious self	Rockford University
Alice Hinman	attention and distraction	University of Nebraska
Lillien Martin	psychophysics	Wellesley College
Anna McKeag	pain	Bardwell School
Naomi Norsworthy	abilities of the child	Columbia Teachers College
Millicent Shinn	child development	unaffiliated
Helen Thompson	mental traits	Mt. Holyoke College
Margaret Washburn	perception	Vassar College
Mabel Williams	visual illusions	unaffiliated

Adapted from Furumoto & Scarborough (1986).

Psychology In Your Life

The Effects of Your Own Culture

Wearing shorts and a sleeveless top on a hot day might seem perfectly acceptable behavior for most American college women, for example, but might be forbidden for many Muslim women.

A cross-cultural psychologist would remind you that, immersed in your own culture, you may take cultural influences for granted, not realizing that what seems "natural" to you can be alien or even shocking to those from another culture. For example, wearing shorts and a tank top on a hot day might seem perfectly acceptable behavior for most American college women, but it would be unthinkable for many Muslim women. Similarly, crossing the street against a red traffic light is common for many New Yorkers, but it would be a breech of cultural norms among Japanese pedestrians in Tokyo. Thus, the sociocultural approach argues that, to predict individual behavior, it is necessary to see the individual as embedded in a social context that includes family, friends, coworkers, social organizations, the larger community, and the values and traditions of the culture.

At the same time, psychologists with multicultural interests are reminding us that we do not need to look outside our own country to find a variety of cultures and viewpoints (Garnets & Kimmel, 1991; Goodchilds, 1991; Jones, 1991; Sue, 1991; Tavris, 1991). Many distinctive cultural groups exist right here at home: Native Americans, Hispanics, Asians, and African Americans, to name a few. Similarly, gender has created its own subcultures. As a result, psychology is beginning to recognize the effects of gender and culture on thoughts and behavior. This important multicultural/cross-cultural/gender awakening in psychology will be a recurrent theme of this book.

1. **APPLICATION:** *Which approach would say that the differences between the behavior of males and females are the result of different survival and reproduction pressures on the two sexes?*
   a. behavioral psychology
   b. evolutionary psychology
   c. humanistic psychology
   d. psychoanalysis

2. **RECALL:** *Mental processes, such as perception and remembering, are sometimes called*
   a. cognitions.
   b. affective events.
   c. neural nets.
   d. dependent variables.

3. **APPLICATION:** *Suppose that your therapist tells you that your problems are caused by urges repressed in your unconscious mind. Which perspective is your therapist using?*
   a. the cognitive perspective
   b. the sociocultural perspective
   c. the humanistic perspective
   d. the psychodynamic perspective

4. **RECALL:** *Which of psychology's seven perspectives would deny that mental events influence our actions?*
   a. the cognitive perspective
   b. the sociocultural perspective
   c. the behavioral perspective
   d. the humanistic perspective

5. **UNDERSTANDING THE CORE CONCEPT:** *Which of psychology's seven perspectives is least grounded in the scientific tradition?*
   a. the biological perspective
   b. the behavioral perspective
   c. the cognitive perspective
   d. the humanistic perspective

ANSWERS: 1. b   2. a   3. d   4. c   5. d

WHAT DO PSYCHOLOGISTS DO?

Not only does psychology have many different viewpoints, but it also has many areas of specialization. You can find psychologists at work in education, industry, sports, prisons, government, churches and temples, private practice, and in psychology departments of colleges and universities. Psychologists also work for athletic teams, engineering firms, consulting firms, and the courts. In these diverse venues they perform an amazing range of duties, including teaching, research, assessment, equipment design, and psychotherapy. (See Figure 1.1.) Our Core Concept for this section groups all these activities under two headings:

> **Psychology is a broad field with many specialities, grouped in two major categories: experimental psychology and applied psychology.**

The many special fields of concentration within psychology provide students with an opportunity, in advanced courses, to study an area of interest in depth. The possibilities are too numerous to cover all of psychology's specialties here, but we can give you the flavor of the field by drawing a few examples from the two major categories mentioned in our Core Concept: *experimental psychology* and *applied psychology*.

Two Main Kinds of Psychology

Most research across the psychological spectrum is done by **experimental psychologists.** Many are faculty members at a college or university, where they also teach. A few work for private industry or the government.

Experimental psychologists: Psychologists who do research on basic psychological processes — as contrasted with *applied* psychologists.

FIGURE 1.1: Work Settings of Psychologists

Shown are percentages of psychologists working in particular settings, according to a survey of American Psychological Association (APA) members holding doctorate degrees in psychology.

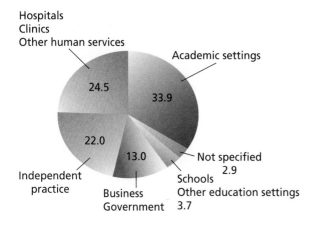

Hospitals
Clinics
Other human services

Academic settings

24.5

33.9

22.0

13.0

Not specified
2.9

Independent
practice

Schools
Other education settings 3.7

Business
Government

Applied psychologists: Psychologists who use the knowledge developed by experimental psychologists to solve human problems.

Clinical psychologists: Psychological practitioners who specialize in the treatment of mental disorders.

Counseling psychologists: Psychological practitioners who help people deal with a variety of problems, including relationships and vocational choice. Counseling psychologists are less likely than clinical psychologists to do long-term therapy with persons having severe mental disorders.

Industrial and organizational psychologists: Applied psychologists who specialize in modifying the work environment to maximize productivity and morale. They are often called *I/O psychologists*.

Engineering psychologists: Applied psychologists who specialize in making objects and environments easier, more efficient, or more comfortable for people to use.

In contrast, **applied psychologists** use the knowledge developed by experimental psychologists to tackle human problems, such as training, equipment design, and psychological treatment. They work in a wide variety of places such as schools, clinics, factories, social service agencies, airports, hospitals, and casinos. All told, some 64 % of the doctoral-level psychologists in the United States work primarily as applied psychologists, and that percentage has been steadily increasing since the 1950s (Kohout & Wicherski, 2000; Rosenzweig, 1992a; Stapp et al., 1985).

And what do they do? Let's have a look at some of the most popular applied specialties.

▶ **Clinical psychologists** and **counseling psychologists** work with people who have problems with social and emotional adjustment or those who face difficult choices in marriages, careers, or education. Nearly half of all doctoral-level psychologists list clinical or counseling psychology as their specialty (American Psychological Association, 1996). The clinician is more likely to have a private practice involving psychological testing and long-term therapy, while the counselor is more likely to work for an agency or school and to spend fewer sessions with each client.

▶ **Industrial and organizational psychologists** (often called *I/O psychologists*) specialize in modifying the work environment to maximize productivity and morale. Some I/O psychologists develop interview and testing procedures to help organizations select new employees. Some develop programs to train and retain employees. Other I/O psychologists specialize in market research.

▶ **Engineering psychologists** often design equipment, such as computers or airplane instrument displays, for easy and reliable human use. Some do psychological detective work to discover what went wrong in accidents attributed to "human error." Engineering psychologists are usually employed by private industry or the government and work on a team with other scientists.

Connection

Chapter 13
Clinical and counseling psychologists use many of the same therapeutic techniques.

► **School psychologists** have expertise in the problems of teaching and learning. Typically, they work for a school district, where they diagnose learning and behavior problems and consult with teachers, students, and parents. School psychologists may spend a good deal of time administering, scoring, and interpreting psychological tests.

► **Rehabilitation psychologists** serve with physicians, nurses, and social workers on teams that may treat patients with both physical and mental disorders, such as stroke, spinal cord injury, alcoholism, drug abuse, or amputation. Some work in a hospital setting. Others work for social service agencies and for sheltered workshops that provide job training for people with disabilities.

A more complete source of information on the career possibilities in psychology can be found in *Psychology: Careers for the Twenty-First Century,* published by the American Psychological Association (1996).

Psychology's Relation to Other Disciplines

Your authors admit to some bias in favor of psychology. (Was it obvious?) Yet, we must quickly tell you that, as broad as psychology is, it cannot claim to have the whole truth about behavior and mental processes. Among the other *social sciences* that study human behavior and mental processes are the following, each with its own emphasis and its own unique contribution to make to our understanding.

► *Sociology* emphasizes the ways that social forces affect *groups* of people. For example, sociologists study religious groups, divorce rates, and causes of poverty. Psychology's emphasis, we have seen, is on the *individual.*

► *Anthropology* comes in two forms. One involves the study of fossils and artifacts to solve the puzzles of human origins and ancient cultures, while the other specializes in describing and comparing existing cultures by observing and recording what people do. The influence of anthropology can be seen in *cross-cultural psychology.*

Medicine, too, has its specialties that deal with understanding behavior and mental processes—and therefore overlap with the interests of psychology. Specifically:

► All **psychiatrists** have MD (Doctor of Medicine) degrees plus specialized training in the treatment of mental and behavioral problems. Therefore, psychiatrists can prescribe medicine and perform other medical procedures. As you might expect, the psychiatrist views patients primarily from a medical or biological perspective. In the public mind, however, psychiatry is often confused with *clinical psychology* because both professions treat people suffering mental disorders (Benjamin, 1986). Psychologists like to point out that psychiatric training emphasizes mental illness, but it devotes relatively little time to basic psychological topics, such as perception, learning, psychological testing, and developmental psychology.

► Most **psychoanalysts** train first as physicians and then as psychiatrists. (Psychoanalytic training institutes also accept some psychologists and social workers with doctorates, but the majority of those trained in psychoanalysis are MDs.) The emphasis in psychoanalytic training is on learning a particular technique of therapy based on the ideas of Sigmund Freud.

School psychologists: Applied psychologists with expertise in the problems of teaching and learning.

Rehabilitation psychologists: Applied psychologists who help people with physical and mental disorders adapt to the problems of everyday life and work.

Psychiatrists: Physicians who specialize in the treatment of mental disorders.

Psychoanalysts: Specialists (usually psychiatrists) who use Freudian methods of treating mental disorders.

Connection

Chapter 13
Psychiatry—unlike clinical psychology—uses the "medical model" of mental disorder.

Connection

Chapter 11
Freud believed that unconscious conflicts drive most of our behavior.

Sigmund Freud (1856–1939), shown here in the office of his Vienna home, developed the psychodynamic approach to behavior.

From this description you can see that psychiatry, psychoanalysis, and some specialties in psychology share a common interest in mental disorders and therapy. What makes psychology unique, however, lies in its broad range of concerns that have no overlap with the interests of psychiatry and psychoanalysis: Psychology is the study of *all* of the individual's behavior — not just of abnormality or mental illness.

Psychology as a Major

In Your Life

Becoming a psychologist requires graduate training beyond the bachelor's degree. While in graduate school, a psychology student takes advanced classes in one or more specialized areas and develops skills as a scholar, researcher, and perhaps as a practitioner. Upon completion the student receives a master's or doctor's degree, usually a PhD (Doctor of Philosophy), or in some cases an EdD (Doctor of Education) or a PsyD (Doctor of Psychology).

Satisfying careers are available at various levels of education in psychology. In most states, licensure as a psychologist requires a graduate degree, usually a doctorate, and an internship in some psychological specialty. Most university teaching or research jobs also require a doctorate.

A master's degree, typically requiring two years of study beyond the bachelor's level, may qualify you for employment as a psychology instructor at the college or high school level or as an applied psychologist in certain specialties, such as counseling. Master's-level psychologists are common in human service agencies, as well as in private practice (although many states do not allow them to advertise themselves as "psychologists"). In addition, many practitioners with master's degrees in the related field of social work offer therapy for emotional problems.

Those holding associate degrees and bachelor's degrees in psychology or related human services fields may find jobs as psychological aides and technicians in agencies, hospitals, nursing homes, and rehabilitation centers. Salaries at this level are relatively low, however (Kohout, 2000). A bachelor's degree in psychology, coupled with training in business or education, can also lead to interesting careers in personnel management or education.

If you would like further information about job prospects and salary levels for psychologists, the U.S. Department of Labor's *Occupational Outlook Handbook* is a good place to look. Your college's career or counseling center undoubtedly has a copy.

1. **RECALL:** *Psychologists are not usually allowed by law to*
   a. do psychotherapy with mentally disturbed individuals.
   b. prescribe medicine.
   c. call themselves "doctor."
   d. do basic research.

2. **RECALL:** *Which one would be considered an applied psychologist?*
   a. an I/O psychologist
   b. a psychologist doing basic research
   c. a professor of psychology at the university
   d. a psychiatrist

3. **APPLICATION:** *Which one of the following would be most likely to do research on learning or memory?*

   a. an applied psychologist
   b. an I/O psychologist
   c. a psychiatrist
   d. an experimental psychologist

Core Concept

4. **UNDERSTANDING THE CORE CONCEPT:**
   One of the main differences between psychology and the other social sciences is that psychology
   a. aims to understand human behavior.
   b. focuses on the individual.
   c. is scientific.
   d. is primarily interested in mental disorders.

   ANSWERS: 1. b   2. b   3. d   4. b

Key Question

HOW DO PSYCHOLOGISTS DEVELOP NEW KNOWLEDGE?

As early as 1880, American psychology had challenged the claims of spiritualists and psychics (Coon, 1992). And today psychology still disputes unfounded claims from the realms of **pseudoscience.** These include astrology, palmistry, graphology, biorhythm analysis, and any number of psychics, seers, and prophets who claim to have special insights into people's personalities and to be able to predict their futures.

So, what makes psychology different from the pseudoscientific approaches to understanding people? Answer: None of the mystical alternatives has survived trial by the *scientific method,* a way of rigorously testing ideas against objective observations. All are based solely on speculation and anecdote (and on an intuitive understanding of human gullibility).

You might think this a snobbish view for psychologists to take. Why can't we make room for many different approaches to the understanding of people? In fact, psychologists have no problem accepting many other approaches to the study of human behavior and mental processes. They are quite willing to accept sociology, anthropology, and psychiatry, for example, as partners in the enterprise of understanding ourselves. Psychologists reject only those approaches that claim to have "evidence" but that really have only opinion.

So, what makes psychology a science? It is the *method*—which psychology shares with all true sciences. As our Core Concept for this section says:

Pseudoscience: Any approach to explaining phenomena in the natural world that does not use empirical observation or other aspects of the scientific method.

Scientific method: A five-step process for empirical investigation of a hypothesis under conditions designed to control biases and subjective judgments.

Core Concept

> **Psychologists, like researchers in all other sciences, use the scientific method to test their ideas empirically.**

What is this marvelous method? Simply put, the **scientific method** is a process for putting ideas to a pass-fail test. At the heart of this testing procedure is

TABLE 1.3

What Questions Can the Scientific Method NOT Answer?

The scientific method is not appropriate for answering questions that cannot be put to an objective, empirical test. Here are some examples of such issues:

TOPIC	QUESTION
Ethics	Should scientists do research with animals?
Values	Which culture has the best attitude toward work and leisure?
Morality	Is abortion morally right or wrong?
Preferences	Is rap music better than blues?
Aesthetics	Was Picasso more creative than Van Gogh?
Existential issues	What is the meaning of life?
Religion	Does God exist?
Law	What should be the speed limit on interstate highways?

Although science can help us understand such issues, the answers ultimately must be settled by logic, faith, legislation, consensus, or other means that lie beyond the scope of the scientific method.

empirical investigation, the collecting of objective information first-hand by making measurements based on sensory experience. Literally, *empirical* means "experience-based" — as contrasted with speculation based on faith, hope, authority, or common sense. To investigate a question empirically is to ask questions and collect information yourself, rather than consulting a second-hand reference or appealing to the opinion of "experts." But the scientific method is not at all appropriate for questions that cannot be put to an objective test. Table 1.3 shows some of the questions that science cannot answer.

Let's see how psychologists use this empirical method.

The Five Steps of the Scientific Method

An empirical investigation begins with a **theory** — a testable explanation for a set of facts or observations (Kerlinger, 1985; Kukla, 1989). This definition contrasts sharply with the way the term is often used to mean "speculation" or "hunch" — an idea that has no evidence to support it. "It's only a theory," we may say in casual conversation .

In science, however, some theories have a great deal of evidence to support them, while others are highly speculative. Examples of well-supported theories include Einstein's theory of relativity, the germ theory of disease, Darwin's theory of natural selection, and, in psychology, the theory of classical conditioning, a common form of learning.

Putting a scientific theory to the test requires following five orderly steps — steps that are essentially the same whether they are being followed in psychology, biology, chemistry, astronomy, or any other scientific discipline. Thus, it is the *method* that makes these fields scientific, not their subject matter. Ideally, a researcher following the scientific method proceeds as follows.

DEVELOPING A HYPOTHESIS The first step calls for formulating an idea, a hunch, or guess about some aspect of a larger theory. Scientists call this idea

Connection

Chapter 6
Classical conditioning explains how fears and phobias can be learned.

Empirical investigation: An approach to research that relies on sensory experience and observation as research data.

Theory: A testable explanation for a set of facts or observations.

a *hypothesis*. (The term *hypothesis* literally means "little theory.") In Emily Rosa's experiment on therapeutic touch, the hypotheses began to take shape this way:

> Emily suspected that the nurses were really detecting their own beliefs and expectations, rather than the "human energy field."

To give a more formal definition, a **hypothesis** is a statement predicting the outcome of a scientific study. You can also think of a hypothesis as a specific prediction that is derived from a larger theory.

For precision, all terms in the hypothesis must be put in the form of **operational definitions**. That is, the researcher must specify the exact procedures (operations) used in establishing the experimental conditions and measuring the results. Moreover, the hypothesis must be stated in such a way that it can be *falsified*—shown to be either correct or incorrect. Thus, Emily Rosa wondered:

> Could TT practitioners accurately detect the presence of her hand when it was placed above one of their hands but out of sight?

She hypothesized that they could not.

So far, so good—but a scientific study must not stop with a mere hypothesis. (The pseudosciences, such as astrology, often generate hypotheses but fail to go on to the other vital steps necessary to complete the study and verify or reject them.) For a scientific hypothesis to be taken seriously by the scientific community, it must be subjected to rigorous testing.

PERFORMING A CONTROLLED TEST   Before a new theory or hypothesis is accepted by scientists, it must undergo an "ordeal of proof"—a test that it can either pass or fail. Here's how Emily Rosa conducted her test:

> She invited each of 21 TT practitioners (varying in experience from 1 to 27 years) to determine which of their two hands (stuck through a screen palms up) was closest to one of hers (palm down a few inches from either of their hands).

In order to control the conditions of her experiment, Rosa varied only one aspect of the situation on each trial: whether her hand was above the subject's left or right hand. We call this variable condition the **independent variable**. It takes its name from the fact that it is a condition that the experimenter changes *independently* of all the other carefully controlled experimental conditions. The independent variable always involves the conditions that the experimenter is evaluating in a study.

In Rosa's experiment, control over the experimental conditions would have been inadequate if she had simply put her hand alternately above the subjects' left and right hands or if she had used some other predictable pattern. In this case, subjects might have just been responding to some expected pattern. The solution was random presentation of the stimulus.

> By a coin flip, Emily randomized the order of presenting her hand above either of the practitioners' hands.

Randomization means that chance alone determined the order in which the stimulus was presented. Randomization is one way of controlling

Hypothesis: A statement predicting the outcome of a scientific study; a statement describing the relationship among variables in a study.

Operational definitions: Specific descriptions of concepts involving the conditions of a scientific study. Operational definitions are stated in terms of how the concepts are to be measured or what operations are being employed to produce them.

Independent variable: A stimulus condition that is so named because the experimenter changes it *independently* of all the other carefully controlled experimental conditions.

Randomization: A process by which chance alone determined the order in which the stimulus was presented.

Emily Rosa's experiment

experimenters' biases that can unexpectedly influence the results of a study. (We will see some other sources of bias later in the chapter.)

GATHERING OBJECTIVE DATA   In the third step of the scientific method the scientist collects objective, *empirical* **data**—data that do not depend on the experimenter's hopes, expectations, or personal impressions. In Emily Rosa's experiment, the data consisted of the nurses' responses during the test:

> The test subjects' task was to say whether they felt energy from the girl's hand above their left or right hand.

These responses are referred to as the **dependent variable.** The term arises from the assumption that the responses of participants in an experiment *depend* directly on the conditions to which they have been exposed—that is, on how the independent variable has been manipulated.

WHAT MAKES STATISTICS UNIQUE IS ITS ABILITY TO *QUANTIFY* UNCERTAINTY, TO MAKE IT PRECISE. THIS ALLOWS STATISTICIANS TO MAKE *CATEGORICAL STATEMENTS*, WITH COMPLETE ASSURANCE—ABOUT THEIR LEVEL OF UNCERTAINTY!

GOOD CHOICE! I'M 95% CONFIDENT THAT *TONIGHT'S* SOUP HAS PROBABILITY BETWEEN 73% AND 77% OF BEING *REALLY DELICIOUS!*

from "The Cartoon Guide to Statistics" by Larry Gonick & Wollcott Smith

No matter what sort of experiment is being performed, the dependent variable must also be given an *operational definition*. That is, the researcher must specify the procedures (operations) that were used in measuring the dependent variable. This is exactly what Emily Rosa did when she described how she required her participants to respond with guesses of "left" or "right."

ANALYZING THE RESULTS AND ACCEPTING OR REJECTING THE HYPOTHESIS

In the fourth step of the scientific method, the scientist examines the results—the data—to see whether the hypothesis passed the test. Based on that analysis, the hypothesis is accepted or rejected. This part can be difficult, especially if the outcome requires a close call. For this reason, scientists usually rely on statistics to analyze their data. Statistical procedures can tell the researcher whether the observed results rise to the level of significance—that is, whether the results are likely due to the independent variable or merely due to chance.

A detailed explanation of statistics is beyond the scope of this book. It is, in fact, a subject for a whole course in itself. Your authors have, however, provided a brief introduction to the use of statistics in the Appendix near the end of this book. There you will find a summary of key points and examples of how psychological concepts are *quantified* (measured and expressed as numbers) and how those quantities can provide meaning and understanding.

In Rosa's experiment, the statistical analysis was not complex. The chances of getting a correct answer by guessing were 50%: Half the time subjects could give the right answer even if they had no ability to sense the "human energy field." So, Rosa set this standard:

> Her subjects would have to perform significantly above the chance level to validate the claim that they can detect a "human energy field."

They did not, so she concluded that practitioners of therapeutic touch were not sensing human energy fields.

PUBLISHING, CRITICIZING, AND REPLICATING THE RESULTS   In the fifth step of the scientific method, scientists must find out whether their research can withstand the scrutiny and criticism of the scientific community. To do so,

Connection

Appendix
A statistical analysis determines whether observed differences between groups are *statistically significant.*

Data: Information, especially information gathered by a researcher to be used in testing a hypothesis. (Singular: *datum.*)

Dependent variable: The measured outcome of a study; the responses of the subjects in a study.

they announce their results to colleagues by publishing them in a professional journal, presenting a paper at a professional meeting, or writing a book. (You may recall that Emily Rosa published her results in *The Journal of the American Medical Association.*) Then they wait for the critics to respond.

If colleagues find the study interesting and important—and especially if it challenges a widely held theory—they may look for flaws in the research design: Did the experimenter choose the participants properly? Were the statistical analyses done correctly? Could other factors account for the results? As we noted earlier, in Rosa's experiment, some critics complained that her study was not an accurate representation of the conditions under which therapeutic touch is done:

> They claim that TT depends on the transfer of emotional energy during a medical crisis, and because Emily was not sick she did not have disturbances in her energy field that could be detected by TT practitioners.

They may also check the work by *replicating* (redoing) the research, perhaps under different control conditions, to see whether they get the same results.

All this is a part of a thorough, and sometimes intimidating, screening process that goes on behind the scientific scenes to filter out poorly conceived and executed research. As a result, fewer than 2% of the papers submitted to psychological journals get into print without major revisions. In fact, the majority never see print at all (Eichorn & VandenBos, 1985). Journal editors and book publishers (including the publishers of this book) nearly always seek the opinion of several expert reviewers for each submission before agreeing to publish it. Different reviewers often will focus their criticism on different facets of the study (Fiske & Fogg, 1990). As a result, the author usually receives helpful, if sometimes painful, suggestions for revision.

Finally, the scientific community hopes, the best and most meaningful work will be published. Only when a hypothesis has survived all these tests will editors put it in print and scholars tentatively accept it as scientific "truth." But, unlike astrology and other pseudoscientific dogma, scientific findings remain forever in jeopardy from a new study that requires a new interpretation and relegates previous work to the scientific scrap heap.

Types of Psychological Research

You're not out of the empirical woods yet—even though you may understand the basic steps of the scientific method. You also need to learn about several forms that psychological research may take. These include *experiments, correlational studies, surveys, naturalistic observations,* and *case studies.* Each has its advantages and limitations.

EXPERIMENTS   Emily Rosa's study was an example of an **experiment,** a kind of research in which the researcher controls all the conditions and directly manipulates them, including the independent variable. Not only did Rosa and her colleagues design the apparatus used in their study, but they established the conditions under which subjects were tested. Virtually everything about the experiment was under their control.

Every experiment, including Rosa's, is designed to answer a question of this form: Does the independent variable *cause* a predicted change in the dependent variable? To determine this, the experimenter designs two or more ways of treating the participants whose responses are being studied. In the therapeutic touch experiment, for example, Rosa created two treatment conditions by varying which of the participants' hands she placed her own hand near. By contrast, in an experiment designed to study a new drug's effective-

Experiment: A kind of research in which the researcher controls all the conditions and directly manipulates the conditions, including the independent variable.

ness, the two treatments would involve giving some volunteers the experimental drug, while others receive a placebo (a "drug" with no medical value, such as a sugar pill). When two or more groups are used, those exposed to the special treatment are said to be in the **experimental condition** of the experiment. These individuals make up the **experimental group.** Meanwhile, those in the **control group** are placed in the **control condition,** where they may receive a placebo or no treatment at all. Thus, the control group can be used as a standard against which to compare the subjects in the experimental condition.

CORRELATIONAL STUDIES   Sometimes the degree of control required for a careful experiment cannot be achieved for practical or ethical reasons. Suppose, for example, that you wanted to test this hypothesis: Children who ingest lead-based paint (common in older homes, especially in low-income urban housing) suffer learning disabilities. You couldn't do an *experiment* to verify this hypothesis. Why? In an experiment you would have to manipulate the independent variable by deliberately feeding toxic lead-based paint to an experimental group of children! Obviously, this would be hazardous and unethical.

Fortunately, we can find a way around this problem—but at the expense of some control over the research conditions. The alternative is a **correlational study.** In correlational research you, in effect, look for an "experiment" that has already occurred by chance, not by design, in the world outside the laboratory. So, in a correlational study on the effects of ingesting lead-based paint, you would find a group of children who had already been exposed to leaded paint and compare them to another group who had not been exposed. As a control, you would try to match the groups so that they were comparable in every conceivable respect (age, family income, gender, etc.) *except* for their exposure to leaded paint.

The big drawback to a correlational study is that you can never be sure that the groups are really similar in every way. Because you can't randomly assign subjects or manipulate the independent variable, you cannot say with certainty that the condition of interest was the *cause* of the effects you observed. So, even if you observe more learning disabilities among children who were exposed to lead-based paint, you *cannot* conclude for certain that

Connection

Chapter 5
Placebos work because of the patient's expectations.

Experimental condition: The stimulus conditions involved in exposing those in the *experimental group* to the special treatment being investigated.

Experimental group: Those subjects in an experiment who are exposed to the treatment of interest.

Control group: Those subjects who are used as a comparison for the experimental group. The control group is not given the special treatment of interest.

Control condition: The stimulus conditions for the control group — conditions that are identical to the experimental condition in every respect, except for the special treatment given to the experimental group.

Correlational study: A form of research in which the relationship between variables is studied, but without the experimental manipulation of an independent variable. Correlational studies cannot determine cause-and-effect relationships.

HIRAM S. DUDSON
1930 – 1993

Member,
Placebo Group

exposure to the paint *caused* the disabilities. The most you can say is that lead-based paint is *correlated* or associated with learning disabilities. As scientists often put it: *Correlation does not imply causation.*

To determine the precise extent of a correlation between two variables, a researcher would first collect two sets of scores, one for each of the two variables. (In the example we used above, you might correlate lead levels in the blood with IQ test scores.) The next step is to calculate a statistic known as a correlation coefficient, often symbolized by the letter *r*. The **correlation coefficient** summarizes the relationship between the two variables. It can range from −1.0 to +1.0.

If the variables have no relationship at all, their coefficient is 0. You would expect a zero correlation between hat size and GPA, for example. If, however, the two variables show a relationship in which they vary in the same direction (as one variable's scores increase, so do the other's) then we say they are *positively* correlated. An example of a positive correlation is the moderate relationship between SAT scores and college grades (which is approximately +0.4).

In contrast, if one variable decreases as the other increases, they are *negatively* correlated, and their correlation coefficient would have a minus sign. You would probably find a negative correlation between the amount of alcohol consumed by college students and their grade-point averages. In our earlier example, a negative correlation would occur if increasing lead levels in the blood were associated with lowered IQ scores.

It is important to note that a correlation can show a strong relationship even when it is negative. Let us suppose that a measure of anxiety has a correlation of −0.7 with time spent studying. Even though it is a negative correlation, it shows a *stronger* relationship than, for example, a positive correlation of +0.4 between SAT scores and grades.

SURVEYS   If you want to know about people's attitudes, preferences, or other characteristics, you may simply *ask* them for the information, using a self-report technique called a **survey.** It is the method used by political pollsters and marketing consultants, as well as by many researchers in psychology and sociology. Surveys typically ask people for their responses to a prepared set of verbal items. A survey often confers the advantage of generating large numbers of respondents with relative ease. But the value of a survey is only as good as the clarity of its questions and the accuracy and honest of the respondents' self-reports (Schwarz, 1999).

NATURALISTIC OBSERVATIONS   When the researchers want to know how individuals behave in their natural surroundings (as opposed to the artificial conditions of a laboratory) they use the method of **naturalistic observation.** The setting for a naturalistic observation could be as varied as a shopping mall, a classroom, a home, or a remote wilderness. But, because the researcher neither controls the conditions or manipulates the independent variable, naturalistic observations are made under far less controlled conditions than are experiments.

Naturalistic observation might be a good choice for studying child-rearing practices, people's shopping habits, or public courting behaviors. The method is also used extensively to study animal behavior in the wild. It was, in fact, the approach used by Jane Goodall in her famous studies of chimpanzee culture.

CASE STUDIES   Yet another type of research, the **case study,** focuses on a few subjects (sometimes just one). It is a method usually reserved for the in-depth study of unusual individuals with rare problems or unusual talents. Psychoanalysts have used this approach, also called the *clinical method,* to gather

Connection

Appendix
The correlation coefficient summarizes the relationship between two variables.

Correlation coefficient: A statistic, *r*, that indicates the relationship between two variables. Correlation coefficients can range from −1.0 to 0 to +1.0.

Survey: A technique used in correlational research that typically involves seeking people's responses to a prepared set of verbal items.

Naturalistic observations: A form of correlational research involving behavioral assessment of people or animals in their home surroundings.

Case study: Research that involves a single subject (or, at most, a few subjects).

material from their psychotherapy patients and develop theories about mental disorder. The disadvantages of the case study method, of course, lie in its subjectivity and its small sample size, which limit the researcher's ability to draw conclusions that can be applied with confidence to other individuals. Nevertheless, the case study can sometimes give us valuable insights that could be obtained by no other method.

Connection

Chapter 11
Psychoanalytic therapy is based on Sigmund Freud's theory of personality.

Sources of Bias

Think of an issue on which you have strong feelings and opinions — perhaps abortion, euthanasia, or capital punishment. Such topics can bring out biases that could affect the ways that an experimenter designs a study, collects the data, or interprets the results. Accordingly, the scientific method, with its public procedures and openness to replication, provides a powerful means to check on an experimenter's bias. Nevertheless, scientists would rather save themselves embarrassment by identifying and controlling their biases before they hit print.

Personal bias can distort one's ability to estimate or evaluate what is observed because of one's long-standing beliefs, characteristics, or past experiences. Often these are not obvious to the individual holding such biases. For example, in his book, *Even the Rat Was White,* psychologist Robert Guthrie (1998) criticizes much of the psychological literature because it is based on studies with the built-in bias of using mainly white subjects.

Likewise, *observer bias* occurs when one's prejudices or opinions act as "filters" to determine whether some events are noticed or seen as meaningful while others are not. For example, an observer studying aggressive behavior in grade school children may expect boys to be more aggressive than girls and so might not notice girls' aggressive behavior.

Expectancy bias also affects observations when the observer expects — and looks for — certain outcomes to follow observed events. We can see the expectancy bias in a classic study in which psychology students were asked to run groups of rats through a maze and record their times (Rosenthal & Jacobson, 1968). The experimenters told some students that their rats were especially bright; other students heard that their rats were slow learners. (In fact, the experimenters had randomly selected both groups of rats from the same litters). Amazingly, the students' data showed that rats believed to be bright outperformed their supposedly duller litter mates.

Sometimes bias can be expensive. Imagine that you are a psychologist working for a pharmaceutical company that wants you to design a test for a new drug. With millions of dollars riding on the outcome, you will want to do it right. But what about the doctors who are going to be prescribing the drug to patients in your study? Surely those doctors will have high hopes for the drug, as will their patients. And so the stage is set to confound your study with people's expectations, along with the real effects of the drug.

A common control strategy for this sort of bias is to keep participants in the research experimentally "blind," or uninformed about the real purpose of the research study or some key part of it. An even stronger strategy is for the design of the study to keep *both* the participants and the researcher uninformed about which group receives which treatment. When both researchers and participants in

Jane Goodall used the method of naturalistic observation to study chimpanzee behavior.

an experiment are uninformed about the nature of the independent variable being administered, we have a **double-blind control.** In such a study, neither those administering the drug nor the volunteers taking the pills will know who is getting the real drug and who is receiving the placebo. Taking this precaution assures that the experimenters will not inadvertently treat the "real drug" subjects differently or scrutinize them more closely, and the subjects will not be able to detect any clue about how they are "supposed" to be responding to the pills.

Researchers must also try to identify other possible influences on the behavior being studied—influences other than the independent variable. Such **confounding variables** are factors that could be confused with the independent variable and thus distort the results. For example, in a study of prescribing a stimulant drug (such as Ritalin) to control hyperactive behavior among schoolchildren, what might be some confounding variables? The drug's effect might differ because of different body weights, eating schedules, and time, method, or setting of administration. Unless arrangements are made to control all such possible confounding variables—that is, to expose all the subjects to identical conditions—the researcher has no way of knowing what factors produced the results.

Ethical Issues in Psychological Research

A final issue we will consider involves the ethics of research. In psychology, ethical issues arise around the possibility that someone might be hurt or unduly distressed by participating in a poorly conceived psychological study. No researcher would want this to happen, yet the issues are not always clear. Is it ethical to cause someone severe frustration in an experiment involving a problem that is impossible to solve? Or, what about deliberately insulting people in an experiment on aggression? What degree of unease is too high a price to pay for the knowledge gained from the experiment? These are difficult, but important, questions, and not all psychologists answer them in exactly the same way.

To provide some guidelines and boundaries for psychological researchers, the American Psychological Association has published *Ethical Principles of Psychologists and Code of Conduct* (1992). This statement advises researchers of their ethical obligation to shield subjects from potentially harmful procedures. Further, the statement admonishes researchers that information acquired about people during a study must be held confidential and must not be published in such a way that individual rights to privacy are compromised. Nevertheless, gray areas still appear, making ethical problems of research a continuing issue (Kimmel, 1991; Pomerantz, 1994; Rosenthal, 1994).

DECEPTION The use of *deception* poses an especially knotty problem. Under most circumstances, the *Ethical Principles of Psychologists* states that participation in research should be voluntary and informed. That is, we should advise volunteers of what challenges they will face and give them a real opportunity to drop out of the study. But what if you are interested the conditions under which people will help a stranger in distress? If you contrive a phony emergency situation and then ask people if they are willing to participate in the research, you will spoil the very effect that you are trying to study. Consequently, the guidelines do allow for deception under some conditions, provided that no substantial risks are likely to accrue to the participants.

But who, you might ask, is to judge the risks? Most places where research is done now have watchdog committees that make these judgments by exam-

Connection

Chapter 13
Stimulants can be effective in treating hyperactive behavior syndrome in children.

Double-blind control: An experimental procedure in which both researchers and subjects are uninformed about the nature of the independent variable being administered.

Confounding variables: Factors that could be confused with the independent variable and thus distort the results of a study.

Connection

Chapter 14
Bystander intervention studies have found interesting reasons why people sometimes fail to help a person in distress.

ining all studies proposed to be carried out under the sponsorship of the institution. When deception is used, the APA guidelines require that subjects be informed of the deception as soon as is possible without compromising the study's research goals. Individuals used in deceptive research must also be *debriefed* after the study to make sure that they suffer no lasting ill effects. Despite these precautions, some psychologists oppose the use of deception in any form of psychological research (Baumrind, 1985; Bower, 1998c).

ANIMAL STUDIES   Another long-standing ethical issue surrounds the use of laboratory animals, such as rats, pigeons, and monkeys. As far back as the mid-1800s, scientists used nonhuman animals for a variety of reasons, including the relative simplicity of their nervous systems and the relative ease with which a large number of subjects can be maintained under controlled conditions. Animals have also served as alternatives to human subjects when a procedure was deemed risky or outright harmful. Concerned about the issue as long ago as 1925, the American Psychological Association established a Committee on Precautions in Animal Experimentation, which adopted guidelines for animal research (Dewsbury, 1990). The American Psychological Association's *Ethical Principles of Psychologists* also directs researchers to provide decent living conditions for animal subjects and to weigh any discomfort caused them against the value of the information sought in the research. A 1985 federal law also imposes legal restrictions on animal research (Novak & Suomi, 1988).

Recent years have seen a renewal of concern, both inside and outside of psychology, about the use of animals as subjects, particularly when the research involves painful or damaging procedures, such as brain surgery, electrode implants, and pain studies. Some people feel that the limitations should be more stringent on studies using humanlike animals, such as chimpanzees. Others believe that limitations or outright bans should apply to all animal research, including studies of simple animals like sea slugs (which are often used in neurological studies). Many psychologists, however, are staunch supporters of animal research, under the APA guidelines (Blum, 1994).

Psychology In Your Life

Getting in Deeper

Whatever your intended major field of study, you will want to learn more about the professional role your field will demand of you. You can do this by taking out student memberships in professional organizations, attending events sponsored by your major department, getting to know your professors personally, and perusing the field's main magazines, journals, and newsletters. And, if you are considering a major in psychology, you will want to investigate the following resources.

PROFESSIONAL ORGANIZATIONS

The largest and oldest professional association for psychologists, the American Psychological Association (APA), has well over 150,000 members and affiliates (American Psychological Association, 1998). The American Psychological Society (APS) was recently formed to give a stronger voice to academic and research psychologists. Although the APS is a much smaller organization, it has won wide respect; many psychologists belong both to the APA and to the APS.

These groups have student memberships that include nearly all privileges at a fraction of full membership costs. If you are thinking of majoring in psychology, ask your instructor for information about student membership in a professional psychology association. Also consider attending a state, regional, or national convention to get a better view of what psychologists are really like. These conventions also offer an opportunity for students to

present their own research. You could do so, too.

PSYCHOLOGY-RELATED JOURNALS, MAGAZINES, AND NEWSLETTERS

Professional groups sponsor newsletters or journals that help keep their members abreast of new developments in the field. Psychology majors should begin looking over a few of the main ones every month. Some, like the *Monitor on Psychology,* publish general and very readable articles, while others contain highly technical reports tailored for those with specialized advanced training. Take your first plunge into the psychological literature with these:

▶ *Monitor on Psychology* — the monthly news magazine of the APA.
▶ *Current Directions in Psychological Science* — a semimonthly APS journal that provides short reviews on trends and controversies in all areas of psychology.
▶ *The American Psychologist* — the flagship journal of the APA.
▶ *Psychological Science* — the main journal of the APS.

In addition, there are several popular magazines in which you may find articles of interest:

▶ *Discover* — a popular general-science magazine that often has articles on psychological topics.
▶ *Scientific American* — another general science magazine that often carries articles on important psychological topics.
▶ *Science News* — a weekly magazine consisting of brief blurbs on new developments in science, including psychology.
▶ *The Skeptical Inquirer* — a delightful pseudoscience-bashing maga-

Dr. Phil Zimbardo, one of your authors, has been elected to a term as president of the American Psychological Association in 2002.

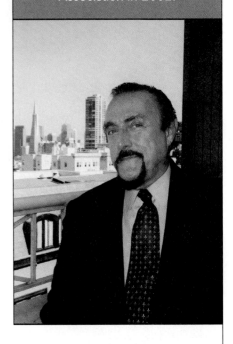

zine published by CSICOP, the Committee for the Scientific Investigation of Claims of the Paranormal.

Don't feel that you must keep up on the entire psychological literature. Nobody can. Read what interests you in these publications.

ELECTRONIC RESOURCES IN PSYCHOLOGY

The printed psychological literature is vast and growing quickly. As a result, anyone wanting to find out what is known on a special topic must know how to access the information on the Internet and in an electronic database. There are several general databases available, such as CARL UnCover (http://uncweb.carl.org/), Expanded Academic Index, and EBSCO Academic

Search Elite, along with some specializing just in psychology. One of the following psychology databases may be available in your campus library:

▶ *PsychLit*—a database containing the recent psychology literature (on CD-ROM). Disks are updated every few months.

▶ *PsychInfo*—an online computer database closely related to Psych-Lit, but continuously updated.

In addition, much free information about psychology is available on the Internet. A good place to start looking would be the American Psychological Association's home page at http://www.apa.org or the American

Psychological Society's home page at http://www.psychologicalscience. org/. Remember that Web addresses often change. Remember, also, that anyone can put anything on the Internet, so you will find some good information and some information of questionable repute. Be skeptical!

CHECK**YOUR**UNDERSTANDING

1. **RECALL:** *A theory is*
   a. an unsupported opinion.
   b. an interpretation of observational data.
   c. the opposite of a fact.
   d. a statement that has not yet been supported with facts.

2. **RECALL:** *A scientific study should begin with*
   a. a controlled test.
   b. a hypothesis.
   c. data collection.
   d. risk/gain assessment.

3. **ANALYSIS:** *The conditions involving the independent variable could also be thought of as*
   a. stimuli.
   b. responses.
   c. cognitions.
   d. experimenter biases.

4. **APPLICATION:** *Which of the following could be an operational definition of "fear"?*
   a. an intense feeling of terror and dread when thinking about some situation
   b. panic
   c. a desire to avoid something
   d. moving away from a stimulus

5. **ANALYSIS:** *Random assignment of subjects to different experimental conditions can control for differences between*
   a. the dependent variable and the independent variable.
   b. the experimental group and the control group.
   c. empirical data and subjective data.
   d. heredity and environment.

6. **RECALL:** *Which is the only form of research that can determine cause and effect?*
   a. a case study
   b. a correlational study
   c. a naturalistic observation
   d. an experimental study

7. **ANALYSIS:** *Which one of the following correlations shows the strongest relationship between two variables?*
   a. +0.4
   b. +0.38
   c. −0.7
   d. 0.05

8. **RECALL:** *In which kind of research does the scientist have the most control over variables that might affect the outcome of the study?*
   a. a case study
   b. a correlational study
   c. an experimental study
   d. a naturalistic observation

9. **UNDERSTANDING THE CORE CONCEPT:**
   Unlike religion, art, the humanities, and the pseudosciences, a science (such as psychology) involves testing its theories against
   a. controlled observations.
   b. expert opinion.
   c. common sense.
   d. intuition and "gut" reactions.

Core Concept

ANSWERS: 1. b 2. b 3. a 4. d
5. b 6. d 7. c 8. c 9. a

Using Psychology to Learn Psychology: Studying with Key Questions and Core Concepts

earning something new can be difficult if it doesn't make sense—and easy if it does. To illustrate, let's turn to a simple demonstration. Examine the string of letters below for about 10 seconds:

TWAIBMFBICIA

Now look away and try to write down the letters in the correct order.

How did you do? Unless you saw some pattern or meaning in the letters, you probably had some difficulty with this task. A close look reveals that the letters are familiar initials of two businesses and two government agencies: TWA, IBM, FBI, and CIA. Discovering this meaning makes them much easier to remember.

In this book, your authors have attempted to help you find meaningful patterns in psychology. To do so, we have built in many learning devices. Among the most important are the Key Questions and the Core Concepts. Let us show you how using these features can make your study of psychology easier.

The Key Questions, which take the place of the familiar section headings in each chapter, give you a "heads up" by signaling what to watch for. For example, one of the Key Questions from this chapter asked: "What Are the Perspectives Psychologists Use Today?" It alerted you to the idea that psychologists have some special ways of looking at mind and behavior that are different from those used in the past. You are much more likely to remember these new concepts if you approach them with an appropriate question in mind (Bransford et al., 1986; Brown & Campione, 1986; Glaser, 1984). You can also use the Key Question as a review-check of your understanding of each section before the next test. If you have a study partner, try asking each other to respond to the key questions.

You can think of Core Concepts as brief responses to the Key Questions. They also highlight the central idea in each chapter section—previews of coming attractions. It is important to realize that a Core Concept is not a complete answer but a capsule summary of ideas to be fleshed out. As you come to understand the meaning of a Core Concept, you will see that the details of the section will fall easily into place. And to reinforce your understanding, it is a good idea to revisit the Core Concept after you have finished reading the section. In fact, this is precisely what the brief end-of-section quizzes (Check Your Understanding) are designed to do.

Another good way to use the Core Concepts is to see if you can explain how the terms in **boldface** link to the Core Concepts. Let's take the second Core Concept in this chapter, which says:

Modern psychologists draw on seven main perspectives: the biological, evolutionary, cognitive, behavioral, psychodynamic, humanistic, and sociocultural.

Can you explain, for example, how the terms *structuralist* and *functionalist* relate to this Core Concept? (Sample answer: Each one of the modern perspectives in psychology employs both the structuralist and functionalist approaches to discover the components and the function of our behavior and mental processes.)

Together, then, the Key Questions and Core Concepts are designed to pose important questions that lead you to the big ideas in the chapter. They will help you step back from the details to see meaningful patterns. To rephrase an old saying: The Key Questions and Core Concepts will help you see the forest through the trees.

Chapter Summary

WHAT IS PSYCHOLOGY, AND WHAT ARE ITS ROOTS?

Psychology has its roots in several often-conflicting traditions stretching back to the ancient Greeks. René Descartes helped the study of the mind to become scientific with his insight that sensations and behaviors are linked to neural activity. The formal beginning as a science is traced to the establishment of the first psychological laboratory in 1879. Wundt's structuralism advocated understanding mental processes such as consciousness by investigating their contents and structure. Functionalism argued that mental processes are best understood in terms of their adaptive purposes and functions.

Psychology is the science of behavior and mental processes, and it has grown out of many, often conflicting, traditions.

WHAT ARE THE PERSPECTIVES PSYCHOLOGISTS USE TODAY?

Modern psychology has seven main viewpoints. The *biological view* looks for the causes of behavior in physical processes such as brain function and genetics. Using cutting-edge technology, psychologists using this perspective have made many discoveries about brain function. The evolutionary view represents a new emphasis in biological psychology, proposing that human mental and behavioral abilities are the result of genetic adaptation for survival and reproductive advantage. It has developed influential theories that explain gender differences and aggressive behavior. The *cognitive view* emphasizes information processing; it has made many discoveries about learning, memory, sensation, perception, language, and thinking. In the *psychodynamic view,* pioneered by Sigmund Freud, behavior and thought are influenced by inner, often unconscious, psychological forces and conflicts. Its impact has been greatest in therapy. The *humanistic view* characterizes human functioning as motivated by a desire to grow, be productive, and fulfill human potential. It has influenced our understanding of personality and the practice of psychotherapy. The *behavioral view* rejects mentalistic explanations and explains behavior in terms of observable stimuli and

responses. It has given us powerful insights into the nature of learning. The *sociocultural view* recognizes the power of society and cultural context on individual thought, feeling, and action, notably through social learning. Cross-cultural psychologists are working to incorporate information about other cultures into a field that has been dominated by psychologists from Europe and the United States.

Seven perspectives dominate modern psychology: the biological, evolutionary, cognitive, behavioral, psychodynamic, humanistic, and sociocultural views.

WHAT DO PSYCHOLOGISTS DO?

Psychology has many areas of specialization. Experimental psychologists do research and often teach. Applied psychologists may be found in many specialties, such as clinical, counseling, engineering, school, and rehabilitation psychology. Other disciplines, especially in the social sciences and in psychiatry, have some overlap with psychology's territory. But only psychology deals with the whole spectrum of behavior and mental processes of the individual. Becoming a psychologist requires graduate study in one or more of psychology's many experimental and applied specialties. Despite having distinctive concerns, psychology also shares interests with other social, behavioral, biological, and health sciences.

Psychology is a broad field with many specialities, grouped in two major categories: experimental psychology and applied psychology.

HOW DO PSYCHOLOGISTS DEVELOP NEW KNOWLEDGE?

Psychology differs from the pseudo-sciences, such as astrology, in that it employs the scientific method to check its ideas empirically—based on firsthand observations. The scientific method consists of five steps: (1) developing a hypothesis, (2) performing a controlled test, (3) gathering objective data, (4) analyzing the results and accepting or rejecting the hypothesis, and (5) publishing, criticizing, and replicating the study. Variations on this scientific method allow for several types of psychological research, including experiments, correlational studies, and case studies. Each differs in the amount of control the researcher has over the conditions being investigated. Everyone, including the scientist, has biases. Common types involve external influences, personal bias, observer bias, expectancy bias, and placebo bias. One way that scientists control for bias in their studies involves the double-blind control method. Psychologists must conduct their work by following a code of ethics, established by the American Psychological Association, for the humane treatment of subjects. Still, some areas of disagreement remain. These especially involve the use of deception and the use of animals as experimental subjects.

 Core Concept

Psychologists, like researchers in all other sciences, use the scientific method to test their ideas empirically.

Review
Test

For each of the following items, choose the single best answer. The answer key appears at the end.

1. Psychology's scientific origins are usually traced to the late 19th century, when _____ established the first psychological laboratory.
   a. William James
   b. Wilhelm Wundt
   c. Sigmund Freud
   d. John B. Watson

2. "To understand consciousness or behavior, you must focus on the probable purpose of an action or process." This statement reflects the arguments of
   a. humanism.
   b. functionalism.
   c. structuralism.
   d. behaviorism.

3. According to the _____ view in psychology, a person's behavior and personality develop as a result of unconscious, inner tensions and conflicts.
   a. biological
   b. cognitive
   c. psychodynamic
   d. behavioral

4. Which of psychology's seven perspectives says that psychology should *not* study mental processes, such as sensation, perception, memory, thinking, motivation, and emotion?

   a. biological
   b. cognitive
   c. psychodynamic
   d. behavioral

5. According to the evolutionary approach in modern psychology, human behavior is the result of the "natural selection" of behaviors that promote:
   a. cultural conformity.
   b. ability to process information.
   c. survival and reproduction.
   d. conflict between individual goals and societal limits.

6. All of the following areas are *applied* psychology specialties, *except:*
   a. social psychology.
   b. counseling psychology.
   c. clinical psychology.
   d. school psychology.

7. Scientific psychology employs empirical investigation methods. This means that the data collected must be based on
   a. firsthand sensory evidence.
   b. reasoned speculation.
   c. the observer's subjective interpretation of events.
   d. established traditions of philosophical inquiry.

8. To study the effects of childhood abuse on adult adjustment patterns, you would do:

a. an experimental study.
b. a correlational study.
c. a double-blind study.
d. an evolutionary study.

9. In psychological research, a _____ is a relationship between the events or variables being studied.
   a. model
   b. base rate
   c. hypothesis
   d. correlation

10. A researcher wonders how to stimulate young schoolchildren to be more creative. She randomly divides a class of first graders in half, reading stories to one group and having members of the other group take turns making up stories to go with the same set of titles. After two weeks, those who made up stories are producing more work in their reading, writing, and art classes than those who merely listened as she read stories to them. Which one of the following statements is *not* true about this study?
   a. The experimental group was the group that made up their own stories.
   b. The dependent variable involves the amount of work produced by the two groups of children.
   c. There are two levels or conditions in the independent variable.
   d. This is an example of a case study.

Answers: 1. b   2. b   3. c   4. d   5. c   6. a
7. a   8. b   9. d   10. d

If You're Interested . . .

ARTICLES

Morgeson, F. P., Seligman, M. E. P., Sternberg, R. J., Taylor, S. E., & Manning, C. M. (1999). Lessons learned from a life in psychological science: Implications for young scientists. *American Psychologist, 54,* 106–115.

Readers interested in becoming psychologists are encouraged to read this article by a panel of well-known psychologists, revealing early career experiences and what they know now that they wish they had known then.

BOOKS

Dawes, R. (2001). *Everyday irrationality: How pseudo-scientists, lunatics, and the rest of us systematically fail to think rationally.* Westview Press.

The author presents an analysis of unscientific thinking as a result of a flawed cognitive style, not merely a failure to think critically about information.

Fancher, R. E. (1996). *Pioneers of psychology, 3rd ed.* W. W. Norton & Co.

This is a collection of biographies of the women and men who established psychology and developed it as a scientific discipline.

Fortey, R. (1998). *Life: A natural history of the first four billion years of life on earth.* Knopf.

A paleontologist describes the exhilaration of scientific discovery and explanation, with colorful imagery and appealing narration.

Gay, P. (1988). *Freud: A life for our time.* W. W. Norton & Co.

This definitive biography by the foremost expert on Freud's life and work is told sympathetically but realistically.

Gonick, L., & Smith, W. (1993). *The cartoon guide to statistics.* New York: HarperPerennial.

This helpful and entertaining comic book introduction to probability, descriptive statistics, sampling, hypothesis testing, and experimental design "invites" the reader to "get it" and should be reassuring to even the most nervous student of research methods.

Hunt, M. (1993). *The story of psychology.* Doubleday.

Here are fascinating anecdotes, summaries, and documentation on the lives and times of what Morton Hunt calls "the Magellans of the mind," from ancient philosophy to modern research.

James, W. (1890/1983). *Principles of psychology.* Harvard University Press.

The 1983 reissue, in one paperback volume, of the great text by William James, father of American psychology, is still engaging and inspiring after more than a century of stunning growth and change in the discipline.

Orkin, M. (2001). *What are the odds?: Chance in everyday life.* W. H. Freeman & Co.

Using minimal mathematics but lots of practical and entertaining examples, Orkin explains probability (the very basis of statistical analysis) and chance by demonstrating how to calculate the likelihood and unlikelihood of a variety of life events (winning the lottery or a variety of gambling exercises) and the very orderliness of the universe.

Popplestone, J. A., & McPherson, M. W. (1994). *An illustrated history of American psychology.* The University of Akron Press.

A friendly sized paperback history richly illustrated with rare photographs and illustrations, this history of psychology in America conveys the strong sense of the people who did the work and generated the ideas that make this profession both interesting and important.

Salsburg, D. (2001). *The lady tasting tea: How statistics revolutionized science in the twentieth century.* W. H. Freeman & Co.

With intriguing stories, Salsburg shows how the mathematics of probability made it possible not only to discover but to test scientific findings.

Shermer, M. (1997). *Why people believe weird things: Pseudoscience, superstition, and other confusions of our time.* W. H. Freeman & Co.

The author gives powerful arguments for developing healthy skepticism about unbelievable and magical "explanations" and for debunking a wide range of bizarre beliefs, from alien abductions to antiscientific creationism and denial of the Holocaust.

Schick, T., Jr., & Vaughn, L. (1999). *How to think about weird things, 2nd edition.* Mayfield.

This book is designed to help readers become good consumers of science by distinguishing good research from bad, keeping both an open mind and high standards in trying to explain baffling or troubling phenomena.

Wilson, E. O. (1998). *Consilience: The unity of knowledge.* Knopf.

The enormously readable, award-winning biologist Edward O. Wilson calls for an ethical and considered approach to science and life in the future.

Wynn, C. M., & Wiggins, A. W. (2001). *Quantum leaps in the wrong direction: Where real science ends . . . and pseudoscience beings.* Joseph Henry Press.

These are stories of influential "scientific" discoveries that turned out to be flawed or false.

VIDEOS

Fast, Cheap, and Out of Control. (1997, color, 82 min.) Directed by Errol Morris; starring Dave Hoover, George Mendonca, Ray Mendez, and Rodney Books.

This documentary interviews four eccentric "geniuses" — a lion tamer, a topiary gardener, an expert on the African naked mole rat, and an MIT robotics scientist — mixed with B-movie footage and running commentary on the nature of life, consciousness, expertise, inspiration, and motivation. Strange and wonderful!

Inherit the Wind. (1960, B&W, 127 min.). Directed by Stanley Kramer; starring Spencer Tracy, Fredric March, Gene Kelly, Dick York.

This classic is a wonderful adaptation of theatrical fictionalization of the 1925 "monkey trial" of John Scopes, a Dayton, Tennessee, schoolteacher prosecuted for teaching evolution in his public school class. Watch the movie — then research the facts about the real people behind the characters.

The Standard Deviants: Psychology. (1996, color, 122 min.) Produced by The Stimulating World of Psychology.

The Standard Deviants take students through major schools of psychology, the brain and nervous system, nature versus nurture, learning theories, psychoanalysis, cognitive science, experimentation, personality, and the scientific method. The film is funny as well as helpful for studying.

HOW ARE GENES AND BEHAVIOR LINKED?

Evolution and Natural Selection
Genes and Inheritance

Behavior consistently found in a species is likely to have a genetic basis that evolved because the behavior has been adaptive.

CHOOSING YOUR CHILDREN'S GENES:
Within your lifetime, parents may be able to select genetic traits for their children. What price will we pay for these choices?

HOW DOES THE BODY COMMUNICATE INTERNALLY?

The Nervous System
The Endocrine System

The body's two communications systems, the nervous system and the endocrine system, both use chemical messengers to communicate with targets throughout the body.

SIDE EFFECTS OF PSYCHOACTIVE DRUGS:
Chemicals that affect behavior usually mimic hormones or neurotransmitters. But they may stimulate unintended targets, where they produce unwanted side effects.

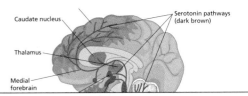

HOW DOES THE BRAIN PRODUCE BEHAVIOR AND MENTAL PROCESSES?

Windows on the Brain
Three Layers of the Brain
Four Lobes of the Cerebral Cortex
Cortical Cooperation and the
    Responsive Brain
Cerebral Dominance
The Split Brain

The brain is composed of many specialized and interconnected modules that work together to create mind and behavior.

BRAIN DAMAGE AND BEHAVIOR:
Everyone knows somebody who has suffered brain damage from an accident, a tumor, or a stroke. The symptoms suggest that part of the brain was damaged.

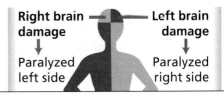

USING PSYCHOLOGY TO LEARN PSYCHOLOGY: Putting Your Knowledge of the Brain to Work

CHAPTER 2

BIOPSYCHOLOGY

I hadn't noticed Dad dragging the toe of his right foot ever so slightly as he walked. But my mother noticed it on their nightly tour of the neighborhood, when he wasn't keeping up with her brisk pace. I just figured that he was slowing down a bit in his later years.

Dad casually dismissed the symptom, but Mom was persistent. She scheduled an appointment with the doctor. In turn, the doctor scheduled a brain scan that showed a remarkably large mass—a tumor—on the left side of Dad's brain. You can see what the neurologist saw in Figure 2.1—an image taken horizontally through the head.

When I saw the pictures, I knew immediately what was happening. The tumor was located in an area that would inter-

fere with Dad's tracking the position of his foot. As I remembered learning in my introductory psychology class, each side of the body communicates directly with the opposite side of the brain—so it made sense that the tumor pressing on the left side of the brain was affecting communications with the right foot.

The neurologist also told us that the diseased tissue was not in the brain itself. Rather, it was in the sacklike layers surrounding the brain and spinal cord. Thus, the mass was occupying space that a portion of the brain should have had. The recommendation was surgery—which was performed after an anxious wait of a few weeks.

(continued)

FIGURE 2.1:   MRI Image of a Brain Tumor

This image shows a large mass on the left side of the brain, in a region involved with tracking the position of the right foot. The scan is of the author's father.

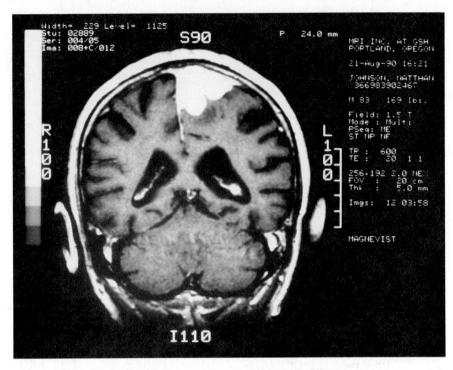

During this time I remember feeling grateful for my professional training. As a psychologist, I knew something about the brain, its disorders, and treatments. This allowed me to shift perspectives—from son to psychologist and back again. It helped me deal with the emotions that rose to the surface when I thought about the struggle for the organ of my father's mind.

Sadly, the operation did not produce the miraculous cure for which we had hoped. Although brain surgery is performed safely on thousands of patients each year—many of whom receive immense benefits in the quality and lengths of their lives—one has to remember that it is a procedure that is usually done on very sick people. In fact, the operation did give Dad some time with us that he may otherwise not have had.

—RJ

When fully matured, a human brain occupies a space the size of a grapefruit, weighs only 3 pounds, and consists of the most common chemical elements. Yet, despite its small size, the human brain is the most complex structure known. Its 100 billion nerve cells, designed to communicate and store information, far outnumber all the transistors and wires in the depths of the biggest, fastest computers. Indeed, the number of nerve cells in the human brain outnumbers the stars in our galaxy.

How can we even begin to understand such a complex object? Psychologists often think of the brain as a sort of biological computer, so powerful that it can learn, interpret, store, and communicate all the information that is possible for the brightest of us to know or the most sensitive of us to experience (Azar, 1997a). Yet, it is much more than the most advanced computer on earth.

Evolutionary shaping of the brain has taken place over millions of years. And now the human brain has turned its attention on itself: This marvelous organ has become the subject of study for a new breed of researchers in **biopsychology,** a rapidly growing specialty that lies at the intersection of biology, behavior, and the environment. Biopsychologists seek to understand the biochemical processes behind the behavior of all living creatures. In general, they want to explain how the *nervous system* and its companion communication network, the *endocrine system,* cooperate to produce all human action. In turn, biopsychologists are part of an emerging interdisciplinary field known as **neuroscience.** This effort involves biologists, psychologists, computer scientists, chemists, and other disciplines interested in the connection between brain and mind (Kandel & Squire, 2000). These disciplines of biopsychology and neuroscience will be the focus of this chapter.

Like biopsychologists, we must use our brains to understand the brain and its mental processes. At first, these processes may seem to exist independently of the tissue inside our heads. But when disease, drugs, or accidents destroy brain cells, the biological basis of the human mind stands out in harsh relief. Then we are forced to recognize the physical matter from which spring sensation and perception, learning and memory, passion and pain, reason and madness.

In this chapter we will first set the scene for our look at the brain by examining how the twin forces of heredity and evolution influence our physical and mental characteristics. Next, we will examine the body's two internal communications systems: the endocrine system and the nervous system, of which the brain is the central component. Finally, we will study the structure and function of the brain itself. Along the way, you will encounter many new terms. We urge you to think of this chapter as a "journey" into the field of psychology. As with most journeys, you may at first find the new territory unfamiliar. But with persistence you will come to know the landmarks and place names of the new territory that lies inside you. On this journey we are asking you to look closely at yourself from a perspective that you may not have taken before—the perspective of biopsychology. By understanding your biological nature, you will better appreciate how brain, mind, behavior, and the environment interact to create the uniqueness of every human being.

HOW ARE GENES AND BEHAVIOR LINKED?

We humans have many **innate** behavioral tendencies, just as fish have an inborn knack for swimming and most birds are built for flight. The human brain is born already programmed for language, social interaction, and many other possibilities. But how did these potentialities become woven into the fabric of the brain?

Understanding the marvelous piece of biology called the brain requires us first to consider **evolution,** the process by which species of organisms gradually change as they adapt to their environments. On a microscopic level, we can observe evolution in action as we see bacteria adapt to antibiotics. Over longer time spans, larger and more complex organisms (such as our ancestors) have also changed, as they adapted to changing temperatures, food supplies, and breeding opportunities. When the environment serves up severe challenges, only those most genetically prepared can compete and pass their genes on to their offspring. In this way, evolution also has an impact on both the

Biopsychology: The specialty in psychology that studies the interaction of biology, behavior, and the environment.

Neuroscience: A new field of study that focuses on the brain and its role in psychological processes.

Innate: Inborn; present at birth; part of the organism's biological heritage.

Evolution: The gradual process of biological change that occurs in a species as it adapts to its environment.

physical attributes of a species and its genetically based behavior. This fact makes evolution an important force in psychology and the basis for the Core Concept for this section:

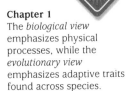

Connection

Chapter 1

The *biological view* emphasizes physical processes, while the *evolutionary view* emphasizes adaptive traits found across species.

Charles Darwin: The British naturalist who first described the evolutionary theory and provided overwhelming evidence for the process of natural selection.

Natural selection: The driving force behind evolution — by which the environment "selects" the fittest organisms.

More than 98% of our genetic material is also found in chimpanzees (Gibbons, 1998). This supports Darwin's idea that humans and apes had a common ancestor.

As you can see, biopsychology makes use of both the biological and evolutionary views. All through this book, the notion of an adaptive, evolutionary basis for behavior will help us understand otherwise puzzling psychological phenomena, including emotions, motives, and intelligence, as well as certain social behaviors and gender differences. After a closer look in the following paragraphs at the way evolution works, we will consider how it has influenced our behavior.

Evolution and Natural Selection

About 170 years ago, British naturalist **Charles Darwin** set sail on HMS *Beagle*, an ocean research vessel commissioned to survey the coastline of South America. During the five-year trip, Darwin made detailed records of the many life-forms and fossils he encountered. The pattern that emerged in Darwin's mind was one of close relationships among species. He explained this pattern in his most famous book, *On the Origin of Species* (1859), where he set forth science's most fundamental and wide-sweeping biological theory, that of the evolution of life. This theory had a revolutionary effect on the way people in the modern world see their relationship to other living things (Mayr, 2000).

Darwin's observations convinced him that some natural mechanism influenced the breeding and survival of organisms from one generation to the next. Species ultimately either adapt to their environments and flourish, or they fail to adapt and die out. Thus the flowers of a plant, the colors of a butterfly's wings, or the hunting instincts of a cat prove adaptive to environmental conditions and are preserved, if the organism survives and breeds. Or, if the characteristics fail to help organisms adapt and reproduce, they may be "selected out." For the fortunate organisms whose ancestors had accumulated new traits that allowed them to adapt and survive, the result "would be the formation of a new species," claimed Darwin (1859).

"Evolution" is, of course, an emotionally loaded term, and many people have a mistaken notion of its meaning. For example, some mistakenly believe that Darwin's theory says humans "come from monkeys." But neither Darwin nor any other evolutionary scientist has ever stated this. Rather, they say we share a common ancestor — a big difference. Another misconception holds that evolution occurs when an animal's behavior alters its genetic inheritance. According to this erroneous view, giraffes evolved long necks from stretching to reach leaves high in the trees. In truth, the ancestors of giraffes that, because of genetic variation, possessed slightly longer necks had a slight survival and reproductive advantage over their shorter-necked cousins. Consequently, the genetic variation behind longer necks came to dominate the gene pool. In the same way, our own traits evolved because they gave our ancestors an advantage in the competitive struggle for survival and reproduction.

You and your unique genetic traits could be an evolutionary dead end — unless you have children who also survive and reproduce. According to Darwin's theory of **natural selection,** the driving force behind evolution is precisely this survival-and-reproduction interaction of organisms and their environment (Buss et al., 1998). Some members of a species produce more offspring that

FIGURE 2.2: How Natural Selection Works

Environmental changes create competition for resources among species members. Individuals that inherit characteristics that promote survival will probably survive and reproduce. The next generation will then have a greater number of individuals possessing these advantageous genes.

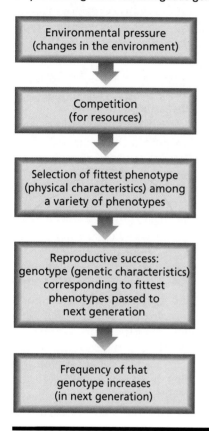

survive and reproduce than do others because environmental conditions favor their inheritable features. For example, birds with larger, stronger beaks may be more likely to survive and reproduce during times of scarcity because they can forage on tougher seeds (Weiner, 1994). Because this characteristic can be inherited, their offspring will carry this genetic advantage, too. In this fashion, individuals with the improved traits survive, reproduce, and pass their adaptive traits on to the next generation more often than do those with less-adaptive traits. Their offspring will, in turn, pass along the survival-promoting traits they possess, and their descendants will eventually outnumber those who have not inherited the helpful features. In evolutionary terms, successful organisms pass their genes along to succeeding generations, while unsuccessful organisms do not. (See Figure 2.2.)

Genes and Inheritance

What else did you inherit from your parents? Your physical characteristics, such as height, weight, facial features, and hair color, all come from the unique combination of your parents' genetic characteristics that were inscribed in every cell in your body. Yet, despite this genetic heritage, you are different from your parents. One source of this difference is the environment in which you grew up—distinct in time and sometimes place from that of your parents.

Connection

Chapter 4
Our genes influence both mental and physical development.

Another source of difference arises from the unique combination of *genes* you possess, coming from both parents, yet different from either one of them.

A mother and father pass on to the offspring a random combination of the genetic traits that past generations of their family lines have given them. This inheritance results in a unique **genotype,** the organism's genetic structure, containing the complete biological plan and timetable for individual development. If the genotype is the blueprint, the resulting physical structure is the **phenotype:** the physical characteristics produced by an individual's genetic makeup.

Remarkably, Darwin knew nothing of genetics. Although he correctly described the process of natural selection, he never knew what the biological basis was for evolutionary change. From our perspective 150 years later, we know that spontaneous genetic variations, or **mutations,** which occur at random, occasionally produce beneficial traits that aid survival. When this occurs, these newly developed traits pass on to the succeeding generations. Occasionally, mutations will also produce troublesome characteristics that generate problems such as mental retardation, hyperaggressiveness, or the extreme emotional turmoil of clinical depression. The same mechanism of mutation that produces beneficial traits may also produce maladaptive ones: Mutations are random, so they do not always work to the individual organism's advantage.

CHROMOSOMES AND DNA   In the film *Jurassic Park,* the genetic code for dinosaurs was recovered from dinosaur blood trapped in fossil amber. Although the story was fiction, the film rested on an important fact: The nucleus of every cell in an organism's body contains the complete genetic code for that individual. In the nucleus a complex molecule, called **DNA** (deoxyribonucleic acid), contains the code of life: the genetic instructions for making thousands of proteins. These proteins, in turn, regulate the body's physical characteristics (the phenotype). The units of DNA that are responsible for specific proteins are called **genes.** The proteins they specify exert biological control over body build, physical strength, intelligence, certain mental disorders, and many other behavior patterns—all of which are part of the individual's phenotype.

The complete package of DNA in a human cell contains approximately 50,000 genes—surprisingly few in view of the complexity of the human brain itself (Netting & Wang, 2001). These genes are assembled end-to-end in long chains to form structures known as **chromosomes.** At the moment you were conceived, cells throughout your body inherited 46 chromosomes from your parents: 23 from your mother paired with 23 from your father. Each of these chromosomes contains thousands of genes. (See Figure 2.3.) Genetic information in a special abbreviated form is written into the ova or sperm cells formed in the reproductive organs.

The **sex chromosomes** warrant special mention because they contain genes for development of a male or female phenotype. An XX combination in this pair codes for femaleness, while an XY combination codes for maleness. Whatever your gender, you inherited one X chromosome from your biological mother. In addition, you received either an X (if you are female) or a Y (if you are male) from your biological father. Thus, your genotype determines your biological sex and the associated phenotypic characteristics in your body structure and chemistry that develop throughout your lifetime.

GENETIC EXPLANATIONS FOR PSYCHOLOGICAL PROCESSES   The influences of both heredity and environment underlie all psychological processes. So, we should avoid attributing everything to genetics (Ehrlich, 2000a, 2000b; Mauron, 2001). Yet, we know that genes exert considerable influence on intelligence, personality, certain mental disorders, and even on certain reading

Genotype: An organism's genetic makeup.

Phenotype: An organism's observable physical characteristics.

Mutations: Genetic variations, which occur randomly, especially during the recombination of chromosomes in sexual reproduction.

DNA: A long, complex molecule that encodes genetic characteristics. The long name for DNA is *deoxyribonucleic acid.*

Genes: Segments of a chromosome that encode the directions for the inherited physical and mental characteristics of an organism. Genes are the functional units of a chromosome.

Chromosomes: Tightly coiled threadlike structures along which the genes are organized, like beads on a necklace. Chromosomes consist primarily of DNA.

Sex chromosomes: The X and Y chromosomes that determine our physical sex characteristics.

Connection

Chapter 4
The *nature–nurture* controversy involves the relative effects of heredity and environment.

FIGURE 2.3: DNA, Genes, and Chromosomes

Each chromosome is made up of thousands of genes. Genes are segments of a long DNA molecule. Each gene contains the complete instructions for making a protein.

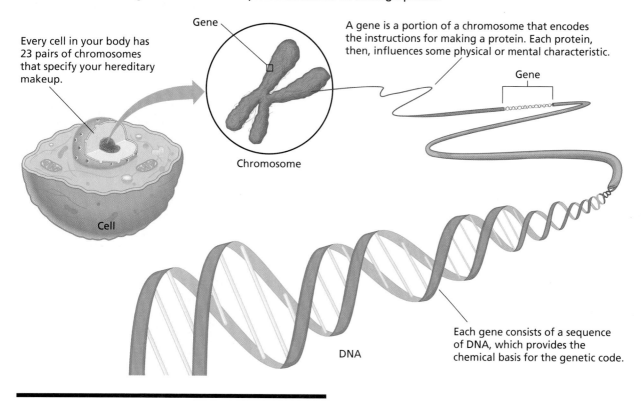

Gene

Every cell in your body has 23 pairs of chromosomes that specify your hereditary makeup.

A gene is a portion of a chromosome that encodes the instructions for making a protein. Each protein, then, influences some physical or mental characteristic.

Gene

Chromosome

Cell

Each gene consists of a sequence of DNA, which provides the chemical basis for the genetic code.

DNA

---

disabilities (Bouchard, 1994; DeAngelis, 1997; Gelernter, 1994; Hamer, 1997; Plomin, Owen, & McGuffin, 1994; Plomin & Rende, 1991; Saudino, 1997). In the hybrid field of **behavior genetics,** geneticists and psychologists collaborate to uncover the genetic influence of still more behavioral characteristics (Plomin, 1997). They also work together to develop environmental interventions, such as training programs, diet, and social interactions, that can modify genetically influenced behavior.

Happily, research in behavior genetics has produced some practical results. Consider, for example, a condition called **Down syndrome,** caused by an extra 21st chromosome fragment. The disorder involves markedly impaired psychomotor and physical development, as well as mental retardation. In an earlier day, people with Down syndrome faced a bleak and unproductive life in which they depended almost wholly on others to fulfill their basic needs. A deeper understanding of the disorder has now changed that outlook. Although no cure has been found, today we know that people with Down syndrome are capable of considerable learning, despite their genetic impairment. With special programs that teach life skills, those with Down syndrome now learn to care for themselves, work, and establish some personal independence.

The science of behavior genetics has had its most striking successes in identifying disorders that involve a single chromosome. To give another example, a rare pattern of impulsive violence found in several members of a Dutch family has been linked to a single gene (Brunner et al., 1993). However, many other genetically based disorders appear to involve multiple genes—or, sometimes, even more than one chromosome (Boomsma, Anokhin, & de Geus, 1997; Plomin, 2000). This is probably the case with schizophrenia, a severe

Behavior genetics: A new field bringing together geneticists and psychologists interested in the genetic basis of behavior and mental characteristics, such as intelligence, altruism, and psychological disorders.

Down syndrome: A genetic disorder that produces one form of mental retardation.

Connection

Chapter 12
Schizophrenia is a psychotic disorder that affects about one out of 100 persons.

Human Genome Project: An international scientific effort to determine the complete human genetic code in all 23 pairs of chromosomes.

mental disorder, and with certain forms of Alzheimer's disease, a disorder involving deterioration of the brain and cognitive processes in some older individuals (Morrison-Bogorad & Phelps, 1997; Plomin, Owen, & McGuffin, 1994; Skoog et al., 1993; St. George-Hyslop, 2000).

Choosing Your Children's Genes

In Your Life

Scientists already have the ability to control and alter the genetics of animals, like Dolly, the famous fatherless sheep that was cloned from one of her mother's cells. But what are the prospects for genetic manipulation in people? Scientists working on the **Human Genome Project** have recently completed a "first draft" of the human genetic code (Pennisi, 2001). Soon we will mine this knowledge for an understanding of the genetic basis for many physical and mental disorders. But not all the promise of human genetics lies in the future. We can already sample fetal cells and search for certain genetic disorders, such as Down syndrome. The Human Genome Project will greatly expand this ability.

Within your lifetime, parents may be able to select genes for their children, much as you select the components of a deli sandwich. It is likely that we will learn to alter the DNA in a developing fetus in order to add or delete certain physical and mental traits (Henig, 1998). This will probably be done by infecting the fetus with a harmless virus containing desirable genes that will alter or replace the genetic blueprint in every cell of the body. But what will be the price of this technology?

Undoubtedly, parents in this brave new genetic world will want their children to be smart and good looking—but, we might wonder, by what standards will intelligence and

looks be judged? And will everyone be able to afford to place an order for their children's genes—or only the very wealthy? What potential for conflict does this newfound "freedom" hold for our species? You can be certain that the problems we face will be simultaneously biological, psychological, political, and ethical (Fackelmann, 1998). One of the most controversial issues surrounding this topic involves cloning. While most people do not favor the cloning of entire humans, the possibility exists for the cloning of specific organs or tissues. Transplants could then potentially cure heart, liver, and kidney failure, as well as diabetes and arthritis. But the difficulty arises from the source of cells for such research. Because donor embryos most often come from surgical abortions, many people oppose this work (Wheeler, 1999).

In general, the more we learn about behavior genetics, the more clearly we know about the powerful biological forces that determine human potential and life experience—and the power we will have when these genetic forces are completely understood. The American Psychological Association has identified genetics as one of the disciplines with the greatest promise for psychology's future (Plomin & McClearn, 1993).

We are also beginning to see the difficult problems genetics will pose. Already, psychologists are called on to provide guidance about how genetic knowledge can best be applied (Plomin, 1997), particularly in helping people assess genetic risks in connection with family

Dolly was cloned from a single cell of her "mother," to which she is genetically identical.

planning. We invite you to assess your own concern with the genetics of parenting by answering the following questions:

▶ If you could select three genetic traits for your children, which ones would you select?

▶ How would you feel about raising children you have adopted or fostered but to whom you are not genetically related?

▶ If a biological child of yours might be born disabled or fatally ill because of your genetic heritage, would you have children anyway? What circumstances or conditions would affect your decision?

▶ If you knew you might carry a gene responsible for a serious medical or behavioral disorder, would you want to be tested before having children? Would it be fair for a prospective spouse to require you to be tested before conceiving children? Would it be fair for the state to make such a requirement?

1. **RECALL:** *Which of the following processes are involved in natural selection, the driving force behind evolution? (More than one may be correct.)*
   a. Individuals best adapted to the environment have a survival advantage.
   b. Some individuals reproduce more successfully than others.
   c. The offspring of some invididuals survive in greater numbers than do those of others.
   d. Individuals with a genetic advantage are more likely to survive and reproduce.

2. **RECALL:** *Which of the following is a characteristic that might be a part of your phenotype?*
   a. your height and eye color
   b. the members of your family
   c. what you have learned in school
   d. the childhood diseases you have had

3. **RECALL:** *Which of the following statements expresses the correct relationship?*
   a. Genes are made of chromosomes.
   b. DNA is made of chromosomes.
   c. DNA is made of genes.
   d. Genes are made of DNA.

4. **ANALYSIS:** *In purely evolutionary terms, which one would be a measure of your own success as an organism?*
   a. your intellectual accomplishments
   b. the length of your life
   c. the number of children you have
   d. the contributions that you make to the happiness of humanity

5. **UNDERSTANDING THE CORE CONCEPT:** *Behavior consistently found in a species is likely to have a genetic basis that evolved because the behavior has been adaptive. Which of the following human behaviors illustrates this concept?*
   a. driving a car
   b. sending astronauts to the moon
   c. Down syndrome
   d. language

ANSWERS: 1. all are correct   2. a   3. d
              4. c   5. d

Core Concept

Key Question

HOW DOES THE BODY COMMUNICATE INTERNALLY?

You are driving on a winding mountain road, and a car is coming directly at you. You and the other driver swerve in opposite directions at the last instant. Your heart is pounding—and it keeps pounding for several minutes after the danger has passed. Externally, you have avoided a potentially fatal accident. Internally, your body has responded to two kinds of messages from its two communication systems.

The fast-acting **nervous system,** a massive network of nerve cells that rapidly relays messages to and from the brain, came to your rescue first. The nervous system's messages rely on the production and release of *neurotransmitters,* chemicals that carry information between nerve cells. This is the system that initially sped up your heartbeat and sent messages to your muscles that you used to swerve the car out of danger.

The body's other communication system, the **endocrine system,** involves a network of glands that also manufacture chemical messengers and secrete them directly into the bloodstream. These chemical messengers, called **hormones,** affect the operation of other glands and organs. (Look ahead to Figure 2.9 for the location of the body's endocrine glands.) Certain components of the slower endocrine system sent follow-up messages that kept your heart pounding, even after the emergency was past.

In general, these two internal message systems work together to help us respond in emergencies. They also act in concert to produce our more usual, everyday behaviors. This is the Core Concept:

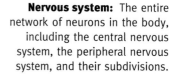

Nervous system: The entire network of neurons in the body, including the central nervous system, the peripheral nervous system, and their subdivisions.

Endocrine system: The hormone system—the body's chemical messenger system, including the following endocrine glands: pituitary, adrenals, gonads, thyroid, parathyroid, pancreas, ovaries, and testes.

Hormones: The chemical messengers used by the endocrine system. Many hormones also serve as neurotransmitters.

> **The body's two communications systems, the nervous system and the endocrine system, both use chemical messengers to communicate with targets throughout the body.**

Core Concept

Connection

Chapter 12
Psychoactive drugs
produce essentially the
same chemical changes in
the brain that occur in
certain mental disorders.

The brain is the "nerve center" of these two communication systems. All its incoming and outgoing messages rely on chemical signals. So do the brain's internal communications, which produce all our thoughts and feelings. As you might expect, psychoactive drugs work by altering these chemical communications. And in later chapters we will note that some psychological disorders also involve disturbances in these communication channels. For now, however, let's focus on the structure and function of the two communication systems: the nervous system and the endocrine system.

The Nervous System

When you stub your toe, the body's fast communication network, the *nervous system,* carries the painful message from your toe to your brain. Processing this message may involve billions of highly specialized **nerve cells,** or **neurons.** These neurons are organized either into densely packed clusters (nuclei) or extended pathways (nerve fibers). Large clusters of nuclei make up much of the brain and spinal cord. Together with the nerve fibers extending throughout the body, these structures make up the entire nervous system.

Nerve cells or **neurons:** Cells specialized to receive and transmit information to other cells in the body. Bundles of many neurons are called *nerves.*

Central nervous system: The brain and the spinal cord.

Peripheral nervous system: All parts of the nervous system lying outside the central nervous system. The peripheral nervous system includes the autonomic and somatic nervous systems.

DIFFERENT PARTS HAVE DIFFERENT FUNCTIONS The nervous system has two major subsystems: the **central nervous system** (CNS) and the **peripheral nervous system.** The CNS is composed of all the neurons in the brain and spinal cord, while the peripheral nervous system is made up of all the nerve fibers that connect the CNS to the rest of the body. Figure 2.4 will help you conceptualize the relationship of the central and peripheral nervous systems.

Like an executive, the central nervous system integrates and coordinates all bodily functions, processes incoming neural messages, and sends out com-

FIGURE 2.4: Organization of the Nervous System

The sensory and motor nerves that make up the peripheral nervous system are linked to the brain by the spinal cord.

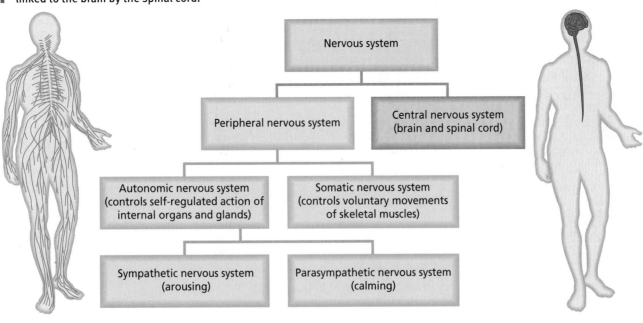

mands to different parts of the body. For example, if a vicious-looking dog approaches you, your CNS signals your legs to run. If a friend greets you, your CNS signals your arms to reach out and your voice to speak. The CNS sends and receives neural messages through the spinal cord, a trunk line of neurons that connects the brain to much of the peripheral nervous system. This trunk line is housed in the spinal column, the central tube running through your backbone.

The spinal cord also is responsible for simple, swift **reflexes** that do not involve the brain (such as the knee-jerk reflex that physicians elicit with a tap on the knee). We know that the brain is not involved in many simple reflexes, because an organism whose spinal cord has been severed from its brain can still respond, for example, by withdrawing its limb from a painful stimulus. Without direction from the brain, however, voluntary movements cannot occur. As a result, damage to the nerves of the spinal cord can produce paralysis of the legs or trunk, as seen in paraplegic individuals. The extent of paralysis depends on how high up on the spinal cord the damage occurred: the higher up the site of damage, the greater the extent of the paralysis. You may recall that, in 1995, American actor Christopher Reeve was paralyzed from the neck down by an injury sustained during a horseback riding accident. Physicians caring for Reeve emphasized that his prognosis (likely future condition) depended on the extent and location of damage to his spinal cord.

Despite their commanding positions, the brain and spinal cord are isolated from any direct contact with the outside world. The central nervous system never directly experiences light waves, sound waves, or surface textures. Instead, it relies on the peripheral nervous system to provide information about the world from sensory receptors, such as those found in the eyes and ears. Likewise, the brain must control our actions by relaying commands through the peripheral nervous system to the muscles. This outgoing division of the peripheral nervous system is actually composed of two parts: the *somatic nervous system* and the *autonomic nervous system* (see Figure 2.4).

The **somatic nervous system** sends messages from the CNS to the body's skeletal muscles. For example, when you type a message on a keyboard, the instruction to move your fingers is carried by the somatic nervous system. As you plan what to type, your brain sends signals about which fingers to use on which keys, and your fingers return feedback about their position and movement. If you strike the wrong *kee,* the somatic nervous system informs the brain, which issues a correction so you can quickly delete the error and hit the right *key.*

The other part of the peripheral nervous system that conveys messages away from the brain is known as the **autonomic nervous system** (*autonomic* means self-regulating or independent). This network carries signals that coordinate functions of the internal organs. It operates constantly, regulating bodily processes we don't usually control consciously, such as respiration, digestion, and arousal. It also works during sleep and even sustains life processes during anesthesia and coma.

Complicating matters, the autonomic nervous system is itself subdivided into the *sympathetic* and *parasympathetic* nervous systems. These two systems work together, in an opposite but complementary fashion, to promote survival by maintaining basic bodily functions and preparing the body to respond to threat. The **sympathetic division** governs responses to stress under conditions of threat or emergency, when action must be quick and powerfully energized. This is the "fight-or-flight" nervous system. It energizes you to respond to a stressor quickly by either fighting what threatens you or taking flight from what you cannot fight. In contrast, the **parasympathetic division** monitors the routine operation of the body's internal functions. This "housekeeping" division returns the body to calmer functioning after sympathetic arousal. The sep-

Connection

Chapter 5
Conscious sensations of pain are realized in the brain.

Reflexes: Simple, unlearned responses triggered by stimuli — such as the knee-jerk reflex set off by tapping the tendon just below your kneecap.

Somatic nervous system: A portion of the peripheral nervous system that sends voluntary messages to the body's skeletal muscles.

Autonomic nervous system: The portion of the peripheral nervous system that sends messages to the internal organs and glands.

Sympathetic division: The part of the autonomic nervous system that sends messages to internal organs and glands that help us respond to stressful and emergency situations.

Parasympathetic division: The part of the autonomic nervous system that monitors the routine operations of the internal organs and returns the body to calmer functioning after arousal by the sympathetic division.

Connection

Chapter 9
Stress messages are carried via the autonomic nervous system.

FIGURE 2.5: Divisions of the Autonomic Nervous System

The parasympathetic nervous system (diagramed at left) regulates day-to-day internal processes and behavior. The sympathetic nervous system (at right) regulates internal processes and behavior in stressful situations. On their way to and from the spinal cord, sympathetic nerve fibers make connections with specialized clusters of neurons called ganglia.

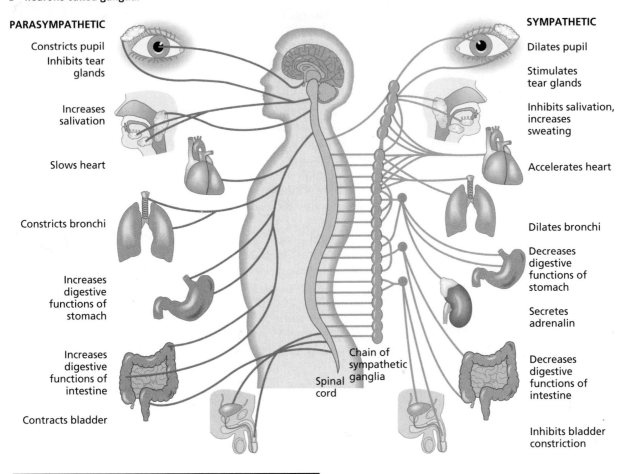

PARASYMPATHETIC

Constricts pupil
Inhibits tear glands

Increases salivation

Slows heart

Constricts bronchi

Increases digestive functions of stomach

Increases digestive functions of intestine

Contracts bladder

Chain of sympathetic ganglia

Spinal cord

SYMPATHETIC

Dilates pupil

Stimulates tear glands

Inhibits salivation, increases sweating

Accelerates heart

Dilates bronchi

Decreases digestive functions of stomach

Secretes adrenalin

Decreases digestive functions of intestine

Inhibits bladder constriction

---

arate duties of the sympathetic and parasympathetic nervous systems are illustrated in Figure 2.5.

THE NEURON: BUILDING BLOCK OF THE NERVOUS SYSTEM How does the nervous system permit us to sense and respond to the world outside our bodies? To answer this question, we will look at the structure and function of the neuron, the basic unit of the nervous system. The neuron is a cell specialized to receive, process, and transmit information to other cells. Neurons vary in shape, size, chemical composition, and function. Although over 200 types have been identified in mammal brains, all neurons have the same basic structure (see Figure 2.6).

We are born with more neurons than we ever use, and many die in the first few years of life. By adolescence, however, the number of neurons stabilizes, and, although the brain apparently generates some new neurons throughout our lifetime, the total remains essentially constant throughout adulthood (Barinaga, 1998a; Kempermann & Gage, 1999; Travis, 1998). This neural sta-

FIGURE 2.6: Major Structures of the Neuron

The neuron receives nerve impulses through its dendrites. These impulses are then transmitted through the cell body to the axon and to the terminal buttons, where neurotransmitters are released to stimulate other neurons.

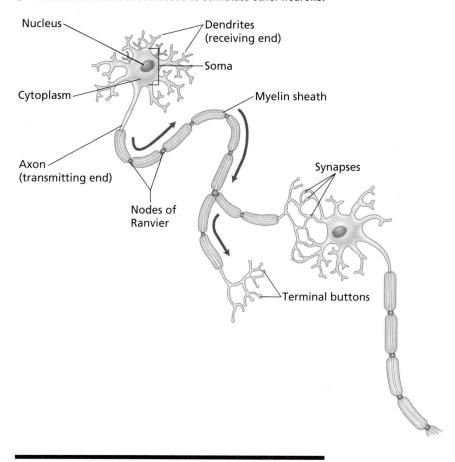

bility may be essential for the continuity of learning and memory over a long lifetime (Rakic, 1985). Surprisingly, however, human neurons do expire in astonishing numbers—about 200,000 will die every day of your life (Dowling, 1992). Fortunately, because we start out with so many neurons, we will lose less than 2% of our original supply in 70 years.

Types of Neurons Biopsychologists distinguish three major classes of neurons: *sensory neurons, motor neurons,* and *interneurons.* **Sensory neurons** transport messages from sense receptor cells toward the central nervous system. Receptor cells are highly specialized sensory neurons that are sensitive to light, sound, or other stimuli. By contrast, **motor neurons** deliver messages from the central nervous system to the muscles and glands.

Except in the simplest of reflexive circuits, sensory neurons do not communicate directly with motor neurons. Instead, they rely on the **interneurons** (shown in Figure 2.7) that make up most of the billions of cells in the brain and spinal cord. Interneurons relay messages from sensory neurons to other interneurons or to motor neurons. For every motor neuron in the body there are as many as 5,000 interneurons in the great intermediate network that forms the CNS's computational system (Nauta & Feirtag, 1979).

Sensory neurons: Nerve cells that carry messages from sense receptors toward the central nervous system.

Motor neurons: Nerve cells that carry messages away from the central nervous system toward the muscles and glands.

Interneurons: Nerve cells that relay messages from between nerve cells, especially in the brain and spinal cord.

FIGURE 2.7:   Sensory and Motor Neurons and the Pain Withdrawal Reflex

Sensory neurons carry information, such as this painful stimulus, from the sense organs to the central nervous system by means of *afferent neurons*. Although the message is relayed to the brain by *interneurons* in the spinal cord, a painful stimulus may set off a simple withdrawal reflex, carried out by *motor neurons*.

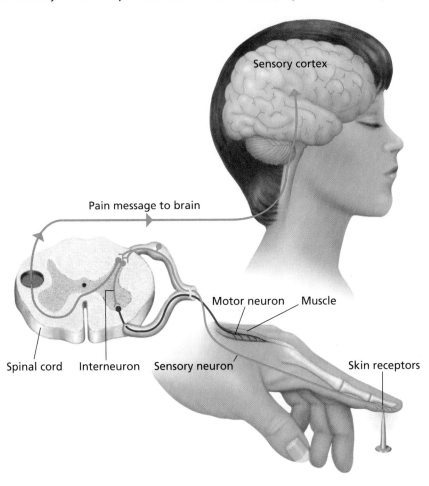

Sensory cortex

Pain message to brain

Motor neuron   Muscle

Spinal cord   Interneuron   Sensory neuron   Skin receptors

Dendrites: Branched fibers that extend outward from the main cell body and carry information into the neuron.

Cell body or soma: The part of a cell (such as a neuron) containing the nucleus, which includes the chromosomes.

Axon: In a nerve cell, an extended fiber that conducts information from the cell body to the terminal buttons. Information travels along the axon in the form of an electric charge.

Terminal buttons: Tiny bulblike structures at the end of the axon, which contain neurotransmitters that carry the neuron's message into the synapse.

The Structure of a Neuron   Neurons typically take in information at one end and send out messages from the other. The parts of the cell that usually receive incoming signals consist of branched fibers called **dendrites,** which extend outward from the cell body. The dendrites receive stimulation from other neurons or sense receptors. They are also modified as a result of learning (Barinaga, 2000; Kennedy, 2000). (A look at Figure 2.6 will help you visualize the parts of a neuron.) The **cell body,** or **soma,** contains the nucleus of the cell and the surrounding material that sustains its life. The soma of a neuron also integrates information about the stimulation received from the dendrites (or in some cases received directly from another neuron) and passes it on to a single, extended fiber, the **axon,** which carries the neural message onward. In the case of neurons connecting the spinal cord and the toes, the axon can be several feet long, while many of those in the brain may be only a tiny fraction of an inch in length. When the neural message arrives at the far end of an axon it opens tiny channels in the swollen, bulblike structures called **terminal buttons,** through which stimulation finally passes on to receptors in glands, muscles, or other neurons (Carlson, 2001).

Neurons generally pass information in only one direction: from the dendrites through the soma to the axon to the terminal buttons. You can see this illustrated by the arrows in Figure 2.6. Because of this one-way flow of information, separate nerve pathways are required to carry messages to and from each part of the body. The sensory and motor systems make up these separate one-way paths.

Interspersed among the brain's vast web of neurons are about five to ten times as many **glial cells.** The name comes from the Greek word for "glue," hinting at one of their major functions. The glia bind neurons to each other. They also seem to help neurons form new connections (Gallo & Chittajallu, 2001). In addition, glial cells form a **myelin sheath,** a fatty insulation around some types of axons, which interacts with the neuron to speed the conduction of internal impulses down the axon (see Figure 2.6). Certain diseases, such as multiple sclerosis, involve destruction of the myelin sheath, with disastrous consequences to neural communications.

The Neural Impulse   The nervous system employs both electrical and chemical signals to process and transmit information. Together these electrical and chemical signals make up a **neural impulse,** the nerve cell's message. Every thought, sensation, or feeling that you have rides through your brain in the form of neural impulses. All of your actions arise from neural impulses delivered to your muscles. In addition, the effects of psychoactive drugs, such as tranquilizers, antidepressants, and painkillers, result from alterations of neural impulses. Typically, a message traveling through the nervous system will involve many neurons sending impulses in synchronized patterns (Deadwyler & Hampson, 1995; Ferster & Spruston, 1995).

At the level of the single neuron, the neural impulse begins when a stimulus, such as a sound or a pinprick, sets off a chemical reaction that causes the cell to become electrically charged and then quickly discharged. As the impulse progresses down the axon, charged particles, called **ions,** are pumped across the cell membrane. This causes the interior of the axon to change from its negative charge, called the **resting potential,** to a positive state, called the **action potential.** When this happens, the cell is said to "fire." After firing, the ion pumping mechanism quickly restores the neuron to its resting potential, and the cell is ready to fire again. The whole cycle may take place in less than a hundredth of a second. But this is not the end of the matter, for the information carried by the action potential still has to traverse a tiny gap to another cell.

Because no two neurons ever touch, they are always separated by a microscopic gap at a junction called the **synapse.** Arrival of the neural impulse at the terminal buttons sets off a whole new process designed to get the neuron's message across the synaptic gap (or *synaptic cleft*). In a remarkable sequence of events known as **synaptic transmission,** information from the electrical impulse in the axon is converted into a chemical message that can traverse the synaptic space between neurons (see Figure 2.8). This occurs in the following way.

Neurotransmitters   At the terminal buttons, the neural impulse activates small chemical packets containing **neurotransmitters,** biochemical substances that stimulate or suppress other neurons. When activated, these packets rupture, spilling their contents—about 5,000 transmitter molecules—into the synaptic cleft (Kandel & Squire, 2000). There some of the neurotransmitters attach themselves to the receiving neuron at its *receptor site*. If the neurotransmitter inputs are sufficiently stimulating at the receptor sites, the receiving neuron will experience a change (either being excited into firing or inhibited from firing). In this fashion, the message carried by the electrical impulse within the neuron can be relayed chemically from cell to cell.

Connection

Chapter 3
Most psychoactive drugs either amplify or inhibit communication between nerve cells in the brain.

Glial cells: These cells bind the neurons together. Glial cells also provide an insulating covering (the myelin sheath) of the axon for some neurons, which facilitates the electrical impulse.

Myelin sheath: A fatty insulation coating some types of neural axons, which biochemically speeds the conduction of neural impulses.

Neural impulse: A brief electric surge generated by a nerve cell and carried down the length of the axon to the terminal buttons. The neural impulse (also called the *action potential*) carries the neuron's message.

Ions: Charged particles. The most important ions for synaptic transmission are sodium, calcium, and potassium.

Resting potential: The electrical charge of the axon in its inactive state, when the neuron is ready to "fire."

Action potential: The nerve impulse caused by a change in the electrical charge across the cell membrane of the axon. When the neuron "fires," this charge travels down the axon and causes neurotransmitters to be released by the terminal buttons.

Synapse: The microscopic gap that serves as a communications link between neurons. Synapses also occur between neurons and the muscles or glands they serve.

Synaptic transmission: The relaying of information across the synapse (from one neuron to another, for example) by means of chemical neurotransmitters.

Neurotransmitters: Chemical messengers that relay neural messages across the synapse. Many neurotransmitters are also hormones.

Michael J. Fox suffers from
Parkinson's disease, caused by a
deficiency of dopamine in his brain.

FIGURE 2.8: Synaptic Transmission

Firing in the presynaptic ("sending") neuron causes neurotransmitters to be
released into the synaptic gap. After crossing the gap, these substances stimulate
receptor molecules in the postsynaptic ("receiving") neuron. A single neuron may
contain many different neurotransmitters.

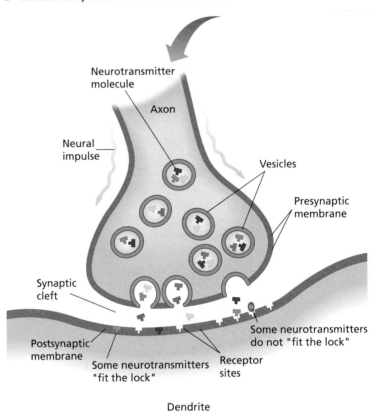

Plasticity: The ability of the
nervous system to adapt or
change as the result of
experience. Plasticity sometimes
can also help the nervous system
adapt to physical damage.

More than 60 hormonelike chemicals are known or suspected to function
as neurotransmitters in the brain. What is their practical importance for our
understanding of human thought and behavior? All nervous system activity
depends on synaptic transmission. And, as we will see, neurotransmitter
imbalances probably underlie certain mental disorders, such as schizophrenia
and depression. Moreover, treatment of these disorders may employ drugs
that act like certain neurotransmitters in order to target certain brain pathways.
Table 2.1 distinguishes seven neurotransmitters that researchers have identified as important in daily brain functioning.

Plasticity The ability of neurons to transmit messages accounts for simple reflexes and other "wired in" responses, but it also involves a much more
powerful process known as **plasticity.** That is, the nervous system—and especially the brain—has the ability to adapt or change as the result of experience
(Kandel & Squire, 2000). This is the process underlying learning and memory.
Plasticity accounts for all the knowledge we have acquired (and forgotten). It
also accounts for the ability for the brain to compensate for injury, as in a
stroke or head trauma, when another part of the brain may sometimes take
over the function of the injured region. Because of plasticity, the brain is constantly being "reprogrammed" by its experience—much as a computer undergoing an upgrade in its software.

Connection

Chapter 7
The study of memory
involves the fate of
learning over time.

Having completed our whirlwind tour of the nervous system, we now turn our attention to the body's other means of internal communication, the endocrine system. You will note that this system makes use of many of the same chemicals that neurons use for communication. In the case of the endocrine system, we call these chemicals *hormones*. (See Figure 2.9.)

The Endocrine System

Did you know that your blood carries *information,* along with oxygen and nutrients? It does so by serving as the information pathway for the endocrine system. The endocrine glands (which take their name from the Greek *endo* for "within" and *krinein* for "secrete") release hormones into the bloodstream, where they affect a wide array of bodily functions and behaviors. For example, hormones from the pituitary influence body growth; hormones from the ovaries and testes influence sexual development; hormones from the adrenals produce arousal; and hormones from the thyroid control metabolism (the body's rate of energy use). The endocrine glands don't operate independently, however. Their action is coordinated by hormones circulating in the bloodstream and by nerve impulses from the brain. Once secreted into the blood, hormones circulate throughout the body until delivered to their targets. Table 2.2 outlines the major glands and the body systems that they regulate.

Connection

Chapter 3
Psychoactive drugs often mimic neurotransmitters.

FIGURE 2.9: Endocrine Glands in Females and Males

The pituitary gland (shown at right) is the "master gland," regulating the endocrine glands, whose locations are illustrated at left. The pituitary gland is under the control of the hypothalamus, an important structure in the limbic system.

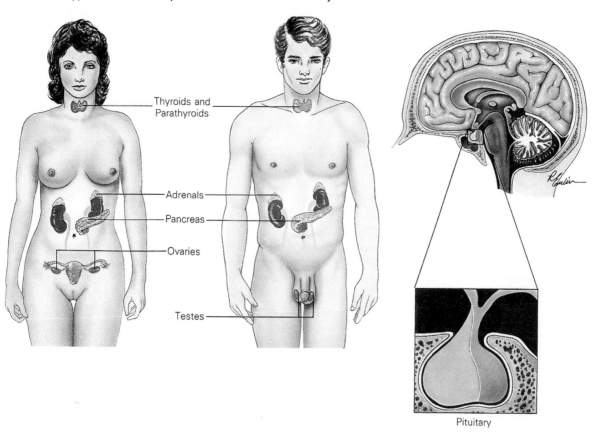

Thyroids and Parathyroids

Adrenals

Pancreas

Ovaries

Testes

Pituitary

			SUBSTANCES THAT AFFECT
NEURO-TRANSMITTER	NORMAL FUNCTION	PROBLEMS ASSOCIATED WITH IMBALANCE	THE ACTION OF THIS NEUROTRANSMITTER
Dopamine	Produces sensations of pleasure and reward Used by CNS neurons involved in voluntary movement	Schizophrenia Parkinson's disease	Cocaine Amphetamine Methylphenidate (Ritalin) Alcohol
Serotonin	Regulates sleep and dreaming, mood, pain, aggression, appetite, and sexual behavior	Depression Certain anxiety disorders Obsessive-compulsive disorder	Fluoxetine (Prozac) Hallucinogenics (e.g., LSD)
Norepinephrine	Used by neurons in autonomic nervous system and by neurons in almost every region of the brain Controls heart rate, sleep, stress, sexual responsiveness, vigilance, and appetite	High blood pressure Depression	Tricyclic antidepressants Beta blockers
Acetylcholine	The primary neurotransmitter used by neurons carrying messages from the CNS Also involved in some kinds of learning and memory	Certain muscular disorders Alzheimer's disease	Nicotine Black widow spider venom Botulism toxin Curare Atropine
GABA	The most prevalent *inhibitory* neurotransmitter in neurons of the CNS	Anxiety Epilepsy	Barbiturates "Minor" tranquilizers (e.g. Valium, Librium) Alcohol
Glutamate	The primary *excitatory* neurotransmitter in the CNS Involved in learning and memory	Release of excessive glutamate apparently causes brain damage after stroke	PCP ("angel dust")
Endorphins	Pleasurable sensations and control of pain	Lowered levels resulting from opiate addiction	Opiates: opium, heroin, morphine, methadone

TABLE 2.1 — *Seven Important Neurotransmitters*

Significantly, endocrine communication not only sustains our normal bodily processes, it also helps the sympathetic nervous system respond in crises. When you encounter a stressor or an emergency (such as a car coming at you), the hormone adrenaline is released into the bloodstream, energizing your body for quick defensive action — for "fight or flight." Your heart pounds, your muscles tense, and you feel impelled to take whatever action your brain tells you makes sense.

The brain and the endocrine system have an intimate relationship. A small brain structure known as the *hypothalamus,* lying near the center of the brain, directs activity in the endocrine system. Specialized cells in the hypothalamus receive messages from other brain cells commanding it to release a number of different chemicals. These chemicals then influence the adjacent **pituitary gland,** the so-called master gland, which can either stimulate or inhibit the release of other glands' hormones. The pituitary gland also releases a hormone that directly influences bodily growth and development.

Connection

Chapter 10
Hormones produce many of the effects of stress.

Pituitary gland: The master gland that produces hormones influencing the secretions of all other endocrine glands, as well as a hormone that influences growth. The pituitary is attached to the brain's hypothalamus, from which it takes its orders.

For only a dollar you can find out how long it takes for the brain to process information and initiate a response.

Hold a crisp dollar bill by the middle of the short side, so that it dangles downward. Have a friend put his or her thumb and index fingers on opposite sides and about an inch away from the center of the bill, as shown in the illustration. Instruct your friend to pinch the thumb and fingers together and attempt to catch the bill when you drop it.

If you drop the bill without warning (being careful not to signal your intentions), your friend's brain will not be able to process the information rapidly enough to get a response to the hand before the dollar bill has dropped safely away.

What does this demonstrate? The time it takes to respond reflects the time it takes for the sensory nervous system to take in the information, for the brain to process it, and for the motor system to produce a response. All of this involves millions of neurons, and even though they respond quickly, their responses do take time.

Do it yourself!

■ Neural Messages and Reaction Time

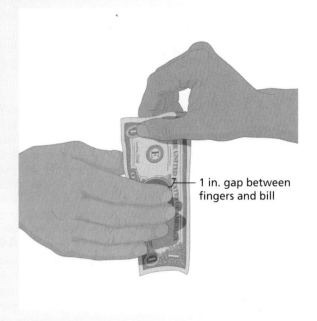

1 in. gap between fingers and bill

TABLE 2.2	Hormonal Functions of Major Endocrine Glands
THESE ENDOCRINE GLANDS . . .	**PRODUCE HORMONES THAT REGULATE . . .**
Anterior pituitary	Ovaries and testes Breast milk production Metabolism Reactions to stress
Posterior pituitary	Conservation of water in the body Breast milk secretion Uterus contractions
Thyroid	Metabolism Physical growth and development
Parathyroid	Calcium levels in the body
Pancreas	Glucose (sugar) metabolism
Adrenal glands	Fight-or-flight response Metabolism Sexual desire (especially in women)
Ovaries	Development of female sexual characteristics Production of ova (eggs)
Testes	Development of male sexual characteristics Sperm production Sexual desire (in men)

Psychology

In Your Life

Side Effects of Psychoactive Drugs

Many psychoactive **drugs** mimic the effects of neurotransmitters in the brain. Others act less directly by enhancing or inhibiting the effects of neurotransmitters. Those that enhance or mimic neurotransmitters are called **agonists.** (Nicotine, for example, is an agonist because it mimics the neurotransmitter acetylcholine.) By contrast, chemicals that *inhibit* the effects of neurotransmitters are known as **antagonists.** (Curare and botulism toxin are antagonists because they interfere with the neurotransmitter acetylcholine.) In general, agonists and antagonists facilitate or inhibit messages in certain parts of the brain.

The well-known antidepressant Prozac does its work as an agonist in the synapses of the brain's serotonin pathways, making more serotonin available (see Figure 2.10). Although Prozac (and related drugs with other brand names) is generally considered safe, undesirable symptoms occasionally occur in some people: anxiety, insomnia, changes in appetite, excitement (mania), seizures, and interference with cognitive performance (*Physician's Desk Reference,* 2001).

Why the unwanted side effects? A main reason involves the brain's design. Within the brain are many bundles of neurons—**neural pathways**—that connect regions having different functions. Each pathway employs only a few specific neurotransmitters. This fact allows drugs that affect or mimic certain transmitters to have a selective effect on brain pathways using those transmitters. Unfortunately for the drug-taking patient, several neural pathways may employ the same neurotransmitter for widely different functions. Thus, serotonin pathways, for example, affect not only mood but sleep, anxiety, and appetite. So, taking Prozac may treat depression but, at the same time, have side effects on other processes. This is the take-away lesson: No psychoactive drug exists that affects only one precise target in the brain.

FIGURE 2.10: Serotonin Pathways in the Brain

Each neurotransmitter is associated with certain neural pathways in the brain. In this cross section of the brain you see the main pathways for serotonin. Drugs that stimulate or inhibit serotonin will selectively affect the brain regions shown in this diagram.

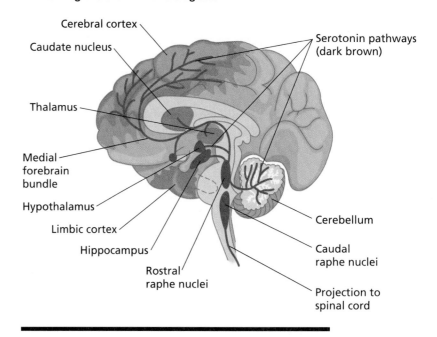

Cerebral cortex

Caudate nucleus

Serotonin pathways (dark brown)

Thalamus

Medial forebrain bundle

Hypothalamus

Limbic cortex

Hippocampus

Rostral raphe nuclei

Cerebellum

Caudal raphe nuclei

Projection to spinal cord

Psychoactive drugs: Chemicals that affect mental processes and behavior by their effects on neurons.

Agonists: Drugs or other chemicals that enhance or mimic the effects of neurotransmitters.

Antagonists: Drugs or chemicals that inhibit the effects of neurotransmitters.

Neural pathways: Bundles of nerve cells that follow generally the same route and employ the same neurotransmitter.

1. **RECALL:** *Of the body's two main communication systems, the _____ is faster, while the _____ sends longer-lasting messages.*

2. **RECALL:** *The _____ division of the autonomic nervous system increases the heart rate during an emergency, while the _____ division slows the heart rate after an emergency is over.*

3. **RECALL:** *Which of the following might carry a neural impulse across the synapse?*
   a. an electrical charge
   b. dopamine
   c. the blood
   d. the cerebrospinal fluid

4. **RECALL:** *Which part of the brain communicates directly with the endocrine system?*
   a. the cortex
   b. the brain stem
   c. the cerebellum
   d. the hypothalamus

5. **RECALL:** *Make a sketch of two connecting neurons. Describe the location and function of the*

dendrites, soma, axon, myelin sheath, terminal buttons, synapse.

6. **APPLICATION:** *Some people seem to have high blood pressure because they have an anxiety response while having their blood pressure taken at the doctor's office. Which part of the nervous system produces this anxiety response?*
   a. the somatic nervous system
   b. the sympathetic nervous system
   c. the parasympathetic nervous system
   d. the spinal cord

Core Concept

7. **UNDERSTANDING THE CORE CONCEPT:**
   The chemical messengers in the brain are called _____, while in the endocrine system they are called _____.

ANSWERS: 1. nervous system/endocrine system
2. sympathetic/parasympathetic   3. b   4. d
5. See Figure 2.6   6. b
7. neurotransmitters/hormones

HOW DOES THE BRAIN PRODUCE BEHAVIOR AND MENTAL PROCESSES?

Key Question

In September of 1848, a 25-year-old American railroad worker named Phineas Gage sustained a horrible head injury when a construction explosion blasted an iron rod up into his face and through his head. Amazingly, he recovered from this injury and lived another 12 years—but as a psychologically changed man (Macmillan, 2000). Those who knew him remarked that he had gone from being an efficient and capable manager to behaving in irresponsible, fitful, and even profane ways. In essence, he was no longer himself (Damasio et al., 1994). Had the site of his injury—the front and top of his brain—been the home of his "old self"?

Humans have probably always recognized the existence of a link between body and mind—although they didn't always know that the brain is the organ of the mind. Even today one might speak of "giving one's heart" to another when falling in love, or of "not having the stomach" for something when describing disgust. Today we know that love does not reside in the heart, nor courage in the digestive system. We now know that emotions, desires, and thoughts flow from the brain. Now, at last, neuroscientists are unraveling this complex neural knot, realizing that it evolved as distinct regions of tissue, each with a special function. This discovery becomes the Core Concept for this section of the chapter:

Connection

Chapter 11
Asian cultures often do not see a "self" as an independent part of the personality.

The brain is composed of many specialized and interconnected modules that work together to create mind and behavior.

As you study the brain in the following pages, you will find that its components have specialized functions that contribute to our psychological makeup. Some specialize in sensory processes, such as vision and hearing. Some parts of the brain influence our emotional lives. Some contribute to memory. And some generate speech and other behaviors. The point is that these specialized parts of the brain usually manage to work together. And they normally do so automatically and without conscious direction. But, when something goes wrong with one or more of the brain's components, as happens to victims of stroke or Alzheimer's disease — or as happened to Phineas Gage — disorders of thought or behavior result.

Let's begin our journey through the brain with a look at the tools neuroscientists use to glimpse the operations of these brain modules.

Windows on the Brain

What would you see if you could peer beneath the bony skull and behold the brain? Superficially, the gray-pinkish appearance of its surface gives no hint of the brain's internal structure or function. Much of what we know about its inner workings comes from disease and head injuries, as in the case of Phineas Gage. Unfortunate as they are, these problems offer the scientist an opportunity to make connections between the abilities lost by brain-injured patients and the site of damage.

We have also learned a great deal from mapping the brain's electrical activity. Using a device called the **electroencephalograph** (or **EEG**), researchers can — without opening the skull — record the patterns of electrical activity called **brain waves,** picked up by electrodes pasted on the scalp. The EEG reveals which areas of the brain are most active during a particular task. It also traces abnormal brain waves caused by brain malfunctions, such as **epilepsy,** a disorder that arises from an electrical "storm" in the brain, often accompanied by seizures.

In the mid-20th century, Canadian neurologist Wilder Penfield opened another window on the brain by mapping its wrinkled surface with an electric probe. During a surgical procedure sometimes used to treat epilepsy, Penfield stimulated patients' exposed brains with an electrode (a thin wire that conducts a mild electric current) and recorded their responses. (Patients were kept awake, but under local anesthesia, so they felt no pain.) His medical purpose was to localize the origin of the seizures and to avoid making surgical **lesions** in other areas vital to the patient's functioning. In the process, he showed that different parts of the brain's surface have different functions. Stimulating a certain region might cause a particular body movement or sensory experience. Stimulating other areas would provoke a specific emotion or even a memory (Penfield & Baldwin, 1952). Later, Walter Hess pioneered the use of electrical stimulation to probe structures deeper in the brain. Hess found that deeply placed electrodes stimulated elaborate sequences of behavior and emotional activity.

Modern advances in brain science have developed even more complex and subtle technologies known as **brain scans.** Many of these techniques rest on the assumption that increased activity by cells in specific parts of the brain will lead to increased blood flow or other biochemical processes in those locations (Posner, 1993). With complex, computer-aided machines that detect and

Electroencephalograph or **EEG:** A device for recording brain waves, typically by electrodes placed on the scalp. The record produced is known as an *electroencephalogram* (also called an *EEG*).

Brain waves: Patterns of electrical activity generated by the brain. The EEG records brain waves.

Epilepsy: A brain disorder that is often marked by seizures and loss of consciousness. Epilepsy is caused by out-of-control electrical activity in the brain.

Lesions: Tissue damage that results from disease or injury. To study the connection between brain and behavior, biopsychologists make precise lesions in the brains of experimental animals and observe the changes in the animals' behavior.

Phineas Gage became a different person after an iron bar blasted through his frontal lobes.

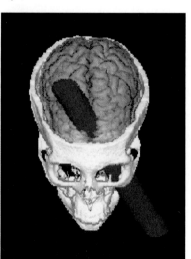

measure these brain events, scientists can study brain activity without needing to expose or physically invade the brain. Images from a brain scan show researchers how specific regions of the brain seem to "light up" when an individual performs certain activities, such as reading or speaking (Raichle, 1994). These methods also help neurosurgeons locate brain abnormalities such as tumors or stroke-related damage.

The most common brain-scanning methods currently used by researchers and clinicians are referred to as *CT scanning, PET scanning,* and *MRI* (Barinaga, 1997a; Mogilner et al., 1993):

▶ **CT scanning,** or **computerized tomography,** creates a computerized image of the brain from X rays passed through the brain at various angles. Tomography (from the Greek *tomos,* "section") detects the soft-tissue structures of the brain that normal X rays do not reveal (see Figure 2.11).

▶ **PET scanning,** or **positron emission tomography,** detects brain cell activity by tracking the movement of radioactive substances in active regions of the brain. PET scans rely on the detection of atomic particles called *positrons* that are emitted by a radioactive dye administered to the patient.

▶ **MRI,** or **magnetic resonance imaging,** relies on the fact that different types of tissue give different responses to powerful pulses of magnetic energy. An even newer technique called *functional magnetic resonance imaging (fMRI)* can distinguish more active tissues from less active ones (Alper, 1993; Collins, 2001). Thus, fMRI allows neuroscientists to determine which parts of the brain are most active during various mental activities.

Figure 2.11 displays the quality and detail possible with various brain scanning techniques. As you can see from the figure, each one provides a different "window" onto brain–mind connections.

Each scanning device also has its particular strengths and weaknesses. For example, PET is good at tracking the brain's activity, but not as good as MRI for distinguishing the fine details of brain structure. In addition, both PET and MRI techniques have difficulty scanning processes that occur at rates faster than hundreds of milliseconds. To track the very fast "conversations" brain cells are capable of conducting, the EEG is required, but it is limited in its detail and accuracy (Raichle, 1994). Currently, no single scanning technique gives biopsychologists the perfect "window" on the brain.

Three Layers of the Brain

Brain scanning shows that some cognitive functions (mental processes) are widely distributed among different brain areas, while other functions are highly localized, or specific to a particular location of brain tissue (Posner, 1993). The picture that emerges shows the brain as a single organ made up of many components collaborating to produce human thought and behavior, as the Core Concept for this section suggests. In our study of the brain, we will recreate this picture by first looking at the brain as a whole and later taking a close-up look at its parts. A good place to begin is with the brain image in Figure 2.12, noting how it is composed of different but interconnected layers of tissue and structures.

Many psychologists would distinguish three especially important layers that appeared in the evolutionary sequence leading to the human brain. These layers consist of paired structures stacked like stereo components. In the bottom layer, at the base of the brain, lie the *brain stem* and *cerebellum,* which

FIGURE 2.11: Windows on the Mind

Images from brain-scanning devices. From top: PET, MRI, EEG. Each scanning and recording device has strengths and weaknesses.

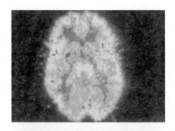

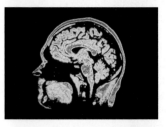

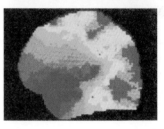

Brain scans: Recordings of the brain's electrical or biochemical activity at specific sites. Typically, the data are formed into visual images by computer. Common brain scanning devices include MRI, CT, and PET.

CT scanning or computerized tomography: A computerized imaging technique that uses X rays passed through the brain at various angles and then combined into an image.

PET scanning or **positron emission tomography:** An imaging technique that relies on the detection of radioactive sugar consumed by active brain cells.

MRI or **magnetic resonance imaging:** An imaging technique that relies on cells' responses in a high-intensity magnetic field.

FIGURE 2.12: Major Structures of the Brain

From an evolutionary perspective, the brain stem and cerebellum represent the oldest part of the brain; the limbic system evolved next; and the cerebral cortex is the most recent achievement in brain evolution.

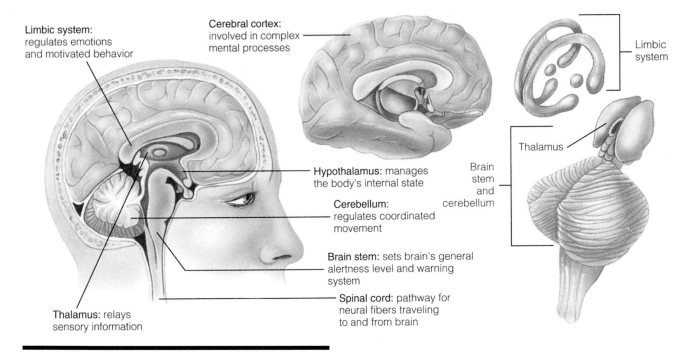

Limbic system: regulates emotions and motivated behavior

Cerebral cortex: involved in complex mental processes

Limbic system

Thalamus

Brain stem and cerebellum

Hypothalamus: manages the body's internal state

Cerebellum: regulates coordinated movement

Brain stem: sets brain's general alertness level and warning system

Spinal cord: pathway for neural fibers traveling to and from brain

Thalamus: relays sensory information

Brain stem: The most primitive of the brain's three major layers. It includes the medulla, pons, and the reticular activating system.

Medulla: A brain-stem region that controls breathing and heart rate. The sensory and motor pathways connecting the brain to the body cross in the medulla.

Pons: A brain-stem region that regulates brain activity during sleep and dreaming. *Pons* derives from the Latin word for "bridge."

Reticular activating system (RAS): A pencil-shaped structure in the brain stem, situated between the medulla and the pons. The RAS arouses the cortex to keep the brain alert and to attend to new stimulation.

drive our vital functions, such as heart rate, breathing, digestion, and motor coordination. The next layer, the *limbic system,* elaborates on these vital functions by adding emotions, complex motives, and increased memory abilities. And at the top is the *cerebrum.* The brain's outermost layer of cells, known as the *cerebral cortex,* enables reasoning, planning, creating, and problem solving. It is the crowning achievement of the human brain's brain evolution. Within this cerebral cortex, networks of nerve cells integrate sensory information, control precise movements of the mouth and hands, and produce abstract thinking and reasoning. Let us examine more closely the structure and function of each of these three important layers.

THE BRAIN STEM AND CEREBELLUM   If you have ever fought to stay awake in class, you have struggled with signals from the brain's most primitive layer, the **brain stem.** This part of the brain also contains modules that regulate the internal state of the body, plus many neural pathways that shuttle information between the brain and spinal cord (see Figure 2.13). Essentially the same equipment is found in the brain stems of all vertebrates (animals with backbones).

At the very top of the spinal cord you will note a slight bulge where the brain stem begins. This is the **medulla,** the region involved in regulating breathing and the beating of the heart. Significantly, nerve fibers connecting the brain and the body cross over at the medulla. Here the left side of the body makes a connection with the right side of the brain and the right side of the body links to the left side of the brain.

Directly above the medulla, the larger bulge of the **pons** regulates brain activity during sleep. Farther back, the **reticular activating system (RAS)** runs

FIGURE 2.13: The Brain Stem and Cerebellum

These structures in the central core of the brain are primarily involved with basic life processes: breathing, pulse, arousal, movement, balance, and early processing of sensory information.

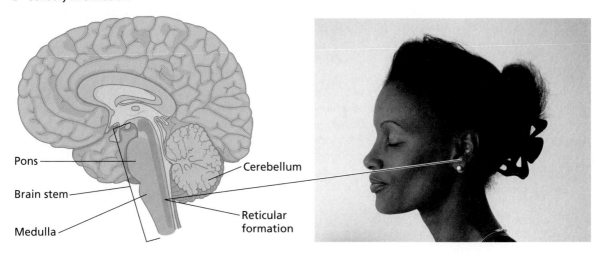

Pons

Brain stem

Medulla

Cerebellum

Reticular formation

the length of the brain stem. This dense network of cells serves as the brain's sentinel by alerting the brain and helping it attend to new stimulation and to stimulation previously tagged as important. Activity in this structure diminishes when you become drowsy.

Nerve fibers run from the reticular activating system both down to the spinal cord and up through a small football-shaped structure called the **thalamus,** perched atop the brain stem. Here, at the very center of the brain, the thalamus serves much the same function as the central processing chip in a computer by receiving sensory information and channeling it to appropriate processing centers. For example, the thalamus relays visual information from the eyes to the visual processing regions at the back of the brain. The thalamus also relays messages from the motor control centers back to organs and muscles. In addition, this structure may play an essential role in learning and in combining sensations, emotions, and memories into the experience of consciousness.

The other major structure lying at the brain's base is a neural knot known as the **cerebellum.** Attached to the brain stem at the rear of the skull, the twin lobes of the cerebellum coordinate movement, control posture, and maintain equilibrium (Wickelgren, 1998b). Your ability to walk, run, and dance reflects the functioning of the cerebellum. Recent research also implicates the cerebellum in an important type of learning, called classical conditioning, which involves learning to give reflexive responses to new cues—as when you begin salivating at the sound of the lunch bell (Raymond et al., 1996).

Taken together, the structures of the brain stem and cerebellum control the most basic functions of life. Note that much of their work is automatic and reflexive. That is, this part of the brain operates largely outside conscious awareness. The next two layers, however, have a heavier impact on our conscious states of mind.

THE LIMBIC SYSTEM All vertebrates have a brain stem and cerebellum, but only mammals and reptiles are equipped with the more recently evolved **limbic system.** (You can see it in Figures 2.12 and 2.14 as a structure that

Thalamus: The brain's central "relay station," situated just atop the brain stem. Nearly all the messages going into or out of the brain go through the thalamus.

Cerebellum: The "little brain" attached to the brain stem. The cerebellum is responsible for coordinated movements.

Limbic system: The middle layer of the brain, involved in emotion and memory. The limbic system includes the amygdala, the hippocampus, the hypothalamus, and other structures.

Connection

Chapter 3
How does the brain create consciousness?

Connection

Chapters 6 & 7
Classical conditioning links old responses to new stimuli.

Connection

Chapter 3
Reward circuits in the limbic system produce sensations of pleasure from certain psychoactive drugs.

Connection

Chapter 9
The limbic system is a collection of brain structures involved in both motivation and emotion.

wraps around the thalamus in the shape of a pair of ram's horns.) The limbic system is yet another collection of brain modules with a variety of functions. Some of its components produce motivated behaviors, such as eating and sexual activity, while some create memories for specific events. Other parts operate more quietly in the background to regulate body temperature, blood pressure, and blood-sugar level. In addition, the limbic system contains "reward circuits" that, when stimulated, produce sensations of pleasure. Because we tend to seek pleasure, these parts of the limbic system play a big part in determining which behaviors we choose.

It is the limbic system's role in emotion that may be its best-known feature. Here in the brain's middle layer lie the neural networks of fear, anger, ecstacy, and despair—the qualities that most clearly distinguish the human brain from the electronic network of a computer. Neuroscientists are just now discovering how these emotional capabilities coordinate with rational thought processes to help us focus attention and tag important memories.

FIGURE 2.14: The Limbic System

The structures of the limbic system are involved with motivation, emotion, and certain memory processes.

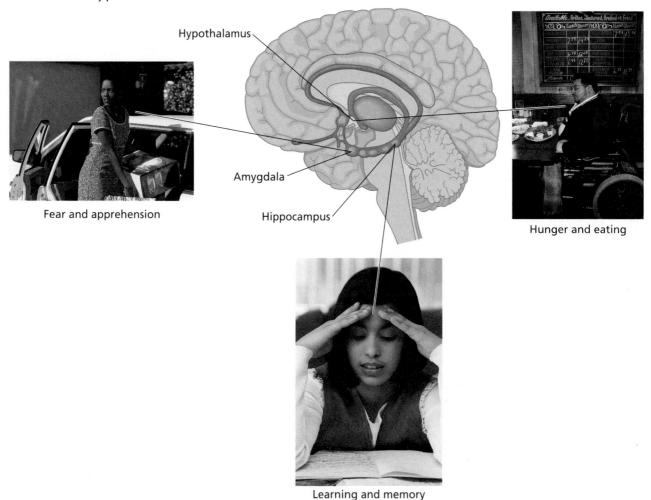

Fear and apprehension

Hypothalamus

Amygdala

Hippocampus

Hunger and eating

Learning and memory

The largest of the limbic system's structures, the **hippocampus** (see Figure 2.14), helps with memory (Galluscio, 1990). The hippocampus gets its name from the ancient Greek word for "seahorse," referring to this structure's distinctively curved ridges. Hippocampal damage impairs the ability to lay down permanent records of newly acquired information. Evidence for this comes mostly from clinical research, notably from studies of a patient referred to as H. M., perhaps psychology's most famous case study (Hilts, 1996). At age 27, H. M. underwent surgery intended to reduce the frequency and severity of his epileptic seizures. During the operation, most of the hippocampus was removed on both sides of his brain. As a result, H. M. can remember only events prior to his surgery: The events of the rest of his life disappear from memory almost as soon as they occur. Long after surgery, H. M. continues to believe he is living in 1953, the year the operation was performed. Similar effects of hippocampal damage occur in monkeys and other experimental animals whose brains contain this structure (Squire, 1992).

The **amygdala,** another part of the limbic system, is known best for its roles in fear, vigilance, and aggression (Whalen, 1998). It also participates in memory and certain basic motivations. Studies with several animal species, including humans, have shown that destroying parts of the amygdala has a calming effect on otherwise mean-spirited individuals, while electrically stimulating the amygdala can trigger aggressive behavior.

One of the smaller structures in the brain, the **hypothalamus** is also one of the most important. Composed of several bundles of nerve cells that continually monitor the blood, this limbic structure regulates a variety of emotional and motivated behaviors, including eating, drinking, temperature control, and sexual arousal. For example, when your body is running low on nutrients, the hypothalamus sends signals to prompt hunger and eating behavior. The hypothalamus also regulates the activities of the endocrine system and influences hormone production. In addition, it houses some of the brain's reward circuits, which generate the good feelings associated with gratifying the hunger, thirst, and sex drives. Because the hypothalamus controls both the arousal of motives and the mechanisms for signaling satisfaction of these motives, it regulates the body's internal balance or equilibrium, a process called **homeostasis.** In general, all the limbic system structures (including the hippocampus, amygdala, and hypothalamus) work together to maintain balance, both within the body and between the individual and the environment.

THE CEREBRUM Evolution has designed the human **cerebrum,** the bulbous cap covering the limbic system, as the seat of higher cognitive functioning. Accounting for two-thirds of the total mass of the human brain, the cerebrum is the major reason why our brains are larger than those of most other species (see Figure 2.15). Its thin outer layer forms the **cerebral cortex** (*cortex* comes from the Latin for "bark" or "shell"). One unique aspect of this structure is its wrinkled or convoluted formation, folding in on itself to enable the billions of cells in this "thinking tissue" to be squeezed into the small space inside the skull.

The two nearly symmetrical halves of the cerebrum, known as the **cerebral hemispheres,** each mediate different cognitive and emotional functions. The two hemispheres normally work in harmony because they are connected by a thick mass of nerve fibers, collectively referred to as the **corpus callosum,** which carries messages back and forth between the hemispheres (Banich, 1998). We will discuss the role of the corpus callosum and the distinct functions of the two hemispheres in more detail later in the chapter.

Connection

Chapters 6 & 7
The hippocampus is needed for making long-term memories of events.

Connection

Chapter 9
The hypothalamus controls several homeostatic drives, such as hunger and thirst, to maintain a balanced condition in the body.

Hippocampus: A component of the limbic system, involved in establishing long-term memories.

Amygdala: (a-MIG-da-la) A limbic system structure involved in memory and emotion, particularly fear and aggression.

Hypothalamus: A limbic structure that serves as the brain's blood-testing laboratory, constantly monitoring the blood to determine the condition of the body.

Homeostasis: The body's tendency to maintain a biologically balanced condition, especially with regard to nutrients, water, and temperature.

Cerebrum: The topmost layer of the brain; the bulbous cap over the limbic system. The cerebrum, particularly the cerebral *cortex,* accounts for most of our thinking and processing of information from our environment.

Cerebral cortex: The thin grey-matter covering of the cerebrum, consisting of a ¼-inch layer dense with cell bodies of neurons. The cerebral cortex carries on the major portion of our "higher" mental processing, including thinking and perceiving.

Cerebral hemispheres: The two walnut-shaped halves of the cerebrum, connected by the corpus callosum.

Corpus callosum: The band of nerve cells that connects the two cerebral hemispheres.

FIGURE 2.15: The Cerebral Cortex

Each of the two hemispheres of the cerebral cortex has four lobes. Different sensory and motor functions have been associated with specific parts of each lobe. The two hemispheres are connected by a thick bundle of fibers called the corpus callosum.

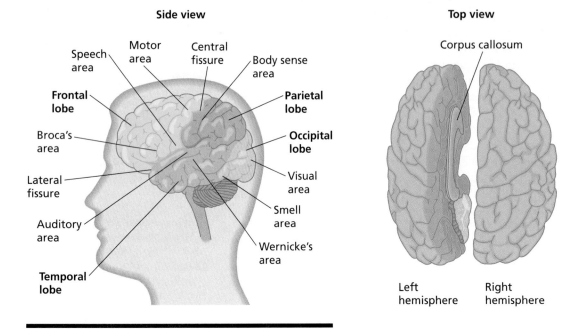

Side view

Speech area
Motor area
Central fissure
Body sense area
Frontal lobe
Parietal lobe
Broca's area
Occipital lobe
Lateral fissure
Visual area
Auditory area
Smell area
Wernicke's area
Temporal lobe

Top view

Corpus callosum

Left hemisphere
Right hemisphere

Central fissure: The prominent vertical groove in the cortex, separating the frontal from the parietal lobes in each hemisphere.

Lateral fissure: The prominent horizontal groove separating the frontal and temporal lobes in each hemisphere.

Frontal lobes: Regions at the front of the brain that are especially involved in movement and in thinking.

Motor cortex: A narrow vertical strip of cortex in the frontal lobes, just in front of the central fissure.

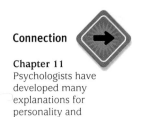

Connection

Chapter 11
Psychologists have developed many explanations for personality and temperament.

Four Lobes of the Cerebral Cortex

Neuroscientists have mapped the cortex of each hemisphere, using two important landmarks as their guides. On each side of the brain, a groove called the **central fissure** divides the cortex almost vertically near the center of each hemisphere. The **lateral fissure** divides the cortex in each hemisphere horizontally. You can see both of these landmarks in Figure 2.15. These vertical and horizontal divisions roughly define four anatomical regions, or lobes, containing structures that serve specific functions. (Note: Each hemisphere has four lobes.) We will now take a closer look at these cortical lobes.

THE FRONTAL LOBES Your choice of major, your plans for the summer, and your ability to answer test questions all depend on the part of your brain lying above the lateral fissure and in front of the central fissure. Here we find the **frontal lobes,** which regulate motor movement and cognitive activities such as planning, deciding, and pursuing goals (Shimamura, 1996). The biological foundations for personality and temperament reside here, too. We know this from accidents that damage the frontal lobes and produce devastating effects, as we saw earlier in the famous case of Phineas Gage.

A special strip of cortex, known as the **motor cortex,** can send messages that control the body's voluntary muscles. As you can see in Figure 2.16, the motor cortex contains an upside-down map of the body. One of its largest areas is devoted to the fingers (especially the thumb), reflecting the importance of manipulating objects. Another major area sends messages to the muscles of the face. In general, commands from the motor cortex on one side of the brain go to muscles on the opposite side of the body, as we saw in our opening vignette. There is, however, one important exception to this rule: The **motor speech area** lies in the left hemisphere in most people.

THE PARIETAL LOBES   If you sit on a tack, your **parietal lobes** will tell you. Located directly behind the central fissure toward the top of the head, these regions process certain incoming sensory information, especially touch and other skin senses. Located in the left and right parietal lobes, just behind the central fissure, the **somatosensory cortex** processes information about temperature, touch, body position, and pain (Helmuth, 2000; Graziano et al., 2000). It was this region that was affected by the tumor described in our opening vignette. You will notice in Figure 2.16 that certain parts of the body are disproportionately represented in the somatosensory cortex, particularly the lips, tongue, thumb, and index fingers—the parts of the body that provide the most

Motor speech area: A part of the left frontal lobe responsible for coordinating the muscles used in producing speech. It is often called Broca's area, after its discoverer.

Parietal lobes: Cortical lobes lying in the upper back of the brain and involved in touch sensation and in perceiving spatial relationships (the relationships of objects in space).

Somatosensory cortex: A strip of the parietal lobe lying just behind the central fissure. The somatosensory cortex is involved with sensations of touch.

 Connection

Chapter 5
The senses process stimulus information, which is passed on to the cortex in the form of nerve impulses.

FIGURE 2.16:   The Motor Cortex and the Somatosensory Cortex

Actions of the body's voluntary muscles are controlled by the motor cortex in the frontal lobe. The somatosensory cortex in the parietal lobe processes information about temperature, touch, body position, and pain. The diagram below shows the proportion of tissue devoted to various activities or sensitivities in each cortex.

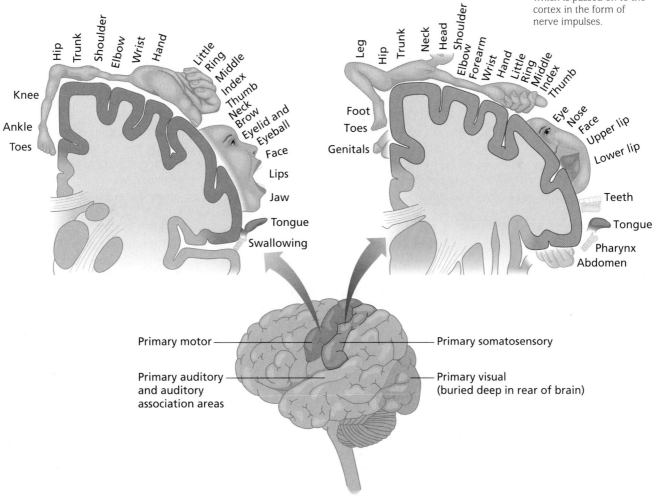

Connection

Chapter 5
Information about light and dark, color, shape, and movement is processed in separate areas of the visual cortex.

Connection

Chapter 5
The auditory cortex extracts information about the frequency and pitch of sound waves.

important input about touch. As with the motor cortex, the right half of the somatosensory cortex communicates with the left side of the body, and the left half with the right side of the body. Note the similarity between the motor cortex and the somatosensory cortex in Figure 2.16.

THE OCCIPITAL LOBES   You see the world with the back of your brain, where the **occipital lobes** serve as the destination for incoming visual information. There we find the **visual cortex,** which processes sensations from the eyes. Input from the center part of the retina at the back of the eye, the area that transmits the most detailed visual information, claims the greatest proportion of the visual cortex. Also within this region are highly specialized areas that process color, movement, shape, shading, and other aspects of visual stimulation, including a patch of cortex responsible solely for the recognition of human faces (Holden, 1997).

THE TEMPORAL LOBES   When the phone rings or a horn honks, it registers in your **temporal lobes,** on the lower side of each cerebral hemisphere. There lies the **auditory cortex,** responsible for processing sounds. In most people, a specialized part of the auditory cortex found on the left side of the brain processes speech sounds. Other parts of the temporal lobes may store long-term memories. This is not surprising, because the hippocampus, which we know to be involved in forming memories, lies directly beneath the temporal lobe.

Cortical Cooperation and the Responsive Brain

No single brain lobe functions in isolation. For example, when you do something as simple as answering a ringing telephone, you hear it in your temporal lobes, visually locate it in your occipital lobes, grasp and handle the receiver with the help of your parietal lobes, and engage in thoughtful conversation through processes in your frontal lobes. The brain's structures normally work in concert to perform all complex functions, although specific structures appear to be necessary for specific activities, such as vision, hearing, language, and memory.

Not all the cerebral cortex, however, is devoted to processing sensory information and commanding the muscles to action. In fact, the largest proportion of the human cortex (those areas that are not specifically labeled in Figures 2.15 and 2.16) has the task of integrating information from various other parts of the brain. Collectively, these regions, known as the **association cortex,** process such mental activities as planning and decision making. We humans have more of the cerebral cortex area devoted to the association cortex than do nonhuman species. Consequently we show much greater flexibility in our behavior. This human associative ability underlies much of our species' adaptive ability to learn, think, anticipate, and solve problems.

Here is a more subtle point: Because of its flexibility, the very structure of the brain can be changed by its interactions with the outside world (Baringa, 1996; Singer, 1995). For example, as a violin player gains expertise, the motor cortex reorganizes itself to devote a larger area to the fingers of the left hand (Juliano, 1998). Increased cortical representation also develops for the index finger used by a blind reader who learns to use Braille (Elbert et al., 1995; Le Doux, 1996). Usually these changes are adaptive, although accumulating evidence suggests that intensely traumatic experiences may also leave a biological imprint on the brain's ability to respond emotionally (Arnsten, 1998; Caldwell, 1995; Mukerjee, 1995). The brains of soldiers who experience com-

Occipital lobes: The cortical lobes at the back of the brain, containing the visual cortex.

Visual cortex: The visual processing areas of cortex in the occipital lobes.

Temporal lobes: Cortical lobes that process sounds, including speech. The temporal lobes are probably involved in storing long-term memories.

Auditory cortex: Portions of the temporal lobe involved in hearing.

Association cortex: Cortical regions that combine information from various other parts of the brain.

bat or women who have been raped may undergo physical changes that can produce a hair-trigger responsiveness. This tends to make them overreact to mild stressors and even to merely unexpected surprises. In general, such findings indicate that the brain is a dynamic system capable of changing both its functions and its physical structure in response to the environment (Sapolsky, 1990).

Connection

Chapter 10
Extremely threatening experiences can cause post-traumatic stress disorder.

Cerebral Dominance

At about the same time that Phineas Gage sustained his frontal-lobe injury, a French neurosurgeon, Paul Broca, was studying the brain's role in language. His research initially focused on a man whose name was derived from the only word he had been able to speak, "Tan." When Tan died, Broca performed an autopsy, which revealed severe damage in the left front portion of Tan's brain. This finding led to the study of the brains of similarly injured patients, where Broca discovered that damage to the same region resulted in similar language impairments. He concluded that language ability depended on the functioning of structures in a specific region of the brain's left frontal lobe (see Figure 2.15). Broca's work was one of the early hints that the two sides of the brain have different tasks. Subsequent work has confirmed and extended Broca's findings:

▶ Patients suffering brain damage that paralyzes the right side of their bodies often develop speech disturbances, suggesting that speech production is usually localized in the left hemisphere.
▶ Patients suffering damage to the left hemisphere often develop problems using and understanding language.
▶ The left hemisphere is usually slightly larger than the right one.

Although the two hemispheres appear to be near-mirror-images of each other, both clinical and experimental evidence indicate dissimilar styles of processing information. This tendency for each hemisphere to dominate the control of different functions is called **cerebral dominance.** Yet, despite the fact that some processes are more under the control of the right hemisphere and others are left-hemisphere dominant, the brain typically functions in an integrated and harmonious fashion.

Much of our knowledge about cerebral dominance comes from observing people, like Tan, who have suffered brain damage on one side of the brain or people whose cerebral hemispheres could not communicate with each other. Patients with right-hemisphere damage are more likely to have perception and attention problems, which can include serious difficulties in **spatial orientation.** For example, they may feel lost in a previously familiar place or be unable to assemble a simple jigsaw puzzle. By contrast, patients with left-hemisphere damage are more likely to have problems with language and logic.

Similarly, studies of both healthy and brain-damaged individuals have shown that the left side of the brain is more involved in controlling speech and other verbal tasks—although the right hemisphere has a role in language comprehension, especially the emotional tone of speech. The right side is more important in directing visual-spatial activities (see Beeman & Chiarello, 1998; Bradshaw, 1989; Bryden, 1982; Davidson, 1992a, b; Lempert & Kinsbourne, 1982; Posner & Raichle, 1994; Springer & Deutsch, 1993). However, the two hemispheres often make different contributions to the same task. That is, they seem to have different processing styles. For example, on matching tasks, the left hemisphere matches objects analytically and verbally—by similarity in

Cerebral dominance: The tendency of each brain hemisphere to exert control over different functions, such as language or perception of spatial relationships.

Spatial orientation: (SPAY-shul) The process of locating one's body or other objects in space.

Left hemisphere   Right hemisphere

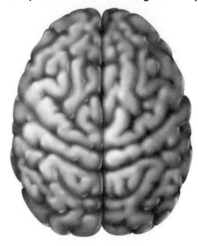

- Positive emotions

- Control of muscles used in speech

- Control of sequence of movements

- Spontaneous speaking and writing

- Memory for words and numbers

- Understanding speech and writing

- Negative emotions

- Responses to simple commands

- Repetitive but not spontaneous speaking

- Memory for shapes and music

- Interpreting spatial relationships and visual images

- Facial recognition

function. The right hemisphere matches things that look alike or fit together to form a visual pattern (Gazzaniga, 1970; Sperry, 1968, 1982). In general, the left hemisphere's processing style could be described as more analytic and sequential, while the right hemisphere interprets experience more holistically and spatially (Reuter-Lorenz & Miller, 1998). The right hemisphere also is more involved in processing emotions (Heller et al., 1998).

The differences between the two sides of the brain have captured popular interest in recent years, and many nonspecialists feel free to speculate whether someone is a "right-brain" or "left-brain" person. You should know, however, that such a distinction is simplistic and misleading. Research findings do not warrant categorizing people in this way. In reality, the differences between the two hemispheres do not outweigh their similarities. Both hemispheres are capable of either analytic (piece-by-piece) or holistic (as-a-whole) processing, and both use one mode or the other depending on the nature of the task (Trope et al., 1992). In their own ways, both hemispheres contribute to communication and memory functions, to perceptual–cognitive functions, and to emotional functions (see Figure 2.17). So, in most people, the hemispheres seem to complement rather than oppose each other.

There are some individuals, however, whose cerebral hemispheres do not work together—because they cannot. These are persons whose brains have been surgically "split." Let's see what their condition can tell us about specialization of the cerebral hemispheres.

The Split Brain

The fact that the two cerebral hemispheres have different processing styles raises an intriguing question: Would each half of the brain act as a different conscious mind if it were, somehow, separated from the other? The answer to this question comes from a rare treatment to relieve the symptoms of severe epilepsy. In this procedure, surgeons sever the *corpus callosum,* the bundle of nerve fibers (discussed earlier) that transfers information between the two hemispheres (Figure 2.18). The goal of the surgery is to prevent abnormal electrical rhythms from echoing between the hemispheres and developing into a

FIGURE 2.18: The Corpus Callosum

Only the corpus callosum is severed when the brain is "split." This medical procedure prevents communication between the cerebral hemispheres. Strangely, split-brain patients act like people with normal brains under most conditions. Special laboratory tests, however, reveal a duality of consciousness in the split brain.

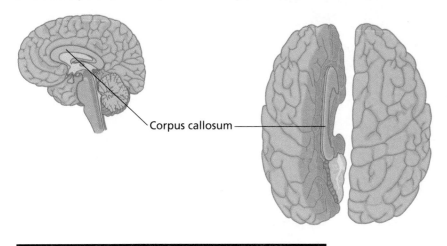

Corpus callosum —

full-blown seizure (Trope et al., 1992; Wilson et al., 1977). After the operation, not only do the seizures usually diminish but the patient's subsequent behavior appears surprisingly normal under all but the most unusual conditions. People who undergo this type of surgery are often referred to as **split-brain patients.**

Early studies comparing the two sides of the brain had focused not on hemispheric independence but on the way the brain combines information. For example, sensory input from each eye automatically divides into two streams and flows to the opposite sides of the brain (right visual field to left hemisphere; left field to right hemisphere), as you can see in Figure 2.19. Thanks to the connecting pathways through the corpus callosum, the information is shared by both hemispheres in the intact brain.

But in the split-brain patient this sharing of information across the corpus callosum can't happen. Surprisingly, however, under conditions outside the laboratory, they get along very well when they can get input from both visual fields into both sides of the brain. (They normally do this by scanning across the visual field with their eyes.) By this means, they can function in their daily lives without noticeable difficulty. But when they must perform special tasks that involve different information presented to each visual field or each hand, the behavior of split-brain patients differs from that of people whose hemispheres can communicate with each other.

This was shown in a series of clever experiments by Roger Sperry (1968) and Michael Gazzaniga (1970). To test the capabilities of the separated hemispheres, Sperry and Gazzaniga devised situations that allowed visual information to be presented separately to each hemisphere (see Figure 2.20). But before they could find out what each side of the brain knew, they had to solve a communication problem: Because the left hemisphere has far better language ability, it could talk to the researchers, but the right hemisphere could not. The solution to this problem involved giving the right hemisphere manual tasks involving identification, matching, or assembly of objects—tasks that did not require the use of words. Once this communication mode was discovered,

Split-brain patients: Individuals who have had the corpus callosum surgically severed, usually as a treatment for severe epilepsy.

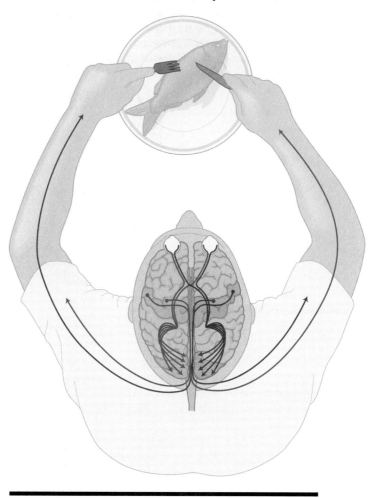

Connection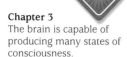

Chapter 3
The brain is capable of producing many states of consciousness.

Duality of consciousness: The condition in which a split-brain patient has a separate consciousness in each hemisphere. The intact brain does not exhibit this duality of consciousness.

the right hemisphere turned out to be better than the left at solving problems involving spatial relationships and pattern recognition (Gazzaniga, 1995).

Because the brain is designed to function as a whole, the result of disconnecting the cerebral hemispheres is a striking **duality of consciousness.** In the split-brain patient, each hemisphere responds independently and simultaneously when stimuli are presented separately to each side. When stimuli are presented to only one side (as in Figure 2.20), responses tend to be more emotional or more analytic, depending on which hemisphere has the task of interpreting the message.

We must be cautious about generalizing such findings from split-brain patients to conclusions about the way a normal brain functions. Does it use a central command system, or is it organized with specialized and independent functions for each hemisphere? Gazzaniga (1998a, b) proposes that the human mind is neither a single entity nor a dual entity but rather a confederation of multiple mind-modules, each one specialized to process a specific kind of information. The input from these many separate "miniminds" is synthesized and

Eye-Hand Coordination in Split-Brain Subjects

When a split-brain patient uses the left hand to find a match to an object appearing in the left visual field, eye-hand coordination is normal, because both are registered in the right hemisphere (left figure). But when asked to use the right hand to match an object seen in the left visual field, the patient cannot perform the task and mismatches a pear with a cup (right figure). This is because sensations from the right hand go to the left hemisphere, and there is no longer a connection between the two hemispheres.

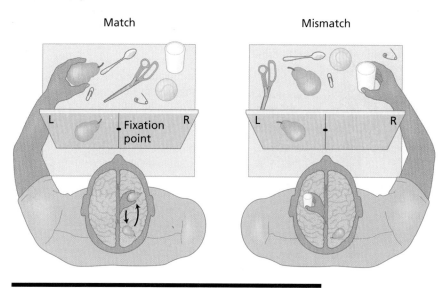

coordinated for action by central, executive processors (Fodor, 1983; Hinton & Anderson, 1981; Ornstein, 1986a). Thus, we come full circle to a Core Concept that we encountered earlier in the chapter: *The brain is composed of many specialized modules that work together to create mind and behavior* (Baynes et al., 1998; Strauss, 1998).

Brain Damage & Behavior

Psychology

In Your Life

Nearly everybody knows someone who has suffered brain damage from an accident, a stroke, or a tumor—such as was described in our opening vignette. Your new knowledge of the brain and behavior will help you understand the problems such people must face. And if you know what abilities have been lost or altered, you can usually make a good guess as to which part of the brain sustained the damage—especially if you bear in mind two simple principles:

▶ Each side of the brain communicates with the opposite side of the body. Thus, if symptoms appear on one side of the body, it is likely that the other side of the brain was damaged. (See Figure 2.21.)
▶ For most people, speech is mainly a left-hemisphere function.

Now use your knowledge of the brain to guess where the damage probably occurred in the brains of these individuals:

1. Edna had a **stroke** (an interruption of blood supply to a part of the brain) and lost her ability to speak (although she could still understand speech). Where did the stroke most likely affect her brain?
2. Theo was in an auto accident, which left him with jerky, unco-

FIGURE 2.21: Effects of Damage to the Cerebral Hemispheres

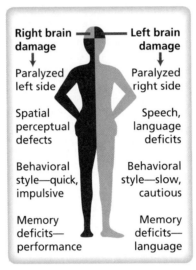

Right brain damage
↓
Paralyzed left side

Spatial perceptual defects

Behavioral style—quick, impulsive

Memory deficits—performance

Left brain damage
↓
Paralyzed right side

Speech, language deficits

Behavioral style—slow, cautious

Memory deficits—language

ordinated movements. Brain scans revealed no damage to his cerebral cortex.
3. Just prior to her seizures, Lydia has a strange sensation (an "aura") that feels like pinpricks on her left leg. What part of her brain generates this sensation?

What is the outlook for people such as these? Depending on her age, physical condition, the extent of the stroke, and how quickly she received medical attention, Edna may get some or all of her speech back. Even if Broca's area in her left frontal lobe has been permanently damaged, other parts of her brain

may be able to take over some of the lost function. Neuroscientists call this the *plasticity* of the brain. Long-term therapy for Edna will emphasize speech therapy.

Theo may also regain some or all of his abilities, especially if the affected neural cells in his cerebellum were merely injured but not severed or destroyed in the accident. Long-term treatment for him will involve physical therapy. Both Edna and Theo may also need psychological therapy to help them cope with any permanent loss of function.

Lydia has epilepsy, originating in her right somatosensory cortex. Like most people with epilepsy, she will probably receive significant help from antiseizure medications. The chances are good that she will be completely symptom free when the drugs are properly adjusted.

A take-away message from all of these cases is that people who suffer from brain damage can often receive significant help. Note, too, that help may come in many forms, both physical and mental. Perhaps the most important long-term therapy, however, is social support—a good thing to remember if you know someone who has sustained brain damage. *(See Chapter 10, Stress, Health, and Well-Being.)*

Stroke: An interruption of blood supply to a part of the brain.

CHECK YOUR UNDERSTANDING

1. **RECALL:** *Which technique for studying the brain relies on the brain's electrical activity?*
   a. EEG
   b. MRI
   c. PET
   d. CT

2. **RECALL:** *Name the three main layers in the human brain:* _____, _____, *and* _____.

3. **RECALL:** *Make a sketch showing the four lobes of the cerebral cortex. Indicate the main functions of each lobe. Which hemisphere of the brain controls language in most people? Which hemisphere of your brain controls your left hand?*

4. **APPLICATION:** *A brain tumor in the limbic system is most likely to produce changes in a person's*
   a. coordination.
   b. vision.
   c. sleep patterns.
   d. emotions.

5. **RECALL:** *In most people, speech is controlled by the brain's*
   a. left hemisphere.
   b. right hemisphere.
   c. corpus callosum.
   d. occipital lobe.

6. **RECALL:** *In the split-brain operation, what part of the brain is split?*
   a. the left hemisphere
   b. the right hemisphere
   c. the corpus callosum
   d. the occipital lobe

7. **ANALYSIS:** *The split-brain patient in Figure 2.20 has trouble using the _____ hand to select the object flashed on the left side of the screen.*
   a. right
   b. left
   (Hints: Which hemisphere controls each hand? Which hemisphere processes information from the left side of the visual field?)

8. **RECALL:** *Unlike the split-brain patient, we do not have two separate consciousnesses because the two hemispheres communicate through*
   a. the brain stem.
   b. the hypothalamus.
   c. the hippocampus.
   d. the corpus callosum.

9. **UNDERSTANDING THE CORE CONCEPT:**
   The brain is composed of many specialized and interconnected modules that work together to create mind and behavior. Can you name at least two specialized parts of the brain that are known to work together? What is the result of the collaboration of the structures you have named?

ANSWERS: 1. a   2. the brain stem and cerebellum, the limbic system, the cerebrum 3. See the location of the four lobes in Figure 2.15. The left hemisphere controls language, and the right hemisphere controls your left hand.
4. d   5. a   6. c   7. a   8. d   9. Examples include the interaction of regions in the four lobes of the cerebral cortex when answering the phone. There are many other examples mentioned in this section.

Core Concept

Using Psychology to Learn Psychology: Putting Your Knowledge of the Brain to Work

The old idea that we use only 10% of our brains is bunk. Every part of the brain gets used every day—but not necessarily for intellectual purposes. We now know that much of the brain merely controls basic biological functions. This tells us that using more of our brains is *not* a route to increased brain power.

So, have neuroscientists found anything that you can use to improve your memory for the concepts you are learning in your classes? Among their most important discoveries is the revelation that many different regions of the cerebral cortex are involved in learning and memory (Kandel & Squire, 2000). Accordingly, if you can bring more of this cerebral circuitry to bear on your studies (about biopsychology, for example), your brain will lay down a wider web of memories.

To be more specific, reading the material in this book will help you form verbal memories, parts of which involve circuits in the temporal cortex. Taking notes brings the motor cortex of the frontal lobes into play, adding a "motor memory" component to your study. Scanning the accompanying photos, charts, and drawings adds visual and spatial memory components in the occipital and parietal lobes. Listening actively to your professor's lectures and discussing the material with a study partner will engage the auditory regions of the temporal cortex and lay down still other memory traces. Finally, study time spent anticipating what questions will appear on the exam will involve regions of the frontal lobes in your learning process.

In general, the more ways that you can deal with the material—the more sensory and motor channels you can employ—the more memory components you will build in your brain's circuitry. As a result, when you need to remember the material, you will have more possible ways of accessing what you have learned. So, put your knowledge of your brain to work in your studying!

Chapter Summary

HOW ARE GENES AND BEHAVIOR LINKED?

Charles Darwin's theory of evolution explains behavior as the result of natural selection. Variation among individuals and competition for resources lead to survival of the most adaptive behavior, as well as the fittest features. This principle accounts for much of our own behavior. In particular, encephalization and language have given humans a distinct evolutionary advantage and promoted the development of human cultures.

Behavior consistently found in a species is likely to have a genetic basis that evolved because the behavior has been adaptive.

HOW DOES THE BODY COMMUNICATE INTERNALLY?

The body's two communication systems are the nervous system and the endocrine system. The nervous system is composed of neurons organized into central and peripheral nervous systems. Each of these is further subdivided for different behavioral and bodily functions. The basic unit of the nervous system is the neuron, which fires when it is stimulated, causing neurotransmitters to be released. These neurotransmitters relay the impulse to other nerve cells throughout the system. The slower endocrine system secretes hormones into the bloodstream, influencing the activity of other glands and bodily structures.

Core Concept

The body's two communications systems, the nervous system and the endocrine system, both use chemical messengers to communicate with targets throughout the body.

Key Question

HOW DOES THE BRAIN PRODUCE BEHAVIOR AND MENTAL PROCESSES?

Early medicine learned about the brain from the study of brain injuries. Later, studies of brain lesions helped to determine more precise brain localization. Recently, electrical stimulation and recording of brain activity have led to brain-scanning techniques that produce images that can reveal both brain structures and mental activity.

We now know that the brain is organized in three integrated layers—the brain stem and cerebellum, the limbic system, and the cerebral cortex—each with distinct functions. Within each of these layers the brain contains many specialized modules, each performing a specific function automatically and without conscious direction.

Different regions of the brain—notably the cerebral cortex—perform different and highly specialized tasks. Language, analytical thinking, and positive emotions are regulated by specific parts of the left hemisphere, while cortical centers in the right hemisphere control spatial interpretation, visual and musical memory, and negative emotions. If the hemispheres are surgically severed, each functions independently of the other and is not directly aware of stimulation or cognitive activities that affect the other.

Core Concept

The brain is composed of many specialized and interconnected modules that work together to create mind and behavior.

Review
Test

For each of the following items, choose the single best answer. The correct answers appear at the end.

1. According to Darwin's theory of *natural selection,*
   a. the environment chooses organisms that are more complex and more advanced.
   b. some members of a species produce more offspring that survive and reproduce because the environment favors their inheritable characteristics.
   c. giraffes evolved longer necks because they were constantly reaching for the tender, higher leaves in the tall trees in their environment.
   d. evolution is a process whereby experience modifies an organism's genes.

2. Evolution takes advantage of adaptive _____ that aid survival and reproduction of the individual.
   a. mutations
   b. environments
   c. thoughts
   d. diseases

3. Which one of the following is an example of behavior controlled primarily by the autonomic nervous system?
   a. typing a sentence accurately on a keyboard
   b. solving a mathematical problem
   c. breathing and swallowing while asleep
   d. feeling hungry

4. During a neural impulse, a neuron "fires" when
   a. it is physically contacted by another cell that is transmitting the signal.
   b. an electric charge travels down the axon.
   c. it contracts and releases powerful chemicals directly into the bloodstream.
   d. signals entering at the axon travel the length of the cell and exit through the dendrites.

5. Neurotransmitters are released by the terminal buttons into the _____, and hormones are released by the endocrine system into the _____.
   a. sympathetic nervous system/parasympathetic nervous system
   b. cortex/brain stem

   c. left hemisphere/right hemisphere
   d. synaptic cleft/bloodstream

6. Which form of brain scanning employs radioactive tracers to reveal the most active regions of the brain?
   a. EEG
   b. CT
   c. PET
   d. MRI

7. Which of the three brain layers is often thought of as the "emotional brain"?
   a. the brain stem and cerebellum
   b. the limbic system
   c. the autonomic nervous system
   d. the cerebrum

8. What part of the cerebral cortex is most involved with initiating and controlling body movements?
   a. the frontal lobes
   b. the hippocampus

   c. the temporal lobes
   d. the occipital lobes

9. Which of the following statements identifying the locations of important brain structures is true?
   a. The hypothalamus is part of the brain stem.
   b. The medulla is part of the limbic system.
   c. The occipital lobe is part of the cerebral cortex.
   d. All of the above.

10. The left hemisphere of the cerebral cortex is more involved than the right hemisphere in experiences such as
   a. recognizing and appreciating visual stimuli.
   b. enjoying and appreciating music.
   c. using spoken and written language.
   d. understanding spatial relationships.

ANSWERS: 1. b   2. a   3. c   4. b   5. d   6. c
7. b   8. a   9. c   10. c

If You're Interested . . .

BOOKS

Amen, D. G. (1999). *Change your brain, change your life.* Random House. Frustrated by some patients who seem resistant to treatment, a psychiatrist using the brain-imaging technique concludes that brain dysfunction, not refusal to change, traps people in unhappy patterns of thought and behavior.

Edelman, G. M. (1992). *Bright air, brilliant fire: On the matter of the mind.* New York: Basic Books. A Nobel Prize–winning immunologist accounts how the brain is "designed" not to mirror reality but to produce a mind that constructs consciousness.

Gazzaniga, M. (2000). *The mind's past.* University of California Press. A noted brain scientist examines the brain's evolution, memory of self, and the nature of consciousness.

Hilts, P. J. (1996). *Memory's ghost: The strange tale of Mr. M. and the nature of memory.* Touchstone. This author describes meeting the famous subject of memory research, whose unusual brain injury left him unable to form new memories.

Kosslyn, S. M., & Koenig, O. (1995). *Wet mind: The new cognitive neuroscience.* Free Press. The mind is less like a computer and more like other physical functions of the body, once its many processes are

appreciated and analyzed like other biological "wetware."

LeDoux, J. (1996). *The emotional brain: The mysterious underpinnings of emotional life.* Touchstone. A well-illustrated and reader-friendly book reviews some of the most complex questions about the human brain: Where do feelings come from, how are they controlled, and in what ways are our feelings distinctly human?

Ray, S. (1998). *5-HTP: Nature's serotonin solution.* Avery Publishing Group. The neurotransmitter serotonin affects a broad range of powerful mental and physical functions, including depression, weight loss, anxiety, and insomnia, whose effects can be understood and treated through a better appreciation of this amazing substance.

Reeve, C. (1999). *Still Me.* Ballantine Books. The author, an actor rendered quadriplegic by an accident, recounts what is changed, the same, and even better since his injury.

Schacter, D. L. (1997). *Searching for memory: The brain, the mind, and the past.* HarperCollins. This work includes brain scans, word games, and how the brain's memory processing makes you the individual you are.

VIDEOS

Awakenings. (1990, color, 121 min.). Directed by Penny Marshall; starring Robin Williams, Robert DeNiro, Julie Kavner. Based on Oliver Sacks' collection of the same title, this is the story of patients suffering from a mysterious "sleeping sickness" whose lives are transformed by a synthetic form of the neurotransmitter dopamine.

My Left Foot. (1989, color, 103 min.). Directed by James Sheridan; starring Daniel Day-Lewis, Brenda Fricker, Ray McAnally, Fiona Shaw. This powerful and wonderful film, featuring Oscar-winning performances, is based on the true story of Christy Brown, an Irish artist-writer born with cerebral palsy and confined lifelong to a wheelchair.

Phenomenon. (1996, color, 124 min.). Directed by Jon Turteltaub; starring John Travolta, Kyra Sedgwick, Forest Whitaker, Robert Duvall, Brent Spiner. This is the touching story of how an ordinary man achieves supernormal brain development and intellectual feats—a blessing that may be a curse.

Regarding Henry. (1991, color, 107 min.). Directed by Mike Nichols; starring Harrison Ford, Annette Bening, Bill Nunn, John Leguizamo. A cold-hearted lawyer, shot in the head during a store holdup, undergoes a change of personality in the course of his rehabilitation. The film provides an intriguing view of how the brain might influence personality as well as intellectual function.

KEY QUESTION		PSYCHOLOGY IN
CHAPTER OUTLINE	CORE CONCEPT	YOUR LIFE

WHAT IS THE NATURE OF CONSCIOUSNESS?

Tools for Studying Consciousness
The Functions and Structures of Consciousness

The brain creates consciousness when it combines external stimulation with internal experience.

YOUR UNCONSCIOUS — RECONSIDERED:

An empirical look suggests a simpler unconscious than the one portrayed by Sigmund Freud.

WHAT ARE THE CYCLES OF EVERYDAY CONSCIOUSNESS?

Daydreaming
Sleep and Dreaming

Consciousness changes in cycles that normally correspond to our biological rhythms and to the patterns of our environment.

SLEEP DISORDERS:

Insomnia, sleep apnea, narcolepsy, and daytime sleepiness can be hazardous to your health — and perhaps even to your life.

WHAT OTHER FORMS CAN CONSCIOUSNESS TAKE?

Hypnosis
Meditation
Psychoactive Drug States

An altered state of consciousness occurs when some aspect of normal consciousness is modified by mental, behavioral, or chemical means.

DEPENDENCE AND ADDICTION:

Psychoactive drugs alter brain chemistry, and they can produce physical or psychological addiction. But is addiction a disease or a character flaw?

USING PSYCHOLOGY TO LEARN PSYCHOLOGY: Connecting Consciousness with Memory

STATES OF MIND

One rainy Swiss summer in the early 19th century, Mary Wollstonecraft Shelley, an 18-year-old bride, and her husband, British poet Percy Bysshe Shelley, were challenged by their friend Lord Byron to write a ghost story. After several days of focused thought and futile effort, Mary Shelley thought she would not be able to complete her assignment. Yet, one night, she woke with ghastly images in her head:

> My imagination, unbidden, possessed and guided me . . . I saw the pale student of unhallowed arts kneeling beside the thing he had put together. I saw the hideous phantasm of a man stretched out, and then . . . show signs of life, and stir with an uneasy, half vital motion . . . [The creator] would rush away from his odious handiwork, horror-stricken.

Early the next day she penned the words: "It was on a dreary night of November . . ." (Shelley, 1831, p. x). Thus began her stunning "ghost story," *Frankenstein, or The Modern Prometheus.*

Dreams as inspiration have been a revered source of knowledge from ancient times, as seen in the Old Testament story of the Israelite Joseph, who interpreted Pharaoh's dreams of fat and lean cattle as predicting first the years of plenty, and then of famine, that lay in store for the Egyptian kingdom (Genesis, 41:i–vii).

Authors, artists, and even scientists have attributed their works to the inspiration of dreams. English poet Samuel Taylor Coleridge attributed the poetic

(continued)

imagery of his 1797 poem "Kubla Khan" to a dream (possibly drug-induced) that he experienced after reading a biography of the famed Mongol warrior. Likewise, painters such as surrealist Salvador Dali have found their dreams to be vivid sources of imagery. Composers as varied as Mozart, Beethoven, the Beatles, and Sting have all credited their dreams with inspiring certain works. In the scientific world, chemist August Kekule's discovery that the benzene molecule has a hexagonal ring-shaped structure was inspired by his dream of a snake rolled into a loop, grasping its own tail tucked in its mouth. Even modern-day horror writer Stephen King claims to have harvested story ideas from his own childhood nightmares.

Can you stimulate your own dreams to help inspire your life and work? Dream "explorer" Robert Moss (1996) cites the work of the 19th-century physicist Herman Heimholtz, who insisted that creative dreaming might result from three practices: (1) *saturating* yourself in your field or topic; (2) letting your creative ideas *incubate* by doing something that is relaxing but not completely distracting; and (3) allowing yourself to experience *illumination,* a sudden flash of insight into the answer you seek.

Moss himself recommends the following technique to find creative guidance in your dreams: First, imagine an admired expert in your field of endeavor. Before you go to sleep, imagine you are asking this person for help in solving your problem; then tell yourself to dream the answer. If you wake from a dream, quickly write or sketch all you can recall. Later, when you review your notes, you may find that your approach to the problem has been "given a distinct tilt" (Moss, 1996, p. 318). Your dreaming thoughts might surprise you with insights you didn't even know you could achieve, just as Mary Wollstonecraft Shelley's nightmare led her to create her infamous horror story.

Perhaps the most dramatic change to our everyday consciousness occurs each night during sleep, when consciousness seems to vanish, only to reemerge later in the bizarre world of dreams. But no matter what form it takes, consciousness always seems to swirl around the center of our being, carrying with it everything we will remember about ourselves and our world.

WHAT IS THE NATURE OF CONSCIOUSNESS?

We can define **consciousness** as our awareness of internal and external stimulation. Thus, consciousness is the brain's model of our experience. But exactly how the brain creates this awareness is, perhaps, psychology's greatest mystery. To understand the mystery, we invite you to try a "thought experiment." Relax. Get comfortable. Now reflect on the contents and limitations of your conscious experience. What does it contain? And what does it exclude?

You will probably notice a mixture of events happening around you is combined with your feelings, desires, and memories. But did it occur to you that much of your brain activity (coordination of eye movements as you read this sentence, for example) takes place outside awareness? Likewise, your head is filled with information that is not caught up in consciousness—but could be, if you pulled it out of memory (the multiplication tables or the events of last night, for example).

Consciousness: The brain's awareness of internal and external stimulation.

Folk wisdom assigns consciousness to an *anima,* a soul or inner life force. A variation on this theme suggests that evil spirits or devils sometimes take over consciousness and cause bizarre behavior. Sigmund Freud's view represents another variant of the anima hypothesis: He put the *ego*—the rational decision-maker part of the mind—at the center of consciousness. There, said Freud, it attempts to keep the powerful forces of the unconscious in check. But was Freud right? While most psychologists today would say that his views were better as metaphors than as science, his ideas are still widely accepted by the general public.

Science first turned its spotlight on consciousness when the structuralists attempted to dissect conscious experience in their laboratories during the late 1800s and early 1900s. Using a simple technique called introspection, subjects were asked to look inside themselves at their own consciousness—much as you did a moment ago. The biggest problem was objectivity. Most psychologists eventually decided that an objective science could not study something so subjective and personal as consciousness.

Finally, early in the 20th century, John Watson's approach to psychology gave up on consciousness altogether. Watson's behaviorism dismissed consciousness as little more than a by-product of behavior and scorned introspection as scientifically useless. In its place, he urged only direct observations of behavior, rather than a search for the mysterious mental processes hidden inside the organism. And, when Watson spoke, everyone listened: In the heyday of behaviorism—from the 1920s to the 1960s—scientists paid scant attention to consciousness.

The psychology of consciousness remained in limbo until the 1960s, when a coalition of cognitive psychologists, neuroscientists, and computer scientists brought the topic back to life. To defend the new science of consciousness, they began using new tools, especially computers, to study internal mental processes, such as memory, perception, and thought. This multidisciplinary effort is now called **cognitive neuroscience.** It eventually won over most psychologists, who defended the view that the conscious mind is a natural process occurring in the brain. After all, the brain has vast resources—approximately 100 billion neurons, each with thousands of interconnections. Surely, with this equipment, the human brain is capable of creating the universe of imagination we think of as consciousness (Chalmers, 1995; Churchland, 1995; Crick, 1994). Our Core Concept puts it this way:

> **The brain creates consciousness when it combines external stimulation with internal experience.**

This insight suggests that we might find the telltale traces of conscious experience if we look at the activity of the brain (see Tononi & Edelman, 1998).

Tools for Studying Consciousness

High-technology tools, such as the MRI, PET, and EEG, have opened new windows through which researchers can look into the brain to see which regions are active during different mental tasks. These imaging devices, of course, do not show the actual contents of conscious experience. To glimpse the underlying mental processes, psychologists have devised other ingenious techniques.

Suppose, for example, that you were asked to fill in the blanks to make a word from the following stem:

Connection

Chapter 11
In Freud's theory, the personality has three parts: the ego, the id, and the superego.

Consciousness can include a rich mixture of memory, fantasy, emotion, and external stimulation.

Core Concept

Cognitive neuroscience: A new, interdisciplinary field involving cognitive psychology, neuroscientists, computer scientists, and specialists from other fields who are interested in the connection between mental processes and the brain.

Connection

Chapter 2
The EEG shows patterns of electrical activity in the brain.

Connection

Chapter 7
Priming is a technique for probing implicit memory.

D E F __ __ __

Using a technique called *priming,* psychologists can have some influence on the answers people give to such problems without subjects being aware that they were influenced. In the example just given, there are a number of possible ways to complete the word stem, including *define, defeat, defect, defile, deform, defray,* and *defuse.* But if you have recently read the paragraph just before our Core Concept, the chance that you might have filled in the blanks to make yet another word is slightly increased. There you were deliberately exposed (twice) to the word *defend* to "prime" your response. With priming methods such as this, psychologists have a powerful tool for probing the interaction of conscious and nonconscious processes. The technique might be used, for example, to study how patients can form memories while under surgical anesthesia.

This brief survey shows that psychologists have a variety of techniques for exploring and illuminating the private world of consciousness. With this in mind, let us turn now to a more detailed consideration of how consciousness is organized and how it works.

Francis Crick says that our consciousness is "no more than the behavior of a vast assembly of nerve cells and their associated molecules."

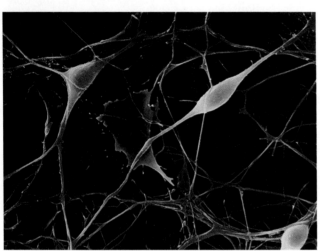

The Functions and Structures of Consciousness

Ordinary waking consciousness consists of the immediate mental experiences that make up our perceptions, thoughts, feelings, and desires. Consciousness includes awareness of ourselves and of stimulation from our environment. We are usually conscious of what we are doing, why we are doing it, and the effect of our behavior on the environment. But neither the fact of consciousness nor a record of its contents tells us what purpose consciousness serves or how it operates. In tackling these problems we will first consider the *functions* of consciousness. Then we will review what research and theory can tell us about how consciousness is *organized*—its forms, structures, and dynamics—in order to perform its functions.

WHAT CONSCIOUSNESS DOES FOR US   Imagine waking up to find yourself in a strange bed, being examined by white-coated strangers who tell you, "You've been in an accident, but you're in a hospital, and you're going to be all right." Your conscious abilities enable you to put this information together with your memories ("A hospital is a place where I will get medical care") to figure out what has happened. In general, consciousness helps us construct both personal realities and culturally shared realities.

The evolutionary perspective reminds us that consciousness must be highly adaptive for it to have become such a prominent feature of human cognition. We can see what makes it so adaptive in the following properties of consciousness:

Connection

Chapter 1
The evolutionary perspective emphasizes how our abilities help us adapt and survive.

▶ *Consciousness restricts our attention.* In this way it controls what we notice and think about. Thus, consciousness keeps our brains from being overwhelmed by stimulation.

▶ *Consciousness combines sensation with learning and memory.* Thus, consciousness is an *interpretation* of the world.

▶ *Consciousness helps us select personally meaningful stimuli from the input of our senses.* In this way, consciousness helps us make a mental record of the most meaningful elements in our lives.

▶ *Consciousness allows us to draw on lessons stored in memory.* Thus, we are not, like simpler organisms, prisoners of the moment. Rather, we can bring both the past and the future into consciousness, as we evaluate alternative responses and imagine the effectiveness of their consequences.

You rely on these four dimensions of consciousness every day. For example, as part of your morning routine, you must restrict attention to certain immediate tasks, such as showering, dressing, and eating. The demands of attention may also rule out other, less pressing tasks, such as a second cup of coffee. Your consciousness also helps you select and store information from the daily weather forecast that helps you consider how to dress for the expected weather. And it helps you draw on memory in order to imagine the consequences of certain choices, such as carrying an umbrella or bringing books and other supplies with you. In general, consciousness offers humans the capacity for flexible, appropriate responses to life's changing demands (Baars, 1988; Baars & McGovern, 1994; Ornstein, 1986b; Rozin, 1976). Let us consider how consciousness works with the nonconscious levels of the mind to perform these functions.

FIGURE 3.1: Structures of Consciousness

If consciousness were represented as an iceberg, conscious processes would be those located above the water's surface, while the unconscious would be submerged. Subconscious and preconscious processes both lie beneath the surface but are accessible through special attention and recall. Nonconscious processes influence bodily processes but never become accessible to consciousness.

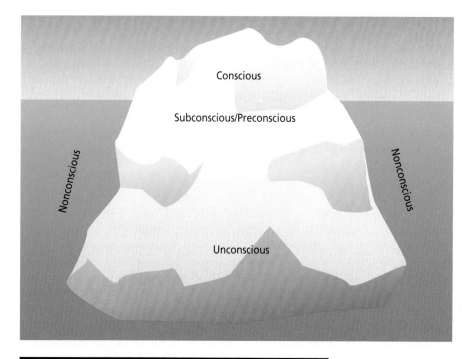

Conscious

Subconscious/Preconscious

Nonconscious

Nonconscious

Unconscious

Nonconscious processes: Any brain process that does not involve conscious processing. Examples include regulation of the heart rate, breathing, and control of the internal organs and glands.

Preconscious memories: Information that is not currently in consciousness but can be recalled to consciousness after something calls attention to them.

Subconscious: A store of information that was registered in memory without being consciously attended to.

Unconscious: In classic Freudian theory, a part of the mind that houses memories, desires, and feelings that would be threatening if brought to consciousness. Recently, many psychologists have come to believe in a simplified, "dumb" unconscious, which stores and processes some information outside of awareness.

Empirical: Relying on direct sensory observation rather than subjective judgment.

LEVELS OF CONSCIOUSNESS Just now, were you aware of your heartbeat? Probably not, for controlling your heartbeat is a function that normally occurs outside of consciousness. Such **nonconscious processes** involve information processed in the brain but not represented in consciousness or memory. In general, the brain automatically and nonconsciously regulates the body's basic life-sustaining functions, such as breathing and the regulation of blood pressure. In addition, certain cognitive operations occur outside of consciousness but exert influence on consciousness. These include *preconsciousness,* the *subconscious,* and the *unconscious.*

Preconsciousness Memories of events, such as your first kiss, have once been the focus of attention, but they now come to consciousness only after something cues their recall. Psychologists call these **preconscious memories.** They lie in the background of your mind until they are needed, and they are retrieved with relative ease. We can bring to mind another example of a preconscious memory by asking: What did you have for breakfast this morning? If you can answer that question, some representation of your meal must have been stored in your mind at the preconscious level of awareness—until just now, when you pulled the memory out to answer the question (Baars & McGovern, 1994). Recalling something consciously is an attention-demanding act, requiring one to seek information and move it from preconsciousness to conscious memory (Jacoby et al., 1989).

Subconscious Processing Just as you began reading this line, you were probably not thinking about background noises, like a clock ticking or traffic on nearby streets. Constantly you must push much of the stimulation around you out of your mind so that you can focus attention on the small remainder that is relevant. But you may be surprised to learn that a great deal of nonattended stimulation gets registered and evaluated below the level of conscious awareness. Most of this **subconscious** information, however, never makes a permanent mark in long-term memory.

On the other hand, research indicates that ongoing consciousness can be influenced by events that have never commanded our attention (Kihlstrom, 1987). In fact, much cognitive processing seems to occur in this way—automatically and without awareness or effort, as when we correctly navigate a familiar route to work or school without apparent thought (Uleman & Bargh, 1989). Priming, which you experienced earlier, also involves subconscious processing.

The Unconscious We use the term *unconscious* in common speech to refer to someone who has fainted, is comatose, or is under anesthesia. In psychology, however, the term **unconscious** has a special meaning. According to psychoanalytic theory, powerful unconscious forces block many of our motives, emotions, and memories from awareness. The founder of psychoanalysis, Sigmund Freud, taught that unconscious thoughts can shape our behavior even though we may have no awareness of their existence (Freud, 1925). According to Freud, the unconscious harbors memories, desires, and emotions that, at a conscious level, would cause one extreme anxiety. Such processes are assumed to stem from the need to *repress* (block) traumatic memories and taboo desires. In this view, the unconscious mind, then, serves as a mental storehouse where terrible urges and threatening memories can be kept out of consciousness. Let us look, however, at another perspective on the unconscious.

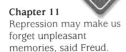

Connection

Chapter 11
Repression may make us forget unpleasant memories, said Freud.

Your Unconscious — Reconsidered

Ever since Freud, the art and literature of the Western world have been captivated by the idea of an unconscious filled with dark and sinister motives and memories. Joseph Conrad's *Heart of Darkness,* for example, tells a story of a person's internal and unconscious struggle with the most evil of desires for power and death. Freud also suggested that raw and unconscious sexual energy motivates most things we do, the relationships we have, and the work we choose. But is this the way your mind really works? Are you merely a pawn in your mind's war with itself—consciousness against the unconscious?

Advances in research methods (such as priming) have made it possible to demonstrate and study nonconscious thought processes in an **empirical** way (Kihlstrom, 1990; Kihlstrom et al., 1992; Rozin, 1976). We now know with certainty what Freud was able to demonstrate only with conjecture: There is a less-than-conscious aspect to your mind. But to cognitive psychologists it doesn't look much like Freud's vision.

For one thing, the less-than-conscious mind does not seem as dramatic or sinister as the Freud portrayal of it. For another, the new view suggests a much simpler structure than the complicated censoring and repressing system that Freud proposed (Greenwald, 1992).

In the cognitive view, the nonconscious mind devotes its resources to simple background tasks such as screening the incoming stream of sights, sounds, smells, and textures, rather than to repressing memories of traumatic experiences. This also provides a quick appraisal of events for their attractiveness or harmfulness (LeDoux, 1996). In these ways, the less-than-conscious mind works *with* consciousness, rather than *against* it. Ironically, the new view of an unconscious that monitors, sorts, discards, and stores the flood of data we encounter may give this portion of the mind a larger role than Freud originally conceived.

CHECK**YOUR**UNDERSTANDING

1. **RECALL:** *Who objected most strenuously to psychology being the science of consciousness?*
   a. the cognitive psychologists
   b. the behaviorists
   c. the humanists
   d. the neurologists

2. **RECALL:** *According to cognitive neuroscience,*
   a. Consciousness does not exist.
   b. Creativity arises from altered states of consciousness.
   c. Consciousness is a product of the brain.
   d. The conscious mind has little access to the larger world of mental activity in the unconscious.

3. **APPLICATION:** *Suppose you wanted to sample the contents of preconsciousness. Which technique would you use?*

   a. MRI
   b. recall
   c. priming
   d. psychoanalysis

4. **UNDERSTANDING THE CORE CONCEPT:**
   Which of the following is a main function of consciousness suggested by the Core Concept for this section?
   a. Consciousness combines sensation with learning and memory.
   b. Consciousness allows us to respond reflexively, without thinking.
   c. Consciousness controls the autonomic nervous system.
   d. Consciousness makes us more alert.

   ANSWERS: 1. b   2. c   3. b   4. a

Core Concept

WHAT ARE THE CYCLES OF EVERYDAY CONSCIOUSNESS?

If you are a "morning person," you are probably at your peak of alertness soon after you awaken. But this mental state doesn't last all day. Like most other people, you probably experience a period of mental lethargy in the afternoon. At this low point in the cycle of wakefulness, you may join much of the Latin world, which wisely takes a siesta. Later, your alertness increases for a time, only to fade again during the evening hours. Punctuating this cycle may be periods of heightened focus and attention (as when you are called on in class) and periods of reverie, known as daydreams. Finally, whether you are a "morning" or "night" person, you eventually drift into that third of your life spent asleep, where conscious contact with the outside world nearly ceases.

Psychologists have traced these cyclic changes in consciousness to find reliable patterns. We will see that the patterns they have found are rooted in our biological nature and in the recurring events of our lives. Our second Core Concept puts it this way:

Core Concept

> **Consciousness changes in cycles that normally correspond to our biological rhythms and to the patterns of our environment.**

In this section we will devote most of our attention to the cyclic changes in consciousness involved in sleep and nocturnal dreaming. First, however, we turn to the sort of dreaming that occurs while we are awake.

Daydreaming

Daydreaming: A mild form of consciousness alteration in which attention shifts to memories, expectations, desires, or fantasies and away from the immediate situation.

In the mild form of consciousness alteration that we call **daydreaming,** attention focuses internally on memories, expectations, and desires. Daydreaming occurs most often when people are alone, relaxed, engaged in a boring or routine task, or just about to fall asleep (Singer, 1966, 1975). But is daydreaming normal? Perhaps you will be relieved to know that most people daydream every day. In fact, it is abnormal if you do not! Research shows, however, that young adults report the most frequent daydreams, with the amount of daydreaming declining significantly with age (Singer & McCraven, 1961).

Daydreaming can serve valuable, healthy functions (Klinger, 1987). Daydreams dwell on practical and current concerns in people's lives: classes, goals (trivial or significant), and interpersonal relationships. Thus, daydreaming can help us make plans and solve problems.

Sometimes daydreams consist of persistent and unwelcome wishes, worries, or fantasies. So, suppose that you decide to stop entertaining a particular thought. What will happen? Research suggests that efforts to suppress unwanted thoughts are likely to backfire. In the "white bear" study (Wegner et al., 1987), subjects spoke into a tape recorder about anything that came to mind. They had been instructed, however, *not* to think about "a white bear." The results: despite their instructions, subjects mentioned a white bear about once per minute! Apparently, trying to suppress a thought or put something out of your mind can result in an obsession with the very thought you seek to escape. Ironically, when you allow your mind to roam freely, as daydreaming and fantasy naturally do,

Daydreaming, common among people of all ages, may be a source of creativity.

unwanted or upsetting thoughts usually become less intrusive and finally cease (Wegner, 1989).

And how do daydreams compare with dreams of the night? No matter how realistic our fantasies may be, daydreams are rarely as vivid as our most colorful night dreams. Neither are they as mysterious — because they are under our control. Nor do they occur (as do night dreams) under the influence of biological cycles and the strange world that we call sleep. It is to this world that we now turn our attention.

Sleep and Dreaming

If you live to be 90, you will have slept for nearly 30 years. Although we spend about a third of our lives sleeping, most of us take this dramatic daily alteration of consciousness for granted. Once the province of psychoanalysts, prophets, and psychics, sleep and dreams have now become a vital area of study for scientific researchers. They have shown that sleep must be understood as one component of our natural biological rhythms. It is a consequence of our world's daylight–dark cycles interacting with our bodies' physical cycles (Beardsley, 1996). We begin our exploration of this realm of altered consciousness with an examination of these biological patterns.

CIRCADIAN RHYTHMS Nearly all creatures fall under the influence of nature's cycles, especially the cycle of light and darkness. Among the most important for humans are those known as **circadian rhythms,** bodily patterns that repeat approximately every 24 hours. (*Circadian* comes from the Latin *circa* for "about" + *dies* for "a day.") Internal control of these circadian rhythms resides in a "biological clock" that sets the cadence of our metabolism, heart rate, body temperature, and hormonal activity. The "clock" itself is not a single mechanism but a coordinated set of physiological operations whose exact cycle may be dictated by an individual's genetic makeup (Dunlap, 1998; Page, 1994; Peretz, 1993). Coordination of these operations seems to be achieved by a group of cells in the thalamus. These thalamic cells are especially sensitive to the light–dark cycles of day and night.

For most people, the normal circadian rhythm is a bit longer than a day in length. But it undergoes continual readjustment by our exposure to light and by our daily routines of sleeping and waking. When people are placed for several days in an environment in which they have no time cues, they usually settle into a circadian cycle of about 25 hours.

Your normal circadian rhythms can be disrupted by air travel, work schedules that shift from day to night, and other disturbances in your sleep–wake habits (Moore-Ede, 1993). In fact, anything that throws off your biological clock affects how you feel and behave. Flying across several time zones results in **jet lag** because the internal circadian rhythm is disrupted by your new temporal environment. If it is 1:00 A.M. to your body but only 10:00 P.M. to the people around you, you must use energy and resources to adapt to your surroundings. The resulting symptoms of jet lag include fatigue, irresistible sleepiness, and temporary cognitive deficits. Air travelers should note that our biological clocks can adjust more readily to longer days than to shorter ones. Therefore, traveling eastbound (losing hours in your day) creates greater jet lag than traveling westbound (gaining hours). Apparently, it is easier to stay awake a bit longer than it is to fall asleep sooner than usual (Klein & Wegmann, 1974).

THE MAIN EVENTS OF SLEEP For most of human history, sleep has been a mystery, made all the more perplexing by the fantastic pageant of our dreams. But now the use of the electroencephalogram (EEG) on sleeping sub-

Circadian rhythms: Physiological patterns that repeat approximately every 24 hours — such as the sleep–wakefulness cycle.

Jet lag: A biological and psychological disruption of the circadian rhythms produced by moving quickly across time zones and attempting to shift one's sleep–wakefulness cycle to the local time.

Connection

Chapter 2
The thalamus is the brain's central "relay station."

Connection

Chapter 2
The EEG shows which regions of the brain are most active.

jects opens the door for researchers seeking an objective look at this formerly subjective world. With the EEG, sleep scientists have been able to record brain activity continuously through the night without disturbing the sleeper. They number among their discoveries the telltale changes in brain waves that begin at the onset of sleep and then cycle in predictable patterns during the rest of the night (Loomis et al., 1937).

The most significant discovery in sleep research first revealed itself in the eyes. About every 90 minutes during the night we enter a period marked by **rapid eye movements (REM)**. These take place for a span of several minutes beneath our closed eyelids (Aserinsky & Kleitman, 1953). The interim periods, without rapid eye movements, are known as **non-REM (NREM) sleep.** And what happens in the brain during these two different phases of sleep? To find out, researchers awakened sleepers during either REM sleep or NREM sleep and asked them to describe their mental activity (Dement & Kleitman, 1957). The NREM reports more often contained either no mental activity or brief descriptions of ordinary daily events, similar to waking thoughts. By contrast, most of the REM reports were filled with vivid cognitions, featuring fanciful, bizarre scenes. Such studies show that rapid eye movements are the best indicator of the mental activity we call dreaming. Strangely, while the eyes dance during REM sleep, the voluntary muscles in the rest of the body are immobile —paralyzed—a condition known as **sleep paralysis.** This probably occurs to keep us from acting out our dreams. (In case you're wondering: Sleepwalking and sleep talking occur during NREM sleep.)

THE SLEEP CYCLE   Now imagine that you are a subject in a laboratory specializing in sleep research. Already connected to EEG recording equipment, you have become comfortable with the wires linking your body to the machinery, and you are settling in for a night's sleep. At the moment, while you are awake and alert, the EEG shows your brain waves pulsing at a rate of about 14 cycles per second (cps). As you begin to relax, they slow to about 8 to 12 cps. When you fall asleep, the EEG shows further changes. In fact, over the course of the night, your brain waves reveal a cycle of activity that repeats itself over and over. A closer look at the recording of this cycle the next morning will show several distinct stages, each with a characteristic EEG signature (see Figures 3.2 and 3.3):

▶ In Stage 1 sleep, the EEG displays fast brain waves similar to the waking state.

▶ During the next phase, Stage 2, the generally slower EEG is punctuated by *sleep spindles* —short bursts of fast electrical activity.

▶ In the following two stages (3 and 4), the sleeper enters a progressively deeper state of relaxed sleep. Brain waves slow dramatically, as do the heart rate and breathing rate. The deepest point in the sleep cycle occurs here, in Stage 4, about a half hour after sleep onset.

▶ As Stage 4 ends, the electrical activity of the brain increases, and the sleeper climbs back up through the stages in reverse order.

▶ As the brain reaches Stage 1 again, waves recorded by the EEG become fast. In addition, the sleeper now enters REM sleep for the first time (see Figure 3.2). Then, after a few minutes of REMing, the entire cycle begins to repeat itself.

Over the course of an average night's sleep, most people make the circuit through the stages of sleep four to six times. But in each successive cycle, the amount of time spent in deep sleep (Stages 3 and 4) decreases, and the amount of time spent in REM sleep increases. During the first cycle, the REM period

Rapid eye movements (REM): Quick bursts of eye movements occurring (under closed eyelids) at periodic intervals during sleep. REM sleep periods are associated with dreaming.

Non-REM (NREM) sleep: The recurring periods when a sleeper is not showing REM.

Sleep paralysis: A condition in which a sleeper is unable to move any of the voluntary muscles, except those controlling the eyes. Sleep paralysis normally occurs during REM sleep.

may last only 10 minutes, while in the last cycle, we may spend as much as an hour REMing. See Figure 3.3 for the pattern of sleep through a typical night. Studying this cyclical pattern will not only help you understand your normal night's sleep but will also provide the framework for understanding the abnormal patterns found in sleep disorders. Again, note three features of normal sleep: (a) the 90-minute cycles, (b) the appearance of deepest sleep during the beginning of the night, and (c) the increase in REM duration as sleep progresses.

What do you suppose would happen if a person were deprived of a substantial part of REM sleep for a night? Laboratory studies show that REM-deprived subjects feel tired and irritable the next day. And during the following night they spend much more time in REM sleep than usual, a condition known as **REM rebound.** This observation suggests that one of the functions of sleep is to satisfy a need for REM. Another function of REM sleep may be the maintenance of emotional balance. Sleep-deprived college students take note: Because we get most of our REM sleep during the last few cycles of the night, we inevitably suffer REM deprivation and REM rebound if we cut our night's sleep short.

THE FUNCTION OF SLEEP   Sleep is so common among animals that it surely must have some essential function, but sleep scientists disagree on what this function is (Pinel, 2000; Rechtschaffen, 1998). There are at least two possibilities: to *conserve* and to *restore*. Evolutionary psychology suggests that sleep may have evolved because it enabled animals to conserve energy at times when there was no need to forage for food, search for mates, or work (Dement & Vaughan, 1999). Sleep also enables the body to restore itself in several ways. During sleep, neurotransmitters build up to compensate for the quantities used in daily activities, and neurons return to their optimal level of sensitivity (Stern & Morgane, 1974).

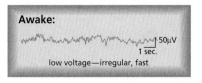

FIGURE 3.2:   EEG Patterns in Stages of Sleep

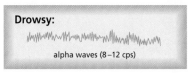
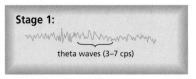
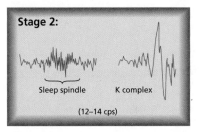
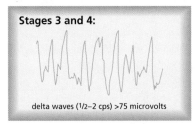
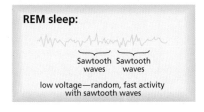

FIGURE 3.3:   Stages of Sleep

In a typical night, the deepest sleep (Stages 3 and 4) occurs mainly in the first few hours. As the night progresses, the sleeper spends more and more time in the stages of light sleep and in REM sleep.

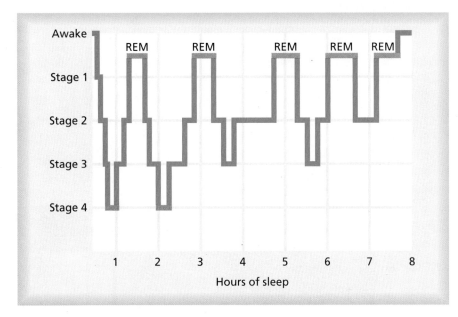

REM rebound: A condition of increased REM sleep following a period of REM-sleep deprivation.

William Shakespeare somewhat more elegantly hypothesized about the restorative function of sleep when he spoke of "Sleep that knits up the ravelled sleave of care." During sleep, "ravelled" material — loose ends of thoughts and emotions — may be either integrated or eliminated.

How does sleep restore us? Consciousness theorists Francis Crick and Graeme Mitchison believe that sleep and dreams help the brain to flush out the day's accumulation of unwanted and useless information — much like reformatting a computer disk. Dreams may also serve to reduce fantasy and obsession, thereby minimizing bizarre connections among our many memories (Crick & Mitchison, 1983).

THE NEED FOR SLEEP How much sleep we need depends on many factors. There is a genetically based need for sleep, different for each species. Sleep duration is also controlled by circadian rhythms, which are in turn linked to the hormone *melatonin* (Barinaga, 1997b; Haimov & Lavie, 1996).

Sleep time also varies with personality. Those who sleep longer than average tend to be more nervous, worrisome, artistic, creative, and nonconforming, while short sleepers tend to be more energetic and extroverted (Hartmann, 1973). Strenuous physical activity during the day increases the amount of time spent in the slow-wave sleep of Stage 4, but, oddly, it has no effect on REM time (Horne, 1988).

Finally, sleep duration and the shape of the sleep cycle change over one's lifetime. As Figure 3.4 shows, we begin life by sleeping about 16 hours per day, with half that time devoted to REM. Young adults typically sleep seven to eight hours (although they may need more), with 20% REM. By old age, we sleep relatively less, with only 15% of sleep spent in REM.

SLEEP DEBT VS. THE CIRCADIAN CLOCK So, how much sleep do we need — and what happens if we don't get enough? Most adults need to sleep

FIGURE 3.4: Patterns of Human Sleep Over a Lifetime

The graph shows changes with age in the total amounts of REM and NREM sleep and in the percentage of time spent in REM sleep. Note that, over the years, the amount of REM sleep decreases considerably, while NREM diminishes less sharply.

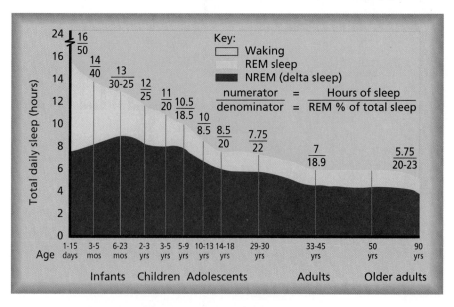

about eight hours, or a bit more, to feel good and function efficiently. The amount varies from person to person, with a range from about six to nine hours. In the sleep laboratory, when people are placed in a dark room and allowed to sleep without interruption, the average adult settles into a pattern that produces about eight and one-half hours of sleep per night. Yet, in their daily lives most Americans get significantly less—night after night (Maas, 1999). This creates a sleep shortage that researcher William Dement calls a **sleep debt** (Dement & Vaughan, 1999).

Oddly, most people who pile up a chronic sleep debt don't realize what they are doing. They may be groggy and sleepy when the alarm clock rouses them in the morning. But they don't see this as a sign of a sleep debt because they "wake up" over the next few hours and begin to feel alert. Afternoon drowsiness may be attributed to a big lunch—which, in truth, does not cause sleepiness. They may also rationalize away their struggle to stay awake in a meeting or class by telling themselves that sleepiness is a normal response to boredom. (In fact, the normal response to boredom is restlessness—unless one is sleep deprived.)

What is actually happening to the sleep-deprived individual is a daily tug-of-war between the *sleep debt* and the *circadian clock*. As we have seen, the circadian clock regulates our sleep–wakefulness cycle and level of alertness. Even when we have not had enough sleep, it can make us feel relatively alert during part of every day. But this alertness can also be illusory. When we run a chronic sleep debt, we are never as alert and mentally efficient as we could be if the sleep debt were paid with a few extended nights of sleep.

Sometimes the sleep debt is "paid" with a tragedy, as happened when a crew member of the *Exxon Valdez* ran the oil tanker aground after having only six hours of sleep in the previous two days (Dement & Vaughan, 1999).

Unfortunately, the pressures and opportunities of modern life cause many of us to underestimate the amount of sleep we need. We may also believe that we can combat sleepiness and successfully reduce our need for sleep by dint of will power and caffeine. But such measures never give us the clarity of mind that a good night's sleep does. As a result, we may operate on a chronic sleep deficit, never realizing why we have a daily struggle with daytime drowsiness.

Sleep debt: A deficiency caused by not getting the amount of sleep that one requires for optimal functioning.

DO IT YOURSELF!   How Much Sleep Do You Need?

Many college students operate in a chronic state of sleep deprivation. Because their schedules are crowded with study, work, and social events, students may convince themselves that they need only a few hours sleep each night. And, in fact, the average college student sleeps only about 6.8 hours a night (Hicks, 1990). Does too little sleep really make a difference in how well you perform in your classes? Psychologist Cheryl Spinweber (1990) has found that sleep-deprived undergraduates get lower grades than their counterparts who get enough sleep.

How can you tell if you need more sleep? Answer the following questions honestly:

1. Do you often get sleepy in your classes?

2. Do you sleep late on weekends?

3. Do you usually get sleepy when you get bored?

4. Do you often fall asleep while reading or watching TV?

5. Do you usually fall asleep within five minutes of going to bed?

6. Do you awake in the morning feeling that you are not rested?

7. Would you oversleep if you did not use an alarm clock to drive you out of bed?

If you answered "Yes" to any of these questions, chances are that you are shorting yourself on sleep. You may also be paying the price in the quality of your learning and in your grades.

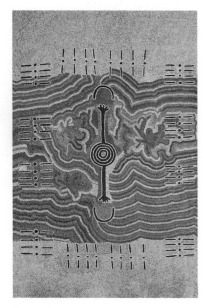

Much of the work by Australian Aboriginal painters depicts a time, long ago, when legend says that the physical features of the landscape were alive. They call this period *Dreamtime.* In the world of Aborigines, the act of making these paintings links the artist and the observer to the ancient Dreamtime. Such artwork has also been used for countless generations to instruct younger people in the ways of their ancestors. The Aborigines believe that those initiated into the mysteries of Dreamtime develop a new level of awareness, or consciousness, that connects the spiritual and material worlds.

Connection

Chapter 13
A major goal of Freud's psychoanalytic therapy is to bring unconscious desires into consciousness.

WHY WE DREAM: A CROSS-CULTURAL PERSPECTIVE   During every ordinary night of your life, you repeatedly experience a spectacular event staged only in the mind: the dream. What produces these fantastic cognitive spectacles?

The ancient Israelites interpreted dreams as messages from God. Their Egyptian contemporaries attempted to influence dreams by sleeping in temples dedicated to the god of dreaming, Serapis. And in India, the sacred Vedas described the religious significance of dreams. Meanwhile, in China dreaming held an element of risk. During a dream, the ancient Chinese believed, the soul wandered about outside the body. For that reason they were reluctant to awaken a sleeper hastily, lest the soul not find its way back to the body (Dement, 1980). From the perspective of many African and Native American cultures, dreams were an extension of waking reality. Consequently, when traditional Cherokee Indians dreamed of snakebite, they received appropriate emergency treatment upon awakening. Likewise, when an African tribal chieftain dreamed of England, he ordered a set of European clothes, and when he appeared in the new togs, his friends congratulated him on making the trip (Dement, 1980).

In contrast with such folk theories, sleep scientists have approached dreaming with this question: What is the function of dreams? Some see dreams as meaningful mental events, serving pressing cognitive needs or reflecting important events or fantasies in the dreamer's mental world. Others argue that dreams are merely the brain's random activity during sleep—and, therefore, their content may have no special meaning. We will consider both of these viewpoints.

DREAMS AS MEANINGFUL EVENTS: AGE, GENDER, AND CULTURE   At the beginning of the 20th century, Sigmund Freud laid out the most complex and comprehensive theory of dreams and their meanings ever developed—a theory that has since enjoyed enormous influence, despite a lack of evidence to support it (Squier & Domhoff, 1998). In this view, dreams represent "the royal road to the unconscious," lined with clues to an individual's hidden mental life. Accordingly, Freud made the analysis of dreams the cornerstone of psychoanalysis with his classic book, *The Interpretation of Dreams* (1900).

In psychoanalytic theory, dreams have two main functions: to guard sleep (by disguising disruptive thoughts with symbols) and to serve as sources of wish fulfillment. Freud believed that dreams play their guardian role by relieving psychic tensions created during the day. They serve their wish-fulfillment function by allowing the dreamer to work through unconscious desires.

Freud also taught that interpreting dreams can help people understand themselves better, and so dream analysis has become a central feature of psychoanalytic therapy. Psychoanalytic therapists mine dreams for clues about motives and conflicts that may lurk in the patient's unconscious. For example, long rigid objects or containers may be sexual symbols in Freudian theory. In the tradition of psychoanalytic practice, however, dream analysis requires extensive training and careful detective work to avoid drawing the wrong conclusions about the hidden meanings of dreams.

But must you be a trained psychoanalyst to understand dreams? Not necessarily. Many of our dreams have fairly obvious meanings that are connected to our waking lives. You have probably noticed that frightening dreams often relate to life stressors that have found their way into your sleeping thoughts. Research has lent support to such observations. For example, one study found that individuals depressed about divorce often had dreams that were fixed on past relationships (Cartwright, 1984). By analyzing the patterns and content of your own dreams, you may find it is not difficult to assign meaning to many of the images and actions you recall (Hall, 1953/1966; Van de Castle, 1994).

Freudian dream analysis has also been challenged on the grounds that Freud was not an experimentalist, nor was he always scrupulous in his data collection. So, for example, when he noted that boys frequently dream of strife with their fathers, he did no careful studies to verify his theoretical suspicions. Instead, he jumped to the conclusion that these dreams were signs of unconscious sexual jealousy. Many other explanations are possible, however, as anthropologists have shown by studying dreams of the Trobriand Islanders. Boys in that culture don't dream of their fathers so much as their uncles, who act as the disciplinarians in that society (Malinowski, 1927; Segall et al., 1990).

Modern sleep scientists have taken a more objective approach to dreams than did Freud (see Domhoff, 1996). They now know, for example, that the content of dreams varies by age, gender, and culture. Women everywhere more commonly dream of children, while men more often dream of aggression, weapons, and tools (Murray, 1995). The highly specific effects of culture can be seen in reports from the West African nation of Ghana, where dreamers often feature attacks by cows (Barnouw, 1963). Likewise, in their dreams, Americans frequently find themselves embarrassed by public nakedness, although such reports rarely occur in cultures where people customarily wear few clothes. Images of death appear more often in the dreams of Mexican-American college students than in the dreams of Anglo-American students, probably because concerns about death are more a part of life in Latin American cultures (Roll et al., 1974). In general, the cross-cultural research lends support to Cartwright's hypothesis (1977) that dreams reflect life events that are important to the dreamer.

Researchers do content analyses of dreams by collecting people's detailed, written descriptions of recent dreams (Hall & Van de Castle, 1966). Then they categorize the settings, characters, objects, and actions described, looking for patterns based on subjects' gender, age group, or other classification. For example, dream researcher Calvin Hall found that, in a sample of over 1,800 dreams, women dreamed about both men and women, while men dreamed about men twice as often as about women. In another sample of over 1,300 dreams, Hall found that hostile interactions between characters outnumbered friendly exchanges, and that 64% of dreamed emotions had a negative complexion, such as anger and sadness (Hall, 1951, 1984). Children are more likely to dream about animals than adults are, and the animals in their dreams are more likely to be large, threatening, and wild. In contrast, college students dream more usually of small animals, pets, and tame creatures. This may mean that children feel less in control of their world than adults do and so may find that world depicted in scarier imagery while they sleep (Van de Castle, 1983, 1994).

Sleep research has also found that dream content frequently relates to recent experience. Typically, the first dream of the night connects with events of the previous day. Then, dreaming in the second REM period (90 minutes later) may build on a theme that emerged during the first REM period. And so it goes through the night—like the childhood game of whispering a message from person to person—the final dream that emerges may have only the remotest relationship to events of the previous day. Ironically, it is this final dream of the night that is most likely to be remembered (Cartwright, 1977; Kiester, 1980).

This connection between dreams and recent experience may belie yet another possible function of dreams. A comparison of subjects who were selectively deprived of REM sleep with those deprived of NREM sleep suggests that REM sleep helps us store information in long-term memory. Those who were deprived of REM sleep performed more poorly than NREM-deprived subjects on tests of material studied the previous day (Kinoshita, 1992; Winson, 1990).

Connection

Chapter 11
Dream interpretation occupies a prominent place in Freudian psychoanalysis.

Connection

Chapter 7
Information is usually processed in short-term memory before it is stored in long-term memory.

Thus, REM sleep may be a normal part of the process for storing memories and fitting recent experiences into networks of previous beliefs or memories (Baringa, 1994; Cartwright, 1978; Dement, 1980; Karni et al., 1994).

DREAMS AS RANDOM ACTIVITY OF THE BRAIN   Not everyone believes that dream content has special importance. Among several such viewpoints, one of the most influential portrays dreams mainly as by-products of biological processes involved in sleep: The **activation-synthesis theory** says that dreams result when the sleeping brain tries to make sense of its own random biological activity (Leonard, 1998; Squier & Domhoff, 1998). According to this theory, the sleeping brain stem periodically emits random electrical discharges. As this energy sweeps over the cerebral cortex, the sleeper experiences impressions of sensation, memory, motivation, emotion, and movement. Although the cortical activation is random, and the images it generates may not be logically connected, the brain tries to make sense of the stimulation it receives. To do so, the brain *synthesizes* or pulls together the separate bursts of electrical *activation* by creating a coherent story — a dream.

The proponents of this theory, J. Allan Hobson and Robert McCarley (1977), argue that REM sleep furnishes the brain with an internal source of needed stimulation. This internal activation promotes the growth and development of the brain at the time when the sleeping brain has blocked out external stimulation. Dream content, therefore, results from brain activation, not unconscious wishes. While Hobson (1988) claims that meaning is added as a "brainstorm afterthought," he says that dream content may nevertheless have some psychological meaning in that the brain is reacting based on cortical patterns influenced by culture, gender, and personality factors. Thus, when activations are synthesized, dreams seem familiar and meaningful.

Activation-synthesis theory:
The theory that dreams begin with random electrical *activation* coming from the brain stem. Dreams, then, are the brain's attempt to make sense of — to *synthesize* — this random activity.

Sleep Disorders

Psychology

In Your Life

You may be among the more than 100 million Americans who get insufficient sleep or poor-quality sleep. While some of these sleep disturbances seem to have a purely biological basis, many are job-related or the result of personal choices. Among people who work night shifts, for example, more than half nod off at least once a week on the job. And it may be no coincidence that some of the world's most serious accidents — the nuclear power plant disasters at Three Mile Island and Chernobyl, the toxic chemical

discharge at Bhopal — have occurred during late evening hours when people are likely to be programmed for sleep. Sleep experts speculate that many accidents occur because key personnel fail to function optimally as a result of insufficient sleep (Dement, 1980; Dement & Vaughan, 1999).

In the following paragraphs, we will examine a sampling of sleep problems of biological and psychological origin. Some are common, while some are both rare and bizarre. The single element that ties them together is a disruption in one or more parts of the normal sleep cycle.

Insomnia, the most common of sleep disorders, is usually the

Insomnia is a complex disorder caused by a variety of psychological, environmental, and biological factors. This college student anxiously contemplates her inability to get enough rest for the next day's classes.

diagnosis when people are dissatisfied with the amount of sleep they get. Its symptoms are chronic inability to fall asleep quickly, frequent arousals during sleep, or early-morning awakening (Bootzin & Nicasio, 1978). Insomnia sufferers include one-third of all adults (Anch et al., 1988; Mellinger et al., 1985).

An occasional bout with insomnia is normal, especially when dealing with exciting or worrisome events in our lives. These incidents pose no special danger in themselves, unless attempts are made to treat the problem with barbiturates or over-the-counter "sleeping pills." Such drugs disrupt the normal sleep cycle by cutting short REM sleep periods (Dement, 1980). As a result, they can actually aggravate insomnia.

Sleep apnea, another common disorder, may be apparent only in a person's complaints of daytime sleepiness and a sleep partner's complaints about snoring. Because sleep apnea often involves problems in the upper respiratory tract, it interferes with breathing during sleep and frequently produces heroic snoring levels (Seligson, 1994). A common form results from collapse of the airway, when muscle tone relaxes during sleep. As a result, breathing stops, the blood's oxygen level drops, and emergency hormones course through the body, causing the sleeper to awaken briefly, begin breathing again, and then fall back to sleep.

Failure to recognize the nature of the problem can cause sufferers — and their families and coworkers — to interpret unusual daytime behavior as laziness or neglect. While this may be disruptive to relationships, sleep apnea can also have dangerous biological effects that include elevated blood pressure, which can put dangerous levels of stress on the blood vessels and heart (Anch et al., 1988; Stavish, 1994).

We should note that occasional episodes of sleep apnea are likely to occur in premature infants, who may need physical stimulation to start breathing again. Obviously, the problem can be lethal, and it is one possible cause of sudden infant death syndrome (SIDS). Until their underdeveloped respiratory systems mature, these infants must remain attached to breathing monitors. For adults with sleep apnea, permanent breathing failure is not a strong concern. Treatment focuses on the hundreds of nightly apnea episodes, which can be alleviated by use of a device that pumps extra air into the lungs and keeps the airway open during sleep.

Narcolepsy, one of the most unusual of sleep disorders, produces sudden daytime sleep attacks, often without warning. These are no ordinary waves of drowsiness, however. So suddenly do narcoleptic sleep attacks appear that victims have reported falling asleep while base running in a softball game or while scuba diving under 20 feet of water.

These sleep attacks may be accompanied by a sudden loss of muscle control, a condition known as **cataplexy.** Oddly, anything exciting can trigger a narcoleptic attack. For example, patients commonly report that they fall asleep while laughing at a joke or while having sex. Obviously, narcolepsy can be dangerous — and not so good for intimate relationships, either.

Assembling the pieces of the narcolepsy puzzle reveals a peculiar disorder of REM sleep. A sleep recording will clinch the diagnosis. It will show that the victim of narcolepsy has an abnormal sleep-onset REM period. Instead of waiting the usual 90 minutes for REM sleep to occur, the narcoleptic individual has a REM period as sleep begins. You may have already guessed what the cataplexy represents: REM sleep paralysis.

Studies of narcoleptic animals show the disorder is a genetic problem based in the brain stem. It has no cure, but there are now effective treatments that rely on drugs to diminish the frequency of both the sleep attacks and the cataplexy. Happily, narcoleptic patients are no longer routinely placed in psychotherapy aimed at searching for the unconscious conflicts that were once assumed to cause the disorder.

What should you do if you suspect that you have a serious sleep disorder, such as narcolepsy or sleep apnea? An evaluation by a sleep expert is the place to start. Many hospitals have sleep disorders clinics to which your physician or clinical psychologist can refer you.

Insomnia: A disorder that involves insufficient sleep, the inability to fall asleep quickly, frequent arousals, or early awakenings.

Sleep apnea: A respiratory disorder in which the person intermittently stops breathing while asleep.

Narcolepsy: A disorder of REM sleep, involving sudden REM-sleep attacks accompanied by cataplexy.

Cataplexy: A sudden loss of muscle control that may occur just before a narcoleptic sleep attack. Cataplexy is a waking form of sleep paralysis.

1. **RECALL:** *Which statement is true about daydreaming?*

   a. Most people can easily suppress unwanted thoughts.
   b. Most people daydream every day.
   c. Daydreams usually serve as an escape from the concerns of real life.
   d. Daydreams are usually more vivid than night dreams.

2. **RECALL:** *All of the following are related to our circadian rhythms, except*

   a. sleep.
   b. dreaming.
   c. jet lag.
   d. daydreaming.

3. **RECALL:** *Suppose that you are working in a sleep laboratory, where you are monitoring a subject's sleep recording during the night. As the night progresses, you would expect to see that*

   a. the four-stage cycle gradually lengthens.
   b. REM periods become longer.
   c. Stage 3 and 4 sleep periods lengthen.
   d. dreaming becomes less frequent.

4. **RECALL:** *According to the activation-synthesis theory, dreams are*

   a. replays of events during the previous day.

   b. an attempt by the brain to make sense of random activity in the brain stem.
   c. a storylike episode that provides clues about problems in the unconscious mind.
   d. wish fulfillments.

5. **APPLICATION:** *Which of the following symptoms suggests the presence of a sleep disorder?*

   a. stopping breathing for several seconds three or four times a night
   b. a REM period at the beginning of sleep
   c. needing nine hours of sleep each night in order to feel rested
   d. not remembering your dreams

6. **UNDERSTANDING THE CORE CONCEPT:**

   Our Core Concept states that consciousness changes in cycles that normally correspond to our biological rhythms and to the patterns of our environment. Which of the following illustrates this concept?
   a. priming
   b. consciousness, preconsciousness, and the unconscious
   c. REM rebound
   d. sleep and dreaming

ANSWERS: 1. b   2. d   3. b   4. b   5. b   6. d

WHAT OTHER FORMS CAN CONSCIOUSNESS TAKE?

Children stand on their heads or spin around to make themselves dizzy. You may get much the same feeling on a wild theme-park ride. But why do we engage in these strange antics? One view says that "human beings are born with a drive to experience modes of awareness other than the normal waking one; from very young ages, children experiment with techniques to change consciousness" (Weil, 1977, p. 37). So, sleep, dreams, fantasies, and wild rides offer compelling alternatives to normal conscious experience. For some people, however, these alternatives may not be wild enough. Their search for mind-altering experiences may lead to drugs that change ordinary awareness. Among the legal substances that alter consciousness, they may be attracted to alcohol, tobacco, and caffeine. On the illegal side, they may turn to heroin, PCP, cannabis, amphetamines, or any of a number of other drugs that exert powerful mental effects. Purely psychological techniques can change consciousness, too. These include procedures such as hypnosis, relaxation training, and meditation.

What is the theme that ties these altered or extended states of consciousness together? The Core Concept of this section says:

> An altered state of consciousness occurs when some aspect of normal consciousness is modified by mental, behavioral, or chemical means

This also suggests that altered states do *not* involve mysterious paranormal or New Age phenomena that defy explanation by science. Rather, altered states are modifications of ordinary consciousness that we can study with the tools of science. Specifically, let us see what these tools can tell us about hypnosis, meditation, and drug states.

Hypnosis

Picture an individual being put into a hypnotic trance. The hypnotist is making suggestions to promote concentration and relaxation. Soon the subject appears to be asleep, although he or she can obviously hear suggestions and carry out requests. The subject also seems to have amazing powers to ignore pain, remember long-forgotten details, and create hallucinations. What mental processes make these things happen? To find out, we will explore the nature of hypnosis as a state of mind, its most important features, and some of its valid psychological uses.

The term "hypnosis" derives from *Hypnos,* the name of the Greek god of sleep. The EEG record tells us, however, that ordinary sleep plays no part in hypnosis, even though subjects may appear to be in a deeply relaxed, sleeplike state. Rather, most authorities would say **hypnosis** involves a state of awareness characterized by deep relaxation, heightened suggestibility, and highly focused attention. (There is, however, no unique EEG signature for hypnosis.) When deeply hypnotized, some people have the special ability to respond to suggestion with dramatic changes in perception, memory, motivation, and sense of self-control (Orne, 1980). After being hypnotized, subjects often report that they experienced heightened responsiveness to the hypnotist's suggestions and felt that their behavior was performed without intention or any conscious effort.

HYPNOTIZABILITY Dramatic stage performances of hypnosis give the impression that the power of hypnosis lies with the hypnotist. However, the real star is the person who is hypnotized. The hypnotist is more like an experienced guide showing the way. Some individuals can even practice self-hypnosis, or *autohypnosis,* by inducing the hypnotic state through self-administered suggestions.

The single most important factor in achieving a hypnotic state is a participant's susceptibility. Experts call this **hypnotizability,** and they measure it by a person's responsiveness to standardized suggestions. Individuals differ in this susceptibility, varying from no responsiveness to any suggestion to total responsiveness to virtually every suggestion. A highly hypnotizable person may respond to suggestions to change motor reactions, experience hallucinations, have amnesia for important memories, and become insensitive to painful stimuli.

Figure 3.5 shows the percentage of college-age subjects at various levels of hypnotizability the first time they were given a hypnotic induction test. For example, a hypnotist may test a new subject's accep-

Hypnosis: An induced alternate state of awareness, characterized by heightened suggestibility and (usually) deep relaxation.

Hypnotizability: The degree to which an individual is responsive to hypnotic suggestions.

A roller coaster ride is one way to alter your consciousness.

FIGURE 3.5: Level of Hypnosis Reached at First Induction

This graph shows the results achieved by 533 subjects hypnotized for the first time. (Hypnotizability was measured by the 12-item Stanford Hypnotic Susceptibility Scale.)

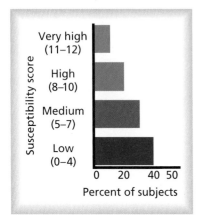

Hypnotic analgesia: Diminished sensitivity to pain while under hypnosis.

Hypnosis can help to control pain in many individuals. Here, a woman is learning hypnotic techniques that she will use in natural childbirth.

tance of suggestion by saying, "Your right hand is lighter than air," and observing whether the subject allows his or her arm to float upward. High scorers are more likely than low scorers to experience pain relief, or **hypnotic analgesia,** and to respond to hypnotic suggestions for experiencing perceptual distortions.

HYPNOSIS AS AN ALTERED STATE   We should maintain a scientific skepticism about the sensational claims made for hypnosis, especially when such claims are based on individual case reports or research that lacks proper control conditions (Barber, 1976, 1986). Even the experts disagree about the psychological mechanisms involved (Fromm & Shor, 1979). Some propose that hypnosis is simply heightened motivation (Barber, 1979). In this view, subjects are not entranced but merely motivated to focus their attention and to channel more energy into suggested activities. They are hypnotized because they want or expect to be, so they focus on expressing and achieving the responses the hypnotist tries to evoke. Other experts think that hypnosis involves social role playing, often to please the hypnotist (Sarbin & Coe, 1972). Still other researchers suggest that hypnosis is a fundamentally different state of consciousness (Fromm & Shor, 1979). Recent theories, however, bring these perspectives closer together by suggesting that hypnosis is actually a range of responses that cover all of these possibilities (Kirsch & Lynn, 1995).

PRACTICAL USES OF HYPNOSIS   Stage tricks aside, what is hypnosis good for? Studies show that hypnosis can exert a powerful influence on many psychological and bodily functions (Bowers, 1983; Hilgard, 1968, 1973; Miller & Bowers, 1993). This makes it a useful tool for researchers. So, instead of being limited to subjects who already have certain conditions or disorders, researchers can recruit normal volunteers and use hypnosis to create hallucinations or mental states, such as anxiety, depression, or euphoria—or physical states, such as sensory loss. In one study, for example, subjects given the hypnotic suggestion to become deaf on cue reported feeling paranoid and excluded because they could not hear what other subjects were saying and assumed they were being deliberately whispered about and excluded (Zimbardo et al., 1981).

Although hypnosis is not used extensively by psychologists or medical practitioners, it does have a place. The medical uses include pain control for procedures in which the patient may be hypersensitive to the usual anesthesia, although we should also note that not everyone can be hypnotized deeply enough for pain relief (Callahan, 1997; Miller & Bowers, 1993; Orne, 1980). In some cases, however, it has been demonstrated that hypnotized subjects can undergo treatments that would otherwise cause excruciating pain without anesthesia (Finer, 1980). For example, the Lamaze method of natural childbirth uses a hypnosis-like procedure as the primary means of pain control. And for some highly suggestible individuals, hypnosis may actually be superior to conventional anesthesia. One study found that, for selected subjects, hypnosis worked better than acupuncture, aspirin, Valium, or even morphine in masking intense pain (Stern et al., 1977). The mechanism by which hypnosis produces such effective pain relief is not known. Experiments show that endorphins, which account for the pain-relieving property of placebos, are *not* responsible for hypnotic analgesia (Grevert & Goldstein, 1985; Mayer, 1979; Watkins & Mayer, 1982).

In psychological treatment, hypnosis can be an effective tool in desensitizing phobic patients to fear-producing stimuli, such as snakes or heights. A variety of other unwanted responses may be eliminated by hypnotherapy, as well. Commonly, hypnotherapists will make posthypnotic suggestions that influence the subject's later eating, drug using, or other behaviors, sometimes for several months (Barnier & McConkey, 1998; Kihlstrom, 1985). Hypnosis can also be a part of a relaxation training program designed to combat stress.

Meditation

Many religions and traditional psychologies of the Asian and Pacific cultures purposely direct consciousness away from immediate worldly concerns and external stimulation. In doing so, they may seek to achieve an inner focus on the mental and spiritual self. In this quest, **meditation** is one technique employed to change consciousness. During meditative states, a person may learn to concentrate on a repetitive behavior (such as breathing), assume certain body positions (yogic postures), minimize external stimulation, and either generate specific mental images or free the mind of all thought.

Meditation produces relaxation and, perhaps, new insights.

To view meditation as an altered state of consciousness may reflect a particularly Western worldview, for Asian beliefs about the mind are typically different from those of Western cultures (Austin, 1998, Rosch, 1999). Buddhism, for example, teaches that the visible universe is an illusion of the senses. To become an enlightened being, a Buddhist tries to control bodily yearnings, to stop the ordinary experiences of the senses and mind, and to discover how to see things in their truest light. Thus, in the Buddhist view, meditation more accurately captures reality. In contrast, the Western scientist views meditation as the altered form of experience.

What exactly are the mental and physical effects of meditation? Changes in EEG patterns during meditation have been reported (Kasamatsu & Hirai, 1966). We lack evidence, however, to show that it produces lasting changes in the brain (Davidson, 2000). Certainly, it produces relaxation (Bjork, 1991). Meditation also reduces anxiety, especially in those who function in stress-filled environments (Benson, 1975; Shapiro, 1985; van Dam, 1996). In some ways, meditating is like resting, because it has been found to reduce some measures of bodily arousal (Dillbeck & Orme-Johnson, 1987; Holmes, 1984; Morrell, 1986). As for some of the more subjective benefits attributed to meditation, such as its power to bring new understandings and meaning to one's life, researchers dispute whether these changes are measurable.

Meditation: A form of consciousness change often induced by focusing on a repetitive behavior, assuming certain body positions, and minimizing external stimulation. Meditation is intended to enhance self-knowledge and well-being by reducing self-awareness.

Psychoactive drugs: Chemicals that affect mental processes and behavior by their effects on the nervous system.

Psychoactive Drug States

For millennia our ancestors have used alcohol, opium, cannabis, mescaline, coca, caffeine, and other drugs to alter their perceptions of reality. Especially under stress, individuals throughout the world take drugs to relax or avoid the unpleasantness of current realities. People also take drugs such as alcohol to help them feel comfortable with each other. And some drugs such as LSD are taken by people seeking the hallucinations they produce.

To some extent, all **psychoactive drugs** impair the emotion-based brain mechanisms that usually help us make good decisions (Gazzaniga, 1998). In addition, we should note that the most widely abused illegal drugs—cocaine, heroin, and amphetamines—are attractive because they stimulate the brain's "reward circuits." From an evolutionary perspective, we know that our brains are built to find pleasure in many substances (such as the taste of sweet or fatty foods) that helped our ancestors survive and reproduce. Cocaine, heroin, and amphetamines can trick us by exploiting these same mechanisms with strong pleasurable signals that makes our bodies "think" that these drugs are good for us (Nesse & Berridge, 1997).

Connection

Chapter 2
The limbic system contains "reward circuits" that produce sensations of pleasure when stimulated.

When psychologists talk about drugs, they include legal substances such as tobacco and caffeine, two extremely popular stimulants in most cultures.

Cultural trends influence drug-taking behavior, too. The United States saw this vividly during the 1960s and 1970s, when the country entered a period of casual experimentation with recreational drugs and other mind-altering techniques. By 1989, nearly 55% of American high school seniors had reported using one or more illegal drugs in their senior year (Johnston et al., 1989). Data from several sources, including emergency room visits, drug arrests, and surveys, indicate that overall illicit drug use has declined since the early 1990s. There has been, however, a rise in drug use among young teenagers (Martin, 1999). Credit for the overall decline in illicit drug use is often awarded to antidrug education programs, although the evidence does not show most of them to be especially effective (Murray, 1997).

Let us now have a closer look at the most commonly used and abused psychoactive drugs. We do so by grouping them in categories: *hallucinogens, opiates, depressants,* and *stimulants* (see Table 3.1). In general, we will find that all the drugs in each category will have similar effects on the mind and brain.

HALLUCINOGENS   Drugs known as **hallucinogens** or **psychedelics** produce changes in consciousness by altering perceptions of the external environment and inner awareness. They often create hallucinations and blur the boundary between self and the external world. For example, an individual experiencing hallucinogenic effects might listen to music and suddenly feel that he or she is producing the music or that the music is coming from within. Most hallucinogenic drugs act in the brain at specific receptor sites for the neurotransmitter serotonin (Jacobs, 1987).

Four of the commonly used hallucinogens are *mescaline* (from a type of cactus), *psilocybin* (from a mushroom), *LSD,* and *PCP* (phencyclidine). Both LSD and PCP are synthetic drugs made in chemical laboratories. PCP, or "angel dust," is a favorite of young people who use hallucinogens. This drug produces a strange dissociative reaction, in which the user feels disembodied or removed from parts of his or her personality. The user may become confused and insensitive to pain and feel separated from the surroundings.

Cannabis, derived from the hemp plant, is also usually classified as a hallucinogen. Its active ingredient is THC (tetrahydrocannabinol), found in both the plant's dried leaves and flowers *(marijuana)* and in the solidified resin of the plant *(hashish).* In the brain, THC causes the release of dopamine, which suggests an effect on the brain's reward system (Carlson, 2001). The experience derived from ingesting THC depends on its dose. Small doses create mild, pleasurable highs, and larger doses result in long hallucinogenic reactions. The positive effects include altered perception, sedation, pain relief, mild euphoria, and

Connection

Chapter 2
Serotonin is a neurotransmitter involved with sleep, memory, and depression.

Hallucinogens or **psychedelics:** Drugs that alter perceptions of the external environment and inner awareness.

Cannabis: A drug, derived from the hemp plant, whose effects include altered perception, sedation, pain relief, and mild euphoria. Cannabis is found in marijuana and hashish.

TABLE 3.1	Psychoactive Drugs: Medical Uses, Effects, Likelihood of Dependence			
			DEPENDENCE	
CATEGORY	MEDICAL USES		PSYCHOLOGICAL	PHYSIOLOGICAL
Opiates				
Morphine	Painkiller, cough suppressant		High	High
Heroin	Under investigation		High	High
Codeine	Painkiller, cough suppressant		Moderate	Moderate
Hallucinogens				
LSD	None		None	Unknown
PCP	Veterinary anesthetic		Unknown	High
Mescaline	None		None	Unknown
Psilocybin	None		Unknown	Unknown
Cannabis	Reduces nausea from chemotherapy		Unknown	Moderate
Depressants				
Barbiturates	Sedative, sleep, anticonvulsant, anesthetic		Moderate–High	Moderate–High
Benzodiazepines	Antianxiety, sleep, anticonvulsant, sedative		Low–Moderate	Low–Moderate
Alcohol	Antiseptic		Moderate	Moderate
Stimulants				
Amphetamines	Weight control, counteract anesthesia		High	High
Cocaine	Local anesthetic		High	High
Nicotine	Gum, patch for cessation of smoking		Low–High	Low–High
Caffeine	Weight control, stimulant in acute respiratory failure, analgesia		Unknown	Unknown

distortions of space and time—quite similar in some respects to the effects of heroin, according to research (Wickelgren, 1997). Depending on the social context and other factors, the psychological effects may also be negative: fear, anxiety, and confusion. Motor coordination is impaired with cannabis use (Julien, 1995), so those who work or drive under its influence suffer a higher risk of accidents (Moskowitz, 1985). Cannabis also produces temporary failures in memory. The potential for physical dependence on this drug, however, is lower than most other psychoactive substances (Grinspoon et al., 1997; Pinel, 2000).

OPIATES The class of drugs known as **opiates**—derivatives of the opium poppy—includes *morphine, heroin,* and *codeine.* All are highly addictive drugs that suppress physical sensation and response to stimulation. Morphine and codeine have excellent analgesic (pain-relieving) properties that result from their similarity to the body's own pain-relieving chemicals, the *endorphins.* Morphine has long been used in postsurgical medicine, and codeine frequently finds application as a cough suppressant.

Derived from morphine, heroin originally was developed in 19th-century Germany by the Bayer Company (of aspirin fame), but it was abandoned because it is even more highly addictive than morphine. For the intravenous heroin user, however, the drug has certain attractive effects that include a rush of pleasurable sensations. These feelings of euphoria supplant all worries and awareness of bodily needs, although—surprisingly—there are no major changes in cognitive abilities. Unfortunately, serious addiction is likely once a person

Connection

Chapter 2
Endorphins are the body's own opiatelike substances.

Opiates: Highly addictive drugs, derived from opium, that can produce a profound sense of well-being and have strong pain-relieving properties.

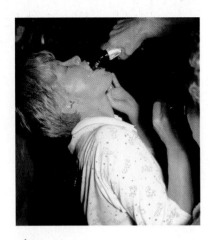

Physical dependence, tolerance, and addiction to alcohol often begin with binge drinking, common on many college campuses.

Connection

Chapter 13
Benzodiazepines are used to treat anxiety-related problems, such as panic disorder and obsessive-compulsive disorder.

Depressants: Drugs that slow down mental and physical activity by inhibiting transmission of nerve impulses in the central nervous system.

begins to inject heroin. To avoid the pain and cravings of withdrawal, the heroin user must take the drug frequently — at least daily — making it a very expensive habit to maintain. Because addicts often steal to support their habit, the use of heroin causes a high proportion of property crime in cities around the world.

Paradoxically, patients who take opiates for pain under medical supervision rarely become addicted. The reason for the difference between the use of opiates for pleasure and for pain is unclear. It appears, however, that the presence of pain causes opiates to affect parts of the brain other than the "reward centers" involved in pleasure. The practical point is this: There is little to fear from the legitimate medical use of these drugs for controlling pain (Melzack, 1990).

DEPRESSANTS Drugs that slow down the mental and physical activity of the body by inhibiting central nervous system activity are collectively known as **depressants.** They include *barbiturates* (usually prescribed for sedation), *benzodiazepines* (antianxiety drugs), and *alcohol* (a social stimulant and nervous system depressant). By inhibiting the transmission of nerve impulses in the central nervous system, depressants tend to slow down the mental and physical activity of the body. In appropriate dosages, depressants can relieve symptoms of pain or anxiety, but overuse or abuse of depressants is dangerous because these drugs impair reflexes and judgment. They may also be addictive.

Barbiturates, a common constituent of "sleeping pills," can induce sleep. Unfortunately, they have the little-known side effect of reducing REM-sleep time. This leaves the user feeling unrested, despite a full night's sleep. In addition, withdrawal from barbiturates causes severe REM rebound, filled with unpleasant dreams. Worse yet, overdoses of barbiturates may cause loss of all sensations, coma, and even death. Fatal reactions to barbiturates are made all the more likely because the lethal dose is relatively low, compared to the effective dose for inducing sleep or other effects. The chance of accidental overdose is further compounded by the additive effects of alcohol or other depressant drugs, which magnify the depressant action of barbiturates (Maisto et al., 1995).

The benzodiazepines (sometimes called "minor tranquilizers"), commonly prescribed to treat anxiety, are safer than barbiturates. Probably the best-known and most widely prescribed benzodiazepine is Valium. While the benzodiazepines (pronounced *BEN-zo-dye-AZ-a-peens*) can calm a patient without causing sleepiness or sedation, they, too, can be overused and abused. Overdoses may cause muscle incoordination, slurred speech, weakness, and irritability, while withdrawal symptoms include increased anxiety, muscle twitching, and sensitivity to sound and light. Because they are so commonly prescribed, and because they can be addictive, the benzodiazepines hold strong potential for abuse. However, these drugs are almost never used recreationally because people who are not anxious do not like their effects (Wesson et al., 1992).

Alcohol, another brain depressant, was one of the first psychoactive substances used by humankind. Under its influence, people have a variety of reactions that involve loosening of inhibitions. They may become talkative or quiet, friendly or abusive, ebullient or depressed. In very small dosages, alcohol can induce relaxation and even slightly improve an adult's reaction speed. However, the body breaks down alcohol at the rate of only one ounce per hour, and greater amounts consumed in short periods impair the central nervous system. When the level of alcohol in the blood reaches a mere 0.1% (1/1000 of the blood), an individual experiences deficits in thinking, memory, and judgment, along with emotional instability and motor incoordination. In most states this level of blood alcohol automatically qualifies a driver as being legally drunk.

Alcoholic beverage makers spend millions of dollars annually depicting the social and personal benefits of drinking alcoholic beverages. And, in fact, many adults use alcohol prudently. Yet, physical dependence, tolerance, and addiction all develop with prolonged heavy drinking—of the sort that often begins with binge drinking, common on many college campuses. When the amount and frequency of drinking alcohol interferes with job or school performance, impairs social and family relationships, and creates serious health problems, the diagnosis of *alcoholism* is appropriate (see Julien, 1995; Vallee, 1998). In general, the abuse of alcohol has become a significant problem for about 15 million Americans (Pinel, 2000). The effects of the problem are much more widespread, however. When ingested by pregnant women, alcohol can affect the fetus. In fact, alcohol use by expectant mothers is a leading cause of mental retardation (Abel & Sokol, 1986). Estimates suggest that 40% of Americans see the effects of alcohol abuse in a family member (Vallee, 1998). For many young Americans aged 15 to 25, the problem becomes a lethal one: Alcohol-related automobile accidents are the leading cause of death in this age group.

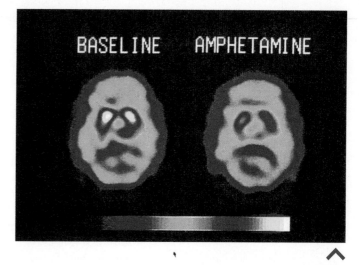

Brain changes during use of drugs can be seen on PET-scan images. Much less activity is seen in the limbic system of the brain under the influence of amphetamines.

STIMULANTS In contrast with depressants, **stimulants** increase central nervous system activity. They speed up both mental and physical rates of activity and enhance attention. Medically, stimulants alleviate symptoms of certain sleep disorders and also *attention-deficit/hyperactivity disorder* (ADHD) in children. They are also used to treat sleep attacks in narcoleptic patients. Recreational users of stimulants such as *amphetamines* and *cocaine* seek other effects: intense pleasurable sensations, increased self-confidence, greater energy and alertness, and euphoria. Cocaine, in particular, packs what may be the most powerful reinforcing punch of any illegal drug (Landry, 1997). *Crack,* an especially addictive form of cocaine, produces a swift high that wears off quickly.

On the down side, heavy amphetamine and cocaine users may experience frightening hallucinations and paranoid delusions (beliefs that others are out to harm them). Special dangers of these drugs include the emotional roller coaster of euphoric highs and depressive lows, which lead users to increase the frequency and dosage, quickly making the use of these drugs spiral out of control. Yet another danger accrues to children who were exposed to cocaine while in the womb: Studies show that such children are at high risk for developing cognitive problems, emotional difficulties, and behavior-control disorders (Vogel, 1997b).

Two other stimulants that you may not even think of as psychoactive drugs are *caffeine* and *nicotine*. Is it accurate to think of these commonplace, legal substances as "drugs"? Their effects are swift and powerful. Within 10 minutes, two cups of strong coffee or tea administer enough caffeine to profoundly affect the heart, blood circulation, and the efficiency of the brain. Nicotine inhaled in tobacco smoke may have similar effects within just seconds. Both are addictive. Both augment the effects of the natural rewarding chemicals released by the brain. Thus, nicotine and caffeine stimulate the same neurons that make us feel good whenever we have done something that aids our survival or reproduction. In this way, both drugs tease the brain's reward centers into responding as if it were good for us to be using these substances. For-

Stimulants: Drugs that arouse the central nervous system, speeding up mental and physical responses.

tunately, the negative effects of caffeine usage appear to be minor for most people. Further, caffeine has a built-in "braking" action that limits its intake: High dosages produce uncomfortable anxiety-like feelings.

On the other hand, nicotine is a much more dangerous drug because it is so addictive and because nicotine and the other ingredients in tobacco have been associated with a variety of health problems, including cancer, emphysema, and heart disease. In fact, the negative impact of smoking on health is greater than that of all other psychoactive drugs combined, including heroin, cocaine, and alcohol. According to the U.S. Public Health Service, smoking is the leading cause of preventable disease, with a human cost of more than 350,000 deaths annually. As a result, in 1995 the American Medical Association formally recommended that the U.S. Food and Drug Administration regard nicotine as a drug to be regulated. Currently, however, nicotine is both legal and actively promoted — with a $2.7 billion budget from the tobacco industry. Although antismoking campaigns have been somewhat effective in reducing the overall level of smoking in the United States, some 47 million Americans still smoke. Most worrisome is the fact that more than 3 million teenagers smoke, and their numbers are increasing by about 3,000 who start every day (Gardyn & Wellner, 2001; Julien, 1995).

Connection

Chapter 10
Smoking is an unhealthy response to stress.

Dependence and Addiction

In Your Life

The line between substance use and abuse is easy to cross for those who become addicted.

We have seen that powerful chemicals called psychoactive drugs can alter the functioning of neurons in your brain and, as a consequence, temporarily change your conscious awareness. Once in your brain, they usually act on synapses to block or stimulate neural messages. In this way, drugs profoundly alter the brain's communication system, affecting perception, memory, mood, and behavior.

Oddly, the continued use of many psychoactive drugs, such as alcohol, lessens their mind-distorting effect on the nervous system, so that greater dosages are required to achieve the same effect. Such reduced effectiveness with repeated use of a drug is called **tolerance.** Hand-in-hand with tolerance goes **physiological dependence**—a process in which the body adjusts to and becomes dependent on the substance, in part because the production of neurotransmitters in the brain is affected by the frequent presence of the drug (Wickelgren, 1998a). **Addiction** is one unfortunate outcome of tolerance and dependence. A person with a physical addiction requires the drug in his or her body and may suffer unpleasant withdrawal symptoms if the drug is not present. **Withdrawal** symptoms can include physical trembling, perspiring, nausea, and,

in the case of extreme alcohol withdrawal, even death. Although heroin and alcohol are the addictive drugs that most commonly come to mind, nicotine and caffeine, as well as certain sleeping pills and "tranquilizing" drugs, actually claim more addicts.

With or without being physically addicted, individuals may find themselves craving or hungering for the drug and its effects, a condition known as **psychological dependence.** This is a result of the powerfully rewarding effects that many psychoactive drugs produce. Psychological dependence can occur with any drug, including caffeine and nicotine, prescription medication, and over-the-counter drugs.

Addiction has its social and economic costs, too. For example, the expense of maintaining an illegal drug habit drives many addicts to crime, including robbery, embezzlement, assault, prostitution, or drug peddling.

Addiction, whether biological or psychological, ultimately affects the brain (Gazzaniga, 1998; Koob & Le Moal, 1997; Nestler, 2001). Consequently, in the view of many public health professionals, this makes both forms of addiction brain *diseases* (Leshner, 1997). On the other hand, the general public has been reluctant to see drug addicts as people suffering from chronic illness. Instead, the public sees addicts as weak or bad individuals who should be punished (MacCoun, 1998). What difference does this

characterization of addiction make? When they are seen as persons suffering from a disease, addicts are

(continued)

Tolerance: The reduced effectiveness a drug has after repeated use.

Physiological dependence: A process by which the body adjusts to, and becomes dependent on, a drug.

Addiction: A physical condition that produces withdrawal when the body lacks a certain drug.

Withdrawal: After addiction, a pattern of painful physical symptoms and cravings experienced when the level of drug is decreased or the drug is eliminated.

Psychological dependence: A pervasive desire to obtain or use a drug—independent of physical addiction.

most logically placed in treatment programs. By contrast, when they are seen as persons with defective characters, addicts are sent to prison for punishment—which does little to break the cycle of drug use, crime, and addiction.

Some observers, however, argue that viewing addiction as a disease may also interfere with the effective treatment of drug addicts. How? The addiction model, with its emphasis on biological causes and medical treatment, does little to deal with the social and economic context in which addictions develop. This may account for the fact that psycho-logically based treatment programs that treat alcohol abuse as a behavioral problem often work better than medically based programs (Miller & Brown, 1997). We can also see the blind spots of the medical/addiction model by comparing the poor record of treatment programs for heroin addicts who have picked up their habits on the streets of the United States with the far greater success rate of treatment for the thousands of veterans who became addicted to heroin in Vietnam. What made the difference? The addicted veterans did not remain in the environment where they had become addicted (the wartime culture of Vietnam). Instead, they returned home to an environment that was not so supportive of a heroin habit. In contrast, heroin users who become addicted in the United States tend to return, after treatment, to the same environment that originally led to their addiction.

Whether physical or psychological, disease or character flaw, drug addiction poses many personal and social problems. Clearly, this is a field that has much room for new ideas and new research.

CHECKYOURUNDERSTANDING

1. **RECALL:** *Hypnosis is sometimes used by psychological researchers to*
   a. study the effects of psychoactive drugs.
   b. induce amnesia for traumatic experiences.
   c. cure patients suffering from severe mental disorders.
   d. create mental states, such as anxiety or euphoria.

2. **RECALL:** *Psychoactive drugs usually create their effects by mimicking _____ in the brain.*
   a. dendrites
   b. neurotransmitters
   c. stress reactions
   d. memories

3. **RECALL:** *Which of the following statements is true?*
   a. Research has proven that addiction is a brain disease.
   b. Most public health professionals view addiction as a character weakness.
   c. Some psychologists suggest that treating addiction as a disease ignores the social and economic factors that surround the problem.
   d. The cycle of addiction is most efficiently broken with a combination of punishment for relapses and drugs that counteract the effects of psychoactive drugs.

4. **APPLICATION:** *Which of the following groups of drugs have the opposite effects on the brain?*
   a. hallucinogens and stimulants
   b. opiates and sedatives
   c. stimulants and depressants
   d. depressants and opiates

5. **UNDERSTANDING THE CORE CONCEPT:**
   An altered state of consciousness occurs when some aspect of normal consciousness is modified either by mental, behavioral, or chemical means. This suggests that:
   a. some states of consciousness are mystical phenomena that cannot ever be explained.
   b. all states of consciousness are controlled by unconscious needs, desires, and memories.
   c. altered states of consciousness are the source of creativity in our minds.
   d. psychologists can study altered states of consciousness with scientific methods.

Core Concept

ANSWERS: 1. d   2. b   3. c   4. c   5. d

108   **CHAPTER 3**   STATES OF MIND   www.ablongman.com/zimbardo

Using Psychology to Learn Psychology: Connecting Consciousness with Memory

expand your consciousness? The fact is that consciousness is a limited resource, as we have seen. What can be expanded, however, is the access your consciousness has to information you have stored outside of consciousness. Learning how to do this can be of tremendous help to students who need to acquire a large amount of information and prove it on an exam.

You will, of course, have an advantage if you face an exam with your consciousness unimpaired by the massive sleep debt that students sometimes incur in an "all-nighter" study session. No amount of caffeine can bring your sleep-deprived consciousness back to optimum functioning. And to know the material, it is smart to spread your studying over several days or weeks, rather than trying to learn everything at once.

It can also help to understand that consciousness is fundamentally the same as *working memory,* a mental "work space" that holds only a few items at once (as we will see in more detail in Chapter 7). Because of its severely limited capacity, you cannot possibly hold all the information you need to remember for an exam in consciousness. Most of the material must be stored outside of consciousness in long-term memory. The trick is to be able to bring it back to consciousness when needed. Here are some strategies that you may find helpful in doing this:

1. *Study for the gist.* Students sometimes think their professors ask "trick questions," although professors almost never do so intentionally. In reality, good exam questions will show whether students understand the meaning of a term — the *gist* — rather than having merely memorized a definition. A twofold study strategy can help you get the gist of a concept. First, paraphrase the definition given in the text or in class. Second, think of an example from your own experience that illustrates the concept.

2. *Look for connections among concepts.* Even if you have the gist of the concepts you have studied, you will probably need to know how those concepts are related to each other. The professor may ask you to explain, for example, what happens to the *sleep cycle* in people with *narcolepsy.* Therefore a good study strategy is to ask yourself: How is this new concept related to what I learned previously?

3. *Anticipate the most likely cues.* Just because you know the material doesn't mean that the exam questions will make the right answer spill from long-term memory back into consciousness. It pays, therefore, to spend some of your study time thinking about the kinds of questions your professor might ask. For example, you may have learned about the effects of various psychoactive drugs, but you could be stumped when the professor asks you to explain why alcohol is more like the barbiturates than the opiates. You can often anticipate such questions by noting what the professor emphasizes in lecture. It also helps to think of the kinds of questions that your professor is known to favor. (A study partner helps a lot with this.) Some of the most frequently seen test questions begin with terms such as "Explain," "Evaluate," or "Compare and contrast."

In general, the relationship between consciousness and memory suggests that learning the kind of material required in your college classes requires that the material be *actively processed* while it is in consciousness. To do so effectively, it must be made meaningful. This requires making connections between new information and information that is already in your memory. It also requires organizing the information so that you see how it is interconnected. And, finally, it requires anticipating the cues that will be used to bring it back to consciousness.

Chapter Summary

WHAT IS THE NATURE OF CONSCIOUSNESS?

Consciousness represents one of the major mysteries of psychology. Cognitive psychologists theorize that consciousness is adaptive because it helps us integrate cognitions with external stimulation. It is also a process that has many distinct levels, including the preconscious, the subconscious, and the unconscious, as well as ordinary awareness. New technologies and techniques have opened windows on conscious processes for researchers. Increasingly, cognitive scientists are disputing the Freudian concept of an unconscious that works in opposition with the conscious mind.

The brain creates consciousness when it combines external stimulation with internal experience.

WHAT ARE THE CYCLES OF EVERYDAY CONSCIOUSNESS?

Consciousness shifts and changes in everyday life, commonly taking the form of daydreaming, sleep, and nocturnal dreams. Sleep researchers have revealed the features of the normal sleep cycle, including the four stages of sleep, which change predictably over the course of the night. The sleep cycle also changes with age. Distortions of the sleep cycle define certain sleep disorders, including insomnia, sleep apnea, and narcolepsy.

Consciousness changes in cycles that normally correspond to our biological rhythms and to the patterns of our environment.

WHAT OTHER FORMS CAN CONSCIOUSNESS TAKE?

Altered states of consciousness include not only sleep but hypnosis, meditation, and the effects of psychoactive drugs. From a neuroscience perspective, these may involve changes in psychological processes rather than entirely new forms of awareness. Hypnosis remains a puzzle, although it is known to block pain and have other uses in therapy and research. Likewise, experts dispute whether meditation is a distinct state of consciousness, even though it has measurable effects on arousal. To understand the effects of psychoactive drugs, it is helpful to group them as hallucinogens, opiates, depressants, and stimulants. Most psychoactive drugs that are abused produce sensations of pleasure and well-being that make the drugs especially attractive and potentially addictive.

An altered state of consciousness occurs when some aspect of normal consciousness is modified by mental, behavioral, or chemical means.

Review Test

For each of the following items, choose the single correct or best answer. The correct answers appear at the end of the test.

1. What was the objection by Watson and other behaviorists to the study of consciousness?
   a. Conscious processes cannot be directly observed and measured.
   b. Consciousness could not be studied by means of introspection.
   c. Consciousness is not affected by rewards and punishments.
   d. Consciousness is the result of an inner life force, which they did not have the tools to study.

2. Imaging techniques, such as MRI and PET scans, allow cognitive scientists to connect mental activity with
   a. cognition.
   b. behavior.
   c. brain activity.
   d. priming.

3. Which of the following is *not* one of the functions of consciousness cited by your text?
   a. restricting attention to what is relevant
   b. combining sensation with memory
   c. imagining and considering alternatives
   d. relinquishing control to enhance self-awareness

4. From a Freudian perspective, which of the following choices correctly pairs an example of an experience or process with its appropriate level of consciousness?
   a. unconscious: repressing traumatic experiences
   b. subconscious: regulation of blood pressure
   c. nonconscious: remembering how to tell time
   d. preconscious: preventing awareness of traumatic memories

5. Rapid eye movements are reliable behavioral signs that
   a. an individual has reached the deepest level of sleep.
   b. one has achieved a genuine meditative state.
   c. a sleeper's mental activity is centered on dreaming.
   d. a subject is very low in hypnotizability.

6. Which one of the following is a sleep disorder characterized by brief interruptions when the sleeper stops breathing, wakens, resumes breathing, and falls back asleep?
   a. apnea
   b. daytime sleepiness
   c. insomnia
   d. analgesia

7. Which of the following statements about hypnosis is true?
   a. Hypnosis is actually a form of NREM sleep.
   b. Hypnotizability relies on a subject's ability to respond to suggestion.
   c. Anyone can be hypnotized if the hypnotist knows the most effective techniques to use.
   d. The less intelligent or educated a person is, the more hypnotizable he or she will be.

8. Psychology has verified that meditation can be useful for producing
   a. a deeper understanding of oneself.
   b. enlightenment.
   c. a state of relaxation.
   d. heightened cognitive arousal.

9. Which of the following is a condition that would lead one to experience hallucinations?
   a. a deep hypnotic state
   b. use of the drug mescaline
   c. withdrawal from alcohol in severe alcoholism
   d. all of the above

10. Three major effects sought by users of _____ are increased alertness, greater self-confidence, and euphoria.
    a. stimulants
    b. depressants
    c. opiates
    d. hallucinogens

ANSWERS: 1. a 2. c 3. d 4. a 5. c 6. a 7. b 8. c 9. d 10. a

If You're
Interested . . .

BOOKS

Bentov, I. (1988). *Stalking the wild pendulum: On the mechanics of consciousness.* Inner Traditions International. Before his untimely death in 1979, Bentov was in the forefront of the new science of consciousness. With this book he questioned the materialistic view of mind, and, with imagination and humor, suggested a moral order based on a new idea about consciousness.

Coren, S. (1996). *Sleep thieves: An eye-opening exploration into the science and mysteries of sleep.* Free Press Paperbacks. Here are the "A to ZZZZs of sleep," including whether dogs and cats dream; determining whether you are getting enough sleep; how to help children sleep better; and the dangers of Daylight Savings Time.

Davich, V. N. (1998). *The best guide to meditation.* Audio Renaissance. An illustrated review of meditation's religious, therapeutic, and New Age origins and influences, the book or audiotape guides the reader through the basics of meditation irrespective of any particular belief system.

Dement, W. C., with Vaughn, C. (1999). *The promise of sleep: A pioneer in sleep medicine explains the vital connection between health, happiness, and a good night's sleep.* Delacorte Press. One of the best experts on sleep asserts that we are a "sleep-sick" society, and explains how we lost our gift for sleep and how we might get it back—and why we will be better for it.

Dennett, D. C. (1992). *Consciousness explained.* Little Brown & Co. We know a lot of things subjectively —how a favorite beverage tastes, what a piece of music "feels" like—that are extremely hard to explain. Dennet shows that consciousness can be explored in an exciting and humorous manner.

Gazzaniga, M. (1998). *The mind's past.* University of California Press. Neuroscientist Michael S. Gazzaniga examines the whethers and whats of the brain's evolutionary advantages and the construction of personal identity and memory.

Mindell, A. (2000). *Dreaming while awake: Techniques for 24-hour lucid dreaming.* Hampton Roads Publishing Company. Dreams weave together our conscious ideas and concerns, so that while awake we may learn to detect the "seeds of dreaming" and influ-

ence their presentation in our dreams, perhaps solving problems and enhancing bodily healing in the process.

Nørretranders, T. (1998). *The user illusion: Cutting consciousness down to size.* Translated by Johnathan Sydenham. Viking Press. In computer science, the "user illusion" is the desktop graphic that conceals the program's inner workings and dynamics. The author writes that our very consciousness is similar to the computer operator's "user illusion," a desktop graphic hiding the machine's inner workings. Our own minds filter and discard an astounding amount of information—what the author calls "exformation." Just how much of reality are we missing out on, after all?

Peacock, R., & Gorman, R. (Eds.). (1998). *Sleep: Bedtime reading.* Universe Publishing. Wide awake and trying not to worry about it? Try some bedtime reading by the best authors. This volume includes short works by authors ranging from Alice Walker to John Updike, along with poetry, pictures, and photographs—all designed to take your mind off what's keeping you awake so you can get some rest.

Ramachandran, V. S., & Blakeslee, S. (1998). *Phantoms in the brain: Probing the mysteries of the human mind.* William Morrow & Co. Based on case studies of patients suffering from a wide array of neurological disorders—from phantom limb pain to stroke-induced disabilities—the authors capture the wonder of people's ability to assert life and individuality beyond the challenges to their bodies and brains.

Svengali (David Geliebter). (1998). *Fun with hypnosis: The complete how-to guide.* Phat Publications. Assuming the name of the frightening fictional hypnotist, the author acknowledges the fascination and fear most of us feel about hypnosis, but also emphasizes that hypnosis, comparable to sleeping or daydreaming, is a *normal* if altered state of mind.

VIDEOS

Altered States. (1980, color, 121 min.). Directed by Ken Russell; starring William Hurt, Blair Brown, Bob Balaban, Charles Haid. This is very dated now but still a good, weird story (especially for a generation of "X Files" fans), with a fantastic plot and high-end vocabulary scripted by the late Paddy Chayefsky, based on his novel. A scientist experiments with sensory deprivation and mind expansion. There is no valid scientific information here, but good imagery and worthwhile questions about the primitive origins and natures of our own states of mind.

Days of Wine and Roses. (1962, black-and-white, 117 min.). Directed by Blake Edwards; starring Jack Lemmon and Lee Remick. This film presents a sentimental but not romanticized view of how alcohol influences a romance, becomes a theme of the marriage, and ultimately destroys the relationship. Included are excellent performances and musical score.

The Lost Weekend. (1945, black-and-white, 101 min.). Directed by Billy Wilder; starring Ray Milland, Jane Wyman, Howard da Silva, Frank Faylen. Ray Milland's Oscar-winning performance riveted audiences with his painful assertion that, "I'm not a drinker—I'm a drunk." A drinking binge takes an articulate, intelligent man from his favorite bar to a psychiatric hospital admission. Harsh and realistic, this was a landmark film in its stark depiction of alcohol abuse.

The Matrix. (1999, color, 136 min.). Directed by Andy Wachowsky & Larry Wachowski; starring Keanu Reeves, Laurence Fishburne, Carrie-Anne Moss. A computer hacker is drafted by a group of techno-rebels in a suspenseful, subversive exploration of mind control and illusion. The movie considers how artificial intelligence might be employed to produce immersion in artificial reality.

Traffic. (2000, color, 137 min.). Directed by Steven Soderbergh; starring Michael Douglas, Catherine Zeta-Jones, Benicio Del Toro (Oscar© for Supporting Actor). America's new "drug czar" discovers his daughter is an addict and becomes enmeshed in the front lines of drug smuggling, crime, and violence. This is less about the psychological effects of illegal drugs than their social and personal consequences.

CD

Gibson, D. (1998). *Natural Sleep Inducement.* This recording incorporates music and natural sounds such as waves and water with biorhythms to support sleep. It was designed with the guidance of a cognitive psychologist with expertise in effects of music.

WEB RESOURCES

http://www.sleepfoundation.org/pressarchives.new_stats.html Sleep is essential for survival, and it is a very important state of consciousness. The National Sleep Foundation presents information on sleep, as well as sleep disorders.

http://www.sleepfoundation.org/epworth/quiz.html Many college students do not get the amount of sleep that the brain and body need to function normally. Use this Web site to test your knowledge of sleep and determine whether or not you are sleep deprived.

http://www.dreamgate.com/dream/resources/online97.htm Dreams combine subconscious and conscious hopes, fantasies, and worries. Visit this massive Web site in order to learn more about dreams.

HOW DO PSYCHOLOGISTS EXPLAIN DEVELOPMENT?

The Nature–Nurture Interaction
Gradual vs. Abrupt Change

Development is a process of growth and change brought about by an interaction of heredity and environment.

PSYCHOLOGICAL TRAITS IN YOUR GENES:
While genes contribute to your thoughts and behaviors, you shouldn't assume that biology is everything.

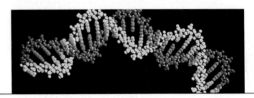

WHAT CAPABILITIES DOES THE NEWBORN POSSESS?

Prenatal Development
Abilities of the Newborn Child
Building on the Neonatal Blueprint

Newborns begin life equipped to deal with three basic survival tasks: finding nourishment, making contacts with people, and avoiding harmful situations.

MILESTONES IN A CHILD'S DEVELOPMENT:
The developmental milestones are averages, but children show great variation in their development.

WHAT ARE THE DEVELOPMENTAL TASKS OF CHILDHOOD?

How Children Acquire Language
Cognitive Development
The Development of Moral Thinking
Social and Emotional Development

Children face especially important developmental tasks in the areas of language, thought processes, and social relationships.

CHILDHOOD INFLUENCES ON YOUR PERSONALITY:
Erikson's theory says that your personality is shaped by a series of developmental crises.

WHAT DEVELOPMENTAL CHANGES OCCUR IN ADOLESCENCE AND ADULTHOOD?

The Transitions of Adolescence
The Developmental Challenges of Adulthood

Nature and nurture continue to produce changes in personality and mental processes throughout the life cycle.

THE LAST DEVELOPMENTAL PROBLEMS YOU WILL FACE:
The final years of life present a challenge, but a new picture of aging is emerging.

USING PSYCHOLOGY TO LEARN PSYCHOLOGY: Cognitive Development in College Students

PSYCHOLOGICAL DEVELOPMENT

fter graduating from college in 1979, Shirley and Reuben ended their long engagement with a traditional wedding ceremony at the campus chapel. Their first son, Bobby, was born later that year, and from day one he was the light of their lives. Although he did not cry often, the young parents jumped at his every sound. As he grew older, Bobby was equally happy leading other children in games or working alone on puzzles and taking things apart to see how they worked. He could be counted on never to make trouble, to be respectful of his elders, and to make sensible decisions that were never influenced solely by his emotions. He excelled in school and went from being teachers' pet to high school

valedictorian and on to college class president in a most natural progression.

Meanwhile, a second child, Billy, had been born to Shirley and Reuben in 1982. By then the proud parents knew a bit more about when to react to a baby's cries. They knew they could count on Bobby to keep him in line and take care of him. Billy Boy always seemed to be in the shadow of his big brother. They got along reasonably well, but Billy felt that he could never quite measure up to his big brother. That feeling may have influenced his progress, which always seemed a little slower on nearly every dimension: walking, talking, problem solving, forming relationships. When he entered school, it

(continued)

didn't help that teachers would remind him how smart and responsible his big brother was. Billy Boy tried hard, was a good student, and had friends, but he could never do or achieve what Bobby did so seamlessly.

Two years after Billy, Benny was born, and with him the peace, quiet, and order of the family household went out the back door. He cried a lot and did whatever it took to get the attention of his parents and those two older lugs. Benny excelled at breaking and messing up things. He found ever new ways to be alternately charming and irritating. But he made friends like bees make honey. What he lacked in smarts, Benny made up for in creativity and daring risk taking that produced novel consequences—some good, some . . . Don't ask.

At this writing, Bobby is majoring in physics. After he graduates from the university in only three years, he plans to be one of the first physicist-astronauts to work in a space station. Billy Boy is a college freshman with ambitions to own a car dealership in his hometown. Benny prefers the beach volleyball circuit but plans to finish high school, if he can take time away from girls. He has some interesting ideas about how to redesign Internet dating services and cyberspace courses that would replace boring teachers with ICIs — Ideally Cyber-Constructed Instructors. The problem is harnessing all that creative energy long enough for Benny to make a marketable product out of his many projects and staying out of trouble long enough for that to happen.

One key to understanding the differences in the behavioral styles of Bobby, Billy, and Benny comes from the analysis of the impact of birth order on personality development. Birth-order expert Frank Sulloway (1996) argues that siblings learn to adapt to the power differences in the family by developing different strategies to compete for parental attention and favor.

People tend to agree about these birth order differences when asked to characterize those they know based on their sibling rank. The common belief is that firstborns are obedient, responsible, outgoing, intelligent, and unemotional. Last-borns are emotional, creative, irresponsible, and very outgoing. Middle-borns like Billy are ranked in the middle on these traits. Later-borns, like Benny, are often rebels. Only-borns? People commonly believe them to be spoiled, academic, and disagreeable (see Baskett, 1985; Musun-Miller, 1993; Nyman, 1995). These expectations, by themselves, can have powerful effects. Not everyone fits these expectations, of course, but Sulloway's large survey of thousands of biographies reveals that throughout history, eminent, successful people tend to be firstborns, like almost all the U.S. astronauts, while later-borns were most likely to lead rebellions and to propose radical theories or be the first to accept those of other scientists and philosophers.

Bobby, Billy, and Benny bring into focus several important forces that influence human development over the course of one's lifetime: heredity, family dynamics, and expectations. Some of these forces like birth order, family dynamics, peer pressure, culture, and economic circumstances, are part of a complex *environment* that shapes us. In addition, we are shaped by *heredity,* which includes all the genetic influences—both physical and behavioral—passed on to us from our parents.

To discover and understand how all these factors interact over the life span is the challenge of **developmental psychology.** We will begin our tour of developmental psychology by considering how psychologists think about

Developmental psychology: The psychological specialty that studies how organisms change over time as the result of biological and environmental influences.

development, starting with the study of newborns. Later we will follow the patterns of development across the life span, from infancy and childhood through adolescence and adulthood and to the end of life itself.

HOW DO PSYCHOLOGISTS EXPLAIN DEVELOPMENT?

What have been the top ten changes in your life?

If you compare your personal list to those of others, you will find some broad similarities: You were born, formed relationships, attended school, and matured both physically and mentally. Your list may also hint at some of the ways you are distinctive: Perhaps you matured socially earlier than your friends, or perhaps you are more self-confident than others you know. In broad terms, however, your developmental story tells of growth and change resulting from the most important influences on your life—both hereditary and environmental. The Core Concept for this section emphasizes the relationship between these two overreaching factors:

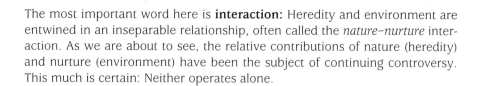

Development is a process of growth and change brought about by an interaction of heredity and environment.

The most important word here is **interaction:** Heredity and environment are entwined in an inseparable relationship, often called the *nature–nurture* interaction. As we are about to see, the relative contributions of nature (heredity) and nurture (environment) have been the subject of continuing controversy. This much is certain: Neither operates alone.

The Nature–Nurture Interaction

It was probably Shakespeare, in *The Tempest,* who first brought the terms *nature* and *nurture* together (Gottesman, 1997). More important, Shakespeare seems to have grasped the idea that nature and nurture can work in partnership—an idea that has not always been obvious to others. Philosophers, educators, scientists, and others who missed this important point have long argued over which of these forces—nature or nurture—is the more important influence on our thoughts and behaviors. This long-running debate has been labeled the **nature–nurture controversy.**

Although the nature–nurture debate continues on talk shows and in the popular press, psychologists today are more interested in understanding how heredity and environment work together to produce our personalities and our mental abilities (Bronfenbrenner & Ceci, 1994; Dannefer & Perlmutter, 1990). We known that virtually every human characteristic (with the trivial exceptions of certain physical traits, such as eye color) is shaped by both an individual's biological inheritance and experience (de Waal, 1999). That is, *nature and nurture interact.* Heredity establishes your potential, but experience determines how your potential will be realized.

Still, we might ask: Which of our characteristics does heredity affect most? And which are most heavily influenced by learning or other environmental factors (such as disease or nutrition)? It is worth noting that the answers to these questions pose some danger. For example, we know that certain genetic disorders, such as Down syndrome, can produce mental retardation, aggressive behavior, or social-emotional deficiencies—and there is no cure. Hearing this, the parents or teachers of children with such problems may sim-

Interaction: A process by which forces work together or influence each other—as in the interaction between the forces of heredity and environment.

Nature–nurture controversy: The long-standing dispute over the relative importance of nature (heredity) and nurture (environment) in their influence on behavior and mental processes.

Connection

Chapter 2
Down syndrome is a genetic disorder caused by an extra 21st chromosome fragment.

Twin studies are one way to study the relative importance of nature and nurture, but they must be interpreted with caution. This photo shows the identical "Bob Twins," who, like the "Jim Twins," grew up not knowing of each other's existence. Both sport mustaches and smoke a pipe; both have engineering degrees; and both married teachers named Brenda. It is unlikely that all the similarities—striking as they may be—are caused by genetics.

Connection

Chapter 1
Correlational studies look for relationships among variables—but not cause and effect.

Connection

Chapter 8
Intelligence is influenced by both heredity and environment.

Twin studies: Developmental investigations in which twins, especially identical twins, are compared in the search for genetic and environmental effects.

Adoption studies: An alternative to twin studies in which the adopted child's characteristics are compared to those of the biological family and of the adoptive family.

ply give up hope. By focusing on the genetic cause, they may overlook effective learning-based treatments that can measurably improve the living skills of these individuals.

Mindful of the dangers, psychologists cautiously study the hereditary and environmental contributions to thought and behavior. To do so, they have invented several methods for weighing the effects of nature and nurture. These include studies of twins and studies of adopted children. Briefly, we will examine the strengths and weaknesses of these two methods.

TWIN STUDIES Twins, especially when they have been separated since birth, can give us some tantalizing clues about the relative importance of nature and nurture. We must interpret these observations with great care, however (Phelps et al., 1997). Consider, for example, the controversial case of the "Jim twins" (Jackson, 1980). Separated in infancy and reunited after nearly 40 years, Jim Springer and Jim Lewis display some remarkable similarities. Both have been married twice, the first time to Lindas and the second time to women named Betty. Both owned dogs named Toy and worked as sheriff's deputies. Both smoke Salem cigarettes, drink Miller Lite beer, and make miniature furniture out of wood. Are these examples of heredity in action? There is no way to know for sure what to ascribe to genetics and what to chance. Critics of **twin studies** correctly point out that the similarities found in *case studies*—no matter how astounding—may well be mere coincidences: Any two people, related or not, are likely to have a number of things in common.

Less striking—but more scientifically robust—are findings that cut across many pairs of twins. These *correlational studies* have found, for example, that twins are more similar than other siblings on measures of intelligence, personality, and interests, as well as in their facial expressions, gestures, and pace of speech (Bouchard et al., 1990; Jackson, 1980). Such findings strongly suggest that these characteristics have at least some genetic basis.

ADOPTION STUDIES If you adopted a baby, would it grow up to resemble you more than its biological parents? This is the sort of question asked by psychologists who do **adoption studies.** With this method, they compare the characteristics of adopted children with those of their biological and adoptive family members. Similarities with the biological family suggest the effects of nature, while similarities with the adoptive family point to the influence of nurture. This work, along with the twin studies, has suggested a genetic contribution to a variety of psychological characteristics, such as intelligence, sexual orientation, temperament, and impulsive behavior (Bouchard, 1994; Dabbs, 2000; Hamer, 1997; Saudino, 1997; Wright & Mahurin, 1997). Likewise, heredity can play a role in a variety of mental disorders, including alcoholism, Alzheimer's disease, schizophrenia, depression, and panic disorder (Eley, 1997; Plomin et al., 1994; Pool, 1997).

Currently behavioral genetics is one of the hottest topics in psychology, an area that has gained momentum from our new insights into the human genome. Despite this enthusiasm (or perhaps because of it) we must guard against attributing any behavior or mental process entirely to heredity. The danger, of course, is that people will mindlessly attribute characteristics they dislike in others solely to "bad genes." In doing so, they will disregard the powerful environmental influences that also shape intelligence, emotional responsiveness, personality traits, and mental disorders—virtually every psychological characteristic that is impacted by genetics (Mann, 1994; Sapolsky, 1997).

Gradual versus Abrupt Change

Taking its place alongside the nature–nurture controversy, a second major issue in developmental psychology deals with the *pattern* of development: Do developmental changes happen abruptly or gradually? Do we go through "stages" or do we continually change throughout our lives?

Consider how a child's ability to think and reason changes during the progression from infancy to adulthood. According to the **continuity view,** children become more skillful in thinking, talking, or acting in much the same way that they become taller: through a gradual developmental process. In contrast, psychologists who take a **discontinuity view** see development as a succession of changes that produce different behavior in different age-specific life periods, or *stages,* such as infancy, childhood, and adolescence. In this view, development can be abrupt, or *discontinuous.* Thus, a child enters a new developmental period when new abilities appear, often rather suddenly, as in the development of walking or talking. (See Figure 4.1.)

You may have heard parents dismissing a child's misbehavior or moodiness as "just going through a stage," such as the "terrible twos," when children are becoming more mobile and independent. But for psychologists who subscribe to the discontinuity view, stages are not simply difficult times. These psychologists define **developmental stages** as periods of life initiated by distinct transitions (changes) in physical or psychological functioning. From a stage perspective, specific abilities, such as walking, talking, or abstract reasoning, appear at specific ages or life periods because different developmental processes come into play. In general, developmental psychologists who take the discontinuity view find that people go through the same stages in the same order—but not necessarily at the same rate.

Connection

Chapter 2
The recently unveiled human genome contains our complete genetic "blueprint."

Continuity view: The perspective that development is gradual and continuous—as opposed to the discontinuity (stage) view.

Discontinuity view: The perspective that development proceeds in an uneven (discontinuous) fashion—as opposed to the continuity view.

Developmental stages: Periods of life initiated by significant transitions or changes in physical or psychological functioning.

Many developmental changes, both physical and psychological, occur across the life span. Here we see Bill Clinton as a boy, as a young man running for office, and during his presidency.

The continuity view sees development as a process of continual change, while the discontinuity view sees development as a series of "steps" or stages.

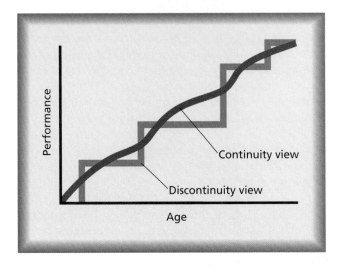

Self-fulfilling prophecy: An expectation that becomes realized because it guides people's behaviors.

Psychology In Your Life

Psychological Traits in Your Genes

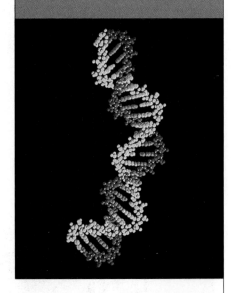

The genetic code, written in DNA, contains our complete hereditary blueprint, grouped into genes and chromosomes.

Eye color and the shape of your earlobes are purely genetic traits — but, as far as we know, heredity by itself determines none of our psychological characteristics (Horgan, 1993). In the psychological domain, heredity always acts in combination with environment. Nevertheless, developmental psychologists and biopsychologists often ask which characteristics have strong genetic links. In fact, they have found a number of traits that have a substantial hereditary basis — including some of your own attributes.

A genetic contribution to general intelligence, for example, is well established — although psychologists disagree over both the strength of heredity's role and the nature of "intelligence" (Plomin et al., 1994). There is also a good possibility that genes contribute to your sexual orientation (Hamer et al., 1993). And it just may be that an interest in skydiving, rock climbing, or other risky behavior has a genetic basis (Hamer, 1997). The evidence suggests that genes also contribute to your basic temperament and personality, including all of the "big five" personality factors (Bouchard, 1994; Plomin, 1997). (See Chapter 11, Personality.)

Some mental and behavioral disorders are associated with genetic abnormalities, too (Eley, 1997; Gibbs, 1995; Mann, 1994; Plomin et al., 1994). One of the first to be discovered was *Huntington's disease,* a rare problem that causes aggressive behavior and mental deterioration beginning in midlife. Depression is among the more common emotional problems that can have an underlying genetic basis. Experts also believe that genetics contributes to *schizophrenia,* a major mental disorder. Fear can have a hereditary basis, as well, especially for those who have a condition known as *panic disorder.* So can repetitive rituals (such as compulsively checking and rechecking the alarm-clock setting) seen in *obsessive–compulsive disorder.* Likewise, the violence of an *antisocial personality* and the uncontrollable outbursts of *Tourette's syndrome* may originate in the genes. And, if you are older, you may worry that every instance of forgetting is a sign of *Alzheimer's disease,* which (in some forms) arises from a genetic flaw that first takes the memory and then the rest of the mind. (See Chapter 12, Psychopathology.)

Thus, it appears that many psychological traits, both desirable and undesirable, have a connection to our genes. But please note: Genetics is not everything. While heredity is involved in nearly all we do, human behaviors also are shaped by environment. This includes learning, as well as factors such as nutrition and physical stress (Brown, 1999).

Unfortunately, people sometimes go to extremes by seeing hereditary effects everywhere. The danger lies in creating a sense of helplessness in those whose parents have undesirable characteristics, such as mental disorders or aggressive personalities. A strong hereditarian stance can also lead to unfair labeling of people as having "bad blood," if they come from troubled families. Just as disturbing, hereditarian expectations can create complacency and self-centeredness in those whose parents have desirable characteristics, such as high intelligence or good looks. Either way, expectations about genetic influences can also create a **self-fulfilling prophecy,** which leads people to live up (or down) to their expectations.

The main idea to remember is that heredity and environment *interact.* In the realm of behaviors and complex traits, neither one acts alone. Rather, genetics offers a basic plan, which learning always modifies.

1. **RECALL:** *Psychologists have resolved the nature–nurture controversy by saying that we are the products of*
   a. heredity.
   b. environment.
   c. both heredity and environment.
   d. neither heredity nor environment.

2. **APPLICATION:** *Which of the following statements is most accurate with regard to the "Jim twins"?*
   a. We cannot say for certain that their similarities are mainly genetic.
   b. It is reasonably certain that their similarities come from shared early experiences.
   c. It has been proven that their similarities are just chance.

   d. They are similar because they were raised in the same family environment.

3. **RECALL:** *Which perspective says that developmental change is a gradual process?*
   a. the continuity view
   b. the discontinuity view
   c. the hereditarian view
   d. the environmental view

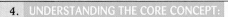

4. **UNDERSTANDING THE CORE CONCEPT:**
   Name a human characteristic that is caused by an interaction of heredity and environment.

ANSWERS: 1. c   2. a   3. a   4. There are many, including language, temperament, and certain mental disorders.

WHAT CAPABILITIES DOES THE NEWBORN POSSESS?

People used to think that babies began life completely helpless and dependent on their caregivers. In recent years, however, that picture has been changing. As we will see, psychologists now know that babies are born with a remarkable set of abilities programmed into their genes. These innate abilities are the focus of the Core Concept for this section:

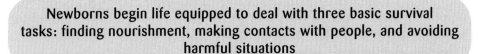

Newborns begin life equipped to deal with three basic survival tasks: finding nourishment, making contacts with people, and avoiding harmful situations

Prenatal period: The developmental period before birth.

Zygote: A fertilized egg.

Embryo: In humans, the name for the developing organism during the first eight weeks after conception.

Differentiation: The process by which cells in the embryo take on specialized functions.

Fetus: In humans, the term for the developing organism between the embryonic stage and birth.

Placenta: The organ separating the embryo or fetus and the mother. The placenta separates the bloodstreams, but it allows the exchange of nutrients and waste products.

Teratogen: Any substance from the environment, including viruses, drugs, and other chemicals, that can damage the developing organism during the prenatal period.

As the brain grows in the developing embryo, it forms 250,000 new neurons per minute.

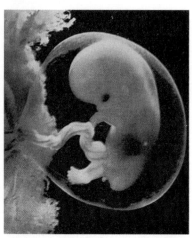

To understand the origins and development of these abilities, we will consider four sets of underlying processes: (1) prenatal development and behavior, (2) maturation, (3) sensory development, and (4) how the developing infant builds on the neonatal blueprint.

Prenatal Development

The **prenatal period** spans the time between conception and birth. It is a time of furious developmental activity that readies the organism for life on its own outside the womb. In this prenatal period, the developing organism successively goes through three stages, during which it is called a *zygote,* then an *embryo,* and finally a *fetus.*

Shortly after conception, the fertilized egg, also known as a **zygote,** begins to grow through cell division. First one cell becomes two; two become four; and when the number reaches about 150, the zygote implants itself in the lining of the uterus — a process that is completed about 10 days after conception. At this point it becomes an **embryo** (along with those cells that will form into the placenta and other supportive structures).

During the embryonic phase, all the structures to be found in the newborn infant begin to form. This occurs because the embryo's cells specialize into components of particular organ systems, a process known as **differentiation.** (Before differentiation, certain embryonic cells, known as *stem cells,* are capable of forming into any type of cell in the body.)

At first, the embryo's cells form distinct layers. Eventually, those in the outer layer become the nervous system and the skin. Cells in the middle layer are programmed to become muscles, bones, blood vessels, and certain internal organs. Those in the inner layer differentiate on a path that will eventually make them into the digestive system, lungs, and glands. By the end of the first month the initial single cell of the zygote has developed into an embryo with millions of specialized cells. Eventually this process of cell division and differentiation, which continues throughout the prenatal period, produces all the tissues and organisms of the body.

The first "behavior" — a heartbeat — appears when the embryo is about three weeks old and a sixth of an inch long. A few weeks later, when it is not yet an inch in length, the embryo makes reflexive responses to stimulation. These behaviors occur long before the brain has developed to the point where it can command behaviors.

After the eighth week, the developing embryo is called a **fetus.** Spontaneous movements begin at about this time, although the mother doesn't usually feel these movements until the 16th week after conception (Carmichael, 1970; Humphrey, 1970). By this point, the fetus has grown to about 7 inches long (the average length at birth is 20 inches).

PRENATAL DANGERS: TERATOGENS We used to think that the womb shielded the developing organism from environmental assaults, but we now know better. Although the **placenta** (an organ that develops between the embryo/fetus and the mother) screens out many potentially dangerous substances, some can pass through this barrier. These toxic substances, called **teratogens,** include viruses, a variety of drugs, and other chemicals. Among the most common teratogens are nicotine and alcohol. The effects of these toxic substances vary from slight to devastating, depending on the amount of exposure and on the stage of prenatal development in which exposure occurs.

PRENATAL DEVELOPMENT OF THE BRAIN   Prenatally, the brain grows new neurons at the amazing rate of up to 250,000 per minute. By birth it has produced over 100 billion (Dowling, 1992). In addition to this cell proliferation, the neurons that build the brain actually migrate, moving into their genetically determined positions. Then, at birth, the brain shifts from producing new cells to a different mode of growth. In the newborn brain, the genetic program emphasizes the branching of axons and dendrites, in order to complete the circuitry of the nervous system (Kolb, 1989). As the dendrites and axons grow and connect, the total mass of neural tissue in the brain continues to increase rapidly—by 50% in the first two years. By four years of age it has nearly doubled its birth size. However, the genetic program (along with the physical limitations imposed by the size of the skull) does not allow this tremendous growth to continue indefinitely. So, the brain's growth rate gradually diminishes, and finally, by about 11 years of age, the brain attains its ultimate mass.

Abilities of the Newborn Child

What is the sensory world like for the newborn? The father of American psychology, William James, believed that, to the newborn infant, everything must be an overwhelming jumble of stimuli—"One great blooming, buzzing confusion" (James, 1890). We now know that his views grossly underestimated infants' capabilities. Long before babies achieve motor coordination and locomotion, they take in vast amounts of information about their surroundings, filtering and processing stimulation that attracts, interests, or upsets them. They also have an amazing behavioral repertoire that they use to manipulate their environment.

During the **neonatal period** (newborn period), which covers the time from birth to one month of age, neonates are capable of responding to stimulation from all of their senses. For example, newborn babies will turn their heads toward anything that strokes their cheeks—a nipple or a finger—and begin to suck it. They can also respond to taste: the sweeter the fluid, the more continuously and forcefully an infant will suck (Lipsitt et al., 1976). And, as early as 12 hours after birth, they show distinct signs of pleasure at the taste of sugar water or vanilla.

What else can newborns do with their senses? Minutes after birth, their eyes scan their surroundings. They turn in the direction of a voice and search inquisitively for the source of preferred sounds or stretch out an exploratory hand. Neonates also express preferences, sometimes quite unmistakably. They smile when they smell banana essence, and they prefer salted to unsalted cereal (Bernstein, 1990; Harris et al., 1990). However, they recoil from the taste of lemon or shrimp or the smell of rotten eggs. They prefer female voices; they attend to familiar sound patterns; and within a few weeks of birth they begin to recognize their mothers' voice (Carpenter, 1973; DeCasper & Fifer, 1980; DeCasper & Spence, 1986; Spelke & Owsley, 1979). In fact, recordings of fetal responses show that some functions, such as hearing, appear even before birth.

Aside from their sensory abilities, babies are born with a remarkable set of behavioral reflexes that sustain life and provide a biological platform for later development. Among these reflexes, the *postural reflex* allows babies to sit with support, and the *grasping reflex* enables them to cling to a caregiver. These and other reflexes equip babies with the essential tools for survival and "instinctive" know-how. In addition, babies are designed to avoid or seek to escape unpleasant stimulation, such as loud noises, bright lights, strong odors, and painful stimuli. All of this, of course, makes much evolutionary sense because these abilities are highly adaptive and promote survival.

Connection

Chapter 2
The brain consists of neurons and other supportive cells, formed into highly specialized yet interdependent modules.

Connection

Chapter 5
Sensation involves the initial stages of information processing by the sense organs and the brain.

Connection

Chapter 2
Reflexes are simple, innate behaviors activated by stimulation.

Neonatal period: In humans, the neonatal (newborn) period extends through the first month after birth.

Building on the Neonatal Blueprint

Following the neonatal period, the child enters **infancy,** a period that lasts until about 18 months, when speech becomes well developed. (The Latin root *infans* means "incapable of speech.") It is a time of rapid, genetically programmed growth and reliance on the repertoire of reflexes and "instinctive" behaviors that we discussed above. But, it is also a period during which youngsters come to depend more and more on their abilities for learning new behaviors.

LEARNING ASSUMES A ROLE IN DEVELOPMENT   Babies start to build up their knowledge of the world by observing relations between sensory events. This represents a fundamental form of learning called *classical conditioning* (the same sort of learning that makes your mouth water at the sight of a pizza). This was shown in an experiment in which newborns were taught to anticipate pleasurably sweet sensations by first stroking the babies' foreheads and then giving them sugar water. After several trials, the stroking alone would cause a baby to turn its head in the direction from which the sweet fluid had been delivered — in anticipation of more of the same (Blass, 1990).

SENSORY ABILITIES AND LIMITATIONS   Despite all their abilities, babies must deal with limitations, particularly with limited vision. In fact, babies are born "legally blind," with a visual acuity of about 20/500 (which means that they can discriminate at 20 feet stimuli that most older children can see clearly at 500 feet). Good vision requires the operation and coordination of a great many receptor cells in the eye's retina, in the visual pathways, and in the occipital cortex of the brain. At birth, relatively few of these connections are laid down. But these immature systems develop very rapidly, and the baby's visual abilities soon become evident (Banks & Bennett, 1988).

Early on, infants can perceive large objects that display a great deal of contrast. By one month a child can detect contours of a head at close distances. At seven weeks the baby can scan the features of the caregiver's face, and, as the caregiver talks, the baby can contact his or her eyes. Just as heredity biases infants to prefer human voices over other sounds, it programs them to prefer human faces to most other visual patterns (Fantz, 1963). At as early as two months, the baby begins to see color, differentiating patterns of white, red, orange, and blue. At three months, the baby can perceive depth and is well on the way to enjoying the visual abilities of adults. And, it may surprise you to know that infants seem to possess a rudimentary ability to "count" objects they see: They know, for example, the difference between two dolls and three (Wynn, 1992, 1995). Such *core knowledge* serves as the foundation for the later development of more complex skills, such as are required for arithmetic (Spelke, 2000).

SOCIAL ABILITIES   Babies are also designed to be sociable, and much of their development during infancy builds on that **innate** sociability. It is important to note that they not only respond to, but also interact with, their caregivers. Film studies of this interaction reveal a remarkable degree of *synchronicity:* close coordination between the gazing, vocalizing, touching, and smiling of mothers and infants (Martin, 1981). And while babies respond and learn, they also send out messages to those willing to listen to and love them. Studies also show that the feelings of mothers and infants are matched in a socially dynamic fashion (Fogel, 1991). So, a three-month-old infant may laugh when his or her mother laughs and frown or cry in response to her display of

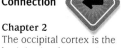

Connection

Chapter 6
Through classical conditioning, organisms learn to associate two different stimuli.

Connection

Chapter 2
The occipital cortex is the brain's visual processing center.

Infancy: In humans, infancy spans the time between the end of the neonatal period and the establishment of language — usually at about 18 months to two years.

Innate: Inborn.

www.ablongman.com/zimbardo

negative emotion (Tronick et al., 1980). Amazingly, even newborns will imitate simple facial expressions, such as sticking out the tongue or rounding the mouth (Meltzoff, 1998; Meltzoff & Moore, 1977, 1983, 1985, 1989).

PHYSICAL ABILITIES The abilities to walk and talk—like the growth of the brain, the growth spurts of adolescence, and the onset of menopause—occur on their own biological time schedules. Psychologists use the term **maturation** for the unfolding of these genetically programmed processes of growth and development over time. When organisms are raised under adequate environmental conditions, their maturation follows a predictable pattern. The systematic changes that we observe in bodily functioning and behavior are influenced by both genetic factors and environmental factors, such as nutrition, touch, and gravity. In humans, maturation generates all of the sequences and patterns of behavior seen in Figure 4.2.

Most of what you do—your voluntary movement and action—requires physical maturation that gives you coordination and strength from many parts of your body. We see maturation in action when children sit without support by seven months of age, pull themselves up to a standing position a month or two later, and walk soon after their first birthday. Once the underlying physical structures are sufficiently developed, proficiency in these behaviors requires only a minimally adequate environment and a little practice.

We must always keep in mind, however, that the sequences of physical and mental growth involve the *interaction* of biology and environment—even though biology may often play the leading role. So, in the sequence for locomotion, as shown in Figure 4.2, a child learns to walk without special training following a time-ordered pattern that is typical of all physically capable members of our species. Indeed, in cultures where children are carried in cradle boards, walking occurs on a similar schedule (Dennis & Dennis, 1940). Despite this hereditary pattern, however, we find that environmental influences can sometimes have an influence on biological tendencies. So, in the West Indies, where infants receive vigorous massage after the daily bath and frequent practice in moving their legs while being held, children sit and walk a little earlier, on the average, than do children in the United States (Hopkins & Westra, 1988). On the other hand, lack of human contact can have the opposite effect: Infants who had spent their lives lying in cribs in Iranian orphanages were observed to be severely retarded in learning to sit and walk (Dennis, 1960).

In general, physical growth in humans has been viewed as a continuous process whose rate changes with age, slowing over time after a very rapid start in the early years. This picture of continuous physical growth has been qualified, however, as the result of research reported during the last few years. Scientists have found that growth in the length of infants' bodies occurs in discontinuous "bursts," a pattern known as *saltation* (from the Latin *saltare,* "to leap"). The data suggest that human physical growth involves an inactive phase and an active growth phase (Lampl et al., 1992).

In general, we have seen that babies seem to come equipped to accomplish three basic tasks of survival: finding sustenance (feeding), maintaining contact with people (for protection and care), and defense against harmful stimuli (withdrawing from pain or threat). Such tasks require a set of innate abilities: These abilities form the foundation on which learning and physical maturation build the perceptual skills, the ability to understand experiences, and basic thinking skills that continue to develop throughout life (von Hofsten & Lindhagen, 1979).

Maturation: The process by which the genetic program manifests itself over time.

FIGURE 4.2: Maturational Timetable for Locomotion

This figure shows average ages at which each behavior is performed. There are considerable individual differences in the *rate* of development, so the time at which each response occurs is variable. Most infants, however, follow the *sequence* of development.

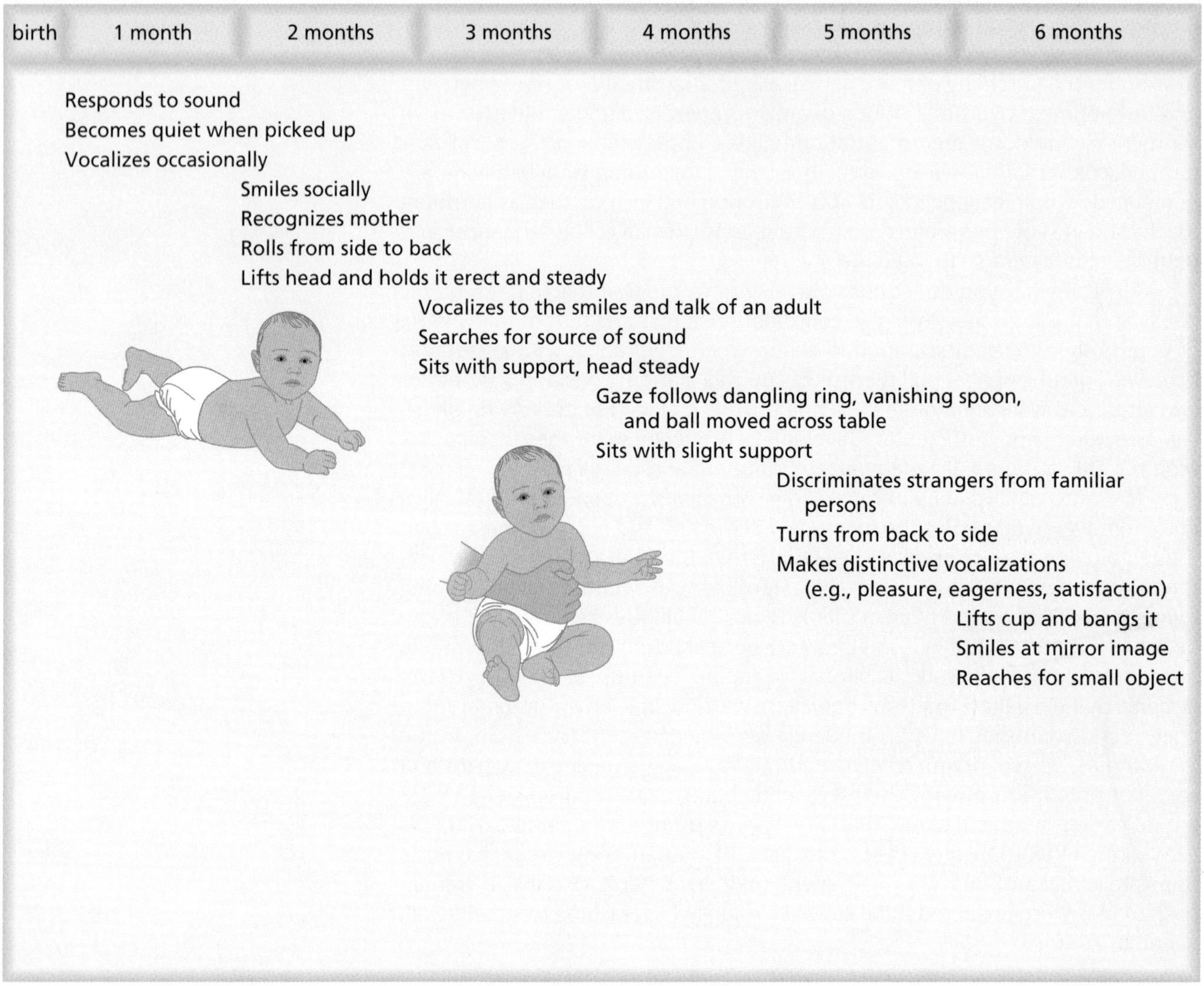

birth	1 month	2 months	3 months	4 months	5 months	6 months

Responds to sound
Becomes quiet when picked up
Vocalizes occasionally

Smiles socially
Recognizes mother
Rolls from side to back
Lifts head and holds it erect and steady

Vocalizes to the smiles and talk of an adult
Searches for source of sound
Sits with support, head steady

Gaze follows dangling ring, vanishing spoon, and ball moved across table
Sits with slight support

Discriminates strangers from familiar persons
Turns from back to side
Makes distinctive vocalizations (e.g., pleasure, eagerness, satisfaction)

Lifts cup and bangs it
Smiles at mirror image
Reaches for small object

7 months	8 months	9 months	10 months	11 months	1 year

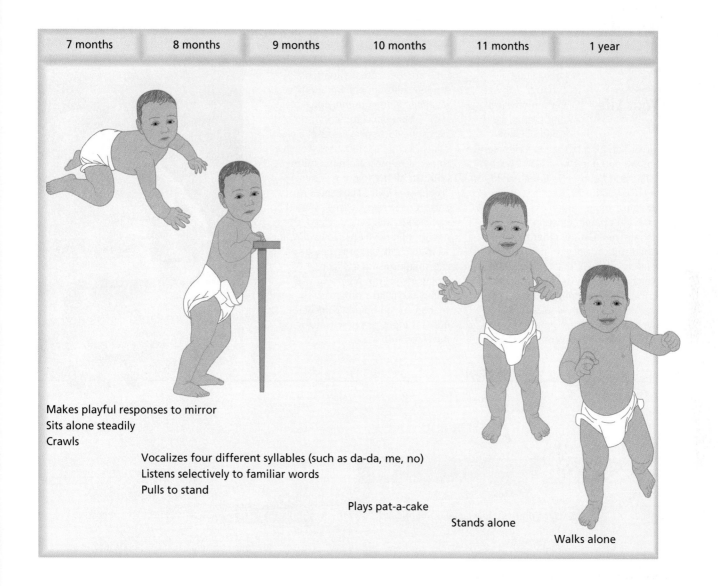

Makes playful responses to mirror
Sits alone steadily
Crawls

Vocalizes four different syllables (such as da-da, me, no)
Listens selectively to familiar words
Pulls to stand

Plays pat-a-cake

Stands alone

Walks alone

Milestones in a Child's Development

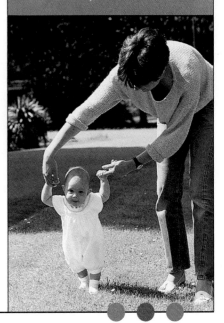

Children show great variation in development, but a child who departs greatly from the norms should be checked by a specialist.

It is risky to discuss the ages by which a child "should" achieve certain physical and mental skills. Children show great variation in their development (as we noted in the cases of Bobby, Billy, and Benny). So if your child, or a child you know, hasn't started walking and talking by age one, you shouldn't panic. Einstein was slow to talk, too. On the other hand, if a child still isn't beginning to walk and talk by age two, the caregiver should consult a specialist, such as a pediatrician or developmental psychologist, to see whether something is wrong. It is well to remember, also, that a delay in one area, such as the onset of speech, does not mean that the child is "retarded" or will be generally slow in other areas. Not only are there great variations among children, but variations occur normally within an individual child.

What developmental standards would a specialist use? Certainly, a child should be responsive to people almost from the moment of birth. All the major reflexes discussed in the previous section should be present. (These should be checked by the pediatrician.) Then, as the child develops, you will want to watch at the appropriate times for the abilities listed in Figure 4.2. Doing so will not only help you follow the child's progress, but it will make you more knowledgeable about the process of psychological development.

CHECK YOUR UNDERSTANDING

1. **RECALL:** *Which of the following does not appear before birth?*
   a. the heartbeat
   b. movement of limbs
   c. growth and migration of neurons
   d. vocalizations

2. **RECALL:** *After birth, brain development emphasizes the*
   a. migration of neurons.
   b. development of connections among neurons.
   c. development of the brain stem.
   d. multiplication of neurons.

3. **RECALL:** *Which of the following is a behavior that appears largely because of maturation?*
   a. the onset of puberty
   b. starting school
   c. moving out of the parents' home
   d. sexual orientation

4. **APPLICATION:** *You would expect your newborn baby to*
   a. quickly learn to recognize the sound of his or her name.
   b. react negatively to a taste of lemon.
   c. prefer the father's deeper voice to the mother's higher voice.
   d. smile when eating.

5. **UNDERSTANDING THE CORE CONCEPT:**
   Which one of the following is an innate ability that promotes survival?
   a. the grasping reflex
   b. recognition of the mother's face
   c. toilet training
   d. sharp vision

ANSWERS: 1. d 2. b 3. a 4. b 5. a

Core Concept

WHAT ARE THE DEVELOPMENTAL TASKS OF CHILDHOOD?

Key Question
?

Three of the greatest accomplishments of your life include acquiring your native language, developing your ability to think and reason, and forming relationships with the important people in your life. Each of these achievements is part of the foundation for adulthood being laid by the child. And, we will see, as children work through these tasks, they undergo profound psychological changes. Here's how our Core Concept states the main idea of this section:

Core Concept

> **Children face especially important developmental tasks in the areas of language, thought processes, and social relationships.**

We will see below that children are developmentally different from adults, but the differences they display in language, thought, and socialization are not simply the result of adults' greater experience or store of information. The differences between children and adults also involve the unfolding of crucial maturational processes. Let us first observe these processes at work on the task of language acquisition.

How Children Acquire Language

Infants know no words at all, yet in only a few years virtually all young children become fluent speakers of any language they hear spoken and have the opportunity to speak. What makes them such adept language learners? Apparently, human infants possess innate (inborn) abilities that help them learn language (Pinker, 1994).

Innate Language Structures in the Brain

According to the **innateness theory of language,** children acquire language not merely by imitating but by following an inborn program of steps to acquire the vocabulary and grammar of the language in their environment. Psycholinguist Noam Chomsky (1965, 1975) says that children are born with mental structures—built into the brain—that make it possible to comprehend and produce speech. Many experts agree with Chomsky that innate mental machinery orchestrates children's language learning. One such mechanism, we have seen, lies in Broca's area, the motor speech "controller" in the cerebral cortex. Chomsky refers to these speech-enabling structures collectively as a **language acquisition device** or **LAD.**

In Chomsky's theory, the LAD—like a computer chip—contains some very basic rules of grammar, common to all human languages, built into its circuits. One such rule might be the distinction between nouns (for names of things) and verbs (for actions). These innate rules, Chomsky argues, make it easier for children to discover patterns in languages to which they are exposed.

What other evidence does Chomsky have to suggest that the foundations of language are innate? Children worldwide proceed through very similar stages of learning their native languages. A logical hypothesis for explaining this pattern would be that children possess inborn "blueprints" for language development that unfold with time and experience. Despite the similarities in the sequence, however, language learning is not precisely the same across cultures. Such variations suggest that children's built-in capacity for language is

Innateness theory of language: The view that children learn language mainly by following an inborn program for acquiring vocabulary and grammar.

Language acquisition device or **LAD:** A biologically organized mental structure in the brain that facilitates the learning of language because (says Chomsky) it is innately programmed with some of the fundamental rules of grammar.

Connection

Chapter 2
Broca's area, in the left frontal lobe, controls the muscles used in speech.

FIGURE 4.3: Growth in Children's Working Vocabulary

The number of words a child can use increases rapidly between 18 months and 6 years of age. This study shows children's average vocabularies at 6-month intervals. (Source: B. A. Moskovitz, "The Acquisition of Language," *Scientific American,* Inc. All rights reserved; reprinted by permission.)

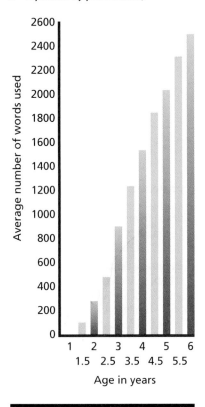

Babbling stage: The time during the first year of life when an infant produces a wide range of sounds but not functional words.

Grammar: The rules of a language, specifying how to use words, morphemes, and syntax to produce understandable sentences.

One-word stage: The first stage of true language, in which children communicate with single words, rather than sentences.

Two-word stage: The second stage of true language, in which two words form rudimentary sentences — showing that the child is beginning to learn syntax.

not a rigid device but a set of "listening rules" or guidelines for perceiving language (Bee, 1994; Slobin, 1985a, 1985b). For example, babies pay attention to the sounds and rhythms of the sound strings they hear others speak (or in sign language, *see*), especially the beginnings, endings, and stressed syllables. Relying on their built-in "listening guides," young children deduce the patterns and rules for producing their own speech.

In general, language researchers have been impressed with the fact that most young children are both ready to acquire language and flexible about its final form and context. This is equally true for children exposed to any of the world's 4,000 spoken languages, as well as to gestural communication systems, such as American Sign Language. Such adaptability suggests that the LAD in children is flexible, not rigidly programmed (Goldin-Meadow & Mylander, 1990; Meier, 1991).

BABBLING   Beside their ability to perceive speech sounds, infants have a tendency to produce language sounds. Part of this tendency arises from a vocal apparatus that is biologically adapted for speech. As a result, infants *babble,* producing speechlike sounds and syllables such as "mamama" or "beebee" well before they begin to use true words. Infants at this stage may also follow conversational "rules," such as taking turns with vocalizations (Jaffe et al., 2001). Amazingly, during this **babbling stage,** babies make nearly all sounds heard in all languages. Eventually, however, learning narrows the repertoire down to the sounds of the language that the baby hears (Clark & Clark, 1977; Mowrer, 1960).

VOCABULARY AND GRAMMAR   Acquiring a basic vocabulary represents an important project for children in their first few years of life, and young children are excellent word learners. By the age of 6, the average child is estimated to understand an astounding 14,000 words (Templin, 1957). Assuming that most of these words are learned between the ages of 18 months and 6 years, this works out to about nine new words a day, or almost one word per waking hour (Bower, 1998b; Carey, 1978). You can see the cumulative growth of a child's working vocabulary in Figure 4.3.

What is the pattern by which children develop vocabulary and **grammar?** Developmental psychologists recognize three initial stages: the *one-word stage,* the *two-word stage,* and *telegraphic speech.* During the **one-word stage,** which begins at about one year of age, children utter single concrete nouns or verbs, such as "Mama" or "doggie." Later, they learn to put words together to express more complex ideas.

NAMES AND WORD COMBINATIONS   At around 18 months, children's word learning accelerates rapidly. At this age, children might point to every object in a room and ask, "What's that?" Researchers have called this phase the "naming explosion" because children begin to acquire new words, especially names for objects, at a rapidly increasing rate. Soon they also discern that some words are not names but actions (verbs) that describe how named objects and persons affect each other.

After the naming explosion occurs between about 18 months and 2 years of age, children begin to use one-word utterances in different sequences to convey more complex meanings. When they enter the **two-word stage,** the range of meanings children can convey increases tremendously. Studies of different languages show that, around the world, children's two-word utterances begin to divide their experience into certain categories. For example, 10 children speaking different languages (English, Samoan, Finnish, Hebrew, and Swedish) were found to talk mostly about three categories of ideas: movers, movable objects, and locations (Braine, 1976). When young Alexis kicks a ball, for example, the mover is Alexis and the movable object is the ball. Alexis can express this relationship in the two-word sequence, "Alexi ball." It is in the two-word stage that children first develop the language rules called *grammar*. This allows them to move past simple naming and combine words into sentences.

The Rules of Grammar   Even if you have a limited vocabulary, you can combine the same words in different sequences to convey a rich variety of meanings. For example, "I saw him chasing a dog" and "I saw a dog chasing him" both use exactly the same words, but switching the order of the words "him" and "dog" yields completely different meanings. Grammar makes this possible: It is a language's set of rules about combining and ordering words to make understandable sentences (Naigles, 1990; Naigles & Kako, 1993). Different languages may use considerably different rules about grammatical combinations. In Japanese, for example, the verb always comes last, while English is much more flexible about verb position.

In their early two- and three-word sentences, children's speech is *telegraphic:* short, simple sequences of nouns and verbs without plurals, tenses, or function words like "the" and "of." For example, "Ball hit Evie cry" is **telegraphic speech.** To develop the ability to make full sentences, children must learn to use other forms of speech, such as modifiers (adjectives and adverbs) and articles (the, those), and they must learn how to put words together—grammatically. In English, this means recognizing and producing the familiar subject-verb-object order, as in "The lamb followed Mary."

Finally, children need to acquire grammatical skill in using **morphemes,** the meaningful units that make up words. Morphemes mark verbs to show tense (walk*ed,* walk*ing*) and mark nouns to show possession (Maria*'s,* the people*'s*) and plurality (fox*es,* child*ren*). Often, however, they make mistakes because they do not know the rule or apply an inappropriate one (Marcus, 1996). One common error, known as **overregularization,** applies a rule too widely and creates incorrect forms. For example, after learning to make past tense verb forms by adding *-d* or *-ed,* children may apply this "rule" even to its exceptions, the irregular verbs, creating such nonwords as "hitted" and "breaked." Learning to add *-s* or *-es* to make plurals, children may apply the rule to irregular nouns, as in "foots" or "mouses."

OTHER LANGUAGE SKILLS   Words and the grammatical rules for combining them are only some of the ingredients of communication. To communicate well, children also need to learn the social rules of conversation. They must learn how to join a discussion, how to take turns talking and listening, and how to make contributions that are relevant. Adult speakers use body language, intonation, and facial expressions to enhance their communication. They also use feedback they get from listeners and are able to take the perspective of the listener. Children must master these skills in order to become successful communicators—to become part of a human language community.

As children grow older, they also begin to express more abstract meanings, going beyond their physical world to talk about their psychological world. For example, after the age of 2, children begin to use words such as *dream, forget, pretend, believe, guess,* and *hope,* as they talk about internal states (Shatz et al., 1983). They also use words such as *happy, sad,* and *angry* to refer to emotional states. Finally, after cognitive advances that occur later in childhood, they understand and use highly abstract words such as *truth, justice,* and *idea.*

What is the major point that stands out amid the complexities of language acquisition? It is implied in our Core Concept: Language is a major developmental task of childhood—for which children are exquisitely prepared. And

Telegraphic speech: Short, simple sentences, typical of young children, who omit plurals, tenses, and function words, such as "the" and "of"; so called because it sounds like a telegram.

Morphemes: The meaningful units of language that make up words. Some whole words are morphemes (example: "word"); other morphemes include grammatical components that alter a word's meaning (examples: "-ed," "-ing," and "un-").

Overregularization: Applying a grammatical rule too widely and creating incorrect forms.

the way they acquire and use language suggests that becoming an adult involves a combination of learning and innate processes that unfold on their own developmental timetables.

Cognitive Development

Connection

Chapter 8
What, besides language, are the components of thought?

If you have ever known a toddler going through the naming explosion, you have seen that children have an insatiable appetite for labeling of things they know. Behind this labeling is their emerging ability for thinking, perceiving, and remembering. The next few pages will focus on the ways that these mental abilities emerge, a process called **cognitive development.**

Psychologists interested in cognitive development ask such questions as these: When do children realize that objects still exist even when they can't see them? Do they know that it is possible to hold ideas that aren't true? Can they understand that people have desires and dreams, but objects do not? Developmental psychologists investigate not only *what* children think but *how* they think.

In this section we will emphasize the pioneering work on cognitive development by the late Swiss psychologist Jean Piaget (although there are other points of view). For nearly 50 years, Piaget observed children's intellectual development and formulated his observations into a comprehensive theory.

Piaget began this quest to understand the nature of the child's mind by carefully observing the behavior of his own three children. His methods were simple: He would pose problems to them, observe their responses, slightly alter the situations, and once again observe their responses. Piaget attended especially to the developmental transitions and changes in his children's thinking, reasoning, and problem solving. This focus led to a *discontinuous stage model* of development, which emphasized Piaget's view that children undergo a revolution in thought at each stage. We will see below that three key ideas distinguish Piaget's approach: (1) *schemes,* (2) the interaction of *assimilation* and *accommodation,* and (3) the *stages of cognitive development.*

Cognitive development: The process by which thinking changes over time.

Schemes: In Piaget's theory, mental structures or programs that guide a developing child's thought.

Assimilation: A mental process that modifies new information to fit it into existing schemes.

SCHEMES To illustrate the concept of *schemes,* think of a four-legged animal. Now think of one that is friendly. Now think of one that barks. You might have started by imagining elephants and tigers (both four-legged), then narrowed your choices down to cats and dogs (four-legged and friendly), and finally to just dogs (which bark). You could do this easily only because you have developed mental structures (mental programs) that enable you to interpret concepts and events. Piaget termed such mental structures **schemes.** We have schemes for concepts, such as "dog" and "development." We have schemes for actions, such as eating with chopsticks. We also have schemes for solving problems, such as finding the area of a circle or dealing with a crying baby. In general, schemes are mental structures that guide thinking. According to Piaget, they are also the building blocks of development. Schemes form and change as we develop and organize our knowledge to deal with new experiences and predict future events. Right now, for example, you are building a scheme about schemes!

ASSIMILATION AND ACCOMMODATION In Piaget's system, two dynamic processes underlie all cognitive growth: *assimilation* and *accommodation.* **Assimilation** is a mental process that modifies new information to fit with existing schemes—with what is already known. So, a baby reflexively knows how to suck from a nipple and will use assimilation to deal with new objects such as a finger or a new toy. Some adult examples: You, too, experience

Although an infant will begin to suck a bottle just the way he or she sucked a breast (assimilation), the infant will soon discover that some changes are necessary (accommodation). The child will make an even greater accommodation in the transitions from bottle to cup.

assimilation when you acquire more information about William Shakespeare or gain skill in using a word-processing program on the computer.

By contrast, **accommodation** is a process of restructuring or *modifying* schemes to incorporate new information. For example, a child's simplistic "bird" scheme, which includes any flying object, undergoes accommodation when the child learns that a butterfly is not a bird. Adults experience accommodation of their mental schemes, too. For example, many computer users in the 1990s had to modify their computer-using schemes when they made the transition from the older, text-based format (DOS) to the graphic Windows format. You, too, may need to modify a scheme when the professor in your psychology course says something that surprises you (such as, "Children have innate language abilities"). As a result, your scheme about newborn children may change to accommodate your new knowledge.

For Piaget, cognitive development results from this constant interweaving of assimilation and accommodation. Through these two processes, the individual's behavior and knowledge become less dependent on concrete external reality and more reliant on internal thought. In general, *assimilation* makes new information fit our existing views of the world, and *accommodation* changes our views to fit new information.

PIAGET'S STAGES OF COGNITIVE DEVELOPMENT The way a child thinks about the world progresses through four revolutionary changes. Piaget described these changes in terms of four *stages* of cognitive growth: the *sensorimotor stage* (infancy), the *preoperational stage* (early childhood), the *concrete operational stage* (middle childhood), and the *formal operational stage* (adolescence). At each stage, distinct styles of thinking emerge as the child progresses from sensory reaction to logical thought. It is important to note that all children progress through these stages in the same sequence, although one child may take longer to pass through a given stage than does another child.

The Sensorimotor Stage (Birth to about age 2) We have seen that children enter the world equipped with many innate and reflexive behaviors, such as those for clinging, sucking, and crying. None of these require thought, in the sense of the complex mental activity seen in problem solving later in childhood. Instead, children in the **sensorimotor stage** give mainly reflexive or "instinctive" motor responses to stimulation, with very little "thinking" involved. Piaget called this **sensorimotor intelligence.** Not everything is automatic, however. As we have seen, children at this stage are also capable of simple learning, even though the circuitry in the cortex is not completely connected yet. They learn to recognize people they see frequently. And they learn to coordinate their body parts to grasp and explore attractive objects (a rattle, perhaps) or to avoid things that they dislike (such as the taste of a lemon wedge).

A major development of significance for later thinking and learning appears in the second year: the ability to make internal **mental representations** of objects. With the power of mental representation, children can now form memories of objects and events that they can retrieve later for use in thinking and problem solving. There is a vast mental difference, for example, between *pointing* to the toy one sees and *knowing* that an unseen toy must be somewhere so that it can be sought or asked for.

Gradually, the child takes mental representation one step farther by realizing that objects continue to exist even when they are out of sight. This ability, called **object permanence,** liberates the child from the present and from his or her immediate surroundings. The basics are in place by one year of age, but the ability of object permanence continues to develop through the second year (Flavell, 1985). At the same time, language begins to appear, and so words

Accommodation: A mental process that restructures existing schemes so that new information is better understood.

Sensorimotor stage: The first stage in Piaget's theory, during which the child relies heavily on innate motor responses to stimuli.

Sensorimotor intelligence: The mental capacity shown in the first schemes an infant displays, which are mainly motor responses to stimuli, with a strong innate basis.

Mental representation: The ability to form internal images of objects and events.

Object permanence: The knowledge that objects exist independently of one's own actions or awareness.

become another way to make mental representations. Together these forms of representational thought become the major accomplishment of the sensori-motor stage.

The Preoperational Stage (From about 2 to 6 or 7 years of age)   The cognitive advances in the next developmental stage, the **preoperational stage,** grow out of the ability to represent objects mentally. One of these advances involves the emerging sense of self as distinctive from other people and objects in the environment. Another advance involves the ability to solve simple problems using mental representation (such as searching different places for a lost toy). Yet, despite these abilities, the child cannot solve problems requiring logical thought. Three other important limiting features of the child's mind in this period are *egocentrism, animistic thinking,* and *centration.*

▶ **Egocentrism,** a self-centered focus, causes children to see the world only in terms of themselves and their own position. Further, they assume that others see the world in the same way that they do. So, when talking to a preoperational child on the phone, she may say, "Look at my new dollie!" assuming you can see things on her end of the line. As a result of this egocentrism, preoperational children are not yet able to fully empathize with others or take others' points of view. For this reason children may act in ways that have destructive or hurtful consequences, even though they don't intend to upset or harm others.

▶ **Animistic thinking** involves the belief that inanimate objects have life and mental processes. For example, if a child slips and bangs her head on the table, she might complain about the "bad table," blaming it for hurting her.

▶ **Centration** involves the inability to understand an event because the child focuses attention too narrowly, while ignoring other important information. So, for example, a thirsty child may insist on drinking a "big glass" of juice, preferring a tall narrow container to a short wide one, mistakenly assuming that the height of the glass ensures that it will hold more juice, while ignoring the other relevant dimension of width. (See the *Do It Yourself* box on p. 136.)

While we might see these as limitations, keep in mind that they are also the characteristics that make children at this stage most charming and interesting —and different from older children and adults.

The Concrete Operational Stage (From about 7 to about 11 years of age)   At the next stage, children understand for the first time that many things may stay essentially the same, even when their superficial appearance changes. In this **concrete operational stage,** they can understand that a short, wide glass can hold as much juice as a tall, narrow one. So, the short-wide versus tall-narrow glass problem that defeated the preoperational child now yields to a new understanding of the way that volume is *conserved.* Similarly, they now understand that a string of red beads is not longer than an identical string of blue beads, even though the red beads are stretched out in a line while the blue beads lie in a small pile. They realize that the beads *look* different in their grouping, but this does not mean that they *are* different in number. This new ability, called **conservation,** represents one of the most important cognitive breakthroughs that most 7-year-olds have made.

Along with the new ability to understand conservation, children at this stage acquire the capability for performing **mental operations.** Now they can solve problems by manipulating concepts entirely in their minds. This allows them to think things through before taking action. As a result, they may be less

Preoperational stage: The second stage in Piaget's theory, marked by well-developed mental representation and the use of language.

Egocentrism: In Piaget's theory, the self-centered inability to realize that there are other viewpoints beside one's own.

Animistic thinking: A preoperational mode of thought in which inanimate objects are imagined to have life and mental processes.

Centration: A preoperational thought pattern involving the inability to take into account more than one factor at a time.

Concrete operational stage: The third of Piaget's stages, when a child understands conservation but still is incapable of abstract thought.

Conservation: The understanding that the physical properties of an object or substance do not change when appearances change but nothing is added or taken away.

Mental operations: Solving problems by manipulating images in one's mind.

impulsive. They are also less gullible, giving up many "magical" notions, such as the belief in Santa Claus.

Using their ability for performing mental operations, concrete operational children begin to use simple logic and inference to solve problems. The symbols they use in reasoning are, however, still mainly symbols for concrete objects and events, not abstractions. The limitations of their concrete thinking are shown in the familiar game of "20 Questions," the goal of which is to determine the identity of an object by asking the fewest possible yes/no questions of the person who thinks up the object. A child of 7 or 8 usually sticks to very specific questions ("Is it a bird?" "Is it a cat?") but does not ask the higher-level questions that more efficiently narrow down the possibilities for the correct answer ("Does it fly?" "Does it have hair?").

The Formal Operational Stage (From about age 12 on)   In the final stage of cognitive growth described by Piaget, the ability for abstract and complex thought appears. In this **formal operational stage** children also begin to ponder problems involving intangible concepts, such as truth, justice, relationships, and existence. Many adolescents begin, at last, to see that their particular reality is only one of several imaginable realities. With these formal operational reasoning powers, adolescents and adults now approach the "20 Questions" game in a way that demonstrates their ability to use abstractions and to adopt an information-processing strategy that is not merely random guesswork. They impose their own structures on the task, starting with broad categories and then formulating and testing hypotheses in light of their knowledge of categories and relationships. Their questioning moves from general categories ("Is it an animal?") to subcategories ("Does it fly?") and then to specific guesses ("Is it a bird?") (Bruner et al., 1966).

BEYOND PIAGET: CONTEMPORARY PERSPECTIVES ON COGNITIVE DEVELOPMENT   Most psychologists accept the broad picture that Piaget painted of the interplay between assimilation and accommodation (Flavell, 1996). However, newer research suggests that the transition between one stage and another is less abrupt than Piaget's theory implies. Also, researchers have shown that children are, in some ways, more intellectually sophisticated at each stage than Piaget had found (Munakata et al., 1997). Studies show, for example, that some mental representation occurs as early as three months of age, rather than in the second year, as Piaget had thought (Gulya et al., 1998). Recent research also shows that by one year of age infants develop the complex idea that people have intentions that may differ from their own (Baldwin, 2000; Tomasello, 2000).

Some psychologists believe that what Piaget saw as limitations on preoperational thought may actually be the inability to *express* thoughts. So, preoperational children may actually *understand* some of the same concepts that older children do, but they may still lack the skills to perform accordingly. For example, a 5-year-old child who has watched her father prepare breakfast in the past can watch him and understand what he is cooking but may not be able to describe it to her visiting grandmother or express why she likes her pancakes "the way Daddy fixes them." Researchers have found, in contrast with Piaget's notion of centration, that young children (ages 3 and 4) understand that the "insides" of objects, although they are invisible, are not necessarily identical to their external appearances (Gelman & Wellman, 1991). And, in contrast with Piaget's claims about animistic thinking, 3- to 5-year-old children are consistently able to distinguish between real and purely mental (imaginary) entities (Wellman & Estes, 1986). Finally, studies of emotional development have shown that preoperational children can understand that other people

Formal operational stage: The last of Piaget's stages, during which abstract thought appears.

Connection

Chapter 8
Problem solving also involves skills that can be learned.

Object permanence, the perception that objects exist independently of one's own actions or awareness, develops gradually during the first stage of cognitive development and is solidly formed before age one. The baby in these pictures clearly believes that the toy no longer exists once it is obscured by the screen.

Playing with Children — Piagetian Style

If you have access to a child, you can try out some of the problems Piaget posed for his children in order to study their thinking. For example, with a preoperational or concrete operational child, it's always fun to give a conservation problem that involves pouring liquid from a tall, narrow container into a short, wide one. Begin by pouring the same amounts into two identical vessels, such as glass measuring cups. Get the child to agree that you are starting with the same amount in each. Then pour the liquid from one cup into a shallow pan. Ask the child, "Does one of these have more than the other, or are they both the same?" Then see if your child's responses fit with Piaget's observations.

Piaget found that the concrete operational child — who understands conservation — will know that the volume of liquid remains the same, regardless of the shape of the container. The preoperational child will think that the shallow pan has less because the liquid does not come up as far on the container. This shows that the younger child does not know that volume is conserved, regardless of the shape of the container. Piaget claimed that it also showed that the younger child cannot reason about both height and width simultaneously.

This 5-year-old girl is aware that the two containers have the same amount of colored liquid. However, when the liquid from one is poured into a taller narrow container, she indicates that there is more liquid in the taller one. She has not yet grasped the concept of conservation, which she will understand by age 6 or 7.

have internal emotional responses that do not always jibe with their outward expressions (Bower, 1997).

Other developmental psychologists counter that Piaget's theory is not as rigid as its critics claim. Rather, it is flexible enough to accommodate new findings. And, say Piaget's supporters, it underwent continual change throughout his long career (Lourenço & Machado, 1996).

What is really needed, says Robert Siegler, is a new metaphor for development (Siegler, 1994). Instead of the abrupt changes implied by stage theories, he proposes that we think of "waves." The wave metaphor, he says, better fits both the scientific data and our everyday experience, which shows the variability of children's behavior. For example, a child may, during a single day, use several different strategies to solve the same linguistic problem: "I ate," "I eated," and "I ated." This is not the pattern we would find if a child were making a sudden leap from one stage to another. Instead, says Siegler, this is a pattern of overlapping developmental waves, where each wave can be thought of as the ebb and flow in the strength of a cognitive strategy (Azar, 1995).

The Development of Moral Thinking

What shapes our sense of right and wrong? The best-known psychological approach to moral development comes from the late Lawrence Kohlberg (1964, 1981), who based his theory squarely on Piaget's theory of cognitive development. After all, reasoned Kohlberg, moral thinking is just a special form of cognition. Mirroring Piaget's views, each stage of moral reasoning proposed in Kohlberg's theory is based on a different moral standard. Table 4.1 summarizes these stages.

You can see how these stages of moral reasoning parallel the stages of Piaget's theory, as the individual moves from concrete, egocentric reasons to more other-oriented, abstract ideas of right and wrong. Accordingly, at the first stages, a child may not steal a cookie for fear of punishment, while at a more advanced level, the child may resist stealing for fear of not living up to the parents' expectations. In general, the earliest stages of moral reasoning are based on self-interest, while later, more advanced stages center on others' expectations or on broader standards of social good. Unfortunately, not all people attain the later, least egocentric stages. In fact, Kohlberg found that many adults never even reach Stage 4.

TABLE 4.1	Kohlberg's Stages of Moral Reasoning	
LEVELS AND STAGES	**REASONS FOR MORAL BEHAVIOR**
I. PRECONVENTIONAL MORALITY	
Stage 1: Egocentric pleasure/pain/profit orientation	Avoid pain or avoid getting caught
Stage 2: Cost/benefit orientation; reciprocity ("I'll scratch your back if you'll scratch mine")	Achieve/receive rewards or mutual benefits
II. CONVENTIONAL MORALITY	
Stage 3: "Good child" orientation	Gain acceptance, avoid disapproval
Stage 4: Law-and-order orientation	Follow rules, avoid penalties
III. POSTCONVENTIONAL (PRINCIPLED) MORALITY	
Stage 5: Social contract orientation	Promote the welfare of one's society
Stage 6: Ethical principle orientation (e.g., Gandhi, Jesus, Mohammed)	Achieve justice, be consistent with one's principles, avoid self-condemnation

CULTURE AND MORALITY Does moral development follow the same developmental sequence everywhere? Yes, said Kohlberg. Cross-cultural work shows that individuals attain the same stages in the same order in all cultures studied, including Turkey, Taiwan, Guatemala, Japan, and the United States (Eckensberger, 1994). However, this research also hints at some limitations of the theory to explain moral development in other cultural contexts: the higher stages, as defined by Kohlberg, have not been found in all cultures. Even in his own U.S. culture, Kohlberg found that Stages 5 and 6 do not always appear. Their emergence appears to be associated with high levels of verbal ability and formal education (Rest & Thoma, 1976).

GENDER AND MORALITY Kohlberg's theory of moral reasoning has generated considerable interest and much controversy. One of the most stinging criticisms has come from Carol Gilligan (1982), a colleague at Kohlberg's own campus. Gilligan argued that Kohlberg's theory has a male bias and ignores uniquely feminine conceptions of morality. For women, says Gilligan, morality is embedded in social relationships and personal caring, which makes them appear to reach a plateau at Stage 3. To his credit, Kohlberg responded by taking a fresh look at his data for Stage 3 and Stage 4. As a result, he redefined Stage 4 by moving militant law-and-order responses (most often given by males) to Stage 3. Most subsequent studies have found no significant sex differences in moral reasoning (Walker, 1989, 1991; Walker & de Vries, 1985; Walker et al., 1987).

Social and Emotional Development

Our moral development is closely linked to our abilities to get along with others. So is a child's very survival, which depends on forming meaningful, effective relationships. This means that children need to learn the rules that their society uses for governing its members' social and political interactions. They must also learn to deal with their own feelings and those of others.

The child must also develop a **theory of mind.** This consists of an awareness that others may have beliefs, desires, and emotions different from one's own and that these mental states underlie their behavior (Frith & Frith, 1999). This accomplishment is fundamental to successful social interaction, whether

Connection

Chapter 14
What factors determine the quality of our social relationships?

Theory of mind: An awareness that other people's behavior may be influenced by beliefs, desires, and emotions that differ from one's own.

Connection

Chapter 9
Some facial expressions of emotion are universal.

it be play, work, or establishing friendships and partnerships. In contrast, we can see the failure to develop a workable theory of mind in autistic children, whose difficulties probably stem from a brain abnormality.

Smiling is one way people begin simple social and emotional interactions. So essential is a smile to human communication that a baby's first smile is probably generated automatically by genetically controlled processes. In fact, smiles occur in babies throughout the world (Gazzaniga, 1998). The delight parents take in a baby's first smile represents the beginning of lifelong lessons in social behavior. People smile not only as a sign of positive feelings but also because their audience expects such a facial expression (Fridlund, 1990). However, social and emotional development involves much more than a winning smile. On the "nurture" side, psychologists have found many environmental factors that influence relationships, particularly the special social relationship called *attachment*. And on the "nature" side, they have found that an innate *temperament* influences our responsiveness to others. We will analyze these important concepts more deeply.

TEMPERAMENT   Psychologists use the term **temperament** for an individual's inherited, enduring pattern of reacting to environmental stimuli and situations. Thus, temperament is the part of personality that is "wired in" at birth. Harvard researcher Jerome Kagan, who has studied temperament in thousands of children, has observed that about 10 to 15% of infants are "born shy" or "born bold" (Kagan, 1994a, b; Kagan et al., 1986; Kagan & Snidman, 1991). The infants in these groups differ in sensitivity to physical and social stimulation. Specifically, the shy baby is more easily frightened and less socially responsive. As a result, people are less likely to interact and be playful with the shy baby, accentuating the child's initial disposition.

While temperaments are in place from birth, they are not written in stone (Kagan, 1996). Experience and parenting styles can modify the way temperament expresses itself. For example, a bold child reared by bold parents will certainly experience and respond to the world differently from a bold child reared by timid or fearful parents. Likewise, if a shy baby's parents recognize the child's withdrawal and gently play with her and encourage her to interact, the child may become more outgoing than her temperament would otherwise have predicted. Thus family members and friends can teach every individual a variety of responses to the world, all within his or her temperamental range. Nor is one temperament ideal for all situations. We should "remember that in a complex society like ours, each temperamental type can find its adaptive niche" (Kagan, quoted in Gallagher, 1994, p. 47).

SOCIALIZATION AND ATTACHMENT   In order to help children find the most adaptive niches for their abilities and temperaments, parents *socialize* their offspring. **Socialization** is the lifelong process of shaping an individual's behavior patterns, values, standards, skills, attitudes, and motives to conform to those regarded as desirable in a particular society (Hetherington & Parke, 1975). Besides parents, many individuals and institutions exert pressure on the individual to adopt socially approved values. Among these, the family is certainly the most influential regulator of socialization, at least during childhood. The patterns of social responsiveness learned in the family form the basis of the individual's habitual style of relating to other people. And of these social response patterns, the most basic is learned in the infant's experience of *attachment*.

Infant Attachment   Ideally, social development begins with the establishment of a close emotional relationship between a child and parent figure. This intense, enduring, relationship is called **attachment**. Developmental psychol-

Temperament: An individual's characteristic manner of behavior or reaction — assumed to have a strong genetic basis.

Socialization: The lifelong process of developing behavior patterns, values, standards, skills, attitudes, and motives that conform to those regarded as desirable in a society.

Attachment: The enduring social-emotional relationship between a child and a parent or other regular caregiver.

ogists find that the attachment relationship is especially important because the quality of attachment lays the foundation for all other relationships that follow.

Attachment behaviors appear to occur "instinctively" in many species, but such behaviors are not necessarily limited to the infant's interactions with its biological parents. One striking example of instinctive attachment occurs in **imprinting,** the powerful attraction of infants of some species to the first moving object or individual they see. A baby chick hatched by a mother duck will form an attachment to this surrogate parent, staying close to her and following her right up to the water's edge when she and her ducklings go for a swim. Thus, the imprinting tendency is an innate predisposition, although the organism's environment and experience determine what form it will take. While imprinting occurs most clearly in birds, a similar, but more complex, process may account for the attachment between human infants and their caregivers.

Although humans apparently have an inborn need for attachment, there is no guarantee that parents will always respond to this need. What, then, can babies do to increase the chances of getting the contact they want? Unlike a baby chick, human babies are not mobile enough at birth to use their own locomotion to get closeness or attention from a caregiver. When they want to get close to the attachment figure (e.g., their mother), they cannot simply crawl or move toward her. But they can emit signals—such as smiling, crying, and vocalizing—to promote responsive behavior (Campos et al., 1983). Who can resist a baby's smile? According to John Bowlby (1973), infants will form attachments to any individual who consistently and appropriately responds to their signals.

Some observers have suggested that attachment begins as early as the first few weeks (Ainsworth, 1973; Ainsworth et al., 1978; Bowlby, 1969, 1973). One study found, for example, that when mothers left the room, their two- to four-month-old babies' skin temperature dropped, a sign of emotional distress (Mizukami et al., 1990). In these youngsters, skin temperature dropped even more when a stranger replaced the mother. In contrast, skin temperature remained steady if the mother stayed in the room—even if the stranger was present. Apparently, children only a few months old rely on their caretakers as a "safe base," even before they can indicate attachment with crying or locomotion (Bee, 1994).

The Strange Situation　Developmental psychologist Mary Ainsworth studied the various forms attachment takes by observing young children in a variety of "strange situations." She did this by separating them by a barrier from their mothers or by putting them in an unfamiliar room (Ainsworth, 1989; Ainsworth et al., 1978; Ainsworth & Wittig, 1969; Lamb, 1999). Using this method in a variety of cultures, Ainsworth found that the children's responses were of two main types: They were either *securely* or *insecurely* attached. Securely attached children felt close to their mothers, safe, and more willing to explore or tolerate a novel experience—confident that they could cry out for help or be reunited with the missing parent. Insecurely attached children were more likely to react to the "strange situation" in one of two ways: with anxiety and **ambivalence** or with avoidance. The anxious-ambivalent children wanted contact but cried with fear and anger when separated and proved difficult to console even when reunited with their mothers. The avoidant children acted as though they were unconcerned about being separated from their mothers, not crying when they left and not seeking contact when they returned. Avoidant children may be showing the effects of repeated rejection, no longer seeking attachment because their efforts have failed in the past (Shaver & Hazan, 1994).

Connection

Chapter 9
"Instinct" refers to behaviors that have a strong genetic basis.

Imprinting: A primitive form of learning in which some young animals follow and form an attachment to the first moving object they see and hear.

Ambivalence: Having conflicting thoughts or feelings.

Children become attached to their caregivers, and parents bond to their children. These bonds of love and responsibility help offset the daily struggles for survival faced by poor families the world over.

Identify which one of the following three self-descriptions you most agree with (adapted from Shaver & Hazan, 1994):

1. I am somewhat uncomfortable being close to others; I find it difficult to trust them completely, difficult to allow myself to depend on them. I am nervous when anyone gets too close, and often, love partners want me to be more intimate than I feel comfortable being.

2. I find that others are reluctant to get as close as I would like. I often worry that my partner doesn't really love me or won't want to stay with me. I want to get very close to my partner, and this sometimes scares people away.

3. I find it relatively easy to get close to others and am comfortable depending on them. I don't often worry about being abandoned or about someone getting too close to me.

WHAT YOUR CHOICE MEANS

We realize that it is probably obvious to you which of the statements above is "best." Nevertheless, just considering the alternatives should help you understand attachment styles — and, perhaps, yourself — a little better. Here's our interpretation: If you selected the first statement, you agreed with the attitude that reflects an avoidant, insecure attachment. This style was chosen by 25% of Shaver and Hazan's respondent sample. The second statement reflects an anxious-ambivalent, insecure attachment style, selected by 20% of the sample. The third statement reflects a secure attachment style, the most common pattern identified, accounting for 55% of respondents (Shaver & Hazan, 1994).

What do these styles signify for later life? Through interviews, observations, and questionnaires, researchers have identified several consequences of attachment style, secure or insecure, in adulthood (see Ainsworth, 1989; Collins & Read, 1990; Hazan & Shaver, 1990; Kirkpatrick & Shaver, 1992; Shaver & Hazan, 1993, 1994; Simpson, 1990):

► Secure individuals have more positive self-concepts and believe that most other people are good-natured and well-intentioned. They see their personal relationships as trustworthy and satisfying.

► Secure respondents are satisfied with their job security, coworkers, income, and work activity. They put a higher value on relationships than on work and derive their greatest pleasure from connections to others.

► Insecure, anxious-ambivalent persons report emotional extremes and jealousy. They feel unappreciated, insecure, and unlikely to win professional advancement. They make less money than those with other attachment styles, working more for approval and recognition than financial gain. They fantasize about succeeding but often slack off after receiving praise.

► Avoidant people fear intimacy and expect their relationships to fail. They place a higher value on work than on relationships and generally like their work and job security. They follow a workaholic pattern, but (not surprisingly) they are dissatisfied with their coworkers.

► Secure individuals tend to choose as partners others who are secure. After breakups, avoidant individuals claim to be less bothered by the loss of the relationship, although this may be a defensive claim, with distress showing up in other ways (e.g., physical symptoms).

Attachment fascinates researchers because patterns established in infancy may persist in a variety of childhood and even adult behaviors, influencing later-life job satisfaction, relationship choices, and intimacy experiences (Bower, 1997; Collins & Read, 1990; Hazan & Shaver, 1990, 1992; Shaver & Hazan, 1993, 1994). As children grow up and become adults, they no longer restrict their attachment to their primary caregiver. While they may retain their childhood attachment style, they gradually widen their attachments to include peers, friends, teachers, coworkers, and others in their community. We should emphasize, however, that — powerful as attachment is — individuals who lack healthy attachments in infancy and childhood are not necessarily doomed to failure in life. While attachment problems are good predictors of later problems with social relationships, many people do succeed in overcoming attachment difficulties (Kagan, 1996, 1998). With that caution in mind, take the quiz on your own attachment style in "Do It Yourself! What's Your Attachment Style?"

Contact Comfort   Why and how do infants become attached to caregivers in the first place? An evolutionary explanation says that attachment safeguards an infant's survival by assuring the support and protection it requires. Through natural selection individuals with genetic tendencies to "attach" will survive, thrive, and pass those tendencies along to their own offspring.

In addition to protection, could attachment also be a child's way of encouraging the parents to provide food, an infant's most basic physical need? This has been dubbed the "cupboard theory" of attachment: Individuals become attached to those who provide the "cupboard" containing the food supply. This view has been a favorite of those who believe that nursing is the basis for healthy relationships. But does the cupboard theory really explain attachment?

Psychologists Harry and Margaret Harlow guessed that a more fundamental cause of attachment involves physical contact (Harlow, 1965; Harlow & Harlow, 1966). To see if they were right, they decided to test this idea against the cupboard theory in an animal model, using infant monkeys who had been separated from their mothers at birth. The Harlows placed orphaned baby monkeys in cages where they had access to two artificial **surrogate mothers.** One was a simple wire figure that provided milk through a nipple—a "cupboard," but little else. The other was a cloth-covered figure providing no milk but offering abundant stimulation from its soft terry-cloth cover. Confirming their expectations, the Harlows observed that their baby monkeys spent many hours nestled close to the cloth mother but little time with the wire model, despite the nourishment the latter provided. Moreover, when the baby monkeys were frightened, they sought comfort by clinging to the cloth figure. They also used it as a base of operations when exploring new situations. With these observations, then, the Harlows were able to show that the infant monkeys become attached to and prefer a "mother" figure that provides **contact comfort,** stimulation and reassurance derived from physical touch.

Human infants need contact comfort, too. The lack of a close, loving relationship in infancy even affects physical growth. We know this from observations of children in emotionally detached or hostile family environments: Such children have slower growth and bone development. They may grow again if removed from the poor environment, but their growth is stunted again if they are returned to it, a phenomenon known as *psychosocial dwarfism.* Accordingly, in some hospitals that recognize the power of contact comfort, premature infants and those born at risk (such as those born to crack-addicted mothers) are scheduled to receive regular holding and cuddling by staff members and volunteers. Clearly, a close, interactive relationship with loving adults is a child's first step toward healthy physical growth and normal socialization.

Effects of Day Care   As families make increasing use of day care for their children, many people have wondered: How necessary is it to have a full-time parent? The question is an urgent one in the United States, where over half of all mothers with children under age 3 are employed, and more children are cared for by paid providers than by relatives (Scarr, 1997; 1998). The research sends us mixed messages (Bower, 1996; Clarke-Stewart, 1989). First the good news: Most children thrive in day care. They do as well—sometimes better—both intellectually and socially as children raised at home by a parent. Now the bad news: Some day care experiences influence children to be aggressive, depressed, or otherwise maladjusted. Fortunately, the overwhelming majority of day care centers do a fine job.

Even though negative effects of day care are uncommon, it is instructive to see what factors are associated with bad outcomes. The research shows that having multiple caregivers does *not* cause psychological problems. Instead, difficulties surface most often in poorly staffed centers where large

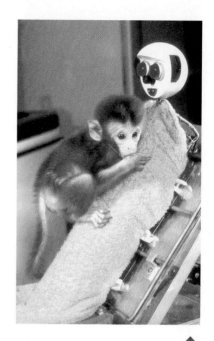

One of Harlow's monkeys and its artificial terry-cloth mother. Harlow found that the contact comfort mothers provide is essential for normal social development.

Surrogate mothers: Mother substitutes, such as the cloth and wire dummies in Harlow's research.

Contact comfort: Stimulation and reassurance derived from the physical touch of a caregiver.

numbers of children get little attention from only a few adults (Howes et al., 1988). Another problem results from the fact that children who are placed in the poorest-quality day care programs are most often from the poorest, most disorganized, and most highly stressed families. Developmental psychologist Laura Berk (2000) concludes that this volatile combination of inadequate day care and family pressure places some children at high risk. Yet, she says, using this evidence to curtail day care services would be mistaken, because forcing a parent on a marginal income to stay home may expose children to an even greater level of risk.

All this means that day care is, in itself, neither good nor bad. It is the *quality of care,* whether given by a parent or a paid provider, that makes all the difference. Development expert Sandra Scarr (1998) says:

> There is an extraordinary international consensus among child-care researchers and practitioners about what quality child care is: It is warm, supportive interactions with adults in a safe, healthy, and stimulating environment, where early education and trusting relationships combine to support individual children's physical, emotional, social, and intellectual development. . . . (p. 102)

Gender Differences   Anyone who has watched young boys and girls playing has noticed gender differences in their social interaction. The sexes usually prefer to segregate themselves—a pattern that holds across cultures (Maccoby, 1998, 2000). Boys are typically more aggressive than girls, although there are certainly exceptions. Girls tend to organize themselves into small, cooperative groups. By contrast, boys often form larger groups that have a hierarchical structure, or "pecking order." In these groups, individual boys continually compete for higher-ranking positions. In doing so, they frequently employ aggressive tactics, such as hitting, shoving, and verbal threats. Evolutionary psychologists believe that these gender differences have an innate basis (Buss, 1999), which may be related to gender differences in testosterone levels (Dabbs, 2000). This does not mean, of course, that environmental factors, such as parenting styles and peer influences, make no differences. Individuals *can* learn to become more aggressive or cooperative.

Psychosocial crises: In Erikson's theory, any of the eight major developmental challenges across the life span, which require an individual to rethink his or her orientation to self and others.

Autonomy: The ability to act independently.

Childhood Influences on Your Personality

Psychology

In Your Life

Your personality and your social relationships are a complex blend of your temperament, attachment style, and many other forces that have acted on you through life. But do these factors produce predictable patterns across the life span? A

theory of personality proposed by psychoanalyst Erik Erikson says yes. (See also Chapter 11, Personality.)

As a middle-aged immigrant to America, Erik Erikson (1963) became aware of conflicts and choices he faced because of his new status. This caused him to reflect on the many such conflicts every individual must face in the continuing process of development. Before reading further, please take a

moment to do as Erikson did: Recall some of the conflicts or crises you have experienced in childhood. These will give you a vantage point from which to understand Erikson's theory—and your own personality.

ERIKSON'S THEORY OF PSYCHOSOCIAL DEVELOPMENT ACROSS THE LIFE SPAN

Erikson saw human development as a sequence of challenges that emerge throughout life, from infancy to old age. His theory says that when people face these **psychosocial crises** they make choices that influence the growth of their personalities. Good choices lay the foundation for healthy growth during later stages of development.

What are the major psychosocial crises that shape our personalities? Erikson identified eight such challenges. With each, a particular conflict comes into focus, as shown in Table 4.2. The conflict must be sufficiently resolved at a given stage if an individual is to cope successfully with the new crises of later stages. Here we will review the psychosocial crises of childhood; in the following section we will review the crises experienced in adolescence and adulthood.

TRUST VERSUS MISTRUST

In the first stage of your psychosocial development, you needed to develop a basic sense of trust in your environment and in those who cared for you. This trust is a natural accompaniment to a strong attachment relationship with a caregiver who provides food, warmth, and the comfort of physical closeness. But if these basic needs were not met, Erikson suggested, you experienced a developmental crisis. At this stage, inconsistent handling, lack of physical closeness and warmth, or the frequent absence of a caring adult may produce a lasting sense of mistrust, insecurity, and anxiety. Children facing such conditions will not be prepared for the second stage in their psychological development.

The healthy personality requires a foundation of trust from which the individual can become more adventurous.

AUTONOMY VERSUS SELF-DOUBT

In the second stage, as you acquired skills in walking and talking, you expanded your exploration and manipulation of objects (and sometimes of people). If you entered this stage with a sense of trust, these activities should have brought you a comfortable sense of **autonomy** (independence) and of being a capable and worthy person. Excessive restriction or criticism at this stage may have led to self-doubts. Demands made on you beyond your ability—such as attempting toilet training too early—could have discouraged your efforts to persevere in mastering new tasks. Such demands also can lead to stormy scenes of confrontation, disrupting the supportive parent–child relationship. In contrast, the 2-year-old who affirms the right to do something without help, in response to appropriate demands, acts out of a need to affirm his or her autonomy and adequacy.

INITIATIVE VERSUS GUILT

If you developed a basic sense of trust and autonomy during your preschool days, you probably became a child who could comfortably initiate intellectual and motor tasks. For example, children in this stage want to do things for themselves, such as pour a glass of juice, choose what to wear, or get dressed. The danger at this stage is that overcontrolling adults will demand an impossible degree of self-control ("Why can't you sit still?"), and the child will be overcome by feelings of inadequacy and guilt. Caregivers' responses to self-initiated activities either encourage or discourage the

freedom and self-confidence needed for the next stage.

COMPETENCE VERSUS INFERIORITY

If you successfully resolved the crises of the three earlier stages, you were ready to go beyond random exploration to develop your skills and competencies in a more systematic way. During the elementary school years, school and sports offer arenas for learning more complex intellectual and motor skills, while peer interaction offers the chance to develop social skills. Successful efforts in these pursuits lead to feelings of competence. Some youngsters, however, become discouraged spectators rather than performers, or they experience discouraging failure that leaves them with a sense of inferiority. Such children will find it more difficult to face continuing challenges and crises of psychosocial development.

THE CURRENT STATUS OF ERIKSON'S THEORY

How much confidence should we place in Erikson? Although widely accepted, his developmental theory does have some shortcomings. Based mainly on clinical observation, it lacks a rigorous scientific basis. Moreover, as some critics point out, Erikson's crises do not capture the problems faced by girls and women as well as they do those faced by boys and men, especially in the later periods of life, which we will cover in the next section. Despite these problems, however, Erikson's work should be seen as a comprehensive pioneering effort that has encouraged us to look at the life cycle as a whole, putting into perspective both the unfolding changes and the continuity of life experience.

1. **RECALL:** *Noam Chomsky has presented evidence supporting his theory that*
   a. children learn language by imitating their parents.
   b. children are born with some rules of grammar programmed into their brains.
   c. vocabulary is innate, but grammar is learned.
   d. different languages may have entirely different rules of grammar.

2. **RECALL:** *Match the ability/limitation with the Piagetian stage at which it appears.*
   a. centration   i. sensorimotor stage
   b. abstract thought   ii. preoperational stage
   c. innate schemes   iii. concrete operational stage
   d. conservation   iv. formal operational stage

3. **RECALL:** *According to Kohlberg, as moral reasoning advances, individuals become less*
   a. emotional.
   b. self-centered.
   c. ruled by instinct.
   d. attached to their parents.

4. **RECALL:** *Mary Ainsworth found two main types of attachment,*
   a. shy and bold.
   b. introverted and extraverted.
   c. secure and insecure.
   d. strong and weak.

5. **APPLICATION:** *You are a psychologist working in a pediatric hospital. What would you recommend as one of the most important things that the staff could do for newborn babies to promote their healthy development?*
   a. Talk to them.
   b. Touch them.
   c. Make eye contact with them.
   d. Feed them on demand.

Core Concept

6. **UNDERSTANDING THE CORE CONCEPT:**
   Children are different from adults with respect to their language, their thought processes, and their social relationships. Can you name one way that young children are different from adults in each of these three areas?

ANSWERS: 1. b   2. a. ii, b. iv, c. i, d. iii   3. b   4. c   5. b   6. Language: both vocabulary and grammar. Thought processes: for example, young children are not capable of abstract reasoning. (Piaget's theory suggests other differences at each stage.) Social relationships: adult attachments broaden to include peers, friends, coworkers, and others.

Key Question
?

WHAT DEVELOPMENTAL CHANGES OCCUR IN ADOLESCENCE AND ADULTHOOD?

Most early theorists assumed that the major work of development occurred before adolescence. After that, they believed, the psyche was set for life and would undergo few important changes. Modern research challenges such notions. Psychologists now agree that we have a remarkable capacity for developmental change throughout our life span (Kagan, 1996, 1998). Accordingly, here is the Core Concept of life-span development:

Core Concept

> **Nature and nurture continue to produce changes in personality and mental processes throughout the life cycle.**

Below we will trace some of the major changes that occur through adolescence, adulthood, and at the end of life.

The Transitions of Adolescence

Do you remember what event first made you think of yourself as an adolescent? Chances are that it had something to do with your sexual maturation,

TABLE 4.2 Erikson's Psychosocial Crises

AGE/PERIOD (APPROXIMATE)	CRISIS	ADEQUATE RESOLUTION	INADEQUATE RESOLUTION
0 to 1½ years	Trust vs. mistrust	Basic sense of safety, security; ability to rely on forces outside oneself	Insecurity, anxiety
1½ to 3 years	Autonomy vs. self-doubt	Perception of self as agent; capable of controlling one's own body and making things happen	Feelings of inadequacy about self-control, control of events
3 to 6 years	Initiative vs. guilt	Confidence in oneself as being able to initiate, create	Feeling of lack of self-worth
6 years to puberty	Competence vs. inferiority	Adequacy in basic social and intellectual skills; acceptance by peers	Lack of self-confidence; feelings of failure
Adolescence	Identity vs. role confusion	Comfortable sense of self as a person, both unique and socially accepted	Sense of self as fragmented, shifting, unclear sense of self
Early adulthood	Intimacy vs. isolation	Capacity for closeness and commitment to another	Feeling of aloneness, loneliness, separation; denial of intimacy needs
Middle adulthood	Generativity vs. stagnation	Focus of concern beyond oneself, to family, society, future generations	Self-indulgent concerns; lack of future orientation
Late adulthood	Ego-integrity vs. despair	Sense of wholeness; basic satisfaction with life	Feelings of futility, disappointment

such as a first menstrual period or a nocturnal ejaculation. Psychologists pinpoint the beginning of **adolescence** as the onset of **puberty,** when sexual maturity, or the ability to reproduce, is attained. However, they cannot so precisely identify the point at which adolescence ends and adulthood begins.

CULTURAL DIFFERENCES   Variations among cultures compound the difficulty of specifying the span of adolescence. Although the physical changes that take place at this stage are universal, the social and psychological dimensions of adolescence depend on the cultural context. For example, if you enter your teen years in a culture that celebrates puberty as the entry to adulthood and rewards you with the power to make responsible choices, you will have a very different experience from someone whose culture condemns teenagers as confused and potentially dangerous troublemakers.

Most nonindustrial societies do not identify an adolescent stage as we know it. Instead, children in these societies move directly into adulthood with **rites of passage.** These rituals usually take place around puberty and serve as a public acknowledgment of the transition from childhood to adulthood. Rites of passage vary widely among cultures, from extremely painful rituals to periods of instruction in sexual and cultural practices or periods of seclusion involving survival ordeals. For example, in some tribal cultures, the young person may be asked to take a meditative journey alone or to submit to symbolic scarring or circumcision surrounded by friends and family. Once individuals have

Adolescence: In industrial societies, a developmental period beginning at puberty and ending (less clearly) at adulthood.

Puberty: The onset of sexual maturity.

Rites of passage: Social rituals that mark the transition between developmental stages, especially between childhood and adulthood.

Body image becomes especially important in the teenage years.

completed the passage, there is no ambiguity about their status: They are adults, and the ties to their childhood have been severed.

Our own society has few transition rituals to help children clearly mark their new adolescent status or for adolescents to know when they have become young adults. One subtle rite of passage for many middle-class teenagers in America is qualifying for a driver's license. Both symbolically and practically, being able to drive a car legally provides a young person with freedom, independence, and mobility that is not available to children.

Although many issues are important in adolescence, we will focus on a few of the most important developmental tasks that confront adolescents in the Western world: coming to terms with physical maturity and adult sexuality; redefining social roles, including achieving autonomy from parents; and deciding upon occupational goals. Each of these issues is a component of the central task of establishing an integrated identity.

PHYSICAL MATURATION IN ADOLESCENCE The first concrete indicator of the end of childhood is the *pubescent growth spurt*. Two to three years after the onset of the growth spurt, puberty, or sexual maturity, is reached. Puberty for males begins with the production of live sperm (usually at about age 14 in the United States), while for girls it begins at **menarche,** the onset of menstruation (between ages 11 and 15).

Physical Attractiveness Unfair as it may be, physical attractiveness influences the way people view each other (Hatfield & Rapson, 1993), and during adolescence an attractive appearance takes on vastly increased importance. Consequently, the adolescent task of developing a personal identity involves coming to terms with one's physical self by developing a realistic yet accepting body image (one's personal and subjective view of one's own appearance). This image is dependent not only on measurable features, such as height and weight, but also on perceptions of other people's assessments and on cultural standards of physical beauty. During adolescence, dramatic physical changes and heightened emphasis on peer acceptance (especially sexually attractive peers) can intensify concern with one's body image.

Appearance and Self-Esteem Approximately 44% of American adolescent girls and 23% of boys claimed that they "frequently felt ugly and unattractive"; similar data have been found across many cultures (Offer et al., 1981, 1988). Physical appearance is clearly one of the biggest concerns among adolescents (Perkins & Lerner, 1995). Girls' self-concepts are particularly tied to perceptions of their physical attractiveness, while boys seem more concerned with their physical prowess, athletic ability, and effectiveness in achieving goals (Lerner et al., 1976; Wade, 1991). Girls and women are more dissatisfied with their weight and shape than are males, and experience more conflict about food and eating (Rolls et al., 1991). These differences probably mirror a cultural preoccupation with female beauty and male strength—an inevitable source of concern because not all adolescents can embody the cultural ideals of attractiveness. There are also cultural influences on self-concept; some research indicates that the self-esteem of white adolescents of both sexes is more tied to physical attractiveness than is that of black adolescents (Wade, 1991). Over time, adolescents seem to become more accepting of their appearances. Nonetheless, the attainment of acceptable body images can be a difficult task.

Behind these changes in thinking are some profound changes occurring inside the body. Levels of the hormones estrogen and testosterone rise to high

Menarche: The onset of menstruation, which signals puberty in girls.

levels. At the same time, the frontal lobes of the brain, a region involved in social and emotional behaviors, is undergoing a "remodel," involving growth of new circuits, loss of some old ones, and changes in the balance of neurotransmitters (Spear, 2000). All of this probably contributes to increases among adolescents in sensation-seeking and risk-taking behaviors, as well as to increasing preoccupation with body image and sex.

SEXUALITY IN ADOLESCENCE A new awareness of sexual feelings and impulses accompanies physical maturity. In one large study, the majority of American adolescent males and females said that they often think about sex (Offer et al., 1981). Yet many still lack adequate knowledge or have misconceptions about sex and sexuality—even if they are sexually active. Sex is a topic parents find difficult to discuss with children, so adolescents tend to be secretive about sexual concerns, making exchange of information and communication even more difficult. The development of a sexual identity that defines sexual orientation and guides sexual behavior thus becomes an important task of adolescence.

Sexual Orientation In early adolescence masturbation is the most common orgasmic expression of sexual impulses (Bell et al., 1981; Coles & Stokes, 1985; Wilson & Medora, 1990). Between 14 and 17% of teenage boys and half that many girls report some homosexual experiences (broadly defined as becoming sexually aroused with a person of the same sex), although most of these individuals ultimately identify with a heterosexual orientation (Hass, 1979; Sorensen, 1973; Wyatt et al., 1988). Exclusively homosexual feelings are much more difficult to resolve during adolescence, when individuals are intensely concerned with the conventions and norms of their society. While most gay and lesbian individuals first become aware of their sexual orientation in early adolescence, many may not attain self-acceptance of their sexual identities until their middle or late twenties (Newman & Muzzonigro, 1993; Riddle & Morin, 1977). The time lag undoubtedly reflects the relative lack of social support for a homosexual orientation and exemplifies the importance of society's role in all aspects of identity development.

Sexual Intercourse in Adolescence The proportion of American adolescents engaging in sexual intercourse rose substantially during the 1970s and 1980s but leveled off in the 1990s (Chilman, 1983; London et al., 1989; Reinisch, 1990; Zeman, 1990). About half of all young Americans have engaged in intercourse before age 17, and about 75% have done so by the age of 20 (Harvey & Spigner, 1995). There is evidence that the initial sexual experiences of males and females differ substantially. For the vast majority of females emotional involvement is an important ingredient of sexual attraction. In contrast, for most males personal relationships appear to be less important than the sex act itself. In fact, the average male reports no emotional involvement with his first sexual partner (Miller & Simon, 1980).

SOCIAL IDENTITY AND THE IDENTITY CRISIS OF ADOLESCENCE Erik Erikson believed that the essential crisis of adolescence is discovering one's true *identity* amid the confusion of playing many different roles for different audiences in an expanding social world. Resolving this **identity crisis** helps the individual develop a sense of a coherent self. Failure to resolve the identity crisis adequately may result in a self-concept that lacks a stable core. This was apparent in Benny's case, which we considered at the beginning of the chapter. Resolution of this issue is both a personal process and a social experience

Connection

Chapter 9
Research has found no link between sexual orientation and parenting styles.

Connection

Chapter 11
The self-concept is a core component of the personality, according to many theorists.

Identity crisis: In Erikson's theory, the developmental crisis of adolescence.

(Erikson, 1963). (Review Table 4.2 for Erikson's concept of the adolescent identity crisis.)

The Increasing Influence of Peers   Several factors influence the move toward an emerging self-identity. Family ties become stretched as the adolescent spends more time outside the home (Paikoff & Brooks-Gunn, 1991). Indeed, some developmental psychologists argue that the effects of parents, family, and childhood become nearly lost as the adolescent peer group gains influence (Harris, 1995). In American society, the adolescent encounters new values, receives less structure and adult guidance, and feels a strong need for peer acceptance. As a result, adolescents report spending more than four times as much time talking to peers as to adults (Csikszentmihalyi et al., 1977). With their peers, adolescents refine their social skills and try out different social behaviors. Gradually, they define their social identities, the kind of people they choose to be, and the sorts of relationships they will pursue.

According to Erikson, during the "identity crisis," adolescents must define their identities as individuals even as they seek the comfort and feeling of belonging that comes from being with friends and family. One compromise might be to experiment with different norms – such as clothing or hairstyles – within the security of supportive relationships with companions, cliques, or romantic partners.

Common Social Problems of Adolescence   Loneliness also becomes significant during adolescence: Between 15 and 25% of adolescents report feeling very lonely (Offer et al., 1981). Similarly, shyness reaches its highest level in early teenage years as the desire for social acceptance markedly increases (Zimbardo, 1990). Studies of adolescent suicide show that the triggering experience for such a tragedy is often a shaming or humiliating event, such as failure in some achievement or a romantic rejection (Garland & Zigler, 1993). The intensity of a young person's social and personal motives can make it hard to keep perspective and recognize that even difficult times will pass and that everyone makes mistakes.

As the need for close friendships and peer acceptance becomes greater, anxiety about the possibility of rejection increases. Many young adolescents may choose the "safe" route of conformity and go along with their friends to avoid weakening those relationships. Females may be especially concerned with personal relationships, but they are less likely than males to give in to group pressure to behave antisocially (Berndt, 1979). Many parents worry that their teenagers will endanger themselves in proving their loyalty to unreasonable friends or norms. Fortunately, research suggests that most adolescents are able to "look before they leap" by considering the wisdom of committing risky acts (Berndt, 1992).

Connection

Chapter 14
Many social factors influence conformity.

The dual forces of parents and peers at times exhibit conflicting influences on adolescents, intensifying the separation from parents and increasing identification with peers. But generally parents and peers serve complementary functions and fulfill different needs in adolescents' lives, and both have influence (Davis, 1985). For example, adolescents look to their families for structure and support, while they look to their friends for acceptance and approval. Having well-adjusted friends helps adolescents face challenges constructively, while having poorly adjusted friends can be a drain on adolescents' psychological resources (Hartup & Stevens, 1999).

But, is adolescence inevitably a period of turmoil? It is a period in which individuals are most likely to have conflicts with their parents, experience extremes of mood, and engage in risky behaviors (Arnett, 1999). For some, adolescence certainly presents overwhelming problems in relationships and in self-esteem. As a survey of the research has concluded, "The adolescent years mark the beginning of a downward spiral for some individuals" (Eccles et al., 1993, p. 90). For most teens, however, these years are *not* a time of anxiety and despair

(Myers & Diener, 1995). While many parents anticipate that the relationship with their children will encounter a rocky road when the children enter adolescence, the more typical experience is relatively tranquil. In fact, the majority of adolescent youth say that they feel close to their parents (Galambos, 1992). In general, those who have the least trouble are adolescents whose parents are responsive and, at the same time, hold their children to high standards. Those adolescents who have the most difficulty are most likely to come from homes where parenting is either permissive or authoritarian (Collins et al., 2000).

THINKING ABOUT OCCUPATIONAL CHOICES According to Erikson, deciding on a vocational commitment is a central issue of adolescent identity formation. The question, "What are you going to be when you grow up?" reflects the common assumption that what you *do* determines what you *are*. It also requires the ability to think about the future and to set realistic goals that are both achievable and likely to be satisfying. Anticipating the future—mentally imagining its possibilities—strongly influences adolescents' motivation and abilities to plan and evaluate life choices (Nurmi, 1991).

While many factors affect vocational interests and achievement, the clearest is socioeconomic background. Adolescents from families of higher socioeconomic status are more likely to pursue and complete education beyond high school and to aspire toward and achieve higher levels of personal and social success. Middle-class and upper-middle-class parents encourage higher achievement motivation in their children, model greater career success, and supply the economic resources unavailable to poorer children (Achenbach, 1982; Featherman, 1980; Gustafson & Magnusson, 1991). We saw another powerful factor in our chapter-opening case, where birth order and family position affected achievement motivation (Sulloway, 1996).

The Developmental Challenges of Adulthood

The transition from adolescence to young adulthood is marked by decisions about advanced education, career, and intimate relationships. Making such decisions and adjusting to the consequences are major tasks of adulthood because they shape the course of adult psychological development. We might ask: What are the psychological forces that shape these decisions?

LOVE AND WORK According to Freud, adult development is driven by two basic needs: *love* and *work*. Abraham Maslow (1970) described these needs as *love* and *belonging,* which, when satisfied, allow the emergence of the needs for *success* and *esteem.* Other theorists divide the basic needs of adulthood into *affiliation* or *social acceptance* needs, *achievement* or *competence* needs, and *power* needs (McClelland, 1975, 1985; McClelland & Boyatzis, 1982). And in Erikson's theory, the early and middle adult years focus on needs for intimacy and "generativity."

Intimacy versus Isolation Erikson's psychosocial crisis of young adulthood poses the problem of establishing close relationships with loved ones (see Table 4.2). Erikson described intimacy as the capacity to make a full commitment—sexual, emotional, and moral—to another person. The individual must resolve the conflict between wanting to establish closeness to another and fearing the risks and losses such closeness can entail. Making intimate commitments requires compromising personal preferences, accepting responsibilities, and yielding some privacy and independence. Failure to resolve this crisis leads to isolation and the inability to connect to others in meaningful ways. Much research supports one of the most practical applications that you can take with you from this text: *Anything that isolates us from sources of social sup-*

In recent years, a growing tolerance for divorce has led many adults to change their ideas about traditional marriage. Communication and affection between modern spouses has also changed, improving over earlier times. Shown here on their wedding day are Ril and Sayoko Bandy with Ril's children from a previous marriage.

Connection

Chapter 9
Maslow suggested that our needs occur in a hierarchy —a priority order.

Connection

Chapter 9
McClelland found that some people have a higher need for achievement than do others.

Connection

Chapter 10
Social support affects your health and your ability to cope with stress.

port—from a reliable network of friends and family—puts us at risk for a host of physical ills, mental problems, and even social pathologies. We are social creatures, and we need each other's help and support to be effective and healthy (Basic Behavioral Science Task Force, 1996).

For Erikson, a young adult must consolidate a clear and comfortable sense of identity (resolving the crisis of adolescence) before being able to cope successfully with the risks and benefits of adult intimacy. In essence, you must know who and what you are before you can begin to love someone else and share your life with that person. However, the sequence from identity to intimacy that Erikson described may not accurately reflect present-day realities. The trend in recent years has been for young adults to live together before marrying, to delay making contractual commitments to lifelong intimacy with one person. Many individuals today must struggle with identity issues (for example, career choices) at the same time they are trying to deal with intimacy issues.

To complicate matters, marriage (one common route to the successful resolution of the search for intimacy) often occurs more than once in an individual's life. In fact, married adults in the United States are now divorcing at a rate four times greater than adults did 50 years ago. Half of all U.S. marriages end in divorce (Doyle, 1999). This situation may result from individuals seeking intimacy before they resolve their own identities. It may also result from unrealistic expectations that members of a couple have of each other and of what constitutes an ideal marriage and family structure (Cleek & Pearson, 1985). On the other hand, there is evidence that communication and affection between spouses is now better than it was in earlier times and that those who have learned good communications skills have substantially improved their chances of avoiding divorce (Caplow, 1982; Markman & Notarius, 1993).

Married people are more likely to see each other as partners and friends and less likely to feel constrained by the stereotype of what society expects of a "husband" or "wife." Partners in "peer marriages" talk with and help each other in ways that work best for their relationship, irrespective of traditional ideas about the man being "boss" or the wife being responsible for "women's work" (Schwartz, 1994). The key to such a fair and satisfying relationship is communication in which both partners feel able to openly express their hopes and fears (Klagsbrun, 1985). A mushrooming of knowledge on how good communication can maintain relationships has helped our culture to view marriage as a worthwhile investment and therapy as a valuable option for supporting such efforts (Gottman, 1994; Notarius, 1996). In brief, relating is no longer viewed as a set of skills that "comes naturally" with the establishment of intimacy. Instead, close relationships are seen as lifelong works-in-progress, worthwhile investments of time and energy whose quality can be improved with clearer self-understanding, effective conflict resolution, and good communication.

Generativity: In Erikson's theory, a process of making a commitment beyond oneself to family, work, society, or future generations.

Demographic: Refers to population characteristics, such as age, gender, or income distribution.

Ego-integrity: In Erikson's theory, the ability to look back on life without regrets and to enjoy a sense of wholeness.

Generativity versus Stagnation   According to Erikson, the next major opportunity for growth occurs in the **generativity** crisis of adult midlife. For those who have successfully met the earlier challenges of identity and intimacy, generativity brings a commitment to make a contribution to family, work, society, or future generations—a crucial challenge of one's thirties, forties, and fifties. Thus, people in this phase of life broaden their focus beyond self and partner, often as volunteers in community service groups. Research confirms that adults who express a strong sense of being generative and productive also report high life satisfaction (McAdams et al., 1993). In contrast, those who have not resolved earlier crises of identity and intimacy may experience a "midlife crisis." Such people question past choices, becoming cynical and stagnant or, at the other extreme, self-indulgent and reckless.

Psychology

In Your Life

The Last Developmental Problems You Will Face

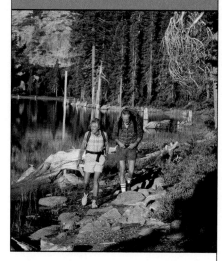

Older people who pursue high levels of environmental stimulation tend to maintain higher levels of cognitive abilities.

At the beginning of the 20th century, only 3% of the U.S. population was over 65. One hundred years later that figure is about 13%. When the baby-boom generation reaches this age in the next few years, nearly one-fourth of our population will be in this oldest group.

If you are now a 20-year-old college student, you will be nearly 50 years old by the year 2030, and you will have witnessed a profound **demographic** shift. By that time, more than 80 million Americans will be over 60 years of age. For the first time in history, the number of people in the 60+ age group will outnumber those under 20 years of age. This represents a dramatic reversal of all previous demographics and a potentially significant shift away from today's youth-oriented culture (Pifer & Bronte, 1986).

With such drastic changes in our society's age distribution, it is more essential than ever to understand the nature of aging as well as the abilities and needs of the elderly (Roush, 1996). The problem of dealing with an aging population is even more pressing in Third World countries, where incomes and standards of living are low and where health care resources are minimal (Holden, 1996a). And, on a personal level, it may be helpful to anticipate some of the developmental challenges you will face in the last phase of your life.

EGO-INTEGRITY VERSUS DESPAIR

According to Erikson, an increasing awareness of your own mortality and of the changes in your body, behavior, and social roles will set the stage for late adulthood. The crisis at this stage involves **ego-integrity,** the ability to look back on life without regrets and to enjoy a sense of wholeness. For those whose previous crises had unhealthy solutions, however, aspirations remain unfulfilled, and these individuals experience futility, despair, and self-deprecation. Sadly, they often then fail to resolve the crisis successfully at this final developmental stage.

In general, Erikson characterizes old age as a time of challenge. What are the tasks of old age, and what resources and limitations must we confront as we look ahead to the autumn of our lives? In a series of interviews with middle-aged and older men and women, Ryff (1989) found that both age groups and sexes defined "well-being" in terms of having an orientation toward others: being a caring, compassionate person and having good relationships. Respondents also emphasized the value of accepting change, enjoying life, and cultivating a sense of humor.

NEW PERSPECTIVES ON AGING

What does aging mean for us? From a biological perspective, aging typically means decline: Energy reserves are reduced, cells decay, and muscle tone diminishes. From a cognitive perspective, however, we know that aging is no longer synonymous with decline (Qualls & Abeles, 2000). In fact, many abilities, including expert skills and some aspects of memory, may improve with age (Azar, 1996; Krampe & Ericsson, 1996). A lifetime's accumulation of experience may finally culminate in wisdom—if the mind remains open and active. Theories of aging are models of balance or trade-offs: In old age, a person may lose energy reserves but gain an ability to control emotional experiences and thereby conserve energy. Thus, we can expect two kinds of changes—gains and losses—as we grow older (Baltes, 1987).

Some of the most obvious changes that occur with age affect people's physical appearances and abilities. As we grow older, we can expect our skin to wrinkle, our hair to thin and gray, and our height to decrease an inch or two. Our hearts and lungs operate less efficiently, so we can expect decreased physical stamina. We can also expect some of our senses to dull. These changes occur and develop gradually, so we have ample opportunity to gauge them and try to adjust. Earlier psychological explanations characterized aging as a change from growth to decline, but a more accurate understanding of aging considers the joint influence of individual potential and realistic limits (Baltes, 1993). Consider how an individual might make the most of the resources he or she has, given each of the changes accompanying aging:

▶ **Vision** As we age, the lenses in our eyes become rigid and discolored, affecting both distance and color vision. Most people over 65 experience some loss of visual acuity, and without corrective lenses half of the elderly would be considered legally blind. Cor-
(continued)

rective lenses do aid in adjusting to these changes in vision, however, especially for night driving or close work such as reading. *(See Chapter 5, Sensation and Perception.)*

▶ *Hearing* Hearing loss is common among those 60 and older, especially the ability to hear high-frequency sounds. Problems can ensue if the loss is undetected or denied (Maher & Ross, 1984; Manschreck, 1989). A person may come to believe that others are deliberately whispering to avoid being heard, leading to a mild form of paranoia (belief that one is being victimized). Those with a hearing loss might explain others' actions inaccurately because they lack information and blame their misinterpretations on evil intentions instead of simple bad hearing (Zimbardo et al., 1981). Fortunately, early hearing-aid therapy can be more effective than later psychotherapy. Hearing aids can compensate for much of one's hearing loss. In addition, those close to someone with a probable hearing loss can help them by speaking in lower tones, enunciating clearly, and reducing background noise. (See Chapter 12, Psychopathology.)

▶ *Intelligence* A great fear about aging is that it is accompanied by the loss of mental abilities. Is this fear justified? In fact, there is little evidence that healthy older adults experience a decline in general cognitive abilities. However, people do acquire information more slowly by the time they are in their seventies and eighties. Performance of tasks requiring imagination, such as vivid imagery strategies for memorizing, also declines with age (Baltes & Kliegl, 1992). However, more general losses are neither inevitable nor necessarily disruptive. There is even evidence that some aspects of intellectual functioning are superior in older people. For example, skilled musicians have been shown to improve well into their nineties

(Krampe & Ericsson, 1996). Psychologists are now exploring age-related gains in wisdom, such as expertise in practical knowledge and life experience (Baltes, 1990).

▶ *Memory* A common complaint among older adults is that their ability to remember things is not as good as it used to be. Most of these age-related memory difficulties appear in a part of the memory system that processes and stores new information (Poon, 1985). Aging does *not* seem to diminish access to knowledge or events that occurred long ago. So, an elderly person may have to ask the name of a new acquaintance once or twice before finally remembering it but may have no trouble recalling the names of old friends or celebrities. A more important concern might be that people explain memory loss differently depending on the age of the forgetful person. Using a double standard, younger adults attribute other young adults' memory failures to lack of effort but those of older adults to loss of ability (Parr & Siegert, 1993). (See Chapter 7, Memory.)

▶ *Sexual Functioning* One myth about aging is that elderly people cannot or should not be sexually active. Belief in such a myth can be a greater obstacle than any physical limitations to experiencing satisfying sex in late adulthood. There is no age, for either men or women, at which the capability for arousal or orgasm ceases. Sex loses its reproductive functions in late adulthood but not its capacity for providing pleasure. Regular sexual practice enhances healthy aging because it provides arousal, aerobic exercise, fantasy, and social interaction (Ornstein & Sobel, 1989). Experience and creativity clearly compensate for minor physical changes or losses of physical stamina. (See Chapter 9, Emotion and Motivation.)

▶ *Social Interaction* An unfortunate consequence of living a long life is outliving some friends and

family members. In addition, the reduced mobility associated with aging can account for the fact that people become somewhat less active socially in later adulthood. While older adults reduce the extent of their social contacts, they remain more invested in those ties they choose to keep. Maintaining even a single intimate relationship can markedly improve personal health, as can living with a beloved pet (Siegel, 1990). Research shows that as people age, they tend to engage in **selective social interaction,** maintaining only the most rewarding contacts for the investment of precious physical and emotional energy (Carstensen, 1987, 1991; Lang & Carstensen, 1994). (See Chapter 14, Social Psychology.)

What can be done for those who experience trouble or personal difficulty in aging? Many elderly people have discovered particular strategies that help them age successfully. For example, older adults can remain both active and close to people by doing volunteer work in the community, joining clubs and classes, or spending time with grandchildren. In addition, we might learn lessons from other cultures where older citizens are respected and venerated for their wisdom. Before this happens, however, people must overcome stultifying stereotypes of the elderly as incapable and incompetent (Brewer et al., 1981).

What, then, would be a good strategy for dealing with the challenges of aging? Perhaps successful aging consists of making the most of gains while minimizing the impact of losses (Schulz & Heckhausen, 1996). Additionally, it is helpful to realize that losses of specific abilities need not represent threats to one's sense of self. As one's physical and psychological resources change, so do one's goals (Carstensen & Freund, 1994). In this fashion, late adulthood may be a time not of increasing frustration, but of increasing fulfillment.

1. **RECALL:** *In recent years, psychologists have come to see that*
   a. adult development is a gradual process of decline of physical and cognitive functions until death.
   b. adults continue to develop in problem-solving skills but not emotionally.
   c. physical and mental development continue throughout the life cycle.
   d. most adults are mildly depressed about the passing of their youth.

2. **RECALL:** *Which one is a stage of life that is not recognized by many cultures?*
   a. childhood
   b. adolescence
   c. adulthood
   d. old age

3. **RECALL:** *Which one is associated with a major crisis of adolescence, according to Erikson?*
   a. identity
   b. intimacy
   c. generativity
   d. ego-integrity

4. **APPLICATION:** *Which of the following individuals is most likely to develop physical or mental problems?*
   a. Mary, who works long hours at a challenging job
   b. Joe, who has an easy job, but no friends
   c. Eduardo, who must study 10 hours a day in graduate school
   d. Lucy, who works in a fast-food restaurant all day and has no prospects for advancement

Core Concept

5. **UNDERSTANDING THE CORE CONCEPT:**
   Nature and nurture continue to produce changes in personality and mental processes throughout the life cycle. In what way have you changed since you were in your previous stage of development?

ANSWERS: 1. c   2. b   3. a   4. b
5. Whatever you say is correct—but you should consider this: Does it jibe with Erikson's theory of life-span development?

Selective social interaction: Choosing to restrict the number of one's social contacts to those who are the most gratifying.

Using Psychology to Learn Psychology: Cognitive Development in College Students

s arrival at the formal operational stage the end of the cognitive line—or will your thinking abilities continue to develop as you go through college? A study by developmental psychologist William Perry suggests that your perspective on learning will change and mature as your college experience unfolds. This prediction is based on a sample of students that Perry followed through their undergraduate years at Harvard and Radcliffe. Specifically, he found that students' views of psychology and their other social science courses changed radically, as did their view of what they were there to learn (Perry, 1970, 1994).

At first, students in Perry's study had the most difficulty coming to grips with the diverse and conflicting viewpoints they encountered in their courses. For example, many confronted, for the first time, the idea that reasonable people can disagree—even about their most cherished "truths" concerning good and evil, God, nature, and human nature. Perry says:

> A few seemed to find the notion of multiple frames of reference wholly unintelligible. Others responded with violent shock to their confrontation in dormitory bull sessions, or in their academic work, or both. Others experienced a joyful sense of liberation. (Perry, 1970, p. 4)

In dealing with this academic culture shock, Perry's students passed through a series of distinct intellectual stages that were reminiscent of Piaget's stages. And, although they arrived at college at different levels of cognitive maturity and continued to develop at different rates, all progressed through the same intellectual stages in the same sequence. Here are some of the highlights of this intellectual journey:

▶ Students at first typically see a college or university as a storehouse of information—a place to learn the Right Answers. Thus, they believe it is the professor's job to help students find these answers.

▶ Sooner or later, students discover an unexpected diversity of opinion, even among the experts. At this stage they are likely to attribute conflicting opinions to confusion among poorly qualified experts.

▶ Eventually, students begin to accept diverse views as legitimate—but only in the fuzzy areas (such as psychology, other social sciences, and humanities) where experts haven't yet found the Right Answers. They decide that, in subjects where the Right Answers haven't been nailed down, professors grade them on "good expression" of their ideas.

▶ Next, some students discover that uncertainty and diversity of opinion are everywhere—not just in the social sciences and humanities. They solve this problem in their minds by dividing the academic world into two realms: (a) one in which Right Answers exist (even though they haven't all been discovered) and (b) another in which anyone's opinion is as good as anyone else's. Often, at this stage, they perceive math and the "hard" sciences as the realm of Right Answers, leaving the social sciences and humanities in the realm of opinion.

▶ Finally, the most mature students come to see that multiple perspectives exist in all fields of study.

The students who achieve this final stage begin to see "truth" as tentative. They now realize that knowledge is always building and changing—even in the "hard" sciences. And they realize that a college education is not just learning an endless series of facts. Rather, it is learning about the important *questions* and major *concepts* of a field. In this book we have called them Key Questions and Core Concepts.

At what stage do you find yourself?

Chapter Summary

HOW DO PSYCHOLOGISTS EXPLAIN DEVELOPMENT?

Developmental psychologists study change and growth in physical and mental functioning throughout the life span. They have resolved the nature–nurture controversy by noting that nature and nurture interact. They employ a variety of methods, including observations of twins and adopted children, to assess the relative contributions of heredity and environment. The resulting studies show that many behaviors have a genetic component.

Another controversy in developmental psychology involves continuity versus discontinuity. Psychologists who speak of developmental stages are taking the discontinuity view.

Development is a process of growth and change brought about by an interaction of heredity and environment.

WHAT CAPABILITIES DOES THE NEWBORN POSSESS?

Physical development, notably of the brain, proceeds at a rapid pace during the prenatal period and during the first few years after birth. Developmental research shows that infants are born with many sensory capabilities, preferences, and motor reflexes, plus the abilities to learn new responses. In addition, they are designed to be sociable. All of these characteristics make newborns highly interactive with the world around them.

Newborns begin life equipped to deal with three basic survival tasks: finding nourishment, making contacts with people, and avoiding harmful situations.

WHAT ARE THE DEVELOPMENTAL TASKS OF CHILDHOOD?

Young children are biologically equipped to learn language and motivated to communicate. Many experts believe that children have "language acquisition devices" built into their brains. Psychologists find that language development proceeds in a predictable fashion, as children acquire both vocabulary and grammar at an almost unbelievable rate.

Piaget's theory says that the twin processes of assimilation and accommodation underlie cognitive development. Piaget also proposed that children's cognitive development goes through four stages: the sensorimotor, the preoperational, the concrete operational, and the formal operational stages. New abilities mark the emergence of each stage. Newer theory and research have, however, modified many of Piaget's ideas. Kohlberg's theory of moral development, built on Piaget's foundation, is also a stage theory. In Kohlberg's view, lower stages involve concerns with personal consequences and higher stages have a broader focus on principles of ethical living.

Social development is built on a foundation of temperament, but it is also strongly influenced by the process of attachment to the caregiver. Ainsworth found that children may become either securely or insecurely attached. Attachment patterns established in infancy often persist into adulthood. Attachment probably evolved to give the infant protection. Harlow's research suggests that infants seek contact comfort in the attachment relationship.

Erikson's theory proposes that personality develops through a series of crises, each focused on resolving an issue about oneself and others. These issues define four stages of psychosocial development in childhood.

Children face especially important developmental tasks in the areas of language, thought processes, and social relationships.

WHAT DEVELOPMENTAL CHANGES OCCUR IN ADOLESCENCE AND ADULTHOOD?

The transitions of adolescence involve rapid physical maturation and development of sexual identity. Adolescents must also forge a social identity and make enduring occupational choices.

The challenges of adulthood focus on achieving intimacy and a sense of generativity. In later adulthood, individuals must maintain a sense of integrity despite some physical changes and losses. Successful resolution of earlier life crises can enable one to face death and loss with acceptance and a willingness to cope.

New perspectives on aging show that this period of life is marked by both gains and losses, notably in vision, hearing, intelligence, memory, sexual functioning, and social interaction. For some aging is very difficult, but for others it is a time of increasing fulfillment.

Core Concept

Nature and nurture continue to produce changes in personality and mental processes throughout the life cycle.

Review
Test

For each of the following items, choose the single correct or best answer. The correct answers appear at the end.

1. "Nature" refers to the effects of _____ and "nurture" refers to the effects of _____.
   a. continuity; discontinuity
   b. parents; peers
   c. assimilation; accommodation
   d. heredity; environment

2. A psychologist taking the discontinuity view might see development as
   a. a gradual process.
   b. a matter of learning.
   c. entirely genetic.
   d. a series of stages.

3. About eight weeks after conception, the developing human organism is known as:
   a. a zygote.
   b. an embryo.
   c. a fetus.
   d. a neonate.

4. Which of the following is true of the physical abilities of the newborn infant?
   a. At birth babies already have preferences for particular tastes and smells and dislikes for others.
   b. Just moments after birth a neonate may turn in the direction of a voice or reach out an exploring hand.
   c. While babies are born legally blind, they soon learn to detect large objects and high-contrast patterns.
   d. all of the above

5. Which of the following utterances illustrates *over-regularization* in language development?
   a. "Babababa."
   b. "Me gots two foots and two handses."
   c. "Drink milk, all gone."
   d. "Want cookie."

6. "Hey! That's not fair," complains Judi. "Tonio has more ice cream than me." Actually, both Judi and Tonio received a single scoop, but Tonio has stirred his around so it seems to fill the dish, while Judi's scoop is more compact. Judi's complaint indicates that she has not yet acquired the concept of _____ that affects how children think about the physical properties of things.
   a. centration
   b. egocentrism
   c. conservation
   d. object permanence

7. Harry and Margaret Harlow conducted landmark studies of the behaviors of baby monkeys who were separated from their mothers and had access only to mother "dummies" in their cages. This work confirmed that
   a. genuine attachment is possible only with the infant's biological mother.
   b. contact comfort and physical touch are important for healthy early development.
   c. the "cupboard theory of attachment" is true for both humans and nonhumans.
   d. nonhuman infants will imprint on and restrict social behavior to the first visually prominent thing they see after birth.

8. For Erikson, the psychosocial crisis of _____ is addressed by skill development and social interaction during the elementary school years, when children must explore their abilities, talents, and peer relationships.
  a. trust vs. mistrust
  b. autonomy vs. doubt
  c. competence vs. inferiority
  d. identity vs. role confusion

9. The briefest summary of the concerns and crises of adult development might simply be
  a. success and security.
  b. power and conquest.
  c. youth and beauty.
  d. love and work.

10. In late adulthood, loss of _____ has often been associated with feelings of paranoia and social isolation.
  a. intellectual abilities
  b. sexual functioning
  c. one's spouse
  d. hearing

ANSWERS: 1. d   2. d   3. c   4. d   5. b   6. c
7. b   8. c   9. d   10. d

If You're Interested . . .

BOOKS

Candland, D. K. (1993). *Feral children and clever animals: Reflections on human nature.* Oxford University Press. This work chronicles "wild children" discovered in the last two centuries and the impact of those discoveries on ideas about nature–nurture and civilization.

Colapinto, J. (2001). *As nature made him: The boy who was raised as a girl.* HarperPerennial. When a newborn boy lost his penis in a botched circumcision, his parents were advised by an "expert" to raise him as a girl, with a girl's name, costumes, and new gender instruction. Originally presented as a successful effort in identity shaping, the treatment became a developmental nightmare for the growing child, who at 14 decided to live life as a male instead. Presenting the family with sympathy and the doctors with disdain, the narrative becomes a gripping story of an individual in the crossfire of nature and nurture.

Eagle, C. J. (1994). *All that she can be: Helping your daughter maintain her self-esteem.* Fireside. Illustrated with anecdotes and sample conversations, this book is concerned about the problems unique to adolescent girls, reviewing what is included in "normal" behavior and how to deal with issues of friendship, sexuality, and body self-awareness.

Kagan, J., Snidman, N., Arcus, D., & Reznick, J. S. (1994). *Galen's prophecy.* HarperCollins. This exploration of temperament, its origins, varieties, and lifelong influence on behavior and personality is told with examples and case studies.

Miller, G. W. (1998). *Toy wars: The epic struggle between G.I. Joe, Barbie, and the companies that make them.* Adams Media Corporation. Toys are *not* child's play—not from the perspective of the corporations that profit from sales to children and their parents. Reading like a mystery thriller, this true account of toy makers' competition reveals a perspective on children-as-consumers that is enlightening and a little scary.

Rymer, R. (1993). *Genie: An abused child's flight from silence.* HarperCollins. Rymer presents the amazing and disturbing true story of Genie, a girl imprisoned and neglected since birth and not discovered and "freed" until adolescence. There are no simple happy endings here; the book documents the chaotic experience of Genie and the plight of those who tried to help her. Should any child, in need of love and care, ever be studied "for science"?

Snowdon, D. (2001). *Aging with grace: What the Nun Study teaches us about leading longer, healthier, and more meaningful lives.* Bantam Doubleday Dell. In the late 1980s, the author undertook a study of aging and disability in a community of elderly Catholic nuns, but eventually found he could not maintain a scholarly distance from them, and began to care and learn about them individually. Here he presents the lessons he learned from them about the blend of community, commitment, activity, and health.

Wallerstein, J. S., Blakeslee, S., & Lewis, J. M. (2001). *The unexpected legacy of divorce: A 25-year landmark study.* Hyperion. Politically correct wisdom has it that divorce is not as hard on children as continuing to live with unhappy, conflicted parents. But when psychologists examined the evidence, they found very un-P.C. evidence that the children of divorce feel, act, and often talk as if their parents ought to have stayed together for their sake. This is a controversial work—not the last word, but required reading for anyone who cares.

VIDEOS

Boy with Green Hair, The. (1948, color, 82 min.). Directed by Joseph Losey; starring Dean Stockwell, Pat O'Brien. A war orphan raised by his grandfather becomes a social outcast when his hair inexplicably turns green, highlighting the fear of "differentness," the tragedies of war, and the dangers of mindless conformity.

Curse of the Cat People. (1944, b&w, 70 min.). Directed by Robert Wise & Gunther von Fritsch; starring Kent Smith, Simone Simon, Ann Carter. Legendary horror-fantasy producer Val Lewton created this moody sequel that is better than its predecessor (*The Cat People*). A little girl's enchantment with her father's cursed former love is dismissed as "childish imagination" by all except an elderly relative who knows better. This is a great horror flick as well as a microcosm of intergenerational myths.

Marvin's Room. (1996, color, 98 min.). Directed by Jerry Zaks; starring Meryl Streep, Diane Keaton, Leonardo DiCaprio. Estranged sisters face family crises as one who is sick calls on help from the other who is losing a continual battle with her teenaged son. This cinematic tangle of family ten-

sions, insights, and oversights still summarizes the messiness of real-life family relationships.

Space Cowboys. (2000, color, 130 min.). Directed by Clint Eastwood; starring Clint Eastwood, Tommy Lee Jones, Donald Sutherland, James Garner. Four men ejected from the original U.S. space program finally get their chance to "take the ride"—four decades later. When NASA needs expertise from their era, the former buddies leave diverse retirements to undergo inhuman NASA qualification trials for the mission. Subplots should not distract entertaining scenes of young men in old bodies: terrific cinematic depictions of what does and does not change as the individual ages.

Stepmom. (1998, color, 125 min.). Directed by Chris Columbus; starring Susan Sarandon, Julia Roberts, Ed Harris. The children's plight is greatest when they are confronted with the triangle of their father, his new bride, and the ex-wife she is "replacing." The film has realistic depictions of the resentment and anxiety experienced when parents impose change on children and when new spouses face the challenges of blended families.

Three Men and a Cradle. (1985, color, 106 min.; French: *Trois hommes et un couffin*). Directed by Coline Serreau; starring Roland Giraud, Michel Boujenah, Andre Dussolier. Much better than the 1987 U.S. remake, this is a funny and instructive story of three bachelors whose lives and lifestyles are disrupted when a baby girl is left on the doorstep of the flat they share—and they become attached to her even as they try to be rid of her. Some interesting insights are presented on the demands of parenthood and the two-sided nature of attachment.

Welcome to the Dollhouse. (1996, color, 87 min.). Directed by Todd Solondz; starring Heather Matarazzo, Brandon Sexton, Jr., Daria Kalinina, Matthew Faber. The pain of puberty is depicted through the eyes of a young woman whose suburban parents are amazingly unsympathetic (favoring her baby sister) and whose school experience seems to be the Seventh Grade from Hell. The film has good performances and a lot of humor.

WEB RESOURCES

http://www.leaderu.com/orgs/tul/psychtoday9809.html This article explains some interesting research and findings in the area of fetal psychology. Are there fewer differences between a newborn baby and a 32-week fetus than scientists once thought?

http://www.heritage.org/library/categories/family/bg111 5.html Child abuse has increased in the United States in recent decades. In an attempt to under-stand this problem, psychologists have studied the relationship between child abuse and family structure. Can you think of the many ways abuse affects psychological development of children and adolescents?

http://www.aoa.dhhs.gov Visit this Web site for information on individuals who are growing old. How do you think changes in technology and science will change the way people view and worry about aging?

HOW DOES STIMULATION BECOME SENSATION?

Transduction
Sensory Adaptation
Thresholds
Signal Detection Theory
Psychology in Your Life: A Critical
    Look at Subliminal Persuasion

The brain senses the world indirectly because the sense organs convert stimulation into the language of the nervous system: neural impulses.

A CRITICAL LOOK AT SUBLIMINAL PERSUASION:
Subliminal perception occurs, but individual differences in perceptual thresholds make widespread use of subliminal persuasion unworkable.

HOW ARE THE SENSES ALIKE? AND HOW ARE THEY DIFFERENT?

Vision: How the Nervous System
    Processes Light
Hearing: If a Tree Falls in the
    Forest . . .
How the Other Senses Are Like Vision
    and Hearing

The senses all operate in much the same way, but each extracts different information and sends it to its own specialized processing region in the brain.

THE EXPERIENCE OF PAIN:
Pain is more than just a stimulus; it is an experience that varies from person to person. Pain control methods include drugs, hypnosis, and — for some — placebos.

WHAT IS THE RELATIONSHIP BETWEEN PERCEPTION AND SENSATION?

The Machinery of Perceptual
    Processing
Perceptual Ambiguity and Distortion
Theoretical Explanations for
    Perception

Perception brings *meaning* to sensation, so perception produces an interpretation of the external world, not a perfect representation of it.

SEEING AND BELIEVING:
Magicians and politicians rely on the fact that we don't merely sense the world, we perceive it.

USING PSYCHOLOGY TO LEARN PSYCHOLOGY: Studying for the Gestalt

CHAPTER

5

SENSATION AND PERCEPTION

an you imagine what your world would be like if you could no longer see colors—but merely black, white, and gray? Such a bizarre sensory loss actually befell Jonathan I., a 65-year-old New Yorker, following an automobile accident (Sacks, 1995). Apparently the trauma of the crash caused damage to a region in his brain that processes color information. At first, Jonathan I. also had some *amnesia* for reading letters of the alphabet, which all seemed like nonsensical markings to him. But, after five days, his inability to read disappeared. His loss of color vision, however, persisted as a permanent condition, known as *cerebral achromatopsia* (pronounced *ay-kroma-TOP-see-a*).

As you might expect, Jonathan I. became depressed by this turn of events in

his life. The problem was aggravated by the fact that Jonathan was a painter whose profession was based on representing his images of the world in vivid colors. Now his world of colors was all gone, all drab, all "molded in lead." When he looked at his own paintings, which had seemed bursting with special meaning and emotional associations, all he now saw were unfamiliar and meaningless objects on canvas.

Curiously, Jonathan also lost his memory of color and eventually the names for colors. He could no longer even imagine, for instance, what "red" once looked like. What Jonathan I.'s experience dramatically demonstrated to the researchers and clinicians who studied him

(continued)

and tried to help him was the nonobvious neurological truth that colors do not really exist "out there" in objects. Rather, our world of color is a construction of the sensory and perceptual processes of the brain.

Fortunately, Jonathan's story has a happy ending, one that reveals much about the resilience of the human spirit. First, Jonathan became a "night person," traveling and working at night, and socializing with other night people. (As we will see in this chapter, good color vision depends on bright illumination such as daylight; most people's color vision is not as acute in the dark of night.) Jonathan also became aware that what remained of his vision was remarkably good, enabling him to read license plates from four blocks away at night. He began to reinterpret his "loss" as a "gift" in which he was no longer distracted by color, so that he could now focus his work more intensely on shape, form, and content. Finally, Jonathan switched to painting only in black and white, and critics acclaimed his "new phase" as a success. He has also become good at sculpting, which he had never attempted before his accident. So, as Jonathan's world of color died, a new world of "pure forms" was born in his perception of the people, objects, and events in his environment.

Sensation: An early stage of perception in which neurons in a receptor create a pattern of nerve impulses that represent the stimulation and pass these signals on to the brain for further processing.

Perception: A process that makes sensory patterns meaningful and more elaborate. Perception draws heavily on memory, motivation, emotion, and other psychological processes.

J onathan's experience shows that the brain has the flexibility to meet severe physical challenges and to adapt psychologically to lost abilities. By examining such losses, we can momentarily slip outside the confines of our own experience to see more clearly how we process sensory information.

Although these very private processes extend deep into the brain, we will begin our tour at the sense organs. This is the territory of *sensory psychology*. Psychologists define **sensation** as the process by which a stimulated receptor (such as the eyes or ears) creates a pattern of neural impulses that represent the stimulus. Thus, sensation gives us our initial experience of the stimulus.

In this chapter we will see how the sense organs transform physical stimulation (such as light waves) into the neural impulses that give us sensations (such as light and dark). Here we will discover the basis for color, odor, sound, texture, and taste. Here we will learn why tomatoes and limes seem to have different hues and why a pinprick feels different from a caress.

Under most conditions our sensory experience is highly reliable. So, when you catch sight of a friend, the sensation usually registers clearly, immediately, and accurately. Nevertheless, we do have our sensory limitations. Humans lack the acute senses that many other species have perfected, such as the vision of hawks, the hearing of bats, the sense of smell of rodents, or the sensitivity to magnetic fields found in migratory birds. So, what's our specialty? Our species has evolved the sensory equipment that enables us to process a wider range and variety of sensory input than any other creature.

Our ultimate destination in this chapter lies in the realm of *perception*. There we will uncover the psychological processes that attach meaning and personal significance to the sensory messages entering our brains. Perceptual psychology will help us understand how we assemble a series of tones into a familiar melody or a collage of shapes and shadings into a familiar face. We will define **perception** as a process that elaborates and assigns meaning to the incoming sensory patterns. Thus, perception creates an *interpretation* of sensation. Is the tomato ripe? Is the bell a church bell or the doorbell? Does the face belong to someone you know?

To hunt small flying objects at night, bats rely on the sensory system of echolocation, a kind of sonar. Bats emit high-frequency sounds that bounce off insects, revealing their locations so the bats can find and eat them.

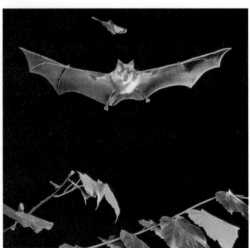

Even more fundamentally, in this chapter you will learn that this inner world of sensation and perception is the only world we can ever know directly. No matter what we do, all the information we get about external events must always be filtered through our sense organs and then combined with our unique mix of memories, emotions, motives, and expectations. You will also learn that many complex acts of sensing and perceiving occur behind the scenes, so effortlessly, continuously, and flawlessly that we pay them little conscious mind.

As you can see, the boundary of sensation blurs into that of perception. Perception is essentially an interpretation and elaboration of sensation. Sensation, then, refers to the initial steps in the processing of a stimulus. It is to these first sensory steps that we now turn our attention.

HOW DOES STIMULATION BECOME SENSATION?

A thunderstorm is approaching, and you feel the electric charge in the air make the hair stand up on your head. Lightning flashes, and a split second later you hear the thunderclap. It was close by, and you smell the ozone left as the bolt sizzled through the air. Your senses are warning you of danger.

Our senses have other adaptive functions, as well. They aid our survival by directing us toward certain sensations, such as tasty foods, which provide nourishment. Our senses also help us locate mates, seek shelter, and recognize our friends. Incidentally, our senses also give us the opportunity to find pleasure in music, art, athletics, food, and sex.

How do our senses accomplish all this? The complete answer is complex, but it involves one simple idea that applies across the sensory landscape: Our sensory impressions of the world involve *neural representations* of stimuli—not the actual stimuli. The Core Concept puts it this way:

> **The brain senses the world indirectly because the sense organs convert stimulation into the language of the nervous system: neural impulses.**

The brain never receives stimulation directly from the outside world. Its experience of a tomato is not the same as the tomato itself—although we usually assume that the two are identical. Neither can the brain receive light from a sunset, reach out and touch velvet, or inhale the fragrance of a rose. It must always rely on secondhand information from the go-between sensory system, which delivers only a coded neural message, out of which the brain must create its own experience. (See Figure 5.1.)

To understand more deeply how stimulation becomes sensation, we will consider three attributes common to all the senses: *transduction, sensory adaptation,* and *thresholds.* They determine which stimuli will actually become sensation, what the quality and impact of that sensation will be, and whether it grabs our interest. These attributes determine whether a tomato actually registers in the sensory system strongly enough to enter our awareness, what its color and form appear to be, and how strongly it bids for our attention.

Transduction

The idea that sensations, such as the redness and flavor of a tomato, are entirely creations of the sense organs and brain may seem incredible to you.

FIGURE 5.1: Stimulation Becomes Perception

For stimulation to become a percept it must undergo several transformations. First, physical stimulation (light waves from the butterfly) are *transduced* by the eye, where information about the wavelength and intensity of the light is coded into neural impulses. Second, the neural impulses travel to the sensory cortex of the brain, where they become *sensations* of color, brightness, form, and movement. Finally, the process of *perception* interprets these sensations by making connections with memories, expectations, emotions, and motives in other parts of the brain.

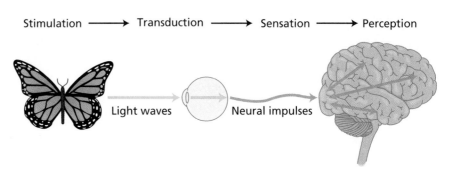

Stimulation ⟶ Transduction ⟶ Sensation ⟶ Perception

Light waves   Neural impulses

Connection

Chapter 2
The brain receives information in the form of neural impulses.

Transduction: Transformation of one form of energy into another — especially the transformation of stimulus information into nerve impulses.

Receptors: Specialized neurons that are activated by stimulation and transduce (convert) it into a nerve impulse.

Sensory pathway: Bundles of neurons that carry information from the sense organs to the brain.

Connection

Chapter 2
Neural pathways involve bundles of neurons taking essentially the same route.

But remember that all sensory communication with the brain flows through neurons in the form of neural impulses: Neurons cannot transmit light or sound waves or any other external stimulus. Accordingly, none of the light bouncing off the tomato ever actually reaches the brain. It only gets as far as the back of the eyes, where the information it contains is converted to neural impulses. Neither do the chemicals that signal taste actually make their way into the brain; they go only as far as the tongue.

In general, it is the job of the sensory receptors to convert stimulus information into electrochemical signals — neural impulses — the only language the brain comprehends. Sensations, such as "red" or "sweet" or "cold," occur when the neural signal reaches the cerebral cortex. In fact, it is here in the specialized regions of the cortex that sensory experience is created. The whole process seems so immediate and direct that it fools us into assuming that the sensation of redness is characteristic of a tomato or the sensation of cold is a characteristic of ice cream. But they are not!

Psychologists use the term **transduction** for the process that converts physical energy, such as light waves, into the form of neural impulses. Transduction begins with the detection by a sensory neuron of the physical stimulus (such as the sound wave made by a vibrating guitar string). When the appropriate stimulus reaches a sense organ, it activates specialized neurons, called **receptors,** which respond by converting their excitation into a *nerve impulse.* Table 5.1 summarizes the main stimuli and receptors for each sense. It is this impulse that carries a code of the sensory event in a form that can be further processed by the brain. This information-carrying impulse travels along a **sensory pathway** to specialized sensory processing areas in the brain (the auditory cortex, in the case of sounds). From neural impulses arriving from these pathways, the brain extracts information about the basic qualities of the stimulus, such as its intensity, pitch, and direction. Please keep in mind that the stimulus itself terminates in the receptor: The only thing that continues on into the nervous system is *information* carried by the neural impulse.

TABLE 5.1
Fundamental Features of Human Senses

SENSE	STIMULUS	SENSE ORGAN	RECEPTOR	SENSATION
Sight	Light waves	Eye	Rods and cones of retina	Colors, patterns, textures
Hearing	Sound waves	Ear	Hair cells of the basilar membrane	Noises, tones
Skin senses	External contact	Skin	Nerve endings in skin	Touch, warmth, cold
Smell	Volatile substances	Nose	Hair cells of olfactory epithelium	Odors (musky, flowery, burnt, minty, etc.)
Taste	Soluble substances	Tongue	Taste buds of tongue	Flavors (sweet, sour, salty, bitter)
Equilibrium	Mechanical and gravitational forces	Inner ear	Hair cells of semi-circular canals and vestibule	Spatial movement, gravitational pull
Pain	Many intense or extreme stimuli: temperature, chem-icals, mechanical stimuli, etc.	Net of pain fibers all over the body	Specialized pain receptors, overactive or abnormal neurons	Acute pain, chronic pain
Kinesthetic and vestibular senses	Body position and movement	Semicircular canals, skeletal muscles, joints, tendons	Hair cells in semi-circular canals; neurons connected to skeletal muscles, joints, and tendons	Position of body parts in space

Sensory Adaptation

If you have ever jumped into a cool pool on a hot day, you know that sensation is critically influenced by change. In fact, a main role of our stimulus detectors is to announce *changes* in the external world such as a flash of light, a splash of water, a clap of thunder, the prick of a pin, or the burst of flavor from a dollop of salsa. Thus, our sense organs are novelty detectors. Their receptors pump information about new and changing events into the barrage of neural messages that the brain uses to interpret environmental conditions.

This great quantity of incoming sensation would soon overwhelm us, if not for a specially evolved function of all sensory systems: *adaptation*. **Sensory adaptation** is the diminishing responsiveness of sensory systems to prolonged stimulation. Stimulation that does not change in intensity or some other qual-ity tends to shift into the background of our awareness, unless it is quite intense or painful. For example, you probably did not realize—until you read these words and considered their meaning—that you had adapted to the press of furniture against your body at this moment. As long as these streams of stimulation remain relatively constant, your attention shifts to other sensa-tions. However, any change in the signals you are receiving (if an air condi-tioner suddenly becomes louder or higher-pitched, for example) will draw your attention. Incidentally, sensory adaptation is why the background music often played in stores is so boring: It has been selected and filtered to remove any large changes in volume or pitch that might distract attention from the mer-

Sensory adaptation: Loss of responsiveness in receptor cells after stimulation has remained unchanged for a while.

chandise. (Do you see why it's not a good idea to listen to interesting music while you are studying?)

Thresholds

What is the weakest stimulus that an organism can detect? How dim can a light be, for instance, and still be visible? These questions refer to the **absolute threshold** for different types of stimulation: the minimum amount of physical energy needed to produce a sensory experience. In the laboratory, a psychologist would define this operationally as the intensity at which the stimulus is detected *half* of the time over many trials. Obviously, this threshold will vary from one person to another. So, if you point out a faint star to a friend who says he cannot see it, the star's light is above your absolute threshold (you can see it) but below that of your friend (who cannot).

Connection

Chapter 1
An operational definition describes a concept in terms of the operations required to produce, observe, or measure it.

A faint stimulus does not abruptly become detectable as its intensity increases. Because of the fuzzy boundary between detection and nondetection, a person's absolute threshold is not absolute! In fact, it varies continually with our mental alertness and physical condition. Table 5.2 shows some typical absolute threshold levels for several familiar natural stimuli.

We can illustrate another kind of threshold with the following imaginary experiment. Suppose you are relaxing by watching television on the one night you don't need to study, while your roommate busily prepares for an early morning exam. Your roommate asks you to "turn it down a little" to eliminate the distraction. You feel that you should make some effort to comply but really wish to leave the volume as it is. What is the least amount you can lower the volume to prove your good intentions to your roommate while still keeping the volume clearly audible? Your ability to make judgments like this one depends on your **difference threshold,** the smallest physical difference between two stimuli that can still be recognized as a difference.

A swimmer must undergo sensory adaptation when jumping into cool water.

If you turn the volume knob as little as possible, your roommate might complain, "I don't hear any difference" or "You haven't turned it down enough." By "enough," your roommate probably means his or her difference threshold. Even if you have adjusted the volume downward slightly, the difference might not be large enough to detect. If you hear the difference, it exceeds your own difference threshold; if your roommate can hear the difference, it exceeds his or hers. Suppose you start adjusting the volume and ask your roommate to "say when" — to stop you when the adjustment is sufficient to be detected. This minimal amount of change in the signal that is still recognizable is the **just noticeable difference (JND).** The terms *difference threshold, just noticeable difference,* and *JND* are used interchangeably by psychologists.

Research on the JND for different senses has yielded some interesting glimpses of how human stimulus detection works. It turns out that *the JND is large when the stimulus intensity is high, and small when the stimulus intensity is low.* Psychologists refer to this notion, that the size of the JND is proportional to the intensity of the stimulus, as **Weber's law.** And what does Weber's law tell us about adjusting the TV volume? If you have the volume turned up very high, you will have to turn the volume down a lot to make the difference noticeable. On the other hand, if you already have the volume set to a very low level, so that you can barely hear it if you listen carefully, a small adjustment

Absolute threshold: The amount of stimulation necessary for the stimulus to be detected. In practice, this means being detected half the time over a number of trials.

Difference threshold: The smallest amount by which a stimulus can be changed and the difference be detected half the time.

Just noticeable difference (JND): Same as the *difference threshold.*

Weber's law: This concept says that the size of a JND is proportional to the intensity of the stimulus; the JND is large when the stimulus intensity is high and small when the stimulus intensity is low.

TABLE 5.2	Approximate Perceptual Thresholds of Five Senses
SENSE MODALITY	**DETECTION THRESHOLD**
Light	A candle flame at 30 miles on a dark, clear night
Sound	The tick of a mechanical watch under quiet conditions at 20 feet
Taste	One teaspoon of sugar in 2 gallons of water
Smell	One drop of perfume diffused into the entire volume of a three-bedroom apartment
Touch	The wing of a bee falling on your cheek from a distance of one centimeter

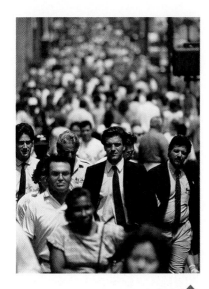

Signal detection theory says that the background stimulation would make it less likely for you to hear someone calling your name on a busy downtown street than in a quiet park.

will probably be noticeable enough for your roommate. The same principle operates across all our senses. Knowing this, you might guess that a weight lifter would notice the difference when small amounts are added to light weights, but it would take a much larger addition to be noticeable with heavy weights.

What does all this mean for our understanding of human sensation? It means that we are built to detect *changes* in stimulation and *relationships* among stimuli. You can see how this works in the box, "Do It Yourself! An Enlightening Demonstration of Sensory Relationships."

Signal Detection Theory

An improvement in our understanding of absolute and difference thresholds comes from **signal detection theory** (Green & Swets, 1966). It works equally well for biological or electronic sensors. Thus, signal detection theory uses the same concepts to explain both the electronic sensing of stimuli by devices, such as your TV set, and by the human senses, such as vision and hearing.

According to signal detection theory, sensation depends on the characteristics of the stimulus, the background stimulation, and the detector. You may have noticed, for example, that you get more out of an 8 o'clock class if your nervous system has been aroused by a strong cup of coffee. Similarly, a person's interests and biases can affect what he or she notices on the evening news. The original theory of thresholds, however, ignored the effects of the per-

Signal detection theory: Explains perceptual judgment as a combination of sensation and decision-making processes. Signal detection theory adds observer characteristics to classical psychophysics.

DO IT YOURSELF! An Enlightening Demonstration of Sensory Relationships

In this simple demonstration, you will see how detection of change depends on the intensity of the background stimulation. Find a three-way lamp equipped with a bulb having equal wattage increments, such as a 50–100–150 watt bulb. (Wattage is closely related to brightness.) Then, in a dark room, switch the light on to 50 watts. This will unmistakably increase brightness. Changing from 50 to 100 watts will also seem like a large increase. But why

does the last 50-watt increase (from 100 to 150 watts) appear only slightly brighter? Your sensory system does not give you a sensation of the exact brightness. Rather, it compares the stimulus *change* to the background stimulation, translating the jump from 100 to 150 watts as a mere 50% increase (50 watts added to 100) compared to the earlier 100% increase (50 watts added to 50). This illustrates how your brain computes *sensory relationships,* rather than absolutes.

ceiver's physical condition, judgments, or biases. Thus, in classical *psychophysics* (the study of stimulation and sensory experience), if a signal were intense enough to exceed one's absolute threshold, it would be sensed; if below threshold, it would be missed. In the view of the new signal detection theory, sensation is not a simple present/absent, "yes/no" experience.

What does signal detection theory offer psychology that was missing in classical psychophysics? One factor is the variability in human judgment. Signal detection theory recognizes that the observer, whose physical and mental status is always in flux, must compare a sensory experience with ever-changing expectations and biological conditions. For example, when something "goes bump in the night" after you have gone to bed, you must decide whether it is the cat, an intruder, or just your imagination. What you decide depends on the keenness of your hearing and what you expect to hear, as well as other noises in the background. By taking into account the variable conditions that affect detection of a stimulus, signal detection theory provides a more accurate portrayal of sensation than did classical psychophysics.

A Critical Look at
Subliminal Persuasion

In Your Life

Can extremely weak stimulation — stimulation that you don't even notice — affect your mind or behavior? The alluring promise that signals can be processed in your sensory system without awareness lies at the basis of the industry that sells "subliminal" tapes and CDs touted as remedies for obesity, shoplifting, smoking, and low self-esteem. But before you put your money in the mail, let's look at a bit of history and some fundamentals of sensory psychology.

Some years ago, an advertising executive, James Vicary, dramatically announced to the press that he had discovered an almost irresistible sales technique now known as "subliminal advertising." Vicary said that his method consisted of projecting very brief messages on the screen of a movie theater, urging the audience to "Drink Coke" and "Buy popcorn." He claimed that the ads presented ideas so fleetingly that the conscious

mind could not perceive them — yet the messages would still lodge in the unconscious mind, where they worked on the viewer's desires unnoticed. Vicary claimed that sales of Coca Cola and popcorn had soared at a New Jersey theater where he tested the technique.

The public was both fascinated and outraged. Subliminal advertising became the subject of intense debate. People worried that they were being manipulated by powerful psychological forces without their consent. As a result, laws were proposed to quash the practice. But aside from the hysteria, was there any real cause for concern? For answers to that question we must return to the concept of *threshold,* the minimum amount of stimulation necessary to trigger a response. The word *subliminal* means "below the threshold" (*limen* = threshold). In the language of perceptual psychology, *subliminal* more specifically refers to stimuli lying near the absolute threshold. Such stimuli may, in fact, be strong enough to affect the sense organs and to enter the sensory system,

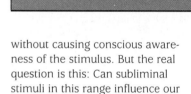

without causing conscious awareness of the stimulus. But the real question is this: Can subliminal stimuli in this range influence our thoughts and behavior?

Several studies have found that subliminal words flashed briefly on a screen (for less than 1/100 second) can "prime" a person's later responses (Merikle & Reingold, 1990). For example, can you fill in the following blanks to make a word?

S N _ _ _ E L

If you had been subliminally primed by a brief presentation of the appropriate word, it would be more likely that you would have found the right answer, even though you were not aware of the priming stimulus. (The answer, by the way, is "snorkel.")

Apparently people *do* respond to stimuli below the absolute threshold, under some circumstances

(Greenwald, Draine, & Abrams, 1996; Reber, 1993). But here is the problem for would-be subliminal advertisers who would attempt to influence us in the uncontrolled world outside the laboratory: Different people have thresholds at different levels. So, what might be *subliminal* for me could well be *supra*liminal (above the threshold) for you. Consequently, the subliminal advertiser runs the risk that some in the audience will notice — and be angry about — a stimulus aimed slightly below the average person's threshold. In fact, *no controlled research has ever shown that subliminal messages delivered to a mass audience can influence people's buying habits.*

But what about those subliminal recordings that some stores play to prevent shoplifting? Again, no reputable study has ever demonstrated their effectiveness. A more likely explanation for any decrease in shoplifting accruing to these tapes lies in increased vigilance from employees who know that management is worried about shoplifting. The same goes for the tapes that claim to help you quit smoking, lose weight, become creative, or achieve other dozens of elusive dreams. In a comprehensive study of subliminal self-help techniques, the U.S. Army found all to be without foundation (Druckman & Bjork, 1991). The simplest explanation for rare successes lies in the purchasers' expectations of success and the desire to prove that they did not spend their money foolishly. And finally, to take the rest of the worry out of subliminal persuasion, you should know that James Vicary eventually admitted that his claims for subliminal advertising were a hoax (Druckman & Bjork, 1991).

CHECK**YOUR**UNDERSTANDING

1. **RECALL:** *The sensory pathways carry information*
   a. from the brain to the muscles.
   b. from the sense organs to the brain.
   c. from the brain to the sense organs.
   d. from the central nervous system to the autonomic nervous system.

2. **RECALL:** *Which one refers to the least amount of stimulation that your perceptual system can detect about half the time?*
   a. the stimulus threshold
   b. the difference threshold
   c. the absolute threshold
   d. the action threshold

3. **APPLICATION:** *Which one would involve sensory adaptation?*
   a. The water in a swimming pool seems cooler at first than it does after you have been in it for a while.
   b. The flavor of a spicy salsa on your taco seems hot by comparison with the blandness of the sour cream.

c. You are unaware of a priming stimulus flashed on the screen at 1/100th of a second.
   d. You prefer the feel of silk to the feel of velvet.

4. **RECALL:** *Which of the following is a process that adds meaning to incoming information obtained by the sensory systems?*
   a. stimulation
   b. sensation
   c. sensory adaptation
   d. perception

Core Concept

5. **UNDERSTANDING THE CORE CONCEPT:**
   When you hear the sound of a tree falling in the forest, the brain has received nothing but
   a. sound waves from the air.
   b. neural impulses in the sensory pathways.
   c. the vibration of the eardrums.
   d. sound waves traveling through the sensory pathways.

ANSWERS: 1. b   2. c   3. a   4. d   5. b

HOW ARE THE SENSES ALIKE? AND HOW ARE THEY DIFFERENT?

Vision, hearing, smell, taste, touch, pain, body position: In many respects all our senses work in the same ways. They all transduce stimulus energy into neural impulses. They are all more sensitive to change than to constant stimulation. And they all provide us information about the world—information that has survival value. But how are they *different?* With the exception of pain, each sense taps a different form of stimulus energy, and each sends the information it extracts to a different part of the brain. These contrasting ideas lead us to the Core Concept of this section:

Core Concept

> The senses all operate in much the same way, but each extracts different information and sends it to its own specialized processing region in the brain.

Each sense organ has a different design, but all of them send neural messages to the brain. So, in the end, *different sensations occur because different areas of the brain become activated.* Whether you hear a bell or see a bell depends ultimately on which part of the brain receives stimulation. We will explore how this all works by looking at each of the senses in turn. First, we will find out how the visual system—the best understood of the senses—transduces light waves into visual sensations of color and brightness.

Vision: How the Nervous System Processes Light

Animals with good vision have an enormous biological advantage. This fact has exerted evolutionary pressure to make vision the most complex, highly developed, and important sense for humans and most other mobile creatures. Good vision helps us detect desired targets, threats, and changes in our physical environment and adapt our behavior accordingly. How does the visual system accomplish this?

THE ANATOMY OF VISUAL SENSATION   You might think of the eye as the camera for the brain's motion pictures of the world (see Figure 5.2). Like a camera, the eye gathers light, focuses it, converts it to neural impulses, and sends these neural signals on their way for subsequent processing into a visual image. The unique characteristic of the eye is its ability to extract the information about the world from light waves—to transduce the characteristics of light into neural signals that the brain can process. This transduction happens in the **retina,** the light-sensitive layer of cells at the back of the eye that acts much like the light-sensitive chip in a digital camera.

The light-sensitive cells in the retina are known as **photoreceptors.** These photoreceptors consist of specialized neurons that absorb light energy and respond by creating neural impulses. The retina does this with two types of photoreceptors known as **rods** and **cones** (see Figure 5.3). Why two kinds of photoreceptors?

Because we sometimes function in darkness and sometimes in bright light, we have evolved two ways of processing, using two distinct receptor cell types, named for their shapes. The 125 million thin rods "see in the dark"—that is, they detect low intensities of light at night, though they cannot discriminate colors. Your rods enable you to find a seat in a darkened movie theatre.

Connection

Chapter 2
Evolutionary pressure comes from *natural selection,* favoring individuals with the most adaptive traits.

Retina: The light-sensitive layer at the back of the eyeball.

Photoreceptors: Light-sensitive cells in the retina that convert light energy to neural impulses.

Rods: Photoreceptors in the retina that are especially sensitive to dim light but not to colors.

Cones: Photoreceptors in the retina that are especially sensitive to colors but not to dim light.

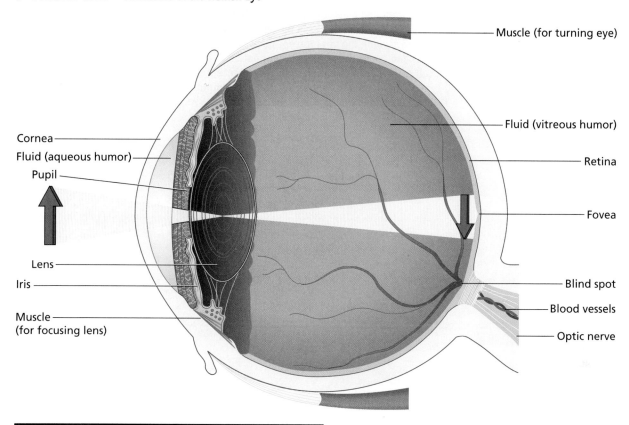

Muscle (for turning eye)

Cornea

Fluid (aqueous humor)

Pupil

Lens

Iris

Muscle
(for focusing lens)

Fluid (vitreous humor)

Retina

Fovea

Blind spot

Blood vessels

Optic nerve

Sensing color is the job of the seven million fat cones that dominate during the bright, color-filled day. Each cone is specialized to detect either the wavelengths corresponding to sensations of blue, red, or green hues. We use these cones to distinguish red from green tomatoes in good light. (You can learn more about these cones by trying the "Do It Yourself!" demonstration on page 176.) The cones concentrate in the very center of the retina, in a small region called the **fovea,** which gives us our sharpest vision. With the fovea we automatically scan whatever interests us visually—the features of a face or, perhaps, a flower.

There are still other types of cells in the retina that do not respond directly to light. Instead, they gather the responses from groups of nearby receptors. These *bipolar cells* collect impulses from many photoreceptors and send them on to *ganglion cells*. Bundled together, the axons of the ganglion cells make up the **optic nerve,** which carries visual information from the eye to the brain. (See Figures 5.3 and 5.4.)

At the point where the optic nerve exits each eye, there is a small area of the retina that has no layer of photoreceptors. This region, therefore, cannot detect light. The result is a gap in the visual field called the **blind spot.** You do not normally experience blindness there because what one eye misses is registered by the other eye, and the brain "fills in" the spot with information that matches the background. You can find your own blind spot by following the instructions in the "Do It Yourself!" box on page 173.

PROCESSING VISUAL SENSATION IN THE BRAIN   At the back of the brain lies a special area for processing incoming neural information from the eyes

Fovea: The area of sharpest vision in the retina.

Optic nerve: The bundle of neurons that carries visual information from the retina to the brain.

Blind spot: The point where the optic nerve exits the eye and where there are no photoreceptors.

FIGURE 5.3: Transduction of Light in the Retina

This simplified diagram shows the pathways that connect three layers of nerve cells in the retina. Incoming light passes through the ganglion cells and bipolar cells first before striking the photoreceptors at the back of the eyeball. Once stimulated, the rods and cones then transmit information to the bipolar cells (note that one bipolar cell combines information from several receptor cells). The bipolar cells then transmit neural impulses to the ganglion cells. Impulses travel from the ganglia to the brain via axons that make up the optic nerve.

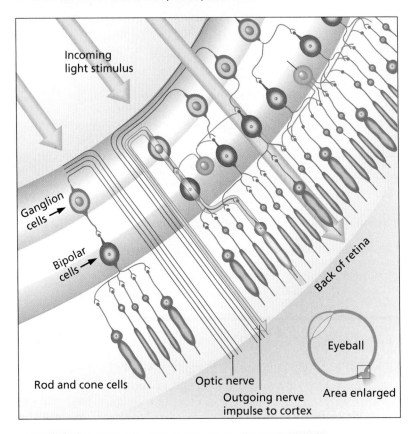

Connection

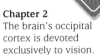

Chapter 2
The brain's occipital cortex is devoted exclusively to vision.

Visual cortex: The part of the brain — in the occipital lobe — where visual sensations are processed.

Color: The psychological sensation derived from the wavelength of visible light. Color, itself, is not a property of the external world.

(see Figure 5.4). This area in the occipital lobe is known as the **visual cortex.** Here the brain transforms the signals from the eyes into visual sensations of color, form, boundary, and movement. Amazingly, the visual cortex also manages to take the two-dimensional patterns from each eye and assemble them into the three-dimensional world of depth (Barinaga, 1998; Dobbins et al., 1998). In addition, the cortex combines these visual sensations with memories, motives, emotions, and sensations of body position and touch to create a representation of the visual world that fits our current concerns and interests (Barinaga, 1999; Batista et al., 1999; de Gelder, 2000; Maunsell, 1995). This suggests why you are strongly attracted by the visual appeal of appetizing foods if you go grocery shopping when you are hungry. In short, we look with our eyes but we *see* with our brains.

How the Visual System Creates Color You may have been surprised to learn that a ripe tomato, itself, has no **color.** Physical objects seen in bright light *seem* to have the marvelous property of being awash with color, but as we have

Find Your Blind Spot

The "blind spot" occurs at the place on the retina where the neurons from the retina bunch together to exit the eyeball and form the optic nerve. There are no light-sensitive cells at this point on the retina. Consequently, you are "blind" in this small region of your visual field. The following demonstrations will help you determine where this blind spot occurs in your visual field.

DEMONSTRATION 1

Hold the book at arm's length, close your right eye, and fix your left eye on the "bank" figure. Keep your right eye closed, and bring the book slowly closer. When it is about 10 to 12 inches away and the dollar sign is in your blind spot, the dollar sign will disappear — but you will not see a "hole" in your visual field. Instead, your visual system "fills in" the missing area with information from the white background. You have "lost" your money!

DEMONSTRATION 2

To convince yourself that the brain fills in the missing part of the visual field with appropriate background, close your right eye again and focus on the cross in the lower part of the figure. Once again, keeping the right eye closed, bring the book closer to you as you focus your left eye on the cross. This time, the gap in the line will disappear and will be filled in with a continuation of the line on either side. This shows that what you see in your blind spot may not really exist!

Find Your Blind Spot

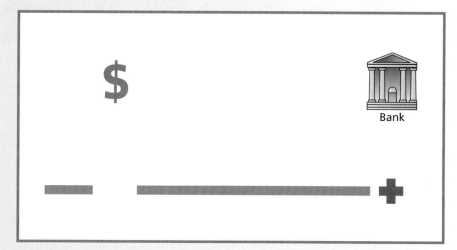

Bank

---

seen, the red tomatoes, green fir trees, blue oceans, and multihued rainbows are, themselves, actually quite colorless. Despite appearances, color does not exist in the external world. It exists only in the mind of the viewer. That is, color is a *psychological* property of your sensory experience, created when specialized areas of your brain process the wavelength information about a beam of light, which has been coded in neural impulses. To understand how this happens, we must first know something of the nature of light.

Our eyes are designed to detect the special form of energy that we call visible light. Actually, the light we see occupies but a tiny segment of the vast **electromagnetic spectrum,** which also includes ultraviolet light, infrared light, X rays, microwaves, radio waves, and television waves. You can see how small our visual "window" is, in comparison with the whole electromagnetic spectrum, by examining Figure 5.5. Because we have no biological receptors sensitive to the other portions of the electromagnetic spectrum, we must employ special detection instruments, such as radios and TVs, to help us convert this energy into signals we can use.

Electromagnetic spectrum: The entire range of electromagnetic energy, including radio waves, X rays, microwaves, and visible light.

FIGURE 5.4: Neural Pathways in the Human Visual System

Light from the visual field projects onto the two retinas; neural messages from the retinas are sent to the two visual centers of each hemisphere.

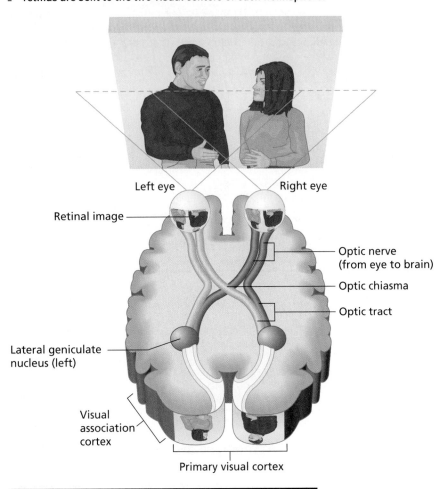

Left eye   Right eye

Retinal image

Optic nerve (from eye to brain)

Optic chiasma

Optic tract

Lateral geniculate nucleus (left)

Visual association cortex

Primary visual cortex

FIGURE 5.5: The Electromagnetic Spectrum

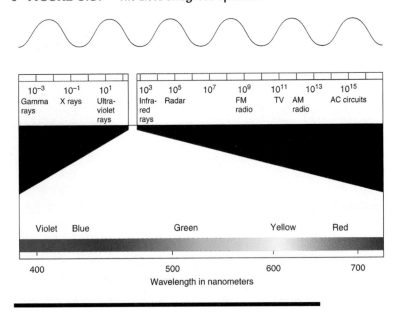

10^{-3}	10^{-1}	10^{1}	10^{3}	10^{5}	10^{7}	10^{9}	10^{11}	10^{13}	10^{15}
Gamma rays	X rays	Ultra-violet rays	Infra-red rays	Radar		FM radio	TV	AM radio	AC circuits

Violet   Blue   Green   Yellow   Red

400   500   600   700

Wavelength in nanometers

Within the tiny portion of the electromagnetic spectrum that our eyes can detect, colors arise from certain characteristic light waves. Specifically, the eyes are highly sensitive to differences in *wavelengths* of light in this **visible spectrum** (see Figure 5.5). It is the wavelength of light from which the eye extracts the information used by the brain to construct colors. Longer waves make us see a tomato as red, and medium-length waves give rise to the sensations of yellow and green in lemons and limes. Shorter waves from a clear sky stimulate sensations of blue.

Colors themselves are realized in a highly specialized region of the occipital cortex, where humans are capable of visually discriminating among about five million different hues. Other nearby cortical areas are responsible for processing information about boundaries, shapes, and movements. Each of these regions is most sensitive to changing or contrasting stimulation. Remarkably, our experiences of color, form, position, and depth are all based on processing the same stream of sensory information from our eyes in different parts of the visual cortex.

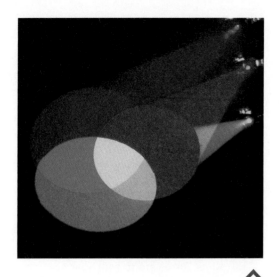

The combination of any two unique hues yields the complement of a third color. The combination of all three wavelengths produces white light, as does the combination of two complementary colors.

Color Blindness   Not everyone sees colors in the same way, because some people are born with a color deficiency. At the extreme, complete **color blindness** is the total inability to distinguish colors. Problems in distinguishing color come in different degrees and forms besides total color blindness. People with one form of *color weakness* can't distinguish pale colors, such as pink or tan. Most color weakness or blindness, however, involves a genetically based difficulty in distinguishing red from green, especially at weak saturations. Those who confuse yellows and blues are rare, about one or two people per thousand. Rarest of all are those who see no color at all and see only variations in brightness. In fact, only about 500 cases of this total color blindness have ever been reported—including Jonathan I., whom we met at the beginning of this chapter. To see whether you have a major color deficiency, look at Figure 5.6 and note what you see. If you see the number 15 in the dot pattern, your color vision is probably normal. If you see something else, you are probably at least partially color blind.

How the Visual System Creates Brightness   Sensations of **brightness** come from the intensity of light, determined by how much light reaches the retina. A bright light creates much neural activity in the retina, while a dim light does not. Ultimately, the brain senses brightness by the level of neural activity produced in the retina and passed along through the optic pathways.

UNDERSTANDING WHAT HAPPENED TO JONATHAN   After his accident, it seemed to Jonathan I. that the color had gone out of his world. In reality, how-

TABLE 5.3	*Visual Stimulation* *Becomes Sensation*	
PHYSICAL STIMULATION	**PSYCHOLOGICAL SENSATION**
Wavelength	color
intensity (amplitude)	brightness

Color and brightness are the psychological counterparts of the wavelength and intensity of a light wave. Wavelength and intensity are characteristics of physical light waves, while color and brightness exist only in the brain.

Visible spectrum: The tiny part of the electromagnetic spectrum to which our eyes are sensitive.

Color blindness: Typically a genetic disorder (although sometimes the result of trauma) that prevents an individual from discriminating certain colors. The most common form is red-green color blindness.

Brightness: A sensation caused by the intensity of light waves.

After you stare at a colored object for a while, the cone cells of your retina will become fatigued, causing an interesting visual effect. When you shift your gaze to a blank surface, you can "see" the object in complementary colors — as a *visual afterimage.* The "phantom flag" demonstration will show you how this works.

Stare at the dot in the center of the green, black, and orange flag for at least 30 seconds. Take care to hold your eyes steady and not to let them scan over the image during this time. Then quickly shift your gaze to the center of a sheet of white paper or to a light-colored blank wall. What do you see? Have your friends try this, too. Do they see the same afterimage? (The effect may not work for people who are color blind.)

Afterimages may be negative or positive. *Positive afterimages* are caused by a continuation of the receptor and neural processes following stimulation. They are brief. An example of positive afterimages occurs when you see the trail of a sparkler twirled by a Fourth of July reveler. *Negative afterimages* are the opposite or the reverse of the original experience, as in the flag example. They last longer. Negative afterimages are caused by the light temporarily depleting the pigments in certain areas of the retina. As a result, white light subsequently coming into the eye can arouse only the previously unstimulated cone cells, which encode for the complementary colors.

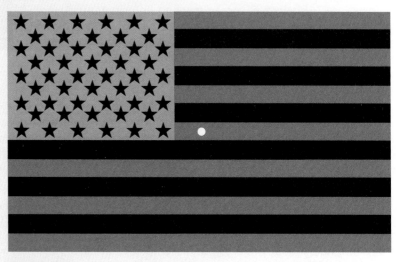

Phantom Flag

FIGURE 5.6: The Ishihani Color Blindness Test

Someone who cannot discriminate between red and green hues will not be able to identify the number hidden in the figure. What do you see? If you see the number 15 in the dot pattern, your color vision is probably normal.

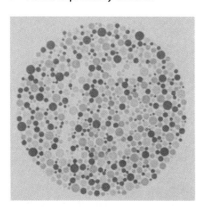

ever, the wavelength reflections that produce color were intact in the objects around him, but the "color" — the ability to sense different hues — was gone from Jonathan's visual system. His experience supports the idea that color is not a quality of objects but an experience constructed in the brain of the viewer (Zeki, 1992).

> Although Mr. I. does not deny his loss, and at some level still mourns it, he has come to feel that his vision has become "highly refined," "privileged," that he sees a world of pure form, uncluttered by color. . . . He feels he has been given "a whole new world," which the rest of us, distracted by color, are insensitive to. (Sacks, 1995, pp. 38–39)

Hearing: If a Tree Falls in the Forest . . .

While vision is the most thoroughly investigated of our senses, the study of hearing has also received much attention from psychologists. Imagine how your world would change if your ability to hear were suddenly and dramatically altered. You would soon realize that hearing, like vision, provides us with reliable spatial information over extended distances. In fact, hearing may be even more important than vision in orienting us toward distant events. We often hear things, such as footsteps coming up behind us, before we see the source of the sounds. Hearing may also tell us of events that we cannot see, including speech, music, or a car approaching from behind.

But there is more to hearing than its *function*. Accordingly, we will look a little deeper to learn *how* we hear. Specifically, in the next few pages we will review what sensory psychologists have discovered about how sound waves are produced, how they are sensed, and how these sensations of sound are interpreted.

THE PHYSICS OF SOUND   Sound waves come from vibrating objects, such as guitar strings, bells, and vocal cords. The vibrational energy transfers to the surrounding medium—usually air—as the vibrating objects push the molecules of the medium back and forth. The resulting changes in pressure spread outward in the form of sound waves that can travel 1,100 feet per second in air. (Sound cannot travel in a true vacuum, such as interplanetary space, because there is no medium there to carry the sound waves. This means that those Hollywood explosions of planets in space movies should be silent!)

A pure tone made by a tuning fork consists of a single, simple sound wave (see Figure 5.7). It has only two characteristics: *frequency* and *amplitude,* the physical properties that determine how it sounds to us. **Frequency** refers to the number of vibrations or cycles the wave completes in a given amount of time; it is usually expressed in *cycles per second (cps)* or *hertz (Hz)*. **Amplitude** measures the physical strength of the sound wave (shown in its peak-to-valley height); it is defined in units of sound pressure or energy. When you turn down the volume on your stereo, you are decreasing the amplitude of the sound waves.

Most sounds, however, are produced not by pure tones. Rather, they consist of complex waves containing a combination of frequencies and amplitudes. This explains why we hear different sound qualities from different sources (clarinet versus piano, for example); the sounds contain different combinations of frequencies and amplitudes.

HOW SOUND WAVES BECOME AUDITORY SENSATIONS   The psychological sensation of sound requires that sound waves be transduced into neural impulses and sent to the brain. This happens in four steps:

1. *Airborne sound waves must be relayed to the inner ear.* In this initial transformation, vibrating air molecules enter the ears and strike the eardrum, or **tympanic membrane** (see Figure 5.8). The eardrum transmits the vibrations to three tiny bones: the hammer, anvil, and stirrup (named for their shapes). These bones pass the vibrations on to the primary organ of hearing, the **cochlea,** located in the inner ear.

2. *The cochlea focuses the vibrations on the basilar membrane.* Here in the cochlea, the formerly airborne sound wave becomes "seaborne," because the coiled tube of the cochlea is filled with fluid. As the bony stirrup vibrates against the oval window at the base of the cochlea, the vibrations set the fluid into wave motion. The fluid wave causes the **basilar membrane,** a thin strip of tissue running through the cochlea, to vibrate.

3. *The basilar membrane converts the vibrations into neural impulses.* Bending of tiny hair cells on the vibrating basilar membrane stimulates sensory nerve endings connected to the hair cells. This transforms the mechanical vibrations of the basilar membrane into neural activity.

4. *Finally, the neural impulses travel to the auditory cortex.* Nerve impulses leave the cochlea in a bundle of neurons called the

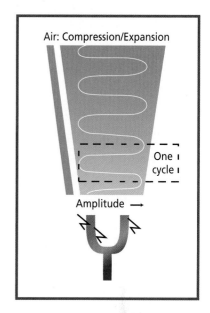

FIGURE 5.7:   Sound Waves
Sound waves produced by the vibration of a tuning fork create waves of compressed and expanded air.

Afterimages: Sensations that linger after the stimulus is removed. Most visual afterimages are *negative afterimages,* which appear in reversed colors.

Frequency: The number of cycles completed by a wave in a given amount of time, usually a second.

Amplitude: The physical strength of a wave. This is usually measured from peak (top) to trough (bottom) on a graph of the wave.

Tympanic membrane: The eardrum.

Cochlea: The primary organ of hearing; a coiled tube in the inner ear, where sound waves are transduced into nerve impulses.

Basilar membrane: A thin strip of tissue sensitive to vibrations in the cochlea. The basilar membrane contains hair cells connected to neurons, which accomplish the final step of converting sound waves to nerve impulses.

FIGURE 5.8: Structures of the Human Ear

Sound waves are channeled by the external ear (pinna) through the external canal, causing the tympanic membrane to vibrate. The vibration activates the tiny bones in the middle ear (hammer, anvil, and stirrup). These mechanical vibrations pass from the oval window to the cochlea, where they set internal fluid in motion. The fluid movement stimulates tiny hair cells along the basilar membrane, inside the cochlea, to transmit neural impulses from the ear to the brain along the auditory nerve.

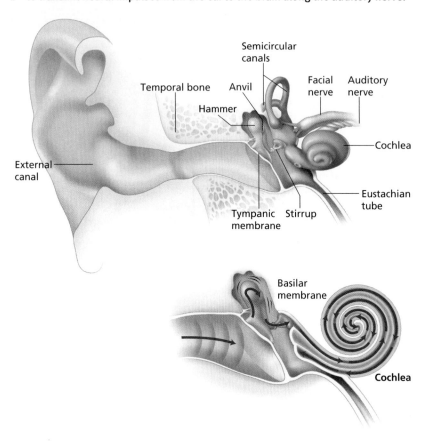

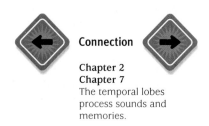

Connection

Chapter 2
Chapter 7
The temporal lobes process sounds and memories.

Auditory nerve: The neural pathway connecting the ear and the brain.

Auditory cortex: A portion of the temporal lobe that processes sounds.

auditory nerve. The neurons from the two ears meet in the brain stem, which passes the auditory information to both sides of the brain. Ultimately, the signals arrive in the **auditory cortex** of the temporal lobes for higher-order processing.

If the auditory system seems complicated, you might think of it as a sensory "relay team." Sound waves are first funneled in by the outer ear, then handed off from the tissue of the eardrum to bones in the middle ear. Mechanical vibrations of these bones are then passed to the cochlea and basilar membrane, where they finally become neural impulses, which are, in turn, passed along to the brain. This series of steps transforms commonplace vibrations and shifts in air pressure into experiences as exquisite and varied as music, doorbells, whispers, shouts, and psychology lectures.

THE PSYCHOLOGICAL QUALITIES OF SOUND No matter where they come from, sounds have only three qualities that we experience: *pitch, loudness,* and *timbre.* In the following discussion, we will learn how the two physical characteristics of a sound wave (frequency and amplitude) produce these

TABLE 5.4	Auditory Stimulation Becomes Sensation	
PHYSICAL STIMULATION	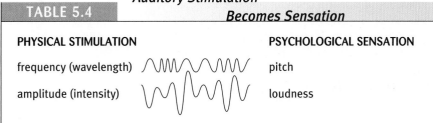	**PSYCHOLOGICAL SENSATION**
frequency (wavelength)		pitch
amplitude (intensity)		loudness

Pitch and loudness are the psychological counterparts of the frequency and amplitude of a sound wave. Frequency and intensity are characteristics of the physical sound wave, while sensations of pitch and loudness exist only in the brain. Compare this table with Table 5.3 for vision.

three psychological sensations. As you read about psychology of sound, please note the similarities between sound and the visual sensations discussed earlier.

Sensations of Pitch   A sound wave's *frequency* determines the highness or lowness of a sound—a quality known as **pitch.** High frequencies produce high pitch, and low frequencies produce low pitch (see Table 5.4). The full range of human auditory sensitivity extends from frequencies as low as 20 cps (the lowest range of a subwoofer in a good stereo system) to frequencies as high as 20,000 cps (produced by a stereo's high-frequency tweeter).

How does the auditory apparatus produce sensations of pitch? Two auditory systems divide the task, affording us much greater sensory precision than either system alone could provide. Here's what happens:

▶ When sound waves are conducted through the inner ear, the basilar membrane vibrates (see Figure 5.8), as we have noted. Different frequencies activate different locations on the membrane. The pitch one hears depends, in part, on which basilar membrane site receives the greatest stimulation. Different *places* on the basilar membrane send neural codes for different pitches to the auditory cortex of the brain—an explanation of pitch perception known as the *place theory*. The place theory accounts for our ability to hear high tones—above about 1,000 Hz (cycles per second).

▶ Neurons on the basilar membrane also respond with different firing rates for different frequencies. And so, the rate of firing provides another code for pitch perception in the brain. This *frequency theory* explains how the basilar membrane transduces frequencies below about 5,000 Hz. (Between 1,000 and 5,000 Hz, hearing is based on *both* place and frequency.)

Why does our auditory system seem designed for double duty for sounds within the range of 1,000 to 5,000 Hz? This range of human speech is an especially important attribute of our species. Further, the shape of the auditory canal amplifies sounds within the speech range. It appears that the auditory system has evolved two mechanisms especially for hearing the human voice.

Sensations of Loudness   The **loudness** of a sound is determined mainly by its physical strength or *amplitude* (much as brightness is determined by the intensity of light). We experience sound waves with large amplitudes (a shout) as loud and those with small amplitudes (a whisper) as soft.

Because our range of hearing is so great, physical intensities of sound are usually expressed in ratios rather than absolute amounts. Specifically, sound

Pitch: A sensory characteristic of sound produced by the frequency of the sound wave.

Loudness: A sensory characteristic of sound produced by the amplitude (intensity) of the sound wave.

  Connection

Chapter 2
Evolution occurs through *natural selection,* which favors adaptive traits.

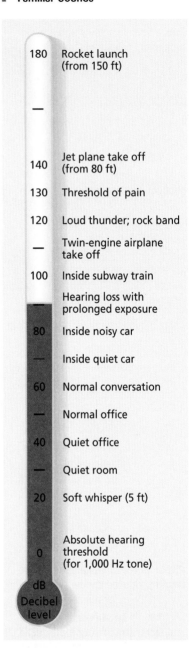

180 | 180 Rocket launch (from 150 ft)

140 | Jet plane take off (from 80 ft)

130 | Threshold of pain

120 | Loud thunder; rock band

— | Twin-engine airplane take off

100 | Inside subway train

 | Hearing loss with prolonged exposure

80 | Inside noisy car

— | Inside quiet car

60 | Normal conversation

— | Normal office

40 | Quiet office

 | Quiet room

20 | Soft whisper (5 ft)

0 | Absolute hearing threshold (for 1,000 Hz tone)

dB Decibel level

Timbre: The quality of a sound wave that derives from the wave's complexity (combination of pure tones).

Vestibular sense: The sense of body orientation with respect to gravity.

intensity is measured in units called *decibels* (dB). Figure 5.9 shows the levels of some representative natural sounds in decibel units.

Sensations of Timbre   The quality of a sound wave's complexity is its **timbre** (pronounced TAM-b'r). It is this property that distinguishes a guitar from a violin or one voice from another. Figure 5.10 shows the waveforms that correspond to the timbre of several familiar sounds.

With all this information about sound in mind, we are in a position to answer an ancient puzzle: If a tree falls in the forest and there is no ear there to hear it, is there a sound? Based on our knowledge of sensory psychology, we can say emphatically, "No." Even though a falling tree makes a physical *sound wave,* we know that it produces no physical sound because sound is not a physical phenomenon. Rather, sound is a purely *psychological sensation* that requires an ear (and the rest of the sensory system) to produce it.

COMPARING AUDITORY AND VISUAL SENSATIONS   Earlier we discussed how visual information is carried to the brain by the optic nerve in the form of neural impulses. Now, we find that auditory information is also conveyed to the brain as neural impulses—but by a different pathway. So, why do we "see" visual impulses and "hear" auditory impulses? As our Core Concept suggested, the answer lies in the region of the cortex receiving the neural message—not on some unique quality of the message itself. In brief, different regions of the brain are designed to produce different sensations. In the "Do It Yourself!" box (on p. 181), we will show you how to use visual sensations known as *phosphenes* to demonstrate this cortical specialization in your own brain.

How the Other Senses Are Like Vision and Hearing

Of all our senses, vision and hearing have been studied the most. However, our survival depends on other senses, too. To conclude our discussion of sensation, we will briefly review the processes involved in our sense of (1) body position and movement, (2) smell, (3) taste, (4) the skin senses, and (5) pain. You will note that each gives us information about a different aspect of our internal or external environment. Yet each operates on similar principles. Each transduces physical stimuli into neural impulses, and each is more sensitive to change than to constant stimulation. And, as was the case with vision and hearing, each of these senses is distinguished by the type of information it extracts and by the specialized regions of the brain devoted to it.

POSITION AND MOVEMENT   To act purposefully and gracefully in our environment, we need constant information about where our limbs and other body parts are in relation to each other and to objects in the environment. Without this knowledge, even our simplest actions would be hopelessly uncoordinated. (You have probably had just this experience when you tried to walk on a leg that had "gone to sleep.")

The sense of body position and movement actually consists of two different systems. The **vestibular sense** is the body position sense that orients us with respect to gravity. It tells us how our bodies—especially our heads—are postured, whether straight, leaning, reclining, or upside down. The vestibular sense also tells us when we are moving or how our motion is changing. The receptors for this information are tiny hairs (much like those we found in the basilar membrane) in the *semicircular canals* of the inner ear (see Figure 5.8). These hairs respond to our movements by detecting corresponding movements in the fluid of the semicircular canals.

The **kinesthetic sense,** the other sense of body position and movement, keeps track of body parts relative to each other. Your kinesthetic sense makes

One of the simplest concepts in perceptual psychology is among the most difficult for most people to understand: The brain and its sensory systems create the colors, sounds, tastes, odors, textures, and pains that you sense.

Skeptical? You can demonstrate this to yourself with an odd perceptual phenomenon called the *phosphene.*

Close your eyes and press gently with your finger on the inside corner of one eye. On the opposite side of your visual field you will "see" a pattern caused by the pressure of your finger — not by light. These **phosphenes** are visual images caused by fooling your visual system with pressure. Just as light does, the pressure on your eye stimulates the optic nerve, making it send messages to your brain, which misinterprets the signals as light. Direct electrical stimulation of the occipital lobe, sometimes done during brain surgery, can have the same effect. This shows that what you sense depends on which part of the brain has been stimulated. It also shows that light waves are not necessary for the sensation of light. The sensory experience of light, therefore, must be a creation of the brain, rather than a property of the external world.

Aside from demonstrating that light sensations are a creation of the brain, phosphenes may have some practical value. It may be possible to use these artificial visual images to create visual sensations for people who have lost their sight (Dobelle, 1977; Leutwyler, 1994). At this point, researchers can connect a TV camera or computer to wires that have been surgically implanted on the surface of the occipital cortex. The "picture" sent to the brain actually consists of electrical impulses that the brain interprets as a coarse array of dots — something like a crude image from a digital camera (Service, 1999). Another approach under development involves replacing a section of the retina with an electronic microchip (Lui et al., 2000).

sensation of light

you aware of crossing your legs, for example, and of which hand is closer to the telephone when it rings. Kinesthesis provides constant sensory feedback about what the muscles in your body are doing during motor activities, such as whether to continue reaching for your cup of coffee or to stop before you knock it over (Turvey, 1996).

Receptors for kinesthesis can be found in the joints and in the muscles and tendons. These receptors, as well as those for the vestibular sense, connect to processing regions in the brain's parietal lobes — which, in general, help us understand the spatial relationship among objects and events. Except when we are learning a new physical skill, this processing is usually accomplished automatically and effortlessly, outside of conscious awareness.

SMELL   The sense of smell, or **olfaction,** involves a chain of biochemical events. Odors, in the form of airborne chemical molecules, interact with receptor proteins on the membrane of specialized hairs in the nose (Axel, 1995; Buck & Axel, 1991; Mombaerts, 1999). This stimulates associated nerve cells. Their impulses convey odor information to the brain, where sensations of smell are realized in the **olfactory bulbs**. These are located on the underside

> **Phosphenes:** Visual sensations that are not caused by light waves but by other forms of stimulation, such as pressure on the eyeball or electrical stimulation of the visual cortex.
>
> **Kinesthetic sense:** The sense of body position and movement of body parts relative to each other (also called *kinesthesis*).
>
> **Olfaction:** The sense of smell.
>
> **Olfactory bulbs:** The brain sites of olfactory processing, located below the frontal lobes, where odor-sensitive receptors send their signals.

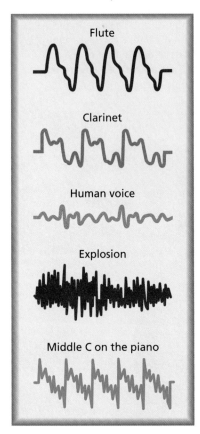

FIGURE 5.10: Waveforms of Familiar Sounds

Each sound is a distinctive combination of several pure tones.

Flute

Clarinet

Human voice

Explosion

Middle C on the piano

Pheromones: Chemical signals released by organisms to communicate with other members of their species; often sexual attractors.

Gustation: The sense of taste.

Taste buds: Receptors for taste, located primarily on the upper side of the tongue.

Skin senses: Sensory systems for processing touch, warmth, and cold.

of the brain just below the frontal lobes (Mori et al., 1999). (See Figure 5.11.) Unlike all the other senses, smell signals are not relayed through the thalamus, suggesting that smell evolved earlier than the other senses.

In humans, olfaction has an intimate connection with memory: Certain smells, such as a favorite perfume, may evoke emotion-laden memories (Azar, 1998a; Holloway, 1999). Originally, however, smell was probably a system in primitive organisms for detecting and locating food (Moncrieff, 1951). A major factor in survival, smell is also used for detecting potential sources of danger. In addition, odors can be used for communication. Members of some species (for example, insects such as ants and termites and vertebrates such as dogs and cats) communicate with each other by secreting and detecting odorous signals. These signals, called **pheromones,** are chemical substances commonly used within a given species to signal sexual receptivity, danger, territorial boundaries, and food sources. Humans seem to use the sense of smell primarily in conjunction with taste to seek and sample food, but there is also some evidence that we may also secrete and sense sexual pheromones and pheromones that help us identify family members by smell (Azar, 1998b; Filsinger & Fabes, 1985; Holden, 1996b).

TASTE   When you eat, the senses of taste and smell work together closely. Having a cold makes food seem tasteless because your nasal passages are blocked and you can't smell the food. Moreover, many of the subtle distinctions you may think of as flavors really come from odors. (Much of the "taste" of an onion is odor, not flavor.) Thus, your sense of taste, or **gustation,** is far from precise in its sensitivity. There are four main taste qualities: sweet, sour, bitter, and salty. In addition, researchers have recently identified a fifth taste quality called *umami* (Chaudhari et al., 2000). Umami is the flavor associated with monosodium glutamate (MSG), often used in Asian cuisine. It also occurs naturally in protein-rich foods, such as meat, seafood, and cheese.

The taste receptor cells are gathered in the **taste buds,** receptors for taste that are located primarily on the upper side of the tongue. Taste buds cluster in very small mucous-membrane projections called *papillae,* as shown in Figure 5.12. Individuals vary in their sensitivity to taste sensations, a function of the density of these papillae on the tongue (Bartoshuk et al., 1994). Those with more taste buds for bitter flavors are "supertasters," more sensitive than regular tasters or extreme "nontasters"—a survival advantage, because most poisons are bitter (Bartoshuk, 1993). Ultimately, taste is realized in a specialized region of the brain's parietal somatosensory cortex, adjacent to the area receiving touch stimulation from the face (Gadsby, 2000).

Taste sensitivity is exaggerated in infants and decreases with age. Consequently, many elderly people complain that food has lost its taste—which really means that they have lost much of their sensory ability to detect differences in the taste and smell of food. In addition, taste receptors can be easily damaged (by alcohol, smoke, acids, or hot foods). Fortunately, they are replaced every few days—even more frequently than the smell receptors. Because of this constant renewal, the taste system is the most resistant to permanent damage of all your senses, and a total loss of taste is extremely rare (Bartoshuk, 1990).

THE SKIN SENSES   Consider the skin's remarkable versatility: It protects us against surface injury, holds in body fluids, and helps regulate body temperature. The skin also contains nerve endings that, when stimulated by contact with external objects, produce sensations of touch, warmth, and cold. Like the other senses, these **skin senses** are ultimately realized in the somatosensory cortex located in the brain's parietal lobes.

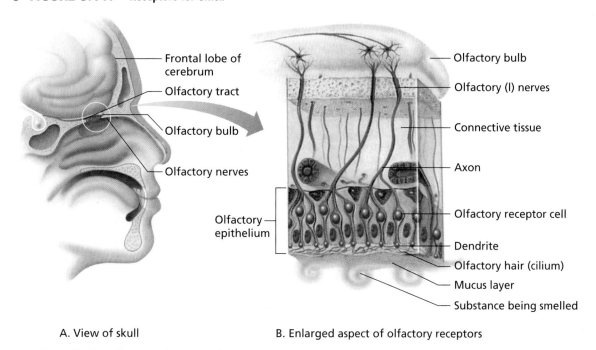

A. View of skull

B. Enlarged aspect of olfactory receptors

■ **FIGURE 5.12:**   Receptors for Taste

(A) Distribution of the papillae on the upper side of the tongue; (B) a single papilla enlarged so that the individual taste buds are visible; (C) one of the taste buds enlarged.

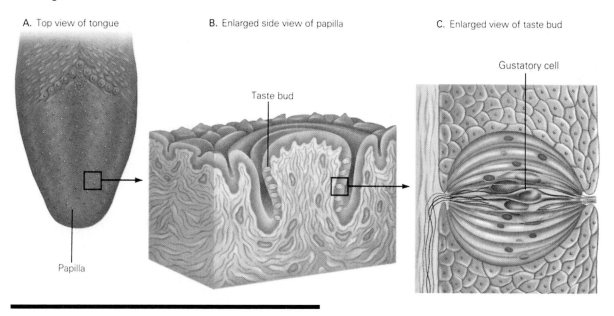

A. Top view of tongue

B. Enlarged side view of papilla

C. Enlarged view of taste bud

The skin's sensitivity to stimulation varies tremendously over the body. For example, we are ten times more accurate in sensing the position of stimulation on our fingertips than the position of stimulation on our backs. In general, our sensitivity is greatest where we need it most — on our faces, tongues, and hands. Precise sensory feedback from these parts of the body permits effective eating, speaking, and grasping.

Placebos: Substances that appear to be drugs but are not.

Placebo effect: A response to a placebo (a fake drug), caused by subjects' belief that they are taking real drugs.

One aspect of skin sensitivity — touch — plays a central role in human relationships. Through touch we communicate our desire to give or receive comfort, support, love, and passion (Fisher, 1992; Givens, 1983; Harlow, 1965; Henley, 1977; Masters & Johnson, 1966; Morris, 1967). Touch also serves as a primary stimulus for sexual arousal in humans. And it is essential for healthy mental and physical development (Field & Schanberg, 1990). On the other hand, deprivation of touch stimulation has been shown to stunt the growth of young animals and human children.

The Experience of Pain

Psychology

In Your Life

If you are in pain, nothing else matters. A wound or a toothache can dominate all other sensations. And if you are among the one-third of Americans who suffer from persistent or recurring pain, the experience can be debilitating and can sometimes even lead to suicide (Wallis, 1984). Yet pain is also part of your body's adaptive mechanism that makes you respond to conditions that threaten damage to your body. Unlike other sensations, pain can arise from intense stimulation in various sensory pathways. Research points to the *anterior cingulate cortex,* located along the fissure separating the frontal lobes, as the site where pain signals from different pathways converge (Craig & Reiman, 1996; Vogel, 1996).

Pain comes in two main forms. *Acute pain* is sharp or sudden. Scientists study it experimentally in laboratories with paid volunteers, who experience varying degrees of a precisely regulated pain stimulus, such as heat applied briefly to a small area of the skin. This procedure can test a subject's tolerance for pain and measure responses to it without causing tissue damage. In contrast, *chronic pain* (prolonged or enduring pain) is typically studied in hospital research clinics as part of treatment programs designed to find new ways to alleviate such pain.

PAIN TOLERANCE

The threshold of pain varies enormously from person to person. One study, for example, found that electric shocks had to be eight times more powerful to produce painful sensations in their least-sensitive subjects as compared with their most-sensitive subjects (Rollman & Harris, 1987). The same study also found that tolerance for intense pain varies by the same amount. This may explain why some people always demand Novocain at the dentist, while others may prefer dental work without the added hassle of an injection.

INTERPRETATIONS OF PAIN

Your response to pain is far from simple, involving an interplay between biochemistry, nerve impulses, and psychological and cultural factors. Remarkably, attitudes, beliefs, emotions, and motives can influence the biological processes associated with pain (Price, 2000; Turk, 1994). To a small child, a bath can be a painful experience. And if someone unexpectedly touches you with an ice cube and says "Hot!" you will feel it as a burn. In contrast, soldiers wounded in the excitement of battle may feel little or no pain from wounds that would, under other circumstances, cause great suffering. Painful stimuli can even be interpreted as pleasurable, as an aficionado of hot salsa or Thai

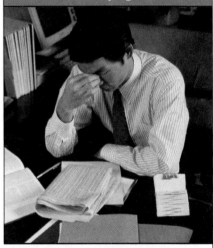

Pain is affected by experience and circumstance. A person who is unhappy may find the pain of a headache unbearable, while another individual, in a more satisfactory job, considers a headache merely annoying.

curry will testify. Thus, pain can be more than a mere signal of danger.

DEALING WITH PAIN

Wouldn't it be nice to banish the experience of pain altogether? Actually, such a condition could easily be deadly. People with congenital insensitivity to pain do not feel what is hurting them, and their bodies often become scarred and their limbs become deformed from injuries that they could have avoided if their brains were able to warn them of danger. In fact, because of their failure to notice and respond to tissue-damaging stimuli, these people tend to die young (Manfredi et al., 1981). In general, pain serves as an essential defense signal: It warns us of potential harm. It helps us to survive in hostile environments and to cope with sickness and injury.

What can you do if you are in pain? Analgesic drugs, ranging from over-the-counter remedies, such as aspirin and ibuprofen, to prescription narcotics, such as morphine, are widely used and effective. These act in a variety of ways. We have seen that morphine, for example, mimics your body's own pain control substances, the endorphins.

All such drugs—especially the narcotics—can have unwanted side effects. These include addiction or damage to the digestive tract. But, to dispel an old concern, studies have shown that if you must use narcotics to control severe pain, the possibility of your becoming addicted is far less than it would be if you were using narcotics recreationally (Melzack, 1990).

Many people can also learn to control pain by treatments that use mental processes, such as hypnosis, deep relaxation, and thought-distraction procedures (Brown, 1998). You also may be among those for whom pain can also be modified by **placebos,** mock drugs made to appear as real drugs. For example, a placebo may be an injection of mild saline solution (salt water) or a pill made of sugar. Such fake drugs are routinely given to a control group in tests of new drugs. The reason, of course, involves the people's *belief* that they are getting real medicine. Because this **placebo effect** frequently occurs, any drug deemed effective must prove itself stronger than a placebo.

But exactly how do placebos produce their effects? Apparently the expectation of pain relief is enough to cause the brain to release painkilling endorphins. We believe this is so because those who respond to placebos report that their pain *increases* when they take the endorphin-blocking drug, *naltrexone* (Fields, 1978; Fields & Levine, 1984). It is likely that endorphins are responsible for the pain-relieving effects of acupuncture (Price et al., 1984; Watkins & Mayer, 1982).

What is the psychological lesson that pain can teach us? Our responses to potentially painful stimuli illustrate a general principle that we will see amplified in the last section of this chapter: *What we perceive may be quite different from the stimulation presented by the world outside us.*

CHECK**YOUR**UNDERSTANDING

1. **RECALL:** *The eyes have two distinct types of photoreceptors: the rods, which detect _____, and the cones, which detect _____.*
   a. low-intensity light/wavelengths corresponding to colors
   b. motion/shape
   c. bright light/dim light
   d. stimuli in consciousness/stimuli outside of consciousness

2. **RECALL:** *The wavelength of light causes sensations of _____, while the intensity of light causes sensations of _____.*
   a. motion/shape
   b. color/brightness
   c. primary colors/secondary colors
   d. depth/color

3. **RECALL:** *The frequency theory best explains _____ sounds, while the place theory best explains _____ sounds.*
   a. low-pitched/high-pitched
   b. loud/soft
   c. pitch/timbre
   d. simple/complex

4. **RECALL:** *Which sense makes use of electromagnetic energy?*
   a. hearing
   b. taste
   c. pain
   d. vision

5. **SYNTHESIS:** *What do all of these forms of sensation have in common: vision, hearing, taste, smell, hearing, pain, equilibrium, and body position?*
   a. They all arise from stimulation that comes only from outside the body.
   b. They all involve location of stimulation in three-dimensional space.
   c. They all are conveyed to the brain in the form of nerve impulses.
   d. They all involve waves having frequency and amplitude.

6. **UNDERSTANDING THE CORE CONCEPT:**
   Different senses give us different sensations mainly because
   a. they involve different stimuli.
   b. they activate different sensory regions of the brain.
   c. they have different intensities.
   d. we have different memories associated with them.

ANSWERS: 1. a   2. b   3. a   4. d
5. c   6. b

WHAT IS THE RELATIONSHIP BETWEEN PERCEPTION AND SENSATION?

So, sensory signals have been transduced and transmitted to specific regions of your brain for further processing: Then what? You must employ the brain's *perceptual* machinery to understand what that sensory information *means* to you. Does a bitter taste mean poison? Does a red flag mean danger? Does a smile signify a friendly overture? The Core Concept of this section emphasizes this perceptual elaboration of sensory information:

> Perception brings *meaning* to sensation, so perception produces an interpretation of the external world, not a perfect representation of it.

Perception is no mirror of reality, says psychologist Richard Gregory (1997). In brief, we might say that the task of perception is to extract sensory input from the environment and organize it into stable, meaningful *percepts*. A **percept** is what is perceived—the experienced outcome of the process of perception. Not a simple task, perception must identify features of the world that are invariant (fixed and unchanging) by sorting through a continual flood of information. For example, as you move about the room, the sights in the environment create a rapidly changing, blurred sequence of images—yet you remain sure that it is you who are moving, while the objects around you remain stationary. As we study this complex process, we will first discuss how perception discerns what is real, and then we will consider the perceptual tasks of attention, organization, and identification.

The Machinery of Perceptual Processing

Suppose that you notice a person, such as the individual pictured in Figure 5.13. Based on what we have learned about visual processing, you know that light reflected from this person produces a retinal image that is processed further by the visual cortex. Ultimately—but very quickly—you compare the incoming image with similar images from memory and identify it. Let's see how this happens.

FEATURE DETECTORS   To help us make such perceptual judgments, our brains employ specialized groups of cells that are dedicated to the detection of specific stimulus features, such as length, slant, color, and boundary (Heeger, 1994; Hubel & Wiesel, 1979; Kandel & Squire, 2000; Lettvin et al., 1959; Maunsell, 1995; Zeki, 1992). There is even a part of the occipital lobe containing cells that are especially sensitive to features of the human face (Carpenter, 1999). Perceptual psychologists call such cells **feature detectors.**

Despite our extensive knowledge of feature detectors, we still don't know exactly how the brain manages to combine (or "bind") the features it detects into a single percept of, say, a face. Psychologists call this puzzle the **binding problem** (Kandel & Squire, 2000). It has been suggested that diverse regions of the brain synchronize the firing pattern of their neurons when they combine information (Bower, 1998; Schechter, 1996).

BOTTOM-UP AND TOP-DOWN PROCESSING   Regardless of the way information may be combined in the brain, perception involves taking sensory data into the system through receptors and sending it "upward" to the cortex

Percept: The meaningful product of perception—often an image that has been associated with concepts, memories of events, emotions, and motives.

Feature detectors: Cells in the cortex that specialize in extracting certain features of a stimulus.

Binding problem: A major unsolved mystery in cognitive psychology, concerning the physical processes used by the brain to combine many aspects of sensation into a single percept.

for analysis based on the characteristics of the stimulus. Psychologists call this **bottom-up processing.** It is also known as *stimulus-driven processing* because the resulting percept is determined, or "driven," by stimulus features. Many of the fundamental attributes of objects that we sense in our world clearly involve this form of processing. Examples include following the motion of a ball, identifying the colors of a banner, and recognizing the sound of a bell. But bottom-up processing is not the only process at work.

Simultaneously, a complementary process is occurring at the "top"—at the highest levels of the cerebral cortex. **Top-down processing** invokes a perceiver's goals, past experience, knowledge, expectations, memory, motivations, or cultural background in the interpretation of an object or event (see Nelson, 1993). It is also known as *conceptually driven* processing, because the system is fed by concepts and other products of the perceiver's own thinking. An example is a sound heard in the middle of the night and interpreted as an intruder—a process driven more by expectations than by characteristics of the stimulus.

PERCEPTUAL CONSTANCIES   We can illustrate another aspect of perception with yet another example of top-down processing. Suppose that you are looking at a door, such as the one pictured in Figure 5.14A. You "know" that the door is rectangular, even though your sensory image of it is distorted when you are not looking at it straight-on. Your brain automatically corrects the sensory distortion, so that you *perceive* the door as in Figure 5.14B.

This ability to see an object as being the same shape from different angles or distances is an example of **perceptual constancy.** In fact, there are many kinds of perceptual constancies. These include *color constancy,* which allows us to see a flower as being the same color in the reddish light of sunset as in the

Bottom-up processing: Perceptual analysis that emphasizes characteristics of the stimulus, rather than our concepts and expectations.

Top-down processing: Perceptual analysis that emphasizes the perceiver's expectations, concept memories, and other cognitive factors, rather than being driven by the characteristics of the stimulus.

Perceptual constancy: The ability to recognize the same object under different conditions, such as changes in illumination, distance, or location.

Connection

Chapter 8
Concepts are fundamental units of thought.

FIGURE 5.13:   Who is this? Perceptual processes help us recognize Tom Cruise by matching the stimulus to images in memory.

FIGURE 5.14:   A Door

(A) A door seen from an angle presents the eye with a distorted rectangle image.
(B) The brain perceives the door as rectangular.

(A)

(B)

white glare of midday. *Size constancy* allows us to perceive a person as the same size at different distances and also serves as a strong cue for depth perception. *Shape constancy* is responsible for our ability to see the door in Figure 5.14 as remaining rectangular from different angles. Together these constancies help us identify and track objects in a changing world.

Perceptual Ambiguity and Distortion

A primary goal of perception is to get an accurate "fix" on the world—to recognize friends, foes, opportunities, and dangers. Survival depends on accurately perceiving the environment, but the environment is not always easy to "read." We can illustrate this difficulty with the photo of black and white splotches in Figure 5.15. What is it? Try to extract the stimulus figure from the background: a Dalmatian sniffing at the ground. The dog is hard to find because it blends with the background. The same problem occurs when you try to single out a voice against a noisy background at a party.

But it is not just the inability to find an image that causes perceptual problems. Sometimes our perceptions can be wildly inaccurate because we misinterpret an image. This is a common response to stimulus patterns known as *illusions.*

WHAT ILLUSIONS TELL US ABOUT SENSATION AND PERCEPTION When your mind deceives you by interpreting a stimulus pattern in a manner that is demonstrably incorrect, you are experiencing an **illusion.** Typically, illusions become more likely when the stimulus is unclear, when information is missing, when elements are combined in unusual ways, or when familiar patterns are not apparent. Such illusions can help us understand some fundamental properties of sensation and perception—particularly the discrepancy between our percepts and external reality (Cohen & Girgus, 1978).

Let's first examine a remarkable illusion that works at the level of sensation: the black-and-white Hermann grid (Figure 5.16). As you stare at the center of the grid, note how dark, fuzzy spots appear at the intersections of the white bars. But when you focus on an intersection, the spot vanishes. Why? The answer lies in the way receptor cells in your visual pathways interact with

FIGURE 5.15: An Ambiguous Picture
What is depicted here? How do you know?

Illusion: The demonstrably incorrect experience of a stimulus pattern, shared by others in the same perceptual environment.

FIGURE 5.16: The Hermann Grid

The Hermann grid is an example of an illusion that occurs at the sensory level (at the level of receptor cells).

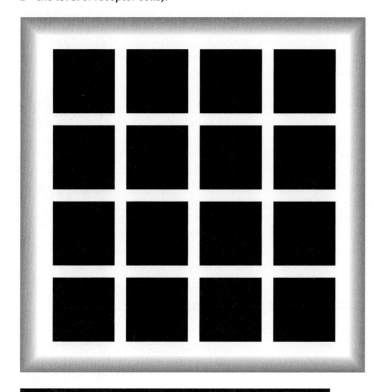

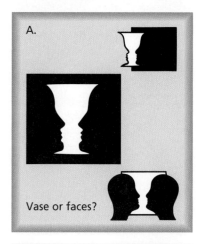

A.

Vase or faces?

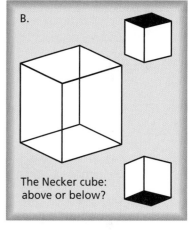

B.

The Necker cube: above or below?

each other. The firing of certain cells sensitive to light and dark boundaries inhibits the firing of adjacent cells. This inhibiting process makes you sense darker regions—the grayish areas—at the white intersections just outside your focus. Even though you know the squares in the Hermann grid are black and the lines are white, this knowledge cannot overcome the illusion, which operates at the more basic, sensory level. Illusions at this level generally occur when receptors have been stimulated in an unusual way and so give rise to a spurious image.

To study illusions at the level of perception, psychologists often employ **ambiguous figures**—stimulus patterns that can be interpreted in two or more distinct ways, as in Figures 5.17A and B. Both the vase/faces figure and the Necker cube are designed to confound your interpretations, not just your sensation. Each suggests two conflicting meanings; and, once you have seen both, your perception will cycle back and forth between them as you look at the figure. Recent studies suggest that these alternating interpretations involve the shifting of perceptual control between the left and right hemispheres of the brain (Gibbs, 2001).

APPLYING THE LESSONS OF ILLUSIONS Several prominent modern artists, fascinated with the visual experiences created by ambiguity, have used perceptual illusion as a central artistic feature of their work. Consider the two examples of art shown here. *Gestalt Bleue* by Victor Vasarely (Figure 5.18) produces depth reversals like those in the Necker cube, with corners that alternately project and recede. In *Sky and Water* by M. C. Escher (Figure 5.19), you can see birds and fishes only through the process of figure–ground reversal, much like

Ambiguous figures: Images that are capable of more than one interpretation.

FIGURE 5.18: Victor Vasarely's Gestalt Bleue

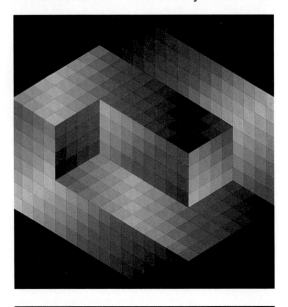

the vase/faces illusion we encountered earlier (Figure 5.17). The effect of these paintings on us underscores the function of human perception to make sense of the world and to fix on the best interpretation we can make.

To make sense of such illusions, we draw on our personal experiences, learning, and motivation. Knowing this, those who understand the principles of perception often can control illusions to achieve desired effects far beyond the world of painting. Architects and interior designers, for example, create illusions that make spaces seem larger or smaller than they really are. They may, for example, make a small apartment appear more spacious when it is painted in light colors and sparsely furnished. Similarly, set and lighting designers in movies and theatrical productions purposely create visual illusions on film and on stage. So, too, do many of us make everyday use of illusion in our choices of cosmetics and clothing (Dackman, 1986). For example, light-colored clothing and horizontal stripes can make our bodies seem larger, while dark-colored clothing and vertical stripes can make our bodies seem slimmer. In these ways, we use illusions to distort "reality" and make our lives more pleasant.

Theoretical Explanations for Perception

The fact that perception is an interpretation and the fact that most people perceive illusions in essentially the same ways suggest that some fundamental psychological principles must be involved. In fact, psychologists looking for these fundamental principles have formulated theories that explain how perception works. Below we will examine two of the classic explanations: *learning-based inference* and the *Gestalt theory* of perception. You will see that these two approaches both emphasize top-down processing, but they take very different positions on a familiar psychological issue—the nature–nurture controversy. Nevertheless, as you will see, we need both perspectives to understand the complexities of perception.

INFERRING FROM LEARNING In 1866, Hermann von Helmholtz pointed out the importance of learning from experience—or nurture—in perception. According to his theory of **learning-based inference,** an observer uses prior learning about the environment to interpret sensory information. Based on this learning the observer makes inferences—reasonable guesses or hunches—about what the sensations mean.

Ordinarily these perceptual inferences are fairly accurate; but, as we have seen, confusing sensations and ambiguous arrangements can create perceptual illusions and erroneous conclusions. Our perceptual interpretations are, in effect, hypotheses about our sensations. For example, as babies we learn to expect that faces have certain features in fixed arrangements (pair of eyes above nose, mouth below nose) and that expressions are most easily perceived in the right-side-up arrangement. In fact, we so thoroughly learn about faces in their usual orientation that we fail to "see" facial patterns that violate our expectations. When you look at the two inverted portraits of Britney Spears (Figure 5.20), do you detect any important differences between them? Turn the book upside down for a surprise.

From a learning perspective, what determines how successful we will be in recognizing and identifying a percept? The most important factors include the *context,* our *expectations,* and *perceptual set.* Each of these involves a way of narrowing our search of the vast store of concepts in long-term memory.

Connection

Chapter 4
The *nature–nurture* controversy centers on the relative importance of heredity and environment.

Learning-based inference: The view that perception is primarily shaped by learning (or experience), rather than innate factors.

FIGURE 5.19: M. C. Escher's *Sky and Water*

FIGURE 5.20: Britney Spears

Although one of these photos clearly has been altered, they look similar when viewed this way. However, turn the book upside down and look again.

Quickly scan this photo. Then look away and describe as much as you recall. Turn to the next page to learn what you, or other perceivers, might not have seen.

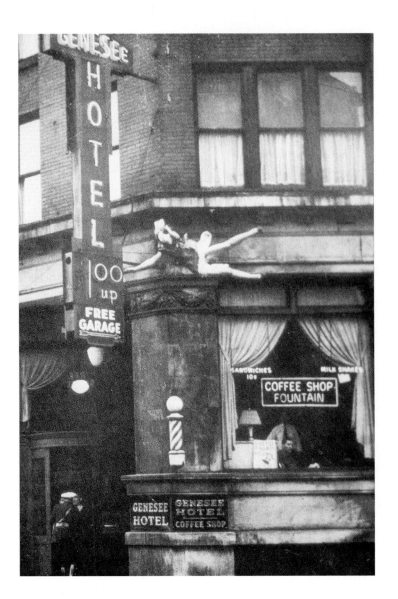

Context and Expectations   Once you identify a *context,* you form *expectations* about what persons, objects, and events you are likely to experience (Biederman, 1989). For example, you have probably had difficulty recognizing people you know in places where you didn't expect to see them, such as in a different city or a new social group. This experience undoubtedly made you realize that it is much harder to recognize people outside their usual context. The problem, of course, is not that they looked different but that the context was unfamiliar: You didn't expect them to be there. Thus, perceptual identification depends on context and expectations as well as on an object's physical properties. To give a more immediate illustration of our expectations being influenced by the context, take a look at the following:

It says THE CAT, right? Now look again at the middle letter of each word. Physically, these two letters are exactly the same, yet you perceived the first as an H and the second as an A. Why? Clearly, your perception was affected by what you know about words in English. The context provided by T__E makes an H highly likely and an A unlikely, whereas the reverse is true of the context of C__T (Selfridge, 1955).

Although context can fool you into misperceiving some stimuli, as in this demonstration, context is an enormously useful cue to identify ambiguous stimuli, such as in recognizing objects in a dimly lit room or deciphering hard-to-read handwriting. So, if you receive a scenic postcard from a friend whose scrawled note describes "having a wonderful time on v_____," you rely on context cues to guess that the V-word is probably *vacation,* and probably not a series of alternatives such as *vacuum, viaduct,* or *Venus!*

Perceptual Set   Another way context and expectation influence your perception comes from your *set,* or readiness to notice and respond to stimulus cues, like a sprinter waiting for the starter's pistol. In general, **perceptual set** is a readiness to detect a particular stimulus in a given context. For example, a new mother is perceptually set to hear the cries of her child. Often, a perceptual set leads you to transform an ambiguous stimulus into the one you were expecting.

To experience perceptual set yourself, read quickly through the series of words that follow in both rows:

FOX; OWL; SNAKE; TURKEY; SWAN; D?CK
BOB; RAY; DAVE; BILL; TOM; D?CK

Notice how the words in the two rows lead you to read D?CK differently in each row. The meanings of the words read prior to the ambiguous stimulus create a perceptual set. Words that refer to animals create a perceptual set that influences you to read D?CK as "DUCK." Names create a perceptual set leading you to see D?CK as DICK. Yet another illustration of perceptual set appears in the "Do It Yourself!" box.

Did you see a woman committing suicide in the photo, entitled "The Moment before Death," on the previous page? Most people have difficulty identifying the falling woman in the center of the photo because of the confusing background and because they have no perceptual schema that makes them expect to see a person positioned horizontally in midair.

Perceptual set: Readiness to detect a particular stimulus in a given context.

DO IT YOURSELF!   You See What You're Set to See

Labels create a context that can impose a *perceptual set* for an ambiguous figure. Have a friend look carefully at the picture of the "young woman" in part A of the accompanying figure, and have another friend examine the "old woman" in part B. (Cover the other pictures while they do this.) Then, have them look together at part C. What do they see? Each will probably see something different, even though it's the same stimulus pattern. Prior exposure to the picture with a specific label will usually affect a person's perception of the ambiguous figure.

A. A Young Woman

B. An Old Woman

C. Now what do you see?

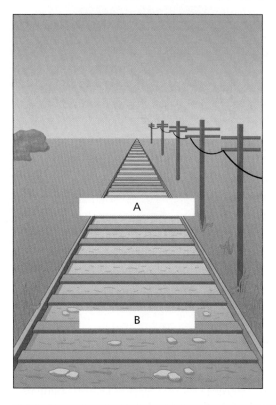

FIGURE 5.21: The Ponzo Illusion

The two white bars superimposed on the railroad track are actually identical in length. Because A appears farther away than B, we perceive it as longer.

People can also develop very different views of the same person when conditions have created different sets. For example, your perception of your psychology professor is probably quite different from that of someone who knows him or her primarily in a social setting. Likewise, context and perceptual set can influence attitudes toward groups of people. So, you can see that sets may underlie the social problem of prejudice. Those who have been taught that certain ethnic groups are cheap, stupid, athletic, dangerous, or musical may have developed perceptual sets that influence their attitudes and behaviors toward those groups.

Cultural Influences on Perception Cross-cultural psychologists have shown that the different everyday experiences of people in different cultures create differences in their perceptions (Deregowski, 1980; Segall, 1994; Segall et al., 1966). Consider, for example, the version of the famous Ponzo illusion seen in Figure 5.21. The question for respondents looking at this figure is: "Which line is longer, the one on top (marked A) or the one on the bottom (marked B)?"

In actuality, both lines are the same length. Research shows, however, that responses to these figures depend strongly on culture-related experiences. Many readers of this book will report that the top lines are longer than the bottom lines. People from certain other cultural backgrounds are not so easily fooled by the Ponzo illusion. Why the difference?

People learn to use a variety of cues in judging size and distance. In particular, the world you have grown up in probably included objects that

Connection

Chapter 14
Perceptual set is just one of many causes of prejudice.

appeared smaller as they moved farther away. In addition, you have probably seen many structures featuring parallel lines that seemed to converge in the distance: long buildings, airport runways, and tunnels. You may even have stood on a straight railroad track and mused how the rails seem to meet at a far-away point. Such learning experiences leave you vulnerable to images, such as the Ponzo illusion, in which cues for size and distance are unreliable.

But what about people from cultures where individuals have had far less experience with these distance cues? Research on this issue has been carried out on the Pacific island of Guam, where there are no Ponzo-like railroad tracks (Brislin, 1974, 1993). There, too, the roads there are so winding, that people have few opportunities to see roadsides "converge" in the distance. People who have spent their entire lives on Guam, then, presumably have fewer opportunities to learn the strong perceptual cue that converging lines indicate distance.

Just as researchers had predicted, adult respondents on Guam were found to be less susceptible to the Ponzo illusion than were respondents from the mainland United States. That is, they were less likely to report that the top line in the figure was longer. These results strongly support the argument that people's experiences affect their perceptions—as Helmholz had suggested.

THE GESTALT APPROACH   A contrasting view of perception arose in Germany in the 1920s. Known as **Gestalt psychology,** this view maintained that the brain is designed to seek patterns (called *Gestalts*). Moreover, they believed that some of these patterns are innate—built into the brain at birth by *nature.* Thus, the brain forms a "whole" percept that is more than just the sum of its sensory "parts" (Prinzmetal, 1995; Rock & Palmer, 1990). For example, we perceive a square as a single Gestalt, rather than merely four lines. Similarly, when you hear a familiar song, you do not focus on the exact duration and pitch of each of its notes. Rather, your brain is "wired" to extract the *melody,* which is your perception of the overall pattern of notes. Such examples, the Gestalt psychologists argued, show that we organize sensory information according to meaningful patterns, some of which are present in our brains at birth. Because this approach has been so influential, we will examine some of the Gestalt discoveries in detail.

Figure and Ground   One of the most basic of perceptual processes identified by Gestalt psychology divides a percept into *figure* and *ground*. A **figure** is a pattern, or Gestalt, that becomes the focus of attention. Everything else becomes **ground,** the backdrop against which we perceive the figure. Visually, the figure might be a word on the background of a page. In the ambiguous faces/vase seen in Figure 5.17A, the figure and ground reverse when the faces and vase alternatively "pop out" as figure. In a similar fashion, a melody becomes a figure heard against a background of complex harmonies.

Filling in the Blanks   Our minds seem to abhor a gap, as you can see in the Do It Yourself! box. Note especially the illusory white triangle—superimposed on red circles and black lines. Moreover, you will note that you have mentally divided the white area into two regions: the triangle and the background. Where this division occurs you perceive **subjective contours:** boundaries that exist not in the stimulus but only in the subjective experience of your mind.

Your perception of these triangles demonstrates another powerful organizing process identified by the Gestalt psychologists. **Closure** makes you see incomplete figures as complete and supplies the missing edges beyond gaps

Picasso's *Weeping Woman* shows separation of figure and ground. One of the techniques pioneered by Picasso was the portrayal of a figure simultaneously from multiple perspectives.

Gestalt psychology: A view of perception that originated in Germany. *Gestalt* is a German word (pronounced *gush-TAWLT*) that means "whole" or "form" or "configuration." The Gestaltists believed that much of perception is shaped by innate factors built into the brain.

Figure: The part of a pattern that commands attention. The figure stands out against the ground.

Ground: The part of a pattern that does not command attention; the background.

Subjective contours: Boundaries that are perceived but do not appear in the stimulus pattern.

Closure: The Gestalt principle that identifies the tendency to fill in gaps in figures and to see incomplete figures as complete.

The tendency to perceive a figure as being in *front* of a ground is strong. It is so strong, in fact, that you can even get this effect when the perceived figure doesn't actually exist! You can demonstrate this with an examination of the accompanying figure. You probably perceive a fir-tree shape against a ground of red circles on a white surface. But, of course, there is no fir-tree figure printed on the page; the figure consists only of three solid red shapes and a black-line base. You perceive the illusory white triangle in front because the wedge-cuts in the red circles seem to be the corners of a solid white triangle. To see an illusory six-pointed star, look at part B. Here, the nonexistent "top" triangle appears to blot out parts of red circles and a black-lined triangle, when in fact none of these is

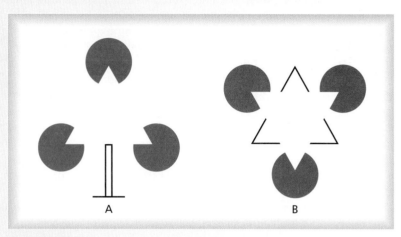

Subjective Contours

(A) A subjective fir tree; (B) a subjective 6-pointed star.

depicted as such complete figures. Again, this demonstrates that we prefer to see the figure as an object that obscures the ground. (That's why we often call the ground a *back*ground.)

and barriers. Similarly, when you see a face peeking around a corner, in your mind you automatically fill in the obscured parts of the face. In general, humans have a natural tendency to perceive stimuli as complete and balanced even when pieces are missing. (Does this ring a _____ with you?) Closure also fills in your "blind spot" (Ramachandran, 1992).

In the foregoing demonstrations we have seen how the perception of subjective contours and closure involves the brain's creation of percepts out of incomplete stimulation. Now let us turn to the Gestalt laws that explain how we group the stimulus elements that are actually present.

The Gestalt Laws of Perceptual Grouping   How does your visual system accomplish this *perceptual grouping,* the perception that separate stimulus elements "belong" together? Consider, for example, how you mentally connect the line segments down the center of a road into a perceived single line or how you put facial features together into a single percept of a face. Gestalt psychologist Max Wertheimer (1923) studied this problem by presenting subjects with arrays of simple geometric figures. By varying a single factor and observing how it affected the way people perceived the structure of the array, he was able to formulate a set of **laws of perceptual grouping**. Figure 5.22 shows three of these Gestalt principles.

According to the **law of similarity,** we group things together that have a similar look (sound, feel, etc.). So, when you watch a football game, you use the colors of the uniforms to group the players into two teams because of their similarity, even when they are mixed together during a play. Likewise, in Figure 5.22A you see that the Xs and Os form distinct columns, rather than rows,

Laws of perceptual grouping:
The Gestalt principles of *similarity, proximity, continuation,* and *common fate.* These ideas suggest how stimulus elements are grouped together perceptually.

Law of similarity: The Gestalt principle that we tend to group similar objects together in our perceptions.

FIGURE 5.22: Gestalt Principles of Perceptual Grouping

(A) similarity, (B) proximity (nearness), and (C) continuity. In (A) you most easily see the Xs grouped together, while Os form a separate Gestalt. So columns appear—not rows. The rows combine dissimilar elements and do not form patterns so easily. In (B) dissimilar elements easily group together when they are near each other. In (C), even though the lines cut each other into many discontinuous segments, it is easier to see just two lines—each of which appears to be continuous as a single line cutting through the figure.

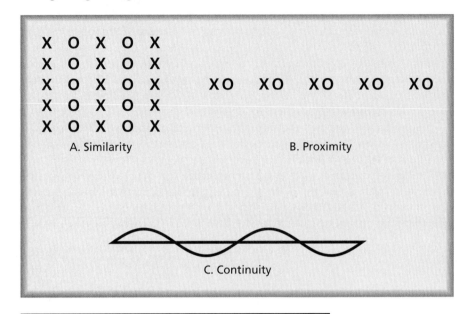

A. Similarity

B. Proximity

C. Continuity

The law of similarity helps us group together players wearing the same color of uniform.

because of similarity. Any such tendency to perceive things as belonging together because they share common features reflects the law of similarity. You can also hear the law of similarity echoed in the old proverb: "Birds of a feather flock together," which is a commentary not only on human and avian behavior but also on the assumptions we make about perceptual grouping.

Now, suppose that, on one drowsy morning, you mistakenly put on two different-colored socks because they were together in the drawer and you assumed that they were a pair. Your mistake was merely Wertheimer's **law of proximity** (nearness) at work. The proximity principle says that we group things together that are near each other, as you can see in the pairings of the Xs with the Os in Figure 5.22B. On the level of person perception, your parents were worried about the law of proximity when they cautioned you, "You're known by the company you keep."

The Gestalt **law of continuity** can be seen in Figure 5.22C, where the straight line is seen as a single, continuous line, even though it is cut repeatedly by the curved line. In general, the law of continuity says that we prefer smoothly connected and continuous figures to disjointed ones. Continuity also operates in the realm of person perception, where we commonly make the assumption of continuity in the personality of an individual whom we haven't seen for some time. So, we expect that he or she will remain essentially the same person we knew earlier.

There is yet another form of perceptual grouping that we cannot easily illustrate in the pages of a book because it involves motion. But you can easily

Law of proximity: The Gestalt principle that we tend to group objects together when they are near each other.

Law of continuity: The Gestalt principle that we prefer perceptions of connected and continuous figures to disconnected and disjointed ones.

FIGURE 5.23: We usually
see what we expect to see—not
what is really there. Look again.

A
BIRD
IN THE
THE HAND

Law of common fate: The Gestalt
principle that we tend to group
similar objects together that
share a common motion or
destination.

Law of Prägnanz: The most
general Gestalt principle, which
states that the simplest
organization, requiring the least
cognitive effort, will emerge as
the figure.

conjure up your own image that exemplifies the **law of common fate:** Imagine a gaggle of geese, a school of fish, or a marching band. When visual elements (the individual geese, fish, or band members) are moving together, you perceive them as a single Gestalt.

According to the Gestalt perspective, each of these examples of perceptual grouping illustrates the profound idea that our perceptions are influenced by innate patterns in the brain. These inborn mental patterns, then, in a top-down fashion, determine the organization of the individual parts of the percept. Moreover, the Gestalt psychologists suggested, all these grouping laws are particular examples of a more general principle — the **law of Prägnanz** ("meaningfulness"), which says that we will perceive the simplest possible pattern, requiring the least cognitive effort. The most general of all the Gestalt principles, Prägnanz (pronounced *PRAYG-nonce*) has also been called the *minimum principle of perception*. The law of Prägnanz is what makes proofreading so hard to do, as you will find when you examine Figure 5.23.

So, which of the two theories about perception that we have been discussing — Helmholtz's learning theory or the Gestaltists' innate theory — is correct? Both of them are. That is, our perceptual processes show the influence of both nature and nurture. While both emphasize top-down processes, Gestalt theory emphasizes that the brain is innately predisposed to influence perception in specific ways. But we can also say with confidence that perception is influenced by experience and learning, as Helmholtz's theory argues.

Seeing & Believing

Psychology

In Your Life

I f you assume, as most people do, that your senses give you an accurate and undistorted picture of the outside world, you are mistaken (Segall et al., 1990). Magicians, who base their careers on the difference between appearance and reality, count on people for whom "seeing is believing." You may have also noticed that politicians rely on influencing people's interpretations of events, too. So we hope that this chapter has shaken your faith in your senses and perceptions . . . just a bit.

Unlike magicians and politicians, perceptual psychologists are happy to reveal how sensation and perception play tricks on all of us (Hyman, 1989). They have developed a number of demonstrations that show how your vivid impressions of the world are really highly processed and interpreted images. We have already seen this in many visual illusions presented in the chapter. But, to drive the point home, consider this statement (which, unfortunately, was printed backwards):

.rat eht saw tac ehT

Please turn it around in your mind: What does it say? At first most people see a sensible sentence that says, "The cat saw the rat." But take another look. The difficulty lies in the power of expectations to shape your interpretation of stimulation.

This demonstration illustrates again that we don't merely *sense* the world as it is, we *perceive* it. The goal of the process by which stimulation becomes sensation and,

Magicians count on the difference between appearance and reality.

finally, perception is to find meaning in our experience. But it is well to remember that we impose our own meanings on sensory experience.

Differences in the ways we interpret our experiences explain why two people can look at the same sunset, the same presidential candidates, or the same religions and perceive them so differently. Perceptual differences make us unique individuals. An old Spanish proverb makes the point elegantly:

En este mundo traidor
No hay verdad ni mentira;
Todo es según el color
Del cristál con que se mira.

In this treacherous world
There is neither truth nor lie;
All is according to the color
Of the lens through which we spy.

CHECK**YOUR**UNDERSTANDING

1. **RECALL:** *Which of the following is an example of the kind of information that* top-down processing *contributes to perception?*
   a. seeing a face in a crowd and realizing it is a friend
   b. having to wait for your eyes to adjust to the dark in a theater
   c. hearing a painfully loud noise
   d. feeling a pinprick

2. **RECALL:** *The illusion in the Hermann grid (Figure 5.16) operates at the level of*
   a. stimulation.
   b. sensation.
   c. figure and ground.
   d. perception.

3. **RECALL:** *The Gestalt theory proposes that many of our perceptions are determined by*
   a. bottom-up factors.
   b. illusions.
   c. ambiguity.
   d. innate factors.

4. **RECALL:** *The faces/vase image (in Figure 5.17) illustrates*
   a. similarity.
   b. closure.
   c. figure and ground.
   d. attention as a gateway to consciousness.

5. **APPLICATION:** *When two close friends are talking, other people may not be able to follow their conversation because it has many gaps, which the friends can mentally fill in from their shared experience. Which Gestalt principle is illustrated by the friends' ability to fill in these conversational gaps?*
   a. similarity
   b. proximity
   c. closure
   d. common fate

6. **UNDERSTANDING THE CORE CONCEPT:**

   Which of the following best illustrates the idea that perception is not an exact internal copy of the external world?
   a. the sound of a familiar tune
   b. the Ponzo illusion
   c. a bright light
   d. jumping in response to a pinprick

ANSWERS: 1. a   2. b   3. d   4. c
5. c   6. b

Using Psychology to Learn Psychology: Studying for the Gestalt

One of the most mistaken notions about studying and learning is that students should set aside a certain amount of time for study every day. This is not to suggest that you shouldn't study regularly. Rather, it is to suggest that you shouldn't focus mainly on putting in your time. So where should you place your emphasis? (And what does this have to do with perceptual psychology?)

Recall the concept of *Gestalt,* the idea of the meaningful pattern, encountered earlier in this chapter. The Gestalt psychologists taught us that we have an innate tendency to understand our world in terms of meaning-ful patterns. Applied to your studying, this means that your emphasis should be on finding meaningful patterns — Gestalts — in your course work.

In this chapter, for example, you will find that your authors have helped you by dividing the material into three major sections. You can think of each section as a conceptual Gestalt, built around a Core Concept that ties it together and gives it meaning.

The psychological message is this: Organize your study around meaningful units of material. That is, identify a major concept or section of your book, and study that until it makes sense.

And forget about the clock.

Chapter Summary

HOW DOES STIMULATION BECOME SENSATION?

The most fundamental step in sensation transduces physical stimuli into neural events. Psychophysics has focused on identifying thresholds for sensations and for just-noticeable differences. A newer approach, signal detection theory, explains sensation as a process involving context, physical sensitivity, and judgment. Sensory adaptation occurs when the senses discontinue processing unchanging stimuli.

The brain senses the world indirectly because the sense organs convert stimulation into the language of the nervous system: neural impulses.

HOW ARE THE SENSES ALIKE? AND HOW ARE THEY DIFFERENT?

All the senses involve transduction of physical stimuli into nerve impulses. Vision and hearing have been the most thoroughly investigated by sensory psychologists. In vision, photoreceptors transduce light into neural codes, which are transmitted to the brain, where they become color sensations. In the ear, vibrations are transduced into neural energy and transmitted to the brain, where qualities of pitch and loudness are experienced. Other senses include position and movement (the vestibular and kinesthetic senses); smell; taste; the skin senses (touch, pressure, and temperature); and pain. Different sensations involve sensory processing by different regions of the brain.

Core Concept The senses all operate in much the same way, but each extracts different information and sends it to its own specialized sensory processing region in the brain.

Key Question

WHAT IS THE RELATIONSHIP BETWEEN PERCEPTION AND SENSATION?

Stimuli are organized and interpreted in stages that involve sensation, perceptual organization, and identification/recognition. We derive meaning from "bottom-up" stimulus cues and from "top-down" processes in the brain. By studying illusions, researchers can learn about the factors that influence and distort the construction of perceptions. Perception has been explained by theories that differ in their emphasis on the role of innate brain processes versus learning—nature versus nurture. Research has identified feature detector cells in the brain, but the "binding problem," or how the pieces of perception are finally bound together meaningfully, remains unsolved. We also know that certain organization processes in perception help us find meaning in sensation: to distinguish figure from ground, to identify contours and apply closure, and to group stimuli that are similar, near each other, or share a common fate. During identification and recognition, percepts are given learning-based meaning through processes involving context, expectation, perceptual set, and cultural and personal factors.

Core Concept Perception brings *meaning* to sensation, so perception produces an interpretation of the external world, not a perfect representation of it.

Review Test

For each of the following items, choose the single correct or best answer. The correct answers appear at the end.

1. What is the process that converts physical energy, such as sound waves, into neural impulses?
   a. sensory adaptation
   b. psychophysics
   c. kinesthesis
   d. transduction

2. Luisa agrees to look after her friends' new baby while they run an errand. Luisa tries to read with the stereo on, but keeps listening for signs that the baby might be crying in the bedroom. Several times, Luisa thinks she can hear whimpering—but when she checks the baby, she finds her still sound asleep. Which of the following best explains why Luisa is hearing imaginary cries?
   a. classical absolute threshold theory
   b. signal detection theory
   c. the law of Prägnanz
   d. Weber's law

3. Which of these sensory structures does *not* belong with the others?
   a. lens
   b. ganglion cells
   c. basilar membrane
   d. visual cortex

4. Place theory and frequency theory are explanations for processes involved in the sensation of
   a. the hue created by a light's wavelength.
   b. the timbre of sound.
   c. different olfactory stimuli.
   d. the pitch of sound.

5. Which one of the following is the only sense that does not relay information through the thalamus?
   a. olfaction
   b. kinesthesis
   c. the vestibular sense
   d. vision

6. At a crime scene, a detective finds a slip of paper with three symbols printed on it in ink. She cannot identify the source of the figures or which orientation is up. Thus she cannot determine if the figures are the numbers *771* or the letters *ILL*. Because she has to guess at the meaning of the figures, her perception of them is
   a. data-driven.
   b. stimulus-driven.
   c. bottom-up.
   d. top-down.

7. Which one of the following is most commonly experienced when a stimulus is ambiguous, information is missing, elements are combined in unusual ways, or familiar patterns are not apparent.
   a. an illusion
   b. common fate
   c. a false alarm
   d. a correct rejection

8. According to Gestalt explanations of how perceptual processes work, when a person encounters an unfamiliar collection of stimuli, he or she will try to
   a. judge whether each stimulus matches a familiar signal.
   b. assemble the parts into a meaningful whole or pattern that makes sense.
   c. analyze each stimulus component separately to ascertain its meaning.
   d. make guesses about its symbolism until finding a matching concept.

9. Research has shown that cultural factors can influence people's perception of
   a. distance.
   b. timbre.
   c. sensory adaptation.
   d. subliminal stimulation.

10. Although the markings in the ceiling tiles are of all different shapes and sizes, you notice that larger, darker spots seem to stand out against a background made up of smaller, lighter ones. Which principle of perceptual grouping explains this distinction?
    a. the law of similarity
    b. the law of proximity
    c. the law of common fate
    d. the principle of closure

ANSWERS: 1. d   2. b   3. c   4. d   5. a   6. d
7. a   8. b   9. a   10. a

If You're Interested . . .

BOOKS

Ackerman, D. (1990). *A natural history of the senses*. Vintage. Poet Diane Ackerman presents a collection of essays on smell, touch, taste, hearing, vision, and synesthesia (experiencing a sensation in the "wrong" sense, such as feeling a color or seeing a sound). The book is vivid and inspiring as well as informative.

Hogan, K. L. (1998). *Tinnitus: Turning the volume down: Proven strategies for quieting the noise in your head*. Network 3000. Ringing in the ears or "noise in the head" is a very real and surprisingly common affliction. This book seeks to reassure sufferers by explaining the origins of this haunting distraction and recommending therapies and treatments that have been increasingly found to relieve the suffering.

Jourdain, R. (1998). *Music, the brain, and ecstasy: How music captures our imagination*. Avon Books. The author, a composer himself, examines the nature of sound, music, the experience of making and listening to music, and its links with emotional appeal, satisfaction, mood, and happiness.

Myers, D. G. (2000). *A quiet world: Living with hearing loss*. Yale University Press. A social psychologist explores the pains and reflections of his own developing deafness through the changes in both his relationships and experiences. Your own hearing is just fine? Well, you probably have a relative or friend whom you'll understand and appreciate better after reading this short, perceptive book.

Ornstein, R. E. (1998). *On the experience of time*. Westview Press. Through a series of experiments, consciousness expert Robert Ornstein demonstrates how the human mind uses a variety of sensations and perceptions in order to construct an experience of past, present, and future.

Rodieck, R. W. (1998). *The first steps in seeing*. Sinauer Associates. The author, a neuroanatomist, is most fascinated with the structure and power of the human retina but deals with the broadest range of biochemical and physiological processes — and challenges — involved in normal vision, providing clear explanations of the "eyeshow" the eyes and brain produce, highlighted with gorgeous illustrations.

Sacks, O. (1998). *The island of the colorblind.* Vintage Books. The latest by the author of *The Man Who Mistook His Wife for a Hat* and *An Anthropologist on Mars,* this fascinating, touching, and funny book describes Sacks' journey to a small island in Micronesia, where all the residents are color blind—yet experience and describe their world with richness, vividness, and acceptance.

Valnet, J., & Tisserand, R. (Eds.). (1990). *The practice of aromatherapy: A classic compendium of plant medicines and their healing properties.* Beekman Publishing. How can natural aromas affect and even heal the body? As alternative therapies become more popular, it's worth taking a look at what is and is not yet known about smell, the most primitive and perhaps powerful sense, and the essences that stimulate it.

VIDEOS

Babette's Feast. (1987, color, 102 min., Danish). Directed by Gabriel Axel; starring Stéphane Audran, Jean-Philippe Lafont, Gudmar Wivesson, Jarl Kulle. This is a story of the pleasures of taste—and of producing those pleasures for others. A French woman working as a servant in 18th century Denmark wins a lottery, and instead of returning to France she uses her winnings to create an elaborate feast for her kindly but unworldly employers. If you don't eat before watching, this film could make you hungry!

Chocolat. (2000, color, 105 min., French). Directed by Lasse Hallstrm; starring Juliette Binoche, Alfred Molina, Judi Dench, Johnny Depp. The award-winning film is a feast not only for "chocaholics," but for anyone interested in how sensory pleasures are often feared and suppressed by controlling institutions and doctrines. A woman's dessert confections amaze and inspire her customers, while their sensory effects seem to threaten the local authorities.

Immortal Beloved. (1994, color, 125 min.). Directed by Bernard Rose; starring Gary Oldman, Jeroen Krabbe, Isabella Rossellini, Johanna Ter Steege. Ludwig van Beethoven's late-life deafness is perhaps explained in this musically rich biography, focusing on the question of the identity of the composer's great love. A few scenes are stunning both to watch and hear, a nice change from films with forgettable scores and soundtracks.

Rashomon. (1950, black-and-white, 88 min.; Japanese). Directed by Akira Kurosawa; starring Toshiro Mifune. A classic film by a master director, *Rashomon* tells the tale of a rape and murder from the perspectives of four very different witnesses, illustrating the intertwining of perception with motivation and emotion. What you see and remember is what you expect, based on your perception of the world—and of yourself.

WEB RESOURCES

http://depts.washington.edu/otoweb/ear_anatomy.html The Web site for the Department of Otolaryngology-Head and Neck Surgery provides a tour of the human ear, as well as description and images of various hearing conditions.

http://www.stlukeseye.com/anatomy.htm St. Luke's Cataract & Laser Institute presents various resources regarding visual anatomy and disease. Explore this site to learn about the details of perception.

http://www.exploratorium.edu/imagery/exhibits.html Visit this Web site for digital versions of Exploratorium exhibits. Think about what you have learned in this chapter in order to understand each of these exhibits.

HOW DOES CLASSICAL CONDITIONING EXPLAIN LEARNING?

The Essentials of Classical Conditioning

Applications of Classical Conditioning

Classical conditioning is a basic form of learning in which a stimulus that produces an innate reflex becomes associated with a neutral stimulus, which acquires the power to elicit the same response.

TASTE AVERSIONS AND CHEMOTHERAPY:
Your friend needs to avoid developing a food aversion when the medicine makes her feel sick.

HOW DO WE LEARN NEW BEHAVIORS BY OPERANT CONDITIONING?

Trial-and-Error Learning

Skinner's Radical Behaviorism

The Power of Reinforcement

The Problem of Punishment

Alternatives to Punishment

Operant and Classical Conditioning Compared

In operant conditioning, rewards and punishments are consequences that influence the likelihood of the behaviors they follow recurring in the future.

A CHECKLIST FOR MODIFYING OPERANT BEHAVIOR:
A combination of reinforcement and extinction is usually the best bet.

HOW DOES COGNITIVE PSYCHOLOGY EXPLAIN LEARNING?

Insight Learning: Köhler in the Canaries with the Chimps

Cognitive Maps: Tolman Finds Out What's on a Rat's Mind

Social Learning: Bandura's Challenge to Behaviorism

Rethinking Behavioral Learning in Cognitive Terms

Brain Mechanisms and Learning

"Higher" Cognitive Learning

According to cognitive psychology, some forms of learning must be explained as changes in mental processes, rather than as changes in behavior alone — but they can still be studied scientifically.

A CRITICAL LOOK AT "LEARNING STYLES":
Many claims are made for different learning styles, but the evidence supporting them is weak.

USING PSYCHOLOGY TO LEARN PSYCHOLOGY: Operant Conditioning Can Help You Study More — and Enjoy It

6

LEARNING

Sabra had just graduated from college with a degree in graphic arts and landed a good job at an advertising firm in San Francisco. The work was interesting and challenging, and Sabra enjoyed her new colleagues. The only negative was that her supervisor had asked her to attend an upcoming conference in Hawaii — and take an extra few days of vacation there at the company's expense. The problem was Sabra's fear of flying.

She hadn't had to deal with her fear previously because there was always an alternative. All her life, Sabra had lived close enough to family members that she could easily drive to see them for visits. And when she went away to college, it was only a 300-mile journey, so she could drive or take the train. But there was no other way to get to Hawaii (except by boat — which would be much too slow for commuting to a business conference). What was she to do?

A friend mentioned having seen an article in the newspaper about a program initiated by one of the airlines to help people overcome their fear of flying. Fortunately, Sabra had a few weeks before the conference started, so she contacted the airline and signed up for three weekend treatment sessions to be held at a local airport.

Sabra arrived at the appointed time, full of expectations and apprehensions — most of which turned out to be wrong.

(continued)

Would she have to see a therapist who would probe her childhood experiences and fantasies? Would they prescribe tranquilizers? Or would they give her some sort of terror-inducing treatment, such as flying upside-down in a small airplane?

In fact, the sessions were organized by a behavioral psychologist who gathered the nine participants in a small conference room. The therapist began by saying that such fears are learned—much as you might learn to cringe when you hear a dentist's drill or the scraping of fingernails on a blackboard. She said that it was not important how such fears got started. This fear-of-flying program would focus on the present, not on the past. Sabra began to feel more relaxed.

After a brief description of the learning-based therapy to be used, the group took a tour of the airport, including the cabin of a passenger jet parked on the tarmac. Then they went back to "class" to learn the basics of how airplanes work and the physical forces that allow them to fly. The group also watched some videos involving routine flights in a commercial airplane. All in all, these first sessions went smoothly, and everyone seemed much more at ease than when they started.

The second weekend began with more classroom discussion. Then, the class went back into the airliner, where they took seats and went through a series of relaxation exercises led by the therapist. This training included deep breathing and progressive relaxation of specific muscle groups all over the body. When everyone in the group reported feeling relaxed, they again watched videos of flight on the plane's TV monitors. This was followed by more relaxation exercises. The final activity for the second weekend involved starting the engines and going through the preflight routine—all the way up to take-off . . . and more relaxation exercises.

The final weekend session was almost identical to the previous one. The only difference was that the "graduation" exercise was an actual flight—a 20-minute trip in an airliner out over the local countryside and back to the airport. It was, of course, voluntary, and only one of the nine people in the class chose not to go. Sabra went, but not without some anxiety. The therapist, however, encouraged everyone to focus on the relaxation exercises they had learned, rather than on their feelings of fear. To the amazement of all who participated, these learning-based techniques helped them through the flight exercise without losing control of their emotional responses. Although no one's fear had vanished completely, everyone was able to bring it under control.

The happiest result was that Sabra was able to go to her meeting in Hawaii—where, by the way, she had a productive conference and a wonderful time. For our purposes we should also note that Sabra has flown several times since then, and she reports that each trip gets just a little easier—just as the psychology of learning would predict.

Learning: A lasting change in behavior or mental processes that results from experience.

What do we mean by *learning?* Psychologists would say that learning results from *experience*—our interaction with objects and events. In brief, we can define **learning** as a process through which experience produces a lasting change in behavior or mental processes. According to this definition, Sabra's "flight training" was learning—just as much as acquiring the skills to play the piano or studying medicine are learning experiences.

To avoid confusion, two aspects of our definition need some elaboration. First, we should emphasize that learning leads to a *lasting change*. Accordingly, a simple, reflexive response, such as jumping when you feel a painful prick by a needle, does *not* qualify as learning because it involves nothing more than a momentary reflex. But, suppose that you had gone to your doctor's office, and the sight of a needle had been associated with a painful injection. As a result of this experience, you might learn to wince at the mere glimpse of a hypodermic needle. This more enduring change in responding involves learning.

Second, our definition says that learning affects *behavior* or *mental processes*. In the example above, it is easy to see how learning affects behavior. Mental processes are more difficult to demonstrate because we cannot directly observe internal events. Because of this, a certain group of psychologists known as behaviorists avoid making inferences about mental processes that they cannot observe directly.

The problem of observing mental events underlies a controversy between the behaviorists and the cognitive psychologists that runs through this chapter. For over 100 years, the behaviorists have steadfastly maintained that psychology could be a true science only if it disregarded mental processes and focused exclusively on objective, observable stimuli and responses. On the other side of the issue, cognitive psychologists have contended that understanding learning requires some inferences about mental processes. In the following pages, we will see that both sides in this dispute have made important contributions to our understanding of learning.

So, what does learning—either behavioral or cognitive learning—do for us? Nearly everything we humans do, from working to playing to interacting with family and friends, involves learning. Without this ability we would have to rely entirely on reflexes and on the innate (inborn) behaviors that are often called "instincts." Instinctive behavior (more properly known as *species-typical behavior*) accounts for bird migrations, animal courtship rituals, and some human response patterns, such as nursing in the newborn. But complex learning represents an evolutionary advance over instincts because it allows quick adjustments to changing environments.

Some forms of learning can be quite simple. For example, if you live near a busy street, you may learn to ignore the sound of the traffic. This simplest of all forms of learning, known as **habituation,** involves learning *not* to respond to stimulation. It occurs in all animals that have nervous systems. Another relatively simple form of learning is most obvious in humans: a preference for stimuli to which we have been previously exposed. This **mere exposure effect** probably accounts for the effectiveness of much advertising (Terry, 2000; Zajonc, 1968, 2001).

Other kinds of learning can be much more complex. These include forming a connection between two stimuli—as when a factory worker associates the 12 o'clock whistle with lunch. We also learn to associate our actions with rewarding and punishing stimuli, such as praise or a reprimand from the boss. The first two sections of the chapter will deal with these two important forms of **behavioral learning,** known as *classical conditioning* and *operant conditioning*.

In the third section of the chapter, the focus shifts from outside to inside the organism—from behavioral learning to cognitive learning. Here we will see how people acquire new behaviors by insight and by imitating responses they have seen in others, as when using a product seen demonstrated on TV. We will also discuss the very complex type of learning involving the acquisition of concepts, such as those taught in your college classes. We will end on a practical note by considering how to use the psychology of learning to help you

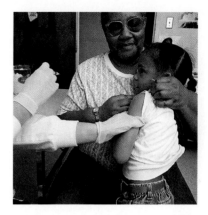

Aversive conditioning has occurred when the mere sight of an object, such as a hypodermic needle, causes an avoidance reaction.

Connection

Chapter 1
Behaviorism asserts that overt behavior is the only proper subject of study for psychology.

Connection

Chapter 9
Instincts are a form of motivated behavior that has a strong biological basis.

Habituation: Learning not to respond to the repeated presentation of a stimulus.

Mere exposure effect: A learned preference for stimuli to which we have been previously exposed.

Behavioral learning: Forms of learning, such as classical conditioning and operant conditioning, that can be described in terms of stimuli and responses.

Connection

Chapter 8
Concepts are mental categories that enable us to organize our knowledge.

To study classical conditioning, Pavlov placed his dogs in a restraining apparatus. The dogs were then presented with a neutral stimulus, such as a tone. Through its association with food, the neutral stimulus became a conditioned stimulus eliciting salivation.

study more effectively — and enjoy it. We begin, however, with a form of learning that accounts for many of your likes and dislikes.

HOW DOES CLASSICAL CONDITIONING EXPLAIN LEARNING?

Ivan Pavlov (1849–1936) would have been insulted if you had called him a psychologist. In fact, he had only contempt for the psychology of his time, which he saw as being hopelessly mired in speculation about subjective mental life (Todes, 1997). Pavlov and his associates (hundreds of student-researchers who passed through Pavlov's research "factory") were famous for their work on the digestive system, for which Pavlov eventually won a Nobel prize.

Unexpectedly, however, the experiments on salivation (the first step in digestion) went awry, sending Pavlov and his crew on a detour into the psychology of learning — a detour that occupied Pavlov for the rest of his life. During measurements of saliva produced by dogs while eating, the researchers noted that the animals began salivating even *before* food was put in their mouths (Dewsbury, 1997). In fact, saliva would start flowing when they saw the food or even when they heard the footsteps of the assistant bringing the food.

Classical conditioning: A form of behavioral learning in which a previously neutral stimulus (CS) acquires the power to elicit the same innate reflex produced by another stimulus.

This response was a puzzle. What, after all, was the function of salivating without food? When Pavlov and his associates turned their attention to understanding these "psychic secretions" they made a series of discoveries that would change the course of psychology (Pavlov, 1928; Todes, 1997). Quite by accident, they had stumbled on an objective model of *learning* — one that could be manipulated in the laboratory to tease out the connections among stimuli and responses. This discovery, now known as **classical conditioning**, forms the Core Concept of this section:

> Classical conditioning is a basic form of learning in which a stimulus that produces an innate reflex becomes associated with a neutral stimulus, which acquires the power to elicit the same response

In the following pages we will see that classical conditioning accounts for learning not only in animals but in people. By means of classical conditioning, organisms learn about cues that warn of danger, as well as cues alerting them to food, sexual opportunity, and other conditions that promote survival. First, however, let's examine some of the fundamental features of classical conditioning.

The Essentials of Classical Conditioning

It is important to note that Pavlov's work focused on simple, automatic responses known as reflexes (Windholz, 1997). Salivation, knee jerks, and eye blinks are examples of such reflexes: They are normally triggered by stimuli that have biological significance. The blinking reflex, for example, protects the eyes; the salivation reflex aids digestion. Pavlov's great discovery, however, was that these reflexive responses could be associated with new stimuli that had no apparent biological relevance. He could, for example, teach his dogs to salivate after hearing a certain sound, such as the tone produced by a tuning fork or a bell.

To understand how these "conditioned reflexes" worked, Pavlov's team employed a simple strategy. They first placed an untrained dog in a harness. Then, at intervals, a tone was sounded, and the dog was given a bit of food. The dog's first reaction to the tone was merely an *orienting response:* It pricked up its ears and turned its head (oriented) to locate the source of the novel sound. But with repeated pairings of the tone and the food, the orienting response stopped, and the dog began to salivate in response to the tone alone. In general, Pavlov found that a **neutral stimulus** (one without any natural eliciting power, such as a tone or a light), when paired with a reflex-producing stimulus (food), will come to elicit a learned response (salivation) that is similar to the original reflex.

The same kind of conditioning has occurred when you salivate at the mere sight of a pizza placed on the table before you. Likewise, classical conditioning has taught us to associate the smell of smoke with fire. It is also the process behind the association of romance with flowers or chocolate.

The main features of Pavlov's classical conditioning procedure are illustrated in Figure 6.1. At first glance, the terms may seem a bit intimidating. Nevertheless, it will help immensely to learn them now so that we can use them later to analyze real-life situations, such as the learning of fears, phobias, and aversions. Here we go . . .

ACQUISITION   Classical conditioning always begins with an **unconditioned stimulus (UCS)** — a stimulus that automatically activates a reflexive response. In Pavlov's experiments, food was the UCS because it provoked a salivation reflex. Therefore, salivation is called an *unconditioned reflex* or, more commonly, an **unconditioned response (UCR),** when it is elicited by the unconditioned stimulus. It is important to realize that there is *no learning* involved in the UCS–UCR connection.

During **acquisition** — the initial learning stage in classical conditioning — a neutral stimulus (a tone, for example) is repeatedly paired with the UCS. After several trials the neutral stimulus will elicit essentially the same response as does the UCS. Thus, in Pavlov's experiment, the tone produced salivation, so we say that this formerly neutral stimulus has become a **conditioned stimulus (CS).** The tone now has the power to elicit the same salivation response as the UCS. Although the response to the CS is essentially the same as the salivation response originally produced by the UCS, we now refer to it as the **conditioned response (CR).** (Look again at Figure 6.1 if this is confusing.)

A graph of the acquisition phase in a classical conditioning experiment appears in the first panel in Figure 6.2. Note that, at first, only weak responses are elicited by the CS. With continued CS–UCS pairings, however, the conditioned response increases in strength.

In conditioning, as in telling a joke, *timing* is critical. In most cases, the CS and UCS must be presented contiguously (close together in time) so that the organism can make the appropriate connection. The range of time intervals

Connection

Chapter 2
Reflexes are simple, innate responses to stimulation.

Neutral stimulus: Any stimulus that produces no conditioned response prior to learning.

Unconditioned stimulus (UCS): In classical conditioning, the stimulus that elicits an unconditioned response.

Unconditioned response (UCR): In classical conditioning, the response elicited by an unconditioned stimulus without prior learning.

Acquisition: The initial learning stage in classical conditioning, during which the conditioned response comes to be elicited by the conditioned stimulus.

Conditioned stimulus (CS): In classical conditioning, a previously neutral stimulus that comes to elicit the conditioned response.

Conditioned response (CR): In classical conditioning, a response elicited by a previously neutral stimulus that has become associated with the unconditioned stimulus.

FIGURE 6.1: Basic Features of Classical Conditioning

Before conditioning, the unconditioned stimulus (UCS) naturally elicits the unconditioned response (UCR). A neutral stimulus, such as a tone, has no eliciting effect. During conditioning, the neutral stimulus is paired with the UCS. Through its association with the UCS, the neutral stimulus becomes a conditioned stimulus (CS) and elicits a conditioned response (CR) that is similar to the UCR. (Gerrig & Zimbardo, 2002.)

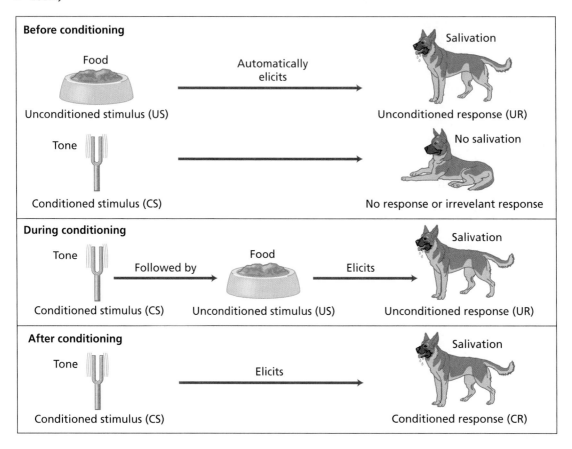

Before conditioning

Food — Automatically elicits → Salivation
Unconditioned stimulus (US) → Unconditioned response (UR)

Tone → No salivation
Conditioned stimulus (CS) → No response or irrevelant response

During conditioning

Tone — Followed by → Food — Elicits → Salivation
Conditioned stimulus (CS) Unconditioned stimulus (US) Unconditioned response (UR)

After conditioning

Tone — Elicits → Salivation
Conditioned stimulus (CS) → Conditioned response (CR)

Connection

Chapter 2
Motor responses involve the skeletal muscles, which move the body.

between the CS and UCS that will produce the best conditioning depends on the response being conditioned. For motor responses, such as eye blinks, a short interval of a second or less is best. For visceral responses, such as heart rate and salivation, longer intervals of 5 to 15 seconds work best. Conditioned fear, which we will discuss below, optimally requires longer intervals of many seconds or even minutes to develop.

These, then, are the building blocks of classical conditioning: the CS, UCS, CR, UCR, and the timing that connects them. So, why did it take Pavlov three decades and 532 experiments to study such a simple phenomenon? There was more to classical conditioning than first met Pavlov's eyes. Along with *acquisition,* he discovered the processes of *extinction, spontaneous recovery, generalization,* and *discrimination.*

EXTINCTION AND SPONTANEOUS RECOVERY Suppose you have learned —by classical conditioning—to fear spiders or to salivate at the sound of the lunch bell. Do such conditioned responses have to remain permanently in your behavioral repertoire? Experiments by Pavlov's group suggested that they do

FIGURE 6.2: Acquisition, Extinction, and Spontaneous Recovery

During acquisition (CS + UCS), the strength of the CR increases rapidly. During extinction, when the UCS no longer follows the CS, the strength of the CR drops to zero. The CR may reappear after a brief rest period, even when the UCS is still not presented; only the CS alone appears. The reappearance of the CR is called "spontaneous recovery."

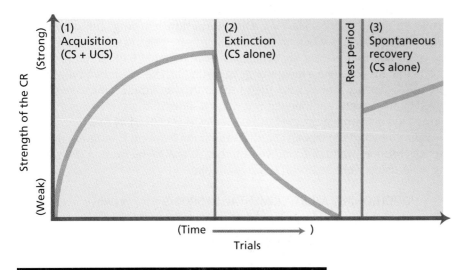

not. Conditioned responses in dogs were easily eliminated by withholding the UCS (food) over several trials in which the CS (the tone) was presented alone. In the language of classical conditioning this is called **extinction**. It occurs when a conditioned response is eliminated by repeated presentations of the CS without the UCS. Figure 6.2 shows how the CR (salivation) becomes weaker and weaker during extinction trials.

Now for the bad news: Even if your fear of spiders has been extinguished, it may reappear some time later when you happen to see a spider crawling across your desk. Pavlov used the term **spontaneous recovery** for this later reappearance of the CR after extinction. Fortunately, the CR reappears at a lower intensity, as you can see in Figure 6.2. Some cases require several extinction sessions before an unwanted response comes under satisfactory control.

The occurrence of spontaneous recovery tells us that extinction does *not* involve a complete elimination of the response from the organism's behavioral repertoire. Rather, extinction causes a *suppression* of the conditioned response. What actually seems to be happening during extinction is the learning of a competing response *not to respond* to the CS.

GENERALIZATION If you fear spiders, you will probably respond the same way to spiders of all sizes and markings. This is called **stimulus generalization,** a process that becomes evident when you give a conditioned response to stimuli that are similar to the CS. Pavlov demonstrated generalization in his laboratory by showing that a well-trained dog would respond to a bell that makes a sound slightly different from the one he had used during conditioning. Naturally, the closer the sound of the new bell was to the original, the stronger the response.

In everyday life, generalization is common in people who have acquired fears as a result of traumatic events. Accordingly, a person who has been bit-

Extinction: In learning, the weakening of a conditioned association in the absence of an unconditioned stimulus or a reinforcer.

Spontaneous recovery: The reappearance of an extinguished conditioned response after a time delay.

Stimulus generalization: The extension of a learned response to stimuli that are similar to the conditioned stimulus.

ten by a dog may develop a fear of dogs in general, rather than a fear only of the dog responsible for the attack. Likewise, generalization accounts for an allergy sufferer's sneeze upon seeing a paper flower. In short, by means of stimulus generalization we learn to apply old reflexes in new situations.

DISCRIMINATION   Although you may have learned to salivate at the sound of the lunch bell, you probably don't drool when the doorbell rings — thanks to *discrimination learning*. **Discrimination learning,** the opposite of generalization, occurs when an organism learns to respond to one stimulus but not to stimuli that are similar. This was demonstrated experimentally when Pavlov and his colleagues taught dogs to distinguish between two tones of different frequencies. Once again, their procedure was simple: One tone was followed by food, while another was not. Over a series of trials, the dogs gradually learned the discrimination, evidenced in salivation elicited by one tone and not the other. Beyond the laboratory, discrimination learning is found in our preferences for one brand of food over another. It is also involved in the continuing advertising battle between Pepsi and Coke.

CONDITIONING AN EXPERIMENTAL NEUROSIS   If you have ever had a class in which you couldn't guess what the teacher wanted, you have faced a vexing problem in discrimination learning. In a laboratory version of this, Pavlov confronted dogs with the task of discriminating between a circle and an ellipse. The task was especially stressful because one stimulus was always paired with food and the other was always paired with a painful electric shock. Over a series of trials, Pavlov gradually changed the ellipse to become more and more circular. And how did the dog respond? As the discrimination became increasingly difficult, the dog's responses grew more erratic. Finally, as the animal grew more confused between the circle and the ellipse, it began snarling and snapping at its handlers. Because such agitated responses resemble behavior of "neurotic" people who become irritable and defensive when they have difficult choices to make, this behavior pattern was dubbed **experimental neurosis.**

Applications of Classical Conditioning

The beauty in classical conditioning is that it offers a simple explanation for many adaptive behaviors across a wide range of species — from the simplest animals to humans. But it is more than an explanation: It also provides us the tools for modifying behaviors. Let's see how this works, beginning with the conditioning of distastes and aversions.

Pavlov's use of food in conditioning his dogs is an example of *appetitive conditioning*. There is, however, another form of classical conditioning that involves an unpleasant or *aversive* UCS, such as a painful electric shock. **Aversive conditioning** occurs when the CS signals the occurrence of an aversive UCS. The typical response is a defensive reflex. For example, you may have seen a child who has had to swallow some bitter-tasting medicine (a UCS) grimace at the sight of the medicine bottle (a CS). Aversive conditioning is also what happens in people who have learned to faint at the sight of blood, which has become a CS.

In aversive conditioning, the organism typically learns a specific conditioned muscle response, such as flinching or crying. It also learns a generalized fear reaction that involves the autonomic nervous system, which governs such internal responses as heart rate and respiration. These changes, both internal and external, become part of an overall conditioned fear response caused by

Discrimination learning: A change in responses to one stimulus but not to stimuli that are similar.

Experimental neurosis: A pattern of erratic behavior resulting from a demanding discrimination learning task, typically one that involves aversive stimuli.

Aversive conditioning: A type of classical conditioning in which the conditioned stimulus predicts the occurrence of an aversive or unpleasant unconditioned stimulus.

Connection

Chapter 2
The autonomic nervous system controls internal organs and glands.

aversive conditioning. Such responses can be easily produced, as was shown in a notorious experiment performed on a young boy named Albert.

THE FAMOUS CASE OF LITTLE ALBERT   Conditioned fear was demonstrated experimentally by John Watson and Rosalie Rayner over 80 years ago. In an experiment that would be considered unethical today, Watson and Rayner (1920/2000) conditioned an infant named Albert to react fearfully to a white laboratory rat. They created Albert's fear by repeatedly presenting the rat paired with an aversive UCS—the loud sound of a steel bar struck with a mallet just behind the child's head. It took only seven trials for "Little Albert" to react with fear at the appearance of the rat (CS) alone. After Albert's response to the rat had become well established, Watson and Rayner showed that his fear readily *generalized* from the rat to other furry objects, such as a Santa Claus mask worn by Watson (Harris, 1979).

Most likely, the experiment caused Little Albert only temporary distress because his fear faded rapidly. In fact, Watson and Rayner found it necessary to strengthen the child's response periodically. This need to recondition Albert threatened the whole experiment when, after five days, Watson and Rayner were attempting to show that Albert's fear could be generalized to a dog, a rabbit, and sealskin coat. Watson decided to "freshen the reaction to the rat" by again striking the steel bar. The noise startled the dog, which began to bark at Albert, scaring both experimenters and their hapless subject (Harris, 1979).

Unlike Little Albert's short-lived aversion to furry objects, some fears learned under extreme conditions can persist for years (LeDoux, 1996). Many sailors were exposed to such conditions during World War II, when the signal used to call them to battle stations was a gong sounding at the rate of 100 rings a minute. For combat personnel aboard ship, this sound was strongly associated with danger—a CS for emotional arousal. The persistent effect of this learning was shown in a study conducted 15 years after the war: Navy veterans who had experienced combat still gave a strong autonomic reaction to the old "call to battle stations" (Edwards & Acker, 1962).

Like those veterans, we may also retain a learned readiness to respond to old emotional cues. Fortunately, however, classical conditioning provides some tools for dealing with conditioned fears (Wolpe & Plaud, 1997). The best therapeutic strategy combines extinction of the conditioned fear response with a conditioning of a relaxation response to the CS. This counterconditioning therapy teaches patients to respond in a relaxed manner to the CS. The technique has been particularly effective in dealing with phobias. It was also part of the treatment used to help Sabra conquer her fear of flying.

CONDITIONED TASTE AVERSIONS   As young children, all three of your authors had bad experiences with specific foods. One of us got sick after eating pork and beans in the grade-school lunchroom. Another developed nausea after eating apple fritters. The third became ill after overdosing on olives. In all three cases, we associated our distress with the distinctive sight, smell, and taste of the food—but not to anything else in our environment. Subsequently, the very smell or appearance of the "culprit" food set off reactions of nausea and avoidance.

Unpleasant as it is, learning to avoid a food associated with illness has real survival value. Humans and many other animals readily form an association between illness and food—much more readily than between illness and a nonfood stimulus, such as a light or a tone. Moreover, while most forms of classical conditioning require a short delay between the CS and the UCS, food aversions are an exception. They can develop when a distinctive taste has been

John Watson and Rosalie Rayner conditioned Little Albert to fear furry objects like this Santa Claus mask (*Discovering Psychology*, 1990).

Connection

Chapter 13
Counterconditioning is a behavior therapy, based on classical conditioning, that is used to treat fears and phobias.

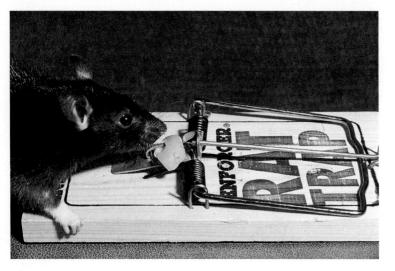

Bait shyness has survival value.

separated by *hours* from the onset of illness. "Must have been something I ate!" we say.

This tendency to connect illness specifically with food seems to run deep. In fact, the tendency for **taste-aversion learning** appears to be a part of our genetic endowment. The peculiar nature of taste aversions, however, has caused us to revise some details of Pavlov's original theory of classical conditioning.

A CHALLENGE TO PAVLOV The problem that conditioned taste aversions pose for classical conditioning is that they are not entirely *learned.* As we have noted, they also seem to require an *innate* disposition to connect the taste of a novel food with a sensation of illness. When an organism acquires a taste aversion, most of the other stimuli present (such as a light or a book on the table) are not conditioned to be avoided. Only those involving taste seem to become conditioned stimuli. We see this, for example, in rats that easily learn an association between the flavor of the bait and a later illness, although they do *not* learn to associate the flavor with a simultaneous pain. Similarly, rats readily learn to associate sound and light cues with a shock-produced pain but do not connect light or sound cues with illness (see Figure 6.3). This probably makes "sense" to the rat's brain, because evolutionary pressure has programmed it to know that illness can follow drinking and pain can follow an event involving light and noise. Taken together, such results suggest that organisms have an inborn preparedness to associate particular stimuli with particular consequences, while other CS–UCS combinations are highly resistant to learning (Garcia & Koelling, 1966).

Connection

Chapter 12
Common fears and phobias may result from a biological predisposition, known as *preparedness.*

FIGURE 6.3: Inborn Tendency to Associate Certain Cues with Certain Consequences

Rats possess an inborn bias to learn that certain cues predict certain outcomes. Rats avoided saccharine-flavored water when it predicted illness, but not when it predicted shock. They avoided the "bright-noisy" water when it predicted shock, but not when it predicted illness (Garcia & Koelling, 1966).

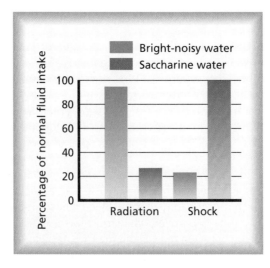

Taste-aversion learning: A biological tendency in which an organism learns, after a single experience, to avoid a food with a certain taste, if eating it is followed by illness.

CONDITIONING COYOTES The principles behind conditioned food aversion have been applied to practical problems in the world outside the laboratory. For example, John Garcia and his colleagues demonstrated that aversive conditioning can dissuade wild coyotes from attacking sheep. The researchers did so by wrapping toxic lamb burgers in sheepskins and stashing them on sheep ranches. When roaming coyotes found and ate these morsels, they became sick and—as predicted—developed a distaste for lamb meat, which resulted in a 30 to 50% reduction in sheep attacks. So powerful was this aversion that, when captured and placed in a cage with a sheep, conditioned coyotes would not get close to it. Some even vomited at the sight of a sheep (Garcia, 1990). Although field trials have demonstrated the effectiveness of aversive conditioning for combating coyote predation on livestock, scientists have been unable to modify the behavior of sheep ranchers—who apparently have a strong aversion to feeding lamb to coyotes!

So, what is the big lesson of taste aversions for our understanding of classical conditioning? Conditioning depends not only on the relationship among stimuli and responses but also on the way an organism is genetically predisposed toward stimuli in its environment (Barker et al., 1978). This is a concept that Pavlov didn't understand. What any organism can—and cannot—learn in a given setting is to some extent a product of its evolutionary history (Garcia, 1993).

Psychology

In Your Life

Taste Aversions and Chemotherapy

I magine that your friend Jena is about to undergo her first round of chemotherapy, just to make sure that any stray cells from the tumor found in her breast will be destroyed. To her surprise, the nurse enters the lab, not with the expected syringe, but with a dish of licorice-flavored ice cream. "Is this a new kind of therapy?" she asks. The nurse replies that it is, indeed. She explains that most patients who undergo chemotherapy experience nausea, which can make them "go off their feed" and quit eating, just when their body needs nourishment to fight the disease. "But," says the nurse, "We have found a way around the problem. If we give patients some unusual food before their chemotherapy, they will usually develop an aversion only to

that food." She continued, "Did you ever hear of Pavlov's dogs?"

Cancer patients like Jena often develop aversions to normal foods in their diets to such an extent that they become anorectic and malnourished. The aversions are conditioned responses in which food (the CS) becomes associated with nausea. The problem is aggravated when chemotherapy treatments, which produce the nausea, are administered right after meals. Therapists trained to understand classical conditioning use their knowledge to prevent the development of aversions to nutritive foods by arranging for meals not to be given just before the chemotherapy. And, as in Jena's case, they also present a "scapegoat" stimulus. Thus, patients are given candies or ice cream with unusual flavors before the treatments so that the taste aversion becomes conditioned only to those special flavors. For some patients,

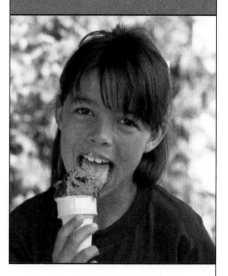

If this child gets sick tonight she may develop a taste aversion to this unusual flavor of ice cream.

this practical solution to problems with chemotherapy may make the difference between life and death (Bernstein, 1988, 1991).

1. **RECALL:** *Classical conditioning is especially useful for understanding which one of the following examples of learning?*

   a. a dog that has learned to "sit up" for a food reward

   b. a psychology student who is learning how memory works

   c. a child who, after a painful dental visit, has learned to fear the dentist

   d. an executive who is afraid that she will lose her job

2. **RECALL:** *The responses in classical conditioning were originally*

   a. innate reflexes.

   b. new behaviors.

   c. premeditated behaviors.

   d. random acts.

3. **APPLICATION:** *If you learned to fear electrical outlets after getting a painful shock, what would be the CS?*

   a. the electrical outlet

   b. the painful shock

   c. the fear

   d. the time period between seeing the outlet and getting the shock

4. **UNDERSTANDING THE CORE CONCEPT:**

   Which of the following would be most likely to be an unconditioned stimulus (UCS) involved in classical conditioning?

   a. food

   b. a flashing light

   c. music

   d. money

ANSWERS: 1. c   2. a   3. a   4. a

HOW DO WE LEARN NEW BEHAVIORS BY OPERANT CONDITIONING?

With classical conditioning you can teach a dog to salivate, but you can't teach it to sit up or roll over. Why? Salivation is a passive, involuntary reflex, while sitting up and rolling over are much more complex behaviors, controlled by rewards—which had no role in classical conditioning. The process at work is another important form of learning called *operant conditioning.*

In **operant conditioning,** behavior change is brought about by consequences that are of significance to the organism—especially rewards and punishments. Accordingly, operant conditioning affects all of our voluntary behavior. The Core Concept of this section puts this notion more succinctly:

> **In operant conditioning, rewards and punishments are consequences that influence the likelihood of the behaviors they follow recurring in the future**

Rewarding consequences that come readily to mind include money, praise, food, or high grades—all of which can encourage the behaviors they follow. By contrast, punishments such as pain, loss of privileges, or low grades can discourage the behaviors with which they are associated.

The notion of operant conditioning is a powerful one for at least two reasons. First, operant conditioning involves a much wider spectrum of behavior than does classical conditioning. And second, it accounts for new and complex behaviors—not just innate reflexes. The germ of this idea implanted itself a century ago in the mind of Edward Thorndike.

Operant conditioning: A form of behavioral learning in which the probability of a responses is changed by its consequences — that is, by the stimuli that follow the response.

To get out of the puzzle box and obtain food, Thorndike's cat had to manipulate a mechanism to release a weight that would then pull the door open. (Gerrig & Zimbardo, 2002.)

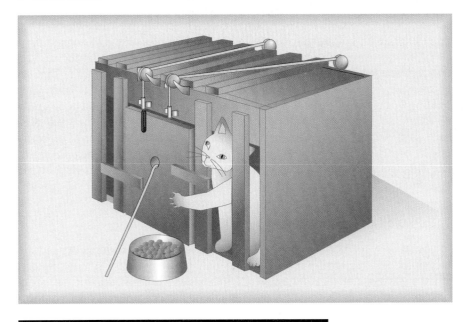

Taking aspirin for pain usually results in negative reinforcement, because the pain diminishes.

Trial-and-Error Learning

At about the same time that Pavlov was conditioning Russian dogs to salivate at the sound of a tone, Edward L. Thorndike (1898/1998) was watching American cats learn to escape from "puzzle boxes" (see Figure 6.4). Unlike Pavlov's dogs, Thorndike's cats faced a problem: how to open the door in the puzzle box to get a food reward lying just outside. To solve this problem, his cats used **trial-and-error learning,** rather than simple reflexes. The consequences of their responses altered their subsequent behavior. You can see this in Thorndike's description of a typical experiment:

> The cat that is clawing all over the box in [its] impulsive struggle will probably claw the string or loop or button so as to open the door. And gradually . . . the particular impulse leading to the successful act will be *stamped in* by the resulting pleasure. . . . (Thorndike, 1898, p. 13).

Thorndike was a careful scientist who based his theories on observations of animal learning (Galef, 1998), but he believed that the laws he discovered applied equally to human learning. His ideas had a major impact on the field of educational psychology, particularly on the notion of "transfer of training." Contrary to the prevailing view of the time, Thorndike's work suggested that learning one subject (such as music) has little carryover effect on a person's ability to learn an unrelated subject (such as English grammar).

Skinner's Radical Behaviorism

Thorndike's successor, B. F. Skinner, also embraced the view that environmental consequences influence the responses that preceded them. However, when Skinner changed his college major from English to psychology he also

Trial-and-error learning: An operant form of learning, described by Thorndike, in which the learner gradually discovers the correct response by attempting many behaviors and noting which ones produce the desired consequences.

B. F. Skinner is shown reinforcing the animal's behavior in an operant chamber, or "Skinner box." The apparatus allows the experimenter to control all the stimuli in the animal's environment.

rejected as subjective and unscientific any speculation about an organism's feelings, intentions, or goals. What an animal "wanted" or the "pleasure" it felt were not important for an objective understanding of the animal's behavior. As a radical behaviorist in the tradition of John Watson, Skinner refused to hypothesize about what happens inside an organism. Such speculation cannot be verified by observation. For example, eating can be observed, but we can't observe the inner experiences of hunger, the desire for food, or pleasure at eating.

Skinner called his system "operant conditioning" because it focused on *operant responses*. An **operant** is an observable, voluntary behavior that an organism emits to "operate" or have an effect on the environment. Thus, your reading this book is an operant behavior if you are doing so to get a good grade on the next test. (Compare this with Pavlov's emphasis on *involuntary* reflexes, such as salivation.) Again, the main feature of operant conditioning lies in the effects of *consequences* of behavior, especially in the forms of *reinforcement* and *punishment*. In large measure, operant conditioning is a theory built on the foundation Thorndike had laid.

The Power of Reinforcement

In casual conversation we often speak of "reward," but Skinner preferred the more precise term **reinforcer.** By this he meant any condition that follows and *strengthens* a response. Food, money, and sex serve this function for most people. So do attention, praise, or a smile. All these are examples of **positive reinforcement,** which strengthens a response by being *presented* after the response. But there is another type of reinforcement that involves the *removal* of an *aversive* stimulus, such as a toothache. Psychologists call this **negative reinforcement.** (Incidentally, "negative" here means *subtract* or *remove;* "positive" means *add* or *apply*.) Using an umbrella to avoid getting wet during a downpour is a behavior learned and maintained by negative reinforcement. That is, you use the umbrella to avoid or remove an unpleasant stimulus (getting wet). Likewise, when a driver buckles the seat belt, negative reinforcement occurs as the annoying sound of the seat-belt buzzer stops. Remember, it is the "subtraction" of the unpleasant sound that provides negative reinforcement.

REINFORCING TECHNOLOGY: THE "SKINNER BOX" One of B. F. Skinner's (1956) most important innovations was a simple technique for studying the effects of reinforcers on laboratory animals. As he was conducting a lengthy experiment that involved rats running down an alley for a food reward, he tired of retrieving them and putting them back at the start of the alley for each new trial. Eventually, it occurred to Skinner that it was unnecessary for the rats to go down the alley to obtain their reward. Instead, he let the rats remain in a single place and devise a task they could perform there to earn their food. Based on this inspiration, he invented a box with a lever that an animal could press to obtain food, and the *operant chamber* or **Skinner box** was born. Since that time, the Skinner box has been used by thousands of psychologists to study the effects of reinforcement — and, as we shall see, the effects of punishment, as well.

Incidentally, Skinner devised a unique baby crib for his daughter, Deborah (Benjamin & Nielsen-Gammon, 1999). The device was an enclosed, temperature-controlled box, which unfortunately bore a superficial resemblance to the operant chambers used in his experiments. The public learned about the "baby tender" from an article by Skinner in the magazine *Ladies' Home Journal.* Many readers (and also people who did *not* read the article) came to wildly erroneous conclusions involving child neglect and heartless experimentation. In later years, stories arose about Deborah's supposed psychotic breakdown,

Operant: An observable, voluntary behavior that an organism emits to "operate" or have an effect on the environment.

Reinforcer: A condition (involving either the presentation or removal of a stimulus) that occurs after a response and strengthens the response.

Positive reinforcement: A stimulus presented after a response that increases the probability of that response happening again.

Negative reinforcement: The removal of an unpleasant or aversive stimulus, contingent upon a particular behavior. Compare with *punishment*.

Skinner box: An operant chamber that can be programmed to deliver reinforcers and punishers contingent on an animal's behavior.

suicide, and lawsuits against her father — none of which were true. In fact, Deborah grew up to be a well-adjusted individual who loved her parents.

PRIMARY AND SECONDARY REINFORCERS   You can't eat money or drink it. So, why does money act as a reinforcer for most people? It is easier to see why stimuli that fulfill basic biological needs or desires will provide reinforcement: Food reinforces a hungry animal, and water reinforces a thirsty one. Similarly, the opportunity for sex becomes a reinforcer for a sexually aroused organism. Psychologists call such stimuli **primary reinforcers.**

On the other hand, neutral stimuli that are associated with primary reinforcers may also acquire a reinforcing effect and become **conditioned reinforcers** or **secondary reinforcers** for operant responses. And that's where money enters the picture. Similarly with grades, praise, smiles of approval, gold stars, and various kinds of status symbols: All are among the numerous conditioned reinforcers that influence our actions. Virtually any stimulus can become a secondary or conditioned reinforcer by being paired with a primary reinforcer. With strong conditioning, secondary reinforcers such as money, status, or awards can even come to be ends in themselves.

The power of conditioned reinforcers has been exploited in mental institutions that have set up so-called token economies to encourage desirable and healthy patient behaviors. Under a token economy, grooming or taking medication, for example, may be reinforced by plastic tokens given by the staff when patients perform these desired behaviors. The tokens can later be exchanged by patients for a wide array of rewards and privileges (Ayllon & Azrin, 1965; Holden, 1978). As an adjunct to other forms of therapy, token economies can help mental patients learn useful strategies for acting effectively in the world (Kazdin, 1994).

CONTINGENCIES OF REINFORCEMENT   College and university students are reinforced for their studying with grade reports two or three times a year. That's too long between reinforcers for most people to maintain their academic behavior — which is why professors schedule exams and papers periodically throughout their courses. They want to encourage continual studying, rather than one big push at the end of the semester.

To a behavioral psychologist it's all a matter of operant conditioning and especially of the frequency, timing, and number of rewards. How often will reinforcement be given? How much work is needed to earn a reinforcer? Will every response be reinforced — or will reinforcement occur only after a certain number of responses? These are the important questions we will pose in our discussion of **reinforcement contingencies,** the many possible connections between responses and reinforcers. As you will see, the answers to these questions determine the behavior patterns of organisms, from laboratory rats to students and their professors.

CONTINUOUS VS. INTERMITTENT REINFORCEMENT   Suppose you want to teach your dog a trick — say, sitting up on command. It would be a good idea to begin the training program with a reward for every correct response. Psychologists call this **continuous reinforcement.** It's a useful tactic early in the learning process because continuous reinforcement gives feedback on how well each response was performed. Your failure to reward a correct response on one trial could easily be misinterpreted as a signal that the response was not correct. Likewise, continuous reinforcement is useful for *shaping* complex new behaviors, such as playing a musical instrument, because it provides feedback telling the learner when performance has improved. In general, we can say

Primary reinforcers: Reinforcers, such as food and sex, that have an innate basis because of their biological value to an organism.

Conditioned reinforcers or **secondary reinforcers:** Stimuli, such as tokens or money, that acquire their reinforcing power by a learned association with primary reinforcers.

Reinforcement contingencies: Relationships between a response and the changes in stimulation that follow the response.

Continuous reinforcement: A type of reinforcement schedule by which all correct responses are reinforced.

Connection

Chapter 13
"Token economies" are a form of behavioral therapy based on operant conditioning.

Chimpanzees will work for conditioned reinforcers. Here a chimp has earned plastic tokens, which it is depositing in a "chimp-o-mat" to obtain raisins, a primary reinforcer.

Parents can use reinforcement contingencies to affect children's behavior.

Intermittent reinforcement: A type of reinforcement schedule by which some, but not all, correct responses are reinforced; also called partial reinforcement.

Extinction: In operant conditioning, a process by which a response that has been learned is weakened by the absence or removal of reinforcement. (Compare with extinction in classical conditioning.)

Schedules of reinforcement: Programs for the timing and frequency of reinforcements.

that continuous reinforcement is the best method for teaching and learning new behaviors.

But once your dog's sitting-up habit is well established, the learning demands of the situation change. The dog no longer needs rewards to discriminate a correct response from an incorrect one. Now is the time to shift to **intermittent reinforcement,** also called *partial reinforcement.* A less frequent schedule of reward—perhaps, after every third correct response—can still serve as an incentive to maintain the behavior. In brief, intermittent reinforcement—the rewarding of some, but not all, responses—is the most efficient way to maintain behaviors that have already been learned (Robbins, 1971; Terry, 2000). This is true for several reasons.

First, a reward for each response may actually take time away from responding. It would be impractical to pay a worker on the assembly line for each correctly placed bolt. Nor could you pay a data-entry clerk for each keystroke. Efficiency dictates waiting until a reasonable block or *chain* of behaviors has occurred. For most employees, this means waiting at least until the end of the week; for a grade-school child the wait may be only until an assignment is completed.

A second reason for the efficiency of intermittent reinforcement lies in its economy. It simply costs less to reward some of the responses rather than all of them. In addition, if you can make the reinforcements unpredictable, the subject often becomes more excited, active, and responsive. As a result, you get an increase in the amount of responding without having to increase the amount of reinforcement. Naturally, labor unions resist management attempts to take advantage of workers by instituting "stretch out" partial reinforcement schemes that would require more work for less pay. These apprehensions also lie behind labor-management clashes over "merit pay" systems.

A third advantage of intermittent reinforcement comes from the resistance to **extinction** that it induces. Under operant conditioning, extinction causes responding to cease as a result of withholding reinforcement. So, why

Continuous reinforcement is useful for *training* animals, but intermittent reinforcement is better for *maintaining* their learned behaviors.

do responses strengthened by partial reinforcement resist extinction much more strongly than do responses that have been rewarded continuously? Imagine two gamblers and two slot machines. One machine inexplicably pays off on every trial and another, a more usual machine, pays on an unpredictable, intermittent schedule. Now, suppose that both devices suddenly stop paying. Which gambler will catch on first? The one who has been rewarded for each pull of the lever (continuous reinforcement) will quickly notice the change, while the gambler who has won only occasionally (on partial reinforcement) may continue playing unrewarded for a long while.

SCHEDULES OF REINFORCEMENT   Now that you are convinced of the power of intermittent reinforcement, you should know that it comes in two main forms or **schedules of reinforcement** (so-called because they describe the contingencies that an experimenter might use to "schedule" the delivery of reinforcers). A **ratio schedule** rewards a subject after a certain *number of responses*. The other, known as an **interval schedule,** provides a reward after a certain *time interval.* Each has its advantages and disadvantages (see Figure 6.5).

Ratio Schedules   If you pay your employees based on the amount of work they perform, you are using a ratio schedule of reinforcement. Ratio schedules occur any time you dispense rewards *based on the number of responses.* Psychologists distinguish between two kinds of ratio schedules: *fixed ratio* and *variable ratio* schedules.

Fixed ratio (FR) schedules are common in industry, where workers are paid on a piecework basis. Suppose that you have a golf ball factory, and you pay your workers a dollar for every ten cartons of golf balls they manufacture; you are using a fixed ratio schedule. Under such a schedule the amount of work (the number of responses) needed for a reward remains constant. Managers like FR schedules because the rate of responding is usually high (Whyte, 1972; Terry, 2000).

Variable ratio (VR) schedules are less predictable. Telemarketers—people who make sales pitches by telephone—work on a VR schedule: They never know how many phone calls they must make before they get the next sale. Slot machine players also respond on a VR schedule. In both cases the variable ratio schedule keeps responses coming at a high rate—so high, in fact, that the VR schedule usually produces more responding than any other schedule of reinforcement. In the laboratory, Skinner demonstrated that a variable ratio schedule could entice a hungry pigeon to peck a disk 12,000 times an hour for rewards given, on the average, for every 110 pecks.

Interval Schedules   On an interval schedule, reinforcement is based on responding after a certain *amount of time has elapsed* since the last reinforcement (instead of on the number of responses given). (See Figure 6.5.) Psychologists distinguish two kinds of interval schedules: *fixed interval* and *variable interval* schedules.

Fixed interval (FI) schedules can produce a monthly paycheck, reward the wait for a train, or reinforce studying for a weekly quiz. On an FI schedule, the time period between rewards remains constant. You may have already guessed that fixed interval reinforcement usually results in a low rate of responding. Ironically, this is the schedule most widely adopted by business. Even a rat in a Skinner box programmed for a fixed interval schedule soon learns that it must produce only a limited amount of work during the interval in order to get its reward. Lever presses beyond the required minimum are just wasted energy.

Both rats and humans on a fixed interval schedule may display only modest productivity until near the end of the interval, when the response rate

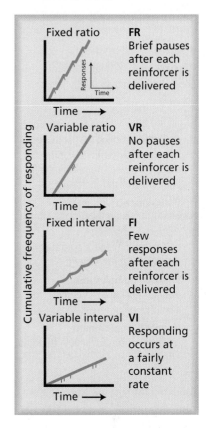

FIGURE 6.5:   Reinforcement Schedules

These different patterns of behavior are produced by four simple schedules of reinforcement. The hash marks indicate when reinforcement is delivered. (Gerrig & Zimbardo, 2002.)

Ratio schedule: A program by which reinforcement depends on the number of correct responses.

Interval schedule: A program by which reinforcement depends on the time interval elapsed since the last reinforcement.

Fixed ratio (FR) schedules: Programs by which reinforcement is contingent upon a certain, unvarying number of responses.

Variable ratio (VR) schedules: Reinforcement programs by which the number of responses required for a reinforcement varies from trial to trial.

Fixed interval (FI) schedules: Programs by which reinforcement is contingent upon a certain, fixed time period.

What schedule of reinforcement encourages this man to buy lottery tickets?

Variable interval (VI) schedules: Programs by which the time period between reinforcements varies from trial to trial.

Punishment: An aversive stimulus which, occurring after a response, diminishes the strength of that response. (Compare with *negative reinforcement*.)

Positive punishment: The *application* of an aversive stimulus after a response.

Negative punishment: The *removal* of an attractive stimulus after a response.

Foods that many people around the world enjoy may not be a source of reinforcement for the typical North American.

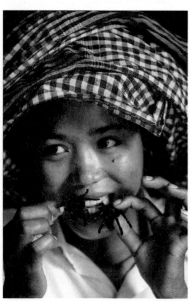

increases rapidly. (Think of college students facing a term paper deadline.) Graphically, in Figure 6.5 you can see the "scalloped" pattern of behavior that results from this flurry of activity near the end of each interval.

Variable interval (VI) schedules are, perhaps, the most unpredictable of all reinforcement schedules. On a VI schedule, the time interval between rewards varies. The resulting rate of responding can be high. For a pigeon or a rat in a Skinner box, it may be a 30-second interval now, 3 minutes next, and a 1-minute wait later. On the job, random visits by the boss (who may deliver reinforcement in the form of praise) occur on a variable interval schedule. Fishing represents still another example: You never know how long it will be before the fish start biting again, but the occasional, unpredictable fish delivers reward enough to encourage fishing behavior over long intervals. And, while waiting for an elevator, it is fun to note which of your companions presses the button as if on a VI schedule.

REINFORCEMENT ACROSS CULTURES   The laws of operant learning apply to all animals with a brain. The biological process underlying reinforcement is, apparently, the same across species. On the other hand, what serves as a reinforcer varies wildly. Experience suggests that food for a hungry organism and water for a thirsty one will act as reinforcers because they satisfy basic needs related to survival. But exactly what will satisfy those needs may depend as much on learning as on survival instincts—especially in humans, where secondary reinforcement is so important. For us, culture plays a powerful role in determining what will act as reinforcers. Accordingly, some people would find eating a cricket reinforcing, while most people of European ancestry would not. Disposing of a noisy cricket might seem both sensible and rewarding to a Baptist and aversive to a Buddhist. And, watching a game of cricket would be rewarding to a British fan—although punishingly dull to most Americans.

While culture shapes preferences in reinforcement, reinforcement also shapes culture. When you first walk down a street in a foreign city, all the differences that catch your eye are merely different ways that people have found to seek reinforcement or avoid punishment. A temple houses cultural attempts to seek rewards from the gods. Clothing may reflect attempts to seek a reinforcing mate or to feel comfortable in the climate. A culture's cuisine evolves from learning to survive on the native plants and animals. Learning shapes all aspects of culture. In this sense, culture is an enduring set of *learned* behaviors shared by a group of people.

The Problem of Punishment

Punishment is a tricky means of influencing behavior, as schoolteachers and prison wardens will attest. In some respects punishment is the opposite of reinforcement: It is an *aversive* consequence that *weakens* the behavior it follows. And, like reinforcement, punishment comes in two main forms. One, called **positive punishment,** requires the *application* of an aversive stimulus—as, when you touch a hot plate, the pain punishes you and reduces the likelihood of your repeating that behavior. The other main form of punishment, known as **negative punishment,** results from the *removal* of a *reinforcer*—as when parents take away a misbehaving teen's car keys.

Unlike reinforcement, however, punishment must be administered consistently. Intermittent punishment is far less effective than punishment delivered after every undesired response. In fact, *not punishing* an occurrence of unwanted behavior can have the effect of rewarding it—as when a supervisor overlooks the late arrival of an employee.

Calvin and Hobbes

by Bill Watterson

Calvin & Hobbes by Bill Watterson/Universal Press Syndicate

The probability of someone making another response can be decreased if the first response is followed by an aversive consequence, such as a loud noise or angry complaint.

PUNISHMENT VS. NEGATIVE REINFORCEMENT You have probably noted that punishment and negative reinforcement both involve unpleasant stimuli. So, to avoid confusion, let's see how they differ, using the following examples. Suppose that an animal in a Skinner box can turn off a loud noise by pressing a lever: This provides negative reinforcement. Compare that with an animal for in which the loud noise serves as a punishment for pressing the lever. (See Figure 6.6.)

Please note that punishment and negative reinforcement have opposite effects on behavior (Baum, 1994). Punishment *decreases* a behavior or reduces its probability of recurring. In contrast, negative reinforcement—like positive reinforcement—always *increases* a response's probability of occurring again.

You will remember that the descriptors "positive" and "negative" mean "add" and "remove." Thus, both positive reinforcement and positive punishment involve administering or "adding" a stimulus. On the other hand, negative reinforcement and negative punishment always involve withholding or removing a stimulus. See Table 6.1 for a summary of the distinctions between positive and negative reinforcement and punishment.

THE USES AND ABUSES OF PUNISHMENT Our society relies heavily on punishment and the threat of punishment to keep people "in line." We put peo-

▌ FIGURE 6.6: Negative Reinforcement and Punishment Compared

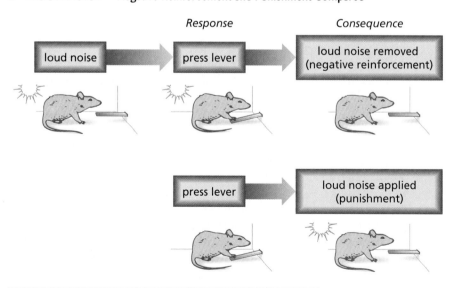

TABLE 6.1 *Four Kinds of Consequences*

	WHAT'S THE CONSEQUENCE?	
	APPLY (ADD) STIMULUS (POSITIVE)	**REMOVE (SUBTRACT) STIMULUS (NEGATIVE)**
The probability of the behavior increases	**Positive reinforcement** *Example:* An employee is given a bonus for good work — and continues to work hard.	**Negative reinforcement** *Example:* Your headache disappears after taking aspirin — so you take aspirin again the next time you have a headache.
The probability of the behavior decreases	**Positive Punishment** *Example:* A speeder is given a traffic ticket — and drives away more slowly.	**Negative Punishment** *Example:* A child who has stayed out late misses dinner — and comes home early next time.

What's the effect of the consequence on behavior?

Three important points to keep in mind as you study this table:

1. "Positive" and "negative" mean that a stimulus (consequence) has been added (presented) or subtracted (removed). These terms have nothing to do with "good" or "bad."

2. We can often predict what effect a particular consequence will have. But the only way to know for sure whether it will be a reinforcer or a punisher is to observe its effect on behavior. For example, we might guess that a spanking would punish a child, but it might actually serve as a reinforcer to strengthen the unwanted behavior.

3. From a cognitive viewpoint, we can see that reinforcement consists of the presentation of a pleasant stimulus or the removal of an unpleasant one. Similarly, punishment entails the presentation of an unpleasant stimulus or the removal of a pleasant one.

ple in jail, fine them, spank them, and give them bad grades, parking tickets, and disapproving looks. And what is the result? Punishment often produces an immediate change in behavior, which is reinforcing to the punisher and a major reason why the use of punishment is so widespread. Several other factors also encourage a punishment habit. For one, punishers may feel good while delivering the punishment, sensing that they are "settling a score" or "getting even" or "making the other person pay." This is why we speak of revenge (a form of punishment) as being "sweet." Completing the vicious circle, these rewards then encourage the use of more punishment. Yet, punishment often doesn't work as well as we would like. Punished children continue to misbehave, reprimanded employees still arrive late for work, and, in the United States, we are sending convicted criminals to prison in numbers that far exceed those of any other Western democracy. Why is punishment so difficult to use effectively? There are several reasons.

First, *the power of punishment to suppress behavior usually disappears when the threat of punishment is removed* (Skinner, 1953). Drivers will observe the speed limit when they know the highway patrol is watching. Johnny will refrain from hitting his little brother when his parents are within earshot. And you will probably give up your wallet to a mugger who puts a gun to your head. That is, most people will comply with a demand accompanied by the threat of strong and certain punishment, but they may act quite differently when they know punishment is unlikely. This explains why motorists rarely slow down for "construction speed" signs on the highways; they know that the police rarely enforce these zones. In general, you can be certain of controlling someone's behavior through punishment or threat of punishment only if you can control the environment all of the time. Such total control is usually not possible, even in a prison.

Second, *punishment often triggers aggression*. When punished, organisms usually seek to flee from further punishment. But if all escape is blocked, they may become aggressive. Corner a wounded animal, and it may savagely attack you. Put two rats in a Skinner box with an electrified floor grid, and the rats will attack each other (Ulrich & Azrin, 1962). Put humans in a harsh prison environment, and they may riot. Further, in a punitive environment, whether it be a prison, a school, or a home, people learn that punishment and aggression are legitimate means of influencing others (Bongiovanni, 1977; Hyman, in Schmidt, 1987). The punishment–aggression link also explains why abusing parents so often come from abusive families and why aggressive delinquents so often come from homes where aggressive behavior toward the children is commonplace (Straus & Gelles, 1980). Unfortunately, the well-documented fact that punishment often leads to aggression remains widely unknown to the general public.

An organism being punished relentlessly may eventually give up its attempts at flight or fight — overwhelmed by a sense of hopelessness. The passive acceptance of a punitive fate is a behavior pattern called *learned helplessness* (Overmier & Seligman, 1967). In people, this reaction can produce the clinical problem known as depression (Terry, 2000).

A third reason why punishment is so often ineffective is that *punishment makes the learner apprehensive, which inhibits learning new and better responses*. Whether it produces escape, aggression, or learned helplessness, punishment focuses learners on their own misery — which interferes with new learning. It also fails to help learners see what *to do* because it focuses attention on what *not to do*. By contrast, individuals who have not been punished feel much freer to experiment with new behaviors.

Fourth, *punishment is often applied unequally*. Boys are punished more often than girls. Children, especially grade-school children, receive more physical punishment than do adults. Our schools (and probably our society at large) more often use punishment to control members of racial minority groups than they do to control members of the Caucasian majority (Hyman, 1996; Hyman et al., 1977).

DOES PUNISHMENT EVER WORK?   In limited circumstances, punishment works remarkably well. For example, punishment can halt the self-destructive behavior of some disturbed children who attempt to injure themselves severely by banging their heads or chewing the flesh off their fingers. In these cases, an electric shock or a splash of cold water in the face can quickly end such acts (Lovaas, 1977; Lovaas et al., 1974).

In general, if punishment is to be effective and its undesirable effects minimized, it should meet the following conditions (Walters & Grusec, 1977):

▶ Punishment should be swift and brief; a delay will decrease its effectiveness.

▶ Punishment should be certain, administered every time the unwanted response occurs. (When it fails to occur, the effect can be rewarding.)

▶ Punishment should be limited in duration and intensity — just enough to stop the behavior.

Prison riots and other aggressive behavior may result from highly punitive conditions.

Connection

Chapter 16
Inescapable punishment can cause *learned helplessness* and *depression*.

- Punishment should clearly target the *behavior*, not the character of the person.
- Punishment should be limited to the situation in which the response occurred.
- Punishment should not give mixed messages to the punished person (e.g., "You are not permitted to hit others, but I am allowed to hit you").
- The most effective punishment is usually *negative* punishment, consisting of penalties (such as loss of privileges) rather than the application of unpleasant stimuli, such as pain.

It is widely accepted in many cultures that punishment is not only necessary but actually necessary for character: "Spare the rod and spoil the child" (not a quote from the Bible, incidentally). Many times, however, people resort to punishment because they can think of no alternative.

Alternatives to Punishment

What does psychology have to offer in lieu of punishment? Operant conditioning suggests several options. We begin with one possibility that has a counterpart in classical conditioning.

EXTINCTION   As we have seen, a response will usually diminish or disappear if it ceases to produce the rewards it once did—that is, it will be *extinguished.* The effect on behavior is the same as we saw in the extinction of a classically conditioned response, but the process is slightly different. Suppose that you have encouraged a professor to make eye contact with you during lecture. Smiling and nodding are behaviors you can use to reinforce your professor's tendency to look at you. Now, once you have the desired behavior well established, you can put the professor on extinction. It's simple: Merely withhold reinforcement by stopping your smiling, nodding, and eye contact. (Don't try this in your psychology class!)

Extinction does not always require deliberate human intervention. For example, if a light switch in your classroom stops working, people will eventually stop flipping the switch as they enter the room. Or, perhaps you have had the experience of dropping money into a vending machine only to get nothing in return. If you kicked the machine and your soda or candy came out, kicking would be reinforced. However, if your kicking produced no soda, candy, or satisfaction, this useless response would soon be extinguished.

For a response to be effectively extinguished, all possible reinforcers must be withheld. In real life this can be harder than you might think. Beyond the control of the laboratory, many stimuli may strengthen or maintain a particular behavior. (Mere attention to a misbehavior can reinforce it.) A parent, teacher, or work supervisor may not be able to identify easily—much less control—all the reinforcers that maintain an unwanted response. Research has also shown that, during extinction, organisms will begin searching for novel strategies to obtain reinforcement (Carpenter, 2001). This means that a parent who stops attending to a child's whining should be ready for the child to change tactics or redouble efforts to regain attention before the behavior is finally extinguished.

For these reasons, real-life extinction outside the laboratory is more likely to take effect when it can be combined with positive reinforcement of a desirable response. So, a child who throws public tantrums to get your attention is more likely to stop the misbehavior if (a) the rewarding attention is withheld (operant extinction) and (b) more desirable behaviors are rewarded with attention and social approval before the tantrum occurs.

REINFORCING PREFERRED ACTIVITIES   The opportunity for certain activities can reinforce behavior just as effectively as food or drink or other primary reinforcers. For example, people who work out regularly might use a daily run or fitness class as a reward for getting other tasks done. Likewise, teachers have found that young children will learn to sit still if that behavior is reinforced with occasional permission to run around and make noise (Homme et al., 1963).

The principle at work here says that a preferred (more frequent) activity, such as running around and making noise, can be used to reinforce a less preferred (less frequent) one, such as sitting still. Psychologists call this the **Premack principle,** after its discoverer, David Premack (1965). He first demonstrated this in water-deprived rats, which learned to increase their running in an exercise wheel when the running was followed by an opportunity to drink. Other rats that were not thirsty, but were exercise-deprived, learned to increase their drinking when that response was followed by a chance to run in the wheel.

Parents and teachers often use the Premack principle to get children to engage in low-probability behavior. For a shy child, the opportunity to read a new book could be used to reinforce the less-frequent (or less-preferred) activity of playing with other children. The preferred activity, used as a reinforcer, increases the probability that the individual will engage in an activity that is less preferred. Over time, the less-favored activities may even become more valued as exposure to them leads individuals to discover their intrinsic worth. The once-shy child might eventually enjoy playing with others and no longer require the promise of a preferred activity to reinforce social interaction.

PROMPTING AND SHAPING   A problem encountered by many behavior analysts is the difficulty of getting the organism to begin performing the desired behavior so that it can be reinforced. Suppose you want to train your dog to roll over on command. Must you wait and watch until the moment finally arrives when the dog spontaneously rolls over? Chances are you will wait a long time for your dog to come up with such a specific sequence of actions on its own. A more efficient option is **prompting** the animal by cuing it or moving it into the desired initial position and **shaping** its behavior by giving reinforcement in steps that get closer and closer to what you want. When shaping begins, any approximation of the target response is reinforced. Once this approximate response occurs regularly, you can make the criterion for reinforcement more strict. Eventually, only responses that are very close to perfect are reinforced. By rewarding more and more specific approximations to the target behavior, a trainer can shape responses quickly and efficiently.

Shaping is of interest to those who would influence human behavior, as well as animal behavior. As you will recall from our chapter-opening vignette, Sabra's behavior was gradually prompted and shaped by the therapist to help her overcome the fear of flying. In fact, we often wish to get other people to make responses that might not appear spontaneously. Perhaps you can think of ways that a teacher might use shaping and prompting to encourage class participation by students who don't usually offer answers or opinions.

Operant and Classical Conditioning Compared

The diagrams in Figure 6.7 show a comparison of operant and classical conditioning, each in its simplest form. Most obviously, you can see that the *consequences* of behavior — rewards and punishments — make operant conditioning different from classical conditioning. In the diagram, a bone rewards the dog for sitting up. Note, however, that the food presented to the dog in the classi-

Animals can learn to do surprising things, with a little help from operant conditioning techniques, such as prompting and shaping.

Premack principle: The concept, developed by David Premack, that a more-preferred activity can be used to reinforce a less-preferred activity.

Prompting: Cuing a response in such a way that the subject knows what response is required. Prompting often involves touching or manipulating a body part to be moved in the desired response or modeling a part of the response.

Shaping: An operant learning technique in which a new behavior is produced by reinforcing responses that approach the desired performance.

FIGURE 6.7: Classical Conditioning and Operant Conditioning Compared

Note that classical conditioning involves the association of two stimuli that occur *before* the response. Operant conditioning involves a reinforcing (rewarding) or punishing stimulus that occurs *after* the response.

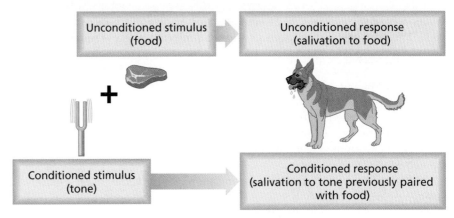

| Unconditioned stimulus (food) | → | Unconditioned response (salivation to food) |

+

| Conditioned stimulus (tone) | → | Conditioned response (salivation to tone previously paired with food) |

Classical Conditioning

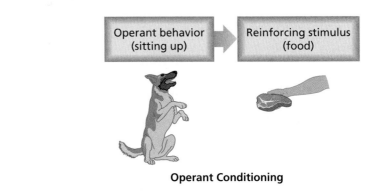

| Operant behavior (sitting up) | → | Reinforcing stimulus (food) |

Operant Conditioning

cal conditioning portion of Figure 6.7 comes *before* the response. Therefore it cannot serve as a reward.

Rewards are especially effective in enticing people to perform a wide variety of *new behaviors* — pulling slot machine levers, making beds, brushing teeth, going to work, or studying for an exam. Classical conditioning, on the other hand, emphasizes giving the *same responses* to *new stimuli* — such as salivating at the sound of a bell or flinching at the sound of a dentist's drill.

Aside from rewards and punishments, operant conditioning and classical conditioning differ in several other important ways. For one, operant behavior is not based on an automatic reflex action, as was the dog's salivation or Little Albert's crying. Accordingly, operant behavior seems more "voluntary" — more under the control of the responder. To paraphrase a proverb: You can stimulate a dog to salivation (a reflex), but you can't make it eat (an operant behavior). In the same sense, when you walk by the ice cream store you can decide whether to stop and treat yourself (an operant behavior), but when you inhale ground pepper you cannot decide against sneezing (a reflex).

Yet another difference between classical conditioning and operant conditioning involves the sequence of stimulus and response. Classically con-

Temper tantrums will last only as long as the child thinks that such displays will be rewarded.

ditioned behavior is largely a response to *past stimulation,* while operant behavior is often directed at attaining some *future condition* (a reinforcer) — or avoiding a punishment. To say it another way, operant conditioning requires a stimulus that follows the response, whereas classical conditioning ends with the response. (See Figure 6.8.)

But don't make the mistake of thinking that classical and operant conditioning are competing explanations of learning. They can be complementary. Frequently, responses that were originally learned by classical conditioning will be maintained by operant conditioning. How might this happen? Consider a

FIGURE 6.8: Classical and Operant Conditioning Can Work Together

A response originally learned through classical conditioning can be maintained and strengthened by operant reinforcement.

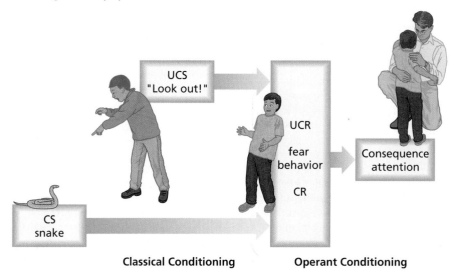

Classical Conditioning   Operant Conditioning

snake phobia. Suppose that the fear of snakes was originally learned by classical conditioning when a snake (CS) was paired with a frightening UCS (someone yelling, "Look out!"). Then, once it was established, the phobic response could be maintained and strengthened by operant conditioning when bystanders give attention to the fearful person (Figure 6.8). In the same fashion, the attention one of your authors gets from refusing to eat olives undoubtedly encourages the dislike of them that was originally learned by classical conditioning.

A Checklist for Modifying Operant Behavior

Psychology In Your Life

Think of someone whose behavior you would like to change. For the sake of illustration, let's assume that you would like to change your nephew Johnny's temper tantrums, which always seem to occur when you take him in public. Operant conditioning offers a variety of tools that can help, provided you have some control over stimuli that are important to Johnny. Let's consider a checklist of these operant tools: positive reinforcement, punishment, negative reinforcement, and extinction.

▶ *Positive reinforcement* is a good bet, especially if you can find some desirable behavior to reinforce before the unwanted behavior occurs. Remember that attention is a powerful reinforcer. If Johnny has not been getting enough attention otherwise, he may produce a tantrum just for the attention.

▶ *Punishment* may be tempting, but it is always chancy. Unfortunately, as we have seen, it usually has a bad effect on the relationship between punisher and the person being punished. It is also dangerous because, unlike positive reinforcement, punishment must be done with unfailing consistency: If you do decide to punish Johnny, do so swiftly, certainly, and without undue harshness. As we said earlier, restriction or loss of privileges is usually far more effective than physical punishment.

▶ *Negative reinforcement* has many of the same drawbacks as punishment because it involves unpleasant stimulation. Parents may try — most often unsuccessfully — to use negative reinforcement as a means of encouraging unlikely behavior that they value (doing homework, taking out the garbage, feeding the dog). In its most common form, the parents nag (an aversive stimulus) their children until the desired behavior occurs, whereupon the nagging presumably stops (negative reinforcement). This tactic rarely works to anyone's satisfaction. Nor is this approach well suited to temper tantrums or any other situation in which one person is trying to alter another's behavior. Negative reinforcement does work well, however, in situations where the aversive conditions were imposed by natural, impersonal conditions — as when taking aspirin removes the aversive stimulus of your headache.

▶ *Extinction* is a guaranteed solution, but only if you control all the reinforcers. In Johnny's case, extinction simply means not giving in to the temper tantrum and not letting him have what he wants (attention, candy, going home). Allow the tantrum to burn itself out. This may be embarrassing for you because children often pick the most public places for such displays — a good sign that they are doing so for attention. The big problem with extinction, however, is that it may take a long time, so extinction is not a good option if the subject is engaging in dangerous behavior, such as playing in a busy street.

The best approach — often recommended by child psychologists — is to use a combination of tactics. Usually they will recommend both reinforcing Johnny's desirable behaviors and extinguishing the undesirable responses.

We recommend memorizing the four items on this checklist: positive reinforcement, punishment, negative reinforcement, and extinction. Whenever you are dealing with someone whose behavior is undesirable, go through the list and see if one or more of these operant tactics will do the trick. And remember: The behavior you may want to change could be your own!

1. **RECALL:** *Thorndike said that animals will learn by trial and error to perform responses that are*
   a. rewarded.
   b. reflexive.
   c. prompted.
   d. preceded by a neutral stimulus.

2. **APPLICATION:** *Which one of the following is an example of* negative reinforcement?
   a. going to the dentist and having a toothache relieved
   b. spanking a child for swearing
   c. taking away a child's favorite toy when the child misbehaves
   d. making a child watch while another child is punished

3. **APPLICATION:** *Suppose that you have taught your dog to roll over for the reward of a dog biscuit. Then, one day you run out of dog biscuits. Which schedule of reinforcement would keep your dog responding longer without a biscuit?*

   a. continuous reinforcement
   b. partial reinforcement
   c. negative reinforcement
   d. noncontingent reinforcement

4. **RECALL:** *Which one of the following is a conditioned reinforcer for most people?*
   a. money
   b. food
   c. sex
   d. a sharp pain in the back

5. **UNDERSTANDING THE CORE CONCEPT:** *Operant conditioning, in contrast with classical conditioning, emphasizes events (such as rewards and punishments) that occur*
   a. before the behavior.
   b. after the behavior.
   c. during the behavior.
   d. at the same time as another stimulus.

ANSWERS: 1. a   2. a   3. b   4. a   5. b

HOW DOES COGNITIVE PSYCHOLOGY EXPLAIN LEARNING?

Key Question

According to J. D. Watson's (1968) account in *The Double Helix*, the genetic code was cracked one day in a flash of insight following months of trial and error. You may have had a similar, if less famous, experience when solving a problem. Such events present difficulties for behavioral learning because they are hard to explain in terms of Pavlovian reflexes or Skinnerian shaping.

Insightful experiences have suggested to some psychologists that another form of learning is at work: *cognitive* learning. According to cognitive psychology, learning does not always cause changes in behavior, but it does produce changes in mental activity. Moreover, this view suggests that such cognitive changes can be examined objectively. As the Core Concept for this section says:

> **According to cognitive psychology, some forms of learning must be explained as changes in mental processes, rather than as changes in behavior alone – but they can still be studied scientifically**

Core Concept

Let's see how this task has been approached.

Insight Learning: Köhler in the Canaries with the Chimps

Marooned in the Canary Islands during World War I, Gestalt psychologist Wolfgang Köhler (KER-ler) brooded about learning. He was convinced that Thorndike's puzzle box was too artificial and restrictive to allow anything other than blind, trial-and- error guessing. And, he thought, Thorndike's cats may not have been smart enough to show the *insightful* learning of which primates are capable. To prove his point, Köhler took advantage of his geographic fortunes to study chimpanzees in situations that encouraged cognitive learning to show itself.

Köhler observed that chimps could, without prompting, solve problems by combining complex behaviors they had previously learned separately. This suggested to him that the animals were not mindlessly using conditioned behaviors but were actually reorganizing their *perceptions* of problems. This was illustrated by Sultan, Köhler's brightest chimp, an animal who had learned to pile up boxes in order to reach fruit suspended high in his cage. Sultan had also learned to use sticks to obtain fruit that was just out of reach. So, when confronted with a novel situation, fruit suspended even higher in the air, this chimp first attacked it unsuccessfully with sticks (trial-and-error fashion). In apparent frustration, Sultan threw the sticks away, kicked the wall, and sat down. According to Köhler's report, the animal then scratched his head and began to stare at some boxes nearby. Suddenly, he jumped up and dragged a box and a stick underneath the fruit, climbed on the box, and knocked down his prize with the stick. Remarkably, Sultan had never before seen or used this combination of responses. Such behavior, Köhler suggested, shows that apes, like humans, learn to solve problems by suddenly perceiving familiar objects in new forms or relationships—a decidedly mental process, rather than a behavioral one. He called this **insight learning** (Köhler, 1925).

Behaviorism, in the mold of Pavlov and Watson, had no convincing stimulus–response explanation for Köhler's demonstration, except to criticize it as poorly controlled. Nevertheless, the feats of Köhler's chimps demanded the *cognitive* explanation of perceptual reorganization. Likewise, rats in the lab of former behaviorist Edward Tolman began behaving in ways that also flew in the face of accepted behavioral doctrine.

Cognitive Maps: Tolman Finds Out What's on a Rat's Mind

If you have ever walked through your house in the dark or given directions to someone, you have some idea of the **cognitive map** that Edward Tolman (1886–1959) and his rats introduced into psychology. Technically, a cognitive map is a mental image that an organism uses to navigate through its environ-

"Well, you don't look like an experimental psychologist to me."

© The New Yorker Collection 1994. Sam Gross from cartoonbank.com. All Rights Reserved.

Insight learning: A form of cognitive learning, originally described by the Gestalt psychologists, in which a problem solving occurs by means of a sudden reorganization of perceptions.

Cognitive map: A mental representation of physical space.

FIGURE 6.9: Using Cognitive Maps in Maze Learning

Subjects preferred the direct path (Path 1) when it was open. When it was blocked at A, they preferred Path 2. When Path 2 was blocked at B, rats usually chose Path 3. Their behavior indicated that they had a cognitive map of the best route to the food box.

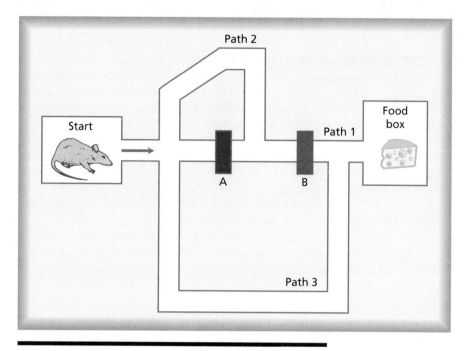

ment. But how could the existence of cognitive maps be demonstrated conclusively?

TAKING A SHORT DETOUR A cognitive map, Tolman argued, was the only way to account for a rat quickly selecting an alternative route in a maze when the preferred path to the goal is blocked. In fact, rats will often select the shortest detour around a barrier, even though taking that particular route was never previously reinforced (Tolman & Honzik, 1930). Rather than blindly exploring different parts of the maze through trial- and-error, as would be predicted by behavioral theory, Tolman's rats behaved as if they had a mental representation of the maze—an internal cognitive map. (Figure 6.9 shows the arrangement of a maze such as Tolman used.)

LEARNING WITHOUT REINFORCEMENT In subsequent research, Tolman (1948) allowed rats to wander freely about a maze for several hours, during which they received no reinforcement at all. Despite the lack of reinforcement (which behaviorists supposed to be essential for maze learning), the rats apparently developed cognitive maps of the maze. How do we know? They could later learn more quickly to run the maze for a food reward than could rats that had never seen the maze before. Moreover, Tolman observed that, before rats made a choice of detours around a blocked route, they sometimes paused and quietly engaged in what he called "VTE"—**vicarious trial-and-error.** That is, the rats appeared to be pondering their options before choosing a new path!

Tolman claimed that learning under these conditions involved not only a cognitive map but also an *expectancy* about the consequences of the chosen response. Thus, his rats were not simply learning a rigid sequence of right and

Connection

Chapter 4
Mental representation involves an internal model of an external object or event.

Vicarious trial-and-error:
Mentally trying alternative behaviors and thinking through their consequences before selecting a physical response. This concept was ridiculed by the behaviorists.

left turns, but they were acquiring some mental representation of the maze's spatial layout (Tolman et al., 1946). Subsequent experiments on cognitive maps in rats, chimpanzees, and humans have supported these notions (Menzel, 1978; Moar, 1980; Olton, 1979). Organisms seem to learn the general layout of their environment by exploration, even if they are not reinforced for learning particular paths. The ability to learn and remember such lessons is obviously adaptive in foraging for food (Kamil et al., 1987).

THE SIGNIFICANCE OF TOLMAN'S WORK What made Tolman's work both significant and controversial was its incompatibility with the prevailing behavioral views of Pavlov, Watson, and—later—Skinner. While Tolman accepted the idea that psychologists must study observable behavior, he had discovered situations in which simple associations between stimuli and responses could not explain the behavior he had observed. Tolman's *cognitive* analysis, therefore, presented a daring challenge to behaviorism (Kesner & Olton, 1990; Olton, 1992; Tolman, 1932).

Later theorists, following in Tolman's footsteps, have shown that even basic forms of behavioral learning, such as operant conditioning, may have cognitive features, such as expectancies, predictions, and judgments (Balsam & Tomie, 1985). An especially important challenge to behaviorism has come more recently from another behaviorist-turned-cognitive-psychologist: Albert Bandura. His work suggests that reinforcement can operate indirectly, through *observation*.

Social Learning: Bandura's Challenge to Behaviorism

Does watching violent behavior make viewers more likely to become violent? A classic study by Albert Bandura suggests that it does—at least in the children he invited to his lab. After observing adults punch, hit, and kick an inflated plastic clown (a BoBo doll), the children later showed similar aggressive behavior toward the doll. Significantly, these children were more aggressive than those in a control condition who had not observed the aggressive models (Bandura et al., 1963). Subsequent studies showed that children will also imitate aggressive behaviors they have seen on film, even when the models were merely cartoon characters.

LEARNING BY IMITATION An important finding in Bandura's study is that imitative learning can serve us in situations where we have not had a chance to gather personal experience. Thus, we learn by *imitation* or *observation*—by watching the behavior of another person, or *model*. If the model's actions appear successful, we may seek to behave in the same way; if they are unsuccessful, we avoid following the example.

Psychologists call this **social learning** or **observational learning**. It accounts for children learning aggressive behavior by imitating aggressive role models who are perceived as successful or admirable or who seem to be enjoying themselves. And it accounts for changes in clothing fashions and for the rapid spread of slang expressions. Observational learning is also a strategy found in nonhuman species, as you may have noticed in a mother cat teaching her kittens how to hunt. One study demonstrates that even a creature as simple as the octopus can learn by example from watching the behavior of other octopi (Fiorito & Scotto, 1992).

Social learning or **observational learning:** A form of cognitive learning in which new responses are acquired after watching others' behavior and the consequences of their behavior.

EFFECTS OF MEDIA VIOLENCE As you might have guessed, much psychological research has been directed at assessing the impact that behavior seen on film and video can have on viewers (Huston et al., 1989; Williams,

In the BoBo doll experiment, a boy and girl imitate the aggressive behavior that they have seen from an adult.

1986). Predictably, the issue is a controversial one (see Freedman, 1984, 1996). Nevertheless, correlational evidence from more than 50 studies shows that observing violence is associated with violent behavior, and more than 100 experimental studies point to a causal relationship (Huesmann & Moise, 1996; Primavera & Heron, 1996). In addition, media violence has been found to cause a reduction in emotional arousal and distress at viewing violence, a condition known as *psychic numbing* (Murray & Kippax, 1979). Finally, according to social psychologist Elliot Aronson, extensive media violence is probably one factor (of many) contributing to widely publicized tragedies, such as the Columbine High School shootings (Aronson, 2000).

Not all imitation is harmful, of course. We also learn from observation about charitable behavior, comforting others in distress, and driving on the customary side of the road. In general, we can say that people learn much — both prosocial (helping) and antisocial (hurting) behaviors — through observation of others. This capacity to learn from watching enables us to acquire behaviors without going through tedious trial-and-error. So, while observational learning seems to be a factor in violent behavior, it also enables us to learn socially useful behaviors by profiting from the mistakes and successes of others.

Rethinking Behavioral Learning in Cognitive Terms

In the last decades of the 20th century, cognitive psychologists ventured into the territory of classical and operant conditioning and gave these theories a more cognitive flavor. One of the big questions they raised concerns the adap-

Connection

Chapter 1
An *experimental study* is required to demonstrate a cause-and-effect relationship.

tive value of classical conditioning for the organism (Hollis, 1997). Particularly influential has been the work of Robert Rescorla, who has shown that the feature of the conditioned stimulus that most facilitates conditioning is its *informativeness*—its reliability in predicting the onset of the unconditioned stimulus (Rescorla, 1972; Rescorla & Wagner, 1972). From a cognitive viewpoint, the CS acts as a *cue* that signals the onset of the UCS. Other stimuli that are present at the same time may not serve this cuing function, however. As we saw in food aversions, a certain taste can serve as a warning of illness, while a flashing light will not.

In the same vein, research by Leon Kamin (1969) has revealed that a learner will form a CS–CR connection only if the CS seems to provide unique information about the UCS. In his experiments, some unconditioned stimuli, such as a shock, were signaled by multiple stimuli, such as lights and tones and tastes. Did his experimental subjects pay attention to *all* of these cues? No. They learned to respond particularly to the stimuli that provided the best *information*. In the wild, this can be seen in butterfly-eating birds that have an aversion for monarch butterflies. (They taste awful.) Their aversion focuses on the insect's unique markings and not on its less distinctive stimuli of shape or size. To give a more personal example, you may see smoke as well as smell the acrid odor of something burning before you actually see the flames of a fire. You have learned from experience that smoke is not always visible during a fire, but the *smell* of something burning is a telltale sign of fire. The smell provides better *information* about whether there is a fire, so you pay closer attention to the smell than to the sight of smoke.

Attempts are also being made by cognitive psychologists to broaden the scope of operant conditioning to include mental processes, as well as behaviors (DeGrandpre, 2000; Ohlsson, 1996). From this perspective, reinforcement changes not just behavior but the individual's *expectations* for future occurrences of similar situations. An example will probably help: If you are rewarded for attending your psychology class, this reward changes your future behavior by changing your expectation that future classes will also be rewarding.

Brain Mechanisms and Learning

On a neural level, learning seems to involve physical changes that strengthen the synapses in groups of nerve cells—a process called **long-term potentiation.** (For a review of the evidence, see Carlson, 2001.) In operant conditioning, the brain's reward circuitry apparently comes into play, involving especially the limbic system and associated brain structures. These circuits are rich in dopamine receptors, leading many experts to believe that this transmitter is the brain's means of sensing reward. (In fact, the highly reinforcing sensations produced by cocaine and amphetamine are due to their action as dopamine agonists in these regions.)

On the level of brain pathways, neuroscientists Eric Kandel and Robert Hawkins (1992) have made a proposal that may bridge the chasm between behavioral learning and cognitive learning. Their insight rests on the discovery that animals with relatively simple nervous systems have a single type of nerve circuit that enables them to learn simple motor responses. In the more complex brains of mammals, however, researchers have found a second type of learning circuitry that apparently facilitates higher forms of learning, such as memory for events.

What is the significance of this finding? Kandel and Hawkins speculate that the two types of learning circuits may divide the task of learning along the line that has long separated behavioral psychologists and cognitive psychologists. The simpler circuit seems to be responsible for the sort of "mindless"

Connection

Chapter 2
The limbic system includes circuits involved in reward.

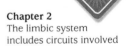
Connection

Chapter 2
An *agonist* is a chemical that mimics or enhances the effects of a neurotransmitter.

Long-term potentiation: A biological process, involving physical changes that strengthen the synapses in groups of nerve cells, which is believed to be the neural basis of learning.

learning that occurs when a dog drools at the sound of a bell or when a person acquires a motor skill, such as riding a bike or swinging a golf club. (See also Clark & Squire, 1998.) This kind of learning occurs slowly and improves with repetition over many trials. Significantly, classical conditioning and much of operant learning fit this description. By contrast, the second type of learning circuit seems to be responsible for more complex forms of learning that require conscious processing—the sort of learning that interests cognitive psychologists: concept formation, insight learning, social learning, and memory for specific events. If further research verifies that this division reflects a fundamental distinction in the nervous system, we will be able to say that those on the behavioral and cognitive extremes were both (partly) right. They were talking about fundamentally different forms of learning.

"Higher" Cognitive Learning

It seems clear to cognitive psychologists that the sort of learning required in college classes, in which you must learn abstract concepts, involves something beyond the sort of behavioral learning that Pavlov, Watson, Thorndike, and Skinner studied. Learning about the field of psychology, for example, involves building mental images and structures and learning how they can be related, compared, and contrasted. Likewise, we saw that Sabra's classes taught her *concepts* about flight and about emotional responses. It's not that conditioning isn't involved in human learning—after all, students *do* work for grades—but the principles of behavioral conditioning don't tell the whole story of "higher" cognitive learning.

It is into this realm of higher learning that we will take you in the next two chapters, where we will discuss thinking, memory, concept formation, problem-solving, and intelligence. There you will learn more about the mental structures that seem to underlie cognitive learning. The problem we face there is exactly the one that the behaviorists were hoping to avoid: When we study cognition, we must make inferences about processes that we cannot measure directly. Cognitive learning is always about processes that are one step removed from behavior. What we will find, however, is that cognitive psychologists have developed some very clever methods to obtain objective data on which to base their inferences. The newest of these—coming fully on line in the last decade or so—is brain imaging, which, as we will see, has brought psychologists very close to an objective glimpse at private mental processes.

Connection

Chapter 8
Concepts are mental categories that enable us to organize our knowledge.

Connection

Chapter 2
PET and fMRI are two imaging techniques that allow researchers to visualize the brain in action.

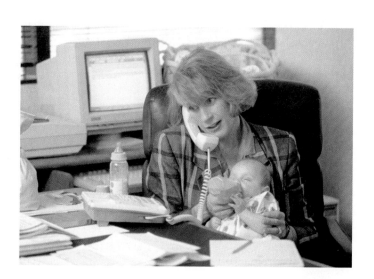

Learning is not efficient when the learner is "multitasking"—trying to perform several tasks that demand attention at the same time.

A Critical Look at "Learning Styles"

In Your Life

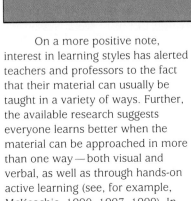

There is no doubt that people differ in the ways that they approach learning. You can see by looking at your classmates that everyone brings a different set of interests, abilities, temperamental factors, developmental levels, social and cultural experiences, and emotions to bear on learning tasks. But, can we say that these constitute distinct "learning styles"?

Some educators have made claims about learning styles that go far beyond any supporting evidence (Terry, 2000). One such claim posits a difference between so-called "left-brained" and "right-brained" individuals. As we have seen, however, this dichotomy is based on a fundamental misinterpretation of split-brain research. (See Chapter 2; both hemispheres work cooperatively in all people with an intact corpus callosum.) What they usually mean is that some people prefer verbal learning, while others prefer materials that are more visual–spatial. Like all learning typologies, however, this one assumes that people can be divided into distinct groups, even though it would be more accurate to see people as gradually shading from one end of the spectrum to the other. This may be one reason why little solid evidence exists to show that people who are described as having different learning styles actually do learn differently.

Many other learning style schemes have been proposed, and with them paper-and-pencil tests have appeared on the market for assessing students' learning styles. Unfortunately, most of these schemes have little supporting data to show that people with different scores learn in different ways. An exception may be an ambitious program developed by Sternberg and Grigorenko to assess students on their abilities for logical, creative, and practical thinking—arguably, three distinct forms of "intelligence" (Sternberg, 1994; Sternberg & Grigorenko, 1997). (See Chapter 8; Sternberg's triarchic theory says that we have three different forms of intelligence.) Students in an introductory psychology course were divided into groups that received instruction emphasizing the form of intelligence on which they had scored highest. (A control group of students was deliberately mismatched.) Tests at the end of the course indicated that students did best when the teaching emphasis matched their intellectual style. As a practical matter, however, such a fine-tuned approach is probably not feasible for implementation on a large scale.

On a more positive note, interest in learning styles has alerted teachers and professors to the fact that their material can usually be taught in a variety of ways. Further, the available research suggests everyone learns better when the material can be approached in more than one way—both visual and verbal, as well as through hands-on active learning (see, for example, McKeachie, 1990, 1997, 1999). In recent years, this has led to the development of a variety of teaching methods to augment the lecture-only method that had previously been used almost exclusively in college classrooms.

The practical lesson is to be skeptical of tests that purport to identify your learning style. Beware also of people who might tell you that you *are* a visual learner, a reflective learner, or some such other type. This sort of thinking erroneously suggests that people learn only in one way—consistent with their supposed learning styles. It also erroneously suggests that the way we learn is fixed and unchanging. In fact, your college experience presents a wonderful opportunity to learn to think and learn in unaccustomed ways.

1. **RECALL:** *When their goal path was blocked, Tolman's rats would take the shortest detour around the barrier. This, said Tolman, showed that they had developed*

   a. trial-and-error learning.
   b. operant behavior.
   c. cognitive maps.
   d. observational learning.

2. **RECALL:** *Cognitive psychologist Robert Rescorla has reinterpreted the process of classical conditioning. In his view, the conditioned stimulus (CS) serves as a*

   a. cue that signals the onset of the UCS.
   b. stimulus that follows the UCS.
   c. negative reinforcement.
   d. cognitive map.

3. **APPLICATION:** *If you were going to use Bandura's findings in developing a program to prevent violence among middle-school children, you might*

   a. have children watch videos of aggressive children who are not being reinforced for their aggressive behavior.

   b. have children role play nonaggressive solutions to interpersonal problems.
   c. have children punch a BoBo doll, to "get the aggression out of their system."
   d. punish children for aggressive acts performed at school.

4. **UNDERSTANDING THE CORE CONCEPT:**

   Which of the following proved to be difficult to explain in purely behavioral terms?

   a. a trained seal doing a trick for a fish
   b. a dog salivating at the sound of a bell
   c. a chimpanzee standing on a box and using a stick to obtain food hung high in its cage
   d. a cat learning to escape from a puzzle box by clawing, trial-and-error fashion, at a rope that would open a door to a food reward

ANSWERS: 1. c   2. a   3. a   4. c

Using Psychology to Learn Psychology: Operant Conditioning Can Help You Study More—and Enjoy It

You may have tried the Premack principle to trick yourself into studying more, perhaps by denying yourself TV time or a trip to the refrigerator until your homework was done. It works for some people, but if it doesn't work for you, try making the studying itself more enjoyable and more reinforcing.

For most of us, being with people we like is reinforcing, regardless of the activity. So, make some (not all) of your studying a social activity. That is, schedule a time when you and another classmate or two can get together to identify and clarify important concepts and to try to predict what will be on the next test.

Don't just focus on vocabulary. Rather, try to discover the big picture—the overall meaning of each section of the chapter. The Core Concepts are a good place to start. Then you can discuss with your friends how the details fit in with the Core Concepts. You will most likely find that the social pressure of an upcoming study group will help motivate you to get your reading done and identify murky points. When you get together for your group study session, you will find that explaining what you have learned reinforces your own learning. The real reinforcement comes, however, from spending some time—studying—with your friends!

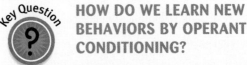

Chapter Summary

Learning produces lasting changes in behavior or mental processes, giving us an advantage over organisms that rely more heavily on reflexes and instincts. Some forms of learning are quite simple, while others, such as classical conditioning, operant conditioning, and cognitive learning, are more complex.

HOW DOES CLASSICAL CONDITIONING EXPLAIN LEARNING?

The earliest learning research focused on classical conditioning, beginning with Ivan Pavlov's discovery of conditioned stimuli that elicit reflexive responses. His experiments showed how conditioned responses could be acquired, extinguished, and undergo spontaneous recovery in laboratory animals. John Watson extended this work to the human learning of fears in his famous experiment on Little Albert. Studies of taste aversions suggest, however, that classical conditioning is not a simple stimulus–response process. In general,

classical conditioning affects basic, survival-oriented responses, including emotions and taste aversions.

 Core Concept

Classical conditioning is a basic form of learning in which a stimulus that produces an innate reflex becomes associated with a neutral stimulus, which acquires the power to elicit the same response.

HOW DO WE LEARN NEW BEHAVIORS BY OPERANT CONDITIONING?

Trial-and-error learning was originally explored by Edward Thorndike. B. F. Skinner expanded that work, now called operant conditioning, to explain how responses are influenced by their environmental consequences. His work examined positive and negative

reinforcement, punishment, extinction, prompting, shaping, and various kinds of reinforcement contingencies. Our society relies heavily on punishment, which usually has undesirable effects on behavior. There are, however, effective alternatives.

Core Concept

In operant conditioning, rewards and punishments are consequences that influence the likelihood of the behaviors they follow recurring in the future.

Key Question

HOW DOES COGNITIVE PSYCHOLOGY EXPLAIN LEARNING?

Much research now suggests that learning is not just a process that links stimuli and responses:

Learning is also cognitive. This was shown in Köhler's work on insight learning in chimpanzees, in Tolman's studies of cognitive maps and place learning in rats, and in Bandura's research on social learning and imitation in humans. In recent years, cognitive scientists have reinterpreted behavioral learning, especially operant and classical conditioning, in cognitive terms.

Core Concept

According to cognitive psychology, some forms of learning must be explained as changes in mental processes, rather than as changes in behavior alone – but they can still be studied scientifically.

Review Test

For each of the following items, choose the single correct or best answer. The correct answers appear at the end.

1. Which one of the following taught that psychology should involve only the analysis of observable stimuli and responses?
   a. Albert Bandura
   b. B. F. Skinner
   c. Sigmund Freud
   d. John Garcia

2. During classical conditioning, for an organism to learn a conditioned association between two stimuli, the UCS must seem to
   a. predict the CS.
   b. be predicted by the CS.
   c. be independent of the CS.
   d. follow the UCR.

3. According to Thorndike, problems are solved by
   a. trial-and-error-learning.
   b. observational learning.
   c. classical conditioning.
   d. extinction.

4. A _____ is a consistent relationship between a response and the changes in the environment it produces.
   a. behavior potential
   b. behavior analysis
   c. reinforcement contingency
   d. conditioned reinforcer

5. "The best part of going to the beach," your friend exclaims as you start your vacation, "is getting away from all the stress of work and school." If this is true, then your friend's vacation-taking behavior has been influenced by
   a. positive reinforcement.
   b. negative reinforcement.
   c. extinction.
   d. punishment.

6. Which of the following is *not* a good way to make punishment effective?
   a. Make it swift and brief.
   b. Make it intense.
   c. Deliver it immediately.
   d. Focus it on the undesirable behavior.

7. According to the Premack principle, a reinforcer can be

a. changes in behavior from its past norms.

b. anything that rewards rather than penalizes behavior.

c. a stimulus that becomes associated with an unconditioned stimulus.

d. the opportunity to engage in any behavior frequently performed by the organism.

8. In his research with rats running mazes, Edward C. Tolman concluded that place learning required each subject to rely on

a. a CS–UCS connection.

b. conditioned reinforcers.

c. a cognitive map.

d. spontaneous recovery.

9. In Bandura's experiment with the BoBo doll, aggressive behavior resulted from

a. painful stimulation.

b. insults.

c. observational learning.

d. negative reinforcement.

10. The biggest problem with the concept of "learning styles" is that

a. there is little evidence showing that people learn in different ways.

b. most people are visual learners—hardly anyone is an auditory learner.

c. people who think with their right brain don't fit into any known learning style.

d. most educators don't believe in learning styles.

ANSWERS: 1. b   2. b   3. a   4. c   5. b   6. b
7. d   8. c   9. c   10. a

If You're Interested . . .

BOOKS

Artiss, K. L. (1996). *Mistake making.* University Press of America. Why doesn't everyone learn from experience? Some experiences may not be memorable—but certain types of people may also have difficulty making the adjustments necessary for each lesson; and, failing to learn, they end up suffering relentless punishment by repeating their errors and failures. Here's why it may happen—and what to do about it.

Baum, W. M. (1994). *Understanding behaviorism: Science, behavior, and culture.* HarperCollins. Baum presents a brief, straightforward, and helpful explanation of the elements of behaviorism—stimuli, responses, reinforcement—and its more complex consequences for life and society, including freedom, responsibility, and justice.

Greven, P. (1992). *Spare the child: The religious roots of punishment and the psychological impact of child abuse.* Vintage Books. Imagine a world in which hitting a child is not only politically incorrect, it is also against the law of both man and God. Greven documents the great weight of evidence against any rationale for corporal punishment of children and asserts that we have a moral obligation to develop humane alternatives to beating our kids.

Hyman, I. A. (1997). *The case against spanking: How to discipline your child without hitting.* Jossey-Bass. Because punishment such as hitting fails to *change* behavior and often models aggression, families need strategies for "positive punishments," contingencies that will reduce unwanted behavior without teaching children even worse habits. Hyman also explores why children seem to know just what will most provoke their parents and argues that the costs of corporal punishment vastly outweigh the convenience and power.

Prochaska, J. O., Norcross, J. C., & Diclimente, C. C. (1995). *Changing for good.* Avon Books. This step-by-step behavior modification program is based on the conclusions of three psychologists that lasting behavior change depends not on fate or fortitude but on a process that can be learned and managed by anyone who can identify first what stage of change he or she is in and next the appropriate change strategy for that stage.

VIDEOS

A Clockwork Orange (1971, color, 137 min.). Directed by Stanley Kubrick; starring Malcolm McDowell, Patrick Magee, Adrienne Corri. This classic and still powerful rendition of Anthony Burgess's novel presents a futuristic society's efforts to reform a psychopathic criminal by applying aversive conditioning—with unexpected results.

WEB RESOURCES

http://www.birthpsychology.com/lifebefore/earlymen.html Scientists are beginning to understand that many aspects of learning begin before birth. This site explains how researchers measure prenatal learning.

http://www.apa.org/monitor/dec99/ss6.html The role of behaviorism in psychology changed during the 20th century; it no longer holds such an important role in the field. Read this article from the *APA Monitor* to learn more about the changes regarding behaviorism.

KEY QUESTION CHAPTER OUTLINE	CORE CONCEPT	PSYCHOLOGY IN YOUR LIFE

WHAT IS MEMORY?

Metaphors for Memory
Memory's Three Essential Functions
The Three Memory Stages

Human memory is a cognitive system composed of three stages that work together constructively to encode, store, and retrieve information.

WOULD YOU WANT A "PHOTOGRAPHIC" MEMORY?
This ability is rare, and those who have it say that the images can sometimes interfere with their thinking.

HOW DO WE FORM MEMORIES?

Processing in Sensory Memory
Processing in Working Memory
Long-Term Memory Processing

Each of the three memory systems encodes and stores memories in a different way, but they work together to transform sensory experience into a lasting record that has a pattern or meaning.

"FLASHBULB" MEMORIES: WHERE WERE YOU WHEN. . . ?
These especially vivid memories usually involve emotionally charged events. Surprisingly, they aren't always accurate.

HOW DO WE RETRIEVE MEMORIES?

Implicit and Explicit Memory
Context and Encoding Specificity:
   Codes and Cues for Better
   Memories

Whether memories are implicit or explicit, the success of their retrieval depends on how they were encoded and how they are cued.

ON THE TIP OF YOUR TONGUE:
It is maddening when you know the word, but you just can't quite say it. But you're not alone. Most people experience this about once a week.

WHY DOES MEMORY SOMETIMES FAIL US?

Transience — When Memories Fade
Absent-Mindedness — When Lapses of
   Attention Cause Forgetting
Blocking — When Memories Encounter
   Interference
Misattribution — When Memories
   Connect with the Wrong Context
Suggestibility — When Cues Distort or
   Create Memories
Bias — When Our Own Characteristics
   Color Our Memories
Persistence — When We Can't Forget
The Advantages of the "Seven Sins"
   of Memory

Most of our memory problems arise from memory's "seven sins" — which are really by-products of otherwise adaptive features of human memory.

IMPROVING YOUR MEMORY WITH MNEMONICS:
There are lots of tricks for learning lists, but another technique works better for mastering the concepts you'll meet in college.

USING PSYCHOLOGY TO LEARN PSYCHOLOGY: How to Avoid Memory Failure on Exams

MEMORY

Some twenty years ago, 12-year-old Donna Smith began to suffer from severe migraine headaches, which left her sleepless and depressed. Her parents, Judee and Dan, agreed to get her psychiatric help. During an evaluation recommended by her therapist, Donna disclosed—for the first time—that she had been sexually molested at the age of 3 by a neighbor. It was concluded that memories of the assault, buried in her mind for so long, were probably responsible for some of Donna's current problems, so she continued with therapy.

As a teenager, Donna began work with a new therapist, a private social worker specializing in child abuse. In their first session, the therapist asked Donna if she had been sexually abused by her father. Donna denied this but did mention the neighbor's assault. The therapist, however, believed there might be more behind Donna's problems. For many months, she repeatedly asked Donna whether her father had abused her. Finally, Donna told her a lie, claiming her father had once "touched" her, hoping this false claim would enable her therapy to move on. The therapist immediately reported Donna's father to the local sheriff and to the Maryland Department of Social Services (ABC News, 1995).

When Donna realized the drastic consequences of her false claim, she tried to set the record straight, but the therapist

(continued)

dismissed the confession, saying that all abuse victims recant their accusations once they learn their therapists are required to report such claims. The therapist was persuasive, and eventually Donna began to entertain the idea that her conscious memory was a self-delusion—a trick of her mind trying to protect itself from the "real" truth. Reluctantly, she concluded that it must have been her father, not the neighbor, who had assaulted her as a toddler. When the therapist convinced her to tell the story to county authorities, Donna was removed from her home and placed in foster care.

To her parents, these sudden accusations were "like a bomb [had] hit"—and it got worse. Still in therapy, Donna became convinced her father had been a chronic abuser, and she began to hate him "wholeheartedly." Committed to a psychiatric hospital, she was diagnosed as having several different personalities, one of which claimed that her parents practiced ritual satanic abuse of Donna's younger brothers. The courts forbade Donna's parents to have contact with her. Judee Smith lost her license to run a day-care center. Dan Smith, a retired naval officer, was arrested at his home and handcuffed in front of their two young sons. Financially ruined, he was tried on charges of abuse, based solely on his daughter's testimony. His two-week trial ended in a hung jury, and Dan Smith went free.

Shortly after the trial, Donna moved to Michigan with her foster family. In these new surroundings, far away from the system that had supported her fabricated story, she gradually regained perspective and found the courage to tell the truth. She admitted the charges had all been fabrications, and her doctor recommended she be sent back to her family. The Smiths had a tearful reunion and began the slow process of rebuilding lost relationships and trust. "She's been a victim of this system, as much as we've been a victim," says Dan Smith. "You know, there's a lot of healing to be done."

According to Johns Hopkins psychiatrist Paul McHugh, erroneous recovered memories are fabricated from suggestions therapists offer in order to blame psychological problems on long-hidden trauma (ABC News, 1995). Memory expert Elizabeth Loftus agrees, noting that some clinicians are all too ready to accept their clients' memories, even fantastic tales of ritualistic abuse (Loftus, 1993). In the book *Making Monsters,* social psychologist Richard Ofshe argues that clients can unknowingly tailor their recollections to fit their therapists' expectations. He adds that "therapists often encourage patients to redefine their life histories based on the new pseudomemories and, by doing so, redefine their most basic understanding of their families and themselves" (Ofshe & Watters, 1994, p. 6).

Today Donna and her family are "in wonderful shape, back together." Still, the memories of the Smith family's ordeal will remain painful shadows in the background of their lives forever. Fortunately, the same flexibility in human learning and remembering that created these problems can also provide the key to forgiving and healing.

● ● ●

We should emphasize that sexual abuse of children *does* occur, and it is a serious problem. While estimates vary, it appears that from 4% to 20% of children in the United States experience at least one incident of sexual abuse (Rathus et al., 2000). The issue raised by Donna's case, however, involves *false* claims of sexual abuse based on faulty "recovered memories." Fortunately, the ordeal that Donna and her family went through is relatively rare. Still, such cases have surfaced often enough to alarm psychologists about the widespread misunderstanding people have about memory. Psychologists know that memory does not always make an accurate record of events.

In fact, Donna's memory works very much like our own. As you will learn in this chapter, our own memories are capable of distortions, too. You will also learn about memory's inner workings and some extraordinary memory abilities. We will end on a practical note by considering some steps you can take to improve your memory.

WHAT IS MEMORY?

The best defense against the tricks that memory can play requires an understanding of memory. We will begin building that defense with a definition: Cognitive psychologists define **memory** broadly as any system that encodes, stores, and retrieves information — a definition that applies equally to an organism or a computer. Unlike a computer's memory, however, human memory is a *cognitive* system — closely related to *perception*. Human memory takes the essentially meaningless barrage of stimulation entering our senses and selectively converts it into meaningful patterns that can be stored and accessed later when needed. Our Core Concept characterizes our memory system this way:

> **Human memory is a cognitive system composed of three stages that work together constructively to encode, store, and retrieve information.**

And how is memory related to learning? You might think of human memory as the biological and mental system that allows us to retain what we have learned for later use.

In a practical sense, what does memory do for us? It confers the ability to adapt quickly to changing conditions. If you had no such capacity, you would have to rely entirely on the innate (inborn) behaviors that we often call *"instincts."* Such genetically based behaviors account for bird migrations, animal courtship rituals, and even a few human behaviors, such as nursing in the newborn. By contrast, the ability to remember represents an evolutionary advance over the limitations of instinctive behavior patterns, because a flexible memory system allows animals with to deal more appropriately with new challenges.

Metaphors for Memory

Human memory has been compared to a library or a storehouse (Haberlandt, 1999), metaphors which capture the ability of our memories to hold large amounts of information. Some metaphors for memory, however, can be misleading. Such is the case with the "video recorder" model of memory: Many people mistakenly believe that human memory works like a video recorder to make a complete and accurate record of everything we experience.

Cognitive psychologists have shown that this "video recorder" metaphor is wrong. Instead, they see human memory as a *constructive* system that *interprets* incoming information, discards many details, and organizes the rest in meaningful patterns. The resulting memory patterns, however, are often only approxima-

Key Question

Memory: Any system — human, animal, or machine — that encodes, stores, and retrieves information.

Core Concept

Connection

Chapter 6
Learning involves changes in behavior or mental processes as a result of experience.

Both people and computers have memory.

NICKERSON AND ADAMS

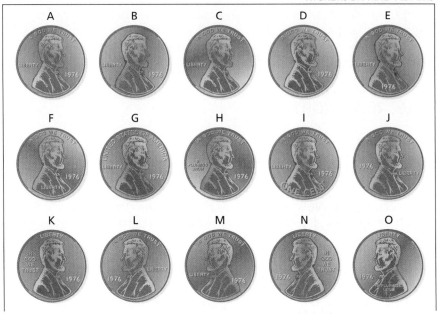

tions of the external stimuli that we have experienced. You can demonstrate this to yourself by looking at Figure 7.1.

Which image in the figure is the most accurate portrayal of a penny? Although pennies are common in our everyday experience, you will probably find that identifying the real penny is difficult. For most of us the details of a penny are unimportant, so we pay little attention to the attributes of these familiar objects. Consequently, the memory image of a penny that usually serves us well enough is sparse on details. Further, when we retrieve such a fragmentary memory image from our memories, we must *reconstruct* it by filling in gaps and details — without realizing how much of the memory we are actually creating while remembering. (The right answer, by the way, is A.)

In general, psychologists have found that human memory usually makes the most accurate records for:

▶ Information on which we have focused our attention — such as a friend's words against the background of a noisy restaurant.

▶ Information in which we are interested — such as the courses in your major field.

▶ Information that arouses us emotionally — such as an experience that is especially enjoyable or painful.

▶ Information that fits with our previous experience — such as a physician learning about a new treatment for a familiar disease.

▶ Information that we rehearse — such as memory for material reviewed the night before an exam.

As you can see, cognitive psychologists use an information-processing approach that takes into consideration the psychological nature of human memory — the ties that memory has to other cognitive processes, such as learning and perceptual processing. In the following pages we will examine this model of memory closely, beginning with the three essential functions that we rely on memory to perform.

Memory's Three Essential Functions

Any memory system, whether in a computer, a laboratory rat, or a person, must perform three essential functions. It must *encode* information in a useful format; it must *store* the information; and it must have a means of *accessing and retrieving* the stored data. We will look at each of these operations in more detail.

Encoding requires that you first *select* some stimulus event from among the vast array of inputs assaulting your senses. Next you *identify* the distinctive features of that input. Is it a sound, a visual image, or a smell? If it's a sound, is it loud, soft, or harsh? Does it fit into some pattern that forms a name, a melody—or a cry for help? Is it a sound you have heard before? Finally, you mentally tag, or *label,* an experience. Some labels are specific and unique ("It's Minerva"), others describe a general category or class ("She's our cat"). These steps involved in encoding are usually so automatic and rapid that you are unaware you are performing them. (If you had trouble with the "penny test," it was probably the result of failure to encode the relevant characteristics of a penny.)

Further encoding entails a process called **elaboration,** which relates the new input to other information you already have in memory or to goals or purposes for which it might later prove useful. Such connections make memories more meaningful. And, because memory is a system built on meaningful connections, elaboration strengthens memories.

Storage, a second essential function of memory, involves the retention of encoded material over time. As we have noted, information is best retained when it has been linked to information already stored. Otherwise it is usually lost. Occasional rehearsal of the material also helps. In general, the more meaningful some item of information is and the more often it is rehearsed, the more likely it is to be retained.

Access and retrieval involve the recovery of stored information, the payoff for your earlier effort involved in encoding and storage. When all goes well, you gain access—sometimes in a split second—to information you stored earlier in your memory banks. (Let's see if your access and retrieval mechanisms are working for the material we just covered. Can you remember which of the three memory functions comes before *storage?*) When a memory is accessed with the appropriate cues, retrieval is usually automatic.

The Three Memory Stages

As the information from a sensory experience (such as reading this sentence) becomes a permanent memory, it must be processed in three stages: first in *sensory memory,* then in *working memory,* and finally in *long-term memory.* At each stage, information receives additional processing. In general, the three stages work together to convert a barrage of initially meaningless incoming stimuli into meaningful patterns that can be stored for later use. Figure 7.2 shows the flow of information through these stages. We will focus our attention on each stage in turn.

Memory encodes the best records for information on which we have focused attention.

Encoding: One of the three basic functions of memory, involving the modification of information to fit the preferred format for the memory system.

Elaboration: A form of encoding that adds meaning to information in working memory so that it can be more easily stored in LTM and later retrieved.

Storage: One of the three basic functions of memory, involving the retention of encoded material over time.

Access and retrieval: Together these form the third basic function of memory, involving the location and recovery of information from memory.

The "standard model" says that memory is divided into three stages. Everything that goes into long-term storage must first be processed by sensory memory and working memory.

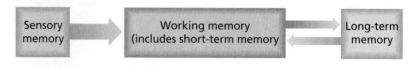

Sensory memory: The first of three memory stages, preserving brief sensory impressions of stimuli; also called *sensory register.*

Working memory or **short-term memory (STM):** The second of three memory stages, and most limited in capacity; preserves recently perceived events or experiences for less than a minute without rehearsal.

Long-term memory (LTM): The third of three memory stages, with the largest capacity and longest duration; LTM stores material organized according to meaning.

Eidetic imagery: An especially clear and persistent form of memory that is quite rare. Sometimes known as "photographic memory."

Connection

Chapter 1
Wundt founded the "school" of psychology known as *structuralism.*

SENSORY MEMORY   Sights, sounds, smells, textures, and other sensory impressions persist only fleetingly in **sensory memory.** You may have experienced a sensory memory trace as you watched a moving Fourth-of-July sparkler that seemed to leave a fading trail of light. The function of these brief images is to store incoming sensory information long enough to be screened for possible access to working memory.

WORKING MEMORY   The second stage of memory, known as **working memory,** takes information from sensory memory and connects it with items already in long-term storage. It also holds information temporarily, making working memory a useful buffer for items such as a phone number you have just looked up. Thus, this stage is sometimes also called **short-term memory (STM)** (Beardsley, 1997; Goldman-Rakic, 1992).

It is noteworthy that everything entering consciousness must also pass into working memory. Likewise, we are conscious of everything that working memory considers. Because of this intimate relationship between working memory and consciousness, some psychologists have suggested that working memory *is* the seat of consciousness (LeDoux, 1996).

LONG-TERM MEMORY   The final stage of processing, known as **long-term memory (LTM),** receives information from working memory and preserves it for retrieval at any later time — sometimes for the rest of a person's life. Information in long-term memory constitutes our knowledge about the world and includes such varied material as the lyrics to your favorite song and the year that Wilhelm Wundt established the first psychology laboratory. (Do you remember what year that was? 18??) Long-term memory constitutes each person's total knowledge of the world and of the self. Material in long-term memory enables you to solve new problems, reason, keep future appointments, and use a variety of rules to manipulate abstract symbols — allowing you to think about situations you have never experienced or that might be impossible.

Would You Want a "Photographic" Memory?

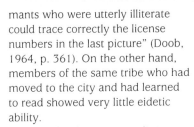

Suppose that your memory were so vivid and accurate that you could "read" paragraphs of this book from it during the next psychology exam. Such was the power of a 23-year-old woman tested by Charles Stromeyer and Joseph Psotka (1970). So vivid was her memory that she could look at the meaningless configuration of dots in the left-hand pattern in the figure in the accompanying "Do It Yourself!" box and combine it mentally with the right-hand image. The combined pattern was the meaningful configuration of dots shown in Figure 7.3. So, wouldn't it be great to have such a "photographic" memory? Not entirely, it turns out.

The technical term for "photographic memory" is **eidetic imagery.** Psychologists prefer this term because eidetic images are, in many important respects, different from images made by a camera (Haber, 1969, 1980). Unlike a photographic image, which renders everything in minute detail, an eidetic image portrays the most interesting and meaningful parts of the scene most accurately.

Eidetic memories also differ in several respects from the long-term memory images that most of us experience. For one thing, *eidetikers* (those who have eidetic imagery) describe their memory images as having the vividness of the original experience (Neisser, 1967). Indeed, research using images such as those in the dot-combining test in the "Do It Yourself!" box suggests this is true.

A second difference between eidetic memories and common long-term memories involves the persistence of the image. Eidetic images often last for several minutes—even for days, in some cases. (The woman tested by Stromeyer & Psotka could pass the dot-combining test even when the images were shown to her 24 hours apart.) Remarkable as this is, the persistence of these images can be a curse. Eidetikers report that their vivid memories may interfere with other things they want to think about. This, then, is one of the drawbacks of having this rare ability: Eidetic imagery can get in the way of new thoughts and new learning (Hunter, 1964).

A third difference between eidetic images and the usual memory images concerns context. The eidetic image is always concrete, never abstract. Whereas most adults can easily draw abstract concepts from long-term memory when they think about ideas such as "freedom," "immoral," "cognition" or "operant conditioning," eidetikers may have trouble with abstractions because their concrete visual images of everyday life interfere with abstract thought.

A fourth difference involves age: Eidetic imagery appears most commonly in children and only rarely in adults. One estimate suggests that up to 5% of children show some eidetic ability—although most are not good enough to pass the dot-combining test (Gray & Gummerman, 1975). Although no one knows why eidetic imagery tends to disappear in adults, it may follow some sort of developmental sequence—like losing one's baby teeth. Possibly its disappearance is related to the child's development of abstract thinking, which begins to develop at about age 11 or 12. Alternatively, a tantalizing study from Nigeria suggests that the loss of eidetic ability may have something to do with acculturation to urban living conditions or, perhaps, education. In the Nigerian study, eidetic imagery was found to be common among adults of the Ibo tribe who were living in rural villages. Tests of these villagers revealed ". . . again and again informants who were utterly illiterate could trace correctly the license numbers in the last picture" (Doob, 1964, p. 361). On the other hand, members of the same tribe who had moved to the city and had learned to read showed very little eidetic ability.

A fifth characteristic distinguishes eidetic images from other kinds of memory: They reportedly appear *outside the head*—out in the external world—rather than in the "mind's eye" inside the head, as is the case with more common memory images. In this respect, eidetic images resemble afterimages, such as the dark spot you momentarily see in front of your eyes after a camera flashes at close range. (See Chapter 3: An afterimage involves a persisting sensation caused by lingering effects in the sensory receptors.) However, *unlike* a negative afterimage, the eidetic image does not appear in negative or reversed colors.

A final difference between eidetic imagery and ordinary long-term memory images involves the ways eidetikers learn to control their memories with language (Haber, 1969). Apparently, describing an eidetic image destroys it. Even naming objects in the image makes them fade from memory. This suggests that verbal information and eidetic imagery may be stored in separate memory systems that interfere with each other (Haber, 1970).

Whatever eidetic memory is, it is clearly rare—so rare, in fact, that some psychologists doubt its existence (Crowder, 1992). The few studies of the phenomenon have portrayed eidetic memory as different from everyday memory, as we have seen. But the fact is that we know relatively little about "photo-

(continued)

graphic memory," and not many psychologists are currently studying it. If it exists, eidetic imagery presents a theoretical problem for the widely accepted three-stage model of memory and a practical problem for those rare individuals who possess it.

A Test of Eidetic Imagery

Look at the dot pattern on the left in the figure for a few moments and try to fix it in your memory. With that image in mind, look at the dot pattern on the right. Try to put the two sets of dots together by recalling the first pattern while looking at the second one. If you are the rare individual who can mentally combine the two patterns, you will see something not apparent in either image alone. Difficult? No problem if you have eidetic imagery — but impossible for the rest of us. If you want to see the combined images, but can't combine them in your memory, look at Figure 7.3.

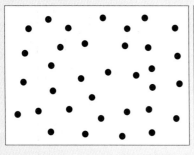 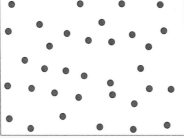

A Test of Eidetic Imagery

People with good eidetic imagery can mentally combine these two images to see something that appears in neither one alone.

CHECK YOUR UNDERSTANDING

1. **ANALYSIS:** *Which of the following is a major objection to the "video-recorder" theory of memory?*
   a. Like perception, memory is an interpretation of experience.
   b. Memories are never accurate.
   c. Unlike a video recorder, memory takes in and stores an enormous quantity of information from all the senses, not just vision.
   d. Unlike a tape-recorded video memory, human memory cannot be edited and changed at a later time.

2. **RECALL:** *Which of the following are the three essential functions of memory?*
   a. encoding, storage, access and retrieval
   b. sensory, working, and long-term
   c. remembering, forgetting, and repressing
   d. recall, recognition, and relearning

3. **ANALYSIS:** *When you get a new cat, you will note her unique markings, so that you can remember what she looks like in comparison with other cats in the neighborhood. What would a cognitive psychologist call this process of identifying the distinctive features of your cat?*
   a. eidetic imagery
   b. encoding
   c. recollection
   d. retrieval

4. **RECALL:** *What is the second stage of memory?*
   a. eidetic imagery
   b. encoding
   c. sensory memory
   d. working memory

5. **UNDERSTANDING THE CORE CONCEPT:**
   Which one of the following memory systems operates constructively?
   a. computer memory
   b. human memory
   c. video recorder memory
   d. information recorded in a book

ANSWERS: 1. a   2. a   3. b   4. d   5. b

Core Concept

FIGURE 7.3: What an Eidetiker Sees

The combined images from the "Do It Yourself" box form a number pattern.

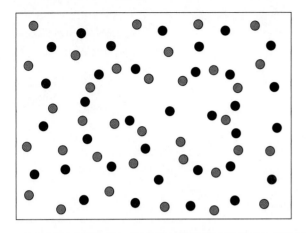

Key Question

HOW DO WE FORM MEMORIES?

Bring to mind a memory of a recent meeting with a close friend. Perhaps the encounter you remember began with a sensory impression of your friend's face or voice. This sensory image was quickly taken into working memory, which compared it with another image of your friend drawn from long-term storage. Finally, a more-or-less permanent memory trace of the meeting with your friend was laid down in your brain—the record that you have just retrieved. As you can see from this exercise, sensory memory, working memory, and long-term memory each perform different tasks. Yet, they work together to transform sensory information into a permanent memory. Our Core Concept says it this way:

Core Concept

> Each of the three memory systems encodes and stores memories in a different way, but they work together to transform sensory experience into a lasting record that has a pattern or meaning.

In this section you will find out just how the three stages of memory accomplish this. And, from a more practical standpoint, you will learn how cognitive psychology's understanding of these memory systems can suggest ways to improve your memory. We begin now with the first of the memory system's three stages.

Processing in Sensory Memory

As you read this book, your senses are filled with information: the words on the page, sounds in the room, the feel of your clothes on your skin, the temperature of the air, the slightly hungry feeling in your stomach. . . . The main task of sensory memory is to hold this flow of sensation just long enough for your brain to decide which stream of information needs your attention. (For visual information, this is usually about $1/4$ second.) But, just how much information can sensory memory hold? Cognitive psychologist George Sperling,

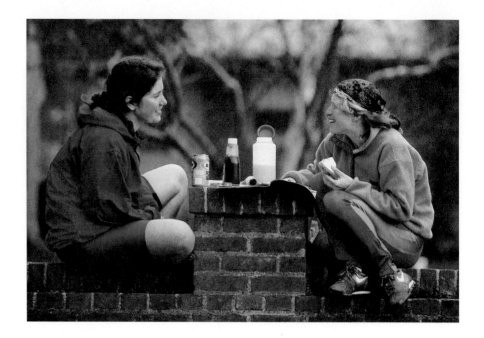

The sensory image of a friend's face is quickly taken into working memory. There it is elaborated with associations drawn from long-term storage.

answered this question by devising one of psychology's simplest and most clever experiments.

THE CAPACITY OF SENSORY MEMORY   In brief, Sperling found that this first stage of memory holds far more information than ever reaches consciousness. His method involved an array of letters, like the one below, flashed on a screen for a fraction of a second.

D   J   B

X   H   G

C   L   Y

First, Sperling asked volunteers to report as many of the letters as they could recall from the array. As you might expect, most people could remember only three or four items from such a brief exposure.

But, was it possible that much more information than these three or four items could have entered a temporary memory buffer and then vanished before it could be reported? Sperling thought so. To test this idea, he modified the experimental task in the following way. Immediately after the array of letters appeared, an auditory cue signaled which row of letters the subject was to report: A high-pitched tone indicated the top row, a medium tone the middle row, and a low tone meant the bottom row. Thus, respondents were asked to report items from only one row, rather than items from the whole array.

Under this "partial report" condition, most people achieved almost perfect accuracy—no matter *which* row was signaled. That is, they could accurately report *any* row, but not *all* rows. This result suggested that the actual capacity of sensory memory is nine or more items—even though all but three or four items usually disappear from sensory memory before they can enter consciousness (Sperling, 1960, 1963).

Would it be better if our sensory memories lasted longer so that we would have more time to scan them? Probably not. New information is constantly coming in, and it must also be monitored. Sensory memories last just

FIGURE 7.4: Multiple Sensory Stores

We have a separate sensory memory for each of our sensory pathways. All feed into short-term (working) memory.

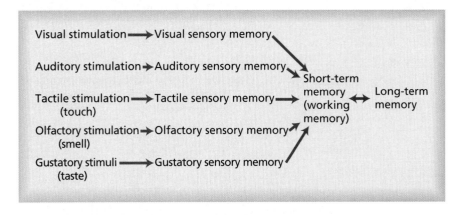

long enough to dissolve into one another and give us a sense of flow and continuity in our experience. But they usually do not last long enough to interfere with new incoming sensory impressions (Loftus et al., 1992). Incidentally, it is this blending of images in sensory memory that allows us to have the impression of motion in a "motion picture" — which is really just a rapid series of still images.

ENCODING AND STORAGE IN SENSORY MEMORY   The only encoding that happens in sensory memory is the transduction of stimuli into the form of neural impulses. But, because there is a separate sensory register for each sense, each part of sensory memory contains a different kind of information. (See Figure 7.4.) The sensory register for vision is called *iconic memory,* and it encodes light patterns that we see as visual images. Similarly, the sensory memory for hearing, known as *echoic memory,* encodes sound waves. In contrast with a visual image, an echoic image may persist for several seconds (Neisser, 1967). Experiments have shown that echoic (auditory) memory, too, holds more information than can pass into consciousness (Darwin et al., 1972).

RETRIEVAL FROM SENSORY MEMORY   As brief as these sensory memories are, they last long enough for the most important sensations to be selected for further processing in working memory. Generally, the sensations selected are those that grab our attention, for one reason or another. They might be especially intense stimuli (a loud noise), stimuli with personal significance (someone calls your name), or perhaps stimuli related to what you were already thinking about (the psychology of memory—right?). Sensory memory is, therefore, essential for holding input just long enough for it to be recognized and passed on for further processing.

THE BIOLOGICAL BASIS OF SENSORY MEMORY   Psychologists now believe that this initial stage of memory relies on the sense organs and the sensory pathways to the brain. Thus, sensory memory consists of the rapidly fading trace of stimulation in our sensory systems (Bower, 2000; Glanz, 1998). Each time the nerve cells in a sensory pathway fires, an old sensory memory is destroyed and a new one created.

Connection

Chapter 5
The senses *transduce* stimulus information into neural impulses.

Look at the following list of numbers and scan the four-digit number, the first number on the list. Don't try to memorize it. Just read it quickly; then look away from the page and try to recall the number. If you remember it correctly, go on to the next longer number, continuing down the list until you begin to make mistakes. How many digits are in the longest number that you can squeeze into your STM?

```
7  4  8  5
3  6  2  1  8
4  7  9  1  0  3
2  3  8  4  9  7  1
3  6  8  9  1  7  5  6
7  4  7  2  1  0  3  2  4
8  2  3  0  1  3  8  4  7  6
```

The result is your *digit span,* or your short-term (working) memory capacity for digits. Studies show that, under ideal testing conditions, most people can remember five to seven digits. If you remembered more, you may have been using special "chunking" techniques.

Processing in Working Memory

The second stage, working memory, is where you process conscious experience (LeDoux, 1996). It is the buffer in which you put the new name you have just heard. It is the momentary storage site for the words at the first part of this sentence as you read toward the end. Working memory provides a mental "work space" where we sort and encode information before adding it to long-term memory (Shiffrin, 1993). It is also the register into which a long-term memory of yesterday's psychology class can be retrieved as you review for tomorrow's test.

To be more precise, working memory is the temporary storage system in which incoming sensory information can be processed for long-term storage. In this role, working memory holds information far longer than does sensory memory—typically about 20 seconds, unless a special effort is made to rehearse the material and keep it active even longer. It is also the mental work space in which we mull over ideas and images pulled from long-term storage in the process that we call thought.

THE CAPACITY OF WORKING MEMORY   This stage of memory is associated with a "magic number": seven. That is, working memory holds about seven items—the number of digits in a phone number (Miller, 1956). This capacity varies slightly from person to person, so you may want to assess how much your own working memory can hold by trying the test in the "Do It Yourself!" box. Surprisingly, the capacity seems to be the same, no matter whether you are dealing with letters, numbers, words, shapes, or sounds. Seven (plus or minus two) items fill up short-term memory for most people. When we try to overload working memory, earlier items are usually lost to accommodate more recent ones. But, when working memory is filled with information that demands attention, we may not even notice new information that may be more important. This limited capacity of working memory, in the opinion of some experts, makes it unsafe to talk on your cell phone while driving (Wickelgren, 2001).

Please note that working memory's meager capacity is significantly smaller than that of sensory memory. In fact, working memory has the smallest capacity of the three memory systems. This limitation, combined with a tendency to discard information after about 20 seconds, makes this part of

Connection

Chapter 8
Thinking is a cognitive process that forms new mental representations.

FIGURE 7.5: The STM Bottleneck

Caught in the middle, with a much smaller capacity than sensory and long-term memories, short-term memory (working memory) becomes an information bottleneck in the memory system. As a result, much incoming information from sensory memory is lost.

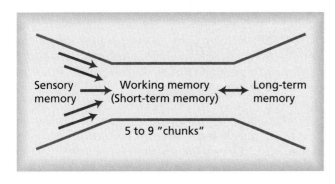

Sensory memory → Working memory (Short-term memory) ↔ Long-term memory

5 to 9 "chunks"

memory the information "bottleneck" of the memory system. (See Figure 7.5.) As you might have suspected, the twin problems of limited capacity and short duration are obstacles for students, who must process and remember large amounts of information when they hear a lecture or read a book. Fortunately, there are ways to work around these difficulties, as we will see below.

ENCODING AND STORAGE IN WORKING MEMORY   There are two important ways of dealing with the limitations of short-term storage: *chunking* and *rehearsal*. With the help of these strategies, information in working memory can be retained and transferred on to long-term memory. Successful students know how to use both strategies.

Chunks and Chunking   In memory, a *chunk* is any pattern or meaningful unit of information. A chunk can be a single letter or number, a group of letters or other items, or even an entire sentence. For example, the sequence 1–4–5–9 consists of four digits that could constitute four chunks. However, if you recognize this sequence as the last four digits of your telephone number — which is already available in your long-term memory — the four numbers need occupy only one chunk in STM. Often, the pattern identified by working memory is simply a pattern of sounds, as we shall see in more detail shortly.

The process of encoding separate items of information into a single pattern is called **chunking.** When you separate the seven digits of a phone number (e.g., 6731459) into two shorter strings of numbers (673-1459), you have transformed seven separate items into two chunks. (The phone company figured this out years ago — which is why they put hyphens in phone numbers.) By chunking you can get more material into the seven slots of working memory.

The Role of Rehearsal   Speaking of phone numbers, suppose that you have just looked up the number mentioned in the preceding paragraph. To keep it alive in working memory, you probably repeat the digits to yourself over and over. This technique is called **maintenance rehearsal,** and it serves well for maintaining information temporarily in working memory. Maintenance rehearsal not only keeps information fresh in working memory, but it prevents competing inputs from crowding it out. However, it is not an efficient way to transfer information to long-term memory — although it is a strategy commonly used for this purpose by people who don't know how memory operates.

Chunking: Organizing pieces of information into a smaller number of meaningful units (or, chunks) — a process that frees up space in working memory.

Maintenance rehearsal: A working-memory process in which information is merely repeated or reviewed to keep it from fading while in working memory. Maintenance rehearsal involves no active elaboration.

A better strategy for getting information into long-term memory involves **elaborative rehearsal.** With this method, information is not merely repeated but is actively connected to knowledge already stored. So, suppose that you own a florist shop, and you want people to remember your phone number. Because numbers are notoriously difficult to remember, you can help your customers with their elaborative rehearsal by using a "number" that makes use of the letters on the phone buttons, such as FLOWERS. The same principle can be used with more complex material, such as you are learning in psychology. For example, if you want to remember that the auditory component of sensory memory is *echoic* memory, you can elaborate this by thinking of an "echo" as an auditory sensation.

Acoustic Encoding   Verbal patterns in working memory often take an *acoustic* (sound) form, even when they come through an individual's eyes rather than ears. As a result, when subjects are asked to recall lists of letters they have just seen, the errors they make tend to involve confusions of letters that have a similar *sound* — such as D and T — rather than letters that have a similar look — such as E and F (Conrad, 1964). **Acoustic encoding** seems to be an essential part of the mechanism that allows us to learn and use spoken language (Schacter, 1999).

Levels of Processing in Working Memory   The more connections you can make with new information while it is in working memory, the more likely you are to remember it later (Craik, 1979). This obviously requires an interaction between working memory and long-term memory. According to the **levels-of-processing theory** proposed by Fergus Craik and Robert Lockhart (1972), "deeper" processing—establishing more connections with long-term memories—makes new information more meaningful and more memorable. An experiment will illustrate this point.

Craik and his colleague Endel Tulving (1975) had volunteer subjects examine a list of 60 common words presented on a screen one at a time. As each word appeared, the experimenters asked questions designed to control how deeply subjects processed each word. For example, when BEAR appeared on the screen, the experimenters would ask one of three questions: "Is it in capital letters?" "Does it rhyme with 'chair?'" "Is it an animal?" Craik and Tulving theorized that merely screening the word for capital letters would not require processing the word as deeply as would comparing its sound with that of another word. The deepest level of processing, they believed, would occur when some aspect of the word's meaning was analyzed, as when they asked whether BEAR was an animal. Thus, Craik and Tulving predicted that items processed more deeply would leave more robust traces in memory. Their prediction was correct. When the subjects were later asked to pick the original 60 words out of a larger list of 180, they remembered the deeply processed words much better than words processed more superficially, as the graph in Figure 7.6 shows.

THE BIOLOGICAL BASIS OF WORKING MEMORY   Recent neuroscience research suggests that circuits in the frontal cortex of the brain are crucial to the operation of working memory (Beardsley, 1997; Smith, 2000). These frontal regions are active across a variety of working memory tasks. And, as we might expect, the working memory circuits have connections with all the sensory parts of the brain and to areas known to be involved in long-term storage.

The research also suggests that the frontal regions house some "executive processes" that are involved in thinking about the information in short-term storage. These mental processes involve attention, setting priorities, planning, updating the contents of working memory, and monitoring the time sequence

Elaborative rehearsal: A working-memory process in which information is actively reviewed and related to information already in LTM.

Acoustic encoding: The conversion of information, especially semantic information, to sound patterns in working memory.

Levels-of-processing theory: The explanation for the fact that information that is more thoroughly connected to meaningful items in long-term memory (more "deeply" processed) will be remembered better.

FIGURE 7.6: Results of Craik and Tulving's Levels-of-Processing Experiment

Words that were processed more deeply (for meaning) were remembered better than words examined for rhymes or for target letters.

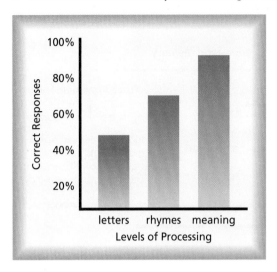

of events. Brain-imaging studies indicate that the executive processes of working memory are anatomically distinct from the sites of short-term storage (Smith & Jonides, 1999).

Long-Term Memory Processing

Can you remember who invented the concept of classical conditioning? What is the name of a play by Shakespeare? How many birthdays have you had? Such information and much more is stored in your long-term memory (LTM), the last of the three memory stages.

Given the vast amount of data stored in LTM, it is a marvel that so much of it is so easily accessible. Your responses to the questions above probably came quickly because of a special feature of long-term memory: Words and concepts are encoded by their *meanings,* which interconnects them with other items that have similar meanings. Consequently, many different *retrieval cues* (stimuli that prompt the activation of a long- term memory) can often help you find the item you want amid all the data stored there.

How much information can long-term memory hold? Apparently, it has unlimited capacity. LTM uses this capacity to store all the experiences, events, information, emotions, skills, words, categories, rules, and judgments that have been transferred to it from working memory. Thus, your LTM contains your total knowledge of the world and of yourself. Material in long-term memory enables you to solve new problems, reason, keep future appointments, and use a variety of rules to manipulate abstract symbols, so that you can think about hypothetical situations or pure fantasies. This versatility of LTM arises from the functions of its two major partitions.

THE PARTITIONS OF LONG-TERM MEMORY   We have two main kinds of LTM, each distinguished by the sort of information it holds. One, a register for the things we know how to *do,* is called *procedural* memory. The other acts as storage for the information that we can *describe*—the facts we know and the experiences we remember. It is called *declarative* memory.

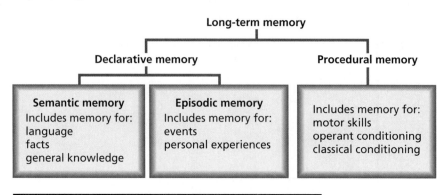

FIGURE 7.7: A Model of Multiple Long-Term Memory Systems

Evidence from humans, rats, and monkeys suggests that semantic, episodic, and procedural memories involve distinct memory systems. Implicit memories in the semantic or procedural systems may influence behavior without conscious processing.

Connection

Chapter 8
An expert's knowledge is both more extensive and more organized than that of a novice.

Procedural memory: A division of LTM that stores memories for how things are done.

Declarative memory: A division of LTM that stores explicit information; also known as *fact memory*. Declarative memory has two subdivisions: *episodic memory* and *semantic memory*.

Episodic memory: A subdivision of declarative memory that stores memory for personal events, or "episodes."

Semantic memory: A subdivision of declarative memory that stores general knowledge, including the meanings of words and concepts.

Procedural Memory   Mental directions, or "procedures," for how things are done are stored in **procedural memory**. We use it to remember skills we have learned, such as riding a bicycle, tying shoelaces, or playing a musical instrument (Anderson, 1982; Tulving, 1983). Most of its operations occur at the fringes of awareness. Typically, we recall the details of our skill memories to consciousness only during the early phases of performance, when we first begin learning a skill. Experts, such as concert pianists, learn to perform tasks requiring advanced skills without conscious recall of the details, much as you can run down a flight of stairs without concentrating on the exact movements of your feet. (See Figure 7.7.)

Declarative Memory   The other major division of LTM, **declarative memory,** stores specific information, such as facts and events. Recalling the directions for driving to a specific location requires declarative memory (although knowing how to drive a car depends on procedural memory). In contrast with procedural memory, declarative memory more often requires some conscious mental effort. You may be able to see evidence of this when people roll their eyes or make facial gestures while searching for material in declarative memory. As they do so, they are searching either of two subdivisions of declarative memory: *episodic* and *semantic* memory.

Episodic memory is the portion of declarative memory that stores personal information: your memory for events, or "episodes" in your life. It also stores *temporal coding* (or time tags) to identify when the event occurred and *context coding* that indicates where it took place. For example, memories of your recent vacation or of an unhappy love affair are stored in episodic memory, along with codes for where and when these episodes occurred. In this way, episodic memory acts as your internal diary or autobiographical record. You consult episodic memory when someone says, "Where were you on New Year's Eve?" or "What did you do in class last Tuesday?"

Semantic memory is the other division of declarative memory. It stores the basic meanings of words and concepts. Usually, semantic memory retains no information about the time and place its contents were acquired. Thus, you keep the meaning of "cat" in semantic memory—but not a recollection of the occasion on which you first learned the meaning of "cat." In this respect, semantic memory more closely resembles an encyclopedia or a database than an autobiography. It stores a vast quantity of facts about names, faces, grammar, history, music, manners, scientific principles, and religious beliefs. All the facts and concepts you know are stored there, and you consult its registry when someone asks you, "Who was the third president?" or "What are the two divisions of declarative memory?"

ENCODING FOR LONG-TERM MEMORY   Anything stored in LTM must be "filed" according to its pattern or meaning. Accordingly, the best way to add material to long-term memory is to associate it in some way with material already stored there, a process that we have called *elaborative rehearsal*. Encoding many such connections gives you more ways of accessing the information, much as a town with many access roads can be approached from many directions.

The role that *meaningful organization* plays in long-term storage is demonstrated when you remember the gist or sense of an idea rather than the actual sentence you heard. For example, you may hear the sentence, "The book was returned to the library by Mary." Later, you are asked if you heard the sentence, "Mary returned the book to the library." You may indeed mistakenly remember having "heard" the second sentence, because even though the two sentences are completely different utterances, they mean the same thing. Thus, human LTM stores *meaning*, rather than an exact replica of the original event (Bransford & Franks, 1971). This is exactly what you would expect from a memory system that relies on the same cognitive processes and brain pathways as does our perceptual system.

The practical application of the fact that LTM is organized according to meaning is this: *If you want to store new information in your LTM, you must make it meaningful while it is in working memory.* This requires you to associate new information with things you already know. That's why it is important in your classes (such as your psychology class) to think of personal examples of the concepts you want to remember. On the other hand, the organization of LTM according to meaning is also the source of memory distortion and inaccuracy because we remember things as we think they *should have been* rather than the way they actually happened. Later in the chapter we shall see how this can cause difficulties in eyewitness testimony.

THE BIOLOGICAL BASIS OF LONG-TERM MEMORY   Research on the biological underpinnings of long-term memory has taken two paths. One involves tracing the brain circuits used by memory. The other path involves searching for the biochemical changes that represent the **engram,** the physical trace of memory.

The search along the first path, for the brain circuits involved in memory, has led to many disappointments. Pioneering brain researcher Karl Lashley approached the problem by surgically removing portions of rats' brains and later testing the animals to see if they had lost memory for a task learned prior to surgery. After years of such work, a frustrated Lashley finally gave up his quest for the engram (Lashley, 1950). Many other researchers efforts have met similar dead ends.

The Tragic Case of H. M.   A breakthrough came in the form of a tragic figure, known only by his initials: H. M. As a result of an unfortunate brain operation in 1953, H. M. lost most of his ability to form episodic memories (Hilts, 1995). Since that time, he has been unable to create new memories of the events in his life. Nevertheless, he has worked extensively with psychologist Brenda Milner, and we owe much of our understanding of memory to their relationship.

Procedural memory allows experts like pitcher Pedro Martinez to perform complex tasks automatically, without conscious recall of the details.

Connection

Chapter 5
Perception involves an *interpretation* of the external world.

Engram: The physical trace, or biological basis, of memory.

In the TV show, *The Weakest Link,* contestants must retrieve facts from the semantic division of declarative memory.

Connection

Chapter 2
The *hippocampus* and *amygdala* are structures in the limbic system of the brain.

Anterograde amnesia: The inability to form memories for new information (as opposed to *retrograde amnesia,* which involves the inability to remember information previously stored in memory).

H. M.'s problem arose from the removal of the hippocampus and amygdala on both sides of his brain. This was done in a surgical procedure that was intended to treat the severe epileptic seizures from which he suffered as a young man (see Figure 7.8). In the nearly 50 years since his surgery, H. M. has not been able to remember someone he met five minutes earlier. Nor has he been able to learn where he lives or who takes care of him. He is always shocked to see an aging face when he looks in the mirror, expecting to see the younger man he was a half century ago (Milner et al., 1968; Rosenzweig, 1992b). He is a man caught in the present moment, which seems to fade without a trace.

Remarkably, H. M. has a normal memory for events prior to his surgery —even though he cannot recall anything that has happened to him since that time 50 years ago. On his medical record, his condition is called **anterograde amnesia.** But, to put the problem in cognitive terms, H. M. can no longer transfer new experiences from short-term storage to long-term memory.

After H. M.'s operation his IQ score actually rose from 101 to 118—probably as a result of fewer seizures. His working memory capacity for digits remained at 6 to 7, well within the normal range. He can still remember with reasonable accuracy the events of his youth and the concepts he learned before the operation. He can also use language well. But when Milner tested his abilities to form new memories, she found that information about events, objects, and people slip away before he can store them in long-term memory—much as you might forget a phone number that you just looked up. As a result of this disabling memory problem, H. M. must live in a nursing home, where his caretakers and his surroundings forever appear unfamiliar. He reads the same magazines over and over. Ironically, he has been able to remember that he has a memory problem.

What have we learned from H. M.? The pattern of his memory loss has shown us that long-term memory is *not* a single entity—not one big mental storage bin. As we will see below, Milner has been able to show that H. M. retains the ability to form *procedural* memories, even though he cannot lay down new *episodic* traces. Just as important, H. M.'s case also brought renewed interest in finding the biological underpinnings of memory. Specifically, H. M.'s case has suggested to neuroscientists that the hippocampus and

FIGURE 7.8: The Hippocampus and Amygdala

The hippocampus and amygdala were surgically removed from both sides of H. M.'s brain. To help yourself visualize where these structures lie, compare the drawing with the MRI image. The MRI shows the brain in cross section, with a slice through the hippocampus visible on each side.

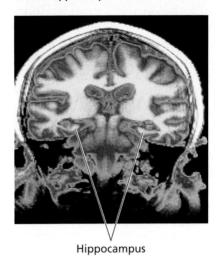
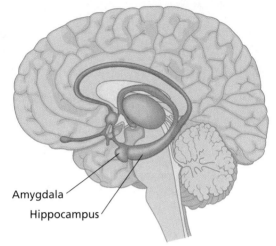

Amygdala

Hippocampus

Hippocampus

amygdala are involved in creating long-term memories of our experiences. This conjecture has also been supported by animal studies and studies of the rare individuals with brain damage similar to H. M.'s (Eichenbaum, 1997; Schacter, 1996). Recent animal research also suggests that the hippocampus plays an especially important role in *place learning* — of the sort that produced cognitive maps in Tolman's rats (Beardsley, 1997).

Neuroscience and Long-Term Memory   Neuroscientists have added much detail to the picture that H. M. has given us of human memory. A part of the brain that deteriorates in Alzheimer's disease (a common cause of memory deficits in elderly persons) is the same structure that was removed from H. M.'s brain. Neuroscientists have also discovered that the brain uses some of the same circuits for memory that it uses for sensation, perception, and motor responses. For example, studies show that the brain's visual cortex is involved in generating visual memory images (Barinaga, 1995; Ishai & Sagi, 1995, 1997; Kosslyn et al., 1995). Further, it has been discovered that a person who sustains damage to a part of the brain involving sensations may lose memories for those sensations. For example, damage to the regions that process color vision may cause memory loss for colors — even to the point of being incapable of imagining what colors might look like (Jacks, 1995; Zeki, 1992). In general, memories of experiences processed by the senses call on parts of the brain used to perceive those experiences in the first place (Martin et al., 1995).

Memories, Neurons, and Synapses   The second approach to the engram — the physical basis of memory — has focused on the chemistry of neurons and their synapses. In brief, neuroscience has shown that memories initially form as fragile chemical traces that gradually consolidate into more permanent records over time (McGaugh, 2000). For this reason, a blow to the head or an electric shock to the brain can cause loss of recent memories that have not yet consolidated.

Connection

Chapter 6
Tolman's demonstration of *cognitive maps* showed that learning can consist of something other than behaviors.

Connection

Chapter 2
Alzheimer's disease involves deterioration of the hippocampus and progressive memory deficits.

Memories can be enhanced by emotional arousal: It is unlikely that the Bush family will forget this moment.

Long-term potentiation: A process underlying memory, by which active pathways in the brain become more likely to respond in the future, as the result of biochemical changes in those pathways.

While memories are forming, they can also be enhanced, particularly by the person's emotional state: Emotionally arousing experiences are usually remembered vividly. This is, of course, highly adaptive. If you survive a frightening encounter with a bear, for example, you are quite likely to remember to avoid bears in the future. The underlying biology involves emotion-related chemicals, such as epinephrine (adrenalin) and certain stress hormones, which have as one of their many roles the ability to enhance memory for such experiences (LeDoux, 1996; McGaugh, 2000).

At the level of synapses and nerve cells, neuroscientists have found memory associated with structural changes in neural circuits (Balter, 2000; Beardsley, 1997; Haberlandt, 1999; Travis, 2000). They have also found that drugs that block these changes interfere with the formation of long-term memories (Lynch & Staubli, 1991). The picture that emerges from such research is this: Memory forms when active pathways in the brain become more likely to respond in the future, as the result of biochemical changes called **long-term potentiation.** Many such neural pathways are probably involved in encoding and storing a single memory.

Psychology

In Your Life

"Flashbulb" Memories: Where Were You When. . . ?

The closest most people will come to having a "photographic memory" is a **flashbulb memory,** an exceptionally clear recollection of an important event. You probably have a few such memories: a tragic accident, a death, a graduation, a victory. It's as though you had made a flash picture in your mind of the striking scene (Brown & Kulik, 1977).

Some events, such as the attacks on New York and Washington, Princess Diana's death, or the shootings at Columbine high school, have such wide impact that many people form flashbulb memories that record precisely where they were at the time, what they were

doing, and the emotions they felt. One study found that most people who were watching the televised explosion of the space shuttle Challenger reported vivid flashbulb memories. Similarly, researchers found that events surrounding the attempted assassination of President Reagan (Pillemer, 1984) and the O. J. Simpson trial verdict (Schmolck et al., 2000) also caused large numbers of people to develop flashbulb memories.

Why are flashbulb memories so vivid? For one thing, they are likely to be remarkable because they record unusual events. For another, flashbulb memories have strong emotional associations that make them distinctive and readily located in LTM. Indeed, accumulating evidence shows that emotion exerts a powerful influence on memory. And, as we have noted, strongly

The attacks on the World Trade Center and the Pentagon were shocking events, and many Americans have "flashbulb" memories that include where they were and what they were doing when they learned of the attacks.

emotional experiences stimulate the release of stress-related hormones which can strengthen memories (Cahill et al., 1994; McGaugh, 2000).

Indeed, flashbulb memories are formed primarily by people who have some sort of personal interest or involvement in the remembered event. Thus, many British people reported flashbulb memories of where they were and what they were doing when Prime Minister Margaret Thatcher resigned (Conway et al., 1994). It is likely, though, that most Americans have nothing more than a hazy memory for the occurrence.

Despite such strong emotional involvement, flashbulb memories can be remarkably accurate (Schmolck et al., 2000). Yet, some studies have found that some flashbulb memories are highly distorted (Neisser, 1991). On the morning after the Challenger disaster, psychologists asked university freshmen to describe the circumstances under which they had heard the news. Three years later they were asked the same question again. Of the latter accounts, about one-third were dead wrong—even though respondents reported a high level of confidence in their accuracy (Winograd & Neisser, 1992).

The discrepancy between these two findings has been recently clarified: The inaccuracies seem to creep in over time. While flashbulb memories up to a year later are usually nearly identical to reports given immediately after the event, recollections gathered after two or three years show substantial distortions (Schmolck et al., 2000). Just because your memory for an important event is accurate now, don't expect it to stay that way. Chances are that, after a year or two, it will undergo a change. What probably won't change, however, is your confidence in your distorted recollection.

CHECK**YOUR**UNDERSTANDING

1. **RECALL:** *Which part of memory has the smallest capacity? (That is, which part of memory is considered the "bottleneck" in the memory system?)*
   a. sensory memory
   b. working memory
   c. long-term memory
   d. implicit memory

2. **RECALL:** *Which part of long-term memory stores autobiographical information?*
   a. semantic memory
   b. procedural memory
   c. recognition memory
   d. episodic memory

3. **RECALL:** *In order to get material into permanent storage, it must be made meaningful while it is in*
   a. sensory memory.
   b. working memory.
   c. long-term memory.
   d. recall memory.

4. **APPLICATION:** *As you study the vocabulary in this book, which method would result in the deepest level of processing?*

   a. learning the definition given in the marginal glossary
   b. marking each term with a highlighter each time it occurs in a sentence in the text
   c. thinking of an example of each term
   d. having a friend read a definition, with you having to identify the term in question form, as on the TV show *Jeopardy*

   Core Concept

5. **UNDERSTANDING THE CORE CONCEPT:**
   As the information in this book passes from one stage of your memory to the next, the information becomes more:
   a. important.
   b. meaningful.
   c. interesting.
   d. accurate.

   ANSWERS: 1. b   2. d   3. b   4. c   5. b

Flashbulb memory: A clear and vivid long-term memory of an especially meaningful and emotional event.

Key Question

?

HOW DO WE RETRIEVE MEMORIES?

Accurate retrieval is obviously the whole point of memory. But there are several quirks of retrieval that are not obvious. One involves the possibility of retrieving a memory that you didn't know you had. Another involves being both quite confident of a memory and quite wrong. Our Core Concept summarizes the retrieval process this way:

Core Concept

> **Whether memories are implicit or explicit, the success of their retrieval depends on how they were encoded and how they are cued.**

We will begin our exploration of retrieval with another lesson from H. M.

Implicit and Explicit Memory

Despite the massive disruption of H. M.'s episodic memory for new events and facts, some parts of his memory remain intact (Milner et al., 1968; Raymond, 1989). Studies by Brenda Milner, the psychologist who has become his guardian and protector, have shown that H. M. can learn new and complex motor skills. For example Milner has taught him the difficult skill of mirror writing—writing while looking at his hands in a mirror. In general, H. M.'s *procedural* memory for such motor tasks is quite normal, even though he cannot remember learning these skills and doesn't know that he knows how to perform them.

You don't have to have brain damage like H. M.'s to have memories of which you are unaware. A normal memory has disconnected islands of information, too. For over a hundred years psychologists have realized that people can know something without knowing that they know it (Roediger, 1990). Memory expert Daniel Schacter (1992, 1996) calls this **implicit memory:** memory that can affect your behavior but which you did not deliberately learn or of which you have no conscious awareness. By contrast, **explicit memory** involves conscious awareness that you know certain information or know how to perform a particular task. In brief, having an explicit memory means *knowing that you know.*

Implicit memories are not limited to procedural memories. Information in your semantic store can be either *explicit* (such as in remembering the material you have studied for a test) or *implicit* (such as knowing the color of the building in which your psychology class is held). Accordingly, there are degrees of implicit memory, ranging from information that was acquired in the background of consciousness (the color of the psychology building) to the nonconscious procedural memories of amnesic patients like H. M. Whatever the degree, implicit memories can affect people's behavior without their realizing it. And, to complicate matters, psychologists have found that we cannot trust our implicit memories to be accurate any more than we can trust our explicit memories (Seger, 1994).

Implicit memory: A memory that was not deliberately learned or of which you have no conscious awareness.

Explicit memory: Memory that has been processed with attention and can be consciously recalled.

Connection

Chapter 5
Priming is a technique used for studying both unconscious processing and implicit memory.

RETRIEVING IMPLICIT MEMORIES BY PRIMING A quirk of implicit memory landed former Beatle George Harrison in court (Schacter, 1996). Lawyers for a singing group known as the Chiffons claimed that the melody in Harrison's song "My Sweet Lord" was nearly identical to that of the Chiffon classic, "He's So Fine." Harrison denied that he deliberately borrowed the melody but conceded that he had heard the Chiffons's tune prior to writing his own. The court agreed, stating that Harrison's borrowing was a product of "subconscious memory."

Everyday life abounds with similar experiences, says Daniel Schacter (1996). You may have proposed an idea to a friend and had it rejected. But, weeks later your friend excitedly proposes the same idea to you, as if it were entirely new.

In such real-life situations it is hard to say what cues an implicit memory to surface. Psychologists have, however, developed ways to "prime" implicit memories in the laboratory (Schacter, 1996). To illustrate, imagine that you have volunteered for a memory experiment. First, you are shown a list of words for several seconds:

assassin, octopus, avocado, mystery, sheriff, climate

Then, an hour later, the experimenter asks you to examine another list and indicate which items you recognize from the earlier list: *twilight, assassin, dinosaur,* and *mystery.* That task is easy for you. But then the experimenter shows you some words with missing letters and asks you to fill in the blanks:

ch – – – – nk, o – t – – – us, – og – y – – –, – l – m – te

It is likely that answers for two of these pop readily into mind: *octopus* and *climate.* But chances are that you will be less successful with the other two words: *chipmunk* and *bogeyman.* The reason for this difference has to do with **priming,** the procedure of providing cues that stimulate memories without awareness of the connection between the cue and the retrieved memory. Because you had been primed with the words *octopus* and *climate,* they more easily "popped out" in your consciousness than did the words that had not been primed.

RETRIEVING EXPLICIT MEMORIES BY RECALL AND RECOGNITION   Retrieval of explicit memories calls for different methods — which we can observe in nearly any classroom: One retrieval method involves essay tests, the other multiple choice tests. **Recall,** required by an essay test, is a retrieval task in which you must create an answer almost entirely from memory, with the help of only minimal cues from the question. "What are the three memory operations?" is a recall question. **Recognition,** on another hand, is the method called for by multiple-choice tests. It is a retrieval task in which you merely identify whether a stimulus has been previously experienced. Normally, recognition is less demanding than recall because the cues available for a recognition task are much more complete.

Recognition is also the method used by police when they ask an eyewitness to identify a suspected robber in a lineup. The witness is required only to match a stimulus from memory (the robber) against a present stimulus (a suspect in the lineup). What would be a comparable recall task? A witness working with a police artist to make a drawing of a suspect must recall, entirely from memory, the suspect's facial characteristics.

Context and Encoding Specificity: Codes and Cues for Better Memories   We have seen that the ability to retrieve information from LTM depends on how information was encoded and rehearsed. You won't be surprised to learn that alertness, stress level, drugs, and general knowledge also affect retrieval. Less well known, however, are influences related to the *context* in which you encoded a memory and the context in which you are remembering. Later in the chapter we will also see how your mood state can also affect what you remember.

Priming: A technique for cuing implicit memories by providing cues that stimulate a memory without awareness of the connection between the cue and the retrieved memory.

Recall: A retrieval method in which one must reproduce previously presented information.

Recognition: A retrieval method in which one must identify present stimuli as having been previously presented.

Perhaps you have encountered your psychology professor at the grocery store, and you needed a moment to recognize who it was. On the other hand, you may have been talking to a childhood friend, and something she said cued a flood of memories that you hadn't thought about for years. These experiences are contrasting examples of **encoding specificity.** That is, they involve situations in which the context affected the way a memory was encoded and stored—which influenced its retrieval at a later time. In general, researchers have found that *the more closely the retrieval cues match the form in which the information was encoded, the better it will be remembered.*

The issue of encoding specificity has not been completely nailed down, however. It seems that context has a bigger effect under some circumstances than others, although researchers are still trying to discover why this is so (Bjork & Richardson-Klavehn, 1989). Apparently, you don't have to worry about a context effect when you study in one setting and take a test in another (Fernandez & Glenberg, 1985; Saufley et al., 1985). Of far more importance to your grade are the kinds of test questions you face. If the exam questions are quite different from anything you have encountered before in class or in your reading, then you may find the exam difficult. For this reason, cognitive psychologist Robert Bjork (2000) suggests that teachers approach the material with their students in a variety of ways. Bjork has even suggested that teachers introduce "desirable difficulties" into their courses. By this he means that students should be induced to grapple with the material in many different ways, rather than just memorizing the material and parroting it back.

Encoding specificity: A process by which memory is encoded and stored with specific cues related to the context in which it was formed. The more closely the retrieval cues match the form in which the information was encoded, the better it will be remembered.

TOT phenomenon: The inability to recall a word, while knowing that it is in memory. People often describe this frustrating experience as having the word "on the tip of the tongue."

On the Tip of Your Tongue

Psychology

In Your Life

Try to answer the following questions before you read further:

▶ What is the North American equivalent of the reindeer?

▶ What do artists call the board on which they mix paints?

▶ What is the name for a tall, four-sided stone monument with a point at the top of its shaft?

▶ What instrument do navigators use to determine latitude by sighting on the stars?

▶ What is the name of the large metal urns used in Russia to dispense tea?

▶ What is the name of a small Chinese boat usually propelled with a single oar or pole?

Unless you have a memory problem like H. M., your response to at least some of these questions was probably either (a) recall of the correct word or (b) the inability to recall the word, accompanied by the strong sense that you have it somewhere in memory. In the second case, the answer was "on the tip of your tongue," an experience that psychologists call the **TOT phenomenon** (Brown, 1991). Surveys show that most people have this experience about once a week. Those who play the board game *Trivial Pursuit* know it well.

The most common TOT experiences come from blocking on the names of personal acquaintances, names of famous persons, and familiar objects (Brown, 1991). About half the time, the target words finally do pop into mind, usually within about one agonizing minute.

Many people know the name for objects like this one—even though they can't quite remember it. Such words are often said to be "on the tip of the tongue."

Most subjects report that the experience is uncomfortable (Brown & McNeill, 1966).

What accounts for the TOT phenomenon? It is the same basic process that causes difficulty in recalling a name when you see a familiar face: the distinction between recall and recognition. Even though you were unable to *recall* some of the correct words (caribou, palette, obelisk, sextant, samovar, sampan) you could probably *recognize* most of them. Some features of the sought-for word may abruptly pop to mind ("I know it begins with an *s!*"), even though the word itself eluded you. Thus, the TOT phenomenon occurs when there is a poor match between retrieval cues and the encoding of the word in long-term memory.

We'll bet you can't name all Seven Dwarfs.

WHY DOES MEMORY SOMETIMES FAIL US?

We forget appointments and anniversaries. During today's test we can't remember what we studied the night before. A familiar name seems just out of our mental reach. And, yet, we cannot rid our minds of an unhappy event. Why does memory play these tricks on us—making us remember what we would rather forget and forget what we want to remember?

According to memory expert Daniel Schacter, the blame falls on what he terms the "seven sins" of memory: *transience, absent-mindedness, blocking, misattribution, suggestibility, bias,* and unwanted *persistence* (Schacter, 1999, 2001). Further, he claims, that these seven problems are really the consequences of some very helpful features of human memory. These are features that stood our ancestors in good stead and so are preserved in our own memory systems. Our Core Concept puts this notion more succinctly:

> **Most of our memory problems arise from memory's "seven sins" — which are really by-products of otherwise adaptive features of human memory.**

Transience: The impermanence of a long-term memory. Transience is based on the idea that long-term memories gradually fade in strength over time.

Relearning: A technique, invented by Hermann Ebbinghaus, used in measuring memory retention by recording the number of trials necessary to relearn certain material. This is then compared with the number of trials necessary to learn the material originally (see *savings method*).

Savings method: Ebbinghaus's approach to measuring memory retention by calculating "savings" in number of trials necessary for relearning after varying amounts of time.

Forgetting curve: A graph plotting the amount of retention and forgetting over time for a certain batch of material, such as a list of nonsense syllables. The typical forgetting curve is steep at first, becoming flatter as time goes on.

Connection

Chapter 2
PET and fMRI are brain scanning techniques that form images of especially active regions in the brain.

As we look into the "seven sins," we will also have the opportunity to consider such practical problems as the reliability of eyewitness testimony and some ways that memory can contribute to certain mental disorders, such as depression. In this section we will also revisit the "memory wars," involving disputes about recovered memories of a sexual abuse — the problem that we encountered in Donna Smith's case at the beginning of the chapter. Finally, we will look at some strategies for improving our memories by overcoming some of Schacter's "seven sins."

Transience — When Memories Fade

Memories seem to weaken with time. (How would you do on a rigorous test of the course work you took a year ago?) Although no one has directly observed a human memory trace fade and disappear, much circumstantial evidence points to the **transience,** or impermanence, of long-term memory — the first of Schacter's "sins."

In a classic study of transience, pioneering psychologist Hermann Ebbinghaus (1908/1973) learned lists of *nonsense syllables* (such as POV, KEB, and RUZ) and tried to recall them over varying time intervals. This worked well to assess his retention over short periods up to a few days. But to measure memory after long delays of weeks or months, when recall had failed completely, Ebbinghaus invented a method that required **relearning** the items on the original list. Because he had kept a record of the number of trials it took him to learn a list the first time, he could compare this with the number of trials required to *relearn* the list. If it took fewer trials to relearn it than to learn it originally, the difference indicated a "savings" that could serve as a measure of memory. By using both the recall and the **savings method,** Ebbinghaus could trace what happened to memory over time. The curve obtained when he plotted the data is shown in Figure 7.9. There you can see how the graph initially plunges steeply and then flattens out over time. This represents one of Ebbinghaus's most important discoveries: *For relatively meaningless material, there is a rapid initial loss of memory, followed by a declining rate of loss.* Subsequent research shows that this **forgetting curve** captures the pattern of transience by which we forget much of the verbal material we learn.

Modern psychologists have built on Ebbinghaus's work, but they are more interested in how we remember *meaningful* material, such as information you read in this book. Much of the modern work uses brain scanning techniques, such as fMRI and PET, to visualize diminishing brain activity during forgetting (Schacter, 1996, 1999). Animal studies also suggest that synaptic connections become weaker over time.

Some memories, however, do not follow this fading pattern. Motor skills, for example, are often retained substantially intact in procedural memory for many years, even without practice — "just like riding a bicycle." The same goes for certain especially memorable experiences, such as "flashbulb" incidents or emotional childhood events. Obviously, the transiency hypothesis — that memories fade over time — doesn't describe the fate of all our memories. As we will see next, even some memories that are forgotten haven't faded away. Instead, they are temporarily lost.

FIGURE 7.9: Ebbinghaus's Forgetting Curve

How many nonsense syllables can people remember when tested over a 30-day period? The curve shows that recall decreases rapidly and reaches a plateau, below which little more is forgotten. The fastest decrease in recall occurs during the first day after learning.

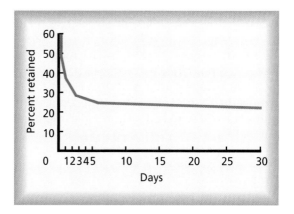

Absent-Mindedness — When Lapses of Attention Cause Forgetting

When you misplace your car keys or forget an anniversary, you have had an episode of **absent-mindedness.** It's not that the memory had disappeared from your brain circuits. Rather, you have suffered a lapse that shifted your attention elsewhere. In the case of a forgotten anniversary, the attention problem occurred on the retrieval end — when you were concentrating on something that took your attention away from the upcoming anniversary. And as for the car keys, your attentive shift probably occurred during the original encoding — when you should have been paying attention to where you laid the keys. In college students, this form of absent-mindedness commonly comes from listening to music or watching TV while studying. In the laboratory, depth-of-processing studies, discussed earlier in the chapter, provide experimental support for this form of absent-mindedness (Schacter, 1999).

Blocking — When Memories Encounter Interference

You are most likely to notice this memory "sin" when you have a "tip-of-the-tongue" experience. It also occurs when you attempt to learn two conflicting things in succession, such as would happen if you had a French class followed by a Spanish class. In general, **blocking** occurs when information has encountered *interference,* when one item interrupts the retrieval of another from memory.

A common source of interference comes from an old habit getting in the way of a new one. This can happen, for example, when people switch from one word-processing program to another. More generally, psychologists distinguish between two main forms of interference: *proactive interference* and *retroactive interference.* Both account for much of our everyday forgetting. We will look more closely at each.

PROACTIVE INTERFERENCE When an old memory disrupts the learning and remembering of new information, **proactive interference** is the culprit. An example of proactive interference occurs when, after moving to a new home,

Absent-mindedness: Forgetting caused by lapses in attention.

Blocking: Forgetting that occurs when an item in memory cannot be accessed or retrieved. Blocking is caused by *interference.*

Proactive interference: A cause of forgetting by which previously stored information prevents learning and remembering new information.

Misplacing your car keys results from a shift in attention. Which of the seven "sins" does this represent?

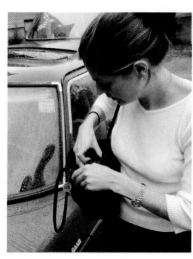

you still look for items in the old places where you used to store them, although no such locations exist in your new environment. *Pro-* means "forward," so in *pro*active interference old memories act forward in time to block your attempts at learning.

RETROACTIVE INTERFERENCE When the opposite happens — when newly learned information prevents the retrieval of previously learned material — we can blame forgetting on **retroactive interference.** *Retro-* means "backward"; the newer material seems to reach back into your memory to block access to old material. Retroactive interference describes what happens when you drive a car with an automatic transmission and then forget to use the clutch when you return to one with a "stick shift." That is, recent experience retroactively interferes with your ability to retrieve an older memory. (See Figure 7.10.)

Retroactive interference: A cause of forgetting by which newly learned information prevents retrieval of previously stored material.

FIGURE 7.10:   Two Types of Interference

In *proactive interference*, earlier learning (Spanish) interferes with memory for later information (French). In *retroactive interference*, new information (French) interferes with memory for information learned earlier (Spanish).

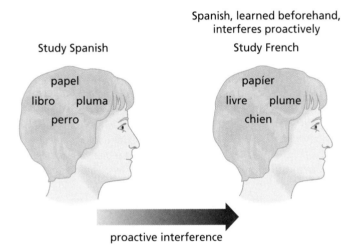

Spanish, learned beforehand, interferes proactively

Study Spanish   Study French

papel   papíer
libro   pluma   livre   plume
perro   chien

French 101
Mid-term exam

proactive interference

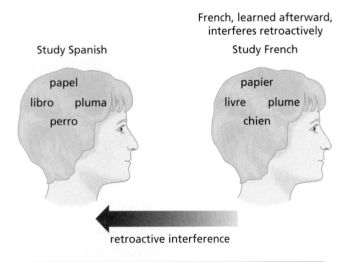

French, learned afterward, interferes retroactively

Study Spanish   Study French

papel   papíer
libro   pluma   livre   plume
perro   chien

Spanish 101
Mid-term exam

retroactive interference

Psychological research has established two important principles that govern interference:

1. The greater the *similarity* between two sets of material to be learned, the greater the interference between them is likely to be.
2. *Meaningless* material is more vulnerable to interference than meaningful material.

Accordingly, classes in French and Spanish would have more potential to interfere with each other more than would French and biology. Likewise, a list of nonsense syllables, such as Ebbinghaus used, would be more vulnerable to interference than would a poem.

THE SERIAL POSITION EFFECT   You may have noticed that the first and last parts of a poem or a vocabulary list are easier to learn and remember than the middle portion. Interference theory explains this **serial position effect** by pointing out that the material in the middle—unlike that at the ends of the poem or list—is exposed to both retroactive and proactive interference. The middle part receives interference from both directions, while material at either end gets interference from only one side. (This suggests that you might find it helpful to pay special attention to the material in the middle of this chapter.)

Misattribution — When Memories Connect with the Wrong Context

All three "sins" discussed so far make memories inaccessible. Sometimes, however, memories are retrievable, but they are associated with the wrong time, place, or person. Schacter (1999) calls this **misattribution.**

In an ironic example of misattribution, psychologist Donald Thompson was accused of rape, based on a victim's detailed, but mistaken, description of her assailant (Thompson, 1988). Thompson's alibi was indisputable, however. At the time of the crime he was being interviewed live on television—about memory distortions. The victim, it turned out, had been watching the interview just before she was raped and had misattributed the assault to Thompson.

To give another example: People sometimes mistakenly believe that other people's ideas are their own. This sort of misattribution occurs when a person hears an idea and keeps it in memory, while forgetting its source. Unintentional plagiarism comes from this form of misattribution, as we saw earlier in the case of Beatle George Harrison.

Another type of misattribution can cause people to remember something they did not experience. Such was the case with volunteers who were asked to remember a set of words associated with a particular theme: *door, glass, pane, shade, ledge, sill, house, open, curtain, frame, view, breeze, sash, screen,* and *shutter.* Under these conditions, many participants later remembered *window,* even though that word was not on the list (Roediger & McDermott, 1995, 2000). This result shows the power of *context cues* in determining the content of memory. It also demonstrates, once again, how people tend to create and retrieve memories based on meaning.

Suggestibility — When Cues Distort or Create Memories

Memories can also be distorted or created by *suggestion.* This possibility is of particular importance to the law, where witnesses may be interviewed by attorneys or by the police, who may deliberately or unintentionally make suggestions about the facts of a case. Concerns about **suggestibility** encouraged

Serial position effect: A form of interference related to the sequence in which information is presented. Generally, items in the middle of the sequence are less well remembered than items presented first or last.

Misattribution: A memory fault that occurs when memories are retrieved, but they are associated with the wrong time, place, or person.

Suggestibility: The process of memory distortion as the result of deliberate or inadvertent suggestion.

Elizabeth Loftus and John Palmer to investigate the circumstances under which memories can be distorted.

MEMORY DISTORTION   Participants in the Loftus and Palmer study first watched a film of two cars colliding. Then, the experimenters asked them to estimate how fast the cars had been moving. The responses, Loftus and Palmer found, depended on how the questions were worded (Loftus & Palmer, 1973; Loftus, 1979, 1984). Half of the respondents were asked, "How fast were the cars going when they *smashed* into each other?" Their estimates, it turned out, were about 25% higher than those given by respondents who were asked, "How fast were the cars going when they *hit* each other?"

Clearly, the Loftus and Palmer study shows that memories can be distorted and embellished by cues and suggestions given at the time of recall. Memories can even be created by similar methods, as we shall see shortly. Moreover, any of this can happen without the rememberer's awareness that memory has been altered.

Along with the other "sins" of memory we have been discussing, the Loftus and Palmer study reminds us of the following general principle about memory: *Retrieval from memory is a **reconstructive** act in which memory fragments are assembled and gaps are filled in without our being conscious of the process.* We first encountered this principle in the "pennies" demonstration at the beginning of the chapter. Remember?

MEMORY CREATION   Not only are our memories subject to distortion, but suggestion may cause us to fabricate recollections without realizing that they are false, much as we saw in our discussion of misattribution. To produce this in the laboratory, Elizabeth Loftus and her colleagues contacted the parents of college students and obtained lists of childhood events, which the students were asked to recall. Added to those lists were plausible events that never happened, such as being lost in a shopping mall, spilling the punch bowl at a wedding, or experiencing a visit by a clown at a birthday party (Hyman et al., 1995; Loftus, 1997a, 1997b; Loftus & Ketcham, 1994). After repeated recall attempts over a period of several days, many of the students claimed to remember the bogus events. In a similar fashion, suggestibility was at work in the case of Donna Smith, discussed at the beginning of the chapter.

Reconstructive: An attribute of the memory system that involves the construction or fabrication of a recollection based on an incomplete memory trace. The rememberer is often unaware that the reconstructed memory is not an accurate rendition of the original experience.

Our criminal justice system relies heavily on eyewitness identifications and descriptions. How well does this system work? You can judge for yourself in the case of a Catholic priest, Father Pagano (right), who was arrested and accused of a series of robberies. The police and the prosecutor were certain that they had the right man, because seven witnesses had identified him as the culprit. Father Pagano was finally exonerated during his trial, when the real robber (left) — hardly a look-alike — confessed.

Cognitive psychologists now see memory as a system susceptible to the same influences and distortions as perception (Payne et al., 1997). All memories — even the most vivid memories, such as the memory of your first kiss — become distorted over time by hopes, expectations, fantasies, motives, emotions, needs, attitudes, and a host of other cognitive factors. In this way, human memory is more like an impressionist painting, rather than the nearly flawless, but mindless, memory of a computer or a video recorder.

Connection

Chapter 5
Perceptions are influenced by memory, emotions, and many other factors.

FACTORS AFFECTING THE ACCURACY OF EYEWITNESSES   Further research has identified the most important factors influencing the accuracy of eyewitness recall (Lindsay, 1990, 1993; Loftus, 1992, 1993; Loftus & Ketcham, 1991, 1994; Weingardt et al., 1995):

► People's recollections are less influenced by leading questions if they are forewarned that interrogations can create memory bias.

► When the passage of time allows the original memory to fade, people are more likely to misremember information.

► The age of the witness matters: Younger children and adults over 65 may be especially susceptible to influence by misinformation in their efforts to recall (see Bruck & Ceci, 1997).

► Confidence in a memory is not a sign of an accurate memory. In fact, misinformed individuals can actually come to believe the misinformation in which they feel confidence.

THE RECOVERED MEMORY CONTROVERSY   At the beginning of the chapter, the Smith family's ordeal began with Donna Smith's claim that she had been sexually abused by her father. Subsequently, Donna came to believe her own claims, although she now insists they were all fabrications. Now we see that research on eyewitness recall confirms the notion that, as a result of suggestion, people not only report false memories, they come to believe them completely (Hyman et al., 1995; Loftus, 1997a, 1997b).

But are all recovered memories suspect? We frequently recover memories — accurate memories — of long-forgotten events. A chance remark, a peculiar odor, or an old tune can cue vivid recollections that haven't surfaced in years. The ones to be especially suspicious of, however, are memories cued by suggestion — as were Donna Smith's recollections.

One notorious source of suggestion in many recovered memory cases is a book, *The Courage to Heal,* which suggests that forgotten memories of incest and abuse may lie behind people's feelings of powerlessness, inadequacy, vulnerability, and a long list of other unpleasant thoughts and emotions (Bass & Davis, 1988). The authors state, "If you . . . have a feeling that something abusive happened to you, it probably did" (pp. 21–22).

The belief that buried memories of traumatic experiences can cause mental and physical symptoms was popularized by Sigmund Freud in his theory of **repression.** Freud taught that threatening memories would be stored in the unconscious mind, where they could indirectly influence our thoughts and behavior. He also taught that the only way to be free of these repressed memories is to root them out during therapy — bringing them into the daylight of consciousness, where they could be dealt with rationally. Yet Freud never offered more than anecdotes to support his repression theory.

In fact, modern cognitive research suggests just the opposite. Memory for emotionally arousing events is usually remembered vividly (Shobe & Kihlstrom, 1997). Most people, however, are unaware of this fact, retaining a strong, but unfounded, belief in repression and in the Freudian unconscious.

Connection

Chapter 11
Psychoanalyst Sigmund Freud taught that most of the mind is not accessible to consciousness.

Repression: The Freudian defense mechanism of forgetting, by which painful or threatening material is blocked off in the unconscious and prevented from reaching consciousness.

We are not suggesting that all therapists use suggestive techniques to recover repressed memories, although some still do (Poole et al., 1995). Patients should be especially wary of therapists who go "fishing" for unconscious causes of mental problem, using such techniques as hypnosis, dream analysis, and repeated leading questions about early sexual experiences. There is *no* evidence to support the validity of these methods for the recovery of accurate memories.

We should note that the issue of recovered memories is both complex and charged with emotion. It is also one that strikes many people close to home. Thus, it remains controversial, even among psychologists, where it has caused bitter dispute between therapists and experimental psychologists. But despite the controversy, most experts agree on the following points.

- ▶ Sexual abuse of children does occur, and it is more prevalent than most professionals had suspected just a few years ago (Herman, 1992).

- ▶ Memories cued by suggestion are particularly vulnerable to distortion and fabrication.

- ▶ Early memories, especially those of incidents that may have happened in infancy, are likely to be fantasies or misattributions. Episodic memories of events before age 3 are extremely rare.

- ▶ There is no infallible way to be sure about memories of sexual abuse (or any other memories) without independent supporting evidence (Ceci & Bruck, 1993).

- ▶ Although unpleasant events can be forgotten, they are much more likely to form persistent and intrusive memories that people would rather forget.

- ▶ There is no solid evidence for *repression* (in the Freudian sense of an unconscious memory that can cause physical and mental symptoms).

Bias — When Our Own Characteristics Color Our Memories

Bias: An attitude, belief, emotion, or experience that distorts memories.

Mood-congruent memory: A memory process that selectively retrieves memories that match (are *congruent* with) one's mood.

The next "sin" of memory — **bias** — is easier to see in another person. But make no mistake: Our own memories also can be colored by beliefs, attitudes, and experiences (Schacter, 1999). You may have noticed this during the last election, when partisans noticed positive things their candidate said or did and neglected the candidate's blunders. Less well known, but just as powerful, is the effect that people's moods can have on their memories.

MOOD AND MEMORY We use the expressions "feeling blue" and "looking at the world through rose-colored glasses" to suggest that moods can bias our perceptions. Likewise, moods can also affect what we pull out of memory. If you have ever had an episode of uncontrollable giggling (usually in a totally inappropriate situation), you know how a euphoric mood can trigger one silly thought after another. At the other end of the mood spectrum, people who are depressed often report that all their thoughts have a melancholy aspect. Thus, depression perpetuates itself through biased retrieval of depressing memories. In general, the kind of information we retrieve from memory heavily depends on our moods (Gilligan & Bower, 1984; Lewinsohn & Rosenbaum, 1987; MacLeod & Campbell, 1992). This phenomenon is known as **mood-congruent memory** (Terry, 2000).

Connection

Chapter 13
Cognitive–behavioral therapy aims to interrupt the process by which depression feeds on itself.

Not just a laboratory curiosity, mood-congruent memory can also have important health implications. Says memory researcher Gordon Bower, "Doctors assess what to do with you based on your complaints and how much you complain" (McCarthy, 1991). Because depressed people are likely to emphasize their medical symptoms, they may receive treatment that is much different from that dispensed to more upbeat individuals with the same disease. This, says Bower, means that physicians must learn to take a person's psychological state into consideration when deciding on a diagnosis and a course of therapy.

SELF-CONSISTENCY BIAS   We don't like to think of ourselves as inconsistent. Instead, most of us nurture the bias that our attitudes, values, beliefs, and behaviors are consistent over time. Research suggests , however, that we are kidding ourselves. For example, one study found that people are less consistent than they believe themselves to be in their support for political candidates (Levine, 1997). Likewise, people exaggerate the consistency of their stands on equality of women, aid to minority groups, and the legalization of marijuana (Marcus, 1986). Most surprising, perhaps, is the finding that people delude themselves about the consistency of their feelings toward their romantic partners, tending to recall earlier evaluations of their partners as being more consistent with their present attitude than they really were (Scharfe & Bartholomew, 1998).

Connection

Chapter 14
A similar *self-serving bias* makes people attribute their mistakes to causes outside themselves.

Persistence — When We Can't Forget

The seventh "sin" of memory, **persistence,** reminds us that memory sometimes works all too well. Intrusive recollections of unpleasant events lie at the heart of certain psychological disorders. Thus, depressed individuals ruminate about depressing episodes in their lives. Similarly, phobic patients (those suffering from extreme and unreasonable fears) have fearful memories triggered by certain cues such as snakes, dogs, crowds, spiders, or lightning. Neuroscience research suggests that, although these persistent memories have been learned, they may provoke physical changes in brain pathways that are extremely resistant to change or extinction (LeDoux, 1996).

Connection

Chapter 6
Phobias may be learned through classical conditioning.

The Advantages of the "Seven Sins" of Memory

Despite the grief they cause us, the "seven sins" are actually by-products of adaptive features of memory, argues Daniel Schacter (1999). Thus, transience — maddening as it is to the student taking a test — is actually a way the memory system prevents itself from being overwhelmed by information that is no longer needed. Similarly, blocking may be viewed as a process that usually allows only the most relevant information (the information most strongly associated with the present cues) to come to mind. Again, this is a process that prevents us from a flood of unwanted and distracting memories.

In contrast, absent-mindedness is the by-product of the useful ability to shift our attention. Similarly, misattributions, biases, and suggestibility result from a memory system built to deal with *meaning* and discard details. (The alternative would be a computerlike memory filled with information at the expense of understanding.) And, finally, we can see that the "sin" of persistence is really a feature of a memory system that is especially responsive to emotional experiences, particularly those involving fear. Thus, persistence allows us to learn lessons from the dangers we survive. In general, then, the picture that emerges of memory's "failures" is also one of a system that is well adapted to the conditions people have faced for thousands of years.

Persistence: A memory problem in which unwanted memories cannot be put out of mind.

Improving Your Memory with Mnemonics

To help yourself remember, try using some of the same tricks the memory experts use: mental strategies called *mnemonics* (pronounced *nee-MON-ix,* from the Greek word meaning "remember"). **Mnemonics** are methods for encoding information to be remembered by associating it with information already in long-term memory. To illustrate, we will take a detailed look at two mnemonic strategies: *the method of loci* and *natural language mediators.*

THE METHOD OF LOCI

Dating back to the ancient Greeks, the **method of loci** (pronounced *LOW-sigh,* from the Latin *locus,* "place"), is literally one of the oldest tricks in this book. It was originally devised to help orators remember the major points of their speeches. You will also find it a practical means of learning and remembering lists.

To illustrate, imagine a familiar sequence of places, such as the bed, desk, and chairs in your room. Then, using the method of loci, mentally move from place to place in your room, and as you go imagine putting one item from your list in each place. To retrieve the series, you merely take another mental tour, examining the places you used earlier. There you will "see" the item you have put in each *locus.* To remember a grocery list, for example, you might mentally picture a can of *tuna* on your bed, *shampoo* spilled on your desktop, and a box of *eggs* open on a chair. Bizarre or unconventional image combinations are usually easier to remember; a can of tuna in your bedroom will

make a more memorable image than tuna in your kitchen (Bower, 1972).

The mental images used in this technique work especially well because they employ both verbal and visual memories (Paivio, 1986). It's worth noting that visual imagery is one of the most effective forms of encoding: You can easily remember things by associating them with vivid, distinctive mental pictures. In fact, you could remember your grocery list by using visual imagery alone. Simply combine the mental images of tuna, shampoo, and eggs in a bizarre but memorable way. So, you might picture a *tuna* floating on an enormous fried *egg* in a sea of foamy *shampoo.* Or you might imagine a politician you dislike eating *tuna* from the can, his hair covered with *shampoo* suds, while you throw *eggs* at him.

NATURAL LANGUAGE MEDIATORS

Memory aids called **natural language mediators** associate meaningful word patterns with new information to be remembered. For instance, you can make up a story to help you remember a grocery list (the same one, consisting of tuna, shampoo, and eggs). The story might link the items this way: "The cat discovers I'm out of *tuna* so she interrupts me while I'm using the *shampoo* and meows to *egg* me on." Similarly, advertisers know that rhyming slogans and rhythmic musical jingles can make it easier for customers to remember their products and brand names ("Oscar Mayer has a way with . . ."). Chances are that a teacher in your past used a simple rhyme to help you remember a spelling rule ("*I* before *E* except after *C*") or the number of days in each month

Mnemonic strategies help us remember things by making them meaningful. Here an elementary school teacher helps students remember the letter "K" by showing that "K does karate."

("Thirty days has September . . ."). In a physics class you may have used a natural language mediator in the form of an *acronym* — a word made up of initials — to learn the colors of the visible spectrum: "Roy G. Biv" stands for red, orange, yellow, green, blue, indigo, violet.

REMEMBERING NAMES

The inability to remember people's names is one of the most common complaints about memory. So, how could you use the power of association to remember names? In the first place, you must realize that remembering names doesn't happen automatically. People who do this well must work at it by making associations between a name and some characteristic of the person — the more unusual the association, the better.

Suppose, for example, you have just met a man whose name is Bob. You might visualize his face framed in a big "O," taken from the middle of his name. To remember his friend Ann, think of her as "Queen Ann," sitting on a throne. And, as for their companion Phil, you might visualize putting a hose in Phil's mouth and "fill"-ing him with water. (It is usually best not to tell people about the mnemonic strategy you are using to remember their names.)

In general, the use of mnemonics teaches us that memory is flexible, personal, and creative. It also teaches us that *memory ultimately works by meaningful associations*. With this knowledge and a little experimentation, you can devise techniques for encoding and retrieval that work well for you based on your own personal associations and, perhaps, on your own sense of humor.

CHECK**YOUR**UNDERSTANDING

1. **RECALL:** *Which one of the following statements best describes forgetting, as characterized by Ebbinghaus's forgetting curve?*
   a. We forget at a constant rate.
   b. We forget slowly at first and then more rapidly as time goes on.
   c. We forget rapidly at first and then more slowly as time goes on.
   d. Ebbinghaus's method of relearning showed that we never really forget.

2. **APPLICATION:** *Which kind of forgetting is involved when the sociology I studied yesterday makes it more difficult to learn and remember the psychology I am studying today?*
   a. decay
   b. retrieval failure
   c. proactive interference
   d. retroactive interference

3. **RECALL:** *What is the term for the controversial notion that memories can be blocked off in the unconscious, where they may cause physical and mental problems?*

   a. interference
   b. repression
   c. persistence
   d. absent-mindedness

4. **RECALL:** *Which one of the seven "sins" of memory involves people's mistaken belief that they are consistent in their attitudes and behaviors?*
   a. blocking
   b. misattribution
   c. bias
   d. persistence

Core Concept

5. **UNDERSTANDING THE CORE CONCEPT:** *Which one of the "sins" of memory probably helps us avoid dangerous situations we have encountered before?*
   a. suggestibility
   b. bias
   c. persistence
   d. misattribution

ANSWERS: 1. c   2. c   3. b   4. c   5. c

Mnemonics: Techniques for improving memory, especially by making connections between new material and information already in long-term memory.

Method of loci: A mnemonic technique that involves associating items on a list with a sequence of familiar physical locations.

Natural language mediators: Words associated with new information to be remembered.

Whole method: The mnemonic strategy of first approaching the material to be learned "as a whole," forming an impression of the overall meaning of the material. The details are later associated with this overall impression.

Distributed learning: A technique whereby the learner spaces learning sessions over time, rather than trying to learn the material all in one study period.

Overlearning: A strategy whereby the learner continues to study and rehearse the material after it has been initially brought to mastery.

Using Psychology to Learn Psychology: How to Avoid Memory Failure on Exams

Mnemonic strategies designed to learn lists of unrelated items won't help much with the material you need to learn in your psychology class. There the important material consists of *concepts*—often *abstract* concepts, such as "operant conditioning" or "retroactive interference." (See Chapter 8; concepts are mental categories that enable us to organize our knowledge.) Such material calls for different mnemonic strategies geared both to concept learning and to avoiding the two memory "sins" feared most by college students: *transience* and *blocking*. Transience, of course, is the problem that makes the memory for material you study today become dimmer by test time. By contrast, blocking makes you unable to access the information you need for the test, even though the information is in your memory. So, let's see what advice cognitive psychologists would give to students for avoiding these two quirks of memory.

STUDYING TO AVOID MEMORY TRANSIENCE

Many studies have shown that memories will remain stronger if the information is approached in a way that makes it meaningful, rather than just a collection of facts and definitions (Baddeley, 1998; Haberlandt, 1999; Terry, 2000). One strategy for doing this involves using the **whole method,** a technique often used by actors who must learn many lines in the shortest possible time. With this approach, the learner begins by getting an overview of all the material to be learned—the "big picture" into which the details can be assimilated. Suppose, for example, that you have a test on this chapter coming up next week. Using the whole method, you would look over the chapter outline, the chapter summary, along with all the Key Questions and Core Concepts on the chapter-opening page before beginning to read the details of the chapter. This approach erects a mental framework on which you can hang the details of encoding, interference, retrieval, and other memory topics. The whole method, of course, takes advantage of the fact that long-term memory most easily stores material that is meaningful.

A second way to build strong memories that are resistant to transience involves **distributed learning** (Baddeley, 1998; Terry, 2000). In less technical terms,

the research suggests that you should study your psychology frequently (distributed, or spaced, learning), rather than trying to learn it all at once in a single "cram" session ("massed" learning). This approach avoids the lowered efficiency of learning brought about by fatigue. One study, for example, found that students could double the amount of information they learned in a given amount of time and also increase their understanding of the material by studying in two separate sessions, rather than in one session (Bahrick et al., 1993). Studies have also shown that distributed learning results in the material being retained longer (Schmidt & Bjork, 1992).

STUDYING TO AVOID BLOCKING ON THE TEST

The strategies mentioned above will help you get to the test with a strong memory for the material you need to know. But, you also will want to avoid blocking, the inability to find and retrieve what you know from memory. To help you achieve this, we suggest some techniques that apply three ideas you have learned in this chapter: *elaborative rehearsal, encoding specificity,* and *interference theory.*

You can't avoid interference altogether, but you can minimize it. For one thing, you should avoid studying for another class after your review session for tomorrow's psychology test. For another, make sure that you understand all the material and have cleared up any potentially conflicting points well before you get to the test. If, for example, you are not sure of the difference is between *declarative memory* and *semantic memory,* you should discuss this with your instructor well before your final review session.

Yet another way to avoid interference is through **overlearning.** Using this technique, you would continue to review the material even after you think you understand it. Overlearning adds to the strength of a memory.

Elaborative rehearsal, you will remember, involves making many associations with the material to be learned. One of the best ways of doing this when studying for the psychology test is to create your own examples of the concepts. So, as you study about proactive interference, think of an example from your own experience. And don't forget to think of examples involving the Core Concepts, too. This approach will help to prevent blocking because adding associations to the material you are learning adds more ways that the material can be accessed in memory.

Finally, by using the principle of *encoding specificity,* you can learn the material in a form that is most likely to be cued by the questions your psychology professor puts on the test. To do this it is helpful to work with a friend who is also studying for the same test. We also recommend that you get together for this purpose a day or two before the test, and after both of you have studied the material thoroughly enough to feel you understand it. Your purpose, at this point, will not be to learn new material but to anticipate the questions on the test. Does your professor prefer essay questions? Short-answer questions? Multiple choice? Try to think up and answer as

many questions as you can of the type most likely to appear on the test. Don't overlook the Key Questions throughout the chapter.

And please don't overlook the other mnemonic features we have included throughout this book to guide you in your study. These include the "Check Your Understanding" quizzes and "Chapter Review" tests, as well as the "Do It Yourself!" demonstrations. You may have noticed, too, that we have taken our own advice and included examples for all the new concepts we have introduced.

All these mnemonic devices are based on well-established principles of learning and memory. Studying this way may sound like a lot of work — and it is. But the results will be worth the mental effort.

Chapter
Summary

WHAT IS MEMORY?

Any memory system involves three important processes: encoding, storage, and retrieval. Human memory, however, is a constructive system that involves three stages: sensory memory, working memory, and long-term memory, each with a distinctive function. Like the perceptual system, our memory systems process and interpret information.

Eidetic imagery is a rare and poorly understood form of memory that produces especially clear and vivid memories that may interfere with abstract thought.

 Human memory is a cognitive system composed of three stages that work together constructively to encode, store, and retrieve information.

HOW DO WE FORM MEMORIES?

 A distinct sensory memory register for each sensory pathway holds material just long enough for important information to be selected for further processing.

Working memory, which has a small capacity, draws information from sensory memory and long-term memory and processes it consciously, often with acoustic encoding.

Information in long-term memory is encoded, stored, and retrieved according to the meaning and con-

text of the material. Further, LTM is not a single entity but is partitioned into declarative memory (for facts and events) and procedural memory (for perceptual and motor skills). Declarative memory can be further divided into episodic and semantic systems.

 Each of the three memory systems encodes and stores memories in a different way, but they work together to transform sensory experience into a lasting record that has a pattern or meaning.

HOW DO WE RETRIEVE MEMORIES?

 Studies of H. M. demonstrated that information can be stored as explicit or implicit memories. Implicit memories can be cued by priming. Explicit memories can be cued by recall or recognition tasks. The accuracy of memory depends on how information is encoded and cued. When cues are not adequate to activate semantic memories, we may experience the TOT phenomenon.

 Whether memories are implicit or explicit, the success of their retrieval depends on how they were encoded and how they are cued.

WHY DOES MEMORY SOMETIMES FAIL US?

Memory failures may involve forgetting, resulting from weakening memory traces (transience), lapses of attention (absent-mindedness), and inability to retrieve a memory (blocking). Much forgetting can also be attributed to a form of blocking called interference.

In addition to forgetting, memory can fail us when recollections are altered through misattribution, suggestibility, and bias. An important example involves eyewitness memories, which are subject to distortion. Suggestibility can also produce false memories that seem believable to the rememberer. This may be the case with some recovered memories.

Sometimes, however, unwanted memories, especially of unpleasant experiences, persist in memory, even though we would like to forget them.

The "seven sins" of memory, however, are by-products of a memory system that is well suited to solv-ing problems of day-to-day living. Some of these problems can be overcome by mnemonic strategies.

Core Concept Most of our memory problems arise from memory's "seven sins" – which are really by-products of otherwise adaptive features of human memory.

USING PSYCHOLOGY TO LEARN PSYCHOLOGY

Learning concepts in a college course requires different mnemonic strategies from those suited to learn lists. By using the whole method and distributed learning, students can overcome the problem of transience. Elaborative rehearsal, overlearning, and anticipation of test items can help to overcome the problem of blocking on a test.

Review
Test

For each of the following items, choose the single correct or best answer. The correct answers appear at the end.

1. Unlike a video recorder, human memory is
   a. accurate.
   b. constructive.
   c. temporary.
   d. fast.

2. Which of the following is *not* one of the three essential functions of memory?
   a. encoding
   b. storage
   c. retrieval
   d. consistency

3. There is no meaning attached to information when it is in:
   a. sensory memory.
   b. working memory.
   c. long-term memory.
   d. declarative memory.

4. Your knowledge of how to use a can opener, boot up your computer, address an envelope, and program a VCR are all examples of _____ memory.
   a. sensory
   b. semantic
   c. procedural
   d. constructive

5. Which part of memory would contain your knowledge of the material you studied in the first chapter of this book?
   a. episodic memory
   b. semantic memory
   c. procedural memory
   d. working memory

6. H. M.'s _____ memory was more profoundly affected by the surgery than was his _____ memory.
   a. episodic / procedural
   b. eidetic / sensory
   c. implicit / explicit
   d. recognition / recall

7. Which one of the following best illustrates the reconstructive nature of retrieval from long-term memory?
   a. the Loftus and Palmer study of eyewitnesses
   b. H. M.'s difficulties with episodic memories
   c. priming of implicit memories
   d. the TOT phenomenon

8. If you wanted to remember the major divisions of long-term memory, which method would be the most effective?

a. repetition: repeating them over and over to yourself

b. elaborative rehearsal: thinking of examples of each division

c. acoustic encoding: trying to remember the sounds associated with each term

d. temporal coding: identifying when you heard of each division

9. Elise used to live in a house with a large kitchen, where all the silverware was stored in a drawer to the right of the sink. Since she moved to her new apartment, she finds that she habitually looks for the silverware in a drawer to the right of the sink, although no such drawer exists. Her behavior reflects forgetting due to

a. absence of retrieval cues.

b. retroactive interference.

c. proactive interference.

d. repression.

10. Studies of eyewitness testimony and recovery of "repressed" memories show that

a. our unconscious minds remember events as they actually happened.

b. distorted memories are a sign of mental disorder.

c. memories can be severely distorted, even when we have confidence in them.

d. the more confident we are of a memory, the more likely it is to be true.

ANSWERS: 1. b 2. d 3. a 4. c 5. b 6. a
7. a 8. b 9. c 10. c

If You're Interested . . .

BOOKS

Rupp, R. (1998). *Committed to memory: How we remember and why we forget*. Crown Publishing. A biochemist well-versed in world literature explains what science knows about memory: how it begins, what goes in, what stays or leaves, why some things cannot be retrieved, and what we can do to improve our memory for the things that matter to us.

VIDEOS

Groundhog Day. (1993, color, 103 min.). Directed by Harold Ramis; starring Bill Murray, Andie MacDowell, Chris Elliott. What if only you had an accurate memory? That's only one of the curses afflicting the protagonist, an arrogant TV weatherman doomed to relive the same day over and over, but while he remembers every conversation and soon every lesson learned in his many "reruns," everyone around him is experiencing them for the first time only. Funny, romantic, and often touching, it illustrates the power of memory to change lives.

Johnny Mneumonic. (1995, color, 98 min.). Directed by Robert Longo; starring Keanu Reeves, Dolph Lundgren, Takeshi, Ice-T, Dina Meyer. Ugly futuristic tale of an "information" courier, who travels the globe with messages stored in his head, who must elude an evil corporation after his latest cargo of "memories."

Total Recall. (1990, color, 109 min.). Directed by Paul Verhoeven; starring Arnold Schwarzenegger, Rachel Ticotin, Sharon Stone, Ronny Cox. Futuristic suspense about a man who realizes his memory — of who he is as well as of events — is a fake record implanted by his enemies. Oscar-winning special effects highlight the film, based on sci-fi writer Philip K. Dick's "We Can Remember It for You Wholesale."

WEB RESOURCES

http://www.apa.org/releases/tv.html Children remember more of what they see on television than what they read. This article examines research that suggests teaching tools could be put on video to teach children in order to help them remember the material.

http://www.exploratorium.edu/exhibits/droodles/index. html How strong is your memory? Visit this site to try to copy simple drawings and keep track of your success.

http://www.apa.org/releases/agingmemory.html This article argues against the assumption that memory declines with age. If people are able to integrate their memories with the context of the experiences, their memory will not decline — and some people can even improve their source memory.

KEY QUESTION **CHAPTER OUTLINE**	**CORE CONCEPT**	**PSYCHOLOGY IN** **YOUR LIFE**
WHAT ARE THE COMPONENTS OF THOUGHT? Concepts Imagery and Cognitive Maps Tools for Studying Thought	Thinking involves manipulation of mental representations, such as concepts, images, schemas, and scripts.	**SCHEMAS AND SCRIPTS HELP YOU KNOW WHAT TO EXPECT:** But sometimes they fill in the blanks — without your realizing it.
WHAT ABILITIES DO GOOD THINKERS POSSESS? Problem Solving Judging and Making Decisions	Good thinkers not only have a repertoire of effective algorithms and heuristics, they know how to avoid the common impediments to problem solving and decision making.	**ON BECOMING A CREATIVE GENIUS:** Such individuals have expertise, certain personality traits, and lots of motivation, but their thought processes are essentially the same as yours.

HOW IS INTELLIGENCE MEASURED?
 	
 Binet and Simon Invent a School
    Abilities Test
 American Psychologists Borrow Binet
    and Simon's Idea
 IQ Testing Today
 Problems with the IQ Formula
 Calculating IQs "on the Curve"
	Intelligence testing has a history of controversy, but most psychologists now view intelligence as a normally distributed trait that can be measured by performance on a variety of tasks — both verbal and nonverbal.	**WHAT CAN YOU DO FOR AN EXCEPTIONAL CHILD?**
		 In both mental retardation and giftedness, children should be encouraged to capitalize on their abilities.

WHAT ARE THE COMPONENTS OF INTELLIGENCE? Psychometric Theories of Intelligence Cognitive Theories of Intelligence Cultural Definitions of Intelligence	Some psychologists believe that the essence of intelligence is a single, general factor, while others believe intelligence is best described as a collection of distinct abilities.	**TEST SCORES AND THE SELF-FULFILLING PROPHECY:** An IQ score can create expectations that have a life of their own.

HOW DO PSYCHOLOGISTS EXPLAIN IQ DIFFERENCES AMONG GROUPS?
 	
 Intelligence and the Politics of
    Immigration
 What Evidence Shows That
    Intelligence Is Influenced by
    Heredity?
 What Evidence Shows That
    Intelligence Is Influenced by
    Environment?
 Heritability and Group Differences
	While most psychologists agree that both heredity and environment affect intelligence, they disagree on the source of IQ differences among racial and social groups.	**HELPING OTHERS THINK CRITICALLY ABOUT GROUP DIFFERENCES:**
		 There are many reasons why the heritability of intelligence doesn't mean that group differences are genetic.

USING PSYCHOLOGY TO LEARN PSYCHOLOGY: Developing Expertise in Psychology — or Any Other Subject

THINKING AND INTELLIGENCE

At the age of 37, newspaper and magazine columnist Bob Greene started to suspect that he "was dumber than [he] had been in high school" (Greene, 1985). At 17 he had been able to add, subtract, and multiply without using a calculator. Twenty years later, those skills seemed to have disappeared completely.

To see if he could still make the grade, Greene decided to retake the Scholastic Assessment Test (SAT), a three-hour examination of verbal and mathematical abilities that many colleges use to select students for admission. Greene sent in his fee, and on the designated Saturday morning, he showed up at his local high school with six sharpened No. 2 pencils

in his pocket. After one hour, "all of us looked dazed, unhappy, and disoriented, although I believe that I was the only student to go to the water fountain and take an Inderal for his blood pressure" (Greene, 1985).

The source of their discomfort, the SAT, was designed to measure high school students' abilities to do college work. It simplifies the job of admissions officers, who have had difficulty comparing grade-point averages from thousands of high schools with different standards and grading policies. But while such tests were intended to be objective evaluations, they have been accused of bias, and, despite many revisions over the years, it has been

(continued)

difficult to quell those accusations (Kohn, 2001).Whites and Asian Americans consistently outperform Mexican Americans, Puerto Ricans, and African Americans (Hacker, 1986). Men on the average score higher than women (Gordon, 1990; Halpern, 1992). And, across all groups, average SAT scores closely parallel family income.

But the SAT is changing. Consider the commonplace use of calculators, for example. When the SAT was introduced in 1941, pocket calculators did not even exist. In the mid-1980s, when Greene took the test for the second time, the proctor instructed that "Calculators or wristwatches with calculator functions may not be used." In 1994, students were permitted to use calculators for the first time, and 20% of the math questions were constructed to require students to produce their own responses rather than merely select from a set of multiple-choice alternatives. Test-takers would have to grapple with questions such as "If the population of a certain country is increasing at the rate of one person every 12 seconds, by how many persons does it increase every half hour?" (Educational Testing Service, 1990a).

When Greene's test results finally arrived in the mail, his hands were shaking. He felt ridiculous. After all, he already had a college degree and a successful career. Nevertheless, he nervously ripped open the envelope. Greene's verbal score had gone up 56 points, not surprising for a writer. But in math, over the two decades since Greene first took the test, his score had nose-dived by 200 points!

Just as it is difficult to know why some groups perform better than others on the SAT, it is impossible to know with certainty why Bob Greene's math score plummeted. Wasn't the test supposed to measure his basic aptitude for math—what he understood, and not just what he had learned? Perhaps his math aptitude had decreased because, in his work as a writer, he no longer used the math he had once practiced regularly in high school. Or perhaps the test itself didn't measure Bob Greene's aptitude or potential to learn and use math. Instead, perhaps the test actually measured his recent accomplishments and practice in the subjects covered on the test—accomplishments made possible because his adult life experience as a professional writer had enhanced his verbal ability, but seldom required use of his early math skills.

Greene (1985) wrote about his experiences with the SAT to document some problems that exist with this system of testing. Standardized group tests —paper-and-pencil instruments, uniformly administered to vast numbers of people—are heavily relied upon, for better or worse, by most college and university admissions offices. Consequently, tests such as the SAT are centrally important to the academic lives of millions of students.

No wonder Bob Greene was anxious. He was trained—as most of us have been trained—to have tests tell us what we know, where our talents lie, and how our personalities work. We are obsessed with tests: SAT tests, IQ tests, achievement tests, abilities tests, interest tests, personality tests—not to mention all the tests in math, history, literature, and biology required in high school and college. To get a driver's license, you must pass a driving test. And, it is likely that you are reading this book, at least in part, because you anticipate a test on it. The problem is that so much of our future can ride on the results of a single test, even though no test gives a perfect measure of our abilities, achievements, or potential.

Are there other ways—better ways—to observe and measure our mental processes? Yes, but only a few of them are designed to predict college success. In this chapter, therefore, we will take a broader look at methods psychologists have developed to study **cognition**—all the mental processes involved in thinking and intelligence. You might think of this chapter as an extension of the material we discussed on learning and memory: The emphasis will be on how we *use* the information acquired by learning and stored in memory.

In the first part of this chapter, we will focus on thinking, particularly the kinds of thinking involved in forming concepts, making decisions, and solving problems. Here we will examine the building blocks of cognition, called *concepts, images, and cognitive maps*. You will also find that the tools psychologists use to study cognition include not only the SAT tests but intelligence tests, brain scans, and a variety of other psychological techniques. (So far, no one has suggested that students submit brain scans along with their college applications!) This excursion into thinking will also give us the opportunity to look at the related topic of creativity and that mysterious quality known as "genius."

In the second half of the chapter, we will turn to **intelligence,** which we will define as the mental abilities involved in reasoning, solving problems, and acquiring knowledge. There you will learn about IQ tests, conflicting perspectives on what intelligence *really* is, and what it means to say that IQ is "heritable." Finally, in the "Using Psychology to Learn Psychology" section, you will learn how to apply the knowledge in this chapter to become an expert in psychology—or any other field you choose.

Only humans—because of their ability for thinking about what might be—can indulge in flights of fancy.

WHAT ARE THE COMPONENTS OF THOUGHT?

What do solving a math problem, deciding what to do Friday night, and indulging a private fantasy all have in common? All involve *thinking*. We can define **thinking** as the cognitive process involved in forming a new mental representation by manipulating available information. Thus, thinking may invoke a combination of mental activities, such as reasoning, imagining, judging, deciding, problem solving, and creativity. Moreover, thinking can make use of information in a variety of forms, as our Core Concept emphasizes:

> **Thinking involves manipulation of mental representations, such as concepts, images, schemas, and scripts.**

Ultimately, thinking *organizes* these building blocks of cognition in meaningful ways.

Concepts

You may have had an experience known as *déjà vu* (from the French for "seen before"). The term refers to a feeling that your present experience jibes with a

Cognition: The mental processes involved in thinking, knowing, perceiving, learning, and remembering; also, the contents of these processes (e.g., thoughts, percepts, concepts).

Key Question

Connection

Chapter 4
Piaget found that children develop *mental representations* of their world by about age 2.

Core Concept

Intelligence: The mental capacity to acquire knowledge, reason, and solve problems effectively.

Thinking: The cognitive process involved in forming a new mental representation by manipulating available information.

Connection

Chapter 7
Explicit memory involves remembering events.

previous experience, even though you cannot retrieve the explicit memory. Perhaps you have visited a new place that seems oddly familiar or had a social conversation that seemed repetitive. While this *déjà vu* feeling can be an illusion, it also reflects the brain's ability to treat new stimuli as instances of familiar categories, even if they are slightly different from anything it has encountered before. Here's the point: The ability to assimilate experiences into familiar mental categories — and to take the same action toward them or give them the same label — is regarded as one of the most basic attributes of thinking organisms (Mervis & Rosch, 1981). We call it *concept formation.*

The mental categories that we form in this way are called **concepts.** Concepts are among the building blocks of thinking, because they enable us to organize knowledge in systematic ways (Goldman-Rakic, 1992). Concepts may represent objects, activities, or living organisms. They may also represent properties, (such as "red" or "large"), abstractions (such as "truth" or "love"), relations (such as "smarter than"), procedures (such as how to tie your shoes), or intentions (such as the intention to break into a conversation) (Smith & Medin, 1981). Because concepts are mental structures, researchers cannot observe them directly but have had to infer their influence in people's thinking indirectly by studying their observable effects on behavior or on brain activity. For example, you cannot be sure that another person shares your concept of "red," but you can observe whether he or she responds in the same way you do to stimuli that you both call "red."

TWO KINDS OF CONCEPTS   Everyone conceptualizes the world in a unique way, so our concepts define who we are. Yet, behind this individual uniqueness, lie similarities in the ways that people form concepts. For example, cognitive psychologists have found that we all distinguish between two different types of concepts: *natural concepts* and *artificial concepts.*

Natural concepts are rather imprecise mental classifications that develop out of our everyday experiences in the world. You may possess a natural concept of "bird" based on your experiences with birds. You probably also have natural concepts associated with Chevrolets, your mother's face, artichokes, and the Statue of Liberty. Likewise, Bob Greene was using natural concepts when he was thinking about "students" and "No. 2 pencils." While each of these examples may involve words, natural concepts also can involve visual images, emotions, and other nonverbal memories.

Your own natural concept of "bird" invokes a mental **prototype,** a generic image that represents a typical bird from your experience (Hunt, 1989; Medin, 1989; Mervis & Rosch, 1981; Rosch & Mervis, 1975). To determine whether some object is a bird or not, you mentally compare the object to your bird prototype. The more sophisticated your prototype, the less trouble you will have with flightless birds, such as ostriches and penguins, or with birdlike flying creatures, such as bats, or with turtles and platypuses, which lay eggs, as do birds. Natural concepts are sometimes called "fuzzy concepts" because of their imprecision (Kosko & Isaka, 1993).

Research support for the idea of a prototype comes from studies showing that people respond more quickly to typical members of a category than to more unusual ones — that is, their reaction times are faster. For example, it takes less time to say whether a robin is a bird than to say whether an ostrich is a bird, because robins resemble most people's prototype of a bird more closely than ostriches do (Kintsch, 1981; Rosch et al., 1976). The prototype is formed on the basis of frequently experienced features. These features are stored in memory, and the more often they are perceived, the stronger their overall memory strength is. Thus, the prototype can be rapidly accessed and recalled.

Concepts: Mental representations of categories of items or ideas, based on experience.

Natural concepts: Mental representations of objects and events drawn from our direct experience.

Prototype: An ideal or most representative example of a conceptual category.

By comparison, **artificial concepts** are those defined by a set of rules or characteristics, such as dictionary definitions or mathematical formulas. The definition of "rectangle" that you learned in math class is an example. Artificial concepts represent precisely defined ideas or abstractions, rather than actual objects in the world. So, if you are a zoology major, you may also have an artificial concept of "bird," which defines it as a "feathered biped." Like these textbook definitions of birds and rectangles, most of the concepts you learn in school are artificial concepts. "Cognitive psychology" is also an artificial concept; so is the concept of "concept"!

Most of the concepts in our everyday lives, however, are natural concepts. We can identify clusters of properties that are shared by different instances of a concept (for example, robins, penguins, and ostriches all are birds and all have feathers), but there may be no one property that is present in all instances. Still, we consider some instances as more representative of a concept — more typical of our mental prototype (more "birdlike") — than others.

CONCEPT HIERARCHIES   We organize much of our declarative memories into **concept hierarchies,** from general to specific, as seen in Figure 8.1. For most people, the broad category of *animal* has several subcategories, such as *bird* and *fish,* which are subdivided, in turn, into their specific forms, such as *canary, ostrich, shark,* and *salmon.* The animal category may itself be a subcategory of the still larger category of *living beings.* We can think of these concepts and categories as arranged in a hierarchy of levels, with the most general and abstract at the top and the most specific and concrete at the bottom, as shown in Figure 8.1. They are also linked to many other concepts: Some birds are edible, some are endangered, some are national symbols. It may help you to understand this if you use the following conceptual model: The connections among concepts seem to work much like the hypertext links you see on your Internet browser.

Connection

Chapter 7
The meaningful categories of declarative memory and the connections among them represent concepts.

Artificial concepts: Concepts defined by rules, such as word definitions and mathematical formulas.

Concept hierarchies: Levels of concepts, from most general to most specific, in which a more general level includes more specific concepts — as the concept of "animal" includes "dog," "giraffe," and "butterfly."

FIGURE 8.1:   Hierarchically Organized Structure of Concepts

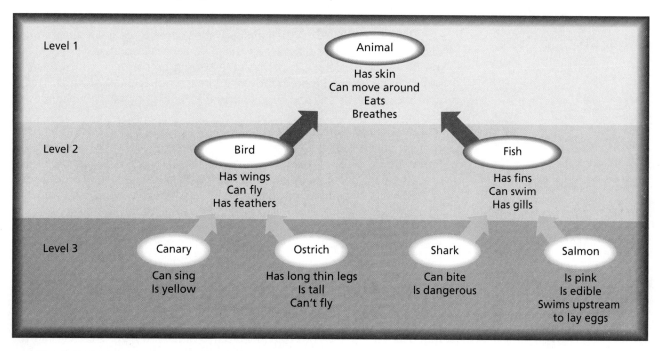

CULTURE, CONCEPTS, AND THOUGHT Most of the research on concept formation has been done by Euro-American psychologists, who have studied how concepts are used in their own culture. But recent work by cross-cultural psychologists cautions us not to assume that thinking works exactly the same way in all parts of the globe. One difference involves the use of logic: Many cultures do not value the use of logical reasoning as much as do Europeans and North Americans (Bower, 2000; Nisbett et al., 2001).

Another difference involves concept formation. Although people everywhere do form concepts, most Asian cultures tend to place less importance on precise definitions and clear-cut conceptual categories than do the dominant cultures of Europe and North America (Nisbett, 2000; Peng & Nisbett, 1999). From an Asian perspective, conceptual boundaries tend to be more fluid, and the focus is more on the relationships among concepts, rather than on their definitions. Thus, Asians might be more interested in the ways in which the terms "masculine" and "feminine" are contrasting ideas, rather than defining the exact meaning of each term.

Imagery and Cognitive Maps

Do you think only in words, or do you sometimes think in pictures and spatial relationships or other sensory images? If you take a moment to think of a face, a tune, or the smell of fresh bread, the answer is obvious. Sensory mental imagery revives information you previously perceived and stored in memory. This revival takes place without immediate sensory input and relies on internal representations of events and concepts in sensory forms, such as visual images.

Consider, for example, the following question: What shape are a German shepherd's ears? Assuming you answered correctly, how did you know? You probably have not intentionally memorized the shapes of dog ears or ever expected to be quizzed about such knowledge. To answer that a German shepherd has pointed ears, you probably consulted a visual image of a German shepherd stored in your memory. In general, thought based on imagery differs from verbal thought because it involves sensory information that is stored in a different part of the brain (Kosslyn, 1983; Paivio, 1983).

VISUAL THINKING Visual imagery adds complexity and richness to our thinking, as do images that involve the other senses (sound, taste, smell, and touch). Visual thinking can be useful in solving problems in which relationships can be grasped more clearly in an image rather than in words. That is why books such as this one often encourage visual thinking with pictures and diagrams.

A cognitive representation of physical space is a special form of visual concept called a cognitive map. You will remember that learning theorist Edward C. Tolman was the first to hypothesize that people form mental maps of their environment and that these internal maps guide their actions toward desired goals. Cognitive maps help people get where they want to go, and they enable them to give directions to others. By using cognitive maps, people can move through their homes with their eyes closed or go to familiar destinations even when their usual routes are blocked (Hart & Moore, 1973; Thorndyke & Hayes-Roth, 1978).

CULTURAL INFLUENCES ON COGNITIVE MAPS Mental maps seem to reflect our subjective impressions of physical reality. The maps often mirror the view of the world that we have developed from the perspective of our own culture. For example, if you were asked to draw a world map, where would you begin and how would you represent the size, shape, and relations between var-

Connection

Chapter 6
Tolman's rats behaved as through they had "cognitive maps" of the mazes they had learned.

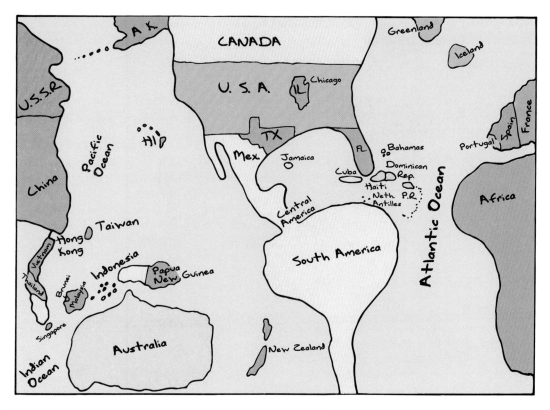

ious countries? This task was given to nearly 4,000 students from 71 cities in 49 countries as part of an international study of the way people of different nationalities visualize the world. The study found that the majority of maps had a Eurocentric world view: Europe was placed in the center of the map and the other countries were arranged around it (probably due to the dominance for many centuries of Eurocentric maps in geography books). But the study also yielded many interesting culture-biased maps, such as the ones by a Chicago student (Figure 8.2) and an Australian student (Figure 8.3). American students, incidentally, did poorly on this task, often misplacing countries, while students from the former Soviet Union and Hungary made the most accurately detailed maps (Saarinen, 1987). This suggests that cultural differences—perhaps in education or world view—have an impact on geographical thinking.

Tools for Studying Thought

As they have studied the inner world of thought, cognitive researchers have had to invent ways of measuring and mapping the territory of the mind with objectivity—methods that can now connect mental activity to brain activity (Ashby & Waldron, 2000; Beardsley, 1997; Behrmann, 2000; Freedman et al., 2001; Thorpe & Fabre-Thorpe, 2001). For example, with the help of the computer, biological scientists have demonstrated that certain thoughts are associated with specific electrical wave patterns in the brain (Garnsey, 1993; Osterhout & Holcomb, 1992). They have demonstrated this by presenting a repeated stimulus (such as the word "dog" flashed on a screen) to a volunteer

FIGURE 8.3: Australiocentric View of the World
Now who's "down under"?

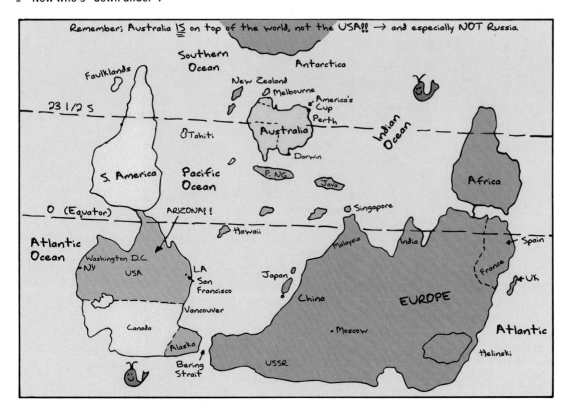

Remember; Australia IS on top of the world, not the USA!! → and especially NOT Russia.

Connection

Chapter 2
The EEG reveals changing patterns, or "waves," of electrical activity generated by the brain.

Connection

Chapter 2
PET scans and functional MRI show parts of the brain that are active.

Event-related potentials: Brain waves shown on the EEG in response to stimulation.

"wired" to record the brain's electrical responses. While the brain waves on one trial may show no clear pattern, a computer can average many brain wave responses to a single, repeated stimulus, eliminating the random background "noise" of the brain and isolating the unique brain wave pattern evoked by that stimulus (Donchin, 1975). These EEG patterns associated with particular stimuli are called **event-related potentials.**

Other methods can also tell us which parts of the brain switch on and off while we think. With PET scans and magnetic resonance imaging (MRI) neuroscientists have identified brain regions that become active during different kinds of mental tasks. Two broad findings have come from this work. First, thinking is an activity involving widely distributed areas of the brain—not just a single "thinking center." Second, brain scans have revealed the brain as a community of highly specialized modules, each of which deals with different components of thought (Posner & McCandliss, 1993; Raichle, 1994; Solso, 1991). In general, the brain generates the images of thought with the same circuitry it uses for sensation and perception. Thus, visual imagery arises from the visual cortex, and auditory images come from the auditory cortex (Behrmann, 2000). Moreover, thinking with words does not use all the same parts of the brain required for thinking with visual images or with musical sounds. The picture of thought coming out of this work reveals thinking as a process composed of many elements.

Particularly exciting is the location of a part of the brain that seems to be associated with what we often call "common sense," or the ability to act on "intuition" (Bechara et al., 1997; Vogel, 1997a). Psychologists have long known that when people make decisions—whether about buying a house or selecting a spouse — they draw on feelings, as well as reason. This emotional component of thinking apparently involves a region of the frontal lobes just above the eyes. This structure allows us unconsciously to add emotional "hunches" to our decisions in the form of information about past rewards and punishments. Individuals with damage to this part of the brain seem to display little emotion. They also lack "intuition" — the ability to know the value of something without conscious reasoning, and they frequently make unwise choices when faced with decisions (Damasio, 1994).

In brief, various forms of brain scanning provide glimpses of cognitive processes through new windows. The task ahead is to figure out what this new information is telling us about cognition. The "big picture" of human cognitive processes is thus still emerging, piece by piece, just as one might assemble a jigsaw puzzle.

Connection

Chapter 2
The frontal lobes are involved in planning and directing behavior.

Schema: A knowledge cluster or general conceptual framework that provides expectations about topics, events, objects, people, and situations in one's life.

Psychology In Your Life

Schemas and Scripts Help You Know What to Expect

Much of your knowledge is stored in your brain as *schemas* (Oden, 1987). A **schema** is a cluster of related concepts that provides a general conceptual framework for thinking about a topic, an event, an object, people, or a situation in one's life. (See Chapter 4; Piaget's *schemes* are a type of schema.) You probably have schemas that represent "college" and "music," for example. Some of these schemas could contain an entire hierarchy of concepts. Let's look at some important ways that schemas are used.

EXPECTATIONS

Schemas provide expectations about the features likely to be found when you encounter familiar people, situations, images, and ideas. For example, to an airline passenger the word "terminal" probably conjures up a schema that includes scenes of crowds, long corridors, and airplanes. For a heart attack victim, however, the schema for "terminal" might include feelings of anxiety and thoughts of death.

MAKING INFERENCES

New information, which is often incomplete or ambiguous, makes more sense when you can relate it to existing knowledge in our stored schemas. So schemas enable you to make inferences about missing information, as the following example will demonstrate. Consider this statement:

> Tanya was upset to discover, upon opening the basket, that she'd forgotten the salt.

With no further information, what can you infer about this event? Salt implies that the basket is a picnic basket. The fact that Tanya is upset that the salt is missing suggests that the food in the basket is food that is usually salted, such as hard boiled eggs or vegetables. You automatically know what other foods might be included and, equally important, what definitely is not: Everything in the world that is larger than a picnic basket and anything that would be inappropriate to take on a picnic — from a boa constrictor to bronze-plated baby shoes. The body of information you now have has been organized around a "picnic-basket" schema. By relating the statement about Tanya to your preestablished

Even though they are not prejudiced, people may avoid interactions with those of other ethnic groups because they don't understand each other's scripts.

schema, the statement has meaning.

How important are schemas to you? According to researchers Donald Norman and David Rumelhart, schemas are the primary units of meaning in the human information-processing system (1975). You comprehend new information by integrating consistent new input with what we already know. (Piaget called this *assimilation*. See Chapter 3. If you find a discrepancy between new input and already-stored schemas, you overcome it by changing what you know or ignoring the new input.

(continued)

Once we interpret information as belonging to a particular schema, we may unwittingly change the information we have taken in. To see how this transformation can occur, try the demonstration in the Do It Yourself! box.

Thus, thinking is a constructive process in which we draw on our existing mental structures to make sense of new information. And, we construct our subjective reality and personal world views from all the information we process. (Thus, thinking involves perception.)

SCRIPTS AS EVENT SCHEMAS

We have schemas not only about objects and events but also about persons, roles, and ourselves. These schemas help us to decide what to expect or how people should behave under specific circumstances. An *event schema* or **script** consists of

knowledge about sequences of inter-related, specific events and actions expected to occur in a certain way in particular settings. We have scripts for going to a restaurant, using the library, listening to a lecture, going on a first date, and even making love.

CULTURAL INFLUENCES ON SCRIPTS

Scripts used in other cultures may differ substantially from ours. For example, during the Persian Gulf War, American women stationed in Arab locales discovered that many behaviors they might take for granted at home—such as walking unescorted in public, wearing clothing that showed their faces and legs, or driving a car—were considered scandalously inappropriate by citizens of their host country. To maintain good relations, these servicewomen had to change their

habits and plans to accommodate local customs. We can see from such examples that the scripts found in diverse cultures have developed from distinct schemas for viewing the world.

CONFLICTING SCRIPTS

When people who follow similar scripts get together, they feel comfortable because they have comprehended the "meaning" of the situation in the same way and have the same expectations of each other (Abelson, 1981; Schank & Abelson, 1977). When people do not all follow similar scripts, however, they may be made uncomfortable by the script "violation" and may have difficulty understanding why the scene was "misplayed." Unfortunately, when scripts clash, people may say, "I tried to interact, but it was so awkward that I don't want to try again" (Brislin, 1993).

CHECKYOURUNDERSTANDING

1. **APPLICATION:** *A dictionary definition would be an example of*
   a. an artificial concept.
   b. a natural concept.
   c. a core concept.
   d. an abstract concept.

2. **APPLICATION:** *Which one of the following would represent a concept hierarchy?*
   a. cat, dog, giraffe, elephant
   b. animal, mammal, dog, cocker spaniel
   c. woman, girl, man, boy
   d. lemur, monkey, chimpanzee, human

3. **APPLICATION:** *Knowing how to check out a book at the library is an example of:*

   a. a natural concept.
   b. an event-related potential.
   c. a cognitive map.
   d. a script.

4. **UNDERSTANDING THE CORE CONCEPT:**
   All of the following are components of thought, except:
   a. concepts.
   b. images.
   c. schemas.
   d. stimuli.

ANSWERS: 1. a   2. b   3. d   4. d

Core Concept

Script: A cluster of knowledge about sequences of events and actions expected to occur in particular settings.

Read the following passage carefully:

> Chief Resident Jones adjusted his face mask while anxiously surveying a pale figure secured to the long gleaming table before him. One swift stroke of his small, sharp instrument and a thin red line appeared. Then the eager young assistant carefully extended the opening as another aide pushed aside glistening surface fat so that the vital parts were laid bare. Everyone stared in horror at the ugly growth too large for removal. He now knew it was pointless to continue.

Stop! Without looking back, please complete the following exercise: Circle below the words that appeared in the passage:

patient   scalpel   blood   tumor

cancer   nurse   disease   surgery

In the original study, most of the subjects who read this passage circled the words patient, scalpel, and tumor. Did you? However, none of the words were there! Interpreting the story as a medical story made it more understandable, but also resulted in inaccurate recall (Lachman et al., 1979). Once the subjects had related the story to their schema for hospital surgery, they "remembered" labels from their schema that were not present in what they had read. Drawing on a schema not only gave the subjects an existing mental structure to tie the new material to but also led them to change the information to make it more consistent with their schema-based expectations.

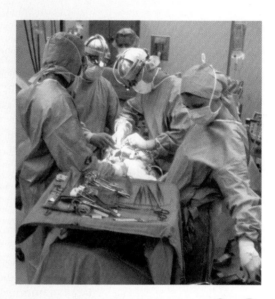

WHAT ABILITIES DO GOOD THINKERS POSSESS?

Key Question

The popularity of lotteries and casino games, in which our chances of winning are small, shows us that human thought is not always purely logical. Nevertheless, our *psycho*logical nature has some advantages: Departures from logic allow us to fantasize, daydream, act creatively, react unconsciously, respond emotionally, and generate ideas that cannot be tested against reality. We are, of course, capable of careful reasoning: After all, our species did invent that most logical of devices, the computer. Still, the psychology of thinking teaches us that we should not expect people to behave always in a strictly logical manner or that good judgment will be based on reason alone. This ability to think *psycho*logically enhances our ability to solve problems and make effective decisions. And, as we will see, good thinking also involves the use of effective thinking strategies and the avoidance of ineffective or misleading strategies. As our Core Concept puts this in more technical language:

Core Concept

Good thinkers not only have a repertoire of effective algorithms and heuristics, they know how to avoid the common impediments to problem solving and decision making.

We will see that such an approach to thinking strategies is useful — more useful than mere logic — because it helps us make decisions rapidly in a changing world that usually furnishes us incomplete information.

Problem Solving

Artists, inventors, Nobel Prize winners, great presidents, successful business executives, world-class athletes, and successful college students — all must be effective problem solvers. And what strategies do effective problem solvers use? No matter what their field, those who are successful share certain characteristics. They, of course, possess the requisite knowledge for solving the problems they face. In addition, they are skilled at (a) *identifying a problem* and (b) *selecting a strategy* to attack the problem. In the next few pages we will examine these two skills, with the aid of some examples.

IDENTIFYING THE PROBLEM   A good problem solver learns to consider all the relevant possibilities, without leaping to conclusions. Suppose that you are driving along the freeway, and your car suddenly begins sputtering and then quits. As you coast over to the shoulder, you notice that the gas gauge says "empty." What do you do? Your action in this predicament depends on the problem you think you are solving. If you assume that you are out of fuel, you may hike to the nearest service station for a gallon of gas. But you may be disappointed. By representing the problem as "out of gas," you may fail to notice a loose battery cable that interrupts the supply of electricity both to the spark plugs and to the gas gauge.

SELECTING A STRATEGY   The second ingredient of successful problem solving requires selecting a strategy that fits the problem at hand (Wickelgren, 1974). Of course, solutions to problems in specialized fields, such as engineering or medicine, may require specialized knowledge and special procedures or formulas. Such problem-solving strategies are called *algorithms*. In contrast, there are more intuitive, but less precise, strategies called *heuristics*. We need both kinds of strategies in our everyday lives.

Algorithms   Whether you are a psychology student or a rocket scientist, selecting the right **algorithms** will guarantee correct solutions for some of your problems. What are these never-fail strategies? Algorithms are formulas or procedures, like those you learned in math classes or in science labs. They are designed to solve particular kinds of problems. For example, you can use algorithms to balance your checkbook, figure your gas mileage, and calculate your grade-point average. If applied correctly, an algorithm *always* works because you merely follow a step-by-step procedure that leads directly from the problem to the solution.

Despite their usefulness, however, algorithms cannot solve every problem you face. Problems involving subjective values (Will you be happier with a red car or a white car? Or which is the best airline to take to Denver?) and problems that are just too complex for a formula (How can you get a promotion? What will the fish bite on today?) do not lend themselves to the use of algorithms. And that is why we also need the more intuitive and flexible strategies called *heuristics*.

Heuristics   Everyone makes a collection of **heuristics** while going through life. Examples: "Don't keep bananas in the refrigerator." "If it doesn't work, see if it's plugged in." "Feed a cold and starve a fever" (or is it the other way around?). Heuristics are simple, basic rules — so-called "rules of thumb" that help us cut through the confusion of complicated situations. Unlike algorithms,

Algorithms: Problem-solving procedures or formulas that guarantee a correct outcome, if correctly applied.

Heuristics: Cognitive strategies or "rules of thumb" used as shortcuts to solve complex mental tasks. Unlike algorithms, heuristics do not guarantee a correct solution.

heuristics do *not* guarantee a correct solution, but they often give us a good start in the right direction. Some heuristics require special knowledge, such as training in medicine or physics or psychology. Other heuristics, such as those you will learn in the following paragraphs, are more widely applicable—and well worth remembering.

SOME USEFUL HEURISTIC STRATEGIES   Here are three essential heuristics that should be in every problem-solver's tool kit. They require no specialized knowledge, yet they can help you in a wide variety of puzzling situations. The common element shared by all three of these heuristics involves getting the problem solver to approach a problem from a different perspective.

Working Backward   Some problems, such as the maze seen in Figure 8.4, may baffle us because they present so many possibilities we don't know where to start. A good way to attack this sort of puzzle is by beginning at the end and *working backward.* (Who says that we must always begin at the beginning?) This strategy can eliminate many of the false starts and dead ends that we would otherwise stumble into by trial-and-error.

In general, working backward is an excellent strategy for problems in which the end-state or goal is clearly specified, such as mazes or certain math problems. This approach can be especially valuable when the initial conditions are vague.

Searching for Analogies   If a new problem is similar to another you have faced before, you may be able to employ a strategy that you learned previously. For example, if you are an experienced cold-weather driver, you use this strategy to decide whether to install tire chains on a snowy day: "Is the snow as deep as it was the last time I needed chains?" The trick is to recognize the similarity, or *analogy,* between the new problem and the old one—a skill that takes practice (Medin & Ross, 1992).

Breaking a Big Problem into Smaller Problems   Are you facing a huge problem, such as an extensive term paper? The best strategy may be to break the big problem down into smaller, more manageable steps. In writing a paper, for example, you might break the problem into the subproblems of selecting a topic, doing your library research, outlining the paper, writing the first draft, and revising the paper. In this way, you will begin to organize the work and

FIGURE 8.4:   Working Backward

Mazes and math problems often lend themselves to the heuristic of working backward. Try solving this maze, as the mouse must do, by starting at the finish (in the center) and working backward to the start.

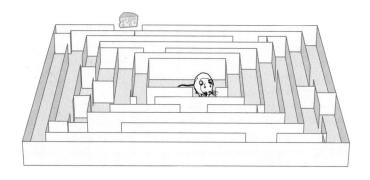

Watson and Crick used the analogy of a spiral staircase to help them understand the structure of the DNA molecule and crack the genetic code.

develop a plan for attacking each part of the problem. And, by tackling a problem in a step-by-step fashion, big problems will seem more manageable. Any large, complex problem—from writing a paper to designing an airplane—may benefit from this approach. In fact, the Wright Brothers deliberately used this heuristic to break down their problem of powered human flight into its components. By using a series of kites, gliders, and models, they studied the component problems of lift, stability, power, and directional control. Later they put their discoveries together to solve the larger problem of powered human flight (Bradshaw, 1992).

OBSTACLES TO PROBLEM SOLVING   Having a good repertoire of strategies is essential to successful problem solving, but people may also get stuck because they latch onto an ineffective strategy. For this reason, problem solvers must learn to recognize when they have encountered an obstacle that demands a new approach. In fact, becoming a successful problem solver has as much to do with recognizing such obstacles as it does with selecting the right algorithm or heuristic. Here are some of the most troublesome obstacles.

Mental Set   Sometimes you may persist with a less-than-ideal strategy simply because it has worked on other problems in the past. In psychological terms, you have an inappropriate **mental set**—the tendency to respond to a new problem in the same way you approached a similar problem previously. It's a case of using the wrong analogy or algorithm. Let's illustrate this with the following puzzle.

Each of the groups of letters in the columns below is a common, but scrambled, word. See if you can unscramble them:

nelin	frsca	raspe	tnsai
ensce	peshe	klsta	epslo
sdlen	nitra	nolem	naoce
lecam	macre	dlsco	tesle
slfal	elwha	hsfle	maste
dlchi	ytpar	naorg	egran
neque	htmou	egsta	eltab

(adapted from Leeper & Madison, 1959)

Mental set: The tendency to respond to a new problem in the manner used for a previous problem.

FIGURE 8.5: Unscrambled Words

The words you found to solve the scrambled word problem may not jibe with the ones listed here—especially in the third and fourth columns. Most people, whether they are aware of it or not, develop an algorithm as they work on the first two columns. While the formula will work on all the words, it interferes with the problem solver's ability to see alternative solutions for the words in the last two columns.

linen	scarf	pears	stain
scene	sheep	talks	poles
lends	train	melon	canoe
camel	cream	colds	steel
falls	whale	shelf	meats
child	party	groan	anger
queen	mouth	gates	bleat

Check your answers against the key in Figure 8.5.

Most people, whether they realize it or not, eventually solve the scrambled word problem with an algorithm by rearranging the order of the letters in all the words in the same way, using the formula 3-4-5-2-1. Thus,

```
n e l i n      becomes      l i n e n
1 2 3 4 5                   3 4 5 2 1
```

Notice, however, that by using that algorithm, your answers for the last two columns won't agree with the "correct" ones given in Figure 8.5. The mental set that you developed while working on the first two columns prevented you from seeing that there is more than one answer for the last fourteen items. The lesson of this demonstration is that a mental set can make you approach new problems in old but restricted ways. While a mental set often does produce results, you should occasionally stop to ask yourself whether you have slipped into a rut that prevents your seeing another answer. (Now can you find some other possible answers to the scrambled words in the last two columns?)

A special sort of mental set occurs when you think you need a screwdriver, but you don't realize that you could tighten the bolt with a dime. Psychologists call this **functional fixedness**. Under this condition, the *function* of a familiar object becomes so set, or *fixed*, in your mind that you cannot see a new function for it. To illustrate, consider this classic problem:

> Your psychology professor has offered you $5 if you can tie together two strings dangling from the ceiling (see Figure 8.6) without pulling them down. But when you grab the end of one string and pull it toward the other one, you find that you cannot quite reach the other string. The only objects available to you in the room are on the floor in the corner: a Ping-Pong ball, five screws, a screwdriver, a glass of water, and a paper bag. How can you reach both strings at once and tie them together?

Connection

Chapter 7
Compare *functional fixedness* with *proactive interference.*

Functional fixedness: The inability to perceive a new use for an object associated with a different purpose; a form of mental set.

FIGURE 8.6: The Two-String Problem

How could you tie the two strings together, using only the objects found in the room?

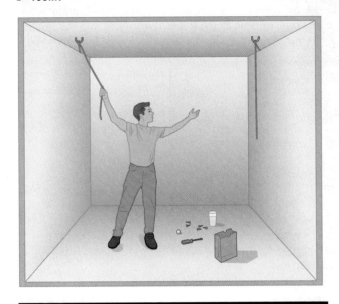

Read the following if you want a hint: In this problem you may have had functional fixedness with regard to the screwdriver. Did you realize that you could use the screwdriver as a pendulum weight to swing one of the strings toward you?

Self-Imposed Limitations We can be our own worst enemies when we limit ourselves unnecessarily. The classic nine-dot problem in Figure 8.7 illustrates this neatly. To solve this one, you must connect all nine dots with no more than four connecting straight lines—that is, without lifting your pencil from the paper. The rules allow you to cross a line, but you may not retrace a line.

FIGURE 8.7: The Nine-Dot Problem

Can you correct all nine dots with four connecting straight lines and without lifting your pencil from the paper?

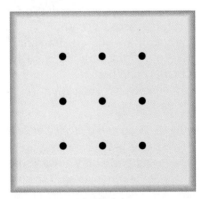

Most people who confront this problem impose an unnecessary restriction on themselves by assuming that they cannot draw lines beyond the square made by the dots. Literally, they don't "think outside the box." Figure 8.8 gives two possible correct answers. Translating this into personal terms, we can find many instances in which people impose unnecessary restrictions on themselves. Students may assume that they have no talent for math or science — thereby eliminating the possibility of a technical career. Or, because of gender stereotypes, a man may never consider that he could be a nurse or a grade school teacher, and a woman may assume that she must be a secretary, rather than an administrator. What real-life problems are you working on in which you have imposed unnecessary limitations on yourself?

Other Obstacles   There are many other obstacles to problem solving that we will simply mention, rather than discuss in detail. These include lack of specific knowledge required by the problem, lack of interest, low self-esteem, fatigue, and drugs (even legal drugs, such as cold medicines or sleeping pills). Arousal and the accompanying stress represent another important stumbling block for would-be problem solvers. When we study emotion and motivation, we will see that there is an optimum arousal level for any task, be it basketball, brain surgery, or survival in Borneo. Beyond that point, further arousal causes performance to deteriorate. Moderate levels of arousal actually facilitate problem solving, but high stress levels can make problem solving impossible.

Connection

Chapter 10
Arousal and stress can help or hinder performance, depending on the task.

In general, our discussion of problem solving shows that we humans are thinkers who readily jump to conclusions, based on our knowledge and biased by our motives, emotions, and perceptions. In view of this, it is surprising that our thinking so often serves us well in day-to-day life. Yet, from another perspective it makes perfect sense: Most of our problem-solving efforts involve drawing on past experience to make predictions about future rewards and punishments. If you think about this for a moment, you will realize that this is exactly what operant conditioning is about — which suggests that this mode of thinking is a fundamental part of our nature. Many of the "flaws" in our reasoning abilities, such as functional fixedness, are actually part of an adaptive (but necessarily imperfect) strategy that helps us use our previous experience to solve new problems.

Connection

Chapter 6
The likelihood of operant behavior recurring is controlled by its consequences.

Judging and Making Decisions

Whether you are a student, a professor, or a corporate president, you will make decisions every day. "How much should I invest?" "What grade does this paper deserve?" "How much time do I need to study tonight?" You can think of each decision as the solution to a problem — a problem for which there may not be a clearly right answer, but a problem requiring judgment. Unfortunately (especially for those who have not studied the psychology of decision making), judgment can be clouded by biases — which are really just faulty heuristics. Let's examine the most common of these causes of poor judgment.

Connection

Chapter 9
The ability for making decisions involves the emotional circuitry of the brain.

THE CONFIRMATION BIAS   Suppose that Fred has strong feelings about raising children: "Spare the rod and spoil the child," he says. How do you suppose Fred will deal with the news that punishment can actually encourage aggressive behavior? Chances are that he will be swayed by the **confirmation bias** to ignore or find fault with information that doesn't fit with his opinions and to seek information with which he agrees. A great deal of evidence shows that the confirmation bias is a powerful and all-too-human tendency (Aronson, 1998; Nickerson, 1998). In fact, we all act like Fred sometimes, especially on

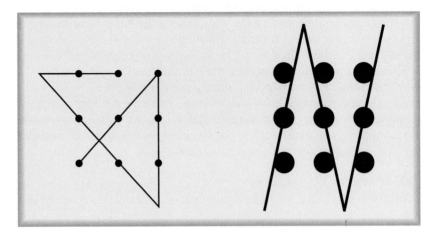

issues on which we hold strong opinions. Watch for the confirmation bias at work when people discuss taxes, abortion, gun control, the environment, national health insurance, religion, and many other emotionally charged issues.

HINDSIGHT BIAS A friend tells you that she lost money investing in "dot-com" stocks. "I thought the Internet was the wave of the future," she says. "I knew the boom in Internet stocks would turn into a bust," you reply. You are guilty of the **hindsight bias,** sometimes called the I-knew-it-all-along effect (Fischhoff, 1975; Hawkins & Hastie, 1990). Just as guilty of hindsight bias are the Monday morning quarterbacks who know what play should have been called at the crucial point in yesterday's big game. This form of distorted thinking appears after an event has occurred and people overestimate their ability to have predicted it. Hindsight bias can flaw the judgment of jurors, historians, newscasters, and anyone else who second-guesses other people's judgments after all the facts are in.

THE ANCHORING BIAS Ask a few of your friends, one at a time, to give a quick, off-the-top-of-the-head guess at the answer to the following simple math problem:

$$1 \times 2 \times 3 \times 4 \times 5 \times 6 \times 7 \times 8 = ?$$

Make them give you an estimate without actually doing the calculation; give them only about five seconds to think about it. Then, pose the problem in reverse to some other friends:

$$8 \times 7 \times 6 \times 5 \times 4 \times 3 \times 2 \times 1 = ?$$

Are the results different for the two groups? Of course, nobody will give precisely the right answer, but it's likely that your friends will respond as volunteers did in Amos Tversky and Daniel Kahneman's (1973, 1974) experiment. It turns out that the answers depended on whether the problem began with larger or smaller numbers. Those who saw the first problem gave a lower estimate than did those who were given the second problem. In Tversky and Kahneman's study, the average answer for the first group was 512, while the average for the second group was 2,250. Apparently, their "first impression"

Confirmation bias: Ignoring or finding fault with information that does not fit with our opinions, and seeking information with which we agree.

Hindsight bias: The tendency, after learning about an event, to "second guess" or believe that one could have predicted the event in advance.

—larger or smaller numbers at the beginning of the problem—biased their responses.

Tversky and Kahneman explain the difference between the two groups on the basis of an **anchoring bias.** That is, people apparently use this flawed heuristic to "anchor" their thinking to the higher or lower numbers that appear at the beginning of the problem. The first group was apparently more influenced by hearing the low numbers at the outset (1 × 2 × 3 ...) and, therefore, gave a lower total than the group that anchored its thinking to the higher numbers (8 × 7 × 6 ...). Multiply it out on your calculator to see how close your own estimate is to the true answer.

THE REPRESENTATIVENESS BIAS   If you assume that all blondes or ministers or psychology professors are alike, your judgment has been affected by **representativeness bias.** One reason people succumb to such prejudices is because the representativeness bias simplifies the task of social judgment. Once something is "categorized," it shares all the features of other members in that category. The fallacy in this heuristic, of course, is that people, events, and objects do not "belong" to categories simply because we find it mentally convenient to give them labels. By relying on category memberships to organize our experiences, we risk ignoring or underestimating the tremendous diversity of individual cases and complexity of people.

When estimating the likelihood that a specific individual belongs to a certain category—"vegetarian," for example—we look to see whether it has the features found in a typical category member. For example, is your new acquaintance, Holly, a vegetarian? Does she resemble your prototype of a "typical" vegetarian? Perhaps you believe that most vegetarians wear sandals, ride bicycles, and support liberal social causes. If so, you might judge that Holly *represents* enough of the characteristics of your concept of "vegetarians" to belong to the same group.

But such an analysis is unreasonable. Although some—perhaps many—vegetarians wear sandals, ride bicycles, and hold liberal views, the opposite may not be true: Because vegetarians are a minority group in the general population, it is unlikely that any particular individual who supports liberal social causes, wears sandals, and rides a bicycle is also vegetarian. That is, by ignoring the *base rate* information—the probability of a characteristic occurring in the general population—you have drawn an erroneous conclusion. Holly may in fact be an omnivore like most of your acquaintances, although if you invite her to dinner she will probably accept the cheese pizza and salad you offer her without complaint. While your representativeness bias—judging Holly by what seems to be her "type"—may not be especially important in this case, the same error underlies the more serious prejudices that result when people classify others solely on the basis of group membership.

THE AVAILABILITY BIAS   Yet another faulty heuristic comes from our tendency to judge probabilities of events by how readily examples come to mind. Psychologists call this the **availability bias.** We can illustrate this by asking you: Do more English words begin with "r" than have "r" in the third position? Most people think so because it is easier to think of words that begin with "r." That is, words beginning with "r" are more *available* to us from long-term memory. Similarly, through observational learning, people who watch a lot of violent crime on television have violent images readily available in their memories. As a result, such people usually judge their chances of being murdered or mugged as being much as higher than do people who watch little television (Singer et al., 1984).

Anchoring bias: A faulty heuristic caused by basing (anchoring) an estimate on a completely unrelated quantity.

Representativeness bias: A faulty heuristic strategy based on the presumption that, once a person or event is categorized, it shares all the features of other members in that category.

Availability bias: A faulty heuristic strategy that estimates probabilities based on information that can be recalled (made available) from personal experience.

Connection

Chapter 6
Models affect behavior through *observational learning.*

On Becoming a Creative Genius

Everyone would agree that Einstein was a creative genius. So were Aristotle and Bach. But what about your Aunt Mabel who does watercolors? What about Seth-the-second-grader who makes horses of modeling clay? These questions illustrate the big problem in creativity research: The experts cannot agree on an exact definition of creativity. Most, however, would go along with the slightly fuzzy notion that **creativity** is a process that produces novel responses that contribute to the solutions of problems. Most would also agree that a "genius" is someone whose insight and creativity are so great that they set that individual apart from ordinary folk. As with creativity, the boundary for genius is not well defined.

DIVERGENT AND CONVERGENT THINKING

Much of the literature connects creativity with **divergent thinking,** the ability to generate many responses to a problem (Guilford, 1967). Consequently, many tests of creativity emphasize divergent thinking tasks, such as listing uses for a burned-out light bulb or ways to improve a wristwatch. The assumption is that the more responses you can give, the more creative you are. Such tests, of course, put a premium on quantity rather than the quality of the responses.

Convergent thinking is the opposite of divergent thinking. It is required in dealing with problems for which there is a single correct answer on which one's thinking "converges." Convergent thinking is not usually thought of as an essential component of creativity.

Scores of consultants have made a living by offering seminars and workshops that purport to open people's minds to divergent thinking. Most emphasize group exercises that encourage people to generate as many ideas as possible—the wilder, the better. In particular, the technique called *brainstorming* is based on the assumption that creativity arises from allowing many ideas to blossom, without making hasty judgments on an idea's worth (Osborn, 1953). Unfortunately, the evidence linking such divergent thinking exercises to other measures of creativity is not impressive (Barron & Harrington, 1981; Goldenberg et al., 1999; Nicholls, 1972).

So, where does this leave you in your quest to become a creative genius? Let's follow the lead of psychologist Robert Weisberg, who offers a novel view of "genius." In brief, he argues that geniuses are merely good problem solvers who also possess certain helpful—but entirely human—characteristics.

CREATIVE GENIUS AS NOT SO SUPERHUMAN

Are the people we label "geniuses" a breed apart from the rest of us? Do they have some extraordinary innate powers of thought or perception that are unavailable to more ordinary mortals? Weisberg (1986) answers these questions this way:

> Our society holds a very romantic view about the origins of creative achievements. . . . This is the genius view, and at its core is the belief that creative achievements come about through great leaps of imagination which occur because creative individuals are capable of extraordinary thought processes. In addition to their intellectual capacities, creative individuals are assumed to possess extra-

There was no question but that Albert Einstein was bright. He also had an independent streak, a sense of humor, an intense interest in the complex problem of gravity, and a willingness to restructure the problem. He also sought the stimulation of other physicists. But he probably did not use thought processes that were altogether different from those used by other thinkers.

> ordinary personality characteristics which also play a role in bringing about creative leaps. These intellectual and personality characteristics are what is called "genius," and they are brought forth as the explanation for great creative achievements. (p. 1)

But, according to Weisberg and some other scholars in this area (Bink & Marsh, 2000), there is surprisingly little evidence supporting this view of creativity. In fact, the notion that creative geniuses are a breed apart may actually discourage creativity by making people feel that it is out of their reach. A more productive portrait, suggests Weisberg, views the thinking of people we call geniuses to be "ordinary thought processes in ordinary individuals" (p. 11). What produces extraordinary creativity, he says, is extensive knowledge, high motivation, and certain personality characteristics — not superhuman talents.

Other psychologists agree with Weisberg that the most highly creative individuals have a highly developed understanding of the basic knowledge in their fields (Gardner, 1993; Who Wants to Be a Genius?, 2001). In fact, you cannot become highly creative without first becoming an *expert:* having extensive and organized knowledge of the field in which you will make your creative contribution. But such mastery is not easily achieved, and it belies a high level of motivation that can sustain intense training and practice. Studies indicate that about ten years of work are required to master the knowledge and skills required for full competence in virtually any field, whether it be skiing, sculpture, singing, or psychology (Ericsson et al., 1993; Sternberg & Lubart, 1991, 1992).

APTITUDES, PERSONALITY CHARACTERISTICS, AND CREATIVITY

In his book *Creating Minds,* Howard Gardner (1993) argues that the extraordinary creativity that we have seen in the work of Freud, Einstein, Picasso, and others is a combination of several factors that include not only expertise and motivation but certain patterns of abilities and personality characteristics. Highly creative individuals, he says, have **aptitudes** — innate potentialities — specific to certain domains. (These potentialities, of course, must be developed by intensive study and practice.) Freud, for example, had a special facility for creating with words and understanding people; Einstein was remarkably good at logic and spatial relationships; and Picasso's creativity arose from a combination of aptitudes comprising spatial relationships and interpersonal perceptiveness.

And what personality characteristics do highly creative people

possess? The literature identifies several (Barron & Harrington, 1981; Csikszentmihalyi, 1996). They include the following:

▶ *Independence* Highly creative people have the ability to resist social pressures to conform to conventional ways of thinking, at least in their area of creative interest (Amabile, 1983, 1987). That is, they have the confidence to strike out on their own. Because of this, perhaps, many creative people describe themselves as loners.

▶ *Intense interest in a problem* Highly creative individuals also must have an all-consuming interest in the subject matter with which they will be creative. They are always tinkering, in their minds, with problems that fascinate them (Weisberg, 1986). External motivators, such as money or a Nobel Prize, may add to their motivation, but the main motivators are internal, otherwise they could not sustain the long-term interest in a problem necessary for an original contribution.

▶ *Willingness to restructure the problem* Highly creative people not only grapple with problems, but they often question the way a problem is presented. (Recall our earlier discussion about defining the problem.) For example, students from the School of the Art Institute of Chicago who later became the most successful creative artists among their class members had one striking characteristic in common: They were always changing and redefining the assignments given by their instructors (Getzels and Csikszentmihalyi, 1976).

▶ *Preference for complexity* Creative people seem drawn to complexity — to what may appear messy or chaotic to others. Moreover, they revel in the challenge of looking for simplicity in complexity. Thus, highly creative

people may be attracted to the largest, most difficult, and most complex problems in their fields (Sternberg & Lubart, 1992).

▶ *Intelligence* This is a tricky issue: High intelligence does not necessarily produce creativity, although low intelligence may inhibit it. Consequently, a person with an IQ of 70 is not likely to be as creative as a person with an IQ of 130, even though the latter's intelligence, by itself, carries no guarantee of creativity. In general, we can say that intelligence and creativity are distinct abilities (Barron & Harrington, 1981; Kershner & Ledger, 1985). We can find plodding, unimaginative persons at all IQ levels, and we can find highly creative persons with only average IQ scores.

▶ *A need for stimulating interaction* Creativity of the highest order almost always grows out of an interaction of highly creative individuals. Early in their careers, creative people usually find a *mentor* — a teacher who brings them up to speed in their chosen field. Highly creative individuals then go on to surpass their mentors and then find additional stimulation from the ideas of others like themselves. Often, this means leaving behind family and former friends (Gardner, 1993).

So, what is the take-home message for our understanding of creativity? Those who have looked closely at this domain agree on two main points. First, creativity requires well-developed knowledge of the field in which the creative contribution will be made. Second, high-level creativity requires certain personal characteristics, such as independence and the motivation required to sustain an interest in an unsolved problem over a very long period of time.

That is your formula for becoming a creative genius.

1. **RECALL:** *What is the first step in problem solving?*
   a. selecting a strategy
   b. avoiding pitfalls
   c. searching for analogies
   d. identifying the problem

2. **APPLICATION:** *A math problem calls for finding the area of a triangle. You know the formula, so you multiply $\frac{1}{2}$ the base times the height. You have used*
   a. an algorithm.
   b. a heuristic.
   c. functional fixedness.
   d. intuition.

3. **RECALL:** *Good problem solvers often use "tricks of the trade" or "rules of thumb" known as*
   a. algorithms.
   b. heuristics.
   c. trial-and-error.
   d. deductive reasoning.

4. **APPLICATION:** *Which one of the following would be an example of the confirmation bias?*
   a. Mary ignores negative information about her favorite political candidate.

   b. Aaron agrees with Joel's taste in music.
   c. Natasha refuses to eat a food she dislikes.
   d. Bill buys a new RV, even though his wife was opposed to the purchase.

5. **RECALL:** *Which of the following is* not *a characteristic that is consistently found among highly creative people?*
   a. independence
   b. a high level of motivation
   c. willingness to restructure the problem
   d. extremely high intelligence

6. **UNDERSTANDING THE CORE CONCEPT:**
   Heuristic strategies show that our thinking is often based on
   a. logic rather than emotion.
   b. experience rather than logic.
   c. trial-and-error rather than algorithms.
   d. common sense rather than learning

ANSWERS: 1. d   2. a   3. b   4. a
5. d   6. b

HOW IS INTELLIGENCE MEASURED?

Creativity: A mental process that produces novel responses that contribute to the solutions of problems.

Divergent thinking: A problem-solving process aimed at producing many appropriate solutions to a single problem. According to Guilford, divergent thinking is also the component of intelligence that is used to generate creative responses.

Convergent thinking: A problem-solving process aimed at producing "correct" answers to problems. According to Guilford, convergent thinking is also a component of intelligence.

Aptitudes: Innate potentialities (as contrasted with abilities acquired by learning).

Psychologists have long been fascinated by the ways people differ in their abilities to reason, solve problems, and think creatively. The assessment of individual differences, however, did not begin with modern psychology. Historical records show that sophisticated assessment techniques were used in ancient China. Over 4,000 years ago, the Chinese employed a program of civil service testing that required government officials to demonstrate their competence every third year at an oral examination. Later, applicants were required to pass written civil service tests to assess their knowledge of law, the military, agriculture, and geography. British diplomats and missionaries assigned to China in the early 1800s described the selection procedures so admiringly that the British, and later the Americans, adopted modified versions of China's system for the selection of civil service personnel (Wiggins, 1973).

Unlike the historical Chinese, modern Americans seem to be more interested in how "smart" people are, as opposed to how much they have learned. It is the interest in this sort of "native intelligence" that spurred the development of intelligence testing as we know it today. But, despite the long history of mental testing and the widespread use of intelligence tests in our society, the exact meaning of the term *intelligence* is still disputed (Neisser et al., 1996). Most psychologists would probably agree with the general definition that we gave at the beginning of the chapter—that intelligence involves abilities to acquire knowledge, reason, and solve problems. They would also agree that a complete picture of an individual's intelligence must be obtained from mea-

Even though the SAT tests are far from perfect predictors of college success, they are widely used. Many items on the SAT are similar to those found on intelligence tests.

surements across a variety of tasks. However, they disagree on exactly what these abilities are or whether they are many or few in number.

It is important to note that all agree that intelligence is a relative term. That is, an individual's level of intelligence is defined in relation to the same abilities in a comparison group, usually of the same age range. Everyone also agrees that intelligence is also a **hypothetical construct:** a characteristic that is not directly observable, but is, instead, inferred from behavior. In practice, this means that intelligence is measured from an individual's responses on an intelligence test. The individual's scores are then compared to those of a reference group. Exactly what these tests should assess is the source of much controversy — and the focus of this section of this chapter. Our Core Concept says:

> **Intelligence testing has a history of controversy, but most psychologists now view intelligence as a normally distributed trait that can be measured by performance on a variety of tasks — both verbal and nonverbal.**

Core Concept

We begin our survey of intelligence and intelligence testing by introducing you to the people who founded the field of intelligence testing.

Binet and Simon Invent a School Abilities Test

Alfred Binet (Bi-NAY) and his colleague Théodore Simon stepped into history in 1904. At that time, a new law required all children to attend school, and the French Government needed a means of identifying those who needed remedial help. Binet and Simon were asked to design a test for this purpose. They responded with 30 problems sampling a variety of abilities that seemed necessary for school (Figure 8.9). The new approach was a success. It did, indeed, predict which children could, or could not, handle normal schoolwork.

Four important features distinguish the Binet-Simon approach (Binet, 1911):

1. Binet and Simon interpreted scores on their test as an estimate of *current performance* and not as a measure of innate intelligence.

Hypothetical construct: A characteristic that is not directly observable but is, instead, inferred from behavior.

FIGURE 8.9:   Sample Items from the First Binet-Simon Test

On the original Binet-Simon test, a child was asked to perform tasks such as the following:

- Name various common objects (such as a clock or a cat) shown in pictures.
- Repeat a 15-word sentence given by the examiner.
- Give a word that rhymes with one given by the examiner.
- Imitate gestures (such as pointing to an object).
- Comply with simple commands (such as moving a block from one location to another).
- Explain the differences between two common objects.
- Use three words (given by the examiner) in a sentence.
- Define abstract terms (such as "friendship").

2. They wanted the test scores to be used to identify children who needed special help and not merely to categorize or label them as bright or dull.

3. They emphasized that training and opportunity could affect intelligence, and they wanted to identify areas of performance in which special education could help these children.

4. They constructed the test empirically—based on how children were observed to perform—rather than tying the test to a particular theory of intelligence.

French Children of various ages were assessed with this test, and the average for children at each age was computed. Then, each child's performance was compared to the averages for children of various ages. Scores were expressed in terms of **mental age (MA):** the average age at which individuals achieve a particular score. So, for example, when a child's score was the same as the average score for a group of 5-year-olds, the child was said to have a *mental age* of 5, regardless of his or her actual **chronological age (CA),** the number of years since the individual's birth. Binet and Simon decided that those most needing remedial help were students whose MA was two years behind CA.

American Psychologists Borrow Binet and Simon's Idea

In the United States, psychologists changed the Binet-Simon test of school abilities into the form we now call an IQ test. They did this by first modifying the scoring procedure, improving the test's content, and obtaining scores from a large normative group of people, including adults. Soon intelligence testing was widely accepted as a technique by which Americans were defining themselves —and each other.

THE APPEAL OF INTELLIGENCE TESTING IN AMERICA   Why did intelligence testing become so popular in the United States? Three forces that were

Connection

Chapter 1
An *empirical* investigation relies on observational data.

Mental age (MA): The average age at which normal (average) individuals achieve a particular score.

Chronological age (CA): The number of years since the individual's birth.

changing the face of the country early in the 20th century conspired to make intelligence testing seem like an orderly way out of growing turmoil and uncertainty. First, the United States was experiencing an unprecedented wave of immigration, resulting from global economic, social, and political crises. Second, new laws requiring universal education — schooling for all children — were flooding schools with students. And third, when World War I began, the military needed a way of assessing and classifying the new recruits. Together, these events resulted in a need for large numbers of people to be identified, documented, and classified (Chapman, 1988). Assessment of intelligence was seen, not only as a way to bring some order to the tumult of rapid social change, but as an inexpensive and democratic way to separate those who could benefit from education or military leadership training from those who could not.

Intelligence Testing Goes to War   In 1917, when the United States declared war on Germany and joined the massive military campaign of World War I, the government commissioned a group of illustrious psychologists to develop psychological instruments that could be used to assess the mental abilities of large numbers of people quickly. They responded by developing the necessary tests in only one month (Lennon, 1985). These new group-administered tests of mental ability were eventually used to evaluate over 1.7 million soldiers.

Civilian Consequences   One consequence of the large-scale group-testing program was that the American public came to accept the idea that intelligence tests could accurately differentiate people in terms of their mental abilities. This acceptance soon led to the widespread use of tests in schools and industry. Another, more unfortunate, consequence was that the tests were used to reinforce prevailing prejudices. Specifically, Army reports suggested that differences in test scores were linked to race and country of origin (Yerkes, 1921). Of course, the same statistics *could* have been used to demonstrate that environmental disadvantages limit the full development of people's intellectual abilities. Instead, immigrants with limited facility in English or even little understanding of how to take such tests were labeled as "morons," "idiots," and "imbeciles" (terms used at the time to specify different degrees of mental retardation).

While these problems are more obvious to us now (with the help of hindsight), at the time they were obscured by the fact that the tests did what most people wanted: Mental tests were simple to administer, and they provided a means of assessing and classifying people according to their scores. Never mind that there were some biases and that some people were treated unfairly. In general, the public perceived that the tests were objective and democratic.

THE STANFORD-BINET INTELLIGENCE SCALE   The most respected of the new American tests of intelligence was developed by Stanford University professor Lewis Terman. His approach was to adapt the Binet and Simon test for U.S. schoolchildren by standardizing its administration and its age-level norms. The result was the Stanford-Binet Intelligence Scale (Terman, 1916), which soon became the standard by which other measures of intelligence were judged. But, because it had to be administered individually, Terman's test was not so economical as were the group tests. Nevertheless, it was better suited for spotting learning problems. Even more importantly, the Stanford-Binet test was designed both for children and adults.

With his new test Terman introduced the concept of the **intelligence quotient (IQ),** a term coined originally by German psychologist William Stern

Intelligence quotient (IQ): A numerical score on an intelligence test, originally computed by dividing the person's mental age by chronological age and multiplying by 100.

in 1914. The IQ was the ratio of mental age (MA) to chronological age (CA), multiplied by 100 (to eliminate decimals):

$$IQ = \frac{\text{mental age}}{\text{chronological age}} \times 100$$

Please follow us through the IQ equation with these examples: Consider a child with a chronological age of 8 years, whose test scores reveals a mental age of 10. Dividing the child's mental age by chronological age (MA/CA = 10/8) gives 1.25. Multiplying that result by 100, we obtain an IQ of 125. In contrast, another 8-year-old child who performs at the level of an average 6-year-old (MA = 6) has an IQ of 6/8 × 100 = 75, according to Terman's formula. Those whose mental age is the same as their chronological age have IQs of 100, which is considered to be the average or "normal" IQ.

Within a short time, the new Stanford-Binet test became a popular instrument in clinical psychology, psychiatry, and educational counseling. With the publication of this test Terman also promoted his belief that intelligence is largely hereditary and that his IQ test could measure it. The implicit message was that an IQ score reflected something fundamental and unchanging about people.

Although the Stanford-Binet became the "gold standard" of intelligence testing, it had its critics. The loudest objection was that it employed an inconsistent concept of intelligence because it measured different mental abilities at different ages. For example, 2- to 4-year-olds were tested on their ability to manipulate objects, whereas adults were tested almost exclusively on verbal items. Test makers heeded these criticisms, and as the scientific understanding of intelligence increased, psychologists found it increasingly important to measure *several* intellectual abilities at *all* age levels. A modern revision of the Stanford-Binet now provides separate scores for several mental skills (Vernon, 1987).

IQ Testing Today

The success of the Stanford-Binet test encouraged the development of other IQ tests. As a result, psychologists now have a wide choice of instruments for

A psychologist administers an intelligence test to a four-year-old child. The performance part of this test includes a block design task, an object completion task, and a shape identification task.

Sample IQ Test Items

Try your hand at the following items adapted from group tests of intelligence. Some of the items are more challenging than others. You will find the correct answers at the end.

VOCABULARY   Select the best definition for each word:

1. **viable**   a. traveled   b. capable of living
                c. V-shaped   d. can be bent

2. **imminent** a. defenseless   b. expensive
                c. impending   d. notorious

ANALOGIES   Examine the relationship between the first two words. Then, find an answer that has the same relationship with the word in **bold letters:**

3. Washington: Lincoln

July: a. January   b. April
                c. May   d. October

4. ocean: canoe

verse: a. poem   b. pen
                c. water   d. serve

SIMILARITIES   Which figure on the right belongs to the same category as the one on the left?

5. J   A M S Z T

6. A   S T U V X

SEQUENCES   Choose the answer that best completes the sequence:

7. a z b y c x d?   e   s   u   w   f

8. 1 3 6 10 15?   16   18   21   27   128

MATHEMATICAL REASONING

9. Portland and Seattle are actually 150 miles apart, but on a map they are two inches apart. If Chicago and Norfolk are five inches apart on the same map, what is the actual distance between those two cities?

   a. 125 miles   b. 250 miles   c. 375 miles   d. 525 miles

ANSWERS: 1. b   2. c   3. d (October comes after July)   4. d (*verse* and *serve* have the same letters)   5. S (the only one with a curve in it)   6. U (the only vowel)   7. W   8. 21   9. 375

---

assessing intelligence. The most prominent of these are the Wechsler Adult Intelligence Scale (WAIS), the Wechsler Intelligence Scale for Children (WISC), and the Wechsler Preschool and Primary Scale of Intelligence (WPPSI). With these instruments, psychologist David Wechsler offers a family of tests that measure a variety of skills, including vocabulary, verbal comprehension, arithmetic ability, similarities (the ability to state how two things are alike), digit span (repeating a series of digits after the examiner), and block design (the ability to reproduce designs by fitting together blocks with colored sides).

Like the Stanford-Binet, the Wechsler tests are *individual* tests. That is, they are given to one person at a time. Also available are *group* tests of intelligence that can be administered to large numbers of students simultaneously. Unlike the Stanford-Binet and the Wechsler tests, these group tests are primarily paper-and-pencil measures, involving booklets of questions and computer-scorable answer sheets. The convenience of group tests—even though they are not as precise as individual tests—has made IQ testing, along with other forms of academic assessment, widespread. It is quite likely that you have taken such tests, perhaps without realizing what they were.

Problems with the IQ Formula

A problem in calculating IQ scores became apparent as soon as psychologists began to use their formula with adults. Here's what happens: By the mid- to late teenage years, gains in mental age scores usually level off, as people develop mentally in many different directions. As a result, mental growth, as measured by a test, appears to slow down. Moreover, Terman's formula for computing IQs makes normal children appear to become mentally retarded adults—at least as far as their test scores are concerned! Note what happens to the average 30-year-old's score if mental age, as measured by a test, stays at the same level as it was at age 15:

$$IQ = \frac{\text{mental age}}{\text{chronological age}} = \frac{15}{30} \times 100 = 50$$

Psychologists quickly realized that this paints an erroneous picture of adult mental abilities. People do not grow less intelligent as they become adults (even though their children sometimes think so!). Rather, adults develop in different directions, which their IQ scores do not necessarily reflect. Prudently, psychologists decided to abandon the original IQ formula and to find another means of calculating IQs. Their solution was similar to the familiar practice of "grading on the curve." This famous curve demands some explanation.

Calculating IQs "on the Curve"

Behind the new method for calculating IQs lay the assumption that intelligence is **normally distributed.** That is, intelligence is assumed to be spread through the population in varying degrees, so that few people fall into the high or low ranges, while most people cluster around a central average. In this respect, intelligence is presumed to be like many physical traits, including height, weight, and shoe size. If you were to measure any of these variables in a large number of people, you would probably get a set of scores that follow the same "curve" teachers use when they grade "on the curve." Let us take women's heights as an example.

Imagine that you have randomly selected a large number of adult women and arranged them in single-file columns, according to their heights (everybody 5′ tall in one column, 5′ 1″ in the next, 5′ 2″ in the next, and so on). You would find most of the women standing in the columns near the group's *average* height (see Figure 8.10). Only a few would be in the columns containing extremely tall women or extremely short women. We could easily describe the number of women at each height by a curve that follows the boundary of each column. We call this bell-shaped curve a **normal distribution.**

Applying this same concept to intelligence, psychologists find that people's IQ test scores (like the women's heights we considered above) fit a normal distribution. (See Figure 8.11.) More precisely, when IQ tests are given to large numbers of individuals, the scores of those at each age level are normally distributed. (Adults are placed in their own group, regardless of age, and the

Normally distributed: Spread through the population in varying degrees, so that few people fall into the high or low ranges, while most people cluster around the middle.

Normal distribution: A bell-shaped curve, describing the spread of a characteristic throughout a population.

Connection

Chapter 1
Random selection means that all potential subjects have an equal chance of being selected.

FIGURE 8.10: An (Imaginary) Normal Distribution of Women's Heights

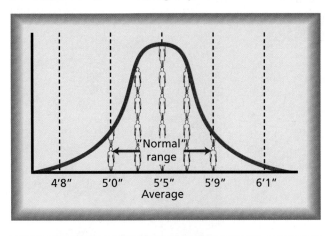

distribution of their scores also fits the bell-shaped curve.) Instead of using the old IQ formula, IQs are now determined from tables that indicate where test scores fall on the normal curve. The scores are statistically adjusted so that the average for each age group is set at 100. Scores between 90 and 110 are considered to be in the **normal range** (see Figure 8.11). At the extreme ends of the distribution, scores below 70 are often said to be in the *mentally retarded* range, while those above 130 are sometimes said to indicate *giftedness*.

Thus, IQ scores are no longer calculated by dividing mental age by chronological age. The concept of a "ratio" expressed as a multiple of 100 (a percentagelike number that is easy to understand) is retained, however. This solves the problem of calculating adult IQs by comparing adults with adults.

FIGURE 8.11: The Normal Distribution of IQ Scores among a Large Sample

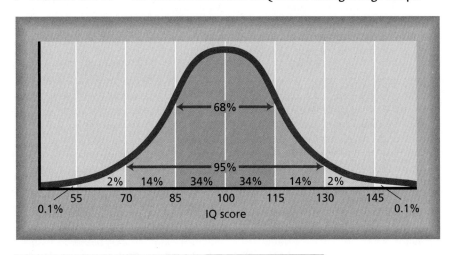

Normal range: Scores falling in (approximately) the middle two-thirds of a normal distribution.

What Can You Do for an Exceptional Child?

The Special Olympics offers mentally retarded children (and others with disabilities) an opportunity to capitalize on their abilities and to build self-esteem.

As we have noted, *mental retardation* and *giftedness* lie at the opposite ends of the intelligence spectrum. As traditionally conceived, **mental retardation** occupies the IQ range below IQ 70 —taking in the scores achieved by approximately 2% of the population (see Figure 8.11). Arbitrarily, **giftedness** begins 30 points above average, at 130 IQ points, comprising another 2% of the population. Now, bearing in mind all we have learned about the limitations of IQ tests, let's take a brief look at these two categories.

MENTAL RETARDATION

The most current view of mental retardation deemphasizes IQ scores by focusing on practical abilities to get along in the world (Baumeister, 1987; Detterman, 1999; Greenspan, 1999; Robinson et al., 2000). In fact, the American Association of Mental Retardation now offers a definition of mental retardation that does not even mention an IQ cutoff score. According to this new perspective, mental retardation involves "significantly subaverage intellectual functioning" that becomes apparent before age 18. It also involves limitations in at least two of the following areas: "communication, self-care, home living, social skills, community use, self-direction, health and safety, functional academics, leisure and work" (Turkington, 1993, p. 26).

Causes of Mental Retardation

Mental retardation has many causes (Daily et al., 2000; Scott & Carran, 1987). Some are known to be genetic because we can point to a specific genetically controlled defect.

This is the case, as we have noted in people who have Down syndrome. (See Chapter 2.) Some causes are environmental, as in *fetal alcohol syndrome,* which involves brain damage incurred before birth, resulting from the mother's abuse of alcohol during pregnancy. Other environmental causes include post-natal accidents that damage the cognitive regions of the brain. Still other causes involve conditions of deprivation or neglect, which fail to give the developing child the experiences needed for advancement up the intellectual ladder. Some cases have no known cause.

Dealing with Mental Retardation

For most types of mental retardation we have no cure, although research has found some preventive measures. For example, a simple test performed routinely on newborn babies can identify a hidden genetic disorder known as PKU. If detected early, the mental retardation usually associated with PKU can be prevented by a special diet. More generally, genetic counseling, pregnancy care services, and education of new parents are other preventive strategies (Scott & Carran, 1987).

Aside from prevention, special education programs can help those who develop mental retardation to learn vocational and independent living skills. Meanwhile, biological scientists hope that one day they will be able to treat genetically based forms of mental retardation with therapies that are just now being conceived. Genetic treatment may involve splicing a healthy gene into a benign virus that would "infect" all of a retarded person's cells and replace the defective gene. At present, genetic therapy is being tried experimentally for the treatment of certain physical diseases, but it is at least a

few years away in the treatment of mental retardation.

For now, what can you do if you have a mentally retarded child? Dealing with mental retardation usually means making the best of a difficult situation. Parents of a retarded child should realize that, because the nervous system is so immature at birth and because so much physical and mental development occurs during the first years of life, interventions that begin early will have the greatest payoffs. Realistically, however, the most intellectual improvement one can expect from an optimal educational program is an IQ gain of about 15 points (Robinson et al., 2000).

Psychological approaches that involve sensory stimulation and social interaction can be enormously important. In fact, an enriched environment may be just as helpful to a mentally retarded child as it is to a gifted child. Teams of special education teachers, speech therapists, educational psychologists, physicians, and other specialists can devise programs that allow mentally retarded persons to capitalize on the abilities they have, rather than being held prisoner of their disabilities (see Schroeder et al., 1987). Behavior modification programs, based on operant conditioning, have been especially successful. (See Chapter 13.) As a result, many retarded citizens have learned to care for themselves and have learned vocational skills that enable them to live independently (Landesman & Butterfield, 1987).

GIFTEDNESS

At the other end of the intelligence spectrum we find the "gifted," with their especially high IQs, typically defined as being in the top 1 or 2% (Robinson et al., 2000). But, you might wonder, what do such people eventually do with their superior intellectual abilities? Does a high IQ give its owner an advantage in life? A 70-year look at gifted individuals suggests that it does.

Terman's Studies of Giftedness

The most extensive project ever undertaken to study gifted individuals began in 1921 under the direction of Lewis Terman, the same person who brought Binet and Simon's IQ test to the United States (Leslie, 2000). From a large pool of children tested in the California schools, Terman selected 1,528 children who scored near the top of the IQ range. His longitudinal research program followed these children as they went through school and on into adulthood. Periodically through their lives, Terman retested them and gathered other information on their achievements and adjustment patterns. The resulting decades of data have taught us much about the nature of giftedness.

Almost uniformly, Terman's gifted children excelled in school—as one might expect from the strong correlation between IQ and academic achievement. Terman also remarked on the good health and happiness of the children in his sample. Apparently, a healthy mind and a healthy body often go together.

As they moved into adulthood, the gifted group continued on the path of success. An unusually high number of scientists, writers, and professionals emerged from its ranks. Together they published more than 2,000 scientific articles, patented 235 inventions, and wrote 92 books. By middle age, more than 86% of the men in Terman's sample had entered high-status professions (Terman & Oden, 1959).

Yet, for all their achievements, no one in this high-IQ sample achieved the level of an Einstein, a Picasso, or a Martha Graham. Nor did a high IQ turn out to be a guarantee of wealth or stature. In fact, many from Terman's sample led ordinary, undistinguished lives. The ones who were most visibly successful seemed to have, in addition to their high IQs, extraordinary motivation and someone at home or at school who was especially encouraging to them (Goleman, 1980; Oden, 1968). You will remember that we previously found these same characteristics to be markers of "genius."

Dealing with Giftedness

Imagine that you are the parent of a child with a very high IQ score, say 145. Which one of the following would be the best course of action?

▶ Enroll your child in special after-school classes.

▶ Hire a tutor to help the child with his or her homework.

▶ Send the child to a private school.

▶ Do nothing special.

What do the experts say?

Don't rush out to enroll your child in special classes or provide other "help" because of his or her IQ score, counsels Csikszentmihalyi (Csikszentmihalyi et al., 1993; Wong & Csikszentmihalyi, 1991). Parents can destroy the spark of curiosity by pushing a child toward goals that do not hold the child's interest, he warns. Chances are you have already provided an environment in which your child's native ability could thrive. So, do not make any rash and radical changes.

Above all, avoid making the child feel like a freak because of the high IQ score. And do not feel smug about your genetic contribution to your child's intellect. Remember that IQ tests sample only a small fraction of human abilities. Other people's kids may have equally amazing abilities in untested regions of their intellects.

Remember, also, that a high IQ is no guarantee of high motivation, high creativity, or success in life. All it guarantees is an intellectual opportunity. So, what should you do with a bright child? Nothing special that you would not have done before you knew the IQ score.

Mental retardation: Often conceived as representing the lower 2% of the IQ range, commencing about 30 points below average (below about 70 points). More sophisticated definitions also take into account an individual's level of social functioning and other abilities.

Giftedness: Often conceived as representing the upper 2% of the IQ range, commencing about 30 points above average—at about 130 IQ points.

CHECKYOURUNDERSTANDING

1. **RECALL:** *One of Binet's great ideas was that of* mental age, *which was defined as*

   a. the average age at which people achieve a particular score on an intelligence test.

   b. an individual's biological age plus the score he or she achieves on a mental test.

   c. an individual's level of emotional maturity, as judged by the examiner.

   d. the variability in scores seen when an individual is tested repeatedly.

2. **APPLICATION:** *You have tested a 12-year-old child and found that she has a mental age of 15. Using the original IQ formula, what is her IQ?*

   a. 75

   b. 100

   c. 115

   d. 125

3. **RECALL:** *The problem with the original IQ formula is that it gave a distorted picture of the intellectual abilities of*

   a. adults.

   b. children.

   c. retarded persons.

   d. gifted students.

4. **UNDERSTANDING THE CORE CONCEPT:**

   If intelligence is a normally distributed characteristic, then you would expect to find it

   a. to be different abilities in different people.

   b. to be spread throughout the population, but with most people clustered near the middle of the range.

   c. to a significant degree only in people whose IQ scores are above 100.

   d. to be determined entirely by hereditary factors.

ANSWERS: 1. a   2. d   3. a   4. b

WHAT ARE THE COMPONENTS OF INTELLIGENCE?

People who show aptitude in one area—language, for example—often score high on other dimensions, such as mathematics or spatial relationships. This fact argues for the idea of a single, general intellectual ability. But there are some glaring exceptions. Persons with **savant syndrome** represent the most extreme cases of this sort. These individuals have a remarkable talent, such as the ability to multiply numbers quickly in their heads or to determine the day of the week for any given date, even though they are mentally slow in other domains. (You may remember Dustin Hoffman's portrayal of one such person in the film *Rainman*.) These cases raise a serious question about the whole concept of a single, general intelligence factor. Obviously, there is no simple solution to the problem of one or many intelligences. Different psychologists have dealt with the issue in different ways, as our Core Concept suggests:

Savant syndrome: Found in individuals having a remarkable talent (such as the ability to multiply numbers quickly in their heads or to determine the day of the week for any given date) even though they are mentally slow in other domains.

> Some psychologists believe that the essence of intelligence is a single, general factor, while others believe intelligence is best described as a collection of distinct abilities.

We will first examine this issue from the viewpoint of psychologists in the *psychometric tradition:* those who have been interested in developing tests to measure mental abilities. Following that excursion, we will look at intelligence from the standpoint of cognitive psychologists who have recently brought a fresh perspective to the problem.

Psychometric Theories of Intelligence

Psychometrics is the field of "mental measurements." It is the psychological specialty that has given us most of our IQ tests, along with achievement tests, personality tests, the SAT, and a variety of other assessment instruments. Many pioneers in psychology carved their professional niches with contributions to psychometrics, including Alfred Binet and Lewis Terman. Yet another famous figure in this field was Charles Spearman, a psychologist who is best known for his work suggesting that intelligence is a single factor.

SPEARMAN'S G FACTOR   By the 1920s there were many tests of intelligence available, and British psychologist Charles Spearman was able to show that individuals' scores on different tests, involving problems of many kind, are often highly correlated (1927). This, he said, points to a single, common factor of *general intelligence* underlying performance across all intellectual domains. Spearman did not deny that some people have outstanding talents or deficits in certain areas. But, he said, these individual differences should not blind us to a single general intelligence factor at work behind all our mental activity. Spearman called this general intellectual ability the **g factor.** He assumed that this general factor is innate, and most psychologists at the time agreed with him (Tyler, 1988, p. 128).

Recently, neuroscientists have found some support for Spearman's theory. John Duncan and his colleagues (2000) have shown that various tests of g all involve a small portion of the brain's frontal lobes. This suggests, they say, a single brain mechanism that controls various forms of intelligent behavior. Could this site be the locus of g? Although Duncan and his group think so, others believe this explanation oversimplifies both the nature of intelligence and of the brain (Sternberg, 2000).

CATTELL'S FLUID AND CRYSTALLIZED INTELLIGENCE   Using sophisticated mathematical techniques, Raymond Cattell (1963) determined that general intelligence can be broken down into two relatively independent components that he called *crystallized* and *fluid* intelligence. **Crystallized intelligence** consists of the knowledge a person has acquired, plus the ability to access that knowledge. Thus, crystallized intelligence relates to the person's ability to store and retrieve information from long-term memory. It is measured by tests of vocabulary, arithmetic, and general information. In contrast, **fluid intelligence** is the ability to see complex relationships and solve problems—abilities that involve using *algorithms* and *heuristics,* which we discussed earlier in this chapter. Fluid intelligence is often measured by tests of block design and spatial visualization, tests that do not rely on the individual possessing certain "crystallized" background information in order to solve a problem. For Cattell, both types of intelligence were essential to adaptive living.

GUILFORD'S STRUCTURE-OF-INTELLECT   Two intelligences—or even a dozen—are still not enough to describe all our mental abilities, according to J. P. Guilford. Accordingly, his theory divides intelligence into 150 separate abilities. As you can see in Figure 8.12, Guilford's model looks like a cube, but you might also think of it as his attempt to create psychology's "periodic table" of the intellect. How did he arrive at 150 components? To begin, he proposed that all intellectual tasks involve three broad attributes (Guilford, 1973, 1985):

▶ *Operations*—which refers to the kind of thinking required (e.g., looking for "correct" answers, as opposed to "creative" answers)

▶ *Contents*—which refers to the kind of information that must be used (e.g., visual, verbal, or mathematical information)

Connection

Chapter 1
A *correlation* shows a relationship.

Connection

Chapter 7
Much of our general knowledge is stored in *declarative memory,* a partition of *long-term memory.*

Psychometrics: The field of mental testing.

g factor: A general ability, proposed by Spearman as the main factor underlying all intelligent mental activity.

Crystallized intelligence: The knowledge a person has acquired, plus the ability to access that knowledge.

Fluid intelligence: The ability to see complex relationships and solve problems.

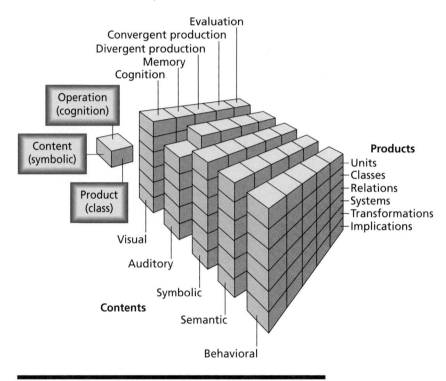

FIGURE 8.12: Guilford's Structure-of-Intellect Model

Guilford's three dimensions of intellect—operations, contents, and products—may be arranged in various combinations to produce 150 separate factors of intellect.

▶ *Products*—which refers to the form that the product of thought will take (e.g., a written report, a painting, or a new surgical procedure)

But Guilford did not stop there. His theory further subdivides the above categories into five kinds of mental operations, five classes of contents, and six types of intellectual products. Thus, each of the 150 small cubes in **Guilford's structure-of-intellect** model contains a different combination of these factors. To give an example: The children's TV program *Sesame Street* often presents viewers with a group of objects (e.g., shirt, socks, shoes, pencil) and asks, "Which one is not like the others?" In Guilford's terms, this problem requires *evaluation* (an operation), *semantic* information (one type of content), and organization of information into *classes* (a product).

While Guilford's model represents the most detailed theory of intelligence yet proposed, it has had little impact on the practice of intelligence testing. Even so, the structure-of-intellect model has helped us realize that there are many ways to be smart. Perhaps his most influential contribution lies in his distinction between two important kinds of mental operations: *convergent thinking* (used to find a correct answer) and *divergent thinking* (used to find solutions to problems that can have many answers). As we saw earlier in this chapter, divergent thinking is believed to be a component of creativity.

Cognitive Theories of Intelligence

Late in the 20th century, when the cognitive view emerged as a major force in psychology, it produced some radical new ideas about intelligence. In brief, the

Guilford's structure-of-intellect: J. P. Guilford's model of intelligence, consisting of some 150 separate factors, generated by five kinds of mental *operations,* five classes of *contents,* and six types of intellectual *products.*

cognitive view of intelligence went well beyond the emphasis on vocabulary, logic, problem solving, and other skills that had been used to predict school success. *Intelligence,* said cognitive psychologists, involves cognitive processes that contribute to success in many areas of life — not just school (Sternberg, 2000). We will focus on two of these cognitive theories.

STERNBERG'S TRIARCHIC THEORY   You may know someone who seems to have plenty of "book smarts" but who has never been very successful in life. Such people often don't know how to "read" others or to deal with unexpected events. Psychologist Robert Sternberg says that they lack **practical intelligence** (also called *contextual intelligence*): the ability to cope with the people and events in their environment. Practical intelligence is sometimes called "street smarts," although it applies just as well at home, on the job, or at school as it does on the street. One study suggests that it can also be thought of as "horse sense": Researchers found that, among regular visitors to racetracks, those who were most successful at picking winning horses had IQs no higher than those who were less successful. This suggests that this very practical ability to pick winners is something different from the form of intelligence measured on standard IQ tests (Ceci & Liker, 1986).

In contrast with practical intelligence, Sternberg refers to the ability measured by most IQ tests as **logical reasoning** (also called *componential intelligence*). It includes the ability to analyze problems and find correct answers. Your grades in college are likely to be closely related to your logical reasoning abilities.

A third form of intelligence described by Sternberg's theory is called **experiential intelligence** — involving insight and creativity. This intelligence helps people see new relationships among concepts. For example, experiential intelligence is thought to be what Picasso used to develop the new form of painting called cubism. It is also the form of intelligence that Sternberg used to develop his new theory of intelligence.

Sternberg's formulation is often called the **triarchic theory** because it combines three (*tri* = three) intelligences. For Sternberg each one in this trio of abilities — practical intelligence, logical reasoning, and experiential intelligence — is relatively independent of the others. That is, a person's ability in one of the three areas doesn't necessarily predict his or her intelligence in the other two. Each represents a different dimension for describing and evaluating human performance. This theory reminds us that it is inaccurate to think of a single IQ score as summarizing all that is important or valuable about people's mental abilities (Sternberg, 1999; Sternberg et al., 1995).

GARDNER'S SEVEN INTELLIGENCES   Like Sternberg, Howard Gardner also believes that traditional IQ tests measure only a limited range of human mental abilities. But, he argues that we have at least seven separate mental abilities, which he calls **multiple intelligences** (Ellison, 1984; Gardner, 1983, 1999):

1. *Linguistic intelligence* — often measured on traditional IQ tests by vocabulary tests and tests of reading comprehension.
2. *Logical-mathematical intelligence* — also measured on most IQ tests with analogies, math problems, and logic problems.
3. *Spatial intelligence* — the ability to form mental images of objects and to think about their relationships in space.
4. *Musical intelligence* — the ability to perceive and create patterns of rhythms and pitches.
5. *Bodily-kinesthetic intelligence* — the ability for controlled movement and coordination, such as that needed by a dancer or a surgeon.

Practical intelligence (also called *contextual intelligence*): According to Sternberg, this is the ability to cope with the environment; sometimes called "street smarts."

Logical reasoning (also called *componential intelligence*): According to Sternberg, this is the ability measured by most IQ tests; includes the ability to analyze problems and find correct answers.

Experiential intelligence: According to Sternberg, the form of intelligence that helps people see new relationships among concepts; involves insight and creativity.

Triarchic theory: The term for Sternberg's theory of intelligence; so called because it combines three ("tri-") main forms of intelligence.

Multiple intelligences: A term used to refer to Gardner's theory, which proposes that there are seven forms of intelligence.

6. *Interpersonal intelligence* — the ability to understand other people's emotions, motives, and actions.

7. *Intrapersonal intelligence* — the ability to know oneself and to develop a sense of identity.

Connection

Chapter 9
Children's *emotional intelligence* can be assessed with the "marshmallow test."

Each of these intelligences arises from a separate module in the brain, Gardner claims. The latter two, interpersonal and intrapersonal intelligence, are similar to a capacity that some psychologists call *emotional intelligence*. People who are high in emotional intelligence are good at "reading" other people's emotional states, as well as being especially aware of their own emotional responses.

Like Sternberg, Gardner sees each component of intelligence as equally important. Yet, the value of each is also culturally determined, according to what is needed by, useful to, and prized by a given society. Gardner notes that Western society promotes the first two intelligences, while other societies value one or more of the other kinds of intelligence. For example, in small island societies, people place a high value on getting along with others (Gardner's *interpersonal ability*). In these restricted social settings, people have no place to go if they get into a quarrel and want to escape or part ways. People cannot move 100 miles away if they live on an island 10 miles long. In such societies, people avoid quarrels by recognizing potential problems at an early stage and modifying behaviors to solve problems quickly.

Assessing these newly recognized kinds of intelligence demands more than the usual paper-and-pencil tests. Gardner's approach requires that examinees be observed and assessed in a variety of life situations. On its face, the notion of multiple intelligences appears to be sound, but it awaits verification through tests that are still in the process of development.

Cultural Definitions of Intelligence

If you had been socialized in a Pacific island culture, which would matter more: your SAT scores or your ability to navigate a boat on the open ocean? Cross-cultural psychologists call our attention to the notion that "intelligence" can have different meanings in different cultures (Kleinfeld, 1994; Neisser et al., 1996; Rogoff, 1990; Segall et al., 1999; Serpell, 1994; Vernon, 1969). In fact, many languages have no word at all for intelligence as we conceive of it: the mental processes associated with logic, vocabulary, mathematical ability, abstract thought, and academic success (Matsumoto, 1996).

On the other hand, people in all cultures prize the ability to solve problems — although the significant problems may differ in different cultures. In addition, many Western cultures associate intelligence specifically with *quick* solutions to problems. This contrasts with the Buganda people in Uganda, who associate intelligence with slow and thoughtful responses. Yet another view is found among the Djerma-Sonhai in Niger (West Africa), who think of intelligence as a combination of social skills and good memory. And for the Chinese, intelligence involves, among other things, extensive knowledge, determination, social responsibility, and ability for imitation.

A NATIVE AMERICAN CONCEPT OF INTELLIGENCE John Berry (1992) has extensively studied the kinds of mental abilities considered valuable among Native Americans. He began by asking adult volunteers among the Cree in northern Ontario to provide him with Cree words that describe aspects of thinking, starting with examples like "smart" or "intelligent." The most frequent responses translate roughly to "wise, thinks hard, and thinks carefully."

One of Gardner's seven intelligences is bodily-kinesthetic intelligence, the ability to coordinate one's body movements with grace and control, as demonstrated by dancers.

Although Cree children attend schools introduced by the dominant Anglo (English-European) culture, the Cree themselves make a distinction between "school" intelligence and the kind of "good thinking" valued in the Cree culture. Such thinking seems to center on being "respectful." As one respondent explained, intelligence "is being respectful in the Indian sense. You need to really know the other person and respect them for what they are" (Berry, 1992, p. 79). This attitude of "respect for others" is widespread in Native American cultures, Berry found.

"BACKWARDS KNOWLEDGE" One term Berry's respondents offered as an example of the opposite of intelligence translates as "lives like a white." This refers disparagingly to behaviors the Cree have observed among some Anglo people. The Cree rate "lives like a white" as a combination of being "stupid" and having "backwards knowledge." A "stupid" person does not know the necessary skills for survival and does not learn by respecting and listening to elders. One has "backwards knowledge" if he or she disrupts relationships, creating disharmony instead of encouraging smooth interactions with others. Such disruption is not necessarily intentional or malicious. For example, an English teacher may ask Cree students to write an essay that would *persuade others* to change certain behaviors. However, in the Cree culture the concept of "persuading" can interfere with the traditional Cree value of "accepting others *as they are*." By encouraging such questioning of elders and traditions—a common practice in Anglo education—the teacher promotes disruption, which may be a path to "wisdom" in Anglo culture, but is "backward" in Cree views of intelligence.

As you can see from these examples, different cultures may define intelligence quite differently. In order to understand and cooperate with people of diverse heritages, we would be most "intelligent" if we resisted the impulse to impose our own definition of "intelligence" on others. Within psychology, cross-cultural psychologists have led the way in urging us to see what is valued —and devalued—in other people's experience.

Connection

Chapter 1
Cross-cultural psychology is a growing specialty within psychology.

Psychology

In Your Life

Test Scores and the Self-Fulfilling Prophecy

I f you have ever been called "dumb" or "slow," "shy," "plain," "bossy," or "unco-ordinated," you know, first hand, the powerful effect that labels and expectations can have. An IQ score is a label, too; and, in our test-conscious society, an IQ score can alter the course of a life. As a nation of test-takers, we sometimes forget that test scores are, at best, statistical measures of current functioning. People too often think of themselves as *being* "an IQ of 110" or "a B student," as if scores or grades were labels stamped permanently on their brains. Such labels may become barriers to advancement, as people come to believe that their mental and personal qualities are unchangeable—that they dictate their lot in life. Two classic studies will bring this fact into stark relief.

EXPECTATIONS INFLUENCE RAT PERFORMANCE

Robert Rosenthal and Lenore Jacobson (1968a,b) asked psychology students to run rats through a maze and record their times. The experimenters told some students that their rats were especially bright; other students heard that their rats were slow learners. (In fact, Rosenthal and Jacobson had randomly assigned rats to the "bright" and "dull" groups.) Amazingly, the students' data showed that rats that were *believed* to be bright outperformed their supposedly duller littermates. Obviously, expectations had influenced the students' observations.

EXPECTATIONS ALSO INFLUENCE STUDENT PERFORMANCE

So, Rosenthal and Jacobson wondered, could a teacher's expectations similarly affect evaluations of a student's performance in school? To find out, they arranged to give grade-school teachers erroneous information about the academic potential of about 20% of their students (approximately five in each classroom). Specifically, the teachers heard that some students had been identified by a standardized test as "spurters," who would blossom academically during the coming year. In fact, testing had revealed no such thing; the "spurters" had been randomly selected by the experimenters.

Knowing what happened to the rats, you can guess what happened to these children. Those whom the teachers expected to blossom did so. The teachers also rated the "spurters" as being more curious and having more potential for success in life than the other children. Socially, the teachers saw these children as happier, more interesting, better adjusted, more affectionate, and needing less social approval. Significantly, when the children again took the original test (actually an IQ test) a year later, the children in the experimental group (who had been arbitrarily assigned a high expectation of mental growth) made substantial gains in IQ points. The gains were especially pronounced among first and second graders. Rosenthal and Jacobson call this effect a **self-fulfilling prophecy.**

You can see it operating anywhere that people live up (or down) to the expectations of others — or of themselves.

THE EFFECTS OF NEGATIVE EXPECTATIONS

Did the self-fulfilling prophecy apply to the students *not* labeled as possible academic "spurters"? Many of these children also gained IQ points during the year of the experiment, but they gained fewer points, and they were rated less favorably by their teachers. Apparently, *not* receiving a promising prophecy can create negative expectations, just as a positive label can create positive expectations.

Please remember the self-fulfilling prophecy the next time you are tempted to place a label on someone.

CHECK**YOUR**UNDERSTANDING

1. **RECALL:** *From the perspective of Cattell's theory, the ability to use algorithms and heuristics would be an aspect of*
   a. convergent thinking.
   b. crystallized intelligence.
   c. logical thinking.
   d. fluid intelligence.

2. **RECALL:** *Guilford's structure-of-intellect model says that creative solutions to problems are found through*
   a. a g factor.
   b. divergent thinking.
   c. convergent thinking.
   d. contextual intelligence.

3. **APPLICATION:** *A friend tells you that he has found a way to improve his grades by stopping by his psychology professor's office once a week to ask questions about the reading. If this is successful, you could say that your friend has shown*
   a. practical intelligence.
   b. logical reasoning.
   c. experiential intelligence.
   d. convergent thinking.

4. **RECALL:** *Which of Gardner's seven intelligences is most like that measured on standard IQ tests?*
   a. linguistic ability
   b. bodily-kinesthetic ability
   c. interpersonal ability
   d. intrapersonal ability

5. **RECALL:** *A self-fulfilling prophecy comes true because of*
   a. innate factors.
   b. most people's lack of substantial logical-mathematical ability.
   c. the lack of precision of IQ tests.
   d. people's expectations.

6. **UNDERSTANDING THE CORE CONCEPT:**
   Which of the following most aptly characterizes the current debate about intelligence?
   a. divergent versus convergent
   b. single versus multiple
   c. practical versus logical
   d. cognitive versus behavioral

Core Concept

ANSWERS: 1. d   2. b   3. a   4. a   5. d   6. b

HOW DO PSYCHOLOGISTS EXPLAIN IQ DIFFERENCES AMONG GROUPS?

Key Question

Connection

Chapter 4
The *nature–nurture controversy* concerns the relative effects of heredity and environment.

It is a fact that a gap of approximately 15 points exists between the average IQ scores of African Americans and Caucasian Americans (Neisser et al., 1996; Vincent, 1991). A similar IQ gap separates children from middle-income homes and low-income homes (Jensen & Figueroa, 1975; Oakland & Glutting, 1990). Nobody disputes that these gaps exist. What the experts disagree about are the *causes* of these IQ discrepancies. As we will see, the disagreement is another example of the nature–nurture controversy. Our Core Concept describes the issue this way:

Core Concept

> **While most psychologists agree that both heredity and environment affect intelligence, they disagree on the source of IQ differences among racial and social groups.**

The controversy over the source of intelligence is potentially of great importance for people's lives—and a politically hot issue. If we assume that intelligence is primarily the result of innate (hereditary) factors, we will most likely conclude that it is fixed and unchangeable. This leads some to the mistaken conclusion that a group having low IQ scores must be innately inferior and should be treated as second-class citizens. On the other hand, if we conclude that intelligence is shaped largely by experience (environment), we are more likely to make a range of educational opportunities available for everyone and to view people of all ethnic, cultural, and economic groups as equals. Either way, our conclusion may become a self-fulfilling prophecy.

In fact, neither the hereditarian nor environmentalist view is completely right. Repeatedly in this book we have seen that psychologists now recognize that *both* heredity and environment play a role in all our behavior and mental processes. But there is more to the issue of group differences than this. In this chapter we add another important dimension to the heredity–environment interaction: While every individual's intelligence is determined, in part, by heredity, this fact does *not* mean that the IQ differences among *groups* have some biological basis. On the contrary, many psychologists have argued that group differences are totally environmental—although this, too, is disputed, as our Core Concept suggests. You will find out why this is so in the following pages.

Self-fulfilling prophecy: Observations or behaviors that result primarily from expectations.

The IQ scores of identical twins show a strong influence of genetics. The identical twins in this photo have gathered for the Twins Days Festival in Twinsburg, Ohio.

Intelligence and the Politics of Immigration

In the early 1900s, Henry Goddard, an influential psychologist who believed that intelligence is a hereditary trait, proposed mental testing for all immigrants and the selective exclusion of those who were found to be "mentally defective" (Strickland, 2000). With encouragement from Goddard and some other assessment-minded psychologists, Congress passed the 1924 Immigration Restriction Act, designed to restrict immigration of groups and nationalities in which people had been "proven" to be of inferior intellect—based largely on Goddard's data. Among the groups restricted were Jews, Italians, and Russians. What

Goddard and the U.S. Congress ignored was the fact that the tests were given in English — often to people with little familiarity with the English language and the culture in which the tests were conceived. Of course many of these immigrants received low scores!

Today we are more aware of the shortcomings of intelligence tests. We also know that, while heredity does have an effect on an *individual's* intelligence, experience does, too. And, we know that Goddard used faulty reasoning when he concluded that heredity accounts for *group* differences in intelligence. To understand how heredity could affect individual differences but not group differences, we need to look first at the evidence supporting the hereditarian and environmentalist arguments.

What Evidence Shows That Intelligence Is Influenced by Heredity?

Many lines of research point to a hereditary influence on intelligence. For example, studies comparing the IQ scores of identical twins with fraternal twins and other siblings show a strong genetic correlation. Another common approach compares adopted children with their biological and adoptive families. These studies find that the correlation between the IQs of children and their biological parents is greater than that with their adoptive parents (Plomin & DeFries, 1998). As Table 8.1 shows, the closer the genetic relationship — from cousins to siblings to twins — the closer the relationship of IQ scores. In general, work on twins and adopted children shows genetic influences on a wide range of attributes as diverse as heart functioning (Brown, 1990), personality traits (Tellegen et al., 1988), hypnotizability (Morgan et al., 1970), and intelligence (Chorney et al., 1998; McClearn et al., 1997; Neisser et al., 1996; Petrill et al., 1998). Work coming out of the Human Genome Project has also lent support to the notion that intelligence has a genetic component. Scientists are careful to point out, however, that the genetic basis of intelligence is complex because it involves the interaction of many genes (Chorney et al., 1998).

Connection

Chapter 4
Twin studies and adoption studies help psychologists identify hereditary and environmental effects.

Connection

Chapter 2
The *Human Genome Project* has recently "read" the DNA code for all the human chromosomes.

Correlation of IQ Scores with Genetic Relationship

TABLE 8.1	
GENETIC RELATIONSHIP	**CORRELATION BETWEEN IQ SCORES**
Identical twins	
Reared together	0.86
Reared apart	0.86
Fraternal twins	
Reared together	0.60
Siblings	
Reared together	0.47
Reared apart	0.24
Parent/child	0.40
Foster parent/child	0.31
Cousins	0.15

Note: A correlation shows the degree of association between variables — in this case, between the IQs of pairs of individuals. The closer to 1.0, the closer the connection. For example, we can see that the IQ scores of identical twins reared together are more closely correlated (.86) than the IQs of mere siblings reared together (.24). The data strongly suggest a genetic component that contributes to intelligence.

While psychologists agree that heredity plays an important part in determining an individual's IQ scores, they also agree that it remains difficult to estimate the relative weights of heredity and environment (Plomin, 1989; Scarr, 1988; Stevenson et al., 1987). One reason for this is that children who live in the same family setting do not necessarily share precisely the same psychological environment. First-born children, for example, are treated differently from the youngest. You probably are aware of this fact if you have siblings.

What Evidence Shows That Intelligence Is Influenced by Environment?

The evidence that the environment influences intellectual development is persuasive, too. Even when we look for genetic effects, we find greater similarities of IQ among people who have been reared together than those reared apart. And, in laboratory animals, a stimulus-enriched habitat early in life has been shown to result in a more complex, complete development of brain cells and cortical regions. The superior performance of these animals on a range of tasks persists through life. In other experiments, we find that young monkeys who are trained to solve problems and are offered the companionship of other monkeys display more active curiosity and higher intelligence than those reared without this environmental stimulation.

Such findings hint that we might boost the intellectual functioning of human infants by enriching their environments. Indeed, we will see that early enrichment programs can raise children's IQ scores. Regular schooling also may boost IQ scores: The amount of schooling children get is directly correlated with their IQ scores (Ceci & Williams, 1997), although we must be cautious about interpreting correlational data. Even in adulthood, environmental factors, such as the cognitive complexity and intellectual demands of one's job, can influence mental abilities throughout life (Dixon et al., 1985). You will recall that columnist Bob Greene's verbal SAT scores increased, undoubtedly because his work called for using verbal skills, while his math SAT scores plummeted, probably due to neglect of his math skills.

Connection

Chapter 1
Correlation does not imply *causation.*

Heritability and Group Differences

Let us acknowledge, then, that heredity has an influence — perhaps a substantial influence — on intelligence. But we should also be clear about another term: *heritability*. This concept is crucial for understanding the idea that hereditary differences among *individuals* do not imply that heredity accounts for the differences we observe among *groups*. In other words, heritability is not the same thing as heredity. Specifically, **heritability** refers to the amount of trait variation *within a group* that can be attributed to genetic differences. It is important to realize that we can speak of heritable differences *only within a group of individuals who have shared the same environment.*

To illustrate, suppose that we examine a group of children who were all raised in an intellectually stimulating environment, with devoted parents who spent lots of time interacting with them and reading to them — things we know improve intellectual abilities. Among these children we would find variation in intellectual abilities. Because they were all treated in essentially the same fashion, however, we could attribute much of the differences in their IQ scores to the effects of heredity. In this group, IQ would have a *high heritability*.

In contrast, suppose that we examine a group of children who had been raised under conditions of neglect (given mere custodial care in an orphanage, with no intellectual stimulation from their caregivers). We would most likely find that these children have relatively little variability among their IQ scores

Heritability: The amount of trait variation *within a group,* raised under the same conditions, that can be attributed to genetic differences. Heritability tells us nothing about between-group differences.

because they are all intellectually stunted. For this group, intelligence would have *low heritability*—because the poor environment did not offer an opportunity for these children's genetic potential to be realized.

Now, what about the differences *between* the two groups? The IQ differences would be real. But—this is the important part—our observations could tell us nothing about the genetic differences (if any) between the groups. For all we know they might have the same genetic potential. But because the environments were so different we cannot tell what role genetics played in determining their IQ scores. By applying this notion to groups of people who are exposed to different cultural traditions or experience different levels of wealth or discrimination, you can see that we have no way to evaluate what proportion of the differences between the groups should be attributed to heredity or to environment. To reiterate: *Heritability is a concept that refers to within-group differences, not between-group differences.* Just because intelligence may be highly heritable does not mean that the environment has no impact (Neisser et al., 1996).

THE JENSEN CONTROVERSY Despite the concerns we have just cited, a few psychologists remain unconvinced that group differences in IQ can be accounted for by environmental factors. In particular, Harvard psychologist Arthur Jensen (1969) has stirred up a hornets' nest of controversy with his contention that racial differences in IQ have a genetic basis. We can boost IQ scores to some extent, said Jensen, by helping the poor and disadvantaged, but there are limits imposed by heredity.

In support of his thesis, Jensen cited several studies showing a strong influence of heredity on IQ. He also presented a complex statistical argument that showed only a weak environmental effect on IQ and achievement. Then, turning his attention to government programs that had attempted to give extra help to disadvantaged black children, Jensen claimed that, while most had shown some positive effects, none had erased racial differences in performance. What remained must be a genetic difference in abilities, he maintained.

Over the next five years more than 100 published articles responded to Jensen's challenge. Sometimes it seemed that the Jensen controversy had generated far more heat than light. The protest occasionally became ugly, with charges of bigotry and racism nearly drowning the scientific debate. Nevertheless, it did have the positive effect of stimulating a new wave of research and theory aimed at gaining greater understanding of black–white IQ differences.

Critics pointed out several factors that Jensen had minimized or ignored, including the effects of racism, lower teacher expectations for black children, lack of opportunity, low self-esteem, and a white, middle-class bias built into IQ and achievement tests. While Jensen holds to his original position (Jensen, 1980, 1985, 1998), many (but not all) psychologists now agree that a combination of environmental factors can explain the differences on which Jensen built his case. Let us now look at some of the post-Jensen discoveries, beginning with a study of children whose environment had been altered by adoption.

THE SCARR AND WEINBERG ADOPTION STUDY A monumental study by Sandra Scarr and Richard Weinberg confronted the issue head-on by comparing black and white children who had been adopted into similar home environments (1976, 1978). Their research focused on educational records and IQ test scores from both the biological families and adoptive families of a 115 white children and 176 black children who had been adopted in Minnesota during the 1950s. All the children had been adopted into white families. For both groups of children, the biological parents had average IQ scores (near 100), while the adoptive parents' IQs were somewhat higher, averaging above 115.

What did Scarr and Weinberg find when they re-examined the IQ scores of these two groups of adoptees in late adolescence? There were *no* differences! *Both* the black group and the white group of adoptees had scores that averaged about 110, significantly higher than their biological parents, although not quite as high as their adoptive parents. Such results testify to a powerful effect of the environment on IQ. The results also contradict Jensen's claim that group differences are genetic.

SOCIAL CLASS AND IQ   Research on the relationship between social class and IQ shows similar environmental effects. Socioeconomic class (as reflected in an individual's financial status and lifestyle) is clearly correlated with IQ. While affluence is associated with higher IQ scores, groups with the lowest average IQ scores are those for whom poverty, illiteracy, and hopelessness are most widespread. Supporters of the environmental position claim that racism and discrimination initially landed many minorities in the impoverished inner cities, and these same factors continue to keep them there today.

How does social class affect IQ? Poverty creates circumstances that limit individual potential in many ways, particularly in terms of nutrition, health care, and education (Brown & Pollitt, 1996; Neisser et al., 1996). Poverty means less-adequate health care, so it should not surprise you that researchers have traced poor health during pregnancy and low birth weight to low mental ability in children. Poverty also means less of other factors known to promote intellectual development. Poor nutrition, lack of access to books and computers, and job schedules that leave parents little time to stimulate a child's intellect all correlate with poverty and can be detrimental to performance on tasks such as those demanded by IQ tests (for example, vocabulary or sentence comprehension). Research also shows that a significant proportion of children with low IQs have been adversely affected by "environmental insults," such as living in homes with lead-based paint chips peeling from walls causing toxic lead levels in children who ingest this material (Needleman et al., 1990).

Poverty has other crippling effects, too. In most parts of the United States, public schools are funded by revenue from local property taxes. Thus, wealthy neighborhoods can provide bigger and better school facilities and amenities, while poorer districts may suffer from crowding, physically deteriorating structures, threats to personal safety, and few "extras" such as media centers or computers. In such environments, even children with the aptitude to learn may find it difficult to rise above their circumstances. Proponents of the view that environment has a strong influence on intelligence usually support equal-opportunity legislation, better schools, and intervention programs which help disadvantaged children build self-confidence and learn the skills necessary to succeed in school (Zigler & Muenchow, 1992; Zigler & Styfco, 1994).

HEAD START: A SUCCESSFUL INTERVENTION PROGRAM   One such intervention program is **Head Start,** designed to provide educational enrichment for disadvantaged children. It grew from the assumption that many children from deprived families need an intellectual boost to prepare them for school. The program is intended to head off problems on several fronts by serving children's physical as well as mental needs with nutritional and medical support, plus a year or two of preschool education. Wisely, Head Start also involves parents in making policy, planning programs, working in classrooms, and learning about parenting and child development. Head Start centers around the country currently serve about 800,000 children yearly — estimated to be 40% of the number who need it (Ripple et al., 1999).

Does it work? Again, there is some controversy (Jensen, 1969; Kantrowitz, 1992), although a great deal of research suggests that Head Start does,

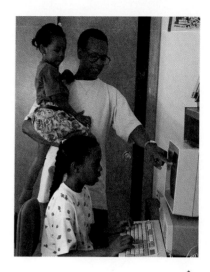

The personal attention children receive can affect their intelligence. This contemporary parent is deeply involved in his children's education.

Head Start: A program providing educational enrichment for children of poor families, launched in the 1960s as a part of the "War on Poverty."

indeed, help disadvantaged children get ready for school (Lazar & Darlington, 1982; Lee et al., 1988; Ripple et al., 1999; Schweinhart & Weikart, 1986; Smith, 1991). Children who were enrolled in the program score higher on IQ tests and have higher school achievement during the early grades than a matched control group who received no such intervention (Zigler & Styfco, 1994). More important, their head start lasts. Although the differences between the Head Start children and the control group diminish over time, the effects are still detectable in adolescence. Compared to the control group, Head Start children are less likely to be placed in special education classes, less likely to fail a grade, and more likely to graduate from high school.

It now appears, however, that such attempts to raise IQ by special environmental interventions may not start early enough. Studies indicate that early educational intervention, starting in the first months of life, can raise infants' scores on intelligence tests by as much as 30% compared to control groups (Ramey & Ramey, 1998a,b; Wickelgren, 1999). Although the gains may diminish with time, especially if supportive programs are withdrawn, significant differences remain when intervention starts in infancy. The best way to summarize these and other relevant findings is to say that the earlier the individual is immersed in an enriched environment, the better.

TEST BIASES   Still other forces influence IQ scores and contribute to differences among groups. A portion of the difference between the average IQ scores of black and white children may reside in problems with the IQ tests themselves. Many psychologists argue that IQ test questions have built-in biases toward a middle- or upper-class background—which favors the white child (Garcia, 1981; Helms, 1992; Miller-Jones, 1989). One source of bias stems from the fact that most IQ tests rely heavily on vocabulary level. This gives a big advantage to children who have been read to and who are encouraged to read. We can see a related bias in a well-known IQ test that asks for a definition of "opulent" (rich), a term one is far less likely to hear in a poor household. Another example of bias emerged from a study which found that children's IQ scores were correlated to experience with a popular—and expensive—game that featured remarkable similarities to items on the IQ test (Dirks, 1982).

Because expectations can also affect IQ scores, psychologists have argued that lowered expectations among some minority groups about their own potential can affect racial differences in IQ scores (Schwartz, 1997). One study found that merely being asked to identify their race produced lower scores for minority students on a test of academic abilities (Steele, 1997). In another study, a group of black women faltered on an IQ test when they were told that white women usually do better on the test. The women, who expected to do poorly, received IQ scores that averaged a full 10 points lower than another group who were told that black women usually receive high scores (Thomas, 1991).

Yet another source of bias has to do with the examiner. Not only does the examiner's attitude influence IQ scores, but so do his or her gender and race. Studies have found that black children receive higher scores when tested by a black examiner (Bodmer & Cavalli-Sforza, 1970; Sattler, 1970). In brief, test takers do best when they perceive the examiner to be similar to themselves.

Finally, Janet Helms (1992) has pointed out that the attempt to explain why African American children deviate from the Caucasian norm may, itself, rest on the biased assumption that one culture is superior to another. Specifically, she says, it "assumes that white-American culture defines the most intellectually rich environment" (p. 1086). Seldom do we ask how well white children learn the norms of other cultures. Helms asks: Why should the Caucasian-American norm be the standard by which everyone else is judged?

Connection

Chapter 1
A well-designed experiment has a *control condition* to serve as a basis of comparison.

THE BELL CURVE: THE LATEST HEREDITARIAN OFFENSIVE   The dispute over causes of racial differences in IQ flared again in 1994. At issue was a book, *The Bell Curve: Intelligence and Class Structure in American Life* by Richard Herrnstein and Charles Murray. The name echoes the shape of the bell-shaped "normal distribution" of IQ scores (see shape of the graph in Figure 8.11). In this volume, Herrnstein and Murray argue that genetic differences in IQ threaten to turn the United States into a split society, with a largely white "elite" at the top of the IQ range and the less intelligent masses at the other end, comprised mainly of African Americans and other minorities. Herrnstein and Murray suggest that acknowledging innate group differences in IQ could lead to more enlightened and humane social policies. Critics immediately identified not only a racist bias but pointed to unsound "science" at the core of *The Bell Curve.*

How is *The Bell Curve*'s argument flawed? The answer will be familiar to you by now: While there is no doubt that heredity influences individual intelligence, Herrnstein and Murray, like hereditarians before them, have offered no proof that differences *between groups* exposed to different environments have a hereditary basis (see Coughlin, 1994; Fraser, 1995). Further, much of the "evidence" they offer is suspect (Kamin, 1994). One study, cited by Herrnstein and Murray, claimed to document the low IQs of black Africans, but it employed tests given in English—a language in which the Zulu subjects of the study were not fluent (Kamin, 1995). The test used in that study also assumed that subjects were familiar with electrical appliances found in urban middle-class homes (rather than Zulu villages) and equipment, such as microscopes, not typically found in Zulu schools.

Compounding the problems in their analysis of the evidence, Herrnstein and Murray commit another scientific error about which you learned early in this book: They confuse correlation with causation. In fact, the Herrnstein and Murray argument is just as plausible when turned around: Poverty and all of the social and economic disadvantages that go with it could just as well be important causes of low IQ scores.

Despite its flaws, *The Bell Curve* has struck a chord with many Americans. It resonates with the preference for simple genetic "causes" for behavior rather than more complex explanations. It also fits with our cultural biases about educational achievement. This is seen in a study that asked Americans and Asians to account for a child's academic success. Predictably, American respondents emphasized "innate ability," whereas Asian respondents emphasized the importance of "studying hard" (Stevenson et al., 1993).

Helping Others Think Critically about Group Differences

In Your Life

So, if someone you know were to claim that the discrepancy between IQ scores of whites and blacks is proof of the genetic intellectual superiority of whites, how would you respond? You might begin with the argument that the influence of genetics on *individual* intelligence tells us nothing about the influence of genetics on *group* differences. You could also point to the evidence showing that, while the group average IQ for African Americans is as much as 10 to 15 IQ points below the group average for U.S. whites, there is much overlapping of scores. That is, the differ-

ence *between* groups is small compared to the spread of scores of individuals *within* each group (Loehlin et al., 1975). And, you could say that biologists have taught

(continued)

us that "race" is not a valid biological concept. Even if we use a social definition, where people define their own racial group, the differences between the gene pools of people who claim to be of different racial groups are very small compared to the genetic differences among individual members of the same group (Gould, 1996; see also Zuckerman, 1990).

Perhaps the most persuasive argument against the genetic interpretation of group differences is that many other variables are confounded with race, including racism, poverty, self-fulfilling prophecies, and differential opportunities for education—each of which can influence IQ scores. For example, in a large-scale, longitudinal study of more than 26,000 children, the best predictors of a child's IQ at age 4, for both black and white children, were the family's socioeconomic status and the level of the mother's education (Broman et al., 1975). When opportunities are made more equal, as we saw in the Scarr-Weinberg study, the differences disappear.

Unfortunately, the fact of group differences in IQ scores has been interpreted as a genetic difference and used to justify racist views. Even today, such data are used to justify discrimination against the disadvantaged poor, women, minorities, and immigrants in providing educational and career opportunities and in formulating public policy (Gould, 1996; Hirsch et al., 1990; Kamin, 1974). In the extreme, racist interpreters of the genetic argument support **eugenics** programs that would limit "breeding" by "undesirable" groups, laws restricting the immigration of certain groups, and legal inequality that favors the group in power. But the science just doesn't support such actions or the beliefs behind them.

In the "separate but equal" schoolroom of 1940s Tennessee, African American children received little attention and a poor education.

CHECK**YOUR**UNDERSTANDING

1. **RECALL:** *Most early American psychologists working on intelligence believed that the dominant influence on intelligence was*

   a. heredity.
   b. experience.
   c. gender.
   d. the size of one's brain.

2. **ANALYSIS:** *It is most accurate to say that*

   a. intelligence is influenced more by heredity than by environment.
   b. intelligence is influenced more by environment than by heredity.
   c. intelligence is the result of an interaction of heredity and environment.
   d. the influence of environment on intelligence is most powerful in the children of minority groups.

3. **RECALL:** *The concept of* heritability *refers to genetic variation*

   a. within an individual's sperm cells or ova.
   b. between one group and another.
   c. within an individual's immediate family.
   d. within a group of individuals that have had the same environment.

4. **UNDERSTANDING THE CORE CONCEPT:**

   Although everyone agrees that heredity affects _____ intelligence, there is no evidence that it accounts for differences among _____.

   a. individual /groups
   b. group/individuals
   c. high/the mentally retarded
   d. academic/practical

   ANSWERS: 1. a   2. c   3. d   4. a

Core Concept

Eugenics: A philosophy and a political movement that encouraged biologically superior people to interbreed and sought to discourage biologically inferior people from having offspring.

Experts: Individuals who possess well-organized funds of knowledge, including the effective problem-solving strategies, in a field.

Using Psychology to Learn Psychology: Developing Expertise in Psychology — or Any Other Subject

Obviously, **experts** are people who know a lot about a particular subject. Unlike a novice, an expert confronting a problem does not have to start from scratch. Experts can often see a solution quickly because they have seen many similar problems before. That is, they are especially good at using the heuristic of finding *analogies*.

Another quality distinguishing expert thinkers from beginners lies in the way their knowledge is organized. While the novice possesses only a collection of disjoint facts and observations, experts have organized their knowledge into elaborate *schemas* (Bédard & Chi, 1992; Bransford et al., 1986; Chi et al., 1982; Glaser, 1990; Greeno, 1989). We can see this quite clearly in a famous study of world-class chess players.

A STUDY OF CHESS EXPERTS

Dutch psychologist Adriaan de Groot found some striking differences when he compared the ways a group of grand master chess players and another group of merely good players responded to a chess problem. Allowed five seconds to view a configuration of pieces as they might appear on a chess board during a match, the grand masters were able to reproduce the pattern far more accurately than the less-expert subjects (de Groot, 1965). Does that mean that the grand masters had better visual memories? No. When confronted with a random pattern of pieces on the chess board—a pattern that would never happen in a match—the grand masters did no better than the other subjects. This suggests that the experts were able to draw on familiar patterns in memory, rather than trying to recall individual pieces and positions.

HOW TO BECOME AN EXPERT

Are experts born, or is expertise learned? Surprisingly, there is little evidence that inborn talent plays a substantial role in expert performance (Ericsson & Charness, 1994). On the other hand, people probably don't make the huge commitment of time and energy to become an expert in a field for which they do not have some initial aptitude.

So, could you, for example, become an expert—in psychology, perhaps? The research shows that, no matter what the field, experts *learn* their expertise (Bédard & Chi, 1992). Aside from facts and specific skills, they also acquire a repertoire of multipurpose heuristics, such as those we discussed earlier. And they know the special problem-solving techniques, or "tricks of the trade," that are unique to their field of expertise. These heuristics help them find solutions more quickly, without having to follow so many blind leads (Gentner & Stevens, 1983; Simon, 1992).

EXPERTISE AS ORGANIZED KNOWLEDGE

Research on experts also shows that learning facts and skills is not enough to produce real expertise (Bransford et al., 1986; Glaser, 1984; Greeno, 1989; Mayer, 1983). In addition, experts also possess a great deal of well-organized information about a field and its important *concepts*, which gives the expert both a fund of knowledge to apply to a problem and a familiarity with the field's common problems and solutions. That is, they know not only the facts but how the facts are interrelated and used.

So, how do you become an expert? Study and practice! But don't just focus on the details. Learn the important schemas and problem-solving strategies in your chosen field, too. How long will it take? Research shows that achieving world-class status in any of a wide gamut of fields—from athletics to academics to chess to music—requires about ten years of intensive study and practice (Ericsson et al., 1993; Gardner, 1993).

What does this suggest for your learning of psychology and other disciplines? You can take the first steps in developing your expertise by attending to the way your professors organize their courses (Gonzalvo et al., 1994). Consider such questions as the following:

- ▶ What are the terms that your psychology professor keeps mentioning over and over? These might be such concepts as "cognitive science," "behaviorism," "developmental," "empiricism," "adaptive," or "alternative theoretical perspectives." For you they may be, at first, unfamiliar and abstract, but for the professor they may represent the core of the course. Make sure you know what the terms mean and why they are important.

- ▶ Around what concepts is the course syllabus organized? What are the new terms that are associated with the main topics?
- ▶ Around what concepts is the textbook organized? You may be able to tell this quickly by looking at the table of contents. Alternatively, the authors may lay out the organizing points in the preface at the beginning of the book. (In this book, we have attempted to help you identify the organizing principles of each chapter in the form of Core Concepts.)

If you can identify the organizing principles for the course, they will simplify your studying. This makes sense, of course, in terms of our earlier study of memory. Long-term memory (as you will remember!) is organized by meaningful associations. Accordingly, when you have a simple and effective way of organizing the material, you will have a framework that will help you store and retain it in long-term memory.

Chapter Summary

WHAT ARE THE COMPONENTS OF THOUGHT?

Thinking is a mental process that forms new mental representations by transforming available information. Natural concepts and artificial concepts are building blocks of thinking; they are formed by identifying properties that are common to a class of objects or ideas. Concepts are often arranged in hierarchies, ranging from general to specific. Other mental structures that guide thinking include schemas, scripts, and visual imagery such as mental maps.

Thinking involves manipulation of mental representations, such as concepts, images, schemas, and scripts.

WHAT ABILITIES DO GOOD THINKERS POSSESS?

Two of the most crucial thinking skills involve defining the problem and selecting a problem-solving strategy. Useful strategies include algorithms and heuristics. Among the most useful heuristics are working backward, searching for analogies, and breaking a bigger problem into smaller problems. Common obstacles to problem solving include mental set, self-imposed limitations. Moreover, judging and decision making can be flawed by biases and faulty heuristics. These include the confirmation bias, hind-

sight bias, the anchoring bias, the representativeness bias, and the availability bias. Those who are often called "creative geniuses" are highly motivated experts who often have certain personality traits. They appear, however, to use ordinary thinking processes.

Good thinkers not only have a repertoire of effective algorithms and heuristics, they know how to avoid the common impediments to problem solving and decision making.

HOW IS INTELLIGENCE MEASURED?

The measurement of intelligence is both common and controversial. Assessment of mental ability has an ancient human history but was not based on scientific practice until the 20th century. In 1904, Binet and Simon developed the first workable test of intelligence, based on the assumption that education can modify intellectual performance. In America, IQ testing became widespread for the assessment of Army recruits, immigrants, and schoolchildren. The original IQ calculation was abandoned in favor of standard scores based on the normal distribution. IQ scores are a key ingredient in identifying mental retardation and giftedness, which are often seen as occupying the extremes of the IQ distribution.

Core Concept Intelligence testing has a history of controversy, but most psychologists now view intelligence as a normally distributed trait that can be measured by performance on a variety of tasks – both verbal and nonverbal.

 Key Question WHAT ARE THE COMPONENTS OF INTELLIGENCE?

Among the first psychometric theories of intelligence, Spearman's analysis emphasized a single, common factor known as g. Later, Cattell separated g into two components: fluid and crystallized intelligence. Others, such as Guilford, have suggested that intelligence was composed of many mental abilities. Cognitive psychologists have also conceived of intelligence as a combination of abilities. Gardner and Sternberg have taken the lead in extending the definition of intelligence beyond school-related tasks. Meanwhile, cross-cultural psychologists have shown that "intelligence" has different meanings in different cultures. In the United States much emphasis is placed on mental tests. In such a climate, however, a big danger lies in test scores becoming mere labels that influence people's behavior through the self-fulfilling prophecy.

 Core Concept Some psychologists believe that the essence of intelligence is a single, general factor, while others believe intelligence is best described as a collection of distinct abilities.

 Key Question HOW DO PSYCHOLOGISTS EXPLAIN IQ DIFFERENCES AMONG GROUPS?

Hereditarian arguments maintain that intelligence is substantially influenced by genetics, a belief endorsed by the U.S. government, which at one time used IQ tests to restrict immigration. Environmental approaches argue that intelligence can be dramatically shaped by influences such as health, economics, and education. While most psychologists now agree that intelligence is heritable, they also know that heritability refers to variation within a group and does not imply that between-group differences are the result of hereditary factors. Nevertheless, the dispute over the nature and nurture of group differences in intelligence flared again in 1969, when Jensen argued that the evidence favored a strong genetic influence. This argument was echoed in the 1994 book, *The Bell Curve*. Critics have pointed out that much of the research cited by the those taking the extreme hereditarian position is flawed. In addition, intelligence testing itself may be biased in favor of those with particular language and cultural experiences. Hereditarian claims, however, have stimulated much research, such as Scarr and Weinberg's research on adopted children and follow-up studies of the Head Start program. This research has shown that the racial and class differences in IQ scores can be eliminated by environmental changes.

 Core Concept While most psychologists agree that both heredity and environment affect intelligence, they disagree on the source of IQ differences among racial and social groups.

Review
Test

For each of the following items, choose the single correct or best answer.

1. Which of the following statements about thinking is true?
   a. It transforms available information to form new mental representations.
   b. It cannot be inferred from observable behavior.
   c. It stores but does not manipulate one's knowledge.
   d. all of the above

2. An alien being from another galaxy has landed on Earth and is overwhelmed by the sensory input it must process. Eventually the alien simplifies its thinking by categorizing sets of experiences and objects according to common features. In other words, the alien learns to form
   a. algorithms.
   b. concepts.
   c. heuristics.
   d. hypotheses.

3. A mental _____ outlines the proper sequence in which actions and reactions might be expected to happen in a given setting, as when you visit a new grocery store.
   a. prototype
   b. script
   c. algorithm
   d. map

4. If you think your chances of being mugged are quite high because you watch a lot of violent videos, then your judgment is flawed because of
   a. anchoring bias.
   b. functional fixedness.
   c. the availability bias.
   d. hindsight bias.

5. Binet and Simon assumed that
   a. intelligence is inherited.
   b. mental age does not increase as fast as chronological age.
   c. social class differences in intelligence should be remedied by governmental programs.
   d. training and opportunity could affect intelligence.

6. According to Lewis Terman's formula, a 9-year-old child with an IQ or 100 would have a *mental age* of
   a. 9.
   b. 10.
   c. 18.
   d. 90.

7. According to Howard Gardner, there are actually seven "intelligences." Which one is most like an ability assessed by traditional IQ tests?
   a. musical
   b. kinesthetic
   c. linguistic
   d. intrapersonal

8. The fact that intelligence is heritable has sometimes been misunderstood by those taking an extreme hereditarian view as meaning that _____ explains _____ differences in IQ scores.
   a. environment / individual
   b. heredity / group
   c. environment / group
   d. heredity / individual

9. The Scarr and Weinberg study supports the idea that racial differences in IQ scores are the result of
   a. genetic differences.
   b. environmental differences.
   c. test biases.
   d. unknown factors.

10. The characteristic that most distinguishes the expert from the novice is
   a. intelligence.
   b. talent.
   c. organized knowledge.
   d. speed of problem solving.

ANSWERS: 1. a   2. b   3. b   4. c   5. d   6. a
7. c   8. b   9. b   10. c

If You're
Interested . . .

BOOKS

Bradbury, R. (1998). *I sing the body electric, and other stories*. Avon Books. The title story, whose name quotes Whitman's *Leaves of Grass,* examines the dilemmas presented when human life and artificial intelligence — including robots — live together. This book is the inspiration for the movie *Bicentennial Man* (see Videos, below) and other works examining the nature of "human" intelligence.

Calvin, W. H. (1998). *The cerebral code: Thinking a thought in the mosaics of the mind.* Bradford Books. The author presents a new theory of how the associative cortex works, building on Darwinian principles and seeking to explain not only concrete information processing but consciousness as well.

Fraser, S. (Ed.). (1995). *The bell curve wars: Race, intelligence, and the future of America.* Basic Books. This is a collection of critical reviews of *The Bell Curve:*

Intelligence and Class Structure in American Life, by Richard J. Herrnstein and Charles J. Murray, a controversial book purporting to prove that intelligence is largely affected by heredity — significantly by racial distinctions.

Johnson, G. (1992). *In the palaces of memory: How we build the worlds inside our heads.* Vintage Books. This rich and enlightening guide describes not only how memory and conceptualization work but also how science is conducted on process at once intensely personal and not directly observable.

Kerr, P. (1992). *A philosophical investigation.* Penguin Books. In this futuristic mystery novel, the government tests all young men for the sex-linked gene indicating the potential to be a serial killer — until one unidentified subject uses his knowledge of genetics, computers, and philosophy to kill those who test positive.

Maisel, E. (2000). *The creativity book: A year's worth of inspiration and guidance.* J. P. Tarcher. The author presents a one-year plan for cultivating your creativity, with weekly exercises and discussions.

Pinker, S. (1999). *How the mind works.* W. W. Norton & Co. MIT psychologist Steven Pinker combines computer technology with evolutionary theory to review modern brain science, with references to love, aggression, illusions, *Star Wars,* and *The Far Side* along the way.

Perkins, D. (2000). *Archimedes' bathtub: The art and logic of breakthrough thinking.* W. W. Norton. Lowering himself into the bath, Archimedes shouted, "Eureka!" ("I have found it!") when he recognized the process of water displacement. This book suggests practical and entertaining strategies for creating such moments of inspiration in our own lives.

Plous, S. (1993). *The psychology of judgment and decision making.* Temple University Press. Psychologist Scott Plous, arguing that common sense is an unreliable guide to modern living, reviews the surprising or silly choices people make, adding recommendations about how to make more logical, successful judgments.

Steward, I., & Cohen, J. (1997). *Figments of reality: The evolution of the curious mind.* Cambridge University Press. A mathematician and a biologist team up to argue that our brains interact with our distinct *social cultures* to produce what we call the "mind."

VIDEOS

Apollo 13. (1995, color, 140 min.). Directed by Ron Howard; starring Tom Hanks, Kevin Bacon, Bill Paxton, Gary Sinise, Kathleen Quinlan, Ed Harris. "Houston, we have a problem . . ." So began astronaut Jim Lovell's report to ground control that the three-man flight had been crippled and would not only not make its lunar landing, but might never return. The story of how the astronauts and their Earth-bound support solved the problem is a fascinating study in applied cognition, as well as a powerful story of courage.

Nell. (1994, color, 113 min.). Directed by Michael Apted; starring Jodie Foster, Liam Neeson, Natasha Richardson. A small-town doctor discovers a young woman who has lived her life in isolation and without recognizable language. In part, this film considers whether such individuals should be left alone, "rescued," or exploited for scrutiny and study.

Searching for Bobby Fischer. (1993, color, 110 min.). Directed by Steve Zaillian; starring Joe Mantegna, Max Pomeranc, Joan Allen, Ben Kingsley. This excellent case, a solid drama based on a true story, depicts a father who discovers his young son has a talent for chess that might earn him a place as successor to the famed American champion of the title.

WEB RESOURCES

http://www.apa.org/monitor/nov99/nl3.html According to this article, children who are imaginative often solve problems more effectively when they are older. Fantasy allows children to generate various ideas about a single topic, and approach problem-solving questions with multiple approaches.

http://www.onlinepsych.com/public/Mind_Games/iq03. htm Do intelligence quotient tests accurately measure intelligence? This simple true-false test will measure intelligence, but some people question the accuracy of these exams.

WHAT DO OUR EMOTIONS DO FOR US?

The Evolution of Emotions

Emotional Expression as a Means of Communication

Counting the Emotions

Emotions have evolved to help us respond to important situations and to convey our intentions to others.

AROUSAL, PERFORMANCE, AND THE INVERTED "U":

Increased arousal improves performance — but only up to a point. That point depends on the task.

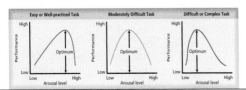

WHERE DO OUR EMOTIONS COME FROM?

The Neuroscience of Emotion

Resolving Some Persistent Issues in the Psychology of Emotion

Emotions result from an interaction of biological, mental, behavioral, and social/cultural processes.

EMOTIONAL DIFFERENCES BETWEEN MEN AND WOMEN DEPEND ON CULTURE:

Culture and socialization account for many of the differences — but not for everything.

HOW MUCH CONTROL DO WE HAVE OVER OUR EMOTIONS?

Developing Emotional Intelligence

Detecting Deception

Although emotional responses are not always consciously regulated, we can learn to control them.

CONTROLLING ANGER:

A common misconception says that it is healthy to ventilate your anger.

MOTIVATION: WHAT MAKES US ACT AS WE DO?

How Psychologists Use the Concept of Motivation

Types of Motivation

Theories of Motivation

Motivation takes many forms, but all involve inferred mental processes that select and direct our behavior.

REWARDS CAN (SOMETIMES) SQUELCH MOTIVATION:

Sometimes extrinsic rewards can dampen intrinsic motivation.

HOW ARE ACHIEVEMENT, HUNGER, AND SEX ALIKE? DIFFERENT?

Achievement Motivation

Hunger Motivation

Sexual Motivation

No single theory accounts for all forms of motivation, because each motive involves its own mix of biological, mental, behavioral, and social/cultural influences.

THE ORIGINS OF SEXUAL ORIENTATION:

We know more about what does *not* influence sexual orientation than what does.

USING PSYCHOLOGY TO LEARN PSYCHOLOGY: Motivating Yourself

EMOTION AND MOTIVATION

lliot presented a puzzle. His life was unraveling, yet he maintained an attitude of composure. Once a model employee, he had let the quality of his work slip to the point that he finally lost his job. If anything, said his supervisors, Elliot had developed a habit of working almost too well. He often latched onto a small task, such as sorting a client's paperwork, and spent the whole afternoon on various classification schemes — never quite getting to the real job he had been assigned (Damasio, 1994).

His personal life also fell apart. A divorce was followed by a short marriage and another divorce. Several attempts at starting his own business involved glar-

ingly flawed decisions that finally ate up all his savings.

Yet, surprisingly, in most respects Elliot seemed normal. He had a pleasant personality and an engaging sense of humor. He was obviously smart — well aware of important events, names, and dates. He understood the political and economic affairs of the day. In fact, examinations revealed nothing wrong with his movements, memory, perceptual abilities, language skills, intellect, or ability to learn.

Complaints of headaches led the family doctor to suspect that the changes in Elliot might be the result of a brain lesion. Tests proved the suspicion correct. Brain scans showed a mass the size of a

(continued)

small orange that was pressing on the frontal lobes just above Elliot's eyes.

The tumor was removed, but not before it had done extensive damage. The impact was limited to the frontal lobes — in a pattern that was remarkably similar to that seen in the famous case of Phineas Gage nearly 150 years earlier (see Chapter 2). Like Gage, Elliot had undergone a profound change as the result of frontal lobe damage. But the effects in Elliot were more subtle than in Gage. As a psychologist who examined him said, "We might summarize Elliot's predicament as *to know but not to feel*" (Damasio, 1994, p. 45). His reasoning abilities were intact, but damage to the circuitry of his frontal lobes disrupted his ability to attach values to the objects, events, and people in his life. In short, Elliot had been emotionally crippled.

Connection

Chapter 8
Cognitive science has largely ignored emotion and motivation until recently.

One of the most pernicious misunderstandings about the human mind is the idea that emotion is the opposite of reason. The case of Elliot, presented in detail in Damasio's 1994 book *Descartes' Error,* makes it clear that emotion is a vital component of making effective personal decisions. With a disruption in his ability to connect concepts and emotions, Elliot could not value one course of action over another.

We must acknowledge, of course, that at times, emotion gets out of control, producing irrational and unwise behavior. We see this in jealous lovers and in severe depression. "Road rage" and "going postal" are terms we use to describe extreme behavior driven by emotions run amok. Yet, as Elliot's case shows, pure reason can also immobilize us.

How is motivation linked to emotion? Think of an emotion — fear, for example — and the behavior it motivates: fight or flight. Or think about your own feelings for a person you love and the way these feelings make you act toward your loved one. In general, psychologists see such motives and emotions as complementary. The concept of emotion emphasizes arousal, both physical and mental, while motivation emphasizes how this arousal becomes action. Note that both words share a common root, "mot-," from the Latin *motus,* meaning "moved." The psychology of motivation and emotion has retained this meaning by viewing emotion and motivation as twin processes that arouse us to deal with important events.

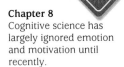

WHAT DO OUR EMOTIONS DO FOR US?

The death of a parent, an insult, rejection by a lover: All induce strong emotions. These emotions have many components that can include feelings of depression, despair, anger, puzzlement, or jealousy. Emotions can also produce behavior, such as crying, grimacing, shouting, lashing out, or running away. At the same time, emotions produce a flurry of internal physical responses, including activity in certain brain circuits, production of hormones, and visceral responses. In short, **emotion** is a three-part process that involves subjective *feelings, behavioral expression,* and *physiological arousal.*

But what functions do emotional responses serve? They become mental markers, pointing to memories of important events. In this way, negatively charged emotions tag memories of real or imagined objects and events to be avoided, such as a snarling dog or an angry neighbor. Positive emotions, on the other hand, call our attention to things to be approached, such as a good friend

Emotion: A three-part process that involves subjective feelings, behavioral expression, and physiological arousal. Emotions help organisms deal with important events.

or a winning lottery ticket. Emotions are never neutral. They may cause us to approach or avoid, but they always direct our attention to something of perceived importance. In doing so, they often send a message to other people about our emotional state, which helps them predict our behavior.

Our Core Concept summarizes the function of emotions this way:

Emotions have evolved to help us respond to important situations and to convey our intentions to others.

In this section, we will look a little deeper into the adaptive functions of emotions. We will also examine how the universal language of emotional expression tells others of our emotional state. Finally, we will see how emotional arousal can affect our performance — say, on a test or in an athletic contest. Let's begin with the evolutionary advantages of emotions.

The Evolution of Emotions

Whether in humans, hyenas, cats, or kangaroos, emotions serve as arousal states that help organisms cope with important recurring situations (LeDoux, 1996). Accordingly, emotions have survival value and so have been shaped by natural selection (Gross, 1998). Fear, for example, undoubtedly helped individuals in your family tree react to situations that could have made them a meal instead of an ancestor. Similarly, the emotion we call "love" may commit us to a family, which helps to continue our genetic line. Likewise, sexual jealousy can be seen as an emotion that evolved to deal with the biologically important problem of mate infidelity, which threatens the individual's chances of producing offspring (Buss & Schmitt, 1993).

Like other inherited characteristics, emotional tendencies enter the human genome through genetic variation and natural selection. Random genetic variations affecting emotional arousal continually occur as organisms reproduce (Gabbay, 1992). In fact, one of the most important facts about emotion is its tremendous variability from one individual to another (Davidson, 2000b). Some of this variability — in emotional responsiveness, or in tendency toward depression versus cheerfulness, for example — results from individual differences in the hormone system, brain circuits, and other physical characteristics.

We should emphasize, however, that emotions are not entirely genetically programmed responses. They also involve learning. Particularly important in setting our emotional temperament are experiences that occur early in life, as well as experiences that have evoked particularly strong emotional responses (Barlow, 2000; LeDoux, 1996). Thus, learned emotional responses can be important components of depression, panic attacks, phobic reactions, and stress-induced disorders.

Emotional Expression As a Means of Communication

You can usually tell when your friends are happy or angry by the looks on their faces or by their actions. This is useful because reading their emotional

Connection

Chapter 1
The evolutionary perspective says that natural selection favors behaviors that help individuals survive and reproduce.

Connection

Chapter 2
Genes encode both mental and physical characteristics.

Sexual jealousy probably has an evolutionary basis because mate infidelity threatens the individual's chances of producing offspring.

expressions helps you to know how to respond to them: As our Core Concept suggests, emotional expressions aid social interaction. But, does raising the eyebrows and rounding the mouth say the same thing in Minneapolis as it does in Madagascar? Much research on emotional expression has centered on such questions.

According to Paul Ekman, the leading researcher in this area, people speak and understand substantially the same "facial language" the world around (Ekman, 1984, 1992; Ekman & Rosenberg 1997). Studies by Ekman's group have demonstrated that humans share a set of universal emotional expressions presumably because our species has a common biological heritage. Cross-cultural research shows, for example, that smiles signal happiness and frowns indicate sadness on the faces of people in such far-flung places as Argentina, Japan, Spain, Hungary, Poland, Sumatra, the United States, Viet-

DO IT YOURSELF! Identifying Facial Expressions of Emotion

Take the facial emotion identification test to see how well you can identify each of the seven emotions that Ekman claims are culturally universal. Do not read the answers until you have matched each of the following pictures with one of these emotions: disgust, happiness, anger, sorrow, surprise, fear, and contempt. Apparently, people everywhere in the world interpret these expressions in the same way. This tell us that certain facial expressions of emotion are probably rooted in our human genetic heritage.

ANSWERS: The facial expressions are (top row from left) surprise, disgust, happiness, and contempt; (bottom row) sadness, anger, and fear.

What emotion is being expressed in each face?

nam, the jungles of New Guinea, and the Eskimo villages north of the Arctic Circle (Biehl et al., 1997; Ekman et al., 1987; Izard, 1994).

More generally, Ekman and his colleagues say that people everywhere can recognize at least seven basic emotions: sadness, fear, anger, disgust, contempt, happiness, and surprise (Ekman, 1993; Ekman & Friesen, 1971, 1986; Ekman et al., 1969, 1987; Keating, 1994). There are, however, huge differences across cultures in the intensity with which people display emotions. In many Asian cultures, for example, children are taught to control emotional responses—especially negative ones—while many American children are encouraged to express their feelings more openly (Matsumoto, 1994, 1996).

Regardless of culture, however, emotions usually show themselves in people's behavior. Even babies, in their first day of life, produce facial expressions that communicate some of their feelings (Ganchrow et al., 1983). The ability to read facial expressions also develops early. Young children attend to facial expressions, and by age 5 they nearly equal adults in their skill at reading them (Nelson, 1987).

This evidence all points to a biological basis for the expression and decoding of a basic set of human emotions. Moreover, as Charles Darwin pointed out over a century ago, some emotional expressions seem to appear across species boundaries. Darwin especially noted the similarity of our own facial expressions of fear and rage to those of chimpanzees and wolves (Darwin, 1998/1862; Ekman, 1984).

But are *all* emotional expressions universal? No. Cross-cultural studies of emotional expressions tell us that certain emotional responses differ from culture to culture (Ekman, 1992, 1994; Ellsworth, 1994). These, therefore, must be learned rather than innate. For example, what emotion do you suppose might be conveyed by sticking out the tongue? For Americans this might indicate disgust, while in China it can signify surprise. Likewise, a grin on an American face may indicate joy, while on a Japanese face it may just as easily mean embarrassment. Clearly, culture influences emotional expression.

Counting the Emotions

How many emotions are there? A long look in the dictionary turns up more than 500 emotional terms (Averill, 1980). Most experts, however, see a more limited number of basic emotions. Often mentioned is Ekman's list of seven—anger, disgust, fear, happiness, sadness, contempt, and surprise—based on the universally recognized facial expressions. Robert Plutchik (1980, 1984) has argued for eight basic emotions that emerged from a mathematical analysis of people's ratings of a large number of emotional terms. You will see in Figure 9.1 that Plutchik's list is similar to Ekman's.

But what about emotions that appear on none of these basic lists? What of envy, regret, pride, or mirth? From the perspectives of Ekman, Plutchik, and others who argue for a simplified list of basic emotions, the wide range of human emotions involves complex blends of the more basic ones.

FIGURE 9.1: The Emotion Wheel

Robert Plutchik's emotion wheel arranges eight primary emotions on the inner ring of a circle of opposite emotions. Pairs of adjacent emotions can combine to form more complex emotions noted on the outer ring of the figure. For example, love is portrayed as a combination of joy and acceptance. Still other emotions, such as envy or regret (not shown) emerge from still other combinations of more basic emotions portrayed on the wheel.

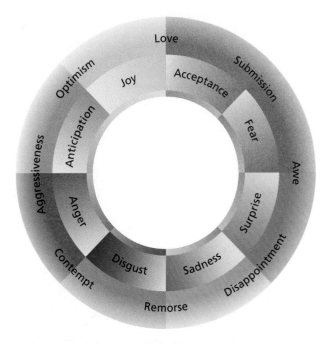

Facial expressions convey universal messages. Although their culture is very different, it is probably not hard for you to tell how this child from New Guinea is feeling.

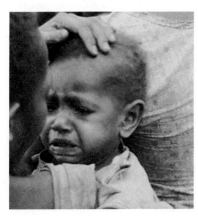

Psychology In Your Life

Arousal, Performance, and the Inverted "U"

Athletes always want to be "up" for a game—but how far up? Cheering sports fans might think that increased arousal will improve performance—but that is not necessarily true. Too much arousal can make an athlete "choke" and performance falter. The same is true for you when you face an examination. Up to a point, increasing levels of arousal can motivate you to study and facilitate your recall during the test, but higher levels can produce test anxiety and a drop in your grade.

This relationship between arousal and behavior has been studied in both laboratory animals and in humans. For hungry and thirsty rats used in experiments on learning, the curve of performance first rises and then later declines with the intensity of arousal. The same pattern holds for the performance of athletes under pressure. Psychologists call this the **inverted "U" function** (so named because the graph resembles an upside-down letter "U," as you can see in the figure). It suggests that either too little or too much arousal can impair performance.

The optimum amount of arousal varies with the task. As you can see in the figure, it takes more arousal to achieve peak performance on simple or well-practiced tasks than it does on complex tasks that require much thinking and planning. Thus, cheers may boost performance at basketball games but not in brain surgery.

The amount of stimulation needed to produce optimal arousal varies with the individual. In fact, some people seem to thrive on the thrill of dangerous sports, such as rock climbing and skydiving—activities that would produce immobilizing levels of arousal in most of us (Zuckerman et al., 1978, 1980). Marvin Zuckerman (1971, 1979), who has studied people he calls **sensation seekers,** believes that such individuals have a biological need for high levels of stimulation. You can test our own sensation-seeking tendencies with Zuckerman's scale, found in the "Do It Yourself!" box below.

The Inverted "U"

Performance varies with arousal level and task difficulty. For easy or well-practiced tasks, a higher level of arousal increases performance effectiveness. However, for difficult or complex tasks, a lower level of arousal is optimal. A moderate level of arousal is generally best for tasks of moderate difficulty. These inverted U-shaped functions show that performance is worst at both low and high extremes.

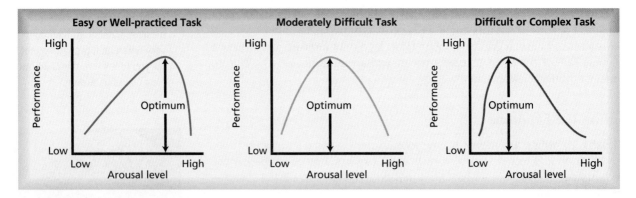

Inverted "U" function: Describes the relationship between arousal and performance. Both low and high levels of arousal produce lower performance than does a moderate level of arousal.

Sensation seekers: In Zuckerman's theory, individuals who have a biological need for higher levels of stimulation than do other people.

From your score on the Sensation Seeking Scale below you can get a rough idea of your own level of sensation seeking. Marvin Zuckerman believes that this trait underlies the need some people have for excitement, stimulation, and arousal. In addition to the need for thrills, sensation seekers may be impulsive, prefer new experiences, and be easily bored (Kohn et al., 1979; Malatesta et al., 1981; Zuckerman, 1974).

You may want to give this scale to some of your friends. Do you suppose that most people choose friends who have sensation-seeking tendencies similar to their own? Wide differences in sensation-seeking tendencies may account for strain on close relationships, when one person is reluctant to take the risks that the other actively seeks.

THE SENSATION-SEEKING SCALE

Choose A or B for each item, depending on which response better describes your preferences. The scoring key appears at the end.

1. A   I would like a job that requires a lot of traveling.

    B   I would prefer a job in one location.

2. A   I am invigorated by a brisk, cold day.

    B   I can't wait to get indoors on a cold day.

3. A   I get bored seeing the same old faces.

    B   I like the comfortable familiarity of every-day friends.

4. A   I would prefer living in an ideal society in which everyone is safe, secure, and happy.

    B   I would have preferred living in the unsettled days of our history.

5. A   I sometimes like to do things that are a little frightening.

    B   A sensible person avoids activities that are dangerous.

6. A   I would not like to be hypnotized.

    B   I would like to have the experience of being hypnotized.

7. A   The most important goal of life is to live it to the fullest and experience as much as possible.

    B   The most important goal of life is to find peace and happiness.

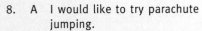

Sensation seekers thrive on stimulation that might terrify others.

8. A   I would like to try parachute jumping.

    B   I would never want to try jumping out of a plane, with or without a parachute.

9. A   I enter cold water gradually, giving myself time to get used to it.

    B   I like to dive or jump right into the ocean or a cold pool.

10. A   When I go on a vacation, I prefer the comfort of a good room and bed.

    B   When I go on a vacation, I prefer the change of camping out.

11. A   I prefer people who are emotionally expressive even if they are a bit unstable.

    B   I prefer people who are calm and even-tempered.

12. A   A good painting should shock or jolt the senses.

    B   A good painting should give one a feeling of peace and security.

13. A   People who ride motorcycles must have some kind of unconscious need to hurt themselves.

    B   I would like to drive or ride a motorcycle.

KEY

Each of the following answers earns one point: 1A, 2A, 3A, 4B, 5A, 6B, 7A, 8A, 9B, 10B, 11A, 12A, 13B. Compare your point total with the following norms for sensation-seeking:

0–3	Very low
4–5	Low
6–9	Average
10–11	High
12–13	Very high

Source: Zuckerman, M. (1978, February). The search for high sensation. *Psychology Today, 12,* 38–46. Copyright © 1978 by the American Psychological Association.

1. **RECALL:** *From the evolutionary perspective, emotions help organisms identify*

   a. their parents.

   b. important and recurring situations.

   c. beauty and wonder in the world around them.

   d. locations in which to find food and mates.

2. **RECALL:** *Which one of the following is not one of the culturally universal emotions identified by Ekman's research?*

   a. anger

   b. surprise

   c. contempt

   d. regret

3. **ANALYSIS:** *Which one is a cognitive process influenced by emotion?*

   a. attention

   b. behavior

   c. threat

   d. rejection

4. UNDERSTANDING THE CORE CONCEPT:

   According to this section of the chapter, what is the adaptive significance of communicating our emotional states?

   a. It helps us to understand our own needs better.

   b. It allows us to deceive others about our emotional states and get what we want.

   c. It allows people to anticipate each other's responses and so to live more easily in groups.

   d. Communicating our emotional state helps us get rid of strong negative emotions, such as fear and anger.

ANSWERS: 1. b   2. d   3. a   4. c

WHERE DO OUR EMOTIONS COME FROM?

What happens inside us when we feel fear, anger, envy, or ecstasy? These and other emotions have their biological roots in our body chemistry and in certain parts of the brain. But biological systems do not act by themselves. In this section you will see that a full explanation of our emotional responses must also include a mental component that involves how we think, both about external events and about our own internal responses — as when we interpret a "Boo!" in a Halloween haunted house. The resulting emotion, of course, can influence behavior, as seen when the startled person jumps. You may be surprised to learn, however, that behavior can also influence emotions. In this section, you will also find that emotions have social/cultural roots that show up strongly in gender differences in emotional expression. This is the Core Concept:

Emotions result from an interaction of biological, mental, behavioral, and social/cultural processes.

In the following pages we will see how the young neuroscience of emotion takes the first three of these factors into account. We will also see how new understandings arising from this work have begun to resolve some long-standing disputes in the field. Then, at the end of this section, we will turn our attention to social/cultural influences that have added yet another dimension to our understanding of emotion.

The Neuroscience of Emotion

People who suffer from phobias, such as a fear of snakes, know that their responses are irrational—yet the fears persist. So, what causes a person to hold two such conflicting mind sets? The answer lies in two distinct emotion processing systems in the brain (LeDoux, 1996). One operates mainly at an unconscious level, where it screens incoming stimuli and helps us respond quickly to cues of potentially important events. This system, linked to the implicit memory system, acts as an early-warning defense that produces, for example, an instantaneous fright response to a loud noise in the middle of the night (Bechara et al., 1995). It relies primarily on deep-brain circuitry that operates automatically, without requiring conscious thought. (See Figure 9.2.)

The unconscious emotion circuits seem to have an innate sensitivity to certain cues (which explains why fears of spiders and snakes are more common than fears of, say, electricity). In addition, this system can quickly learn emotional responses through classical conditioning. But the unconscious emotion system can be slow to forget. Because of this, a person may quickly learn to fear dogs after being bitten, yet the fear may be quite difficult to extinguish.

The other emotional system involves conscious processing and is linked to explicit memory (LeDoux, 1996). Its circuitry can create, for example, the fear you feel in anticipation of giving a speech or the excitement you experi-

Connection

Chapter 7
Implicit memories involve material of which we are unaware—but which can affect behavior.

Connection

Chapter 7
Explicit memory holds material of which we are aware or which can readily be brought to consciousness.

FIGURE 9.2: Two Emotion-Processing Pathways

Two emotion systems are at work when the hiker sees a snake. The unconscious (implicit) system routes incoming visual information through the visual thalamus to the amygdala, which quickly initiates fear and avoidance responses. The slower pathway involves the visual cortex, which makes a more complete appraisal of the stimulus and also sends an emotional message to the amygdala and other lower brain structures.

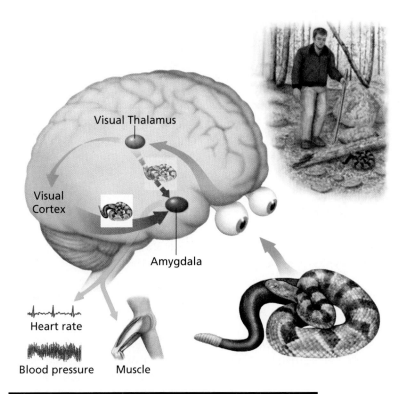

ence on your first whitewater rafting trip. This system generates emotions more slowly, as you consciously think over your experiences, choices, and expectations. It attaches emotional reactions to concepts and experiences that you find especially interesting, attractive, or repulsive. Relying heavily on the cerebral cortex, its view of events can differ significantly from that of the unconscious processing system. Thus, the phobic person can feel fear, despite "knowing" that there is no sensible basis for the feeling.

Although these two emotional systems are distinct, they do interact. The feelings that we associate with an emotion such as fear, for example, well up into consciousness from the unconscious system (LeDoux, 1996). Conversely, the conscious emotional system can tell the unconscious circuits to produce, for example, the knot in your stomach just before giving a speech.

Now, with these two emotional systems in mind, let us take a more detailed look at their biological substrates.

THE ROLE OF THE RETICULAR ACTIVATING SYSTEM There is no single "emotion center" in the brain (Davidson, 2000a). Nevertheless, many emotional reactions such as anger and fear may begin with the nearly instantaneous arousal of the brain as a whole, triggered by the reticular activating system (RAS). This structure, strategically located in the brain stem, monitors incoming information. If it detects a potential threat, it sets off a cascade of automatic responses that can make your heart accelerate, your respiration increase, your mouth get dry, and your muscles become tense. All these responses evolved to mobilize the body quickly for an emergency reaction. Either of the two emotion systems may signal the RAS to produce a general arousal of the brain.

THE ROLE OF THE LIMBIC SYSTEM The hormonal and neural responses to emotional arousal are coordinated by circuits in the brain's limbic system, operating largely outside of consciousness. Situated above the brain stem, the limbic structures probably evolved as control systems for behaviors used in attack, defense, and retreat: the "fight-or-flight" response (Caldwell, 1995; LeDoux, 1994, 1996). Evidence for this comes from lesioning (cutting) or electrically stimulating parts of the limbic system, which can produce dramatic changes in emotional responding. Tame animals with altered limbic systems may become killers, while prey and predators with limbic lesions may become peaceful companions (Delgado, 1969). Particularly well documented is the importance of the amygdala in the emotion of fear (LeDoux, 1996; Whalen, 1998). (See Figure 9.2.) Neuroscientists believe, however, that this structure is a major player in all unconscious emotional processing.

THE ROLE OF THE CEREBRAL CORTEX The cerebral cortex — the outermost layer of brain tissue and our "thinking cap" — also contributes to our emotional responses by interpreting events and associating them with emotions. Just as distinct patches of cortex produce different sensations, positive and negative emotions are produced by different cortical regions. In general, the right hemisphere specializes in negative emotions, such as anger and depression, while the left processes happier emotions (Davidson, 1992a,b; 2000a,b; Heller et al., 1998).

This discovery — that the two cerebral hemispheres specialize in different classes of emotion — has been dubbed **lateralization of emotion.** Lateralization has also been found in EEG recordings of normal people's emotional reactions, as well as in studies relating brain damage in the right or left hemisphere

Connection

Chapter 2
The RAS is involved in attention and alerting the brain to important stimuli.

Connection

Chapter 2
The limbic and the cerebral cortex are the middle and upper layers of the brain.

Lateralization of emotion:
Different influences of the two brain hemispheres on various emotions. The left hemisphere apparently influences positive emotions (for example, happiness), and the right hemisphere influences negative emotions (anger, for example).

TABLE 9.1	Responses Associated with Emotion	
COMPONENT OF EMOTION	**TYPE OF RESPONSE**	**EXAMPLE**
Physiological arousal	Neural, hormonal, visceral, and muscular changes	Increased heart rate, blushing, becoming pale, sweating, rapid breathing
Subjective feelings	The private experience of one's internal affective state	Feelings of rage, sadness, happiness
Cognitive interpretation	Attaching meaning to the emotional experience by drawing on memory and perceptual processes	Blaming someone, perceiving a threat
Social/behavioral reactions	Expressing emotion through gestures, facial expressions, or other actions	Smiling, crying, screaming for help

to specific disturbances in facial expression (Ahern & Schwartz, 1985; Borod et al., 1988).

Mental disorders can also tell us something about the source of emotions. Brain scans of volunteers suffering from schizophrenia (SKITS-oh-FREN-ya), a major disorder of thoughts and emotions, were made with PET scanning technology while the patients were hearing voices. These hallucinations, which the patients heard saying such things as, "How horrible!" and "Don't act stupid," showed up in the PET scans as brain regions of intense abnormal activity. At the same time, the part of the frontal lobes that normally checks the accuracy of sensations showed diminished activation. Apparently, this distorted pattern of brain functioning allowed the patients' private mental experiences to careen out of control (Begley, 1995; Silbersweig et al., 1995). The patients had no way of knowing whether their sensations were real or their emotional responses were reasonable. "The brain . . . is creating its own reality," commented one observer (Begley, 1995, p. 77).

Connection

Chapter 12
Schizophrenia is a serious mental disorder involving loss of contact with reality.

THE ROLE OF THE AUTONOMIC NERVOUS SYSTEM What makes your heart race when you are startled? The first messages that the internal organs receive when you become emotionally aroused are routed through the autonomic nervous system (Levenson, 1992). In pleasant emotions, the parasympathetic division dominates. But when you are startled or when you experience some unpleasant emotion, the sympathetic division becomes more active (see Table 9.1).

Suppose an emergency — or merely the memory of an emergency — occurs (a speeding car is coming directly at you!). The brain alerts the body by means of messages carried along pathways of the sympathetic system. Some messages direct the adrenal glands to release stress hormones. Others make the heart race and blood pressure rise. At the same time, the sympathetic system directs certain blood vessels to constrict, diverting energy to the voluntary muscles and away from the stomach and intestines. (This causes the feeling of a "knot" in your stomach.) Then, when the emergency has passed, the parasympathetic division takes over, carrying instructions that counteract the emergency orders of a few moments earlier. You may, however, remain aroused for some time after experiencing a strong emotional activation because hormones continue to circulate in the bloodstream. If the emotion-provoking situation is prolonged (as when you work every day for a boss whom you detest), the emergency response can sap your energy and cause both physical and mental deterioration.

Connection

Chapter 2
The sympathetic and parasympathetic divisions of the autonomic nervous system control automatic responses by internal organs and glands.

Connection

Chapter 10
Stress can produce both physical and mental disorders.

Connection

Chapter 2
The "fight-or-flight"
response involves the
production of adrenal
hormones.

THE ROLE OF HORMONES   Your body produces dozens of hormones, but among the most important for your emotions are adrenaline, noradrenaline, and serotonin. Serotonin is associated with feelings of depression; adrenaline is the hormone produced in fear; noradrenaline is more abundant in anger. Steroid hormones (sometimes abused by bodybuilders and other athletes) can also exert a powerful influence on emotions. In addition to their effects on muscles, steroids act on nerve cells, causing them to change their excitability. This is a normal part of the body's response to emergency situations. But when additional doses of steroid drugs are ingested over extended periods, these potent chemicals can produce dangerous side effects, including tendencies to rage or depression (Majewska et al., 1986). The mood changes associated with stress, pregnancy, and the menstrual cycle may also be related to the effects that steroid hormones have on brain cells.

Resolving Some Persistent Issues in the Psychology of Emotion

James-Lange theory of emotion:
The theory that an emotion-
provoking stimulus produces a
physical response that, in turn,
produces an emotion.

Just how biology, cognition, and behavior interact to produce an emotion has long been a source of controversy in psychology. Is one the cause of the others? Are emotion and cognition separate? Let's look briefly at these controversies and how insights drawn from neuroscience have begun to resolve them.

DO OUR PHYSICAL RESPONSES CAUSE OUR EMOTIONS?   A century ago, William James taught that our physical responses underlie our emotions. "We feel sorry *because* we cry, angry *because* we strike, afraid *because* we tremble," James said (1890/1950, p. 1006). This view, simultaneously proposed by the Danish psychologist Carl Lange, became known as the **James-Lange theory of emotion.**

Other psychologists, notably Walter Cannon, objected that physical changes in our behavior or our internal organs occur too slowly to account for split-second emotional reactions, such as those we feel in the face of danger.

After crossing a scary bridge, your
level of physiological arousal may be
heightened. You might be more
likely to misattribute your arousal to
some other cause—and some other
emotion, such as romantic
attraction.

They also objected that our physical responses are not varied enough to account for the whole palate of human emotion. In their view, the emotional feeling and the internal physical response occurred simultaneously.

Which side was right? Both had part of the truth. On the one hand, modern neuroscience has confirmed that our physical state *can* influence our emotions—much as the James-Lange theory argued (LeDoux, 1996). You may have noted edgy feelings after drinking too much coffee or grumpiness when hungry. Similarly, drugs such as the antidepressant Prozac can influence the physical condition of our brains and, hence, alter our moods. These emotional responses arise from circuits deep in the brain responding unconsciously to our physical condition.

On the other hand, our physical responses are not the only cause of our emotions—as Walter Cannon had suggested. As we have seen, emotions can also be generated by external cues detected by our unconscious emotional system. Thus, an unexpected loud noise or the sight of blood can trigger a reflexive emotional response that simultaneously makes you jump and produces a visceral response. Many psychologists now believe that depression and phobic reactions can result from conditioned responses of this unconscious emotional system.

WHEN DOES COGNITION PRODUCE EMOTION?   You can make yourself emotional just by thinking. This happens to students who are victims of "test anxiety": The more they think about the dire consequences of failing a test, the more their anxiety builds. Actors take advantage of this fact to make themselves feel real emotions on stage by recalling an incident from their own experience that produced the emotion they want to portray, such as grief, joy, or anger.

Stanley Schachter's (1971) **two-factor theory** adds an interesting complication. It suggests that the emotions we feel depend on our appraisal of both (a) our internal *physical state* and (b) the external *situation* in which we find ourselves. Strange effects occur when these two factors conflict—as they did in the following study.

A female researcher interviewed male subjects who had just crossed one of two footbridges. One was a safe, sturdy structure; the other was wobbly and precarious—selected to elicit physical arousal. The researcher, pretending to be interested in the effects of scenery on creativity, asked the men to write brief stories about a picture of a woman. She also invited them to call her if they wanted more information about the research. As predicted, those men who had just crossed the wobbly bridge (and were, presumably, more physically aroused) wrote stories containing more sexual imagery than those who used the safer structure. And four times as many of them called the female researcher "to get more information"! Apparently, the men who had crossed the shaky bridge misinterpreted their increased arousal as emotional attraction to the female researcher (Dutton & Aron, 1974).

Under what conditions are we most likely to misinterpret our emotions? Normally, external events confirm what our biology tells us, without much need for elaborate interpretation—as when you feel fear during a rollercoaster ride. But what happens when we experience physical arousal from not-so-obvious sources, such as exercise, heat, or drugs? When we know (or think we know) that one of these is the source of our feelings, we will most likely make no emotional interpretation. Misattribution is much more likely in a complex environment where many stimuli are competing for our attention (as in the bridge study, above). It is also likely in an environment where we have faulty information about our physical arousal (as when the unsuspected caffeine in a soft drink makes us edgy).

Numerous attempts to test the two-factor theory have produced conflicting results (Leventhal & Tomarken, 1986; Sinclair et al., 1994). Suppose that you suddenly feel an increase in heart rate and respiration, and you are alone. How would you interpret it: excitement or anxiety? The majority of adult experimental subjects experiencing those arousal symptoms interpreted them as anxiety-based and negative—and searched for ways to control the feelings (Marshall & Zimbardo, 1979; Maslach, 1979). Other experiments show that people can apparently experience emotions without any physical arousal. For example, when confronted by emotion-provoking stimuli, such as an insult, experimental subjects who have received beta-blockers (drugs that reduce heart rate) still can experience intense anger or anxiety.

CAN WE SEPARATE COGNITION AND EMOTION? Some experts have argued that emotion and cognition are separate, independent brain processes (Izard, 1989, 1993; Zajonc, 1980, 1984). In panic disorder, for example, panic attacks can occur suddenly and without warning—in the absence of a threatening situation and without emotion-provoking thoughts.

The two-factor theory would predict that a decaffeinated-coffee drinker who accidentally drank coffee with caffeine could mistake the resulting physical arousal for an emotion.

Two-factor theory: The proposal claiming that emotion results from the cognitive appraisal of both physical arousal (Factor #1) and an emotion-provoking stimulus (Factor #2).

Depression is more common in women, but men are more prone to violence. This sketch is by Vincent Van Gogh, no stranger to depression himself.

Connection

Chapter 13
Cognitive therapies
assume a link between
emotions and thoughts.

An opposing view has been argued by those who specialize in cognitive psychotherapy. This perspective asserts that cognition and emotion have an intimate connection. Richard Lazarus (1984, 1991a), for example, argues that we can conquer negative emotional responses by changing the way we *think* about events. In this view, cognition and emotion are components of a single mental system.

Insights from neuroscience can again help us resolve this conflict—and, again, both sides have part of the truth (LeDoux,1996). Whether emotion and cognition are separate or intertwined depends on which of the two main emotion circuits in the brain is involved. The emotion-and-cognition-are-separate view has recognized the distinction between the conscious and the unconscious emotion systems. In contrast, the emotion-and-cognition-are-connected view has focused on the conscious emotion pathways.

Emotional Differences between Men and Women Depend on Culture

Psychology

In Your Life

Some emotional differences between males and females probably have a biological basis. This would explain, for example, why certain emotional disturbances, such as panic disorder and depression, occur more commonly in women. And hormonal differences may explain why men show more anger and display more physiological signs of emotional arousal during interpersonal conflicts than do women (Gottman, 1994; Gottman & Krokoff, 1989; Gottman & Levenson, 1986; Polefrone & Manuck, 1987; Rusting & Nolen-Hoeksema, 1998). Men also commit most of the world's violent acts.

Other gender differences, however, may depend as much on culture as on biology. For instance, in the United States, males and females often learn different lessons about emotional control. Gender stereotypes may dictate that men and boys receive reinforcement for emotional displays of dominance, anger, and aggressive behavior (Fischer, 1993). On the other hand, they may be punished for emotional displays that show weakness: crying, depression, and sadness (Gottman, 1994). Meanwhile, the pattern of reinforcement and punishment may be reversed for females. Women and girls receive encouragement for emotions that show vulnerability. But they may be punished for displaying emotions that suggest dominance.

Not only does culture affect the emotional displays of men and women differently, but different cultures teach different **display rules** —the permissible ways of showing emotions (Ekman, 1984). In fact, researchers have found neither sex to be more emotionally expressive overall. Rather, cultures differ in emotional expression much more than do the sexes.

In Israel and Italy, for example, men more often than women hide their feelings of sadness. The opposite holds true in Britain, Spain, Switzerland, and Germany, where women are more likely than men to hide their emotions. In many Asian cultures both sexes learn to restrain all their emotional expressions (Wallbott et al., 1986).

A note of caution: It is difficult to distinguish biological from cultural influences. We know that men and women often give different emotional interpretations to the same situation—but only when the situation involves an encounter between a man and a woman (Lakoff, 1990; Stapley & Haviland, 1989).

Overall, we can say that the sexes often differ in their emotional experiences, both within and across cultures. We cannot conclude, however, that one sex has more emotional intensity than the other (Baumeister et al., 1990; Fischer et al., 1993; Oatley & Duncan, 1994; Shaver & Hazan, 1987; Shields, 1991).

1. **RECALL:** *During emotional arousal, the _____ nervous system sends messages to the internal organs.*
   - **a.** somatic
   - **b.** sensory
   - **c.** autonomic
   - **d.** cerebellar

2. **APPLICATION:** *We would be most likely to misattribute the source of our arousal under which of the following circumstances?*
   - **a.** taking a drug, such as a diet pill, that has the unexpected side effect of physical arousal
   - **b.** taking a drug, such as caffeine, that we know produces arousal
   - **c.** winning a race
   - **d.** feeling depressed after the death of a loved one

3. **RECALL:** *In the field of emotion there is currently intense debate about whether*
   - **a.** biological arousal can cause emotional responses.
   - **b.** cognition can cause emotional arousal.
   - **c.** cognition and emotion are independent of each other.
   - **d.** men or women are more emotional.

4. **RECALL:** *In which respect do men and women differ in their emotional expressions?*
   - **a.** Women are, overall, more emotionally expressive than men.
   - **b.** Certain emotional disorders, such as depression, occur more often in women.
   - **c.** In Asian countries, men are more open about their feelings than are women.
   - **d.** Men are more rational than women.

Core Concept

5. **UNDERSTANDING THE CORE CONCEPT:**
   Emotions result from an interaction of biological, mental, behavioral, and social/cultural processes. Which two of these is emphasized in the two-factor theory of emotion?
   - **a.** biological and behavioral
   - **b.** mental and behavioral
   - **c.** biological and mental
   - **d.** biological and social/cultural

ANSWERS:　　1. c　　2. a　　3. c　　4. b　　5. c

HOW MUCH CONTROL DO WE HAVE OVER OUR EMOTIONS?

Key Question ?

The boss says something critical of your work—unfairly, you think. Suddenly anger and defensiveness well up inside you. You can't express these emotions to the boss, but your face betrays your feelings. Is such a response as automatic and uncontrollable as the knee-jerk reflex? Richard Lazarus (1991a,b) has shown that training can help people not only to modify and control their private feelings but also to control the expression of them. In many situations, aside from work, it may be desirable to mask or modify what you are feeling. If you dislike a professor, you might be wise to disguise your emotions. If you have strong romantic feelings toward someone, more than he or she realizes, it might be safest to reveal your feelings gradually. In business negotiations, you will do better if you can prevent yourself from signaling too much emotional arousal. Even in leisure activities like playing poker or planning your next move in chess, you will be most successful if you keep your real feelings, beliefs, and intentions a secret.

In this section, we look at emotional control. We will begin with the concept of "emotional intelligence," the ability to understand your emotions and those of others, as well as to control them. Then we will look at the other side of emotional control: the detection of deception—which is really a problem in detecting emotions that someone is trying to hide. Here is the Core Concept that ties these topics together:

Display rules: The permissible ways of displaying emotions in a particular society.

> **Although emotional responses are not always consciously regulated, we can learn to control them.**

The practical, take-away message from this section is that, while emotions do sometimes slip out of control, we are not simply at their mercy. Emotional control is a skill that can be learned.

Developing Emotional Intelligence

It takes a certain sort of intelligence to understand and control one's own emotions. According to psychologists Peter Salovey and John Mayer, **emotional intelligence** involves the ability to understand and use emotions effectively (1990; Mayer & Salovey, 1997). Often, however emotional intelligence is overshadowed by the academic forms of intelligence assessed by traditional IQ tests.

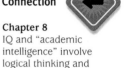

Connection

Chapter 8
IQ and "academic intelligence" involve logical thinking and problem-solving.

THE PREDICTIVE POWER OF EMOTIONAL INTELLIGENCE   Those with high emotional intelligence are not only tuned in to their own emotions and those of others, but they can manage their negative feelings and curtail inappropriate expression of their impulses. The power of this ability can be seen in the results of the "marshmallow test," says Daniel Goleman in his 1995 book, *Emotional Intelligence:*

> Just imagine you're four years old, and someone makes the following proposal: If you'll wait until after he runs an errand, you can have two marshmallows for a treat. If you can't wait until then, you can have only one — but you can have it right now.

How did the children in this experiment respond to the temptation of the marshmallow which sat before them, within reach, while the researcher was away? Goleman continues:

> Some four-year-olds were able to wait what must surely have seemed an endless fifteen to twenty minutes for the experimenter to return. To sustain themselves in their struggle they covered their eyes so they wouldn't have to stare at temptation, or rested their heads in their arms, talked to themselves, sang, played games with their hands and feet, even tried to go to sleep. These plucky preschoolers got the two-marshmallow reward. But others, more impulsive, grabbed the one marshmallow, almost always within seconds of the experimenter's leaving the room on his "errand." (pp. 80–81)

The power of the marshmallow test to predict later adjustment was revealed when these same children were tracked down in adolescence. As a group, those who had curbed their impulse to grab the single marshmallow were better off on all counts. They were more self-reliant, more effective in interpersonal relationships, better students, better able to handle frustration and stress. By contrast, the children who had given in to temptation had lives marked by troubled relationships, shyness, stubbornness, and indecisiveness. They also were much more likely to hold low opinions of themselves, to mistrust others, and to be easily provoked by frustrations. In the academic sphere, they were more likely to be uninterested in school. The marshmallow test also correlated clearly with SAT scores: Those who, as 4-year-olds, were able to delay gratification scored, on the average, 210 points higher than did their counterparts who had grabbed the single marshmallow years earlier.

Emotional intelligence: In Goleman's theory, the ability to understand and control emotional responses.

Emotional intelligence, however, is not a perfect predictor of success, cautions John Mayer (1999). Nor should we think of it as a replacement for traditional IQ scores. Rather, says Mayer, emotional intelligence is merely another variable that can help us refine our understanding and our predictions of behavior.

THE NATURE AND NURTURE OF EMOTIONAL INTELLIGENCE   Is this sort of savvy fixed by heredity or is it influenced by early experience? Goleman believes that emotional intelligence is not rigid. Like academic intelligence, he says, emotional intelligence can be learned. Based on programs already in place in visionary schools across the country, Goleman has a plan for adding emotional training to the curriculum. The result, he predicts, will bring improved relationships, increased self-respect, and even, perhaps, gains in academic achievement.

But emotional control has its dark side, too. Just as some people get into trouble when they let their emotions — particular negative emotions — go unchecked, others take emotional control to the opposite extreme. They become so guarded that they never convey affection, humor, or honest displeasure. Studies also show that overcontrolling emotions interferes with memory for emotionally charged events (Carpenter, 2000; Richards & Gross, 2000).

Still others learn to control their emotions in order to deceive. This is the skill practiced by con artists. Their victims are people who believe that physical or behavioral cues are never-fail indicators of people's private feelings. Let's turn now to the branch of psychology that studies these deceptive tactics of emotional control.

Detecting Deception

You might think you can spot deception when someone fails to "look you in the eye" or fidgets nervously. If so, you could be setting yourself up to be duped. Most of us are poor lie detectors — or truth detectors, for that matter. One reason is that social interactions often occur in familiar situations, where we pay little attention to nonverbal cues. Nevertheless, experts who study deception find that a person who deliberately tries to hoodwink us may "leak" uncontrolled nonverbal signals of deception. Knowing how to read these cues could help you decide whether a salesperson or politician is lying to you or whether a physician might be concealing something about your medical condition.

DECEPTION CUES   The key to effective deception detection lies in perceiving patterns of a person's behavior over time. Without the chance for repeated observations, you are much less able to judge a person's honesty (Marsh, 1988). Still, you may find yourself in a situation where even a little help in deception detection might be better than none at all — such as when buying a used car or listening to a political speech. Here are some helpful guidelines that psychology can offer (from Kleinke, 1975; Marsh, 1988; Zuckerman et al., 1981):

> ► When a lie involves false information, the effort to hide the truth costs the liar some cognitive effort. This results in heightened attention (evident in dilation of the pupils), longer pauses in speech (to choose words carefully), and more constrained movement and gesturing (in an attempt to avoid "giving away" the truth).

> ► Conversely, when a lie involves hiding one's true feelings, the liar may become physically and behaviorally more aroused. This becomes evident in postural shifts, speech errors, nervous gestures (such as preening by touching or stroking the hair or face), and shrugging (as if to dismiss the lie).

The polygraph, often called a "lie detector," relies on the assumption that people display physical signs of arousal when lying.

Polygraph: A device that records or graphs many ("poly") measures of physical arousal, such heart rate, breathing, perspiration, and blood pressure. A polygraph is often called a "lie detector," even though it is really an arousal detector.

▶ The face is easier to control than the body, so a deceiver may work on keeping a "poker face" but forget to restrain bodily clues. A smart deception detective might therefore concentrate on a speaker's body movements: Are they rhythmic? Are they calculated? Do the hands move freely or nervously?

▶ The ability to "look you straight in the eye" is, in fact, a reasonably good indicator of truth-telling—but only when dealing with people who usually tell the truth. When they do lie, their amateurish efforts to deceive often show up in averted gaze, reduced blinking (indicating concentration of attention elsewhere), and less smiling. Remember, however, that a practiced liar can look you straight in the eye while relating complete fiction.

DO "LIE DETECTORS" REALLY WORK?   The **polygraph**, often called a "lie detector," relies on the assumption that people display physical signs of arousal when lying—even though this is not always true. The device really acts as an emotional arousal detector, rather than a direct indicator of truth or lies. Most such devices make a record of the suspect's heart rate, breathing rate, perspiration, and blood pressure. Occasionally, voice-print analysis is also employed.

Critics have pointed out several problems with the polygraphic procedure (Aftergood, 2000; Holden, 2001; Saxe, 1991, 1994). Subjects know when they are suspects, so some will give heightened responses to the critical questions, whether they are guilty or innocent. Some people, however, can give deceptive responses because they have learned to control or distort their emotional responses. To do so they may employ simple physical movements, drugs, or biofeedback training—a procedure in which people are given information on their biological responses (Saxe et al., 1985). Thus, a polygraph examiner risks incorrectly identifying innocent people as liars. For this reason, many courts have banned or severely restricted the use of polygraph examinations (Patrick & Iacono, 1991).

Connection

Chapter 10
Biofeedback is an operant conditioning procedure that can help people control stress responses.

Psychology

In Your Life

Controlling Anger

"Anger has long been a problem for me," writes Melvyn Fein. "Over the years it has cost me a great deal of pain and denied me much happiness" (1993, p. ix). Failing at various efforts to control and constructively express his anger, Fein himself became a clinician and developed an approach to anger disorders. Fein's program,

Integrated Anger Management (I.A.M.), involves five stages:

▶ Learning to express anger safely, so that it will not spin out of control;

▶ Developing tolerance by accepting feelings of anger without becoming enraged and violent;

▶ Identifying the underlying goals of one's anger, such as frustration with injustice or the inability to achieve a valued goal;

▶ Letting go of unrealistic goals that feed the anger, such as the naive

belief that expressing anger will motivate others to "do the right thing"; and

▶ Using anger constructively to reach more realistic, achievable goals.

This analysis counters popular myths about anger. On television talk shows, for example, you can see people attacking and humiliating others, as if the public venting of feelings and the act of revenge will eliminate their anger. In fact, retaliation for a real or imagined wrong is likely to bring only the most fleeting feeling of satisfaction. The overwhelming result of venting anger is to increase the tendency to become enraged at ever smaller provocations. Solid psychological research indicates that, when you are angry with someone, "getting it off your chest" by aggressively confronting or hurting that individual will *not* neutralize your bad feelings. Rather, it will more likely *intensify* them. And, from a social perspective, retaliation is not likely to end a feud but to fuel it — a reality obvious throughout human history, filled with wars about pride, power, status, and honor. A saner and safer strategy is to keep your feelings to yourself, at least until the passion of your anger has subsided and you can be more rational about the nature of your real complaint and what might be done to solve the problem (Tavris, 1983, 1995). Often, all it takes to defuse a tense and angry situation is to communicate the facts and your feelings to the person toward whom you feel anger.

CHECK**YOUR**UNDERSTANDING

1. **RECALL:** *People with emotional intelligence*
   a. feel no emotions.
   b. are extremely emotionally responsive.
   c. know how to control their emotional responses.
   d. can deceive those with less emotional intelligence.

2. **RECALL:** *When lying by giving false information, you are likely to*
   a. become more animated in your gesturing.
   b. become more constrained in your gesturing.
   c. control your body more easily than you control your face.
   d. look someone "straight in the eye."

3. **RECALL:** *"Lie detectors" detect*
   a. feelings.
   b. arousal.
   c. motivation.
   d. untruthfulness.

4. **RECALL:** *Many psychologists have become concerned about the widespread use of polygraphy because*
   a. polygraph testing is not done under the supervision of qualified psychologists.
   b. hypnosis is much more accurate than polygraphy in the detection of lying.
   c. innocent people can be incorrectly identified as lying.
   d. people who are lying can be incorrectly identified as innocent.

5. **APPLICATION:** *Psychological research suggests that it might be best to handle your feelings of anger toward a friend by*
   a. hitting a punching bag.
   b. ventilating your anger by yelling at your friend.
   c. calmly telling your friend that you feel angry.
   d. doing nothing except "stewing" in your angry feelings.

6. **UNDERSTANDING THE CORE CONCEPT:**
   Research suggests that the ability to control one's emotional responses is
   a. a personality trait that varies from person to person.
   b. largely a matter of hormones.
   c. closely connected to IQ.
   d. a skill that can be learned.

ANSWERS: 1. c   2. b   3. b   4. c   5. c   6. d

MOTIVATION: WHAT MAKES US ACT AS WE DO?

Why do some people climb mountains, while others rob banks, or join the Peace Corps? What drives anorectic individuals to starve themselves—sometimes to their deaths? Why do some of us feel a need to achieve, while others seek security? Such questions lie in the domain of the psychology of motivation, which deals with the internal processes that cause us to move toward a goal or away from a situation we judge to be unpleasant. As you will remember, motivation is the complement of emotion. While emotion arouses us, motivation channels that arousal into action.

Motivation is the general term for all the processes involved in starting, directing, and maintaining physical and psychological activities. Motivational processes determine which of many possible responses you will choose at any moment. Will it be laughing or crying? Fight or flight? Studying or playing? The motivational menu always offers multiple choices. The Core Concept for this section puts it this way:

> **Motivation takes many forms, but all involve inferred mental processes that select and direct our behavior.**

We begin our study of motivation with a look at the ways in which we use the concept of motivation.

How Psychologists Use the Concept of Motivation

Professors may think that students who do poorly on exams are "not motivated enough." Sports commentators speculate that winning teams were "hungrier" or "more motivated" than their opponents. Detectives seek to establish a motive in building a case against a criminal suspect. In everyday language, we use the term *motivation* to refer to a variety of mental states involving intentions, energy, or effort.

Psychologists, like everyone else, often need to explain behavior that cannot be attributed to external conditions. Therefore, they may make inferences about internal processes that select and direct behavior. Such inferences are formalized in the concept of motivation, which psychologists find useful in the following circumstances:

Connection

Chapter 14
The common mistake of attributing behavior to personal characteristics (rather than the environment) is known as the *fundamental attribution error*.

Motivation: Refers to all the processes involved in starting, directing, and maintaining physical and psychological activities.

▶ *Motivation connects observable behavior to internal states.* When we see someone eating, we may infer that a hunger drive is at work. We must be careful about drawing such inferences too quickly, though, because eating might be caused by something else (e.g., social pressure, the availability of a favorite food, or a desire to gain weight). So a motive, such as hunger, can be identified with confidence only when other influences have been ruled out.

▶ *Motivation accounts for variability in behavior.* Psychologists use motivational explanations when the variations in people's performances are not obviously due to differences in physical or mental abilities or to differing environmental demands. For example, the intensity of your motivation may explain why you play tennis well one day but poorly another. It also may explain why some people do better than others of comparable skill in competitive situations, such as in a basketball game.

▶ *Motivation explains perseverance despite adversity.* Motivation helps us understand why organisms continue to perform reliably even under difficult or variable conditions. Motivation gets you to work on time, even when you had a sleepless night or had to drive through a blizzard. When highly motivated, you persist, even if you realize the chances of success are slim — as does one of your authors when facing a tough whitewater challenge in his kayak.

▶ *Motives relate biology to behavior.* We are biological organisms with complex internal mechanisms that automatically regulate bodily functions to promote survival. States of deprivation (such as needing food) automatically trigger these mechanisms, which then influence bodily functioning (such as feeling hungry), creating motivational states.

In each of these cases, an internal motivational process channels the organism's energies into a particular pattern of behavior.

The fact that some people do better in competition than others can be explained in part by different degrees of motivation. These men are participating in the international Games for the Disabled.

Types of Motivation

Psychologists often distinguish between *motives* and *drives.* They prefer the term **drive** for motivation that is assumed to have a strong biological component and, therefore, plays an important role in survival or reproduction. Hunger and thirst are examples of such biological drives. In contrast, many psychologists reserve the term **motive** for urges that are learned, such as the need for achievement or the desire to play video games. Obviously, however, many motivated behaviors — such as eating, drinking, and sexual behavior — can have roots in both biology and learning.

Psychologists also distinguish between *intrinsic* and *extrinsic* motivation. **Intrinsic motivation** comes from within the individual who engages in an activity for its own sake, in the absence of external reward. Leisure activities, such as cycling, kayaking, or playing the guitar, are usually intrinsically motivated. Intrinsic motivation arises from inner qualities, such as personality traits or special interests. On the other hand, **extrinsic motivation** comes from outside the person. It involves behavior aimed at some external consequence, such as money or praise, rather than at satisfying an internal need.

In addition, motives and drives can arise either from **conscious motivation** or **unconscious motivation.** That is, motivated individuals may or may not be aware of the drives or motives underlying their behavior. Freud took this idea a step further, suggesting that the unconscious mind harbors complex motives arising from traumatic experiences and sexual conflicts. Modern-day psychologists, however, stand divided on Freud's teachings (see, for example, Bruner, 1992; Erdelyi, 1992; Greenwald, 1992; Jacoby et al., 1992; Kihlstrom et al., 1992; Loftus & Klinger, 1992).

Theories of Motivation

No single explanation of motivation adequately accounts for the whole gamut of human motives and drives. Hunger, for example, seems to obey different motivational rules from those regulating sex or achievement or attachment. Much of the difficulty arises because of our dual nature: We are simultaneously creatures driven by our biology (as when you are ravenous because you haven't eaten all day) and by learning (as when you associate the lunch bell with food). Let's first focus on the biological side of our nature with a look at the common ancestor of all modern motivational theories.

Drive: Biologically instigated motivation.

Motive: An internal mechanism that selects and directs behavior. The term *motive* is often used in the narrower sense of a motivational process that is learned, rather than biologically based (as are drives).

Intrinsic motivation: The desire to engage in an activity for its own sake, rather than for some external consequence, such as a reward.

Extrinsic motivation: The desire to engage in an activity to achieve an external consequence, such as a reward.

Conscious motivation: Having the desire to engage in an activity and being aware of the desire.

Unconscious motivation: Having a desire to engage in an activity but being consciously unaware of the desire. Freud's psychoanalytic theory emphasized unconscious motivation.

INSTINCT THEORY   According to **instinct theory,** organisms are born with a set of biologically based behaviors essential for survival. Instinct accounts reasonably well for regular cycles of animal activity, as seen in salmon that travel thousands of miles back to the stream where they were spawned. Although such instinctive behavior does not depend heavily on learning, the environment can often modify the behavior. This is seen when bees communicate the location of food to other bees, army ants embark on synchronized hunting expeditions, or birds use landmarks in their annual migrations.

The term *instinct* has migrated from the scientific vocabulary to the speech of everyday life. We speak casually of "maternal instincts," of an athlete who "instinctively catches the ball," and of a "killer instinct" in a competitive entrepreneur. In fact, we use the term in so many ways that its meaning has become vague and conflicted. And, much the same problem has occurred in scientific discourse. As a result, the term *instinct* has dropped out of favor among psychologists. And ethologists, who study animal behavior in natural habitats, now prefer the term **fixed-action patterns,** more narrowly defined as unlearned behavior patterns that occur throughout a species and are triggered by identifiable stimuli. Examples of fixed-action patterns include bird migration and dominance displays in baboons.

Do instincts — perhaps in their new guise as fixed-action patterns — retain any value in explaining human behavior? They do seem to motivate some of the behaviors, such as nursing, that we see in newborns. But we stand on shakier ground when using the term to explain more complex human behaviors. So, while we might speculate that the motivation of a hard-driving executive could involve some basic biological instinct, this explanation is weak, at best.

DRIVE THEORY   The concept of "drive" refers to the state of energy or tension that moves an organism to meet a biological need (Woodworth, 1918). Thus, an animal that needs water is driven to drink. Likewise, a need for food drives it to eat. In drive theory, a biological **need** produces a drive. The drive, then, motivates the animal to act to reduce the drive level. You have felt this buildup and release of tension if you have been extremely thirsty and then drank your fill.

According to drive theory, the desirable state that organisms seek is a balanced condition called **homeostasis** (Hull, 1943, 1952). Organisms that have a biological imbalance (caused, say, by lack of fluids) are driven to seek a homeostatic balance (by drinking). Similarly, we can understand hunger as an imbalance in the body's energy supply. This imbalance drives an animal that has been deprived of food to eat in order to restore a condition of equilibrium.

Unfortunately for drive theory, however, the story of motivation has proved not to be that simple. For instance, drive theory cannot explain why, in the absence of any apparent deprivation or drives, organisms act merely to increase stimulation. Accordingly, both humans and animals engage in play — behavior that is satisfying in itself, rather than a means of reducing a drive. And in the laboratory, rats will cross an electrified grid to reach nothing on the other side, except a novel environment. Even animals deprived of food and water, when placed in unfamiliar surroundings with plenty of opportunities to eat or drink, may choose to explore instead. Only after they have satisfied their curiosity do they begin to satisfy their hunger and thirst (Berlyne, 1960; Fowler, 1965; Zimbardo & Montgomery, 1957). And, as for human motivation, it is hard to imagine a basic need or a biological drive that could propel people out of airplanes or force them up the face of Yosemite's El Capitán. Apparently, for both people and animals, exploring and taking an interest in the world are rewarding experiences in themselves. For these reasons, psychologists have concluded that drive theory does not hold all the answers to motivation. Still,

Connection

Chapter 6
Fixed-action patterns can put limitations on the kinds of behaviors an organism can learn.

Instinct theory: The now-outmoded view that certain behaviors are determined by innate factors. The instinct theory was flawed because it overlooked the effects of learning and because it employed instincts merely as labels, rather than as explanations for behavior.

Fixed-action patterns: Genetically based behaviors, seen across a species, that can be set off by a specific stimulus. The concept of fixed-action patterns has replaced the older notion of instinct.

Need: In drive theory, a need is a biological imbalance (such as dehydration) that threatens survival, if the need is left unmet. Biological needs are believed to produce drives.

Homeostasis: The body's tendency to maintain a biologically balanced condition, especially with regard to nutrients, water, and temperature.

they have been reluctant to abandon the concept of drive, which, as we noted earlier, has come to mean a biologically based motive that plays an important role in survival or reproduction.

COGNITIVE THEORY AND LOCUS OF CONTROL   We have seen that many of our motives depend more on learning and thinking than on biological drives or instincts. Watching TV, reading a book, listening to music, climbing a mountain: All get their push from cognitive processes that we have studied earlier in this book. One of the most influential cognitive theories emphasizes the importance of *expectations* in motivating behavior.

In his cognitive *social-learning theory* (1954), Julian Rotter (pronounced ROH-ter) asserted that the likelihood of someone selecting a certain behavior (such as studying for an exam instead of partying) is determined by two factors: (1) the expectation of attaining a goal (getting a good grade) with that behavior and (2) the personal value of the goal. But what determines these expectations? Rotter says that they depend largely on our **locus of control,** our belief about our ability to control the events in our lives. If, for example, you believe that studying hard will lead to good grades, you have an *internal locus of control,* and you will behave differently from those who believe that grades depend on luck or on the teacher's biases. People who believe that their fate hangs on whim or luck have an *external locus of control.* Rotter's theory would also predict that people who exercise, save money, or use seat belts have an internal locus of control. Those who buy lottery tickets or smoke cigarettes have an external locus of control. Such predictions have been supported by hundreds of studies.

MASLOW'S HUMANISTIC THEORY   What happens when you must choose between meeting a biological need and fulfilling a desire based on learning? How do you choose whether to eat, sleep, visit friends, or study? Abraham Maslow (1970) said that you act on your most pressing needs, and some of these needs take priority over others. Unlike the other theories of motivation we have considered, Maslow's humanistic theory attempts to span the whole gamut of human motivation from biological drives to social motives to creativity. Specifically, Maslow's theory proposes a **needs hierarchy:** a listing of needs arranged in priority order (Figure 9.3). The "higher" needs have little influence on our behavior, said Maslow, until the more basic need are fulfilled:

▶ *Biological needs,* such as hunger and thirst, fall at the base of the hierarchy and must be satisfied before higher needs make themselves felt. When biological needs are pressing, other concerns are put on hold.

▶ *Safety needs* motivate us to avoid danger, when biological needs are reasonably well satisfied. Note that a hungry animal (with unmet biological needs) may risk its physical safety for food, until it gets its belly full; then the safety needs take over.

▶ *Attachment and affiliation needs* energize us when we are no longer concerned about danger. These needs make us want to belong, to affiliate with others, to love, and to be loved.

▶ *Esteem needs* follow next in the hierarchy. These include the needs to like oneself, to see oneself as competent and effective, and to do what is necessary to earn the respect of oneself and others.

▶ *Self-actualization* lies at the top of the needs hierarchy, motivating us to seek the fullest development of our creative human potential. Self-actualizing persons are self-aware, self-accepting, socially responsive, spontaneous, and open to novelty and challenge.

Locus of control: An individual's sense of where his or her life influences originate — internally or externally.

Needs hierarchy: In Maslow's theory, the notion that needs occur in priority order, with the biological needs as the most basic.

FIGURE 9.3: Maslow's Hierarchy of Needs

According to Maslow, needs at the lower level of the hierarchy dominate an individual's motivation as long as they are unsatisfied. Once these are adequately satisfied, the higher needs occupy an individual's attention.

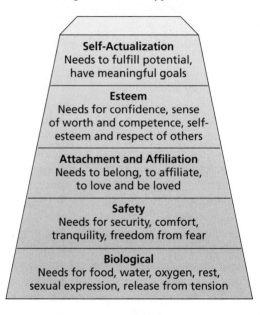

How does Maslow's theory square with observation? It does explain why we may neglect our friends or our career goals in favor of meeting pressing biological needs signaled by pain, thirst, sleepiness, or sexual desire. Yet—in contradiction to Maslow's theory—people frequently neglect their basic biological needs in favor of social ones, as we saw in rescue workers during the terrorist attack on New York. To Maslow's credit, however, he called our attention to the important role of social motivation in our lives. A great body of work now demonstrates this need we have for relationships with others (Baumeister & Leary, 1995; Brehm, 1992; Hatfield & Rapson, 1993; Kelley et al., 1983; Weber & Harvey, 1994a,b).

Exceptions to Maslow's theory have also been pointed out by cross-cultural psychologists, who see his ideas as applicable only to self-oriented (individualistic) cultures, rather than to group-oriented (collectivistic) cultures. Other critics point out that some important human behaviors do not fit Maslow's hierarchy. It fails to explain, for example, why you might miss a meal when you are absorbed in an interesting book. It fails to explain why sensation seekers, as we saw earlier, would pursue risky interests (such as whitewater kayaking) that override their safety needs. And it fails to explain the behavior of people who deliberately take their own lives. The critics will admit, however, that Maslow's theory was, at least, a step toward a comprehensive theory of motivation.

Overall, Maslow's influence has been greater in the spheres of psychotherapy and education than in motivational research. Business, too, has been especially receptive to Maslow's ideas. Many dollars have been made by consultants using this theory as the basis for seminars on motivating employees. The main idea they have promoted is that humans have an innate need to grow and actualize their highest potentials. Such an upbeat approach was also welcomed by psychologists who had wearied of the negative motivational emphasis on hunger, thirst, anxiety, and fear.

Connection

Chapter 10
Chapter 13
Humanistic psychotherapy
draws on Maslow's ideas.

Rewards Can (Sometimes) Squelch Motivation

It's likely that you have had to take a test in a subject that didn't interest you. If you were a conscientious student, you learned the material anyway, in order to get a good grade or, perhaps, to avoid disappointing your parents. Psychologists say that such behavior is *extrinsically motivated* because it aims at getting an external reward (or avoiding aversive consequences). Teachers often use grades as extrinsic motivators, hoping to get students more involved in their studies. Extrinsic motivation also explains why people take vitamins, marry for money, pay their taxes, and use deodorant.

But what do you suppose would happen if people were given extrinsic rewards (praise, money, or other incentives) for *intrinsically* motivated behavior — that they already find enjoyable? Would the reward make the activity even more — or less — enjoyable?

OVERJUSTIFICATION

To find out, psychologists studied two groups of school children who enjoyed drawing pictures (Lepper et al., 1973). One group agreed to draw pictures for a reward certificate, while a control group made drawings without the expectation of reward. Both groups made drawings enthusiastically. Some days later, however, when given the opportunity to draw pictures again, the rewarded children were significantly less enthusiastic about drawing than those who had not been rewarded. (The group who had received no rewards were actually more interested in drawing than they had been before!)

The experimenters reasoned that external reinforcement had squelched the internal motivation in the group that been rewarded. They called this **overjustification.** As a result of overjustification, they reasoned, the children's motivation had changed from intrinsic to extrinsic. Consequently, the children were less interested in making pictures in the absence of reward.

A JUSTIFICATION FOR REWARDS

But do rewards always have this effect? Many studies of this issue have been done since the drawing study, and it is now clear that rewards do not necessarily interfere with intrinsic motivation (Covington, 2000; Eisenberger & Cameron, 1996). This is consistent with the fact that many professionals both love their work and get paid for it.

Overjustification occurs when extrinsic rewards for doing something enjoyable take the intrinsic fun out of the activity. It is likely that this person would not enjoy video games as much if he were paid for playing.

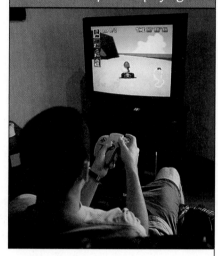

Specifically, the research shows that overjustification occurs only *when the reward is given without regard for quality of performance.* In fact, this is just what happened to the children who were all given certificates for their drawings. The same effect can occur in a business when employees are given year-end bonuses regardless of their work. Happily, we now have proof that rewards can be used effectively to motivate people — if the rewards are given not as a bribe but for a job well done.

Overjustification: The process by which extrinsic (external) rewards can sometimes displace internal motivation, as when a child receives money for playing video games.

1. **RECALL:** *Psychologists use the concept of motivation in several important ways. Which of the following is not among them?*
   a. to connect observable behavior to internal states
   b. to account for variability in behavior
   c. to explain perseverance despite adversity
   d. to explain reflexive responses

2. **RECALL:** *One reason the term instinct has dropped out of favor with psychologists is that*
   a. human behavior has no genetic basis.
   b. all behavior is learned.
   c. the term became a label for behavior, rather than an explanation for behavior.
   d. *instinct* applies to animal behavior, but not to human behavior.

3. **ANALYSIS:** Incentives *are different from* drives *because*
   a. incentives are external and drives are internal.
   b. incentives are homeostatic and drives are not.
   c. incentives are innate and drives are learned.

   d. incentives are emotions and drives are motives.

4. **ANALYSIS:** *What makes Maslow's theory of motivation different from most other theories?*
   a. It deals with biological motives.
   b. It deals with a wide range of motives.
   c. It helps us understand both animal behavior and human behavior.
   d. It deals with both emotion and motivation.

5. **UNDERSTANDING THE CORE CONCEPT:**
   Motivation takes many forms, but all involve inferred mental processes that select and direct our behavior. *Thus, the psychology of motivation attempts to explain why a certain _____ is selected.*
   a. emotion
   b. action
   c. sensation
   d. reward

ANSWERS: 1. d   2. c   3. a   4. b   5. b

HOW ARE ACHIEVEMENT, HUNGER, AND SEX ALIKE? DIFFERENT?

Now that we have reviewed some essential motivational concepts and theories, we will examine three diverse and important motives: achievement, hunger, and sex. We will see how each of these motives differs from the others, not just in the behavior it produces, but in deeper ways as well. The Core Concept expresses the point:

> **No single theory accounts for all forms of motivation, because each motive involves its own mix of biological, mental, behavioral, and social/cultural influences.**

We will see that each of the three motives discussed in this section differs in its mix of nature and nurture. We will also see that they differ in their sensitivity to internal and environmental cues, in the reinforcers that satisfy them, and in the social/cultural influences to which they respond. So far, no one—not even Maslow—has been clever enough to devise a theory that encompasses the whole range of motivations, takes all these factors into account, and still fits the facts.

Recent developments in evolutionary psychology, however, show promise in explaining drives heavily rooted in biology, such as hunger and the sex drive (Buss, 1999, 2001). Evolutionary theory suggests that each motivational mechanism evolved in response to different environmental pressures. And as we will see, the evolutionary perspective has offered some particularly strong and controversial proposals to explain gender differences.

Yet, we still have no complete and comprehensive theory of motivation. For the moment, we must be content with an array of specific theories that each explains a different motive. The contrasts between hunger, sex, and achievement will make this point clear.

Achievement Motivation

Before you read the caption, imagine what might be happening in Figure 9.4. The story you tell about the boy and his violin may reveal your own *need for achievement,* a psychological motive that accounts for a wide range of behaviors in our culture. Achievement, of course, can be motivated by a desire for recognition, fame, praise, money, or other incentives. But, for most of us, a deep satisfaction also comes with meeting a challenge and attaining a goal of personal significance. Whatever its source, the need for achievement is an important source of human motivation.

MEASURING THE NEED FOR ACHIEVEMENT Psychologists Henry Murray and David McClelland pioneered the measurement of achievement motivation with an instrument called the Thematic Apperception Test (TAT). On this test, people are asked to tell stories in response to a series of ambiguous pictures. Each story, Murray and McClelland theorized, represents a **projection** of the respondent's psychological needs. That is, they assumed that the stories would reflect the themes that were psychologically important for the storyteller. From responses to several of these TAT pictures, Murray and McClelland worked out

Projection: The process by which people attribute their own unconscious motives to other people or objects. The concept of projection originally comes from Freud's theory.

FIGURE 9.4: Alternative Interpretations of a TAT Picture

Story Showing High n Ach: The boy has just finished his violin lesson. He's happy at his progress and is beginning to believe that all his sacrifices have been worthwhile. To become a concert violinist he will have to give up much of his social life and practice for many hours each day. Although he knows he could make more money by going into his father's business, he is more interested in being a great violinist and giving people joy with his music. He renews his personal commitment to do all it takes to make it.

Story Showing Low n Ach: The boy is holding his brother's violin and wishes he could play it. But he knows it isn't worth the time, energy, and money for lessons. He feels sorry for his brother, who has given up all the fun things in life to practice, practice, practice. It would be great to wake up one day and be a top-notch musician, but it doesn't happen that way. The reality is boring practice, no fun, and the likelihood that he'll become just another guy playing a musical instrument in a small-town band.

measures of the **need for achievement *(n Ach),*** which they saw as the desire to attain a difficult, but desired, goal. Figure 9.4 shows an example of how a high *n Ach* individual and a low *n Ach* individual might interpret a TAT picture.

What characteristics distinguish people with a high need for achievement? People high in *n Ach* show more persistence on difficult tasks than do people with low achievement needs (Cooper, 1983; French & Thomas, 1958; McClelland, 1987b). In school, those with high *n Ach* tend to get better grades (Raynor, 1970). In their career paths, they take more competitive jobs (McClelland, 1965), assume more leadership roles, and earn more rapid promotions (Andrews, 1967). As entrepreneurs, those with high *n Ach* become more successful (McClelland, 1987a, 1993).

A CROSS-CULTURAL PERSPECTIVE ON ACHIEVEMENT   From a global viewpoint, American psychology's emphasis on achievement motivation may reflect a Western bias. Cross-cultural psychologist Harry Triandis points out that cultures differ in the value they place on achievement motivation. This difference, in turn, involves a fundamental psychological distinction among cultures: their emphasis on *individualism* or *collectivism* (1990). Western cultures, including the United States, Canada, Britain, and Western Europe, emphasize **individualism.** People growing up in these cultures learn to place a high premium on individual achievement (along with the companion concepts of freedom and equality). By contrast, says Triandis, the cultures of Latin America, Asia, Africa, and the Middle East often emphasize **collectivism,** the values of group loyalty and subordination of self to the group. This means that the collectivistic cultures often discourage individual achievement. Even in the collectivist cultures of Japan, Hong Kong, and South Korea, where very high values are placed on achievement in school and business, the expectation is not of achieving individual honors but of bringing honor to the family.

Without a cross-cultural perspective, it would be easy for Americans to jump to the erroneous conclusion that motivation for individual achievement is a "natural" part of the human makeup. But Triandis's insight suggests that this is not true. Rather, collectivist cultures seem to value *group* achievement over *individual* achievement. More generally, cross-cultural research tells us that a complete understanding of motives—particularly those that involve learning—must always take cultural influences into account.

Hunger Motivation

You will survive if you don't achieve, but you will die if you don't eat. Unlike achievement motivation, hunger serves as part of our biological maintenance and survival mechanisms (Rozin, 1996). And if eating were a behavior that had to be entirely learned, many people might starve to death before they mastered its complexities. Instead, when food is available and we are hungry, eating seems to come naturally. But biology isn't the whole story: hunger motivation and eating behavior have turned out to be far more complex than had originally been thought. So psychologists now incorporate the complexities of hunger and eating into a view we will call the *multiple systems approach.*

THE MULTIPLE-SYSTEMS APPROACH TO HUNGER   Your brain combines hunger-related information of many kinds: your body's energy requirements and nutritional state, your food preferences, food cues in your environment, and cultural demands. For example, your readiness to eat a slice of pizza depends on factors such as how long it has been since you last ate, whether you like pizza, what time of day it is (breakfast?), whether your friends are

 Connection

Chapter 4
Chapter 14
Individualism and collectivism also have an effect on moral development and on social attributions.

Need for achievement *(n Ach):* In Murray and McClelland's theory, a mental state that produces a psychological motive to excel or to reach some goal.

Individualism: The view, common in the Euro-American world, that places a high value on individual achievement and distinction.

Collectivism: The view, common in Asia, Africa, Latin America, and the Middle East, that values group loyalty and pride over individual distinction.

encouraging you to have a slice, and whether pizza is an acceptable food in your culture. Assembling all these data, the brain sends signals to neural, hormonal, organ, and muscle systems to start or stop food-seeking and eating. Here are the main biological factors involved (see also Figure 9.5):

▶ Receptors in the brain monitor sugar and fat levels in the blood, sending signals to the *lateral hypothalamus*. If the sugar level in your blood is low, for example, this brain structure sends out signals that produce the feeling of hunger (Nisbett, 1972).

▶ An internal biological "scale" continually weighs the body's fat stores and informs the central nervous system of the result. Whenever deposits stored in specialized fat cells fall below a certain level, or **set point,** signals triggers eating behavior (Keesey & Powley, 1975). Work with mice suggests that one cause of obesity may be the lack of certain proteins that signal when the set point has been reached. Mice lacking this protein continue to eat even when not hungry (Adler & Salzhauer, 1995; Gura, 2000; Woods et al., 1998).

Set point: Refers to the tendency of the body to maintain a certain level of body fat and body weight.

❘ FIGURE 9.5: Multiple-System Model of Hunger and Eating

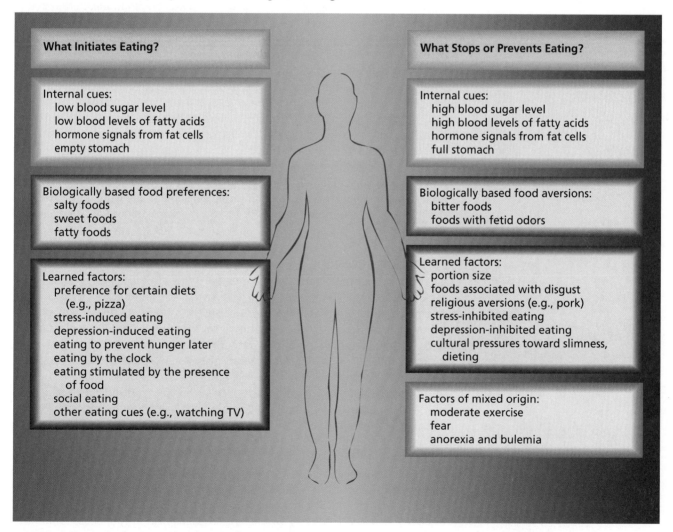

What Initiates Eating?

Internal cues:
  low blood sugar level
  low blood levels of fatty acids
  hormone signals from fat cells
  empty stomach

Biologically based food preferences:
  salty foods
  sweet foods
  fatty foods

Learned factors:
  preference for certain diets
    (e.g., pizza)
  stress-induced eating
  depression-induced eating
  eating to prevent hunger later
  eating by the clock
  eating stimulated by the presence
    of food
  social eating
  other eating cues (e.g., watching TV)

What Stops or Prevents Eating?

Internal cues:
  high blood sugar level
  high blood levels of fatty acids
  hormone signals from fat cells
  full stomach

Biologically based food aversions:
  bitter foods
  foods with fetid odors

Learned factors:
  portion size
  foods associated with disgust
  religious aversions (e.g., pork)
  stress-inhibited eating
  depression-inhibited eating
  cultural pressures toward slimness,
    dieting

Factors of mixed origin:
  moderate exercise
  fear
  anorexia and bulimia

- Pressure detectors in the stomach signal fullness or a feeling of emptiness. These messages are sent to the brain, where they combine with information about blood nutrients and the status of the body's fat cells.

- Other mechanisms give us preferences for sweet and high-fat foods. These preferences have a biological basis that evolved to steer our ancestors toward the calorie-dense foods that enabled them to survive when food supplies were unpredictable. This tendency has been exploited in modern times by the manufacturers of sweet and fatty snack foods.

- Physical activity also contributes to hunger and satiation. Extreme exercise provokes hunger, but studies show that moderate exercise actually suppresses appetite (Hill & Peters, 1998).

These hunger mechanisms usually work together to keep fat stores and body weight within a narrow range, specified by the biological set point. The set point doesn't always keep weight in a desirable range, however. According to the Centers for Disease Control, half of the U.S. population is overweight, and nearly a quarter is clinically obese (Taubes, 1998; Wickelgren, 1998).

In addition to the biological mechanisms we have been discussing, our emotional state can encourage or discourage eating. For example, both humans and animals refrain from eating when they are fearful. Stress and depression can affect appetite, too, although the effects are variable: Some people respond by eating more, and some by eating less.

Likewise, learning can influence hunger and eating. This can be seen in societies, such as the United States, where social norms promote thinness. Images of ultrathin fashion models can especially influence women and girls to believe they are "supposed" to look as if they do not eat much — a distorted ideal that has been linked to self-destructive eating disorders, such as anorexia nervosa and bulemia (Haller, 1992).

We also associate certain situations with eating, so we feel hungry regardless of our biological needs. This explains why you may feel hungry when you notice that the clock says it is lunch time. It also explains why you may feel a desire to snack when you watch TV or want a third helping at Thanksgiving dinner.

Connection

Chapter 12
Anorexia and bulimia are most common in Western cultures.

WEIGHT CONTROL   Among Americans, the problem of obesity has grown at an alarming rate since the early 1980s (Taubes, 1998; Wickelgren, 1998). Worse yet, people in most industrialized nations are following the American lead. Unfortunately, the causes of this obesity epidemic are not altogether clear. Most experts believe, however, that they include lack of exercise, poor diet (including an increasing amount of "junk food"), and genetic factors (Comuzzie & Allison, 1998; Gura, 1998; Hill & Peters, 1998; Levine et al., 1999; Ravussin & Danforth, 1999).

The problem is not caused by lack of concern. Americans, especially, seem obsessed by weight and weight loss, as a glance at the magazine headlines on the newsstand will show. At any given time, one-third of adult Americans say that they are on some sort of weight-control diet (Callaway, 1987; Gibbs, 1996; Jeffery, 1987).

Yet, despite all we know about hunger and weight control, no one has yet discovered a weight-loss scheme that really works. Notwithstanding nationally advertised claims, *no diet, surgical procedure, drug, or other weight-loss gimmick has ever produced long-term weight loss for a majority of the people who have tried it.* It is encouraging to know, however, that several potentially effective weight-control chemicals are being tested as you read this, although it will be several years before any come to market (Campfield et al., 1998). In the meantime, the experts suggest that the best pathway to long-term weight control involves maintaining a well-balanced diet and a program of moderate exercise.

Sexual Motivation

Our cultural lessons and life experiences influence the meaning of sex in our lives.

Sex is a most unusual drive. Unlike hunger or thirst, arousal of the sex drive is usually pleasurable. Even so, sexually aroused individuals typically seek to reduce the tension by sexual activity. And again unlike hunger and thirst, sex is not a homeostatic drive because it does not return the body to an equilibrium condition. Sexual motivation, however, can serve many other goals, including pleasure, reproduction, and social bonding.

In one respect, sexual motivation does have a kinship with hunger and thirst: It has its roots in survival. But even in this respect, sex is unique among biological drives because lack of sex poses no threat to the individual's survival. We can't live for long without food or water, but some people live their lives without sexual activity. Sexual motivation involves the survival of the *species,* not the individual.

All the biological drives—sex included—exert such powerful influences on behavior that they have led to numerous social constraints and taboos, such as prohibitions on eating certain meats or drinking alcohol. In the realm of sexuality, we find extensive culture-specific rules and sanctions involving a wide variety of sexual practices. In fact, all societies regulate sexual activity, but the restrictions vary widely. For example, homosexuality has been historically suppressed in American culture, but it is widely accepted in Polynesian cultures. Even the discussion of sex can become mired in taboo, misinformation, and embarrassment. Scientists who study human sexuality have felt intense social and political pressures, which show no signs of abating in the present. The result is that the scientific understanding of sexuality, which we examine below, has been hard won.

THE SCIENTIFIC STUDY OF SEXUALITY The first major scientific study of human sexuality was initiated by Alfred Kinsey and his colleagues (1948, 1953) in the mid-20th century, with interviews of some 17,000 Americans concerning their sexual behavior. To a generally shocked public these researchers revealed that many behaviors (oral sex, for example) previously considered rare, and even abnormal, were actually quite widespread—or at least reported to be. Kinsey's interviews continue to be an important source of information about human sexual behavior, as seen in the major survey of American sexual behavior entitled *The Social Organization of Sexuality: Sexual Practices in the United States* (Laumann et al., 1994) and in a smaller, more readable companion volume called *Sex in America* (Michael et al., 1994). (See Table 9.2.)

But it was sex researchers William Masters and Virginia Johnson (1966, 1970, 1979) who really broke with tradition and taboo by bringing sex into their laboratory. There they studied sex by directly observing and recording the physiological patterns of people engaging in sexual activity of various types, including masturbation and intercourse. By doing so, they discovered not what people *said* about sex (which carries obvious problems of response bias) but how people actually *reacted physically* during sex. In the wake of Masters and Johnson's daring departure from tradition, the study of human sexual behavior has become much more accepted as a legitimate field of scientific inquiry.

Based on their observations, Masters and Johnson described four phases of human sexual responding, which they collectively called the **sexual**

TABLE 9.2 — Sexual Preferences and Behaviors of Adult Americans*

FREQUENCY OF INTERCOURSE	NOT AT ALL	A FEW TIMES PER YEAR	A FEW TIMES PER MONTH	TWO OR MORE TIMES PER WEEK
Percentage by gender:				
Men	14	16	37	34
Women	10	18	36	37
Percentage by age:				
Men				
18–24	15	21	24	40
25–29	7	15	31	45
30–39	8	15	37	39
40–49	9	18	40	33
50–59	11	22	43	23
Women				
18–24	11	16	32	41
25–29	5	10	38	47
30–39	9	16	36	39
40–49	15	16	44	25
50–59	30	22	35	14

NUMBER OF SEXUAL PARTNERS SINCE AGE 18

	0	1	2–4	5-10	10–20	21+
Percentage of Men	3	20	21	23	16	17
Percentage of Women	3	31	31	20	6	3

INFIDELITY WHILE MARRIED		SEXUAL ORIENTATION	MALES	FEMALES
Men	15.1%	Heterosexual	96.9	98.6
Women	2.7%	Homosexual	2.0	.9
		Bisexual	.8	.5

*Adapted from Michael et al, 1994. Table based on survey of 3,432 scientifically selected adult respondents.

response cycle (see Figure 9.6). These are the distinguishing events of each phase:

▶ In the *excitement phase,* blood vessel changes in the pelvic region cause the clitoris to swell and the penis to become erect. Blood and other fluids also become congested in the testicles and vagina.

▶ During the *plateau phase,* a maximal level of arousal is reached. Rapid increases occur in heartbeat, respiration, blood pressure, glandular secretions, and muscle tension.

▶ When they reach the *orgasm phase,* males and females experience a very intense and pleasurable sense of release from the cumulative

Sexual response cycle: The four-stage sequence of arousal, plateau, orgasm, and resolution occurring in both men and women.

FIGURE 9.6: Phases of Human Sexual Response

The phases of sexual response in males and females have similar patterns. The primary differences are in the time it takes for males and females to reach each phase and in the greater likelihood that females will achieve multiple orgasms.

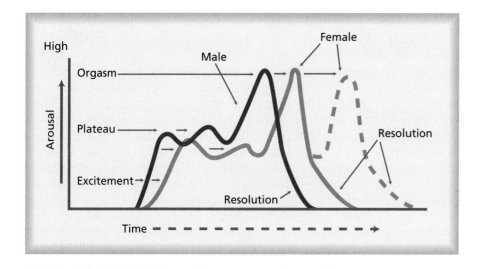

sexual tension. Orgasm, characterized by rhythmic genital contractions, culminates in ejaculation of semen in men and can involve clitoral and vaginal sensations in women.

▶ During the *resolution phase,* the body gradually returns to its preexcitement state, as fluids dissipate from the sex organs. At the same time, blood pressure and heart rate, which had increased dramatically, drop to their customary levels. Note how similar men's and women's physical responses are at each phase of the cycle.

Note that Masters and Johnson focused on physiological arousal and responses. They did not emphasize the psychological aspects of sexuality — for example, emotional responses, sexual desire, or the motivation to seek out a partner or make oneself available for sexual experience. Still, from their biological observations of subjects' sexual behavior, Masters and Johnson drew several significant conclusions:

▶ Men and women have remarkably similar patterns of biological response, regardless of the source of sexual arousal — whether it be intercourse or masturbation. This is clearly seen in the four phases of the sexual response cycle.

▶ Although the phases of the sexual response cycle are similar in the two sexes, women tend to respond more slowly but often remain aroused longer.

▶ Many women can have multiple orgasms in a short time period, while men rarely do.

▶ Size of the genitals or other physical sex characteristics (such as vagina, breasts, penis) is generally unrelated to any aspect of sexual performance (except, perhaps, attitude about one's sexual capability).

In addition, Masters and Johnson used their discoveries about sexual behavior to develop effective behavioral therapies for a variety of sexual disorders,

Connection

Chapter 13
Behavior therapy is effective for a variety of other problems, such as phobias and other anxiety disorders.

including male erectile disorder (inability to achieve or maintain an erection), premature ejaculation, and female orgasmic disorder.

While Masters and Johnson focused on the physiological side of sex, other researchers have studied the cognitive and social components. Much of this work has emphasized how our sexual lives are influenced by learning. We see this, for example, in responses to cues that provoke sexual arousal.

SEXUAL CUES   Human sexual motivation does not come primarily from the genitals. In fact, the brain is the major human sex organ. What turns you on is what your brain finds sexually arousing, and how you respond is determined both by your inherited sexual tendencies and by what your brain has learned. The sequence of sexual activities that may lead to orgasm can begin with a single unconditioned stimulus—usually touch—but may also involve a variety of conditioned stimuli. In the form of genital caresses, touch is a universal component of sexual foreplay (Ford & Beach, 1951). Virtually any stimulus that becomes associated with genital touch and orgasm can become a conditioned stimulus that motivates sexual activity—whether the stimulus is present physically or only in memory or fantasy.

Research shows that both stimuli (such as erotic pictures) and sexual fantasies during masturbation often determine what a person finds sexually stimulating (Storms, 1980, 1981). Inanimate objects, textures, sounds, visual images, odors—any tangible or imagined stimulus—can become the focus of arousal through this conditioned association. For reasons that are poorly understood, some people learn to become aroused only by conditioned stimuli, such as pain or the sight of undergarments (Rachman, 1966).

SEXUAL SCRIPTS   Generalized sexual arousal can be channeled into specific behaviors (such as kissing or masturbation) that depend on how the individual has learned to think about sexual matters. **Sexual scripts** are socially learned programs of sexual interpretation and responsiveness. How do you know how you are "supposed" to feel when aroused? What do you do when you feel that way? Your culture provides you with many clues from which you develop the sexual scripts for your own behavior. Images from movies and television suggest the importance of kissing and touching, and how to engage in these activities—or at least how beautiful actors and actresses (with many hours of "method" rehearsal) manage to engage in these displays. Advertisements, MTV, and conversations with friends also contribute to many young people's sexual scripts. Unfortunately, while these scripts suggest images and goals, they can provide unreliable and unrealistic information. We assemble aspects of these scripts through social interaction over a lifetime. The attitudes and values embodied in one's sexual scripts define one's general approach to sexuality.

When people have different scripts for an interaction, problems can develop. For example, touch can differ in meaning for men and women. Whether they are mates or coworkers, one person's comment or "friendly touch" may be perceived by the other as a "sexual advance." In fact, research supports the idea that men and women frequently perceive sexually related behaviors differently (U.S. Merit Systems Protection Board, 1995).

AN EVOLUTIONARY PERSPECTIVE ON SEXUALITY   While the theory of sexual scripts says that sexual behavior patterns can be learned, the evolutionary perspective looks for the origins of sexual motivation in our genes. Some observers (Archer, 1996; Buss, 1999, 2001; Buss & Schmitt, 1993) argue that genetic pressures have resulted in different mating strategies and, therefore, different gender roles, for males and females. (These views are a matter of

Connection

Chapter 6
Classical conditioning involves learning to give an old response to a new (conditioned) stimulus.

Sexual scripts: Socially learned ways of responding in sexual situations.

emphasis: All theorists recognize that both learning and genetics affect our sexual behaviors.)

Biologically speaking, the goal of both sexes is to leave as many offspring as possible. Yet, the potential physical costs of mating differ for males and females (Bjorklund & Shackelford, 1999). As a result, the sexes have evolved different—and sometimes conflicting—mating strategies. Because females can produce only a few children over a lifetime and because they make a huge biological investment in pregnancy and a substantial commitment of time and energy in child-rearing, the best sexual strategy for females involves caution in mate selection. For males, however, the costs and benefits are much different because they cannot become pregnant. For males, the theory says, the biggest payoff results from copulating as often as possible with mates who are in prime breeding condition. As a result, men tend to seek young and physically well-developed partners, while females may see somewhat older mates who can offer resources, status, and protection for offspring. Not incidentally, these agendas often produce conflict, promiscuity, and sexual jealousy.

Although the evolutionary perspective may seem cold and harsh in its view of sexual motivation, it does account for many gender differences in mating behaviors, such as the larger number of sexual partners typically reported by men than women. Even so, biology does not prohibit the learning of alternative sex roles and scripts, nor does it explain the social pressures that cast men and women in different roles (Eagly & Wood, 1999). A complete understanding of sexual motivation must include both its evolutionary roots and, especially in humans, the many variations that occur through learning.

Connection

Chapter 1
Evolutionary theory says that adaptive traits will spread through the population by natural selection.

Sexual orientation: One's erotic attraction toward members of the same sex (a homosexual orientation), the opposite sex (heterosexual orientation), or both sexes (a bisexual orientation).

Psychology

In Your Life

The Origins of Sexual Orientation

Hetero-sexuality and homo-sexuality represent two forms of **sexual orientation,** which refers to the direction or object of one's sexual interests. Ever since Alfred Kinsey's first reports, we have known that human sexual orientation is a complex issue. To complicate matters, cross-cultural studies reveal considerable variability in sexual customs. In parts of New Guinea, for example, homosexuality is nearly universal among young males (Money, 1987). Among Americans, estimates put the figure between about 1 and 10 percent—depending on whether homosexuality is defined as one's primary orientation or as any same-sex erotic behavior during one's lifetime (see Table 9.2).

What does the available evidence tell us about the origins of sexual orientation? The notion that parenting styles or family configurations cause children to turn toward heterosexuality or homosexuality has *not* found strong research support (see Bailey et al., 1995; Bell et al., 1981, Golombok & Tasker, 1996; Isay, 1990). Similarly, researchers have come up empty handed in their attempts to link human sexual orientation to early sexual experiences. A controversial theory proposed by Daryl Bem, however, asserts that we become attracted to the sex that we, as young children, consider most unlike us. Bem has amassed considerable evidence in support of this "exotic becomes erotic" theory (Bem, 1996, 2001). (For an oppos-

The origins of sexual orientation are unclear, although some evidence points to biological factors. What is clear is that research on sexual orientation often generates controversy.

ing viewpoint, however, see Peplau et al. [1998], who dispute Bem's

(continued)

interpretation of the evidence and argue that his theory does not take women's experiences into account.)

At the same time, attempts to identify biological origins of sexual feelings in the genes and the brain have also shown promise. For example, Richard Pillard and Michael Bailey (1991) studied sexual orientation of male identical twins. They discovered that when one twin is homosexual the chances of the other being homosexual is about 50% — as compared with an incidence of roughly 5 or 6% in the general population. This study also found that the rate drops to 22% for fraternal twins and 11% for adoptive brothers of homosexuals. Encouraged by these results, the researchers later studied female twin pairs — with essentially the same results (Bower, 1992).

Looking through a different biological window on sexual orientation, neurobiologist Simon LeVay (1991; LeVay & Hamer, 1995) found that a part of the hypothalamus in the brains of homosexual men was smaller than the same structure in heterosexual men. Critics of LeVay's research warn of confounding due to the fact that most of his homosexual subjects were AIDS victims and that the disease may have affected the structure under study.

Research in this area remains controversial because of the strong feelings, political issues, and prejudices involved (Herek, 2000) Further, it has attracted scientific criticism because it is correlational — rather than experimental — so the data cannot establish cause and effect with certainty. Also, some observers question whether gay men and lesbians should have to justify their behavior by seeking a biological root for it (Byne, 1995). On one small biological point all agree: Sexual orientation is *not* due to variations in levels of testosterone in adults (Meyer-Bahlburg, 1977, 1979).

In general, psychological research has given us a deeper understanding of sexual orientation. While we currently know much about what does *not* influence sexual orientation, we can see that, with human sexuality in general, sexual orientation grows developmentally out of multiple influences in biology, conditioning, and culture.

CHECK YOUR UNDERSTANDING

1. **RECALL:** *Which of the following is often considered a biological drive?*
   a. hunger
   b. safety
   c. *n Ach*
   d. fear

2. **RECALL:** *How did Murray and McClelland measure n Ach?*
   a. with a polygraph
   b. with the Thematic Apperception Test
   c. by measuring achievement-related hormones in the blood
   d. by using grade-point averages (GPAs)

3. **RECALL:** *According to Masters and Johnson's research, the sexual response cycles of men and women are essentially the same, except for:*
   a. women's ability for multiple orgasms.
   b. men's sexual receptivity at any time of the month.
   c. men's responsiveness to many kinds of stimulation.
   d. women's need for commitment in a sexual relationship.

4. **ANALYSIS:** *Which of the following motives would most likely be influenced by living in an individualistic culture versus a collectivist culture?*
   a. hunger
   b. thirst
   c. sex
   d. *n Ach*

5. **UNDERSTANDING THE CORE CONCEPT:**
   In which of the following would biological factors be least important in accounting for the motivational differences between individuals?
   a. hunger
   b. thirst
   c. sex
   d. *n Ach*

ANSWERS: 1. a   2. b   3. a   4. d   5. d

Core Concept

Flow: In Csikszentmihalyi's theory, an intense focus on an activity, accompanied by increased creativity and near-ecstatic feelings. Flow involves intrinsic motivation.

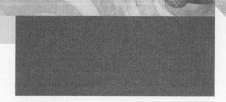

Using Psychology to Learn Psychology: Motivating Yourself

The world's greatest achievements in music, art, science, business, and countless other pursuits often stem from the intrinsic motivation of people pursuing ideas in which they are deeply interested. You achieve this state of mind when focusing intently on some problem or activity that makes you lose track of time and become oblivious to events around you. Psychologist Mihaly Csikszentmihalyi calls this **flow** (1990, 1998).

Although some people turn to drugs or alcohol to experience an artificial flow feeling, meaningful work produces more satisfying and more sustained flow experiences. In fact, one type of flow experience identified by Csikszentmihalyi (1990) is very similar to the goal of *n Ach* as identified by McClelland (1987b), namely the pleasure of mastering a challenging task.

What is the link with studying and learning? If you find yourself lacking in motivation to learn the material for some class, the extrinsic promise of grades may not be enough to prod you to study. You may, however, be able to trick yourself into developing intrinsic motivation and "flow" by posing this question: What do people who are specialists in this field find interesting? Among other things, the experts are fascinated by an unsolved mystery, a theoretical dispute, or the possibility of an exciting practical application. A psychologist, for example, might wonder: What motivates violent behavior? Or, how can we increase people's motivation to achieve? Once you find such an issue, try to find out what solutions have been proposed. In this way, you will share the mind set of those who are leaders in the field. And— who knows?— perhaps you will become fascinated with the field, too.

Chapter Summary

WHAT DO OUR EMOTIONS DO FOR US?

Emotion and motivation are complementary processes that arouse the organism and direct its behavior. Emotions are normally adaptive, but if too intense or prolonged they may be destructive. From an evolutionary standpoint, the function of motives and emotions is to help organisms make responses that promote their survival and reproduction. Socially, emotional expressions serve to communicate feelings and intentions. Research shows that certain basic facial expressions are understood across cultures.

Emotions have evolved to help us respond to important situations and to convey our intentions to others.

WHERE DO OUR EMOTIONS COME FROM?

Neuroscience has revealed two distinct emotion systems in the brain. One operates mainly at an unconscious level and relies on deep limbic structures, especially the amygdala; the other involves conscious processing in the cortex. Emotions also involve visceral changes in response to messages transmitted by the autonomic nervous system and the hormone system. Understanding how the two emotion systems work has begun to resolve some controversies involving the roles of physical responses and cognition in emotion. Research also shows that culture has a role, accounting for some gender differences observed in emotional displays.

Core Concept

Emotions result from an interaction of biological, mental, behavioral, and social/cultural processes.

Key Question

HOW MUCH CONTROL DO WE HAVE OVER OUR EMOTIONS?

Emotional intelligence, the ability to keep one's emotions from getting out of control, is vital for maintaining good social relationships. It is distinct from the characteristics measured by traditional IQ tests. Emotional control can be achieved by learning, which has been demonstrated in anger management programs.

People can also control their emotions to deceive, and no sure method of detecting such deception exists, even though the use of "lie detectors" is widespread. The polygraph industry is built on the dubious premise that people who are lying will show certain signs of emotional arousal, although no verified and accepted standards exist for such examinations.

Core Concept

Although emotional responses are not always consciously regulated, we can learn to control them.

Key Question

MOTIVATION: WHAT MAKES US ACT AS WE DO?

The concept of motivation refers to unobservable internal processes that guide behavior. Psychologists often distinguish psychological motives from biological drives, intrinsic motivation from extrinsic motivation, and conscious motivation from unconscious motivation.

Theorists have explained motivation in terms of instincts, drives, and cognitive states, such as perceived locus of control. Maslow's theory attempted to tie together the whole range of human motivation—from biological drives to psychological motives—into a hierarchy of needs. Many exceptions to his theory have been pointed out.

Extrinsic rewards are widely used as motivators. Research has shown, however, that extrinsic rewards can dampen intrinsic motivation, when rewards are given without regard for the quality of performance.

Core Concept

Motivation takes many forms, but all involve inferred mental processes that select and direct our behavior.

Key Question

HOW ARE ACHIEVEMENT, HUNGER, AND SEX ALIKE? DIFFERENT?

Some motives rely heavily on learning, while others depend more heavily on biological factors. Moreover, motives differ in their sensitivity to environmental cues, reinforcers, and social/cultural influences. No comprehensive theory of motivation takes all these factors into account, although an evolutionary perspective suggests that each distinct motive evolved independently, in response to environmental pressures.

Achievement is a psychological motive that accounts for an important segment of human behavior, both in school and on the job. Individuals and societies vary in the intensity of their need for achievement. In contrast, hunger and eating are motivated at many levels—by biological processes, external cues, social influences, and learning. Many Americans seek to control their appetite and body weight, although no weight-loss scheme is effective for most people over the long run. Unlike hunger and weight control, the sex drive is not homeostatic, even though sexual motivation is heavily influenced by biology. Sexual behavior in humans also depends on learning—of various sexual scripts. Most evidence suggests, however, that sexual orientation also has its origins in biology, as well as learning.

Core Concept

No single theory accounts for all forms of motivation, because each motive involves its own mix of biological, mental, behavioral, and social/cultural influences.

Review Test

For each of the following items, choose the single best answer. The answer key appears at the end.

1. While emotion emphasizes _____, motivation emphasizes _____.
   a. behavior/cognition
   b. arousal/action
   c. neural activity/hormones
   d. needs/drives

2. According to the evolutionary perspective, emotions
   a. help organisms survive in important, recurring situations.
   b. add color and interest to our otherwise drab lives.
   c. give us strong feelings about our experiences.
   d. occur in humans, but not in "lower" animals.

3. Which of the following is a brain structure involved in emotions, attack, self-defense, and flight?
   a. the occipital cortex
   b. the limbic system
   c. the endocrine system
   d. the cerebellum

4. Which theory of emotion first called attention to the idea that our physical responses can influence our emotions?
   a. the instinct theory
   b. Maslow's theory
   c. Ekman's theory
   d. the James-Lange theory

5. Psychologists use the concept of motivation for five basic purposes. Which of the following is *not* one of them?
   a. to relate behavior to internal biological mechanisms
   b. to infer internal states from observable behavior
   c. to explain perseverance despite adversity
   d. to make people work harder

6. Which approach is most compatible with the concept of *homeostasis?*
   a. instinct theory
   b. drive theory
   c. locus-of-control theory
   d. Maslow's humanistic theory

7. Which one of the following is an example of *intrinsic* motivation?
   a. studying because there is a test tomorrow
   b. studying because your friend asked you to study with her
   c. studying because you want to get good grades
   d. studying because you find the subject interesting

8. Unlike achievement motivation, hunger and sex have a strong _____ basis.
   a. cognitive
   b. environmental
   c. biological
   d. perceptual

9. Sexual motivation is different from the other basic drives because it
   a. is not a homeostatic drive.
   b. is more intense.
   c. has no biological basis.
   d. is the only drive for which satisfaction of the drive can be pleasurable.

10. People who are high in the need for achievement have been found to be more likely to
   a. demand immediate gratification for their desires.
   b. persist in monotonous tasks.
   c. have excellent interpersonal skills.
   d. get better grades in school.

ANSWERS: 1. b   2. a   3. b   4. d   5. d   6. b
7. d   8. c   9. a   10. d

If You're Interested . . .

BOOKS

Abramson, E. (1998). *Emotional eating: What you need to know before starting another diet.* Jossey-Bass. This book provides a good introduction to the basic mechanisms of eating disorders such as anorexia, bulimia and the compulsive eating that can lead to obesity — and the personal, emotional underpinnings of "hungering" for control, perfection, or love.

Ackerman, D. (1994). *A natural history of love.* Random House. Poet Ackerman tours of the history of love, ancient and modern ideas of romance, the behavioral impact of love, and love's many shapes and experiences.

Barer-Stein, T. (1999). *You eat what you are: People, culture, and food traditions.* Culture Concepts. The author explores how our culture determines not only what we eat but what we want to eat, how we hunger, and the role of food in our individual lives.

Csikszentmihalyi, M. (1998). *Finding flow: The psychology of engagement with everyday life. (Masterminds Series).* Basic Books. This easy-to-read book guides the reader to becoming engaged in living here and now, overcoming boredom and preventing frustration, and enjoying work as well as play.

Evans, D. (2001). *Emotion: The science of sentiment.* Oxford University Press. A philosopher explores the role of feelings in life and in our lives, including discussions of complex states such as love and happiness, and whether nonemotional intellect is superior — or disabled.

Goleman, D. (1995). *Emotional intelligence.* Bantam Books. A behavioral science reporter documents the many forms and expressions of human feeling, including the range of emotions, self-control, temperament, family and intimacy, and whether emotional intelligence can be learned.

Jamison, K. R. (1999). *On moods.* Random House. The doctor-author who revolutionized writing about manic-depressive illness (bipolar disorder) in her book *An Unquiet Mind* now explores the range and power of lasting emotions and moods in general.

Masson, J. M. (1995). *When elephants weep: The emotional lives of animals.* Delacorte Press. A casebook of evidence and arguments demonstrates the broad range and complexity of the emotions of nonhuman species, ranging from anger, grief, and vengeance to joy, playfulness, compassion, and love.

Provine, R. R. (2000). *Laughter: A scientific investigation.* Viking Press. From the animal origins of laughter to considerations of public laughter, laugh "measurement," and impacts on health, the author takes an unprecedented serious look at our reactions to humor and surprise.

Tuan, Y.-F. (1998). *Escapism.* Johns Hopkins University Press. "A human being," writes the author, "is an animal who is congenitally indisposed to accept reality as it is." When we cannot accept reality, we seek to escape, setting in motion a range of behaviors, from appreciating nature to irrational wishful thinking.

VIDEOS

Emotional Intelligence with Daniel Goleman. (1998). (color, PBS Home Video). Featuring writer Daniel Goleman. Vignettes and interviews show how real people experience and express emotions, how emotional skills affect work, and how animal behavior teaches us about human feelings.

The Fight Club. (1999, color, 139 min.) Directed by David Fincher; starring Edward Norton, Brad Pitt, Meat Loaf. An unusual new acquaintance introduces a disillusioned young man to a new way of life — through fighting. Does manhood (or personhood) depend on a willingness to harm and be harmed? The unusual story, with a surprising psychological twist, made for a surprisingly popular film.

Shallow Hal. (2001, color, 113). Directed by Bobby Farrelly and Peter Farrelly; starring Gwyneth Paltrow, Jack Black. A superficial man falls in love with a 300-pound woman (played by the slim Paltrow in a "fat suit") when he learns to see and appreciate her "inner beauty." Silly situations and neurotic characters are mingled with a consideration of whether looks inevitably matter in sexual attraction.

WEB RESOURCES

http://www.nimh.nih.gov/publicat/baschap1.cfm   This Web site, from the National Institute of Mental Health, provides a thorough introduction of the field of emotion and motivation. Read about the research being done in this field on these subjects.

http://eqi.org/ The information on this site is divided into two groups: academic information on emotions and practical information on emotional intelligence. This site also includes a discussion on personal growth and addresses the escalation of fear and violence around the world.

http://www.top-education.com/Management/motivationtheories1.asp This site offers a multitude of information on several theories of motivation.

Think about how these theories could be applied to a corporate environment versus an academic setting.

http://www.apa.org/pubinfo/anger.html From the American Psychological Association, this Web site offers information on anger. This emotional state varies from mild irritation to rage, and the site offers information on the various stages of anger.

KEY QUESTION CHAPTER OUTLINE	CORE CONCEPT	PSYCHOLOGY IN YOUR LIFE

IS IT THE STRESS OR THE STRESSOR?

Stressors Ancient and Modern

The effects of stress (an internal response) depend more on the intensity and duration of stress than on its source (the stressor).

CHANGE CAN BE HAZARDOUS TO YOUR HEALTH:
Some changes count more than others, but they all count.

HOW DOES STRESS AFFECT US PHYSICALLY?

Biological and Behavioral Responses to Stress

Stress can help us meet challenges and grow stronger, but too much stress — distress — can have harmful physical consequences.

WHEN STRESS IS GOOD FOR YOU:
When stress is mild and brief it can become *eustress,* which has beneficial effects.

HOW DO WE RESPOND PSYCHOLOGICALLY TO STRESS?

Personality and Stress
Learned Helplessness
Diminished Hedonic Capacity
The Stockholm Syndrome
Posttraumatic Stress Disorder

Our psychological responses under stress depend on personality, perceptions, and the ways we have learned to respond.

EGO DEFENSES UNDER STRESS:
Freud called our attention to some common reactions seen in people under stress.

WHAT STRATEGIES CAN PROMOTE HEALTH — RATHER THAN DISTRESS?

Psychological Resources for Coping with Stress
Biophysical Resources for Coping with Stress
Health Psychology and Behavioral Medicine
Prevention: The Example of Heart Disease

All the factors that promote health and well-being will also combat distress — and they are largely under our control.

HAPPINESS AND WELL-BEING:
As far as happiness is concerned, some things are more important than money.

27%   4%   2%

USING PSYCHOLOGY TO LEARN PSYCHOLOGY: Coping with Test Anxiety

STRESS, HEALTH, AND WELL-BEING

any astonishing stories came out of the September 11th attacks on New York and Washington, DC. One of them concerns Genelle Guzman, who was working on the 64th floor of the World Trade Center's Tower 1 when the airplane slammed into the building a few floors above (Cloud, 2001).

Just after the impact, Genelle called her boyfriend, Roger McMillan, to tell him that she would remain at her desk, following instructions that had come over a loudspeaker in the building. McMillan, who could see the horror unfolding from his workplace 20 blocks away, told her to get out and meet him in front of a nearby clothing store.

When he arrived at the rendezvous point, McMillan's heart sank as he gazed on nothing but rubble. A check of his voice mail retrieved a message from Guzman, stating that she had decided to stay at her desk, as directed.

He had no way of knowing that Genelle was still alive somewhere in the mountain of broken concrete and twisted steel. When the word came to evacuate, she had started down the stairs and gotten as far as the 13th floor. Then the building collapsed. There her head was caught between two pillars, where she lay for hours next to a man who died as she listened helplessly to his cries.

Genelle Guzman was among the few lucky victims of the World Trade Center

(continued)

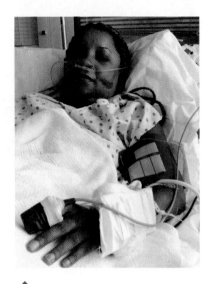

attack. Eventually, a rescuer opened the small cavity in which Genelle was trapped, making her one of only five victims pulled alive from the remains of the World Trade Center. Physically, the trauma was relatively minor: She emerged with a swollen head and legs that required surgery. Psychologically, she had experienced stress in the extreme.

She, of course, feels lucky to be alive and speaks of a renewed spiritual commitment. A psychologist would be concerned, however, that the events of September 11th could leave lasting emotional scars. Although it is too soon to know, we can be confident that the psychological outcome for Genelle Guzman will depend on many factors that we will discuss in this chapter relating to stress, distress, health, and disease.

▲

Roger McMillan was certain that his girlfriend, Genelle Guzman, had been killed in the attack on the World Trade Center. She was one of five persons found alive in the rubble.

Connection ←

Chapter 9
Emotions are normally adaptive responses.

The emotional arousal we call stress usually works to our advantage. It brings threatening events into focus and readies us to respond. Yet, extreme or prolonged emotional arousal carries a threat to our health. Too much arousal can turn our defenses against us in a destructive form of the stress response — often called *distress*. The result can be high blood pressure, a stroke, a heart attack, or any of many life-threatening physical conditions. We see these consequences, for example, among workers in the pressure-cooker environment of corporate offices and air traffic control towers. And we also see among such workers the psychological consequences when stress leads to mental confusion, chronic anxiety, or depression.

But have you ever wondered why some people roll easily through stressful events, while others are derailed by even minor hassles? Stuck in an endless traffic jam, some drivers calmly daydream or listen to their radios; others frantically hit their horns or crane their necks for a better view of the obstruction. The stressful effects of an unpleasant event are, to a large extent, a personal matter. How much stress we experience is determined not only by the quality and intensity of the stressful situation but by how we interpret it, the resources we have available to deal with it, and the consequent difficulty of meeting the demands placed on us. Figure 10.1 shows an overview of the whole stress process — stressors, stress, cognitive appraisal (mental evaluation of the situation), resources, and stress responses.

IS IT THE STRESS OR THE STRESSOR?

What images come to mind when you hear the word *stress?* Most people think of the pressures in their lives: difficult jobs, unhappy relationships, financial woes, health problems, and final exams. You may have some visceral associations with stress, too: a churning stomach, perspiration, headache, or high blood pressure. And, as we have noted, stress is also linked with physical illness. In fact, stress is associated with many aspects of modern society, and it is also associated with our internal reactions. This is what makes stress a slippery concept.

We use the word *stress* loosely in everyday conversation (Lazarus et al.,1985). In common usage, *stress* refers to a *situation*. For example, if your employer or professor has been giving you a difficult time, you may say that you are "under stress," as though you were being squashed by a heavy object. In this sense, stress means an external threat or pressure, an unpleasant event.

Psychologists, however, use the term in a more specific way: For them, stress is a *response*. They see **stress** as the physical and mental changes that occur in response to a challenging or threatening situation (Krantz et al., 1985). This is not hair-splitting: It is useful to make a distinction between stressful stimuli or situations, which we call **stressors,** and the response to those stimuli, which we call *stress* or a *stress response*. So, a *stressor* is the large, angry man climbing out of the car you just bashed into; *stress* is your response to that large, angry man: the knot in your stomach, your racing heart, and the cold sweat on your palms. A *stressor* is your demanding boss; *stress* is your headache.

In this section of the chapter we will look at the stressors that have drawn the most attention of psychologists. These include everything from petty hassles to natural disasters. The Core Concept for this section emphasizes the connection among the many conditions that can produce stress:

> **The effects of stress (an internal response) depend more on the intensity and duration of stress than on its source (the stressor).**

In the following pages, we will see that the problem is not stress, but *excessive* stress and the ways we deal with it. Basic stress is an unavoidable part of living. Every organism faces challenges from its external environment and from its personal needs; these are the challenges that organisms must solve to survive and thrive.

Stressors Ancient and Modern

Early humans survived mortal dangers by responding quickly and decisively to potentially lethal attacks by predators or hostile tribes, and some of the ways we respond to stressors in modern times are the result of their evolutionary legacy. Modern life, of course, adds some new dangers: demanding jobs, financial worries, and computer crashes. Most recently we have faced the stressors of international terrorism. Yet, while we are exposed to new stressors, our stress response reflects the body's millennia-old ability to become quickly aroused to meet emergencies. So, when the power company threatens to cut off your power or your boss criticizes your work, your muscles may tighten, your hormones may surge, and you may feel an urge to flee or fight. Unfortunately, these old remedies don't work as well with the new problems.

Some of the problems of our ancestors, however, are still with us — including war, famine, flood, fire, earthquake, and hurricane, to name a few. We will begin our survey of the human stress response by grouping these ancient and devastating maladies under the heading of *catastrophe*. But we will see that certain distinctive behavior patterns emerge under all sources of stress.

CATASTROPHE   Stress in the extreme can accompany catastrophic events. Anyone caught in a war, hurricane, fire, flood, or earthquake may suddenly lose loved ones and a lifetime of possessions. What is not always obvious, however, is that our response to a catastrophic experience can also have a devastating effect on our physical and mental health.

Psychologists have learned much about stress from people who have undergone catastrophic losses and traumas (Baum,

Stress: A physical and mental response to a challenging or threatening situation.

Stressors: Stressful stimuli or situations.

Traffic can be a hassle — and a significant source of stress for some people.

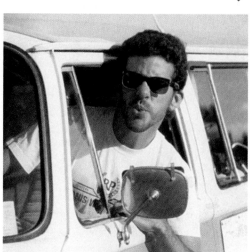

FIGURE 10.1: A Model of Stress

Cognitive appraisal of the stress situation interacts with the stressor and the physical, social, and personal resources available for dealing with the stressor. Individuals respond to threats on various levels—physical, behavioral, emotional, and cognitive. Some responses are adaptive, and others are maladaptive or even lethal.

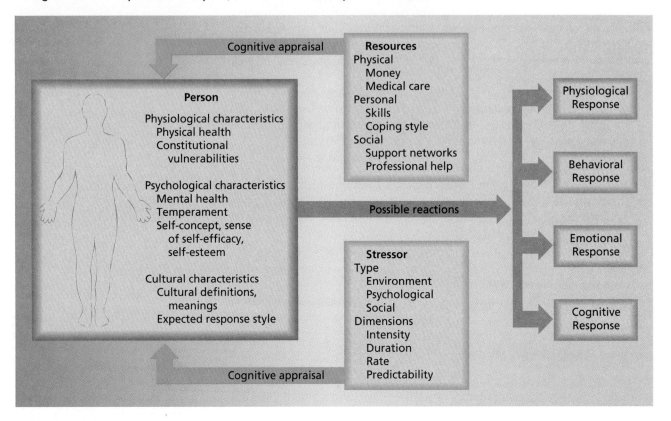

1990). One such opportunity to understand how people respond to extreme ordeals presented itself just as the 1989 World Series was about to begin at San Francisco's Candlestick Park. As spectators settled into their seats, the entire stadium started to shake violently, the lights went out, and the scoreboard turned black. Sixty thousand fans fell silent. They had just experienced a major earthquake. Elsewhere in the city, fires erupted, a bridge collapsed, highways were crushed—and people were dying.

One week after the quake, a team of research psychologists began interviewing approximately 800 people chosen randomly from the San Francisco area and from several comparison cities some distance away. Subjects completed a ten-minute phone survey about their thoughts, social behavior, and health. For the next year, these same subjects were interviewed again every few weeks.

These surveys revealed a pattern: The lives of people who had been through the quake revolved around the disaster for about a month. After this period, the obsessive thoughts about the quake rather abruptly moved out of the center of consciousness. At about the same time, people reported an increase in other stress-related symptoms, such as earthquake dreams and troubled relationships. Most of these symptoms diminished during the ensuing one or two months, although as many as 20% of San Francisco area residents remained distressed about the quake a year later (Pennebaker & Harber, 1991).

Catastrophic events, like the terrorist attack on the World Trade Center, are particularly stressful because they are life threatening, out of our control, and difficult to explain.

In general, researchers have found that the psychological responses to disasters, such as the San Francisco quake, tend to occur in five stages (see Cohen & Ahearn, 1980):

▶ First, there comes a period of shock, confusion, and even *psychic numbness,* during which people cannot fully comprehend what has happened. This period may last only a few moments, or it can linger several days.

▶ In the next phase, people engage in *automatic action.* They respond to the disaster with little awareness of their actions and later show poor recall of these experiences. However, the numbness of the first stage may, under some conditions, linger and paralyze victims into dangerous inaction. For example, when an earthquake shattered the city of Kobe, Japan, in January 1995, the citizens' shock and lack of preparedness prevented timely rescues. This delay in automatic action was later blamed for many of the almost 6,000 related deaths.

▶ In the third stage, people often have a sense of great accomplishment and *communal effort.* Also in this phase, they may feel weary and are aware that they are using up their reserves of energy. This phase builds on automatic action, but without conscious planning and collaboration people may lose hope and take no initiative in rebuilding their lives.

▶ During the fourth phase, people often experience a *letdown;* their energy is depleted, and they finally comprehend and feel the impact of the tragedy emotionally. For example, in recent years victims of hurricane damage have felt frustrated and abandoned when, weeks after the natural disasters occurred, the rest of the country appeared to forget their continuing state of emergency.

▶ An extended final period of *recovery* follows, as people adapt to the changes brought about by the disaster. A flood may leave a small town so changed that some businesses are permanently shut down, while others move in and change the appearance and social activity of the postflood community.

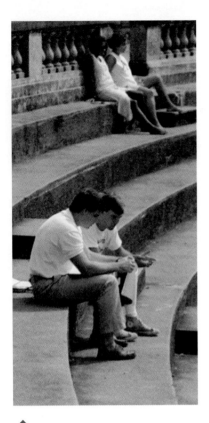

Confiding in others is helpful in working through feelings generated by trauma and loss.

In the wake of catastrophic experiences, we formulate accounts, or stories, that explain what happened and what it means. These accounts are an important part of efforts to explain ourselves to each other. Forming and transmitting such accounts may even reflect a more general human need to tell our stories and be understood by those close to us (Harvey, 1996; Harvey et al., 1990). We especially like to tell of surprising and/or unpleasant experiences (Holtzworth-Munroe & Jacobson, 1985). An important part of working through the pain of loss is formulating an account and confiding it to others (Weber & Harvey, 1994b).

The stress response under catastrophic conditions has a physical side, as well. This was reflected in the health records of people living in Othello, Washington, which was covered by a blanket of gray volcanic ash during the eruption of Mount Saint Helens in 1980. During the six months just after the eruption, these people had a nearly 200% increase in stress-related disorders. The death rate for the period also jumped by 19% (Adams & Adams, 1984). In general, people who undergo any sort of trauma become more susceptible to physical illness. We will look more closely at the physical basis for this response to stress in the second section of this chapter. Significantly, however, research shows that those who discuss the experience in detail with others suffer fewer health problems (Pennebaker, 1990; Pennebaker & Harber, 1993; Pennebaker et al., 1989).

SOCIETAL STRESSORS   Much of our stress comes not from sudden catastrophic events but from **societal stressors,** which are pressures in our social, cultural, and economic environment. These societal stressors often involve chronic home-, work-, or school-related difficulties. For example, a study of unemployed men revealed more depression, anxiety, and worries about health than in men who are employed. These symptoms usually disappeared, however, when the unemployed individuals found work (Liem & Rayman, 1982). Prejudice and discrimination, too, can be significant sources of stress (Contrada et al., 2000). For example, high blood pressure among African Americans—long thought to be primarily genetic—is correlated with the chronic stress caused by menial jobs, limited education, and low socioeconomic status (Klag et al., 1991).

The times and circumstances into which we are born may also deal us a hand of particularly difficult cards. Imagine, for example, the stress experienced by those involved in the attacks on the World Trade Center and the Pentagon. At this writing, it is too soon to know the long-term effects of these events on the survivors.

BURNOUT   The greatest source of chronic stress for many people involves the pressures of work. Continually stressful work can lead to **burnout,** a syndrome of emotional exhaustion, depersonalization, and reduced personal accomplishment, says Christina Maslach (1998), a leading researcher on this widespread problem. It was first recognized in workers from professions that demand high-intensity interpersonal contact with patients, clients, or the public, but we now know that burnout can occur anywhere—even among college students. In the health-care field, practitioners experiencing job burnout treat patients in detached and even dehumanized ways. The effect then feeds on itself, when these practitioners begin to feel bad about themselves and worry that they are failures. Regardless of the field, burnout is correlated with greater absenteeism and job turnover, impaired job performance, poor relations with

Societal stressors: Stressful conditions arising from our social and cultural environment.

Burnout: A syndrome of emotional exhaustion, depersonalization, and reduced personal accomplishment — often related to work.

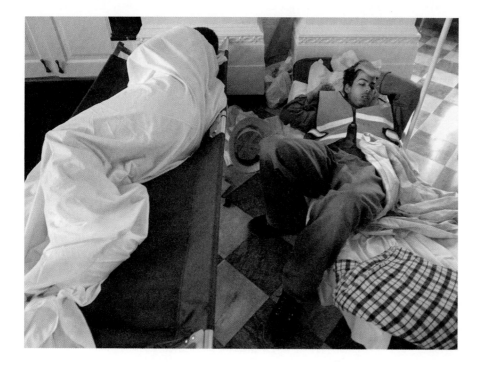

coworkers, family problems, and poor personal health (Leiter & Maslach, 1988; Maslach, 1982; Maslach & Leiter, 1997; Schaufeli et al., 1993).

Burnout can arise from a variety of conditions, including long working hours, high workloads, abusive managers or coworkers, and concerns about losing one's job. The extent of the problem can be seen in surveys showing that nearly three-quarters of all employees identify the worst aspect of their job as their immediate supervisor (Hogan et al., 1994). One's personal life and relationships can also create burnout, so that friends, spouse, and children are seen as unreasonably demanding and draining of one's dwindling energy. Burned-out spouses find their marriages unsatisfactory, and burned-out parents find no joy in their children.

Every job, of course, has its stressors, so an employee's attitudes and **coping strategies** (ways of dealing with stressful situations) can make a big difference in how job stressors affect the individual. We will focus on these coping strategies — healthy and unhealthy — in the last two sections of the chapter. We should emphasize, however, that the employee should not assume that burnout is a sign of personal weakness. Instead, it may signify a weakness in the organization (Leiter & Maslach, 2000; Maslach & Leiter, 1997). In an era of stiff competition and corporate "downsizing," employers may be reluctant to deal with obvious sources of stress and burnout, such as poor management and the threat of losing one's job. Often companies will use Band-Aid measures, such as providing stress-management workshops, rather than addressing the situations that cause the job stress. What this does, in effect, is to shift the blame for burnout from the company to the employees. Some employees may accept this shifted responsibility by assuming that it is, somehow, their own shortcoming for not being able to cope more effectively with job-related stress.

HASSLES   It was a long day at work, and on the way home you stop at the grocery store, where they are out of the very thing you went there to buy.

Coping strategies: Ways of dealing with stressful situations.

TABLE 10.1

Severity of Hassles as Perceived and Ranked by Four Groups

In these New Zealand samples, each group displayed its own pattern when ranking the severity of hassles. In the student group and the elderly group the rankings was almost opposite. For students time pressures were most important, while neighborhood and health pressures were the most important sources of hassles for the elderly. Note also the hassle rankings for mothers in this sample, who had one or more young children at home and no household help.

HASSLE TYPE	STUDENTS (N = 561)	MOTHERS (N = 94)	COMMUNITY (N = 20)	ELDERLY (N = 50)
Time pressure	1*	2	3	4
Future security	2	4	1	3
Finances	3	1	2	4
Household	3	1	2	4
Neighborhood	4	3	2	1
Health	4	3	2	1

*A ranking of 1 means that this item was seen as the most severe hassle by this group.

You get to the checkout with a consolation candy bar, and the clerk is impatient with your fumbling for change. These minor irritations and frustrations, known as **hassles,** don't seem like much in comparison to an earthquake or a burnout job. But psychologists have found that their effects can accumulate, especially when they are frequent and involve interpersonal conflicts (Bolger et al., 1989).

Any annoying incident can be a hassle, but some of the most common hassles involve *frustrations*—the blocking of some desired goal—at home, work, or school. As you can see in Table 10.1, hassles can arise from a variety of sources, including time pressures, finances, health, and problem relationships.

You will recall our Core Concept—that the cumulative impact of stress and our skills for coping with it matter more than its source. In a diary study, a group of white, middle-class, middle-aged men and women kept track of their daily hassles over a one-year period. They also recorded major life changes and physical symptoms. A clear relationship emerged between hassles and health problems: The more frequent and intense the hassles people reported, the poorer was their health, both physical and mental (Lazarus, 1981; 1984). The opposite was also true: As daily hassles diminish, people's sense of well-being increases (Chamberlain & Zika, 1990). Thus, a life filled with hassles can exact a price as great as that of a single, more intense, stressor (Weinberger et al., 1987).

If you interpret these hassles as important, harmful, or threatening to your well-being, they can affect you more than you might imagine (Lazarus, 1984). Moreover, some people may be especially prone to see the world as hassle-filled. One study showed that college students with a more pessimistic outlook experienced both more hassles and poorer health (Dykema et al., 1995).

What is a hassle or an annoyance to you, however, may be unnoticed—or even amusing—to someone else. If you find your life hassle-filled, reappraisal of the situations that provoke feelings of irritation can save you mental and physical wear and tear. In the last section of the chapter we will have more to say about how you might approach such cognitive reappraisal.

Hassles: Situations that cause minor irritation or frustration.

Social Readjustment Rating Scale (SRRS): A psychological rating scale designed to measure stress levels by means of values attached to common life changes.

Change Can Be Hazardous to Your Health

In Your Life

The beginning or end of a relationship is always a time of tension and turmoil. Likewise, any change can cause stress: a new job, starting college, even a vacation. Although change puts spice in our lives, all change demands some adjustment. But did you realize that too much change of nearly any sort can jeopardize your health? Even events that we welcome may require major changes in our routines and adaptation to new requirements. For example, one of the most desired changes in a married couple's life, the birth of their first child, can be a source of stress, contributing to reduced marital satisfaction for many couples (Cowan & Cowan, 1988).

In general, significant levels of stress can result from any important life change, whether it be positive or negative (Dohrenwend & Dohrenwend, 1974; Dohrenwend & Shrout, 1985; Holmes & Rahe, 1967). Yet people vary considerably in the ways they respond to change in their lives, depending on their resources and the contexts in which stress occurs.

THE SRRS

How can we measure the stress of our everyday lives? And how much stress does it take before a person develops a stress-related illness? Thomas Holmes and Richard Rahe (1967) developed a psychological instrument, the **Social Readjustment Rating Scale (SRRS),** to answer these questions. Beginning with a list of 43 common stressful events, Holmes and Rahe assigned "marriage" an arbitrary middle value (50 on a 100-point scale) as a starting point. Then, they had a large number of people rate the other 42

events in comparison with the stress of marriage. The degree of stress associated with different kinds of change experienced in a given period was measured in *life-change units (LCU)*. To measure your current stress level (and risk for stress-related problems) with the SRRS, you would merely total the LCU ratings accumulated in recent life experiences.

Research has shown that the number of life-change units accumulated during the previous year become a modest predictor of changes in a person's health (Holmes & Masuda, 1974; Rahe & Arthur, 1978). More specifically, studies have shown relationships between scores on the SRRS and heart attacks, bone fractures, diabetes, multiple sclerosis, tuberculosis, complications of pregnancy and birth, decline in academic performance, employee absenteeism, and many other difficulties (Holmes & Masuda, 1974). They even found that high SRRS scores among federal prisoners were associated with the length of their prison sentences. Note that these results are also consistent with our Core Concept, which emphasizes the cumulative impact of the stressors in our lives.

Although it was originally validated on an all-male sample, the SRRS has proved useful with both male and female subjects. Both sexes rate events with quite similar scores (Holmes & Masuda, 1974). In addition, the investigators have validated the ratings with Japanese, Latin American, European, and Malaysian samples. Remarkably, the SRRS has transferred well across cultures.

You can assess yourself on the SRRS in the "Do It Yourself!" box. You may want to compare your score with those of classmates and consider whether you detect the same sort of relationship between life changes and well-being that Holmes and Rahe found. Before you

do so, though, please read the following critique of the SRRS.

CRITICAL ANALYSIS OF THE HOLMES-RAHE SRRS

There is no doubt that the Holmes-Rahe scale and its successors have helped us learn about the relationship between stressful life changes and illness. In the first 15 years after it was published, the SRRS was used in more than 1,000 studies worldwide (Holmes, 1979). Yet the Holmes-Rahe scale has been criticized, particularly for the implication that stressful events might *cause* illness (Dohrenwend & Shrout, 1985; Rabkin & Struening, 1976). In fact, the scale gives us *correlational* data. That is, it merely shows a relationship between certain life changes and health changes. So, even though the scale has some power to predict illness (Johnson & Sarason, 1979), the research does not show that life changes are the *cause* of illness. It could just as well be true that some as yet undiscovered factor might be the cause of *both* the life changes and illnesses.

For another thing, while the anchor point of the Holmes-Rahe SRRS is the stress of marriage, we now have substantial evidence that getting married is correlated with longer life. How can we reconcile this apparent contradiction? It appears that *getting married* can be a stressful experience, but once the stress of a wedding has dissipated, *being married* can provide a buffer against stress. In fact, any stable, long-term relationship seems to offer some protection against stress (Friedman et al., 1995). We will see,

(continued)

below, that other forms of social support also are associated with longevity.

Finally, critics point out that the correlations between life changes and health changes are moderate. A high score does not mean that illness is certain, nor does a low score guarantee health. Then too, certain groups, such as students, who are at change points in their lives, tend to get high scores, although it is not clear that they are more at risk for illness. Their youth may offer some protection. In general, people's chances of incurring an illness may be more related to their *interpretations* and *responses* to life changes than to the changes themselves (Lazarus et al., 1985). People differ in their abilities to deal with change, presumably because of genetic differences, general physical condition, lifestyles, and coping skills. The SRRS takes none of these factors into account—although we will in the final section of this chapter. Still, the SRRS does a fair job of measuring stress, and it remains the most widely used measure of stress that we have.

CHECKYOURUNDERSTANDING

1. **RECALL:** *In everyday conversation people often think of stress as a _____, while psychologists refer to stress as a _____.*

   a. situation/mental and physical response
   b. response/stimulus
   c. disease/feeling
   d. result of heredity/result of environment

2. **RECALL:** *Burnout is a source of stress that comes from*

   a. catastrophic events.
   b. work.
   c. chronic disease.
   d. divorce.

3. **APPLICATION:** *You have taken the Holmes-Rahe SRRS and have a high score—say 400 points. How should you interpret this score?*

   a. You will almost certainly have a major health problem within the next year.

   b. Your chances of having a major health problem are low if you are married.
   c. Your chances of developing a health problem depend not only on your score but on your physical condition, lifestyle, and coping skills.
   d. There is no proven relationship between life changes and health.

Core Concept

4. **UNDERSTANDING THE CORE CONCEPT:** *Which of the following is most likely to cause a high level of stress?*

   a. a catastrophic event, such as a major earthquake
   b. burnout
   c. a large number of life changes
   d. all of the above may cause a high level of stress

ANSWERS: 1. a   2. b   3. c   4. d

The Social Readjustment Rating Scale

For each of the following events that has occurred in your life during the past year, write the number of "life-change units" in the blank at the right. Then, add up your life-change units to determine your total score.

> Marriage was given a score of 50 life change units on the SRRS.

	LIFE-CHANGE UNITS	YOUR SCORE		LIFE-CHANGE UNITS	YOUR SCORE
Death of spouse	100	_____	Beginning or ending school	26	_____
Divorce	73	_____	Change in living conditions	25	_____
Marital separation	65	_____	Revision of personal habits	24	_____
Jail term	63	_____	Trouble with one's boss	23	_____
Death of close family member	63	_____	Change in work hours or conditions	20	_____
Personal injury or illness	53	_____	Change in residence	20	_____
Marriage	50	_____	Change in schools	20	_____
Being fired	47	_____	Change in recreation	19	_____
Marital reconciliation	45	_____	Change in church activities	19	_____
Retirement	45	_____	Change in social activities	18	_____
Change in the health of family member	44	_____	*Mortgage or loan of less than $100,000	17	_____
Pregnancy	40	_____	Change in sleeping habits	16	_____
Sex difficulties	39	_____	Change in number of family get-togethers	15	_____
Gain of new family member	39	_____	Change in eating habits	15	_____
Business readjustment	39	_____	Vacation	13	_____
Change in financial state	38	_____	Celebrated Christmas	13	_____
Death of close friend	37	_____	Minor violations of the law	11	_____
Change to a different line of work	36	_____	**Your total:**		_____
Change in number of arguments with spouse	35	_____			
*Home mortgage over $100,000	31	_____			
Foreclosure of a mortgage or loan	30	_____			
Change in responsibilities at work	29	_____			
Son or daughter leaving home	29	_____			
Trouble with in-laws	29	_____			
Outstanding personal achievement	28	_____			
*Spouse beginning or stopping work	26	_____			

How should you interpret your score? With caution. A total of 150 or less is good, suggesting a low level of stress in your life and a low probability of developing a stress-related disorder. But for people scoring between 150 and 200, Holmes and Masuda (1974) found a 50–50 chance of problems: Half the people they found in this range developed a significant physical or mental disorder in the next few months. About 70% of those scoring over 300 became ill. (Adapted from Holmes & Rahe, 1967.)

*These items have been updated.

HOW DOES STRESS AFFECT US PHYSICALLY?

We have no scientific evidence that the mind can affect external events—such as the roll of dice or a phone call from someone you love. Internal events, however, are another story: The influence of the mind on the body lies fully within mainstream psychological and medical science. Mental processes occurring in the brain continually influence our internal physical responses. How this works—to our advantage and disadvantage—when we are under stress is the subject of this section of the chapter. Here is the Core Concept:

> Stress can help us meet challenges and grow stronger, but too much stress—distress—can have harmful physical consequences.

We have seen that stress has many sources, and it can have serious health consequences. Now we will learn *how* it works on us biologically and psychologically.

Biological and Behavioral Responses to Stress

Imagine that you have a highly stressful job, such as being an air traffic controller at a busy metropolitan airport. On this job, you soon learn that keeping track of dozens of aircraft in a crowded airspace—knowing that hundreds of lives depend on your decisions—can extract a mental and physical toll. You may have more colds than you used to. You may find yourself taking medicine for indigestion and diarrhea more frequently. And, your friends may find you less jovial or more irritable. What is happening to you?

In this section, we will focus on the physical side of the response to stressful situations, such as your new job in air traffic control. (We will come back to the psychological consequences of stress after a few pages.) You are about to see that the physical response to nearly any stressor follows this sequence: (1) an initial arousal, (2) a protective behavioral reaction that often takes the form of a "fight-or-flight" response, (3) an internal response of the autonomic nervous system and the endocrine system, and (4) decreased effectiveness of the immune system. As we examine each of these physical responses, please note that they involve the same basic processes that we saw in emotion. Thus, the stress response is essentially one form of emotional response.

Connection

Chapter 2
The brain is composed of many specialized modules that work together to create mind and behavior.

Acute stress: A temporary pattern of arousal caused by a stressor with a clear onset and offset.

Chronic stress: A continuous state of stressful arousal persisting over time.

AROUSAL   If a stressful situation begins suddenly—as when an air traffic controller first hears a pilot's emergency call—the stress response is likely to begin with abrupt and intense arousal, including accelerated heart rate, quickened breathing, a jump in blood pressure, and profuse perspiration. This response involves the same unconscious brain circuits that we found to be involved in emotional arousal. It illustrates **acute stress,** a temporary pattern of arousal caused by a stressor with a clear onset and a limited duration.

Sometimes, however, arousal may merely fester, or it may grow slowly, as when jealousy first tugs at you, then distracts you, and finally disrupts your life with fear or outrage. The second case, of persistent strain, is an example of **chronic stress.** It involves a continuous state of stressful arousal persisting over time, in which demands are perceived to be greater than one's resources for dealing with them.

Arousal does us no good if it creates panic and confusion that keep us from responding to a threat. Fortunately, the human brain evolved to coordi-

Connection

Chapter 9
One of the brain's two emotion circuits relies on lower-brain structures that operate outside of consciousness.

nate several simultaneous reactions involving the nervous system, the endocrine system, and the muscles. As a result, we are biologically equipped to make efficient and effective responses to changing environmental demands. So, when one perceives an external threat, these bodily mechanisms are set in motion. Many are automatic or reflexive because instant action and extra strength may be required if the organism is to survive. We turn now to the most easily observed and best known of such mechanisms, the *fight-or-flight response*.

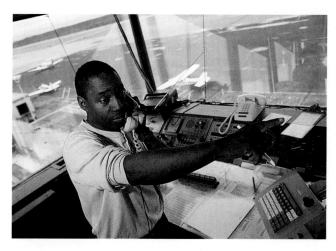

Working in an air traffic control tower at a busy airport is a high-stress occupation.

FIGHT OR FLIGHT Consider this stressful situation: At a meeting for which you have thoroughly prepared, the chair criticizes you and accuses you of failing to attend to tasks that were, in reality, someone else's responsibility. As all eyes turn on you, you feel your face getting hot, your jaw tightening, and your fist clenching. You would not shout or hit anyone, but you feel like it. Now consider another stressful situation: You walk into class a few moments late, only to find everyone putting books and notes away—apparently preparing for a test you did not realize had been scheduled for today. Your heart seems to stop, your mouth is dry, your knees feel weak, and you momentarily consider hurrying back out the door. Your life is not really in danger, and running away will not solve your problem—so why should you feel a physical urge to escape?

These two scenarios illustrate the two poles of the **fight-or-flight response,** a sequence of internal processes that prepares the aroused organism for struggle or escape. It occurs when a situation is interpreted as threatening. (Interestingly, women are not as likely as men to show the classic fight-or-flight response. Instead, they may respond to stressful situations with nurturing behaviors and by forming protective alliances [Azar, 2000; Taylor et al., 2000b].) Nevertheless, when a fight-or-flight reaction does occur, its pattern depends on how the organism has *learned* to deal with threat, as well as on an *innate* fight-or-flight "program" built into the brain.

Learning to Fight or Flee Evidence that the "fight" response can be learned is seen, for example, in studies showing that reactions to a perceived insult are strongly dependent on culture. In the United States this learned "fight" response has been nurtured in the "culture of honor" that developed in the South—which some experts believe may account for the southern states' much higher murder rate in comparison to the northern states (Nisbett, 1993). Learning can also affect our internal responses to stress. For example, in a study of patients with high blood pressure (which can be a stress response), those who took placebos along with their medication for high blood pressure maintained a healthy blood pressure after the medication was removed, as long as they continued taking the placebo (Ader & Cohen, 1993; Suchman & Ader, 1989). This suggests that the expectation that the placebos would control their blood pressure was enough to reduce the emergency response of the blood vessels.

Innate Tendencies Toward Fight or Flight While the fight-or-flight response can be learned, it also involves an innate reaction that operates largely outside consciousness. This was first recognized in the 1920s by physiologist Walter Canon, whose research showed that a threat stimulates a sequence of activities in the organism's nerves and glands. We now know that the amyg-

Fight-or-flight response: A sequence of internal processes that prepares the organism for struggle or escape and is triggered when a situation is interpreted as threatening.

Connection

Chapter 5
Placebos contain no real medicines. They only work because of the patient's expectations.

Connection

Chapter 2
The hypothalamus is a deep brain structure that controls many automatic responses.

Connection

Chapter 2
The autonomic nervous system operates outside of consciousness and sends messages to the internal organs.

dala and the hypothalamus control this response by initiating a cascade of events in the autonomic nervous system (ANS), endocrine system, and immune system (Jansen et al., 1995; LeDoux, 1996).

As you will recall, the autonomic nervous system regulates the activities of our internal organs. When an individual perceives a situation as threatening, the hypothalamus sends an emergency message to the ANS, which sets in motion several bodily reactions to stress. See Figure 10.2 for a detailed list of how the ANS and endocrine (internal gland) system prepare the body for an emergency response. The response can be helpful when you need to escape a hungry bear, confront a hostile rival, or protect your children. It served our ancestors well, but it has a cost. As our Core Concept suggests, staying physiologically "on guard" against a threat eventually wears down the body's natural defenses. In this way, suffering from frequent stress—or frequently *interpreting* experiences as stressful—can create a serious health risk: An essentially healthy stress response can become *distress*.

In sudden emergencies, these automatic responses can be helpful. They may save the life of a soldier in combat. They may also speed you out of danger if you think you might be mugged by the person following you on a dark street. But, as we have seen, modern living has produced a different class of stressors—*psychological stressors*—that act over far longer periods and threaten not our immediate survival but our status, lifestyles, health, or self-

▌FIGURE 10.2:   Bodily Reactions to Stress

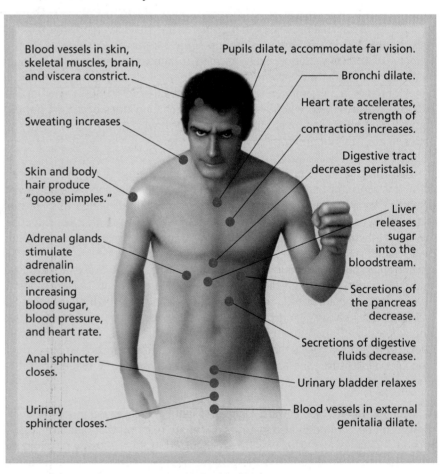

respect. In the face of chronic psychological stressors, our emergency response may offer little help — or may even backfire. Again, stress may become *distress*.

While the fight-or-flight syndrome and other responses to stress are most visible in our behavior, the accompanying autonomic and endocrine responses occur inside us. Like fight-or-flight, these internal processes are adaptive for dealing with acute, life-threatening stressors. But, if stress is chronic, our internal responses can produce the *general adaptation syndrome* — an insidious condition that can weaken us with its powerful attempts to counteract the stressors of life.

THE GENERAL ADAPTATION SYNDROME We now know how people who experience persistently negative emotions associated with stress become candidates for disease. Our understanding is based on the work of Canadian endocrinologist Hans Selye (pronounced *SELL-ya*). In brief, he discovered that different stressors trigger essentially the same systemic reaction, or *general* physical reaction, that mobilizes the body's resources to deal with the threat. Moreover, he found, all stressors provoke some attempt at *adaptation,* or adjustment of the body to the stressor. Normally, these responses are helpful, but under chronically stressful conditions, they can lead to heart disease, asthma, headache, gastric ulcers, arthritis, and a variety of other disorders (Carlson, 2001; Friedman & Booth-Kewley, 1988; Salovey et al., 2000).

Selye termed this bodily response to stress the **general adaptation syndrome (GAS).** His model of the GAS describes a three-stage response to any threat, consisting of an *alarm reaction,* a stage of *resistance,* and a stage of *exhaustion* (Selye, 1956). These three stages of Selye's GAS are shown in Figure 10.3.

General adaptation syndrome (GAS): A general pattern of physical responses that takes essentially the same form in response to any serious, chronic stressor.

FIGURE 10.3: The General Adaptation Syndrome

In stage 1, the body produces an emergency arousal response to a stressor. Then, in stage 2, the body adapts for a while to the continuing presence of the stressor. Finally, in stage 3, the body's defenses against the stressor become exhausted, with catastrophic results.

Stage 1: Alarm reaction

General arousal caused by:
• increase of adrenal hormones.
• reaction of sympathetic nervous system.

If stressor is not removed, organism moves to Stage 2.

Stage 2: Resistance

Arousal subsides because of:
• decrease in adrenal output.
• counter reaction of parasympathetic nervous system.

If stressor is not removed, the organism moves to Stage 3.

Stage 3: Exhaustion

General arousal of Stage 1 reappears.

Powerful parasympathetic response opposes arousal.

If stressor is not removed in time, death occurs.

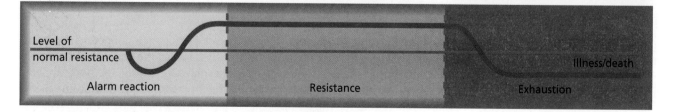

Level of normal resistance

Alarm reaction   Resistance   Exhaustion   Illness/death

▌ FIGURE 10.4: The Alarm Reaction Pathway

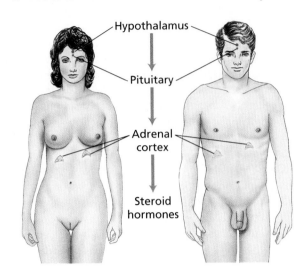

▌ FIGURE 10.5: Sympathetic Pathways for Responses to Stress

Hypothalamus
↓
Sympathetic division of the autonomic nervous system

→ Internal organs

→ Adrenal medulla
↓
Epinephrine
↓

• Heart rate increases.
• Blood pressure increases.
• Blood sugar rises.
• Blood flow to gut decreases.
• Blood flow to heart, brain, and muscles increases.
• Perspiration increases.
• Pupils dilate.

The Alarm Reaction   In the first stage of stress, the body's warning system activates and begins to mobilize its resources against the stressor. In this **alarm reaction,** the hypothalamus sets off an emergency response in the hormone system, especially in the adrenal glands, through the pathway shown in Figure 10.4. The result is a flood of steroid hormones into the bloodstream. (Athletes sometimes use steroid hormones to induce an artificial stress response, which fools the body into mobilizing its emergency resources. This practice, however, has dangerous side effects—similar to the body's reactions in the later stages of the GAS.)

Simultaneously, the hypothalamus sends emergency messages through the sympathetic division of the autonomic nervous system to internal organs and glands, arousing the body for action. This mechanism probably underlies stories of people in emergencies lifting massive objects, leaping high barriers, or running with extraordinary swiftness—feats they could not duplicate later. This autonomic response acts through the pathways shown in Figure 10.5.

As our Core Concept says, if the stress lasts over a long period, this initially adaptive alarm reaction can become *distress,* as it depletes much of the body's energy and defensive resources. It can also cause high blood pressure, deterioration of the immune system, fatty deposits in the blood vessels, bleeding ulcers, and a variety of other symptoms. These reactions also make the person under stress a prime candidate for infections or other diseases. In addition, studies suggest that prolonged or repeated stress may produce long-term changes in the brain that provoke depression (Sapolsky, 1996; Schulkin, 1994). Research has also revealed that stress hormones can damage the brain and interfere with its ability to regenerate neurons, especially in the hippocampus (Gould et al., 1998; Sapolsky, 1996).

The Stage of Resistance   If the stressor persists but is not so strong that it overwhelms the organism during the first stage, the individual begins to rebound during stage 2, the **stage of resistance.** Outwardly, the body appears to be gaining the advantage—resisting the stressor, as the symptoms of the alarm reaction fade. The adrenal glands, swollen earlier, now return to normal size, diminishing their output of emergency steroids. Yet, the hormone response does persist at a lower level, as an almost unnoticed internal struggle against the stressor continues.

Surprisingly, the resistance that the body displays in this stage applies *only* to the original stressor. When an experimental animal had adapted to a stressor, it soon died when Selye switched stressors (say, from electric shocks to cold). Apparently stress had so depleted the animal's resources that it could not mobilize a defense against the new stressor. In general, if a second stressor is introduced in the second stage of the GAS, the organism may not be able to adapt. (Think of the "straw that broke the camel's back.") A human example might involve a soldier who suddenly dies in response to the new stress of a prison camp after surviving months of stressful combat.

The Stage of Exhaustion   If relief from the stressor doesn't arrive during the stage of resistance, the symptoms of the alarm reaction inevitably reappear. This time, however, a powerful autonomic response accompanies them. In this third stage, the **stage of exhaustion,** the autonomic nervous system overcompensates in its attempt to moderate the resurgent hormone response. Soon the organism may approach the point of no return: Exhaustion and eventual death overtake it if the stressor is not removed quickly. You can see again why it is not healthy for an athlete to take high doses of stress hormones for a long period. Prolonged use of steroids (except under certain medical conditions) can, in effect, put the body into Selye's stage 3, a stage of perilous deterioration—even death.

STRESS AND THE IMMUNE SYSTEM   Since Selye, researchers have found other consequences of stress that illustrate the influence of mental processes on the body. For example, scientists have discovered the influences of our mental processes on the immune system—a finding that has established a new field known as **psychoneuroimmunology** (Ader & Cohen, 1993; Maier et al., 1994; Solvason et al., 1988).

How do mental processes affect the immune system? The brain sends messages to the autonomic nervous system and endocrine system, which have links to organs that produce the immune response. The brain also receives feedback from the immune system via neural and endocrine pathways (Maier & Watkins, 2000). At the same time, receptors for stress hormones, located on white blood cells, respond to the presence of a stressor by sending out a widespread chemical alarm, which alerts the brain.

During stress, messages carried along these pathways can have important effects on health (Pert, 1997). For example, the dissolving of interpersonal relationships, such as happens following a death or divorce, can result in suppression of the immune response, making people more vulnerable to disease (Cohen & Syme, 1985; Kiecolt-Glaser & Glaser, 1987). Studies also show that men with wives dying of breast cancer and recently widowed women are less able to fight disease and face an increased risk of illness and premature death (Irwin et al., 1987; Schleifer et al., 1983). Similarly, depression has also been shown to produce **immunosuppression,** a diminished effectiveness of

Stage of exhaustion: The third stage of the GAS, during which the body depletes its resources.

Psychoneuroimmunology: A relatively new field that studies the influence of our mental states on the immune system.

Immunosuppression: Diminished effectiveness of the immune system caused by impairment (suppression) of the immune response.

Stress can affect physical health through its effects on the endocrine and immune systems.

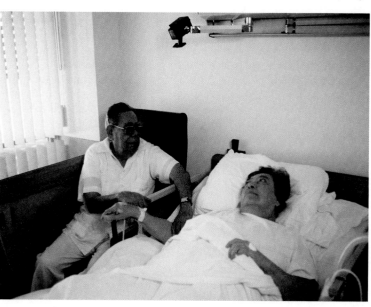

the immune response. The health risks are especially great in older people (Kiecolt-Glaser & Glaser, 2001).

An understanding of the general adaptation syndrome and immunosuppression has proven valuable in explaining disorders, such as heart disease, that formerly baffled physicians. However, most of this work has focused on reactions to *physical* stressors among experimental animals. As a result, medicine has had little to say about the *psychological* stressors so prevalent among humans. In the third section of this chapter, we will fill some of this gap.

Psychology

When Stress Is Good for You

In Your Life

Would this be eustress for you?

Sometimes stress can be pleasurable, as when we play a game, visit an exotic culture, or take a thrilling white-water rafting trip. In fact, these episodes of relatively mild and brief stress can be healthful, rather than harmful. When we experience stress in this form, it actually strengthens us, both physically and mentally. Athletes use this principle to their advantage when they build their bodies with the brief intervals of stress they call "training." Unless overdone, such stress can make nearly anyone more resilient.

In his book *Stress without Distress,* Selye (1974) noted that it is not possible, or even desirable, to have a stress-free life. He later observed that "complete freedom from stress is death" (Selye, 1980, p. 128). Putting the point more positively: A modest level of stress motivates us to live, work, play, and love well, as our Core Concept implies. Selye (1980) called this optimal level of stress **eustress** (from the Greek prefix "eu," which means "good").

Consider how you might apply the concept of "good" stress — *eustress* — in your own life. For example, if you are studying for a career in business management, think about how you might structure the work environment to reduce distress and increase eustress for your future employees (Douglas, 1996). First, an employer should know the three most common sources of employee distress: (1) conflicting expectations from supervisors, (2) unclear expectations and goals, and (3) erratic changes in workload, swinging from overwork to underwork. The first suggests poor communication within management ranks, while the second problem involves poor communication between management and the work force. The third may have any of several causes, but it also calls for dialogue between workers and their managers to find ways of smoothing out the workload.

After addressing these problems, the employer should consider steps to create eustress in the place of distress. For example, jobs can be made more interesting and challenging when workers are assigned to teams that are given workplace problems to solve, rather than being handed management-imposed solutions. And employees should be given increased authority as they are given increased responsibility.

In your personal life, you should remember that eustress can be an antidote for distress. For your own physical and mental health, remember to monitor your stress level. When you sense that stress is taking away your effectiveness, diminishing your emotional responsiveness, or making you feel generally "run down," seek a dose of eustress.

Eustress: An optimum level of stress; "good" stress.

1. **APPLICATION:** *An oncoming car swerves into your lane and heads directly for you. At the last possible moment it swerves again, missing you by inches. Your heart pounds, your blood pressure rises, you begin perspiring. This is an example of*
   a. acute stress.
   b. eustress.
   c. chronic stress.
   d. the GAS.

2. **RECALL:** *Which one of the following is most likely to be influenced by cultural factors?*
   a. the fight-or-flight response
   b. the general adaptation syndrome
   c. the effect of stress on the immune system
   d. the autonomic nervous system

3. **RECALL:** *If a chronic stressor is not removed, the stressed organism may eventually die during*
   a. the alarm reaction.
   b. the stage of resistance.
   c. the stage of exhaustion.
   d. eustress.

4. **UNDERSTANDING THE CORE CONCEPT:**
   The biological mechanisms that helped our ancestors deal with stress are often poorly adapted to the _____ *of the modern world.*
   a. acute stress
   b. eustress
   c. chronic stress
   d. autonomic stress

ANSWERS: 1. a   2. a   3. c   4. c

HOW DO WE RESPOND PSYCHOLOGICALLY TO STRESS?

The consequences of stress are not limited to the body. People also react to stressful situations, such as an upcoming surgical procedure or a final examination, with acute anxiety or depression. And, if the stress is extreme or prolonged, as in a rape or near-death automobile crash with serious injuries, the psychological consequences can be chronic and just as debilitating as the physical ones we examined earlier. In this section we will emphasize several other, more complex psychological reactions to stressful situations. Our Core Concept suggests that these reactions vary widely:

> **Our psychological responses under stress depend on personality, perceptions, and the ways we have learned to respond.**

Thus, different people may respond quite differently to the same stressful situation.

Personality and Stress

Mr. A is an executive who always works over lunch. He makes business calls on his cellular phone as he drives to and from work. He carries a briefcase full of papers home every night, where he pours over them until bedtime, when he takes a pill to slow down his frenetic mind and get him to sleep. He would tell you that he thrives on stress. By contrast, Ms. B, who works in the same office, rarely takes work home, doesn't own a cell phone, and receives evaluations from her manager that are as good or better than Mr. A's. These two executives obviously have different working styles. If these styles are of long standing, if

Connection

Chapter 11

Types are clusters of traits that are found in essentially the same pattern in many people.

A basketball coach displays some Type A behaviors.

Type A: A behavior pattern characterized by an intense, angry, competitive, or perfectionistic response to life.

Type B: A behavior pattern characterized by a relaxed, unruffled response to life.

they are pervasive in these individuals' lives, and if they are similar to patterns found in many other people, we might be justified in calling them *personality types*. In fact, the two we have just described represent two opposite patterns known as *Type A* and *Type B*—patterns of behavior that have some intriguing associations with disease and health.

TYPE A AND B BEHAVIOR PATTERNS   When an upholsterer commented that the front edges of the chairs in their waiting rooms showed unusually high wear, cardiologists Meyer Friedman and Ray Rosenman (1974) realized that a certain coping style might be associated with heart disease. It was as if people with heart disease were always "on the edge of their seats." Subsequent interviews with Friedman and Rosenman's patients revealed a striking pattern of impatience, competitiveness, aggressiveness, and hostility—all stress-related responses. Many said they were notorious workaholics. Friedman and Rosenman dubbed this the **Type A** behavior pattern, and they found that this pattern was predictive of heart disease. In their studies, the Type A individual had twice as much risk of heart disease as the **Type B**, an individual who takes a relaxed approach to life (Matthews, 1982).

Many Type A characteristics, however, are valued in our mobile, competitive society: Speed, perfectionism, and time-urgency may actually help one to succeed in the workplace and in the interpersonal "marketplace," where people are admired for being strong, independent, and self-promoting. But, in the long run, the Type A style can be dysfunctional, unhealthy, and self-defeating. One study showed that Type A businessmen are stricken with coronary heart disease more than twice as often as men in the general population (Friedman & Rosenman, 1974; Jenkins, 1976). Other studies show that Type A individuals are at greater risk for all forms of cardiovascular disease, including heart attack and stroke (Dembroski et al., 1978; Dembroski & Costa, 1987; Haynes & Feinleib, 1980).

In addition to cardiovascular risks, research links Type A habits to other illnesses: allergies, head colds, headaches, stomach disorders, and mononucleosis (Suls & Marco, 1990; Suls & Sanders, 1988). Currently, researchers are focusing on identifying which specific dimensions of the Type A syndrome are its most deadly components. A tendency toward anger and hostility is particularly suspect (Clay, 2001; Whiteman & Fowkes, 1997). So, when a slow-moving vehicle blocks you in traffic, it is reasonable to become momentarily piqued, but it is Type A behavior—and potentially dangerous to your health—to become enraged. Another risky Type A quality, perfectionism, has been linked to anxiety (about reaching impossible goals) and depression (from failing to reach them) (Joiner & Schmidt, 1995).

How does the Type A behavior pattern get translated into a heart attack or other physical disease? The details are not yet clear, but a hint comes from another study by Friedman and Ulmer (1984). As the April 15th tax deadline approached, these researchers drew blood samples from a group of accountants. The closer they came to the filing date, the higher the accountants' cholesterol and clotting factors climbed, in many cases rising to dangerous levels. You will notice the similarity between this response to stress and the "alarm reaction" that Selye found in the first stage of the general adaptation syndrome.

A word of caution: All the fuss in the popular press may lead you to conclude—erroneously—that you must be either a Type A or Type B. The truth is, most people have neither a Type A or Type B personality. The majority of us fall somewhere between these extremes.

Nor is it always bad to be a Type A. If you do have a heart attack, being Type A may save your life. In one study of 257 males who had heart attacks, death rates were equal among Type As and Type Bs. But among the first-day survivors, the Type As were twice as likely to be alive 13 years later. Stress experts suggest that the Type As may have an advantage because they are more aggressive about following medical advice to quit smoking, change their diets, and get more exercise than were the more easygoing Type Bs (Ragland & Brand, 1988).

An understanding of the Type A link with heart disease has led to the development of a remarkably effective approach to the prevention of second heart attacks. In a group of heart attack survivors, Friedman and Ulmer (1984) showed that those given stress management training had half as many heart attacks in the next three years as a control group who had received no such training. The researchers concluded: "No drug, food, or exercise program ever devised, not even a coronary bypass surgical program, could match the protection against recurrent heart attacks" afforded by learning to manage stress (p. 141). Success in preventing heart attacks was also reported in a similar study by Friedman, Thoresen, and Gill (1981).

More recently, a new personality pattern, dubbed *Type D,* has been associated with heart disease in a large Belgian study. The Type D personality is characterized by a need to suppress emotional distress. Among the 303 patients (268 men and 35 women) in the study, the risk of death from a heart attack was four times as high for those with Type D personalities (Denollet & Sys, 1996). Corroborating this finding in a sample of 83 women with heart disease, another study has found that those who react slowly to events and who suppress their anger are more likely to have fatal heart attacks (Powell et al., 1993). The results of these preliminary studies still need to be digested and replicated by other researchers.

In summary, such reports have caused a stir, both among health professionals and in the press (Lesperance & Frasure-Smith, 1996). But the last line of the Type A/B/D story has not yet been written. At this moment, it appears that those who are most at risk may be the ones who are depressed, those who display lots of anger, and (paradoxically) those who suppress their negative emotions (Clay, 2001; Friedman et al., 1994; Whiteman & Fowkes, 1997; Wright, 1988).

HARDINESS   Now consider another personality pattern that has received much attention as a stress moderator: **hardiness,** a resilient quality based on distinctive attitudes toward stress and how to manage it. In contrast with the Type A or D behavior patterns, this is one of the healthy coping styles, as shown in a study by psychologist Suzanne Kobasa (1984). She identified two groups of subjects from a pool of managers working for a big public utility in a large city. The members of one group experienced high levels of stress but were seldom ill, while the members of the second group had high stress and frequently experienced illness (Kobasa et al., 1979). Those who were seldom ill possessed three distinctive attitudes or perspectives, called the "three C's of hardiness":

▶ *Challenge:* Hardy people welcome change as a challenge, not necessarily a threat.

▶ *Commitment:* Hardy individuals make a focused commitment to engaging in purposeful activity, solving problems, and meeting the challenges they face.

▶ *Control:* Hardy persons have an internal sense of control over their actions and experiences.

For example, suppose that on the day you must prepare for a major test, a friend confides in you about a terrible problem and begs for your help. These two stressors—an important test and a needy friend—could be overwhelm-

Hardiness: A resilient quality based on the "three Cs" of health: challenge (welcoming change), commitment (involvement in purposeful activity), and control (internal guide for actions).

Connection

Chapter 9
Locus of control is a personality factor that predicts how much control a person senses over life events.

ing, especially if you feel you are already stretching some of your resources to the limit. But a hardy individual would employ the "three C's" to reduce the stress of the situation: *challenge* ("I want to be fully prepared for this test; how can I reassure my friend that I'll help as well?"); *commitment* ("I'm committed to my friend and to preparing for this test; I'll find a way to meet my obligations in both areas"); and *control* ("I can't take time out from studying, but I can plan to spend the evening discussing the problem; once the test is over I can give my friend my undivided attention").

The key to hardiness is not luck. Nor is it an inherited ability to face stress with a smile. Rather, hardiness is a learned approach to stress, based on *interpreting* or *perceiving* stressful events in an adaptive way (Kobasa, 1984).

Learned Helplessness

Another learned response to stress follows a pattern that is very much the opposite of hardiness. Imagine a child who has grown up in a dysfunctional or abusive family — a child who received no emotional or intellectual support. All his life he has been told how "dumb" he was, and when he gets to school, he stumbles on his initial attempts with words and numbers. The teacher gives him poor grades; the other kids make fun of him. After only a few more such attempts he gives up permanently. This passive resignation following recurring failure or punishment is termed **learned helplessness.**

Evidence of learned helplessness originally came from animal studies performed by Martin Seligman and his colleagues. This work showed that dogs receiving inescapable electric shocks soon gave up their attempts to avoid the punishment and passively resigned themselves to their fate (Seligman, 1975, 1991; Seligman & Maier, 1967). Later, when given the opportunity to escape, the dogs typically did nothing but whimper and take the shock. In contrast, a control group of dogs that had not been subjected to previous punishment were quick to escape. Seligman concluded that the experimental group of animals had already learned that nothing they did mattered or altered the consequences, so they "gave up and lay down" (Seligman, 1991, p. 23) and passively accepted their fate (Seligman & Maier, 1967).

An experiment by Donald Hiroto (1974) employed human subjects in a variation of Seligman's dog research. Subjects were first placed in a room where they were bombarded by a loud noise. Some quickly learned to turn off the noise by pressing buttons on a control panel, but for other subjects, the panel was rigged so that they could not find any pattern of button-pressing to stop the noise. When the subjects were placed in a new situation, in which a different annoying "whooshing" noise could be easily stopped by a simple hand movement, only those who had learned to stop the loud noise attempted to stop the whooshing sound. The veterans of inescapable noise just sat in the new room, making no effort to stop the latest stressor. They had already learned to be helpless. Seligman sees symptoms of the same learned helplessness syndrome in human populations, such as abused and discouraged children, battered wives, prisoners of war, and depressed patients (Seligman, 1975).

We also see learned helplessness in nursing homes (Baltes, 1995). In fact, we may overestimate the physical deterioration of older people in nursing homes because they have learned to feel and to act helpless, say Judith Rodin and Ellen Langer (Buie, 1988). Most nursing homes, geared to routine care of large numbers of patients, do not encourage patients to make decisions or take control of their lives. So, residents are awakened, fed, bathed, toileted, cached in front of television sets, and cycled back to bed, on a routine that offers little variety or choice. This treatment robs patients of individual responsibility and makes them seem incapable of even the simplest tasks.

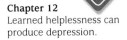

Connection

Chapter 12
Learned helplessness can produce depression.

Connection

Chapter 1
The experimental group (but not the control group) receives some special treatment.

Learned helplessness: A pattern of not responding to noxious stimuli after an organism learns that its behavior has no effect.

But Rodin and Langer have shown that learned helplessness need not be hopeless. They arranged for an experimental group of elderly patients to make more choices about day-to-day events, such as meals and activities. Meanwhile, for a control group the staff took full charge of their care, as usual. After 18 months, the group given more responsibility were more active and alert and reported a more positive outlook than the controls. More significantly, during the follow-up period, 25% of the control group died, while deaths claimed only 15% of the group given increased responsibility (Rodin, 1986).

Diminished Hedonic Capacity

Obviously, severe trauma, such as war and crime, can lower victims' post-trauma quality of life. But even garden-variety stress, such as that caused by persistent pressure and hassles, can rob one of **hedonic capacity,** the ability to experience emotions, particularly those of pleasure and joy. For those with diminished hedonic capacity, the defense against negative emotions, such as anxiety, irritation, depression, frustration, anger, and despair, is an emotional reserve—a numbness. College students, for example, report less pleasure in their everyday activities during final exam week than at a less stressful time (Berenbaum & Connelly, 1993). Stress especially reduces hedonic capacity for individuals whose families have a history of depression. You can see how such negative emotional responses can lead to a vicious cycle: Stress leads to joy-lessness, which prevents people from enjoying life or seeking pleasure, so that they lose hope that anything worth looking forward to will appear in their lives —which creates more stress.

Diminished hedonic capacity—a numbed ability to feel pleasure, joy, and happiness—can result from the chronic stress of being unemployed. Similarly, chronic disease, poverty, homelessness, or any other long-term source of stress can diminish one's capacity to experience positive emotions.

The Stockholm Syndrome

Victimization can also produce a bizarre stress response known as the **Stockholm syndrome.** This reaction occurs when people who have been hostages and prisoners come to identify and sympathize with their captors. The term refers to a 1974 bank robbery in Stockholm, Sweden, where, after five days' imprisonment in the bank vault, the hostages expressed warmth, sympathy, and even attraction for the robbers who had locked them up. In a more recent example, Russian hostages in the breakaway republic of Chechnya had only kind words for their Chechen captors, whom they described as "good," "serious," and kind to children, but they had only harsh criticism for the Russian soldiers who stormed the town to liberate them (National Public Radio, 1995a).

What mysterious emotional process made the captives bond so strongly to their captors? Remember that becoming the hostage of terrorists is a grave stressor that can place overwhelming demands on the captives' emotional repertoire. The captives are isolated from the outside world. They know nothing of outsiders' efforts to free them, and they must depend on their captors for contact and information. Forming ties to and ultimately caring about their captors may be hostages' only effective way to respond to their fear and loss. In order to adjust to the new (if tragic) reality of their confinement, prisoners must begin to see their captors as human, approachable, and friendly (Auerbach et al., 1994). Only then might the captivity be endured and survived. A sad example of this process is found in the attachment abused children sometimes feel for their abusive parents (Goddard & Stanley, 1994).

Hedonic capacity: The ability to experience pleasure and joy.

Stockholm syndrome: A psychological reaction in which hostages and prisoners identify and sympathize with their captors.

Posttraumatic stress disorder (PTSD): A delayed stress reaction in which an individual involuntarily reexperiences emotional, cognitive, and behavioral aspects of past trauma.

Posttraumatic Stress Disorder

Individuals who have undergone severe ordeals may experience a belated pattern of stress symptoms that can appear months, or even years, after their trauma. In **posttraumatic stress disorder (PTSD),** the individual reexperiences

Connection

Chapter 12
Posttraumatic stress disorder is one of the anxiety disorders.

Ego defense mechanisms: According to Freud, these are unconscious strategies that we use to defend ourselves against threat and trauma, reduce internal conflict, and diminish anxiety.

Denial: Freud's ego defense mechanism that allows a person consciously to ignore a problem or to conclude that there is no problem at all.

Rationalization: Giving socially acceptable reasons for actions that are really based on motives that the person believes to be unacceptable.

Projection: Attributing one's own unacceptable motives to another person or thing.

Repression: Freud's ego defense mechanism responsible for forgetting.

Reaction formation: The ego defense mechanism that makes us overreact in a manner opposite to our unconscious desires.

Displacement: The ego defense mechanism by which we shift our reaction from the real source of distress to another individual or object.

Regression: The ego defense mechanism that makes us revert to immature behavior in the face of threat.

mental and physical responses that accompanied the trauma. Victims typically become distracted, disorganized, and experience memory difficulties (Arnsten, 1998). They suffer a psychic numbing to everyday events (a reaction we also called *diminished hedonic capacity* earlier). They may also feel alienated from other people. The emotional pain of this reaction can result in various symptoms, such as problems with sleeping, guilt about surviving, difficulty concentrating, and an exaggerated "startle response" (wide-eyed, gasping, surprised behavior displayed when one perceives a sudden threat). Rape survivors, for example, may experience a barrage of psychological aftereffects, including feelings of betrayal by people close to them, anger about having been victimized, and fear of being alone (Baron & Straus, 1985; Cann et al., 1981).

Posttraumatic stress disorder can also have lasting biological consequences (Arnsten, 1998; Caldwell, 1995; Mukerjee, 1995; Sapolsky, 1996). We have seen that the brain may undergo physical changes when the stress is extreme in intensity or duration. Not only can stress prevent normal regeneration of cells, but it can cause the brain's system that governs hormones to develop a hair-trigger responsiveness. This makes the victim of posttraumatic stress disorder overreact to mild stressors or even to innocuous surprises or unexpected, but harmless, stimulation. Based on these clues, researchers are searching for a treatment that might counteract these malfunctioning brain pathways.

Psychology

In Your Life

Ego Defenses under Stress

Some of our psychological defenses against threatening situations operate unconsciously, said that keen observer of human nature, Sigmund Freud. While many psychologists disagree with the details of Freud's explanation, most agree that he called our attention to some important reactions frequently seen in people under stress (Cramer, 2000). Freud called these unconscious maneuvers **ego defense mechanisms.** *(See also Chapter 11, Personality.)* Most of them, he taught, are unhealthy because they don't really solve our problems but

leave them to fester in the unconscious mind. Here are some of the commonest of the ego defense mechanisms identified by Freud:

▶ **Denial:** "I don't have a problem." This defense avoids a difficult situation by simply denying that it exists. Denial is a defense frequently seen, for example, in alcoholics, child abusers, people who have problems managing anger, and people who engage in risky behavior, such as casual, unprotected sex.

▶ **Rationalization:** A person using this defense mechanism gives socially acceptable reasons for actions that are really based on motives that he or she believes to be unacceptable. So, a student

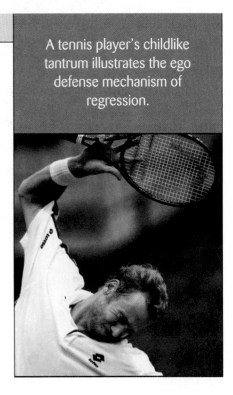

A tennis player's childlike tantrum illustrates the ego defense mechanism of regression.

who feels stressed by academic pressures may decide to cheat on a test, rationalizing it by saying that "everyone does it."

▶ **Projection:** This one involves attributing one's own unacceptable motives to another person or thing. An example of projection might occur when two people are competing with each other for a promotion, and one accuses the other of trying to make her look bad in the supervisor's eyes.

▶ **Repression:** Many people deal with stressful situations by trying to put them out of their minds. If this is done deliberately and consciously, it is called *suppression*. Freud believed, however, that people may also *repress* memories by burying them in the unconscious mind. Freud thought that repressed memories could

disguise themselves as symptoms of mental disorders, such as phobias, depression, or a psychotic break with reality.

▶ **Reaction formation:** This ego defense mechanism occurs when people act in exact opposition to their true feelings. Accordingly, people troubled by their own sexual desires may initiate a crusade against "dirty books" in the city library. Or a child with low self-esteem may become a bully.

▶ **Displacement:** When your boss makes you angry, you may later displace your anger by yelling at your mate or kicking the dog. This ego defense mechanism involves shifting your reaction from the real source of your distress to a safer individual or object.

▶ **Regression:** Under stress, some people hide; others cry, throw

things, or even wet their pants. That is, they adopt immature, juvenile behaviors that were effective ways of dealing with stress when they were younger.

Did you recognize yourself in this list? If so, the traditional remedy has been a long course of psychoanalysis, because Freud believed that these mechanisms must be carefully teased out of the unconscious. While modern psychologists believe that Freud put his finger on some unhealthy responses that people often use under stress, they do not necessarily agree that these reactions come from the unconscious. Therefore, contemporary psychologists are more likely to recommend a less extensive form of counseling or therapy — and, perhaps, a bit of eustress.

CHECK**YOUR**UNDERSTANDING

1. **RECALL:** *The Type A personality is most likely to be*
   a. aggressive and angry.
   b. humorous.
   c. calm and unruffled.
   d. disconnected from reality.

2. **RECALL:** *Which of the following are the "three C" characteristics of hardiness?*
   a. character, contentment, and charisma
   b. challenge, commitment, and control
   c. clarity, compassion, and cleverness
   d. careful, centered, and cautious

3. **APPLICATION:** *Which of the following persons would be most likely to develop a posttraumatic stress disorder?*
   a. a person who narrowly escaped an auto accident
   b. a soldier who had been in combat
   c. an air traffic controller at a busy airport
   d. a person who works for a difficult boss

4. **RECALL:** *Which ego defense mechanism is apt to make you speak sharply to a friend when you are angry at your supervisor?*

   a. repression
   b. reaction formation
   c. displacement
   d. regression

Core Concept

5. **UNDERSTANDING THE CORE CONCEPT:**
   Which of the following best illustrates the Core Concept for this section?
   a. Neither Mary nor Michiyo was worried about the upcoming exam, because they knew that it would be easy.
   b. They both knew the exam would be difficult, but Michiyo was confident, while Mary was a nervous wreck.
   c. The exam was easy, so both Mary and Michiyo were confident that they had done well.
   d. The exam was difficult, and neither Mary nor Michiyo felt that she would receive a good grade.

ANSWERS: 1. a   2. b   3. b   4. c   5. b

WHAT STRATEGIES CAN PROMOTE HEALTH — RATHER THAN DISTRESS?

Do you want to live a long and healthy life? Or, would you prefer a shorter-than-average life ended by heart disease, cancer, stroke, diabetes, cirrhosis of the liver, AIDS, accident, or suicide? While some important factors, such as genetics and access to health care, can have an impact on your health and longevity, the two alternatives are, to a large extent, a matter of lifestyle choices (Elliott & Eisdorfer, 1982; Taylor, 1995). As you can see by "reading between the lines" in Table 10.2, many early deaths derive directly from behaviors that people have voluntarily selected. Stress, of course, is part of the lifestyle equation, too. In this section of the chapter, we will explore resources that can help us become healthier and ward off the devastating effects of stress. As our Core Concept puts it:

Core Concept

> **All the factors that promote health and well-being will also combat distress — and they are largely under our control.**

Social support: The resources others provide to help an individual cope with stress.

We will begin this section of the chapter by examining psychological stress reducers, such as social support and humor. Then we will consider physical tactics associated with stress reduction and disease prevention. Finally, we will look at the characteristics of people who say they have found happiness and a sense of well-being.

Psychological Resources for Coping with Stress

Earlier in the chapter we saw how the Types A and D behavior patterns, learned helplessness, and certain ego defense mechanisms aggravate the unhealthy effects of stress. But, as our Core Concept suggests, many techniques and resources exist for dealing effectively with stress. We will examine a menu of possibilities. Perhaps the most important fact is this: Nearly all the stress-related factors in our lives can be modified. We begin with a little help from our friends.

In addition to grief over lost comrades, delayed posttraumatic stress syndrome has been a special problem for Vietnam veterans. Feeling rejected by the American public seemed to heighten their difficulty in adjusting to civilian life.

SOCIAL SUPPORT One of the best antidotes for stress is **social support:** the psychological and physical resources that others provide to help an individual cope with adversity. Research shows that people who encounter major life stresses, such as the loss of a spouse or job, come through the ordeal more easily if they have an effective network of friends or family for social support (Billings & Moos, 1985). Similarly, social support has demonstrable health benefits for those suffering from physical disease (Davison et al., 2000; Kelley et al., 1997). By contrast, people with few close relationships die younger, on the average, than people with good social support networks (Berkman & Syme, 1979; Cohen, 1988; Gottlieb, 1981; House et al., 1988; Pilisuk & Parks, 1986). In fact, the lack of a reliable support network increases the risk of dying from disease, suicide, or accidents by about the same percentage as does smoking (House et al., 1988).

Social support can take many forms. First, *socioemotional support* gives you the message that you are loved, cared for, esteemed, and connected to other people in a network of communication and mutual oblig-

TABLE 10.2	Leading Causes of Death in the United States (1998)		
RANK	PERCENTAGE OF DEATHS	CAUSE OF DEATH	CONTRIBUTORS TO CAUSE OF DEATH (D = diet; S = smoking; A = alcohol)
1	31.0	Heart disease	DS
2	23.2	Cancers	DS
3	6.8	Strokes	DS
4	4.8	Chronic obstructive lung diseases	S
4	4.2	All accidents	A
	1.9	Accidents; motor vehicles	A
6	3.9	Pneumonia and influenza	S
7	2.8	Diabetes	D
8	1.3	Suicide	A
9	1.1	Kidney diseases	
10	1.1	Chronic liver disease	A

ation (Cobb, 1976; Cohen & Syme, 1985). At times, other people can also provide *tangible support* (money, transportation, housing) and *informational support* (advice, personal feedback, expert guidance). Anyone with whom you have a significant relationship can be part of your social support network in time of need.

Much research points to the power of social support in moderating vulnerability to a variety of stressful situations (Cohen & McKay, 1983). When people can turn to other people, they are psychologically better able to handle unemployment, marital disruption, and serious illness, as well as the everyday problems of living (Gottlieb, 1981; Pilisuk & Parks, 1986). In contrast, lack of a social support system clearly increases one's vulnerability to disease and death (Berkman & Syme, 1979). Moreover, decreased social support in family and work environments is related to increases in psychological problems.

RELAXATION TRAINING AND BIOFEEDBACK   Another approach to coping with stress involves relaxation and leisure. The problem is that our ability to relax is, to a large extent, influenced by activity in the hormone system and the autonomic nervous system—neither of which is normally under direct voluntary control. One way around this problem relies on a technique called **biofeedback** to help people whose internal biological responses have surged out of control. Biofeedback devices measure a variety of physical responses, such as muscle tone, perspiration, skin temperature, and brain waves. The device then gives the user immediate information, or *feedback,* about subtle changes in these responses—changes of which they are not usually aware. With this feedback, subjects can learn relaxation techniques and see how they affect their physical responses.

How effective is biofeedback? Despite some early, overblown claims for its effectiveness, biofeedback has not proved to be the cure-all that some hoped it would be. More realistically, it may help as one component of a multidimensional therapy package (Miller & Brucker, 1979; Paran et al., 1996; Roberts, 1985; Roush, 1997) through which people learn to relax in the face of stress.

Biofeedback: A therapy technique for learning relaxation and new visceral responses to stress, involving devices that sense small physical changes and provide immediate feedback to the individual.

Giving the elderly an opportunity to continue to make a difference in the lives of those around them greatly improves their health and mood.

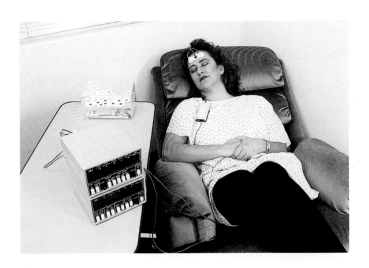

Biofeedback can help people learn how to relax.

OPTIMISTIC THINKING   An optimist sees the glass as half full, while the pessimist sees it as half empty. The optimist sees opportunity, where the pessimist sees potential disaster. The optimist enjoys the smooth sailing, as the pessimist sees only a calm before the storm. Which approach has the advantage under stress? "Life inflicts the same setbacks and tragedies on the optimist as on the pessimist," says psychologist Martin Seligman (1991), "but the optimist weathers them better." In general, optimistic people have fewer physical symptoms of illness, recover more quickly from certain disorders, are healthier, and live longer than pessimists do (Peterson et al., 1988; Taylor et al., 2000a).

A long-term research program by Seligman and his associates at the University of Pennsylvania indicates that an *optimistic style of thinking* has three general characteristics:

▶ It attributes an unpleasant experience to *specific causes* rather than global problems: "I feel fine except for this headache."

▶ It blames problems on *external* rather than internal conditions: "I probably got the headache from reading too long without a break; next study session, I'll remember to stop and stretch every half hour."

▶ It assumes that the causes of pain or illness are *unstable* or temporary; for example, "I don't usually have headaches for very long, so I'm sure I'll feel better soon."

Seligman believes that an optimistic thinking style can be learned. Specifically, he advises those who feel depressed or helpless to acquire an optimistic outlook by *talking to themselves*. This self-talk, says Seligman, should concentrate on the meaning and causes of personal setbacks. For example, if a dieter splurges on a piece of dessert, instead of thinking, "Since I've ruined my whole diet—I might as well eat the whole cake!" she or he should think, "Well, I enjoyed that, but I know I'm strong enough to stick to this diet most of the time." In essence, Seligman argues that optimism is learned by adopting a *constructive* style of thinking, self-assessment, and behavioral planning.

A psychotherapy technique, known as *cognitive restructuring,* is based on the constructive reappraisal of stressors (Swets & Bjork, 1990). The approach recognizes two especially important ways people can reduce stress: They can reduce their *uncertainty* about stressful events by finding out as much as they can in advance, and they can increase their *sense of control* by learning healthy coping techniques. Cognitive restructuring is especially suitable for people who are having problems with chronic stress.

You can apply the lesson of reappraisal if, for example, you are worried about giving a speech to a large audience. Try imagining your potential critics in some ridiculous situation—say, sitting there in the nude—and they become less intimidating. If you are anxious about being shy at a social function you must attend, think about finding someone who is more shy than you and reducing his or her social anxiety by starting a conversation. That is, you can learn to reappraise and restructure nearly any situation to make yourself feel less anxious and more in control.

Connection

➡

Chapter 13
Psychotherapy includes a variety of psychological treatments for mental disorders.

CAN HUMOR HEAL?   In a famous book, *The Anatomy of an Illness* (1979), Norman Cousins described his refusal to succumb to the orthodox routine of hospital treatment for a grave form of rheumatoid arthritis. He objected to the regimen of painkilling and tranquilizing drugs and the bland hospital diet.

Instead, with the help of a sympathetic physician, Cousins checked himself out of the hospital and into happier surroundings: a hotel room, where he stopped taking his painkillers and tranquilizers. In their place, he substituted large doses of vitamin C and a nearly continuous diet of old *Candid Camera* tapes, Marx Brothers films, and other favorite comedies. Remarkably, he not only survived, but he reversed many of his symptoms. Cousins credited his success to taking control over his environment and his illness and to replacing toxic negative emotions with healthful laughter. He concluded that laughter helps renew the adrenal glands, which can become exhausted from fighting disease.

EVALUATING THE EVIDENCE ON ATTITUDES AND HEALTH   In evaluating the claims of Norman Cousins, we must remember that anecdotes are not reliable data. Cousins conducted no controlled experiments. So, there is no way to know whether he might have recovered just as rapidly had he remained in the hospital and followed the usual medical routine. Others with a more scientific frame of mind have conducted controlled experiments, however. In fact, these studies offer little support for the healing power of humor (Martin, 2001).

More generally, research has provided some support for a connection between mental states and physical health (Berk, 1996; Wooten, 1994, 1996). We have seen, for example, that mental stressors and hassles can be hazardous to our health, while optimism can help us stay healthy. Yet attitudes may have limited power to affect serious diseases: One study of 359 cancer patients turned up *no* evidence that patients' attitudes had any effect on the course of the disease (Cassileth et al., 1985). This prompted an editorial in the influential *New England Journal of Medicine,* noting that a happiness-can-make-you-well stance can lead to blaming patients who do not get well (Angell, 1985). This caution has since been echoed by others who have noted a tendency to attribute poor attitudes to people who become ill or fail to recover from a disease (Becker, 1993).

Clearly, the issue is complex. It seems likely that extremely negative attitudes and prolonged emotional arousal can aggravate physical disease processes, while positive attitudes can work with our bodies' natural tendencies to heal themselves. It is probably a mistake, however, to think that attitude is *everything.* It takes more than a healthy attitude to have a healthy body.

Connection

Chapter 1
A controlled experiment is done under conditions that rule out alternative explanations for the results.

Biophysical Resources for Coping with Stress

So far, we have looked primarily at psychological strategies for dealing with the adverse effects of stress. In addition to these, several physical and biological strategies are available for reducing stress. Some are highly effective. Others, we will see, must be approached with caution. We begin with the health-promoting effects of exercise.

EXERCISE   Unfortunately, we have bodies that are better adapted to the strenuous, Stone-Age demands of hunting and foraging than to life in a digital, urban world. Spending our days in relative inactivity behind a desk or computer terminal is not a formula for fitness or mental health.

Without a doubt, a program of regular exercise can be good for you. Not only can it increase muscle tone and eliminate fat, but exercise can help you relax and interact with others. It can also reduce stress (McDonald, 1998). And, it may prolong your life (Lloyd, 1993). A long-term study of 17,000 middle-aged men showed that those who were on an exercise regimen, the equivalent of walking five hours a week, had mortality rates that were almost one-third lower than their couch-potato counterparts (Paffenbarger et al.,

1986). Even smokers who exercised reduced their death rate by about 30%. An exercise-for-health program has several big pluses. Exercise usually requires a change of environment, removing people from their daily hassles and other sources of stress. It also it has a physical training effect by putting short-term stress on the body, which causes the body to rebound and become physically stronger. (Remember *eustress?*)

In addition, it now appears that an exercise program can also make a person *mentally* stronger. In one study, regular aerobic exercise improved the emotional health of female college students who were mildly depressed (McCann & Holmes, 1984). Another study found that a 20-week physical fitness course could produce measurably lower levels of anxiety in sedentary women (Popejoy, 1967). Exercise programs have also been shown to have a positive effect on self-concept (Folkins & Sime, 1981).

Despite these advantages, most resolutions to get more exercise have short lives. People often find it difficult to maintain their motivation. Nevertheless, studies show that people can *learn* to make exercise a regular part of their lives (Myers & Roth, 1997). The keys are (a) finding an activity you like to do and (b) fitting exercise sessions into your schedule several times a week. Having an exercise partner often provides the extra social support people need to stick with their program.

NUTRITION AND DIET Good health and the ability to cope effectively with stress require a brain that has the nutrients it needs to function well. Fortunately, a balanced diet can provide all the nutrients the brain needs. Many people, however, follow a fast-food diet that has excessive fat and can be deficient in other nutrients. You can see in Table 10.3 that, among students surveyed in 21 European countries, only about half say they attempt to follow healthy eating practices. Note, also, that women are more likely to be conscious of good nutrition than are men.

When chronic nutritional deficiencies occur in childhood—when the brain is growing fastest—development can be retarded (Stock & Smythe, 1963; Wurtman, 1982). Poor nutrition can have adverse affects on adults, too. For example, pernicious anemia, a failure to absorb vitamin B_{12}, causes physical and mental slowness. Potassium deficiency can cause listlessness and exhaustion. However, one should be cautious about going to the other extreme by ingesting large quantities of vitamins and minerals. Overdoses of certain vitamins (especially vitamin A) and minerals (such as iron) are easy to achieve and can cause problems that are even more severe than deficiencies.

What can you do to nurture your heath through nutrition? The categories in Table 10.3 are good places to start. We suggest, also, that you beware of nutritional fads, including dietary supplements that come with miraculous promises that seem almost too good to be true. Nutrition is a science in its infancy, and much remains to be discovered about its connections to physical and mental health.

DRUGS AS STRESS RELIEVERS For millennia, people have used alcohol to cope with—or escape from—the stresses of their lives. Illicit drugs, such as cocaine, heroin, and methamphetamine can serve the same purpose. The problem, of course, is that the use of alcohol and other drugs can create new and even more stressful problems through their potential for addiction and distortion of thought processes, not to mention their interpersonal and economic impact.

Physicians may prescribe *antianxiety drugs* (sometimes called "minor tranquilizers") to help their patients cope with stress. While there are valid medical reasons for prescribing these drugs, many psychologists believe that antianxiety

Connection

Chapter 13
Minor tranquilizers (antianxiety drugs) have legitimate therapeutic uses.

TABLE 10.3	Eating Practices of European Students	
	PERCENTAGE WHO FOLLOW EACH PRACTICE	
	MEN	WOMEN
Avoid fat	29	49
Eat fiber	32	50
Eat fruit daily	43	62
Limit red meat	46	62
Limit salt	69	68

Based on Wardle et al. (1997) and a sample of 16,485 students from 21 European countries.

Exercise is a good way to reduce stress and improve your general health.

drugs are too often given to patients who want to ignore problems, rather than face them constructively. In addition to their potential for addiction, all such drugs reduce feelings of anxiety and stress at the cost of impaired cognition.

Smoking, too, can become a drug addiction, as well as a stress-related habit. Blood analysis shows that smokers smoke to maintain a constant nicotine level in their systems (Schachter, 1977). When nicotine levels drop, smokers feel nervous, light-headed, and dizzy. They may develop cramps, tremors, heart palpitations, and cold sweats. The nicotine in a cigarette reverses these symptoms. Stress, however, increases the rate at which the body uses and excretes nicotine. Therefore, individuals addicted to nicotine must smoke more to maintain their accustomed level of this drug.

As a habit, smoking can also become associated with many aspects of a smoker's life that have nothing to do with stress. So, when a smoker attempts to quit, the world seems to come alive with stimulus cues that suggest smoking. Smoking becomes associated with finishing a meal, driving to work, taking a coffee break, going to a bar, watching television—with almost everything but showering and sleeping. Quitting, then, becomes both a matter of building new nonsmoking associations to all the situations in which the person once smoked and at the same time going through the biological discomfort of withdrawal.

Despite the difficulties, an estimated 35 million smokers have kicked the habit (U.S. Department of Health and Human Services, 2000). Most quit on their own, without formal stop-smoking programs. In recent years, the use of nicotine gum or a nicotine patch as part of a plan for quitting has made it much easier for smokers to endure the withdrawal process.

Connection

Chapter 6
The relief of nicotine withdrawal symptoms by smoking is an example of negative reinforcement.

Health Psychology and Behavioral Medicine

Amazingly, 93% of patients don't follow the treatment plans prescribed by their doctors (Taylor, 1990). Obviously, this can have terrible consequences. Accordingly, the need to understand why people fail to take their medicine, get little exercise, eat too much fat, and cope poorly with stress has stimulated the development of two new fields: *behavioral medicine* and *health psychology*.

Behavioral medicine is the medical field that links lifestyle and disease. **Health psychology** is the comparable psychological specialty. Practitioners in both fields are devoted to understanding the psychosocial factors influencing health and illness (Taylor, 1990, 1992). Among their many concerns are health promotion and maintenance; prevention and treatment of illness; causes and correlates of health, illness, and dysfunction; and improvement of the health care system and health policy (Matarazzo, 1980).

Behavioral medicine: The medical field specializing in the link between lifestyle and disease.

Health psychology: The psychological specialty devoted to understanding how people stay healthy, why they become ill, and how they respond when ill.

Both fields are actively involved in the prevention and treatment of trauma and disease that result from stressful or dangerous environments and from poor choices with regard to nutrition, exercise, and drug use. Both are emerging disciplines in countries all over the world (Holtzman, 1992). The two fields overlap, and any differences between them are ones of emphasis. Psychologists have brought increased awareness of emotions and cognitive factors into behavioral medicine, making it an interdisciplinary field rather than an exclusively medical specialty (Miller, 1983; Rodin & Salovey, 1989). Both fields also recognize the interaction of mind and body and place emphasis on preventing illness, as well as changing unhealthy life styles after illness strikes (Taylor, 1986, 1990).

Helping patients to change their lifestyles is difficult. Persuasive strategies identified by social psychologists are now being used to encourage patients' cooperation with their health practitioners (Zimbardo & Leippe, 1991). For example, research shows that people are more likely to comply with requests when they feel they have freedom of choice. Therefore, instead of demanding that a patient strictly adhere to one course of treatment, a physician could offer the patient several options and ask him or her to choose one. Studies also suggest that patients are most likely to adhere to physicians' requests when they are informed of their options and get active social support from friends and family (Gottlieb, 1987; Patterson, 1985). In addition, patients are more satisfied with their health care—and are therefore more likely to comply with a treatment regimen—when they believe that the cost of treatment is outweighed by its effectiveness, and when their practitioners communicate clearly, act courteously, and convey caring and support. Based on these findings, some physicians argue that doctors' attitudes play a large role in their patients' noncompliance. Thus, doctors must first be taught to *care* in order to *cure* (Siegel, 1988).

To continue advancing the quality of life, health practitioners must seek to decrease those deaths and disabilities associated with lifestyle factors (see Table 10.2). Smoking, weight problems, high intake of fat and cholesterol, unsafe sex, drug and alcohol abuse, and stress contribute to heart disease, kidney disease, cancer, strokes, cirrhosis, accidents, and suicide. Changing the behaviors associated with these *diseases of civilization* will prevent much illness and premature death. People are more likely to stay well if they practice good health habits such as those listed in Table 10.4.

Connection

Chapter 14
Social psychologists have studied the factors associated with persuasion, obedience, and compliance.

TABLE 10.4	*Ten Steps to Personal Wellness*
1. Exercise regularly.	
2. Eat nutritious, balanced meals (high in vegetables, fruits, and grains, low in fat and cholesterol).	
3. Maintain a sensible weight.	
4. Sleep 7 to 8 hours nightly; rest/relax daily.	
5. Wear seat belts and bike helmets.	
6. Do not smoke or use drugs.	
7. Use alcohol in moderation, if at all.	
8. Engage only in protected, safe sex.	
9. Get regular medical/dental checkups; adhere to medical regimens.	
10. Develop an optimistic perspective and supportive friendships.	

Prevention: The Example of Heart Disease

We can illustrate some of the problems and accomplishments of health psychology and behavioral medicine with a brief look at a major study to prevent heart disease that was conducted in three towns in California. The goals of the study were (1) to persuade people to reduce their cardiovascular risk via changes in smoking, diet, and exercise; and (2) to determine which method of persuasion was more effective. In one town a two-year advertising campaign was conducted through the mass media. A second town received the same two-year media campaign plus a series of special workshops on modifying health habits for high-risk individuals. The third town served as a control group and received no persuasive campaign. Results showed that the people in the town that had received only the mass-media campaign were more knowledgeable than the controls about the links between lifestyle and heart disease. But, as seen in Figure 10.6, the media blitz produced only modest changes in behaviors and health status. As compared with people in the other two groups, those in the town that received both the workshops and the media campaign showed more substantial and long-lasting effects in changing health habits, particularly in reducing smoking (Farquhar et al., 1984; Maccoby et al., 1977).

The good news from this study is that lifestyle factors can be modified. The bad news is that it is difficult and expensive to do so. Although mass-media campaigns are relatively inexpensive and can increase people's knowledge

Smoking is a stress-related habit.

FIGURE 10.6: Promoting Healthy Change

Knowledge of cardiovascular disease risk factors was greater among residents of Town B, who were exposed to a two-year mass-media health campaign, than among residents of Town A, who were not exposed to the campaign. Knowledge gain was greater still in residents of Town C, who participated in intense workshops and instruction sessions for several months during the media blitz. As knowledge increased, bad health habits (risk behaviors) and signs (indicators) decreased, with Town C leading the way, followed by Town B.

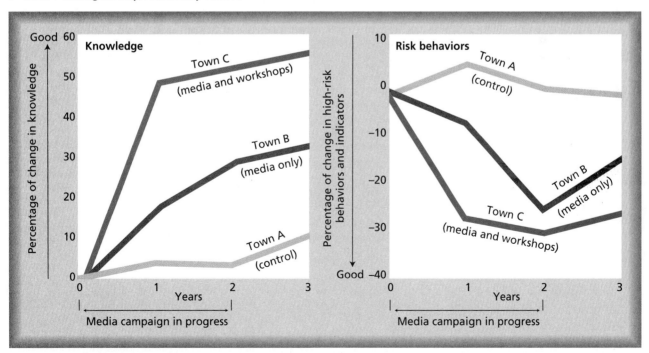

about healthy behaviors, apparently they are not very effective in changing behaviors.

An ambitious program aimed at helping more than a thousand cardiac patients learn to manage stress has been under way since 1978. The project directors have tested several promising methods aimed at reversing the symptoms of the Type A personality, using different combinations of techniques with different groups of volunteer subjects. What have they found to be the best approach? The benefits from participating in small psychotherapy/discussion groups have been the most dramatic. After four and a half years of treatment, patients who had participated in the group therapy program had 44% fewer heart attacks than did a control group of cardiac patients enrolled in an educational program run by a cardiologist (Thoresen, 1990).

What can you do to make your own lifestyle more healthy—and, in the process, perhaps, prevent a heart attack? Table 10.4 gives some specific suggestions. Again, we would like to emphasize the idea contained in our Core Concept: The route to wellness is also the route that leads away from the debilitating effects of excessive stress.

Subjective well-being (SWB): An individual's evaluative response to his or her life, including cognitive and emotional reactions.

Psychology

Happiness and Well-Being

In Your Life

Following the suggestions on the list in Table 10.4 can lead to a feeling-good state that researchers call **subjective well-being (SWB).** Do you usually have that feeling? Studies of SWB ask respondents to rate experiences in their lives, answer questions about factors that affect satisfaction, well-being, mood, or success, or simply rate themselves on a scale like the one in the accompanying figure (Diener, 1984, 2000; Diener & Diener, 1996). The research on happiness (Myers, 2000; Myers & Diener, 1995) shows that, despite many individual differences, SWB is defined by three central components:

► *Satisfaction with present life:* People who are high in SWB like their work and are satisfied with their current personal relationships. They are *sociable,* outgoing, and willing to open up to others (Pavot et al., 1990). Just as important, high SWB people *like*

themselves, and they enjoy good health and high self-esteem (Janoff-Bulman, 1989, 1992).

► *Relative presence of positive emotions:* High SWBs more frequently feel pleasant emotions, mainly because they evaluate the world around them in a generally positive way. They have an *optimistic outlook,* and they expect success in what they undertake (Seligman, 1991).

► *Relative absence of negative emotions:* Individuals with a strong sense of subjective well-being experience fewer and less severe episodes of negative emotions such as anxiety, depression, and anger. On the positive side, they *like what they do,* have a good sense of control in life events, and are able to enjoy the "flow" of engaging work (Crohan et al., 1989; Csikszentmihalyi, 1990; Larson, 1989).

What underlies a healthy response on these dimensions? Twin studies show that feelings of well-being are influenced by genetics (Lykken & Tellegen, 1996), but other research shows that SWB is also

influenced by cognitions and circumstances. Csikszentmihalyi (1999) argues that *flow* experiences are essential for sustained happiness. In addition, studies have found that people who lack social support, who are pressured to pursue goals set by others, and who infrequently receive positive feedback on their performance are likely to rate themselves as relatively unhappy. Accordingly, Richard Ryan and Edward Deci (2000) suggest that feelings of well-being require the satisfaction of (a) a need to feel *competent,* (b) a need for social connection or *relatedness,* and (c) a need for *autonomy* or a sense of self-control.

So, who has feelings of subjective well-being and happiness? Before reading further, take a moment to consider whether you think some groups of people are happier than others. If so, which ones? From their review of the SWB literature, Myers and Diener (1995) have exploded several myths and misunderstandings about happiness:

▶ *There is no "happiest age" of life.* SWB cannot be predicted from someone's age. Most age groups studied exhibit similar levels of life satisfaction, for example, although the causes of their happiness do change with age (Inglehart, 1990).

▶ *Happiness has no "gender gap."* While women are more likely than men to suffer from anxiety and depression, and men are more at risk for alcoholism and certain personality disorders, approximately equal numbers of men and women report being fairly satisfied with life (Fujita et al., 1991; Haring et al., 1984; Inglehart, 1990).

▶ *There are minimal racial differences in happiness.* African Americans and European Americans report nearly the same levels of happiness, and African Americans are even slightly less vulnerable to depression (Diener et al., 1993). Despite racism and discrimination, members of disadvantaged minority groups

generally seem to "think optimistically" by making realistic self-comparisons and attributing problems less to themselves than to unfair circumstances (Crocker & Major, 1989).

▶ *Money does not buy happiness.* At the level of nations, wealthier societies report greater well-being. But within countries — except for very poor, desperate nations such as Bangladesh and India — once the necessities of food, shelter, and safety are provided, there is only a very weak correlation between income and happiness. Having *no* money is a cause of misery, but wealth itself cannot guarantee happiness (Diener & Diener, 1996; Diener et al., 1993). The secret here is that happy people are not those who get what they want — but rather those who want what they have (Myers & Diener, 1995).

▶ Those who have a spiritual dimension in their lives most often report being happy (Myers & Diener, 1995). This may result from many factors, including a healthier life style, social support,

and optimistic thinking . Whatever the reasons, spiritually involved people enjoy, on the average, better mental and physical health (Seybold & Hill, 2001).

These findings tell us that life circumstances — one's age, sex, race, nationality, or income — do not predict happiness. The key factors in subjective well-being appear to be psychological traits and processes. It is sometimes startling to discover how well many people are able to adapt to major changes in their lives — and still feel happy. One study found, for example, that while the moods of victims of spinal cord injuries were extremely negative shortly after their accidents, several weeks later they reported feeling much happier than they had been *before* sustaining their injuries (Silver, 1983).

Life events can alter our moods and change and almost seem to destroy our lives. Not all life events can be forgotten; some people will find it daunting or impossible to recover from tragedies such as losing a loved one to war, violent crime, or disease (Bard & Sangrey, 1979; Janoff-Bulman, 1992; Silver et al., 1983; Silver & Wortman, 1980; Vitaliano et al., 1991). Even more common losses such as the death of a spouse are likely to be deeply painful and sometimes require years for bereavement and healing. But studies of happiness and well-being show that people are exceedingly resilient. Those who undergo severe stress usually manage to adapt. Typically they return to a mood and level of well-being similar to — or even better than — that prior to the traumatic event (Headey & Wearing, 1992).

The Faces Scale: "Which Face Comes Closest to Expressing How You Feel About Your Life as a Whole?" Researchers often use this simple scale to obtain people's ratings of their level of well-being. As the percentages indicate, most people select one of the happy faces. The scale and data are from *Social Indicators of Well-Being: Americans' Perceptions of Life Quality* (p. 207 and p. 306), by F. M. Andrews and S. B. Withey, 1976, New York, Plenum. Copyright 1976 by Plenum.

| 20% | 46% | 27% | 4% | 2% | 1% | 0% |

1. **RECALL:** *All the following are healthy ways to cope with stress, except*
   a. relaxation training.
   b. cognitive restructuring.
   c. exercise.
   d. reaction formation.

2. **RECALL:** *Biofeedback can help people learn*
   a. to relax.
   b. to get rid of ego defense mechanisms.
   c. to do an appraisal of their life goals.
   d. to engage in regular exercise.

3. **RECALL:** *Norman Cousins is well known for his belief in the healing power of*
   a. exercise.
   b. humor.
   c. social support.
   d. drugs.

4. **APPLICATION:** *If you have a very sick friend, you should avoid saying,*
   a. "Social support can help people cope with illness."
   b. "Good nutrition is an essential part of a healthy lifestyle."
   c. "Relaxation training and biofeedback can reduce stress."
   d. "A good attitude can make you well."

Core Concept

5. **UNDERSTANDING THE CORE CONCEPT:**

   Exercise, good nutrition, social support, and relaxation training can help people
   a. cope with stress.
   b. achieve a more healthy lifestyle.
   c. both a and b
   d. none of the above

ANSWERS: 1. d   2. a   3. b   4. d   5. c

Using Psychology to Learn Psychology: Coping with Test Anxiety

The test is being passed down the row, and your heart starts racing. You can feel your pulse pounding in your temples. A knot forms in the pit of your stomach. The pen feels slippery as your hands begin to perspire. You have studied for the test, but suddenly you can't remember "general adaptation syndrome" from "psychoneuroimmunology." You have a full-blown attack of test anxiety! What can you do?

Prevention rather than cure is the best way to deal with this problem. And that's where you can use psychology on yourself. Your authors recommend that you take the following steps well before the test:

▶ *Remember that a moderate degree of arousal is helpful.* It can help you think more clearly. (Remember Selye's concept of *eustress*.) So don't mistake a bit of nervousness for debilitating test anxiety.

▶ *Learn the material thoroughly.* Feeling confident that your head contains the information you need is a great anxiety reducer. To do so, you need to know not only the important terms but how these terms are connected to the important issues and concepts (such as the Core Concepts in this book). You will also want to "psych out" your professor: What does he or she see as the important terms, issues, and concepts? Learning the material and identifying the important concepts can be hard work — but not impossible. Don't be surprised if it requires two or more hours of study outside class for every hour you spend in class.

▶ *Take advantage of social support.* Of all the techniques discussed in this chapter, this may be the most useful. You will find social support in other students who are taking the same course. Seek them out and schedule a few group study sessions. Use these sessions to clarify concepts and to anticipate what will be on the next examination.

▶ *Use relaxation training techniques.* Relaxation training will help you calm both mind and body. Someone on your campus probably has some expertise in this area and would be happy to help you: Ask in your counseling center, psychology department, or learning resources center. Once you acquire some of the techniques, you can apply them before a test or whenever you feel that anxiety threatens to run away with you.

Test anxiety is a common problem. Nearly everyone has experienced it at one time or another, but it doesn't have to spiral out of control and ruin your grade. By using a bit of psychology on yourself, you can change the *distress* of tests into *eustress*.

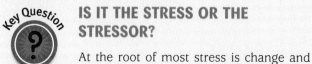

Chapter Summary

IS IT THE STRESS OR THE STRESSOR?

At the root of most stress is change and the need to adapt to environmental, physical, psychological, and social demands. Primitive stressors included mortal threats such as starvation, exposure to the elements, attack, and natural catastrophes. Modern life still may include catastrophes, but it also exposes us to the cumulative effects of stressors acting over the long term: societal stressors, hassles, burnout, and various life changes. The Holmes-Rahe SRRS has been used extensively to measure life changes and to correlate them with changes in health, although this work has been criticized on several counts.

Core Concept

The effects of stress (an internal response) depend more on the intensity and duration of stress than on its source (the stressor).

HOW DOES STRESS AFFECT US PHYSICALLY?

Stress involves the effect of mental processes on the body. Stress arouses us physiologically and often produces a fight-or-flight response. This may serve us well in acute but not chronic stress. Selye found that chronic stress from any source produces the three stages of the general adaptation syndrome: the alarm reaction, resistance, and exhaustion. Stress can also have effects on the immune system—sometimes stimulating it and sometimes suppressing it. Selye also taught that some forms of stress—eustress—can have healthy effects by promoting growth and resilience.

Stress can help us meet challenges and grow stronger, but too much stress – distress – can have harmful physical consequences.

HOW DO WE RESPOND PSYCHOLOGICALLY TO STRESS?

Certain personality variables can help or hinder an individual's ability to cope with stress. Those with Type A personality traits risk adverse stress reactions, although the specific traits associated with this risk are still under dispute. Some people, however, display a resistance to stress stemming from hardiness, a learned trait. When punishment or failure are unavoidable, the result is often learned helplessness and diminished hedonic capacity. There are no gender differences in coping styles, although there are differences in the causes of stress. Extreme stress sometimes produces a delayed stress reaction, known as posttraumatic stress disorder. Those who have undergone a hostage ordeal may come to identify with their captors, a condition known as the Stockholm syndrome. Sigmund Freud identified several more common means of coping with threat that he called ego defense mechanisms. These include denial, rationalization, projection, repression, reaction formation, displacement, and regression.

Our psychological responses under stress depend on personality, perceptions, and the ways we have learned to respond.

WHAT STRATEGIES CAN PROMOTE HEALTH – RATHER THAN DISTRESS?

Many psychological techniques and resources are available to help us cope with stress and promote a healthy lifestyle: social support, relaxation training, the modification of thought processes, optimism, and humor. Critics caution against uncritical acceptance of claims for the effects of attitudes on health. Among the physical factors that can help us cope with stress are exercise and good nutrition. Caution is in order, however, in using drugs to cope with stress. The relatively new fields of health psychology and behavioral medicine focus on coping with stress and encouraging healthy lifestyles. People who are happy or who have subjective well-being tend to have positive emotions and a general satisfaction with their lives. Happiness can be found in people of all ages, genders, racial groups, and income levels.

All the factors that promote health and well-being will also combat distress – and they are largely under our control.

Review
Test

For each of the following items, choose the single correct or best answer.

1. Which of the following would a psychologist call *stress?*
   a. an earthquake that destroys all your possessions
   b. an angry neighbor who is demanding that you turn down your stereo
   c. an adrenaline response that makes your heart pound, your face pale, and your palms sweaty
   d. an extremely frightening experience

2. Which of the following experiences would be considered a chronic *societal stressor?*
   a. an earthquake
   b. a jail term
   c. being stuck in traffic
   d. widespread unemployment

3. Which one would be most likely to produce *learned helplessness?*
   a. frequent and inescapable punishment
   b. as much money as you could ever spend
   c. a situation in which you were fearful
   d. the death of your spouse

4. Malcolm does not get upset when he encounters problems, seeing them as challenges to be overcome rather than threats to his well-being. Which of the following terms best describes Malcolm's approach to possible stressors?
   a. hardiness
   b. learned helplessness
   c. the Type A personality
   d. hedonic capacity

5. The fight-or-flight syndrome involves
   a. PTSD.
   b. ego defense mechanisms.
   c. activity in the autonomic nervous system.
   d. GAS stage 2.

6. Which of the following is *not* a stage in the general adaptation syndrome described by Hans Selye?
   a. alarm
   b. withdrawal
   c. resistance
   d. exhaustion

7. Nursing home patients had more positive moods, better health, and longer survival compared to others when they were provided with
   a. round-the-clock medical care.
   b. busywork and entertaining activities.
   c. responsibilities that gave them control.
   d. service that relieved them of all aspects of self-care.

8. What is the medical specialty that is related to *health psychology?*
   a. rehabilitation medicine
   b. psychoneuroimmunology
   c. behavioral medicine
   d. eustress

9. A good friend of yours has recently suffered the loss of a close family member. To help your friend cope with this trauma, you should encourage her to
   a. use her ego defense mechanisms.
   b. hit a punching bag to "get it out of her system."
   c. exercise until she is exhausted.
   d. seek the social support of friends and relatives.

10. Research on subjective well-being indicates that _____ are happier than _____.
    a. women/men
    b. wealthy Americans/middle-class Americans
    c. young people/older adults
    d. none of the above

ANSWERS: 1. c   2. d   3. a   4. a   5. c   6. b
7. c   8. c   9. d   10. d

If You're Interested . . .

BOOKS

Adams, P., with an introduction by Robin Williams. (1998). *House calls: How we can all heal the world one visit at a time.* Robert D. Reed. This primer on wellness includes suggestions to visit loved ones, how to make healthy choices, how to be a good doctor, and how to be a successful hospital patient. The key, says Adams, is having a meaningful connection between doctor and patient—a healing bond for both of them.

Bennett-Goleman, T. (2001). *Emotional alchemy: How the mind can heal the heart.* Harmony Books. The author recommends a blend of mindfulness, meditation, and cognitive therapy to identify and change the emotional patterns that turn habitual feelings into illness, bringing them to awareness so that their hold can be broken, and healing can begin.

Cousins, N. (1979). *The anatomy of an illness as perceived by a patient: Reflections on healing and rejuvenation.* Norton. Norman Cousins revolutionized popular and professional thinking about modern medicine when he reacted to a frightening diagnosis with his own self-prescription of happiness and laughter, contributing powerfully to the modern science of health promotion.

Hendricks, G. (1995). *Conscious breathing: Breathwork for health, stress release, and personal mastery.* Bantam Books. A bit New-Agey in appearance, yet based on sound principles and practices, this well-illustrated workbook reviews techniques for relaxation, meditation, and body awareness/biofeedback that can be immediately applied to make one feel better, more focused *and* relaxed, and healthier.

Kabat-Zinn, J. (1990). *Full catastrophe living: Using the wisdom of your body and mind to face stress, pain, and illness.* (Preface by Thich Nhat Hanh). Delta Publishing. The title refers to a line from *Zorba the Greek,* the main character's description of the ups and downs of family life. The author, founder of the Stress Reduction Clinic and a major proponent of meditation in stress management, here recommends focusing attention on being in the present in order to listen to the body and participate completely in one's own wellness.

Maslach, C. , & Leiter, M. P. (1997). *The truth about burnout: How organizations cause personal stress and what to do about it.* Jossey Bass. The first author, the original burnout researcher, examines the helplessness and frustration individuals experience in large organizations. The authors profile the problem based on recent research and recommend how to prevent suffering or worsening burnout by understanding it, setting new goals, dealing with crises, and looking to the future.

Paul, M. (1998). *The healing mind: The vital links between brain and behavior, immunity, and disease.* Dunne Books. A medical doctor, writing more like a novelist than a scientist, offers an overview of the connection between health and consciousness, ranging from topics as light as the benefits of keeping pets to those as heavy as dealing with terminal cancer.

Price, R. (1995). *A whole new life: An illness and a healing.* Plume/Penguin. The celebrated novelist Reynolds Price reflects on his own experiences with the discovery of a cancerous tumor "certain to kill" him, his "refusal to die," and his explorations of traditional and alternative medicine, encounters with professionals and fellow patients, the callous and the sympathetic, and the challenges of weaving together the elements of his own life and past to face the crisis of his future.

Rothschild, B. (2000). *The body remembers: The psychophysiology of trauma and trauma treatment.* W. W. Norton & Co. A psychotherapist reviews therapies of stress response, applied to her experience with clients and case studies.

Sapolsky, R. M. (1998). *Why zebras don't get ulcers: An updated guide to stress-related diseases, and coping.* W. H. Freeman. Cutting-edge research-based advice laced with humor and insight, this work examines the utterly human dilemma of life-threatening stress and how it can be understood, modified, and controlled.

Selzer, R. (1998). *The doctor stories.* Picador USA. This selection of short fiction was written by physicians and surgeons, whose stories show the complex challenges and changes inherent in illness and the struggles of both patient and doctor to survive and heal.

Siegel, B. S. (1986). *Love, medicine, and miracles.* Harper & Row. Here are stories of people who made remarkable recoveries, their new perspectives on life, and the characteristics that may have helped them to become survivors.

VIDEOS

The Doctor. (1991, color, 123 min.). Directed by Randa Haines; starring William Hurt, Christine Lahti, Elizabeth Perkins, Mandy Patinkin. Based on *A Taste of My Own Medicine* by Ed Rosenbaum, M.D., the story tells of a cold though brilliant physician whose feeling about his life and work are changed forever when he is diagnosed with cancer and views the world from the patient's perspective.

Falling Down. (1993, color, 115 min.). Directed by Joel Schumacher; starring Michael Douglas, Robert Duvall, Barbara Hershey, Tuesday Weld. A businessman stuck in a traffic jam is stressed to the limit and goes on a rampage of rage at the pressures and disappointments that he feels have victimized him.

Fearless. (1993, color, 122 min.). Directed by Peter Weir; starring Jeff Bridges, Rosie Perez, Isabella Rossellini, Tom Hulce. When he is one of very few passengers to survive an airplane crash, a man loses perspective on his life and becomes convinced he cannot be destroyed. Initially reckless, his feelings prove helpful to the healing of fellow guilt-ridden, grieving survivors.

God Said, "Ha!" (1999, color, 85 min.). Directed by Julia Sweeney; starring Julia Sweeney and Quentin Tarantino as themselves. Former *Saturday Night Live* cast comedian Julia Sweeney survived a terrible period during which both she and her brother were diagnosed with cancer and their families' lives went into an upheaval of anxiety, relocation, and uncertainty that they characteristically treated with dark humor and comic hope. This film, her one-woman show, is based on her book of the same name (Bantam/Doubleday/Dell, 1998).

Patch Adams. (1998, color, 103 min.). Directed by Tom Shadyac; starring Robin Williams, Monica Potter, Daniel London, Bob Gunton, Peter Coyote. This film is based on the true story of Hunter "Patch" Adams, M.D., who became a physician despite his irreverence regarding the power and money of modern medicine and his desire to make medical care reassuring and even fun for patients. (See Adams's book, listed above).

Unbreakable. (2000, color, 106 min.). Directed by M. N. Shyamalan; starring Bruce Willis, Samuel L. Jackson, Robin Wright Penn, Spencer Treat Clark. At the urging of an eccentric stranger, a man born with extreme physical vulnerabilities, a security guard slowly realizes that he appears to be invulnerable to sickness and injury.

WEB RESOURCES

http://www.stress.org/ From the American Institute of Stress, this Web site offers information on the role of stress in health and disease. Read the monthly newsletter and explore the informational packets on stress and health.

http://www.centering.org/ This site is available to people who are recovering from a strong emotional loss. Visit the various pages for specific types of loss, such as suicide survivors or the loss of a child.

http://www.queendom.com/tests/health/social_anxiety_r_access.html This Social Anxiety Test contains 25 questions to test whether or not a person has social anxiety. What determines whether or not someone has social anxiety?

http://www.med.nus.edu.sg/pcm/stress/ How should students manage their stress? Visit this Web site to read some stress management tips for students. Visit the links for relief and treatment information.

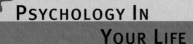
WHAT FORCES SHAPE OUR PERSONALITIES?

Psychodynamic Theories
Humanistic Theories
Cognitive Theories
Current Trends

According to the psychodynamic, humanistic, and cognitive theories, personality is a developmental process, shaped by our internal needs and cognitions and by external pressures from the social environment.

EXPLAINING UNUSUAL PEOPLE AND UNUSUAL BEHAVIOR:
You don't need a theory of personality to explain why people do the expected.

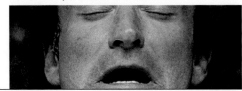

WHAT PATTERNS ARE FOUND IN PERSONALITY?

Personality and Temperament
Personality as a Composite of Traits

Some theories attribute personality to stable patterns known as traits, types, and temperaments.

FINDING YOUR TYPE:
When it comes to classifying personality according to types, a little caution may be in order.

WHAT "THEORIES" DO PEOPLE USE TO UNDERSTAND EACH OTHER?

Implicit Personality Theories
Personality across Cultures

People everywhere develop implicit assumptions ("folk theories") about personality, but these assumptions vary in important ways across cultures.

DEVELOPING YOUR OWN THEORY OF PERSONALITY:
You'll probably want to be eclectic.

USING PSYCHOLOGY TO LEARN PSYCHOLOGY: Your Academic Locus of Control

PERSONALITY

What drove Margaret Sanger? A psychologist trying to understand this powerful and charismatic figure might conclude that the balance in her life shifted on a sweltering day in July of 1912. She had responded to a call from the slums in New York City's Lower East Side, where Jake Sachs had found his wife, Sadie, unconscious and bleeding on the kitchen floor. The cause: Sadie had attempted to give herself an abortion. It was Sanger's job as an emergency-response nurse to save Sadie's life.

In those days, unwanted pregnancy —and botched abortions—were often the result of ignorance. Giving medical advice on sex was illegal, and birth control devices, such as condoms and diaphragms, were nearly impossible to obtain. As a result, some 100,000 illegal abortions were performed in the state every year—many of them by dangerous quack practitioners. People like Sadie, the poor and uneducated—those least able to bear the costliness of many children—had nowhere to turn for competent help with reproduction and family planning (Asbell, 1995).

Thanks to swift action by Margaret Sanger, Sadie Sachs survived. Nevertheless, Sanger was angry that she could do nothing to help *prevent* unwanted pregnancies. She was limited by the law to providing after-the-fact treatment for the victims of incompetent abortionists. It

(continued)

only added fuel to her inner fire when she later heard Sachs ask the doctor, "What can I do to stop having babies?" and heard his sarcastic reply, "Better tell Jake to sleep on the roof" (Sanger, 1971).

Sanger saw Sadie Sachs only one more time: Three months later, pregnant once again, Sadie died of another abortion attempt. This needless death spurred Sanger to seek an answer to her patients' pleas for safe contraception, "no matter what it might cost" (Sanger, 1938, in Conway, 1992, p. 567).

The cost was high. Sanger left the nursing profession and put her own family in the background as she began to research and promote contraception full-time. In 1914 the threat of a prison term for "indecency" forced her to flee for England, where she spent a year waiting for the charges to be dropped. But she couldn't avoid jail altogether: In 1916, when she opened a public birth-control clinic, Sanger had to serve several jail sentences for illegally distributing information about contraception.

For 40 years, Sanger persistently challenged laws making contraception a criminal act and insisted that women take control of—and responsibility for—their bodies, sexuality, and childbearing (Kennedy, 1970; Sanger, 1971). But her single-minded focus on the cause of birth control eventually cost her a marriage to a man who had adored her and supported her work. Finally, in 1952, Sanger, then in her 70s, joined forces with philanthropist Katharine McCormick to commission the development of an oral contraceptive. The result: The first birth-control pills for women were approved for prescription eight years later.

Connection

Chapter 12
More than 300 mental disorders are recognized.

The pattern of dogged determination seen in Sanger across these 40 years of struggle illustrates the central idea of this chapter: **Personality** consists of the psychological qualities that bring *continuity* to an individual in different situations and at different times. Thus, personality is the thread of consistency that runs through our lives (Cervone & Shoda, 1999). And when that thread breaks, we see certain mental disorders involving extreme inconsistencies in personality: bipolar disorder, schizophrenia, and so-called "multiple personality" disorder.

What processes were at work to provide the continuity and consistency that we see in the life of Margaret Sanger? Was her personality shaped primarily by the events and people in her life? Those were often so chaotic that we are forced to consider another possibility—that her strength and determination arose from internal traits—from her basic make-up? You may recognize these alternatives as another instance of the nature–nurture question. The answer, of course, is *both:* Experience *and* innate factors shaped Margaret Sanger's personality, just as they shape our own.

Connection

Chapter 4
The nature–nurture issue concerns the relative effects of heredity and environment.

In this chapter we will examine a number of theoretical explanations for personality. As we do so, you will find that some place more emphasis on nature and others on nurture. You will also find that particular theories are suited to dealing with particular kinds of problems:

Personality: The psychological qualities that bring continuity to an individual's behavior in different situations and at different times.

> ▶ If your goal is to understand a depressed friend, a troublesome child—any individual—as a developing, changing being, you will probably find one of the *psychodynamic, humanistic,* or *cognitive* theories of personality most helpful. These theories are described in the first part of the chapter.

Personality is the thread of continuity in an individual in different situations.

▶ If what you need is a snapshot of a person's current personality characteristics — as you might want if you were screening job applicants for your company — a theory of *traits, types,* or *temperaments* may be your best bet. You will find these in the second section of the chapter.

▶ If you are most interested in how people understand each other — as you might be if you were providing marriage counseling or conflict management — you will want to know the assumptions people make about each other. That is, you will want to know their *implicit theories* of personality. These will be discussed in the final section of the chapter.

▶ And, if you are wondering whether people understand each other in the same ways the world around, you will want to know about the *cross-cultural* work in personality. Such issues are also discussed in the last section of the chapter.

WHAT FORCES SHAPE OUR PERSONALITIES?

Key Question

If you have ever attended a family or high school reunion, you know that people relentlessly change and grow. They develop new interests and new friends, they move to new places, and they have new experiences. In this section we will consider three ways of accounting for the paths their personalities take: the *psychodynamic,* the *humanistic,* and the *cognitive* theories. Each describes personality from a different perspective, but all portray it as a dynamic, developing process. And all emphasize the interplay of internal mental processes and social interactions — as our Core Concept says:

> According to the psychodynamic, humanistic, and cognitive theories, personality is a developmental process, shaped by our internal needs and cognitions and by external pressures from the social environment.

Core Concept

Although the three viewpoints we will consider in this section of the chapter share some common ground, each emphasizes a different combination of factors. The *psychodynamic theories* of personality call attention to the power of the unconscious and the lasting influence of early childhood experience. *Humanistic theories* emphasize our present, subjective reality: what we believe

Sigmund Freud was the founder of psychoanalysis and the psychodynamic perspective. He is seen here walking with his daughter Anna Freud, who later became a psychoanalyst in her own right.

Connection

Chapter 12

Conversion disorder is one of the somatoform disorders, which produce physical symptoms without a physical cause.

Connection

Chapter 13

Psychoanalysis is Freud's method of psychotherapy.

Psychoanalysis: Freud's theory of personality and his system of treatment for mental disorders.

Unconscious: The psychic domain of which the individual is not aware but which is the storehouse of repressed impulses, drives, and conflicts that are unavailable to consciousness.

Eros: The unconscious force that drives people toward acts that are sexual, life-giving, and creative.

Libido: The Freudian concept of psychic energy that drives individuals to experience sensual pleasure.

is important now and how we think of ourselves in relation to others. According to the *cognitive theories,* personality is influenced by perception and social experience. Note that, in these respects, the three approaches complement rather than contradict each other: Our lives include past, present, and future; our minds have both conscious and unconscious levels; our behaviors are sometimes emotional and impulsive and at other times cooler and more calculated. Which theory we choose will depend, to some extent, on what aspect of personality and behavior we want to explain. Let us look closely at each perspective.

Psychodynamic Theories

The psychodynamic approach originated in the late 1800s with a medical puzzle that was called *hysteria,* now known as *conversion disorder.* In this condition, the physician finds physical symptoms, such as a muscle weakness, loss of sensation in a part of the body, or even paralysis—but no apparent physical cause, such as nerve damage. The psychological nature of hysteria finally became apparent when the French physician Jean Charcot demonstrated that he could make hysterical symptoms disappear by suggestion. He did this while his patients were in a hypnotic trance.

Sigmund Freud (1856–1939), a young and curious doctor, heard of this work and traveled to Paris to watch Charcot's renowned hypnotic demonstrations. Inspired, Freud returned to Vienna, resolving to try the hypnotic cure on his own patients. But to his dismay, Dr. Freud found that many could not be hypnotized deeply enough to affect their symptoms. Moreover, even the ones who lost their symptoms under hypnosis regained them after the trance was lifted. Finally, a frustrated Freud resolved to find another way to understand and treat the mysterious illness. The new approach he created became known as **psychoanalysis.**

FREUD'S PSYCHOANALYTIC THEORY At center stage in the new psychoanalytic theory, Freud placed the concept of the **unconscious,** which he saw as the source of powerful impulses, drives, and conflicts that energize the personality. We are normally unaware of this psychic domain, said Freud, because its contents are too threatening and anxiety provoking. Only by using the special techniques of psychoanalysis would we find that a person who had, for example, been sexually molested in childhood holds these memories in the unconscious. From there they may reemerge in disguised form—perhaps as a dream or a symptom of a mental disorder, such as depression or a phobia. Even in the healthiest of us, said Freud, behavior originates in unconscious drives that we don't want to acknowledge. Consequently, we go about our daily business without knowing the real motives behind our behavior. Today, many psychologists consider this concept of the unconscious to be Freud's most important contribution to psychology. (See Figure 11.1)

Drives and Instincts The actions of the unconscious mind are powered by psychological energy—thought by Freud to be the mental equivalent of steam in a boiler. Psychoanalysis focuses on how mental energy is exchanged, transformed, and expressed. For example, the "mental steam" of the sex drive could be expressed directly through sexual activity or indirectly through joking or creative pursuits. Freud named this drive **Eros,** for the Greek god of passionate love. And the energy behind this drive he called **libido,** from the Latin word for "lust." It is libidinal energy that fuels not only our sexual behavior but our work and our leisure activities: drawing, dancing, reading, body building—nearly everything we do.

FIGURE 11.1: Freud's Model of the Mind

For Freud, the mind is like an iceberg. Only a small portion, the Ego, is apparent, while the vast mass of the unconscious lurks beneath the surface.

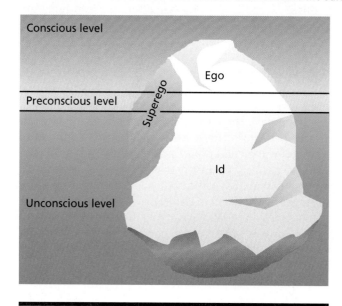

But Eros did not explain everything that fascinated Freud. Specifically, it did not explain acts of human aggression and destruction. It also did not explain the symptoms of the war veterans he saw who continued to relive their wartime traumas in nightmares and hallucinations. Such misery could only be explained with another drive, which he called **Thanatos** (from the Greek word for "death"). Freud conceived of Thanatos as the "death instinct" that drives the aggressive and destructive acts that humans commit against each other and themselves.

Was Freud right about Eros and Thanatos? You might gauge his theory against your own experience. Have you observed any human behavior that could not, broadly speaking, be assigned to one of these two categories: life and death—or, if you prefer, creation and destruction?

Psychic Determinism   For the psychoanalyst, Freud's discoveries mean that the significance of symptoms such as fears and phobias must be interpreted as signs of unconscious difficulties. Similarly, a so-called **Freudian slip** occurs when "accidental" speech or behavior belies an unconscious conflict or desire. You might commit such a slip, as you leave a boring social function, by telling your host, "I really had a terrible—I mean *terrific*—time." Likewise, being consistently late for a date with a particular person is no accident, Freud would have said. Rather, it expresses the way you feel unconsciously.

Freud believed that nothing we do is accidental. All our acts are determined by unconscious forces. This concept is known as the doctrine of **psychic determinism**. For example, consistently forgetting a certain person's name is a sign of inner conflicts or threatening memories.

In his work with hysterical patients, Freud observed that the particular physical symptom often seemed related to a traumatic event that had been "forgotten." For instance, a patient who was hysterically "blind" might, during therapy, suddenly recall seeing her parents having intercourse when she was a small child. How had this produced blindness? As she becomes an adult, she may have anticipated her first sexual encounter, which aroused powerful feel-

Connection

Chapter 9
Other drive theories are not based on unconscious motivation.

Thanatos: The unconscious force that drives people toward aggressive and destructive behaviors.

Freudian slip: "Accidental" speech (a slip of the tongue) or behavior that reveals an unconscious desire.

Psychic determinism: Freud's assumption that all mental and behavioral reactions are caused by earlier life experiences.

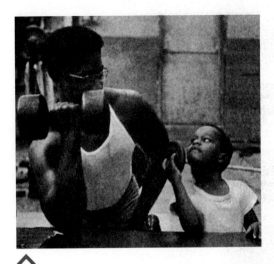

During the phallic stage, a child must resolve feelings of conflict and anxiety by identifying more closely with the same-sex parent—said Freud.

Connection

Chapter 4
Compare Freud's *psychosexual* stages with Erikson's *psychosocial* stages.

Connection

Chapter 9
Most modern psychologists find that gender has a basis in both biology and in learning.

Psychosexual stages: Successive, instinctive patterns of associating pleasure with stimulation of specific bodily areas at different times of life.

Oedipus complex: According to Freud, a largely unconscious process whereby boys displace an erotic attraction toward their mother to females of their own age and, at the same time, identify with their fathers.

Penis envy: According to Freud, the female desire to have a penis—a condition that usually results in their attraction to males.

Fixation: Occurs when psychosexual development is arrested at an immature stage.

ings associated with that upsetting memory. Thus, the young woman's blindness could represent an unconscious attempt to undo her vision of the original event—and to deny her own sexual feelings. Blindness would also bring her attention, comfort, and sympathy from others. In this way, her inner psychic motives both determine and maintain her condition.

Early Childhood Experiences   Such cases suggested to Freud that personality continues to develop throughout childhood and adolescence. He concluded, however, that experiences in infancy and early childhood have the strongest impact on personality formation and later behavior. These early experiences continue to influence the mind as the child progresses through a series of **psychosexual stages:** successive, instinctive patterns of associating pleasure with stimulation of specific bodily areas at different times of life. These stages are detailed in Table 11.1.

Among the issues that Freud was trying to understand with his theory of psychosexual development were those of gender identity and gender roles. Why is it that boys usually develop a masculine identity, even though most boys are raised primarily by their mothers? Why do girls, as they become adults, most often develop a sexual attraction to males—and boys to females? And why do some *not* follow this pattern?

Freud's answers to these questions were convoluted and, many psychologists would say, contrived. His inside-the-mind perspective ignored the influence of vastly different forms of socialization for boys and girls. It also ignored the possibility of differences in genetic programming, about which little was known in Freud's day. Instead, he invoked the notion of the **Oedipus complex,** whereby boys *displace* (shift) an erotic attraction toward their mother to females of their own age and, at the same time, identify with their fathers. Girls, he proposed, develop **penis envy** (because they don't have one!) and are usually attracted to males (who do). Most psychologists today reject these Freudian notions of psychosexual development because they lack scientific support. It is important, however, to remember two things: First, these Freudian concepts continue to have a wide impact outside psychology, particularly in the humanities. Second, while Freud may have been wrong about the details of psychosexual development, he may have been right about other aspects of human personality (Bower, 1998a).

Freud might have been right, for example, in his assertion that certain difficulties early in life lead to **fixation:** arrested psychological development. An *oral stage* fixation, caused by a failure to throw off the dependency of the first year of life, may lead to dependency on others in later childhood and adulthood. We also see an oral fixation in certain behaviors involving the mouth, such as overeating, alcoholism, and tendencies toward sarcasm. Among these diverse problems we find a common theme: using the mouth as the way to connect with what one needs. Fixation in the *anal stage* is presumed to come from problems associated with the second year of life when toilet training is a big issue. Anal fixations can result in a stubborn, compulsive, stingy, or excessively neat pattern of behavior—all related to common themes of "holding on" and not losing control of one's body or life. In Table 11.1 you will find examples of fixation at other developmental stages.

Personality Structure   Freud assembled these ideas about drives and stages into a theory that describes how the parts and processes of personality work together. In the resulting theory, Freud pictured a continuing battle

TABLE 11.1
Freud's Stages of Psychosexual Development

PSYCHOSEXUAL STAGE	LATER SIGNS OF PROBLEMS BEGINNING AT THIS STAGE	
Oral Stage (1st year)	Smoking	Obesity
Desires: Oral stimulation by sucking, eating, crying, babbling	Nail-biting	Talkativeness
Challenge: Overcoming dependency	Chewing	Dependency
	Gluttony	Gullibility
Anal Stage (approximately 1–3 years)	Messiness	
Desires: Anal stimulation by bladder and bowel function	Temper tantrums	Excessive cleanliness
Challenges: Toilet training	Destructiveness	Stinginess
Self-control	Cruelty	Coldness, distance, aloofness
Phallic Stage (approximately 3–6 years)	Masturbation (not considered abnormal by modern psychology and psychiatry; see Chapter 8)	
Desires: Stimulation of genitals	Jealousy	
Challenge: Resolving Oedipus complex, involving erotic attraction to parent of opposite sex and hostility to parent of same sex	Egocentric sex	
	Sexual conquests	
	Problems with parents	
Latency (approximately 6 years to puberty)	Excessive modesty	
Desires: Repression of sexual and aggressive desires, including those involved in the Oedipus complex	Prefers company of same sex	
Challenges: Consciously: learning modesty and shame	Homosexuality (considered by Freud to be a disorder, but not by modern psychology and psychiatry; see Chapter 9)	
Unconsciously: dealing with repressed Oedipal conflict		
Genital Stage (puberty and adulthood)	(none)	
Desires: Mature sexual relationships		
Challenges: Displacement of energy into healthy activities		
Establishing new relationship with parents		

between two antagonistic parts of the personality, the *id* and the *superego,* moderated by yet another part of the mind, the *ego.* (See Figure 11.1.)

He conceived of the **id** as the primitive, unconscious part of the personality that houses the basic drives. The id always acts on impulse and pushes for immediate gratification—especially sexual, physical, and emotional pleasures —to be experienced here and now without concern for consequences. It is the *only* part of the personality present at birth.

By contrast, the **superego** serves as the mind's "police force" in charge of values and morals learned from parents and from society. The superego corresponds roughly to our common notion of *conscience.* It develops as the child forms an internal set of rules based on the external rules imposed by parents and other adults. It is the inner voice of "shoulds" and "should nots." The superego also includes the *ego ideal,* an individual's view of the kind of person

Id: The primitive, unconscious portion of the personality that houses the most basic drives and stores repressed memories.

Superego: The mind's storehouse of values, including moral attitudes learned from parents and from society; roughly the same as the common notion of the conscience.

"All right, deep down it's a cry for psychiatric help—but at one level it's a stick-up."

© Punch/Rothco

Connection

Chapter 3
Preconscious processes operate just below the level of awareness.

Connection

Chapter 10
Most ego defense mechanisms are unhealthy responses to stress.

Ego: The conscious, rational part of the personality, charged with keeping peace between the superego and the id.

Ego defense mechanisms: Largely unconscious mental strategies employed to reduce the experience of conflict or anxiety.

Repression: An unconscious process that excludes unacceptable thoughts and feelings from awareness and memory.

Projection: An unconscious process by which we rid ourselves of tension, as we attribute our own impulses and fantasies to something or someone else.

Projective tests: Personality assessment instruments based on Freud's concept of projection.

he or she should strive to become. Understandably, the superego frequently conflicts with the id's desires because the id wants to do what feels good, while the superego insists on doing what is right and moral.

Resolving these conflicts is the job of the third major part of the personality, the **ego,** which is the *conscious,* rational aspect of our minds. The ego must choose actions that will gratify the id's impulses but without violating one's moral principles or incurring undesirable consequences. For example, if you found that you had been given too much change at the grocery store, the superego would insist that you give it back, while the id might urge you to spend it on ice cream. The ego, then, would try to find a compromise, which might include returning the money and buying ice cream with your own money. That is, when the id and superego conflict, the ego tries to satisfy both. However, as pressures from the id, superego, and environment intensify, it becomes more difficult for the ego to find workable compromises. The result may be disordered thoughts or behaviors that signify mental disorder.

Ego Defenses   The ego has an arsenal of **ego defense mechanisms** for dealing with conflict between the id's impulses and the superego's demand to deny them. All operate at the preconscious level, according to Freud. Under mild pressure from the id we may, for example, rely on simple defenses, such as fantasy or rationalization. But if unconscious desires become too insistent, the ego may solve the problem by "putting a lid on the id." To do so, the ego must push extreme desires and threatening memories out of conscious awareness and into the recesses of the unconscious mind. **Repression** is the name for this process that excludes unacceptable thoughts and feelings from awareness. So, for example, repression may explain the behavior of a student who suspects she failed an important test and "forgets" to attend class the day the graded tests are returned. This memory lapse protects her from feeling upset or anxious—at least temporarily. In fact, that is the problem with repression and most of the other **ego defense mechanisms:** They solve the problem only for the moment, leaving the underlying conflict unresolved. You will remember that we saw a variety of ego defense mechanisms at work in our responses to stress, discussed in the previous chapter.

Repression can block access to feelings, as well as memories. For example, if a child has strong feelings of anger toward her father—which, if acted out, would risk severe punishment—repression may take over. The repressed hostile impulse can no longer consciously press for satisfaction. But, although the impulse is not consciously felt, it is not gone, said Freud. At an unconscious level it continues to influence behavior, but in less direct ways, perhaps disguised as dreams, fantasies, or symptoms of mental disorder.

To understand another important ego defense mechanism, consider the common experience of looking at a cloud and seeing a face or the shape of an animal. It is likely that a friend looking at the same cloud would see something different, because the shape of the cloud is ambiguous and therefore open to interpretation. What people see projected in the cloud, of course, are their own wishes, needs, or desires (Piotrowski et al., 1985, 1993). The underlying mechanism is the ego defense mechanism called **projection.** In a similar way, when we are upset or aroused, we may use the defense of projection to attribute our own unconscious desires to other people or objects. This idea led to the development of *projective tests,* which have been used extensively in clinical psychology for evaluating personality and mental disorders.

Projective Tests   What do you see in Figure 11.2? Ambiguous images such as these are used in **projective tests,** which Freudian clinicians often employ to probe their patients' innermost feelings, motives, conflicts and desires. The

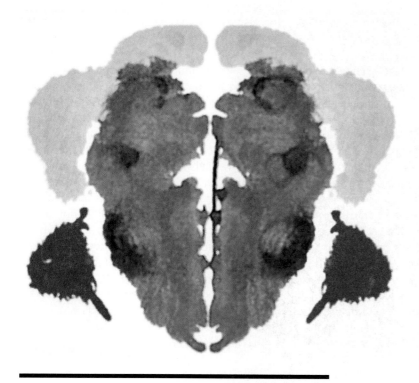

assumption is that people will *project* their hidden psychological processes onto the images. Thus, a person troubled by aggression might report seeing dangerous animals, weapons, blood, or people fighting.

In the most famous of projective techniques, the **Rorschach inkblot technique** (pronounced *ROAR-shock*), the ambiguous stimuli are symmetrical inkblots (Rorschach, 1942). The technique calls for showing the blots one at a time and asking the respondent, "What do you see? What does this seem to be?" The examiner usually interprets responses in light of psychoanalytic theory by noting how they might reflect unconscious sexual and aggressive impulses (Erdberg, 1990).

The Rorschach's value as a testing instrument has been questioned because objective studies of its accuracy have been disappointing (Anastasi, 1988; Lilienfeld et al., 2000a,b; Wood et al., 1996). Moreover, critics claim that the test is based on theoretical concepts (such as unconscious motives) that are impossible to demonstrate objectively. Despite these criticisms, many clinicians have continued to champion the Rorschach, arguing that it can provide unique insights as part of a broader personality assessment (Exner, 1974, 1978; Exner & Weiner, 1982).

By comparison, the **Thematic Apperception Test (TAT),** developed by Henry Murray, is a projective test that stands on somewhat firmer scientific ground. This test involves a series of ambiguous pictures, and respondents are instructed to generate a story about each (see Figure 11.3). The story should describe what the characters in the scenes are doing and thinking, what led up to each event, and how each situation will end. According to the theory behind the TAT, the respondent perceives the elements in the actual picture and further *apperceives* (fills in) personal interpretations and explanations, based on his or her own thoughts, feelings, and needs. The examiner then interprets the

Rorschach inkblot technique: A projective test requiring subjects to describe what they see in a series of ten inkblots.

Thematic Apperception Test (TAT): A projective test requiring subjects to make up stories that explain ambiguous pictures.

Connection

Chapter 9
The TAT is used to assess achievement motivation.

responses by looking for psychological themes, such as aggression, sexual needs, and relationships among people mentioned in the stories. The TAT has proved to be especially useful for assessing achievement motivation (McClelland, 1987b).

Evaluating Freud's Work   Freud's observations were often astute, and his ideas have had an enormous impact on the way psychologists think about normal and abnormal aspects of personality (Fisher & Greenberg, 1985). But psychologists today give Freud mixed reviews (Azar, 1997). One problem is that many Freudian concepts, such as "libido," "anal stage," or "repression," are vague. Because they lack clear operational definitions, much of the theory is difficult to evaluate scientifically. We have seen the results of this lack of objectivity in the controversy over recovery of repressed memories—a notion that arises directly from Freud's theory but that has no solid empirical support. Elizabeth Loftus warns that, by blithely accepting vague Freudian notions of repression and "recovery" of memories, society risks dangerous levels of paranoia, persecution of the innocent, and self-inflicted misery (Loftus & Ketcham, 1991, 1994). It should be noted, however, that efforts are being made to put Freud's concepts on a scientific footing (Cramer, 2000).

A second criticism is that Freudian theory is a seductive explanation for the past but a poor predictor of future responses. That is, its focus is on *retrospective* explanation. By overemphasizing historical origins of current behavior, the theory directs attention away from current events that may be responsible for maintaining the behavior.

A third criticism says that Freud gave short shrift to women. For example, we have seen that he portrayed women as suffering from "penis envy." In fact, Freud's theory may simply describe the attitudes that permeated the male-dominated world of psychiatry of his time.

A final criticism claims that the unconscious mind is not as smart or purposeful as Freud believed (Loftus & Klinger, 1992). In this view, the unconscious acts reflexively, sometimes based on innate response patterns and sometimes based on conditioned responses. Research in the neuroscience of emotion has, as we have seen, supported this new view of an unconscious emotional processing system in the brain—much less malign and deliberate than anything that Freud imagined (LeDoux, 1996).

Freud's ideas have found a receptive audience with the public at large (Gray, 1993, p. 47). Much of his appeal may be explained by his accessibility to nonpsychologists and by his emphasis on sexuality, a topic that interests everyone. Freudian images and symbols abound in the art and literature of the 20th century. His ideas have had an enormous influence on marketing as well. For example, advertisers often promote new products by associating them with a sexy model and hinting that the product will bring sexual satisfaction to its owner. Alternatively, some advertisers capitalize on Freud's destructive instinct. Television commercials for everything from mouthwash and cake mix to laxatives and life insurance work by first reminding you of threats to your happiness (social rejection, irregularity, untimely death) and then offering products and services to reduce your anxiety and restore hope.

Let us end our discussion of Freud by seeing whether his theory can give us a new perspective on Margaret Sanger. A psychoanalyst interpreting her drive and sense of mission would examine her childhood, looking for conflicts with parents and anxiety about sexual feelings. The analyst might also focus on her mother's death, which occurred when Sanger was 19, and on her later claim that

Connection

Chapter 1
Operational definitions are stated in objective, observable, and measurable terms.

Connection

Chapter 7
Evidence for recovery of long-repressed memories is anecdotal.

Connection

Chapter 9
The brain has two emotional pathways: One operates mainly at an unconscious level.

❙ FIGURE 11.3:   **Sample Card from the TAT**

Those who take the third route, moving *away from others* to protect themselves from imagined hurt and rejection, are likely to close themselves off from intimacy and support.

What analysis would Horney have made of Margaret Sanger? We suspect that she would have focused on Sanger's achievements, attempting to determine whether they were the result of a healthy drive to fulfill her potential or a neurotic need for power, status, self-respect, achievement, and independence. Undoubtedly, Horney would have reminded us that society often praises these needs in men and punishes them in women. So, from this point of view, it is likely that Horney may have seen in Sanger a robust and healthy personality.

Evaluating Horney's Work   Neglect engulfed Karen Horney's ideas during midcentury (Monte, 1980). Then, her 1967 book, *Feminine Psychology,* appeared at just the right time to elevate her among those seeking a feminist perspective within psychology and psychiatry. But, having attracted renewed interest, will Horney eventually slip again into oblivion? Her theory suffers from the same flaw that plagues the other psychodynamic theories: a weak scientific foundation. It awaits someone to translate her concepts into verifiable form so that they can be put to a scientific test.

OTHER POST-FREUDIAN THEORIES   Sigmund Freud's revolutionary ideas attracted many others to the psychoanalytic movement — some of whom, like Erik Erikson and Alfred Adler, also broke from Freud to develop their own ideas. For the most part, the post-Freudian theorists accepted the basic psychodynamic notions of psychic determinism and unconscious motivation. But they did not always agree with Freud on the details, especially about the sex and death instincts or the indelible nature of early life experiences. In general, the post-Freudians made several significant changes in the course of psychoanalysis:

Connection

Chapter 4
Erikson proposed a life-span theory of psychosocial development.

▶ They put greater emphasis on ego functions, including ego defenses, development of the self, and conscious thought — whereas Freud focused primarily on the unconscious.

▶ They viewed social variables (culture, family, and peers) as having an important role in shaping personality — whereas Freud focused mainly on instinctive urges.

▶ They extended personality development beyond childhood to include the entire life span — whereas Freud focused mainly on early childhood experiences.

In doing so, the post-Freudians broke Freud's monopoly on personality theory and paved the way for new ideas from the humanistic and cognitive theorists.

Humanistic Theories

With its emphasis on internal conflict and mental disorder, psychoanalysis failed to provide a workable theory of the healthy personality. The humanistic perspective arose to fulfill that need. Its theories are optimistic about the core of human nature. For humanists, personality is not driven by unconscious conflicts and defenses against anxiety, but rather by needs to adapt, learn, grow, and excel. Mental disorders, when they do occur, are seen as stemming from unhealthy *situations* that cause low self-esteem and unmet needs, rather than from unhealthy *individuals*.

Once people are freed from negative situations and negative self-evaluations, the tendency to be healthy should actively guide them to life-

How would Karen Horney have interpreted Margaret Sanger's personality? Margaret Sanger had a flair for publicity. Here she has her lips sealed with tape so that she cannot be accused of preaching birth control in Boston — where she will write her message on a blackboard.

Maslow considered Eleanor Roosevelt to be a self-actualizing person.

Connection

Chapter 1
Behaviorism asserts that our actions are controlled by the environment, rather than by free will.

Connection

Chapter 9
Maslow's theory of motivation is based on a hierarchy of needs.

Self-actualizing personalities: Healthy individuals who have met their basic needs and are free to pursue an interest in "higher" ideals, such as truth, justice, and beauty.

Fully functioning person: Carl Roger's term for a self-actualizing individual, who has a self-concept that is both positive and congruent with reality.

Incongruence: Occurs when a negative emotional experience affects one's ability to perceive accurately.

Phenomenal field: Our psychological reality, composed of perceptions.

enhancing choices. These ideas brought a new respect for the individual's own view of the *self* and subjective interpretation of reality, rather than the external perspective of an observer or therapist.

ABRAHAM MASLOW AND THE HEALTHY PERSONALITY   Maslow often referred to the humanistic view as psychology's "third force," to contrast his ideas with the Freudian and behavioristic movements that had dominated psychology during most of his lifetime. He was especially concerned by the Freudian fixation on mental disturbance and maladjustment. Instead, Maslow argued, we need a theory that describes mental health as something more than just the absence of illness. That theoretical need became his life's quest. He sought the ingredients of the healthy personality where no one had ever looked for them before: in people who had lived especially full and productive lives.

Maslow's subjects included the historical figures Abraham Lincoln and Thomas Jefferson, plus several persons of stature during his own lifetime: Albert Einstein, Albert Schweitzer, and Eleanor Roosevelt. In these individuals Maslow found personalities whose basic needs had been met (e.g., needs for food, shelter, love, and respect) and who had become free to pursue an interest in "higher" ideals, such as truth, justice, and beauty — a penchant that sometimes engaged them in causes about which they felt deeply. (We hope you're thinking about Margaret Sanger at this point.) They could act independently because they had no neurotic need for the approval of others. Maslow called these people **self-actualizing personalities.** He found his self-actualizers to be creative, full of good humor, and given to spontaneity — but, at the same time, accepting of their own limitations and those of others. In brief, self-actualizers are those who feel free to fulfill their potentialities.

Although Maslow was most interested in the healthy, self-actualizing personality, his theory of a *hierarchy of needs* also offers an explanation of maladjustment. A long-unfulfilled "deficiency" need, such as a need for love or esteem, can produce maladjustment, while freedom from such needs allows the person to pursue interests that promote growth and fulfillment. Indeed, the research shows that people who are self-accepting lead happier lives, while people who have low self-esteem may go through life feeling fearful, angry, or depressed (Baumeister, 1993; Brown, 1991).

CARL ROGERS'S FULLY FUNCTIONING PERSON   In contrast with Maslow, Carl Rogers was a therapist who often worked with dysfunctional people rather than self-actualizers (1951, 1961, 1980). Yet he did not overlook the healthy personality, which he called the **fully functioning person.** Such a person is distinguished by a self-concept that is *positive* and *congruent* with reality. That is, the fully functioning person has high self-esteem, which is consistent (congruent) with the messages he or she receives from others, who express their approval, friendship, and love. Negative experiences, however, can produce **incongruence,** a threat to one's self-esteem. For example, a boy who thinks of himself as "smart" has a positive self-concept, but he experiences incongruence when the teacher returns his paper with a C on it.

Rogers insisted that psychology recognize the reality of perceptions and feelings, which he called the **phenomenal field.** We respond, he said, to this phenomenal field, not to an "objective" reality. Thus, how a student reacts to a grade depends entirely on the student's perception: Receiving a C may shock a superior student but thrill one who has been failing. In Rogers's system, the phenomenal field becomes a part of the personality. It contains our interpretations of both the external world and our inner experience. It also contains the *self,* the humanists' version of the Freudian *ego,* which is the part of the phenomenal field that defines who we are.

Rogers believed that everyone has the capacity for growth in a supportive and nurturing environment. This assumption probably grew from his reaction to an isolated and unhappy childhood dominated by the rigid rules of his parents' strict religious beliefs. So restrictive was this environment that he even felt "wicked" when he first tasted a bottle of pop without his parents' knowledge (Rogers, 1961). Later, from an adult perspective, Rogers concluded that children from homes where parental love is *conditional* (dependent) on good behavior may grow up with anxiety and a strong sense of guilt that leads to low self-esteem and mental disorder. Instead of guilt-mongers, he believed, we need people in our lives who can give us **unconditional positive regard**—love without conditions attached.

Unlike the psychodynamic theorists who focused on unhealthy, self-destructive motives, Rogers, Maslow, and other humanistic personality theorists believe that our deepest motives are for positive growth. In its healthiest form, self-actualization is a striving to realize one's potential—to develop fully one's capacities and talents. According to the humanistic theorists, this innate quest is a constructive, guiding force that moves each person toward positive behaviors and the enhancement of the self.

Connection

Chapter 9
The most basic levels in Maslow's hierarchy must be met before the person is motivated by self-actualization.

How would humanistic theorists characterize Margaret Sanger? They would probably begin by asking, "How does Margaret Sanger see her world? What matters to her? Where is she, where does she want to be, and how does she believe she can get there?" The answers to these questions would identify her motives. Perhaps Sanger saw her life as an opportunity to change the miserable and often deadly consequences of unwanted pregnancy. But why, then, did she claim credit for the success of the birth-control movement, despite the fact that it was a team effort? A humanistic perspective would not assume that her motives were necessarily self-centered. If she believed the cause needed a figurehead, she may have felt that too many personalities associated with the movement would diffuse the effort. Ultimately, they would judge her healthy if her motives were healthy, that is, if she were self-actualizing. In everyday language this means moving toward fulfilling her potential.

EVALUATING THE HUMANISTIC THEORIES The upbeat humanistic view of personality brought a welcome change for many therapists who had become accustomed to the more pessimistic Freudian perspective, with its emphasis on unspeakable desires and repressed traumas. They liked its focus on making one's present and future life more palatable, rather than dredging up painful memories of an unalterable past. They also liked its attention to mental health rather than mental disorder.

But not everyone jumped on the humanists' bandwagon. Behaviorists criticized humanistic concepts for being fuzzy: What exactly is "self-actualization," they asked? Is it an inborn tendency or is it created by one's culture? The behaviorists also noted that humanistic psychologists had neglected the influence of important environmental variables by emphasizing the role of the self in behavior. Experimental psychologists contended that too many concepts in humanistic psychology are so unclear that they defy objective testing. And the psychoanalytic theorists criticized the humanistic emphasis on present conscious experience, arguing that the humanistic approach does not recognize the power of the unconscious. Finally, cross-cultural psychologists criti-

Connection

Chapter 6
The behaviorists have emphasized that psychology should include only those things that we can observe and measure.

Unconditional positive regard:
Love or caring without conditions attached.

Children develop a clearer sense of identity by observing how men and women behave in their culture.

cized the humanists' emphasis on the *self*—as in *self*-concept, *self*-esteem, and *self*-actualization. This "self-centered" picture of personality may simply be the viewpoint of observers looking through the lens of an individualistic Western culture (Heine et al., 1999).

Recently, a movement known as **positive psychology** has formed to pursue essentially the same goals established by the humanists. The difference is that those allied with positive psychology are more concerned than were the humanists about laying a scientific foundation for their theories. This effort has produced the solid work we have seen on optimism, happiness, social support, and health (Buss, 2000; Diener, 2000; Myers, 2000; Peterson, 2000; Seligman & Csikszentmihalyi, 2000; Volz, 2000). But, despite these successes, the positive psychology movement is limited as an explanation of personality by its restricted focus on desirable aspects of human functioning.

So, is there an alternative view that overcomes the problems we have seen in the psychodynamic, humanistic, and the new positive psychology theories? Let's consider the cognitive approach.

Cognitive Theories

Neither the humanists nor psychoanalysts showed much interest in putting their ideas on a firm experimental foundation. Their work came out of a clinical tradition of working with individuals who sought their help. Cognitive psychology, however, arose from a different source—a solidly scientific tradition with an emphasis on research. The trade-off is that the cognitive theories are not as comprehensive as those of the humanists or psychodynamic theorists. The cognitive approach zeroes in on specific influences on personality and behavior, without assuming to explain everything, as we shall see in our sampling of cognitive ideas below.

SOCIAL LEARNING AND PERSONALITY   In Albert Bandura's view, we are driven not by inner forces or environmental influences alone but also by our *expectations* of how our actions might affect other people, the environment, and ourselves (Bandura, 1986). A distinctive feature of the human personality is the ability to foresee the consequences of actions. So, you don't have to yell "Fire!" in a crowded theatre to know what would happen if you did. In addition, we can learn *vicariously* (by observing other people) to see what rewards and punishments their behaviors bring. Thus, our personalities are shaped by our interactions with others—by *social* learning.

Perhaps the most important contribution of Bandura's theory is this focus on **observational learning,** the process by which people learn new responses by watching each others' behavior. Through observational learning, children and adults acquire an enormous range of information about their social environment—what gets rewarded and what gets punished or ignored. Skills, attitudes, and beliefs may be acquired simply by noting what others do and the consequences that follow. In this vein, psychological problems can be acquired by observing poor role models or by exposure to environments that reward unhealthy behaviors.

Note how Bandura's theory points to an interaction of cognitions, behav-

Connection

Chapter 6
Bandura's "Bobo doll" experiment showed the power of observational learning.

Positive psychology: A movement within psychology, focusing on desirable aspects of human functioning, as opposed to an emphasis on psychopathology.

Observational learning: The process of learning new responses by watching others' behavior.

ior, and the environment. Each of these three factors can influence or change the others, and the direction of change is rarely one way; it is *reciprocal* or bidirectional. Bandura calls this **reciprocal determinism** (Bandura, 1981, 1999). The simple but powerful relationship of these variables is summarized in Figure 11.4. How does it work in real life? If, for example, you like sailing, your interest (a cognition) will probably lead you to spend time on the waterfront (an environment) interacting with people (social behavior) who share your interest. To the extent that this is stimulating and rewarding, this activity will reciprocally strengthen your interest in sailing and encourage you to spend more time with your friends on the waterfront. This, then, is one instance of the reciprocal determinism among cognition (interest in sailing), environment (the waterfront) and behavior (interacting with other sailors).

LOCUS OF CONTROL Another cognitive psychologist, Julian Rotter (rhymes with *voter*) tells us that the way we act depends on our sense of personal power or **locus of control.** Do you feel you can control the grade you achieve in your psychology class? If so, you have an *internal* locus of control, and you probably work hard to get good grades. If you have the feeling that the professor will arbitrarily give you whatever she or he wants you to have—regardless of how much studying you do or the quality of your work—you have an *external* locus of control, and you probably study relatively little.

Scores on Rotter's *Internal-External Locus of Control Scale* correlate with people's emotions and behavior in many situations (Rotter, 1990). For example, those with an internal locus of control are not only more likely to get good grades, but they also are more likely to exercise and watch their diets than are externals (Balch & Ross, 1975; Findley & Cooper, 1983). As you might expect, externals are more likely to be depressed (Benassi et al., 1988).

While we may feel more in control of certain situations than others, many studies suggest that locus of control is a general characteristic of our personalities. That is, people tend to approach different situations with assumptions about their ability to control their fate. Therefore, an internal or external disposition seems to be a reliable characteristic of personality—although Rotter resists calling this a *trait* because he believes the term conveys the erroneous idea that internality–externality is fixed and unchangeable. You can evaluate your own locus of control by following the instructions in the "Do It Yourself!" box on page 438.

EVALUATING THE COGNITIVE APPROACH TO PERSONALITY Critics argue that the cognitive theories generally overemphasize rational information processing and overlook *emotion* as an important component of personality. For those who feel that emotions and motives are central to the functioning of human personality, the cognitive approaches to personality are flawed. However, because emotion has assumed a greater role in cognitive psychology recently, we can anticipate a new generation of cognitive theories of personality that do take emotion into account.

How would a cognitive psychologist explain Margaret Sanger? A cognitive interpretation of Sanger's work and personality would focus on how she interpreted the rewards and punishments she experienced and how these interpretations shaped her behavior. Each time she gave a public lecture about birth-control methods or printed and distributed an illegal pamphlet, Sanger's actions brought punitive consequences—but she was also rewarded with public attention and admiration, press coverage, and ultimately the revocation of unjust laws. Margaret Sanger learned that by enduring hardships, she raised public awareness and changed the social climate. In turn, these successes shaped her, making her less a private citizen and more a public figure.

FIGURE 11.4: Reciprocal Determinism

In reciprocal determinism, the individual's cognitions, behavior, and the environment all interact.

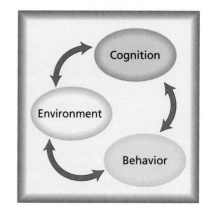

Connection

Chapter 9
Rotter's locus-of-control theory is also a motivational theory.

Connection

Chapter 10
Compare *external locus of control* with Seligman's concept of *learned helplessness.*

Connection

Chapter 8
Emotion is increasingly recognized as a component of cognition.

Reciprocal determinism: The process in which the person, situation, and environment mutually influence each other.

Locus of control: An individual's sense of where his or her life influences originate.

Julian Rotter (1966) has developed a test that assesses a person's sense of internal or external control over events. The test items consist of pairs of contrasting statements, and subjects must choose one statement with which they most agree from each pair. This format is called a *forced choice test*. Unlike many other personality tests, the scoring for each item on Rotter's Internal–External Scale is transparent: The test-taker can easily tell in which direction most items are scored. Here are some items from a preliminary version of the test (Rotter, 1971):

1a. Promotions are earned through hard work and persistence.

1b. Making a lot of money is largely a matter of getting the right breaks.

2a. In my experience I have noticed that there is usually a direct connection between how hard I study and the grades I get.

2b. Many times the reactions of teachers seem haphazard to me.

3a. If one knows how to deal with people they are really quite easily led.

3b. I have little influence over the way other people behave.

4a. People like me can change the course of world affairs if we make ourselves heard.

4b. It is only wishful thinking to believe that one can really influence what happens in society at large.

5a. I am the master of my fate.

5b. A great deal that happens to me is probably a matter of chance.

You can see which direction you lean by counting up the number of statements with which you agreed in each column. Agreement with those in the left column suggests an internal locus of control.

A cognitive personality theorist would also call attention to the lessons Sanger learned in her social relationships. As she became a celebrity—someone whom others saw as a symbol of a movement rather than a mere individual—she acquired a sense of personal power and an internal locus of control that had eluded her in her early efforts to speak about health education. In her 1938 autobiography, she styled herself as a heroine and martyr, interweaving fanciful stories with accurate information about her life. A cognitive theorist would wonder whether she had come to believe the legendary side of the personality that she had strived to create.

Current Trends

Gone are the days when Freud, Jung, Erikson, Horney, and others were building the grand, sweeping theories of personality that attempted to explain everything we humans do. The humanistic and cognitive theorists arose and pointed out blind spots in the older psychodynamic theories. Now the emphasis has shifted again, as psychologists have brought elements of the psychodynamic, humanistic, and cognitive perspectives together with new knowledge about the impact of culture, gender, and family dynamics. You should be especially aware of three important trends in our thinking about personality.

In *family systems theory,* for example, the basic unit of analysis is not the individual but the family (Gilbert, 1992). This perspective says that personality is shaped by the ways people interacted first in the family and, later, in the peer group. While Freud and others did recognize that parents influence children, the new emphasis is on *interaction*—on the ways that members of the family or the peer group influence each other. This has led to viewing people with psychological problems as individuals embedded in dysfunctional groups, rather than as "sick" persons. This emphasis has also given us a new interpersonal language for personality. We often speak now of *codependence* (instead of *dependent* personalities) and *communication* (instead of mere *talk*). We also have a heightened awareness of *relationships* and *process* (the changes that occur as relationships develop).

A second trend comes from psychology's increasing awareness of cultural differences. As Stanley Sue (1991) reminds us, our society is becoming ethnically more diverse. No longer can we assume that everyone shares the same cultural experience or the same values. Harry Triandis (1995) has warned us, for example, that people who grow up in *collectivistic* societies may not have the need for individual achievement learned by those who grow up in *individualistic* societies. Triandis also tells us that no culture's approach is superior to the others: They are merely different. We will consider the question of personality differences across cultures in more detail near the end of this chapter.

A third trend comes from an increasing appreciation of gender influences. While we do not know the weights to assign nature and nurture in our attempts to understand gender differences, we do know that males and females often perceive situations differently (Tavris, 1991). For example, males tend to be more physically aggressive than females. Females tend to form close relationships in small, equal-status groups, while males tend to connect in larger groups (teams) organized hierarchically with leaders and followers.

Together these three trends have enlarged our understanding of the forces that shape personality. The new emphasis is on diversity and group processes, rather than on commonalities and individuals. As a result, the picture of personality has become much more complex — but it has undoubtedly become far more accurate.

Connection

Chapter 14
Individualism and collectivism represent one of the fundamental differences among cultures.

Connection

Chapter 9
There are gender differences in the ways that people express emotions.

Psychology

In Your Life

Explaining Unusual People and Unusual Behavior

You don't need a theory of personality to explain why people usually get to work on time, go to concerts, or spend weekends with their family and friends. That is, you don't need a theory of personality to explain why people do what you would expect them to do. But when they behave in odd and unexpected ways a personality theory becomes handy. A good theory can help you understand interesting and unusual people whom you read about in the newspaper — those who risk their lives to save another, politicians embroiled in scandal, a serial killer, the charismatic leader of a religious cult, and the controversial CEO of a Fortune 500 company.

Which approach to personality offers the best explanations? Unfortunately, none has the whole truth. But each perspective we have covered so far — the psychodynamic, the humanistic, and the cognitive — can help you see personality from a different angle, so you will need to use them all to get the whole picture. To illustrate, let's suppose that you are a counseling psychologist, working at a college counseling center, and a client, a young woman, tells you that she is contemplating suicide. How can your knowledge of personality help you understand her?

The cognitive perspective, with its emphasis on perception and social learning, suggests that her

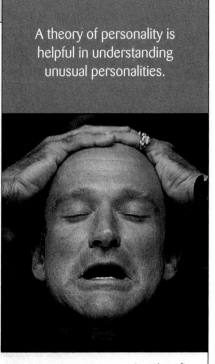

A theory of personality is helpful in understanding unusual personalities.

(continued)

difficulty may lie in her interpretation of some depressing or threatening event. It also alerts you to the possibility that her suicidal thoughts reflect a suicidal role model—perhaps a friend or a family member.

The humanistic view suggests that you explore her unmet needs, such as feeling alone, unloved, or not respected. This view also calls your attention to the possibility of suicidal thoughts arising from low self-esteem.

The psychodynamic perspective suggests that you consider your client's internal motivation. Is she a hostile person who has turned her hostility on herself? Does she have some unfinished emotional business from an earlier developmental stage, such as guilt for angry feelings toward her parents? Does she have an unresolved identity crisis?

No one has a simple answer to the problem of understanding why people do what they do. That is for the counselor and client to work out together. What these theories of personality can do, however, is call your attention to factors you might otherwise overlook.

CHECK**YOUR**UNDERSTANDING

1. **RECALL:** *The psychodynamic theories emphasize*
   a. motivation.
   b. learning.
   c. consciousness.
   d. the logical basis of behavior.

2. **RECALL:** *Freud believed that mental disorders stem from conflicts and drives that are repressed in the*
   a. ego.
   b. superego.
   c. id.
   d. Eros.

3. **APPLICATION:** *Which of the following behaviors would a Freudian say is driven by Thanatos?*
   a. sexual intercourse
   b. a violent assault
   c. dreaming
   d. flying an airplane

4. **RECALL:** *What is the ego defense mechanism on which the Rorschach and TAT are based?*
   a. displacement
   b. fantasy
   c. regression
   d. projection

5. **APPLICATION:** *If you react strongly to angry outbursts in others, you may be struggling with which Jungian archetype?*
   a. the anima
   b. the shadow
   c. introversion
   d. the hero

6. **RECALL:** *Karen Horney believed that the main forces behind our behaviors are*
   a. social.
   b. sexual.
   c. aggressive and destructive.
   d. the result of the Oedipus complex.

7. **RECALL:** *The humanistic theorists were very different from the psychodynamic theorists because of their emphasis on*
   a. the cognitive forces behind behavior.
   b. the healthy personality.
   c. mental disorder.
   d. emotional intelligence.

8. **RECALL:** *Our expectations of reward, punishment, and control over forces in our environment play a major role in*
   a. the psychodynamic theories.
   b. the humanistic theories.
   c. the cognitive theories.
   d. none of the above theories of personality.

9. **UNDERSTANDING THE CORE CONCEPT:** *What do the psychodynamic, humanistic, and cognitive theories of personality have in common?*
   a. They all view personality as largely unconscious.
   b. They all acknowledge the internal mental processes underlying our personality characteristics.
   c. They all say that men and women have entirely different motives underlying their behaviors.
   d. They all have a strong basis in psychological research.

Core Concept

ANSWERS: 1. a   2. c   3. b   4. d
5. b   6. a   7. b   8. c   9. b

WHAT PATTERNS ARE FOUND IN PERSONALITY?

Key Question

Connection

Chapter 12
Hippocrates' theory also explained mental disorders.

Long before academic psychology appeared, people were classifying each other according to four *temperaments,* based on a theory proposed by the Greek physician Hippocrates. A person's temperament, he suggested, resulted from the balance of the four **humors,** or fluids, secreted by the body. A *sanguine,* or cheerful, person was characterized by strong, warm blood. A *choleric* temperament, marked by anger, came from yellow bile (called *choler*), believed to flow from the liver. Hippocrates thought that the liver also produced black bile, from which arose a *melancholic,* or depressed, temperament. Finally, if the body's dominant fluid is phlegm, or mucus, the person will have a *phlegmatic* temperament: cool, aloof, slow, and unemotional. Hippocrates' biology may have been a little off the mark, but his notion of temperaments established themselves as "common sense." Even today you will occasionally encounter his terms used to describe people's temperaments.

Since the days of Hippocrates, many other personality classification systems have been developed. If fat, then jolly; if an engineer, then conservative; if female, then sympathetic. Such systems have traditionally had much popular appeal—and they still do in the mass media. Unfortunately, they oversimplify the very complicated problem of understanding the patterns found in personality.

Something in human nature seems to encourage us to group people by categories, according to certain distinguishing features. This habit is apparently universal—although the specific characteristics and categories may vary. College students might group people according to college class, major, sex, ethnicity, and qualities such as honesty, shyness, or sense of humor. In modern psychology, some personality theorists do something similar: They describe people in terms of *traits,* enduring characteristics in the personality. Others group people according to their personality *types,* or clusters of traits. Most, however, agree on certain fundamental dimensions of personality. Our Core Concept says:

Core Concept

> **Some theories attribute personality to stable patterns known as traits, types, and temperaments.**

Trait, type, and temperament theories all give us a "snapshot" of the personality, portraying it as relatively fixed and unchanging. Unlike the developmental perspectives we considered in the first part of the chapter, the trait, type, and temperament theories typically say little about the underlying mechanisms or *processes* of personality. As a result, these approaches are of more interest to personnel managers and others who want to identify people with certain characteristics. The trait, type, and temperament theories are of less value in counseling and psychotherapy than are the psychodynamic, or "process," theories considered earlier in this chapter.

Personality and Temperament

Psychologists define **temperament** as the inherited personality dispositions that are apparent in early childhood and that establish the tempo and mood of the individual's behaviors (Hogan et al., 1996; Mischel, 1993). When they speak of temperaments, psychologists are usually referring to a single, domi-

Humors: Four body fluids—blood, phlegm, black bile, and yellow bile—that, according to an ancient theory, control personality by their relative abundance.

Temperament: The basic, inherited personality dispositions that are apparent in early childhood and that establish the tempo and mood of the individual's behaviors.

Connection

Chapter 2
Phineas Gage had a dramatic change in his personality when an iron rod blasted through his frontal lobes.

Connection

Chapter 2
Neurotransmitters are chemicals used for communication between neurons.

Connection

Chapter 12
Shyness is not a mental disorder, but there are effective therapies for overcoming it.

Some shyness is inherited and some is learned through experience.

nant "theme," such as shyness or moodiness, that characterizes a person's personality. Modern psychology has, of course, abandoned the four humors theory of temperament, but it has retained its most basic concept: Biological factors do affect our basic personalities. In support of this view, psychologists can point to chemicals and structures in the brain that are known to regulate fundamental aspects of personality (Craik et al., 1999; Zuckerman, 1995). You will recall, for example, the case of Phineas Gage, who received an accidental lobotomy and thereby demonstrated the role of the frontal lobes in social interaction and the suppression of impulsive behavior.

Biological psychologists now suspect that some individual differences in disposition also arise from the balance of chemicals in the brain, which may also have a genetic basis (Sapolsky, 1992). In this sense, the theory of humors still lives, but in different clothes: Modern biological psychology has replaced the humors with neurotransmitters. So, depression—which characterizes most suicidal people—may result from an abundance or deficiency of certain transmitters. Likewise, anxiety, anger, and euphoria may each arise from other neurochemical patterns. As developmental psychologist Jerome Kagan says (in Stavish, 1994a), "We all have the same neurotransmitters, but each of us has a slightly different mix" (p. 7). That, says Kagan, is what accounts for many of the temperamental differences among people, especially with regard to negative traits, such as fearfulness, sadness, and shyness.

In fact, Kagan runs a fascinating research program focusing on the inherited basis of shyness (Kagan et al., 1994). This program has clearly demonstrated that on the very first day of life, newborns already differ in the degree to which they are "inhibited" or "uninhibited"—that is, shy versus bold. About 10 to 15% of all children appear to be born shy or introverted, while a similar percentage appear to be born bold or extraverted, as assessed by a variety of measures. These initial differences in temperament persist over time, with the majority of children being classified with the same temperament in measurements taken over an 11-year interval. On the other hand, we know that the percentage of shy college-age students—40% or more—is much higher than the percentage of shy children (Zimbardo, 1990). It is thus reasonable to assume that some shyness is inherited, while some is learned through negative experiences in one's social life. It is also the case that if a child is withdrawn, startles easily, is unlikely to smile, and is fearful of both strangers and novelty, then that child will create an environment that is not friendly, playful, or supportive. In this way, heredity and environment interact, with initially inherited characteristics becoming amplified—or perhaps muted—over time, because they produce social signals telling others to either approach or stay away.

So does biology determine your destiny? An inherited temperament may set the *range* of your responses to some life situations. However, temperament by itself does not fully determine your life experiences (Kagan & Snidman, 1998). Even among your biological relatives, your unique family position, experiences, and sense of self guarantee that your personality pattern is unlike that of anyone else (Bouchard et al., 1990).

Personality as a Composite of Traits

If you were to describe a friend, you might speak of temperament —a single dominant theme in his or her personality. But you might also describe your friend on several dimensions, using the language of *traits:* moody, cheerful, melancholy, enthusiastic, volatile, friendly, or smart. **Traits** are stable personality characteristics that are presumed to exist within the individual and guide his or her thoughts and actions under various conditions.

We can see the close kinship between trait theory and biological psychology in the book *The Biological Basis of Personality,* by British trait theorist Hans Eysenck (1967). In this manifesto Eysenck declares, "Personality is determined to a large extent by a person's genes" (p. 20). He believes that especially strong evidence points to a biological basis for the traits of introversion and extraversion and for emotional stability (Eysenck, 1992; Eysenck & Eysenck, 1985).

THE "BIG FIVE" TRAITS   By restricting the definition of personality to motivational and emotional characteristics (excluding such attributes as IQ, skills, and creativity), trait theorists are building a consensus on the major components of personality. Using the mathematical tool of *factor analysis* (which helps an investigator look for relationships, or clusters, among personality test items), many researchers have found five dominant personality factors, sometimes called the **"Big Five"** (Carver & Scheier, 2000; Digman, 1990; Goldberg, 1981, 1993). As yet, we have no universally accepted names for these factors, although the first term in the list below may be the most widely used. (You will note that each dimension is *bipolar,* describing a range from high to low on that trait. The first term we have listed is a label referring to the "high" pole for each trait.)

- ▶ *Extraversion* (also called *social adaptability, assertiveness, sociability, boldness,* or *self-confidence,* and, at the opposite pole, *introversion*)
- ▶ *Agreeableness* (also called *conformity, likeability, friendly compliance, warmth,* or, at the opposite pole, *coldness* or *negativity*)
- ▶ *Neuroticism* (also called *anxiety* or *emotionality* and, at the opposite pole, *emotional stability* or *emotional control*)
- ▶ *Openness to experience* (also called *inquiring intellect, curiosity, independence,* or, at the opposite pole, *closed-mindedness*)
- ▶ *Conscientiousness* (also called *dependability, cautiousness, perseverance, superego strength, prudence,* or *constraint,* and, at the opposite pole, *impulsiveness, carelessness,* or *irresponsibility*)

The five-factor theory is important because it greatly simplifies a formerly confusing picture. Various theorists, such as Freud, Jung, Adler, Horney, Erikson, and Maslow, had suggested a wide array of "fundamental" personality dimensions. In addition, the dictionary gives us several hundred terms commonly used to describe personality (Allport & Odbert, 1936). While psychologists had attempted to simplify this daunting list of personality characteristics, it wasn't until the last decade or so that agreement has emerged on which traits were fundamental. Although debate still continues about the details, a broad coalition of theorists has now concluded that we can describe people with reasonable accuracy by specifying their position on each of these five dimensions. The five-factor theory also offers the advantage of describing personality in the familiar terms of everyday language.

Significantly, the five-factor model also seems to have validity across cultures. An Israeli sample produced the same five factors as those found in Americans (Birenbaum & Montag, 1986). A study drawing on people from Canada, Germany, Finland, and Poland also supported the five-factor theory (Paunonen et al., 1992), as did still other studies of individuals from Germany, Portugal, Israel, China, Korea, and Japan (McCrae & Costa, 1997), as well as Japanese university students (Bond et al., 1975) and Filipino students (Guthrie & Bennet,

Connection

Chapter 2
Biological psychology has shown that genes influence some of our behaviors.

Traits: Stable personality characteristics that are presumed to exist within the individual and guide his or her thoughts and actions under various conditions.

Big Five: A group of apparently fundamental personality traits: extraversion, agreeableness, conscientiousness, emotional stability, and openness to new experience.

1970). Note that the same five factors stood out in each of these cultures as the basic framework of personality. Digman (1990) notes that these strikingly consistent results, coming in from such diverse cultures, lead to the suspicion "that something quite fundamental is involved here" (p. 433).

ASSESSING TRAITS If you were a clinical or counseling psychologist, you would have your choice of dozens of instruments for measuring personality. We have already met some of these in our discussion of the Rorschach inkblot technique, along with its projective cousin, the TAT, which came to us from the psychodynamic perspective. Now, let us examine some of the personality tests spawned by the trait theories.

One of the newer trait-based instruments comes from the five-factor theory: the NEO-PI or "Big Five Inventory" (Caprara et al., 1993; Costa & McCrae, 1992a,b). This personality assessment device has been used to study personality stability across the life span and the relationship of personality characteristics to physical health and various life events. It is also useful in career counseling.

The most widely used of the trait inventories is the Minnesota Multiphasic Personality Inventory, usually called the **MMPI-2.** (The "2" means it is a revised form of the original MMPI.) The instrument was developed to measure serious mental problems, such as depression and schizophrenia (Butcher et al., 1989; Butcher & Williams, 1992; Greene, 1991; Helmes & Reddon, 1993). It consists of 567 statements dealing with attitudes, habits, fears, preferences, physical health, beliefs, and general outlook. Here are some items similar to those found on the MMPI-2:

> ▶ I am often bothered by thoughts about sex.
> ▶ Sometimes I like to stir up some excitement.
> ▶ If people had not judged me unfairly, I would have been far more successful.

Respondents are asked to indicate whether each statement describes them, and their answers are scored on the ten clinical dimensions listed in Table 11.2.

Connection

Chapter 10
Personality variables are related to people's physical and mental responses under stress.

Connection

Chapter 12
Depression, paranoia, hypochondriasis, hysteria, and schizophrenia are examples of serious mental disorders.

MMPI-2: A widely used personality assessment instrument that gives scores on ten important clinical traits. Also called the *Minnesota Multiphasic Personality Inventory.*

TABLE 11.2	*MMPI-2 Clinical Scales*

Hypochondriasis (Hs): Abnormal concern with bodily functions

Depression (D): Pessimism; hopelessness; slowing of action and thought

Conversion hysteria (Hy): Unconscious use of mental problems to avoid conflicts or responsibility

Psychopathic deviate (Pd): Disregard for social custom; shallow emotions; inability to profit from experience

Masculinity–femininity (Mf): Differences between men and women

Paranoia (Pa): Suspiciousness; delusions of grandeur or persecution

Psychasthenia (Pt): Obsessions; compulsions; fears; low self-esteem; guilt; indecisiveness

Schizophrenia (Sc): Bizarre, unusual thoughts or behavior; withdrawal; hallucinations; delusions

Hypomania (Ma): Emotional excitement; flight of ideas; overactivity

Social introversion (Si): Shyness; disinterest in others; insecurity

Attempting to fake a good or bad score on the MMPI-2 is not a smart idea. The test has four "lie" scales that will most likely signal that something is amiss. All are sensitive to unusual responses. Here are some items similar to those on the lie scales:

- ▶ Sometimes I put off doing things I know I ought to do.
- ▶ On occasion I have passed on some gossip.
- ▶ Once in a while, I find a dirty joke amusing.

Too many attempts to make yourself look good or bad will boost your lie scale scores into the questionable range.

As a diagnostic instrument, the MMPI-2 has a good record — although it must be used with care in non-Western cultures (Lonner, 1990). Clinicians should also be cautious when giving the MMPI-2 to members of ethnic minorities in the United States, because minority groups were not well represented in the original sample used in developing the test (Butcher & Williams, 1992; Graham, 1990). Nevertheless, the instrument does a credible job of identifying depressed or psychotic persons (Greene, 1991). On the other hand, the MMPI-2 is of less value in understanding the normal personality.

EVALUATING TRAIT AND TEMPERAMENT THEORIES The biggest criticisms of trait theories are that (1) they portray personality as fixed and static, rather than as a dynamic and changing process, and (2) they oversimplify our complex natures by describing personality on just a few dimensions. As evolution scholar Stephen Jay Gould has remarked, "The world does not come to us in neat little packages" (1996, p. 188). And what would we gain, for example, by judging Margaret Sanger as "passionate" or by finding that she scored high on traits such as outgoingness and dominance but low on agreeableness or conventional thinking? Such judgments would validate others' observations of her, and even her own self-descriptions. But brief labels and concise categories also leave out important detail. Although many women may have possessed similar traits, no one else did what Margaret Sanger did when she did it. A simple sketch of personality cannot provide the insight of a more complex portrait.

On the positive side, trait theories give us some ability to *predict* behavior in common situations, such as work settings. But trait theories suffer from the same problem as the instinct theories. Both *describe* behavior with a label but do not *explain* it. For example, we can attribute depression to a depressive trait or an outgoing personality to extraversion without really understanding the behavior. In short, trait theories identify common traits, but they do not tell us much about their source or how they interact (McAdams, 1992; Pervin, 1985). Moreover, because most people display a trait only to a moderate degree, we must ask how useful traits are for understanding all but the extreme cases. In contrast, dynamic theories of personality (which we examined in the first part of this chapter) emphasize changing, developing forces within the individual and the environment.

Finally, with trait theory we again encounter the problem of the *self-fulfilling prophecy*. When given trait labels, people may begin to act as those labels suggest, making it more difficult for them to change. A child labeled "shy," for example, may have to struggle against both the label and the trait.

TRAITS AND THE PERSON–SITUATION DEBATE Cognitive theorist Walter Mischel dropped a scientific bombshell on the trait theorists with evidence suggesting that we behave far less consistently from one situation to another than most had assumed (1968, 1973). A person who is extraverted in one sit-

Connection

Chapter 9
The instinct theory foundered because it merely labeled behavior, rather than explaining it.

Connection

Chapter 4
A self-fulfilling prophecy can come true because expectations can influence behavior.

Often the situation is a more powerful predictor of behavior than are personality traits.

THE FAR SIDE®   **By GARY LARSON**

The four basic personality types

uation can become shy and retiring in another; an emotionally stable person may fall apart when the situation changes radically. Therefore, Mischel argued, knowledge of the *situation* is more important in predicting behavior than knowing a person's traits. The ensuing tumult within the field has become known as the **person–situation controversy** (Pervin, 1985).

Mischel's position challenged the very foundations of most personality theories. After all, if people do act inconsistently in different situations, then what good is a theory of personality? Critics mounted withering attacks on Mischel's thesis, pointing out that his methods underestimated a thread of consistency across situations (Epstein, 1980). Bem and Allen (1974) have also pointed out that some people behave more consistently than others. Moreover, people are most consistent when others are watching (Kenrick & Stringfield, 1980) and when in familiar situations (Funder, 1983a, b; Funder & Ozer, 1983).

Nevertheless, it is true that personality traits as measured by personality tests typically account for less than 10% of all the factors that affect behavior (Digman, 1990) — a small number, indeed! But don't make the mistake of assuming that the situation accounts for the remaining 90%. Correlations between situations and behaviors are relatively weak, too. The lesson to be learned here is that the majority of factors affecting behavior simply cannot be assigned to one category or the other. Behavior seems to result from an *interaction* of trait and situational variables (Kenrick & Funder, 1988). In fact, Mischel has never suggested that we abandon theories of personality. Rather, he sees behavior as a function of the situation, the individual's *interpretation* of the situation, and personality (1990; Mischel & Shoda, 1995).

Mischel has argued that personality variables have their greatest impact on behavior when cues in the situation are *weak* or *ambiguous*. When situations are strong and clear, there will be less individual variation in response. For example, suppose that one day when you are in class, a student collapses, apparently unconscious, onto the floor. After a stunned silence, the instructor asks the class to keep their seats and then points *at you,* demanding loudly, "Go to the office, call 911, and get an ambulance here!" What do you do? This is a "strong" situation: Someone is in control, an instructor you already see as an authority figure; that person has told you unambiguously what to do. You are likely to comply—as would most people in that situation. In Mischel's characterization of person–situation interactions, there would be very little variation in how individuals respond to these circumstances.

But now suppose that you are walking leisurely through campus and you see a crowd gathered to listen to a figure giving an impassioned speech. Will you stop to listen? This is a "weak" situation, and your actions are likely to depend more strongly on your interests and on such personality variables as independence, curiosity, and extraversion.

▲

Extraversion is thought by some to represent a major personality type.

Finding Your Type

In Your Life

The notion of **type** refers to especially important dimensions or clusters of traits that are found in essentially the same pattern in many people. As we saw earlier, Carl Jung made the concept of type a feature of his theory of personality. (Thus, we can see Jung as both a psychodynamic theorist and a trait/type theorist.) Jung's typology scheme, especially his notions of introversion and extraversion, have enjoyed wide influence and, as we have seen, is now recognized as one of the Big Five trait dimensions. Of particular importance is the use of Jung's typology as the foundation for the world's most widely used test of personality: the Myers-Briggs Type Indicator.

You are likely to have taken the **Myers-Briggs Type Indicator (MBTI)** because it is given to nearly two million people each year (Druck-

man & Bjork, 1991). It is used in many college counseling centers, where students may be advised to select a career that fits with their personality type. It is also used in relationship counseling, where couples are taught to accommodate to each other's personality styles. And, the MBTI is commonly used by consultants in management training sessions to convey the message that people have distinct personality patterns that suit them for different kinds of jobs.

We pause to give the MBTI a close look for two reasons. First, as the only objective measure of personality based on Jung's type theory, it presents an opportunity to examine some of his ideas critically. Second, as one of the most widely used of psychological instruments, the MBTI deserves critical scrutiny. We suggest that there are some good reasons to be cautious when interpreting the results on an MBTI profile.

On the Myers-Briggs test, examinees answer a series of ques-

tions about how they make judgments, perceive the world, and relate to others (Myers, 1962, 1976, 1987; Myers & Myers, 1995). Based on these responses, a scoring system assigns an individual to a four-dimensional personality type, derived from the Jungian dimensions of *Introversion–Extraversion, Thinking–Feeling, Sensation–Intuition,* and *Judgment–Perception.* Remember that, according to Jung, personality types are stable patterns over time.

So, what does the Myers-Briggs Type Indicator tell us about the stability or **reliability** of types? A *reliable* test gives consistent results, but the reliability of the MBTI is questionable. One study found that less than half of those tested on the MBTI had exactly the same type when retested five weeks later (McCarley & Carskadon, 1983). Another study found a change in at least one of the four type categories in about 75% of respondents (see Druckman & Bjork, 1991). Such results certainly raise questions about the fundamental concept of "type."

A second issue concerns the **validity** of the Myers-Briggs test (Pittenger, 1993). A *valid* test actually measures what it is being used to measure. And again the research on the MBTI gives a mixed picture (Druckman & Bjork, 1991). As you might expect, people who work with people—entertainers, counselors, managers, and sellers—tend to score higher on extraversion. By comparison, librarians, computer specialists, and physicians number many introverts in their ranks. The danger lies, however, in turning averages into stereotypes. In fact,

the data show a diversity of types within occupations. Further, we have a conspicuous lack of evidence documenting a relationship between personality type and occupational success. Although proponents of the MBTI claim that it is useful in vocational counseling, a review of the literature by a team from the National Academy of Sciences found no relationship between personality type, as revealed by the MBTI, and performance on a particular job (Druckman & Bjork, 1991). This report has, however, been hotly disputed by users of the instrument (Pearman, 1991). Clearly, the Myers-Briggs Type Indicator needs more validity work before we can confidently encourage people to make life choices on the basis of its results.

Counselors using the Myers-Briggs to assess Jungian personality types often argue that its value lies not in its accuracy but in its ability to suggest new avenues for exploration. And those who take the test often report that they have gained insight into themselves from the experience. Thus, the instrument may have some value in counseling, especially when counselors resist the temptation to interpret the results rigidly. Unfortunately, no research has been done that documents these benefits over the long term. Says the National Academy of Sciences Report (Druckman & Bjork, 1991), "Lacking such evidence, it is a curiosity why the instrument is used so widely" (p. 99).

CHECK**YOUR**UNDERSTANDING

1. **RECALL:** *Temperament refers to personality characteristics that*
   a. cause people to be "nervous" or unpredictable.
   b. are learned, especially from one's parents and peers.
   c. have a substantial biological basis.
   d. cause mental disorders.

2. **APPLICATION:** *A friend of yours always seems calm and unruffled, even in circumstances where other people feel stress. Which one of the Big Five traits applies to this characteristic of your friend?*
   a. introversion
   b. agreeableness
   c. emotional stability
   d. conscientiousness

3. **RECALL:** *Walter Mischel argues that _____ is (are) less important than _____.*

   a. traits/the situation
   b. traits/temperament
   c. the conscious mind/the unconscious
   d. emotions/reason

4. **UNDERSTANDING THE CORE CONCEPT:**
   What is found in most psychodynamic, humanistic, and cognitive theories, but is not found in most trait, type, and temperament theories?
   a. a description of the components of the personality
   b. labels for common mental disorders
   c. concepts that are useful for individuals involved in personnel selection decisions
   d. a description of the processes of development and change underlying personality

Core Concept

ANSWERS: 1. c   2. c   3. a   4. d

Key Question

WHAT "THEORIES" DO PEOPLE USE TO UNDERSTAND EACH OTHER?

We have seen how psychologists view personality. But how do people who are *not* psychologists think about people? This is an important matter because we all regularly make assumptions—right or wrong—about other people's personalities. You do so when you meet someone new at a party, when you apply for a job, and when you form your first impression of a professor or classmate. Do people make similar assumptions about each other in other cultures? These questions are significant because the "folk theories," or *implicit personality theories,* that people use to understand each other can support or undermine relationships among individuals — or even among nations. Our Core Concept says:

> People everywhere develop implicit assumptions ("folk theories")
> about personality, but these assumptions vary in important ways
> across cultures.

In this section we will examine the assumptions commonly found in implicit theories.

Implicit Personality Theories

Think of someone who has been a role model for you. Now think of someone you can't stand to be around. In both cases, what immediately springs to mind are personal attributes — traits — that you have learned to use to describe people: honesty, reliability, sense of humor, generosity, outgoing attitude, aggressiveness, moodiness, or pessimism, for example. Even as a child, you had a rudimentary system for appraising personality. You tried to determine which new acquaintances would be friend or foe; you worked out ways of dealing with your parents or teachers based on how you read their personalities. You have probably also spent a great deal of time trying to get a handle on who *you* are — on what qualities distinguish you from others, which ones to develop, and which to discard.

In each case, your judgments were personality assessments reflecting your **implicit personality theory,** your personal explanation of how people's qualities and experiences influence their response patterns. Implicit theories simplify the task of understanding other people (Fiske & Neuberg, 1990; Macrae et al., 1994). Some observers believe that certain aspects of our implicit theories are innate, especially the tendency to interpret others' mental states (Lillard, 1997).

Implicit theories often rely on naive assumptions about traits. For example, people tend to assume that certain clusters of traits go together — creativity and emotional sensitivity, for example. Consequently, when they observe one of these traits, they may assume that the person possesses the other (Hochwalder, 1995). People's personal experiences and motives can also influence their judgment of others. So, if you have had your heart broken by someone who was attractive but unwilling to make a commitment, you may quickly judge other attractive persons to be "insincere" or "untrustworthy."

Americans and Europeans also tend to make the **fundamental attribution error,** the assumption that another person's behavior, especially clumsy, inappropriate, or otherwise undesirable behavior, is the result of a flaw in the personality, rather than in the situation. For example, if you spill your coffee in an American restaurant, people are liable to assume that you are a clumsy person, rather than assuming that some external cause, such as someone bumping you, caused the spill. Cross-cultural research shows that the fundamental attribution error is less common in group-oriented "collectivistic" cultures, such as are found in China and India (Lillard, 1997; Miller, 1984; Morris & Peng, 1994).

Validity: An attribute of a psychological test that actually measures what it is being used to measure.

Implicit personality theory: Assumptions about personality that are held by people (especially nonpsychologists) to simplify the task of understanding others.

Fundamental attribution error: The assumption that another person's behavior, especially clumsy, inappropriate, or otherwise undesirable behavior, is the result of a flaw in the personality, rather than in the situation.

Connection

Chapter 14
The fundamental attribution error is not so fundamental in some other cultures.

Personality across Cultures

The very concept of personality theory is a Western (Euro-American) invention (Draguns, 1979). Therefore, it is not surprising that all formal theories of personality have been created by people trained in the framework of the Western social sciences, with a built-in bias toward individualism (Guisinger & Blatt, 1994; Segall et al., 1999). Other cultures, however, address many of the same issues in their own ways. Most of these non-Western perspectives have originated in religion (Walsh, 1984). Hindus, for example, see personality as a union of opposing characteristics (Murphy & Murphy, 1968). The Chinese concept of complementary opposite forces, *yin* and *yang,* provides a similar perspective (which influenced Carl Jung's *principle of opposites*).

INDIVIDUALISM, COLLECTIVISM, AND PERSONALITY   According to Harry Triandis (1989, 1990, 1994), cultures differ most fundamentally on the dimension of *individualism* versus *collectivism,* which we alluded to above. For those raised in the Euro-American tradition, the individual is the basic unit of society, while those raised in many Asian and African cultures emphasize the family or other social groups. In *collectivistic cultures* people tend to form identities that blend harmoniously with the group, and they expect that others are motivated to do the same. In *individualistic cultures,* a person tends to form a unique identity and assume that others are similarly motivated to stand out from the crowd (Pedersen, 1979). Thus, for Euro-Americans, the self is a whole, while for many Asians and Africans the self is only a part (Gardiner et al., 1998; Markus & Kitayama, 1994). For Euro-Americans, a group is composed of separate individuals; when they work together they become a "team." By contrast, for Asians and Africans the group is the natural unit; the individual is incomplete without the group. Much of the conflict and misunderstanding arising from business dealings and political negotiations across cultures stems from different expectations about personality and the individual's relationship to the group.

Many aspects of peoples' personalities and behavior are related to their culture's position on the individualism versus collectivism dimension. We have already seen how the fundamental attribution error is more common in individualistic cultures. Two other topics related to individualism versus collectivism and to personality have received special emphasis by cross-cultural psychologists: (1) competition versus cooperation and (2) the need for achievement. In brief, when given the choice of competition or cooperation, individualistic Americans characteristically choose to compete (Aronson, 1999; Gallo & McClintock, 1965). Americans, on the average, also score higher on measures of need for achievement than do people in collectivist cultures.

Cultural change that produces a clash between the values of individualism and collectivism may also cause conflict *within* a culture. One can see this conflict developing in Japan, the archetypal collectivist culture, as its youth experiments with individualist values imported along with American music, television, and film. One can also find generational conflicts over individualistic and collectivistic values in Hispanic, Asian, and Afro-American groups in the Unites States.

OTHER CULTURAL DIFFERENCES   Cultures differ on other personality-related dimensions that are not so obviously related to individualism–collectivism. These include:

> ▶ *Status of different age groups and sexes:* The status of the elderly is higher in many Asian cultures than in the United States; women

Connection

Chapter 9
Achievement motivation is affected by the culture's tendency toward individualism or collectivism.

have second-class status in many traditional societies (Segall et al., 1999).

▶ *Romantic love:* The assumption that romantic love should be the basis for marriage is a recent European invention and is most often found in individualistic cultures (Rosenblatt, 1966).

▶ *Stoicism:* Asian cultures teach people to suppress the expression of intense feelings (Tsai & Uemura, 1988), while Euro-Americans are much more likely to express strong emotions (although there are pronounced gender differences).

▶ *Locus of control:* Persons in industrialized nations, such as the United States and Canada, more often have an internal locus of control than those in developing countries, such as Mexico or China (Berry et al., 1992; Draguns, 1979).

▶ *Thinking versus feeling:* Many cultures (e.g., in Latin America) do not make the strong distinction between thoughts and emotions that Americans do (Fajans, 1985; Lutz, 1988).

▶ *Attribution:* Americans often attribute behavior to internal traits, while Asians are more likely to explain people's actions in terms of the external situation (Lillard, 1997).

Cultures even differ in their views of the ideal personality (Matsumoto, 1996). In the Western psychological tradition, mental health consists of integrating opposite and conflicting parts of the personality. This can be seen especially clearly in Freudian and Jungian theory. By contrast, some Asian psychologies, particularly those associated with Buddhism, seek the opposite: to dissociate consciousness from sensation and from memories of worldly experience (Pedersen, 1979).

Despite these differences, can we say that people are fundamentally the same the world over? On the level of neurons and brain circuits, the answer is almost certainly "Yes." But personality is also locked in the embrace of culture, so a more comprehensive answer would be "No — but perhaps they can be described on the same Big Five dimensions." In the words of Erika Bourguignon (1979), "It is one of the major intellectual developments of the twentieth century to call into question the concept of a universal human nature."

Even though personality and culture are partners in a perpetual dance, we can make this distinction between them:

"Culture" refers to those aspects of a society that all its members share, are familiar with, and pass on to the next generation. "Personality" refers to unique combinations of traits (which all people in a culture know about, even though a given trait does not describe a given person) which differentiate individuals within a culture. (Brislin, 1981, pp. 51–52)

But don't forget that culture and personality interact. A culture shapes the personalities of the individuals within it, just as individuals can influence a culture (Draguns, 1979). So, your personality is, to a certain extent, a product of your society's values, attitudes, beliefs, and customs about morality, work, child-rearing, aggression, achievement, competition, death, and dozens of other matters important to humans everywhere. And, in a larger sense, a culture is the personality of a society (Benedict, 1934).

Connection

Chapter 14
The American assumption of romantic love as the basis for a long-term commitment is not universal.

Eclectic: Either switching theories to explain different situations or building one's own theory of personality from pieces borrowed from many perspectives.

Most Asian cultures have a collectivist tradition that affirms the group, rather than the individual, as the fundamental social unit.

Developing Your Own Theory of Personality

Psychology In Your Life

Each of the theories we have examined has its limitations and strengths (see Table 11.3). Consequently, most psychologists become **eclectic.** That is, they either switch theories as the situation requires or construct a theory of personality by borrowing ideas from many perspectives. While an eclectic approach may appear to offer the easiest route, it presents difficulties that arise from certain fundamental conflicts among theories. To give one example: How could we reconcile Freud's concept of our behavior being driven by primitive instincts with humanism's assumption of the innate goodness of our nature?

It may help to think of a personality theory as a map showing the major pathways through a person's psychological landscape. As you formulate your own theory, you must decide how to weight the forces that determine which paths we select—the forces of conditioning, motivation and emotion, heredity and environment, individualism and collectivism, cognition, traits, culture, self-concept, and potential. We propose the following questions, which will help you sort out the assumptions in your implicit theory of personality.

▶ In your opinion, are people more rational and logical (as the cogni-

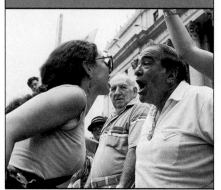

Some views of personality assert that anger comes from an inner drive that arises in the unconscious mind. Other views emphasize conscious cognitions of environmental stimuli. Do you think these people are conscious of the reasons for their behavior?

TABLE 11.3	**Comparison of the Major Psychological Theories of Personality**			
PERSPECTIVE	**EMPHASIS**	**CAUSES OF PSYCHOLOGICAL DISORDER**	**MAJOR FIGURES**	**IMPORTANT TERMS**
Psychodynamic theories	Unhealthy motivation	Unconscious drives and conflicts	Sigmund Freud	Id, ego, superego Ego defense mechanisms: repression, projection Rorschach, TAT Eros, Thanatos, libido Psychic determinism Psychosexual stages
			Carl Jung	Collective unconscious Archetypes Introversion, extraversion Personality types
			Erik Erikson	Psychosocial stages
Humanistic theories	Healthy motivation	Unhealthy situations, low self-esteem, unmet needs	Abraham Maslow	Hierarchy of needs
			Carl Rogers	Self-actualization Self-esteem
Cognitive theories	Cognitive learning, expectations	Poor role models, unhealthy situations	Albert Bandura	Observational learning Reciprocal determinism Locus of control
			Julian Rotter	
			Walter Mischel	Person–situation controversy

PERSPECTIVE	EMPHASIS	CAUSES OF PSYCHOLOGICAL DISORDER	MAJOR FIGURES	IMPORTANT TERMS
Trait, type, and temperament theories	Enduring personality characteristics	Maladaptive traits, conflicts of different personality types, extremes of temperament	Jerome Kagan Hans Eysenck Various theorists	Temperament Extraversion, neuroticism, psychoticism "Big Five" personality traits MMPI-2 MBTI
Implicit and cross-cultural theories	"Common sense" theories Cultural differences	Many views — depending on culture	Harry Triandis	Individualistic versus collectivistic cultures Fundamental attribution error

tive theories contend), or do they more often act on the basis of feelings and emotions (as the psychodynamic theories argue)?

▶ Are people usually conscious of the reasons for their behavior, as many of the post-Freudians claimed? Or, are their actions mainly caused by unconscious needs, desires, and urges (as Freud suggested)?

▶ What are the basic motives behind human behavior: sex,

aggression, power, love, spirituality. . . ?

▶ Are human motives essentially egocentric and self-serving? Or are they altruistic, unmotivated by the desire for personal gain (as the humanists suggest)?

▶ When you try to understand another person's actions, which of the following do you consider to be most important: the situation (as Mischel says); the person's inner needs, drives, motives, and emotions (as the

psychodynamic theories say); or the person's basic personality characteristics (as the trait and type theories say)?

▶ Is our basic, inner nature essentially healthy and good (as the humanists see it) or composed of primitive and self-serving desires (as Freud saw it)?

No one has yet found the "right" answers, but the answers *you* give say a great deal about your own personality.

CHECK**YOUR**UNDERSTANDING

1. **APPLICATION:** *You would expect to find the concept of* self *emphasized in*
   a. the culture of an industrialized society.
   b. a wealthy culture.
   c. an individualistic culture.
   d. a collectivistic culture.

2. **RECALL:** *Cross-cultural psychologists say that the most basic distinction among cultures is their emphasis on*
   a. capitalism or socialism.
   b. external or internal locus of control.
   c. thoughts or feelings.
   d. individualism or collectivism.

3. **APPLICATION:** *You are making the fundamental attribution* error *(which is not so fundamental, after all) when*
   a. you decide to dislike someone who speaks angrily to you.

   b. you see someone who is nice looking and assume that she is self-centered and arrogant.
   c. you go to a foreign country and assume that everyone thinks the same way you do.
   d. you think someone is clumsy when he trips and drops his books.

4. **UNDERSTANDING THE CORE CONCEPT:**
   Implicit personality theories involve
   a. the assumptions that people make about each other's motivations and intentions.
   b. assumptions about themselves that people want to hide from others.
   c. unconscious instincts, memories, and conflicts.
   d. opinions that people privately hold about others but will not say openly.

ANSWERS: 1. c   2. d   3. d   4. a

Using Psychology to Learn Psychology: Your Academic Locus of Control

Although an internal or external locus of control can be a central feature of your personality, your perceived locus of control can also change from situation to situation. When you are speaking in front of a group, for example, you may feel that the situation is beyond your control, but when you are on skis, you may feel that your are fully the master of your fate. And what about your education? Do you have a sense of internal or external control with regard to, say, your grade in psychology?

An external locus of control concerning grades poses a danger for the college student because college life is so full of distractions and temptations. If you believe that your grades are largely beyond your control, you can easily be driven by the enticements of the moment and let your studies slide. This attitude can, of course, become a self-fulfilling prophecy that ruins your grades not only in psychology but across the board.

The following questions will help you discover your academic locus of control.

1. On a test do you often find that, even if you know the material, anxiety wipes the information from your memory?
2. On a test do you often know the material well but find that the test is unfair or covers material that the teacher did not indicate would be on the test?
3. Do you feel poorly motivated to cope with college-level work?
4. Are you so easily distracted that you can never quite get around to studying?
5. Do you believe that some people are born to be good students and some are not?

6. Do you feel that you have no control over the grades you receive?
7. Do you feel that you are not smart enough to cope with college-level work?
8. Do you feel that success in college is largely a matter of luck?

If you answered "yes" to several of these questions, then you probably have an *external* locus of control with respect to your college work—an attitude that can hamper your chances of college success. What can be done? Nothing, if you are completely convinced that your success in college is beyond your control. If, however, you are open to the idea of establishing more control over your college experience, here are several suggestions.

▶ Get help with test anxiety from your counseling center or learning resources center.
▶ Find a tutor either among friends or at your learning resources center.
▶ Talk to your professors individually: Ask them to give you some pointers on what they consider to be especially important (and testable) in their classes.
▶ Go to your counseling center or learning resources center and get an assessment of your strengths and weaknesses and of your interest patterns. Then make a plan to correct your weaknesses (e.g., with remedial classes in your weak areas) and build on your strengths. Select a major that capitalizes on your interests.

We would wish you good luck—but that's only of concern to externalizers!

Chapter Summary

WHAT FORCES SHAPE OUR PERSONALITIES?

The psychodynamic, humanistic, and cognitive theories all seek to explain the influences that mold our personalities. Psychodynamic theories, such as those proposed by Freud, Jung, and Horney, assume that personality is driven by unconscious forces and shaped by early childhood experience. Humanistic theories, such as those of Maslow and Rogers, argue that people are naturally driven toward self-actualization, but this tendency can be suppressed by unhealthy conditions and perceptions. According to the cognitive theories, such as those of Bandura and Rotter, behavior is a function of situational and personal variables, direct and observational learning, and expectations.

 Core Concept

According to the psychodynamic, humanistic, and cognitive theories, personality is a developmental process, shaped by our internal needs and cognitions and by external pressures from the social environment.

 Key Question

WHAT PATTERNS ARE FOUND IN PERSONALITY?

Type, trait, and temperament theories are descriptive approaches to personality with a long history stretching back to the ancient Greeks. Modern trait/type/temperament theories are frequently used as the basis for diagnosis, personnel selection, and psychological testing. Temperament refers to innate personality dispositions, which may be tied to factors in the brain. Traits give personality consistency across situations and may be influenced by both heredity and learning. Many psychologists now agree on the Big Five

traits. The person–situation controversy, however, has raised questions about the relative contribution of personality traits and situations to behavior. Type theory is seen especially in the controversial and widely used MBTI, based on Jung's personality typology.

 Core Concept

Some theories attribute personality to stable patterns known as traits, types, and temperaments.

 Key Question

WHAT "THEORIES" DO PEOPLE USE TO UNDERSTAND EACH OTHER?

People everywhere deal with each other on the basis of their implicit personality theories, which simplify the task of understanding others. Implicit theories may rely on naive assumptions, such as the fundamental attribution error. Moreover, cross-cultural psychologists have found that the assumptions people make about personality and behavior vary widely across cultures.

 Core Concept

People everywhere develop implicit assumptions ("folk theories") about personality, but these assumptions vary in important ways across cultures.

Review Test

For each of the following items, choose the single best answer. The correct answers appear at the end.

1. Which sort of personality theory would most likely emphasize unconscious motivation?
   a. psychodynamic theory
   b. trait theory
   c. humanistic theory
   d. cognitive theory

2. Which one of the following is an ego defense mechanism that causes us to forget unpleasant or threatening experiences?
   a. displacement
   b. projection
   c. regression
   d. repression

3. Critics fault Freud's psychoanalytic theory because it
   a. does not explain the source of mental disorders.
   b. has no theory of psychological development.
   c. has little basis in scientific research.
   d. has had little impact on popular culture.

4. One of the biggest differences between Freud and Jung can be seen in Jung's idea of
   a. the collective unconscious.
   b. locus of control.
   c. implicit personality theories.
   d. shyness.

5. The humanistic theorists were the first to emphasize
   a. unconscious motives.
   b. mental disorder.
   c. the healthy personality.
   d. how people are similar to other animals.

6. According to Rogers, children may grow up with feelings of guilt and anxiety in homes where
   a. parents are not good role models.
   b. one of the parents is absent most of the time.
   c. parental love is conditional on good behavior.
   d. the parents are in conflict with each other.

7. Reciprocal determinism involves the interaction of
   a. the id, ego, and superego.
   b. self-actualization, unconditional positive regard, and the phenomenal field.
   c. the conscious mind, the conscience, and the collective unconscious.
   d. cognitions, behavior, and the environment.

8. Explaining why a new classmate does not seem attractive, your friend remarks, "I don't much like thin people, because they're too nervous!" This assumption reveals that your friend favors a _____ theory of personality.
   a. type

b. psychodynamic
c. cognitive
d. collectivistic

9. Which of the following is *not* one of the Big Five personality factors?
   a. neuroticism
   b. intelligence
   c. conscientiousness
   d. openness to experience

10. Your *implicit theory of personality* would help you
    a. know that a friend needs comforting when she loses her job.
    b. laugh at a joke.
    c. shout at a friend when you are angry at your employer.
    d. feel rewarded when you receive your paycheck.

ANSWERS: 1. a   2. d   3. c   4. a   5. c   6. c
7. d   8. a   9. b   10. a

If You're Interested . . .

BOOKS

Albom, M. (1997). *Tuesdays with Morrie: An old man, a young man, and life's greatest lesson.* Doubleday. This is the true story of the friendship between Mitch Albom and his aging mentor, an open-minded and compassionate sociology professor dying of ALS (amyotrophic lateral sclerosis). For Morrie Schwartz's own perspective see *Morrie: In His Own Words* (2000).

Carducci, B. J., with Golant, S. (1999). *Shyness: A bold new approach.* HarperCollins. Not a workbook for "changing" shy people into extroverts, but rather a set of strategies for living a "successfully shy life," this book includes managing shyness when meeting others, working, falling in love, making small talk, and caring for shy children.

Conroy, P. (1976). *The great Santini.* Houghton-Mifflin; reissued 1987, Bantam Books. This novel about an intense, complex military man and the family who find him impossible to either love or hate, emphasizes the perspective of the oldest son, a born athlete who nevertheless can never please his demanding, derisive father. (The character of Col. Bull Meecham was poignantly portrayed by actor Robert Duvall in the 1979 film version.)

Fiffer, S. (1999). *Three quarters, two dimes, and a nickel: A memoir of becoming whole.* Free Press. Paralyzed from the neck down by a high-school wrestling accident, Steve Fiffer (pronounced FYE-fer) dealt with denial, deceit, depression, and rejection before he finally found a coach who could bully him into independence and mobility. (The title, implying that a dollar bill is worth the same amount in change, sums up his response to being rejected: He might be different, but he is *whole*.

Hales, D. (1999). *Just like a woman: How gender science is redefining what makes us female.* Bantam. Writer Diane Hales reviews research findings regarding differences and similarities between the genders, with an emphasis on how women can overcome stereotypes and prejudices that block their potential for growth.

Nohria, N., & Lawrence, P. R. (2001). *Driven: The four key drives to understanding why we choose to do what we do.* Jossey-Bass. Two Harvard Business School professors synthesize research in the biological and social sciences, proposing a new theory of why people behave as they do in the workplace, focusing on four goals: getting, loving, learning, and defending.

Riso, R., & Hudson, R. (1996). *Personality types: Using the enneagram for self-discovery.* Mariner Books. Here is a revised and expanded edition of the best-selling book offering and analyzing a lengthy self-test along nine distinctive patterns of personality traits and patterns: Reformer, Helper, Status Seeker, Artist, Thinker, Loyalist, Generalist, Leader, and Peacemaker.

Rosenbaum, R. (1999). *Explaining Hitler: The search for the origins of evil.* HarperCollins. Instead of another biography or history of the life of the Nazi dictator, this book seeks to understand why Adolf Hitler became the monster behind World War II and the Holocaust. What emerges is no single, comprehensive explanation, but many faces of one man, much like any other person with private and public personas.

VIDEOS

Billy Elliott. (2000, color, 100 min.). Directed by Stephen Daldry; starring Jamie Bell, Julie Walters, Gary Lewis. During northern England's 1984 coal miners' strike, a young boy from a disintegrating family abandons the "acceptable" sport of boxing and makes the provocative choice of studying ballet. Here is a provocative depiction of what happens when personality and talent clash with culture and family.

Citizen Kane. (1941, b&w, 199 min.). Directed by Orson Welles; starring Orson Welles, Joseph Cotton, Agnes Moorehead, Dorothy Comingore. One of the best films ever, based on the life of newspaper magnate William Randolph Hearst, this is a retrospective on the influences, choices, and accomplishments that have shaped the life of an unhappy, reclusive, self-made millionaire.

Gattaca. (1997, color, 112 min.). Directed by Andrew Niccol; starring Ethan Hawke, Uma Thurman, Jude Law, Alan Arkin, Tony Shalhoub. This science-fiction film views a future where parents can eliminate genetic defects from their unborn children, so that they will be "Valid" for their destinies. An "In-Valid" (genetically imperfect) young man dreams of becoming an astronaut, so swaps identities with a Valid acquaintance in order to qualify —and must now elude detection as well as the penalties for "passing" as perfect.

La Cage aux Folles (Birds of a Feather). (1978, color, 91 min., French-Italian). Directed by Edouard Molinaro; starring Ugo Tognazzi, Michel Serrault, Michel Galabru, Claire Maurier. Somewhat better than the 1996 U.S. remake *The Birdcage,* this tells the story of a boy raised by his gay father and his father's effeminate partner, who try to pose as a straight couple to impress the conservative parents of their son's fiancee. It includes some outrageous and some touching scenes about the difficulty of changing one's role or behavior through an act of will alone.

Talented Mr. Ripley, The. (1999, color, 139 min.). Directed by Anthony Minghella; starring Matt Damon, Jude Law, Gwyneth Paltrow, Philip Seymour Hoffman. Mistaken for an Ivy League graduate, a sincere young man deceives his wealthy new friends, only to find himself tempted by the good life into considering more serious crimes. Who is the "real" Tom Ripley?

Truman Show, The. (1998, color, 102 min.). Directed by Peter Weir; starring Jim Carrey, Laura Linney, Ed Harris, Noah Emmerich. Truman Burbank was born and raised on a TV production set, an enormous sound stage peopled entirely by actors and extras, all so his life can be broadcast 24 hours a day on television, while he is unaware that this is all a show. This film raises more questions than it answers about what makes him the person he is, given that his "parents," "friends" and "teachers" are all constantly conning and persuading him. Nonetheless it is eerie, well-acted, and absorbing.

WEB RESOURCES

http://bill.psyc.anderson.edu/perth/freud.htm Visit this Web site for an extensive list of links to major individuals and theories in the study of personality.

http://www.wynja.com/personality/theorists.html This Web site includes many major personality theorists, such as Sigmund Freud, Carl Rogers, or Alfred Adler. Detailed material on their theories is also included.

http://www.2h.com/Tests/personality.phtml Numerous personality tests are offered on this site, including the Keirsey Temperament Sorter. This site also includes tests for anxiety, self-esteem, attention deficit disorder, and type A personality.

http://www.shyness.com/ This Web site explores shyness, with an emphasis on how to learn new behaviors in order to eliminate shyness. Various resources are offered to help individuals overcome their timidity.

WHAT IS MENTAL DISORDER?

Evolving Concepts of Mental Disorder
Indicators of Abnormality

The medical model takes a "disease" view, while psychology sees mental disorder as an interaction of biological, cognitive, social, and other environmental factors.

A CAUTION TO READERS:
If you find that you have some signs of mental disorder, don't jump to conclusions.

HOW ARE MENTAL DISORDERS CLASSIFIED?

Overview of the *DSM-IV* Classification
System
Mood Disorders
Anxiety Disorders
Somatoform Disorders
Dissociative Disorders
Eating Disorders
Schizophrenic Disorders
Personality Disorders
Adjustment Disorders and Other
Conditions
Psychology in Your Life: Shyness

The most widely used system, found in the *DSM-IV,* classifies disorders by their mental and behavioral symptoms.

SHYNESS:
If you have it, it doesn't have to be permanent. (And, by the way, it's not a mental disorder.)

WHAT ARE THE CONSEQUENCES OF LABELING PEOPLE?

Diagnostic Labels Can Compound the
Problem
The Cultural Context of Mental
Disorder
Psychology in Your Life: The Plea of
Insanity

Ideally, accurate diagnoses lead to proper treatments, but diagnoses may also become labels that depersonalize people and ignore the social and cultural contexts in which their problems arise.

THE PLEA OF INSANITY:
It's not a psychological or psychiatric term, and, contrary to popular opinion, it is a defense that is seldom used.

USING PSYCHOLOGY TO LEARN PSYCHOLOGY: Diagnosing Your Friends and Family

PSYCHOPATHOLOGY

he volunteers knew they were on their own. If they managed to get into the hospital, the five men and three women could only get out by convincing the staff that they were sane. None had ever been diagnosed with a mental illness, but perhaps they were not so "normal" after all: Would a normal person lie to get into such a place? In fact, all were collaborators in an experiment designed to find out whether normality would be recognized in a mental hospital.

The experimenter, David Rosenhan —himself one of the pseudopatients— suspected that terms such as "sanity," "insanity," "schizophrenia," "mental illness," and "abnormal" might have fuzzier boundaries than the psychiatric community thought. He also suspected that some strange behaviors seen in mental patients might originate in the abnormal atmosphere of the mental hospital, rather than in the patients themselves. To test these ideas, Rosenhan and his collaborators decided to see how mental hospital personnel would deal with patients who were not mentally ill.

Individually, they applied for admission at different hospitals, complaining that they had recently heard voices that seemed to say "empty," "hollow," and "thud." Aside from this, they claimed no other symptoms of mental disorder. All used false names, and the four who were mental health professionals gave false

(continued)

459

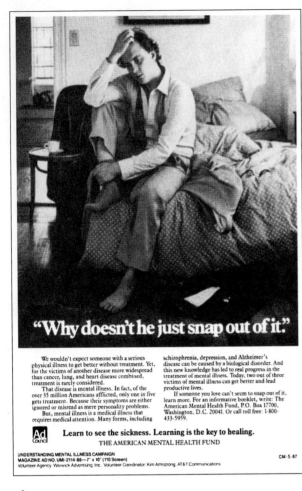

"Why doesn't he just snap out of it."

We wouldn't expect someone with a serious physical illness to get better without treatment. Yet, for the victims of another disease more widespread than cancer, lung, and heart disease combined, treatment is rarely considered.

That disease is mental illness. In fact, of the over 35 million Americans afflicted, only one in five gets treatment. Because their symptoms are either ignored or misread as mere personality problems.

But, mental illness is a medical illness that requires medical attention. Many forms, including schizophrenia, depression, and Alzheimer's disease can be caused by a biological disorder. And this new knowledge has led to real progress in the treatment of mental illness. Today, two out of three victims of mental illness can get better and lead productive lives.

If someone you love can't seem to snap out of it, learn more. For an informative booklet, write: The American Mental Health Fund, P.O. Box 17700, Washington, D.C. 20041. Or call toll free: 1-800-433-5959.

 Learn to see the sickness. Learning is the key to healing.
THE AMERICAN MENTAL HEALTH FUND

UNDERSTANDING MENTAL ILLNESS CAMPAIGN
MAGAZINE AD NO. UMI-2114-86—7" x 10" (110 Screen)
Volunteer Agency: Warwick Advertising, Inc. Volunteer Coordinator: Kim Armstrong, AT&T Communications

CM-5-87

▲

Advertisements, like the one shown here, have gone a long way toward correcting our views of mental illness and creating sympathy for its sufferers.

Connection

Chapter 14
Social psychology has also taught us about the "power of the situation."

occupations—but apart from these fibs, the subjects answered all questions truthfully. They tried to act normally, although the prospect of entering the alien hospital environment made them feel anxious; they also worried about not being admitted and—worse yet—being exposed as frauds. Their concerns vanished quickly, for all readily gained admittance at 12 different hospitals (some did it twice). All but one were diagnosed with "schizophrenia," a major mental disorder often accompanied by hearing imaginary voices.

After admission, the pseudopatients made no further claims of hearing voices or any other abnormal symptoms. Indeed, all wanted to be on their best behavior to gain release. Their only apparent "deviance" involved taking notes on the experience—at first privately and later publicly, when they found that the staff paid little attention. The nursing records indicated that, when the staff did notice, they interpreted the note-taking as part of the patient's illness. (One comment: "Patient engages in writing behavior.") But in spite of the absence of abnormal symptoms, it took an average of 19 days for the pseudopatients to convince the hospital staff that they were ready for discharge. One unfortunate subject wasn't released for almost two months.

Two main findings from this classic study jarred the psychiatric community to its core. First, *no professional staff member at any of the hospitals ever realized that any of Rosenhan's pseudopatients was a fraud.* Of course, the staff may have assumed that the patients had been ill at the time of admission and had improved during their hospitalization. But that possibility did not let the professionals off Rosenhan's hook: Despite apparently normal behavior, not one pseudopatient was ever labeled as "normal" or "well" while in the hospital. And, upon discharge, they were still seen as having schizophrenia—but "in remission."

The mistaken diagnosis does not suggest that the hospital staff members were unskilled or unfeeling. The fact that they did not detect the pseudopatients' normal behavior is probably because they spent little time observing and interacting with the patients. Most of the time they kept to themselves in a glassed-in central office that patients called "the cage." As Rosenhan (1973) said:

> It could be a mistake, and a very unfortunate one, to consider that what happened to us derived from malice or stupidity on the part of the staff. Quite the contrary, our overwhelming impression of them was of people who really cared, who were committed and who were uncommonly intelligent. Where they failed, as they sometimes did painfully, it would be more accurate to attribute those failures to the environment in which they, too, found themselves than to personal callousness. Their perceptions and behavior were controlled by the situation . . . (p. 257)

A second finding tells us volumes about the patients and the nature of mental disorder itself: To everyone's surprise, *the hospital patients readily detected the ruse, even though the professional staff did not.* The pseudopatients reported that the other patients regularly voiced their suspicions: "You're not crazy. You're a journalist or a professor. . . . You're checking up on the hospital." In his report of this experience, entitled "On Being Sane in Insane Places," Rosenhan (1973) noted dryly: "The fact that the patients often recognized normality when staff did not raises important questions" (p. 252). You will hear the echo of these "important questions" as we critically examine the medical view of mental disorder in this chapter.

Please note that Rosenhan did not deny the existence of mental abnormalities. People *do* suffer the anguish of psychopathology. According to a study conducted by the National Institutes of Mental Health, about 15.4% of the population suffers from diagnosable mental health problems. Another study found that, during any given year, the behaviors of over 56 million Americans meet the criteria for a diagnosable mental disorder (Carson et al., 1996; Regier et al., 1993). Over the life span, as many as 32% of Americans will suffer from some psychological disorder (Regier et al., 1988).

Neither did Rosenhan deny that the initial diagnoses given his pseudopatients were justified. After all, they claimed to be hearing voices—a strong indicator of abnormality. Rosenhan's quarrel with mental hospitals centered on the dehumanizing atmosphere and the assumptions made by hospital staff members about "mental illness." These conditions, he argued, blinded caregivers to the needs of their patients. As we look at the problem of diagnosing and describing mental disorder in this chapter, it will be helpful to keep Rosenhan's study in mind.

WHAT IS MENTAL DISORDER?

Distinguishing "normal" from "abnormal" is no simple task. Consider, for example, how you would classify such eccentric personalities as Robin Williams or Madonna or Dennis Rodman. And what about a soldier who risks his or her life in combat: Is that "normal"? Or consider a grief-stricken woman who is unable to return to her normal routine three months after her husband died: Does she have a mental disorder?

Three classic symptoms suggest severe mental disorder: *hallucinations, delusions,* and extreme *affective disturbances.* **Hallucinations** are false sensory experiences, such as hearing nonexistent voices (as Rosenhan's pseudopatients said they did). **Delusions** are extreme disorders of thinking that involve persistent false beliefs. If you think you are the President of the United States (and you are not), you have a symptom of psychopathology. Similarly, those whose **affect** (emotion) is, for no apparent reason, depressed, anxious, or manic—or those who seems to have no emotional response at all—have yet other signs of mental disorder. The clinician, however, must be aware that any of these may also arise from other causes, such as drug reactions.

Beyond such signs of distress, the experts do not always agree, however. What is abnormal and what is not becomes a judgment call, a judgment made more difficult because no sharp boundary separates normal from abnormal thought and behavior. It may be helpful to think of mental disorder as part of a *continuum* ranging from the absence of disorder to severe disorder, as shown in Table 12.1.

The "abnormal" region of this continuum is sometimes referred to as the region of *psychopathology* or *mental disorder*—or even *mental illness*. In general, we can define **psychopathology** as any pattern of emotions, behaviors, or thoughts inappropriate to the situation and leading to personal distress or the inability to achieve important goals. In everyday terms, this may mean unhap-

Hallucinations: False sensory experiences that may suggest mental disorder. Hallucinations can have other causes, such as drugs or sensory isolation.

Delusions: Extreme disorders of thinking, involving persistent false beliefs. Delusions are the hallmark of paranoid disorders.

Affect: A term referring to emotion or mood.

Psychopathology: Any pattern of emotions, behaviors, or thoughts inappropriate to the situation and leading to personal distress or the inability to achieve important goals.

piness, anxiety, despair, worries, addiction, anger, or loss of contact with the surrounding world. Of course, occasional periods of worry, self-doubt, sadness, and escapism are all part of normal life. But taken to excess, these same experiences become symptoms of mental disorder. It is a matter of degree; it is a matter of judgment.

In this section of the chapter, we will focus on two contrasting views of mental disorder. One, coming to us from the profession of psychiatry, is sometimes called the "medical model" of mental disorder. It portrays mental problems much as it does physical disorders: as a sickness. The other view, a psychological view, sees mental disorders as the result of multiple factors both inside and outside the person. As our Core Concept puts it:

> **The medical model takes a "disease" view, while psychology sees mental disorder as an interaction of biological, cognitive, social, and other environmental factors.**

No matter how we conceptualize psychopathology, nearly everyone agrees that mental disorder is widespread. It touches the daily lives of millions. It can be insidious, working its way into thoughts and feelings, diminishing its victims' emotional and physical well-being, along with their personal and family relationships. And it can create an enormous financial burden through lost productivity, lost wages, and the high costs of prolonged treatment. Yet, the way people conceptualize psychopathology does have a consequence: It determines how they will attempt to treat it—with drugs, charms, rituals, talk, torture, surgery, hospitalization, or commitment to an "insane asylum."

In this section of the chapter, we will find that the two main ways of looking at psychopathology, the medical model and the psychological view, are often at odds. Some of this conflict is territorial, resulting from professional infighting. But some of the conflict has historical roots, as we shall see next.

TABLE 12.1	*The Spectrum of Mental Disorder*

Mental disorder occurs on a spectrum that ranges from the absence of signs of pathology to severe disturbances, such as is found in schizophrenia. The important point is that there is *no* sharp distinction that divides those with mental disorders from those who are "normal."

NO DISORDER	MILD DISORDER	MODERATE DISORDER	SEVERE DISORDER
• Absence of signs of mental disorder • Absence of behavior problems • No problems with interpersonal relationships	• Few signs of unease or distress • Few problem behaviors • Few difficulties in interpersonal relationships	• Signs of unease or distress that are more pronounced or occur more frequently • More distinct behavior problems • More frequent difficulties with relationships	• Clear signs of mental disorder meeting *DSM-IV* criteria • Severe behavior problems meeting *DSM-IV* criteria • Many poor relationships or lack of relationships with others

Evolving Concepts of Mental Disorder

In the ancient world, people assumed that supernatural powers were every-where, accounting for good fortune, disease, and disaster—even for the rise and fall of nations. In this context, psychopathology was caused by demons and spirits that had taken possession of the person's mind and body (Sprock & Blashfield, 1991). If you had been living at that time, your daily routine would have included rituals aimed at outwitting or placating these supernatural beings.

In about 400 B.C., the Greek physician Hippocrates (Hip-POCK-ra-teez) may have taken humanity's first step toward a scientific view of mental disturbance when he declared that abnormal behavior has physical causes. He taught his disciples to interpret the symptoms of psychopathology as an imbalance among four body fluids called "humors": blood, phlegm (mucus), black bile, and yellow bile. Those with an excess of black bile, for example, were inclined to melancholy or depression, while those who had an abundance of blood were sanguine, or warmhearted. With this revolutionary idea, Hippocrates incorporated mental disorder into medicine, and his view influenced educated people in the Western world until the end of the Roman Empire.

Then, in the Middle Ages, superstition eclipsed the Hippocratic model of mental disorder. Under the influence of the Church, physicians and clergy reverted to the old ways of explaining abnormality in terms of demons and witchcraft. In these harsh times, the Inquisition was driven by the belief that unusual behavior was the work of the Devil. The "cure" involved attempts to drive out the demons who possessed the unfortunate victim's soul. As a result, thousands of mentally disturbed people were tortured and executed all across the European continent. And, in 1692, the same view of mental disorder led the young colony in Salem, Massachusetts, to convict and execute a group of its residents for witchcraft (Karlsen, 1987). A group of young girls had frightened the community with a rash of convulsions and reports of sensory disturbances that were interpreted as signs of demonic possession. A modern analysis of the Salem witch trials has concluded that the girls were probably suffering from poisoning by a fungus growing on rye grain—the same fungus that produces the hallucinogenic drug LSD (Caporeal, 1976; Matossian, 1982, 1989).

Even today the ancient ideas about spirit possession, witchcraft, and mental disturbance are held by some people. A well-known American evangelist has declared on television that the Devil causes mental illness. Many other Americans believe that the full moon drives people to "lunacy." (It does not.) Similar folk beliefs permeate many cultures. Some Africans, for example, believe that mental disorder results from sorcery (Sow, 1977); the Haitian belief in voodoo has the same origins. Likewise, Thais assert that clever spirits called *pi* can create mental disturbances, while peoples of the northern Mediterranean credit the "evil eye" with supernatural powers that cause physical or mental affliction.

THE MEDICAL MODEL   In the latter part of the 18th century, the "illness" view that originated with Hippocrates reemerged with the rise of science. The resulting **medical model** held that mental disorders are *diseases* of the mind that, like ordinary physical diseases, have objective causes and require specific treatments. People began to perceive individuals with psychological problems as *sick* (suffering from illness), rather than as demon-possessed or immoral. And what a difference a new theory made! It no longer made sense to treat mental disorder by torture and abuse. The new view of mental illness brought

Connection

Chapter 11
Hippocrates' *humor* theory was a theory of temperaments.

Connection

Chapter 3
Hallucinogenic drugs change consciousness by altering perceptions.

Medical model: The view that mental disorders are diseases that, like ordinary physical diseases, have objective causes and require specific treatments.

A painting of the Salem witchcraft trials, Salem, Massachusetts, 1692. Twenty people were executed before the hysteria subsided.

sweeping reforms that were implemented in "asylums" for the "insane." In this supportive atmosphere, many patients actually improved—even thrived—on rest, contemplation, and simple but useful work (Maher & Maher, 1985). Unfortunately, the initially therapeutic asylums turned into warehouses of neglect, as a result of overcrowding and political pressures.

Despite such problems, however, the medical model was unquestionably an improvement over the demon model. Yet, modern psychologists think that the medical model has its own weaknesses. They point out that the assumption of "illness" leads to a doctor-knows-best approach in which the therapist takes all the responsibility for diagnosing the illness and prescribing treatment. The patient becomes a passive recipient of medication and advice, rather than an active treatment participant learning how to manage his or her thoughts and behaviors. Psychologists believe that this attitude wrongly encourages dependency on the doctor, encourages unnecessary drug therapy, and does little to help the patient develop good coping skills.

Not incidentally, the doctor-knows-best approach also takes responsibility away from psychologists and gives it to psychiatrists. Psychologists bristle at the medical model's implication that their treatment of mental "illnesses" should be done under the supervision of a physician. In effect, the medical model assigns psychologists to second-class professional status. As you can see, ownership of the whole territory of mental disorder is hotly contested.

PSYCHOLOGICAL MODELS   What do psychologists have to offer in place of the medical model? The psychological alternative gives equal footing to cognitive, environmental, and biological explanations. Thus, if you are depressed, your problem is seen as a disorder of thought and circumstances, as well as the brain. This view opens up the possibility of treatment on many fronts.

Like the medical model, this psychological perspective emerged most clearly at the end of the 18th century, helped along by the flamboyant work of Franz Anton Mesmer (1734–1815). Mesmer believed (incorrectly) that many disorders were caused by disruptions in the flow of a mysterious force that he called *animal magnetism.* He unveiled several new techniques to study animal magnetism, including one originally called *mesmerism,* which we now call hypnosis (Darnton, 1968; Pattie, 1994).

Mesmer's animal magnetism theory was eventually discredited by scientists, but his hypnotic techniques were embraced by many clinicians, including a prominent French neurologist, Jean-Martin Charcot (1825–1893). With the aid of hypnosis, Charcot dramatically demonstrated that he could remove the symptoms of "hysteria," a mysterious disorder that presented physical symptoms, such as paralysis of a limb, but no neurological disease. Moreover, Charcot showed that hypnosis could produce the symptoms of hysteria even in healthy individuals. This work suggested that the disorder was **psychogenic** (psychologically caused).

One of Charcot's students, the brilliant young Sigmund Freud, began his own experiments with hypnosis. These experiments eventually led to Freud's revolutionary idea that psychopathology arises from pressures originating in the unconscious mind. Eventually Freud abandoned hypnosis, replacing it with

Connection

Chapter 3
When hypnotized, some people respond to suggestion with changes in perception, memory, and motivation.

Psychogenic: Caused by psychological factors.

his "talking cure," which he claimed to be a more effective system for revealing unconscious conflicts and for treating psychological disorders.

The modern psychological approach, however, goes well beyond these prescientific theories. Their primary legacy in clinical psychology is the conviction that psychopathology involves disturbances in thoughts and emotions — disturbances that the victim may not fully understand. In the place of Freud's psychoanalytic theory of mental disorder, most clinical psychologists have now turned to a combination of psychological perspectives including *behaviorism*, *cognitive psychology*, and *biological psychology*. We will look at both of these more closely.

The Cognitive–Behavioral Approach One new approach to psychopathology combines what were once the two warring camps of cognitive psychology and behaviorism. In brief, cognitive psychology looks inward, emphasizing mental processes, while behaviorism looks outward, emphasizing the influence of the environment. A major shift in psychological thinking in recent years sees these two traditions as opposite sides of the same coin.

The **behavioral perspective** tells us that abnormal behaviors can be acquired in the same fashion as healthy behaviors — through behavioral learning. This view focuses on our behavior and the environmental conditions, such as rewards and punishments, that maintain it. For example, the behavioral perspective would suggest that a fear of public speaking could result from a humiliating public speaking experience and a subsequent avoidance of any opportunity to develop public speaking skills.

By discovering the conditions that initiate and maintain an undesirable behavior, the clinician can recommend an effective treatment (Emmelkamp, 1986). Thus, a behavioral therapist treating a fear of public speaking would focus on the conditions under which the individual felt fearful. Does the fear occur in a group of friends or only with strangers? How big does the group have to be to produce symptoms? Is the fearful response rewarded in some way — with attention or sympathy? In general, behavioral therapy identifies problem behaviors, analyzes the conditions that keep them in place, and seeks ways to encourage new behaviors, especially through reinforcement. Instead of probing for memories of long-repressed traumas, as a Freudian analyst might, the behavioral perspective deals with the present conditions that keep the disorder alive.

The **cognitive perspective,** the other half of the new cognitive–behavioral view, suggests that we must also consider how people *perceive* or *think about* themselves and their relations with other people. Among the important cognitive variables are these: whether people believe they have control over events in their lives (an internal or external locus of control), how they cope with threat and stress, and whether they attribute behavior to situational or personal factors (Bandura, 1986).

The **cognitive–behavioral approach,** then, combines both the cognitive and behavioral perspectives. From this view, a fear of public speaking can be understood as a product of both behavioral and cognitive learning. Thus, the complete picture of the problem involves factors both inside and outside the person.

The Biopsychology of Madness Although most psychologists reject the medical model, they do not deny the influence of biology on thought and behavior. Modern biopsychology assumes that mental disturbances involve the biology of the brain or nervous system in some way, and this view is taking an increasingly prominent position. An explosion of research in neuroscience during the past decade confirms the role of the brain as a complex organ whose mental functions depend on a delicate balance of chemicals and ever-changing

Connection

Chapter 13
Freud's "talking cure" was also called
"psychoanalysis."

Connection

Chapter 6
Behavioral learning includes operant conditioning and classical conditioning.

Connection

Chapter 11
Rotter's locus-of-control theory comes from the cognitive perspective in learning and personality.

Behavioral perspective: The psychological view suggesting that abnormal behaviors can be acquired through behavioral learning, especially by operant conditioning and classical conditioning.

Cognitive perspective: The psychological view suggesting that abnormal behaviors are influenced by mental processes — by how people perceive or think about themselves and their relations with other people.

Cognitive–behavioral approach: A psychological view that combines both the cognitive and the behavioral perspectives in attempting to understand behavior and mental processes.

Connection

Chapter 2
Neurotransmitters are chemicals used for communication between neurons across the synapse.

Connection

Chapter 2
Psychologists caution against assuming that behavioral genetics will fully explain mental disorders.

Connection

Chapter 10
Social support and hardiness allow some people to deal with stress better than others.

circuits. Subtle alterations in the brain's tissue or in its chemical messengers — the neurotransmitters — can profoundly alter thoughts and behaviors. Genetic factors, brain injury, infection, and learning are a few factors that can tip the balance toward psychopathology.

Many links between psychological disorders and specific brain abnormalities have been revealed by brain scanning techniques, such as PET scans and MRI (Gur & Pearlson, 1993). Such work has, for example, linked certain cases of violence with brain tumors located in the amygdala, a part of the limbic system associated with aggressive behavior. Psychology also recognizes that drug therapies alleviate certain symptoms of psychological disorders (Elkin et al., 1989; Kane & Marder, 1993; Papolos & Papolos, 1987; Schatzberg, 1991).

On the heredity front, advances in the field of behavioral genetics may eventually allow researchers to identify genes associated with specific psychological disorders (Joyce, 1989; Kendler & Diehl, 1993; Rutter et al., 1990). So far, however, only a few genetic abnormalities have been linked with specific mental problems, despite the fact that some of the most severe pathologies, such as schizophrenia and bipolar disorder, do run in families. Most such disorders are likely to result from multiple genes interacting with forces in the environment (Boomsma et al., 1997). Stay tuned for further developments.

An Interactionist View   Psychologists today increasingly view psychopathology as the product of an *interaction* among biological, behavioral, and cognitive factors (Cowan, 1988). For example, a genetic predisposition may make a person vulnerable to depression by affecting neurotransmitter levels or hormone levels. At the same time, psychological or social stressors, such as the loss of a love or certain learned grief behaviors, may be required for the disorder to develop fully. And why does one person seem to get over a relationship breakup fairly quickly, while another suffers prolonged grief reaction? A quick recovery may be attributable to a supportive social environment, mental "hardiness," or good coping skills. Additionally, one individual may be genetically better equipped than another to deal with stress. Effective treatment must, therefore, reflect these individual differences in biology, cognition, and environment.

Indicators of Abnormality

Clinicians often disagree about the **etiology** (causes) of mental disorders. Yet, they usually agree on the indicators of abnormality (Rosenhan & Seligman, 1995). What are these indicators?

▶ *Distress.* Does the individual show unusual or prolonged levels of unease or anxiety? For example, almost anyone will get nervous before an important test, but feeling so overwhelmed with unpleasant emotions that concentration becomes impossible is a sign of abnormality.

▶ *Maladaptiveness.* Does the person act in ways that interfere with his or her well-being or the needs of society? We can see this, for example, in someone who drinks so heavily that she or he cannot hold down a job or drive a car without endangering others.

▶ *Irrationality.* Does the person act or talk in ways that are irrational or incomprehensible to others? A woman who converses with her long-dead sister, whose voice she hears in her head, is behaving irrationally. Likewise, behavior or emotional responses that are inappropriate to the situation, such as laughing at the scene of a tragedy, show irrational loss of contact with one's social environment.

Etiology: The causes of, or factors related to, the development of a disorder.

- *Unpredictability*. Does the individual behave erratically and inconsistently at different times or from one situation to another, as if experiencing a loss of control? For example, a child who suddenly smashes a fragile toy with his fist for no apparent reason is behaving unpredictably. Similarly, a manager who treats employees compassionately one day and abusively the next is acting unpredictably.

- *Unconventionality and undesirable behavior*. Does the person behave in ways that are statistically rare and violate social norms of what is legally or morally acceptable or desirable? Being merely "unusual" is not a sign of abnormality—so feel free to dye your hair red and green at Christmastime. But if you decide to act beyond the bounds of social acceptability by strolling naked in the mall, that would be considered abnormal.

- *Observer discomfort*. Does the person create discomfort in others by making them feel threatened or distressed? Bullying behavior is abnormal on this count. So is the behavior of a stranger who sits down beside you in a restaurant and questions you loudly.

Is the presence of just one indicator enough to demonstrate abnormality? Clinicians are more confident in labeling behavior as "abnormal" when two or more of the six indicators are present. Moreover, none of these six criteria is a condition shared by all forms of disorder. Different diagnoses, we shall see later in the chapter, include different combinations from the above list. The more extreme and prevalent the indicators are, the more confident psychologists can be about identifying an abnormal condition.

While these indicators may suggest a disorder, the clinician still must decide which disorder it is. This can be difficult, because psychopathology takes many forms. Some disorders may have a familiar ring: *depression, phobias,* and *panic disorder*. You may be less well acquainted with others, such as *Tourette's disorder, conversion disorder,* or *catatonic schizophrenia*. In all, a bewildering 300-plus varieties of psychopathology are described in the *Diagnostic and Statistical Manual of Mental Disorders* (4th edition), known by clinicians and researchers as the *DSM-IV* ("DSM-four"), used by mental health professionals of all backgrounds to describe and diagnose psychopathology. So influential is this system that we will devote the entire middle section of this chapter to an explanation of it.

Behaviors that make other people feel uncomfortable or threatened may be a sign of abnormality.

Psychology In Your Life

A Caution to Readers

As you read about the symptoms of mental disorder, you are likely to wonder about your own mental health. All students studying abnormal psychology face this hazard. To see what we mean, you might answer the following questions, which are based on the six indicators of abnormality discussed earlier.

1. Have you had periods of time when you felt "blue" for no apparent reason? (distress)

2. Have you ever gone to a party on a night when you knew you should be studying? (maladaptiveness)

3. Have you had an experience in which you thought you heard or saw something that wasn't really there? (irrationality)

4. Have you had a flash of temper in which you said something that you later regretted? (unpredictability)

5. Have you had unusual thoughts that you told no one about? (unconventionality)

6. Have you distressed someone because of something you said or did? (observer discomfort)

The fact is that almost everyone will answer "yes" to at least one—and perhaps all—these questions. This does not necessarily mean abnormality. Whether you, or anyone else, is normal or abnormal is a matter of degree and frequency—and opinion.

So, as we take a close look at specific mental disorders in the next section of the chapter, you will most likely find some symptoms that you have experienced. So will your classmates. Even though they may not say so, most other students will find themselves in one or more of the disorders that we will be studying. (A similar problem is common among medical students, who begin to notice that they, too, have symptoms of the physical diseases they learn about.) You should realize that *this is normal,* although it may cause readers some distress. One reason, of course, that you may see yourself in this chapter arises from the fact that no sharp line separates psychopathology from normalcy. All psychological disorders involve exaggerations of normal tendencies. Healthy people may become depressed, for example—although they do not *stay* depressed or

Sadness or crying is not necessarily a sign of abnormality. Some occasions call for sadness and tears.

develop the depths of despair that clinically depressed people do. We are not suggesting that concerns about mental disorder should be taken lightly, however. If, after reading this chapter, you suspect that you may have a problem, you should discuss it with a professional.

CHECK**YOUR**UNDERSTANDING

1. **RECALL:** *In Rosenhan's study, who discovered that the "pseudopatients" were feigning mental illness?*

   a. psychiatrists
   b. psychologists
   c. nurses and aides working on the ward
   d. other patients

2. **APPLICATION:** *Which of the following symptoms most clearly suggests the presence of abnormality?*

   a. hallucinations
   b. worries
   c. unusual behavior
   d. creativity

HOW ARE MENTAL DISORDERS CLASSIFIED?

Imagine that you have entered a music store looking for a particular CD. Anything you could possibly want is there, but the employees do not bother grouping albums by musical category: They just dump everything randomly into the bins. With so many selections, but no organization, shopping there would be impossible—which is why record stores never operate this way. Instead, they organize selections into categories, such as rock, blues, classical, rap, country, and jazz. In much the same way, the *Diagnostic and Statistical Manual of Mental Disorders* (4th ed.) brings order to the more than 300 recognized mental disorders. Because it is the most widely used system for classifying mental disorders, we will use it as the scheme for organizing the disorders discussed in this chapter.

What is the organizing pattern employed by the **DSM-IV?** It groups nearly all recognized forms of psychopathology into categories, according to mental and behavioral symptoms, such as anxiety, depression, sexual problems, and substance abuse. Our Core Concept states:

> **The most widely used system, found in the *DSM-IV*, classifies disorders by their mental and behavioral symptoms.**

It would be impossible to cover all the recognized mental disorders in this chapter. Therefore we must focus on those that you are most likely to encounter in daily life and in the study of psychopathology in more advanced courses. All the disorders discussed in this chapter appear in Table 12.2. (Please note, however, that Table 12.2 also includes a few disorders that are discussed elsewhere in this book.)

Overview of the *DSM-IV* Classification System

The fourth edition of the *Diagnostic and Statistical Manual of Mental Disorders,* the *DSM-IV,* was published in 1994 by the American Psychiatric Association. Then, in 2000, that volume was given a midedition update, the *DSM-IV-TR* (*TR* means *Text Revision*). It offers practitioners a common and concise language for the description of mental disorders. It also contains criteria for diagnosing

DSM-IV: The fourth edition of the *Diagnostic and Statistical Manual of Mental Disorders,* published by the American Psychiatric Association; the most widely accepted classification system in the United States.

TABLE 12.2 — Some Important DSM-IV Disorders

DSM-IV CATEGORY	PRIMARY SYMPTOMS
AFFECTIVE DISORDERS	Excitement or depression (extreme forms may be psychotic)
Depressive disorders	
Bipolar disorder	
ANXIETY DISORDERS	Fears, panic attacks, anxiety
Panic disorder	
Agoraphobia	
Specific phobias	
Obsessive–compulsive disorder	
Posttraumatic stress disorder (Chapter 10)	
SOMATOFORM DISORDERS	Physical symptoms or overconcern with physical health
Conversion disorders	
Hypochondriasis	
DISSOCIATIVE DISORDERS	Nonpsychotic fragmentation of the personality
Dissociative fugue	
Depersonalization disorder	
Dissociative identity disorder	
EATING DISORDERS	Extreme dieting or binging and purging
Anorexia nervosa	
Bulimia	
SCHIZOPHRENIA AND OTHER PSYCHOTIC DISORDERS	Psychotic deterioration of the personality or paranoid disturbances of logic and reasoning
Disorganized schizophrenia	
Catatonic schizophrenia	
Paranoid schizophrenia	
Undifferentiated schizophrenia	
PERSONALITY DISORDERS	Chronic disorders affecting all parts of the personality
Narcissistic personality disorder	
Antisocial personality disorder	
ADJUSTMENT DISORDERS AND OTHER CONDITIONS THAT MAY BE A FOCUS OF CLINICAL ATTENTION	The patient has problems, but not a major mental disorder

each of the more than 300 disorders it covers. Even though the manual was developed primarily by psychiatrists, its terminology has been adopted by clinicians of all stripes, including psychiatrists, psychologists, and social workers. In addition, most health insurance companies use *DSM-IV* standards in determining what treatments they will pay for—a fact that gives this manual enormous economic influence.

The fourth edition of the *DSM* has brought with it some big changes. For example, it has banished the term *neurosis* from the official language of psychiatry (although you will frequently hear the term used in more casual conversation). Originally, a **neurotic disorder** or **neurosis** was conceived of as a relatively common pattern of subjective distress or self-defeating behavior that did not show signs of brain abnormalities or grossly irrational thinking. In short, a "neurotic" was someone who might be unhappy or dissatisfied, but not considered dangerously ill or out of touch with reality. In the *DSM-IV,* the term

Neurotic disorder or **neurosis:** Before the *DSM-IV,* these were terms used to describe a pattern of subjective distress or self-defeating behavior that did not show signs of brain abnormalities or grossly irrational thinking.

neurosis has been replaced by the term *disorder* (Carson et al., 1996; Holmes, 1994).

In contrast, a **psychotic disorder** or **psychosis** was previously thought to differ from neurosis in both the quality and severity of symptoms. A condition was designated as psychotic if it involved profound disturbances in perception, rational thinking, or affect (emotion). Using previous editions of the *DSM,* a clinician would have been more likely to diagnose severe depression, for example, as "psychotic." In the *DSM-IV,* the term "psychotic" is restricted mainly to a loss of contact with reality, as is found in the *schizophrenic* disorders, which we shall discuss below (Carson et al., 1996; Holmes, 1994).

As you may have surmised from its origins in psychiatry, the *DSM-IV* has close ties to the medical model of mental illness. Its language is the language of medicine — symptoms, syndromes, diagnoses, and diseases — and its final form is a curious mixture of science and tradition. (Note: It contains no diagnosis of "normal.") Yet, in contrast with early versions of the manual, which had a distinctly Freudian flavor, the *DSM-IV* manages, for the most part, to avoid endorsing theories of cause or treatment. It also differs from early versions of the *DSM* by giving extensive and specific descriptions of the symptoms of each disorder. So, while the *DSM-IV* has its critics, the need for a common language of mental disorder has brought it wide acceptance.

Let us turn now to a sampling of disorders described in the *DSM-IV*. A look at Table 12.2 will give you an overview of the scheme the manual uses to classify these disorders. We begin with those that involve extremes of emotion: the *mood disorders*.

Mood Disorders

Everyone, of course, experiences occasional strong or unpleasant emotional reactions. Emotionality is a normal part of our ability to interpret and adapt to our world. However, when moods career out of control, soaring to extreme elation or plunging to deep depression, the diagnosis will probably be one of the **mood disorders.** The clinician will also suspect an affective disorder when an individual's moods are consistently inappropriate to the situation. Here we will discuss the two best-known of these affective disturbances: *bipolar disorder* and *unipolar depression*.

BIPOLAR DISORDER   Wide swings of mood, unexplained by events in a person's life, signify a form of mood disturbance, often called *manic–depressive disorder*. The *DSM-IV* calls it **bipolar disorder.** The alternating periods of **mania** (excessive elation or manic excitement) and the profound sadness of **depression** represent the two "poles." During the manic phase, the individual becomes euphoric, energetic, hyperactive, talkative, and emotionally wound tight like a spring.

It is not unusual for people, swept up in mania, to spend their life savings on extravagant purchases or to engage promiscuously in a number of sexual liaisons or other potentially high-risk actions. When the mania diminishes, they are left to deal with the damage they have created during their frenetic period. Soon, in the depressive phase, a dark wave of melancholy sweeps over the mind, producing symptoms indistinguishable from the "unipolar" depression we will discuss below. Biologically speaking, however, these two forms of depression differ: We know this because the antidepressant drugs that work well on unipolar depression are not usually effective for bipolar disorder.

Dutch artist Vincent Van Gogh showed signs of bipolar disorder. This problem seems to have a high incidence among highly creative people.

Connection

Chapter 9
Mental disorders tell psychologists much about emotional processes.

Psychotic disorder or **psychosis:** A disorder involving profound disturbances in perception, rational thinking, or affect.

Mood disorders: Abnormal disturbances in emotion or mood, including bipolar disorder and unipolar disorder. Mood disorders are also called *affective disorders*.

Bipolar disorder: A mental abnormality involving swings of mood from mania to depression.

Mania: Pathologically excessive elation or manic excitement.

Depression: Pathological sadness or despair.

The duration and frequency of the mood disturbances in bipolar disorder vary from person to person. Some people function normally for long periods, punctuated by occasional, brief manic or depressive episodes. A small percentage of unfortunate individuals go right from manic episodes to clinical depression and back again in continuous, unending cycles that are devastating to them and to their families, friends, and coworkers.

A genetic component in bipolar disorder is well established, although the exact genes involved have not been pinpointed (Bradbury, 2001; Plomin et al., 1994). While only 1% of the general population has bipolar attacks, having an identical twin afflicted with the problem inflates one's chances to about 70% (Allen, 1976; Tsuang & Faraone, 1990). The fact that bipolar disorder usually responds well to medication also suggests biological factors at work.

UNIPOLAR DEPRESSION   If you fail an important examination, lose a job, or lose a love, it is normal to feel depressed. If a close friend dies, it is also normal to feel depressed. But if you remain depressed for weeks or months, long after the depressing event has passed, then you may have the clinically significant depressive disorder called **unipolar depression,** the commonest of all major mental disturbances. Novelist William Styron (1990) writes movingly about his own experience with severe depression. The pain he endured convinced him that clinical depression is much more than a bad mood: He characterized it as "a daily presence, blowing over me in cold gusts" and "a veritable howling tempest in the brain" that can begin with a "gray drizzle of horror." Unipolar depression does not give way to manic periods.

Incidence   Psychologist Martin Seligman (1973, 1975) has called depression the "common cold" of psychological problems because nearly everyone has suffered it at some time. In the United States, depression accounts for the majority of all mental hospital admissions, but it is still believed to be underdiagnosed and undertreated (Robins et al., 1991). *The Wall Street Journal* estimates that depression costs Americans about $43 billion each year, including the costs of hospitalization, therapy, and lost productivity (Miller, 1993). But the human cost cannot be measured in dollars. Countless people in the throes of depression may feel worthless, lack appetite, withdraw from friends and family, have difficulty sleeping, lose their jobs, and become agitated or lethargic. In severe cases, they may also have psychotic distortions of reality. Most worrisome of all, suicide claims one in 50 depression sufferers (Bostwick & Pankratz, 2000).

Cross-cultural studies indicate that depression is the single most prevalent form of disability around the globe (Holden, 2000), although the incidence of major depression varies widely throughout the world, as Table 12.3 shows. While some of the variation may be the result of differences in reporting and in readiness or reluctance to seek help for depression, other factors seem to be at work, too. In Taiwan and Korea, for example, these factors include low rates of marital separation and divorce—factors known to be associated with high risk of depression in virtually all cultures. On the other hand, the stresses of war have undoubtedly inflated the rate of depression in the Middle East (Horgan, 1996; Weissman et al., 1996).

Causes of Depression   Some cases of unipolar depression almost certainly have a genetic predisposition. Severe bouts with depression often run in families (Andreasen et al., 1987; Plomin et al., 1994; Weissman et al., 1986). Further indication of a biological basis for depression comes from the favorable response that many depressed patients have to drugs that affect the brain's neurotransmitters norepinephrine, serotonin, and dopamine (Hirschfeld &

Unipolar depression: A form of depression that does not alternate with mania.

TABLE 12.3	Lifetime Risk of a Depressive Episode Lasting a Year or More
Taiwan	1.5%
Korea	2.9%
Puerto Rico	4.3%
United States	5.2%
Germany	9.2%
Canada	9.6%
New Zealand	11.6%
France	16.4%
Lebanon	19%

Goodwin, 1988; Nemeroff, 1998). Evidence also indicates that depression is related to lower brain wave activity in the left frontal lobe (Davidson, 1992a,b, 2000; Robbins, 2000). In a few cases, depression may be caused by viral infection (Bower, 1995). Such evidence leads some observers to believe that depression is really a collection of disorders having a variety of causes (Kendler & Gardner, 1998).

A special form of unipolar depression seems to be related to sunlight deprivation. It appears most frequently during the long, dark winter months among people who live in high latitudes (Wehr & Rosenthal, 1989). (See Figure 12.1.) Aptly named, **seasonal affective disorder,** or **SAD,** is related to levels of the light-sensitive hormone *melatonin,* which regulates our internal biological clocks (Campbell & Murphy, 1998; Oren & Terman, 1998). Based on this knowledge, researchers have developed an effective therapy that regulates melatonin by exposing SAD sufferers daily to bright artificial light (Lewy et al., 1987).

Biology alone cannot entirely explain depression, however. We must also understand it as a mental and behavioral condition. Initially, a negative event, such as losing a job, can make anyone feel depressed, but low self-esteem and

Connection

Chapter 3
The "biological clock," located in the thalamus, regulates our circadian rhythms.

FIGURE 12.1: Seasonal Affective Disorder

People who suffer from seasonal affective disorder are most likely to experience symptoms of depression during months with shortened periods of sunlight.

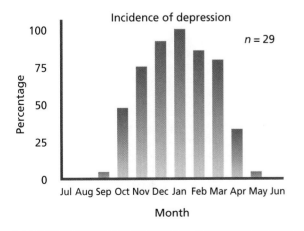

Seasonal affective disorder or **SAD:** A form of depression believed to be caused by deprivation of sunlight.

a pessimistic attitude can fuel a cycle of depressive thought patterns (Abramson et al., 1989; Sweeney et al., 1986; Wood et al., 1990a,b). (See Figure 12.2.) Probably because of low self-esteem, depression-prone people are more likely to perpetuate the depression cycle by attributing negative events to their own personal flaws or external conditions that they feel helpless to change (Azar, 1994b; Robins, 1988; Seligman, 1991; Seligman et al., 1979). Martin Seligman calls this *learned helplessness.* The resulting negative self-evaluation generates a depressed mode, which leads in turn to negative behaviors such as crying. These behaviors encourage others to avoid the depressed individual. Consequently, depressed people feel rejected and lonely, which also feeds the cycle of their despair (Coyne et al., 1991).

The cognitive approach to depression points out that negative thinking styles are learned and modifiable. This implies that, if you work on changing the way you *think,* perhaps blaming yourself less and focusing more on constructive plans for doing better, you can ultimately change your feelings and your performance. Indeed, Peter Lewinsohn and his colleagues (Lewinsohn et al., 1980, 1990; Lewinsohn & Gottlib, 1995) have found that they can treat many cases of depression effectively with cognitive–behavioral techniques. Their approach intervenes at several points in the cycle of depression to teach people how to change their helpless thinking, to cope adaptively with unpleasant situations, and to build more rewards into their lives.

Who Becomes Depressed?   Clinicians have noted that depression rates are higher for women than for men (Leutwyler, 1995; Strickland, 1992; Turkington, 1992; Weissman et al., 1996). According to Susan Nolen-Hoeksema (1987, 1990), the response styles of men and women once they begin to experience negative moods may account for the difference. In this view, when women experience sadness, they tend to think about the possible causes and implications of their feelings. In contrast, men attempt to distract themselves

Connection

Chapter 10
People suffering from *learned helplessness* passively accept unpleasant conditions.

Connection

Chapter 14
Compare this attribution style with the *self-serving bias* of nondepressed individuals.

❚ **FIGURE 12.2:**   The Cognitive–Behavioral Cycle of Depression

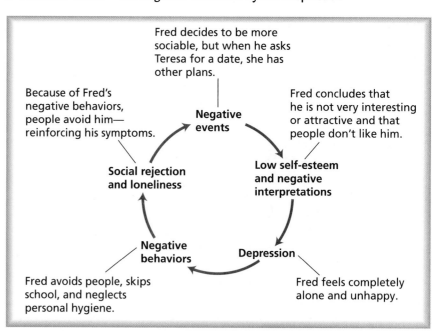

from depressed feelings, either by shifting their attention to something else or by engaging in a physical activity that will take their minds off their mood. This model suggests that the more *ruminative* response of women — characterized by a tendency to concentrate on problems — increases women's vulnerability to depression (Shea, 1998).

The incidence of depression and the age at which it strikes are changing — at least in the United States. According to Martin Seligman, depression is between 10 and 20 times as common as it was 50 years ago (National Press Club, 1999). At midcentury, most casualties of depression were middle-aged women, but now it has become a teenage problem — still more prevalent in females than in males. Currently, the average age of individuals diagnosed with depression in the United States is between 14 and 15 years. Seligman, who has studied depression extensively, blames this increase in occurrence and decrease in age to three factors: (1) an out-of-control individualism and self-centeredness that focuses on individual success and failure, rather than group accomplishments; (2) the self-esteem movement, which has taught a generation of schoolchildren that they should feel good about themselves, irrespective of their efforts and achievements; and (3) a culture of *victimology,* which reflexively points the finger of blame at someone or something else.

Connection

Chapter 14
The self-serving bias, which attributes mistakes and failures to external causes, is more common in individualistic cultures.

Anxiety Disorders

Would you pick up a snake or let a tarantula rest on your shoulder? For some people the mere thought of snakes or spiders is enough to send chills of fear down their spines. Everyone, of course, has experienced anxiety or fear in threatening or dangerous situations. But pathological anxiety is far more severe than the normal anxiety associated with life's challenges. It is also relatively common — even more common than depression (Barlow, 2000). One estimate

---

DO IT YOURSELF!　　**A Depression Check**

Most people think that depression is marked by outward signs of sadness, such as weeping. But depression affects other aspects of thought and behavior, as well. For a quick check on your own tendencies to depression, please answer "yes" or "no" to each of the following questions, all adapted from the *DSM-IV:*

1. Do you feel deeply depressed, sad, or hopeless most of the day?

2. Do you feel you have lost interest in most or all activities?

3. Have you experienced any major change in appetite or body weight, though not from dieting?

4. Have you experienced a significant change in your sleeping patterns?

5. Do you feel more restless than usual — or more sluggish than usual?

6. Do you feel more fatigued than you ought to?

7. Do you feel persistently hopeless or inappropriately guilty?

8. Have you been finding it increasingly difficult to think or concentrate?

9. Do you have recurrent thoughts of death or suicide?

Your answers to these items do not constitute any proof that you are or are not depressed. While there is no "magic number" of items you must answer "yes" to in order to qualify as depressed, if you answered "yes" to some of them and if you are concerned, you might want to seek a professional opinion. Remember that it is the *pattern* and the *quality* of your life, experience, and behavior that determine whether or not you are depressed. Remember also that self-report is always subject to some bias. A competent examination by a mental health professional would take into account not only your self-descriptions but also observable behaviors and performance.

says that 15% of the general population has, at some time, experienced the symptoms that are serious enough to qualify as one of the **anxiety disorders** recognized in the *DSM* (Regier et al., 1988).

Here we will review three major problems that have anxiety as their main feature: (1) panic disorder, (2) phobic disorder, and (3) obsessive–compulsive disorder. You will note that the major difference among them has to do with the focus of anxiety. Does the anxiety seem to come from nowhere—unrelated to the individual's environment or behavior? Does it come from an external object or situation, such as the sight of blood or a snake? Does it involve the victim's own ritualistic behavior, as in a person who compulsively avoids stepping on cracks in the sidewalk?

PANIC DISORDER   While calmly eating lunch, an unexpected wave of panic sweeps over you, seemingly from nowhere. Your heart races, your body shakes, you feel dizzy, your hands become clammy and sweaty, you are afraid that you might be dying. You are having a *panic attack.*

The distinguishing feature of **panic disorder** is a feeling of panic that has no connection with present events (Barlow, 2001). The feeling is one of "free-floating anxiety." Attacks usually last for only a few minutes and then subside (McNally, 1994). Because of the unexpected nature of these "hit-and-run" attacks, *anticipatory anxiety* often develops as an added complication. The dread of the next attack and of being helpless and suddenly out of control can lead a person to avoid public places, yet fear being left alone. Cognitive–behavioral theorists view panic attacks as conditioned responses to physical sensations that may have initially been learned during a period of stress (Antony et al., 1992).

Biologically, we have evidence of a genetic influence in panic disorder (Plomin et al., 1994). However, the brain mechanism responsible for this condition lies in the limbic system—especially in the amygdala, which appears abnormal on PET scans of many patients (Barlow, 2000, 2001; Resnick, 1992). Significantly, it is this part of the brain that houses the unconscious emotional-arousal circuits described by Joseph LeDoux (1996). Overstimulation of these circuits can produce lasting physical changes that make the individual more susceptible to anxiety attacks in the future (Rosen & Schulkin, 1998).

To complicate matters, many victims of panic disorder have additional symptoms of **agoraphobia.** This condition involves panic that develops when they find themselves in situations from which they cannot easily escape, such as crowded public places or open spaces (Antony et al., 1992; Magee et al., 1996). The term *agoraphobia* is a literal translation from the ancient Greek for "fear of the marketplace." Victims of agoraphobia often fear that, if they experience an attack in one of these locations, help might not be available or the situation will be embarrassing to them. These fears deprive afflicted persons of their freedom, and some become prisoners in their own homes. If the disorder becomes this extreme, they cannot hold a job or carry on normal daily activities.

You may know someone who has panic disorder or agoraphobia. These disorders occur in about 2% of the population (McNally, 1994) and are much more common in women than in men. Fortunately, the treatment outlook is good. Medical therapy involves antianxiety drugs to relieve the panic attacks. Purely psychological treatment is also effective: Studies have shown that cognitive–behavioral therapy may equal or outperform drug therapy in combating panic attacks ("Cognitive–Behavior Therapy," 1991; Craske et al., 1991).

PHOBIC DISORDERS   In contrast with panic disorder, **phobia,** or **phobic disorder,** involves a persistent and irrational fear of a specific object, activity,

Anxiety disorders: Mental problems characterized mainly by anxiety. Anxiety disorders include panic disorder, specific phobias, and obsessive–compulsive disorder.

Panic disorder: A disturbance marked by panic attacks that have no connection with events in the person's present experience.

Agoraphobia: A fear of public places and open spaces, commonly accompanying panic disorder.

Phobia or **phobic disorder:** An anxiety disorder involving a pathological fear of a specific object or situation.

Connection

Chapter 9
The brain has two main emotional pathways: One operates mainly at an unconscious level.

Connection

Chapter 13
Many psychologists believe that antianxiety drugs are prescribed too frequently in the United States.

or situation — a response all out of proportion to the circumstances. Many of us respond fearfully to certain stimuli, such as spiders or snakes — or perhaps to multiple-choice tests! But these emotional responses become full-fledged phobic disorders only when they cause substantial disruption to our lives.

Phobias are relatively common. Studies suggest that 12.5% of Americans suffer from some form of phobia at some point in their lives (Regier et al., 1988). Some phobias are oddly specific, such as a fear of a certain type of insect; others are so common, such as fear of public speaking, that they seem almost normal (Stein et al., 1996). Nearly any stimulus can come to generate a phobic avoidance reaction (see Table 12.4), although some phobias are much more common than others. Among the most common phobic disorders are *social phobias,* irrational fears of normal social situations such as interacting with others or appearing in front of a group (Magee et al., 1996). Phobic responses to heights (acrophobia), snakes (ophidiophobia), and closed-in spaces (claustrophobia) are also common.

What causes phobias? Long ago, John Watson demonstrated that fears can be learned. We also have abundant evidence that fears and phobias can be *unlearned* through cognitive–behavioral therapy based on conditioning. But learning may not tell the whole story. Martin Seligman (1971) contends that humans are biologically disposed to learn some kinds of fears more easily than others. This **preparedness hypothesis** suggests that we carry an innate tendency, acquired through natural selection, to respond quickly and automatically to stimuli that posed a survival threat to our ancestors (Seligman, 1971). This explains why we develop phobias for snakes and lightning much more easily that we develop fears for automobiles and electrical outlets — objects that have posed a danger only in recent times.

OBSESSIVE–COMPULSIVE DISORDER   Just a year ago, 17-year-old Jim seemed to be a normal adolescent with many talents and interests. Then, almost overnight, he was transformed into a lonely outsider, excluded from social life by his psychological disabilities. Specifically, he developed an obsession with washing. Haunted by the notion that he was dirty — in spite of what his senses told him — Jim began to spend more and more time cleansing himself. At first his ritual ablutions were confined to weekends and evenings, but soon they consumed all his time, forcing him to drop out of school (Rapoport, 1989).

Jim suffers from **obsessive–compulsive disorder,** a condition characterized by patterns of persistent, unwanted thoughts and behaviors. Obsessive–compulsive disorder (OCD) affects about 2.5% of Americans at some point during their lives (Regier et al., 1988). Nearly everyone has had some of its symptoms in a mild form.

The *obsession* component of OCD consists of thoughts, images, or impulses that recur or persist despite a person's efforts to suppress them. For example, a person with an obsessive fear of germs may avoid using bathrooms outside his or her home or refuse to shake hands with strangers. And, because sufferers realize that their obsessive thoughts and compulsive rituals are senseless, they often go to great lengths to hide their compulsive behavior from other people. This, of course, places restrictions on their domestic, social, and work lives. Not surprisingly, OCD patients have extremely high divorce rates.

You probably have had some sort of mild obsessional experience, such as petty worries ("Did I remember to lock the door?") or a haunting phrase or melody that kept running through your mind. Such thoughts are normal if they occur only occasionally and have not caused significant disruptions of your life. As we have noted in other disorders, it is a matter of degree.

A common form of social phobia involves an extreme fear of public speaking.

Connection

Chapter 6
Watson's infamous experiment with Little Albert showed that fears could be learned by classical conditioning.

Connection

Chapter 2
Natural selection favors organisms possessing genetic traits that have survival value.

Preparedness hypothesis: The notion that we have an innate tendency, acquired through natural selection, to respond quickly and automatically to stimuli that posed a survival threat to our ancestors.

Obsessive–compulsive disorder: A condition characterized by patterns of persistent, unwanted thoughts and behaviors.

TABLE 12.4 *Phobias*

	OBJECT/SITUATION	PERCENTAGE OF ALL PHOBIAS	GENDER DIFFERENCES	TYPICAL AGE OF FIRST OCCURRENCE
Agoraphobia	Crowds, open spaces	10–50	Large majority among women	Early adulthood
Social phobias	Fear of being observed or doing something humiliating	10	Majority are women	Adolescence
Specific phobias *Animals*	Cats (ailurophobia) Dogs (cynophobia) Insects (insectophobia) Spiders (arachnophobia) Birds (avisophobia) Horses (equinophobia) Snakes (ophidiophobia) Rodents (rodentophobia)	5–15	Vast majority are women	Childhood
Inanimate objects or situations	Closed spaces (claustrophobia) Dirt (mysophobia) Thunder (brontophobia) Lightning (astraphobia) Heights (acrophobia) Darkness (nyctophobia) Fire (pyrophobia)	20	None	Any age
Illness-injury	(nosophobia) Death (thanatophobia) Sight of blood (hematophobia) Cancer (cancerophobia) Venereal disease (venerophobia)	15–25	None	Middle age
Other specific phobias	Numbers (numerophobia) The number 13 (triskaidekaphobia) Strangers, foreigners (xenophobia) String (linonophobia) Books (bibliophobia) Work (ergophobia)	rare		

Note: Hundreds of phobias have been described and given scientific names; this table provides only a sample. Some of the rare and strange-sounding phobias may have been observed in a single patient.

Compulsions, the other half of obsessive–compulsive disorder, are repetitive, purposeful acts performed according to certain private "rules," in response to an obsession. Victims feel that their compulsive behavior will reduce the tension associated with their obsessions. Typical compulsions include irresistible urges to clean, to check that lights or appliances have been turned off, and to count objects or possessions. When they are calm, people with obsessive–compulsive disorder view the compulsion as senseless, but when their anxiety rises, they can't resist performing the compulsive behavior ritual to relieve tension. Part of the pain experienced by people with this problem is that they are frustrated by the irrationality of their obsessions and their powerlessness to eliminate them.

The tendency for OCD to run in families suggests a genetic link. Another hint comes from the finding that many people with OCD also display **tics**, unwanted involuntary movements, such as exaggerated eye blinks. In these

Tics: Unwanted involuntary movements and twitches, such as exaggerated eye blinks.

patients, brain imaging often shows oddities in the deep motor control areas, suggesting something amiss in the brain (Resnick, 1992). OCD expert Judith Rapoport tells us to think of compulsions as "fixed software packages" programmed in the brain. Once activated, she theorizes, the patient gets caught in a behavioral "loop" that cannot be switched off (Rapoport, 1989).

Curiously, certain drugs that are commonly prescribed for depression can alleviate both the obsessions and the compulsive rituals (Poling et al., 1991). In further support of a biological basis for OCD, investigators have found that these drugs can reverse compulsive behavior in dogs that display a compulsion for grooming themselves (Ross, 1992).

Again, however, we must note that biology cannot explain everything. Some victims of OCD have clearly *learned* that their anxiety-provoking thoughts are connected to harmful consequences (Barlow, 2000). Further evidence that learning plays a role can be seen in the results of behavioral therapy, which is effective in reducing compulsive actions. The behavioral strategy for treating compulsive hand-washing, for example, calls for a form of extinction, in which the therapist soils the patient's hands and prevents him or her from washing them for progressively longer periods. Indeed, behavioral therapy can produce changes that show up in PET scans of OCD sufferers' brains (Schwartz et al., 1996). Thus, when we change behavior, we inevitably change the wiring of the obsessive–compulsive brain. This disorder shows us, once again, that biology and behavior are inseparable.

Somatoform Disorders

"Soma" means *body*. Thus, we use the term **somatoform disorders** for psychological problems appearing in the form of bodily symptoms or physical complaints, such as weakness or excessive worry about disease. Because these symptoms have no apparent biological cause, clinicians call them *psychogenic:* The cause originates in the mind. The *DSM-IV* recognizes several types of somatoform disorders, but we will cover only two: *conversion disorder* and *hypochondriasis.* (Note that the *DSM-IV* places the *psychosomatic disorders,* in which mental conditions—especially stress—lead to physical disease, under a separate heading called Psychological Factors Affecting Medical Condition.)

CONVERSION DISORDER   Paralysis, weakness, or loss of sensation—with no discernible physical cause—distinguishes **conversion disorder** (formerly called "hysterical neurosis"). Patients with this diagnosis may, for example, be blind, deaf, unable to walk, or insensitive to touch in part of their bodies. Yet they have no organic disease that shows up on neurological examinations, laboratory tests, or X rays. In conversion disorder, the problem really is "all in the mind."

"Glove anesthesia" represents a classic form of conversion disorder. As you can see in Figure 12.3, the pattern of insensitivity to touch or pain fits the patient "like a glove." The tip-off that the problem is psychogenic, not physical, comes from the pattern of the patient's symptoms: They do not match any possible pattern of nerve impairment. Other cases, however, are not always so clear-cut. Therefore, conversion disorder may be merely a convenient diagnosis when the neurologist has ruled out everything else. Some physicians, too, may diagnose conversion disorder when they are confronted with baffling

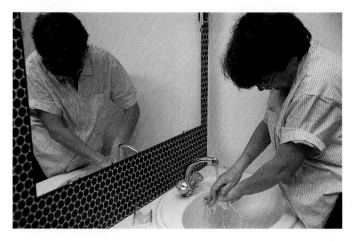

Obsessive-compulsive disorder makes people engage in senseless, ritualistic behaviors, such as repetitive handwashing.

Connection

Chapter 6
This is slightly different from Pavlov's original form of extinction: It calls for presenting the conditioned stimulus without allowing the conditional response.

Connection

Chapter 10
Stress demonstrates the effect of the mind (psyche) on the body (soma).

Somatoform disorders: Psychological problems appearing in the form of bodily symptoms or physical complaints, such as weakness or excessive worry about disease. The somatoform disorders include conversion disorder and hypochondriasis.

Conversion disorder: A type of somatoform disorder, marked by paralysis, weakness, or loss of sensation, but with no discernible physical cause.

FIGURE 12.3: Glove Anesthesia

The form of conversion disorder known as "glove anesthesia" (a) involves a loss of sensation in the hand, as though the patient were wearing a thick glove. This cannot be a neurological disorder because the pattern of "anesthesia" does not correspond to the actual pattern of nerves in the hand, shown in (b).

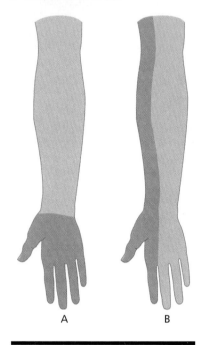

A   B

symptoms or especially difficult patients. Concluding that the problem is "all in their heads" conveniently tosses it into somebody else's lap. Women, particularly, have charged that physicians dismiss their physical complaints as "just a hysterical reaction" and refer the patient to a psychiatrist. Clearly, conversion disorder, like many other labels for mental problems, is a diagnosis that can be abused.

We should point out that the term *conversion disorder* carries with it some baggage from the Freudian past. "Conversion" implies an unconscious displacement (conversion) of anxiety into physical symptoms—although many clinicians no longer subscribe to that explanation. Some cases of conversion disorder are now thought to be physical stress responses.

Mysteriously, conversion disorder was much commoner several decades ago in Europe and the United States. As we saw earlier, both Charcot and Freud diagnosed many cases of conversion disorder. For unknown reasons, the problem has declined in industrialized countries (American Psychiatric Association, 1994), but it still occurs frequently in economically undeveloped regions, such as China (Spitzer et al., 1989) and Africa (Binitie, 1975).

HYPOCHONDRIASIS   "Hypochondriacs" worry about getting sick. Every ache and pain signals a disease. Because of their exaggerated concern about illness, patients with **hypochondriasis** often bounce from physician to physician until they find one who will listen to their complaints and prescribe some sort of treatment—often tranquilizers or placebos. Naturally, these individuals represent easy marks for health fads and scams. They also find their way to the fringes of the medical community, where they may buy extensive treatment packages from disreputable practitioners.

The flip side of the problem is a mistaken diagnosis of hypochondriasis (similar to the problem we found with conversion disorder). Clinicians may sometimes be too ready to conclude that the patient's concerns are imaginary. This can have disastrous consequences, such as overlooking the symptoms of very real and very serious physical diseases, such as cancer or a chronic infection.

Dissociative Disorders

The common denominator for all the **dissociative disorders** is "fragmentation" of the personality—a sense that parts of the personality have detached (dissociated) from others. Among the dissociative disorders, we find some of the most fascinating forms of mental pathology, including *dissociative fugue, depersonalization disorder,* and the controversial *dissociative identity disorder* (formerly called "multiple personality"), made famous by the fictional Dr. Jekyll and Mr. Hyde. Their underlying causes remain unclear.

Dissociative Fugue

Consider the case of "Jane Doe," a woman who was found to be incoherent, suffering the effects of exposure, and near death in a Florida park. She had no memory of her identity nor any ability to read or write. Therapy revealed general information about the kind of past she must have had, but no good clues to her origins. After a nationwide television appeal, Jane Doe and her doctors were flooded with calls from possible relatives, the most promising of which was an Illinois couple, certain she was their daughter. They had not heard from her for over four years, since she had moved from Illinois to Florida. Despite their confidence that they had found her, she was never able to remember her past or what had happened to her (Carson et al., 1996).

Hypochondriasis: A somatoform disorder involving excessive concern about health and disease.

Dissociative disorders: A group of pathologies involving "fragmentation" of the personality, in which some parts of the personality have become detached, or dissociated, from other parts. Forms of dissociative disorder include amnesia, fugue, depersonalization disorder, and dissociative identity disorder.

These two paintings by Sybil, a dissociative identity disorder (DID) victim, illustrate the differences between the personalities. The painting on the left was done by Peggy, Sybil's angry, fearful personality. The painting above was done by Mary, a home-loving personality.

Jane Doe had **dissociative fugue,** which is a combination of **amnesia** and *fugue,* or "flight." Persons with dissociative fugue not only lose their sense of identity, but they abruptly flee their homes, families, and jobs. Some appear disoriented and perplexed. Others may travel to distant locations and take up new lives, appearing unconcerned about the unremembered past. Usually the fugue state lasts only hours or days, followed by complete and rapid recovery. A few cases may continue for months — or, as with Jane Doe, for years.

Heavy alcohol use may predispose a person to dissociative fugue. This suggests that it may involve some brain impairment — although no certain cause has been established. Like dissociative amnesia, fugue occurs more often in those under prolonged high stress, especially in times of war and other calamities. Some psychologists also suspect memory dissociation and repression accompany instances of sexual and physical childhood abuse (Spiegel & Cardeña, 1991). This conjecture, however, is disputed.

DEPERSONALIZATION DISORDER Yet another form of dissociation involves a sensation that mind and body have separated. Patients with **depersonalization disorder** commonly report "out-of-body experiences" or feelings of being external observers of their own bodies. Some patients feel as if they were in a dream. People undergoing severe physical trauma, such as a life-threatening injury in an auto accident, may report symptoms of depersonalization, as do some patients who have had near-death experiences. Usually the sensation passes quickly, although it can recur. Investigators have attributed the disorder to hallucinations and to natural changes in the brain that occur during shock (Siegel, 1980).

DISSOCIATIVE IDENTITY DISORDER Robert Louis Stevenson's famous story of Dr. Jekyll and Mr. Hyde has become a misleading stereotype of **dissociative identity disorder.** In reality, most cases of dissociative identity disorder occur in women, and most display more than two identities (Ross et al., 1989). Unlike the homicidal Mr. Hyde, rarely do they pose a danger to others.

Connection

Chapter 7
Compare with *anterograde* amnesia in the case of H. M.

Connection

Chapter 9
Recovery of repressed memories is a controversial topic.

Dissociative fugue: Essentially the same as dissociative amnesia, but with the addition of "flight" from one's home, family, and job. *Fugue* means "flight."

Amnesia: A loss of memory for personal information, such as one's identity or residence.

Depersonalization disorder: An abnormality involving the sensation that mind and body have separated, as in an "out-of-body" experience.

Dissociative identity disorder: A condition in which an individual displays multiple identities, or personalities; formerly called "multiple personality disorder."

Once thought to be rare, some specialists now believe that dissociative identity disorder has always been common, but hidden or misdiagnosed. It usually first appears in childhood (Vincent & Pickering, 1988), and its victims frequently report having been sexually abused (Putnam et al., 1986; Ross et al., 1990). The formation of multiple identities or selves may be a form of defense by the dominant self to protect itself from terrifying events.

Dissociative identity disorder (DID) has now become a familiar diagnosis because of its portrayal in fact-based books and movies, such as *The Three Faces of Eve* (Thigpen & Cleckley, 1957), *Sybil* (Schreiber, 1973), and *The Flock* (Casey & Wilson, 1991). Although the original personality is unaware of the others, the others are usually aware of the host and often of each other. Each emerging personality contrasts in some significant way with the original self. For example, they might be outgoing if the original personality is shy, tough if the original is weak, and sexually assertive if the other is fearful and sexually naive. Each personality has a unique identity, name, behavior pattern, and even characteristic brain-wave activity. In some cases, dozens of characters emerge to help the person deal with a difficult life situation. These alternate personalities, each with its own consciousness, emerge suddenly—usually under stress.

What lies behind this mysterious disturbance? Psychodynamic theories explain it as a fracturing of the ego, as a result of ego defense mechanisms that do not allow energy from conflicts and traumas to escape from the unconscious mind. Cognitive theories see it as a form of role-playing or mood-state dependency, a form of memory bias in which events experienced in a given mood are more easily recalled when the individual is again in that mood state (Eich et al., 1997). Others suggest that at least some cases are frauds (as in the case of a student, charged with plagiarizing a term paper, who claimed that he had multiple personalities and that one of them copied the paper without the knowledge of his dominant personality).

Until about 30 years ago, only some 100 cases had been documented worldwide. Since then the numbers have gone up rapidly, possibly because more patients are being misdiagnosed with DID or more are feigning the symptoms—or because the trauma and abuse associated with the syndrome have increased along with a variety of other societal "sicknesses" (Carson et al., 1996). Alternatively, through social learning people may become convinced that they have DID when they hear of it on talk shows and see it featured in television soap operas.

In an unfortunate choice of terms, dissociative identity disorder is sometimes called "split personality." This causes confusion because *schizophrenia,* which literally means "split mind," has no relationship to dissociative identity disorder. In schizophrenia, the "split" refers to a psychotic split from reality, not to a fracturing of one personality into many personalities. Dissociative identity disorder, on the other hand, is *not* a psychotic disorder. We suggest that the reader avoid confusion by avoiding the term "split personality."

We might add a note of caution here about what is and is not yet understood about dissociative disorders. There is an ongoing debate in psychology, psychiatry, and the public arena about the validity of the recent increase in cases of DID that are based on adult women's claims to have been abused as children. Some observers have even suggested that the disorder exists only in the minds of a few therapists (Piper, 1998). In this view, patients may initially be led by the suggestive questioning of their therapists, who seek to uncover what they suspect are repressed memories of trauma and molestation. Then, based on the therapists' expectations, some patients may be reinforced for generating not only repressed memories but also multiple personalities (Loftus, 1993; Loftus & Ketcham, 1994; Ofshe & Watters, 1994).

Connection

Chapter 7
Mood-congruent memory is a related form of memory bias.

Connection

Chapter 6
Social learning, or observational learning, involves expectations of rewards and punishments learned through social interaction and the observation of others.

Connection

Chapter 7
Recall the case of Donna, who fabricated memories of abuse.

Eating Disorders

Like a drug addiction, Carla's eating disorder is so powerful that she cannot resume healthy eating patterns without great difficulty. She (it is usually a *she*) has always felt overweight, and recently she has put herself on a severe diet — a starvation diet. Little does Carla realize that she has become the victim of an eating disorder that will ultimately alter her body in undesirable, and even lethal, ways. After some months, she may become dangerously underweight. Food has become repugnant. She feels "full" after eating only a bite or two. The original motivation may have been the same with Carla's friend Jennifer, but Jennifer has resorted to another extreme method of weight control: She often overeats, but she makes herself vomit after a meal. Eventually, her teeth and the tissues in her mouth and esophagus come under attack by the action of refluxed stomach acid. And she, like Carla, may become dangerously malnourished.

Significantly, such eating disorders are most prevalent in Western cultures in which hunger is not widespread. They are especially likely to develop among middle- and upper-middle-class young women. Here we examine the two best-known eating disorders, exemplified above: *anorexia nervosa* and *bulimia*.

ANOREXIA NERVOSA   The condition called *anorexia* (persistent lack of appetite) may develop as a consequence of certain physical diseases or conditions, such as shock, nausea, or allergic reactions. However, when loss of appetite that endangers an individual's health stems from emotional or psychological causes, the syndrome is called **anorexia nervosa** ("nervous anorexia"). A person suffering from anorexia nervosa may act as though she is unconcerned with her condition, although she is emaciated. Commonly, anorexia nervosa is associated with extreme dieting, as in Carla's case. (Most dieters, by contrast, have an increased desire for food.)

What causes anorexia nervosa? A strong hint comes from the finding that most anorectic persons are young white females from middle-class American homes. They typically have backgrounds of good behavior and academic success, but they starve themselves, hoping to become acceptably thin and attractive (Brumberg, 1988; Gilbert & DeBlassie, 1984). While cultural ideals of feminine beauty change over time, in recent decades the mass media — including fashion magazines and MTV — have promoted extremely slim models and celebrities (Andersen & DiDomenico, 1992; Rolls et al., 1991). Especially during adolescence, when people tend to evaluate themselves in terms of physical attractiveness, they judge themselves harshly for failing to live up to cultural ideals (Conger & Petersen, 1984). A victim of anorexia typically holds a distorted body image, believing herself to be unattractively fat, and rejects others' reassurances that she is not overweight (Bruch, 1978; Fallon & Rozin, 1985). In an effort to lose imagined "excess" weight, the anorectic victim rigidly suppresses her appetite, feeling rewarded for such self-control when she does lose pounds and inches — but never feeling quite thin enough. (See Figure 12.4.)

BULIMIA   In the "binge-and-purge" syndrome known as **bulimia,** the sufferer overeats (binges) and then attempts to lose weight (purges) by means of self-induced vomiting, laxative use, or fasting (Rand & Kuldau, 1992). Those who suffer from bulimia usually keep their disorder inconspicuous and may even be supported in their behavior patterns by peers and by competitive norms in their academic, social, and athletic lives (Polivy & Herman, 1993; Rodin et al., 1985; Squire, 1983; Striegel-Moore et al., 1993).

Eating disorders are often associated with other forms of psychopathology. For example, bulimia is a predictor of depression (Walters et al., 1992). Further, while hungry normal people look forward to eating and enjoying a

Billboards, magazines, TV, and the movies promote images of body shapes that are unrealistic for most people — yet people often judge themselves against these standards

Connection

Chapter 9
Anorexia nervosa shows that cognitions and emotional states can affect the hunger drive.

Anorexia nervosa: An eating disorder involving persistent loss of appetite that endangers an individual's health and stemming from emotional or psychological reasons rather than from organic causes.

Bulimia (pronounced *boo-LEE-me-uh*): An eating disorder characterized by eating binges followed by "purges," induced by vomiting or laxatives; typically initiated as a weight-control measure.

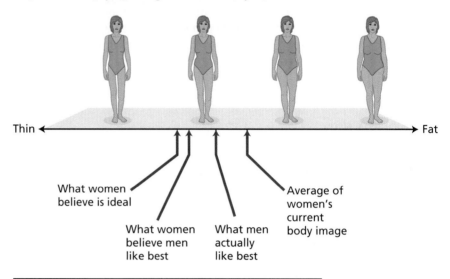

FIGURE 12.4: Women's Body Images

April Fallon and Paul Rozin (1985) asked female college students to give their current weight, their ideal weight, and the weight they believed men would consider ideal. The results showed that the average woman felt that her current weight was significantly higher than her ideal weight—and higher than the weight she thought men would like. To make matters worse, women also see their bodies as looking larger than they actually are (Thompson, 1986). When men were asked to rate themselves on a similar questionnaire, Fallon and Rozin found no such discrepancies between ideal and actual weights. But, when asked what they saw as the ideal weight for women, they chose a higher weight than women did. No wonder women go on diets more often than men and are more likely to have a major eating disorder (Mintz & Betz, 1986; Striegel-Moore et al., 1986).

Thin ← → Fat

What women believe is ideal

What women believe men like best

What men actually like best

Average of women's current body image

good meal, eating-disordered individuals do not associate pleasure with food and may even dread having to eat. In comparison with control subjects, bulimic patients in one study took longer to begin eating a scheduled meal, ate more slowly, and reported significantly more negative moods during eating (Hetherington et al., 1993). Although their original rationale might have been to lose weight, anorectic and bulimic individuals apparently take little joy in their slimmer states.

Cognitive explanations for eating disorders analyze how the individual sees herself and thinks about food, eating, and weight. Accordingly, many successful treatments of eating disorders employ strategies that alter self-perception and boost feelings of self-efficacy (Baell & Wertheim, 1992).

Schizophrenic Disorders

Literally, the word *schizophrenia* means "split or broken mind." In psychological terms, a **schizophrenia** is a severe form of psychopathology in which personality seems to disintegrate and perception is distorted. Schizophrenia is the disorder we usually mean when we refer to "madness," "psychosis," or "insanity."

For the victim of schizophrenia, the mind is distorted in terrible ways. The world may become bleak and devoid of meaning, or it may become so filled with sensation that everything appears in a confusion of multiple realities layered with hallucinations and delusions. In schizophrenia, emotions may

Schizophrenia (pronounced *skits-o-FRENNY-a*)**:** A psychotic disorder involving distortions in thoughts, perceptions, and/or emotions.

become blunted, thoughts turn bizarre, and language takes strange twists. Memory may also become fragmented (Danion et al., 1999). The disorder breaks the unity of the mind, sending its victims on meaningless mental detours, riding trains of "clang" associations (associations involving similar-sounding words), and producing confused verbalizations that clinicians call "word salads." Here is an example of schizophrenic speech:

> The lion will have to change from dogs into cats until I can meet my father and mother and we dispart some rats. I live on the front of Whitton's head. You have to work hard if you don't get into bed . . . It's all over for a squab true tray and there ain't no squabs, there ain't no men, there ain't no music, there ain't no nothing besides my mother and my father who stand alone upon the Island of Capri where is no ice. Well it's my suitcase sir. (Rogers, 1982)

Those suffering from the catatonic type of schizophrenia may hold unusual poses for long periods . . . as if frozen in action

Between two and three million living Americans have suffered from this tragic mental disorder (Regier et al., 1988). In a lifetime, more than one of every 100 Americans—more than two million over the age of 18—will become afflicted (Holmes, 1994; McGuire, 2000; Regier et al., 1993). For as yet unknown reasons, the first occurrence of schizophrenia typically occurs for men before they are 25 and for women between 25 and 45 years of age (Lewine et al., 1981).

For years, schizophrenia has consistently been the primary diagnosis for about 40% of all patient admissions to public mental hospitals—far out of proportion to all other possible categories of mental illness (Manderscheid et al., 1985). Because schizophrenic patients require prolonged or recurrent treatment, they can be expected to occupy about half of all mental hospital beds in the nation (Carson et al., 1996). Most sobering, about one-third of all schizophrenic patients will never fully recover, even with the best therapy available.

MAJOR TYPES OF SCHIZOPHRENIA Many investigators consider schizophrenia a constellation of separate disorders. Here are the five most common:

- ▶ **Disorganized type** represents everyone's image of mental illness, featuring incoherent speech, hallucinations, delusions, and bizarre behavior. A patient who talks to imaginary people most likely has this diagnosis.
- ▶ **Catatonic type,** involving a spectrum of motor dysfunctions, appears in two forms. Persons with the more common *catatonic stupor* may remain motionless for hours—even days—sometimes holding rigid, statuelike postures. In the other form, called *catatonic excitement,* patients become agitated and hyperactive.
- ▶ **Paranoid type** features delusions and hallucinations, but no catatonic symptoms and none of the incoherence of disorganized schizophrenia. The delusions found in paranoid schizophrenia are typically less well organized—more illogical—than those of the patient with a purely delusional disorder.
- ▶ **Undifferentiated type** serves as a catchall category for schizophrenic symptoms that do not clearly meet the requirements for any of the other categories above.

Disorganized type: A form of schizophrenia featuring incoherent speech, hallucinations, delusions, and bizarre behavior.

Catatonic type: A form of schizophrenia involving stupor or extreme excitement.

Paranoid type: A form of schizophrenia in which a combination of delusions and hallucinations is the prominent feature.

Undifferentiated type: A category used to designate persons displaying a combination of schizophrenic symptoms that do not clearly fit in one of the other categories of schizophrenia.

Connection

Chapter 13
Antipsychotic drugs work by reducing the activity of the neurotransmitter dopamine in the brain.

▶ **Residual type** is the diagnosis for individuals who have suffered from a schizophrenic episode in the past but currently have no major symptoms such as hallucinations or delusional thinking. Instead, their thinking is mildly disturbed, or their emotional lives are impoverished. The diagnosis of residual type may indicate that the disease is entering *remission,* or becoming dormant.

Our understanding of schizophrenia suffers from the fact that most schizophrenic patients display such a hodgepodge of symptoms that they drop into the "undifferentiated" category. Trying to make more sense of the problem, many investigators now merely divide the schizophrenias into "positive" and "negative" types. **Positive schizophrenia** involves active symptoms, such as delusions and hallucinations, while **negative schizophrenia** is distinguished by deficits, such as social withdrawal and poverty of thought processes. Patient responses to drug therapy support this division: Those with positive schizophrenia usually respond to antipsychotic drugs, while those with negative schizophrenia do not (Heinrichs, 1993). But even this distinction has its problems. Negative schizophrenia often looks like major depression. In addition, both positive and negative symptoms may occur in a single patient. All these difficulties have led some researchers to conclude that schizophrenia is a name for many separate disturbances.

POSSIBLE CAUSES OF SCHIZOPHRENIA   No longer do most theorists look through the Freudian lens to see schizophrenia as the result of defective parenting or repressed childhood trauma (Johnson, 1989). Studies show that adopted children with *no* family history of the disorder run no increased risk of developing schizophrenia when placed in a home with a schizophrenic parent (Gottesman, 1991). Thus, an emerging consensus among psychiatrists and psychologists views schizophrenia as fundamentally a brain disorder—or a group of disorders.

Support for this brain-disorder view comes from many quarters. As we have noted, the antipsychotic drugs (sometimes called *major tranquilizers*)—which interfere with the brain's dopamine receptors—can suppress the symptoms of positive schizophrenia (Carlsson, 1978; Snyder, 1986). On the other hand, drugs that stimulate dopamine production (e.g., the amphetamines) can actually produce schizophrenic symptoms (Dracheva et al., 2001; Lewis et al., 2001; Smith et al., 2001). Other evidence of a biological basis for schizophrenia comes in the form of brain abnormalities shown by computerized imaging techniques (Mesulam, 1990; Raz & Raz, 1990; Resnick, 1992; Suddath et al., 1990). (See Figure 12.5.)

Yet another line of evidence for the biological basis of schizophrenia comes from family studies (Lencer et al., 2000; Plomin et al., 1994). As we found with the mood disorders, the closer one's relationship to a person with schizophrenia, the greater one's chances of developing it (Gottesman, 1991; Heston, 1970; Nicol & Gottesman, 1983). This conclusion comes from impressive studies of identical twins reared apart and from adoption studies of children having schizophrenic blood relatives. While only about 1% of us in the general population become schizophrenic, the child of a schizophrenic parent incurs a risk about 14 times higher. The worst case would be to have an identical twin who has developed the condition. In that event, the other twin's chances of becoming schizophrenic jump to nearly 50%.

As with the mood disorders, genetics does not tell the whole story of schizophrenia. We can see the effect of the environment, for example, in the fact that 90% of the relatives of schizophrenic patients do not have schizophrenia (Barnes, 1987). Even in identical twins who share *exactly* the same

Residual type: A diagnostic category used for individuals who have suffered from a past episode of schizophrenia but are currently free of symptoms.

Positive schizophrenia: Any form of schizophrenia in which the person displays active symptoms, such as delusions or hallucinations.

Negative schizophrenia: Any form of schizophrenia distinguished by deficits, such as withdrawal and poverty of thought processes, rather than by active symptoms.

FIGURE 12.5: MRI Scans of a Twin with Schizophrenia and a Twin without Schizophrenia

The normal twin is on the left. Note the enlarged ventricles (fluid-filled spaces) in the brain of the schizophrenic twin on the right.

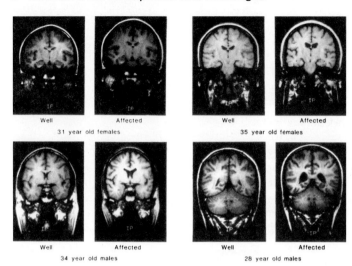

genes, the **concordance rate** for schizophrenia is only about 50%. That is, in half the cases in which schizophrenia strikes identical twins, it leaves one twin untouched. A hopeful Finnish study found that being raised in a healthy family environment can actually lower the risk of schizophrenia in adopted children who have a genetic predisposition to the disease (Tienari et al., 1987). Apparently, schizophrenia requires a biological predisposition plus some unknown environmental agent to "turn on" the hereditary tendency (Cromwell, 1993; Iacono & Grove, 1993). This agent could be a chemical toxin, stress, or some factor we have not yet dreamed of. Taken as a whole, this research suggests that genetic factors may not themselves be sufficient for the disorder to develop (Nicol & Gottesman, 1983). (See Figure 12.6.) Despite all the biological evidence, we must remember that mental disorder is always an interaction of biological, cognitive, and environmental factors, as our first Core Concept of the chapter suggested.

This broader perspective is often called the **diathesis–stress hypothesis.** It says that biological factors may place the individual at risk, but environmental stressors transform this potential into an actual schizophrenic disorder (Walker & Diforio, 1997). (The word *diathesis* refers to a predisposition or physical condition that makes one susceptible to disease.) Thus, schizophrenia can be seen as a stress response. However, individuals who are genetically predisposed to develop schizophrenia may never do so if they are spared certain damaging conditions or stressors that might push them "over the edge."

Connection

Chapter 10
Stress can cause both physical and mental disorders.

Personality Disorders

A way of life characterized by distrust, lack of feelings for others, attention-seeking, hypersensitivity, submissiveness, perfectionism, impulsivity, unstable relationships, or a pathological need for admiration suggests one of the **personality disorders.** These conditions involve a chronic, pervasive, inflexible, and maladaptive pattern of thinking, emotion, social relationships, or impulse control. The key is that the condition derives from a personality pattern of long

Connection

Chapter 11
Personality brings continuity to a person's thoughts and actions in different situations.

The graph shows average risks for developing schizophrenia. Data were compiled from family and twin studies conducted in European populations between 1920 and 1987; the degree of risk correlates highly with the degree of genetic relatedness.

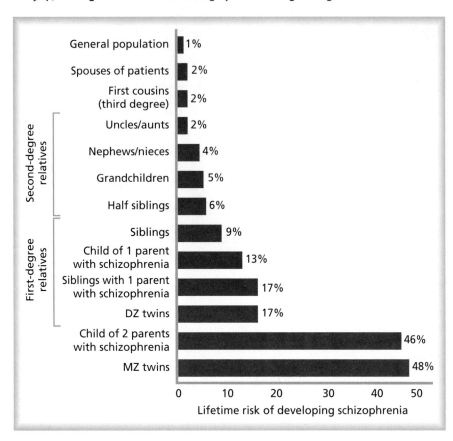

standing. These patterns can seriously impair an individual's ability to function in social or work settings and can cause significant distress.

Ten types of personality disorder are recognized in the *DSM-IV*. Here we will consider two of the better known: *narcissistic personality disorder* and *antisocial personality disorder*.

People with a **narcissistic personality disorder** have a grandiose sense of self-importance, a preoccupation with fantasies of success or power, and a need for constant attention or admiration. These people often respond inappropriately to criticism or minor defeat, either by acting indifferent or by overreacting. They have problems in interpersonal relationships, feel entitled to favors without obligations, exploit others selfishly, and have difficulty understanding how others feel. For example, an individual with narcissistic personality disorder might express annoyance—but not empathy—when a friend has to cancel a date because of a death in the family.

Antisocial personality disorder is marked by a long-standing pattern of irresponsible or harmful behavior that indicates a lack of conscience and a diminished sense of responsibility to others. Chronic lying, stealing, and fighting are common signs. People with antisocial personality disorder may not experience shame or any other sort of intense emotion. They can "keep cool"

Narcissistic personality disorder: Characterized by a grandiose sense of self-importance, a preoccupation with fantasies of success or power, and a need for constant attention or admiration.

Antisocial personality disorder: Characterized by a long-standing pattern of irresponsible behavior indicating a lack of conscience and a diminished sense of responsibility to others.

The films *Silence of the Lambs* and *Hannibal* portray an extreme antisocial personality in the character of Hannibal Lecter.

in situations that would arouse and upset normal people. Violations of social norms begin early in their lives—disrupting class, getting into fights, and running away from home. Individuals who show a criminal pattern of antisocial personality disorder, such as committing murders and other serious crimes, are popularly referred to as "psychopaths" or "sociopaths."

Although carriers of the antisocial type of personality disorder can be found among street criminals and con artists, they are also well represented among successful politicians and businesspeople who put career, money, and power above everything and everyone. Two to three percent of the population in the United States may have antisocial personality disorder. Men are four times more likely to be so diagnosed than women (Regier et al., 1988, 1993).

Adjustment Disorders and Other Conditions

Although the large majority of everyday psychological problems involve making choices and dealing with confusion, frustration, and loss, the *DSM-IV* gives these problems short shrift under **adjustment disorders** and under the awkwardly named **"other conditions that may be a focus of clinical attention."** Together, these categories represent a catch basin for relatively mild problems that do not fit well under other headings. They span a diverse range of conditions that include mild depression, physical complaints, marital problems, academic problems, job problems, parent–child problems, bereavement, and even *malingering* (faking an illness). Consequently, the largest group of people suffering from mental problems may fit these headings—even though the *DSM-IV* devotes disproportionately little space to them. Ironically, because these adjustment difficulties are so prevalent, sufferers who turn to psychologists and psychiatrists account for a large proportion of the patient load seen by professionals in private practice.

Adjustment disorders and other conditions that may be a focus of clinical attention: A diverse group of relatively mild problems that do not fit under other headings. These categories include mild depression, physical complaints, marital problems, academic problems, job problems, parent–child problems, bereavement, malingering, and a number of other conditions.

"Wait! Come back! I was just kidding about wanting to be happy."

Shyness

Psychology In Your Life

Being shy is a common problem, but it is not a *DSM-IV* disorder. Rather, **shyness** is a distressing pattern of avoiding or withdrawing from social contact. Shy behavior may resemble the social phobias, as afflicted individuals seek to limit or escape from social interactions. As we have seen many times before, it is a matter of degree. Shy people are not utterly incapacitated by fear, yet they may suffer from loneliness and from lost opportunities to pursue interests and relationships.

What are the origins of this painful problem? For some people it may begin at birth: Shyness is one of three basic temperaments that have been observed among infants and traced through adult life (Kagan et al., 1988, 1994). But shyness and other forms of social anxiety are also *learned* responses, so that even those who are not "born shy" can acquire shy behavior patterns. Several social forces and societal changes in recent decades have reduced people's experience of daily, casual, face-to-face interaction. Consider five social forces that have diminished social contact among Americans (National Public Radio, 1995b; Zimbardo, 1995):

▶ *Automation* in the workplace and in human services replaces people with more efficient, but non-human, computer chips. We conduct transactions with ATMs (automatic teller machines) instead of human bank tellers, and we fill our gas tanks by sliding credit cards into automated gas pumps without having to speak to a clerk or mechanic.

▶ *The perception of widespread,* *uncontrolled crime* has frightened citizens into hiding indoors. Fearful for their children's safety, parents either restrict their outdoor play or supervise them closely. Turning to video games instead, children are lulled into passivity by television and may even come to regard their computers as their "best friends."

▶ *Changes in family structure* such as divorce, single parenting, and households where both parents work outside the home have led many children to become "prematurely mature." Because they see less interaction among their parents or other adults, they end up with no real-life models for their own social behavior and may rely too much on stereotyped media imagery.

▶ *Perceptions of a culture-wide "time crunch"* lead individuals to feel busier and more pressured than ever — an irony since we have more time-saving options than any previous generation. When we take less time for hobbies, social groups, leisure, and household chores, we lose valuable opportunities for unique interactions with family and friends. We also develop a prejudice against such socializing as time-wasting and unproductive, so we continue to minimize its value.

▶ *Computer technology and the Internet* make it possible for people to engage in faster and more numerous exchanges with people they never actually meet, see, or touch. Faxes and electronic mail enable us to focus on others' words without the experience of their facial expressions, tone of voice, or nonverbal gestures.

This mixture of social forces diminishes the opportunity to acquire interpersonal skills and

Shyness may be painful, but it is not a DSM-IV disorder.

more and more people respond to their discomfort with shyness. Since the mid-1980s, the number of Americans who describe themselves as shy has increased from 40% to almost 50% (Carducci & Zimbardo, 1995). It appears that the conveniences of high technology and the challenges of living in a complex society have *taught* people to be shy.

On a hopeful note, shyness does not have to be a permanent condition. Many people overcome it on their own. Organizations such as Toastmasters help people build verbal skills and confidence in social situations. And many others have found the help they need in cognitive–behavioral therapy groups. If you suffer from shyness, we recommend Dr. Philip Zimbardo's (1990) book *Shyness* as a good place to look for help.

1. **RECALL:** *The DSM-IV is based on the*
   a. cognitive perspective.
   b. behavioral perspective.
   c. medical model.
   d. psychoanalytic view.

2. **RECALL:** *Which disorder involves extreme swings of mood from elation to depression?*
   a. panic disorder
   b. bipolar disorder
   c. schizophrenia
   d. unipolar depression

3. **APPLICATION:** *According to the* biological preparedness hypothesis, *which (one) of the following phobias would you expect to be most common?*
   a. fear of snakes (ophidophobia)
   b. fear of cancer (cancerophobia)
   c. fear of horses (equinophobia)
   d. fear of the number 13 (triskaidekaphobia)

4. **RECALL:** *Which of the following disorders involves a deficiency in memory?*
   a. phobia
   b. antisocial personality
   c. dissociative fugue
   d. obsessive–compulsive disorder

5. **RECALL:** *Which of the following is a disorder in which the individual displays more than one distinct personality?*
   a. schizophrenia
   b. depersonalization disorder
   c. bipolar disorder
   d. dissociative identity disorder

6. **RECALL:** *Which of the following is primarily a disorder of young American women?*
   a. bipolar disorder
   b. schizophrenia
   c. anorexia nervosa
   d. antisocial personality disorder

7. **RECALL:** *Which category of disorder is most common?*
   a. schizophrenic disorders
   b. dissociative disorders
   c. eating disorders
   d. the adjustment disorders and "other conditions that may be a focus of clinical attention"

8. **RECALL:** *Hallucinations and delusions are symptoms of*
   a. positive schizophrenia.
   b. negative schizophrenia.
   c. anxiety disorders.
   d. depersonalization disorder.

9. **UNDERSTANDING THE CORE CONCEPT:**
   The DSM-IV groups most mental disorders by their
   a. treatments.
   b. causes.
   c. symptoms.
   d. theoretical basis.

Core Concept

ANSWERS: 1. c   2. b   3. a   4. c
5. d   6. c   7. d   8. a   9. c

The Insanity Plea: How Big Is the Problem?

How often is the plea of insanity used? Before you read about the insanity defense in the next part of the chapter, try to guess the approximate percentage of accused criminals in the United States who use a plea of insanity in court: _____%. You will find the correct answer in the "Psychology in Your Life" section below. (An answer within 10% indicates that you have an exceptionally clear grasp of reality!)

Hint: Research shows that the public has an exaggerated impression of the problem.

Shyness: A distressing pattern of avoiding or withdrawing from social contact; not a *DSM-IV* disorder.

WHAT ARE THE CONSEQUENCES OF LABELING PEOPLE?

Mad. Maniac. Mentally ill. Crazy. Insane. Disturbed. Psychotic. Neurotic. These, along with all the diagnostic terms that appear in the *DSM-IV,* are labels used by the public, the courts, and mental health professionals to describe people who display mental disturbances. Ideally, an accurate diagnosis leads to an effective treatment program for the afflicted individual. Sometimes, however, labels create confusion and hurt. They can turn people into stereotypes, masking their personal characteristics and the unique circumstances that contribute to their disorders. And, if that is not enough, labels can provoke prejudices and social rejection.

In this section we will begin with the problem of labeling as it affects the individual. Then we will pursue the issue of labeling in a larger context: Does mental disorder mean the same thing in all cultures? Finally, we will look critically at the label "insanity" as used by the courts. The Core Concept, around which all of this is organized, says:

Core Concept

> Ideally, accurate diagnoses lead to proper treatments, but diagnoses may also become labels that depersonalize people and ignore the social and cultural contexts in which their problems arise.

Diagnostic Labels Can Compound the Problem

Labeling a person as mentally disturbed can have both serious and long-lasting consequences, aside from the mental disturbance itself. People may suffer a broken leg or an attack of appendicitis, but when they recover, the diagnosis moves into the past. Not so with mental disorders. A label of "depression" or "mania" or "schizophrenia" can be a stigma that follows a person forever (Farina et al., 1996; Wright et al., 2000). But what about a *mistaken* diagnosis? As Rosenhan pointed out, a mistaken diagnosis of cancer is cause for celebration, but almost never is a diagnosis of mental disorder found to be wrong. As you will recall in the "pseudopatient" study, discussed at the beginning of the chapter, the glaring fact of normalcy never emerged because of the label *schizophrenia.*

The diagnostic label may also become part of a cycle of neglect resulting from the inferior status accorded people with mental disorders. Sadly, in our society, to be mentally disordered is to be publicly degraded and personally devalued. This, of course, lowers self-esteem and reinforces disordered behavior. Thus, society extracts costly penalties from those who deviate from its norms (see Figure 12.7)—and in the process it perpetuates the problem of mental disorder.

Perhaps the most extreme reaction against labeling comes from radical psychiatrist Thomas Szasz, who says that mental illness is a "myth" (1961, 1977). Szasz argues that the symptoms used as evidence of mental illness are merely medical labels that give professionals an excuse to intervene in what are really social problems: deviant people violating social norms. Once labeled, these people can be treated for their "problem of being different," with no threat of disturbing the existing order.

We must keep in mind, therefore, that the goal of diagnosis is not simply to fit a person into a diagnostic box. Instead, a diagnosis should initiate a process that leads to a greater understanding of a person and to the development of a plan to help. A diagnosis should be a beginning, not an end.

FIGURE 12.7: Penalties for Unacceptable Behavior

This figure illustrates a continuum of behaviors that are deemed increasingly unacceptable and are responded to with increasing severity. In essence, each reaction is a punishment for deviance. Thus behavior toward those who suffer from psychopathology can be seen to resemble behavior toward criminals or other deviants.

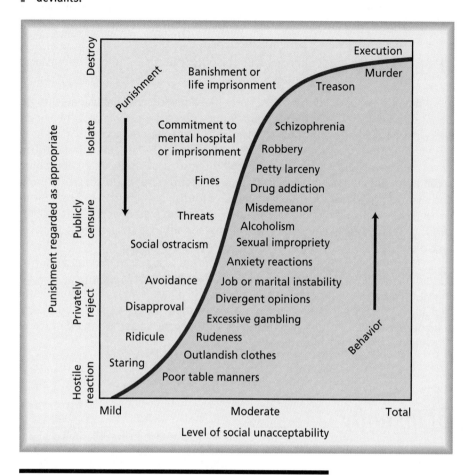

The Cultural Context of Mental Disorder

Few other clinicians would go as far as Thomas Szasz, but many advocate an *ecological model* that takes the individual's external world into account (Levine & Perkins, 1987). In this model, abnormality is viewed as an interaction between individuals and the social and cultural context. Disorder results from a mismatch between a person's behavior and the needs of the situation. If you are a private investigator, for example, it might pay to have a slightly suspicious, or "paranoid," complexion to your personality, but if you are a nurse, this same characteristic might be called "deviant."

In support of an ecological model, studies show that culture influences both the prevalence of mental disorders and the symptoms that disturbed people display (Jenkins, 1994; Manson, 1994; Matsumoto, 1996). For example, work done by the World Health Organization (1973, 1979) in Colombia, Czechoslovakia, Denmark, India, Nigeria, Taiwan, Britain, the United States, and the then-USSR established that the incidence of schizophrenia varies substantially from culture to culture. It also showed that schizophrenic symptoms, such as auditory hallucinations, show cultural variability.

Psychiatry, too, is beginning to note the effects of culture on psychopathology. The *DSM-IV*, in fact, has a section devoted to culture-specific disorders (although this section recognizes no disorders that are found specifically in the United States). According to psychiatrists Arthur Kleinman and Alex Cohen (1997), psychiatry has clung too long to three persistent myths:

▶ The myth that mental disorders have a similar prevalence in all cultures

▶ The myth that biology creates mental disorder, while culture merely shapes the way a person experiences it

▶ The myth that culture-specific disorders occur only in exotic places, rather than here at home

But, are cultural differences so great that a person who hallucinates might be labeled schizophrenic in our culture but visionary or *shaman* (a healer or seer) in another? Jane Murphy (1976) set out to answer this question in a study of two non-Western groups, the Eskimos of northwest Alaska and the Yorubas of rural tropical Nigeria, societies selected because of their wide geographic separation and cultural dissimilarity. In both groups she found separate terms and distinct social roles for the shaman and for the psychotic individual. Similar findings have since come from studies of cultures all over the world (Draguns, 1980). If mental illness is a socially defined myth, as psychiatrist Thomas Szasz asserts, it is a myth nurtured by cultures everywhere.

The incidence of specific mental disorders also varies among cultures. Abundant evidence shows that, while schizophrenia, for example, can be found everywhere, American clinicians use the diagnosis far more frequently than their counterparts in other countries. In the United States we apply the schizophrenic label to nearly all patients with psychotic symptoms (Sprock & Blashfield, 1991).

The Plea of Insanity

Psychology In Your Life

Now let's look at another label: the plea of insanity. What is your opinion: Does the insanity plea really excuse criminal behavior and put thousands of dangerous people back on the streets? Let's look at the facts.

In 1843, Daniel M'Naughten, a deranged woodcutter from Glasgow, thought he had received "instructions from God" to kill the British Prime Minister, Robert Peel. Fortunately for Peel, this would-be assassin struck down his secretary by mistake. Apprehended and tried, M'Naughten was found "not guilty

by reason of insanity." The court reasoned that M'Naughten's mental condition prevented him from knowing right from wrong. The public responded with outrage. Neither did the public like the outcome of the modern-day case involving John Hinckley, the young man who shot and wounded then-President Ronald Reagan. Hinckley pled insanity, and the court agreed. As a result, he was placed in a mental hospital, where he remains today.

Such infamous cases have molded a low public opinion of the insanity defense. The citizenry blames psychologists and psychiatrists for clogging the courts with insanity pleas, allowing homicidal maniacs back on the streets, and

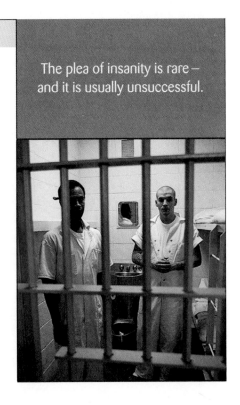

The plea of insanity is rare—and it is usually unsuccessful.

letting criminals go to hospitals for "treatment" instead of prisons for punishment. But this public image of insanity has several problems.

For one thing, "insanity" appears nowhere among the *DSM-IV* listing of disorders recognized by psychologists and psychiatrists. Technically, **insanity** is not a psychological nor psychiatric term. It is a *legal* term, which only a court—not psychologists or psychiatrists—can officially apply. By law, insanity can include not only psychosis, but jealous rage, mental retardation, and a wide variety of other conditions in which a person might not be able to control his or her behavior or distinguish right from wrong (Thio, 1995).

So, why can we not simply abolish the laws that allow this technicality? The answer to that question turns on the definition of a crime. Legally, a crime requires two elements: (1) an illegal *act* (just wanting to commit a crime is not enough) and (2) the *intent* to commit the act. Merely wishing your boss dead is no crime (because you committed no illegal act). Neither is flattening the boss who accidentally steps in front of your moving car in the parking lot (assuming you had not planned the deed). But, if you lie in wait and willfully run over the scoundrel, you have committed an intentional and illegal act—and the courts can convict you of murder.

From this example, you can see why no one wants to give up the legal requirement of intent. But you can also see why this safeguard leaves the door open for the controversial plea of insanity.

With these things in mind, take a moment to recall your estimate of the percentage of accused criminals who use the insanity plea. (See the earlier "Do It Yourself!" box.) In reality, accused criminals use the insanity defense far less often than the public realizes. According to David Rosenhan (1983), it occurs in only about two of 1,000 criminal cases, and of this tiny number, only a fraction are successful. Also contrary to popular belief, most successful insanity pleas do *not* occur in murder cases. Still, public concern about abuses of the insanity plea have led several states to experiment with alternatives. Some now require separate verdicts on the act and the intent, allowing a jury to reach a verdict of "guilty but mentally ill" (Savitsky & Lindblom, 1986).

CHECK**YOUR**UNDERSTANDING

1. **RECALL:** *Which one of the following statements is true?*
   a. Mental disorders have a similar prevalence in all cultures.
   b. In general, biology creates mental disorder, while culture merely shapes the way a person experiences it.
   c. Culture-specific stressors occur primarily in developing countries.
   d. Cultures around the world seem to distinguish between people with mental disorders and people who are visionaries or prophets.

2. **RECALL:** *The term "insanity" is a*
   a. psychological term.
   b. psychiatric term, found in the *DSM-IV* under "psychotic disorders."
   c. legal term.
   d. term that refers either to "neurotic" or "psychotic" symptoms.

Core Concept

3. **UNDERSTANDING THE CORE CONCEPT:**
   This section of the chapter emphasizes which unfortunate consequence of diagnosing mental disorders?
   a. the inaccuracy of diagnosis.
   b. stigmatizing those with mental disorders.
   c. adding to the already overcrowded conditions in mental hospitals.
   d. that some cultures do not recognize mental disorders.

ANSWERS: 1. d   2. c   3. b

Insanity: A legal term, not a psychological or psychiatric one, referring to a person who is unable, because of a mental disorder or defect, to conform his or her behavior to the law.

Using Psychology to Learn Psychology: Diagnosing Your Friends and Family

D on't do it! Don't use your new knowledge of mental disorders to diagnose your family and friends. This is a common source of grief among psychology students.

We realize how tempting it is to apply what you are learning to the people in your life. Some of the disorders that we have considered here are common, so it would be surprising if they sounded completely alien. As you go through this chapter, you will almost certainly notice signs of anxiety, paranoia, depression, mania, and various other impairments of perception, memory, or emotion in your friends and relatives. It is a variation on the tendency, discussed earlier, to see signs of mental disorder in oneself. You should recognize this as a sign that you are assimilating some new knowledge of mental disorder. But we suggest that you keep these thoughts to yourself.

You must remember that reading one chapter does not make you an expert on psychopathology. So, you should be cautious about making amateur diagnoses. What you especially should *not* do is to tell someone that you think he or she is schizophrenic, bipolar, obsessive–compulsive — or any other diagnostic label.

Having said that, we should also note that erring too far in the opposite direction by ignoring signs of pathology could also be hazardous. If someone you know is struggling with significant mental problems — and if he or she asks for your opinion — you should refrain from putting a label on the problem, but you can encourage that person to see a competent professional for diagnosis and possible treatment. We will discuss more about how that is done — in the next chapter.

Chapter Summary

WHAT IS MENTAL DISORDER?

Our conception of abnormality has evolved from one of demon possession to the current medical model, which sees psychopathology as "illness," and the broader psychological model, which includes mental and contextual factors as well as biological ones. In practice, abnormality is judged by the degree to which a person exhibits distress, maladaptiveness, irrationality, unpredictability, and unconventionality, or prompts observer discomfort.

The medical model takes a "disease" view, while psychology sees mental disorder as an interaction of biological, cognitive, social, and other environmental factors.

HOW ARE MENTAL DISORDERS CLASSIFIED?

The most widely used system for classifying mental disorders is the *DSM-IV,* which derives from psychiatry and has a bias toward the medical model. The *DSM-IV* recognizes more than 300 specific disorders, categorized by symptom patterns, but it has no category for "normal" functioning.

Among the *DSM-IV* categories are the *affective disorders,* which involve disturbances of mood. Unipolar depression is the most common affective disorder, while bipolar disorder is much rarer. The *anxiety disorders* include panic disorder, phobic disorders, and obsessive–compulsive disorder. The *somatoform disorders* involve the mind–body relationship in various ways. Those with conversion disorder have physical symptoms, but no organic disease, while those with hypochondriasis suffer from exaggerated concern about illness. The *dissociative disorders* include dissociative amnesia, fugue, depersonalization disorder, and dissociative identity disorder. All disrupt the integrated functioning of memory, consciousness, or personal identity. Two patterns of *eating disorder* are common: anorexia nervosa (self-starvation) and bulimia (binging and purging). Both are related to unrealistic, negative body images and are difficult to treat. *Schizophrenia* is characterized by extreme distortions in perception, thinking, emotion, behavior, and language. Schizophrenia takes five forms: disorganized, catatonic, paranoid, undifferentiated, and residual types. Evidence for the causes of schizophrenia has been found in a variety of factors including genetics, abnormal brain structure, and biochemistry. *Personality disorders* are patterns of perception, thinking, or behavior that are long-standing and inflexible and that impair an individual's functioning. The most common forms of disorder are classified in the *DSM-IV* as the *adjustment disorders* and *"other conditions that may be a focus of clinical attention."* These include a wide range of problems in living. *Shyness* is a widespread problem—and a treatable one—but it is not officially a disorder, unless it goes to the extreme of a social phobia.

Core Concept

The most widely used system, found in the *DSM-IV*, classifies disorders by their mental and behavioral symptoms.

Key Question

?

WHAT ARE THE CONSEQUENCES OF LABELING PEOPLE?

Labeling someone as psychologically or mentally disordered is ultimately a matter of human judgment. Therefore, even professional judgments can be biased by prejudices. Those labeled with psychological disorders are often depersonalized in ways that most physically ill people are not. Culture has an effect on whether a behavior is called normal, abnormal, or merely unusual. Cross-cultural research suggests that people everywhere distinguish between psychotic individuals and those whom they label shamans, prophets, or visionaries. Insanity, however, is a special sort of label that is awarded by the courts: Insanity is not a psychological or psychiatric term.

Core Concept

Ideally, accurate diagnoses lead to proper treatments, but diagnoses may also become labels that depersonalize people and ignore the social and cultural contexts in which their problems arise.

Review
Test

For each of the following items, choose the single correct or best answer. The answer key appears at the end.

1. The medical model views mental disorder as
   a. a character defect.
   b. a disease or illness.
   c. an interaction of biological, cognitive, behavioral, social, and cultural factors.
   d. normal behavior in an abnormal context.

2. Which of the following is *not* one of the six indicators of possible abnormality agreed upon by psychologists?
   a. chronic physical illness
   b. observer discomfort
   c. unconventionality
   d. irrationality

3. The *DSM-IV* refers to
   a. a personality inventory.
   b. the most widely used classification system for mental disorders.

   c. the neurochemical implicated in anxiety disorders.
   d. a class of psychoactive drugs effective in the treatment of schizophrenia.

4. A long-standing pattern of irresponsible behavior that hurts others without causing feelings of guilt or remorse is typical of
   a. an obsessive–compulsive disorder.
   b. an antisocial personality disorder.
   c. a narcissistic personality disorder.
   d. paranoid schizophrenia.

5. A young woman wanders into a hospital, claiming not to know who she is, where she came from, or how she got there. Her symptoms indicate that she might be suffering from a(n) _____ disorder.
   a. anxiety
   b. affective
   c. personality
   d. dissociative

6. Which of the following statements about phobic disorders is true?
   a. Any extreme and irrational fear, such as of spiders, is considered a "phobia."
   b. The "preparedness hypothesis" suggests that some people learn their fears from their parents at an early age.
   c. Phobias represent one form of affective disorders.
   d. all of the above

7. _____ has been called the "common cold of psychopathology," because it occurs so frequently and because almost everyone has experienced it at some time.
   a. Obsessive–compulsive disorder
   b. Bipolar disorder
   c. Unipolar depression
   d. Paranoid schizophrenia

8. A person who suffers from _____ cannot eat normally but engages in a ritual of "binging"—overeating fattening foods—followed by "purging" with induced vomiting or use of laxatives.
   a. anorexia nervosa
   b. bulimia
   c. inhibition
   d. mania

9. The _____ type of schizophrenia is characterized by delusions.
   a. disorganized
   b. catatonic
   c. paranoid
   d. undifferentiated

10. Rosenhan believes that his "pseudopatients" were not recognized as normal because
   a. the staff members in the mental hospitals were stupid and foolish.
   b. the staff members in the mental hospitals were just as disturbed as the patients.
   c. mental illness is a myth.
   d. many situational factors depersonalize mental patients.

ANSWERS: 1. b   2. a   3. b   4. b   5. d   6. a
7. c   8. b   9. c   10. d

If You're Interested . . .

BOOKS

Colas, E. (1998). *Just checking: Scenes from the life of an obsessive-compulsive.* Pocket Books. The author frankly and humorously discusses her incessant worrying about *everything,* one hallmark of the obsessive–compulsive personality, who may be unable to resist the urge to check and double-check every threat and possible action in everyday life, from electric lights and appliances to the dangers of driving accidents.

Jamison, K. R. (1996). *Touched with fire: Manic depressive illness and the artistic temperament.* Free Press. Best-selling psychiatrist-author Kay Redfield Jamison, who chronicled her own manic–depressive illness in *An Unquiet Mind* (1995), examines the many cases of lives whose genius in music, art, and the sciences were also afflicted—not coincidentally—with extreme and uncontrollable moods.

Lyden, J. (1997). *Daughter of the Queen of Sheba: A Memoir.* Houghton Mifflin. National Public Radio journalist Jacki Lyden turns her journalistic attention to her own childhood, growing up with a "mad mother" whose bipolar disorder made her by turns impossible to live with and hysterically funny and delightful.

Markway, B. G., & Markway, G. P. (2001). *Painfully shy: How to overcome social anxiety and reclaim your life.* St. Martin's Press. By whatever name—social anxiety or painful shyness—the fear of social interaction or conversation prevents millions of Americans from having good relationships or satisfying work. The authors' program cites case histories, practical exercises, a directory of resources, and plenty of tips for overcoming shyness

Secunda, V. (1998). *When madness comes home: Help and hope for the children, siblings, and partners of the mentally ill.* Hyperion. This is a well-researched and well-written description of what can be expected by the loved ones of those afflicted by psychological disorders, and strategies for coping, by a sympathetic author whose own sister is schizophrenic.

Sheehan, S. (1982). *Is there no place on earth for me?* Vintage. Journalist Susan Sheehan lived with a young schizophrenic woman and her family members off and on for several years in order to compose this chronicle of the life, times, and marginally helpful treatment of a complex, colorful, difficult disorder.

Styron, W. (1990). *Darkness visible: A memoir of madness*. Random House. *Sophie's Choice* author William Styron was the first in a line of distinguished celebrities to admit to suffering from depression, but his brief book — really an essay about his experiences — is still one of the easiest to read, most affecting, and most helpful.

VIDEOS

A Beautiful Mind. (2001, color). Directed by Ron Howard; starring Russell Crowe, Ed Harris, Jennifer Connelly, Paul Bettany. This true story of the early career of mathematician John Forbes Nash, Jr., diagnosed as paranoid schizophrenic, who later won the Nobel Prize for his work on game theory, is based on the biography by Sylvia Nasar.

As Good as It Gets. (1997, color, 138 min.). Directed by James Brooks; starring Jack Nicholson, Helen Hunt, Greg Kinnear, Cuba Gooding, Jr. An obsessive–compulsive writer becomes entangled, much against his will and inclinations, in the lives of a neighbor, a waitress, and their families, in his efforts to keep his world predictable and protected. For all its funny as well as tragic moments, the film makes clear the struggle of those who suffer from anxiety disorders.

The Fisher King. (1991, color, 137 min.). Directed by Terry Gilliam; starring Robin Williams, Jeff Bridges, Amanda Plummer, Michael Jeter. When a talk-radio announcer's flip remark to an unstable caller has tragic consequences, he seeks to make amends by helping one of the victims. The powerful imagery of fantastic visions, paranoid delusions, and post-traumatic stress has poignant and comic moments, too.

Harvey. (1950, b&w, 104 min.). Directed by Henry Koster; starring James Stewart, Josephine Hull, Peggy Dow. An harmless eccentric with an alcohol problem — and a 6-foot-tall rabbit pal no one else can see — is presumed crazy by family and friends. This humorous film shows that even benign nonconformity can frighten others.

K-Pax. (2001, color, 120 min.). Directed by Iain Softley; starring Kevin Spacey, Jeff Bridges, Mary McCormack. A mental hospital patient claiming to be an alien from the planet K-Pax baffles his psychiatrist, who searches for clues to a human past. This is another view (contrasted with *Harvey,* above) of the mentally ill as Other.

Mr. Jones. (1993, color, 114 min.). Directed by Mike Figgis; starring Richard Gere, Lena Olin, Delroy Lindo. The melodrama of a romance between a psychiatrist and her bipolar patient allows Richard Gere to portray the high highs of mania and the low lows of depression. The manic extremes are especially affecting as "Mr. Jones" enjoys life "too much"

with dangerous risk-taking, impulsive spending, and concerning those around him.

One Flew Over the Cuckoo's Nest. (1975, color, 133 min.). Directed by Milos Forman; starring Jack Nicholson, Louise Fletcher, Brad Dourif, Will Sampson, Danny Devito, Christopher Lloyd. Long before *As Good as It Gets,* Nicholson won the Oscar for his portrayal of McMurphy, a con artist and petty criminal whose "soft sentence" in a psychiatric hospital turns into a war between the patients and the controlling nurse who supervises their ward. The film has inaccurate depictions of electroconvulsive therapy and psychosurgery — for dramatic effect — but wonderful performances by stars, some at the beginning of their careers.

The Three Faces of Eve. (1957, b&w, 91 min.). Directed by Nunnally Johnson; starring Joanne Woodward, Lee J. Cobb, David Wayne. The film is based on the true story of a woman found to have at least three distinct personalities, and the efforts she and her therapists made to find the source — and the resolution — of her dissociative disorder. Woodward won the Oscar for her astonishing performance.

Vertigo. (1958, color, 128 min.). Directed by Alfred Hitchcock; starring James Stewart, Kim Novak, Barbara Bel Geddes. A police detective with a fear of heights (acrophobia) is lured into a mysterious romance and then a crime in this dramatic cinematic portrayal of anxiety and terror.

WEB RESOURCES

http://www.counselingnet.com This Web site offers information for anxiety, depression, stress, sexual problems, and other issues. Explore the various resources available on this site and think about whether or not it is appropriate to offer counseling over the Internet.

http://www.nimh.nih.gov/anxiety/ The Anxiety Disorders Educational Program is a national education campaign from the National Institute of Mental Health to increase awareness of anxiety disorders. Explore the objectives of this organization, as well as recent news and research regarding these disorders.

http://www.ncpamd.com/psychopharm.htm The Northern County Psychiatric Associates Psychiatric Services for Children, Adolescents, Adults and Families has put together a list of psychopharmacology resources.

http://www.schizophrenia.com/ Visit this site to learn more about schizophrenic disorders by exploring the links on causes, diagnoses, and medications. Message boards are also available for individuals suffering from schizophrenia.

WHAT IS THERAPY?

Entering Therapy

The Therapeutic Relationship and the
    Goals of Therapy

Therapy in Historical and Cultural
    Context

Therapy takes a variety of
forms, but the common
element is a relationship
focused on altering
behavior or mental
processes.

**PARAPROFESSIONALS DO THERAPY,
TOO:**
Some studies show that amount of
training is not the main factor in
therapeutic effectiveness.

HOW DO PSYCHOLOGISTS TREAT MENTAL DISORDERS?

Behavioral Therapies

Insight Therapies

Cognitive–Behavioral Therapy: A
    Synthesis

Evaluating the Psychological
    Therapies

Psychologists employ two
main forms of treatment:
the behavioral therapies
and the insight therapies.

**WHERE DO MOST PEOPLE GET
HELP?**
A lot of therapy is done by friends,
hairdressers, and bartenders.

HOW IS THE BIOMEDICAL APPROACH USED TO TREAT MENTAL DISORDERS?

Drug Therapy

Psychosurgery

Electroconvulsive and Magnetic
    Therapies

Hospitalization and the Alternatives

Biomedical therapies seek
to alter the structure or
function of the brain
through drugs, surgery, or
electromagnetic
stimulation.

**WHAT SORT OF THERAPY WOULD
YOU RECOMMEND?**
If a friend asks for a
recommendation, you have a wide
range of therapeutic possibilities to
consider.

USING PSYCHOLOGY TO LEARN PSYCHOLOGY: How Is Education Like Therapy?

THERAPIES FOR MENTAL DISORDER

ost of the time, my work as a therapist is enormously challenging," Laura admits. "Even when a new client claims not to have serious problems, or says he just has one specific issue he wants to focus on, the reality is that no one is ever completely 'fixed.' Everyone has work to do: unresolved grievances to deal with, new challenges to face — and we face them together. For me, being a therapist means, most of all, being aware of *my own* internal world, so that I can be more present, be more conscious of what I bring to the relationship, and share more with the individual who has placed this trust in me. But even then, therapy is usually no quick fix."

Laura, a petite woman in her forties,

with a contagious smile, speaks intently about her profession. Yes, she says, once your therapeutic practice is established, you might enjoy greater flexibility, autonomy, and meaningfulness than in many other careers. But no, it's not easy work, and it demands both an intellectual and an emotional investment. Moreover, Laura protests, dispelling a common myth about therapy, "A therapist is *not* a 'paid friend'! A therapist is a trained professional who knows the art of establishing a helping relationship and knows how to apply the knowledge of psychology to an individual struggling with problems and choices."

When she was young, Laura recalls, she was "always the listener. Friends came

(continued)

to me with their problems. I seemed to have a knack for that interaction. It seemed natural to me, interesting, and it brought me closer to people." Laura confesses, though, that she always felt insecure. This lack of confidence led her to seek therapy herself when she was in college. "I wanted to find out why I was in pain," Laura reflects. "My life had seemed to be good, even enviable—so why didn't I like myself? I wanted to figure that out. My therapist was very helpful, and we had a good interaction. Later, when I considered becoming a therapist myself, I remembered what he was like, how helpful my own experience had been. It gave me direction in seeking the training I needed."

Laura's orientation is in humanistic therapy, an approach aimed at helping clients see themselves clearly. Humanistic therapies are designed for individuals who seek to be more adaptive, healthy, and productive in their lives. "Early in the therapeutic relationship, my role might be somewhat parental," Laura explains. "Perhaps my client never had the opportunity to grow up with real support. As a child, this client may have created a way to function that worked for her. But now, she needs to be an adult—not a child—and she gets pushed back into those old ways of reacting. It becomes self-sabotaging. The client feels stuck." Laura sits quietly for a few moments, then goes on. "Since I've been there myself, I recognize it. When the client finally trusts me enough, I point these issues out to her, and she can begin to take charge of her life in a healthier way."

Today, practicing psychotherapists may hold any of dozens of degrees and certifications, choosing from hundreds of therapeutic techniques. For all that training, however, Laura insists that working as a therapist is not purely a science. "Therapy is an art," asserts Laura, "It's experiential. We may know the skills required to be an effective therapist, like listening well. And we know the central issues, like trust between therapist and client. But these aren't enough to make someone a good therapist. You also need personal experience and insight. You need to be able to sense what your client cannot communicate. And there's no science for that—it's intuitive.

"In some ways, the best therapists are people who have been wounded themselves. They have dealt with pain in their lives and can now provide a safe relationship for someone else. I guess I'm making it sound very stressful," Laura says as she smiles wryly. She thinks for a moment. "And there are stressful times—times when my gut response is that I don't know what to do." Fortunately, at such times, Laura has a whole body of research and theory to turn to—the science part of therapy.

But there's still more to having a psychotherapy practice, Laura points out: "It's not only challenging cases that are difficult! Sometimes just dealing with health insurance paperwork will get to you." Laura grins. "But when the therapeutic relationship is real, and our work together progresses, it's very satisfying—even, sometimes, fun! Once we finally 'get it,' my client and I can laugh together.

"I do love it. I love the intensity of it," Laura concludes. "As a therapist, I am there for my clients—*with* my clients. I see them clearly. They come to me with the gift of their trust. It's awe-inspiring. And they wouldn't come if they didn't have the strength and the love to keep going and keep growing."

As Laura makes clear, therapists work at the interface between psychological science and the art of helping and healing. While their training is based on a solid foundation of knowledge about human behavior, this knowledge is derived from groups and averages. That is the nature of science. Accordingly, the therapist's job is to apply the impersonal science to individuals who want to change the course of their lives.

As you will see in this chapter, the story of psychological therapy is largely a success story. The overwhelming majority of people who enter **therapy** receive significant help, even though each individual who seeks treatment is different. Not only do they come to therapy with the full range of problems found in the *DSM-IV,* but they come from diverse backgrounds and with varied goals for therapy. These are some of the things that make evaluating therapy difficult.

Not everyone who enters therapy, of course, becomes a success case. Some people wait too long, until their problems become intractable. Some do not end up with the right sort of therapy for their problems. And many people who could benefit from therapy do not have access to it because of financial constraints. Yet, despite these shortfalls, the development of a wide range of effective therapies is one of the success stories in modern psychology.

In this next-to-last chapter of our journey through *Psychology: Core Concepts,* we begin our overview of therapy by discussing what it is, who seeks it, what sorts of problems they bring to therapy, and who the therapists are. We will also see how therapeutic practices are influenced by history and culture. In the second section of the chapter, we consider the major types of psychological treatments currently used and how well they work. In the final section we will look at medical treatments for mental disorders, including drug therapy, psychosurgery, and "shock treatment." We will also consider when it is appropriate to place people who need treatment in institutions, such as mental hospitals, as opposed to delivering therapy in the community. As you read through the chapter, we hope you will weigh the advantages and disadvantages of each therapy, keeping in mind that you may sometime be asked by a friend or relative to use what you have learned here to recommend an appropriate therapy—or you may need therapy yourself.

WHAT IS THERAPY?

When you think of "therapy," chances are that a stereotypic scene, taken from countless cartoons and movies, pops into mind: a "neurotic" patient lying on the analyst's couch, with a bearded therapist sitting at the patient's head, scribbling notes and making interpretations. In fact, this is a scene from classic Freudian therapy, which is a rarity today. The reality of modern therapy differs from the stereotype on several counts. First, most therapists don't use a couch. Second, people now seek therapeutic help for a wide range of problems: making difficult choices, dealing with academic problems, and coping with unhappy relationships. And third, many forms of therapy involve far more than talk and interpretation.

In modern therapy for mental disorders—as with physical illnesses—the form that treatment takes is determined by the nature and severity of the problem. Some difficulties, such as schizophrenia, may require long-term, intensive treatment in special institutional settings. A less overwhelming prob-

Many people could benefit from some form of therapy. Most people who enter therapy receive significant help.

Connection

Chapter 12
The *DSM-IV* contains the most widely accepted listing of mental disorders.

Key Question

Therapy: A general term for any treatment process; in psychology and psychiatry, *therapy* refers to a variety of psychological and biomedical techniques.

"You are a very sick rabbit."

lem, such as making a career decision, may require only short-term counseling. Between the extremes of severe and mild lie a variety of disorders. Because the experience of abnormality affects each individual uniquely and subjectively, people's willingness to consider therapy will vary widely even for similar problems. As we will see in this chapter, when it is appropriate for the problem, therapy can be a great source of help and reassurance.

For those who do seek therapy, help may appear in a bewildering menu of possibilities, which can involve talk and interpretation, behavior modification, drugs, and, in some cases, even "shock treatment," or brain surgery. No matter what form therapy takes, however, there is one constant, as our Core Concept suggests:

Core Concept

> **Therapy takes a variety of forms, but the common element is a relationship focused on altering behavior or mental processes.**

In this chapter, as we examine a sample from the therapeutic universe, we will see that each form of therapy is based on different assumptions about mental disorder. Yet all involve relationships designed to change a person's functioning in some way. Let's begin our exploration of therapy by looking at the variety of people who enter treatment and the problems they bring with them to the therapeutic relationship.

Entering Therapy

Why would *you* go into therapy? Why would anyone? Most often, people enter therapy when they have a problem that they are unable to resolve by themselves. They may seek therapy on their own initiative, or they may be advised to do so by family, friends, a physician, or a coworker.

The problems that people bring to therapy run the gamut of life's difficulties. People seek therapy to cope with sudden life changes due to unemployment, death of a loved one, or a divorce. They seek treatment for help with problems associated with long-term physical illnesses. Students who seek therapy from college mental health facilities often do so because of difficulties in their interpersonal relationships and concerns about academic performance. In

Cathy □ Cathy Guisewite

Cathy by Cathy Guisewite/Universal Press Syndicate

a few cases, persons whose behavior is judged as dangerous to themselves or others can be committed by a state court to a mental institution for therapy.

Obviously, you don't have to be "crazy" to seek therapy. If you do enter therapy, however, you may be referred to as either a patient or a client. The term *patient* is often used by professionals who take a biological or medical approach to treatment and for those who are hospitalized for their treatment. The term *client* may be used by professionals who think of psychological disorders not as mental *illnesses* but rather as *problems in living* for which people seek the assistance of professionals trained in various forms of **psychotherapy** (Rogers, 1951; Szasz, 1961).

One's ability to obtain therapy can be affected by a variety of factors. As we have noted, therapy is far easier to obtain if you have money or adequate health insurance. The poor, especially poor ethnic minorities, often lack access to adequate mental health care (Bower, 1998d; Nemecek, 1999). Another problem can be lack of qualified therapists. In many communities, it is still much easier to get help for physical health problems than for psychological problems. Even the nature of a person's psychological problems can interfere with getting help. An individual with agoraphobia, for example, finds it hard, even impossible, to leave home to seek therapy. Paranoid persons may not seek help because they don't trust mental health professionals. And extremely shy people cannot call for an appointment or go to an initial diagnostic interview precisely because of the problem for which they desire help.

The Therapeutic Relationship and the Goals of Therapy

Sometimes you only need to talk out a problem with a sympathetic companion, perhaps to "hear yourself think" or to receive reassurance that he or she still cares for you. But friends have needs and agendas of their own that may not always coincide with yours. Sometimes they may be a part of the problem. For whatever reason, when friends or family cannot offer the help you need, it may be appropriate to seek the help of a professionally trained therapist. You might also want professional help if you wish to keep your problems and concerns confidential. Moreover, professional therapists have expertise in identifying mental disorders and in using therapeutic techniques that a friend would probably not know about and certainly would not have the skills to employ. In all these ways, a professional relationship with a therapist differs from a friendship.

Still, the essence of therapy is a *relationship* between the therapist and the patient/client seeking assistance — as our Core Concept indicates. You must be able to trust your therapist, just as you would a reliable friend. You and your therapist must be able to work as *allies,* on the same side, joining forces to cope with and solve the problems that have brought you to therapy (Horvath & Luborsky, 1993). And you must share concerns, values, and goals with the therapist. It also helps if you *believe* that therapy will be effective for your problem.

Connection

Chapter 12
The *medical model* assumes that mental disorders are similar to physical diseases.

Connection

Chapter 12
Agoraphobia commonly involves a fear of public places and open spaces, from which there is no easy escape.

Psychotherapy: A term for any of the psychologically based therapies, including behavioral therapies and insight therapies.

In addition to the relationship between therapist and client, the therapeutic process typically involves the following four tasks or goals:

1. *Identifying the problem.* This may mean merely agreeing on a simple description of circumstances or feelings to be changed, or, in the case of a *DSM-IV* disorder, this step may call for a formal *diagnosis* about what is wrong.

2. *Identifying the etiology, or cause, of the problem.* This involves identifying its probable origins, its development, and the reasons for the symptoms.

3. *Making a prognosis.* This is the prediction of the course the problem will take and the outlook for improvement or recovery.

4. *Deciding on and carrying out some form of treatment.* This involves selecting a specific type of therapy designed to minimize or eliminate the troublesome symptoms and, perhaps, also their sources.

Although more people seek out therapy now than in the past, people usually turn to trained mental health professionals only when their psychological problems become severe or persist for extended periods. When they do, they usually choose one of seven main types of professional therapists: counseling psychologists, clinical psychologists, psychiatrists, psychoanalysts, psychiatric nurse practitioners, clinical social workers, or pastoral counselors. The differences among these specialties are detailed in Table 13.1. As you examine that table, note that each has its area of expertise. For example, the only therapists licensed to prescribe drugs are psychiatrists, psychoanalysts (with medical degrees), and psychiatric nurse practitioners. Currently some psychologists are seeking to obtain prescription privileges, but this is a highly political issue that is not likely to be resolved soon in most states (Clay, 1998; Sleek, 1996). On the other hand, we will see later in the chapter that psychologists have developed therapeutic alternatives that are in many cases equal or superior to drug treatment.

Incidentally, we should note that little practical difference exists between the processes called *counseling* and *psychotherapy*. Some see counseling as a shorter problem-solving process, while psychotherapy involves a longer-term overhaul of the personality. The difference, if any, is one of degree.

Therapy in Historical and Cultural Context

People with psychological problems may encounter anything from sympathetic understanding to avoidance to scorn and even abuse. How we respond depends on the way we think about mental disorder. Do you believe, for example, that mental problems are diseases, the mark of a character flaw, a "problem in living," or a sign of demon possession? How society responds—including the treatment options it provides—depends on its prevailing beliefs about mental disorders and on the economic resources it has available for treatment.

CONTEMPORARY APPROACHES TO THERAPY   Modern mental health professionals have abandoned the old demon model and frankly abusive treatments in favor of therapies based on psychological and biological theories of mind and behavior. Yet the professionals often disagree on the exact causes and appropriate treatments. This situation is reflected in the abundance of therapies available: Each theory and its accompanying treatment emphasize some aspects of mind and behavior and de-emphasize others. To help you sort them out, here is a preliminary sketch of the modern therapeutic landscape—a picture that will also serve as a preview of things to come in this chapter.

The **psychological therapies**, as we have noted, are often collectively

Connection

Chapter 12
Diagnostic labels can be dehumanizing, and they can create harmful expectations.

Connection

Chapter 12
Demon possession was the medieval explanation for mental disorder.

Psychological therapies:
Therapies based on psychological principles (rather than on the biomedical approach); often called "psychotherapy."

TABLE 13.1

Types of Mental Health Care Professionals

PROFESSIONAL TITLE	SPECIALTY AND COMMON WORK SETTINGS	CREDENTIALS AND QUALIFICATIONS
Counseling psychologist	Provides help in dealing with the common problems of normal living, such as relationship problems, childrearing, occupational choice, and school problems. Typically counselors work in schools, clinics, or other institutions.	master's in counseling, PhD (Doctor of Philosophy), EdD (Doctor of Education), or PsyD (Doctor of Psychology)
Clinical psychologist	Trained primarily to work with those who have more severe disorders; practice often overlaps considerably with that of all other mental health professionals. Usually in private practice or employed by mental health agencies or by hospitals. Not licensed to prescribe drugs.	PhD or PsyD
Psychiatrist	A specialty of medicine; deals with severe mental problems — most often by means of drug therapies. May be in private practice or employed by clinics or mental hospitals.	MD (Doctor of Medicine)
Psychoanalyst	Practitioners of Freudian therapy. Usually in private practice.	MD (some practitioners have doctorates in psychology, but most are psychiatrists who have taken additional training in psychoanalysis)
Psychiatric nurse practitioner	A nursing specialty; licensed to prescribe drugs for mental disorders. May work in private practice or in clinics and hospitals.	RN (Registered Nurse) — Plus special training in treating mental disorders and prescribing drugs.
Clinical social worker	Social workers with a specialty in dealing with mental disorders, especially from the viewpoint of the social and environmental context of the problem.	MSW (Master of Social Work)
Pastoral counselor	A member of a religious order or ministry who specializes in treatment of psychological disorders. Combines spiritual guidance with practical counseling.	varies

called simply "psychotherapy." They focus on changing disordered thoughts, feelings, and behavior using psychological techniques rather than biological interventions. No matter what the name, all the psychological therapies consist principally of (a) helping people change their behavior or (b) helping people achieve *insight* into their problems. Let's look at some specific differences.

Behavioral therapy treats the problem behaviors themselves as disturbances that must be modified. Disorders are viewed as learned habit patterns rather than as the symptoms of some underlying mental disease. Behavior therapists believe that changing problematic behavior corrects the disorder.

Connection

Chapter 6
Behavioral therapy is based on the principles of behavioral learning.

In this engraving from the 1730s, we see the chaos of a cell in the London hospital St. Mary of Bethlehem. Here the upper classes have paid to see the horrors, the fiddler who entertains, and the mental patients chained, tortured, and dehumanized. The chaos of Bethlehem eventually became synonymous with the corruption of its name—Bedlam.

Among the insight therapies, *cognitive therapy* tries to restructure how a person thinks about a problem. Cognitions (including thoughts, beliefs, emotions, and attitudes) are viewed as the focus of therapy. As compared with behavior therapy, the emphasis in cognitive therapy is internal, rather than on external circumstances and behaviors.

Another group of insight therapies, the *psychodynamic approaches,* view mental disorders as the outer symptoms of unresolved childhood traumas and inner conflicts. The best-known psychodynamic treatment is Freudian *psychoanalysis,* the so-called "talking cure" in which a therapist helps a person develop insights about the relationship between the overt symptoms and the unresolved hidden conflicts that presumably cause those symptoms.

Insight therapies in the humanistic tradition emphasize the self-concept, needs, and values of the patient. *Humanistic therapies* are directed toward self-actualization and psychological growth. Humanistic therapists emphasize the development of more meaningful interpersonal relationships and the enhancement of freedom of choice and a healthier view of oneself.

In contrast with psychotherapy, the **biomedical therapies** focus on treating mental problems by changing the underlying biology of the brain. To do so, a physician or nurse practitioner can call on a variety of drugs, including antidepressants, "tranquilizers," and stimulants. Occasionally the brain may be treated with electrical stimulation or even surgery. In general, biomedical therapies try to alter brain functioning with chemical or physical interventions.

As we have noted, laws specify which professions are licensed to provide biomedical therapy. So, clinical psychologists, who cannot prescribe medicine in most states, often work closely with physicians who can prescribe medication when necessary.

HEALING IN CULTURAL CONTEXT   Individualistic Western (European and North American) views and practices generally regard psychological disorders to be the result of disease processes, abnormal genetics, distorted mental processes, unhealthy environments, or stressors. But collectivist cultures often

Connection

Chapter 11
Psychoanalysis is based is Freud's theory of personality.

Connection

Chapter 11
The *hierarchy of needs* is part of Maslow's humanistic theory of personality.

Biomedical therapies:
Treatments that focus on altering the brain, especially with drugs, psychosurgery, or electroconvulsive therapy.

have quite different perspectives (Triandis, 1990). For example, many Africans believe that mental disorder results when an individual becomes estranged from nature and the community, including the community of ancestral spirits (Nobles, 1976; Sow, 1977). In such cultures, treating mentally disturbed individuals by removing them from society is unthinkable. Instead, healing takes place in a social context, emphasizing a distressed person's beliefs, family, work, and life environment. The African use of group support in therapy has been expanded into a procedure called "network therapy," where a patient's entire network of relatives, coworkers, and friends becomes involved in the treatment (Lambo, 1978). Similar views have begun to work their way into therapies in the United States and other individualistic countries.

In many places around the world, the treatment of mental and physical disease is also bound up with religion and the supernatural. Certain persons—priests, ministers, shamans, sorcerers, and witches—are assumed to have special mystical powers to help distressed fellow beings. Their methods involve ceremonies and rituals that bring emotional intensity and meaning into the healing process. Combined with the use of symbols, they connect the individual sufferer, the shaman, and the society to supernatural forces to be won over in the battle against madness (Devereux, 1981; Wallace, 1959). In some cases this approach is similar to the old demon-possession model that was dominant in medieval Europe, although we should note that attributing disorders to supernatural forces has more often led to personal blame and abusive treatment in individualist cultures than in collectivist societies.

In many cultures, treatments for mental and physical disorders are closely allied with religious beliefs. Here, a Native American healer concentrates on spiritual forces that are presumed to have a role in the woman's discomfort.

Paraprofessionals Do Therapy, Too

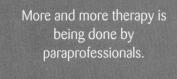

More and more therapy is being done by paraprofessionals.

Does the best therapy always require a highly trained (and expensive) professional? Or can *paraprofessionals*—who may have received on-the-job training in place of graduate training and certification—be effective therapists? If you are seeking treatment, these questions are important because hospitals, clinics, and agencies are increasingly turning to paraprofessionals as a cost-cutting measure: Those who lack full professional credentials can be hired at a fraction of the cost of those with professional degrees. They are often called "aides" or "counselors" (although many counselors do have professional credentials).

Surprisingly, a review of the literature has failed to find substan-tial differences in the effectiveness of the two groups across a wide spectrum of psychological problems (Christensen & Jacobson, 1994). The implications of this conclusion are not yet clear, but it is good news in the sense that the need for mental health services is far greater than the number of professional therapists can possibly provide. And, because paraprofessional therapists can be effective, highly trained professionals may be freed for other roles, including prevention and community education programs, assessment of patients, training and supervision of paraprofessionals, and research. The reader should be cautioned about over-interpreting this finding, however. Professionals and paraprofessionals have been found to be equivalent only in the realm of the insight therapies (Zilbergeld, 1986). Such differences have not been demonstrated in the

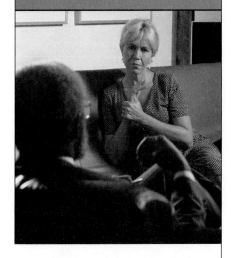

areas of behavioral therapies, which require extensive knowledge of operant and classical conditioning and of social learning theory.

1. **RECALL:** *People in collectivist cultures are likely to view mental disorder as a symptom of something wrong in*
   a. the unconscious mind.
   b. the person's behavior, rather than in the mind.
   c. the person's relationship with family or community.
   d. a person's character.

2. **RECALL:** *A therapist, but not necessarily a friend, can be relied on to*
   a. maintain confidentiality.
   b. give you good advice.
   c. offer sympathy when you are feeling depressed.
   d. give you social support.

3. **APPLICATION:** *Which of the following therapists would be most likely to treat an unwanted response,* such as nail biting, as merely a bad habit, rather than as a symptom of an underlying disorder?
   a. a psychoanalyst
   b. a psychiatrist
   c. an insight therapist
   d. a behavioral therapist

4. **UNDERSTANDING THE CORE CONCEPT:**
   All therapies are alike in this respect:
   a. All may be legally administered only by licensed, trained professionals.
   b. All make use of insight into a patient's problems.
   c. All involve the aim of altering the mind or behavior.
   d. All focus on discovering the underlying cause of the patient's problem, which is often hidden in the unconscious mind.

ANSWERS: 1. c   2. a   3. d   4. c

Connection

Chapter 11
An *eclectic* theorist combines ideas from many different perspectives.

HOW DO PSYCHOLOGISTS TREAT MENTAL DISORDERS?

Psychologists have developed an impressive array of therapies. Some are based on the assumption that psychopathology is learned — and can be unlearned. Others emphasize the roles of emotion, personality traits, or the social context. The boundaries between the various forms of therapies, however, are becoming blurred. As therapists become more *eclectic,* they are assembling their therapeutic tool kits with a blend of methods. These include the psychodynamic theories, cognitive theories, existential–humanistic theories, and the behavioral learning theories — all of which we have studied earlier in this book. Our Core Concept will help you organize in your mind these approaches to therapy:

> **Psychologists employ two main forms of treatment: the behavioral therapies and the insight therapies.**

Connection

Chapter 6
The behavioral learning theories include *classical conditioning* and *operant conditioning.*

The insight therapies, we shall see, were the first truly psychological treatments developed; and for a long time they were the only psychological therapies available. But in recent years they have been joined by the behavioral therapies, which are now in many cases the most effective tools we have. Frequently they equal or surpass the more highly publicized drug therapies. It is with these behavioral methods that we begin.

Behavioral Therapies

If the problem is overeating, bed-wetting, shyness, antisocial behavior, or anything else that can be described in behavioral terms, the chances are good that it can be modified by one of the behavioral therapies, derived from behavioral learning theories. **Behavioral therapy** (also called **behavior modification**) applies the well-established principles of conditioning and reinforcement to a wide range of undesirable behavior patterns that, in addition to those listed above, include fears, compulsions, depression, addictions, aggression, and delinquent behaviors. Behavioral therapists focus on problem *behaviors* (rather than inner thoughts or emotions), examining how these behaviors might have been learned and, more important, how they can be eliminated and replaced by more effective patterns. We will look first at the techniques they borrow from classical conditioning.

CLASSICAL CONDITIONING TECHNIQUES The development of irrational fear responses and other undesirable emotionally based behaviors seems to follow the classical conditioning model. As you will recall, classical conditioning involves the association of a new stimulus with a powerful and familiar stimulus, so that the person responds the same way to both. For example, when a claustrophobic woman walks into an elevator (a conditioned stimulus), she may experience an anxiety response (e.g., shaking, turning pale), learned originally when she was trapped in a locked closet as a child (the frightening confinement served as the unconditioned stimulus for fear and anxiety).

When a problem behavior such as this arises from classical conditioning, a favored treatment is **counterconditioning,** a set of techniques designed to substitute a new response for the unwanted one. Counterconditioning is most often applied when an individual has an anxiety disorder such as a phobia, an irrational fear reaction directed at a harmless object or situation, such as a spider, a confined space, or social contact. From our discussion of classical conditioning, we know that *any* neutral stimulus may acquire the power to elicit strong conditioned reactions if it has been associated with an unconditioned stimulus. To weaken the strength of these learned associations, behavioral therapists often use a form of therapeutic *extinction*. Let us see how this is done in a special form of counterconditioning called *reciprocal inhibition therapy*.

RECIPROCAL INHIBITION AND SYSTEMATIC DESENSITIZATION The nervous system cannot be relaxed and agitated at the same time because these two incompatible processes cannot be activated simultaneously. This simple notion is the basis for the technique of **reciprocal inhibition,** developed by South African psychiatrist Joseph Wolpe (1958, 1973).

Wolpe has used reciprocal inhibition extensively to treat fears and phobias. He begins with a training program that teaches his patients to relax their muscles and their minds. While they are in this deeply relaxed state, he *desensitizes* them to their fear by having them imagine the feared situation. They do so in gradual steps that move from remote associations of the feared situation to direct images of it. Wolpe calls this part of the treatment **systematic desensitization.**

In the process of desensitization, the therapist and client first identify the stimuli that provoke anxiety and arrange them in a *hierarchy* ranked from weakest to strongest (Shapiro, 1995). For example, a patient suffering from severe fear of public speaking constructed the hierarchy in Table 13.2. During desensitization, the relaxed client vividly imagines the *weakest* anxiety stimulus on the list. If the stimulus can be visualized without discomfort, the client goes on to the next stronger one. After a number of sessions, the client can

Professor Gallagher and his controversial technique of simultaneously confronting the fear of heights, snakes and the dark.

 Connection

Chapter 6
Classical conditioning techniques can alter conditioned responses (CR) to conditioned stimuli (CS).

Behavioral therapy: Any form of psychotherapy based on the principles of behavioral learning, especially operant conditioning and classical conditioning.

Behavior modification: Another term for behavioral therapy.

Counterconditioning: A set of classical conditioning techniques for substituting a new response for an unwanted response; used especially in treating phobias.

Reciprocal inhibition: Joseph Wolpe's counterconditioning technique, involving relaxation training and systematic desensitization therapy.

Systematic desensitization: A behavioral therapy technique in which anxiety is extinguished by exposing the patient to an anxiety-provoking stimulus.

Exposure therapy: A form of desensitization therapy in which the patient directly confronts the anxiety-provoking stimulus (as opposed to imagining the stimulus).

In "virtual reality," phobic patients can confront their fears safely and conveniently in the behavioral therapist's office. On a screen inside the headset, the patient sees computer-generated images of feared situations, such as seeing a snake, flying in an airplane, or looking down from the top of a tall building.

Aversion therapy: As a classical conditioning procedure, aversive counterconditioning involves presenting individuals with an attractive stimulus paired with unpleasant (aversive) stimulation in order to condition a repulsive reaction.

FIGURE 13.1: Conditioning an Aversion for Cigarette Smoke

Aversion therapy for smoking might simultaneously pair a foul odor with cigarette smoke blown in the smoker's face. The foul odor (such as rotten eggs) produces nausea. This response then becomes the conditioned response associated with cigarette smoke.

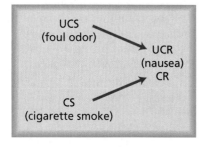

TABLE 13.2	A Sample Anxiety Hierarchy

The following is typical of anxiety hierarchies that a therapist and a patient might develop to desensitize a fear of public speaking. The therapist guides the deeply relaxed patient in imagining the following situations:

1. Seeing a picture of another person giving a speech.
2. Watching another person give a speech.
3. Preparing a speech that I will give.
4. Having to introduce myself to a large group.
5. Waiting to be called upon to speak in a meeting.
6. Being introduced as a speaker to a group.
7. Walking to the podium to make a speech.
8. Making a speech to a large group.

imagine the most distressing situations on the list without anxiety (Lang & Lazovik, 1963). In some forms of desensitization, called **exposure therapy,** the therapist may actually have the patient confront the feared object or situation, such as flying.

A number of evaluation studies have shown that this behavioral therapy works remarkably well with most phobic patients (Smith & Glass, 1977). Desensitization has also been successfully applied to a variety of fears, including stage fright and anxiety about sexual performance (Kazdin, 1994; Kazdin & Wilcoxin, 1976). Recently, some psychologists have been using computer-generated images that expose phobic patients to fear-producing situations in a safe virtual-reality environment (Rothbaum & Hodges, 1999; Rothbaum et al., 2000).

AVERSION THERAPY Desensitization therapy helps clients deal with stimuli that they want to *avoid.* But what can be done to help those who are *attracted* to stimuli that are harmful or illegal? For example, drug addiction, sexual paraphilias, and uncontrollable violence are human problems in which deviant behavior is elicited by tempting stimuli. A classical conditioning form of **aversion therapy** uses a counterconditioning procedure designed to make tempting stimuli less tempting by pairing the attractive stimuli with noxious (aversive) stimuli. These noxious stimuli might include electric shocks or nausea-producing drugs, whose effects are highly unpleasant but not in themselves destructive or dangerous to the client. In time, the negative reactions (unconditioned responses) associated with the aversive stimuli are elicited by the conditioned stimuli (such as an addictive drug), and the person develops an aversion that replaces the desire.

To give an example, persons who elect aversion therapy to help them quit smoking may be required to chain-smoke cigarettes (sometimes more than one cigarette at a time) while having a foul-smelling odor blown in their faces—until smoking is associated with nausea and vomiting (see Figure 13.1). A similar conditioning effect occurs in alcoholics who drink while taking the drug Antabuse. The drug has no side effects—unless the patient drinks even a small amount of alcohol; then he or she becomes severely nauseated. Often a daily dose of Antabuse is prescribed for alcoholics who want help with their resolve to quit drinking. With the single daily decision to take Antabuse, the patient can significantly strengthen the determination *not* to take a drink.

In some ways, aversion therapy resembles nothing so much as torture. So why would anyone submit voluntarily to it? Usually people do so only because they have unsuccessfully tried other treatments. In some cases, people may be required to enter aversion therapy by the courts or as part of a prison treatment program.

Critics are concerned that the painful procedures in aversion therapy may give too much power to the therapist, can be more punitive than therapeutic, and are most likely to be used in situations where people have the least freedom of choice about what is done to them. As a result, aversion therapy is now regulated by state laws and professional association guidelines.

OPERANT CONDITIONING TECHNIQUES Johnny has a screaming fit when he goes to the grocery store with his parents and they refuse to buy him candy. His behavior is an example of a problem that has been acquired by *operant conditioning* — as the result of previously rewarded responses (his parents have occasionally given in to his demands) rather than by the paired association of classical conditioning. Accordingly, a therapist would most likely modify Johnny's behavior by *contingency management.* Contingency management involves using operant conditioning techniques to alter the rewards and punishers that have shaped the individual's behavior. In other cases, the problem behavior arises not from direct rewards but from observing someone else who is rewarded. This is an extension of operant learning known as *social learning.* Social learning therapy changes people's expectations of reward and punishment by letting them observe the desired behavior in others. Let us consider both of these techniques in more detail.

Contingency Management Changing behavior by modifying its consequences is the essence of **contingency management.** This approach has

A patient undergoes a simplified form of aversion therapy in which overexposure to smoke makes the patient nauseous. The smell of smoke and smoking behavior then take on unpleasant associations.

Contingency management: An operant conditioning approach to changing behavior by altering the consequences, especially rewards and punishments, of behavior.

FIGURE 13.2: Fear Reactions in Monkeys

After young monkeys raised in laboratories observe unrelated adult monkeys showing a strong fear of snakes, they are vicariously conditioned to fear real snakes and toy snakes with an intensity that persists over time.

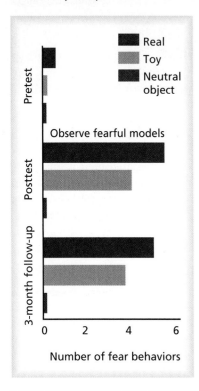

Number of fear behaviors

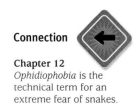

Connection

Chapter 12
Ophidiophobia is the technical term for an extreme fear of snakes.

Social learning therapy: An approach to therapy based on social learning theory, which teaches that behavior is influenced by observation and imitation of others.

Participant modeling: A social learning technique in which a therapist demonstrates and encourages a client to imitate a desired behavior.

proved effective in managing behavior problems found in schools, prisons, and mental hospitals. It is also useful in treating *autism,* a developmental condition marked by extreme difficulties in social interaction and, often, by repetitive, self-destructive behavior (Frith, 1997).

Perhaps the widest use of contingency management has been in helping parents deal with their children's behavior problems. For example, Johnny's parents may learn to extinguish his fits at the grocery store by withdrawing their attention. On the other hand, they learn to give him attention when he is being good. Over time, the changing contingencies will work to extinguish the old, undesirable behaviors (throwing a fit) and help to keep the new ones in place.

One caution is in order: While some people misbehave merely because they aren't getting enough reinforcement in their lives, this is not always the case. For example, overzealous parents and teachers may be tempted to praise children lavishly, even when their performance has been mediocre—under the mistaken impression that the extra praise will increase low self-esteem and boost performance. But in such cases, increasing rewards inappropriately can aggravate behavior problems (Viken & McFall, 1994). How could this be? The subject may learn that more rewards can be "earned" by producing fewer and fewer desirable behaviors. One must, therefore, take care in simply piling on more rewards. The key to success lies in tying rewards more closely to (making them *contingent* on) desirable behaviors.

Social Learning Therapy "Monkey see—monkey do," we say. And sure enough, monkeys learn fears by observation and imitation. One study showed that laboratory monkeys with no previous aversion to snakes could acquire a simian version of *ophidiophobia* by observing their parents reacting fearfully to real snakes and toy snakes. The more disturbed the parents were at the sight of the snakes, the greater the resulting fear in their offspring (Mineka et al., 1984). A follow-up study showed that such fears were not just a family pattern. When other monkeys that had previously shown no fear of snakes were given the opportunity to observe unrelated adults responding to snakes fearfully, they quickly acquired the same fear. (See Figure 13.2.) This fear persisted but was less strong and more variable than that of the other young monkeys who had observed their own parents' fearful reactions (Cook et al., 1985).

Like monkeys, we also learn by observing the behavior of others. Fears, in particular, are often learned in this way. **Social learning therapy** takes advantage of this capacity by having the client observe and imitate other persons—called *models*—while being reinforced for the desired response. This therapy has proved of special value in overcoming phobias and in building social skills.

Many new responses, especially complex ones, can be acquired more readily if a person can observe and imitate another person performing the desired behavior. In **participant modeling,** the therapist may model the behavior and encourage the client to imitate it. For example, in treating a phobia for snakes, a therapist might first approach a caged snake, then touch the snake, and so on. (Snake phobias have often been the subject of behavioral therapy demonstrations.) The client is urged and helped to imitate each modeled behavior, but at no time is the client forced to perform. Resistance at any level is overcome by having the client return to a previously successful, less-threatening approach behavior.

The power of participant modeling can be seen in a study that compared the participant modeling technique with several other approaches: (1) *symbolic modeling,* a technique in which subjects receive indirect exposure by watching a film or video in which models deal with a feared situation; (2) desensitization

FIGURE 13.3: Participant Modeling Therapy

The subject shown in the photo first watches a model make a graduated series of snake-approach responses and then repeats them herself. Eventually, she can pick up the snake and let it move about on her. The graph compares the number of approach responses subjects made before and after receiving participant modeling therapy (most effective) with the behavior of those exposed to two other therapeutic techniques and a control group.

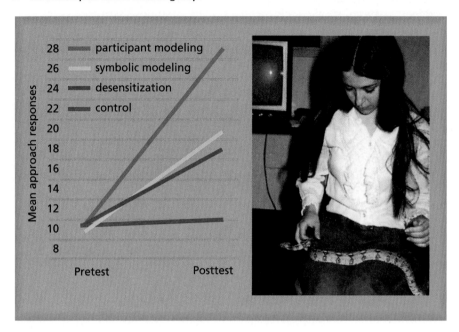

therapy, which, as you will remember, involves exposure to an imagined fearful stimulus; and (3) no therapeutic intervention (the control condition). As you can see in Figure 13.3, participant modeling was the most successful. A snake phobia was eliminated in 11 of the 12 subjects in the participant modeling group (Bandura, 1970).

Token Economies   A special form of reinforcement therapy called the **token economy** is applied to groups of people in classrooms and institutions (Ayllon & Azrin, 1968; Martin & Pear, 1999). The therapy takes its name from the plastic tokens sometimes awarded by therapists (or teachers) as immediate reinforcers for desirable behaviors. Later, recipients may redeem the tokens for food, merchandise, or privileges. "Points" or other objects may be used in place of tokens. The important thing is that subjects receive *something* as a reinforcer immediately after giving desired responses. Immediate reward is the key to the success of token economies—or any reinforcement therapy, for that matter.

The token economy approach has been found to work especially well in encouraging prosocial behaviors among mental patients and prisoners (Schaefer & Martin, 1966). It also can stimulate academic performance among primary and secondary school students (Packard, 1970). And, it has been tried on college professors: At the institution where one of your authors teaches, the president has established a variation on the token economy to encourage staff participation in college events, such as athletic events and theatrical productions. Every staff member receives a special card, called a "college spirit pass." Then, those attending college-sponsored events receive "token" reinforcers in

Token economy: An operant technique applied to groups, such as classrooms or mental hospital wards, involving the distribution of "tokens" or other indicators of reinforcement contingent on desired behaviors. The tokens can later be exchanged for privileges, food, or other reinforcers.

Connection

Chapter 11
The psychodynamic theories include those developed by Freud. Jung, Adler, Horney, and Erikson.

Connection

Chapter 11
Repression is the Freudian mechanism of forgetting by blocking threatening material in the unconscious.

Connection

Chapter 11
Projection is the ego defense mechanism involved in attributing one's unconscious desires to someone else.

Connection

Chapter 3
Introspection is a subjective technique that involves describing one's own private mental processes.

the form of punches in their spirit passes. At the end of the year, those having the most punches receive merchandise prizes from the campus store. It works.

Insight Therapies

In contrast with the behavioral therapies, which focus on external behavior, the **insight therapies** attempt to change people on the *inside* — the way they think and feel. Sometimes called *talk therapies,* these methods share the assumption that distressed patients need to develop an understanding of the disordered thoughts, emotions, and motives that underlie their mental difficulties.

There are many forms of insight therapy, but all offer techniques for revealing and changing a patient's disturbed mental processes through discussion and interpretation. Some, like Freudian psychoanalysis, assume that problems lie hidden deep in the unconscious, so they employ elaborate and time-consuming techniques to draw them out. Others, like Albert Ellis's *rational–emotive therapy,* assume that problems lie closer to the surface of awareness and, therefore, require correspondingly shorter and more direct courses of treatment. Because these therapies come in dozens of "brands," we will have space to examine only a sampling of the most influential ones, beginning with the legendary methods developed by Sigmund Freud.

Psychodynamic Therapies   So called because they emphasize the *energy* within the personality, the **psychodynamic therapies** are based on the psychodynamic theories of personality that originated with Sigmund Freud. In the classic Freudian view, the psychological tension created by forbidden impulses and threatening memories locked in the unconscious cause the patient's problems. Therefore, Freudian therapy, known as **psychoanalysis,** requires intensive and prolonged exploration of patients' unconscious. Psychoanalytic techniques were designed to help neurotic, anxiety-ridden individuals to change their disruptive, often self-defeating patterns of thinking and acting by understanding the "true" causes of their problems. The major goal of psychoanalysis, therefore, is to reveal the unconscious mind's contents.

Of central importance to the psychoanalyst is understanding how a patient uses the ego defenses to handle conflicts, impulses, and memories. Symptoms are considered to be messages from the unconscious that something is wrong. But whatever the problem is, the ego blocks it from consciousness by repression. A psychoanalyst's task, then, is to help a patient bring these repressed thoughts to consciousness. By doing so, the patient gains *insight* into the relationship between the current symptoms and the repressed conflicts. In the final stages of psychoanalysis, patients learn how their relationship with the therapist reflects unresolved problems with their parents at earlier stages in their lives. This *projection* of parental attributes onto the therapist is called *transference,* and this final phase of therapy is known as the **analysis of transference.** According to psychoanalytic theory, patients will recover when they are "released" from repression established in early childhood (Munroe, 1955).

The goals of psychoanalysis are ambitious. They involve not just the elimination of the immediate symptoms of psychopathology but a reorganization of the personality. Because traditional psychoanalysis is an attempt to reconstruct long-standing repressed memories and then work through painful feelings to an effective resolution, it takes a long time. Patients must be highly motivated, introspective, verbally fluent, and able to bear the considerable expense in time and money. Classic psychoanalysis might involve three to five sessions of analysis per week over a period of years. Modern psychoanalytic techniques usually involve fewer sessions.

POST-FREUDIAN PSYCHODYNAMIC THERAPIES Freud's followers have retained some of his basic ideas and techniques but modified others. Classical Freudian psychoanalysis emphasizes the importance of three factors: unconscious motivation and conflict; the power of early childhood development; and the dynamics within one's personality. In contrast, **post-Freudian psychodynamic theories** generally emphasize:

- ▶ The importance of the individual's current social environment.
- ▶ The ongoing influence of life experiences beyond childhood.
- ▶ The role of social and interpersonal relationships.
- ▶ The significance of one's conscious self-concept.

These post-Freudian (or *neo-Freudian*) approaches include therapies developed by Adler, Jung, Horney, and Erikson.

HUMANISTIC THERAPIES The primary symptoms for which college students seek therapy include low self-esteem, feelings of alienation, failure to achieve all they feel they should, and general dissatisfaction with their lives. These problems in everyday existence are commonly called *existential crises*. This term underscores the idea that many problems deal with questions about the meaning and purpose of one's existence. The humanistic psychologists have developed therapies aimed specifically at these problems. This is the approach preferred by Laura, the therapist we met at the beginning of the chapter.

Humanistic therapists dispute Freud's assumption of a personality divided into warring parts, dominated by a selfish id, and driven by hedonistic instincts and repressed conflicts. Instead, they emphasize the concept of a *whole person* who engages in a continual process of changing and becoming. Despite the restrictions of environment and heredity, we remain free to choose what we will become. Along with this *freedom to choose,* however, comes the *burden of responsibility.* This burden may lead to anxiety and despair. We also suffer from guilt over lost opportunities. **Humanistic therapies** attempt to help clients con-

Connection

Chapter 11
Adler, Jung, Horney, and Erikson all modified Freud's ideas about personality and mental disorder.

Post-Freudian psychodynamic therapies: Therapies for mental disorder that were developed by psychodynamic theorists who disagreed with some aspects of Freud's theories and methods of treatment.

Humanistic therapies: Treatment techniques based on the assumption that people have a tendency for positive growth and self-actualization, which may be blocked by an unhealthy environment that can include negative self-evaluation and criticism from others.

Humanistic therapist Carl Rogers (right center) facilitates a therapy group.

Connection

Chapter 11
Rogers's method of treatment is based on his person-centered theory of personality.

front these problems by recognizing their own freedom, enhancing their self-esteem, and realizing their fullest potential (see Schneider & May, 1995).

Among the most influential of the humanistic therapists, Carl Rogers (1951, 1977) developed a method called **person-centered therapy,** which assumes that all people have the need to self-actualize, that is, to realize their potential. But healthy development can be hindered by a conflict between one's desire for a positive self-image and criticism by self and others. This conflict creates anxiety and unhappiness. The task of Rogerian therapy, then, is to create a nurturing environment in which clients can work through their conflicts to achieve self-enhancement and self-actualization.

One of the main techniques used by Rogerian therapists involves **reflection of feeling** to help clients understand their emotions. With this technique therapists paraphrase their clients' words, attempting to capture the emotional tone expressed and acting as a sort of psychological "mirror" in which clients can see themselves. Notice how the Rogerian therapist uses reflection of feeling in the following extract from a therapy session with a young woman (Rogers, 1951, p. 152):

CLIENT: It probably goes all the way back into my childhood. . . . My mother told me that I was the pet of my father. Although I never realized it—I mean, they never treated me as a pet at all. And other people always seemed to think I was sort of a privileged one in the family. . . . And as far as I can see looking back on it now, it's just that the family let the other kids get away with more than they usually did me. And it seems for some reason to have held me to a more rigid standard than they did the other children.

THERAPIST: You're not so sure you were a pet in any sense, but more that the family situation seemed to hold you to pretty high standards.

CLIENT: M-hm. That's just what has occurred to me; and that the other people could sorta make mistakes, or do things as children that were naughty . . . but Alice wasn't supposed to do those things.

THERAPIST: M-hm. With somebody else it would be just—oh, be a little naughtiness; but as far as you were concerned, it shouldn't be done.

CLIENT: That's really the idea I've had. I think the whole business of my standards . . . is one that I need to think about rather carefully, since I've been doubting for a long time whether I even have any sincere ones.

THERAPIST: M-hm. Not sure whether you really have any deep values which you are sure of.

CLIENT: M-hm. M-hm.

In Rogers's humanistic therapy, people are assumed to have basically healthy motives—which may be stifled by pressures from others. The therapist's task is mainly to remove barriers that limit the expression of this natural positive tendency and help the client clarify and accept his or her own feelings. This is accomplished within an atmosphere of **unconditional positive regard** —nonjudgmental acceptance and respect for the client. In addition, the therapist tries to experience the client's feelings. Such total empathy requires that the therapist care for the client as a worthy, competent individual—not to be judged or evaluated but to be assisted in discovering his or her individuality

Person-centered therapy: A humanistic approach to treatment developed by Carl Rogers, emphasizing an individual's tendency for healthy psychological growth through self-actualization.

Reflection of feeling: Carl Rogers's technique of paraphrasing the clients' words, attempting to capture the emotional tone expressed.

Unconditional positive regard: Rogers's term for the therapist's attitude of nonjudgmental acceptance and respect for the client.

(Meador & Rogers, 1979). Unlike practitioners of other therapies, who interpret, give answers, or instruct, the client-centered therapist is a supportive listener who reflects and clarifies the client's feelings. Thus, person-centered therapy strives to be **nondirective.** The client determines the direction of therapy, and the therapist merely facilitates the patient's search for self-awareness and self-acceptance.

GROUP THERAPIES   All the treatment approaches we have discussed so far involve one-to-one relationships between a patient or client and therapist. However, **group therapy** can have value in treating a variety of concerns, particularly problems with social behavior and relationships. This can be done in many ways — there are even therapy groups available on the Internet (Davison et al., 2000). Most commonly, therapy groups employ the humanistic perspective: Humanistic therapies have most often made use of group contexts in order to provide clients with social support or evidence that they are not alone. Other benefits of group therapy include opportunities to observe and imitate new social behaviors in a forgiving, supportive atmosphere. We will examine only a small sample of group therapies below: *self-help groups* and *marital and family therapy*.

Self-Help Groups   The most dramatic development in group therapy has been the surge of interest and participation in **self-help groups.** It is estimated that there are 500,000 such groups, which are attended by 15 million Americans every week (Leerhsen, 1990). Many of these sessions are free, especially those that are not directed by a health care professional. These groups give people a chance to meet others with similar problems who are surviving and sometimes thriving (Christensen & Jacobson, 1994; Jacobs & Goodman, 1989). Such groups are most effective when the participants feel compatible with each other (Schiff & Bargal, 2000).

One of the oldest, Alcoholics Anonymous (AA), pioneered the self-help concept, beginning in the mid-1930s. Central to the original AA structure was the concept of "12 steps" to recovery from alcohol addiction, based not on psychological theory but on the trial-and-error experience of early AA members. The first step begins with recognizing that one has become powerless over alcohol; the second affirms that faith in a "greater power" is necessary for recovery. In the remaining steps the individual seeks help from God and sets goals for making amends to those who have been hurt by his or her actions. Members are urged and helped by the group to accept as many of the steps as possible in order to maintain recovery.

The feminist consciousness-raising movement of the 1960s extended the reach of self-help groups beyond the arena of alcoholism. Today, such support groups deal with four basic categories of problems:

▶ Managing life transition or other crises, such as divorce or death of a child.
▶ Coping with physical and mental disorders, such as depression or heart attack.
▶ Dealing with addiction, such as alcohol, gambling, and drug dependency.
▶ Handling the stress felt by relatives or friends of those who are dealing with addictions.

Group therapy has also made valuable contributions to the treatment of terminally ill patients. The goals of such therapy are to help patients and their families live their lives as fully as possible, to cope realistically with impending

Nondirective: Rogers's term for a therapeutic approach in which the client, rather than the therapist, takes the lead in determining the direction of therapy.

Group therapy: Any form of psychotherapy done with more than one client/patient at a time. Group therapy is often done from a humanistic perspective.

Self-help groups: Therapy groups, such as Alcoholics Anonymous, that are organized and run by laypersons, rather than professional therapists.

A cognitive therapist would say that this student, depressed about a poor grade, may well stay depressed if he berates his own intelligence rather than reattributing the blame to the situation—a tough test.

death, and to adjust to the terminal illness (Adams, 1979; Yalom & Greaves, 1977). One general focus of such support groups for the terminally ill is to help them learn "how to live fully until you say goodbye" (Nungesser, 1990).

Marital and Family Therapy Sometimes the best group in which to learn about relationships is a group beset by problem relationships—as we see in groups composed of dysfunctional couples and families. *Couples counseling* (or therapy), for example, seeks to clarify the typical communication patterns of the partners and then to improve the quality of their interaction (Napier, 2000). By seeing a couple together (and sometimes videotaping and playing back their interactions) a therapist can help both partners appreciate the verbal and nonverbal styles they use to dominate, control, or confuse each other. Each party is taught how to reinforce desired responses in the other and withdraw reinforcement for undesirable reactions; they are also taught nondirective listening skills to help the other person clarify and express feelings and ideas (Dattilio & Padesky, 1990; O'Leary, 1987).

Couples therapy focuses not on the personalities involved but on the *processes* of their relationship, particularly their patterns of conflict and communication (Gottman, 1994; Greenberg & Johnson, 1988; Notarius & Markman, 1993). Ideally, both partners are willing to make some changes in the ways they think and behave and to take responsibility for their part in the relationship. Difficult as this may be, couples therapy can be much "easier" and more effective than efforts to change the basic personalities of the people involved. And, because both participants work together and support each other in reaching mutually desired goals, couples therapy is more effective in resolving marital problems and keeping marriages intact than is individual therapy with only one partner (Gottman, 1994).

In *family therapy,* the "client" is an entire nuclear family, and each family member is treated as a member of a *system* of relationships (Fishman, 1993). A family therapist helps troubled family members perceive the issues or patterns that are creating problems for them. The focus is on altering the psychological "spaces" between people and the interpersonal *dynamics* of people acting as a unit (Foley, 1979; Schwebel & Fine, 1994).

Family therapy can reduce tensions within a family and improve the functioning of individual members by helping them recognize the positives as well as the negatives in their relationships. Virginia Satir, an innovative developer of family therapy approaches, noted that the family therapist plays many roles, acting as an interpreter and clarifier of the interactions that take place in the therapy session and as influence agent, mediator, and referee (Satir, 1983; Satir et al., 1991). Family therapists focus on the *situational* rather than the *dispositional* aspects of a family's problem—for example, how one family member's unemployment affects everyone's feelings and relationships—rather than seeking to assign blame or label anyone as lazy or selfish. The goal of a family therapy meeting is not to have a "gripe session," but to develop constructive, cooperative problem solving together.

COGNITIVE THERAPY Most insight therapies emphasize changing people's emotional and motivational disturbances, while **cognitive therapy** sees rational *thinking* as the key to therapeutic change. Cognitive therapy does not neglect feelings or motives, but it does not focus on them directly. The underlying assumption of such therapy is that abnormal behavior patterns and emotional distress start with problems in *what* we think (cognitive content) and *how*

Cognitive therapy: Emphasizes rational thinking (as opposed to subjective emotion, motivation, or repressed conflicts) as the key to treating mental disorder.

we think (cognitive process). Cognitive therapy takes several forms, but we will discuss only two examples here: Aaron Beck's *cognitive therapy for depression* and Albert Ellis's *rational–emotive therapy*.

Connection

Chapter 12
Along with bipolar disorder, depression is one of the *mood disorders*.

Cognitive Therapy for Depression   Depressed patients commonly repeat to themselves such self-destructive thoughts as, "Nobody would like me if they really knew me" and "I'm not smart enough to make it in this competitive school." Aaron Beck believes that their depression occurs because of negative self-talk. Accordingly, "The therapist helps the patient to identify his warped thinking and to learn more realistic ways to formulate his experiences" (Beck, 1976, p. 20). Beck and his followers may instruct depressed individuals to write down negative thoughts about themselves, figure out why these self-criticisms are unjustified, and come up with more realistic (and less destructive) self-cognitions. From here, cognitive therapists rely on specific tactics to change the cognitive foundation that supports the depression. These tactics include the following suggestions from Beck and his colleagues (1979):

▶ Evaluating the *evidence* the patient has for and against these automatic thoughts ("But I always did well in math before; I can't be stupid")

▶ Reattributing blame to *situational factors* rather than to the patient's incompetence ("I had a disagreement with my roommate the night before the math test")

▶ Openly discussing *alternative solutions* to the problem ("I could study math between my two afternoon classes")

Research shows that such an approach can be at least as effective in the treatment of depression as is medication (Antonuccio, 1995).

Rational–Emotive Behavior Therapy   Another form of cognitive therapy is that developed by Albert Ellis (1987, 1990, 1996) to help a broad spectrum of unhappy clients eliminate ineffective, self-defeating thought patterns. Ellis dubbed his treatment **rational–emotive behavior therapy (REBT).** The name derives from its aim to change troubling emotional problems by attacking and modifying the client's basic "irrational" beliefs and behaviors.

What are these irrational beliefs, and how do they lead to maladaptive feelings and actions? According to Ellis, maladjusted individuals base their lives on a set of unrealistic values and unachievable goals. These "neurotic" goals and values lead people to hold unrealistic expectations that they should *always* succeed, that they should *always* receive approval, that they should *always* be treated fairly, and that their experiences should *always* be pleasant. (You can see the most common irrational beliefs in the accompanying box, "Do It Yourself! Examining Your Own Beliefs.") For example, in your own daily life, you may frequently tell yourself what you "should" get an A in math or that you "ought to" spend an hour exercising every day. If you are unable to meet your goals and seldom question this neurotic self-talk, it may come to control your actions or even prevent you from choosing the life you want. If you were to enter REBT, your therapist would teach you to recognize such assumptions, question how rational they are, and replace faulty ideas with more valid ones. Don't "should" on yourself, says Ellis.

A rational–emotive behavior therapist attempts to alter a client's irrational thinking by showing that an emotional reaction to an event may spring from unrecognized *beliefs* about the event, rather than the event itself. For example, a client behaves in a possessive and clingy way toward a romantic partner when that partner seems less interested or is distracted. According to Ellis, this emotional overreaction may be activated by a neurotic need for continual reminders of love and approval. Signs that the other person is pulling

It may be obvious that the following are not healthy beliefs, but Albert Ellis finds that many people hold them. Do you? Be honest: Put a check mark beside each of the following statements that accurately describes how you feel about yourself.

_____ 1. I must be loved and approved by everyone.

_____ 2. I must be thoroughly competent, adequate, and achieving.

_____ 3. It is catastrophic when things do not go the way I want them to go.

_____ 4. Unhappiness results from forces over which I have no control.

_____ 5. People must always treat each other fairly and justly; those who don't are nasty and terrible people.

_____ 6. I must constantly be on my guard against dangers and things that could go wrong.

_____ 7. Life is full of problems, and I must always find quick solutions to them.

_____ 8. It is easier to evade my problems and responsibilities than to face them.

_____ 9. Unpleasant experiences in my past have had a profound influence on me. Therefore, they must continue to influence my current feelings and actions.

_____ 10. I can achieve happiness by just enjoying myself each day. The future will take care of itself.

In Ellis's view, all these statements are irrational beliefs that can cause mental problems. His cognitive approach to therapy, known as rational–emotive behavior therapy, concentrates on helping people see that they "drive themselves crazy" with these irrational beliefs. For example, a person who is depressed about not landing a certain job probably holds irrational belief #3 above. You can obtain more information on Ellis's system from his books.

---

away are unreasonably interpreted to mean, "My partner will leave me if I don't take emergency action." Experiencing a real breakup may prompt the irrational thought that "Without this person to love me, I'll have no one in my life at all!" In REBT, these beliefs are openly disputed through rational confrontation and examination of alternative reasons for the event.

Now research suggests that these cognitive therapies may enable the mind to change the brain itself, not only for problems with relationships, but for conditions such as obsessive–compulsive disorder. Patients who suffered from obsessions about whether they had turned off their stoves, for example, were given cognitive behavior modification (Schwartz et al., 1996). When they felt an urge to run home and check the stove, they were trained to *relabel* their experience as an obsession or compulsion—not a rational concern. They then focused on waiting out this "urge" rather than giving in to it, by distracting themselves with other activities for about 15 minutes (Begley & Biddle, 1996). Positron emission tomography (PET) scans of the brains of subjects who were trained in this technique indicated that, over time, the part of the brain responsible for that nagging fear or urge gradually became less active (Schwartz et al., 1996). Thus, the mind can apparently "fix the brain."

Cognitive–Behavioral Therapy: A Synthesis

Suppose you are having difficulty controlling feelings of jealousy every time your mate is friendly with someone else. Chances are that the problem origi-

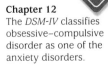

Connection

Chapter 12
The *DSM-IV* classifies obsessive–compulsive disorder as one of the anxiety disorders.

Rational-emotive behavior therapy (REBT): Albert Ellis's brand of cognitive therapy, based on the idea that irrational thoughts and behaviors are the cause of mental disorders.

nates in your *cognitions* about yourself and the others involved ("Marty is stealing Terry away from me!") But these thoughts probably affect your *behavior,* too—making you act in ways that could drive Terry away from you. A dose of therapy aimed at *both* your cognitions and behaviors may be a better bet than either one alone. This is the two-pronged thrust of **cognitive–behavioral therapy.**

In brief, cognitive–behavioral therapy combines a cognitive emphasis on thoughts and attitudes with behavioral strategies that alter reinforcement contingencies. This approach assumes that an irrational *self-statement* is the cause of maladaptive behavior. For example, an addicted smoker might automatically tell himself, "One more cigarette won't hurt me," "I'll go crazy if I don't have a smoke now," or even "I can quit any time I want—I just don't want to." Before unacceptable behavior patterns can be modified, the individual's irrational self-statements must be changed or replaced with rational, constructive coping statements. ("I can get through this craving if I distract myself with something else I like to do, like going to a movie.") Then, the therapist and client work together to set attainable goals, develop realistic strategies for attaining them, and evaluate the results. In this way, people change the way they approach problems and gradually develop a sense of mastery and *self-efficacy* (Bandura, 1986, 1992; Schwarzer, 1992). Indeed, PET scans show that cognitive–behavioral therapy can produce fundamental changes in the way the brain responds to events (Schwartz et al., 1996).

Evaluating the Psychological Therapies

Now that we have looked at a variety of psychotherapies (see Figure 13.4), let us step back and ask how well psychotherapy works. Does it make a difference? Are some kinds better than others? The issue of therapy's effectiveness has been disputed for over a half century, but we now have evidence that it works (Kopta et al., 1999; Shadish et al., 2000).

The dispute came to a head in 1952, when British psychologist Hans Eysenck (1952) shook the therapeutic world with the claim that roughly two-thirds of all people with nonpsychotic problems recover spontaneously within two years of the onset of the problem, whether they get therapy or not. If true, this meant that psychotherapy was essentially worthless—little better than no treatment at all. Eysenck's evidence came from a review of several outcome studies of various kinds of insight therapy.

As you might expect, Eysenck's claim hit a raw nerve with therapists. But, right or wrong, it had a most important result: It stimulated therapists to respond with a flurry of research on the effectiveness of therapy. One of the main questions they put to the test was this: Does therapy *really* help—or is therapy simply a kind of *placebo,* a behavioral sugar pill that only "works" because the individual expects it to?

In fact, the placebo effect probably accounts for some of the success in therapy. After all, for therapies to work, people must believe in them. Many psychologists and psychiatrists believe that the key placebo ingredients in any therapy's success are a patient's belief that therapy will help and a therapist's social influence in conveying this suggestion (Fish, 1973). For psychiatrist Jerome Frank (Frank, 1973, 1990; Frank & Frank, 1991), "belief is really crucial . . . because without the belief the person does not participate in any real way" (Frank, 1990).

Reviews of the research on therapeutic effectiveness were reported in 1970 (by Meltzoff & Kornreich) and in 1975 (by Luborsky et al.). And, by 1977, the list of outcome studies numbered some 375, all of which were surveyed in

Connection

Chapter 5
Placebos may imitate psychological treatments —not just drugs. Either way, they work because of expectations.

Cognitive-behavioral therapy: A newer form of psychotherapy that combines the techniques of cognitive therapy with those of behavioral therapy.

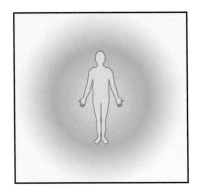

Behavior therapy
aims to change things *outside the individual*: rewards, punishments, and cues in the environment in order to change the person's external behaviors

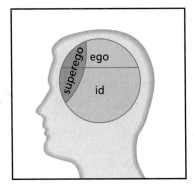

Psychodynamic therapies
aim to make changes *inside the person's mind*, especially the unconscious.

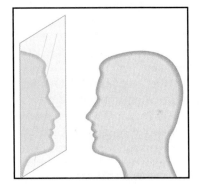

Humanistic therapies
aim to change the way people *see themselves.*

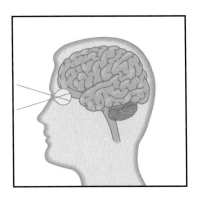

Cognitive therapies
aim to change the way people *think and perceive.*

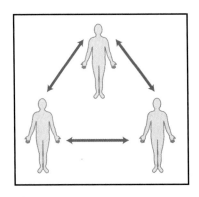

Group therapies
aim to change the way people *interact.*

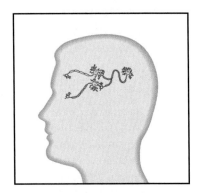

Biomedical therapies
aim to change the structure or function of the brain.

a monumental analysis by Smith and Glass. While their work substantiated Eysenck's estimate of improvement in two-thirds of those in therapy, Smith and Glass found that he had *over*estimated the improvement rate in no-therapy controls. Everything pointed to the conclusion that therapy is, after all, more effective than no therapy. By 1980 a consensus supporting the value of psychotherapy had emerged (Meredith, 1986; VandenBos, 1986). More recent evaluations of psychotherapy have also reported positive results in a variety of cultural settings throughout the world (Beutler & Machado, 1992; Lipsey & Wilson, 1993). A number of writers caution, however, that therapists must be sensitive to cultural differences and adapt their techniques appropriately (Matsumoto, 1996; Shiraev & Levy, 2001).

The new studies have, however, raised new issues. First, while they found that therapy is often effective, they also found most forms of insight therapy essentially equivalent in their effectiveness. This may be because effective therapists share a common core of characteristics and methods. Carl Rogers (1957) suggested the "necessary and sufficient conditions" for therapy: warmth (*unconditional positive regard*), empathy, and genuineness. Others would add another requirement: An effective therapist helps clients organize their thoughts about their problems (Frank, 1973, 1982). Using the *meta-analysis* technique, which combines information from many studies, researchers find that a common element in successful therapy is a caring, hopeful relationship and a new way of looking at oneself and the world (Barker et al., 1988; Jones et al., 1988). This conclusion has been supported by a more recent study which found that the effectiveness of therapy depended less on the specific *type* of therapy employed and more on the *quality of the relationship* between therapist and client (Blatt, Sanislow, & Pilkonis, 1996).

Based on their broad survey of the research, Smith and Glass (1977) found the behavioral therapies had an advantage over insight therapies for the treatment of many disorders. More recent evaluations have found insight therapies can also be used effectively to treat certain problems, such as marital discord and depression (see Table 13.3). In general, the trend in psychological therapy is toward matching specific therapies to specific conditions — such as behavior therapy for the treatment of phobias.

It is important to realize, however, that these therapeutic techniques do not necessarily "cure" psychological disorders. In some cases — schizophrenia, mental retardation, or autism, for example — psychological therapies may be deemed effective when people suffering from these afflictions learn more adaptive behaviors (Hogarty et al., 1997; Lovaas, 1993; Wolpe, 1985).

The past decade has also seen a trend toward blending psychological and medical therapies. As we have noted, some studies suggest that for depression, cognitive–behavioral therapy and drug therapy combined can have a greater effect than either treatment alone (Keller et al., 2000). Currently, therapists are testing combination medical and psychological therapies for schizophrenia, obsessive–compulsive disorder, drug and alcohol problems, panic disorder, and a variety of other disorders.

Whatever the approach, most patients or clients seem to *like* therapy. This was shown in a survey involving thousands of subscribers of *Consumer Reports* (1995). Respondents indicated how much their treatment helped, how satisfied they were with the therapist's treatment of their problems, how much their "overall emotional state" changed following therapy, as well as what kind of therapy they had undergone. For about 3,000 of the 7,000 respondents, therapy consisted of talking to friends, to relatives, or to clergy (as might be expected from our discussion earlier in this chapter). Another 2,900 saw a mental health professional; the rest saw family doctors or support groups. Among the results: (a) Therapy works — that is, it was perceived to have helped clients diminish or eliminate their psychological problems; (b) long-term therapy is better than short-term therapy; and (c) all forms of therapy are about equally effective for improving clients' problems (see Jacobson & Christensen, 1996; Kazdin, 1986; Seligman, 1995). We can't give a thumbs-up, however, to therapy merely because patients say they like it or that it helped them (Hollon, 1996).

During the past decade, the American Psychological Association has sponsored a special task force charged with evaluating psychological therapies (Chambless et al., 1996; Nathan, 1998; "Task Force," 1993). The thrust of the task force reports is that more and more specific disorders — literally dozens of them — can be treated successfully by specific therapies, as demonstrated in well-designed experiments (Barlow, 1996). (Many of the disorders for which psychological therapies exist are listed in Table 13.3.) Still, the number of disorders with clearly proven treatments is small, compared to the list in the *DSM-IV*. In addition, most people who seek psychotherapy do not do so because they suffer from a *DSM-IV* disorder but rather to find purpose and meaning in their lives (Strupp, 1996).

Connection

Chapter 9
Masters and Johnson developed effective behavioral therapies for a variety of sexual disorders.

TABLE 13.3	Demonstrably Effective Therapies	
TYPE OF THERAPY	**PROBLEM OR DISORDER**	**SUPPORTING REFERENCES**
Behavior therapy	Specific phobias	Leitenberg & Callahan (1973)
	Generalized anxiety disorder	Kazdin & Wilcoxin (1976)
	Alcohol and drug addictions	Barlow et al. (1992)
	Enuresis (bedwetting)	Miller & Brown (1997)
	Autism	Kupfersmid (1989)
	Male erectile dysfunction	Lovaas (1993)
	Female orgasmic dysfunction	Auerbach & Kilmann (1977)
	Panic disorder	LoPiccolo & Stock (1986)
	Obsessive–compulsive disorder	Barlow et al. (1989)
	Posttraumatic Stress Disorder	Marks & O'Sullivan (1988)
		Fals-Stewart et al. (1993)
		Foa et al. (1991)
		Keane et al. (1989)
Cognitive–behavioral therapy	Depression	Antonuccio (1995)
	Bulimia	Dobson (1989)
	Panic disorder	Lewinsohn et al. (1989)
	Generalized anxiety disorder	Thackwray et al. (1993)
	Chronic pain	Barlow et al. (1989)
	Agoraphobia	Butler et al. (1991)
	Social phobia	Keefe et al. (1992)
	Marital discord	Clark et al. (1994)
		Heimberg et al. (1990)
		Jacobson & Follette (1985)
		Gottman (1999)
Insight therapy	Bulimia	Fairburn et al. (1993)
	Depression	Elkin et al. (1989)
	Marital discord	Snyder et al. (1991)

Note: This is only a sampling of effective psychological therapies and the supporting literature. Readers interested in more extensive listings are directed to Chambless et al. (1996) and the report of the Task Force on Promotion and Dissemination of Psychological Procedures (1993).

Psychology

In Your Life

Where Do Most People Get Help?

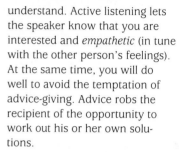

The effectiveness of psychotherapy for a variety of problems seems to be established beyond doubt. Having said that, we should again acknowledge that most people experiencing mental distress do not turn to professional therapists for help. Rather they turn to "just people" in the community (Wills & DePaulo, 1991). Those suffering from mental problems often look to friends, ministers, hairdressers, bartenders, and others with whom they have a trusting relationship. In fact, for some types of problems — perhaps the commonest problems of every-day living — a sympathetic friend may be just as effective as a trained professional therapist (Berman & Norton, 1985; Christensen & Jacobson, 1994). To put this in a different way: Most mental problems are not the crippling disorders described in the previous chapter. The psychological difficulties most of us face result from lost jobs, difficult marriages, misbehaving children, friendships gone sour, loved ones dying . . . In brief, the most familiar problems involve chaos, confusion, choice, frustration, stress, and loss. People who find themselves in the throes of these difficulties may not need extensive psychotherapy, medication, or some other special treatment. They need someone to help them sort through the pieces of their problems. Usually this means that they turn to someone like you.

So, what can you do when someone asks you for help? First, you should realize that some problems may require professional emergency treatment. These include a suicide threat or an indication of intent to harm others. You should not delay getting competent help for someone with such tendencies. Second, remember that some therapy methods *do* require special training, especially those methods that call for drugs, cognitive–behavioral therapy techniques, or major intervention in peoples' lives and personalities, such as attempts to unveil unconscious conflicts. We urge you to learn as much as you can about these methods — but we strongly recommend that you leave them to the professionals. Some other techniques, however, are simply extensions of good human relationships, and they fall well within the layperson's abilities for mental "first aid." Briefly, we will consider three of these:

▶ *Listening.* You will rarely go wrong if you just listen. Sometimes listening is all the therapy a person in distress needs. It works by encouraging the speaker to organize a problem well enough to communicate it. As a result, those who talk out their problems frequently arrive at their own solutions. As an **active listener,** you take the role a step farther by giving the speaker *feedback:* nodding, maintaining an expression that shows interest, paraphrasing, and asking for clarification when you don't

understand. Active listening lets the speaker know that you are interested and *empathetic* (in tune with the other person's feelings). At the same time, you will do well to avoid the temptation of advice-giving. Advice robs the recipient of the opportunity to work out his or her own solutions.

▶ *Acceptance.* Nondirective therapists call this a *nonjudgmental attitude.* It means accepting the person and the problem as they are. It also means suppressing shock, disgust, or condemnation that would create a hostile climate for problem-solving.

▶ *Exploration of alternatives.* People under stress may see only one course of action, so you can help by identifying other potential choices and exploring the consequences of each. (You can point out that *doing nothing* is also a choice.) Remember that, in the end, the choice of action is not up to you but to the individual who owns the problem.

Beyond these basic helping techniques lies the territory of the trained therapist. We strongly advise you against trying out the therapy techniques discussed in this chapter for any of the serious psychological disorders discussed in the previous chapter or listed in the *DSM-IV.*

Active listener: A person who gives the speaker feedback in such forms as nodding, paraphrasing, maintaining an expression that shows interest, and asking questions for clarification.

1. **RECALL:** *Counterconditioning is based on the principles of*
   a. operant conditioning.
   b. classical conditioning.
   c. social learning.
   d. cognitive learning.

2. **APPLICATION:** *You could use contingency management to change the behavior of a child who comes home late for dinner by*
   a. pairing food with electric shocks.
   b. having the child observe someone else coming home on time and being rewarded.
   c. refusing to let the child have dinner.
   d. having the child relax and imagine being home on time for dinner.

3. **RECALL:** *The primary goal of psychoanalysis is to*
   a. change behavior.
   b. reveal problems in the unconscious.
   c. overcome low self-esteem.
   d. learn how to get along with others.

4. **RECALL:** *Carl Rogers invented a technique to help people see their own thinking more clearly. Using this technique, the therapist paraphrases the client's statements. Rogers called this*
   a. person-centered therapy.
   b. reflection of feeling.
   c. unconditional positive regard.
   d. self-actualization.

5. **RECALL:** *Which form of therapy directly confronts a client's self-defeating thought patterns?*
   a. humanistic therapy
   b. behavioral therapy
   c. social–learning therapy
   d. rational–emotive therapy

6. **RECALL:** *Eysenck caused a furor with his claim that people who receive psychotherapy*
   a. are just looking for a paid friend.
   b. really should seek medical treatment for their disorders.
   c. are usually just pampered rich people who have nothing better to do with their lives.
   d. get better no more often than people who receive no therapy at all.

7. **UNDERSTANDING THE CORE CONCEPT:**
   A phobia would be best treated by _____, while a problem of choosing a major would be better suited for _____.
   a. behavioral therapy/insight therapy
   b. cognitive therapy/psychoanalysis
   c. insight therapy/behavioral therapy
   d. humanistic therapy/behavioral therapy

ANSWERS: 1. b   2. c   3. b   4. b
5. d   6. d   7. a

Key Question

HOW IS THE BIOMEDICAL APPROACH USED TO TREAT MENTAL DISORDERS?

The ecology of the mind is held in a delicate biological balance. It can be upset by irregularities in our genes, hormones, enzymes, and metabolism, as well as by damage from accidents and disease. When something goes wrong with the brain, we can see the consequences in abnormal patterns of behavior or peculiar cognitive and emotional reactions. Based on these assumptions, the biomedical therapies attempt to treat mental disorders by treating the dysfunctional brain. As our Core Concept says, they do this in three ways:

Core Concept

> Biomedical therapies seek to alter the structure or function of the brain through drugs, surgery, or electromagnetic stimulation.

Each of the biomedical therapies emerges from the *medical model* of abnormal mental functioning, which assumes an organic basis for mental illnesses and treats them as diseases. We begin our examination of these biomedical therapies with the powerful arsenal of prescription psychoactive drugs.

Drug Therapy

In the history of the treatment of mental disorder, nothing has ever rivaled the revolution created by the discovery of drugs that could calm anxious patients, restore contact with reality in withdrawn patients, and suppress hallucinations in psychotic patients. This new therapeutic era began in 1953 with the introduction of "tranquilizing" drugs, notably *chlorpromazine* (Thorazine), into mental hospital treatment programs. As more psychoactive drugs came on line, unruly, assaultive patients became cooperative, calm, and sociable. Thought-disordered patients who had been absorbed in their delusions and hallucinations began to respond to the real physical and social environment around them. No longer did mental hospital staff have to act as guards, putting patients in seclusion or straitjackets, so staff morale also improved (Swazey, 1974).

The effectiveness of drug therapy had a pronounced effect on the census of the nation's mental hospitals. In 1955, over half a million Americans were living in mental institutions, staying an average of several years. Then, with the introduction of *chlorpromazine* and other drugs, the numbers began a steady decline. In just over ten years, less than half the country's mental patients actually resided in mental hospitals, and those who did were institutionalized for an average of only a few months.

Drug therapy has long since steamrolled out of the mental hospital and into our everyday lives. Currently, millions of people take drugs for anxiety, stress, depression, hyperactivity, insomnia, fears and phobias, obsessions and compulsions, addictions, and numerous other problems.

Who can prescribe psychoactive drugs? Most prescriptions are filled by physicians (often by general practitioners who lack expertise in mental disorder). The law also allows psychiatric nurse practitioners to prescribe. In addition, a few clinical psychologists have earned prescription privileges through special medical programs (Hayes & Heiby, 1996; Rabasca, 1999; Smith, 2000).

Clearly, a drug-induced revolution occurred. But what are these miraculous drugs? You have probably heard of Prozac and Valium, but these are just two of scores of psychoactive drugs that can alter your mood, your perceptions, your desires, and perhaps your basic personality. Here we will consider four major categories of drugs used today: *antipsychotics, antidepressants, antianxiety drugs,* and *stimulants.* We will look at each category in turn.

ANTIPSYCHOTIC DRUGS By dampening delusions, hallucinations, social withdrawal, and agitation, the **antipsychotic drugs** diminish the symptoms of psychosis (Dawkins et al., 1999; Gitlin, 1990; Holmes, 2001; Kane & Marder, 1993). Most work by reducing the activity of the neurotransmitter dopamine in the brain. Specifically, *chlorpromazine* (Thorazine) and *haloperidol* (Haldol), for example, are known to block dopamine receptors in the synapse between nerve cells. A newer antipsychotic drug, *clozapine* (Clozaril), both decreases dopamine activity and increases the activity of another neurotransmitter, serotonin, which inhibits the dopamine system. Though these drugs reduce overall brain activity, they do not merely "tranquilize" the patient. They reduce the positive symptoms of schizophrenia that we have listed, although they do little for the social distance, jumbled thoughts, and poor attention spans seen in

Connection

Chapter 12
The *medical model* approaches mental disorders much as medicine deals with physical diseases.

Connection

Chapter 3
All drugs used to treat mental disorders are psychoactive drugs.

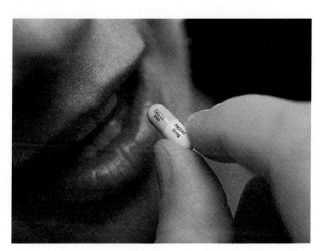

What will be the effect of prescribing mood-altering drugs such as Prozac to millions of people?

Antipsychotic drugs: Medicines that diminish psychotic symptoms, usually by their effect on the dopamine pathways in the brain.

Connection

Chapter 2
Dopamine is a transmitter used in many parts of the brain, notably the "pleasure centers."

Connection

Chapter 12
"Positive" symptoms of schizophrenia include active hallucinations, delusions, and extreme emotions.

patients with "negative" symptoms of schizophrenia (Wickelgren, 1998b). Because of their powerful and wide-reaching effects on behavior and personality, these drugs are sometimes called "major tranquilizers."

Unfortunately, long-term administration of antipsychotic drugs has several negative side effects. Physical changes in the brain have been noted (Gur & Maany, 1998). Most worrisome is **tardive dyskinesia,** an incurable disturbance of motor control (especially of the facial muscles) caused by antipsychotic drugs. Although the newer drug, clozapine, has reduced motor side effects because of its more selective dopamine blocking, its use involves a small risk of *agranulocytosis,* a rare blood disease caused by bone marrow dysfunction. With the possibility of such side effects, are antipsychotic drugs worth the risk? There is no easy answer. The risks must be weighed against the severity of the patient's current suffering. And, while it is true that there is no *cure* for schizophrenia, appropriate drug treatments can promote great relief and symptom reduction in many cases.

ANTIDEPRESSANT AND ANTIMANIC DRUGS   The drug therapy arsenal includes several compounds that have revolutionized the treatment of depression and bipolar disorder. The **antidepressant drugs** work by "turning up the volume" among neurons using the transmitters norepinephrine and serotonin (Holmes, 2001). *Tricyclic* compounds such as Tofranil and Elavil reduce the body's reabsorption of neurotransmitters after they have been released in the synapse between brain cells. The famous antidepressant, Prozac (fluoxetine), is part of a group of drugs that allow serotonin to work longer in the synapse. For many people, this prolonged serotonin effect dramatically lifts depressed moods (Hirschfeld, 1999; Kramer, 1993). But some critics warn it may also "relieve" patients of their personality and creativity (Breggin & Breggin, 1994). Another group of antidepressant drugs includes *monoamine oxidase (MAO) inhibitors,* which limit the activity of the enzyme MAO, a chemical that breaks down norepinephrine. When MAO is inhibited, more norepinephrine is available in the body.

A simple chemical, **lithium carbonate** has proved highly effective in the treatment of bipolar disorder (Schou, 1997). Lithium is not just an antidepressant, however, because it affects both ends of the emotional spectrum, dampening swings of mood from uncontrollable periods of hyperexcitement to the lethargy and despair of depression. Lithium, unfortunately, has its drawbacks: In high concentrations, it has proved toxic. Physicians have learned that safe therapy requires that small doses be given to build up therapeutic concentrations of lithium in the blood over a period of a week or two. Then, as a precaution, patients must have periodic blood analyses to assure that lithium concentrations have not risen to dangerous levels. Additionally, the drug can cause stomach problems and other physical complications for some patients. Aside from these side effects, the other difficulty with lithium therapy is the reluctance of some patients to take their medicine. Why? Some enjoy the "high" feeling that accompanies the manic excitement phase of their disorder.

In a welcome development, researchers have found a promising alternative to lithium for the treatment of bipolar disorder (Azar, 1994a; Walden et al., 1998). A drug called *divalproex sodium* (sold under the brand name Depakote), originally developed to treat epilepsy, seems to be more effective than lithium, but with fewer dangerous side effects (Bowden et al., 2000).

The wide and enthusiastic use of mood-altering medications, including those for depression and bipolar disorder, has provoked controversy. Some studies suggest that these drugs simply have a placebo effect (Eserink, 1999; Fisher & Greenberg, 1995; Horgan, 1999; Kirsch & Sapirstein, 1998). Never-

Connection

Chapter 2
The synapse is a microscopic gap between a neuron and an organ or muscle.

Connection

Chapter 12
Bipolar disorder causes mood swings, from mania to depression.

Tardive dyskinesia: An incurable disorder of motor control, especially involving muscles of the face and head, resulting from long-term use of antipsychotic drugs.

Antidepressant drugs: Medicines that affect depression, usually by their effect on the serotonin and/or norepinephrine pathways in the brain.

Lithium carbonate: a simple chemical compound that is highly effective in dampening the extreme mood swings of bipolar disorder.

theless, drug therapy has changed psychiatry by shifting the emphasis away from traditional psychotherapy (Barondes, 1994).

In his book *Listening to Prozac,* psychiatrist and Prozac advocate Peter Kramer (1993) encourages the use of the drug to deal not only with depression but with general feelings of social unease and fear of rejection. Such claims have brought heated replies from therapists who fear that drugs may merely mask the psychological problems that people need to face and resolve. Some worry that the wide use of antidepressants may produce fundamental changes in the personality structure of a huge segment of our population — changes that could bring unanticipated, and possibly unwelcome, social consequences (Sleek, 1994). In fact, more prescriptions are being written for antidepressants than there are people who are clinically depressed (Coyne, 2001). With an estimated 900,000 prescriptions for Prozac filled in the United States each month (Brown & Epperson, 1993), we must ask: What are the potential dangers of altering the brain chemistry of large numbers of people over long periods?

ANTIANXIETY DRUGS   To reduce stress and suppress anxiety associated with everyday hassles, untold millions of Americans take pills. In general, these **antianxiety drugs** work by sedating the user (Holmes, 2001; Schatzberg, 1991). And, if used over long periods, these drugs can be physically and psychologically addicting. Many psychologists believe that the antianxiety drugs, like the antidepressants, are too often prescribed for problems that people should face, rather than mask with chemicals. Nevertheless, antianxiety compounds can be useful in helping people deal with specific situations, such as anxiety prior to major surgery.

Certain drugs work best to alleviate certain disorders (Spiegel et al., 2000). Oddly, some antidepressant drugs have also been found useful for reducing the symptoms of certain anxiety disorders such as panic disorders, agoraphobia, and obsessive–compulsive disorder. Because these problems may arise from low levels of serotonin, they may also respond well to drugs like Prozac that specifically affect serotonin function. The most commonly prescribed classes of antianxiety compounds, however, are *barbiturates* and *benzodiazepines.* Barbiturates are central nervous system (CNS) depressants; they have a relaxing effect, but they can be dangerous if taken in excess or in combination with alcohol. Benzodiazepine drugs, such as Valium and Xanax, work by increasing the activity of the neurotransmitter GABA, thereby decreasing activity in brain regions more specifically involved in feelings of anxiety. The benzodiazepines are sometimes called "minor tranquilizers."

Here are some *cautions* to bear in mind about the antianxiety drugs (Hecht, 1986):

▶ These medicines should not be taken to relieve anxieties that are part of the ordinary stresses of everyday life.

▶ When used for extreme anxiety, these drugs should not normally be taken for more than a week or two at a time. If used longer than this, their dosage should be gradually reduced by a physician. Abrupt cessation can lead to *withdrawal symptoms,* such as convulsions, tremors, and abdominal and muscle cramps.

▶ Because the antianxiety drugs depress the central nervous system, they can impair one's ability to drive, operate machinery, or perform other tasks that require alertness (such as studying or taking exams).

▶ In combination with alcohol (also a central nervous system depressant) or with sleeping pills, antianxiety drugs can lead to unconsciousness and even death.

Connection

Chapter 10
Stress can cause both physical and mental disorders.

Connection

Chapter 3
Many critics believe that the "minor tranquilizers" are overprescribed by physicians.

Antianxiety drugs: A category of drugs that includes the *barbiturates* and *benzodiazepines,* drugs that diminish feelings of anxiety.

Connection

Chapter 3
Narcolepsy is a REM-sleep disorder involving sudden daytime sleep attacks.

Connection

Chapter 3
Stimulants increase activity level in the brain.

STIMULANTS We have noted that **stimulants** find some use in the treatment of *narcolepsy.* They also have an accepted niche in treating **attention-deficit/hyperactivity disorder (ADHD),** a common problem in children who have difficulty controlling their behavior and focusing their attention. While it may seem odd to prescribe stimulants for hyperactive children, studies comparing stimulant therapy with behavior therapy and with *placebos* have shown a clear advantage for stimulants (Henker & Whalen, 1989; Poling et al., 1991; Welsh et al., 1993). They may work in hyperactive children by increasing the availability of dopamine and/or serotonin in their brains (Barkley, 1998; Gainetdinov et al., 1999; Wu, 1998).

As you can imagine, the use of stimulants to treat hyperactive children has generated heated controversy (Whalen & Henker, 1991). Some objections, of course, stem from ignorance of the well-established calming effect these drugs have in children with this condition. But some of the controversy also arises from the legitimate concern that the causes and boundaries of ADHD are vague and that a potential exists for excessive diagnosis (Alford & Bishop, 1991; Angold et al., 2000; Marshall, 2000). Critics charge that any troublesome youngster risks being labeled with attention-deficit/hyperactivity disorder and started on stimulant therapy. They also worry that the prescription of stimulants might encourage drug abuse in children.

As with any drug therapy, it is important to monitor the patient's progress when prescribing stimulants to treat ADHD. For some, the drug will interfere with normal sleep patterns. For others, especially when the dosage is too high, the patient will become withdrawn and engage in repetitive, autistic-like behaviors (Solanto & Connors, 1982). Additionally, there is some controversial evidence that stimulant therapy might slow the growth of children taking these drugs (Klein et al., 1988).

EVALUATING THE DRUG THERAPIES The drug therapies have caused a revolution in the treatment of severe mental disorders, starting in the 1950s, when virtually the only treatments available were talk therapies, hospitalization, restraints, "shock treatment," and lobotomies. Drugs don't "cure" mental disorders, of course, but they sometimes alter the brain's chemistry to reduce or eliminate people's symptoms. Currently, millions of people have prescriptions for one of these drugs. Many cannot imagine facing their lives without their Prozac or Valium.

But is all the enthusiasm warranted? No, says neuroscientist Elliot Valenstein (Rolnick, 1998; Valenstein, 1998). The closer we look at the evidence, the more gaps we find. Valenstein credits the wide acceptance of drug therapy to the huge investment drug companies have made in marketing their products.

The apparent advantages of drug therapy over psychotherapy are quick results and lower cost. New research, however, questions these assumptions. For many conditions, including depression, anxiety disorders, and eating disorders, specifically tailored psychotherapy is both more effective and economical in the long run (Clay, 2000). From the medical therapist's perspective, however, it can be far more profitable to prescribe medication to six patients in an hour (each for a 10-minute visit) than to proffer psychotherapy to one person per hour (Karon, 1999).

Another reason to dampen our enthusiasm for drug therapies comes from the lack of effective drugs for some of the most common psychological problems, such as stress on the job or child-rearing difficulties. For many other problems, such as depression and obsessive–compulsive disorder, purely psychological treatments may do as well or better than drugs (Barlow, 1996; Hollon, 1996). In fact, both approaches to treatment may have similar effects on

Stimulants: Drugs that normally increase activity level by encouraging communication among neurons in the brain. Stimulants, however, have been found to suppress activity level in persons with attention-deficit/hyperactivity disorder.

Attention-deficit/hyperactivity disorder (ADHD): A common problem in children who have difficulty controlling their behavior and focusing their attention.

In medieval times, those suffering from madness were sometimes treated by cutting "the stone of folly" from their brains.

the brain (Miller, 1995). The moral of the story — as it is written in the research so far — is not to put all your faith in drug therapies.

Psychosurgery

The headline in the *Los Angeles Times* read, "Bullet in the Brain Cures Man's Mental Problem" (February 23, 1988). The article revealed that a 19-year-old man suffering from severe obsessive–compulsive disorder had shot a .22 caliber bullet through the front of his brain in a suicide attempt. Remarkably, he survived, his pathological symptoms were gone, and his intellectual capacity was not affected, even though some of the underlying causes of his problems remained.

This case illustrates the potential effects of physical intervention in the brain. With scalpels in place of bullets, surgeons have attempted to treat mental disorders by severing connections between parts of the brain or by removing small sections of brain. **Psychosurgery,** the general term for such procedures, is often considered a method of last resort to treat psychopathologies that have proven intractable with other, less extreme forms of therapy. Ongoing, heated controversy surrounds their usefulness and their side effects, as well as the ethics of taking such drastic measures to change behavior.

Psychosurgery has a long history, dating back to Stone Age openings of the skull, presumably to release pressure caused by head wounds (Maher & Maher, 1985). In medieval times, surgeons opened the skull to cut "the stone of folly" from the brains of those suffering from madness, as shown vividly in engravings and paintings from that era. (There is, of course, no such "stone" — and there was no anesthetic for these procedures.) Miraculously, many of the patients survived these treatments.

In modern times, the best-known form of psychosurgery involved the now-abandoned prefrontal lobotomy — an operation that severed certain nerve fibers connecting the frontal lobes with deep brain structures, especially those of the thalamus and hypothalamus — much as happened to Phineas Gage by accident. The original candidates for lobotomy were agitated schizophrenic patients and patients who were compulsive and anxiety ridden. The effects of this rather crude operation were often dramatic. A new personality emerged,

Psychosurgery: The general term for surgical intervention in the brain to treat psychological disorders.

Connection

Chapter 2
Phineas Gage survived — with a changed personality — after a steel rod was driven through his frontal lobe.

with less intense emotional arousal. However, the operation permanently destroyed basic aspects of their mental functioning — and of their human nature. Lobotomized patients usually lost something special: their unique personalities. Specifically, the lobotomy resulted in inability to plan ahead, indifference to the opinions of others, childlike actions, and the intellectual and emotional flatness of a person without a coherent sense of self. Because the new drug therapies promised to control psychotic symptoms with less risk of permanent damage, the era of lobotomy came to a close in the 1950s (Valenstein, 1980).

Psychosurgery is still occasionally done, but it is now much more limited to precise and proven procedures. We have seen, for example, that severing the fibers of the corpus callosum can reduce violent seizures in certain cases of epilepsy, with few side effects. Psychosurgery is also done on portions of the brain involved in pain perception in cases of otherwise incurable pain. However, no *DSM-IV* diagnoses are routinely treated with psychosurgery.

Electroconvulsive and Magnetic Therapies

Electrical stimulation of the brain in the form known as **electroconvulsive therapy (ECT)** is still widely used. The therapy consists of applying weak electric current (75 to 100 volts) to a patient's temples for a period of time from one-tenth to a full second, until a convulsion occurs. The convulsion usually runs its course in 45 to 60 seconds. Patients are prepared for this traumatic intervention by sedating them with a short-acting barbiturate and a muscle relaxant. This renders the patient unconscious and minimizes violent, uncontrolled physical spasms during the seizure (Abrams, 1992; Malitz & Sackheim, 1984). While ECT is not a panacea or cure-all, some studies have shown it to be useful in the treatment of certain psychiatric disorders, particularly severe depression (Sackheim et al., 2000).

One benefit of ECT, according to its practitioners, is that it works quickly: Typically the symptoms of depression are reduced in a three- or four-day course of treatment, in contrast with the one- to two-week period required for drug therapy to be effective. Speed can be a major concern in depression, where suicide is always a possibility. Nonetheless, because of its occasional side effects, many therapists regard ECT with suspicion, reserving it for depressed patients for whom drug therapy is ineffective. Critics also fear it might be abused — used to silence dissent or punish patients who are uncooperative (Holmes, 2001). Among scientists themselves, suspicion of ECT comes from the fact that its effects are not well understood. To date no definitive theory "explains" why inducing a mild convulsion should alleviate disordered symptoms.

What are the unwanted side effects of ECT? They include temporary disorientation and a variety of memory deficits (Breggin, 1979, 1991). However, proponents claim that patients generally recover their specific memories within months of the treatment (Calev et al., 1991). One study found that patients who had received over 100 ECT treatments showed no deficit in functioning compared with those who had never received ECT (Devanand et al., 1991). To minimize even short-term side effects, however, ECT is now often administered "unilaterally" to only the right temple, in order to reduce the possibility of speech impairment (Scovern & Kilmann, 1980). In the face of such concerns, the National Institute of Mental Health (1985) investigated the use of ECT and gave it a cautious endorsement for treating a narrow range of disorders. In 1990, the American Psychiatric Association followed suit. In fact, its use is now limited largely to the treatment of depression.

A promising new therapeutic tool for stimulating the brain with magnetic fields seems to offer the benefits of ECT without the unwanted side effects of

Connection

Chapter 2
The "split-brain" operation severs the corpus callosum — the fibers connecting the cerebral hemispheres.

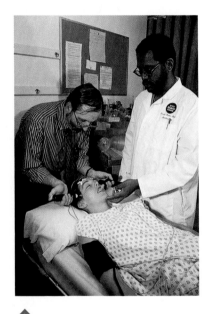

A sedated patient about to receive ECT. Electroconvulsive therapy applies a weak electrical current to a patient's temples, until a convulsion occurs. Some psychiatrists have found ECT successful in alleviating symptoms of severe depression, but it remains a treatment of last resort for most therapists.

Electroconvulsive therapy (ECT): A treatment used primarily for depression and involving the application of an electric current to the head, producing a generalized seizure. Sometimes called "shock treatment."

memory loss. Still in the experimental stages, **transcranial magnetic stimulation (TMS)** involves directing magnetic stimulation to specific parts of the brain. Studies indicate that TMS may be useful for treating not only depression but schizophrenia and bipolar disorder (George et al., 1999; Travis, 2000; Wassermann & Lisanby, 2001). Because most applications of TMS therapy do not require the induction of a seizure, researchers hope that it offers a safer alternative to ETC.

Hospitalization and the Alternatives

Originally mental hospitals were designed as places of refuge—"asylums"—where disturbed people could escape the pressures of normal living. In fact, they often worked very well (Maher & Maher, 1985). But by the 20th century these hospitals had become overcrowded and, at best, little more than warehouses for the mentally ill. A feeble form of "group therapy" was often done with a whole ward—perhaps 50 patients—at a time. But too many patients and too few therapists meant little, if any, real therapy occurred. The drugs that so profoundly altered treatment in mental hospitals did not appear until the 1950s, so prior to that time institutionalized patients were often controlled by straitjackets and locked rooms.

THE THERAPEUTIC COMMUNITY   Finally, in 1953—at about the time antipsychotic drugs were introduced—psychiatrist Maxwell Jones launched a frontal attack on the mental hospital system. He proposed its replacement with a **therapeutic community** designed to interrupt the cycle of illness and institutionalization. Jones intended that the daily hospital routine could, itself, become a therapy designed to help patients learn to cope with the world outside. With this goal in mind, he abolished the dormitory accommodations that had been typical of mental hospitals, and gave patients more private living quarters. He required that they make decisions about meals and daily activities. Then, as they were able to take more responsibilities, patients assumed the tasks of everyday living, including laundry, housekeeping, and maintenance. Further, Jones involved them in helping to plan their own treatment, which included not only group psychotherapy but occupational therapy and recreational therapy (Jones, 1953).

Eventually, variations on the therapeutic community concept were adopted across the United States, Canada, Britain, and Europe—often more on paper than in fact, as we saw in Rosenhan's "pseudopatient" study. But the changes did not come cheaply. The newer approach obviously required more staff and more costly facilities. The high costs led to a search for still another alternative, which came in the form of community-based treatment. Thus, more mental patients entered psychiatric wards at general medical hospitals in their own communities. As a result, hospital care continued to consume most funding for mental health in the United States. Currently, mental patients account for about 25% of all hospital days (Kiesler, 1982a,b, 1993).

And what has become of the therapeutic community? Most mental hospitals and mental wards in general hospitals have become holding places for patients whose medication is being adjusted. Although the abuse and gross neglect of earlier times is gone, very little nonmedical therapy occurs in most mental hospitals today.

DEINSTITUTIONALIZATION AND COMMUNITY MENTAL HEALTH   For mental health professionals of all stripes, the goal of **deinstitutionalization,** begun in the 1950s, was to remove patients from mental hospitals as quickly as possible and return them to their communities. The concept of deinstitutionaliza-

Transcranial magnetic stimulation (TMS): A treatment that involves magnetic stimulation of specific regions of the brain. Unlike ECT, TMS does not produce a seizure.

Therapeutic community: Jones's term for a program of treating mental disorder by making the institutional environment supportive and humane for patients.

Deinstitutionalization: The policy of removing patients, whenever possible, from mental hospitals.

Connection

Chapter 12
None of Rosenhan's pseudopatients was ever discovered to be normal by any hospital staff member.

Deinstitutionalization put mental patients back in the community— but often without adequate resources for continued treatment.

tion also gained popularity with politicians, who saw large sums of money being poured into mental hospitals (filled, incidentally, with nonvoting patients). Thus, a consensus formed among politicians and the mental health community that the major locus of treatment should shift from mental hospitals back to the community. There therapy would be dispensed from outpatient clinics, and recovering patients could live with their families, in foster homes, or in group homes. This vision became known as the **community mental health movement.**

Unfortunately, the reality did not match the vision (Torrey, 1996, 1997). Community mental health clinics—the centerpieces of the community mental health movement—never received full funding. Chronic patients were released from mental hospitals, but they often returned to communities that could offer them few therapeutic resources and to families ill-equipped to cope with them (Arnhoff, 1975; Smith et al., 1993). As a result, an estimated 150,000 patients, especially those with chronic schizophrenia, have ended up as homeless persons with no network of support (Torrey, 1997). Although estimates vary widely, up to 52 % of homeless men and 71 % of homeless women in the United States probably suffer from psychological disorders (Fischer & Breakey, 1991). Many also have problems with alcohol or other drugs (Drake et al., 1991). Under these conditions, they survive by shuttling from agency to agency. With no one to monitor their behavior, they usually stop taking their medication, and so their condition deteriorates until they require a period of rehospitalization. In fact, about 50 % of all patients released from public mental hospitals find their way back to a hospital again within a year (Kiesling, 1983).

Despite this dismal picture, community treatment has not proved altogether unsuccessful. When patients become integrated back into the community, it can be highly effective (McGuire, 2000). After a review of ten studies in which mental patients were randomly assigned to hospital treatment or to various community-based programs, Kiesler (1982a) reported that patients more often improved in the community treatment programs. Further, those given community-based treatment were less likely to be hospitalized at a later date. These results suggest that community treatment programs can work when they have been given the resources needed to extend a helping hand.

Community mental health movement: An effort to deinstitutionalize mental patients and to provide therapy from outpatient clinics. Proponents of community mental health envisioned that recovering patients could live with their families, in foster homes, or in group homes.

Psychology

In Your Life

What Sort of Therapy Would You Recommend?

Now that we have looked at both the psychological and medical therapies, consider the following situation. A friend tells you about some personal problems he or she is having and requests your help in finding a therapist. Because you are studying psychology, reasons your friend, you might know what kind of treatment would be best. How do you respond?

First, you can lend a friendly ear, using the techniques of active listening, acceptance, and exploration of alternatives, which we discussed earlier in the chapter. In fact, this may be all that your troubled friend needs. But, if the situation looks in any way like one that requires professional assistance, you can use your knowledge of mental disorders and therapies to help your friend decide what sort of therapist might be most appropriate.

To take some of the burden off your shoulders, both you and your friend should realize that any competent therapist will always refer the client elsewhere if the required therapy lies outside the therapist's specialty. Most cities and towns have specialists in marriage counseling, career counseling, treatment of phobic reactions, alcohol and drug treatment, sexual dysfunctions, and grief therapy.

A THERAPY CHECKLIST

Here, then, are some questions you will want to consider before you recommend a particular type of therapist.

▶ Is medical treatment needed? You should not try to make a diagnosis. Nevertheless, you should encourage your friend to see a psychiatrist for medical treatment if you suspect that the problem involves psychosis, extreme depression, mania, bipolar disorder, or the like. Medical evaluation is also indicated if you suspect narcolepsy, sleep apnea, epilepsy, Alzheimer's disease, or other problems that have a known biological basis. If your suspicion is confirmed, the psychiatrist may employ a combination of drug therapy and psychotherapy.

Even if you suspect a disorder that needs medical attention, however, you might refer your friend first to a clinical psychologist. Clinical psychologists all have extensive training in working on the psychological aspects of such problems. And most have established a work-

■ **Which therapy would you recommend to a friend?**

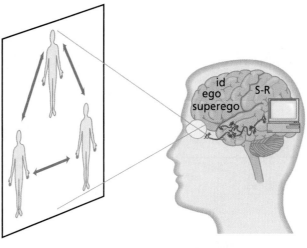

ing relationship with a physician, who can prescribe medication when necessary. You and your friend can get some guidance from *Talk to Someone Who Can Help,* available online from the APA at http://helping.apa.org/forms/brochure.cfm.

▶ Is there a specific behavioral problem? For example, does your friend want to eliminate a fear of spiders or a fear of flying? Is the problem a rebellious child? A sexual problem? Is she or he depressed—but not psychotic? If so, behavioral therapy (or cognitive–behavioral therapy) with a psychologist is probably the best bet. (Most psychiatrists and other medical practitioners are not trained in these procedures.) Call the prospective therapist's office and ask for information on specific areas of training and specialization.

▶ Would group therapy be helpful? Many people find valuable help and support in a group setting, where they can learn not only from the therapist but also from other group members. Groups can be especially helpful in dealing with shyness, lack of assertiveness, addictions, and with complex problems of interpersonal relationships. (As a bonus, group therapy is often less expensive than individual therapy.) Professionals with training in several disciplines, including

psychology, psychiatry, and social work, run therapy groups. Again, your best bet is a therapist who has had special training in this method and about whom you have heard good things from former clients.

▶ Is the problem one of stress, confusion, or choice? Most troubled people don't fall neatly into one of the categories that we have discussed in the previous paragraphs. More typically, they need help sorting through the chaos of their lives, finding a pattern, and developing a plan to cope. This is the territory of the insight therapies.

SOME CAUTIONS

We now know enough about human biology, behavior, and mental processes to know some treatments to avoid. People with problems should be especially wary of therapies that may produce addictions or unwanted side effects. Some specifics follow.

▶ *Drug therapies to avoid.* The minor tranquilizers are too frequently prescribed for patients leading chronically stressful lives (Alford & Bishop, 1991). As we have said, because of their addicting and sedating effects, these drugs should only be taken for short periods—if at all. Similarly, some physicians ignore the dangers of sleep-inducing medications for their patients who suffer from insomnia. While these drugs have legitimate uses, many such prescriptions carry the possibility of drug dependence and of interfering with the person's ability to alter the conditions that may have caused the original problem.

▶ *Advice and interpretations to avoid.* Although psychodynamic therapy can be helpful, patients should also be cautioned that

(continued)

some therapists may give ill-advised counsel in problems of anger management. Traditionally, Freudians have believed that individuals who are prone to angry or violent outbursts harbor deep-seated aggression that needs to be vented. But, as we have seen, research shows that trying to empty one's aggressions through aggressive behavior, such as shouting or punching a pillow, may actually increase the likelihood of later aggressive behavior.

Another danger in some therapies lies in digging up the psychological bones of the patient's past and fixing blame on people for human frailties. A replay of our grievances can renew feelings of resentment and ill will toward parents, relatives, and friends. A good therapist will help patients work through such feelings. A good therapist will also remind patients of the *reconstructive* nature of memory, pointing out that memory is notoriously unreliable and that sudden recollections of "repressed" emotional material from childhood may not accurately reflect actual events.

CHECKYOURUNDERSTANDING

1. **APPLICATION:** *Imagine that you are a psychiatrist. Which type of drug would you prescribe to a patient who has obsessive–compulsive disorder?*
   a. an antipsychotic drug
   b. lithium carbonate
   c. an antianxiety drug
   d. a stimulant

2. **RECALL:** *Which class of drugs blocks dopamine receptors in the brain?*
   a. antipsychotics
   b. antidepressants
   c. antianxiety drugs
   d. stimulants

3. **RECALL:** *A controversial treatment for attention-deficit/hyperactivity disorder involves*
   a. antipsychotics.
   b. antidepressants.
   c. antianxiety drugs.
   d. stimulants.

4. **RECALL:** *Which of the following medical treatments for mental disorder has now been largely abandoned as ineffective and dangerous?*
   a. electroconvulsive therapy
   b. lithium carbonate
   c. prefrontal lobotomy
   d. the "split-brain" operation

5. **RECALL:** *The community mental health movement followed a deliberate plan of _____ mental patients.*
   a. hospitalizing
   b. deinstitutionalizing
   c. administering insight therapy to
   d. removing stressful events in the lives of

6. **UNDERSTANDING THE CORE CONCEPT:**
   Drug therapies, psychosurgery, and ECT all are methods of treating mental disorder
   a. by changing the chemistry of the body.
   b. by removing stress in the patient's life.
   c. by directly altering the function of the brain.
   d. that have no scientific basis.

ANSWERS: 1. c   2. a   3. d   4. c
5. b   6. c

Using Psychology to Learn Psychology: How Is Education Like Therapy?

Consider the ways in which psychotherapy is like your classroom experiences in college:

▶ Most therapists, like most professors, are professionals with special training in what they do.

▶ Most patients/clients are like students in that they are seeking professional help to change their lives in some way.

▶ Much of what happens in therapy and in the classroom involves learning: new ideas, new behaviors, new insights, new connections.

It may help you learn psychology (and other subjects, as well) to think of teaching and learning in therapeutic terms. As we have seen, therapy seems to work best when therapist and client have a good working relationship and when the client believes in the value of the experience—and the same is almost certainly true for the student–professor relationship. You can take the initiative in establishing a personal-but-professional relationship with your psychology professor by doing the following two things: (1) asking questions or otherwise participating in class (at appropriate times and without dominating, of course) and (2) seeking your instructor's help on points you don't understand or on course-related topics you would like to pursue in more detail (doing so during regular office hours). The result will be learning more about psychology, because you will be taking a more active part in the learning process. Incidentally, an active approach to the course will also help you stand out from the crowd in the professor's mind, which could be helpful if you later need a faculty recommendation.

Now consider a parallel between education and group therapy. In group therapy, patients learn from each other, as well as from the therapist. Much the same can occur in your psychology course, if you consider other students as learning resources. As we noted earlier in this book, the most successful students often spend part of their study time sharing information in groups.

One other tip for learning psychology we can borrow from the success of behavioral therapies: the importance of changing behavior, not just thinking. It is easy to "intellectualize" a fact or an idea passively when you read about it or hear about it in class. But you are likely to find that the idea makes little impact on you ("I know I *read* about it, but I can't *remember* it!") if you don't *use* it. The remedy is to *do* something with your new knowledge: Tell someone about it, come up with illustrations from your own experience, or try acting in a different way. For example, after reading about *active listening* in this chapter, try it the next time you talk to a friend. Educators sometimes speak of this as "active learning." And it works!

Chapter Summary

WHAT IS THERAPY?

People seek therapy for a variety of problems. Treatment comes in many forms, both psychological and biomedical, but all involve diagnosing the problem, finding the source of the problem, making a prognosis and carrying out treatment. A variety of professionals work under this model. In earlier times, treatments for those with mental problems were usually harsh and dehumanizing. Only recently have people with emotional problems been treated as individuals with "illnesses" or "problems" to be dealt with. This view of mental disorder has led to more humane treatment. Many cultures have their own ways of understanding and treating mental disorders, although some "universals" hold true for all forms of therapy.

Therapy takes a variety of forms, but the common element is a relationship focused on altering behavior or mental processes.

HOW DO PSYCHOLOGISTS TREAT MENTAL DISORDERS?

Behavioral therapy applies the principles of learning to problem behaviors. Among the classical conditioning techniques, counterconditioning and systematic desensitization are commonly employed to treat fears. Aversion therapy may also be used for eliminating unwanted responses. Operant techniques include contingency management to modify behavior, primarily through positive reinforcement and extinction strategies. Social learning therapy involves the use of models and social skills training to help individuals gain confidence about their abilities.

The first of the insight therapies, psychoanalysis grew out of Sigmund Freud's theory of personality. Its goal is to release repressed material from the unconscious. Neo-Freudians emphasize the patient's current social situation, interpersonal relationships, and self-concept.

Among other insight therapies, humanistic therapy focuses on individuals becoming more fully self-actualized. Therapists strive to be nondirective in helping their clients establish a positive self-image. Group therapy has many applications, including community self-help groups and support groups. Family and marital therapy concentrate on situational difficulties and interpersonal dynamics as a total system in need of improvement.

Another form of insight therapy, cognitive therapy concentrates on changing negative or irrational thought patterns about oneself and one's social relationships. The client must learn more constructive thought patterns in reference to a problem and apply the new technique to other situations. Rational–emotive therapy helps clients recognize that their irrational beliefs about themselves interfere with life and helps them learn how to change those thought patterns. In recent years a synthesis of cognitive and behavioral therapies has emerged, combining the techniques of insight therapy with methods based on learning theory.

Research shows that psychotherapy is effective for a variety of psychological problems. Often it is more effective than drug therapy. As the research on mental disorders becomes more refined, we are learning to match specific psychotherapies to specific disorders.

Psychologists employ two main forms of treatment: the behavioral therapies and the insight therapies.

HOW IS THE BIOMEDICAL APPROACH USED TO TREAT MENTAL DISORDERS?

Biomedical therapies concentrate on changing the physiological aspects of mental illness. Drug therapy includes antipsychotic, antidepressant, antianxiety, and stimulant medicines. Together these drugs have caused a revolution in the medical treatment of mental disorder, although critics warn of their abuse, particularly in treating the ordinary stress of daily living. Psychosurgery has lost much of its popularity in recent years because of its radical, irreversible side effects. Electroconvulsive therapy is used primarily with depressed patients, but it remains controversial. A new and promising alternative involves magnetic brain stimulation. In all of this, hospitalization has been a mainstay of medical treatment, although the trend is away from mental hospitals to community-based treatment. The policy of deinstitutionalization was based on the best intentions, but many mental patients have been turned back into their communities with few resources and little treatment. When the resources are available, however, community treatment is often successful.

Biomedical therapies seek to alter the structure or function of the brain through drugs, surgery, or electromagnetic stimulation.

Review Test

For each of the following items, choose the single correct or best answer. The answer key appears at the end of the test.

1. Despite the differences between various types of therapy, all therapeutic strategies are designed to
   a. make the client feel better about him- or herself.
   b. help the individual fit better into his or her society.
   c. change the individual's functioning in some way.
   d. educate the person without interfering with his or her usual patterns of behavior.

2. While professionals with somewhat different training and orientations can provide similar forms of therapy, only _____ on the list below are qualified to prescribe medications for the treatment of mental or behavioral disorders.
   a. psychiatrists
   b. psychiatric social workers
   c. psychologists
   d. psychotherapists

3. Because a central goal of the therapist is to guide a patient toward understanding the connections between past origins and present symptoms, psychodynamic therapy is often called _____ therapy.
   a. insight
   b. cognitive
   c. existential
   d. rational–emotive

4. A patient finds herself feeling personally fond of her therapist, who reminds her of her father. This is an example of the psychoanalytic process known as
   a. resistance.
   b. transference.
   c. countertransference.
   d. negative transference.

5. Lola has an irrational fear of speaking in front of others. With the support of her instructor and her entire psychology class, Lola confronts her fear by standing alone in front of her classmates and talking about her phobia. This strategy of placing the individual in the dreaded situation is called
   a. exposure therapy.
   b. catharsis.
   c. insight therapy.
   d. social-learning therapy.

6. To teach his young daughter not to be afraid to swim, a father tells her to "Watch me!" as he wades into the surf, then rolls with the waves, and finally invites her to join him if she wants to try. In behavioral therapy, this technique is known as
   a. clinical ecology.
   b. counterconditioning.
   c. behavioral rehearsal.
   d. participant modeling.

7. Which of the following problems might best be corrected through rational–emotive behavior therapy (REBT)?
   a. An addicted smoker wants to quit.
   b. A young man has an extreme fear of heights.
   c. An average-weight woman diets constantly, believing that she must be thin in order to have anyone love her.
   d. A patient complains of continual "voices" in his head telling him that people are trying to harm him.

8. Which of the following statements about electroconvulsive therapy (ECT) is true?
   a. Proper ECT applies a very strong electric current to a patient's brain without the interference or insulation of sedatives or anesthetic medication.
   b. Some studies have found ECT to be effective in the treatment of severe depression.
   c. It is known to work by increasing the stimulation of a particular neurotransmitter in the brain.
   d. It works best with manic patients.

9. Valium, a drug with a high "abuse potential," is classified as an _____ medication.
   a. antianxiety
   b. antidepressant
   c. antipsychotic
   d. antihistamine

10. Psychiatrist Jerome Frank argues that, like religious and political indoctrination programs, all healing processes rely on a common crucial element:
    a. deception.
    b. fear of authority.
    c. rejection of culture.
    d. belief in the experience.

ANSWERS: 1. c   2. a   3. a   4. b   5. a   6. d
7. c   8. b   9. a   10. d

If You're Interested . . .

BOOKS

Berger, L., & Vuckovic, A. (1995). *Under observation: Life inside the McLean Psychiatric Hospital.* Penguin Books. This vivid portrayal of life in psychiatric institutions is illustrated with the case histories and personal stories of patients who emerge not as characters but as real people, disturbingly familiar and similar to ourselves.

Breggin, P. R. (2001). *The anti-depressant fact book: What your doctor won't tell you about Prozac, Zoloft, Paxil, Celexa, and Luvox.* Perseus Books. The renowned author and psychiatrist discusses the biochemical nature of depression, the brain impact of the SSRI drugs, and issues important to patients, including deceptions by drug companies, public misconceptions about medication, and alternatives to drug treatment.

Gillick, M. R. (1999). *Tangled minds: Understanding Alzheimer's disease and other dementias.* Plume/Penguin. A Harvard medical school professor reviews the stages of Alzheimer's disease, its history, research into its causes, and treatments now in use to alleviate symptoms. She also offers advice about diagnosing dementia, caring for Alzheimer's patients, mediating its effects on family members, promoting public advocacy and funding, and preserving dignity and individuality in the face of debilitating loss of cognitive function.

Graham, H. (1998). *Discover color therapy: A first-step handbook to better health.* Ulysses Press. This short, interesting approach to self-improvement is based on a topic that interests everyone — the colors of our world and our specific preferences for certain colors.

Hagerty, J. W., & Hagerty, J. G. (2001). *Rent two films and let's talk in the morning: Using popular movies in psychotherapy,* 2nd edition. John Wiley & Sons. Comparable to Gary Solomon's two excellent works, *The Motion Picture Prescription* (1995, Aslan) and *Reel Therapy* (2001, Lebhorn-Friedman Books), this is a wonderful guide to getting more out of viewing feature films whose messages, themes, and scenes provide information about psychological disorders and treatment.

Imber-Black, E. (1998). *The secret life of families: Truth-telling, privacy, and reconciliation in a tell-all society.* Bantam Doubleday Dell. The author, a psychiatry professor, critiques the phenomenon of indiscriminate self- and other-disclosure popularized by tabloids and talk shows, noting that every secret is different, and while some revelations may be relieving and inconsequential for others, other secrets create lasting pain and no relief. This book provides a valuable examination of the difference between therapy and "entertainment."

Kaysen, S. (1993). *Girl, interrupted.* Turtle Bay Books. Susanna Kaysen gives the reader an honest account of her years in the McLean Hospital (see Berger & Vuckovic, above) when she was 18 to 20 years old, including dark and funny stories of herself and others she encountered there. (See the video listing in recommended viewing, below).

Kramer, P. D. (1993). *Listening to Prozac: A psychiatrist explores antidepressant drugs and the remaking of the self.* Viking. When an antidepressant drug relieves your symptoms, are you becoming *more* or *less* "yourself"? Kramer's bestseller reviews before-and-after accounts of patients who themselves were touched or changed by Prozac, the most popular of the new class of antidepressants.

Leahy, R. L. (1996). *Cognitive therapy: Basic principles and applications.* Jason Aronson. With pressure from HMOs and government agencies to devise shorter courses of treatment for complex disorders, therapists are combining elements of cognitive and psychodynamic treatments — and achieving surprising success, according to Leahy's review of treatments for depression, anxiety, anger, and relationship conflict.

Rogers, C. R. (1995). *A way of being.* Mariner Books. Here is a new edition of a wonderful introduction to humanistic psychology, by the founder of client-centered therapy. Readable, engaging, richly informative, Rogers engages in a personal dialogue with the reader, offering not a correction or quick fix, but a vision of human living.

Schiller, L., & Bennett, A. (1996). *The quiet room: A journey out of the torment of madness.* Warner Books. This true story of the first author's descent into schizophrenia and, with help from therapists and family, her return to reality is a vivid, acclaimed account.

Yalom, I. D. (1997). *Lying on the couch.* HarperPerennial. This psychological thriller is based on the premise that the relationship between therapist and client is fraught not only with secrets and expectations, but perhaps lying, betrayal, and treachery as well. Existential analyst Irving Yalom's fictional tale is also filled with information and insights about types and techniques of psychotherapy, presented in the form of a novel, far more engaging than a section in (most) psychology textbooks.

VIDEOS

Analyze This. (1999, color, 103 min.). Directed by Harold Ramis; starring Robert DeNiro, Billy Crystal, Lisa Kudrow. This is a comedy about a normally arrogant mob boss who becomes overwhelmed by life problems and seeks the help of a psychotherapist —but how much can he reveal without disclosing vital criminal secrets? It provides a funny satire of every gangster role DeNiro has played, counterpointed by Crystal's nervous and wry commentary.

Benny & Joon. (1993, color, 98 min.). Directed by Jeremiah S. Chechik; starring Johnny Depp, Mary Stuart Masterson, Aidan Quinn. This offbeat, touching comedy presents a misfit named Sam in love with a mentally unbalanced young woman in the care of her protective brother, who hopes Sam might be just the one for her.

Girl, Interrupted. (1999, color, 127 min.). Directed by James Mangold; starring Winona Ryder, Angelina Jolie, Whoopi Goldberg. Based on Susanna Kaysen's memoir of her two years in a psychiatric hospital as a young adult, this film is an intense, dramatic depiction of the environment, treatments, and relationships in a modern mental institution.

Good Will Hunting. (1997, color, 126 min.). Directed by Gus Van Sant; starring Matt Damon, Robin Williams, Ben Affleck, Minnie Driver, Stellan Skarsgård. A working-class youth with a genius for mathematics must confront a painful past and a belligerence about intimacy in order to hone his gifts, with the help of an MIT professor, sympathetic friends, and a sensitive, offbeat psychotherapist (Williams in his Oscar-winning role).

My Name Is Bill W. (1989, color, 100 min.). Directed by Daniel Petrie; starring James Garner, James Woods, JoBeth Williams, Fritz Weaver, Gary Sinise. The true story of the founding of Alcoholics Anonymous, the first support group, in the 1930s, by two alcoholics who formed a partnership to help each other quit drinking is superbly acted, depicting the therapeutic possibilities of friendship, empathy, and loyalty.

Ordinary People. (1980, color, 123 min.). Directed by Robert Redford; starring Donald Sutherland, Mary Tyler Moore, Timothy Hutton, Judd Hirsch. A young man's suicide attempt and subsequent treatment confront his parents with their own troubled relationships as an insightful therapist brings to light the unusual problems suffered by this "normal American" family.

The Snake Pit. (1948, B&W, 108 min.). Directed by Anatole Litvak; starring Olivia de Havilland, Mark Stevens, Leo Genn. A telling contrast with "Girl, Interrupted" (above), this drama shows the breakdown and recovery of a young married woman in the 1940s, whose symptoms have landed her in a state mental hospital. It presents an accurate and frightening picture of how such patients were warehoused and disciplined in decades before the development of psychiatric drugs and public enlightenment about the mentally ill.

Spellbound. (1945, B&W, 111 min.). Directed by Alfred Hitchcock; starring Gregory Peck, Ingrid Bergman, Leo G. Carroll. The classic suspense mystery tells the tale of an amnesiac who may or may not be a murderer, helped by the psychoanalyst with whom he has fallen in love. The surreal dream sequences were designed by artist Salvador Dali.

What about Bob? (1991, color, 99 min.). Directed by Frank Oz; starring Bill Murray, Richard Dreyfuss, Julie Hagerty. A professional psychiatric patient proves the undoing of a pompous psychiatrist, pursued by the needy, neurotic man to his family summer vacation — where the patient proceeds to charm everyone, clarifying the psychiatrist's own inabilities as a father and husband. The sometimes disturbing comedy exposes the artificial barriers blocking the unique therapist–client relationship.

WEB RESOURCES

http://www.aboutpsychotherapy.com Visit this Web site to learn about psychotherapy. The multiple links provide information on the various types of psychotherapy, as well as coverage of meditation and hypnosis.

http://site.health-center.com/brain/therapy/default.htm Cognitive psychotherapy focuses on changing negative thinking patterns. People with depression think negative thoughts about the world, and cognitive psychologists attempt to alter this way of thinking in order to alleviate depressive feelings. This Web site explains the concept of behavior therapy, which can be used for recurring behaviors, such as drug and alcohol problems, eating disorders, or anxiety disorders.

http://www.apa.org/monitor/mar99/depress.html What is the most effective form of treatment? This article argues that a combined treatment of psychotherapy and drug therapy is effective in treating depressed individuals. Do you think that this theory would be applicable to other disorders as well? Why or why not?

HOW DOES THE SOCIAL SITUATION AFFECT OUR BEHAVIOR?

Social Standards of Behavior
Conformity
Obedience
The Bystander Problem

We usually adapt our behavior to the demands of the social situation, and in ambiguous situations we take our cues from the behavior of others.

NEED HELP? ASK FOR IT!
In an emergency, giving simple instructions can turn bystander bewilderment into helping behavior.

WHAT INFLUENCES OUR JUDGMENTS OF OTHERS?

Interpersonal Attraction
Making Attributions
Prejudice and Discrimination

The judgments we make about others depend not only on their behavior but on our interpretation of the social situation.

LOVING RELATIONSHIPS:
The end of a relationship can be difficult for everyone. Social psychologists have begun to study what it takes to keep people together.

WHAT ARE THE ROOTS OF VIOLENCE AND TERRORISM?

The Social Psychology of Aggression and Violence
The Robbers Cave: An Experiment in Conflict
A Personal Endnote

The power of the situation can help us understand violence and terrorism, but a broader under-standing requires multiple perspectives that go beyond the boundaries of psychology.

MULTIPLE PERSPECTIVES ON TERRORISM:
An experiment on groups of Boy Scouts holds lessons for dealing with conflict in the Middle East.

USING PSYCHOLOGY TO LEARN PSYCHOLOGY: Persuasion in the Classroom

SOCIAL PSYCHOLOGY

On a summer Sunday in California, a siren shattered the serenity of college student Tommy Whitlow's morning. A police car screeched to a halt in front of his home. Within minutes, Tommy was charged with a felony, informed of his constitutional rights, frisked, and handcuffed. After he was booked and fingerprinted, Tommy was blindfolded and transported to the Stanford County Prison, where he was stripped, sprayed with disinfectant, and issued a smock-type uniform with an I.D. number on the front and back. Tommy became Prisoner 647. Eight other college students were also arrested and assigned numbers.

The prison guards were not identified by name, and their anonymity was en-

hanced by khaki uniforms and reflector sunglasses—Prisoner 647 never saw their eyes. He referred to each of his jailers as "Mr. Correctional Officer, Sir"; to them, he was only number 647.

The guards insisted that prisoners obey all rules without question or hesitation. Failure to do so led to the loss of a privilege. At first, privileges included opportunities to read, write, or talk to other inmates. Later, the slightest protest resulted in the loss of the "privileges" of eating, sleeping, and washing. Failure to obey rules also resulted in the assignment of menial, unpleasant work such as cleaning toilets with bare hands, doing push-ups while a guard stepped on the prisoner's

(continued)

Scenes from the Stanford prison experiment.

back, and spending hours in solitary confinement. The guards were always devising new strategies to make the prisoners feel worthless. Every guard Prisoner 647 encountered engaged in abusive, authoritarian behavior.

Less than 36 hours after the mass arrest, prisoner 8412, the ringleader of an aborted prisoner rebellion that morning, began to cry uncontrollably. He experienced fits of rage, disorganized thinking, and severe depression. On successive days, three more prisoners developed similar stress-related symptoms. A fifth prisoner developed a psychosomatic rash all over his body when the parole board rejected his appeal.

At night, Prisoner 647 tried to remember what Tommy Whitlow had been like before he became a prisoner. He also tried to imagine his tormentors before they became guards. He reminded himself that he was a college student who had answered a newspaper ad and agreed to be a subject in a two-week experiment on prison life. He had thought it would be fun to do something unusual, and he could always use some extra money.

Everyone in the prison, guard and prisoner alike, had been selected from a large pool of student volunteers. On the basis of extensive psychological tests and interviews, the volunteers had been judged as law-abiding, emotionally stable, physically healthy, and "normal-average" on all psychological measures. In this mock prison experiment, assignment of participants to "guard" or "prisoner" roles had been determined by the flip of a coin. The prisoners lived in the jail around the clock, and the guards worked standard eight-hour shifts.

As guards, students who had been pacifists and "nice guys" in their usual life settings behaved aggressively — sometimes even sadistically. As prisoners, psychologically stable students soon behaved pathologically, passively resigning themselves to their unexpected fate of learned helplessness. The power of the simulated prison situation had created a new social reality — a real prison — in the minds of the jailers and their captives. The situation was so powerful that the researchers decided to terminate the two-week study after only six days.

Although Tommy Whitlow said he wouldn't want to go through it again, he valued the personal experience because he learned so much about himself and about human nature. Fortunately, he and the other students were basically healthy, and debriefing showed that they readily bounced back from the prison experience. Follow-ups over many years revealed no lasting negative effects. The participants had all learned an important lesson: Never underestimate the power of a bad situation to overwhelm the personalities and good upbringing of even the best and brightest among us (Haney et al., 1973; Haney & Zimbardo, 1998; Zimbardo, 1973, 1975; Zimbardo et al., 1999; replicated in Australia by Lovibond et al., 1979).

Suppose *you* had been a subject in the Stanford prison experiment. Would you have been a "nice guy" guard — or a sadist? A model prisoner — or a rebel? Could you have resisted the pressures and stresses of these circumstances? We'd all like to believe we would be good guards and heroic prisoners or that we could keep things in perspective, knowing that it was "just an experiment." But the best bet is that we would react the way the participants did. In all likelihood, many of us would fall short of our own standards.

Welcome to *social psychology,* the field that investigates how individuals affect each other. It may be a relief to hear that not all of social psychology brings such bad news about ourselves as does the Stanford prison experiment. It also explores the forces that bring people together for friendships and loving relationships. As you study **social psychology** in this chapter, you will learn how people's thoughts, feelings, perceptions, motives, and behavior are influenced by interactions with others. That is, social psychologists try to understand behavior within its *social context.* Defined broadly, this context includes the real, imagined, or symbolic *presence of other people;* the *activities and interactions* that take place among people; the *settings* in which behavior occurs; and the *expectations and norms* governing behavior in a given setting (Sherif, 1981).

Most of all, the Stanford prison experiment conducted by Philip Zimbardo (one of your authors) underscores the *power of social situations* to control human behavior. This is a major theme to emerge from social psychologists research of the past 50 years. In the first part of this chapter, you will see how seemingly minor features of social settings can have a huge impact on what we think and how we feel and act. In these studies you will see how the situation can produce conformity to group standards—even when the group is clearly "wrong." Other studies will demonstrate how the situation can lead people blindly to follow orders—perhaps even orders to harm others.

Yet, as powerful as the situation can be, psychologists know that it is not objective reality to which we respond. Rather, we respond to our *subjective interpretation* of the situation, which can differ significantly from person to person. This, then, is the second great theme in social psychology: the construction of a *subjective social reality.* We must grasp this world of expectations and perceptions in order to understand the attractive forces at work in friendships and romantic relationships as well as the repulsive forces underlying prejudice.

Our examination of prejudice will set the stage for a third theme that will combine the first two. We will see how social psychologists have experimented with altering the situation to change subjective social reality. This, we will discover, has important implications for resolving conflicts among individuals, groups, and even nations. We begin now with the first of these three themes, the power of the situation.

Connection

Chapter 5
Perception normally gives us useful—but not always entirely accurate—interpretations of events.

HOW DOES THE SOCIAL SITUATION AFFECT OUR BEHAVIOR?

Suppose that you have just graduated from college. You find yourself in an interview, with the very real possibility of being hired for the job of your dreams. Afterward, the department head suggests that you go to lunch together in the company cafeteria. Will you order a sandwich, a salad, or a full-course meal? Will you leave the plastic tray under your plate as you eat? Will you put the tiny paper napkin in your lap? If you are like most people in an unfamiliar situation such as this, you will take your cues from those around you.

Social psychologists believe that, even when the situation is a familiar one, such as a college classroom, the primary determinant of individual behavior is the social situation in which that behavior occurs. So powerful is the situation that it can sometimes dominate our personalities and override our past history of learning, values, and beliefs. We will see that the pressures of the situation can create powerful psychological effects, such as prejudice, blind obedience, and violence. Social roles, competition, or the mere presence of others can profoundly influence how we behave. Often, these subtle situational vari-

Social psychology: The branch of psychology that studies the effects of social variables and cognitions on individual behavior and social interactions.

ables affect us without our awareness. Our Core Concept emphasizes this point:

> **We usually adapt our behavior to the demands of the social situation, and in ambiguous situations we take our cues from the behavior of others.**

In this section, we will review some research that explores this concept, called **situationism**. Situationism assumes that the environment can have both subtle and forceful effects on people's thoughts, feelings, and behaviors. Here we will look particularly at the power of the situation to create conformity, obedience, and sometimes even the willingness to inflict harm on others.

Social Standards of Behavior

A job interview, such as the one we discussed above, provides an example of a situational influence on your behavior. You will also notice the power of the situation when you compare the way students talk to their friends versus their professors. That is, most people learn to size up their social circumstances and conform their behavior to situational demands. The responses they make depend heavily on two factors: the *social roles* they play and *norms* of the group. Let us look at both of these closely.

Situationism: The view that environmental conditions influence people's behavior as much or more than their personal dispositions do.

Social role: One of several socially defined patterns of behavior that are expected of persons in a given setting or group.

SOCIAL ROLES Whether you are at a concert, a department meeting, or a pizza parlor, you will see that people operate by different rules, depending on their *social roles.* You can see this more clearly by responding to the question: Who are you? Almost certainly you and other readers of this book are students or professors of psychology—social roles that imply different sets of behaviors. (One, for example, takes exams; the other grades them.) It is likely that you take on several other social roles, too. Are you a part-time employee? Someone's parent? A cyclist? A musician? A friend? A **social role** is one of several socially defined patterns of behavior that are expected of persons in a given setting or group. The roles you assume may result from your interests, abilities, and goals—or they may be imposed on you by the group or by cultural, economic, or biological conditions beyond your control. In any case, social roles prescribe your behavior.

The situations in which you live and function also determine the roles that are available to you and the behaviors others expect of you. Being a college student, for example, is a social role that carries certain implicit assumptions about attending classes, studying, and handing in papers. In addition, the adoption of this role makes other roles less likely. Thus, your role as college student diminishes the chances that you will assume the role of homeless person, drug pusher, or shaman, for example. By the same token, because you have college experience, numerous other roles (such as manager, teacher, airline pilot, and politician) are available to you.

The Stanford prison experiment cast guards and prisoners in different social roles. Yet, just a week before, their roles (college students) were very similar. Chance, in the form of random assignment, had decided their new roles as guards or prisoners, and these roles created status and power differences that came out in the prison situation.

Social norms can define rigid dress codes for group members.

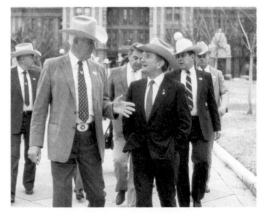

Remember that no one taught the participants to play their roles. Each student called upon *scripts* about those roles. A **script** involves a person's knowledge about the sequence of events and actions that are expected of a particular social role. So, if an individual understands the role of "guard" as someone who uses coercive rules to limit the freedom of "prisoners," then that person is likely to use a script derived from that schema to become an authoritarian guard under conditions such as the Stanford prison experiment. In fact, many students in the guard role were surprised at how easy it was for them to enjoy controlling other people.

In trying to understand what happened in the Stanford prison experiment, we should note that all the prisoners and guards were male. Would it have made any difference if women had been in the roles of prisoner and guard? We will never know because the unanticipated negative impact of the experiment on both the guards and prisoners would make it unethical to do the experiment again. The possibility of gender differences, however, is raised by this fact: The experiment was called off after a female graduate student, Christina Maslach, visited the "prison" and was shocked by what she saw. Immediately she conferred with Dr. Zimbardo, whom she implored to end the study. After some discussion, he agreed to do so. (Drs. Maslach and Zimbardo were later married.)

SOCIAL NORMS   In addition to specific social roles, groups develop many "unwritten rules" for the ways that members should act. These expectations, called **social norms,** dictate socially appropriate attitudes and behaviors. Social norms can be broad guidelines, such as ideas about which political or religious attitudes are considered acceptable. Social norms can also be quite specific, embodying standards of conduct such as being quiet in the library or shining your shoes for a job interview. Norms can guide conversation, as when they restrict discussion of sensitive or taboo subjects in certain company. And norms can define dress codes, whether requiring uniforms or business suits or prohibiting shorts and tank tops. In the Stanford prison experiment, the guards quickly developed norms for abusive behavior.

When a person joins a new group, such as a work group or a group of friends, there is always an adjustment period during which the individual tries to discover how best to fit in. Adjustment to a group typically involves discovering its social norms. Individuals experience this adjustment in two ways: by noticing the *uniformities* in certain behaviors and by observing the *negative consequences* when someone violates a social norm. For example, a child whose parents move her to a new school sees that her new classmates all wear jeans and baggy T-shirts. If this girl wears a frilly dress, the others may laugh at her, penalizing her "mistake."

We can also see the power of social norms in a famous study of students attending Vermont's Bennington College in the 1930s. At that time, Bennington's campus culture had a prevailing norm of political and economic liberalism, encouraged by a young, dynamic, and liberal faculty. By contrast, most of the young women attending Bennington came from privileged, conservative homes—and brought decidedly nonliberal values with them. Social psychologist Theodore Newcomb wondered: Which forces shape students' attitudes? His data showed that the norms of the campus won the war of influence against the norms of the family. In most women, the initial attitude of conservatism steadily waned as they progressed through their college years, so that by their senior year they had clearly converted to liberal thinking and causes (Newcomb, 1943).

Twenty years later, the marks of the Bennington experience were still evident, Newcomb discovered. Women who had graduated as liberals were still

Connection

Chapter 8
Schemas are cognitive structures that integrate knowledge and expectations about a topic or concept.

"GOSH, ACKERMAN, DIDN'T ANYONE IN PERSONNEL TELL YOU ABOUT OUR CORPORATE CULTURE ?"
© Ted Goff

Connection

Chapter 6
Bandura demonstrated that we acquire many social behaviors through observational learning.

Script: Knowledge about the sequence of events and actions that is expected in a particular setting.

Social norms: A group's expectations regarding what is appropriate and acceptable for its members' attitudes and behaviors.

liberals; those who had resisted the prevailing liberal norm had remained conservative. Most had married husbands with values similar to their own and created supportive new home environments. In the 1960 presidential election, the liberal Bennington allegiance was evident when 60% of the class Newcomb had studied voted for liberal John F. Kennedy, rather than conservative Richard M. Nixon—in contrast to less than 30% support for Kennedy among graduates of comparable colleges at that time (Newcomb et al., 1967).

Campus culture is not the only source of norms and group pressure, of course. One's workplace, neighborhood, religious group, and family all communicate standards for behavior—and threaten sanctions (such as firing, social rejection, or excommunication) for violating those norms. But a college or university environment can have a powerful impact on young people. This is especially true if they have had narrow life experiences and not previously encountered attitudes radically different from their own. For example, a new student may adopt classmates' political opinions, as in the Bennington study, as well as religious beliefs and attitudes about sex and alcohol (Prentice & Miller, 1993; Schroeder & Prentice, 1995).

Conformity

How powerful are these social pressures? We can see the effects of social pressure in people's moods, clothing styles, and leisure activities (Totterdell, 2000; Totterdell et al., 1998). This tendency to mimic other people is called the *chameleon effect* (Chartrand & Bargh, 1999). We can also see social pressure in political attitudes, as with Bennington College students. But, can social influence be strong enough to make people follow a group norm that is clearly and objectively wrong? Could the power of that situation prove stronger than the evidence of your own eyes?

THE ASCH STUDIES   Solomon Asch (1940; 1956) set out to answer just such questions with a group rigged to make subjects think that their eyes were deceiving them. In Asch's study, male college students were told they would be participating in a study of visual perception. They were shown cards with three lines of differing lengths and asked to indicate which of the three lines was the same length as a separate, standard line (see Figure 14.1). The problem was simple: The lines were different enough so that mistakes were rare in subjects responding alone. But in a group of seven to nine students, where others had been coached to give wrong answers, everything changed.

Here's how the experiment worked. On the first three trials, everyone agreed on the correct answer. But the first person to respond on the fourth trial reported an obviously incorrect judgment, reporting as equal two lines that were clearly different. So did the next person and so on, until all members of the group but the remaining one (the only real subject in the experiment) had unanimously agreed on an erroneous judgment. The subject then had to decide whether to go along with everyone else's view of the situation and conform, or remain independent, standing by the evidence of his own eyes. This group pressure was imposed on 12 of the 18 trials.

What did he and others in his position finally do? As you might expect, subjects showed signs of disbelief and discomfort when faced with a majority who saw the world so differently from the way they did. But the group pressure usually prevailed. Three-quarters of the subjects conformed to the false judgment of the group one or more times, while only one-fourth remained completely independent on all trials. In various related studies, between 50 and 80% of the subjects conformed with the majority's false estimate at least once; a third of the subjects yielded to the majority's wrong judgments on half or

Connection

Chapter 5
Asch made us realize that perceptual interpretation involves the social situation.

FIGURE 14.1: Conformity in the Asch Experiments

In this photo from Asch's study, the naive subject, number 6, displays obvious concern about the majority's erroneous judgment. At top right, you see a typical stimulus array. At top left, the graph illustrates conformity across 12 critical trials, when subjects were grouped with a unanimous majority, or had the support of a single dissenting partner. (A lower percentage of correct estimates indicates a greater degree of conformity with the group's false judgment.)

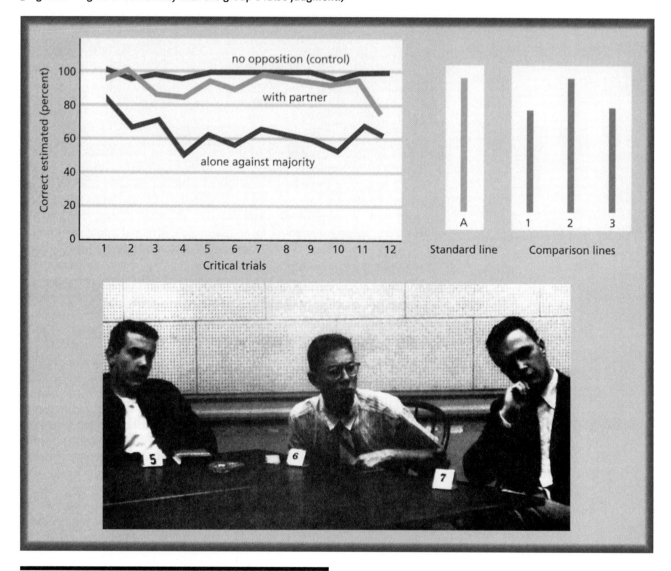

more of the critical trials. Social psychologists call this the **Asch effect:** the influence of a group majority on the judgments of an individual. The Asch effect has become the classic illustration of **conformity**—the tendency for people to adopt the behavior and opinions presented by other group members. Even though subjects were judging matters of fact, not merely personal opinions, most caved in to conformity pressures.

At the same time, we should recognize that the Asch effect, powerful as it is, still does not make everyone conform. Conformity researchers do regularly find "independents," individuals who are bothered and even dismayed to find themselves in disagreement with the majority, but who nonetheless stand

Asch effect: A form of conformity in which a group majority influences individual judgments.

Conformity: The tendency for people to adopt the behaviors, attitudes, and opinions of other members of a group.

their ground and "call 'em as they see 'em" — even to the point of deliberately giving a wrong answer when the group gives a correct one (Friend et al., 1990).

GROUP CHARACTERISTICS THAT PRODUCE CONFORMITY In further experiments, Asch identified three factors that influence whether a person will yield to group pressure: (1) *the size of the majority,* (2) *the presence of a partner who dissented* from the majority, and (3) *the size of the discrepancy* between the correct answer and the majority's position. He found that subjects tended to conform with a unanimous majority of as few as three people, but not if they faced only one or two. However, even in a large group, giving the subject one ally who dissented from the majority opinion sharply reduced conformity (as shown in Figure 14.1). With such a "partner," nearly all subjects resisted the pressures to conform. Remarkably, however, some individuals continued to yield to the group even with a partner present. All who yielded underestimated the influence of the social pressure and the frequency of their conformity; some even claimed that they really had *seen* the lines as the majority had claimed (Asch, 1955, 1956).

Numerous studies have revealed additional factors that influence conformity. (These experiments have included both female and male subjects.) Specifically, a person is likely to conform under the following circumstances:

Connection

Chapter 8
Our judgments are often affected by biases.

▶ When a judgment task is difficult or ambiguous (Deutsch & Gerard, 1955; Lott & Lott, 1961; Saltzstein & Sandberg, 1979);

▶ When the group members are perceived as especially competent;

▶ When responses are given publicly rather than privately;

▶ When the group majority is unanimous: Once that unanimity is broken, the rate of conformity drops dramatically (Allen & Levine, 1969; Morris & Miller, 1975).

For example, when you vote in a group, as is common in clubs or on boards of directors, you are more likely to go along with the majority if: (a) the issue being decided is complex or confusing, (b) others in the group seem to know what they are talking about, (c) you must vote by raising your hand instead of casting an anonymous ballot, and (d) the entire group, without exception, votes in a certain way.

The Asch situation has given us abundant information about the pressure to conform. Now let us take the question of social influence a step farther: Under what conditions will social pressure produce *obedience?* Specifically, could a situation be contrived in which ordinary people would be willing to follow orders that would cause harm to another person? The answer to these questions, unfortunately, is "Yes."

Obedience

So far, we have seen how groups influence individuals. But the arrow of influence also points the other way: Certain individuals, such as leaders and authorities, can command the obedience of groups — even large masses of people. The ultimate demonstration of this effect was seen in the World War II era, with the emergence of Adolf Hitler in Germany and Benito Mussolini in Italy. These dictators transformed the rational citizens of whole nations into loyal followers of a hideous fascist ideology bent on world conquest.

Modern social psychology had its origins in this wartime crucible of fear and prejudice. The early social psychologists focused on the personalities of people drawn into fascist groups. Specifically, they looked for an *authoritarian personality* behind the fascist group mentality (Adorno et al., 1950). Let us

Connection

Chapter 11
Most personality theories focus on internal processes, while social psychology now emphasizes the external situation.

reflect for a moment on some more recent examples of unquestioning obedience to authority.

In 1978, a group of American citizens left California to relocate their Peoples Temple in South America. There, following the orders of their charismatic leader, Reverend Jim Jones, over 900 members of the Peoples Temple willingly administered lethal doses of cyanide to their children and then to themselves. Then in 1993, 100 members of a religious sect in Waco, Texas, joined their leader, David Koresh, in defying federal agents who had surrounded their compound. After a standoff of several weeks, the Branch Davidians set fire to their quarters rather than surrender to authorities. In the resulting conflagration, scores of men, women, and children perished. Four years later the members of another group calling itself Heaven's Gate followed their leader's command to commit mass suicide in order to achieve a "higher plane" of being. And, on September 11, 2001, followers of Osama bin Laden commandeered commercial airliners and piloted them into the Pentagon and the World Trade Center. Were these people subhuman monsters or mentally deranged—altogether unlike us? Are there any conditions under which you would blindly obey an order from a person you love and respect (or fear)? Would you, for example, obey an authority figure who told you to electrocute a stranger?

Your answer is most likely, "No! What kind of person do you think I am?" After reading this chapter, you may be more likely to answer, "I hope not—but I have a better understanding of the social forces that can pressure ordinary people to commit horrible acts." And, your authors hope, your study of social psychology will make you more resistant to the forces that produce unquestioning obedience and conformity.

On that note, let us now turn to the most convincing demonstration of situational power ever created in the laboratory. In a dramatic experiment, Stanley Milgram (1965, 1974) showed that a willingness to follow brutal, and even potentially lethal, orders is not confined to a few extreme personalities or deranged individuals. This finding, along with certain ethical issues that the experiment raises, places Milgram's work at the center of one of the biggest controversies in psychology (Blass, 1996; Miller, 1986; Ross & Nisbett, 1991). Let us begin with a look at the controversial methods Milgram used.

MILGRAM'S OBEDIENCE EXPERIMENT The volunteers thought that they were participating in a scientific study of memory and learning. Specifically, the experimenter told them that the purpose of the experiment was to discover how learning and memory could be improved through the proper balance of reward and punishment. Cast in the role of "teacher," a volunteer subject was instructed to punish memory errors made by another person (actually a confederate of the experimenter) playing the role of "learner." To administer punishment, the teacher was told to throw a switch that would deliver an electric shock to the learner each time the learner made an error. Moreover, the teacher was told to increase the level of shock by a fixed amount for every new error. Overseeing the whole procedure was a white-coated experimenter. This authority figure presented the rules, arranged for the assignment of roles (by a rigged drawing of lots), and ordered the teachers to do their job whenever they hesitated or dissented.

The real question driving the experiment was this: How far would subjects go before they defied the authority figure by refusing to obey? The depen-

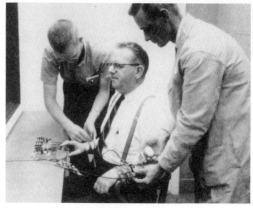

Milgram's obedience experiment. Top, generator; bottom, the "learner" being strapped into his electrified chair. Experts incorrectly predicted the behavior of Milgram's subjects because they failed to consider the influence of the special situation created in the experiment. Although many of the subjects in Milgram's study dissented verbally, the majority obeyed.

dent variable was the subject's response, measured by the shock level the subject was willing to deliver. The level of shock could be clearly seen on a "shock generator" that featured a row of 30 switches that apparently could deliver shocks in 15-volt steps up to a whopping 450 volts.

To make the situation realistic, Milgram gave each "teacher" a mild sample shock. This convinced his subjects that the apparatus was actually delivering shocks and that they would be causing the "learner" increasing pain and suffering each time they flipped a switch. Except for this demonstration shock, however, no shocks were actually administered: You will remember that the learner was actually a part of the experimental team.

The part of the learner was played by a pleasant, mild-mannered man, about 50 years old. He mentioned having a "heart condition" but said he was willing to go along with the procedure. The experimenter obliged by strapping him into an "electric chair" in the next room. As the learner, his task was to memorize pairs of words, then choose the correct response for each stimulus word from a multiple-choice listing. Following the experimental script, the learner soon began making mistakes.

At 75 volts, the script called for the learner to moan and grunt; at 150 volts he would demand to be released from the experiment. At 180 volts he would cry out that he could not stand the pain any longer. The plan then called for the learner's protests to increase with increasing shock levels. For any subjects still delivering punishment at the 300-volt level, the learner would shout that he would no longer take part in the experiment and must be freed. He would also whimper about a heart condition and refuse to reply any further. As you might imagine, this situation was stressful. If the teacher hesitated or protested about delivering the required shock at any level, the experimenter interrupted, stating that the experiment "must continue" and asking the teacher to "please continue." The experiment ended only when the shock level reached the 450-volt maximum — or when the teacher refused to obey.

THE SHOCKING RESULTS   Suppose for a moment that *you* were the subject-teacher. Ask yourself the following questions:

▶ How far up the shock scale would you go?
▶ At which level would you refuse to continue?

In fact, the majority of subjects obeyed the authority fully! Nearly two-thirds delivered the maximum 450 volts to the learner. Most of those who refused to give the maximum shock obeyed until reaching about 300 volts. And no subject who got within five switches of the end refused to go all the way. By then their resistance was broken; they had resolved their own conflicts and just tried to get it over with as quickly as possible.

These were not sadistic people who obeyed happily. Most dissented verbally, even though they continued to deliver shocks. One subject complained to the unwavering experimenter, "He can't stand it! I'm not going to kill that man in there! You hear him hollering? He's hollering . . . Who is going to take the responsibility if anything happens to that gentleman?" Clearly upset, this subject added, "You mean I've got to keep going up with that scale? No sir, I'm not going to kill that man!" (1965, p. 67). But, the shocks continued. When the learner simply stopped responding to the teacher's questions, some subjects called out to him, urging him to get the answer right so they would not have to con-

This Chinese man risked his life by defying authority. Would you have done so?

▼

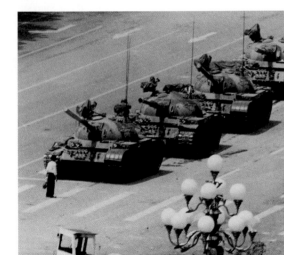

tinue shocking him. All the while they protested loudly to the experimenter, but the experimenter responded with stern commands: "You have no other choice, you *must* go on." Even when there was only silence from the learner's room, the teacher was ordered to keep shocking him more and more strongly, all the way up to the button that was marked "Danger: Severe Shock XXX (450 volts)." Most subjects obeyed.

Of course, no shocks were ever delivered to the learner. The "victim" of the "shocks" was an accomplished actor who congenially chatted with his "teacher" after the experiment and assured him he was fine and had never felt any shocks at all. The controversy about Milgram's research concerns the ethics of deception and the potentially devastating effects on those in the role of teacher.

WHY DO WE OBEY AUTHORITY?   You may wonder whether Milgram's subjects were unusual in some way. His initial obedience experiments were conducted at Yale University with male college students and then with male residents of New Haven who received payment for their participation. In later variations, Milgram set up a storefront research unit in Bridgeport, Connecticut, recruiting through newspaper ads a broad cross section of the population. Subjects eventually included both sexes and varied widely in age, occupation, and education. In all, Milgram tested more than 1,000 subjects.

From the many variations Milgram conducted on his original study, we can conclude that subjects tended to be obedient under the following conditions (Milgram, 1965, 1974; Rosenhan, 1969):

▶ *When a peer modeled obedience* by complying with the authority figure's commands

▶ *When the victim was remote from the subject* and could not be seen or heard

▶ *When the teacher was under direct surveillance of the authority figure* so that the teacher was aware of the authority's presence

▶ *When a subject acted as an intermediary bystander* — merely "assisting" the one who was delivering the shock, rather than actually throwing the switches

▶ *When the authority figure had higher relative status than the subject*, as when the subject was a student and the experimenter was billed as "professor" or "doctor"

If you carefully review these conditions (Figure 14.2), you can see that the obedience effect results from situational variables and not personality variables. In fact, personality tests administered to the subjects did *not* reveal any traits that differentiated those who obeyed from those who refused, nor did they identify any psychological disturbance or abnormality in the obedient punishers. These findings enable us to rule out personality as a variable in obedient behavior. And what about gender? Milgram found that women were just as obedient as men (Milgram, 1974).

Like the Stanford prison study, obedience research challenges the myth that evil lurks in the minds of evil people — that the bad "they" differ from the good "us" who would never do such things. The purpose in recounting these findings is not to debase human nature or to excuse evil deeds, but to make clear that even normal, well-meaning individuals can give in to strong situational and social influences to do wrong.

The Bystander Problem

Harm doesn't always come from a hurtful act. It can also come from *inaction* when someone needs help. We can illustrate this fact with a news event that

Connection

Chapter 4
Moral judgments depend not only on the situation but on one's stage of moral development.

FIGURE 14.2: Obedience in Milgram's Experiments

The graph shows a profile of weak of strong obedience effects across situational variations of Milgram's study of obedience to authority.

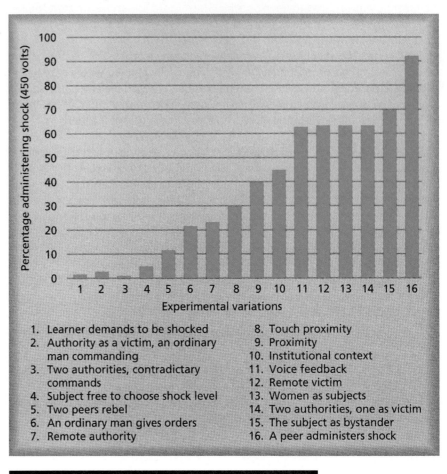

1. Learner demands to be shocked
2. Authority as a victim, an ordinary man commanding
3. Two authorities, contradictary commands
4. Subject free to choose shock level
5. Two peers rebel
6. An ordinary man gives orders
7. Remote authority
8. Touch proximity
9. Proximity
10. Institutional context
11. Voice feedback
12. Remote victim
13. Women as subjects
14. Two authorities, one as victim
15. The subject as bystander
16. A peer administers shock

Kitty Genovese was murdered in her neighborhood, while 38 of her neighbors watched. Why didn't somebody help? The answer is not what most people think.

stunned the nation and loosed a flood of psychological research: In Queens, New York, 38 ordinary citizens watched a man stalk and stab Kitty Genovese for more than half an hour, in three separate attacks. Two times the sound of the bystanders' voices and the sudden glow of their bedroom lights interrupted the assailant and frightened him. Each time, however, he returned and stabbed her again. Not a single person telephoned the police during the assault. Only one witness called the police—after the woman was dead (*New York Times,* March 13, 1964, cited in Darley & Latané, 1968). The newspaper and TV accounts of this murder played up the angle of bystander "apathy" and bewildered the nation.

Why didn't bystanders help? Is it something in the *person* or something in the *situation?* Come let us see again how social psychology is done.

CONTRIVED EMERGENCIES Soon after hearing of the Kitty Genovese murder and the analysis in the press, social psychologists Bibb Latané and John Darley began a series of studies of the bystander intervention problem. These studies all ingeniously created laboratory analogues of the problem faced by bystanders in real emergency situations. In one such experiment, a college student, placed alone in a room with an intercom, was led to believe that he was communicating with one or more students in adjacent rooms. During a discussion about personal problems, this individual heard what sounded like another student having a seizure and gasping for help. During the "seizure" the subject couldn't talk to the other students or find out what, if anything, they were doing about the emergency. The dependent variable—the response of interest in the experiment—was the speed with which he reported the emergency to the experimenter. The independent variable was the number of people he believed were in the discussion group with him.

It turned out that the speed of response by subjects in this situation depended on the number of bystanders they thought were present. The more other people they believed to be listening in on the situation in other rooms, the slower they were to report the seizure, if they did so at all. As you can see in Figure 14.3, all subjects in a two-person situation intervened within 160 seconds, but only 60% of those who believed they were part of a large group ever informed the experimenter that another student was seriously ill (Latané & Darley, 1968).

Was it the person or the situation? Personality tests showed no significant relationship between particular personality characteristics and speed or likelihood of intervening. The best predictor of bystander intervention was the situational variable of *group size* present. By way of explanation, Darley and Latané proposed that the likelihood of intervention *decreases* as the group

Connection

Chapter 1
The *independent variable* refers to the various conditions for different groups in an experiment.

FIGURE 14.3: Bystander Intervention in an Emergency

The more people present in a crisis, the less likely it is that any one bystander will intervene. As this summary of research findings shows, bystanders act most quickly in two-person groupings.

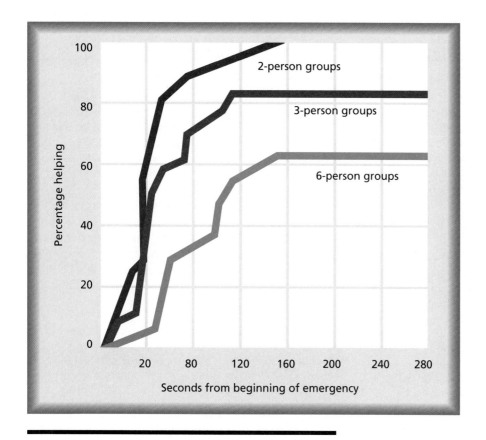

increases in size, because each person assumes that others will help, so he or she does not have to make that commitment. Individuals who perceive themselves as part of a large group of potential interveners experience a **diffusion of responsibility**: a dilution or weakening of each group member's obligation to help. You may have experienced moments of diffused responsibility if you have driven past a disabled car beside a busy highway because "surely someone else" would stop and help.

Another factor was undoubtedly also at work: conformity. As you will remember from our Core Concept and from Asch's studies of conformity, when people don't know what to do, they take their cues from others. The same thing occurred in the bystander studies, where subjects who failed to intervene were observing and conforming to the behavior of other people who were doing nothing.

DOES TRAINING ENCOURAGE HELPING?   Two studies suggest that the bystander problem can be countered with appropriate training. Ted Huston and his colleagues (1981) found no personality traits that distinguished people who had helped in actual emergency situations from those who had not. But they did find that helpers more often had had some medical, police, first-aid, or CPR training in dealing with emergency situations. And another study shows that even a psychology class lecture on the bystander problem can help (Beaman et al., 1978). Students had an opportunity to help a "victim" slumped in a doorway while walking by with a nonresponsive confederate of the experimenter. Those who had attended a lecture on bystander intervention were twice as likely to stop and attempt to help as those who did not receive the lecture on helping. Education apparently makes a difference.

Diffusion of responsibility:
Dilution or weakening of each group member's obligation to act when responsibility is perceived to be shared with all group members.

DOITYOURSELF!   ## What Makes a Samaritan Good or Bad?

Now that you know something about bystander intervention, let's see how good you are at picking the crucial variable out of a bystander situation inspired by the biblical tale of the Good Samaritan (see Luke 10:30–37). In the biblical account, several important people are too busy to help a stranger in distress. He is finally assisted by an outsider, a Samaritan, who takes the time to offer aid. Could the failure of the distressed individual's countrymen to help be due to character flaws or personal dispositions? Or was it determined by the situation?

Social psychologists decided to put students at the Princeton Theological Seminary into a similar situation. It was made all the more ironic because they thought that they were being evaluated on the quality of the sermons they were about to deliver on the parable of the Good Samaritan. Let's see what happened when these seminarians were given an opportunity to help someone in distress.

With sermon in hand, each was directed to a nearby building where the sermon was to be recorded. But as a subject walked down an alley

between the two buildings, he came upon a man slumped in a doorway, in obvious need of help. The student now had the chance to practice what he was about to preach. What would you guess was the crucial variable that predicted how likely a seminarian — ready to preach about the Good Samaritan — was to help a person in distress? Choose one:

a. how religious the seminarian was (as rated by his classmates)

b. how "neurotic" the seminarian was (as rated on the "Big Five" personality traits)

c. how much of a hurry the seminarian was in

d. how old the seminarian was

Let's see . . .

All of the *dispositional variables* (personal characteristics) of the seminarians were controlled by random assignment of subjects to three different conditions. Thus, we know that personality was not the determining factor. Rather, it was a *situational variable:* time. Before subjects left the briefing

---

room to have their sermons recorded in a nearby building, each was told how much time he had to get to the studio. Some were assigned to a *late condition*, in which they had to hurry to make the next session; others to an *on-time condition*, in which they would make the next session just on time; and a third group to an *early condition*, in which they had a few spare minutes before they would be recorded.

What were the results? Of those who were in a hurry, only 10% helped. Ninety percent failed to act as Good Samaritans! If they were on time, 45% helped the stranger. The greatest bystander intervention came from 63% of those who were not in any time bind (Darley & Batson, 1973).

Remarkably, the manipulation of time urgency made those in the "late" condition six times less likely to help than those in the "early" condition. While fulfilling their obligation to hurry, these individuals appeared to have a single-minded purpose that blinded them to other events around them. Again, it was the power of the situation.

Results of the "Good Samaritan" Study

Even with a sermon on the Good Samaritan in hand, seminary students who were in a hurry didn't usually stop to help.

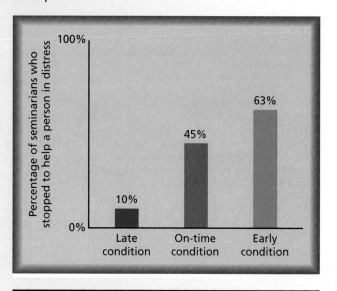

Need Help? Ask for It!

In Your Life

To demonstrate the positive effects of situational power, social psychologist Tom Moriarity (1975) arranged two fascinating experiments. In the first study, New Yorkers watched as a thief snatched a woman's suitcase in a restaurant when she left her table. In the second, they watched a thief grab a portable radio from a beach blanket when the owner left it for a few minutes. What did these onlookers do? Some did nothing, letting the thief go on his merry way. But others did intervene. What were the conditions under which some helped and others did not?

In each experiment, the would-be theft victim (the experimenter's accomplice) had first asked the soon-to-be observer of the crime either "Do you have the time?" or "Will you please keep an eye on my bag (radio) while I'm gone?" The first interaction elicited no personal responsibility, and the bystander stood by idly as the theft unfolded. However, of those who had agreed to watch the victim's property, almost every bystander intervened. They called for help, and some even tackled the runaway thief on the beach.

The encouraging message is that we can convert apathy to action and transform callousness to kindness just by asking for it. The act of requesting a favor forges a special

human bond that involves other people in ways that materially change the situation. It makes them responsible to you, and thereby responsible for what happens in your shared social world. You can use this knowledge to increase your chances of getting aid from would-be helpers in several ways (Schroeder et al., 1995):

▶ *Ask for help.* Let others know you need it rather than assuming they realize your need or know what is required.

(continued)

▶ Reduce the ambiguity of the situation by clearly explaining the problem and what should be done: "She's fainted! Call an ambulance right away," or "Someone broke into my house —call the police and give them this address!"

▶ Identify specific individuals so they do not diffuse responsibility with others present: "You, in the red shirt: Call 911!" or "Will the person in the blue Toyota please call for a tow truck right away?"

None of these tactics guarantees the safety of your person or possessions, of course. (Kitty Genovese did call for help.) Nevertheless they probably represent your best hope if you find yourself, alone in a crowd, facing a real emergency.

CHECK YOUR UNDERSTANDING

1. **RECALL:** *The Stanford prison experiment illustrates the power of _____ to influence people's behavior.*
   a. personality
   b. heredity
   c. childhood experiences
   d. the situation

2. **RECALL:** *Which of the following would be a social role?*
   a. prisoner
   b. student
   c. professor
   d. all of the above

3. **RECALL:** *In the Asch studies, which of the following produced a decrease in conformity?*
   a. The task was seen as difficult or ambiguous.
   b. The subject had to respond publicly, rather than privately.
   c. The majority was not unanimous in its judgment.
   d. The group was very large.

4. **RECALL:** *In Milgram's original study, about what proportion of the subjects gave the maximum shock?*

   a. about two-thirds
   b. about 10 %
   c. about 3 %
   d. nearly all

5. **APPLICATION:** *In an emergency situation, you would have the best chance of getting help from a*
   a. lone bystander.
   b. large group of people.
   c. group of people who are friends of each other.
   d. group of six people.

6. **UNDERSTANDING THE CORE CONCEPT:**
   Which of the following best illustrates how people in ambiguous situations take their cues from others?
   a. the majority of subjects in the Asch experiments
   b. those who disobeyed Milgram
   c. helpers who have had CPR training
   d. the experimenter in the Latané & Darley study of bystander intervention

ANSWERS: 1. d   2. d   3. c   4. a
5. a   6. a

WHAT INFLUENCES OUR JUDGMENTS OF OTHERS?

Powerful as the social situation is, it doesn't account for everything that people do. For example, it does not account for the individual differences we see in people's choices of friends and romantic partners, nor does it account for their prejudices. To explain the patterns we find in social interaction, we must also look at cognitive processes. In the language of social psychology, we need to understand how we construct our **social reality**—our subjective interpretations of other people and of our relationships. Thus, the social reality that we construct determines whom we find attractive, whom we find threatening,

Social reality: An individual's subjective interpretation of other people and of relationships with them.

whom we seek out, and whom we avoid. This, then, leads us to the second lesson of social psychology, captured in our next Core Concept:

The judgments we make about others depend not only on their behavior but on our interpretation of the social situation.

We will illustrate how these cognitive factors operate by analyzing how they affect our attitudes toward other people. We will commence on the positive end of the scale by asking a simple question: What makes people like each other? Then we will move to the opposite end with a look at the negative feelings that lie at the heart of *prejudice.*

Interpersonal Attraction

It is no surprise that we are attracted to people who have something to offer us (Brehm, 1992; Simpson & Harris, 1994). We like those who give us gifts, agree with us, act friendly toward us, share our interests, entertain us, and help us in times of need—unless, of course, we suspect that their behavior is self-serving. Although we don't necessarily mind giving something back—a social exchange—we may shrink from relationships that merely take from us and offer nothing in return. In the best of relationships—be it a friendship, partnership, marriage, or business relationship—both parties receive rewards. You might consider whether this is true in your own relationships as we look at the reward theory of attraction in the following paragraphs.

REWARD THEORY: WE (USUALLY) PREFER REWARDING RELATIONSHIPS

Most relationships can be seen as an exchange of benefits (Batson, 1987; Clark et al., 1989). The benefits could be some combination of money, cars, clothes, or other material possessions. Or the exchange might involve something intangible like praise, status, information, sex, or emotional support.

Social psychologist Elliot Aronson (1999) summarizes this in a **reward theory of attraction,** which says that attraction is a form of social learning. By looking at the social costs and benefits, claims Aronson, we can usually understand why people are attracted to each other. In brief, reward theory says that we like best those who give us maximum rewards at minimum cost. After we look at the evidence, we think you will agree that this theory explains (almost) everything about interpersonal attraction.

What is it about another person that we find most rewarding? Social psychologists have found four especially powerful sources of reward that predict interpersonal attraction: *proximity, similarity, self-disclosure,* and *physical attractiveness.* Most of us choose our friends, associates, and lovers because they offer some combination of these factors at a relatively low social cost. Let's see how each of these affects our relationships.

Proximity   An old saying advises, "Absence makes the heart grow fonder." Another contradicts with "Out of sight, out of mind." Which one is correct? Studies show that frequent contact best predicts our closest relationships (Simpson & Harris, 1994). In college dormitories, residents more often become close friends with the person who lives in the next room than they do with the person who lives two doors down (Priest & Sawyer, 1967). Residents of apartments make more friendships among people who live on the same floor than among those who live on other floors (Nahemow & Lawton, 1975). Those who live in neighborhoods more often become friends with the occupants of the

Connection

Chapter 6
Social learning involves expectations of rewards and punishments learned through social interaction and the observation of others.

Reward theory of attraction: A social learning view that says we like best those who give us maximum rewards at minimum cost.

The principle of proximity predicts that coworkers are likely to become friends.

house next door than with people living two houses away (Festinger, Schachter, & Back, 1950). This **principle of proximity** (nearness) also accounts for the fact that many people end up married to the boy or girl next door (Ineichen, 1979). And it correctly predicts that people at work will make more friends among those with whom they have the most contact (Segal, 1974).

Although you don't have to like your neighbors, the proximity rule says that when you know two individuals who are equally attractive, you will probably find it easier to make friends with the nearest one: The rewards are equal, but the cost is less in time and trouble. Apparently, the old saying that familiarity breeds contempt should be revised in light of social psychological research: Familiarity more often breeds friendship. Increased contact, itself, often increases peoples' liking for each other (Bornstein, 1989).

Similarity   People usually find it more rewarding to strike up a friendship with someone who shares their attitudes, interests, values, and experiences than to have their thinking challenged by people who are disagreeable or merely different (Hatfield & Rapson, 1993; Hendrick & Hendrick, 1992; Kelley et al., 1983; Simpson & Harris, 1994). If we have just discovered that we share tastes in music, politics, and attitudes toward education, we will probably hit it off because we have, in effect, exchanged compliments that reward each other for our tastes and attitudes (Byrne, 1969). The **similarity principle** also explains why teenagers are most likely to make friends among those who share their political and religious views, educational aspirations, and attitudes toward alcohol and drugs (Kandel, 1978). Likewise, similarity accounts for the fact that most people find marriage partners of the same age, race, social status, attitudes, and values (Brehm, 1992; Hendrick & Hendrick, 1992). In general, similarity—like proximity—makes the heart grow fonder.

Self-Disclosure   Good friends and lovers share intimate details about themselves (Sternberg, 1998). This practice not only allows people to know each other more deeply, but it sends signals of trust. It is as if I say, "Here is a piece of information that I want you to know about me, and I trust you not to hurt me with it." Friends and lovers usually find such exchanges highly rewarding. When you observe people exchanging confidences and details about their lives, you can predict that they are becoming more and more attracted to each other.

Physical Attractiveness   A cliché tells us that beauty is only skin deep. Nevertheless, people usually find it more rewarding to associate with people they consider physically attractive than with those they consider to be plain or homely (Patzer, 1985). Fair or not, good looks are a real social asset. Potential employers, for example, prefer good-looking job candidates to plainer applicants (Cash & Janda, 1984). Looks also affect people's judgments of children. Attractive children are judged as happier and more competent than their peers (Dion, 1986; Eagly et al., 1991; Hatfield & Sprecher, 1986). Even babies judge people by their appearances. We know this because babies gaze longer at pictures of normal faces than at those of distorted faces (Langlois et al., 1987).

Most people are repelled by the idea that they might make judgments based only on looks. Indeed, when asked what they look for in a dating partner, college students rank physical attractiveness last. But what people *say*

Connection

Chapter 5
The Gestalt principle of *similarity* refers to perceptual grouping of objects that share common features.

Principle of proximity: The notion that people at work will make more friends among those who are nearby — with whom they have the most contact. *Proximity* means "nearness."

Similarity principle: The notion that people are attracted to those who are most similar to themselves.

does not match their actions—at least as far as their first impressions go. Across many studies, involving a variety of characteristics—including intelligence, sincerity, masculinity, femininity, and independence—physical attractiveness overwhelmed everything else as the best predictor of how well a person would be liked after a first meeting (Aronson, 1999; Feingold, 1990; Tesser & Brodie, 1971).

Other research shows that the principle of attractiveness applies equally to same-sex and opposite-sex relationships (Maruyama & Miller, 1975). Gender differences do exist, however. While both males and females are strongly influenced by physical attractiveness, men seem to be *more* influenced by looks than are women (Cash & Killcullen, 1985; Feingold, 1990; Folkes, 1982; Hatfield & Sprecher, 1986).

These findings may come as bad news for the majority of us, who consider ourselves rather average-looking—or worse. But we can take some comfort in a study that suggests that people actually consider "average" features to be the most attractive. Investigators fed images of many students' faces into a computer that allowed them to manipulate the facial features. Surprisingly, they found that people usually liked best the images having features closest to the average size and shape (Langlois & Roggman, 1990; Langlois et al., 1994; Rhodes et al., 1999).

Now some bad news for exceptionally attractive readers: While we usually associate positive qualities with attractive individuals (Calvert, 1988), extreme attractiveness can also be a liability. Although physically attractive people are seen as more poised, interesting, sociable, independent, exciting, sexual, intelligent, well-adjusted, and successful, they are also perceived as more vain and materialistic (Brigham, 1980; Cash & Duncan, 1984; Hassebrauck, 1988; Moore et al., 1987). A "double standard" also comes into play. For example, the public favors good-looking male politicians but disparages their attractive female counterparts (Sigelman et al., 1986).

These studies on the effects of physical attractiveness hint that reward, as powerful as it is, does not account for everything. We will see this more clearly below, as we explore some important exceptions to the reward theory of attraction.

EXCEPTIONS TO THE REWARD THEORY OF ATTRACTION   While the rules of proximity, similarity, self-disclosure, and physical attractiveness may explain a lot about interpersonal attraction, a casual look around reveals lots of relationships that don't seem especially rewarding. Why, for example, might a woman be attracted to a man who abuses her? Or, why would a person want to join an organization that requires a difficult or degrading initiation ritual? Such relationships pose most interesting puzzles (Aronson, 1999). Could some people actually feel *more* attraction when they find that another person has *less* to offer them? Let's try to uncover the principles of social cognition operating behind some interesting exceptions to a reward theory of attraction.

Expectations and the Influence of Self-Esteem   We have seen that reward theory predicts our attraction to smart, good-looking, nearby, self-disclosing, like-minded, and powerful people. Yet, you have probably observed that most people end up with friends and mates whom you would judge to be of about their same level of attractiveness—the so-called **matching hypothesis** (Feingold, 1988; Harvey & Panwels, 1999). How does this happen? Is our selection of associates the result of a sort of bargaining for the best we can get in the interpersonal marketplace?

Yes, says **expectancy-value theory**. People usually decide whether to pursue a relationship by weighing the *value* they see in another person (includ-

Matching hypothesis: The prediction that most people will find friends and mates that are of about their same level of attractiveness.

Expectancy-value theory: A theory in social psychology that states how people decide whether or not to pursue a relationship by weighing the potential *value* of the relationship against their *expectation* of success in establishing the relationship.

Cognitive dissonance theory predicts that these recruits will increase their loyalty to the Marine Corps as a result of their basic training ordeal.

ing such qualities as physical attractiveness, wit, interests, and intelligence) against their *expectation* of success in the relationship (Will the other person be attracted to me?). Most of us don't waste too much time on interpersonal causes we think are lost. Rather, we initiate relationships with the most attractive people we think will probably like us in return. In this sense, expectancy-value theory is not so much a competitor of reward theory as it is a refinement of it.

One noteworthy exception to this argument involves people who suffer from low self-esteem. Sadly, people with low opinions of themselves tend to establish relationships with people who share their views — that is, with people who devalue them. Such individuals generally feel a stronger commitment to a relationship when their partner thinks poorly of them than they do when the partner thinks well of them (Swann et al., 1992).

Those individuals who appear to be extremely competent can also be losers in the expectancy-value game. Why? Most of us keep such people at a distance — probably because we fear that they will reject our approaches. But, if you happen to be one of these stunningly superior people, do not despair: Social psychologists have found hope! When highly competent individuals commit minor blunders — spilling a drink or dropping a sheaf of papers — other people actually like them *better,* probably because blunders bring them down to everyone else's level (Aronson et al., 1966, 1970). Don't count on this, however, unless you are so awesomely competent as to be unapproachable. The latté-in-the-lap trick only makes most of us look like klutzes that people like *less.*

Attraction and Self-Justification   "Semper fidelis," says the Marine Corps motto: "Always faithful." Considering the discomforting experiences that people must go through to become Marines (grueling physical conditioning, loss of sleep, lack of privacy, being yelled at, suffering punishment for small infractions of rules), it may seem remarkable that recruits routinely develop so much loyalty to their organization. Obviously, some powerfully attractive and interesting forces are at work.

Cognitive dissonance theory offers a compelling explanation for the mental adjustments that occur in people who voluntarily undergo unpleasant experiences (Festinger, 1957). The theory says that when people voluntarily act in ways that produce discomfort or otherwise clash with their attitudes and values, they develop a highly motivating mental state, called **cognitive dissonance.** A Republican politician who makes a public statement agreeing with a Democratic opponent is likely to feel cognitive dissonance. The same holds true for people who find themselves acting in ways that cause them physical discomfort. Thus, our Marine recruits may feel cognitive dissonance when they find that they have volunteered for an experience that is far more punishing than they had imagined.

According to cognitive dissonance theory, people are motivated to avoid the uncomfortable state of dissonance. If they find themselves experiencing cognitive dissonance, they attempt to reduce it in ways that are predictable — if not always entirely logical. The two main ways of reducing dissonance are to change either one's behavior or one's cognitions. So, in civilian life, if the boss is abusive, you might avoid dissonance by simply finding find another job. But in the case of a Marine recruit, changing jobs is not an option: It is too late to

Cognitive dissonance: A highly motivating state in which people have conflicting cognitions, especially when their voluntary *actions* conflict with their *attitudes.*

Connection

Chapter 9
Social psychologists view cognitive dissonance as a powerful psychological motive.

turn back once basic training has started. A recruit experiencing cognitive dissonance therefore is motivated to adjust his or her thinking. Most likely the recruit will resolve the dissonance by rationalizing the experience ("It's tough, but it builds character!") and by developing a stronger loyalty to the organization ("Being a member of such an elite group is worth all the suffering!").

In general, cognitive dissonance theory says that *when people's cognitions and actions are in conflict (dissonance) they often reduce the conflict by changing their thinking to fit their behavior.* Why? People don't like to see themselves as being inconsistent. So, to explain their own behavior to themselves, people are motivated to change their attitudes. Otherwise, it would threaten their self-esteem.

One qualification on this theory has recently come to light. In Japan—and, perhaps, in other parts of Asia—studies show that people have a lesser need to maintain high self-esteem than do North Americans (Bower, 1997; Heine et al., 1999). As a result, cognitive dissonance was found to have less power to change attitudes among Japanese. Apparently, cognitive dissonance is yet another psychological process that operates differently in collectivist and individualistic cultures.

Despite cultural variations, cognitive dissonance theory explains many things that people do to justify their behavior and thereby avoid dissonance. For example, it explains why smokers so often rationalize their habit. It explains why people who have put their efforts into a project, whether it be volunteering for the Red Cross or writing a letter of recommendation, become more committed to the cause as time goes on—in order to justify their effort. It also explains why, if you have just decided to buy a Chevrolet, you will attend to new information supporting your choice (such as Chevrolet commercials on TV), but you will tend to ignore dissonance-producing information (such as a Chevy broken down alongside the freeway).

Cognitive dissonance theory also helps us understand certain puzzling social relationships—for example, a woman who is attracted to a man who abuses her. Her dissonance might be summed up in this thought: "Why am I staying with someone who hurts me?" Her powerful drive for self-justification may make her reduce the dissonance by focusing on his good points and minimizing the abuse. And, if she has low self-esteem, she may also tell herself that she deserved his abuse. To put the matter in more general terms: *Cognitive dissonance theory predicts that people are attracted to those for whom they have agreed to suffer.* A general reward theory, by contrast, would never have predicted that outcome.

To sum up our discussion on interpersonal attraction: You usually will not go far wrong if you use a reward theory to understand why people are attracted to each other. People initiate social relationships because they expect some sort of benefit. It may be an outright reward, such as money or status or sex, or it may be an avoidance of some feared consequence, such as pain. But social psychology also shows that a simple reward theory cannot, by itself, account for all the subtlety of human social interaction. A more sophisticated and useful understanding of attraction must take into account such cognitive factors as expectations, self-esteem, and cognitive dissonance. That is, a complete theory must take into account the ways that we *interpret* our social environment. This notion of interpretation also underlies other judgments that we make about people, as we shall see next in our discussion of *attributions*.

Making Attributions

We are always trying to explain to ourselves why people do what they do. Suppose you are riding on a bus when a middle-aged woman with an armload of

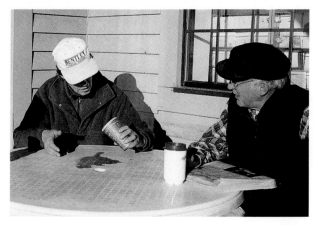

If this observer attributes his blunder to clumsiness or carelessness, he commits the fundamental attribution error. This is more likely in Western cultures, such as those of Canada and the United States, than in Eastern cultures, such as those of China and Japan.

Connection

Chapter 4
Collectivist cultures socialize people to put the needs of the group before the desires of the individual.

Fundamental attribution error: The tendency to emphasize internal causes and ignore external pressures. The FAE is more common in individualistic cultures than in collectivistic cultures.

Self-serving bias: An attributional pattern in which one takes credit for success but denies responsibility for failure. (Compare with the *fundamental attribution error.*)

packages gets on. In the process of finding a seat, she drops everything on the floor as the bus starts up. How do you explain her behavior? Do you think of her as the victim of circumstances—or is she a klutz?

Social psychologists have found that we tend to *attribute* other people's actions and misfortunes to their personal traits, rather than to situational forces, such as the unpredictable lurching of the bus. This helps explain why we often hear attributions of laziness or low intelligence to the poor or homeless, rather than an externally imposed lack of opportunity (Furnham, 1982; Pandey et al., 1982; Zucker & Weiner, 1993). It also helps us understand why most commentators on the Kitty Genovese murder attributed the inaction of the bystanders to defects in character, rather than to social influence.

On the other side of the attributional coin, we find that people use the same process to explain each other's successes. So, you may ascribe the success of a favorite singer, athlete, or family member to personal traits, such as exceptional talent or intense motivation. In doing so, we tend to ignore the effects of situational forces, such as the influence of family, coaches, a marketing blitz, or just a "lucky break."

Psychologists call this tendency to emphasize personal traits and ignore situational influences the **fundamental attribution error.** Despite its name, however, the fundamental attribution error is not as fundamental as psychologists at first thought. Cross-cultural research has suggested that it is more pervasive in individualistic cultures, as found in the United States or Canada, than in collectivist cultures, as found in Japan or China (Fletcher & Ward, 1988; Miller, 1984; Norenzayan & Nisbett, 2000; Triandis, 1996). Even within the United States, urban children are more susceptible to the fundamental attribution error than are their country cousins (Lillard, 1999).

The fundamental attribution error (FAE) is not always an "error," of course. If the causes really are dispositional, the observer's guess is correct. So the FAE is best thought of as a *bias* rather than a mistake. However, the FAE is an error in the sense that an observer may overlook legitimate, situational explanations for another's actions. For example, if the car in front of you brakes suddenly so that you almost collide, your first impression may be that the other driver is at fault, a dispositional judgment. But what if the driver slowed down in order to avoid hitting a dog that ran into the road? Then the explanation for the near-accident would be situational, not dispositional. By reminding ourselves that circumstances may account for seemingly inexplicable actions, we are less likely to commit the FAE.

Oddly, you probably judge yourself by a different standard—depending on whether you have experienced success or failure. When things go well, most people attribute their own success to internal factors, such as motivation, talent, or skill ("I am good at taking multiple-choice tests."). But when things go poorly, they attribute failure to external factors beyond their control ("The professor asked trick questions.") (Smith & Ellsworth, 1987). Psychologists have dubbed this tendency the **self-serving bias** (Bradley, 1978; Fletcher & Ward, 1988). Self-serving biases are probably rooted in the need for self-esteem, a preference for interpretations that save face and cast our actions in the best possible light (Epstein & Feist, 1988; Ickes & Layden, 1978; Schlenker et al., 1990). Social pressures to excel as an individual make the self-serving bias, like the fundamental attribution error, more common in individualist cultures than in collectivist cultures (Markus & Kitayama, 1994).

Prejudice and Discrimination

While attribution can be positive or negative, prejudice, as social psychologists use the term, is always negative. Prejudice can make an employer discriminate against women (or men) for a management job. It can make a teacher expect poor work from a minority student. And, some places in the world, it can still lead to *genocide,* the systematic extermination of a group of people because of their racial or ethnic origins. We will define **prejudice** as a negative attitude toward an individual based solely on his or her membership in a particular group. Prejudice may be expressed as negative emotions (such as dislike or fear), negative attributions or stereotypes that justify the attitude, and/or the attempt to avoid, control, dominate, or eliminate those in the target group. Prejudiced attitudes serve as filters that influence the way others are perceived and treated. Thus, prejudice exerts a powerful force for selectively processing, organizing, and remembering pertinent information about people.

We should distinguish prejudice from *discrimination,* a related concept. While prejudice is an *attitude,* discrimination is a *behavior.* We will define **discrimination,** then, as a negative action taken against an individual as a result of his or her group membership. Racial profiling, for example, is often considered a discriminatory procedure because it singles out people based solely on racial features. But, while discrimination can arise from prejudice, we will see that this is not always the case.

CAUSES OF PREJUDICE   Prejudice and discrimination can grow from many sources (Aronson, 1999). Some we acquire at an early age. Some are defensive reactions when we feel threatened. Some are the result of conformity to social customs. And some help us distinguish strangers (and possible foes) from friends (Whitley, 1999). An understanding of these sources of prejudice and discrimination will provide us with the foundation necessary for thinking about possible "cures." Here are some common sources that link with concepts we have already studied.

Dissimilarity and Social Distance   If similarity breeds liking, then dissimilarity can breed disdain. So, if you wear baggy shorts and a nose ring, it's a good bet that some middle-aged people from a traditional background feel just a bit uncomfortable around you. They are likely to perceive you as a part of a social group that flaunts values and behaviors quite distinct from those of their own group. This perceived difference can easily become fertile ground for the growth of prejudice.

What psychological principles are at work? When you perceive someone to be unlike the people in your **in-group,** you mentally place that person at a greater **social distance** than members of your own group. You are then less likely to view that individual as a social equal (Turner & Oakes, 1989). This inequality easily translates into inferiority, making it easier for you to treat members of an **out-group** with contempt. Historically, more powerful groups have discriminated against out-groups by withholding privileges, sending members of out-groups to different schools, making them sit in the back of the bus, forcing them into low-wage jobs, and otherwise treating them punitively.

Economic Competition   Highly competitive situations, where one group wins economic benefits or jobs at the other group's expense, can easily fan the flames of prejudice. For example, in the Pacific Northwest, where competition over old-growth forests threatens jobs and wildlife habitat, prejudice breeds among both timber workers and environmentalists. Likewise, prejudice may develop between groups of adults who see themselves in competition for the

Prejudice: A negative attitude toward an individual based solely on his or her membership in a particular group.

Discrimination: A negative action taken against an individual as a result of his or her group membership.

In-group: The group with which an individual identifies.

Social distance: The perceived difference or similarity between oneself and another person.

Out-group: Those outside the group with which an individual identifies.

Connection

Chapter 6
Aggression often results from punishment or the threat of punishment.

Probable causes of prejudice at work here include conformity to group norms, role models, and a sense of threat.

same jobs, especially if one group seems to have received preferential treatment. Surveys have found, for example, prejudice against black Americans to be greatest among white groups poised at an economic level just above the black American average—precisely the ones who would feel their jobs most threatened by black Americans (Greeley & Sheatsley, 1971).

Scapegoating The Hebrew priests of old performed a ritual that symbolically transferred the sins of the people to a goat—the *scapegoat*. The animal was then driven into the desert to carry its burden of guilt away from the community. The term *scapegoat* has been applied in modern times to an innocent person or group who receives blame when others feel threatened. On a large and horrifying scale, German Jews served as scapegoats for the Nazis in World War II. **Scapegoating** may also explain why the number of lynchings in the southern United States between 1882 and 1930 was related to the price of cotton. When cotton prices dropped, lynchings increased, and when cotton prices rallied, the number of lynchings fell (Hovland & Sears, 1940).

Conformity to Social Norms The source of discrimination and prejudice that is perhaps the most pervasive is an unthinking tendency to maintain conditions the way they are—even when those conditions involve unfair assumptions, prejudices, and customs (see Aronson, 1999). For example, in many offices it is the norm for secretaries to be female and executives to be male. Because of this norm, it may be difficult for a woman to break into the executive ranks. We may find the same process where the norm says that nurses should be females, engineers should be males, or basketball players should be African Americans.

So, conformity to social norms can cause discrimination, but can discrimination also cause prejudice? Imagine that you were the male executive who discriminated against a woman applying for an executive position. Or, imagine that you were the white bus driver in the mid-20th-century South who routinely sent black passengers to a special section in the back of the bus. In either case, you would have had to justify your own behavior to yourself. And if you have just treated people as second-class citizens because of their gender or ethnicity, it will be difficult—perhaps impossible—for you to think of them as anything other than inferior beings (without having a severe attack of cognitive dissonance). In this way, your discriminatory behavior can cause or strengthen prejudices.

Media Stereotypes The images used to depict groups of people in film, in print, and on television may reflect and reinforce prejudicial social norms. But they can also change those norms. Until the Black Power movement gained media attention, Africans and African Americans were most often portrayed in movies and on TV as simple, slow, comic characters, perpetuating the "Sambo" image that many whites held. Fortunately, the most blatant racial stereotypes have disappeared from the national media in the past few decades. Such images were far from harmless, because people learned many of their prejudices from the stereotypes they saw on TV and in books, movies, and magazines (Greenberg, 1986). Media distortions still occur, of course, but they are more subtle. Prime time features three times as many male as female characters (Aronson, 1999). Most are shown in professional and managerial positions, even though two-thirds of the U.S. work force is employed in blue-collar and service jobs (Aronson, 1999). The proportion of nonwhites and older persons who appear on TV is also much smaller than in the general population. For viewers, the result is a biased picture of the world.

Scapegoating: Blaming an innocent person or a group for one's own troubles.

COMBATING PREJUDICE During the civil rights struggles of the 1950s and 1960s, educators expressed a belief that prejudice could be overcome through a gradual process of information campaigns and education. The idea was to change prejudiced attitudes, and then a change in discriminatory behavior would follow. But experience provided no encouragement for this hope. In fact, these approaches have been found to be among the *least effective* tools for combating prejudice. The reason? Prejudiced people (like everyone else) usually avoid information that conflicts with their view of the world. Even for those who want to change their prejudiced attitudes, erasing the emotions associated with long-standing prejudices is difficult (Devine & Zuwerink, 1994). The process is even more difficult for those who cherish their prejudices.

So, how can one attack the prejudices of people who do not want to listen to another viewpoint? Research in social psychology suggests several possibilities. Among them are the use of *new role models, equal status contact,* and (surprisingly) *legislation.*

Connection

Chapter 6
Through social learning we acquire behaviors observed in our role models.

New Role Models Tiger Woods, Connie Chung, and many others serve as role models in prestigious jobs and leadership positions where few of their race or gender have appeared before. Certainly having such role models must encourage people in these groups who might never have considered such careers. What we do not know much about, however, is the ability of role models to change the minds of people who are already prejudiced. Role models may serve better to prevent prejudice than to cure it.

Equal Status Contact Slave owners have always had plenty of contact with their slaves, but they have always managed to hang onto their prejudices. Obviously, mere contact with people from an out-group is not enough to erase prejudices against them. Evidence, however, from integrated public housing (where the economic threat of lowered property values is not an issue) suggests that when people are placed together under conditions of equal status, where neither wields power over the other, the chances of developing understanding increase (Deutsch & Collins, 1951; Wilner et al., 1955).

Legislation You can't legislate morality. Right? The evidence of several studies suggests, however, that the old cliché may be wrong (Aronson, 1999). One of the most convincing of these studies was an experiment, done in the late 1940s, comparing the attitudes of white tenants toward black tenants in public housing projects. In one project, white and black occupants were assigned to different buildings — that is, the project was racially segregated. In another project the two racial groups were mixed (integrated) by being assigned housing in the same buildings. Only in the racially integrated project did prejudicial attitudes sharply decrease (Deutsch & Collins, 1951). This result strongly suggests that rules requiring equal-status contact can diminish prejudice.

This notion is reinforced by a larger social "experiment" that, unfortunately for social psychologists, was done under far less controlled conditions. During the past half century, the United States has adopted laws abolishing racial discrimination. The consequences were sometimes unhappy, even violent, but prejudice and discrimination have gradually diminished (although they have not been eliminated). Evidence for this shift comes from polls showing that, in the 1940s, fewer than 30% of white Americans favored desegregation. That percentage has steadily climbed to well above 90% today (Aronson, 1999).

Because these changes in public opinion were not part of a carefully controlled experiment, we cannot say that the data *prove* that legislation has

Golfer Tiger Woods is a new role model in a sport that has traditionally had few representatives of minority groups.

Romantic love: A temporary and highly emotional condition based on infatuation and sexual desire.

Triangular theory of love: A theory that describes various kinds of love in terms of three components: passion (erotic attraction), intimacy (sharing feelings and confidences), and commitment (dedication to putting this relationship first in one's life).

caused peoples' prejudices to diminish. Nevertheless, we can argue that the increased number of white Americans favoring desegregation is exactly what one might predict from cognitive dissonance theory: When the law requires people to *act* in a less discriminatory fashion, people have to justify their new behavior by softening their prejudiced attitudes. From this vantage point, it appears that legislation can affect prejudiced attitudes, after all (Aronson, 1999).

Loving Relationships

Psychology

In Your Life

e return to the positive end of the attitude spectrum to consider the form of attraction called "love." How do we know when attraction becomes love? To a large extent, our culture tells us. That is, each culture has certain common themes defining love — such as sexual arousal, attachment, concern for the other's welfare, and a willingness to make a commitment. But the idea of "love" can vary greatly from culture to culture (Aron & Aron, 1994; Beall & Sternberg, 1995; Berscheid, 1988; Fehr, 1988; Hatfield, 1988; Sprecher & McKinney, 1994; Sternberg, 1998).

There are also many kinds of love. The love that a parent has for a child differs from the love that long-time friends have for each other. Both differ from the commitment found, say, in a loving couple who have been married for 40 years. Yet, for many Americans, the term "love" brings to mind yet another form of attraction based on infatuation and sexual desire: **romantic love,** a temporary and highly emotional condition that generally fades after a few months (Hatfield et al., 1995; Hatfield & Rapson, 1993, 1998). But the American assumption that romantic love is the basis for a long-term intimate commitment is not universal. In many other cultures marriage is seen as an eco-

nomic bond or, perhaps, as a political relationship linking families.

A well-known view, proposed by Robert Sternberg (1998) in his **triangular theory of love,** says that love can have three components: passion (erotic attraction), intimacy (sharing feelings and confidences), and commitment (dedication to putting this relationship first in one's life). Various forms of love can be understood in terms of different combinations of these three components. Thus, Sternberg suggests that

▶ *Romantic love* is high on passion and intimacy, but low on commitment

▶ *Liking* and *friendship* are characterized by intimacy but not by passion and commitment

▶ *Infatuation* has a high level of passion, but it has not developed into intimacy or a committed relationship

▶ *Complete love (consummate love)* involves all three: passion, intimacy, and commitment

The need to understand what strengthens and weakens loving relationships in our own culture has acquired some urgency because of the "divorce epidemic" in the United States (Brehm, 1992; Harvey & Pauwels, 1999). If current rates hold, approximately half of all today's first marriages — and up to 60% of second marriages — will end in divorce. Much research stimulated by concern about high divorce rates has focused on the effects of divorce

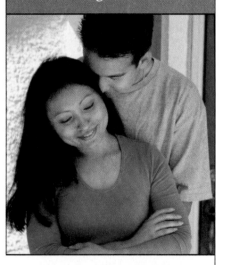

Is it love? Social psychologists have been exploring the psychology of the human heart, collecting and interpreting data about how people fall in love and strengthen their bonds of intimacy. Most recently the emphasis has shifted to the factors that keep relationships together.

on children (Ahrons, 1994; Edwards, 1995b).

In the past decade or so, however, research emphasis has shifted to the processes by which couples maintain loving relationships and the environments that challenge relationships (Berscheid, 1999; Brehm, 1992; Duck, 1992; Hatfield & Rapson, 1993). We now know, for example, that for a relationship to stay healthy and to thrive both partners must see it as rewarding and equitable. As we saw in our discussion of reward theory, both must, over the long run, feel that they are getting something out of the relationship, not just giving. What they get — the rewards of the relationship — can involve many things, including adventure, status, laughter, mental stimulation, and material goods, as well as nurturance, love, and social support.

In addition, for a relationship to thrive, communication between partners must be open, ongoing, and mutually validating (Gottman et al., 1998; Gottman & Silver, 1994; Harvey & Omarzu, 1997; Monaghan, 1999). Research shows that couples in lasting relationships have five times more positive inter-actions than negative ones — including exchanges of smiles, loving touches, laughter, and compliments (Gottman, 1994). Yet, because every relationship experiences an occasional communication breakdown, the partners must know how to deal with conflicts effectively. Conflicts must be faced early and resolved fairly and effectively. Ultimately, each partner must take responsibility for his or her own identity, self-esteem, and commitment to the relationship — rather than expect the partner to engage in mind reading or self-sacrifice. (We will say more about dealing with conflicts in the next section of the chapter.)

This has been the briefest sampling from the growing social psychology of relationships. Such research has practical applications. Teachers familiar with research findings can now inform their students about the basic principles of healthy relationships. Therapists apply these principles in advising clients on how to communicate with partners, negotiate the terms of their relationships, and resolve inevitable conflicts. More immediately, as you yourself learn about the factors that influence how you perceive and relate to others, you should gain a greater sense of self-control and well-being in your own intimate connections with others (Harvey, 1996; Harvey et al., 1990).

CHECK YOUR UNDERSTANDING

1. **RECALL:** *According to Aronson, we can explain almost everything about interpersonal attraction with a theory of*
   a. love.
   b. rewards.
   c. genetics.
   d. gender.

2. **RECALL:** *Which of the following does the research say is most important in predicting initial attraction?*
   a. physical attractiveness
   b. money
   c. personality
   d. nurturing qualities

3. **RECALL:** *Which theory of attraction best explains why people who are considered to be extremely competent are often not the people we are most attracted to?*
   a. reward theory
   b. expectancy-value theory
   c. cognitive dissonance theory
   d. psychoanalytic theory

4. **APPLICATION:** *According to cognitive dissonance theory, which of the following would be the best strategy for getting people to like you?*
   a. Give them presents.
   b. Show interest in their interests.
   c. Tell them that you like them.
   d. Persuade them to perform a difficult or unpleasant task for you.

5. **RECALL:** *Prejudice is a(n) _____, while discrimination is a(n) _____.*
   a. behavior/attitude
   b. instinct/choice
   c. attitude/behavior
   d. stimulus/response

6. **RECALL:** *The evidence suggests that one of the most effective techniques for eliminating racial prejudice has been*
   a. education.
   b. threat and force.
   c. legislation.
   d. tax incentives.

7. **UNDERSTANDING THE CORE CONCEPT:**
   Reward theory, expectancy-value theory, cognitive dissonance theory, and attribution theory all tell us that we respond not just to situations but to
   a. our cognitive interpretations.
   b. our social instincts.
   c. the intensity of the stimuli.
   d. our biological needs and drives.

Core Concept

ANSWERS: 1. b   2. a   3. b   4. d
5. c   6. c   7. a

WHAT ARE THE ROOTS OF VIOLENCE AND TERRORISM?

The terrorist attacks of September 11, 2001, raise questions for which there are no easy answers. In this section, however, we will see that social psychology's findings on the *power of the situation* offer a useful starting point for understanding why people commit violent acts. But, your authors will argue, a complete picture of violence and terrorism requires the combined insights of many perspectives—and not just those from psychology. Issues of money, power, resources, and ancient grudges must be considered as well. Our Core Concept says:

> **The power of the situation** can help us understand violence and terrorism, but a broader understanding requires multiple perspectives that go beyond the boundaries of psychology.

Before we plunge into these chilling waters, however, let us clarify two basic terms, **violence** and **aggression,** that have overlapping definitions. In the following discussion, we will use these terms interchangeably for any behavior that is intended to cause harm to others (whether or not harm actually results). A key component of this definition is *intent,* but it is also important to note that violence and aggression are social—or, perhaps more aptly, *antisocial*—phenomena.

The Social Psychology of Aggression and Violence

In this chapter we have seen repeatedly that the pressures of a social situation can make ordinary people commit horrible acts (Zimbardo, 2001). Social influence was at work in Milgram's obedience studies, where subjects obeyed orders to deliver apparently lethal shocks to a stranger. Likewise, the social situation provoked aggression in the Stanford prison study, where ordinary students acting as guards behaved with brutality toward fellow students in the role of prisoners. Still other research has shown that aggressive behavior can be induced by situations that create prejudice, conformity, frustration, threat, or wounded pride (Aronson, 1999; Baumeister et al., 1996). Now, let us take a detailed look at another important study that showed how aggression could arise out of intergroup conflict—again caused by the power of the situation.

The Robbers Cave: An Experiment in Conflict

The setting was a Boy Scout Camp known as the Robbers Cave. There, the experimenters, Muzafer Sherif and his colleagues (1961) randomly assigned 11- and 12-year-old boys to two groups, dubbed the Eagles and the Rattlers. The experiment called for conditions similar to those at many other summer camps for boys: days filled with competitive games and activities. Competition, the experimenters hoped, would create conflict between the two groups.

Initially, the Eagles and Rattlers were kept apart, allowing within-group activities to build group **cohesiveness** (solidarity, loyalty, and a sense of group membership). Later the experimenters brought the two groups together for competitions, such as tug-of-war and football. Prizes for the winners heightened the competitive atmosphere. The final straw was a "party" at which the experimenters arranged to have the Eagles arrive an hour early. Half the food was mouth watering, and half was deliberately unappealing. As you might

Violence and **aggression:** Terms that refer to behavior that is intended to cause harm.

Cohesiveness: Solidarity, loyalty, and a sense of group membership.

expect, when the Rattlers arrived they found that the Eagles had devoured the more desirable food. This led to name calling and scuffling, which culminated in a food fight.

With a rancorous atmosphere well established, Sherif and his colleagues tried various tactics for promoting cooperation between the groups. Their initial attempts were, however, complete failures. In particular, it did *not* help merely to bring the Eagles and Rattlers together for social events, such as movies or eating in the same dining room. Such occasions just offered opportunities for more hostility.

What *did* help was to contrive situations in which the groups had to cooperate in order to serve their own interests. First, however, the experimenters called a halt to the competitive games. Then, they assembled the boys to inform them of a "problem" that had developed with the camp's vital water line. Both groups agreed to search the line for the trouble spot, which they did together—harmoniously. On another day, the experimenters arranged for the camp's truck to break down—which meant that it could not go to town for food. To get the truck running, the two groups had to work cooperatively by pulling it with the same rope previously used for the divisive tug-of-war game.

To serve its own needs, each group had to cooperate with the "enemy." And, as dissonance theory would predict, hostility changed to friendliness. The change in behavior led directly to a change in attitude. That is, the attitude change resulted from a need to justify the altered behavior.

It took several such crises to break down the hostile barriers between the two groups and to build a sense of **mutual interdependence,** a working relationship based on shared goals. But, in the end, the groups actively sought opportunities to mingle with each other, and friendships developed between members of the Eagles and Rattlers. One group even used its own money to buy treats for members of the other group.

Competition can promote aggressive behavior.

Mutual interdependence: A shared sense that individuals or groups need each other in order to achieve common goals.

How does this apply to our understanding of the terrorist attacks of September 11? Admittedly, it is a stretch between experiments in the laboratory and conflicts on the international stage. Nevertheless, please consider the following ideas.

First, understanding terrorism does not mean condoning or accepting it—any more than understanding prejudice means approving of it. There can be no moral justification for the vicious attacks on the United States—or any other terrorist

attacks. But—like it or not—many people in the world perceive the United States as the enemy. Understanding this perception—and dealing constructively with it—demands that we see the conflict from someone else's point of view: those who consider the United States to be the enemy. Doing so involves a *cultural perspective*.

Second, the Eagles and Rattlers study suggests that effective conflict resolution can come from identifying goals of mutual benefit and persuading the antagonistic groups to pursue these shared goals. This task requires leadership of exceptional vision and skill. At this writing, it remains uncertain

Third-world poverty generates conditions that can nurture terrorism.

whether such leadership will emerge in the conflict resulting from the

(continued)

terrorist attacks on the United States.

Third, we must realize that terrorism does not always involve international conflict. The shootings at Columbine high school were terrorist acts, as was the bombing of the Federal Building in Oklahoma City, along with thousands of racial/ethnic hate crimes, attacks against gays, and violence directed at abortion providers that have made news in recent years (Doyle, 2001). It would be a mistake to believe that terrorism is always a threat from foreigners: Every culture can breed violent people—although some cultures are more violent than others (Moghaddam et al., 1993; Shiraev & Levy, 2001)

Fourth, as in other areas of psychology, understanding the problem of violence and terrorism requires application of *multiple perspectives*—perhaps the most profound and far-reaching idea in psychology. In an earlier chapter, for example, we viewed aggression from a *biological perspective,* noting its association with testosterone and with certain parts of the brain (Davidson et al., 2000; Enserink, 2000; Holden, 2000). From a *behavioral perspective,* we saw how aggression often results from pain or punishment (Shiraev & Levy, 2001). From an *evolutionary perspective,* we can see that aggression involves an impulse built into our genetic make-up and triggered by fear, threat, scarce resources, and sexual rivalry. Experiments in social learning have also shown how role models can stimulate aggression. And in this chapter, we have seen how other forms of social influence can lead to aggression and violence.

A complete picture, however, necessitates taking perspectives that extend beyond psychology (Segall et al., 1999). When we expand our view of terrorism, we can see that long-standing hostilities arise from religious, ethnic, and racial prejudices and from poverty, powerlessness, and hopelessness. To arrive at this understanding, however, we must view terrorism from *historical, economic,* and *political perspectives*—again, not to excuse violent acts

but to understand their origins. In the following section, we discuss the roles these factors may have played in producing the events of September 11.

FUEL FOR TERRORISM

The flammable combination of poverty, powerlessness, and hopelessness are the tinder that the September 11 attacks were intended to ignite, says Jonathan Lash, president of the World Resources Institute in Washington, D.C. (2001). Much of the world lives in poverty and hunger and sees no way out. Ethnic hatred and wars aggravate their plight. Moreover, the number of people living in these miserable conditions is increasing, as most of the world's population explosion is occurring in poorer countries. And, to make matters more volatile, says Lash, a large proportion of these desperate people depend directly on resources that are rapidly being depleted: fisheries, forests, soils, and water resources. As a result, every day, thousands flee their traditional homelands and stream into the largest and poorest cities. Most are young—a result of the high birth rates in the Third World. Mr. Lash warns that urban slums, filled with restless, jobless young men, are "tinderboxes of anger and despair; easy recruiting grounds for bin Laden or those who may come after him" (p. 1789). Consider this warning in light of Milgram's obedience studies: If ordinary, well-fed people can be induced to deliver apparently lethal shocks, how much easier it would be to persuade angry, hopeless young men to commit violent acts.

Thus, says Lash, removing the flint that sets off the spark is not sufficient; we must also deal with the tinder. In other words, even if we strike down the terrorists' leaders and capture their resources, the anger and despair of the world's poor and desperate people will continue to pose a threat to the United States and other wealthy nations. As psychologists, we can understand this threat as a political restatement of the pain–aggression relationship.

Understanding the tinderbox conditions that arise from poverty and despair and the tension between rich and poor nations, then, requires that we take economic and political perspectives. In addition, we must see that many of the conflicts that breed terrorism have historical roots. We cannot understand, for example, the tensions between Christianity and Islam without knowing about the 200-year war that we call the Crusades (1095–1291) or the fall of the six-centuries-old Ottoman empire (1300–1922) at the end of World War I. Although such events may seem remote, they changed the trajectory of history, and their impact continues to fuel conflict in the Middle East today.

WHAT CAN *WE* DO ABOUT TERRORISM?

Your authors believe that taking multiple perspectives can provide important insights on the problems of aggression, violence, and terrorism. In this vein, please consider the following suggestions.

As citizens, each of us can demand better of politicians, journalists, and others who supply easy, single-perspective answers to complex problems. Meeting aggression with aggression may be necessary, but it is never sufficient. We should encourage our political representatives to consider responses based on multiple perspectives. More specifically, we can support efforts to find common goals—in much the same way as Sherif and his colleagues reduced conflict among the Eagles and Rattlers.

Unfortunately, the easiest and most simplistic response is to demonize those who perpetrate evil deeds —but that is merely name-calling, and we should resist it. This tactic blinds us to the power of the situation to create aggression in ordinary people. More important, it prevents us from dealing with the situations that nurture violence.

A related mistake is to think of violence and terrorism as "senseless." On the contrary, destructive deeds always make sense from the perpetrator's frame of reference. As Shakespeare's Hamlet said, there is "method" in madness: We must understand the method in the minds of potential terrorists, if we are to deter them.

Finally, as individuals and as a society, we must refuse to adopt the terrorists' devaluing of human life. If we act on the desire to destroy our enemy at any cost, we have succumbed to the power of the situation. Moreover, we will have played into the hands of the ones we would destroy.

ONE PSYCHOLOGIST'S APPROACH

The hope that the psychology of cooperation and conflict reduction might ease international tensions lies behind a quiet program currently operating in Israel. There,

social psychologist Herbert Kelman applies the lessons of the Eagles and Rattlers to the long-standing hostilities and prejudices between the Israelis and the Palestinians (Kelman, 1997, 1999; Rouhana & Kelman, 1994). His approach involves bringing community leaders from both sides together for small-group discussions of mutual problems. Not just anyone could have started such a program: Kelman's credibility with both sides is a product of his stature as a scholar and the prestige of his affiliation with Harvard University.

Kelman's approach was carefully planned to encourage cooperation and minimize the rewards for hostile behaviors. Representatives of both groups are invited to attend a series of meetings. These are not the usual, high-profile public negotiation sessions, however. Kelman has found that the process works best when the participants are midlevel community leaders, who have some

power and status but who are in close touch with ordinary, grassroots citizens. Also important is the fact that meetings are held in private to avoid competitive posturing for the press. Removed from the public spotlight, tensions between the two factions have eased, and earnest communication has developed.

Proof that this approach works is difficult to come by, especially in these times of political crisis and upheaval, although Kelman can recite case studies in which old hatreds have been soothed. In fact, several participants in these workshops have later become involved in other peace efforts in their communities. While the method is inspired by solid science, Kelman is performing no laboratory experiment. Rather, he is applying principles of social psychology to the world beyond the laboratory, where most of the variables remain uncontrolled.

CHECK**YOUR**UNDERSTANDING

1. **RECALL:** *Conflict between the groups in the Robbers' Cave experiment was encouraged by*
    a. punishing nonaggressive boys.
    b. showing movies featuring hostile role models.
    c. competitive games.
    d. putting a particularly aggressive boy in charge of each group.

2. **RECALL:** *In Kelman's work in the Middle East, he removed much of the incentive for competitive responses by*
    a. punishing those who responded competitively.
    b. holding the meetings in private.
    c. taking hostages from both sides.

    d. publicly denouncing those who responded competitively.

3. **UNDERSTANDING THE CORE CONCEPT:**
    In both the Robbers Cave experiment and Kelman's work in the Middle East, helping people to build a sense of mutual interdependence encouraged them to
    a. alter their perceptions of each other.
    b. punish those who had encouraged hostilities.
    c. become more creative.
    d. adopt new personality traits.

ANSWERS: 1. c   2. b   3. a

Core Concept

A PERSONAL ENDNOTE

And so we come to the end of our journey together through psychology. If you are a curious people-watcher, perhaps you will continue on to the next phase of the journey into more advanced courses and into the books and films we have suggested at the end of each chapter. If you scan back through the Core Concepts in this book, you will realize that you have learned much already. Yet, because people are so complex, we have scarcely scratched the surface of the excitement and challenges that the field offers.

One day you may be among those who contribute to this dynamic enterprise as a scientific researcher. (Your name could appear as a reference in a future edition of this book. Please send us word of your discoveries!) Or perhaps you will decide to be a practitioner who applies what is known in psychology to the solution of personal and social problems. (Again, we would like to know if your career in psychology began with our journey together.) But, even if you don't become a professional psychologist, your authors hope that this introduction to psychology has sparked a lasting interest in mind and behavior.

Playwright Tom Stoppard reminds us that "Every exit is an entry somewhere else." We would like to believe that the entry into the next phase of your life will be facilitated by what you have learned from *Psychology: Key Questions and Core Concepts* and from your introductory psychology course. In that next journey, may you infuse new life into the study of human nature, while strengthening the human connections among all people you encounter. Till we meet again,

Phil Zimbardo

Ann Weber

Bob Johnson

Using Psychology to Learn Psychology: Persuasion in the Classroom

You may associate persuasion with advertising and politics, but persuasion does not stop there. It is woven into all human interaction —including the exchanges of ideas that occur in the classroom. There, your professors and fellow students will attempt to persuade you with reasoned arguments, and they will expect you to set out your points of view in the same fashion. But, aside from the open exchange of ideas and opinions, there are other, more subtle persuasive pressures of which you should be aware, says social psychologist Robert Cialdini (2001a, b). If you don't know about these, you run the risk of letting other people make up your mind for you. We will discuss three such subtle forms of influence that you will encounter in your college or university experience.

SOCIAL VALIDATION

Although you may choose to see the most popular movie of the year, going along with the crowd is a poor basis for judging the theories you encounter in your classes. Many of the world's discarded ideas were once accepted by nearly everyone. In psychology, these include the false notions that we use only 10% of our brain, that personality is determined by the first two years of life, and that IQ tests are a good measure of innate abilities. So, rather than accepting what you hear and read, questioning even the most widely held concepts is a good habit. In fact, most famous scientists have built their careers on challenging ideas that everyone else accepted.

AUTHORITY

The lectures you hear and the textbooks you read are full of authority figures. Every parenthetical reference in this book, for example, cites an authority. Most are given, in part, to persuade you that the argument being offered is credible. The problem, of course, is that ideas are not true merely because some authority says so. For example, just a few years ago, every introductory psychology text in print taught that no new neurons were created in the brain after birth. Now we know that the textbooks and the experts they cited were wrong. Real proof of such assertions, however, requires more objective evidence obtained by the scientific method—not just the declaration of an authority.

THE POISON PARASITE ARGUMENT

In advertising, a good way to undermine a competitor, says Cialdini, is with a message that calls into question the opponent's credibility. Then, to get people to remember what you have said, you can infect your opponent with a "parasite"—a mnemonic link that reminds people of your message every time they hear your opponent's pitch (Brookhart, 2001). A classic example involved antismoking ads that looked like Marlboro commercials, except that they featured a coughing, sickly "Marlboro Man." You may encounter the same sort of poison parasite argument in a lecture or a textbook that attempts to hold someone's ideas up to ridicule. That's not necessarily bad: In the academic world, weak ideas should perish. The sneaky, dishonest form of this technique, however, involves a misrepresentation or oversimplification of the opponent's arguments. The antidote is to be alert for ridicule and to check out the other side of the argument yourself.

The social psychology of persuasion, of course, involves much more than we have discussed here. A good place to look for more information is Cialdini's book, *Influence: Science and Practice* (2001a). Perhaps the most important idea is that some knowledge of persuasion can forearm you against the persuasive techniques you will encounter, both in and out of the classroom. When you know how effective persuaders operate, you are less likely to donate money to causes you don't care about, buy a car you don't really like, or accept a theory without examining the evidence critically.

Chapter
Summary

HOW DOES THE SOCIAL SITUATION AFFECT OUR BEHAVIOR?

The Stanford prison experiment demonstrated how norms and social roles can be major sources of situational influence. The Asch studies demonstrated the powerful effect of the group to produce conformity, even when the group is clearly wrong. Another shocking demonstration of situational power came from Stanley Milgram's controversial experiments on obedience to authority. Situational influence can also lead to inaction: The bystander studies showed that individuals are inhibited by the number of bystanders, the ambiguity of the situation, and their resultant perception of their social role and responsibility.

We usually adapt our behavior to the demands of the social situation, and in ambiguous situations we take our cues from the behavior of others.

WHAT INFLUENCES OUR JUDGMENTS OF OTHERS?

The situation, by itself, does not determine behavior. Rather, it is our *interpretation* of the situation—our constructed social reality—that regulates behavior, including our social interactions. Usually we are attracted to relationships that we find rewarding, although there are exceptions, predicted by expectancy-value theory and cognitive dissonance theory. Attribution theory predicts that we will attribute other people's blunders to their traits (the fundamental attribution error) and our own to the situation (the self-serving bias), although this tendency depends on one's culture. Prejudice and discrimination also demonstrate how we construct our own social reality through such cognitive processes as the perception of social distance and threats, the influence of media stereotypes, scapegoating, and self-justification. Healthy loving relationships also demonstrate the social construction of reality, because there are many kinds of love and many cultural variations in the understanding of love.

The judgments we make about others depend not only on their behavior but on our interpretation of the social situation.

WHAT ARE THE ROOTS OF VIOLENCE AND TERRORISM?

Many studies in social psychology—particularly those dealing with obedience and conformity—show that the *power of the situation* can pressure ordinary people to commit horrible acts. In the Robbers Cave experiment, conflict between groups arose from an intensely competitive situation. Cooperation, however, replaced conflict when the experimenters contrived situations that fostered mutual interdependence and common goals for the groups.

The Robbers Cave experiment may hold a valuable lesson about dealing with violence and terrorism: the need for leadership that will find common goals for groups in conflict. A fuller understanding of violence and terrorism, however, requires taking *multiple perspectives*—including those that go beyond the boundaries of psychology to include the historical, economic, and political roots. Unfortunately, the easiest responses involve demonizing those who commit violent acts or labeling such acts as "senseless"—responses that interfere with our understanding them and dealing with them effectively.

A constructive approach, based on understanding conflict from multiple perspectives, is now underway in the Middle East. There, social psychologist Herbert Kelman has created noncompetitive situations in which Israeli and Palestinian community leaders are seeking solutions that benefit all sides.

The power of the situation can help us understand violence and terrorism, but a broader understanding requires multiple perspectives that go beyond the boundaries of psychology.

Review
Test

For each of the following items, choose the single correct or best answer. The answer key appears at the end.

1. Which of the following is the social psychological principle illustrated by the Stanford prison experiment and its findings about participants' behavior?
   a. Social situations have powerful influences on human behavior.
   b. An experience is only socially real when the group is unanimous about interpreting it.
   c. Because everyone is basically different, no two people will respond to the same circumstances in the same way.
   d. Even in healthy circumstances, disturbed people will behave in unhealthy ways.

2. Theodore Newcomb's study of the attitudes of Bennington College students showed that, 20 years after they were first studied,
   a. all the women had gradually shifted to more conservative attitudes.
   b. all the women had gradually shifted to more liberal attitudes.
   c. the liberals were still liberal, and the conservatives still conservative.
   d. none of the above.

3. According to research on the Asch effect, which of the following is *not* a condition that encourages greater conformity?
   a. The task being judged is difficult or ambiguous.
   b. Each group member votes privately and anonymously.
   c. The group is extremely cohesive.
   d. The group members perceive each other to be highly competent.

4. Which of the following statements about Milgram's obedience experiments is true?
   a. All subjects were unable to resist the authority figure's orders, no matter how high the level of shock they believed they were administering.
   b. The majority of subjects delivered increasingly intense shocks until the learner complained of a heart condition, at which point most subjects refused to go on.
   c. Although most subjects verbally dissented and complained, most obeyed.
   d. Despite predictions by human nature experts that no one would comply, subjects enjoyed the experiment and had no trouble obeying the authority figure's commands.

5. Research on the factors that influence helping behavior suggests that the best predictor of bystander intervention is
   a. each individual's measurable level of personal altruism.
   b. the appearance or attractiveness of the victim.
   c. an individual's degree of religiousness or agreement with conventional religious values.
   d. the size of the group of bystanders to the emergency.

6. According to research on interpersonal attraction and close relationships, which of the following is *false*?
   a. The more you interact with someone, the more likely you are to like him or her.
   b. We form friendships on the basis of our similarity of backgrounds and attitudes.
   c. As far as first impressions go, a pleasing personality counts more than good looks.
   d. If you voluntarily undergo a hardship or suffering at someone's request, you will probably like them more than you did before.

7. Which of the following situations would be likely to create a feeling of cognitive dissonance in the mind of the individual described?
   a. A woman who has said she is on a diet declines the offer of dessert.
   b. A young man who says he loves his girlfriend spends a great deal of time choosing just the right valentine card to send her.
   c. When a man finds out the car he wants costs more than he can afford, he decides not to buy it and looks instead for a less expensive vehicle.
   d. A woman with a prejudice against Jews finds herself agreeing to do a favor for a Jewish neighbor.

8. Which of the following illustrates the effects of the fundamental attribution error?
   a. Explaining why he is turning his paper in late, a student tells the professor that he had car trouble on the way to campus.
   b. Watching an acquaintance hurry from the dining hall, a woman remarks, "Amy's in such a hurry — she must be a pretty impatient person."
   c. After waiting an unusually long time to be waited on in a restaurant, a customer thinks there must be something wrong in the kitchen that is interfering with the waitress's ability to work as quickly as usual.

d. All of the above illustrate the fundamental attribution error.

9. In the Robbers Cave experiment, hostility between the groups was reduced by
   a. having the groups engage in social activities with each other.
   b. creating crisis situations that the groups had to work on cooperatively.
   c. punishing aggressive behavior.
   d. allowing the groups to take out their hostilities in competitive sports.

10. In an application of social psychological findings on promoting cooperation between hostile groups, Herbert Kelman has

a. used the power of conformity (the Asch effect) to reduce hostilities.
b. advocated the use of rewards for peaceful actions and punishments for hostile actions.
c. brought community officials on both sides together for private discussions of mutual problems.
d. promoted "friendly" athletic competition as a means of displacing harmful aggressions and "burning off" energy that could explode into violence.

ANSWERS: 1. a   2. c   3. b   4. c   5. d   6. c
7. d   8. b   9. b   10. c

If You're Interested . . .

BOOKS

Aronson, E. (2000). *Nobody left to hate: Teaching compassion after Columbine.* Worth Publishers. Renowned social psychologist Elliot Aronson argues that violent shootings by young students are in part fostered by the pressures and negativity in the schools themselves, including bullying, taunting, and exclusion. To end the tragedy, he offers strategies by which students, teachers, and communities might work to make schools humane, compassionate, and respectful.

Beck, A. T. (1999). *Prisoners of hate: The cognitive basis of anger, hostility, and violence.* HarperCollins. The author, an expert on cognitive therapy and depression, finds parallels between the crimes of terrorists and extremists and the genocides perpetrated by warring nations. The book can be taken as a primer on the cognitive distortions that justify violence and destruction.

Cialdini, R. B. (1993). *Influence: The psychology of persuasion.* Quill. Noted social psychologist Robert Cialdini summarizes the key principles of social influence, by which you get others to do what you want — or they get *you* to obey, agree, or buy. Whether you're selling, buying, or trying *not* to buy, this review arms you with the principles and research explaining how ideas and relationships alter behavior.

Coplin, W. D. (2000). *How you can help: An easy guide to doing good deeds in your everyday life.* Routledge.

Since September 11, 2001, many citizens want to "do good" but aren't sure how to start. This guide lists needy groups and worthwhile causes, strategies and principles for efficient helping, and brief, inspiring case histories of people who have made a difference in ways both large and small.

Gay, P. (1994). *The cultivation of hatred.* W. W. Norton & Co. This is volume 3 of a series exploring the bourgeois experience at the turn of the last century, examining the Victorians' ambivalence about aggression, so that it becomes channeled into sports, duels, wars of "honor," myths of "manliness," and finally old-fashioned warfare, prejudice, racism, sexism, and repression.

Friday, N. (1996). *Our looks, our lives: Sex, beauty, power, and the need to be seen.* Harper. Best-selling author Nancy Friday takes a careful, critical look at life in the "age of the empty package," when looks take precedence over personal qualities and everyone lusts for beauty.

Kohn, A. (1990). *The brighter side of human nature: Altruism and empathy in everyday life.* Basic Books. Kohn provides an uplifting review of the many ways in which people help and cooperate with each other and the challenge this poses for more cynical views of human nature as "naturally" warlike and selfish.

Pope, H. G., Phillips, K. A., & Olivardia, R. (2000). *The Adonis complex: The secret crisis of male body obsession.* The Free Press. Much has been written about the damage done to girls and women by society's unreal expectations and impossible images of female thinness and beauty. But what about males? This book examines a pressure to be not anorexic but "bigorexic," pumped up and bulging with muscles to achieve the look of strength and power, a pressure the authors relate to women's gains in social power and men's inability to define masculinity in new ways. It includes recommendations for identifying and treating symptoms of dangerously disordered behavior.

VIDEOS

Ghosts of Mississippi. (1996, color, 130 min.). Directed by Rob Reiner; starring Alec Baldwin, Whoopi Goldberg, James Woods. This is the involving drama of the murder of civil rights leader Medgar Evers, the campaign by his widow to arrest and convict Byron De La Beckwith (the admitted but not confessed killer), and the attorney who finally agreed to prosecute the case at great cost to his own life. It is a portrait of a culture's doomed efforts to protect their prejudices and resist change.

Fahrenheit 451. (1966, color, 111 min.). Directed by François Truffaut; starring Oskar Werner, Julie Christie, Cyril Cusack. Based on the Ray Bradbury novel, this is a futuristic tale of a book-burning society (paper burns at 451 degrees Fahrenheit) in which a conforming "fireman" is tempted to explore the illicit, underground world of book-reading nonconformists.

Pay It Forward. (2001, color, 123 min.). Directed by Mimi Leder; starring Kevin Spacey, Helen Hunt, Haley Joel Osment. Challenged by a talented but afflicted new teacher, a young boy initiates a program of helping others in threes, with each recipient obligated to do the same for others in need. The engaging plot about the personalities and relationships of the principal characters also shows how such a plan might work and suggests that altruism might yet prevail.

Ridicule. (1992, color, 102 min. [French w/subtitles]). Directed by Patrice Leconte; starring Charles Berling, Jean Rochefort, Fanny Ardant. In the reign of Louis XVI, an environmentally conscious landowner seeking an audience with the king learns that he must meet social norms for sardonic wit and putdown in order to win influence and attention.

Separate but Equal. (1991, color, 193 min.). Directed by John Stevens, Jr., starring Sidney Poitier, Richard Kiley, Burt Lancaster. Originally a two-part TV movie, this docudrama tells the story of a young Thurgood Marshall's 1954 argument of Brown v. Board of Education before the Supreme Court, of which he was later to become the first black justice. Includes depiction of classic research by black psychologists Kenneth and Mamie Clark, who discovered that segregated children's self-concepts had been harmed, even to the point of preferring white dolls to black ones.

Six Degrees of Separation. (1993, color, 111 min.). Directed by Fred Schepisi; starring Stockard Channing, Donald Sutherland, Will Smith. Social psychologist Stanley Milgram once demonstrated that a letter with only an unknown addressee and city, but no address, could be hand delivered via a series of only five or six go-betweens, each of whom knew each other if no one else in the "chain." In this film, based on John Guare's stage play, an affluent urban couple find their lives surprisingly connected to and affected by a young man impersonating a celebrity's son.

Sliding Doors. (1998, color, 108 min.). Directed by Peter Howitt; starring Gwyneth Paltrow, John Hannah, John Lynch, Jeanne Tripplehorn, Zara Turner. This romantic comedy explores how situations and chance events—like catching or not catching a subway home—can set in motion a sequence of life-changing events. Two parallel stories are told of a woman's experiences after she either does or does not get through the sliding doors in time to catch the departing train.

To Kill a Mockingbird. (1962, b&w, 129 min.). Directed by Robert Mulligan; starring Gregory Peck, Mary Badham, Philip Alford, Brock Peters, Robert Duvall. This dramatization of Harper Lee's novel about a small-town Southern lawyer defending a black man falsely accused of rape shows the impact of his unpopular efforts on his young children and his community.

12 Angry Men. (1957, b&w, 95 min.). Directed by Sidney Lumet; starring Henry Fonda, Lee J. Cobb, E. G. Marshall, Ed Begley, Jack Klugman, Jack Warden, Robert Webber. In this absorbing drama of 12 jurors' deliberation over a verdict in a murder trial, their own prejudices, eyewitness memory, and group influence all play a part.

WEB RESOURCES

http://www.influenceatwork.com/ Influence is a field of psychological inquiry that examines how people change. Explore how social psychology can be applied to a corporate environment, through consulting or training, or an academic setting, through influence and persuasion.

http://www.sesp.org The Social of Experimental Social Psychology is a scientific organization focused on the advancement of social psychology.

http://www.telecom.csuhayward.edu/ ~ psy3500/key03 a.html How do people fall in love? Visit this Web site to learn about the stages of attraction and love.

http://www.socialpsychology.org/social.htm Visit this Web site to learn about prejudice and discrimina-tion. This site on social psychology also covers the psychology of gender, social influence, and inter-personal relations, as well as many other topics.

http://www.stanleymilgram.com This Web site is cre-ated by Dr. Thomas Blass, a social psychologist and biographer of Stanley Milgram. Visit the vari-ous links that provide accurate information on the life and work of this social psychologist.

UNDERSTANDING GRAPHS & STATISTICS: ANALYZING DATA & FORMING CONCLUSIONS

OUTLINE

How Do Psychologists Analyze Their Data?

GRAPHIC REPRESENTATION

STATISTICAL ANALYSIS

How Can You Be Misled by Statistics?

Connection

Chapter 1
Theories provide explanations for patterns observed or predicted in the data.

All scientists make measurements. In psychology, the measurements often describe people's behavior or other attributes, such as extraversion, romantic attraction, memory, aggression, or shyness. To look for patterns in these measurements, psychologists may put their data in visual form—as graphs. In addition, they use a set of mathematical techniques called **statistics** to organize the data and draw inferences from them. In the next few pages, we will give you a glimpse of graphic presentation and statistical analysis by walking you through the details of some real psychological research. For this purpose, we have selected a study designed to understand people who commit violent crimes:

> Relatives, coworkers, and acquaintances described Fred Cowan as a "nice, quiet man," a "gentle man who loved children," and a "real pussy-cat." The principal of the parochial school Cowan had attended as a child reported that his former student had received A grades in courtesy, cooperation, and religion. According to a coworker, Cowan "never talked to anybody and was someone you could push around." Cowan, however, surprised everyone who knew him when, one Valentine's Day, he strolled into work toting a semiautomatic rifle and shot and killed four coworkers, a police officer, and, finally, himself.

How could a habitually "gentle man" suddenly become a murderer? A team of researchers had a hunch that there might be a link between violent behavior and certain personal characteristics, such as shyness (Lee et al., 1977). They reasoned that seemingly nonviolent people who suddenly commit murders might be individuals who keep strong passions and impulses under tight control. But, thought the researchers, these "sudden murderers" are probably also individuals who never learned how to deal comfortably with others. For most of their lives, they may silently suffer slights and indignities. Seldom do they express anger, regardless of how angry they really feel. According to this theory, such people appear unbothered on the outside, but on the inside they may be fighting a long and losing battle to control their emotions. They give the impression that they are quiet, passive, responsible people, both as children and as adults. But, because they are shy, they do not let others get close to them, so no one knows how they really feel. Then, suddenly, something "snaps." At a slight provocation—one more small insult, one more little rejection, one more bit of social pressure—they explode, releasing the suppressed violence that has been building for so long. Because they did not learn to deal with interpersonal conflicts through discussion and verbal negotiation, they are driven to act out their anger explosively and physically.

This line of reasoning led to three specific hypotheses:

1. A measure of impulse control should show that these *sudden murderers*—people who had engaged in homicide without any prior history of violence or antisocial behavior—usually exert higher levels of control over their impulses than would *habitual-criminal murderers*—those who had not only committed homicide but also had previous records of violent criminal behavior.

2. Shyness should be more characteristic of sudden murderers—who may have always felt themselves alienated from others—than of habitual-criminal murderers.

3. Finally, the researchers predicted that sudden murderers would be found to have personalities characterized by passivity and dependence.

(Take a moment to decide which of these hypotheses you agree with.)

To test their hypotheses, the researchers administered three psychological questionnaires to inmates serving time for murder in California prisons. Nineteen inmates (all male) agreed to participate in the study. Prior to committing murder, some had committed a series of crimes, while the others had had no previous criminal record.

The first hypothesis was tested with a questionnaire that was a portion of the Minnesota Multiphasic Personality Inventory (MMPI), an instrument that was originally designed to measure many aspects of personality. The sudden-murderers study used only the "ego-overcontrol" scale, which measures the degree to which a person controls impulses. The higher the score on this scale, the more the subject attempts to suppress, or "overcontrol," the urge to act impulsively.

To assess shyness, involved in the second hypothesis, they used the Stanford Shyness Survey (Zimbardo, 1990). The most important item on this instrument simply asked if the subject considered himself to be shy. The answer could be either yes or no. Other items on the scale tapped degree and kinds of shyness and a variety of dimensions related to origins and triggers of shyness.

Finally, to test the third hypothesis, the researchers used the Bem Sex-Role Inventory (BSRI) to assess passivity and dependence. This instrument presents a list of adjectives, such as *aggressive* and *affectionate*, and asks how well each adjective describes the subject (Bem, 1974, 1981). Some adjectives are typically associated with being "feminine" because women more often use them to describe themselves than do men. The total score of these adjectives was a subject's femininity score. Other adjectives were considered "masculine," and the total score of those adjectives was a subject's masculinity score. The so-called "feminine" traits generally involve more passive and dependent characteristics than do the "masculine" traits. The final "sex-role difference score," which you see in Table A.1, was calculated by subtracting the masculinity score from the femininity score. If the researchers' hypothesis was correct, the sudden murderers should choose more "feminine" characteristics to describe themselves, and this should result in a higher sex-role difference score.

Connection

Chapter 1
A *hypothesis* is a statement predicting the outcome of a scientific study.

Connection

Chapter 11
The MMPI-2 is a widely used trait inventory designed to detect serious disorders.

Statistics: A set of mathematical techniques used to organize data and to draw inferences from them. Numbers derived from these mathematical procedures are also called statistics.

	MMPI (MINNESOTA MULTIPHASIC PERSONALITY INVENTORY)	STANFORD SHYNESS SURVEY	BSRI (BEM SEX-ROLE INVENTORY)
SUBJECT NUMBER	**EGO OVERCONTROL**		**FEMININITY MINUS MASCULINITY**
Group 1: Sudden Murderers			
1	yes	+5	17
2	no	−1	17
3	yes	+4	13
4	yes	+61	17
5	yes	+19	13
6	yes	+41	19
7	no	−29	14
8	yes	+23	9
9	yes	−13	11
10	yes	+5	14
Group 2: Habitual-Criminal Murderers			
11	no	−12	15
12	no	−14	11
13	yes	−33	14
14	no	−8	10
15	no	−7	16
16	no	+3	11
17	no	−17	6
18	no	+6	9
19	no	−10	12

TABLE A.1 — *Raw Data from the Sudden-Murderers Study*

To summarize, the researchers predicted that sudden murderers would (1) score higher in ego overcontrol, (2) more often describe themselves as shy on the shyness survey, and (3) select more "feminine" traits than "masculine" ones on the sex-role scale. What did they discover? Before you find out, you need to understand some of the basic procedures that were used to analyze these data.

HOW DO PSYCHOLOGISTS ANALYZE THEIR DATA?

For most researchers, analyzing the data is both an exciting and anxiety-filled step. At this point they discover whether their predictions were correct. Analysis of the data will tell them if their results will contribute to our understanding of behavior or if they have to go back to the drawing board and develop new hypotheses.

To illustrate how this process works, we will go step-by-step through an analysis of some of the data from the sudden-murderers study. You do not need to be highly skilled in math to understand the concepts we will discuss. You just need the courage to see a few graphical conventions and mathemati-

TABLE A.2	Rank Ordering of Sex-Role Difference Scores	
SUDDEN MURDERERS		**HABITUAL-CRIMINAL MURDERERS**
Highest	+61	+6
	+41	+3
	+23	−7
	+19	−8
	+5	−10
	+5	−12
	+4	−14
	−1	−17
	−13	−33
Lowest	−29	

Note: Difference scores represent the femininity score minus the masculinity score, so + scores are more "feminine"; − scores are more "masculine."

cal symbols for what they are—a shorthand for presenting ideas and conceptual operations.

Graphic Representation

The **raw data**—the actual scores or other measures obtained—from the 19 inmates in the murderers study are listed in Table A.1. As you can see, there were ten inmates in the sudden-murderers group and nine in the habitual-criminal murderers group. When first glancing at these data, any researcher would feel what you probably feel: puzzled. What do all these scores mean? Do the two groups of murderers differ from one another on these various personality measures? It is difficult to know just by examining this disorganized array of numbers. To make sense of the results, psychologists often organize their data in graphic form so that they can get a visual impression of the numbers. To do so, they often begin with a *frequency distribution*.

FREQUENCY DISTRIBUTIONS A summary picture of the various scores can be quickly drawn from a **frequency distribution,** which shows how often each score occurs in the sample data. The first step in preparing a frequency distribution is to *rank order* the scores in each group from highest to lowest. The rank ordering for the sex-role scores is shown in Table A.2. The second step is to group these rank-ordered scores into a smaller number of categories called *intervals*. In the sudden-murderers study, 11 intervals were used, with each interval covering 10 possible scores. This gives us a frequency distribution table, listing the intervals from highest to lowest and noting the *frequencies*— the number of scores within each interval (see Table A.3). This frequency distribution shows us that the sex-role scores for both groups fall mainly between −20 and +9. You will notice, however, that different patterns appear in the data from the two groups. Of the sudden murderers, 70% (7 of the 10) chose adjectives that were more feminine than masculine (scores in the plus range). In comparison, only 22% of the habitual criminals (2 of 9) said that the feminine adjectives described them more accurately than did the masculine ones.

Constructing a frequency distribution for the shyness data is simpler because there are only two "intervals": *yes* (shy) and *no* (not shy). As you can

Raw data: The unanalyzed scores or other quantitative measures obtained from a study; the data on which statistical procedures are performed.

Frequency distribution: A summary chart, showing how frequently each of the various scores in a set of data occurs.

TABLE A.3	Frequency Distribution of Sex-Role Difference Scores	
CATEGORY	SUDDEN MURDERERS FREQUENCY	HABITUAL-CRIMINAL MURDERERS FREQUENCY
+60 to +69	1	0
+50 to +59	0	0
+40 to +49	1	0
+30 to +39	0	0
+20 to +29	1	0
+10 to +19	1	0
0 to +9	3	2
−1 to −10	1	3
−11 to −20	1	3
−21 to −30	1	0
−31 to −40	0	1

see in Table A.4, the sudden murderers and the habitual-criminal murderers do seem to differ on the shyness variable. Most sudden murderers described themselves as shy, while most habitual-criminal murderers did not. Of the 19 scores, we can see 9 *yes* and 10 *no* responses; almost all the *yes* responses are in the sudden murderers group, and almost all the *no* responses are in the habitual-criminal murderers group. You may be interested to know that, by comparison, 40% of people in the United States describe themselves as shy. The researchers also noticed a difference in the circumstances that precipitated the murders committed by the shy men. In virtually every case, the precipitating incidents for the sudden murderers were minor, compared with the incidents that triggered the violence of the habitual-criminal murderers.

Inspection of the ego-overcontrol scores of the two groups shows no clear trend (see Table A.5). While sudden murderers scored higher in overcontrolling their impulses than did habitual-criminal murderers, their scores were not much higher (Lee et al., 1977). Clearly, we need more powerful techniques in order to tell whether the groups differ significantly in their overcontrol tendencies.

Although summaries of data such as this are compelling, we must look at a number of other analyses before we can state our conclusions with any certainty. The researchers' next step was to plot the distributions graphically.

HISTOGRAMS AND BAR GRAPHS   Distributions are often easier to understand when they are displayed as graphs. The simplest type of graph is a *bar graph*. We can use a bar graph to illustrate how many more sudden murderers

TABLE A.4	Frequency Distribution of Shyness in the Sudden-Murderers Study	
Shy:	SUDDEN MURDERERS	HABITUAL-CRIMINAL MURDERERS
Yes	8	1
No	2	8

TABLE A.5	Frequency Distribution of Ego-Overcontrol Scores	
CATEGORY	SUDDEN MURDERERS FREQUENCY	HABITUAL-CRIMINAL MURDERERS FREQUENCY
1 to 5	0	0
6 to 10	1	3
11 to 15	5	5
16 to 20	4	1

than habitual-criminal murderers described themselves as shy (see Figure A.1). The bar graph reveals a striking difference in the number of shy inmates in each group—at least in the sample used for the study.

For a more complex array of data, such as the sex-role scores, we can use a *histogram,* as in Figure A.2. This sort of graph is similar to a bar graph except that the histogram's bars represent data *intervals.* That is, a histogram represents *number* categories (e.g., "–40 to –31" or "0 to +9") instead of the *name* categories used in the bar graph (e.g., "sudden murderers" or "habitual-criminal murderers"). In other words, a histogram gives a visual picture of the number of scores falling in each interval of a distribution. It is easy to see from the sex-role scores shown in the histograms in Figure A.2 that the distribution of scores differs in the two groups of murderers. Note how the sudden murderers are represented in almost every interval from –30 to +69, with a spike in the 0 to +9 interval. Habitual murderers, on the other hand, all cluster in the intervals below +9.

Statistical Analysis

To complement this visual picture of the data, researchers customarily paint a mathematical picture, using two kinds of statistics. They begin with **descriptive statistics,** which involve a numerical *description* of their subjects' characteristics and responses. (If you have ever computed your grade-point average, you have used a descriptive statistic to summarize your grades.) Then, they use **inferential statistics** to assess whether the results of a study are reliable or whether they might be simply the result of chance. (Inferential statistics are often used to determine whether the scores from two or more groups are essentially the same or different.) Let's look first at descriptive statistics.

DESCRIPTIVE STATISTICS Researchers form a summary picture of basic patterns in the data with *descriptive statistics.* Descriptive statistics may indicate the frequency of certain behaviors. Alternatively, descriptive statistics may summarize sets of scores collected from a group of subjects. These could be, for example, scores on a questionnaire or a personality test. Descriptive statistics may also be used to describe relationships among variables, such as the relationship between grades and time spent studying. In general, you might think of descriptive statistics as a way to simplify the data.

Three kinds of descriptive statistics can help us understand and compare the data for the two groups in the sudden-murderers study. One kind indicates the scores that are most *typical* for each group. A

Descriptive statistics:
Statistical procedures used to describe characteristics and responses of groups of subjects.

Inferential statistics:
Statistical techniques (based on probability theory) used to assess whether the results of a study are reliable or whether they might be simply the result of chance. Inferential statistics are often used to determine whether two or more groups are essentially the same or different.

FIGURE A.1: Shyness for Two Groups of Murderers (a Bar Graph)

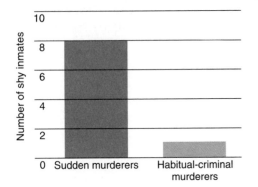

FIGURE A.2: Sex-Role Scores (Histograms)

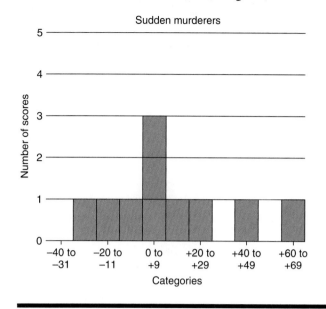

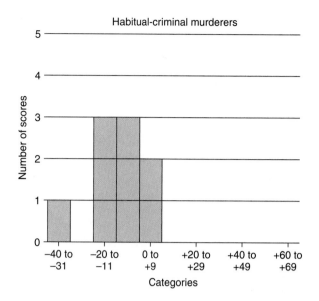

second shows the extent to which the individual scores are spread out or clustered closely together. The third shows how closely related are the different measures used in the study—whether they are measuring the same traits or different traits. These three types of descriptive statistics are known as *measures of central tendency, measures of variability,* and *correlation.*

MEASURES OF CENTRAL TENDENCY In order to compare the scores of sudden murderers and habitual-criminal murderers, one could summarize each group with the one score on each scale that is most typical of it. Then, one could compare the typical scores of the two groups rather than trying to compare their entire distributions. Such a single, *representative* score that can be used to describe a group of subjects is called a **measure of central tendency.** It is located near the center of the distribution, and other scores tend to cluster around it. Psychologists often use three statistical measures of central tendency: the *mode,* the *median,* and the *mean.*

The simplest of these measures of central tendency is the **mode:** the score that occurs more often than any other. On the shyness variable, the modal response of the sudden murderers was *yes:* Eight out of ten said yes, they were shy. Among habitual-criminal murderers, the modal response was *no* (not shy). The sex-role scores for the sudden murderers had a mode of +5. Can you figure out what the modes of their ego-overcontrol scores are?

While the mode is the easiest index of central tendency to determine, it is often the least useful. You will see one reason for this relative lack of usefulness if you notice that only one overcontrol score lies above the mode of 17, while six lie below it. Although 17 is the score obtained most often, it may not fit your idea of "typical" or "central."

The **median** is more clearly a central score. It is the score that separates the upper half of the scores in a distribution from the lower half. The number of scores larger than the median is the same as the number of scores that are smaller. If you look at the rank-ordering of the sex-role difference scores of the sudden murderers (Table A.2), you will see that the median score is +5 (in this

Measure of central tendency: A single, representative score that can be used as an index of the most typical score obtained by a group of subjects in a distribution. Measures of central tendency include the *mean, median,* and *mode.*

Mode: A measure of central tendency for a distribution, represented by the score that occurs more often than any other.

Median: A measure of central tendency for a distribution, represented by the score that separates the upper half of the scores in a distribution from the lower half.

case, the same as the mode, although this is not always true). Four scores are higher than +5, and four scores are lower. The median is quite simply the score in the middle of the distribution.

A big advantage in using the median is that it is not affected by extreme scores. For example, even if the highest sex-role score had been 129 instead of 61, the median value would still have been 5. That score would still separate the upper half of the data from the lower half.

The **mean** is what most people think of when they hear the word *average*. It is also the statistic most often used to describe sets of data. To calculate the mean, you add up all the scores in a distribution and divide by the total number of scores. The operation is summarized by the following formula:

$$M = \Sigma X \div N$$

In this formula, M is the mean, X is each individual score, Σ (the Greek letter *sigma*) is the summation of what immediately follows it, and N is the total number of scores. Because the summation of all the scores (ΣX) is 115 and the total number of scores (N) is 10, the mean (M) of the sex-role scores of the sudden murderers would be calculated as follows:

$$M = 115 \div 10 = +11.5$$

The mean sex-role score for the habitual murderers is

$$M = (-92) \div 9 = -10.22$$

You can see from these scores that there is a big difference between the two groups.

Unlike the median, the mean *is* affected by the specific values of all scores in the distribution. An extreme score *does* change the value of the mean. For example, if the sex-role score of inmate 4 happened to be 101 instead of 61, the mean for the whole group of sudden murderers would increase from 11.5 to 15.5.

Now try to calculate the mean overcontrol scores for the two groups yourself. You should find that the mean for the sudden murderers is 14.4. The mean for the habitual murderers is 11.56.

MEASURES OF VARIABILITY   In addition to knowing which score is most representative of the distribution as a whole, it is useful to know how representative that measure of central tendency really is. Are most of the other scores fairly close to it or widely spread out? **Measures of variability** are statistics that describe the distribution of scores around some measure of central tendency.

Can you see why measures of variability are important? Another example may help. Suppose you are a second-grade teacher, and it is the beginning of the school year. Knowing that the average child in your class can read a first-grade-level book will help you to plan your lessons. You could plan better, however, if you knew how *similar* or how *divergent* the reading abilities of the 30 children are. Do they all read at about the same level (low variability)? If so, then you can plan a fairly standard second-grade lesson. But what if the group has high variability, with several that can read fourth-grade material and others that can barely read at all? Now the mean reading level is not so representative of the entire class, and you will have to plan a variety of lessons to meet the children's varied needs.

The simplest measure of variability is the **range,** the difference between the highest and the lowest values in a frequency distribution. Returning to the study of murderers, let us look at the range of scores in Table A.1. For the sudden murderers' sex-role scores, the range is 90: from +61 to –29. The range

Mean: The measure of central tendency most often used to describe a set of data—calculated by adding all the scores and dividing by the number of scores.

Measures of variability: Statistics that describe the distribution of scores around some measure of central tendency. Measures of variability include the *range* and the *standard deviation*.

Range: The simplest measure of variability, represented by the difference between the highest and the lowest values in a frequency distribution.

of their overcontrol scores is 10: from 19 to 9. To compute the range, you need to know only two of the scores: the highest and the lowest.

The range is simple to determine, but psychologists often prefer measures of variability that are more sensitive and that take into account all the scores in a distribution, not just the extremes. One widely used measure is the **standard deviation** (SD), a measure of variability that indicates an *average* difference between each score and the mean. To figure out the standard deviation of a distribution, you need to know the mean of the distribution, along with the individual scores. Although the arithmetic involved in calculating the standard deviation is easy, the formula is a bit more complicated than the one used to calculate the mean and, therefore, will not be presented here. (Many calculators have a button for computing the standard deviation of a set of scores.) The general procedure, however, involves subtracting the value of each individual score from the mean and then determining an average of those mean deviations.

The standard deviation is relatively easy to interpret, however. The larger the standard deviation, the more spread out the scores are. In our example, the standard deviation of the sex-role scores for the sudden murderers is 24.6 points, but the standard deviation for the habitual criminals is only 10.7. This shows that there was less variability in the habitual-criminals group. Their scores clustered more closely about their mean than did those of the sudden murderers. When the standard deviation is small, the mean is a good representative index of the entire distribution. When the standard deviation is large, the mean is less typical of the whole group.

CORRELATION   Another useful tool in interpreting psychological data is the **correlation coefficient,** a measure of the relationship between two variables (such as height and weight). A correlation coefficient tells us the extent to which scores on one measure are associated with scores on the other. If people with high scores on one variable tend to have high scores on the other variable, the correlation coefficient will be positive (greater than 0). If, however, people with high scores on one variable tend to have *low* scores on the other variable, then the correlation coefficient will be negative (less than 0). If there is *no* consistent relationship between the scores, the correlation will be close to 0.

Correlation coefficients range from + 1.00 (a perfect positive correlation) to −1.00 (a perfect negative correlation). The further a correlation coefficient lies from 0 in *either* direction, the more closely the two variables are related, positively or negatively. Higher coefficients permit better predictions of one variable, given knowledge of the other.

In the sudden-murderers study, the correlation coefficient (symbolized as *r*) between the sex-role scores and the overcontrol scores turns out to be + 0.35. The sex-role scores and the overcontrol scores are, thus, *positively correlated:* In general, subjects describing themselves in more feminine terms also tend to be higher in overcontrol. However, the correlation is modest compared with the highest possible value of + 1.00, telling us that there are many exceptions to this relationship. (If we had also measured the self-esteem of these inmates and found a correlation of, say, −0.68 between overcontrol scores and self-esteem, it would mean that there was a *negative correlation*. If this were the case, we could say that the subjects who had high overcontrol scores tended to be lower in self-esteem. It would be a stronger relationship than the relationship between the sex-role scores and the overcontrol scores, because −0.68 is farther from 0, the point of no relationship, than is + 0.35.)

INFERENTIAL STATISTICS   We have used several kinds of descriptive statistics to characterize the data from the sudden-murderers study, and now we

Connection

Chapter 1
The correlation coefficient summarizes the relationship between the two variables.

Connection

Chapter 1
Correlational research can show a relationship, but it cannot show which variable is the *cause* and which is the *effect*.

Standard deviation: A measure of variability that indicates the *average* difference between the scores and their mean.

Correlation coefficient: A measure of the relationship between two variables.

Normal curve: A bell-shaped curve that describes distributions of IQ scores in the general population, as well as other sets of data in which most subjects score near the center of the distribution and only a few have extreme scores.

Connection

Chapter 8
IQ stands for "intelligence quotient" and is an index of general intelligence.

Connection

Chapter 8
The Stanford-Binet is a widely used IQ test developed at Stanford University and based on Binet's original intelligence test.

Connection

Chapter 8
IQ scores falling more than two standard deviations from the mean are associated with "mental retardation" and "giftedness."

have an idea of the pattern of results. We have compared the average responses and the variability in the two groups, and they appear to display some differences. However, some basic questions remain unanswered. How do we know if the differences are large enough to be reliable or meaningful? To put it another way, if we repeated this study, with other samples of sudden murderers and habitual-criminal murderers, would we be likely to find the same patterns, or could these results have been merely the work of chance? Or, if we could somehow measure the entire population of sudden murderers and habitual-criminal murderers, would the means and standard deviations be essentially the same as those we found for these small samples?

Inferential statistics are used to answer these kinds of questions. They tell us what *inferences* we can make from our samples and which conclusions we can legitimately draw from our data. Inferential statistics use probability theory to determine the likelihood that a set of sample data occurred simply by chance variation.

THE NORMAL CURVE In order to understand how inferential statistics work, we must look first at the properties of a special distribution called the *normal distribution*. A normal distribution occurs when data on a variable (height, IQ, or overcontrol, for example) collected from a large number of subjects fit a bell-shaped curve similar to that shown for IQ scores in Figure A.3 on page 593. (This is essentially the same bell curve used by teachers who grade "on the curve.") Notice that the curve is symmetrical (the left half is a mirror image of the right) and bell shaped—high near the middle, where most scores are, and lower the farther you get from the mean. This type of curve is also called a **normal curve** because it describes a *normal distribution*. (By contrast, a *skewed* distribution is one in which scores cluster toward one end instead of around the middle.)

If the measurements you have made fit a normal curve, then the median, mode, and mean values are the same. Moreover, a specific percentage of the scores can be predicted to fall under different sections of the curve. Figure A.3 shows a normal curve generated by IQ scores on the Stanford-Binet Intelligence Test. These scores have a mean of 100 and a standard deviation of 16—telling us that most scores on this test cluster within 16 points on either side of 100. If you mark off standard deviation units as distances from the mean along the baseline of the graph in Figure A.3, you find that about 68% of all the scores lie between the mean of 100 and 1 standard deviation above and below—between IQs of 84 and 116 on the Stanford-Binet. Roughly another 27% of the scores are found between the first and second standard deviations below the mean (IQ scores between 68 and 84) and above the mean (IQ scores between 116 and 132). Fewer than 5% of the scores fall in the third standard deviation above and below the mean, and very few scores fall beyond—only about 0.25%.

Using the statistics associated with the normal curve, researchers can judge whether two groups of scores have been drawn from groups that are truly different. That is, if each group's scores represent a sample from a normal distribution, but the averages of the two groups differ—say, the mean of one group is 100, whereas for the other it's 84—the researchers can feel confidence in saying that the scores reflect a real difference between the larger groups.

For example, if you hypothesize that time spent studying is associated with the grades students receive, you could use means and standard deviations to compare the amount of study time in a sample of students with high grades and low grades. To be sure that any differences you find are real, however, you must look at the distribution of scores in both groups (do the sample scores

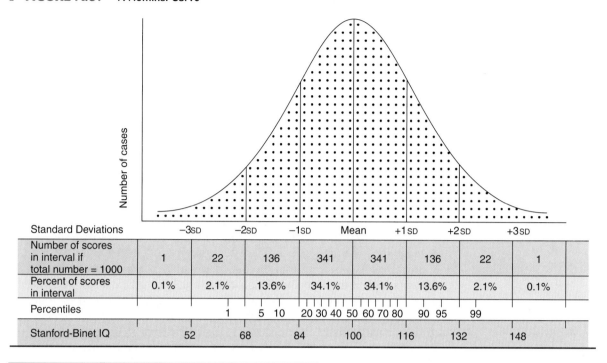

Standard Deviations	−3SD	−2SD	−1SD	Mean	+1SD	+2SD	+3SD		
Number of scores in interval if total number = 1000	1	22	136	341	341	136	22	1	
Percent of scores in interval	0.1%	2.1%	13.6%	34.1%	34.1%	13.6%	2.1%	0.1%	
Percentiles		1	5 10	20 30 40 50 60 70 80		90 95	99		
Stanford-Binet IQ	52	68	84	100	116	132	148		

approximate a normal distribution?) and you must factor in the size of the sample you used (is the sample large enough?). As you might expect, with a small sample, a relatively large difference in grades between the two sample groups is required before you can conclude that the samples represent truly different populations. You will learn how to perform these statistical tests in a course on research design and statistics.

You must, of course, also make sure that your sample was selected in an unbiased manner. The safest way is to select subjects *at random,* by a method such as drawing names from a hat. Sometimes obtaining a **random sample** is not practicable (imagine trying to get a random sample of all college students). Then, a *representative sample* is often used. A **representative sample** is obtained in such a way that it reflects the important variables in the larger population in which you are interested—variables such as age, income level, ethnicity, and geographic distribution. Remarkably, a carefully selected representative sample of only a few hundred persons is often sufficient for public-opinion pollsters to obtain a highly accurate reflection of the political opinions of the entire population of a country. (A weakness in the sudden-murderers study is that the sample was not random. Nor do we know how representative it is of all sudden murderers and habitual-criminal murderers.)

STATISTICAL SIGNIFICANCE   As noted earlier, a researcher who finds a difference between the mean scores for two samples must ask if it represents a *real* difference between the two groups from which the samples were drawn or if it occurred simply because of chance. A simple example will help illustrate the point. Suppose your psychology professor wants to see if the gender of a person proctoring a test makes a difference in the test scores obtained from male and female students. For this purpose, the professor randomly assigns half the students to a male proctor and half to a female proctor. The professor then compares the mean score of each group. If the proctor's gender makes *no*

Random sample: A sample group of subjects selected by chance (without biased selection techniques).

Representative sample: A sample obtained in such a way that it reflects the distribution of important variables in the larger population in which the researchers are interested—variables such as age, income level, ethnicity, and geographic distribution.

difference at all, then you would expect that the two mean scores would be fairly similar, and any slight difference the professor might find in the samples would be due to chance.

But, what if the difference between the scores for the two groups is large? As you have learned, less than a third of the scores in a normal distribution should be greater than one standard deviation above or below the mean (see Figure A.3). So, if there is no real difference between the male-proctor group and the female-proctor group (that is, if they come from the same larger group), the chances of getting a sample with a male-proctor mean score that is more than three standard deviations above or below the female-proctor mean would be very small. Thus, a researcher who *does* get a difference that great would feel fairly confident that the difference is a real one and is somehow related to the gender of the test proctor. The next question would be *how* that variable influences test scores.

If male and female students were randomly assigned to each type of proctor, it would be possible to analyze whether an overall difference found between the proctors was consistent across both student groups or was limited to only one sex. Imagine that the data show that male proctors grade female students higher than do female proctors, but both grade male students the same. Our professor could use a statistical inference procedure to estimate the probability that an observed difference could have occurred by chance. This computation is based on the sample size, the size of the difference, and the spread of the scores. (The details of this computation are beyond the scope of this book, but you will learn how to do the computation in an introductory statistics class.)

By common agreement, psychologists accept a difference between the groups as "real" when the probability that it might be due to chance is less than 5 in 100 (indicated by the notation p < .05). A **significant difference** is one that meets this criterion. However, in some cases, even stricter probability levels are used, such as $p < .01$ (less than 1 in 100) and $p < .001$ (less than 1 in 1,000).

If we were to carry out the appropriate calculations on the murderers' data, we would find that the differences between the groups on their sex-role scores were *statistically significant*. That is, there is only a very slim possibility—less than 5 in 100 ($p < .05$) of the difference between groups shown in our data being merely due to a chance. Therefore, we can feel more confident that the difference is real. The sudden murderers did rate themselves as more "feminine" than did the habitual-criminal murderers. Likewise, the difference in shyness, analyzed using another statistical test for frequency of scores, is highly significant, as we had suspected from inspection of the frequency distributions and graphs.

On the other hand, the difference between the two groups of murderers' overcontrol scores turns out not to be statistically significant ($p < .10$), so we must be more cautious in talking about this difference. There is a *trend* in the predicted direction—the difference in overcontrol scores is one that would occur by chance only 10 times in 100—but the difference is not within the accepted standard 5-in-100 range. This may mean that the hypothesis about sudden murderers holding in their impulses is mistaken.

In this way, you can see that inferential statistics can help us answer some of the basic questions with which we began, and we are closer to understanding the psychology of people who suddenly change from mild-mannered, shy individuals into mass murderers. Any conclusion, however, is only a statement of the *probable* relationship between the events that were investigated; it is never one of absolute certainty. Truth in science is provisional, always open to revision by later data from better studies, developed from better hypotheses.

Connection

Chapter 1
Only science bases its conclusions on empirical observations, which are subject to revision as new data become available.

Significant difference:
Psychologists accept a difference between the groups as "real," or *significant,* when the probability that it might be due to an atypical sample drawn by chance is less than 5 in 100 (indicated by the notation *p* < .05)

HOW CAN YOU BE MISLED BY STATISTICS?

Now that we have considered the nature of statistics, how they are used, and what they mean, we should talk about how they can be misused. Many people accept unsupported "facts" when they are bolstered by the air of authority lent by a statistic. Unfortunately, they may not know how to examine critically the numbers that are presented in support of a product, politician, or proposal.

Statistics can give a misleading impression in many ways. For example, characteristics of the group of subjects used in the research can make a large difference that can easily remain undetected when the results are reported. Thus, a survey of views on abortion rights will yield very different results if conducted in a small, conservative community in the South rather than a university in New York City. Likewise, a prolife group surveying the opinions of its membership will very likely arrive at conclusions that differ from those obtained by the same survey conducted in a prochoice group.

Even if the subjects are randomly selected, the statistics can produce misleading results if the necessary assumptions behind the statistics are violated. For example, suppose 20 people take an IQ test; 19 of them receive scores between 90 and 110, and 1 receives a score of 220. The mean of the group will be strongly elevated by that one high score. With such a data set, the median or the mode would more accurately report the group's generally average intelligence, while the mean would make it look as if the average member of this group had a high IQ. This bias is especially powerful in a small sample. On the other hand, if the number of people in this group was 2,000 instead of 20, the one extreme score would make virtually no difference, and the mean would be a good representation of the group's intelligence.

You can avoid falling for this sort of deception by checking the size of the sample: Large samples are less likely to be misleading than small ones. Another approach involves checking the median or the mode as well as the mean: The results can be interpreted with confidence if those statistics are similar.

Yet another way to avoid being misled by statistics is to examine the methodology of the research. Check to see if the experimenters report their sample size and significance levels. Try to find out if the methods they used accurately and consistently measure whatever they claim to be investigating.

Statistics are the backbone of psychological research. They are used to understand observations and to determine whether findings are, in fact, correct and significant. Through the methods we have described, psychologists can prepare frequency distributions of their data and find the central tendencies and variability of the scores. They can use the correlation coefficient to determine the strength and direction of the association between sets of scores. Finally, psychological investigators can find out how representative the observations are and whether they differ significantly from what is observed among the general population. But, statistics can also be used poorly or deceptively, misleading those who do not understand them. Yet, when statistics are applied correctly and ethically, they allow researchers to expand the body of psychological knowledge.

GLOSSARY

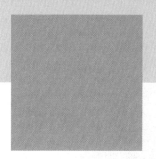

Absent-mindedness: Forgetting caused by lapses in attention.

Absolute threshold: The amount of stimulation necessary for the stimulus to be detected. In practice, this means being detected half the time over a number of trials.

Access and retrieval: Together these form the third basic function of memory, involving the location and recovery of information from memory.

Accommodation: A mental process that restructures existing schemes so that new information is better understood.

Acoustic encoding: The conversion of information, especially semantic information, to sound patterns in working memory.

Acquisition: The initial learning stage in classical conditioning, during which the conditioned response comes to be elicited by the conditioned stimulus.

Action potential: The nerve impulse caused by a change in the electrical charge across the cell membrane of the axon. When the neuron "fires," this charge travels down the axon and causes neurotransmitters to be released by the terminal buttons.

Activation-synthesis theory: The theory that dreams begin with random electrical *activation* coming from the brain stem. Dreams, then, are the brain's attempt to make sense of—to *synthesize*—this random activity.

Active listener: A person who gives the speaker feedback in such forms as nodding, paraphrasing, maintaining an expression that shows interest, and asking questions for clarification.

Acute stress: A temporary pattern of arousal caused by a stressor with a clear onset and offset.

Addiction: A physical condition that produces withdrawal when the body lacks a certain drug.

Adjustment disorders and other conditions that may be a focus of clinical attention: A diverse group of relatively mild problems that do not fit under other headings. These categories include mild depression, physical complaints, marital problems, academic problems, job problems, parent–child problems, bereavement, malingering, and a number of other conditions.

Adolescence: In industrial societies, a developmental period beginning at puberty and ending (less clearly) at adulthood.

Adoption studies: An alternative to twin studies in which the adopted child's characteristics are compared to those of the biological family and of the adoptive family.

Affect: A term referring to emotion or mood.

Afterimages: Sensations that linger after the stimulus is removed. Most visual afterimages are *negative afterimages,* which appear in reversed colors.

Agonists: Drugs or other chemicals that enhance or mimic the effects of neurotransmitters.

Agoraphobia: A fear of public places and open spaces, commonly accompanying panic disorder.

Alarm reaction: The first stage of the GAS, during which the body mobilizes its resources to cope with a stressor.

Algorithms: Problem-solving procedures or formulas that guarantee a correct outcome, if correctly applied.

Ambiguous figures: Images that are capable of more than one interpretation.

Ambivalence: Having conflicting thoughts or feelings.

Amnesia: A loss of memory for personal information, such as one's identity or residence.

Amplitude: The physical strength of a wave. This is usually measured from peak (top) to trough (bottom) on a graph of the wave.

Amygdala: (a-MIG-da-la) A limbic system structure involved in memory and emotion, particularly fear and aggression.

Analysis of transference: The Freudian technique of analyzing and interpreting the patient's relationship with the therapist, based on the assumption that this relationship mirrors unresolved conflicts in the patient's past.

Anchoring bias: A faulty heuristic caused by basing (anchoring) an estimate on a completely unrelated quantity.

Anima: The female archetype.

Animistic thinking: A preoperational mode of thought in which inanimate objects are imagined to have life and mental processes.

Animus: The male archetype.

Anorexia nervosa: An eating disorder involving persistent loss of appetite that endangers an individual's health and stemming from emotional or psychological reasons rather than from organic causes.

Antagonists: Drugs or chemicals that inhibit the effects of neurotransmitters.

Anterograde amnesia: The inability to form memories for new information (as opposed to *retrograde amnesia*, which involves the inability to remember information previously stored in memory).

Antianxiety drugs: A category of drugs that includes the *barbiturates* and *benzodiazepines,* drugs that diminish feelings of anxiety.

Antidepressant drugs: Medicines that affect depression, usually by their effect on the serotonin and/or norepinephrine pathways in the brain.

Antipsychotic drugs: Medicines that diminish psychotic symptoms, usually by their effect on the dopamine pathways in the brain.

Antisocial personality disorder: Characterized by a long-standing pattern of irresponsible behavior indicating a lack of conscience and a diminished sense of responsibility to others.

Anxiety disorders: Mental problems characterized mainly by anxiety. Anxiety disorders include panic disorder, specific phobias, and obsessive–compulsive disorder.

Applied psychologists: Psychologists who use the knowledge developed by experimental psychologists to solve human problems.

Aptitudes: Innate potentialities (as contrasted with abilities acquired by learning).

Archetypes: The ancient memory images in the collective unconscious. Archetypes appear and reappear in art, literature, and folk tales around the world.

Artificial concepts: Concepts defined by rules, such as word definitions and mathematical formulas.

Asch effect: A form of conformity in which a group majority influences individual judgments.

Assimilation: A mental process that modifies new information to fit it into existing schemes.

Association cortex: Cortical regions that combine information from various other parts of the brain.

Attachment: The enduring social-emotional relationship between a child and a parent or other regular caregiver.

Attention-deficit/hyperactivity disorder (ADHD): A common problem in children who have difficulty controlling their behavior and focusing their attention.

Auditory cortex: Portions of the temporal lobe involved in hearing.

Auditory nerve: The neural pathway connecting the ear and the brain.

Autonomic nervous system: The portion of the peripheral nervous system that sends messages to the internal organs and glands.

Autonomy: The ability to act independently.

Availability bias: A faulty heuristic strategy that estimates probabilities based on information that can be recalled (made available) from personal experience.

Aversion therapy: As a classical conditioning procedure, aversive counterconditioning involves presenting individuals with an attractive stimulus paired with unpleasant (aversive) stimulation in order to condition a repulsive reaction.

Aversive conditioning: A type of classical conditioning in which the conditioned stimulus predicts the occurrence of an aversive or unpleasant unconditioned stimulus.

Axon: In a nerve cell, an extended fiber that conducts information from the cell body to the terminal buttons. Information travels along the axon in the form of an electric charge.

Babbling stage: The time during the first year of life when an infant produces a wide range of sounds but not functional words.

Basilar membrane: A thin strip of tissue sensitive to vibrations in the cochlea. The basilar membrane contains hair cells connected to neurons, which accomplish the final step of converting sound waves to nerve impulses.

Behavior genetics: A new field bringing together geneticists and psychologists interested in the genetic basis of behavior and mental characteristics, such as intelligence, altruism, and psychological disorders.

Behavior modification: Another term for behavioral therapy.

Behavioral learning: Forms of learning, such as classical conditioning and operant conditioning, that can be described in terms of stimuli and responses.

Behavioral medicine: The medical field specializing in the link between lifestyle and disease.

Behavioral perspective: The psychological view suggesting that abnormal behaviors can be acquired through behavioral learning, especially by operant conditioning and classical conditioning.

Behavioral therapy: Any form of psychotherapy based on the principles of behavioral learning, especially operant conditioning and classical conditioning.

Behavioral view or **behaviorism:** A psychological perspective that finds the source of our actions in environmental stimuli, rather than in inner mental processes.

Bias: An attitude, belief, emotion, or experience that distorts memories.

Big Five: A group of apparently fundamental personality traits: extraversion, agreeableness, conscientiousness, emotional stability, and openness to new experience.

Binding problem: A major unsolved mystery in cognitive psychology, concerning the physical processes used by the brain to combine many aspects of sensation into a single percept.

Biofeedback: A therapy technique for learning relaxation and new visceral responses to stress, involving devices that sense small physical changes and provide immediate feedback to the individual.

Biological view: The psychological perspective that searches for the causes of behavior in the functioning of genes, the brain and nervous system, and the endocrine (hormone) system.

Biomedical therapies: Treatments that focus on altering the brain, especially with drugs, psychosurgery, or electroconvulsive therapy.

Biopsychology: The specialty in psychology that studies the interaction of biology, behavior, and the environment.

Bipolar disorder: A mental abnormality involving swings of mood from mania to depression.

Blind spot: The point where the optic nerve exits the eye and where there are no photoreceptors.

Blocking: Forgetting that occurs when an item in memory cannot be accessed or retrieved. Blocking is caused by *interference.*

Bottom-up processing: Perceptual analysis that emphasizes characteristics of the stimulus, rather than our concepts and expectations.

Brain scans: Recordings of the brain's electrical or biochemical activity at specific sites. Typically, the data are formed into visual images by computer. Common brain scanning devices include MRI, CT, and PET.

Brain stem: The most primitive of the brain's three major layers. It includes the medulla, pons, and the reticular activating system.

Brain waves: Patterns of electrical activity generated by the brain. The EEG records brain waves.

Brightness: A sensation caused by the intensity of light waves.

Bulimia (pronounced ***boo-LEE-me-uh***): An eating disorder characterized by eating binges followed by "purges," induced by vomiting or laxatives; typically initiated as a weight-control measure.

Burnout: A syndrome of emotional exhaustion, depersonalization, and reduced personal accomplishment—often related to work.

Cannabis: A drug, derived from the hemp plant, whose effects include altered perception, sedation, pain relief, and mild euphoria. Cannabis is found in marijuana and hashish.

Case study: Research that involves a single subject (or, at most, a few subjects).

Cataplexy: A sudden loss of muscle control that may occur just before a narcoleptic sleep attack. Cataplexy is a waking form of sleep paralysis.

Catatonic type: A form of schizophrenia involving stupor or extreme excitement.

Cell body or soma: The part of a cell (such as a neuron) containing the nucleus, which includes the chromosomes.

Central fissure: The prominent vertical groove in the cortex, separating the frontal from the parietal lobes in each hemisphere.

Central nervous system: The brain and the spinal cord.

Centration: A preoperational thought pattern involving the inability to take into account more than one factor at a time.

Cerebellum: The "little brain" attached to the brain stem. The cerebellum is responsible for coordinated movements.

Cerebral cortex: The thin grey-matter covering of the cerebrum, consisting of a 1/4-inch layer dense with cell bodies of neurons. The cerebral cortex carries on the major portion of our "higher" mental processing, including thinking and perceiving.

Cerebral dominance: The tendency of each brain hemisphere to exert control over different functions, such as language or perception of spatial relationships.

Cerebral hemispheres: The two walnut-shaped halves of the cerebrum, connected by the corpus callosum.

Cerebrum: The topmost layer of the brain; the bulbous cap over the limbic system. The cerebrum, particularly the cerebral *cortex,* accounts for most of our thinking and processing of information from our environment.

Charles Darwin: The British naturalist who first described the evolutionary theory and provided overwhelming evidence for the process of natural selection.

Chromosomes: Tightly coiled threadlike structures along which the genes are organized, like beads on a necklace. Chromosomes consist primarily of DNA.

Chronic stress: A continuous state of stressful arousal persisting over time.

Chronological age (CA): The number of years since the individual's birth.

Chunking: Organizing pieces of information into a smaller number of meaningful units (or, chunks)—a process that frees up space in working memory.

Circadian rhythms: Physiological patterns that repeat approximately every 24 hours—such as the sleep–wakefulness cycle.

Classical conditioning: A form of behavioral learning in which a previously neutral stimulus (CS) acquires the power to elicit the same innate reflex produced by another stimulus.

Clinical psychologists: Psychological practitioners who specialize in the treatment of mental disorders.

Closure: The Gestalt principle that identifies the tendency to fill in gaps in figures and to see incomplete figures as complete.

Cochlea: The primary organ of hearing; a coiled tube in the inner ear, where sound waves are transduced into nerve impulses.

Cognition: The mental processes involved in thinking, knowing, perceiving, learning, and remembering; also, the contents of these processes (e.g., thoughts, percepts, concepts).

Cognitive–behavioral approach: A psychological view that combines both the cognitive and the behavioral perspectives in attempting to understand behavior and mental processes.

Cognitive-behavioral therapy: A newer form of psychotherapy that combines the techniques of cognitive therapy with those of behavioral therapy.

Cognitive development: The process by which thinking changes over time.

Cognitive dissonance: A highly motivating state in which people have conflicting cognitions, especially when their voluntary *actions* conflict with their *attitudes*.

Cognitive map: A mental representation of physical space.

Cognitive neuroscience: A new, interdisciplinary field involving cognitive psychology, neuroscientists, computer scientists, and specialists from other fields who are interested in the connection between mental processes and the brain.

Cognitive perspective: The psychological view suggesting that abnormal behaviors are influenced by mental processes—by how people perceive or think about themselves and their relations with other people.

Cognitive therapy: Emphasizes rational thinking (as opposed to subjective emotion, motivation, or repressed conflicts) as the key to treating mental disorder.

Cognitive view: The psychological perspective that emphasizes mental processing and interpretation of experience.

Cohesiveness: Solidarity, loyalty, and a sense of group membership.

Collective unconscious: Jung's addition to the unconscious, involving a reservoir for instinctive "memories," including the archetypes, which exist in all people.

Collectivism: The view, common in Asia, Africa, Latin America, and the Middle East, that values group loyalty and pride over individual distinction.

Color: The psychological sensation derived from the wavelength of visible light. Color, itself, is not a property of the external world.

Color blindness: Typically a genetic disorder (although sometimes the result of trauma) that prevents an individual from discriminating certain colors. The most common form is red-green color blindness.

Community mental health movement: An effort to deinstitutionalize mental patients and to provide therapy from outpatient clinics. Proponents of community mental health envisioned that recovering patients could live with their families, in foster homes, or in group homes.

Concept hierarchies: Levels of concepts, from most general to most specific, in which a more general level includes more specific concepts—as the concept of "animal" includes "dog," "giraffe," and "butterfly."

Concepts: Mental representations of categories of items or ideas, based on experience.

Concordance rate: The percentage of relatives who show the same trait.

Concrete operational stage: The third of Piaget's stages, when a child understands conservation but still is incapable of abstract thought.

Conditioned reinforcers or **secondary reinforcers:** Stimuli, such as tokens or money, that acquire their reinforcing power by a learned association with primary reinforcers.

Conditioned response (CR): In classical conditioning, a response elicited by a previously neutral stimulus that has become associated with the unconditioned stimulus.

Conditioned stimulus (CS): In classical conditioning, a previously neutral stimulus that comes to elicit the conditioned response.

Cones: Photoreceptors in the retina that are especially sensitive to colors but not to dim light.

Confirmation bias: Ignoring or finding fault with information that does not fit with our opinions, and seeking information with which we agree.

Conformity: The tendency for people to adopt the behaviors, attitudes, and opinions of other members of a group.

Confounding variables: Factors that could be confused with the independent variable and thus distort the results of a study.

Conscious motivation: Having the desire to engage in an activity and being aware of the desire.

Consciousness: The brain's awareness of internal and external stimulation.

Conservation: The understanding that the physical properties of an object or substance do not change when appearances change but nothing is added or taken away.

Contact comfort: Stimulation and reassurance derived from the physical touch of a caregiver.

Contingency management: An operant conditioning approach to changing behavior by altering the consequences, especially rewards and punishments, of behavior.

Continuity view: The perspective that development is gradual and continuous—as opposed to the discontinuity (stage) view.

Continuous reinforcement: A type of reinforcement schedule by which all correct responses are reinforced.

Control condition: The stimulus conditions for the control group—conditions that are identical to the experimental condition in every respect, except for the special treatment given to the experimental group.

Control group: Those subjects who are used as a comparison for the experimental group. The control group is not given the special treatment of interest.

Convergent thinking: A problem-solving process aimed at producing "correct" answers to problems. According to Guilford, convergent thinking is also a component of intelligence.

Conversion disorder: A type of somatoform disorder, marked by paralysis, weakness, or loss of sensation, but with no discernible physical cause.

Coping strategies: Ways of dealing with stressful situations.

Corpus callosum: The band of nerve cells that connects the two cerebral hemispheres.

Correlation coefficient: A statistic, r, that indicates the relationship between two variables. Correlation coefficients can range from -1.0 to 0 to $+1.0$.

Correlational study: A form of research in which the relationship between variables is studied, but without the experimental manipulation of an independent variable. Correlational studies cannot determine cause-and-effect relationships.

Counseling psychologists: Psychological practitioners who help people deal with a variety of problems, including relationships and vocational choice. Counseling psychologists are less likely than clinical psychologists to do long-term therapy with persons having severe mental disorders.

Counterconditioning: A set of classical conditioning techniques for substituting a new response for an unwanted response; used especially in treating phobias.

Creativity: A mental process that produces novel responses that contribute to the solutions of problems.

Crystallized intelligence: The knowledge a person has acquired, plus the ability to access that knowledge.

CT scanning or computerized tomography: A computerized imaging technique that uses X rays passed through the brain at various angles and then combined into an image.

Culture: A term referring to a complex blend of language, beliefs, customs, values, and traditions developed by a group of people and shared with others in the same environment.

Data: Information, especially information gathered by a researcher to be used in testing a hypothesis. (Singular: *datum*.)

Daydreaming: A mild form of consciousness alteration in which attention shifts to memories, expectations, desires, or fantasies and away from the immediate situation.

Declarative memory: A division of LTM that stores explicit information; also known as *fact memory*. Declarative memory has two subdivisions: *episodic memory* and *semantic memory*.

Deinstitutionalization: The policy of removing patients, whenever possible, from mental hospitals.

Delusions: Extreme disorders of thinking, involving persistent false beliefs. Delusions are the hallmark of paranoid disorders.

Demographic: Refers to population characteristics, such as age, gender, or income distribution.

Dendrites: Branched fibers that extend outward from the main cell body and carry information into the neuron.

Denial: Freud's ego defense mechanism that allows a person consciously to ignore a problem or to conclude that there is no problem at all.

Dependent variable: The measured outcome of a study; the responses of the subjects in a study.

Depersonalization disorder: An abnormality involving the sensation that mind and body have separated, as in an "out-of-body" experience.

Depressants: Drugs that slow down mental and physical activity by inhibiting transmission of nerve impulses in the central nervous system.

Depression: Pathological sadness or despair.

Developmental psychology: The psychological specialty that studies how organisms change over time as the result of biological and environmental influences.

Developmental stages: Periods of life initiated by significant transitions or changes in physical or psychological functioning.

Diathesis–stress hypothesis: In reference to schizophrenia, the proposal that says that genetic factors place the individual at risk, but environmental stress factors transform this potential into an actual schizophrenic disorder.

Difference threshold: The smallest amount by which a stimulus can be changed and the difference be detected half the time.

Differentiation: The process by which cells in the embryo take on specialized functions.

Diffusion of responsibility: Dilution or weakening of each group member's obligation to act when responsibility is perceived to be shared with all group members.

Discontinuity view: The perspective that development proceeds in an uneven (discontinuous) fashion—as opposed to the continuity view.

Discrimination: A negative action taken against an individual as a result of his or her group membership.

Discrimination learning: A change in responses to one stimulus but not to stimuli that are similar.

Disorganized type: A form of schizophrenia featuring incoherent speech, hallucinations, delusions, and bizarre behavior.

Displacement: The ego defense mechanism by which we shift our reaction from the real source of distress to another individual or object.

Display rules: The permissible ways of displaying emotions in a particular society.

Dissociative disorders: A group of pathologies involving "fragmentation" of the personality, in which some parts of the personality have become detached, or dissociated, from other parts. Forms of dissociative disorder include amnesia, fugue, depersonalization disorder, and dissociative identity disorder.

Dissociative fugue: Essentially the same as dissociative amnesia, but with the addition of "flight" from one's home, family, and job. *Fugue* means "flight."

Dissociative identity disorder: A condition in which an individual displays multiple identities, or personalities; formerly called "multiple personality disorder."

Distributed learning: A technique whereby the learner spaces learning sessions over time, rather than trying to learn the material all in one study period.

Divergent thinking: A problem-solving process aimed at producing many appropriate solutions to a single problem. According to Guilford, divergent thinking is also the component of intelligence that is used to generate creative responses.

DNA: A long, complex molecule that encodes genetic characteristics. The long name for DNA is *deoxyribonucleic acid.*

Double-blind control: An experimental procedure in which both researchers and subjects are uninformed about the nature of the independent variable being administered.

Down syndrome: A genetic disorder that produces one form of mental retardation.

Drive: Biologically instigated motivation.

***DSM-IV*:** The fourth edition of the *Diagnostic and Statistical Manual of Mental Disorders,* published by the American Psychiatric Association; the most widely accepted classification system in the United States.

Duality of consciousness: The condition in which a split-brain patient has a separate consciousness in each hemisphere. The intact brain does not exhibit this duality of consciousness.

Eclectic: Either switching theories to explain different situations or building one's own theory of personality from pieces borrowed from many perspectives.

Ego: The conscious, rational part of the personality, charged with keeping peace between the superego and the id.

Ego defense mechanisms: According to Freud, these are unconscious strategies that we use to defend ourselves against threat and trauma, reduce internal conflict, and diminish anxiety.

Egocentrism: In Piaget's theory, the self-centered inability to realize that there are other viewpoints beside one's own.

Ego-integrity: In Erikson's theory, the ability to look back on life without regrets and to enjoy a sense of wholeness.

Eidetic imagery: An especially clear and persistent form of memory that is quite rare. Sometimes known as "photographic memory."

Elaboration: A form of encoding that adds meaning to information in working memory so that it can be more easily stored in LTM and later retrieved.

Elaborative rehearsal: A working-memory process in which information is actively reviewed and related to information already in LTM.

Electroconvulsive therapy (ECT): A treatment used primarily for depression and involving the application of an electric current to the head, producing a generalized seizure. Sometimes called "shock treatment."

Electroencephalograph or **EEG:** A device for recording brain waves, typically by electrodes placed on the scalp. The record produced is known as an *electroencephalogram* (also called an *EEG*).

Electromagnetic spectrum: The entire range of electromagnetic energy, including radio waves, X rays, microwaves, and visible light.

Embryo: In humans, the name for the developing organism during the first eight weeks after conception.

Emotion: A three-part process that involves subjective feelings, behavioral expression, and physiological arousal. Emotions help organisms deal with important events.

Emotional intelligence: In Goleman's theory, the ability to understand and control emotional responses.

Empirical: Relying on direct sensory observation rather than subjective judgment.

Empirical investigation: An approach to research that relies on sensory experience and observation as research data.

Encoding: One of the three basic functions of memory, involving the modification of information to fit the preferred format for the memory system.

Encoding specificity: A process by which memory is encoded and stored with specific cues related to the context in which it was formed. The more closely the retrieval cues match the form in which the information was encoded, the better it will be remembered.

Endocrine system: The hormone system—the body's chemical messenger system, including the following endocrine glands: pituitary, adrenals, gonads, thyroid, parathyroid, pancreas, ovaries, and testes.

Engineering psychologists: Applied psychologists who specialize in making objects and environments easier, more efficient, or more comfortable for people to use.

Engram: The physical trace, or biological basis, of memory.

Epilepsy: A brain disorder that is often marked by seizures and loss of consciousness. Epilepsy is caused by out-of-control electrical activity in the brain.

Episodic memory: A subdivision of declarative memory that stores memory for personal events, or "episodes."

Eros: The unconscious force that drives people toward acts that are sexual, life-giving, and creative.

Etiology: The causes of, or factors related to, the development of a disorder.

Eugenics: A philosophy and a political movement that encouraged biologically superior people to interbreed and sought to discourage biologically inferior people from having offspring.

Eustress: An optimum level of stress; "good" stress.

Event-related potentials: Brain waves shown on the EEG in response to stimulation.

Evolution: The gradual process of biological change that occurs in a species as it adapts to its environment.

Evolutionary view: A relatively new perspective in psychology that views behavior and mental processes in terms of genetic adaptations for survival and reproduction.

Expectancy-value theory: A theory in social psychology that states how people decide whether or not to pursue a relationship by weighing the potential *value* of the relationship against their *expectation* of success in establishing the relationship.

Experiential intelligence: According to Sternberg, the form of intelligence that helps people see new relationships among concepts; involves insight and creativity.

Experiment: A kind of research in which the researcher controls all the conditions and directly manipulates the conditions, including the independent variable.

Experimental condition: The stimulus conditions involved in exposing those in the *experimental group* to the special treatment being investigated.

Experimental group: Those subjects in an experiment who are exposed to the treatment of interest.

Experimental neurosis: A pattern of erratic behavior resulting from a demanding discrimination learning task, typically one that involves aversive stimuli.

Experimental psychologists: Psychologists who do research on basic psychological processes—as contrasted with *applied* psychologists.

Experts: Individuals who possess well-organized funds of knowledge, including the effective problem-solving strategies, in a field.

Explicit memory: Memory that has been processed with attention and can be consciously recalled.

Exposure therapy: A form of desensitization therapy in which the patient directly confronts the anxiety-provoking stimulus (as opposed to imagining the stimulus).

Extinction: In learning, the weakening of a conditioned association in the absence of an unconditioned stimulus or a reinforcer. In operant conditioning, a process by which a response that has been learned is weakened by the absence or removal of reinforcement. (Compare with extinction in classical conditioning.)

Extraversion: The Jungian personality dimension involving turning one's attention outward, toward others.

Extrinsic motivation: The desire to engage in an activity to achieve an external consequence, such as a reward.

Feature detectors: Cells in the cortex that specialize in extracting certain features of a stimulus.

Fetus: In humans, the term for the developing organism between the embryonic stage and birth.

Fight-or-flight response: A sequence of internal processes that prepares the organism for struggle or escape and is triggered when a situation is interpreted as threatening.

Figure: The part of a pattern that commands attention. The figure stands out against the ground.

Fixation: Occurs when psychosexual development is arrested at an immature stage.

Fixed-action patterns: Genetically based behaviors, seen across a species, that can be set off by a specific stimulus. The concept of fixed-action patterns has replaced the older notion of instinct.

Fixed interval (FI) schedules: Programs by which reinforcement is contingent upon a certain, fixed time period.

Fixed ratio (FR) schedules: Programs by which reinforcement is contingent upon a certain, unvarying number of responses.

Flashbulb memory: A clear and vivid long-term memory of an especially meaningful and emotional event.

Flow: In Csikszentmihalyi's theory, an intense focus on an activity, accompanied by increased creativity and near-ecstatic feelings. Flow involves intrinsic motivation.

Fluid intelligence: The ability to see complex relationships and solve problems.

Forgetting curve: A graph plotting the amount of retention and forgetting over time for a certain batch of material, such as a list of nonsense syllables. The typical forgetting curve is steep at first, becoming flatter as time goes on.

Formal operational stage: The last of Piaget's stages, during which abstract thought appears.

Fovea: The area of sharpest vision in the retina.

Frequency: The number of cycles completed by a wave in a given amount of time, usually a second.

Freudian slip: "Accidental" speech (a slip of the tongue) or behavior that reveals an unconscious desire.

Frontal lobes: Regions at the front of the brain that are especially involved in movement and in thinking.

Fully functioning person: Carl Roger's term for a self-actualizing individual, who has a self-concept that is both positive and congruent with reality.

Functional fixedness: The inability to perceive a new use for an object associated with a different purpose; a form of mental set.

Functionalism: A historical school of psychology that believed mental processes could best be understood in terms of their adaptive purpose and function.

Fundamental attribution error: The assumption that another person's behavior, especially clumsy, inappropriate, or otherwise undesirable behavior, is the result of a flaw in the personality, rather than in the situation. The FAE is more common in individualistic cultures than in collectivistic cultures.

g factor: A general ability, proposed by Spearman as the main factor underlying all intelligent mental activity.

General adaptation syndrome (GAS): A general pattern of physical responses that takes essentially the same form in response to any serious, chronic stressor.

Generativity: In Erikson's theory, a process of making a commitment beyond oneself to family, work, society, or future generations.

Genes: Segments of a chromosome that encode the directions for the inherited physical and mental characteristics of an organism. Genes are the functional units of a chromosome.

Genotype: An organism's genetic makeup.

Gestalt psychology: A view of perception that originated in Germany. *Gestalt* is a German word (pronounced *gush-TAWLT*) that means "whole" or "form" or "configuration." The Gestaltists believed that much of perception is shaped by innate factors built into the brain.

Giftedness: Often conceived as representing the upper 2% of the IQ range, commencing about 30 points above average—at about 130 IQ points.

Glial cells: These cells bind the neurons together. Glial cells also provide an insulating covering (the myelin sheath) of the axon for some neurons, which facilitates the electrical impulse.

Grammar: The rules of a language, specifying how to use words, morphemes, and syntax to produce understandable sentences.

Ground: The part of a pattern that does not command attention; the background.

Group therapy: Any form of psychotherapy done with more than one client/patient at a time. Group therapy is often done from a humanistic perspective.

Guilford's structure-of-intellect: J. P. Guilford's model of intelligence, consisting of some 150 separate factors, generated by five kinds of mental *operations,* five classes of *contents,* and six types of intellectual *products.*

Gustation: The sense of taste.

Habituation: Learning not to respond to the repeated presentation of a stimulus.

Hallucinations: False sensory experiences that may suggest mental disorder. Hallucinations can have other causes, such as drugs or sensory isolation.

Hallucinogens or **psychedelics:** Drugs that alter perceptions of the external environment and inner awareness.

Hardiness: A resilient quality based on the "three Cs" of health: challenge (welcoming change), commitment (involvement in purposeful activity), and control (internal guide for actions).

Hassles: Situations that cause minor irritation or frustration.

Head Start: A program providing educational enrichment for children of poor families, launched in the 1960s as a part of the "War on Poverty."

Health psychology: The psychological specialty devoted to understanding how people stay healthy, why they become ill, and how they respond when ill.

Hedonic capacity: The ability to experience pleasure and joy.

Heritability: The amount of trait variation *within a group,* raised under the same conditions, that can be attributed to genetic differences. Heritability tells us nothing about between-group differences.

Heuristics: Cognitive strategies or "rules of thumb" used as shortcuts to solve complex mental tasks. Unlike algorithms, heuristics do not guarantee a correct solution.

Hindsight bias: The tendency, after learning about an event, to "second guess" or believe that one could have predicted the event in advance.

Hippocampus: A component of the limbic system, involved in establishing long-term memories.

Homeostasis: The body's tendency to maintain a biologically balanced condition, especially with regard to nutrients, water, and temperature.

Hormones: The chemical messengers used by the endocrine system. Many hormones also serve as neurotransmitters.

Human Genome Project: An international scientific effort to determine the complete human genetic code in all 23 pairs of chromosomes.

Humanistic therapies: Treatment techniques based on the assumption that people have a tendency for positive growth and self-actualization, which may be blocked by an unhealthy environment that can include negative self-evaluation and criticism from others.

Humanistic view: A viewpoint that emphasizes human ability, growth, potential, and free will.

Humors: Four body fluids—blood, phlegm, black bile, and yellow bile—that, according to an ancient theory, control personality by their relative abundance.

Hypnosis: An induced alternate state of awareness, characterized by heightened suggestibility and (usually) deep relaxation.

Hypnotic analgesia: Diminished sensitivity to pain while under hypnosis.

Hypnotizability: The degree to which an individual is responsive to hypnotic suggestions.

Hypochondriasis: A somatoform disorder involving excessive concern about health and disease.

Hypothalamus: A limbic structure that serves as the brain's blood-testing laboratory, constantly monitoring the blood to determine the condition of the body.

Hypothesis: A statement predicting the outcome of a scientific study; a statement describing the relationship among variables in a study.

Hypothetical construct: A characteristic that is not directly observable but is, instead, inferred from behavior.

Id: The primitive, unconscious portion of the personality that houses the most basic drives and stores repressed memories.

Identity crisis: In Erikson's theory, the developmental crisis of adolescence.

Illusion: The demonstrably incorrect experience of a stimulus pattern, shared by others in the same perceptual environment.

Immunosuppression: Diminished effectiveness of the immune system caused by impairment (suppression) of the immune response.

Implicit memory: A memory that was not deliberately learned or of which you have no conscious awareness.

Implicit personality theory: Assumptions about personality that are held by people (especially nonpsychologists) to simplify the task of understanding others.

Imprinting: A primitive form of learning in which some young animals follow and form an attachment to the first moving object they see and hear.

Incongruence: Occurs when a negative emotional experience affects one's ability to perceive accurately.

Independent variable: A stimulus condition that is so named because the experimenter changes it *independently* of all the other carefully controlled experimental conditions.

Individualism: The view, common in the Euro-American world, that places a high value on individual achievement and distinction.

Industrial and organizational psychologists: Applied psychologists who specialize in modifying the work environment to maximize productivity and morale. They are often called *I/O psychologists.*

Infancy: In humans, infancy spans the time between the end of the neonatal period and the establishment of language—usually at about 18 months to two years.

In-group: The group with which an individual identifies.

Innate: Inborn; present at birth; part of the organism's biological heritage.

Innateness theory of language: The view that children learn language mainly by following an inborn program for acquiring vocabulary and grammar.

Insanity: A legal term, not a psychological or psychiatric one, referring to a person who is unable, because of a mental disorder or defect, to conform his or her behavior to the law.

Insight learning: A form of cognitive learning, originally described by the Gestalt psychologists, in which a problem solving occurs by means of a sudden reorganization of perceptions.

Insight therapies: Psychotherapies in which the therapist helps the patient understand (gain *insight* into) the causes of his or her problems.

Insomnia: A disorder that involves insufficient sleep, the inability to fall asleep quickly, frequent arousals, or early awakenings.

Instinct theory: The now-outmoded view that certain behaviors are determined by innate factors. The instinct theory was flawed because it overlooked the effects of learning and because it employed instincts merely as labels, rather than as explanations for behavior.

Intelligence: The mental capacity to acquire knowledge, reason, and solve problems effectively.

Intelligence quotient (IQ): A numerical score on an intelligence test, originally computed by dividing the person's mental age by chronological age and multiplying by 100.

Interaction: A process by which forces work together or influence each other—as in the interaction between the forces of heredity and environment.

Intermittent reinforcement: A type of reinforcement schedule by which some, but not all, correct responses are reinforced; also called partial reinforcement.

Interneurons: Nerve cells that relay messages from between nerve cells, especially in the brain and spinal cord.

Interval schedule: A program by which reinforcement depends on the time interval elapsed since the last reinforcement.

Intrinsic motivation: The desire to engage in an activity for its own sake, rather than for some external consequence, such as a reward.

Introspection: The process of reporting on one's own inner conscious experience.

Introversion: The Jungian dimension that focuses on inner experience—one's own thoughts and feelings, making the introvert less outgoing and sociable than the extravert.

Inverted "U" function: Describes the relationship between arousal and performance. Both low and high levels of arousal produce lower performance than does a moderate level of arousal.

Ions: Charged particles. The most important ions for synaptic transmission are sodium, calcium, and potassium.

James-Lange theory of emotion: The theory that an emotion-provoking stimulus produces a physical response that, in turn, produces an emotion.

Jet lag: A biological and psychological disruption of the circadian rhythms produced by moving quickly across time zones and attempting to shift one's sleep–wakefulness cycle to the local time.

Just noticeable difference (JND): Same as the *difference threshold.*

Kinesthetic sense: The sense of body position and movement of body parts relative to each other (also called *kinesthesis*).

Language acquisition device or **LAD:** A biologically organized mental structure in the brain that facilitates the learning of language because (says Chomsky) it is innately programmed with some of the fundamental rules of grammar.

Lateral fissure: The prominent horizontal groove separating the frontal and temporal lobes in each hemisphere.

Lateralization of emotion: Different influences of the two brain hemispheres on various emotions. The left hemisphere apparently influences positive emotions (for example, happiness), and the right hemisphere influences negative emotions (anger, for example).

Law of common fate: The Gestalt principle that we tend to group similar objects together that share a common motion or destination.

Law of continuity: The Gestalt principle that we prefer perceptions of connected and continuous figures to disconnected and disjointed ones.

Law of Prägnanz: The most general Gestalt principle, which states that the simplest organization, requiring the least cognitive effort, will emerge as the figure.

Law of proximity: The Gestalt principle that we tend to group objects together when they are near each other.

Law of similarity: The Gestalt principle that we tend to group similar objects together in our perceptions.

Laws of perceptual grouping: The Gestalt principles of *similarity, proximity, continuation,* and *common fate.* These ideas suggest how stimulus elements are grouped together perceptually.

Learned helplessness: A pattern of not responding to noxious stimuli after an organism learns that its behavior has no effect.

Learning: A lasting change in behavior or mental processes that results from experience.

Learning-based inference: The view that perception is primarily shaped by learning (or experience), rather than innate factors.

Lesions: Tissue damage that results from disease or injury. To study the connection between brain and behavior, biopsychologists make precise lesions in the brains of experimental animals and observe the changes in the animals' behavior.

Levels-of-processing theory: The explanation for the fact that information that is more thoroughly connected to meaningful items in long-term memory (more "deeply" processed) will be remembered better.

Libido: The Freudian concept of psychic energy that drives individuals to experience sensual pleasure.

Limbic system: The middle layer of the brain, involved in emotion and memory. The limbic system includes the amygdala, the hippocampus, the hypothalamus, and other structures.

Lithium carbonate: A simple chemical compound that is highly effective in dampening the extreme mood swings of bipolar disorder.

Locus of control: An individual's sense of where his or her life influences originate—internally or externally.

Logical reasoning (also called *componential intelligence*): According to Sternberg, this is the ability measured by most IQ tests; includes the ability to analyze problems and find correct answers.

Long-term memory (LTM): The third of three memory stages, with the largest capacity and longest duration; LTM stores material organized according to meaning.

Long-term potentiation: A biological process, involving physical changes that strengthen the synapses in groups of nerve cells, which is believed to be the neural basis of learning.

Loudness: A sensory characteristic of sound produced by the amplitude (intensity) of the sound wave.

Maintenance rehearsal: A working-memory process in which information is merely repeated or reviewed to keep it from fading while in working memory. Maintenance rehearsal involves no active elaboration.

Mania: Pathologically excessive elation or manic excitement.

Matching hypothesis: The prediction that most people will find friends and mates that are of about their same level of attractiveness.

Maturation: The process by which the genetic program manifests itself over time.

Medical model: The view that mental disorders are diseases that, like ordinary physical diseases, have objective causes and require specific treatments.

Meditation: A form of consciousness change often induced by focusing on a repetitive behavior, assuming certain body positions, and minimizing external stimulation. Meditation is intended to enhance self-knowledge and well-being by reducing self-awareness.

Medulla: A brain-stem region that controls breathing and heart rate. The sensory and motor pathways connecting the brain to the body cross in the medulla.

Memory: Any system—human, animal, or machine—that encodes, stores, and retrieves information.

Menarche: The onset of menstruation, which signals puberty in girls.

Mental age (MA): The average age at which normal (average) individuals achieve a particular score.

Mental operations: Solving problems by manipulating images in one's mind.

Mental representation: The ability to form internal images of objects and events.

Mental retardation: Often conceived as representing the lower 2% of the IQ range, commencing about 30 points below average (below about 70 points). More sophisticated definitions also take into account an individual's level of social functioning and other abilities.

Mental set: The tendency to respond to a new problem in the manner used for a previous problem.

Mere exposure effect: A learned preference for stimuli to which we have been previously exposed.

Method of loci: A mnemonic technique that involves associating items on a list with a sequence of familiar physical locations.

Misattribution: A memory fault that occurs when memories are retrieved, but they are associated with the wrong time, place, or person.

MMPI-2: A widely used personality assessment instrument that gives scores on ten important clinical traits. Also called the *Minnesota Multiphasic Personality Inventory*.

Mnemonics: Techniques for improving memory, especially by making connections between new material and information already in long-term memory.

Mood-congruent memory: A memory process that selectively retrieves memories that match (are *congruent* with) one's mood.

Mood disorders: Abnormal disturbances in emotion or mood, including bipolar disorder and unipolar disorder. Mood disorders are also called *affective disorders*.

Morphemes: The meaningful units of language that make up words. Some whole words are morphemes (example: "word"); other morphemes include grammatical components that alter a word's meaning (examples: "-ed," "-ing," and "un-").

Motivation: Refers to all the processes involved in starting, directing, and maintaining physical and psychological activities.

Motive: An internal mechanism that selects and directs behavior. The term *motive* is often used in the narrower sense of a motivational process that is learned, rather than biologically based (as are drives).

Motor cortex: A narrow vertical strip of cortex in the frontal lobes, just in front of the central fissure.

Motor neurons: Nerve cells that carry messages away from the central nervous system toward the muscles and glands.

Motor speech area: A part of the left frontal lobe responsible for coordinating the muscles used in producing speech. It is often called Broca's area, after its discoverer.

MRI or **magnetic resonance imaging:** An imaging technique that relies on cells' responses in a high-intensity magnetic field.

Multiple intelligences: A term used to refer to Gardner's theory, which proposes that there are seven forms of intelligence.

Mutations: Genetic variations, which occur randomly, especially during the recombination of chromosomes in sexual reproduction.

Mutual interdependence: A shared sense that individuals or groups need each other in order to achieve common goals.

Myelin sheath: A fatty insulation coating some types of neural axons, which biochemically speeds the conduction of neural impulses.

Myers-Briggs Type Indicator (MBTI): A widely used personality test based on Jungian types.

Narcissistic personality disorder: Characterized by a grandiose sense of self-importance, a preoccupation with fantasies of success or power, and a need for constant attention or admiration.

Narcolepsy: A disorder of REM sleep, involving sudden REM-sleep attacks accompanied by cataplexy.

Natural concepts: Mental representations of objects and events drawn from our direct experience.

Natural language mediators: Words associated with new information to be remembered.

Natural selection: The driving force behind evolution—by which the environment "selects" the fittest organisms.

Naturalistic observations: A form of correlational research involving behavioral assessment of people or animals in their home surroundings.

Nature–nurture controversy: The long-standing dispute over the relative importance of nature (heredity) and nurture (environment) in their influence on behavior and mental processes.

Need: In drive theory, a need is a biological imbalance (such as dehydration) that threatens survival, if the need is left unmet. Biological needs are believed to produce drives.

Need for achievement (n Ach): In Murray and McClelland's theory, a mental state that produces a psychological motive to excel or to reach some goal.

Needs hierarchy: In Maslow's theory, the notion that needs occur in priority order, with the biological needs as the most basic.

Negative punishment: The *removal* of an attractive stimulus after a response.

Negative reinforcement: The removal of an unpleasant or aversive stimulus, contingent upon a particular behavior. Compare with *punishment*.

Negative schizophrenia: Any form of schizophrenia distinguished by deficits, such as withdrawal and poverty of thought processes, rather than by active symptoms.

Neonatal period: In humans, the neonatal (newborn) period extends through the first month after birth.

Nerve cells or **neurons:** Cells specialized to receive and transmit information to other cells in the body. Bundles of many neurons are called *nerves*.

Nervous system: The entire network of neurons in the body, including the central nervous system, the peripheral nervous system, and their subdivisions.

Neural impulse: A brief electric surge generated by a nerve cell and carried down the length of the axon to the terminal buttons. The neural impulse (also called the *action potential*) carries the neuron's message.

Neural pathways: Bundles of nerve cells that follow generally the same route and employ the same neurotransmitter.

Neuroscience: A new field of study that focuses on the brain and its role in psychological processes.

Neurotic disorder or **neurosis:** Before the *DSM-IV,* these were terms used to describe a pattern of subjective distress or self-defeating behavior that did not show signs of brain abnormalities or grossly irrational thinking.

Neurotransmitters: Chemical messengers that relay neural messages across the synapse. Many neurotransmitters are also hormones.

Neutral stimulus: Any stimulus that produces no conditioned response prior to learning.

Nonconscious processes: Any brain process that does not involve conscious processing. Examples include regulation of the heart rate, breathing, and control of the internal organs and glands.

Nondirective: Rogers's term for a therapeutic approach in which the client, rather than the therapist, takes the lead in determining the direction of therapy.

Non-REM (NREM) sleep: The recurring periods when a sleeper is not showing REM.

Normal distribution: A bell-shaped curve, describing the spread of a characteristic throughout a population.

Normal range: Scores falling in (approximately) the middle two-thirds of a normal distribution.

Normally distributed: Spread through the population in varying degrees, so that few people fall into the high or low ranges, while most people cluster around the middle.

Object permanence: The knowledge that objects exist independently of one's own actions or awareness.

Observational learning: The process of learning new responses by watching others' behavior.

Obsessive–compulsive disorder: A condition characterized by patterns of persistent, unwanted thoughts and behaviors.

Occipital lobes: The cortical lobes at the back of the brain, containing the visual cortex.

Oedipus complex: According to Freud, a largely unconscious process whereby boys displace an erotic attraction toward their mother to females of their own age and, at the same time, identify with their fathers.

Olfaction: The sense of smell.

Olfactory bulbs: The brain sites of olfactory processing, located below the frontal lobes, where odor-sensitive receptors send their signals.

One-word stage: The first stage of true language, in which children communicate with single words, rather than sentences.

Operant: An observable, voluntary behavior that an organism emits to "operate" or have an effect on the environment.

Operant conditioning: A form of behavioral learning in which the probability of a responses is changed by its consequences—that is, by the stimuli that follow the response.

Operational definitions: Specific descriptions of concepts involving the conditions of a scientific study. Operational definitions are stated in terms of how the concepts are to be measured or what operations are being employed to produce them.

Opiates: Highly addictive drugs, derived from opium, that can produce a profound sense of well-being and have strong pain-relieving properties.

Optic nerve: The bundle of neurons that carries visual information from the retina to the brain.

Out-group: Those outside the group with which an individual identifies.

Overjustification: The process by which extrinsic (external) rewards can sometimes displace internal motivation, as when a child receives money for playing video games.

Overlearning: A strategy whereby the learner continues to study and rehearse the material after it has been initially brought to mastery.

Overregularization: Applying a grammatical rule too widely and creating incorrect forms.

Panic disorder: A disturbance marked by panic attacks that have no connection with events in the person's present experience.

Paranoid type: A form of schizophrenia in which a combination of delusions and hallucinations is the prominent feature.

Parasympathetic division: The part of the autonomic nervous system that monitors the routine operations of the internal organs and returns the body to calmer functioning after arousal by the sympathetic division.

Parietal lobes: Cortical lobes lying in the upper back of the brain and involved in touch sensation and in perceiving spatial relationships (the relationships of objects in space).

Participant modeling: A social learning technique in which a therapist demonstrates and encourages a client to imitate a desired behavior.

Penis envy: According to Freud, the female desire to have a penis—a condition that usually results in their attraction to males.

Percept: The meaningful product of perception—often an image that has been associated with concepts, memories of events, emotions, and motives.

Perception: A process that makes sensory patterns meaningful and more elaborate. Perception draws heavily on memory, motivation, emotion, and other psychological processes.

Perceptual constancy: The ability to recognize the same object under different conditions, such as changes in illumination, distance, or location.

Perceptual set: Readiness to detect a particular stimulus in a given context.

Peripheral nervous system: All parts of the nervous system lying outside the central nervous system. The peripheral nervous system includes the autonomic and somatic nervous systems.

Persistence: A memory problem in which unwanted memories cannot be put out of mind.

Person-centered therapy: A humanistic approach to treatment developed by Carl Rogers, emphasizing an individual's tendency for healthy psychological growth through self-actualization.

Person–situation controversy: A theoretical dispute concerning the relative contribution of personality factors and situational factors in controlling behavior.

Personal unconscious: Jung's term for that portion of the unconscious corresponding roughly to the Freudian id.

Personality: The psychological qualities that bring continuity to an individual's behavior in different situations and at different times.

Personality disorders: Conditions involving a chronic, pervasive, inflexible, and maladaptive pattern of thinking, emotion, social relationships, or impulse control.

PET scanning or **positron emission tomography:** An imaging technique that relies on the detection of radioactive sugar consumed by active brain cells.

Phenomenal field: Our psychological reality, composed of perceptions.

Phenotype: An organism's observable physical characteristics.

Pheromones: Chemical signals released by organisms to communicate with other members of their species; often sexual attractors.

Phobia or **phobic disorder:** An anxiety disorder involving a pathological fear of a specific object or situation.

Phosphenes: Visual sensations that are not caused by light waves but by other forms of stimulation, such as pressure on the eyeball or electrical stimulation of the visual cortex.

Photoreceptors: Light-sensitive cells in the retina that convert light energy to neural impulses.

Physiological dependence: A process by which the body adjusts to, and becomes dependent on, a drug.

Pitch: A sensory characteristic of sound produced by the frequency of the sound wave.

Pituitary gland: The master gland that produces hormones influencing the secretions of all other endocrine glands, as well as a hormone that influences growth. The pituitary is attached to the brain's hypothalamus, from which it takes its orders.

Placebo effect: A response to a placebo (a fake drug), caused by subjects' belief that they are taking real drugs.

Placebos: Substances that appear to be drugs but are not.

Placenta: The organ separating the embryo or fetus and the mother. The placenta separates the bloodstreams, but it allows the exchange of nutrients and waste products.

Plasticity: The ability of the nervous system to adapt or change as the result of experience. Plasticity sometimes can also help the nervous system adapt to physical damage.

Polygraph: A device that records or graphs many ("poly") measures of physical arousal, such heart rate, breathing, perspiration, and blood pressure. A polygraph is often called a "lie detector," even though it is really an arousal detector.

Pons: A brain-stem region that regulates brain activity during sleep and dreaming. *Pons* derives from the Latin word for "bridge."

Positive psychology: A movement within psychology, focusing on desirable aspects of human functioning, as opposed to an emphasis on psychopathology.

Positive punishment: The *application* of an aversive stimulus after a response.

Positive reinforcement: A stimulus presented after a response that increases the probability of that response happening again.

Positive schizophrenia: Any form of schizophrenia in which the person displays active symptoms, such as delusions or hallucinations.

Post-Freudian psychodynamic therapies: Therapies for mental disorder that were developed by psychodynamic theorists who disagreed with some aspects of Freud's theories and methods of treatment.

Posttraumatic stress disorder (PTSD): A delayed stress reaction in which an individual involuntarily reexperiences emotional, cognitive, and behavioral aspects of past trauma.

Practical intelligence (also called *contextual intelligence*): According to Sternberg, this is the ability to cope with the environment; sometimes called "street smarts."

Preconscious memories: Information that is not currently in consciousness but can be recalled to consciousness after something calls attention to them.

Prejudice: A negative attitude toward an individual based solely on his or her membership in a particular group.

Premack principle: The concept, developed by David Premack, that a more-preferred activity can be used to reinforce a less-preferred activity.

Prenatal period: The developmental period before birth.

Preoperational stage: The second stage in Piaget's theory, marked by well-developed mental representation and the use of language.

Preparedness hypothesis: The notion that we have an innate tendency, acquired through natural selection, to respond quickly and automatically to stimuli that posed a survival threat to our ancestors.

Primary reinforcers: Reinforcers, such as food and sex, that have an innate basis because of their biological value to an organism.

Priming: A technique for cuing implicit memories by providing cues that stimulate a memory without awareness of the connection between the cue and the retrieved memory.

Principle of opposites: A Jungian concept that portrays each personality as a balance between opposing pairs of unconscious tendencies, such as introversion and extroversion.

Principle of proximity: The notion that people at work will make more friends among those who are nearby—with whom they have the most contact. *Proximity* means "nearness."

Proactive interference: A cause of forgetting by which previously stored information prevents learning and remembering new information.

Procedural memory: A division of LTM that stores memories for how things are done.

Projection: The process by which people attribute their own unconscious motives to other people or objects. The concept of projection originally comes from Freud's theory.

Projective tests: Personality assessment instruments based on Freud's concept of projection.

Prompting: Cuing a response in such a way that the subject knows what response is required. Prompting often involves touching or manipulating a body part to be moved in the desired response or modeling a part of the response.

Prototype: An ideal or most representative example of a conceptual category.

Pseudoscience: Any approach to explaining phenomena in the natural world that does not use empirical observation or other aspects of the scientific method.

Psychiatrists: Physicians who specialize in the treatment of mental disorders.

Psychic determinism: Freud's assumption that all mental and behavioral reactions are caused by earlier life experiences.

Psychoactive drugs: Chemicals that affect mental processes and behavior by their effects on neurons and the nervous system.

Psychoanalysis: The form of psychodynamic therapy developed by Sigmund Freud. The goal of psychoanalysis is to release conflicts and memories from the unconscious.

Psychoanalysts: Specialists (usually psychiatrists) who use Freudian methods of treating mental disorders.

Psychodynamic therapies: Any of the insight therapies based on the assumption that mental disorder is caused by powerful mental forces and conflicts. Freudian *psychoanalysis* was the first form of psychodynamic therapy to be developed.

Psychodynamic view: A viewpoint that emphasizes the understanding of mental disorders in terms of unconscious needs, desires, memories, and conflicts.

Psychogenic: Caused by psychological factors.

Psychological dependence: A pervasive desire to obtain or use a drug—independent of physical addiction.

Psychological therapies: Therapies based on psychological principles (rather than on the biomedical approach); often called "psychotherapy."

Psychology: The science of individual behavior and mental processes.

Psychometrics: The field of mental testing.

Psychoneuroimmunology: A relatively new field that studies the influence of our mental states on the immune system.

Psychopathology: Any pattern of emotions, behaviors, or thoughts inappropriate to the situation and leading to personal distress or the inability to achieve important goals.

Psychosexual stages: Successive, instinctive patterns of associating pleasure with stimulation of specific bodily areas at different times of life.

Psychosocial crises: In Erikson's theory, any of the eight major developmental challenges across the life span, which require an individual to rethink his or her orientation to self and others.

Psychosurgery: The general term for surgical intervention in the brain to treat psychological disorders.

Psychotherapy: A term for any of the psychologically based therapies, including behavioral therapies and insight therapies.

Psychotic disorder or **psychosis:** A disorder involving profound disturbances in perception, rational thinking, or affect.

Puberty: The onset of sexual maturity.

Punishment: An aversive stimulus which, occurring after a response, diminishes the strength of that response. (Compare with *negative reinforcement*.)

Randomization: A process by which chance alone determined the order in which the stimulus was presented.

Rapid eye movements (REM): Quick bursts of eye movements occurring (under closed eyelids) at periodic intervals during sleep. REM sleep periods are associated with dreaming.

Ratio schedule: A program by which reinforcement depends on the number of correct responses.

Rational-emotive behavior therapy (REBT): Albert Ellis's brand of cognitive therapy, based on the idea that irrational thoughts and behaviors are the cause of mental disorders.

Rationalization: Giving socially acceptable reasons for actions that are really based on motives that the person believes to be unacceptable.

Reaction formation: The ego defense mechanism that makes us overreact in a manner opposite to our unconscious desires.

Recall: A retrieval method in which one must reproduce previously presented information.

Receptors: Specialized neurons that are activated by stimulation and transduce (convert) it into a nerve impulse.

Reciprocal determinism: The process in which the person, situation, and environment mutually influence each other.

Reciprocal inhibition: Joseph Wolpe's counterconditioning technique, involving relaxation training and systematic desensitization therapy.

Recognition: A retrieval method in which one must identify present stimuli as having been previously presented.

Reconstructive: An attribute of the memory system that involves the construction or fabrication of a recollection based on an incomplete memory trace. The rememberer is often unaware that the reconstructed memory is not an accurate rendition of the original experience.

Reflection of feeling: Carl Rogers's technique of paraphrasing the clients' words, attempting to capture the emotional tone expressed.

Reflexes: Simple, unlearned responses triggered by stimuli—such as the knee-jerk reflex set off by tapping the tendon just below your kneecap.

Regression: The ego defense mechanism that makes us revert to immature behavior in the face of threat.

Rehabilitation psychologists: Applied psychologists who help people with physical and mental disorders adapt to the problems of everyday life and work.

Reinforcement contingencies: Relationships between a response and the changes in stimulation that follow the response.

Reinforcer: A condition (involving either the presentation or removal of a stimulus) that occurs after a response and strengthens the response.

Relearning: A technique, invented by Hermann Ebbinghaus, used in measuring memory retention by recording the number of trials necessary to relearn certain material. This is then compared with the number of trials necessary to learn the material originally (see *savings method*).

Reliability: An attribute of a psychological test that gives consistent results.

REM rebound: A condition of increased REM sleep following a period of REM-sleep deprivation.

Representativeness bias: A faulty heuristic strategy based on the presumption that, once a person or event is categorized, it shares all the features of other members in that category.

Repression: The Freudian defense mechanism of forgetting, by which painful or threatening material is blocked off in the unconscious and prevented from reaching consciousness.

Residual type: A diagnostic category used for individuals who have suffered from a past episode of schizophrenia but are currently free of symptoms.

Resting potential: The electrical charge of the axon in its inactive state, when the neuron is ready to "fire."

Reticular activating system (RAS): A pencil-shaped structure in the brain stem, situated between the medulla and the pons. The RAS arouses the cortex to keep the brain alert and to attend to new stimulation.

Retina: The light-sensitive layer at the back of the eyeball.

Retroactive interference: A cause of forgetting by which newly learned information prevents retrieval of previously stored material.

Reward theory of attraction: A social learning view that says we like best those who give us maximum rewards at minimum cost.

Rites of passage: Social rituals that mark the transition between developmental stages, especially between childhood and adulthood.

Rods: Photoreceptors in the retina that are especially sensitive to dim light but not to colors.

Romantic love: A temporary and highly emotional condition based on infatuation and sexual desire.

Rorschach inkblot technique: A projective test requiring subjects to describe what they see in a series of ten inkblots.

Savant syndrome: Found in individuals having a remarkable talent (such as the ability to multiply numbers quickly in their heads or to determine the day of the week for any given date) even though they are mentally slow in other domains.

Savings method: Ebbinghaus's approach to measuring memory retention by calculating "savings" in number of trials necessary for relearning after varying amounts of time.

Scapegoating: Blaming an innocent person or a group for one's own troubles.

Schedules of reinforcement: Programs for the timing and frequency of reinforcements.

Schema: A knowledge cluster or general conceptual framework that provides expectations about topics, events, objects, people, and situations in one's life.

Schemes: In Piaget's theory, mental structures or programs that guide a developing child's thought.

Schizophrenia (pronounced *skits-o-FRENNY-a*): A psychotic disorder involving distortions in thoughts, perceptions, and/or emotions.

School psychologists: Applied psychologists with expertise in the problems of teaching and learning.

Scientific method: A five-step process for empirical investigation of a hypothesis under conditions designed to control biases and subjective judgments.

Script: A cluster of knowledge about sequences of events and actions expected to occur in particular settings.

Seasonal affective disorder or **SAD:** A form of depression believed to be caused by deprivation of sunlight.

Selective social interaction: Choosing to restrict the number of one's social contacts to those who are the most gratifying.

Self-actualizing personalities: Healthy individuals who have met their basic needs and are free to pursue an interest in "higher" ideals, such as truth, justice, and beauty.

Self-fulfilling prophecy: An expectation that becomes realized because it guides people's behaviors.

Self-help groups: Therapy groups, such as Alcoholics Anonymous, that are organized and run by laypersons, rather than professional therapists.

Self-serving bias: An attributional pattern in which one takes credit for success but denies responsibility for failure. (Compare with the *fundamental attribution error*.)

Semantic memory: A subdivision of declarative memory that stores general knowledge, including the meanings of words and concepts.

Sensation: An early stage of perception in which neurons in a receptor create a pattern of nerve impulses that represent the stimulation and pass these signals on to the brain for further processing.

Sensation seekers: In Zuckerman's theory, individuals who have a biological need for higher levels of stimulation than do other people.

Sensorimotor intelligence: The mental capacity shown in the first schemes an infant displays, which are mainly motor responses to stimuli, with a strong innate basis.

Sensorimotor stage: The first stage in Piaget's theory, during which the child relies heavily on innate motor responses to stimuli.

Sensory adaptation: Loss of responsiveness in receptor cells after stimulation has remained unchanged for a while.

Sensory memory: The first of three memory stages, preserving brief sensory impressions of stimuli; also called *sensory register*.

Sensory neurons: Nerve cells that carry messages from sense receptors toward the central nervous system.

Sensory pathway: Bundles of neurons that carry information from the sense organs to the brain.

Serial position effect: A form of interference related to the sequence in which information is presented. Generally, items in the middle of the sequence are less well remembered than items presented first or last.

Set point: Refers to the tendency of the body to maintain a certain level of body fat and body weight.

Sex chromosomes: The X and Y chromosomes that determine our physical sex characteristics.

Sexual orientation: One's erotic attraction toward members of the same sex (a homosexual orientation), the opposite sex (heterosexual orientation), or both sexes (a bisexual orientation).

Sexual response cycle: The four-stage sequence of arousal, plateau, orgasm, and resolution occurring in both men and women.

Sexual scripts: Socially learned ways of responding in sexual situations.

Shadow: The archetype representing the destructive and aggressive tendencies that we don't want to recognize in ourselves.

Shaping: An operant learning technique in which a new behavior is produced by reinforcing responses that approach the desired performance.

Shyness: A distressing pattern of avoiding or withdrawing from social contact; not a *DSM-IV* disorder.

Signal detection theory: Explains perceptual judgment as a combination of sensation and decision-making processes. Signal detection theory adds observer characteristics to classical psychophysics.

Similarity principle: The notion that people are attracted to those who are most similar to themselves.

Situationism: The view that environmental conditions influence people's behavior as much or more than their personal dispositions do.

Skin senses: Sensory systems for processing touch, warmth, and cold.

Skinner box: An operant chamber that can be programmed to deliver reinforcers and punishers contingent on an animal's behavior.

Sleep apnea: A respiratory disorder in which the person intermittently stops breathing while asleep.

Sleep debt: A deficiency caused by not getting the amount of sleep that one requires for optimal functioning.

Sleep paralysis: A condition in which a sleeper is unable to move any of the voluntary muscles, except those controlling the eyes. Sleep paralysis normally occurs during REM sleep.

Social distance: The perceived difference or similarity between oneself and another person.

Social learning or **observational learning:** A form of cognitive learning in which new responses are acquired after watching others' behavior and the consequences of their behavior.

Social learning therapy: An approach to therapy based on social learning theory, which teaches that behavior is influenced by observation and imitation of others.

Social norms: A group's expectations regarding what is appropriate and acceptable for its members' attitudes and behaviors.

Social psychology: The branch of psychology that studies the effects of social variables and cognitions on individual behavior and social interactions.

Social Readjustment Rating Scale (SRRS): A psychological rating scale designed to measure stress levels by means of values attached to common life changes.

Social reality: An individual's subjective interpretation of other people and of relationships with them.

Social role: One of several socially defined patterns of behavior that are expected of persons in a given setting or group.

Social support: The resources others provide to help an individual cope with stress.

Socialization: The lifelong process of developing behavior patterns, values, standards, skills, attitudes, and motives that conform to those regarded as desirable in a society.

Societal stressors: Stressful conditions arising from our social and cultural environment.

Sociocultural view: A psychological perspective that emphasizes the importance of social interaction, social learning, and a cultural perspective.

Somatic nervous system: A portion of the peripheral nervous system that sends voluntary messages to the body's skeletal muscles.

Somatoform disorders: Psychological problems appearing in the form of bodily symptoms or physical complaints, such as weakness or excessive worry about disease. The somatoform disorders include conversion disorder and hypochondriasis.

Somatosensory cortex: A strip of the parietal lobe lying just behind the central fissure. The somatosensory cortex is involved with sensations of touch.

Spatial orientation: (SPAY-shul) The process of locating one's body or other objects in space.

Split-brain patients: Individuals who have had the corpus callosum surgically severed, usually as a treatment for severe epilepsy.

Spontaneous recovery: The reappearance of an extinguished conditioned response after a time delay.

Stage of exhaustion: The third stage of the GAS, during which the body depletes its resources.

Stage of resistance: The second stage of the GAS, during which the body seems to adapt to the presence of the stressor.

Stimulants: Drugs that arouse the central nervous system, speeding up mental and physical responses. Such drugs normally increase activity level by encouraging communication among neurons in the brain. Stimulants, however, have been found to suppress activity level in persons with attention-deficit/hyperactivity disorder.

Stimulus generalization: The extension of a learned response to stimuli that are similar to the conditioned stimulus.

Stockholm syndrome: A psychological reaction in which hostages and prisoners identify and sympathize with their captors.

Storage: One of the three basic functions of memory, involving the retention of encoded material over time.

Stress: A physical and mental response to a challenging or threatening situation.

Stressors: Stressful stimuli or situations.

Stroke: An interruption of blood supply to a part of the brain.

Structuralism: A historical school of psychology devoted to uncovering the basic structures that make up mind and thought. Structuralists sought the "elements" of conscious experience.

Subconscious: A store of information that was registered in memory without being consciously attended to.

Subjective contours: Boundaries that are perceived but do not appear in the stimulus pattern.

Subjective well-being (SWB): An individual's evaluative response to his or her life, including cognitive and emotional reactions.

Suggestibility: The process of memory distortion as the result of deliberate or inadvertent suggestion.

Superego: The mind's storehouse of values, including moral attitudes learned from parents and from society; roughly the same as the common notion of the conscience.

Surrogate mothers: Mother substitutes, such as the cloth and wire dummies in Harlow's research.

Survey: A technique used in correlational research that typically involves seeking people's responses to a prepared set of verbal items.

Sympathetic division: The part of the autonomic nervous system that sends messages to internal organs and glands that help us respond to stressful and emergency situations.

Synapse: The microscopic gap that serves as a communications link between neurons. Synapses also occur between neurons and the muscles or glands they serve.

Synaptic transmission: The relaying of information across the synapse (from one neuron to another, for example) by means of chemical neurotransmitters.

Systematic desensitization: A behavioral therapy technique in which anxiety is extinguished by exposing the patient to an anxiety-provoking stimulus.

Tardive dyskinesia: An incurable disorder of motor control, especially involving muscles of the face and head, resulting from long-term use of antipsychotic drugs.

Taste-aversion learning: A biological tendency in which an organism learns, after a single experience, to avoid a food with a certain taste, if eating it is followed by illness.

Taste buds: Receptors for taste, located primarily on the upper side of the tongue.

Telegraphic speech: Short, simple sentences, typical of young children, who omit plurals, tenses, and function words, such as "the" and "of"; so called because it sounds like a telegram.

Temperament: An individual's characteristic manner of behavior or reaction—assumed to have a strong genetic basis; the basic, inherited personality dispositions that are apparent in early childhood and that establish the tempo and mood of the individual's behaviors.

Temporal lobes: Cortical lobes that process sounds, including speech. The temporal lobes are probably involved in storing long-term memories.

Teratogen: Any substance from the environment, including viruses, drugs, and other chemicals, that can damage the developing organism during the prenatal period.

Terminal buttons: Tiny bulblike structures at the end of the axon, which contain neurotransmitters that carry the neuron's message into the synapse.

Thalamus: The brain's central "relay station," situated just atop the brain stem. Nearly all the messages going into or out of the brain go through the thalamus.

Thanatos: The unconscious force that drives people toward aggressive and destructive behaviors.

Thematic Apperception Test (TAT): A projective test requiring subjects to make up stories that explain ambiguous pictures.

Theory: A testable explanation for a set of facts or observations.

Theory of mind: An awareness that other people's behavior may be influenced by beliefs, desires, and emotions that differ from one's own.

Therapeutic community: Jones's term for a program of treating mental disorder by making the institutional environment supportive and humane for patients.

Therapy: A general term for any treatment process; in psychology and psychiatry, *therapy* refers to a variety of psychological and biomedical techniques.

Thinking: The cognitive process involved in forming a new mental representation by manipulating available information.

Tics: Unwanted involuntary movements and twitches, such as exaggerated eye blinks.

Timbre: The quality of a sound wave that derives from the wave's complexity (combination of pure tones).

Token economy: An operant technique applied to groups, such as classrooms or mental hospital wards, involving the distribution of "tokens" or other indicators of reinforcement contingent on desired behaviors. The tokens can later be exchanged for privileges, food, or other reinforcers.

Tolerance: The reduced effectiveness a drug has after repeated use.

Top-down processing: Perceptual analysis that emphasizes the perceiver's expectations, concept memories, and other cognitive factors, rather than being driven by the characteristics of the stimulus.

TOT phenomenon: The inability to recall a word, while knowing that it is in memory. People often describe this frustrating experience as having the word "on the tip of the tongue."

Traits: Stable personality characteristics that are presumed to exist within the individual and guide his or her thoughts and actions under various conditions.

Transcranial magnetic stimulation (TMS): A treatment that involves magnetic stimulation of specific regions of the brain. Unlike ECT, TMS does not produce a seizure.

Transduction: Transformation of one form of energy into another—especially the transformation of stimulus information into nerve impulses.

Transience: The impermanence of a long-term memory. Transience is based on the idea that long-term memories gradually fade in strength over time.

Trial-and-error learning: An operant form of learning, described by Thorndike, in which the learner gradually discovers the correct response by attempting many behaviors and noting which ones produce the desired consequences.

Triangular theory of love: A theory that describes various kinds of love in terms of three components: passion (erotic attraction), intimacy (sharing feelings and confidences), and commitment (dedication to putting this relationship first in one's life).

Triarchic theory: The term for Sternberg's theory of intelligence; so called because it combines three ("tri-") main forms of intelligence.

Twin studies: Developmental investigations in which twins, especially identical twins, are compared in the search for genetic and environmental effects.

Two-factor theory: The proposal claiming that emotion results from the cognitive appraisal of both physical arousal (Factor #1) and an emotion-provoking stimulus (Factor #2).

Two-word stage: The second stage of true language, in which two words form rudimentary sentences—showing that the child is beginning to learn syntax.

Tympanic membrane: The eardrum.

Type: Refers to especially important dimensions or clusters of traits that are not only central to a person's personality but are found with essentially the same pattern in many people.

Type A: A behavior pattern characterized by an intense, angry, competitive, or perfectionistic response to life.

Type B: A behavior pattern characterized by a relaxed, unruffled response to life.

Unconditional positive regard: Rogers's term for the therapist's attitude of nonjudgmental acceptance and respect for the clien; love or caring without conditions attached.

Unconditioned response (UCR): In classical conditioning, the response elicited by an unconditioned stimulus without prior learning.

Unconditioned stimulus (UCS): In classical conditioning, the stimulus that elicits an unconditioned response.

Unconscious: In classic Freudian theory, a part of the mind that houses memories, desires, and feelings that would be threatening if brought to consciousness. Recently, many psychologists have come to believe in a simplified, "dumb" unconscious, which stores and processes some information outside of awareness.

Unconscious motivation: Having a desire to engage in an activity but being consciously unaware of the desire. Freud's psychoanalytic theory emphasized unconscious motivation.

Undifferentiated type: A category used to designate persons displaying a combination of schizophrenic symptoms that do not clearly fit in one of the other categories of schizophrenia.

Unipolar depression: A form of depression that does not alternate with mania.

Validity: An attribute of a psychological test that actually measures what it is being used to measure.

Variable interval (VI) schedules: Programs by which the time period between reinforcements varies from trial to trial.

Variable ratio (VR) schedules: Reinforcement programs by which the number of responses required for a reinforcement varies from trial to trial.

Vestibular sense: The sense of body orientation with respect to gravity.

Vicarious trial-and-error: Mentally trying alternative behaviors and thinking through their consequences before selecting a physical response. This concept was ridiculed by the behaviorists.

Violence and **aggression:** Terms that refer to behavior that is intended to cause harm.

Visible spectrum: The tiny part of the electromagnetic spectrum to which our eyes are sensitive.

Visual cortex: The visual processing areas of cortex in the occipital lobes.

Weber's law: This concept says that the size of a JND is proportional to the intensity of the stimulus; the JND is large when the stimulus intensity is high and small when the stimulus intensity is low.

Whole method: The mnemonic strategy of first approaching the material to be learned "as a whole," forming an impression of the overall meaning of the material. The details are later associated with this overall impression.

Withdrawal: After addiction, a pattern of painful physical symptoms and cravings experienced when the level of drug is decreased or the drug is eliminated.

Working memory or **short-term memory (STM):** The second of three memory stages, and most limited in capacity; preserves recently perceived events or experiences for less than a minute without rehearsal.

Zygote: A fertilized egg.

REFERENCES

ABC News. (1995). "My Family, Forgive Me." *20/20*, Transcript #1526, June 30, pp. 6–10. New York: American Broadcasting Companies, Inc.

Abel, E. L., & Sokol, R. J. (1986). Fetal alcohol syndrome is now a leading cause of mental retardation. *Lancet, 2,* 1222.

Abelson, R. P. (1981). Psychological status of the script concept. *American Psychologist, 36,* 715–729.

Abrams, A. R. (1992). *Electroconvulsive therapy.* New York: Oxford University Press.

Abramson, L. Y., Metalsky, G. I., & Alloy, L. B. (1989). Hopelessness depression: A theory-based subtype. *Psychological Review, 96,* 358–372.

Achenbach, T. M. (1982). *Developmental psychopathology* (2nd ed.), New York: Wiley.

Adams, J. (1979). Mutual-help groups: Enhancing the coping ability of oncology clients. *Cancer Nursing, 2,* 95–98.

Adams, P. R., & Adams, G. R. (1984). Mount Saint Helens' ashfall: Evidence for a disaster stress reaction. *American Psychologist, 39,* 252–260.

Ader, R., & Cohen, N. (1993). Psychoneuroimmunology: Conditioning and stress. *Annual Review of Psychology, 44,* 53–85.

Adler, J., & Salzhauer, A. (1995). Escaping the diet trap. *Newsweek, 126*(6), 54.

Adorno, T. W., Frenkel-Brunswick, E., Levinson, D. J., & Sanford, R. N. (1950). *The authoritarian personality.* New York: Harper.

Aftergood, S. (2000, November 3). Polygraph testing and the DOE National Laboratories. *Science, 290,* 939–940.

Ahern, G. L., & Schwartz, G. E. (1985). Differential lateralization for positive and negative emotion in the human brain: EEG spectral analysis. *Neuropsychologia, 23,* 744–755.

Ahrons, C. R. (1994). *The good divorce: Keeping your family together when your marriage comes apart.* New York: HarperCollins.

Ainsworth, M. D. S. (1973). The development of infant–mother attachment. In B. M. Caldwell & H. N. Ricciuti (Eds.), *Review of child development research* (Vol. 3). Chicago: University of Chicago Press.

Ainsworth, M. D. S. (1989). Attachments beyond infancy. *American Psychologist, 44,* 709–716.

Ainsworth, M. D. S., Blehar, M., Water, E., & Wall, S. (1978). *Patterns of attachment.* Hillsdale, NJ: Erlbaum.

Ainsworth, M. D. S., & Wittig, B. A. (1969). Attachment and exploratory behavior of one-year-olds in a strange situation. In B. M. Foss (Ed.), *Determinants of infant behavior* (Vol. 4). London: Methuen.

Alford, G. S., & Bishop, A. C. (1991). Psychopharmacology. In M. Hersen, A. E. Kazdin, & A. S. Bellack (Eds.), *The clinical psychology handbook* (2nd ed., pp. 667–694). New York: Pergamon Press.

Allen, M. G. (1976). Twin studies of affective illness. *Archives of General Psychiatry, 33,* 1476–1478.

Allen, V. S., & Levine, J. M. (1969). Consensus and conformity. *Journal of Experimental Social Psychology, 5,* 389–399.

Allport, G. W., & Odbert, H. S. (1936). Trait-names, a psycho-lexical study. *Psychological Monographs, 47* (1, Whole No. 211).

Alper, J. (1993). Echo-planar MRI: Learning to read minds. *Science, 261,* 556.

Amabile, T. M. (1983). *The social psychology of creativity.* New York: Springer-Verlag.

Amabile, T. M. (1987). The motivation to be creative. In S. Isaksen (Ed.), *Frontiers in creativity: Beyond the basics.* Buffalo, NY: Bearly Limited.

American Psychiatric Association. (1994). *Diagnostic and statistical manual of mental disorders,* 4th edition. Washington, DC: American Psychiatric Association.

American Psychiatric Association. (2000). *Diagnostic and statistical manual of mental disorders,* 4th edition, text revision. Washington, DC: Author.

American Psychological Association. (1992). Ethical principles of psychologists and code of conduct. *American Psychologist, 47,* 1597–1611.

American Psychological Association. (1996). *Psychology: Careers for the twenty-first century.* Washington, DC: Author.

American Psychological Association. (1998). Association report. *American Psychologist, 53,* 836–853.

Anastasi, A. (1988). *Psychological testing* (6th ed.). New York: Macmillan.

Anch, A. M., Browman, C. P., Mitler, M. M., & Walsh, J. K. (1988). *Sleep: A scientific perspective.* Englewood Cliffs, NJ: Prentice Hall.

Anderson, A. E., & DiDomenico, L. (1992). Diet vs. shape content of popular male and female magazines: A dose-response relationship to the incidence of eating disorders? *International Journal of Eating Disorders, 11,* 283–287.

Anderson, J. R. (1982). Acquisition of cognitive skill. *Psychological Review, 89,* 369–406.

Andreasen, N. C., Rice, J., Endicott, J., Coryell, W., Grove, W. W., & Reich, T. (1987). Familial rates of affective disorder. *Archives of General Psychiatry, 44,* 461–472.

Andrews, J. D. W. (1967). The achievement motive and advancement in two types of organization. *Journal of Personality and Social Psychology, 6,* 163–168.

Angell, M. (1985). Disease as a reflection of the psyche. *New England Journal of Medicine, 312,* 1570–1572.

Angold, A., Erkanli, A., Egger, H. L., & Costello, E. J. (2000). Stimulant treatment for children: a community perspective. *Journal of the American Academy of Child and Adolescent Psychiatry, 39,* 975–984.

Antonuccio, D. (1995). Psychotherapy for depression: No stronger medicine. *American Psychologist, 50,* 450–452.

Antony, M. M., Brown, T. A., & Barlow, D. H. (1992). Current perspectives on panic and panic disorder. *Current Directions in Psychological Science, 1,* 79–82.

Archer, J. (1996). Sex differences in social behavior: Are the social role and evolutionary explanations compatible? *American Psychologist, 51,* 909–917.

Arnett, J. J. (1999). Adolescent storm and stress, reconsidered. *American Psychologist, 54,* 317–326.

Arnhoff, F. N. (1975). Social consequences of policy toward mental illness. *Science, 188,* 1277–1281.

Arnsten, A. F. T. (1998, June 12). The biology of being frazzled. *Science, 280,* 1711–1712.

Aron, A., & Aron, E. (1994). Love. In A. L. Weber & J. H. Harvey (Eds.), *Perspectives on close relationships* (Chapter 7), pp. 131–152. Boston: Allyn & Bacon.

Aronson, E. (1995). *The Social Animal* (7th ed.). New York: W. H. Freeman.

Aronson, E. (1999). *The social animal* (8th ed.). New York: W. H. Freeman.

Aronson, E. (2000). *Nobody left to hate: Teaching compassion after Columbine.* New York: W. H. Freeman & Company.

Aronson, E., Helmreich, R., & LeFan, J. (1970). To err is humanizing—sometimes: Effects of self-esteem, competence, and a pratfall on interpersonal attraction. *Journal of Personality and Social Psychology, 16,* 259–264.

Aronson, E., Willerman, B., & Floyd, J. (1966). The effect of a pratfall on increasing interpersonal attractiveness. *Psychonomic Science, 4,* 227–228.

Asbell, B. (1995). *The Pill: A biography of the drug that changed the world.* New York: Random House.

Asch, S. E. (1940). Studies in the principles of judgments and attitudes: 11. Determination of judgments by group and by ego standards. *Journal of Social Psychology, 12,* 433–465.

Asch, S. E. (1955). Opinions and social pressure. *Scientific American, 193*(5), 31–35.

Asch, S. E. (1956). Studies of independence and conformity: A minority of one against a unanimous majority. *Psychological Monographs, 70* (9, Whole No. 416).

Aserinsky, E., & Kleitman, N. (1953). Regularly occurring periods of eye mobility and concomitant phenomena during sleep. *Science, 118,* 273–274.

Ashby, F. G., & Waldron, E. M. (2000). The neurpsychological bases of category learning. *Current Directions in Psychological Science, 9,* 10–14.

Auerbach, R., & Kilman, P. R. (1977). The effects of group systematic desensitization on secondary erectile failure. *Behavior Therapy, 8,* 330–339.

Auerbach, S. M., Kiesler, D. J., Strentz, T., & Schmidt, J. A. (1994). Interpersonal impacts and adjustment to the stress of simulated captivity: An empirical test of the Stockholm syndrome. *Journal of Social and Clinical Psychology, 13,* 207–221.

Austin, J. H. (1998). *Zen and the brain: Toward an understanding of meditation and consciousness.* Cambridge, MA: MIT Press.

Averill, J. A. (1980). A constructivist view of emotion. In R. Plutchik & H. Kellerman (Eds.), *Emotion: Theory, research, and experience: Vol. 1. Theories of emotion.* New York: Academic Press.

Axel, R. (1995, October). The molecular logic of smell. *Scientific American, 273,* 154–159.

Ayllon, T., & Azrin, N. H. (1965). The measurement and reinforcement of behavior of psychotics. *Journal of Experimental Analysis of Behavior, 8,* 357–383.

Ayllon, T., & Azrin, N. H. (1968). *The token economy: A motivational system for therapy and rehabilitation.* New York: Appleton-Century-Crofts.

Azar, B. (1995, June). New cognitive research makes waves. *APA Monitor,* p. 16.

Azar, B. (1996, November). Some forms of memory improve as people age. *APA Monitor,* p. 27.

Azar, B. (1997a, March). Human brain inspires new computer models. *APA Monitor,* p. 22.

Azar, B. (1997b, October). Was Freud right? Maybe, maybe not. *American Psychological Association Monitor, 28,* 30.

Azar, B. (1998a, January). Certain smells evoke stronger memories. *APA Monitor,* 10.

Azar, B. (1998b, January). Communicating through pheromones. *APA Monitor,* 1, 12.

Azar, B. (2000a, July/August). How do parents matter? Let us count the ways. *Monitor on Psychology,* pp. 62–66.

Azar, B. (2000b, July/August). A new stress paradigm for women. *Monitor on Psychology,* 42–43.

Baars, B. J. (1988). *A cognitive theory of consciousness.* Cambridge, England: Cambridge University Press.

Baars, B. J., & McGovern, K. (1994). Consciousness. *Encyclopedia of Human Behavior, 1,* 687–699. San Diego: Academic Press.

Baddeley, A. (1998). *Human memory: Theory and practice.* Boston: Allyn and Bacon.

Baell, W. K., & Wertheim, E. H. (1992). Predictors of outcome in the treatment of bulimia nervosa. *British Journal of Clinical Psychology, 31*(3), 330–332.

Bahrick, H. P., Bahrick, L. E., Bahrick, A. S., & Bahrick, P. E. (1993). Maintenance of foreign language vocabulary and the spacing effect. *Psychology Science, 4,* 316–321.

Bailey, J. M., Bobrow, D., Wolfe, M, & Mikach, S. (1995). Sexual orientation of adult sons of gay fathers. *Developmental Psychology, 31,* 124–129.

Balch, P., & Ross, A. W. (1975). Predicting success in weight reduction as a function of locus of control: A uni-dimensional and multi-dimensional approach. *Journal of Consulting and Clinical Psychology, 43,* 119.

Baldwin, D. A. (2000). Interpersonal understanding fuels knowledge acquisition. *Current Directions in Psychological Science, 9,* 40–45.

Balsam, P. D., & Tomie, A. (Eds.). (1985). *Context and learning.* Hillsdale, NJ: Erlbaum.

Balter, M. (2000, October 20). Celebrating the synapse. *Science, 290,* 424.

Baltes, M. M. (1995). Dependency in old age: Gains and losses. *Current Directions in Psychological Science, 4,* 14–19.

Baltes, P. B. (1987). Theoretical propositions on life-span developmental psychology: On the dynamics between growth and decline. *Developmental Psychology, 23,* 611–626.

Baltes, P. B. (1990, November). *Toward a psychology of wisdom.* Invited address presented at the annual convention of the Gerontological Society of America, Boston, MA.

Baltes, P. B. (1993). The aging mind: Potential and limits. *The Gerontologist, 33,* 580–594.

Baltes, P. B., & Kliegl, R. (1992). Further testing of limits of cognitive plasticity: Negative age differences in a mnemonic skill are robust. *Developmental Psychology, 28,* 121–125.

Bandura, A. (1970). Modeling therapy. In W. S. Sahakian (Ed.), *Psychopathology today: Experimentation, theory and research.* Itasca, IL: Peacock.

Bandura, A. (1981). In search of pure unidirectional determinants. *Behavior Therapy, 12,* 30–40.

Bandura, A. (1986). *Social foundations of thought and action: A social cognitive theory.* Englewood Cliffs, NJ: Prentice-Hall.

Bandura, A. (1992). Exercise of personal agency through the self-efficacy mechanism. In R. Schwarzer (Ed.), *Self-efficacy: Thought control of action* (pp. 3–38). Washington: Hemisphere.

Bandura, A. (1999). Social cognitive theory of personality. In L. A. Pervin & O. P. John (Eds.), *Handbook of personality: Theory and research* (2nd ed.) (pp. 154–196). New York: Guilford Press.

Bandura, A., Ross, D., & Ross, S. A. (1963). Imitation of film-mediated aggressive models. *Journal of Abnormal and Social Psychology, 66,* 3–11.

Banich, M. T. (1998). Integration of information between the cerebral hemispheres. *Current Directions in Psychological Science, 7,* 32–37.

Banks, M. S., & Bennet, P. J. (1988). Optical and photoreceptor immaturities limit the spatial and chromatic vision of human neonates. *Journal of the Optical Society of America, 5,* 2059–2079.

Barber, T. X. (1976). *Hypnosis: A scientific approach.* New York: Psychological Dimensions.

Barber, T. X. (1979). Suggested ("hypnotic") behavior: The trance paradigm versus an alternative paradigm. In E. Fromm & R. E. Shor (Eds.), *Hypnosis: Developments in research and new perspectives.* New York: Aldine.

Barber, T. X. (1986). Realities of stage hypnosis. In B. Zilbergeld, M. G. Edelstein, & D. L. Araoz (Eds.), *Hypnosis: Questions and answers.* New York: Norton.

Bard, M., & Sangrey, D. (1979). *The crime victim's book.* New York: Basic Books.

Barinaga, M. (1994, July 29). To sleep, perchance to . . . learn? New studies say yes. *Science, 265,* 603–604.

Barinaga, M. (1995, December 1). Brain researchers speak a common language. *Science, 270,* 1437–1438.

Barinaga, M. (1996, January 19). Social status sculpts activity of crayfish neurons. *Science, 271,* 290–291.

Barinaga, M. (1997, July 25). How jet-lag hormone does double duty in the brain. *Science, 277,* 480.

Barinaga, M. (1998a, March 27). No-new-neurons dogma loses ground. *Science, 270,* 2041–2042.

Barinaga, M. (1998b, July 24). How the brain sees in three dimensions. *Science, 281,* 500–501.

Barinaga, M. (1999, July 9). The mapmaking mind. *Science, 285,* 189, 191–192.

Barinaga, M. (2000, October 27). Synapses call the shots. *Science, 290,* 736–738.

Barker, L. M., Best, M. R., & Domjan, M. (Eds.). (1978). *Learning mechanisms in food selection.* Houston: Baylor University Press.

Barker, S. L., Funk, S. C., & Houston, B. K. (1988). Psychological treatment versus nonspecific factors: A meta-analysis of conditions that engender comparable expectations for improvement. *Clinical Psychology Review, 8,* 579–594.

Barkley, R. A. (1998, September). Attention-deficit hyperactivity disorder. *Scientific American, 279*(9), 66–71.

Barlow, D. H. (1996). Health care policy, psychotherapy research, and the future of psychotherapy. *American Psychologist, 51,* 1050–1058.

Barlow, D. H. (2000). Unraveling the mysteries of anxiety and its disorders from the perspective of emotion theory. *American Psychologist, 55,* 1247–1263.

Barlow, D. H. (2001). A modern learning theory perspective on the etiology of panic disorder. *Psychological Review, 108,* 4–32.

Barlow, D. H. (2000). Unraveling the mysteries of anxiety and its disorders from the perspective of emotion theory. *American Psychologist, 55,* 1247–1263.

Barlow, D. H., Craske, M. G., Cerny, J. A., & Klosko, J. S. (1989). Behavioral treatment of panic disorder. *Behavior Therapy, 20,* 261–282.

Barlow, D. H., Rapee, R. M., & Brown, T. A. (1992). Behavioral treatment of generalized anxiety disorder. *Behavior Therapy, 23,* 551–570.

Barnes, D. M. (1987). Biological issues in schizophrenia. *Science, 235,* 430–433.

Barnier, A. J., & McConkey, K. M. (1998). Posthypnotic responding away from the hypnotic setting. *Psychological Science, 9,* 256–262.

Barnouw, V. (1963). Culture and personality. Homewood, IL: Dorsey Press.

Baron, L., & Straus, M. A. (1985). *Four theories of rape in American society: A state-level analysis.* New Haven, CT: Yale University Press.

Barondes, S. H. (1994, February 25). Thinking about Prozac. *Science, 263,* 1102–1103.

Barron, F., & Harrington, D. M. (1981). Creativity, intelligence and personality. *Annual Review of Psychology, 32,* 439–476.

Bartoshuk, L. M. (1990, August–September). Psychophysiological insights on taste. *Science Agenda,* 12–13.

Bartoshuk, L. M. (1993). The biological basis of food perception and acceptance. *Food Quality and Preference, 4,* 21–32.

Bartoshuk, L. M., Duffy, V. B., & Miller, I. J. (1994). PCT/PROP tasting: Anatomy, psychophysics and sex effects. *Physiology and Behavior, 56,* 1165–1171.

Basic Behavioral Science Task Force of the National Advisory Mental Health Council (1996). Basic behavioral science research for mental health: Family processes and social networks. *American Psychologist, 51,* 622–630.

Baskett, L. (1985). Sibling status: Adult expectations. *Developmental Psychology, 21,* 441–445.

Bass, E., & Davis, L. (1988). *The courage to heal.* New York: Harper-Collins.

Batista, A. P., Buneo, C. A., Snyder, L. H., & Andersen, R. A. (1999, July 9). Reach plans in eye-centered coordinates. *Science, 285,* 257–260.

Batson, C. D. (1987). Prosocial motivation: Is it ever truly altruistic? In L. Berkowitz (Ed.), *Advances in experimental social psychology* (Vol. 20). Orlando, FL: Academic Press.

Baum, A. (1990). Stress, intrusive imagery, and chronic distress. *Health Psychology, 9,* 653–675.

Baum, W. M. (1994). *Understanding behaviorism: Science, behavior, and culture.* New York: HarperCollins.

Baumeister, A. A. (1987). Mental retardation: Some conceptions and dilemmas. *American Psychologist, 42,* 796–800.

Baumeister, R. F. (Ed.). (1993). *Self-esteem: The puzzle of low self-regard.* New York: Plenum.

Baumeister, R. F., & Leary, M. R. (1995). The need to belong: Desire for interpersonal attachments as a fundamental human motivation. *Psychological Bulletin, 117,* 427–529.

Baumeister, R. F., Smart, L., & Boden, J. M. (1996). Relation of threatened egotism to violence and aggression: The dark side of high self-esteem. *Psychological Review, 103,* 5–33.

Baumeister, R. F., Stillwell, A. M., & Wotman, S. R. (1990). Victim and perpetrator accounts of interpersonal conflict: Autobiographical narratives about anger. *Journal of Personality and Social Psychology, 59,* 994–1005.

Baumrind, D. (1985). Research using intentional deception: Ethical issues revisited. *American Psychologist, 40,* 165–174.

Baynes, K., Eliassen, J. C., Lutsep, H. L., & Gazzaniga, M. S. (1998). Modular organization of cognitive systems masked by interhemispheric integration. *Science, 280,* 902–905.

Beall, A. E., & Sternberg, R. J. (1995). The social construction of love. *Journal of Social and Personal Relationships, 12* (3), 417–438.

Beaman, A. L., Barnes, P. J., Klentz, B., & McQuirk, B. (1978). Increasing helping rates through information dissemination: Teaching pays. *Personality and Social Psychology Bulletin, 4,* 406–411.

Beardsley, T. (1996, July). Waking up. *Scientific American, 14,* 18.

Beardsley, T. (1997a, August). The machinery of thought. *Scientific American, 277,* 78–83.

Beardsley, T. (1997b, March). Memories are made of . . . *Scientific American,* pp. 32–33.

Bechara, A., Damasio, H., Tranel, D., & Damasio, A. R. (1997, February 28). Deciding advantageously before knowing the advantageous strategy. *Science, 275,* 1293–1295.

Bechara, A., Tranel, D., Damasio, H., Adolphs, R., Rockland, C., & Damasio, A. R. (1995, August 25). Double dissociation of conditioning and declarative knowledge relative to the amygdala and hippocampus in humans. *Science, 269,* 1115–1118.

Beck, A. T. (1976). *Cognitive therapy and emotional disorders.* New York: International Universities Press.

Beck, A. T., Rush, A. J., Shaw, B. F., & Emery, G. (1979). *Cognitive therapy of depression.* New York: Guilford Press.

Becker, M. H. (1993). A medical sociologist looks at health promotion. *Journal of Health and Social Behavior, 34,* 1–6.

Bédard, J., & Chi, M. T. H. (1992). Expertise. *Current Directions in Psychological Science, 1,* 135–139.

Bee, H. (1994). *Lifespan Development.* New York: HarperCollins.

Beeman, M. J., & Chiarello, C. (1998). Complementary right- and left-hemisphere language comprehension. *Current Directions in Psychological Science, 7,* 2–8.

Begley, S. (1995). Lights of madness. *Newsweek, CXXVI* (21), November 20, pp. 76–77.

Begley, S., & Biddle, N. (1996). For the obsessed, the mind can fix the brain. *Newsweek, Vol. CXXVII* (9), p. 60.

Behrmann, M. (2000). The mind's eye mapped onto the brain's matter. *Current Directions in Psychological Science, 9,* 50–54.

Bell, A. P., Weinberg, M. S., & Hammersmith, S. K. (1981). *Sexual preference.* Bloomington: Indiana University Press.

Bem, D. J. (1974). The measurement of psychological androgyny. *Journal of Consulting and Clinical Psychology, 42,* 155–162.

Bem, D. J. (1981). *The Bem Sex Role Inventory: Professional manual.* Palo Alto, CA: Consulting Psychology Press.

Bem, D. J. (1996). Exotic becomes erotic: A developmental theory of sexual orientation. *Psychological Review, 103,* 320–335.

Bem, D. J. (2001). *Interplay of theory and politics in explaining the enigma of sexual orientation.* Address given at the annual convention of the American Psychological Association in San Francisco, CA.

Bem, D. J., & Allen, A. (1974). On predicting some of the people some of the time: The search for cross-situational consistencies in behavior. *Psychological Review, 81*(6), 506–520.

Benassi, V. A., Sweeney, P. D., & Dufour, C. L. (1988). Is there a relation between locus of control orientation and depression? *Journal of Abnormal Psychology, 97,* 357–367.

Benedict, R. (1934). *Patterns of culture.* Boston: Houghton Mifflin.

Benedict, R. (1959). *Patterns of culture.* Boston: Houghton Mifflin.

Benjamin, L. T., Jr. (1986). Why don't they understand us? A history of psychology's public image. *American Psychologist, 41,* 941–946.

Benjamin, L. T., Jr., & Nielsen-Gammon, E. (1999). B. F. Skinner and psychotechnology: The case of the heir conditioner. *Review of General Psychology, 3,* 155–167.

Benson, H. (1975). *The relaxation response.* New York: Morrow.

Berenbaum, H., & Connelly, J. (1993). The effect of stress on hedonic capacity. *Journal of Abnormal Psychology, 102,* 474–481.

Berk, L. (1996). The laughter–immune connection: New discoveries. *Humor and Health Journal, 5,* 1–5.

Berk, L. E. (1991). *Child development.* Boston: Allyn & Bacon.

Berk, L. E. (2000). *Child development* (5th ed.). Boston: Allyn & Bacon.

Berkman, L. F., & Syme, S. L. (1979). Social networks, host resistance, and mortality: A nine-year follow-up study of Alameda County residents. *American Journal of Epidemiology, 109,* 186–204.

Berlyne, D. E. (1960). *Conflict, arousal, and curiosity.* New York: McGraw-Hill.

Berman, J. S., & Norton, N. C. (1985). Does professional training make a therapist more effective? *Psychological Bulletin, 98,* 401–407.

Berndt, T. J. (1979). Developmental changes in conformity to peers and parents. *Developmental Psychology, 15,* 608–616.

Berndt, T. J. (1992). Friendship and friends' influence in adolescence. *Current Directions in Psychological Science, 1,* 156–159.

Bernstein, I. L. (1988). What does learning have to do with weight loss and cancer? *Proceedings of the Science and Public Policy Seminar of the Federation of Behavioral, Psychological and Cognitive Sciences.* Washington, DC.

Bernstein, I. L. (1990). Salt preference and development. *Developmental Psychology, 26,* 552–554.

Bernstein, I. L. (1991). Aversion conditioning in response to cancer and cancer treatment. *Clinical Psychology Review, 11,* 185–191.

Berry, J. (1992). Cree conceptions of cognitive competence. *International Journal of Psychology, 27,* 73–88.

Berry, J. W., Poortinga, Y. H., Segall, M. H., & Dasen, P. R. (1992). *Cross-cultural psychology: Research and applications.* New York: Cambridge University Press.

Berscheid, E. (1988). Some comments on love's anatomy: or, Whatever happened to old-fashioned lust? In R. J. Sternberg & M. L. Barnes (Eds.), *The psychology of love.* New Haven, CT: Yale University Press.

Berscheid, E. (1999). The greening of relationship science. *American Psychologist, 54,* 260–266.

Beutler, L. E., & Machado, P. P. (1992). Research on psychotherapy. In M. R. Rosenzweig (Ed.), *International psychological science: Progress, problems, and prospects* (pp. 227–252). Washington, DC: American Psychological Association.

Biederman, I. (1989). Higher-level vision. In D. N. Osherson, H. Sasnik, S. Kosslyn, K. Hollerbach, E. Smith, & N. Block (Eds.), *An invitation to cognitive science.* Cambridge, MA: MIT Press.

Biehl, M., Matsumoto, D., Ekman, P., Hearn, V., Heider, K., Kudoh, T., & Ton, V. (1997). Matsumoto and Ekman's Japanese and Caucasian facial expressions of emotion (JACFEE): Reliability data and cross-national differences. *Journal of Nonverbal Behavior, 21,* 3–21.

Billings, A. G., & Moos, R. H. (1985). Life stressors and social resources affect posttreatment outcomes among depressed patients. *Journal of Abnormal Psychology, 94,* 140–153.

Binet, A. (1911). *Les idées modernes sur les enfants.* Paris: Flammarion.

Binitie, A. (1975). A factor-analytical study of depression across cultures (African and European). *British Journal of Psychiatry, 127,* 559–563.

Bink, M. L., & Marsh, R. L. (2000). Cognitive regularities in creative activity. *Review of General Psychology, 4,* 59–78.

Birenbaum, M., & Montag, I. (1986). On the location of the sensation seeking construct in the personality domain. *Multivariate Behavioral Research, 21,* 357–373.

Bjork, R. (1991, November). How do you improve human performance? *APS Observer,* 13–15.

Bjork, R. A. (2000). Creating desirable difficulties for the learner. Implications for theory and practice. Address given at the American Psychological Society's annual convention, Miami Beach, FL.

Bjork, R. A., & Richardson-Klarehn, A. (1989). On the puzzling relationship between environmental context and human memory. In C. Izawa (Ed.), *Current issues in cognitive processes: The Tulane-Floweree symposium on cognition.* Hillsdale, NJ: Erlbaum.

Bjorklund, D. F., & Shackelford, T. K. (1999). Differences in parental investment contribute to important differences between men and women. *Current Directions in Psychological Science, 8,* 86–89.

Blass, E. M. (1990). Suckling: Determinants, changes, mechanisms, and lasting impressions. *Developmental Psychology, 26,* 520–533.

Blass, T. (1996). Experimental invention and controversy: The life and work of Stanley Milgram. *The General Psychologist, 32,* 47–55.

Blatt, S. J., Sanislow III, C. A., & Pilkonis, P. A. (1996). Characteristics of effective therapists: Further analyses of data from the National Institute of Mental Health treatment of depression collaborative research program. *Journal of Consulting and Clinical Psychology, 64,* 1276–1284.

Blum, D. (1994). *The monkey wars.* New York: Oxford University Press.

Bodmer, W. F., & Cavalli-Sforza, L. L. (1970, October). Intelligence and race. *Scientific American,* pp. 19–29.

Bolger, N., DeLongis, A., Kessler, R. C., & Schilling, E. A. (1989). Effects of daily stress on negative mood. *Journal of Personality and Social Psychology, 57,* 808–818.

Bond, M. H., Nakazato, H. S., & Shiraishi, D. (1975). Universality and distinctiveness in dimensions of Japanese person perception. *Journal of Cross-Cultural Psychology, 6,* 346–355.

Bongiovanni, A. (1977). A review of research on the effects of punishment in the schools. *Conference on Child Abuse,* Children's Hospital National Medical Center, Washington, DC.

Boomsma, D., Anokhin, A., & de Geus, E. (1997, August). Genetics of electrophysiology: Linking genes, brain, and behavior. *Current Directions in Psychological Science, 6,* 106–110.

Boone, D. E. (1994). Validity of the MMPI-2 depression content scale with psychiatric inpatients. *Psychological Reports, 74,* 159–162.

Bootzin, R. R., & Nicasio, P. M. (1978). Behavioral treatments for insomnia. In M. Hersen, R. Eisler, & P. Miller (Eds.), *Progress in behavior modification.* New York: Academic Press.

Bornstein, R. F. (1989). Exposure and affect: Overview and meta-analysis of research, 1968–1987. *Psychological Bulletin, 106,* 265–289.

Borod, C., Koff, E., Lorch, M. P., Nicholas, M., & Welkowitz, J. (1988). Emotional and nonemotional facial behavior in patients with unilateral brain damage. *Journal of Neurological and Neurosurgical Psychiatry, 5,* 826–832.

Bostwick, J. M., & Pankratz, V. S. (2000). Affective disorders and suicide risk: a reexamination. *American Journal of Psychiatry, 157,* 1925–1932.

Bouchard, T. J., Jr. (1994, June 17). Genes, environment, and personality. *Science, 264,* 1700–1701.

Bouchard, T. J., Lykken, D. T., McGue, M., Segal, N. L., & Tellegen, A. (1990). Sources of human psychological differences: The Minnesota study of twins reared apart. *Science, 250,* 223–228.

Bourguignon, E. (1979). *Psychological anthropology: An introduction to human nature and cultural differences.* New York: Holt, Rinehart and Winston.

Bowden, C. L., Calabrese, J. R., McElroy, S. L., Gyulai, L. Wassef, A., Petty, F., Pope, H. G. Jr., Chou, J. C., Keck, P. E. Jr., Rhodes, L. J., Swann, A. C., Hirschfeld, R. M., & Wozniak, P. J. (2000). A randomized, placebo-controlled 12-month trial of divalproex and lithium in treatment of outpatients with bipolar I disorder. Divalproex Maintenance Study Group. *Archives of General Psychiatry, 57,* 481–489.

Bower, B. (1992, August 22). Genetic clues to female homosexuality. *Science News, 142,* 117.

Bower, B. (1995, March 4). Virus may trigger some mood disorders. *Science News, 147,* 132.

Bower, B. (1996, April 27). Mom–child relations withstand day care. *Science News, 149,* 261.

Bower, B. (1997a, October 18). My culture, my self: Western notions of the mind may not translate to other cultures. *Science news, 152,* 248–249.

Bower, B. (1997a, August 9). The ties that bond: Adult romantic and sexual styles may grow out of parent–child affiliations. *Science News, 152,* 94–95.

Bower, B. (1997b). Preschoolers get grip on hidden emotions. *Science news, 152,* 70.

Bower, B. (1998a, February 21). All fired up: Perception may dance to the beat of collective neuronal rhythms. *Science News, 153,* 120–121.

Bower, B. (1998b). Dr. Freud goes to Washington. *Science News, 154,* 347–349.

Bower, B. (1998c, April 25). The name game: Young kids grasp new words with intriguing dexterity. *Science News, 153,* 268–269.

Bower, B. (1998d, June 20). Psychology's tangled web. *Science News, 153,* 394–395.

Bower, B. (2000a, January 22). Cultures of reason: Thinking styles may take Eastern and Western routes. *Science News, 157,* 56–58.

Bower, B. (2000b, September, 30). Memory echoes in brain's sensory terrain. *Science News, 158,* 213.

Bower, G. H. (1972). A selective review of organizational factors in memory. In E. Tulving & W. Donaldson (Eds.), *Organization of memory.* New York: Academic Press.

Bower, G. H. (1981). Mood and memory. *American Psychologist, 36,* 129–148.

Bower, G. H., & Mayer, J. D. (1980). In search of mood-dependent retrieval. *Journal of Social Behavior and Personality, 4,* 133–168.

Bower, G. H., Monteiro, K. P., & Gilligan, S. G. (1978). Emotional mood as a context of learning and recall. *Journal of Verbal Learning and Verbal Behavior, 17,* 573–585.

Bowers, K. S. (1983). *Hypnosis for the seriously curious* (2nd ed.) New York: Norton.

Bowlby, J. (1969). *Attachment and loss: Vol. 1. Attachment.* New York: Basic Books.

Bowlby, J. (1973). *Attachment and loss: Vol. 2. Separation, anxiety and anger.* London: Hogarth.

Bradbury, J. (2001, May 19). Teasing out the genetics of bipolar disorder. *Lancet, 357,* 1596.

Bradley, G. W. (1978). Self-serving biases in the attribution process: A re-examination of the fact or fiction question. *Journal of Personality and Social Psychology, 35,* 56–71.

Bradshaw, G. (1992). The airplane and the logic of invention. In R. N. Giere (Ed.). *Minnesota studies in the philosophy of science* (pp. 2239–250). Minneapolis: University of Minnesota Press.

Bradshaw, J. L. (1989). *Hemispheric specialization and psychological function.* New York: Wiley.

Braine, M. D. S. (1976). Children's first word combinations. *Monographs of the Society for Research in Child Development, 41* (Serial No. 164).

Bransford, J., Sherwood, R., Vye, N., & Rieser, J. (1986). Teaching thinking and problem solving: Research foundations. *American Psychologist, 41,* 1078–1089.

Bransford, J. D., & Franks, J. J. (1971). The abstraction of linguistic ideas. *Cognitive Psychology, 2,* 331–350.

Breggin, P. R. (1979). *Electroshock: Its brain disabling effects.* New York: Springer.

Breggin, P. R. (1991). *Toxic psychiatry.* New York: St. Martin's Press.

Breggin, P. R., & Breggin, G. R. (1994). *Talking back to Prozac.* New York: St. Martin's Press.

Brehm, S. S. (1992). *Intimate relationships,* 2nd edition. Boston, MA: McGraw-Hill.

Brewer, M. B., Dull, V., and Lui, L. (1981). Perceptions of the elderly: Stereotypes and prototypes. *Journal of Personality and Social Psychology, 41,* 656–670.

Brigham, J. C. (1980). Limiting conditions of the "physical attractiveness stereotype": Attributions about divorce. *Journal of Research in Personality, 14,* 365–375.

Brislin, R. (1974). The Ponzo illusion: Additional cues, age, orientation, and culture. *Journal of Cross-Cultural Psychology, 5,* 139–161.

Brislin, R. (1993). *Understanding culture's influence on behavior.* Fort Worth, TX: Harcourt Brace Jovanovich.

Brislin, R. W. (1981). *Cross-cultural encounters: Face-to-face interaction.* Boston: Allyn and Bacon.

Broman, S. H., Nichols, P. I., & Kennedy, W. A. (1975). *Preschool IQ: Prenatal and early developmental correlates.* Hillsdale, NJ: Erlbaum.

Bronfenbrenner, U., & Ceci, S. J. (1994). Nature–nurture reconceptualized in developmental perspective: A bioecological model. *Psychological Review, 101,* 568–586.

Brookhart, S. (2001). Persuasion and the 'poison parasite.' *APS Observer, 14*(8), 7.

Brown, A. L., & Campione, J. C. (1986). Psychological theory and the study of learning disabilities. *American Psychologist, 41,* 1059–1068.

Brown, A. M. (1990). *Human universals.* Unpublished manuscript, University of California, Santa Barbara.

Brown, B. (1999). Optimizing expression of the common human genome for child development. *Current Directions in Psychological Science, 8,* 37–41.

Brown, D. E., & Epperson, S. E. (1993, October 11). The personality pill. *Time, 142,* 61–62.

Brown, J. D. (1991). Accuracy and bias in self-knowledge. In C. R. Snyder & D. F. Forsyth (Eds.), *Handbook of social and clinical psychology: The health perspective.* New York: Pergamon.

Brown, J. L., & Pollitt, E. (1996, February). Malnutrition, poverty and intellectual development. *Scientific American, 274* (2), 38–43.

Brown, R., & Kulik, J. (1977). Flashbulb memories. *Cognition, 5,* 73–99.

Brown R., & McNeill, D. (1966). The "tip of the tongue" phenomenon. *Journal of Verbal Learning and Verbal Behavior, 5,* 325–337.

Brown, W. A. (1998, January). The placebo effect. *Scientific American,* 90–95.

Bruch, H. (1978). *The golden cage: The enigma of anorexia nervosa.* Cambridge, MA: Harvard University Press.

Bruck, M., & Ceci, S. (1997). The suggestibility of young children. *Current Directions in Psychological Science, 6,* 75–79.

Brumberg, J. J. (1988). *Fasting girls: The history of anorexia nervosa.* New York: Plume.

Bruner, J. (1992). Another look at new look 1. *American Psychologist, 47,* 780–783.

Bruner, J. S. (1973). *Beyond the information given.* New York: Norton.

Bruner, J. S., Olver, R. R., & Greenfield, P. M. (1966). *Studies in cognitive growth.* New York: Wiley.

Brunner, H. G., Nelen, M., Breakefield, X. O., Ropers, H. H., & van Oost, B. A. (1993). Abnormal behavior associated with a point mutation in the structural gene for monoamine oxidase A. *Science, 262,* 578.

Bryden, M. P. (1982). *Laterality: Functional asymmetry in the intact brain.* New York: Academic Press.

Buck, L., & Axel, R. (1991). A novel multigene family may encode odorant receptors: A molecular basis for odor recognition. *Cell, 65,* 175–187.

Buie, J. (1988, July). "Control" studies bode better health in aging. *APA Monitor,* p. 20.

Buss, D. M. (1999). *Evolutionary psychology: The new science of the mind.* Boston: Allyn and Bacon.

Buss, D. M. (2000). The evolution of happiness. *American Psychologist, 55,* 15–23.

Buss, D. M. (2001). *Human mating strategies and human nature.* Address given at the annual convention of the American Psychological Association, San Francisco, CA.

Buss, D. M., Haselton, M. G., Shackelford, T. K., Bleske, A. L., and Wakefield, J. C. (1998). Adaptations, exaptations, and spandrels. *American Psychologist, 53,* 533–548.

Buss, D. M., & Schmitt, D. P. (1993). Sexual strategies theory: An evolutionary perspective on human mating. *Psychological Review,* 100, 204–232.

Butcher, J. N., Graham, J. R., Williams, C. L., & Ben-Porath, Y. (1989). *Development and use of the MMPI-2 content scales.* Minneapolis: University of Minnesota Press.

Butcher, J. N., & Williams, C. L. (1992). *Essentials of MMPI-2 and MMPI-A interpretation.* Minneapolis: University of Minnesota Press.

Byne, W. (1995). The biological evidence challenged. *Scientific American, 270*(5), 50–55.

Byrne, D. (1969). Attitudes and attraction. In L. Berkowitz (Ed.), *Advances in experimental social psychology* (Vol. 4). New York: Academic Press.

Cahill, L., Prins, B., Weber, M., & McGaugh, J. L. (1994). β-Adrenergic activation and memory for emotional events. *Nature, 371,* 702–704.

Caldwell, M. (1995, June). Kernel of fear. *Discover, 16,* 96–102.

Calev, A., Nigal, D., Shapira, B., Tubi, N., Chazan, S., Ben-Yehuda, Y., Kugelmass, S., & Lerer, B. (1991). Early and long-term effects of electroconvulsive therapy and depression on memory and other cognitive functions. *Journal of Nervous and Mental Disorders, 179,* 526–533.

Callahan, J. (1997, May/June). Hypnosis: Trick or treatment? *Health, 11* (1), 52–55.

Callaway, C. W. (1987). Obesity. *Public Health Reports Supplement,* 102, 26–29.

Calvert, J. D. (1988). Physical attractiveness: A review and reevaluation of its role in social skill research. *Behavioral Assessment, 10,* 29–42.

Campbell, S. S., & Murphy, P. J. (1998, January 16). Extraocular circadian phototransduction in humans. *Science, 279,* 396–399.

Campfield, L. A., Smith, F. J., & Burn, P. (1998, May 29). Strategies and potential molecular targets for obesity treatment. *Science, 280,* 1383–1387.

Campos, J. J., Barrett, K. C., Lamb, M. E., Goldsmith, H. H., & Stenberg, C. (1983). *Socioemotional development* (Vol. 2). New York: Wiley.

Candland, D. K. (1993). *Feral children and clever animals: Reflections on human nature.* New York: Oxford University Press.

Cann, A., Calhoun, L. G., Selby, J. W., & Kin, H.

E. (Eds.). (1981). Rape. *Journal of Social Issues, 37* (Whole No. 4).

Caplow, T. (1982). *Middletown families: Fifty years of change and continuity.* Minneapolis: University of Minnesota Press.

Caporeal, L. R. (1976). Ergotism: The Satan loosed in Salem? *Science, 192,* 21–26.

Caprara, G. V., Barbaranelli, C., Borgoni, L., & Perugini, M. (1993). The Big Five Questionnaire: A new questionnaire for the measurement of the five-factor model. *Personality and Individual Differences, 15,* 281–288.

Carducci, B. J., & Zimbardo, P. G. (1995). Are you shy? *Psychology Today, 28,* 34–40ff.

Carey, S. (1978). The child as word learner. In M. Halle, J. Bresnan, & G. A. Miller (Eds.), *Linguistic theory and psychological reality* (pp. 265–293). Cambridge, MA: MIT Press.

Carlson, N. R. (2001). *Physiology of behavior* (7th ed.). Boston: Allyn and Bacon.

Carlsson, A. (1978). Antipsychotic drugs, neurotransmitters, and schizophrenia. *American Journal of Psychiatry, 135,* 164–173.

Carmichael, L. (1970). The onset and early development of behavior. In P. H. Mussen (Ed.), *Carmichael's manual of child psychology* (3rd ed., Vol. 1). New York: Wiley.

Carpenter, G. C. (1973). Differential response to mother and stranger within the first month of life. *Bulletin of the British Psychological Society, 16,* 138.

Carpenter, S. (1999, August 14). A new look at recognizing what people see. *Science News, 156,* 102.

Carpenter, S. (2000, September). Stoicism reconsidered. *Monitor on Psychology, 31*(8), 58–61.

Carpenter, S. (2001, January). When at last you don't succeed . . . *Monitor on Psychology, 32*(1), 70–71.

Carson, R. C., Butcher, J. N., & Mineka, S. (1996). *Abnormal psychology and modern life,* 10th ed. New York: HarperCollins.

Carstensen, L. L. (1987). Age-related changes in social activity. In L. L. Carstensen & B. A. Edelstein (Eds.), *Handbook of clinical gerontology* (pp. 222–237). New York: Pergamon Press.

Carstensen, L. L. (1991). Selectivity theory: Social activity in life-span context. In K. W. Schaie (Ed.), *Annual Review of Geriatrics and Gerontology* (Vol. 11). New York: Springer.

Carstensen, L. L., and Freund, A. M. (1994). Commentary: The resilience of the aging self. *Developmental Review, 14,* 81–92.

Cartwright, R. D. (1977). *Night life: Explorations in dreaming.* Englewood Cliffs, NJ: Prentice Hall.

Cartwright, R. D. (1978). *A primer on sleep and dreaming.* Reading, MA: Addison-Wesley.

Cartwright, R. D. (1984). Broken dreams: A study of the effects of divorce and depression on dream content. *Psychiatry, 47,* 251–259.

Carver, C. S., & Scheier, M. F. (1992). *Perspectives on personality.* Boston: Allyn and Bacon.

Carver, C. S., & Scheier, M. F. (2000). *Perspectives on personality* (4th ed.). Boston: Allyn and Bacon.

Casey, J. F., & Wilson, L. (1991). The flock. New York: Fawcett Columbine.

Cash, T. F., & Duncan, N. C. (1984). Physical attractiveness stereotyping among Black American college students. *Journal of Social Psychology, 122,* 71–77.

Cash, T. F., & Janda, L. H. (1984, December). The eye of the beholder. *Psychology Today, 18,* 46–52.

Cash, T. F., & Kilcullen, R. N. (1985). The aye of the beholder: Susceptibility to sexism and beautyism in the evaluation of managerial applicants. *Journal of Applied Social Psychology, 15,* 591–605.

Cassileth, B. R., Lusk, E. J., Miller, D. S., Brown, L. L., & Miller, C. (1985). Psychosocial correlates of survival in advanced malignant disease. *New England Journal of Medicine, 312,* 1551–1555.

Cattell, R. B. (1963). Theory of fluid and crystallized intelligence: A critical experiment. *Journal of Educational Psychology, 54,* 1–22.

Ceci, S. J., & Bruck, M. (1993). Suggestibility of the child witness: A historical review and synthesis. *Psychological Bulletin, 113,* 403–439.

Ceci, S. J., & Liker, J. K. (1986). A day at the races: A study of IQ, expertise, and cognitive complexity. *Journal of Experimental Psychology: General, 115,* 255–266.

Ceci, S. J., & Williams, W. M. (1997). Schooling, intelligence, and income. *American Psychologist, 52,* 1051–1058.

Cervone, D., & Shoda, Y. (1999). Beyond traits in the study of personality coherence. *Current Directions in Psychological Science, 8,* 27–32.

Chalmers, D. J. (1995, December). The puzzle of conscious experience. *Scientific American, 273*(6), 80–86.

Chamberlain, K., & Zika, S. (1990). The minor events approach to stress: Support for the use of daily hassles. *British Journal of Psychology, 81,* 469–481.

Chambless, D. L., Sanderson, W. C., Shoham, V., Johnson, S. B., Pope, K. S., Crits-Christoph, P., Baker, M., Johnson, B., Woody, S. R., Sue, S., Beutler, L., Williams, D. A., & McCurry, S. (1996). An update on empirically validated therapies. *The Clinical Psychologist, 49,* 5–18.

Chapman, P. D. (1988). *Schools as sorters: Lewis M. Terman, applied psychology, and the intelligence testing movement, 1890–1930.* New York: New York University Press.

Chartrand, T. L.; Bargh, J. A. (1999). The chameleon effect: The perception-behavior link and social interaction. *Journal of Personality & Social Psychology, 76,* 893–910.

Chase, W. G., & Simon, H. A. (1973). The mind's eye in chess. In W. G. Chase (Ed.), *Visual information processing* (pp. 215–281). new York: Academic Press.

Chaudhari, N., Landin, A. M., & Roper, S. D. (2000). A metabotropic glutamate receptor variant functions as a taste receptor. *Nature Neuroscience, 3,* 113–119.

Chi, M., Glaser, R., & Rees, E. (1982). Expertise in problem solving. In R. Sternberg (Ed.), *Advances in the psychology of human intelligence* (Vol. 1). Hillsdale, NJ: Erlbaum.

Chilman, C. S. (1983). *Adolescent sexuality in a changing American society* (2nd ed.). New York: Wiley.

Chomsky, N. (1957). *Syntactic structures.* The Hague: Mouton.

Chomsky, N. (1965). *Aspects of a theory of syntax.* Cambridge, MA: MIT Press.

Chomsky, N. (1972). *Language and mind.* New York: Harcourt Brace Jovanovich.

Chomsky, N. (1975). *Reflections on language.* New York: Pantheon Books.

Chorney, M. J., Chorney, N. S., Owen, M. J., Daniels, J., McGuffin, P., Thompson, L. A., Detterman, D. K., Benbow, C., Lubinski, D., Eley, T., & Plomin, R. (1998). A quantitative trait locus associated with cognitive ability in children. *Psychological Science, 9,* 159–166.

Christensen, A., & Jacobson, N. S. (1994). Who (or what) can do psychotherapy: The status and challenge of nonprofessional therapies. *Psychological Science, 5,* 8–14.

Churchland, P. M. (1995). *The engine of reason, the seat of the soul: A philosophical journey into the brain.* Cambridge, MA: MIT Press.

Cialdini, R. B. (2001a). *Influence: Science and practice* (4th ed.). Boston: Allyn and Bacon.

Cialdini, R. B. (2001b, February). The science of persuasion. *Scientific American, 284,* 76–81.

Clark, H. H., & Clark, E. V. (1977). *Psychology and language: An introduction to psycholinguistics.* New York: Harcourt Brace Jovanovich.

Clark, D. M., Salkovskis, P. M., Hackman, A., Middleton, H., Anastasiades, P., & Gelder, M. (1994). A comparison of cognitive therapy, applied relaxation, and imipramine in the treatment of panic disorder. *British Journal of Psychiatry, 164,* 759–769.

Clark, M. S., Mills, J. R., & Corcoran, D. M. (1989). Keeping track of needs and inputs of friends and strangers. *Personality and Social Psychology Bulletin, 15,* 533–542.

Clark, R. E., & Squire, L. R. (1998, April 3). Classical conditioning and brain systems: The role of awareness. *Science, 280,* 77–81.

Clarke-Stewart, K. A. (1989). Infant day care: Maligned or malignant? *American Psychologist, 44,* 266–273.

Clay, R. A. (1998, November). Preparing for the future: Practitioners seek training for prescribing medication. *APA Monitor,* p. 22–23.

Clay, R. A. (2000, January). Psychotherapy *is* cost-effective. *Monitor on Psychology, 31*(1) 40–41.

Clay, R. A. (2001, January). Research to the heart of the matter. *Monitor on Psychology, 32*(1), 42–49.

Cleek, M. B., & Pearson, T. A. (1985). Perceived causes of divorce: An analysis of interrelationships. *Journal of Marriage and the Family, 47,* 179–191.

Cloud, J. (2001, September 24). In a dark time, light. *Time, 158*(13), 70–71.

Cobb, S. (1976). Social support as a moderator of stress. *Psychosomatic Medicine, 35,* 375–389.

Cognitive–behavior therapy effective for panic disorder. (1991, November). *APS Observer,* p. 8.

Cohen, R. E., & Ahearn, F. L., Jr. (1980). *Handbook for mental health care of disaster victims.* Baltimore: Johns Hopkins University Press.

Cohen, S. (1988). Psychosocial models of the role of social support in the etiology of physical disease. *Health Psychology, 7,* 269–297.

Cohen, S., & Girgus, J. S. (1973). Visual spatial

illusions: Many explanations. *Science, 179,* 503–504.

Cohen, S., & McKay, G. (1983). Social support, stress, and the buffering hypotheses: A theoretical analysis. In A. Baum, S. E. Taylor, & J. Singer (Eds.), *Handbook of psychology and health* (Vol. 4). Hillsdale, NJ: Erlbaum.

Cohen, S., & Syme, S. L. (Eds.). (1985). *Social support and health.* Orlando, FL: Academic Press.

Cole, M. (1984). The world beyond our borders: What might our students need to know about it? *American Psychologist, 39,* 998–1005.

Coles, R., & Stokes, G. (1985). *Sex and the American teenager.* New York: Harper & Row.

Collins, A. W., Maccoby, E. E., Steinberg, L., Hetherington, E. M., & Bornstein, M. H. (2000). Contemporary research on parenting: The case for nature *and* nurture. *American Psychologist, 55,* 218–232.

Collins, G. P. (2001, October). Magnetic revelations: Functional MRI highlights neurons *receiving* signals. *Scientific American,* 21.

Collins, N. L., & Read, S. J. (1990). Adult attachment, working models, and relationship quality in dating couples. *Journal of Personality and Social Psychology, 58,* 644–663.

Comuzzie, A. G., & Allison, D. B. (1998, May 29). The search for human obesity genes. *Science, 280,* 1374–1377.

Conger, J. J., & Peterson, A. C. (1984). *Adolescence and youth,* 3rd edition. New York: Harper & Row.

Conrad, R. (1964). Acoustic confusions in immediate memory. *British Journal of Psychology, 55,* 75–84.

Consumer Reports. (1995, November). Mental health: Does therapy help? 734–739.

Contrada, R. J., Ashmore, R. D., Gary, M. L., Coups, E., Egeth, J. D., Sewell, A., Ewell, K., Goyal, T. M., & Chasse, V. (2000). Ethnicity-related sources of stress and their effects on well-being. *Current Directions in Psychological Science, 9,* 136–139.

Conway, J. K. (1992). *Written by herself: Autobiographies of American women: An anthology.* New York: Vintage.

Conway, M. A., Anderson, S. J., Larsen, S. F., Donnelly, C. M., McDaniel, M. A., McClelland, A. G. R., & Rawles, R. E. (1994). The formation of flashbulb memories. *Memory and Cognition, 22,* 326–343.

Cook, M., Mineka, S., Wolkenstein, B. & Laitsch, K. (1985). Observational conditioning of snake fear in unrelated rhesus monkeys. *Journal of Abnormal Psychology, 94,* 591–610.

Coon, D. J. (1992). Testing the limits of sense and science: American experimental psychologists combat spiritualism, 1880–1920. *American Psychologist, 47,* 143–151.

Cooper, W. H., (1983). An achievement motivation normological network. *Journal of Personality and Social Psychology, 44,* 841–861.

Costa, P. T., Jr., & McCrae, R. R. (1992a). Four ways five factors are basic. *Personality and Individual Differences, 13,* 653–665.

Costa, P. T., Jr., & McCrae, R. R. (1992b). *Revised NEO Personality Inventory (NEO-PI-R) and NEO Five-Factor Inventory (NEO-FFI) professional manual.* Odessa, FL: Psychological Assessment Resources.

Coughlin, E. K. (1994, October 26). Class, IQ, and heredity. *The Chronicle of Higher Education,* pp. A12, A20.

Cousins, N. (1979). *The anatomy of an illness as perceived by a patient: Reflections on healing and rejuvenation.* New York: Norton.

Covington, M. V. (2000). Intrinsic versus extrinsic motivation in schools: A reconciliation. *Current Direction in Psychology Science, 9,* 22–25.

Cowan, P., & Cowan, P. A. (1988). Changes in marriage during the transition to parenthood. In G. Y. Michaels & W. A. Goldberg (Eds.), *The transition to parenthood: Current theory and research.* Cambridge, England: Cambridge University Press.

Cowan, P. A. (1988). Developmental psychopathology: A nine-cell map of the territory. In E. Nannis & P. A. Cowan (Eds.), *Developmental psychopathology and its treatment: New directions for child development* (No. 39, pp. 5–29). San Francisco: Jossey Bass.

Coyne, J. C., Burchill, S. A. L., & Stiles, W. B. (1991). An interactional perspective on depression. In C. R. Snyder & D. O. Forsyth (Eds.), *Handbook of social and clinical psychology: The health perspective* (pp. 327–349). New York: Pergamon Press.

Coyne, K. J. C. (2001, February). Depression in primary care: Depressing news, exciting research opportunities. *APS Observer, 14*(2), 1, 18.

Craig, A. D., & Reiman, E. M. (1996, November 21). Functional imaging of an illusion of pain. *Nature, 384,* 258–260.

Craik, F. I. M. (1979). Human memory. *Annual Review of Psychology, 30,* 63–102.

Craik, F. I. M., & Lockhart, R. S. (1972). Levels of processing: A framework for memory research. *Journal of Verbal Learning and Verbal Behavior, 11,* 671–684.

Craik, F. I. M., Moroz, T. M., Moscovitch, M., Stuss, D. T., Winocur, G., Tulving, E., & Shitij, K. (1999). In search of the self: A positron emission tomography study. *Psychological Science, 10,* 26–34.

Craik, F. I. M., & Tulving, E. (1975). Depth of processing and the retention of words in episodic memory. *Journal of Experimental Psychology: General, 104,* 268–294.

Cramer, P. (2000). Defense mechanisms in psychology today. *American Psychologist, 55,* 637–646.

Craske, M. G., Brown, T. A., & Barlow, D. H. (1991). Behavioral treatment of panic disorder: A two year follow-up. *Behavior Therapy, 19,* 577–592.

Crick, F. (1994). *The astonishing hypothesis: The scientific search for the soul.* New York: Charles Scribner's Sons.

Crick, F., & Mitchison, G. (1983). The function of dream sleep. *Nature, 304,* 111–114.

Crocker, J., & Major, B. (1989). Social stigma and self-esteem: The self-protective properties of stigma. *Psychological Review, 96,* 608–630.

Crohan, S. E., Antonucci, T. C., Adelmann, P. K., & Coleman, L. M. (1989). Job characteristics and well-being at mid-life. *Psychology of Women Quarterly, 13,* 223–235.

Cromwell, R. L. (1993). Searching for the origins of schizophrenia. *Psychological Science, 4,* 276–279.

Crowder, R. G. (1992). Eidetic images. In L. R. Squire (Ed.), *The encyclopedia of learning and memory* (pp. 154–156). New York: MacMillan.

Csikszentmihalyi, M. (1990). *Flow: The psychology of optimal experience.* New York: Harper & Row.

Csikszentmihalyi, M. (1996, July/August). The creative personality. *Psychology Today, 29*(4), 34–40.

Csikszentmihalyi, M. (1998). *Finding flow.* New York: Basic Books.

Csikszentmihalyi, M. (1999). If we are so rich, why aren't we happy? *American Psychologist, 54,* 821–827.

Csikszentmihalyi, M., Larson, R., & Prescott, S. (1977). The ecology of adolescent activity and experience. *Journal of Youth and Adolescence, 6,* 281–294.

Csikszentmihalyi, M., Rathunde, K. R., Whalen, S., & Wong, M. (1993). *Talented teenagers: The roots of success and failure.* New York: Cambridge University Press.

Cushman, P. (1990). Why the self is empty: Toward a historically situated psychology. *American Psychologist, 45,* 599–611.

Dabbs, J. M. (2000). *Heroes, rogues, and lovers: Testosterone and behavior.* New York: McGraw-Hill.

Dackman, L. (1986). Everyday illusions. *Exploratorium Quarterly, 10,* 5–7.

Daily, D. K., Ardinger, H. H., & Holmes, G. E. (2000). Identification and evaluation of mental retardation. *American Family Physician, 61,* 1059–1067.

Damasio, A. B. (1994). *Descartes' error: Emotion, reason, and the human brain.* New York: Avon Books.

Damasio, H., Grabowski, T., Frank, R., Balaburda, A. M., & Damasio, A. R. (1994). The return of Phineas Gage: Clues about the brain from the skull of a famous patient. *Science, 264,* 1102–1105.

Danion, J., Rizzo, L., & Bruant, A. (1999). Functional mechanisms underlying impaired recognition memory and conscious awareness in patients with schizophrenia. *Archives of General Psychiatry, 56,* 639–644.

Dannefer, D., & Perlmutter, M. (1990). Developmental as a multidimensional process: Individual and social constituents. *Human Development, 33,* 108–137.

Darley, J. M., & Batson, C. D. (1973). From Jerusalem to Jericho: A study of situational and dispositional variables in helping behavior. *Journal of Personality and Social Psychology, 27,* 100–108.

Darley, J. M., & Latané, B. (1968) Bystander intervention in emergencies: Diffusion of responsibility. *Journal of Personality and Social Psychology, 8,* 377–383.

Darnton, R. (1968). *Mesmerism and the end of the Enlightenment in France.* Cambridge, MA: Harvard University Press.

Darwin, C. (1963). *On the origin of species.* London: Oxford University Press. (Original work published in 1859).

Darwin, C. (1998). *The expression of the emotions in man and animals* (3rd ed., with Introduction, Afterword, and Commentaries by P. Ekman). New York: Oxford University Press. (Original work published in 1862).

Darwin, C. J., Turvey, M. T., & Crowder, R. G. (1972). The auditory analogue of the Sperling partial report procedure: Evidence for brief auditory stage. *Cognitive Psychology, 3,* 255–267.

Dattilio, F. M., & Padesky, C. A. (1990). *Cognitive therapy with couples.* Sarasota, FL: Professional Resource Exchange.

Daum, I., & Schugens, M. M. (1996). On the cerebellum and classical conditioning. *Current Directions in Psychological Science, 5,* 58–61.

Davidson, R. J. (1992a). Anterior cerebral asymmetry and the nature of emotion. *Brain and Cognition, 20,* 125–151.

Davidson, R. J. (1992b). Emotion and affective style: Hemispheric substrates. *Psychological Science, 3,* 39–43.

Davis, I. P. (1985). *Adolescents: Theoretical and helping perspectives.* Boston: Kluwer-Nijhoff Publishing.

Davison, K. P., Pennebaker, J. W., & Dickerson, S. S. (2000). Who talks? The social psychology of illness support groups. *American Psychologist, 55,* 205–217.

Davison, R. J. (2000a). *Affective neuroscience.* Address given at the American Psychological Association's annual convention, Washington, DC.

Davison, R. J. (2000b). Affective style, psychopathology, and resilience: Brain mechanisms and plasticity. *American Psychologist, 55,* 1196–1214.

Davison, R. J., Putnam, K. M., & Larson, C. L. (2000, July 28). Dysfunction in the neural circuitry of emotion regulation—a possible prelude to violence. *Science, 289,* 591–594.

Dawkins, K., Lieberman, J. A., Lebowitz, B. D., & Hsiao, J. K. (1999). Antipsychotics: Past and future. *Schizophrenia Bulletin, 25,* 395–405.

Deadwyler, S. A., & Hampson, R. E. (1995, November 24). Ensemble activity and behavior: What's the code? *Science, 270,* 1316–1318.

DeAngelis, T. (1997, January). Chromosomes contain clues on schizophrenia. *APA Monitor,* p. 26.

DeCasper, A. J., & Fifer, W. P. (1980). Of human bonding: Newborns prefer their mothers' voices. *Science, 208,* 1174–1176.

DeCasper, A. J., and Spence, M. J. (1986). Prenatal maternal speech influences newborns' perception of speech sounds. *Infant Behavior and Development, 9,* 133–150.

de Gelder, B. (2000, August 18). More to seeing than meets the eye. *Science, 289,* 1148–1149.

DeGrandpre, R. J. (2000). A science of meaning: Can behaviorism bring meaning to psychological science? *American Psychologist, 55,* 721–739.

de Groot, A. D. (1965). *Thought and choice in chess.* The Hague: Mouton.

Delgado, J. M. R. (1969). *Physical control of the mind: Toward a psychocivilized society.* New York: Harper & Row.

Dembroski, T. M., & Costa, P. T., Jr. (1987). Coronary prone behavior: Components of the Type A pattern and hostility. *Journal of Personality, 55,* 211–235.

Dembroski, T. M., Weiss, S. M., Shields, J. L. et al. (1978). *Coronary-prone behavior.* New York: Springer-Verlag.

Dement, W. C. (1980). *Some watch while some must sleep.* San Francisco: San Francisco Book Co.

Dement, W. C., & Kleitman, N. (1957). Cyclic variations in EEG during sleep and their relations to eye movement, body mobility and dreaming. *Electroencephalography and Clinical Neurophysiology, 9,* 673–690.

Dement, W. C., & Vaughan, C. (1999). *The promise of sleep.* New York: Delacorte Press.

Dennis, W. (1960). Causes of retardation among institutionalized children: Iran. *Journal of Genetic Psychology, 96,* 47–59.

Dennis, W., & Dennis, M. G. (1940). The effect of cradling practices upon the onset of walking in Hopi children. *Journal of Genetic Psychology, 56,* 77–86.

Denollet, J., & Sys, S. U. (1996, February 17). Personality as independent predictor of long-term mortality in patients with coronary heart disease. *Lancet, 347,* 417–421.

Denton, L. (1987, November). Mood's role in memory still puzzling. *APA Monitor,* p. 18.

Deregowski, J. B. (1980). *Illusions, patterns and pictures: A cross-cultural perspective* (pp. 966–977). London: Academic Press.

Detterman, D. K. (1999). The psychology of mental retardation. *International Review of Psychiatry, 11,* 26–33.

Deutsch, M., & Collins, M. E. (1951). *Interracial housing: A psychological evaluation of a social experiment.* Minneapolis: University of Minnesota Press.

Deutsch, M., & Gerard, H. B. (1955). A study of normative and informational social influence upon individual judgment. *Journal of Abnormal and Social Psychology, 51,* 629–636.

Devereux, G. (1981). Mohave ethnopsychiatry and suicide: The psychiatric knowledge and psychic disturbances of an Indian tribe. *Bureau of American Ethology Bulletin 175.* Washington, DC: Smithsonian Institution.

Devine, P. G., & Zuwerink, J. R. (1994). Prejudice and guilt: The internal struggle to overcome prejudice. In W. J. Lonner & R. Malpass (Eds.), *Psychology and culture* (pp. 203–207). Boston: Allyn & Bacon.

de Waal, F. B. M. (1999, December). The end of nature versus nurture. *Scientific American,* 94–99.

Dewsbury, D. A. (1990). Early interactions between animal psychologists and animal activists and the founding of the APA Committee on Precautions in Animal Experimentation. *American Psychologist, 45,* 315–327.

Dewsbury, D. A. (1997). In celebration of the centennial of Ivan P. Pavlov's (1897/1902) The work of the digestive glands. *American Psychologist, 52,* 933–935.

Dewsbury, D. A. (1998). Celebrating E. L. Thorndike a century after *Animal Intelligence. American Psychologist, 53,* 1121–1124.

Diamond, J. (1990). The great leap forward. *Discover* (Special Issue), pp. 66–77.

Diener, E. (1984). Subjective well-being. *Psychological Bulletin, 95,* 542–575.

Diener, E. (2000. Subjective well-being: The science of happiness and a proposal for a national index. *American Psychologist, 55,* 34–43.

Diener, E., & Diener, C. (1996). Most people are happy. *Psychological Science, 7,* 181–189.

Diener, E., Sandvik, E., Seidlitz, L., & Diener, M. (1993). The relationship between income and subjective well-being: Relative or absolute? *Social Indicators Research, 28,* 195–223.

Digman, J. M. (1990). Personality structure: Emergence of the five-factor model. *Annual Review of Psychology, 41,* 417–440.

Dillbeck, M. C., & Orme-Johnson, D. W. (1987). Physiological differences between transcendental meditation and rest. *American Psychologist, 42* (9), 879–881.

Dion, K. K. (1986). Stereotyping based on physical attractiveness: Issues and conceptual perspectives. In C. P. Herman, M. P. Zanna, & E. T. Higgins (Eds.), *Physical appearance, stigma, and social behavior: The Ontario symposium on personality and social psychology* (Vol. 3). Hillsdale, NJ: Erlbaum.

Dirks, J. (1982). The effect of a commercial game on children's Block Design scores on the WISC-R test. *Intelligence, 6,* 109–123.

Discovering Psychology. (1990). PBS Video Series. Washington, DC: Annenberg/CPB Project.

Dixon, R. A., Kramer, D. A., & Baltes, P. B. (1985). Intelligence: A life-span developmental perspective. In B. B. Wolman (Ed.), *Handbook of intelligence* (pp. 301–352). New York: Wiley.

Dobbins, A. C., Jeo, R. M., Fiser, J., & Allman, J. M. (1998, July 24). Distance modulation of neural activity in the visual cortex. *Science, 281,* 552–555.

Dobelle, W. (1977). Current status of research on providing sight to the blind by electrical stimulation of the brain. *Journal of Visual Impairment and Blindness, 71,* 290–297.

Dobson, K. S. (1989). A meta-analysis of the efficacy of cognitive therapy for depression. *Journal of Consulting and Clinical Psychology, 57,* 414–419.

Dohrenwend, B. P., & Shrout, P. E. (1985). "Hassles" in the conceptualization and measurement of life stress variables. *American Psychologist, 40,* 780–785.

Dohrenwend, B. S., & Dohrenwend, B. P. (1974). *Stressful life events: Their nature and effects.* New York: Wiley.

Domhoff, G. W. (1996). *Finding meaning in dreams: A quantitative approach.* New York: Plenum Press.

Donchin, E. (1975). On evoked potentials, cognition, and memory. *Science, 790,* 1004–1005.

Doob, L. W. (1964). Eidetic images among the Ibo. *Ethnology, 3,* 357–363.

Douglas, M. E. (1996, October). Creating eustress in the workplace: A supervisor's role. *Supervision, 57,* 6–9.

Dowling, J. E. (1992). *Neurons and networks: An introduction to neuroscience.* Cambridge, MA: Harvard University Press.

Doyle, R. (1999, December). The decline of marriage. *Scientific American,* 36–37.

Doyle, R. (2001, June). The American terrorist. *Scientific American, 285*(6), 28.

Dracheva, S., Marras, S. A. E., Elhakem, S. L., Kramer, F. R., Davis, K. L., & Haroutunian, V. (2001). *N*-methyl-*d*-aspartic acid receptor expression in the dorsolateral prefrontal cortex of elderly patients with schizophrenia. *American Journal of Psychiatry, 158,* 1400–1410.

Draguns, J. (1980). Psychological disorders of clinical severity. In H. Triandis & J. Draguns (Eds.), *Handbook of cross-cultural psychology, Vol. 6: Psychopathology* (pp. 99–174). Boston: Allyn & Bacon.

Draguns, J. G. (1979). Culture and personality. In A. J. Marsella, R. G. Tharp, & T. J. Ciborowski (Eds.), *Perspectives on cross-cultural psychology* (pp. 179–207). New York: Academic Press.

Drake, R. E., Osher, F. C., & Wallach, M. A. (1991). Homelessness and dual diagnosis. *American Psychologist, 46,* 1149–1158.

Druckman, D., & Bjork, R. A. (1991). *In the mind's eye: Enhancing human performance.* Washington, DC: National Academy Press.

Duck, S. (1992). *Human relationships,* 2nd edition. Newbury Park, CA: Sage.

Duncan, J., Seitz, R. J., Kolodny, J., Bor, D., Herzog, H., Ahmed, A., Newell, F. N., & Emslie, H. (2000, July 21). A neural basis for general intelligence. *Science, 289,* 457–460.

Dunlap, J. (1998, June 5). Circadian rhythms: An end in the beginning. *Science, 280,* 1548–1549.

Dutton, D. G., & Aron, A. P. (1974). Some evidence for heightened sexual attraction under conditions of high anxiety. *Journal of Personality and Social Psychology, 30,* 510–517.

Dykema, J., Bergbower, K., & Peterson, C. (1995). Pessimistic explanatory style, stress, and illness. *Journal of Social and Clinical Psychology, 14,* 357–371.

Eagly, A. H., Ashmore, R. D., Makhijani, M. G., & Kennedy, L. C. (1991). What is beautiful is good, but. . . : A meta-analytic review of the social psychological literature. *Psychological Bulletin, 100,* 283–308.

Eagly, A. H., & Wood, W. (1999). The origins of sex differences in human behavior: Evolved dispositions versus social roles. *American Psychologist, 54,* 408–423.

Eccles, J. S., Midgley, C., Wigfield, A., Buchanan, C. M., Reuman, D., Flanagan, C., & Mac Iver, D. (1993). Development during adolescence: The impact of stage-environment fit on young adolescents' experiences in schools and in families. *American Psychologist, 48,* 90–101.

Eckensberger, L. H. (1994). Moral development and its measurement across cultures. In W. J. Lonner & R. Malpass (Eds.), *Psychology and culture* (pp. 71–78). Boston, MA: Allyn & Bacon.

Educational Testing Service. (1990a, October 31). Background on the new SAT-I and SAT-II. Announcement at the College Board National Forum.

Edwards, A. E., & Acker, L. E. (1962). A demonstration of the long-term retention of a conditioned galvanic skin response. *Psychosomatic Medicine, 24,* 459–463.

Ehrlich, P. R. (2000a). *Genes, cultures and the human prospect.* Washington, DC: Island Press.

Ehrlich, P. R. (2000b, September 22). The tangled skeins of nature and nurture in human evolution. *The Chronicle of Higher Education,* B7–B11.

Eich, E. (1995). Searching for mood dependent memory. *Psychological Science, 6,* 67–75.

Eich, E., Macaulay, D., Loewenstein, R. J., & Dihle, P. H. (1997). Memory, amnesia, and dissociative identity disorder. *Psychological Science, 8,* 417–422.

Eichenbaum, H. (1997, July 18). How does the brain organize memories? *Science, 277,* 330–332.

Eichorn, D. H., & VandenBos, G. R. (1985). Dissemination of scientific and professional knowledge: Journal publication within the APA. *American Psychologist, 40,* 1309–1316.

Eisenberger, R., & Cameron, J. (1996). Detrimental effects of reward: Reality or myth? *American Psychologist, 51,* 1153–1166.

Ekman, P. (1984). Expression and the nature of emotion. In K. R. Scherer & P. Ekman (Eds.), *Approaches to emotion.* Hillsdale, NJ: Erlbaum.

Ekman, P. (1992). Facial expressions of emotion: New findings, new questions. *Psychological Science, 3,* 34–38.

Ekman, P. (1993). Facial expression and emotion. *American Psychologist, 48,* 384–392.

Ekman, P. (1994). Strong evidence for universals in facial expressions: A reply to Russell's mistaken critique. *Psychological Bulletin, 115,* 268–287.

Ekman, P., & Friesen, W. V. (1971). Constants across cultures in the face and emotion. *Journal of Personality and Social Psychology, 17,* 124–129.

Ekman, P., & Friesen, W. V. (1975). *Unmasking the face: A guide to recognizing emotions from facial clues.* Englewood Cliffs, NJ: Prentice-Hall.

Ekman, P., & Friesen, W. V. (1986). A new pancultural facial expression of emotion. *Motivation and Emotion, 10,* 159–168.

Ekman, P., Friesen, W. V., O'Sullivan, M., Chan, A., Diacoyanni-Tarlatzis, I., Heider, K., Krause, R., LeCompte, W. A., Pitcairn, T., Ricci-Bitti, P. E., Scherer, K., Tomita, M., & Tzavaras, A. (1987). Universal and cultural differences in the judgments of facial expressions of emotion. *Journal of Personality and Social Psychology, 53,* 712–717.

Ekman, P., & Rosenberg, E. (1997). *What the face reveals.* New York: Oxford University Press.

Ekman, P., Sorenson, E. R., & Friesen, W. V. (1969). Pan-cultural elements in facial displays in emotion. *Science, 764,* 86–88.

Elbert, T., Pantev, C., Wienbruch, C., Rockstroh, B., & Taub, E. (1995, October 13). Increased cortical representation of the fingers of the left hand in string players. *Science, 270,* 305–307.

Eley, T. C. (1997). General genes: A new theme in developmental psychopathology. *Current Directions in Psychological Science, 6,* 90–95.

Elkin, I., Shea, M. T., Watkins, J. T., Imber, S. D., Sotsky, S. M., Collins, J. F., Glass, D. R., Pilkonis, P. A., Leber, W. R., Kocherty, J. P., Fiester, S. J. & Parloff, M. B. (1989). National Institutes of Mental Health treatment of depression collaborative research program: General effectiveness of treatments. *Archives of General Psychiatry, 46,* 971–982.

Elliott, G. R., & Eisdorfer, C. (Eds.). (1982). *Stress and human health: Analysis and implications of research* (A study by the Institute of Medicine/National Academy of Sciences). New York: Springer.

Ellis, A. (1987). *The practice of rational emotive therapy (RET).* New York: Springer.

Ellis A. (1990). *The essential Albert Ellis: Seminal writings on psychotherapy.* New York: Springer.

Ellis, A. (1996). *Better, deeper, and more enduring brief therapy: The rational emotive behavior therapy approach.* New York: Brunner/Mazel Publishers.

Ellison, J. (1984, June). The seven frames of mind. *Psychology Today, 18,* 21–24, 26.

Ellsworth, P. C. (1994). William James and emotion: Is a century of fame worth a century of misunderstanding? *Psychological Review, 101,* 222–229.

Emmelkamp, P. M. (1986). Behavior therapy with adults. In S. L. Garfield & A. E. Bergin (Eds.), *Handbook of psychotherapy and behavior change* (pp. 385–442). New York: Wiley.

Enserink, M. (1999, April 9). Can the placebo be the cure? *Science, 284,* 238–240.

Enserink, M. (2000, July 28). Searching for the mark of Cain. *Science, 289,* 575–579.

Epstein, S. (1980). The stability of confusion: A reply to Mischel and Peake. *Psychological Review, 90,* 179–184.

Epstein, S., & Feist, G. J. (1988). Relation between self- and other-acceptance and its moderation by identification. *Journal of Personality and Social Psychology, 54,* 309–315.

Erdberg, P. (1990). Rorschach assessment. In G. Goldstein & M. Hersen (Eds.), *Psychological assessment* (2nd ed.). New York: Pergamon.

Erdelyi, M. H. (1992). Psychodymanics and the unconscious. *American Psychologist, 47,* 784–787.

Ericsson, K. A., & Charness, N. (1994). Expert performance: Its structure and acquisition. *American Psychologist, 49,* 725–747.

Ericsson, K. A., Krampe, R. T., & Tesch-Römer, C. (1993). The role of deliberate practice in the acquisition of expert performance. *Psychological Review, 100,* 363–406.

Erikson, E. H. (1963). *Childhood and society* (2nd. ed.). New York: Norton.

Erikson, K. A., & Simon, H. A. (1993). Protocol analysis: Verbal reports as data (rev. ed.) Cambridge, MA: MIT Press.

Exner, J. E., Jr. (1974). *The Rorschach: A comprehensive system: Vol. 1.* New York: Wiley.

Exner, J. E., Jr. (1978). *The Rorschach: A comprehensive system: Vol. 2: Current research and interpretation.* New York: Wiley.

Exner, J. E., Jr., & Weiner, I. B. (1982). *The Rorschach: A comprehensive system: Vol. 3: Assessment of children and adolescents.* New York: Wiley.

Eysenck, H. J. (1952). The effects of psychotherapy: An evaluation. *Journal of Consulting Psychology, 16,* 319–324.

Eysenck, H. J. (1967). *The biological basis of personality.* Springfield, IL: Charles C. Thomas.

Eysenck, H. J. (1992). Four ways five factors are *not* basic. *Personality and Individual Differences, 13,* 667–673.

Eysenck, H. J., & Eysenck, M. W. (1985). *Personality and individual differences: A natural science approach.* New York: Plenum.

Facklemann, K. (1998, November 28). It's a girl! Is sex selection the first step to designer children? *Science News, 154,* 350–351.

Fadiman, J., & Frager, R. (2001). *Personality and Personal Growth.* Upper Saddle River, NJ: Prentice-Hall.

Fairburn, C. G., Jones, R., Peveler, R. C., Hope, R. A., & O'Conner, M. (1993). Psychotherapy and bulimia nervosa: Longer-term effects of interpersonal psychotherapy, behavior therapy, and cognitive behavior therapy. *Archives of General Psychiatry, 50,* 419–428.

Fajans, J. (1985). The person in social context: The social character of Baining "psychology." In G. M. White & J. Kirkpatrick (Eds.), *Person, self, and experience* (pp. 367–400). Berkeley: University of California Press.

Fallon, A., & Rozin, P. (1985). Sex differences in perceptions of desirable body states. *Journal of Abnormal Psychology, 94,* 102–105.

Fals-Stewart, W., Marks, A. P., & Schafer, J. (1993). A comparison of behavioral group therapy and individual behavioral therapy in treating obsessive–compulsive disorder. *Journal of Nervous and Mental Disease, 181,* 189–193.

Fantz, R. L. (1963). Pattern vision in newborn infants. *Science, 140,* 296–297.

Farina, A., Fischer, E. H., Boudreau, L. A., & Belt, W. E. (1996). Mode of target presentation in measuring the stigma of mental disorder. *Journal of Applied Social Psychology, 26,* 2147–2156.

Farquhar, J. W., Maccoby, N., & Solomon, D. S. (1984). Community applications of behavioral medicine. In W. D. Gentry (Ed.), *Handbook of behavioral medicine* (pp. 437–478). New York: Guilford Press.

Featherman, D. L. (1980). Schooling and occupational careers: Constancy and change in worldly success. In O. G. Brim, Jr., and J. Kagan (Eds.), *Constancy and change in human development.* Cambridge, MA: Harvard University Press.

Fehr, B. (1988). How do I love thee? Let me consult my prototype. *Journal of Personality and Social Psychology, 55* (4), 557–579.

Fein, M. L. (1993). *I.A.M.: A common sense guide to coping with anger.* Westport, CT: Praeger/Greenwood.

Feingold, A. (1988). Matching for attractiveness in romantic partners and same-sex friends: A meta-analysis and theoretical critique. *Psychological Bulletin, 104,* 226–235.

Feingold, A. (1990). Gender differences in effects of physical attractiveness on romantic attraction: A comparison across five research paradigms. *Journal of Personality and Social Psychology, 59,* 981–993.

Fernandez, A., & Glenberg, A. M. (1985). Changing environmental context does not reliably affect memory. *Memory and Cognition, 13,* 333–345.

Ferster. D., & Spruston, N. (1995, November 3). Cracking the neuronal code. *Science, 270,* 756–757.

Festinger, L. (1957). *A theory of cognitive dissonance.* Stanford, CA: Stanford University Press.

Festinger, L., Schachter, S., & Back, K. (1950). *Social pressures in informal groups: A study of a housing community.* New York: Harper & Row.

Field, T. F., & Schanberg, S. M. (1990). Massage alters growth and catecholamine production in preterm newborns. In N. Gunzenhauser (Ed.), *Advances in touch* (pp. 96–104). Skillman, NJ: Johnson & Johnson Co.

Fields, H. L. (1978, November). Secrets of the placebo. *Psychology Today,* p. 172.

Fields, H. L., & Levine, J. D. (1984). Placebo analgesia: A role for endorphins. *Trends in Neuroscience, 7,* 271–273.

Filsinger, E. E., & Fabes, R. A. (1985). Odor communication, pheromones, and human families. *Journal of Marriage and the Family, 47,* 349–359.

Findley, M. J., & Cooper, H. M. (1983). Locus of control and academic achievement: A literature review. *Journal of Personality and Social Psychology, 44,* 419–427.

Finer, B. (1980). Hypnosis and anaesthesia. In G. D. Burrows & L. Donnerstein (Eds.), *Handbook of hypnosis and psychosomatic medicine.* Amsterdam: Elsevier/North Holland Biomedical Press.

Fiorito, G., & Scotto, P. (1992). Observational learning in *Octopus vulgaris. Science, 256,* 545–547.

Fischer, A. H. (1993). Sex differences in emotionality: Fact or stereotype? *Feminism & Psychology, 3,* 303–318.

Fischer, P. C., Smith, R. J., Leonard, E., Fuqua, D. R., Campbell, J. L., & Masters, M. A. (1993). Sex differences on affective dimensions: Continuing examination. *Journal of Counseling and Development, 71,* 440–443.

Fischer, P. J., & Breakey, W. R. (1991). The epidemiology of alcohol, drug, and mental disorders among homeless persons. *American Psychologist, 46,* 1115–1128.

Fischhoff, B. (1975). Hindsight ≠ foresight: The effect of outcome knowledge on judgment under uncertainty. *Journal of Experimental Psychology: Human Perception and Performance, 1,* 288–299.

Fish, J. M. (1973). *Placebo therapy.* San Francisco: Jossey-Bass.

Fisher, H. E. (1992). *Anatomy of love: The natural history of monogamy, adultery, and divorce.* New York: W. W. Norton and Company.

Fisher, S., & Greenberg, R. P. (1985). *The scientific credibility of Freud's theories and therapy.* New York: Columbia University Press.

Fisher, S., & Greenberg, R. P. (1995, September/October). Prescriptions for happiness? *Psychology Today, 28,* 32–37.

Fishman, H. C. (1993). *Intensive structural therapy: Treating families in their social context.* New York: Basic Books.

Fiske, D. W., & Fogg, L. (1990). But the reviewers are making different criticisms of my paper! Diversity and uniqueness in reviewer comments. *American Psychologist, 45,* 591–598.

Fiske, S. T., & Neuberg, S. L. (1990). A continuum of impression formation, from category-based to individuating processes: Influences of information and motivation on attention and interpretation. In M. P. Zanna (Ed.), *Advances in experimental social psychology* (Vol. 23). San Diego, CA: Academic Press.

Flavell, J. H. (1985). *Cognitive development* (2nd ed.). Englewood Cliffs, NJ: Prentice-Hall.

Flavell, J. H. (1996). Piaget's legacy. *Psychological Science, 7,* 200–203.

Fletcher, G. J. O., & Ward, C. (1988). Attribution theory and processes: A cross-cultural perspective. In M. H. Bond (Ed.), *The cross-cultural challenge to social psychology* (pp. 230–244). Newbury Park, CA: Sage.

Foa, E. B., Rothbaum, B. O., Riggs, D. S., & Murdock, T. B. (1991). Treatment of post-traumatic stress disorder in rape victims: A comparison between cognitive–behavioral procedures and counseling. *Journal of Consulting and Clinical Psychology, 59,* 715–723.

Fodor, J. (1983). *The modularity of mind.* Cambridge, MA: MIT Press.

Fogel, A. (1991). Movement and communication in human infancy: The social dynamics of development. *Human Movement Science, 11,* 387–423.

Foley, V. D. (1979). Family therapy. In R. J. Corsini (Ed.), *Current psychotherapies* (2nd ed., pp. 460–469). Itasca, IL: Peacock.

Folkes, V. S. (1982). Forming relationships and the matching hypothesis. *Journal of Personality and Social Psychology, 8,* 631–636.

Folkins, C. H., & Sime, W. (1981). Physical fitness training and mental health. *American Psychologist, 36,* 373–389.

Ford, C. S., & Beach, F. A. (1951). *Patterns of sexual behavior.* New York: Harper & Row.

Fowers, B. J., & Richardson, F. C. (1996). Why is multiculturalism good? *American Psychologist, 31,* 609–621.

Fowler, H. (1965). *Curiosity and exploratory behavior.* New York: Macmillan.

Frank, J. (1990). In *Discovering Psychology,* Program 2 [PBS video series]. Washington, DC: Annenberg/CPB Project.

Frank, J. D. (1973). *Persuasion and healing: A comparative study of psychotherapy* (Rev. ed.) Baltimore: Johns Hopkins University Press.

Frank, J. D. (1982). Therapeutic components shared by all psychotherapies. In J. H. Harvey & M. M. Parks (Eds.), *Psychotherapy research and behavior change.* Washington, DC: American Psychological Association.

Frank, J. D., & Frank, J. B. (1991). *Persuasion and healing: A comparative study of psychotherapy* (3rd ed.) Baltimore: Johns Hopkins University Press.

Fraser, S. (Ed.). (1995). *The bell curve wars: Race, intelligence, and the future of America.* New York: Basic Books.

Freedman, D. J., Riesenhuber, M., Poggio, T., & Miller, E. K. (2001, January 12). Categorical representation of visual stimuli in the primate prefrontal cortex. *Science, 291,* 312–316.

Freedman, J. L. (1984) Effect of television violence on aggression. *Psychological Bulletin, 96,* 227–246.

Freedman, J. L. (1996, May). Violence in the mass media and violence in society: The link is unproven. *Harvard Mental Health Letter, 12* (11), 4–6.

French, E. G. & Thomas, F. H. (1958). The relation of achievement motivation to problem-solving effectiveness. *Journal of Abnormal and Social Psychology, 56,* 46–48.

Freud, S. (1915). Instincts and their vicissitudes. In S. Freud, *The collected papers.* New York: Collier.

Freud, S. (1925). The unconscious. In S. Freud, *The collected papers* (Vol. 4). London: Hogarth.

Freud, S. (1953). *The interpretation of dreams.* New York: Basic Books. (Original edition published in 1900).

Fridlund, A. J. (1990). Evolution and facial action in reflex, social motive, and paralanguage. In P. K. Ackles, J. R. Jennings, & M. G. H. Coles (Eds.), *Advances in psychophysiology.* Greenwich, CT: JAI Press.

Friedman, H. S., & Booth-Kewley, S. (1988). Validity of the Type A construct: A reprise. *Psychological Bulletin, 104,* 381–384.

Friedman, H. S., Hawley, P. H., & Tucker, J. S. (1994). Personality, health, and longevity. *Current Directions in Psychological Science, 3,* 37–41.

Friedman, H. S., Tucker, J. S., Schwartz, J. E., Tomlinson-Keasey, C., Martin, L. R., Wingard, D. L., & Criqui, M. H. (1995). Psychosocial and behavioral predictors of longevity: The aging and death of the "termites." *American Psychologist, 50,* 69–78.

Friedman, M., & Rosenman, R. F. (1974). *Type A behavior and your heart.* New York: Knopf.

Friedman, M., Thoresen, C. E., & Gill, J. J. (1981). Type A behavior: Its possible role, detection, and alteration in patients with ischemic heart disease. In J. W. Hurst (Ed.), *The heart: Update V.* Hightstown, NJ: McGraw-Hill.

Friedman, M., & Ulmer, D. (1984). *Treating Type A behavior—and your heart.* New York: Knopf.

Friend, R., Rafferty, Y., & Bramel, D. (1990). A puzzling misinterpretation of the Asch "conformity" study. *European Journal of Social Psychology, 20,* 29–44.

Frith, C. D., & Frith, U. (1999, November 26). Interacting minds—A biological basis. *Science, 286,* 1692–1695.

Frith, U. (1997). Autism. *Scientific American* (Special Issue: The Mind), 7(1), 92–98.

Fromm, E., & Shor, R. E. (Eds.). (1979). *Hypnosis: Developments in research and new perspectives* (2nd ed.). Hawthorne, NY: Aldine.

Fujita, F., Diener, E., & Sandvik, E. (1991). Gender differences in dysphoria and well-being: The case for emotional intensity. *Journal of Personality and Social Psychology, 61,* 427–434.

Funder, D. C. (1983a). Three issues in predicting more of the people: A reply to Mischel & Peake. *Psychological Review, 90,* 283–289.

Funder, D. C. (1983b). The "consistency" controversy and the accuracy of personality judgments. *Journal of Personality, 51,* 346–359.

Funder, D. C., & Ozer, D. J. (1983). Behavior as a function of the situation. *Journal of Personality and Social Psychology, 44,* 107–112.

Furnham, A. (1982). Explanations for unemployment in Britain. *European Journal of Social Psychology, 12,* 335–352.

Furumoto, L. (1991). From "paired associates" to a psychology of self: The intellectual odyssey of Mary Whiton Calkins. In G. A. Kimble, M. Wertheimer, & C. White (Eds.), *Portraits of pioneers in psychology* (pp. 57–72). Washington, DC: American Psychological Association; and Hillsdale, NJ: Erlbaum.

Furumoto, L., & Scarborough, E. (1986). Placing women in the history of psychology: The first American women psychologists. *American Psychologist, 41,* 35–42.

Gabbay, F. H. (January, 1992). Behavior-genetic strategies in the study of emotion. *Psychological Science, 3*(1), 50–54.

Gadsby, P. (2000, July). Tourist in a taste lab. *Discover, 21,* 70–75.

Gainetdinov, R. R., Wetsel, W. C., Jones, S. R., Levin, E. D., Jaber, M., & Caron, M. G. (1999). Role of serotonin in the paradoxical calming effect of psychostimulants on hyperactivity. *Science, 283,* 397–401.

Galambos, N. L. (1992). Parent–adolescent relations. *Current Directions in Psychological Science, 1,* 146–149.

Galef, B. G. (1998). Edward Thorndike: Revolutionary psychologist, ambiguous biologist. *American Psychologist, 53,* 1128–1134.

Gallagher, W. (1994, September). How we become what we are. *The Atlantic Monthly, 39–55.*

Gallo, P. S., & McClintock, C. G. (1965). Cooperative and competitive behavior in mixed-motive games. *Journal of Conflict Resolution, 9,* 68–78.

Gallo, V., & Chittajallu, R. (2001, May 4). Unwrapping glial cells from the synapse: What lies inside? *Science, 292,* 872–873.

Galluscio, E. H. (1990). *Biological Psychology.* New York: Macmillan.

Ganchrow, J. R., Steiner, J. E., & Daher, M. (1983). Neonatal facial expressions in response to different qualities and intensities of gustatory stimuli. *Infant Behavior and Development, 6,* 189–200.

Garcia, J. (1981). The logic and limits of mental aptitude testing. *American Psychologist, 36,* 1172–1180.

Garcia, J. (1990). Learning without memory. *Journal of Cognitive Neuroscience, 2,* 287–305.

Garcia, J. (1993). Misrepresentations of my criticisms of Skinner. *American Psychologist, 48,* 1158.

Garcia, J., & Koelling, R. A. (1966). The relation of cue to consequence in avoidance learning. *Psychonomic Science, 4,* 123–124.

Gardiner, H. W., Mutter, J. D., & Kosmitzki, C. (1998). *Lives across cultures: Cross-cultural human development.* Boston: Allyn & Bacon.

Gardner, H. (1983). *Frames of mind.* New York: Basic Books.

Gardner, H. (1985). *The mind's new science: A history of the cognitive revolution.* New York: Basic Books.

Gardner, H. (1993). *Creating minds: An anatomy of creativity seen through the lives of Freud, Einstein, Picasso, Stravinsky, Eliot, Graham, and Gandhi.* New York: Basic Books.

Gardner, H. (1999, February). Who owns intelligence? *The Atlantic Monthly,* pp. 67–76.

Gardyn, R., & Wellner, A. S. (2001, February). Blowin' smoke. *American Demographics, 23*(2), 20–22.

Garland, A., & Zigler, E. (1993). Adolescent suicide prevention: Current research and social policy implications. *American Psychologist, 48,* 169–182.

Garnsey, S. M. (1993). Event-related brain potentials in the study of language: An introduction. *Language and Cognitive Processes, 8,* 337–356.

Gazzaniga, M. (1970). *The bisected brain.* New York: Appleton-Century-Crofts.

Gazzaniga, M. S. (1995). Consciousness and the cerebral hemispheres. In M. S. Gazzaniga (Ed.), *The cognitive neurosciences.* Cambridge, MA: MIT Press.

Gazzaniga, M. S. (1998a, July). The split brain revisited. *Scientific American, 279,* 50–55.

Gazzaniga, M. S. (1998b). *The Mind's Past.* Berkeley: University of California Press.

Gelernter, J. (1994, June 17). Behavioral genetics in transition. *Science, 264,* 1684–1689.

Gelman, S. A., & Wellman, H. M. (1991). Insides and essences: Early understandings of the non-obvious. *Cognition, 38,* 213–244.

Gentner, D., & Stevens, A. L. (1983). *Mental models.* Hillsdale, NJ: Erlbaum.

George, M. S., Nahas, Z., Kozel, F. A., Goldman, J., Molloy, M., & Oliver, N. (1999). Improvement of depression following transcranial magnetic stimulation. *Current Psychiatry Reports, 1,* 114–124.

Gergen, K. J., Gulerce, A., Lock, A., & Misra, G. (1996). Psychological science in cultural context. *American Psychologist, 51,* 496–503.

Getzels, J. W., & Csikszentmihalyi, M. (1976). *The creative vision.* New York: Wiley.

Gibbons, A. (1998, September 4). Which of our genes make us human? *Science, 281,* 1432–1434.

Gibbs, W. W. (1995, March). Seeking the criminal element. *Scientific American,* pp. 100–107.

Gibbs, W. W. (1996, August). Gaining on fat. *Scientific American, 275*(2), 88–94.

Gibbs, W. W. (2001). Side splitting. *Scientific American, 284,* 24–25.

Gilbert, E. H., & DeBlassie, R. R. (1984). Anorexia nervosa: Adolescent starvation by choice. *Adolescence, 19,* 839–853.

Gilbert, R. M. (1992). *Extraordinary relationships: A new way of thinking about human interactions.* New York: Wiley.

Gilligan, C. (1982). *In a different voice: Psychological theory and women's development.* Cambridge, MA: Harvard University Press.

Gilligan, S. G., & Bower, G. H. (1984). Cognitive consequences of emotional arousal. In C. Izard, J. Kagan, & R. Zajonc (Eds.), *Emotions, cognitions and behavior.* New York: Cambridge University Press.

Gitlin, M. J. (1990). *The psychotherapist's guide to psychopharmacology.* New York: The Free Press.

Givens, D. B. (1983). *Love signals: How to attract a mate.* New York: Crown.

Glanz, J. (1998, April 3). Magnetic brain imaging traces a stairway to memory. *Science, 280,* 37.

Glaser, R. (1984). Education and thinking: The role of knowledge. *American Psychologist, 39,* 93–104.

Glaser, R. (1990). The reemergence of learning theory within instructional research. *American Psychologist, 45,* 29–39.

Goddard, C. R., & Stanley, J. R. (1995). Viewing the abusive parent and the abused child as captor and hostage: The application of hostage theory to the effects of child abuse. *Journal of Interpersonal Violence, 9,* 258–269.

Goldberg, L. R. (1981). Language and individual differences: The search for universals in personality lexicons. In L. Wheeler (Ed.), *Review of personality and social psychology* (Vol. 2, pp. 141–165). Beverly Hills, CA: Sage.

Goldberg, L. R. (1993). The structure of phenotypic personality traits. *American Psychologist, 48,* 26–34.

Goldenberg, J., Mazursky, D., & Solomon, S. (1999, September 3). Creative sparks. *Science, 285,* 1495–1496.

Goldin-Meadow, S., & Mylander, C. (1990). Beyond the input given: The child's role in the acquisition of language. *Language, 66,* 323–355.

Goldman-Rakic, P. S. (1992, September). Working memory and the mind. *Scientific American, 267,* 110–117.

Goleman, D. (1980, February). 1528 little geniuses and how they grew. *Psychology Today, 14,* 28–53.

Goleman, D. (1995). *Emotional intelligence.* New York: Bantam Books.

Golombok, S., & Tasker, F. (1996). Do parents influence the sexual orientation of their children? Findings from a longitudinal study of lesbian families. *Developmental Psychology, 32,* 3–11.

Gonzalvo, P., Cañas, J. J., & Bajo, M. (1994). Structural representations in knowledge acquisition. *Journal of Educational Psychology, 86,* 601–616.

Goodchilds, J. D. (Ed.). (1991). *Psychological perspectives on human diversity in America.* Washington, DC: American Psychological Association.

Gordon, L. (1990, September 2). Proposal to overhaul SAT to consider relevance, bias. *The Seattle Times/Post-Intelligencer.*

Gorman, J. (1999, January). The 11-year-old debunker. *Discover, 20*(1), 62–63.

Gottesman, I. I. (1991). *Schizophrenia genesis: The origins of madness.* New York: Freeman.

Gottesman, I. I. (1997, June 6). Twins: En route to QTLs for cognition. *Science, 276,* 1522–1523.

Gottlieb, B. H. (Ed.). (1981). *Social networks and social support.* Beverly Hills, CA: Sage.

Gottlieb, B. H. (1987). Marshalling social support for medical patients and their families. *Canadian Psychology, 28,* 201–217.

Gottman, J., Coan, J., Carrere, S., & Swanson, C. (1998). Predicting marital happiness and stability from newlywed interactions. *Journal of Marriage and the Family, 60,* 5–22.

Gottman, J., & Silver, N. (1994). *Why marriages succeed or fail.* New York: Simon and Schuster.

Gottman, J. M. (1994). *What predicts divorce?* Hillsdale, NJ: Erlbaum.

Gottman, J. M. (1999). *Seven principles for making marriages work.* New York: Crown.

Gottman, J. M., & Krokoff, L. J. (1989). Marital interaction and satisfaction: A longitudinal view. *Journal of Consulting & Clinical Psychology, 57,* 47–52.

Gottman, J. M., & Levenson, R. W. (1986). Assessing the role of emotion in marriage. *Behavioral Assessment, 8,* 31–48.

Gould, E., Tanapat, P., McEwen, B. S., Flüge, G., & Fuchs, E. (1998). Proliferation of granule cell precursors in the dentate gyrus of adult monkeys is diminished by stress. *Proceedings of the National Academy of Science, 99,* 3168–3171.

Gould, S. J. (1996). *The mismeasure of man* (2nd ed.). New York: Norton.

Graham, J. R. (1990). *MMPI-2: Assessing personality and psychopathology.* New York: Oxford University Press.

Gray, C. R., & Gummerman, K. (1975). The enigmatic eidetic image: A critical examination of methods, data, and theories. *Psychological Bulletin, 82,* 383–407.

Gray, P. (1993, November 29). The assault on Freud. *Time, 142* (23), 46–51.

Graziano, M. S. A., Cooke, D. F., & Taylor, C. S. R. (2000, December 1). Coding the location of the arm by sight. *Science, 290,* 1782–1786.

Greeley, A., & Sheatsley, P. (1971). The acceptance of desegregation continues to advance. *Scientific American, 225*(6), 13–19.

Green, D. M. & Swets, J. A. (1966). *Signal detection theory and psychophysics.* New York: Wiley.

Greenberg, B. S. (1986). Minorities and the mass media. In J. Bryant & D. Zillman (Eds.), *Perspectives in media effects* (pp. 17–40). Hillsdale, NJ: Erlbaum.

Greenberg, L. S., & Johnson, S. (1988). *Emotionally focused therapy for couples.* New York: Guilford.

Greene, B. (1985). A testing time. In B. Greene, *Cheeseburgers* (pp. 56–61). New York: Ballantine.

Greene, R. L. (1991). *The MMPI-2/MMPI: An interpretive manual.* Boston: Allyn and Bacon.

Greeno, J. G. (1989). A perspective on thinking. *American Psychologist, 44,* 134–141.

Greenspan, S. (1999, February). What is meant by mental retardation? *International Review of Psychiatry, 11,* 6–18.

Greenwald, A. G. (1992). New Look 3: Unconscious cognition reclaimed. *American Psychologist, 47* (6), 766–779.

Greenwald, A. G., Draine, S. C., & Abrams, R. L. (1996, September 20). Three cognitive markers of unconscious semantic activation. *Science, 273,* 1699–1702.

Gregory, R. (1997). *Mirrors in mind.* New York: W. H. Freeman.

Grevert, P., & Goldstein, A. (1985). Placebo analgesia, naloxone, and the role of endogenous opioids. In L. White, B. Turks, & G. E. Schwartz (Eds.), *Placebo,* (pp. 332–351). New York: Guilford.

Grinspoon, L., Bakalar, J. B., Zimmer, L., & Morgan, J. P. (1997, August 8). Marijuana addiction. (1997). *Science, 752,* 748.

Gross, J. J. (1998). The emerging field of emotion regulation: An integrative review. *Review of General Psychology, 2,* 271–299.

Guilford, J. P. (1967). *The nature of human intelligence.* New York: McGraw-Hill.

Guilford, J. P. (1973). Theories of intelligence. In B. B. Wolman (Ed.), *Handbook of general psychology* (pp. 630–643). Englewood Cliffs, NJ: Prentice-Hall.

Guilford, J. P. (1985). The Structure-of-Intellect model. In B. B. Wolman (Ed.), *Handbook of intelligence* (pp. 225–266). New York: Wiley.

Guisinger, S., & Blatt, S. J. (1994). Individuality and relatedness: Evolution of a fundamental dialectic. *American Psychologist, 49,* 104–111.

Gulya, M., Rovee-Collier, C., Galluccio, L., & Wilk, A. (1998). Memory processing of a serial list by young infants. *Psychological Science, 9,* 303–307.

Gur, R. E., & Maany, V. (1998). Subcortical MRI volumes in neuroleptic-naive and treated patients with schizophrenia. *American Journal of Psychiatry, 155,* 1711–1718.

Gur, R. E., & Pearlson, G. D. (1993). Neuroimaging in schizophrenia research. *Schizophrenia Bulletin, 19,* 337–353.

Gura, T. (1998, May 29). Uncoupling proteins provide new clue to obesity's causes. *Science, 280,* 1369–1370.

Gura, T. (2000, March 10). Tracing leptin's partners in regulating body weight. *Science,* 1738–1741.

Gustafson, S. B., & Magnusson, D. (1991). *Female life careers: A pattern approach.* Hillsdale, NJ: Erlbaum.

Guthrie, G. M., & Bennett, A. B. (1970). Cultural differences in implicit personality theory. *International Journal of Psychology, 6,* 305–312.

Guthrie, R. V. (1998). *Even the rat was white.* Boston: Allyn & Bacon.

Haber, R. N. (1969, April). Eidetic images. *Scientific American,* pp. 36–44.

Haber, R. N. (1970, May). How we remember what we see. *Scientific American,* 104–112.

Haber, R. N. (1980, November). Eidetic images are not just imaginary. *Psychology Today, 14,* 72–82.

Haberlandt, K. (1999). *Human memory: Exploration and application.* Boston: Allyn & Bacon.

Hacker, A. (1986, February 13). The decline of higher learning. *The New York Review.*

Haimov, I., & Lavie, P. (1996). Melatonin—A soporific hormone. *Current Directions in Psychological Science, 5,* 106–111.

Hall, C., (1951). What people dream about. *Scientific American, 184,* 60–63.

Hall, C. (1953/1966). *The meaning of dreams.* New York: Harper & Row/McGraw-Hill.

Hall, C., & Van de Castle, R. L. (1966). *The content analysis of dreams.* New York: Appleton-Century-Crofts.

Hall, C. C. I. (1997). Cultural malpractice: The growing obsolescence of psychology with the changing U.S. population. *American Psychologist, 52,* 642–651.

Hall, C. S. (1984). "A ubiquitous sex difference in dreams" revisited. *Journal of Personality and Social Psychology, 46,* 1109–1117.

Haller, E. (1992). Eating disorders: A review and update. *Western Journal of Medicine, 157,* 658–662.

Halpern, D. F. (1992). *Sex differences in cognitive abilities* (2nd ed.). Hillsdale, NJ: Erlbaum.

Hamer, D. (1997). The search for personality genes: Adventures of a molecular biologist. *Current Directions in Psychological Science, 6,* 111–112.

Hamer, D. H., Hu, S., Magnuson, V. L., Hu, N., & Pattatucci, A. M. L. (1993, December 24). Male sexual orientation and genetic evidence. *Science, 261,* 2863–2865.

Haney, C., Banks, W. C., & Zimbardo, P. G. (1973). Interpersonal dynamics in a simulated prison. *International Journal of Criminology and Penology, 1,* 69–97.

Haney, C., & Zimbardo, P. (1998). The past and future of U.S. prison policy: Twenty-five years after the Stanford prison experiment. *American Psychologist, 53,* 709–727.

Haring, M. J., Stock, W. A., & Okun, M. A. (1984). A research synthesis of gender and social class as correlates of subjective well-being. *Human Relations, 37,* 645–657.

Harlow, H. F. (1965). Sexual behavior in the rhesus monkey. In F. Beach (Ed.), *Sex and behavior.* New York: Wiley.

Harlow, H. F., & Harlow, M. K. (1966). Learning to love. *American Scientist, 54,* 244–272.

Harris, B. (1979). Whatever happened to Little Albert? *American Psychologist, 34,* 151–160.

Harris, G., Thomas, A., & Booth, D. A. (1990). Development of salt taste in infancy. *Developmental Psychology, 26,* 534–538.

Harris, J. R. (1995). Where is the child's environment? A group socialization theory of development. *Psychological Review, 102,* 458–489.

Hart, R. A., & Moore, G. I. (1973). The development of spatial cognition: A review. In R. M. Downs & D. Stea (Eds.), *Image and environment.* Chicago: Aldine.

Hartmann, E. L. (1973). *The functions of sleep.* New Haven, CT: Yale University Press.

Hartup, W. W., & Stevens, N. (1999). Friendships and adaptation across the life span. *Current Directions in Psychological Science, 8,* 76–79.

Harvey, J. H. (1996) Embracing their memory: Loss and the social psychology of storytelling. Needham Heights, MA: Allyn & Bacon.

Harvey, J. H., & Omarzu, J. (1997). Minding the close relationship. *Personality and Social Psychology Review, 1,* 224–240.

Harvey, J. H., & Pauwels, B. G. (1999). Recent developments in close-relationships theory. *Current Directions in Psychological Science, 8,* 93–95.

Harvey, J. H., Weber, A. L., & Orbuch, T. L. (1990). Interpersonal accounts: A social psychological perspective. Cambridge, MA: Basil Blackwell.

Harvey, S. M., & Spigner, C. (1995). Factors associated with sexual behavior among adolescents: A multivariate analysis. *Adolescence, 30,* 253–264.

Hass, A. (1979). *Teenage sexuality: A survey of teenage sexual behavior.* New York: Macmillan.

Hassebrauck, M. (1988). Beauty is more than "name" deep: The effect of women's first names on ratings of physical attractiveness and personality attributes. *Journal of Applied Social Psychology, 18,* 721–726.

Hatfield, E. (1988). Passionate and compassionate love. In R. J. Sternberg & M. L. Barnes (Eds.), *The psychology of love.* New Haven, CT: Yale University Press.

Hatfield, E., & Rapson, R. (1993). *Love, sex, and intimacy: Their psychology, biology, and history.* New York: HarperCollins.

Hatfield, E., & Rapson, R. (1998). On love and sex in the 21ˢᵗ century. *The General Psychologist, 33*(2), 45–54.

Hatfield, E., Rapson, R. L., & Rapson, R. (1995). *Love and sex: Cross-cultural perspectives.* Needham Heights, MA: Allyn & Bacon.

Hatfield, E., & Sprecher, S. (1986). *Mirror, mirror: The importance of looks in everyday life.* New York: State University of New York Press.

Hawkins, S. A., & Hastie, R. (1990). Hindsight: Biased judgments of past events after the outcomes are known. *Psychological Bulletin, 108,* 311–327.

Hayes, S. C., & Heiby, E. (1996). Psychology's drug problem: Do we need a fix or should we just say no? *American Psychologist, 51,* 198–206.

Haynes, S. G., & Feinleib, M. (1980). Women, work, and coronary heart disease: Prospective findings from the Framingham Heart Study. *American Journal of Public Health, 70,* 133–141.

Hazan, C., & Shaver, P.R. (1990). Love and work: An attachment-theoretical perspective. *Journal of Personality and Social Psychology, 59,* 270–280.

Hazan, C., & Shaver, P. R. (1992). Broken attachments: Relationship loss from the perspective of attachment theory. In T. L. Orbuch (Ed.), *Close relationship loss: Theoretical approaches* (pp. 90–108). New York: Springer Verlag.

Headey, B., & Wearing, A. (1992). *Understanding happiness: A theory of well-being.* Melbourne: Longman Cheshire.

Hecht, A. (1986, April). A guide to the proper use of tranquilizers. *Healthline Newsletter,* pp. 5–6.

Heeger, D. J. (1994). The representation of visual stimuli in primary visual cortex. *Current Directions in Psychological Science, 3,* 159–163.

Heimberg, R. G., Dodge, C. S., Hope, D. A., Kennedy, C. R., & Zollo, L. J. (1990). Cognitive behavioral group treatment for social phobia: Comparison with a credible placebo control. *Cognitive Therapy and Research, 14,* 1–23.

Heine, S. J., Lehman, D. R., Markus, H. R., & Kitayama, S. (1999). Is there a universal need for positive self-regard? *Psychological Review, 106,* 766–794.

Heinrichs, R. W. (1993). Schizophrenia and the brain: Conditions for a neuropsychology of madness. *American Psychologist, 48,* 221–233.

Heller, W., Nitschke, J. B., & Miller, G. A. (1998). Lateralization in emotion and emotional disorders. *Current Directions in Psychological Science, 7,* 26–32.

Helmes, E., & Reddon, J. R. (1993). A perspective on developments in assessing psychopathology: A critical review of the MMPI and MMPI-2. *Psychological Bulletin, 113,* 453–471.

Helms, J. E. (1992). Why is there no study of cultural equivalence in standardized cognitive ability testing? *American Psychologist, 47,* 1083–1101.

Helmuth, L. (2000, December 1). Where the brain monitors the body. *Science, 290,* 1668.

Hendrick, S. S., & Hendrick, C. (1992). *Liking, loving, and relating,* (2nd ed.) Pacific Grove, CA: Brooks/Cole.

Henig, R. M. (1998, May). Tempting fates. *Discover,* 58.

Henker, B., & Whalen, C. K. (1989). Hyperactivity and attention deficits. *American Psychologist, 44,* 216–223.

Henley, N. (1977). *Sexual politics: Power, sex, and nonverbal communication.* Englewood Cliffs, NJ: Prentice-Hall.

Herek, G. M. (2000). The psychology of sexual prejudice. *Current Directions in Psychological Science, 9,* 19–22.

Herman, J. L. (1992). *Trauma and recovery.* New York: Basic Books.

Hernstein, R. J., Nickerson, R. S., Sánchez, & Swets, J. A. (1986). Teaching thinking skills. *American Psychologist, 41,* 1279–1289.

Herrnstein, R. J., & Murray, C. (1994). *The bell curve.* New York: Free Press.

Heston, L. L. (1970). The genetics of schizophrenic and schizoid disease. *Science, 167,* 249–256.

Hetherington, E. M., & Parke, R. D. (1975). *Child psychology: A contemporary viewpoint.* New York: McGraw-Hill.

Hetherington, M. M., Spalter, A. R., Bernat, A. S., Nelson, M. L. et al. (1993). Eating pathology in bulimia nervosa. *International Journal of Eating Disorders, 13*(1), 13–24.

Hicks, R. A. (1990). *The costs and benefits of normal insomnia.* Paper presented at the annual meeting of the Western Psychological Association, Los Angeles, CA.

Hilgard, E. R. (1968). *The experience of hypnosis.* New York: Harcourt Brace Jovanovich.

Hilgard, E. R. (1973). The domain of hypnosis with some comments on alternative paradigms. *American Psychologist, 28,* 972–982.

Hill, J. O., & Peters, J. C. (1998, May 29). Environmental contributions to the obesity epidemic. *Science, 280,* 1371–1374.

Hilts, P. J. (1995). *Memory's ghost: The strange tale of Mr. M. and the nature of memory.* New York: Simon & Schuster.

Hinton, G. F., & Anderson, J. A. (1981). *Parallel models of associative memory.* Hillsdale, NJ: Erlbaum.

Hiroto, D. S. (1974). Locus of control and learned helplessness. *Journal of Experimental Psychology, 102,* 187–193.

Hirsch, J., Harrington, G., & Mehler, B. (1990). An irresponsible farewell gloss. *Educational Theory, 40,* 501–508.

Hirschfeld, R. M. A. (1999). Efficacy of SSRIs and newer antidepressants in severe depression: Comparison with TCAs. *Journal of Clinical Psychiatry, 60,* 326–335.

Hirschfeld, R. M. A., & Goodwin, F. K. (1988). Mood disorders. In J. A. Talbott, R. E. Hales, & S. C. Yudofsky (Eds.), *The American Psychiatric Press textbook of psychiatry.* Washington, DC: American Psychiatric Press.

Hobson, J. A. (1988). *The dreaming brain.* New York: Basic Books.

Hobson, J. A., & McCarley, R. W. (1977). The brain as a dream state generator: An activation-synthesis hypothesis of the dream process. *American Journal of Psychiatry, 134,* 1335–1348.

Hochwalder, J. (1995). On stability of the structure of implicit personality theory over situations. *Scandinavian Journal of Psychology, 36,* 386–398.

Hogan, R., Curphy, G. J., & Hogan, J. (1994). What we know about leadership: Effectiveness and personality. *American Psychologist, 49,* 493–504.

Hogan, R., Hogan, J., & Roberts, B. W. (1996). Personality measurement and employment decisions: Questions and answers. *American Psychologist, 51,* 469–477.

Hogarty, G. E., Kornblith, S. J., Greenwald, D., DiBarry, A. L., Cooley, S., Ulrich, R. F., Carter, M., & Flesher, S. (1997). Three-year trials of personal therapy among schizophrenic patients living with or independent of family, I: Description of study and effects on relapse rates. *American Journal of Psychiatry, 154,* 1504–1513.

Holden, C. (1978). Patuxent: Controversial prison clings to belief in rehabilitation. *Science, 199,* 665–668.

Holden, C. (1996a, July 5). New populations of old add to poor nations' burdens. *Science, 273,* 46–48

Holden, C. (1996b, July 19). Sex and olfaction. *Science, 273,* 313.

Holden, C. (1997, October 3). A special place for faces in the brain. *Science, 278,* 41.

Holden, C. (2000, April 7). Global survey examines impact of depression. *Science, 288,* 39–40.

Holden, C. (2000, July 28). The violence of the lambs. *Science, 289,* 580–581.

Holden, C. (2001, February 9). Panel seeks truth in lie detector debate. *Science, 291,* 967.

Hollis, K. L. (1997). Contemporary research on Pavlovian conditioning. *American Psychologist, 52,* 956–965.

Hollon, S. D. (1996). The efficacy and effectiveness of psychotherapy relative to medications. *American Psychologist, 51,* 1025–1030.

Holloway, M. (1999, November). The ascent of scent. *Scientific American, 281,* 42, 44.

Holmes, D. S. (1984). Meditation and somatic arousal: A review of the experimental evidence. *American Psychologist, 39,* 1–10.

Holmes, D. S. (1994). *Abnormal psychology.* New York: HarperCollins.

Holmes, D. S. (2001). *Abnormal psychology* (4th ed.). Boston: Allyn and Bacon.

Holmes, T. H. (1979). Development and application of a quantitative measure of life change magnitude. In J. E. Barrett, R. M. Rose, & G. L. Klerman (Eds.), *Stress and mental disorder.* New York: Raven.

Holmes, T. H., & Masuda, M. (1974). Life change and stress susceptibility. In B. S. Dohrenwend & B. P. Dohrenwend, (Eds.), *Stressful life events: Their nature and effects* (pp. 45–72). New York: Wiley.

Holmes, T. H., & Rahe, R. H. (1967). The social readjustment rating scale. *Journal of Psychosomatic Research, 11*(2), 213–218.

Holtzman, W. H. (1992). Health psychology. In M. A. Rosenzweig (Ed.), *International psychological science* (pp. 199–226). Washington, DC: American Psychological Association.

Holtzworth-Munroe, A., & Jacobson, N. S. (1985). Causal attributions of marital couples: When do they search for causes? What do they conclude when they do? *Journal of Personality and Social Psychology, 48,* 1398–1412.

Homme, L. E., de Baca, P. C., Devine, J. V., Steinhorst, R., & Rickert, E. J. (1963). Use of the Premack principle in controlling the behavior of nursery school children. *Journal of the Experimental Analysis of Behavior, 6,* 544.

Hopkins, B., & Westra, T. (1988). Maternal handling and motor development: An intracultural study. *Genetic, Social and General Psychology Monographs, 14,* 377–420.

Horgan, J. (1993, June). Eugenics revisited. *Scientific American,* pp. 122–131.

Horgan, J. (1996, November). Multicultural studies: Rates of depression vary widely throughout the world. *Scientific American, 275*(6), 24–25.

Horgan, J. (1999). The undiscovered mind: How the human brain defies replication, medication, and explanation. *Psychological Science, 10,* 470–474.

Horne, J. A. (1988). *Why we sleep: The functions of sleep in humans and other mammals.* Oxford, U. K.: Oxford University Press.

Horney, K. (1939). *New ways in psychoanalysis.* New York: Norton.

Horney, K. (1942). *Self-analysis.* New York: Norton.

Horney, K. (1967). *Feminine psychology.* New York: W. W. Norton.

Horvath, A. O., & Luborsky, L. (1993). The role of the therapeutic alliance in psychotherapy. *Journal of Consulting and Clinical Psychology, 61,* 561–573.

House, J. S., Landis, K. R., & Umberson, D. (1988). Social relationships and health. *Science, 241,* 540–545.

Hovland, C. I., & Sears, R. (1940). Minor studies of aggression: Correlation of lynchings with economic indices. *Journal of Psychology, 9,* 301–310.

Howard, A., Pion, G. M., Gottfredson, G. D., Flattau, P. E., Oskamp, S., Pfafflin, S. M., Bray, D. W., & Burstein, A. G. (1986). The changing face of American psychology: A report from the committee on employment and human resources. *American Psychologist, 41,* 1311–1327.

Howes, C., Rodning, C., Galluzzo, D. C., & Myers, L. (1988). Attachment and child care: Relationships with mother and care-giver. *Early Childhood Research Quarterly, 3,* 403–416.

Hubel, D. H., & Wiesel, T. N. (1979, September). Brain mechanisms of vision. *Scientific American, 241,* 150–162.

Huesman, L. R., & Moise, J. (1996, June). Media violence: A demonstrated public health threat to children. *Harvard Mental Health Letter, 12*(12), 5–7.

Hull, C. L. (1943). *Principles of behavior: An introduction to behavior theory.* New York: Appleton-Century-Crofts.

Hull, C. L. (1952). *A behavior system: An introduction to behavior theory concerning the individual organism.* New Haven, CT: Yale University Press.

Humphrey, T. (1970). The development of human fetal activity and its relation to postnatal behavior. In H. W. Reese & L. P. Lipsitt (Eds.), *Advance in child development and behavior* (Vol. 5). New York: Academic Press.

Hunt, E. (1989). Cognitive science: Definition, status, and questions. *Annual Review of Psychology, 40,* 603–629.

Hunter, I. (1964). *Memory.* Baltimore: Penguin.

Huston, A. C., Watkins, B. A., & Kunkel, D. (1989). Public policy and children's television. *American Psychologist, 44,* 424–433.

Huston, T. L., Ruggiero, M., Conner, R., & Geis, G. (1981). Bystander intervention into crime: A study based on naturally-occurring episodes. *Social Psychology Quarterly, 44,* 14–23.

Hyman, I. A. (1996). Using research to change public policy: Reflections on 20 years of effort to eliminate corporal punishment in schools. *Pediatrics, 98,* 818–821.

Hyman, I. A., McDowell, E., & Raines, B. (1977). Corporal punishment and alternatives in the schools: An overview of theoretical and practical issues. In J. H. Wise (Ed.), *Proceedings: Conference on corporal punishment in the schools* (pp. 1–18). Washington, DC: National Institutes of Education.

Hyman, I. E., Jr., Husband, T. H., & Billings, F. J. (1995). False memories of childhood experiences. *Applied Cognitive Psychology, 9,* 181–197.

Hyman, R. (1989). The psychology of deception. *Annual Review of Psychology, 40,* 133–154.

Iacono, W. G., & Grove, W. M. (1993). Schizophrenia reviewed: Toward an integrative genetic model. *Science, 4,* 273–276.

Ickes, W., & Layden, M. A. (1978). Attributional styles. In J. H. Harvey, W. Ickes, & R. F. Kidd (Eds.), *New directions in attributional research* (Vol. 2). Hillsdale, NJ: Erlbaum.

Ineichen, B. (1979). The social geography of marriage. In M. Cook & G. Wilson (Eds.), *Love and attraction.* New York: Pergamon Press.

Inglehart, R. (1990). *Culture shift in advanced industrial society.* Princeton, NJ: Princeton University Press.

Irwin, M., Daniels, M., Smith, T. L., Bloom, E., & Weiner, H. (1987). Impaired natural killer cell activity during bereavement. *Brain Behavior Immunology, 1,* 98–104.

Isay, R. A. (1990). Psychoanalytic theory and the therapy of gay men. In D. P. McWhirter, S. A. Sanders, & J. M. Reinisch (Eds.), *Homosexuality/heterosexuality: Concepts of sexual orientation* (pp. 283–303). New York: Oxford University Press.

Ishai, A., & Sagi, D. (1995). Common mechanisms of visual imagery and perception. *Science, 268,* 1772–1774.

Ishai, A., & Sagi, D. (1997). Visual imagery: Effects of short- and long-term memory. *Journal of Cognitive Neuroscience, 9,* 734–742.

Izard, C. E. (1989). The structure and functions of emotions: Implications for cognition, motivation, and personality. In I. S. Cohen (Ed.), *The G. Stanley Hall lecture series* (Vol. 9, pp. 39–73). Washington, DC: American Psychological Association.

Izard, C. E. (1993). Four systems for emotion activation: Cognitive and noncognitive processes. *Psychological Review, 100,* 68–90.

Izard, C. E. (1994). Innate and universal facial expressions: Evidence from developmental and cross-cultural research. *Psychological Bulletin, 115,* 288–299.

Jackson, D. D. (1980, October). Reunion of identical twins, raised apart, reveals some astonishing similarities. *Smithsonian,* pp. 48–57.

Jacobs, B. L. (1987). How hallucinogenic drugs work. *American Scientist, 75,* 386–392.

Jacobs, M. K., & Goodman, G. (1989). Psychology and self-help groups: Predictions on a partnership. *American Psychologist, 44,* 536–545.

Jacobson, N. S., & Christensen, A. (1996). Studying the effectiveness of psychotherapy: How well can clinical trials do the job? *American Psychologist, 51,* 1031–1039.

Jacobson, N. S., & Follette, W. C. (1985). Clinical significance of improvement resulting from two behavioral marital therapy components. *Behavior Therapy, 16,* 249–262.

Jacoby, L. L., Lindsay, D. S., Toth, J. P. (1992). Unconscious influences revealed: Attention, awareness, and control. *American Psychologist, 47,* 802–809.

Jacoby, L. L., Woloshyn, V., & Kelley, C. (1989). Becoming famous without being recognized: Unconscious influences of memory produced by divided attention. *Journal of Experimental Psychology: General, 118* (2), 115–125.

Jaffe, J., Beebe, B., Feldstein, S., Crown, C. L., & Jasnow, M. D. (2001. Rhythms of dialogue in infancy: Coordinated timing in development. *Monographs of Society for Research in Child Development, 66,* vii, 1–132.

James, W. (1950). *The principles of psychology* (2 vols.). New York: Holt, Rinehart & Winston. (Original work published 1890).

Janoff-Bulman, R. (1989). The benefits of illusions, the threat of disillusionment, and the limitations of inaccuracy. *Journal of Social and Clinical Psychology, 8,* 158–175.

Janoff-Bulman, R. (1992). *Shattered assumptions: Towards a new psychology of trauma.* New York: The Free Press.

Jansen, A. S. P., Nguyen, X. V., Karpitskiy, V., Mettenleiter, T. C., & Loewy, A. D. (1995, October 27). Central command neurons of the sympathetic nervous system: Basis of the fight-or-flight response. *Science, 270,* 644–646.

Jeffery, R. W. (1987). Behavioral treatment of obesity. *Annals of Behavioral Medicine, 9,* 20–24.

Jenkins, C. D. (1976). Recent evidence supporting psychologic and social risk factors for coronary disease. *New England Journal of Medicine, 294,* 987–994, 1033–1038.

Jenkins, J. H. (1994). Culture, emotion, and psychopathology. In S. Kitayama & H. R. Markus (Eds.), *Emotion and culture: Empirical studies of mutual influence.* Washington, DC: American Psychological Association.

Jensen, A. R. (1969). How much can we boost IQ and scholastic achievement? *Harvard Educational Review, 39,* 1–123.

Jensen, A. R. (1980). *Bias in mental testing.* New York: Free Press.

Jensen, A. R. (1985). Methodological and statistical techniques for the chronometric study of mental abilities. In C. R. Reynolds & V. L. Wilson (Eds.), *Methodological and statistical advances in the study of individual difference* (pp. 51–116). New York: Plenum.

Jensen, A. R. (1998). The *g* factor and the design of education. In R. J. Sternberg & W. M. Williams (Eds.), *Intelligence, instruction, and assessment: Theory into practice.* Mahwah, NJ: Lawrence Erlbaum Associates.

Jensen, A. R., & Figueroa, R. A. (1975). Forward and backward digit-span interaction with race and IQ: Predictions from Jensen's theory. *Journal of Educational Psychology, 67,* 882–893.

Johnson, D. L. (1989). Schizophrenia as a brain disease: Implications for psychologists and families. *American Psychologist, 44,* 553–555.

Johnson, J. H., & Sarason, I. B. (1979). Recent developments in research on life stress. In V. Hamilton & D. M. Warburton (Eds.), *Human stress and cognition: An information processing approach* (pp. 205–233) Chichester, England: Wiley.

Johnson, M. K., & Hasher, L. (1987). Human learning and memory. *Annual Review of Psychology, 38,* 631–638.

Johnston, L. D., O'Malley, P. M., & Bachman, J. G. (1989). *Drug use, drinking, and smoking: National survey results from high school, college, and young adult populations, 1975–1988.* Rockville, MD: U.S. Department of Health and Human Services.

Joiner, T. E., Jr., & Schmidt, N. B. (1995). Dimensions of perfectionism, life stress, and depressed and anxious symptoms: Prospective support for diathesis-stress but not specific vulnerability among male undergraduates. *Journal of Social and Clinical Psychology, 14,* 165–183.

Jones, E. E., Cumming, J. D., & Horowitz, M. J. (1988). Another look at the nonspecific hypothesis of therapeutic effectiveness. *Journal of Consulting and Clinical Psychology, 56,* 48–55.

Jones, J. M. (1991). Psychological models of race: What have they been and what should they be? In J. D. Goodchilds (Ed.), *Psychological perspectives on human diversity in America* (pp. 3–46). Washington, DC: American Psychological Association.

Jones, M. (1953). *The therapeutic community.* New York: Basic Books.

Joyce, L. (1989, Fall). Good genes, bad genes. *Stanford Medicine,* pp. 18–23.

Juliano, S. L. (1998, March 13). Mapping the sensory mosaic. *Science, 279,* 1653–1654.

Julien, R. M. (1995). *A primer of drug action: A concise, nontechnical guide to the actions, uses, and side effects of psychoactive drugs.* New York: W. H. Freeman.

Jung, C. G. (1959). The concept of the collective unconscious. In *The archetypes and the collective unconscious, collected works* (Vol. 9, Part 1, pp. 54–77). Princeton, NJ: Princeton University Press. (Original work published 1936)

Kagan, J. (1994a). *Galen's prophecy: Temperament in human nature.* New York: Basic Books.

Kagan, J. (1994b, October 5). The realistic view of biology and behavior. *The Chronicle of Higher Education,* p. A64.

Kagan, J. (1996). Three pleasing ideas. *American Psychologist, 51,* 901–908.

Kagan, J. (1998). *Three seductive ideas.* Cambridge, MA: Harvard University Press.

Kagan, J., Reznick, J. S., & Snidman, N. (1986). Temperamental inhibition in early childhood. In R. Plomin & J. Dunn (Eds.), *The study of temperament: Changes, continuities, and challenges.* Hillsdale, NJ: Erlbaum.

Kagan, J., Reznick, J. S., & Snidman, N. (1988). Biological basis of childhood shyness. *Science, 20,* 167–171.

Kagan, J., & Snidman, N. (1991). Infant predictors of inhibited and uninhibited profiles. *Psychological Science, 2,* 40–44.

Kagan, J., & Snidman, N. (1998). Childhood derivatives of high and low reactivity in infancy. *Child Development, 69,* 1483–1493.

Kagan, J., Snidman, N., Arcus, D., and Reznick, J. S. (1994). *Galen's prophecy: Temperament in human nature.* New York: Basic Books.

Kamil, A. C., Krebs, J., & Pulliam, H. R. (1987). *Foraging behavior.* New York: Plenum.

Kamin, L. (1994, November 23). Intelligence, IQ tests, and race. *Chronicle of Higher Education,* p. B5.

Kamin, L. J. (1969). Predictability, surprise, attention, and conditioning. In B. A. Campbell & R. M. Church (Eds.), *Classical conditioning: A symposium.* New York: Appleton-Century-Crofts.

Kamin, L. J. (1974). *The science and politics of IQ.* Potomac, MD: Erlbaum.

Kamin, L. J. (1995, February). Book review: Behind the curve. *Scientific American, 272,* pp. 99–103.

Kandel, D. B. (1978). Similarity in real-life adolescent friendship pairs. Journal of *Personality and Social Psychology, 36,* 306–312.

Kandel, E. R., & Hawkins, R. D. (1992, September). The biological basis of learning and individuality. *Scientific American, 267,* 79–86

Kandel, E. R., & Squire, L. R. (2000, November 10). Neuroscience: Breaking down scientific barriers to the study of brain and mind. *Science, 290,* 1113–1120.

Kane, J. M., & Marder, S. R. (1993). Psychopharmacologic treatment of schizophrenia. *Schizophrenia Bulletin, 19,* 287–302.

Kantrowitz, B. (1992, January 27). A Head Start does not last. *Newsweek, 119,* 44–45.

Karlsen, C. F. (1998). The devil in the shape of a woman: Witchcraft in colonial New England. New York: W. W. Norton & Company.

Karni, A., Tanne, D., Rubenstein, B. S., Askenasy, J. J. M., & Sagi, D. (1994, July 29). Dependence on REM sleep of overnight improvement in perceptual skill. *Science, 265,* 679–682.

Karon, B. P. (1999, Spring). The tragedy of schizophrenia. *The General Psychologist, 34,* 1–12.

Kasamatsu, A., & Hirai, T. (1966). An electroencephalographic study on the Zen meditation (Zazen). *Folia Psychiatrica et Neurological Japonica, 20,* 315–336.

Kazdin, A. E. (1986). Comparative outcome studies of psychotherapy: Methodological issues and strategies. *Journal of Consulting and Clinical Psychology, 54,* 95–105.

Kazdin, A. E. (1994). *Behavior modification in applied settings* (5th ed.). Pacific Grove, CA: Brooks/Cole.

Kazdin, A. E., & Wilcoxin, L. A. (1976). Systematic desensitization and nonspecific treatment effects: A methodological evaluation. *Psychological Bulletin, 83,* 729–758.

Keane, T. M., Fairbank, J. A., Caddell, J. M., & Zimering, R. T. (1989). Implosive (flooding) therapy reduces symptoms of PTSD in Vietnam combat veterans. *Behavior Therapy, 20,* 245–260.

Keating, C. F. (1994). World without words: Messages from face and body. In W. J. Lonner & R. Malpass (Eds.), *Psychology and culture* (pp. 175–182). Boston: Allyn and Bacon.

Keefe, F. J., Dunsmore, J., & Burnett, R. (1992). Behavioral and cognitive–behavioral approaches to chronic pain: Recent advances and future directions. *Journal of Consulting and Clinical Psychology, 60,* 528–536.

Keesey, R. E., & Powley, T. L. (1975). Hypothalamic regulation of body weight. *American Scientist, 63,* 558–565.

Keller, M. B., McCullough, J. P., Klein, D. N., Arnow, B., Dunner, D. L., Gelenberg, A. J., Markowitz, J. C., Nemeroff, C. B., Russell, J. M., Thase, M. E., Trivedi, M. H., & Zajecka, J. (2000, May 18). A comparison of nefazodone, the cognitive behavioral-analysis system of psychotherapy, and their combination for the treatment of chronic depression. *New England Journal of Medicine, 342,* 1462–1461.

Kelley, H. H., Berscheid, E., Christensen, A., Harvey, J., Huston, T., Levinger, G., McClintock, E., Peplau, A., & Peterson, D. (1983). *Close relationships.* San Francisco: Freeman.

Kelley, J. E., Lumley, M. A., & Leisen, J. C. C. (1997). Health effects of emotional disclosure in rheumatoid arthritis patients. *Health Psychology, 16,* 331–340.

Kelman, H. C. (1997). Group processes in the resolution of international conflicts: Experiences from the Israeli-Palestinian case. *American Psychologist, 52,* 212–220.

Kelman, H. C. (1999). Interactive problem solving as a metaphor for international conflict resolution: Lessons for the policy process. *Peace & Conflict: Journal of Peace Psychology, 5,* 201–218.

Kelsoe, J. R., Ginns, E. I., Egeland, J. A., Gerhard, D. S., Goldstein, A. M., Bale, S. J., Pauls, D. L., Long, R. T., Kidd, K. K., Conte, G., Housman, D. E., & Paul, S. M. (1989). Reevaluation of the linkage relationship between chromosome 11p loci and the gene for bipolar affective disorder in the Old Order Amish. *Nature, 342,* 238–243.

Kempermann, G., & Gage, F. H. (1999, May). New nerve cells for the adult brain. *Scientific American, 280,* 48–53.

Kendler, K. S., & Diehl, S. R. (1993). The genetics of schizophrenia: A current, genetic–epidemiologic perspective. *Schizophrenia Bulletin, 19,* 261–285.

Kendler, K. S., & Gardner, C. O., Jr. (1998). Boundaries of major depression: An evaluation of DSM-IV criteria. *American Journal of Psychiatry, 155,* 172–177.

Kennedy, D. M. (1970). *Birth control in America: The career of Margaret Sanger.* New Haven, CT: Yale University Press.

Kennedy, M. B. (2000, October 27). Signal-processing machines at the postsynaptic density. *Science, 290,* 750–754.

Kennedy, S. H., & Garfinkel, P. E. (1992). Advances in diagnosis and treatment of anorexia nervosa and bulimia nervosa. *Canadian Journal of Psychiatry, 37*(5), 309–315.

Kenrick, D. T., & Funder, D. C. (1988). Profiting from controversy: Lessons from the person-situation debate. *American Psychologist, 43,* 23–34.

Kenrick, D. T., & Stringfield, D. O. (1980). Personality traits and the eye of the beholder: Crossing some traditional philosophical boundaries in the search for consistency in all of the people. *Psychological Review, 87,* 88–104.

Kerlinger, F. N. (1985). *Foundations of behavioral research* (3rd ed.). New York: Holt, Rinehart & Winston.

Kershner, J. R., & Ledger, G. (1985). Effect of sex, intelligence, and style of thinking on creativity: A comparison of gifted and average IQ children. *Journal of Personality and Social Psychology, 48,* 1033–1040.

Kesner, R., & Olton, D. S. (1990). *The neurobiology of comparative cognition.* Hillsdale, NJ: Erlbaum.

Kiecolt-Glaser, J. K., & Glaser, R. (1987). Psychosocial moderators of immune function. *Annals of Behavioral Medicine, 9,* 16–20.

Kiecolt-Glaser, J. K., & Glaser, R. (2001). Stress and immunity: Age enhances the risks. *Current Directions in Psychological Science, 10,* 18–21.

Kiesler, C. A. (1982a). Mental hospitals and alternative care: Noninstitutionalization as potential public policy for mental patients. *American Psychologist, 37,* 349–360.

Kiesler, C. A. (1982b). Public and professional myths about mental hospitalization. *American Psychologist, 37,* 1323–1339.

Kiesler, C. A. (1993). Mental health policy and mental hospitalization. *Current Directions in Psychological Science, 2,* 93–95.

Kiesling, R. (1983). Critique of Kiesler articles. *American Psychologist, 38,* 1127–1128.

Kiester, E. (1980, May/June). Images of the night. *Science 80,* pp. 36–42.

Kihlstrom, J. F. (1985). Hypnosis. *Annual Review of Psychology, 36,* 385–418.

Kihlstrom, J. F. (1987). The cognitive unconscious. *Science, 237,* 1445–1452.

Kihlstrom, J. F. (1990). The psychological unconscious. In L. Pervin (Ed.), *Handbook of personality: Theory and research* (pp. 445–464). New York: Guilford Press.

Kihlstrom, J. F., Barnhardt, T. M., & Tartaryn, D. J. (1992). The psychological unconscious: Found, lost, and regained. *American Psychologist, 47,* 788–791.

Kimmel, A. J. (1991). Predictable biases in the ethical decision making of American psychologists. *American Psychologist, 46,* 786–788.

Kinoshita, J. (1992, July). Dreams of a rat. *Discover, 13,* pp. 34–41.

Kinsey, A. C., Pomeroy, W. B., & Martin, C. E. (1948). *Sexual behavior in the human male.* Philadelphia: Saunders.

Kinsey, A. C., Pomeroy, W. B., Martin, C. E., & Gebhard, P. H. (1953). *Sexual behavior in the human female.* Philadelphia: Saunders.

Kintsch, W. (1981). Semantic memory: A tutorial. In R. S. Nickerson (Ed.), *Attention and performance* (Vol. 8). Hillsdale, NJ: Erlbaum.

Kirkpatrick, L. A., & Shaver, P. R. (1992). An attachment-theoretical approach to romantic love and religious belief. *Personality and Social Psychology Bulletin, 18,* 266–275.

Kirsch, I., & Lynn, S. J. (1995). The altered state of hypnosis: Changes in the theoretical landscape. *American Psychologist, 50,* 846–858.

Kirsch, I., & Sapirstein, G. (1998, June 26). Listening to Prozac but hearing placebo: A meta-analysis of antidepressant medication. *Prevention & Treatment, 1,* Article 0002a. [http://journals.apa.org/prevention/volume1/pre0010002a.htm]

Klag, M. J., Whelton, P. K., Grim, C. E., & Kuller, L. H. (1991). The association of skin color with blood pressure in U.S. blacks with low socioeconomic status. *Journal of the American Medical Association, 265,* 599–602.

Klagsbrun, F. (1985). *Married people: Staying together in the age of divorce.* New York: Bantam Books.

Klein, K. E., & Wegmann, H. M. (1974). The resynchronization of human circadian rhythms after transmeridian flights as a result of flight direction and mode of activity. In L. E. Scheving, F. Halberg, & J. E. Pauly (Eds.), *Chronobiology* (pp. 564–570). Tokyo: Igaku.

Klein, R. G., Landa, B., Mattes, J. A., & Klein, D. F. (1988). Methylphenidate and growth in hyperactive children: A controlled withdrawal study. *Archives of General Psychiatry, 45,* 1127–1130.

Kleinfeld, J. (1994). Learning styles and culture. In Lonner, W. J. & Malpass, R. *Psychology and culture* (pp. 151–156). Boston: Allyn & Bacon.

Kleinke, C. (1975). *First impressions: The psychology of encountering others.* Englewood Cliffs, NJ: Prentice Hall.

Kleinman, A., & Cohen, A. (1997). Psychiatry's global challenge. *Scientific American, 276* (3), 86–89.

Klinger, E. (1987, May). The power of daydreams. *Psychology Today,* pp. 37–44.

Kobasa, S. O. (1984). How much stress can you survive? *American Health, 3,* 64–77.

Kobasa, S. O., Hilker, R. R., & Maddi, S. R. (1979). Who stays healthy under stress? *Journal of Occupational Medicine, 21,* 595–598.

Kohlberg, L. (1964). Development of moral character and moral ideology. In M. L. Hoffman & L. W. Hoffman (Eds.), *Review of child development research* (Vol. 1). New York: Russell Sage Foundation.

Kohlberg, L. (1981). *The philosophy of moral development.* New York: Harper & Row.

Köhler, W. (1925). *The mentality of apes.* New York: Harcourt Brace Jovanovich.

Kohn, A. (2001, March 9). Two cheers for an end to the SAT. *The Chronicle of Higher Education,* B12–B13.

Kohn, P. M., Barnes, G. E., & Hoffman, F. M. (1979). Drug-use history and experience seeking among adult male correctional inmates. *Journal of Consulting and Clinical Psychology, 47,* 708–715.

Kohout, J. (2000, January). A look at recent baccalaureates in psychology. *Monitor on Psychology,* p. 13.

Kohout, J. (2001, February). Who's earning those psychology degrees. *Monitor on Psychology,* p. 42.

Kohout, J., & Wicherski, M. (2000, December). Where are the new psychologists working? *Monitor on Psychology,* p. 13.

Kolb, B. (1989). Development, plasticity, and behavior. *American Psychologist, 44,* 1203–1212.

Koob, G. F., & Le Moal, M. (1997, October 3). Drug abuse: Hedonic homeostatic dysregulation. *Science, 278,* 52–58.

Kopta, S. M., Lueger, R. J., Saunders, S. M., & Howard, K. I. (1999). Individual psychotherapy outcome and process research: Challenges leading to greater turmoil or a positive transition? *Annual Review of Psychology, 30,* 441–469.

Kosko, B., & Isaka, S. (1993, July). Fuzzy logic. *Scientific American, 269,* 76–81.

Kosslyn, S., Thompson, W., Kim, I., & Alpert,

N. (1995). Topographical representations of mental images in primary visual cortex. *Nature, 378,* 496–498.

Kosslyn, S. M. (1983). *Ghosts in the mind's machine: Creating and using images in the brain.* New York: Norton.

Kramer, P. D. (1993). *Listening to Prozac: A psychiatrist explores antidepressant drugs and the remaking of the self.* New York: Viking.

Krampe, R. T., & Ericsson, K. A. (1996). Maintaining excellence: Deliberate practice and elite performance in young and older pianists. *Journal of Experimental Psychology: General, 125,* 331–359.

Krantz, D. S., Grunberg, N. E., & Baum, A. (1985). Health psychology. *Annual Review of Psychology, 36,* 349–383.

Kukla, A. (1989). Nonempirical issues in psychology. *American Psychologist, 44,* 785–794.

Kupfersmid, J. (1989). Treatment of nocturnal enuresis: A status report. *The Psychiatric Forum, 14,* 37–46.

Lachman, R., Lachman, J. L., & Butterfield, E. C. (1979). *Cognitive psychology and information processing: An introduction.* Hillsdale, NJ: Erlbaum.

Lakoff, R. T. (1990). *Talking power.* New York: Basic Books.

Lamb, M. E. (1999, May/June). Mary D. Salter Ainsworth 1913–1999 attachment theorist. *APS Observer, 32,* 34–35.

Lambo, T. A. (1978). Psychotherapy in Africa. *Human Nature, 1*(3), 32–39.

Lampl, M., Veldhuis, J. D., & Johnson, M. L. (1992). Saltation and stasis: A model of human growth. *Science, 258,* 801–803.

Landesman, S., & Butterfield, E. C. (1987). Normalization and deinstitutionalization of mentally retarded individuals: Controversy and facts. *American Psychologist, 42,* 809–816.

Landry, D. W. (1997, February). Immunotherapy for cocaine addiction. *Scientific American,* 42–45.

Lang, F. R., & Carstensen, L. L. (1994). Close emotional relationships in late life: Further support for proactive aging in the social domain. *Psychology and Aging, 9,* 315–324.

Lang, P. J., & Lazovik, D. A. (1963). The experimental desensitization of a phobia. *Journal of Abnormal and Social Psychology, 66,* 519–525.

Langlois, J. H., & Roggman, L. A. (1990). Attractive faces are only average. *Psychological Science, 1,* 115–121.

Langlois, J. H., Roggman, L. A., Casey, R. J., Ritter, J. M., Rieser-Danner, L. A., & Jenkins, V. Y. (1987). Infant preferences for attractive faces: Rudiments of a stereotype. *Developmental Psychology, 23,* 363–369.

Langlois, J. H., Roggman, L. A., & Musselman, L. (1994). What is average and what is not average about attractive faces? *Psychological Science, 5,* 214–220.

Larson, R. (1989). Is feeling "in control" related to happiness in daily life? *Psychological Reports, 64,* 775–784.

Lash, J. (2001). Dealing with the tinder as well as the flint. *Science, 294,* 1789.

Lashley, K. S. (1950). In search of the engram. In *Physiological mechanisms in animal behavior: Symposium of the Society for Experi-*

mental Biology, Vol. 4. New York: Academic Press.

Latané, B., & Darley, J. M. (1968). Group inhibition of bystander intervention in emergencies. *Journal of Personality and Social Psychology, 10,* 215–221.

Laumann, E. O., Gagnon, J. H., Michael, R. T., & Michaels, S. (1994). *The social organization of sexuality: Sexual practices in the United States.* Chicago: University of Chicago Press.

Lazar, I., & Darlington, R. (1982). Lasting effects of early education: A report from the Consortium for Longitudinal Studies. *Monographs of the Society for Research in Child Development, 47*(2–3, Serial No. 195).

Lazarus, R. S. (1981, July). Little hassles can be hazardous to your health. *Psychology Today,* pp. 58–62.

Lazarus, R. S. (1984). On the primacy of cognition. *American Psychologist, 39,* 124–129.

Lazarus, R. S. (1991a). Cognition and motivation in emotion. *American Psychologist, 46,* 352–367.

Lazarus, R. S. (1991b). Progress on a cognitive-motivational-relational theory of emotion. *American Psychologist, 46,* 819–834.

Lazarus, R. S., DeLongis, A., Folkman, S., & Gruen, R. (1985). Stress and adaptational outcomes: The problem of confounded measures. *American Psychologist, 40,* 770–779.

LeDoux, J. (1996). *The emotional brain: The mysterious underpinnings of emotional life.* New York: Touchstone (Simon & Schuster).

LeDoux, J. E. (1994). Emotion, memory and the brain, *Scientific American, 270*(6), 50–57.

LeDoux, J. E. (1996). *The emotional brain: The mysterious underpinnings of emotional life.* New York: Simon & Schuster.

Lee, M., Zimbardo, P., & Bertholf, M. (1977, November). Shy murders. *Psychology Today,* pp. 68–70, 76, 148.

Lee, V. E., Brooks-Gunn, J., & Schnur, E. (1988). Does Head Start work? A 1-year follow-up of disadvantaged children attending Head Start, no preschool. *Developmental Psychology, 24,* 210–222.

Leeper, R. W., & Madison, P. (1959). *Toward understanding human personalities.* New York: Appleton-Century-Crofts.

Leerhsen, C. (1990, February 5). Unite and conquer: America's crazy for support groups. *Newsweek,* pp. 50–55.

Lefcourt, H. M., & Martin, R. A. (1986). *Humor and life stress: Antidote to adversity.* New York: Springer-Verlag.

Leitenberg, H., & Callahan, E. J. (1973). Reinforced practice and reduction of different kinds of fears in adults and children. *Behavior Research and Therapy, 11,* 19–30.

Leiter, M. P., & Maslach, C. (1988). The impact of interpersonal environment on burnout and organizational commitment. *Journal of Organizational Behavior, 9,* 297–308.

Leiter, M. P., & Maslach, C. (2000). *Preventing burnout and building engagement: A complete program for organizational renewal.* San Francisco, CA: Jossey-Bass.

Lempert, H., & Kinsbourne, M. (1982). Effect of laterality of orientation on verbal memory. *Neuropsychologia, 20,* 211–214.

Lencer, R., Malchow, C. P., Trillenberg-Krecker, K., Schwinger, E., & Arolt, V. (2000). Eye-tracking dysfunction (ETD) in families with

sporadic and familial schizophrenia. *Biological Psychiatry, 47,* 391–401.

Lennon, R. T. (1985). Group tests of intelligence. In B. B. Wolman (Ed.), *Handbook of intelligence* (pp. 825–847). New York: Wiley.

Leonard, J. (1998, May-June). Dream-catchers: Understanding the biological basis of things that go bump in the night. *Harvard Magazine, 100,* 58–68.

Lepper, M. R., Greene, D., & Nisbett, R. E. (1973). Undermining children's intrinsic interest with extrinsic reward: A test of the over-justification hypothesis. *Journal of Personality and Social Psychology, 28*(1), 129–137.

Lerner, R. M., Orlos, J. R., & Knapp, J. (1976). Physical attractiveness, physical effectiveness and self-concept in adolescents. *Adolescence, 11,* 313–326.

Leshner, A. I. (1997, October 3). Addiction is a brain disease, and it matters. *Science, 278,* 45–47.

Leslie, M. (2000, July/August). The vexing legacy of Lewis Terman. *Stanford, 28*(4), 44–51.

Lesperance, F., & Frasure-Smith, N. (1996, February 17). Negative emotions and coronary heart disease: Getting to the heart of the matter. *Lancet, 347,* 414–415.

Lettvin, J. Y., Maturana, H. R., McCulloch, W. S., & Pitts, W. H. (1959). What the frog's eye tells the frog's brain. *Proceedings of the Institute of Radio Engineers, 47,* 1940–1951.

Leutwyler, K. (1994, March). Prosthetic vision: Workers resume the quest for a seeing-eye device. *Scientific American, 270,* 108.

Leutwyler, K. (1995, June). Depression's double standard. *Scientific American, 272,* 23–24.

LeVay, S. (1991). A difference in hypothalamic structure between heterosexual and homosexual men. *Science, 253,* 1034–1037.

LeVay, S., & Hamer, D. (1995). Evidence for a biological influence in male homosexuality. *Scientific American, 270* (5), 44–49.

Levenson, R. W. (1992). Autonomic nervous system differences among emotions. *Psychological Science, 3,* 23–27.

Leventhal, H., & Tomarken, A. J. (1986). Emotion: Today's problems. *Annual Review of Psychology, 37,* 565–610.

Levine, J. A., Eberhardt, N. L., & Jensen, M. D. (1999, January 8). Role of nonexercise activity thermogenesis in resistance to fat gain in humans. *Science, 283,* 212–214.

Levine, L. J. (1997). Reconstructing memory for emotions. *Journal of Experimental Psychology: General, 126,* 165–177.

Levine, M., & Perkins, D. V. (1987). *Principles of community psychology: Perspectives and applications.* New York: Oxford University.

Lewine, R. R., Strauss, J. S., & Gift, T. E. (1981). Sex differences in age at first hospital admission for schizophrenia: Fact or artifact? *American Journal of Psychiatry, 138,* 440–444.

Lewinsohn, P. M., Clarke, G. N., Hops, H., & Andrews, J. A. (1990). Cognitive-behavioral treatment for depressed adolescents. *Behavior Therapy, 21,* 385–401.

Lewinsohn, P. M., & Gotlib, I. H. (1995). Behavioral theory and treatment of depression. In E. E. Beckham, & W. R. Leber (Eds.),

Handbook of depression (2nd ed.) (pp. 352–375). New York: Guilford Press.

Lewinsohn, P. M., Hoberman, H. M., & Clarke, G. N. (1989). The coping with depression course: Review and future directions. *Canadian Journal of Behavioural Science, 21,* 470–493.

Lewinsohn, P. M., & Rosenbaum, M. (1987). Recall of parental behavior by acute depressives, remitted depressives, and nondepressives. *Journal of Personality and Social Psychology, 52,* 611–619.

Lewinsohn, P. M., Sullivan, J. M., & Grosscup, S. J. (1980). Changing reinforcing events: An approach to the treatment of depression. *Psychotherapy: Theory, Research and Practice, 17,* 322–334.

Lewis, D. A., Cruz, D. A., Melchitzky, D. S., & Pierri, J. N. (2001). Lamina-specific deficits in parvalbumin-immunoreactive varicosities in the prefrontal cortex of subjects with schizophrenia: Evidence for fewer projections from the thalamus. *American Journal of Psychiatry, 158,* 1411–1422.

Lewy, A. J., Sack, R. L., Miller, S., & Hoban, T. M. (1987). Antidepressant and circadian phase-shifting effect of light. *Science, 235,* 352–354.

Liem, R., & Rayman, P. (1982). Health and social costs of unemployment: Research and policy considerations. *American Psychologist, 37,* 1116–1123.

Lilienfeld, S. O., Wood, J. M., & Garb, H. N. (2000a). The scientific status of projective techniques. *Psychological Science in the Public Interest, 1,* 27–66.

Lilienfeld, S. O., Wood, J. M., & Garb, H. N. (2000b). What's wrong with this picture? *Scientific American, 284*(5), 80–87.

Lillard, A. (1999). Developing a cultural theory of mind: The CIAO approach. *Current Directions in Psychological Science, 8,* 57–61.

Lillard, A. S. (1997). Other folks' theories of mind and behavior. *Psychological Science, 8,* 268–274.

Lindsay, D. S. (1990). Misleading suggestions can impair eyewitnesses' ability to remember event details. *Journal of Experimental Psychology: Learning, Memory, and Cognition, 16* (6), 1077–1083.

Lindsay, D. S. (1993). Eyewitness suggestibility. *Current Directions in Psychological Science, 2,* 86–89.

Lipsey, M. W., & Wilson, D. B. (1993). The efficacy of psychological, educational, and behavioral treatment: Confirmation from meta-analysis. *American Psychologist, 48,* 1181–1209.

Lipsitt, L. P., Reilly, B., Butcher, M. G., & Greenwood, M. M. (1976). The stability and interrelationships of newborn sucking and heart rate. *Developmental Psychobiology, 9,* 305–310.

Lloyd, P. (1993). Hedonistic long-range planning: The psychology of exercise. *The General Psychologist, 29,* 75–77.

Loehlin, J. C., Lindzey, G., & Spuhler, J. N. (1975). *Race differences in intelligence.* San Francisco: Freeman.

Loftus, E. F. (1979). *Eyewitness testimony.* Cambridge, MA: Harvard University Press.

Loftus, E. F. (1984). The eyewitness on trial. In B. D. Sales & A. Alwork (Eds.), *With liberty and justice for all.* Englewood Cliffs, NJ: Prentice Hall.

Loftus, E. F. (1992). When a lie becomes memory's truth: Memory distortion after exposure to misinformation. *Current Directions in Psychological Science, 1,* 121–123.

Loftus, E. F. (1993). The reality of repressed memories. *American Psychologist, 48,* 518–537.

Loftus, E. F. (1997a, September). Creating false memories. *Scientific American, 227,* 70–75.

Loftus, E. F. (1997b). Memory for a past that never was. *Current Directions in Psychological Science, 6,* 60–65.

Loftus, E. F., & Ketcham, K. (1991). *Witness for the defense: The accused, the eyewitness, and the expert who puts memory on trial.* New York: St. Martin's Press.

Loftus, E. F., & Ketcham, K. (1994). *The myth of repressed memory: False memories and allegations of sexual abuse.* New York: St. Martin's Griffin.

Loftus, E. F., & Klinger, M. R. (1992). Is the unconscious smart or dumb? *American Psychologist, 47,* 761–765.

Loftus, E. F., & Loftus, G. R. (1980). On the permanence of stored information in the human brain. *American Psychologist, 35,* 409–420.

Loftus, E. F., & Palmer, J. C. (1973). Reconstruction of automobile destruction: An example of the interaction between language and memory. *Journal of Verbal Learning and Verbal Behavior, 13,* 585–589.

Loftus, G. R., Duncan, J., & Gehrig, P. (1992). On the time course of perceptual information that results from a brief visual presentation. *Journal of Experimental Psychology: Human Perception and Performance, 18* (2), 530–549.

London, K. A., Mosher, W. D., Pratt, W. F., & Williams, L. B. (1989, March). Preliminary findings from the National Survey of Family Growth, Cycle IV. Paper presented at the annual meeting of the Population Association of America, Baltimore, MD.

Lonner, W. J. (1990). An overview of cross-cultural testing and assessment. In R. W. Brislin (Ed.), *Applied cross-cultural psychology.* Newbury Park, CA: Sage.

Loomis, A. L., Harvey, E. N., & Hobart, G. A. (1937). Cerebral states during sleep as studied by human brain potentials. *Journal of Experimental Psychology, 21,* 127–144.

LoPiccolo, J., & Stock, W. E. (1986). Treatment of sexual dysfunction. *Journal of Consulting and Clinical Psychology, 54,* 158–167.

Lott, A. J., & Lott, B. E. (1961). Group cohesiveness, communication level, and conformity. *Journal of Abnormal and Social Psychology, 62,* 408–412.

Lourenço, O., & Machado, A. (1996). In defense of Piaget's theory: A reply to 10 common criticisms. *Psychological Review, 103,* 143–164.

Lovaas, O. I. (1977). *The autistic child: Language development through behavior modification.* New York: Halstead Press.

Lovaas, O. I. (1993). The development of a treatment-research project for developmentally disabled and autistic children. *Journal of Applied Behavior Analysis, 26,* 617–630.

Lovaas, O. I., Schreibman, L., & Koegel, R. L. (1974). A behavior modification approach to the treatment of autistic children. *Journal of Autism and Childhood Schizophrenia, 4,* 111–129.

Lovibond, S. H., Adams, M., & Adams, W. G. (1979). The effects of three experimental prison environments on the behavior of non-conflict volunteer subjects. *Australian Psychologist, 14,* 273–285.

Luborsky, L., Singer, B., & Luborsky, L. (1975). Comparative studies of psychotherapies: Is it true that everyone has won and all must have prizes? *Archives of General Psychiatry, 32,* 995–1008.

Lui, W., McGuecken, E., Clements, M., DeMarco, C., Vichienchom, K., Hughes, C., Humayun, M., Weiland, J., Greenber, R., & de Juan, E. (2000). Multiple-unit artificial retina chipset system to benefit the visually impaired. *IEEE Transactions on Rehabilitation Engineering,* in press.

Lutz, C. (1988). *Unnatural emotions.* Chicago: University of Chicago Press.

Lykken, D., & Tellegen, A. (1996). Happiness is a stochastic phenomenon. *Psychological Science, 7,* 186–189.

Lynch, G., & Staubli, U. (1991). Possible contributions of long-term potentiation to the encoding and organization of memory. *Brain Research Reviews, 16,* 204–206.

Maas, J. B. (1999). *Power sleep: The revolutionary program that prepares your mind for peak performance.* New York: HarperPerennial.

Macaluso, E., Firth, C. D., & Driver, J. (2000, August 18). Modulation of human visual cortex by crossmodal spatial attention. *Science, 289,* 1206–1208.

Maccoby, E. (1998). *The two sexes: Growing up apart, coming together.* Cambridge, MA: Belknap Press.

Maccoby, E. (2000). *Gender differentiation in childhood: Broad patterns and their implications.* Address given at the American Psychological Association annual convention, Washington, DC.

Maccoby, N., Farquhar, J. W., Wood, P. D., & Alexander, J. K. (1977). Reducing the risk of cardiovascular disease: Effects of a community-based campaign on knowledge and behavior. *Journal of Community Health, 3,* 100–114.

MacCoun, R. J. (1998). Toward a psychology of harm reduction. *American Psychologist, 53,* 1199–1208.

MacLeod, C., & Campbell, L. (1992). Memory accessibility and probability judgments: An experimental evaluation of the availability heuristic. *Journal of Personality and Social Psychology, 63,* 890–902.

Macmillan, J. C. (2000). *An odd kind of fame: Stories of Phineas Gage.* Cambridge, MA: MIT Press.

Macrae, C. N., Milne, A. B., & Bodenhausen, G. V. (1994). Stereotypes as energy-saving devices: A peek inside the cognitive toolbox. *Journal of Personality and Social Psychology, 66,* 37–47.

Magee, W. J., Eaton, W. W., Wittchen, H.-U., McGonagle, K. A., Kessler, R. C. (1996). Agoraphobia, simple phobia, and social phobia in the national comorbidity survey. *Archives of General Psychiatry, 53,* 159–168.

Maher, B. A., & Maher, W. B. (1985). Psychopathology: II. From the eighteenth century to modern times. In G. A. Kimble & K. Schlesinger (Eds.), *Topics in the history of psychology* (Vol. 2) (pp. 295–329). Hillsdale, NJ: Erlbaum.

Maher, B. A., & Ross, J. S. (1984). Delusions. In H. E. Adams & P. B. Sutker (Eds.), *Comprehensive handbook of psychopathology* (pp. 383–987). New York: Plenum.

Maier, S. F., & Watkins, L. R. (2000). The immune system as a sensory system: Implications for psychology. *Current Directions in Psychological Science, 9,* 98–102.

Maier, S. F., Watkins, L. R., & Fleshner, M. (1994). Psychoneuroimmunology: The interface between behavior, brain, and immunity. *American Psychologist, 49,* 1004–1017.

Maisto, S. A., Galizio, M., & Connors, G. J. (1995). *Drug use and abuse* (2nd ed). Fort Worth, TX: Harcourt Brace.

Majewska, M. D., Harrison, N. L., Schwartz, R. D., Barker, J. L., & Paul, S. M. (1986). Steroid hormone metabolites are barbiturate-like modulators of the GABA receptor. *Science, 232,* 1004–1007.

Malatesta, V. J., Sutker, P. B., & Treiber, F. A. (1981). Sensation seeking and chronic public drunkenness. *Journal of Consulting and Clinical Psychology, 49,* 282–294.

Malinowski, B. (1927). *Sex and repression in savage society.* London: Humanities Press.

Malitz, S., & Sackheim, H. A. (1984). Low dosage ECT: Electrode placement and acute physiological and cognitive effects. *American Journal of Social Psychiatry, 4,* 47–53.

Manderscheid, R. W., Witkin, M. J., Rosenstein, M. J., Milazzo-Sayre, L. J., Bethel, H. E., & MacAskill, R. L. (1985). In C. A. Taube & S. A. Barrett (Eds.), *Mental Health, United States, 1985.* Washington, DC: National Institute of Mental Health.

Manfredi, M., Bini, G., Cruccu, G., Accornero, N., Beradelli, A., & Medolago, L. (1981). Congenital absence of pain. *Archives of Neurology, 38,* 507–511.

Mann, C. C. (1994, June 17). Behavioral genetics in transition. *Science, 264,* 1686–1689.

Manschreck, T. C. (1989). Delusional (paranoid) disorders. In H. I. Kaplan & B. J. Sadock (Eds.), *Comprehensive textbook of psychiatry* (pp. 816–829). Baltimore: Williams & Wilkins.

Manson, S. M. (1994). Culture and depression: Discovering variations in the experience of illness. In W. J. Lonner & R. Malpass (Eds.), *Psychology and culture* (pp. 285–290). Boston: Allyn and Bacon.

Marcus, G. B. (1986). Stability and change in political attitudes: Observe, recall, and "explain." *Political Behavior, 8,* 21–44.

Marcus, G. F. (1996). Why do children say "breaked"? *Current Directions in Psychological Science, 3,* 81–85.

Markman, H. J., & Notarius, C. I. (1993). *We can work it out.* Berkeley, CA: Berkeley Publishing Group.

Marks, I., & O'Sullivan, G. (1988). Drugs and psychological treatments for agoraphobia/panic and obsessive-compulsive disorders: A review. *British Journal of Psychiatry, 153,* 650–658.

Markus, H. R., & Kitayama, S. (1994). The cultural construction of self and emotion: Im-
plications for social behavior. In H. R. Markus & S. Kitayama (Eds.), *Emotion and culture: Empirical studies of mutual influence* (pp. 89–130). Washington, DC: American Psychological Association.

Marsh, P. (1988). Detecting insincerity. In Marsh, P. (Ed.), *Eye to eye: How people interact.* (Ch. 14, pp. 116–119). Oxford, England: Oxford Andromeda Ltd.

Marshall, E. (2000, August 4). Duke study faults overuse of stimulants for children. *Science, 289,* 721.

Marshall, G. D., & Zimbardo, P. G. (1979). Affective consequences of inadequately explained physiological arousal. *Journal of Personality and Social Psychology, 37,* 970–988.

Martin, A., Haxby, J. V., Lalonde, F. M., Wiggs, C. L., & Ungerleider, L. G. (1995). Discrete cortical regions associated with knowledge of color and knowledge of action. *Science, 270,* 102–105.

Martin, G., & Pear, J. (1999). *Behavior modification: What it is and how to do it* (6th ed.). Upper Saddle River, NJ: Prentice-Hall.

Martin, J. A. (1981). A longitudinal study of the consequences of early mother-infant interaction: A microanalytic approach. *Monographs of the Society for Research in Child Development, 46* (203, Serial No. 190).

Martin, R. A. (2001). Humor, laughter, and physical health: Methodological issues and research findings. *Psychological Bulletin, 127,* 504–519.

Martin, S. (1999, February). Drug use appears to be easing among teens. *APA Monitor,* 8.

Maruyama, G., & Miller, N. (1975). *Physical attractiveness and classroom acceptance* (Research Report 75–2). Los Angeles: University of Southern California, Social Science Research Institute.

Maslach, C. (1979). Negative emotional biasing of unexplained arousal. *Journal of Personality and Social Psychology, 37,* 953–969.

Maslach, C. (1982). *Burnout: The cost of caring.* Englewood Cliffs, NJ: Prentice-Hall.

Maslach, C. (1998, April). The truth about burnout. The G. Stanley Hall Lecture given at the Western Psychological Association convention in Albuquerque, NM.

Maslach, C., & Leiter, M. P. (1997). *The truth about burnout: How organizations cause personal stress and what to do about it.* San Francisco: Jossey-Bass Publishers.

Maslow, A. H. (1968). *Toward a psychology of being* (2nd ed.). New York: Van Nostrand.

Maslow, A. H. (1970). *Motivation and personality* (Rev. ed.). New York: Harper & Row.

Maslow, A. H. (1971). *Farther reaches of human nature.* New York: Viking Penguin.

Masters, W. H., & Johnson, V. E. (1966). *Human sexual response.* Boston: Little, Brown.

Masters, W. H., & Johnson, V. E. (1970). *Human sexual inadequacy.* Boston: Little, Brown.

Masters, W. H., & Johnson, V. E. (1979). *Homosexuality in perspective.* Boston: Little, Brown.

Matarazzo, J. D. (1980). Behavioral health and behavioral medicine: Frontiers for a new health psychology. *American Psychologist, 35,* 807–817.

Matossian, M. K. (1982). Ergot and the Salem witchcraft affair. *American Scientist, 70,* 355–357.
Matossian, M. K. (1989). *Poisons of the past: Molds, epidemics, and history.* New Haven: Yale University Press.

Matsumoto, D. (1994). *People: Psychology from a cultural perspective.* Pacific Grove, CA: Brooks/Cole.

Matsumoto, D. (1996). *Culture and psychology.* Pacific Grove, CA: Brooks/Cole.

Matthews, K. A. (1982). Psychological perspectives on the Type-A behavior pattern. *Psychological Bulletin, 91,* 293–323.

Maunsell, J. H. R. (1995, November 3). The brain's visual world: Representation of visual targets in cerebral cortex. *Science, 270,* 764–769.

Mauron, A. (2001, February 2). Is the genome the secular equivalent of the soul? *Science, 291,* 831–833.

Mayer, D. J. (1979). Endogenous analgesia systems: Neural and behavioral mechanisms. In Bonica, J. J. (Ed.), *Advances in pain research and therapy* (Vol. 3). New York: Raven Press.

Mayer, J. D. (1999, September). Emotional intelligence: Popular or scientific psychology? *American Psychological Association Monitor,* 50.

Mayer, J. D., & Salovey, P. (1997). What is emotional intelligence? In P. Salovey & D. J. Sluyter (Eds.), *Emotional development and emotional intelligence: Educational implications.* New York: Basic Books.

Mayer, R. E. (1983). *Thinking, problem solving, and cognition.* San Francisco: W. H. Freeman.

Mayr, E. (2000, July). Darwin's influence on modern thought. *Scientific American,* pp. 79–83.

McAdams, D. P. (1992). The five-factor model in personality: A critical appraisal. *Journal of Personality, 60,* 239–361.

McAdams, D. P., de St. Aubin, E., & Logan, R. L. (1993). Generativity among young, midlife, and older adults. *Psychology and Aging, 8,* 221–230.

McCann, I. L., & Holmes, D. S. (1984). Influence of aerobic exercise on depression. *Journal of Personality and Social Psychology, 46,* 1142–1147.

McCarley, N., & Carskadon, T. G. (1983). Test-retest reliabilities of scales and subscales of the Myers-Briggs Type Indicator and of criteria for clinical interpretive hypotheses involving them. *Research in Psychological Type, 6,* 24–36.

McCarthy, K. (1991, August). Moods—good and bad—color all aspects of life. *APA Monitor,* 13.

McClearn, G. E., Johansson, B., Berg, S., Pedersen, N. L., Ahern, F., Petrill, S. A., & Plomin, R. (1997, June 6). Substantial genetic influence on cognitive abilities in twins 80 or more years old. *Science, 276,* 1560–1563.

McClelland, D. C. (1965). Achievement and entrepreneurship: A longitudinal study. *Journal of Personality and Social Psychology, 1,* 389–392.

McClelland, D. C. (1975). *Power: The inner experience.* New York: Irvington.

McClelland, D. C. (1985). *Human motivation.* New York: Scott Foresman.

McClelland, D. C. (1987a). Characteristics of

successful entrepreneurs. *The Journal of Creative Behavior, 21,* 219–233.

McClelland, D. C. (1987b). *Human motivation.* New York: Cambridge University Press.

McClelland, D. C. (1993). Intelligence is not the best predictor of job performance. *Current Directions in Psychological Science, 2,* 5–6.

McClelland, D. C., & Boyatzis, R. E. (1982). Leadership motive pattern and long-term success in management. *Journal of Applied Psychology, 67,* 737–743.

McCrae, R. R., & Costa, P. T., Jr. (1997). Personality trait structure as a human universal. *American Psychologist, 52,* 509–516.

McDonald, K. A. (1998, August 14). Scientists consider new explanations for the impact of exercise on mood. *The Chronicle of Higher Education,* p. A15–A16.

McGaugh, J. L. (2000, January 14). Memory—a century of consolidation. *Science, 287,* 248–251.

McGuire, P. A. (2000, February). New hope for people with schizophrenia. *Monitor on Psychology, 31*(2), 24–28.

McKeachie, W. J. (1990). Research on college teaching: The historical background. *Journal of Educational Psychology, 82,* 189–200.

McKeachie, W. J. (1997). Good teaching makes a difference—and we know what it is. In R. B. Perry & J. C. Smart (Eds.), *Effective teaching in higher education: Research and practice* (pp. 396–408). New York: Agathon Press.

McKeachie, W. J. (1999). *McKeachie's teaching tips: Strategies, research, and theory for college and university teachers* (10th ed.). Boston: Houghton Mifflin.

McNally, R. J. (1994, August). Cognitive bias in panic disorder. *Current Directions in Psychological Science, 3,* 129–132.

Meador, B. D., & Rogers, C. R. (1979). Person-centered therapy. In R. J. Corsini (Ed.), *Current psychotherapies* (2nd ed., pp. 131–184). Itasca, IL: Peacock.

Medin, D. L. (1989). Concepts and conceptual structure. *American Psychologist, 44,* 1469–1481.

Medin, D. L., & Ross, B. H. (1992). *Cognitive psychology.* Fort Worth, TX: Harcourt Brace Jovanovich.

Meier, R. P. (1991). Language acquisition by deaf children. *American Scientist, 79,* 60–70.

Mellinger, G. D., Balter, M. B., & Uhlenhuth, E. H. (1985). Insomnia and its treatment: Prevalence and correlates. *Archives of General Psychiatry, 42,* 225–232.

Meltzoff, A. N. (1998). *The nature of the preverbal mind: Towards a developmental cognitive science.* Paper presented at the Western Psychological Association/Rocky Mountain Psychological Association joint convention, Albuquerque, NM.

Meltzoff, A. N., & Moore, M. K. (1977). Imitation of facial and manual gestures by human neonates. *Science, 198,* 75–78.

Meltzoff, A. N., & Moore, M. K. (1983). Newborn infants imitate adult facial gestures. *Child Development, 54,* 702–709.

Meltzoff, A. N., & Moore, M. K. (1985). Cognitive foundations and social functions of imitation and intermodal representation in infancy. In J. Mehler & R. Fox (Eds.), *Neonate cognition: Beyond the blooming buzzing confusion* (pp. 139–156). Hillsdale, NJ: Erlbaum.

Meltzoff, A. N., & Moore, M. K. (1989). Imitation in newborn infants: Exploring the range of gestures imitated and the underlying mechanisms. *Developmental Psychology, 25,* 954–962.

Meltzoff, J., & Kornreich, M. (1970). *Research in psychotherapy.* New York: Atherton.

Melzack, R. (1990, February). The tragedy of needless pain. *Scientific American, 262,* 27–33.

Menzel, E. M. (1978). Cognitive mapping in chimpanzees. In S. H. Hulse, H. Fowler, & W. K. Honzig (Eds.), *Cognitive processes in animal behavior* (pp. 375–422). Hillsdale, NJ: Erlbaum.

Meredith, N. (1986, June). Testing the talking cure. *Science 86, 7,* 30–37.

Merikle, P. M., & Reingold, E. M. (1990). Recognition and lexical decision without detection: Unconscious perception? *Journal of Experimental Psychology: Human Perception & Performance, 16,* 574–583.

Mervis, C. B., & Rosch, E. (1981). Categorization of natural objects. *Annual Review of Psychology, 32,* 89–115.

Mesulam, M. M. (1990). Schizophrenia and the brain. *New England Journal of Medicine, 322,* 842–845

Meyer-Bahlburg, H. F. L. (1977). Sex hormones and female homosexuality: A critical examination. *Archives of Sexual Behavior, 8,* 297–326.

Meyer-Bahlburg, H. F. L. (1979). Sex hormones and female homosexuality: A critical examination. *Archives of Sexual Behavior, 8,* 101–120.

Michael, R. T., Gagnon, J. H., Laumann, E. O., & Kolata, G. (1994). *Sex in America: A definitive survey.* New York: Little, Brown.

Milgram, S. (1965). Some conditions of obedience and disobedience to authority. *Human Relations, 18,* 56–76.

Milgram, S. (1974). *Obedience to authority.* New York: Harper & Row.

Miller, A. G. (1986). *The obedience paradigm: A case study in controversy in social science.* New York: Praeger.

Miller, G. A. (1956). The magic number seven plus or minus two: Some limits in our capacity for processing information. *Psychological Review, 63,* 81–97.

Miller, J. (1984). Culture and the development of everyday social explanation. *Journal of Personality and Social Psychology, 46,* 961–978.

Miller, M. E., & Bowers, K. S. (1993). Hypnotic analgesia: Dissociated experience of dissociated control? *Journal of Abnormal Psychology, 102,* 29–38.

Miller, M. W. (1993, December 2). Dark days: The staggering cost of depression. *The Wall Street Journal,* p. B1.

Miller, N. E. (1983). Behavioral medicine: Symbiosis between laboratory and clinic. *Annual Review of Psychology, 34,* 1–31.

Miller, N. E. (1995). Clinical–experimental interactions in the development of neuroscience: A primer for nonspecialists and lessons for young students. *American Psychologist, 50,* 901–911.

Miller, N. E., & Brucker, B. S. (1979). A learned visceral response apparently independent of skeletal ones in patients paralyzed by spinal lesions. In N. Birbaumer & H. D. Kimmel (Eds.), *Biofeedback and self-regulation.* Hillsdale, NJ: Erlbaum.

Miller, P. Y., & Simon, W. (1980). The development of sexuality in adolescence. In J. Adelson (Ed.), *Handbook of adolescent psychology.* New York: Wiley.

Miller, W. R., & Brown, S. A. (1997). Why psychologists should treat alcohol and drug problems. *American Psychologist, 52,* 1269–1279.

Miller-Jones, D. (1989). Culture and testing. *American Psychologist, 44,* 360–366.

Milner, B., Corkin, S., & Teuber, H. H. (1968) Further analysis of the hippocampal amnesic syndrome: 14-year follow-up study of H. M. *Neuropsychologia, 6,* 215–234.

Mineka, S., Davidson, M., Cook, M., & Keir, R. (1984). Observational conditioning of snake fear in rhesus monkeys. *Journal of Abnormal Psychology, 93,* 355–372.

Mintz, L. B., & Betz, N. E. (1986). Sex differences in the nature, realism, and correlates of body image. *Sex Roles, 15,* 185–195.

Mischel, W. (1968). *Personality and assessment.* New York: Wiley.

Mischel, W. (1973). Toward a cognitive social learning conceptualization of personality. *Psychological Review, 80,* 252–283.

Mischel, W. (1990). Personality dispositions revisited and revised: A view after three decades. In L. A. Pervin (Ed.), *Handbook of personality: Theory and research.* New York: Guilford Press.

Mischel, W. (1993). *Introduction to personality* (5th ed.). Fort Worth, TX: Harcourt Brace Jovanovich College Publishers.

Mischel, W., & Shoda, Y. (1995). A cognitive-affective system theory of personality: Reconceptualizing situations, dispositions, dynamics, and invariance in personality structure. *Psychological Review, 102,* 246–268.

Mizukami, K., Kobayashi, N., Ishii, T., and Iwata, H. (1990). First selective attachment begins in early infancy: A study using telethermography. *Infant Behavior and Development, 13,* 257–271.

Moar, I. (1980). The nature and acquisition of cognitive maps. In D. Cantor & T. Lee (Eds.), *Proceedings of the international conference on environmental psychology.* London: Architectural Press.

Moghaddam, F. M., Taylor, D. M., & Wright, S. C. (1993). *Social psychology in cross-cultural perspective.* New York: W. H. Freeman.

Mogilner, A., Grossman, J. A. I., & Ribary, W. (1993). Somatosensory cortical plasticity in adult humans revealed by magnetoencephalography. *Proceedings of the National Academy of Sciences, 90*(8), 3593–3597.

Mombaerts, P. (1999, October 22). Seven-transmembrane proteins as odorant and chemosensory receptors. *Science, 286,* 707–711.

Monaghan, P. (1999, February 26). Lessons from the "marriage lab." *The Chronicle of Higher Education,* p. A9.

Moncrieff, R. W. (1951). *The chemical senses.* London: Leonard Hill.

Money, J. (1987). Sin, sickness, or status? Homosexual gender identity and psychoneuroendocrinology. *American Psychologist, 42,* 384–399.

Monte, C. F. (1980). *Beneath the mask: An introduction to theories of personality* (2nd ed.). New York: Holt, Rinehart and Winston.

Moore, J. S., Graziano, W. G., & Millar, M. G. (1987). Physical attractiveness, sex role orientation, and the evaluation of adults and children. *Personality and Social Psychology Bulletin, 13,* 95–102.

Moore-Ede, M. (1993). *The twenty-four-hour society: Understanding human limits in a world that never stops.* Reading, MA: Addison-Wesley.

Morgan, A. H., Hilgard, E. R., & Davert, E. C. (1970). The heritability of hypnotic susceptibility of twins: A preliminary report. *Behavior Genetics, 1,* 213–224.

Mori, K., Nagao, H., & Yoshihara, Y. (1999). The olfactory bulb: Coding and processing of odor molecule information. *Science, 286,* 711–715.

Moriarity, T. (1975). Crime, commitment and the responsive bystander: Two field experiments. *Journal of Personality and Social Psychology, 31,* 370–376.

Morrell, E. M. (1986). Meditation and somatic arousal. *American Psychologist, 41*(6), 712–713.

Morris, D. (1967). *The naked ape.* New York: McGraw-Hill.

Morris, M. W., & Peng, K. (1994). Culture and cause: American and Chinese attributions for social and physical events. *Journal of Personality & Social Psychology, 8,* 949–971.

Morris, W. N., & Miller, R. S. (1975). The effects of consensus-breaking and consensus-preempting partners on reduction of conformity. *Journal of Experimental Social Psychology, 11,* 215–223.

Morrison-Bogorad, M., & Phelps, C. (1997, March 12). Alzheimer disease research comes of age. *JAMA: Journal of the American Medical Association, 277,* 837–840.

Moskovitz, B. A. (1978, November). The acquisition of language. *Scientific American,* p. 94D.

Moskowitz, H. (1985). Marihuana and driving. *Accident Analysis & Prevention, 17,* 323–345.

Moss, R. (1996). *Conscious dreaming: A spiritual path to everyday life.* New York: Crown Publishing.

Mowrer, O. (1960). *Learning theory and symbolic processes.* New York: Wiley.

Mukerjee, M. (1995, October). Hidden scars: Sexual and other abuse may alter a brain region. *Scientific American, 273*(4), 14, 20.

Munakata, Y., McClelland, J. L., Johnson, M. H., & Siegler, R. S. (1997). Rethinking infant knowledge: Toward an adaptive process account of successes and failures in object permanence tasks. *Psychological Review, 104,* 686–713.

Munroe, R. L. (1955). *Schools of psychoanalytic thought.* New York: Dryden.

Murphy, G., & Murphy, L. B. (Eds.). (1968). *Asian psychology.* New York: Basic Books.

Murphy, J. M. (1976, March 12). Psychiatric labeling in cross-cultural perspective. *Science, 191,* 1019–1028.

Murray, B. (1995, October). Americans dream about food, Brazilians dream about sex. *APA Monitor,* p. 30.

Murray, B. (1997, September). Why aren't antidrug programs working? *APA Monitor,* 30.

Murray, D. J., Kilgour, A. R., & Wasylkiw, L. (2000). Conflicts and missed signals in psychoanalysis, behaviorism, and Gestalt psychology. *American Psychologist, 55,* 422–426.

Murray, J. P., & Kippax, S. (1979). Children's social behavior in three towns with differing television experience. *Journal of Communication, 28,* 19–29.

Musun-Miller, L. (1993). Sibling status effects: Parents' perceptions of their own children. *The Journal of Genetic Psychology, 154,* 189–198.

Myers, D. G. (2000). The funds, friends, and faith of happy people. *American Psychologist, 55,* 56–67.

Myers, D. G., & Diener, E. (1995). Who is happy? *Psychological Science, 6,* 10–19.

Myers, I. B. (1962). *The Myers-Briggs type indicator.* Palo Alto, CA: Consulting Psychologists Press.

Myers, I. B. (1976). *Introduction to type* (2nd ed.). Gainesville, FL: Center for Applications of Psychological Type.

Myers, I. B. (1987). *Introduction to type: A description of the theory and applications of the Myers-Briggs Type Indicator.* Palo Alto, CA: Consulting Psychologists Press.

Myers, I. B., & Myers, P. B. (1995). *Gifts differing: Understanding personality type.* Palo Alto, CA: Consulting Psychologists Press.

Myers, R. S., & Roth, D. L. (1997). Perceived benefits of and barriers to exercise and stage of exercise adoption in young adults. *Health Psychology, 16,* 277–283.

Nahemow, L., & Lawton, M. P. (1975). Similarity and propinquity in friendship formation. *Journal of Personality and Social Psychology, 32,* 205–213.

Naigles, L. (1990). Children use syntax to learn verb meanings. *Child language, 17,* 357–374.

Naigles, L. G., & Kako, E. T. (1993). First contact in verb acquisition: Defining a role for syntax. *Child Development, 64,* 1665–1687.

Napier, A. Y. (2000). Making a marriage. In W. C. Nichols, M. A. Pace-Nichols, D. S. Becvar, & A. Y. Napier (Eds.), *Handbook of family development and intervention* (pp. 145–170). New York: Wiley.

Nathan, P. E. (1998). Practice guidelines: Not yet ideal. *American Psychologist, 53,* 290–299.

National Press Club. (1999, Summer). Seligman on positive psychology: A session at the National Press Club. *The General Psychologist, 34*(2), 37–45.

National Public Radio. (1995a, June 25). The Stockholm syndrome: Empathy with captors discussed. *Weekend Edition.* Washington, DC: National Public Radio.

National Public Radio. (1995b, August 30). Americans are generally shy, and getting shyer. *Morning Edition.* Washington, DC: National Public Radio.

Nauta, W. J. H., & Feirtag, M. (1979). The organization of the brain. *Scientific American, 241* (9), 88–111.

Needleman, H., Schell, A., Belinger, D., Leviton, A., & Allred, E. (1990). The long-term effects of exposure to low doses of lead in childhood: An 11-year follow-up report. *New England Journal of Medicine, 322,* 83–88.

Neisser, U. (1967). *Cognitive psychology.* New York: Appleton-Century-Crofts.

Neisser, U. (1991). A case of misplaced nostalgia. *American Psychologist, 46,* 34–36.

Neisser, U., Boodoo, B., Bouchard, T. J., Jr., Boyukin, A. W., Brody, N., Ceci, S. J., Halpern, D. F., Loehlin, J. C., Perloff, R., Sternberg, R. J., & Urbina, S. (1996). Intelligence: Knowns and unknowns. *American Psychologist, 51,* 77–101.

Nelson, C. A. (1987). The recognition of facial expressions in the first two years of life: Mechanisms of development. *Child Development, 58,* 889–909.

Nelson, T. D. (1993). The hierarchical organization of behavior: A useful feedback model of self-regulation. *Current Directions in Psychological Science, 2,* 121–126.

Nemacek, S. (1999, January). Unequal health. *Scientific American, 280*(1), 40–41.

Nemeroff, C. B. (1998, June). The neurobiology of depression. *Scientific American, 278,* 42–49.

Nesse, R. M., & Berridge, K. C. (1997, October 3). Psychoactive drug use in evolutionary perspective. *Science, 278,* 63–66.

Nestler, E. J. (2001, June 22). Total recall—the memory of addiction. *Science, 292,* 2266–2267.

Netting, J., & Wang, L. (2001, February 17). The newly sequenced genome bares all. *Science News, 159,* 100–101.

Neuringer, A., Kornell, N., & Olufs, M. Stability and variability in extinction. *Journal of Experimental Psychology: Animal Behavior Processes, 27,* 79–94.

Newcomb, T. M. (1943). *Personality and social change.* New York: Holt.

Newcomb, T. M., Koenig, D. E., Flacks, R., & Warwick, D. P. (1967). *Persistence and change: Bennington College and its students after twenty-five years.* New York: Wiley.

Newman, B. S., & Muzzonigro, P. G. (1993). The effects of traditional family values on the coming out process of gay male adolescents. *Adolescence, 28,* 213–226.

Nicholls, J. G. (1972). Creativity in the person who will never produce anything original and useful: The concept of creativity as a normally distributed trait. *American Psychologist, 27,* 717–727.

Nickerson, R. S. (1998). Confirmation bias: A ubiquitous phenomenon in many guises. *Review of General Psychology, 2,* 175–220.

Nickerson, R. S., & Adams, M. J. (1979). Long-term memory for a common object. *Cognitive Psychology, 11,* 287–307.

Nicol, S. E., & Gottesman, I. I. (1983). Clues to the genetics and neurobiology of schizophrenia. *American Scientist, 71,* 398–404.

Nisbett, R. E. (1972). Hunger, obesity, and the ventromedial hypothalamus. *Psychological Review, 79,* 433–453.

Nisbett, R. E. (1993). Violence and U.S. regional culture. *American Psychologist, 48,* 441–449.

Nisbett, R. E. (2000). *Culture and systems of thought: Holistic versus analytic cognition in East and West.* Master Lecture presented at the annual convention of the American Psychological Association, Washington, DC.

Nisbett, R. E., Peng, K., Choi, I., & Norenzayan, A. (2001). Culture and systems of thought:

Holistic versus analytic cognition. *Psychological Review, 108,* 291–310.

Nobles, W. W. (1976). Black people in white insanity: An issue for black community mental health. *Journal of Afro-American Issues, 4,* 21–27.

Nolen-Hoeksema, S. (1987). Sex differences in unipolar depression: Evidence and theory. *Psychological Bulletin, 101,* 259–282.

Nolen-Hoeksema, S. (1990). *Sex differences in depression.* Stanford, CA: Stanford University Press.

Norenzayan, A., & Nisbett, R. E. (2000). Culture and causal cognition. *Current Directions in Psychological Science, 9,* 132–135.

Norman, D. A., & Rumelhart, D. E. (1975). *Explorations in cognition.* San Francisco: Freeman.

Notarius, C. I. (1996). Marriage: Will I be happy or sad? In N. Vanzetti and S. Duck's *A lifetime of relationships.* Pacific Grove, CA: Brooks/Cole Publishing Company.

Notarius, C., & Markman, H. (1993). *We can work it out: Making sense of marital conflict.* New York: G. P. Putnam's Sons.

Novak, M. A., & Suomi, S. J. (1988). Psychological well-being of primates in captivity. *American Psychologist, 43,* 765–773.

Nungesser, L. G. (1990). *Axioms for survivors: How to live until you say goodbye.* Santa Monica, CA: IBS Press.

Nurmi, J.E. (1991). How do adolescents see their future? A review of the development of future orientation and planning. *Developmental Review, 11,* 1–59.

Nyman, L. (1995). The identification of birth order personality attributes. *The Journal of Psychology, 129,* 51–59.

Oakland, T., & Glutting, J. J. (1990). Examiner observations of children's WISC-R test-related behaviors: Possible socioeconomic status, race, and gender effects. *Psychological Assessment, 2,* 86–90.

Oatley, K., & Duncan, E. (1994). The experience of emotions in everyday life. *Cognition and Emotion, 8,* 369–381.

Oden, G. C. (1968). The fulfillment of promise: 40-year follow-up of the Terman gifted group. *Genetic Psychology Monographs, 77,* 3–93.

Oden, G. C. (1987). Concept, knowledge, and thought. *Annual Review of Psychology, 38,* 203–227.

Offer, D., Ostrov, E., & Howard, K. I. (1981). *The adolescent: A psychological self-portrait.* New York: Basic Books.

Offer, D., Ostrov, E., Howard, K. I., & Atkinson, R. (1988). *The teenage world: Adolescents' self-image in ten countries.* New York: Plenum Medical.

Ofshe, R., & Watters, E. (1994). *Making monsters: False memories, psychotherapy, and sexual hysteria.* New York: Charles Scribner's Sons.

Ohlsson, S. (1996). Learning from performance errors. *Psychological Review, 103,* 241–262.

O'Leary, K. D. (Ed.). (1987). *Assessment of marital discord: An integration for research and clinical practice.* Hillsdale, NJ: Erlbaum.

Olton, D. S. (1979). Mazes, maxes, and memory. *American Psychologist, 34,* 583–596.

Olton, D. S. (1992). Tolman's cognitive analyses: Predecessors of current approaches in psychology. *Journal of Experimental Psychology: General, 121,* 427–428.

Oren, D. A., & Terman, M. (1998, January 16). Tweaking the human circadian clock with light. *Science, 279,* 333–334.

Orne, M. T. (1980). Hypnotic control of pain: Toward a clarification of the different psychological processes involved. In J. J. Bonica (Ed.), *Pain* (pp. 155–172). New York: Raven Press.

Ornstein, R., & Sobel, D. (1989). *Healthy pleasures.* Reading, MA: Addison-Wesley.

Ornstein, R. E. (1986a). *Multimind: A new way of looking at human behavior.* Boston: Houghton Mifflin.

Ornstein, R. E. (1986b). *The psychology of consciousness* (Rev. ed.). New York: Penguin Books.

Osborn, A. (1953). *Applied imagination* (Rev. ed.). New York: Charles Scribner's Sons.

Osterhout, L., & Holcomb, P. J. (1992). Event-related brain potentials elicited by syntactic anomaly. *Journal of Memory and Language, 31,* 785–806.

Overmier, J., & Seligman, M. (1967). Effects of inescapable shock upon subsequent escape and avoidance learning. *Journal of Comparative and Physiological Psychology, 63,* 23–33.

Packard, R. G. (1970). The control of "classroom attention": A group contingency for complex behavior. *Journal of Applied Behavior Analysis, 3,* 13–28.

Page, T. L. (1994). Time is the essence: Molecular analysis of the biological clock. *Science, 263,* 1570–1572.

Paikoff, R. L., & Brooks-Gunn, J. (1991). Do parent–child relationships change during puberty? *Psychological Bulletin, 110,* 47–66.

Paivio, A. (1983). The empirical case for dual coding. In J. C. Yuille (Ed.), *Imagery, memory and cognition* (pp. 307–332). Hillsdale, NJ: Erlbaum.

Paivio, A. (1986). *Mental representations: A dual coding approach.* New York: Oxford University Press.

Pandey, J., Sinha, Y., Prakash, A., & Tripathi, R. C. (1982). Right-left political ideologies and attribution of the causes of poverty. *European Journal of Social Psychology, 12,* 327–331.

Papolos, D. F., & Papolos, J. (1987). *Overcoming depression.* New York: Harper & Row.

Paran, E., Amir, M., & Yaniv, N. (1996). Evaluating the response of mild hypertensives to biofeedback-assisted relaxation using a mental stress test. *Journal of Behavior Therapy and Experimental Psychiatry, 27,* 157–167.

Parr, W. V., and Siegert, R. (1993). Adults' conceptions of everyday memory failures in others: Factors that mediate the effects of target age. *Psychology and Aging, 8,* 599–605.

Patrick, C. J., & Iacono, W. G. (1991). Validity of the control question polygraph test: The problem of sampling bias. *Journal of Applied Psychology, 76,* 229–238.

Patterson, J. M. (1985). Critical factors affecting family compliance with home treatment for children with cystic fibrosis. *Family Relations, 34,* 74–89.

Pattie, F. A. (1994). *Mesmer and animal magnetism: A chapter in the history of medicine.* New York: Edmonston.

Patzer, G. L. (1985). *The physical attractiveness phenomena.* New York: Plenum Press.

Paunonen, S. P., Jackson, D. N., Trzebinski, J., & Fosterling, F. (1992). Personality structure across cultures: A multimethod evaluation. *Journal of Personality and Social Psychology, 62,* 447–456.

Pavlov, I. P. (1928). *Lectures on conditioned reflexes: Twenty-five years of objective study of higher nervous activity (behavior of animals)* (Vol. 1, W. H. Gantt, Trans.). New York: International Publishers.

Pavot, W., Diener, E., & Fujita, F. (1990). Extraversion and happiness. *Personality and Individual Differences, 1,* 1299–1306.

Pawlik, K., & d'Ydewalle, G. (1996). Psychology and the global commons: Perspectives of international psychology. *American Psychologist, 51,* 488–495.

Payne, D. G., Neuschatz, J. S., Lampinen, J. M., & Lynn, S. J. (1997). Compelling memory illusions: The qualitative characteristics of false memories. *Current Directions in Psychological Science, 6,* 56–60.

Pearman, R. R. (1991, November 13). Disputing a report on "Myers-Briggs" test. *Chronicle of Higher Education,* p. B7.

Pedersen, P. (1979). Non-Western psychology: The search for alternatives. In A. J. Marsella, R. G. Tharp, & T. J. Ciborowski (Eds.), *Perspectives on cross-cultural psychology* (pp. 77–98). New York: Academic Press.

Penfield, W. (1959). The interpretive cortex. *Science, 129,* 1719–1725.

Penfield, W., & Baldwin, M. (1952). Temporal lobe seizures and the technique of subtotal lobectomy. *Annals of Surgery, 136,* 625–634.

Peng, K., & Nisbett, R. E. (1999). Culture, dialectics, and reasoning about contradiction. *American Psychologist, 54,* 741–754.

Pennebaker, J. W. (1990). *Opening up: The healing power of confiding in others.* New York: William Morrow.

Pennebaker, J. W., Barger, S. D., & Tiebout, J. (1989). Disclosure of traumas and health among Holocaust survivors. *Psychosomatic Medicine, 51,* 577–589.

Pennebaker, J. W., & Harber, K. D. (1991, April). *Coping after the Loma Prieta earthquake: A preliminary report.* Paper presented at the Western Psychological Association Convention, San Francisco, CA.

Pennisi, E. (2001, February 16). The human genome. *Science, 291,* 1177–1180.

Peplau, L. A., Garnets, L. D., Spalding, L. R., Conley, T. D., & Veniegas, R. C. (1998). Critique of Bem's "Exotic becomes erotic" theory of sexual orientation. *Psychological Review, 105,* 387–394.

Peretz, L. (1993). *The enchanted world of sleep.* (Trans. by Anthony Berris). New Haven, CT: Yale University Press.

Perkins, D. F., & Lerner, R. M. (1995). Single and multiple indicators of physical attractiveness and psychosocial behaviors among young adolescents. *Journal of Early Adolescence, 15,* 268–297.

Perry, W. G., Jr. (1970). *Forms of intellectual and ethical development in the college years: A scheme.* New York: Holt, Rinehart and Winston.

Perry, W. J., Jr. (1994). Forms of intellectual and ethical development in the college years:

A scheme. In Puka, B. (Ed.), *Defining perspectives in moral development: Vol. 1. Moral development: A compendium* (pp. 231–248). New York: Garland Publishing.

Pert, C. (1997). *Molecules of emotion.* New York: Scribner.

Pervin, L. A. (1985). Personality: Current controversies, issues, and directions. *Annual Review of Psychology, 36,* 83–114.

Peterson, C. (2000). The future of optimism. *American Psychologist, 55,* 44–55.

Peterson, C., Seligman, M. E. P., & Valliant, G. E. (1988). Pessimistic explanatory style is a risk factor for physical illness: A thirty-five year longitudinal study. *Journal of Personality and Social Psychology, 55,* 23–27.

Petrill, S. A., Plomin, R., Berg, S., Johansson, B., Pedersen, N. L., Ahern, F., & McClearn, G. E. (1998). Specific cognitive abilities in twins age 80 and older. *Psychological Science, 9,* 183–195.

Phelps, J. A., Davis, J. O., & Schartz, K. M. (1997). Nature, nurture, and twin research strategies. *Current Directions in Psychological Science, 6,* 117–121.

Physician's desk reference (55th ed.). (2001). Montvale, NJ: Medical Economics Company.

Pifer, A., & Bronte L. (Eds.). (1986). *Our aging society: Paradox and promise.* New York: Norton.

Pilisuk, M., & Parks, S. H. (1986). *The healing web: Social networks and human survival.* Hanover, NH: University Press of New England.

Pillard, R., & Bailey, M. (1991). A genetic study of male sexual orientation. *Archives of General Psychiatry, 48,* 1089–1096.

Pillemer, D. B. (1984). Flashbulb memories of the assassination attempt on President Reagan. *Cognition, 16,* 63–80.

Pinel, J. P. J. (2000). *Biopsychology* (4th ed.). Boston: Allyn & Bacon.

Piotrowski, C., Keller, J. W., & Ogawa, T. (1993). Projective techniques: An international perspective. *Psychological Reports, 72,* 179–182.

Piotrowski, C., Sherry, D., & Keller, J. W. (1985). Psychodiagnostic test usage: A survey of the Society for Personality Assessment. *Journal of Personality Assessment, 49,* 115–119.

Piper, A., Jr. (1998, May/June). Multiple personality disorder: Witchcraft survives in the twentieth century. *Skeptical Inquirer, 22*(3), 44–50.

Pittenger, D. J. (1993). The utility of the Myers-Briggs Type Indicator. *Review of Educational Research, 63,* 467–488.

Plomin, R. (1989). Environment and genes: Determinants of behavior. *American Psychologist, 44,* 105–111.

Plomin, R. (1997, August). Current directions in behavioral genetics: Moving into the mainstream. *Current Directions in Psychological Science, 6,* 85.

Plomin, R. (2000, September). Psychology in a post-genomics world: It will be more important than ever. *American Psychological Society Observer, 3,* 27.

Plomin, R., & DeFries, J. C. (1998). The genetics of cognitive abilities and disabilities. *Scientific American, 278*(5), 62–69.

Plomin, R., & McClearn, G. E. (Eds.). (1993). *Na-*

ture, nurture, and psychology. Washington, DC: American Psychological Association.

Plomin, R., Owen, M. J., & McGuffin, P. (1994). The genetic basis of complex human behaviors. *Science, 264,* 1733–1739.

Plomin, R., & Rende, R. (1991). Human behavioral genetics. *Annual Review of Psychology, 42,* 161–190.

Plutchik, R. (1980). *Emotion: A psychoevolutionary synthesis.* New York: Harper & Row.

Plutchik, R. (1984). Emotions: A general psychoevolutionary theory. In K. Scherer & P. Ekman (Eds.), *Approaches to emotion.* Hillsdale, NJ: Erlbaum.

Polefrone, J. M., & Manuck, S. B. (1987). Gender differences in cardiovascular and neuroendocrine response to stressors. In R. C. Barnett, L. Biener, & G. K. Baruch (Eds.), *Gender and stress.* New York: Free Press.

Poling, A., Gadow, K. D., & Cleary, J. (1991). *Drug therapy for behavior disorders: An introduction.* New York: Pergamon Press.

Polivy, J., & Herman, C. P. (1993). Etiology of binge eating: Psychological mechanisms. In C. G. Fairburn & G. T. Wilson (Eds.), *Binge eating: Nature, assessment, and treatment* (pp. 173–205). New York: Guilford Press.

Pomerantz, J. R. (1994). On criteria for ethics in science: Commentary on Rosenthal. *Psychological Science, 5,* 135–136.

Pool, R. (1997, October). Portrait of a gene guy. *Discover,* pp. 51–55.

Poole, D. A., Lindsay, D. S., Memon, A., & Bull, R. (1995). Psychotherapy and the recovery of memories of childhood sexual abuse: U.S. and British practitioners' opinions, practices, and experiences. *Journal of Consulting and Clinical Psychology, 63,* 426–437.

Poon, L. W. (1985). Differences in human memory with aging: Nature, causes, and clinical implications. In J. E. Birren & W. K. Schaie (Eds.), *Handbook of the psychology of aging* (pp. 427–462). New York: Van Nostrand Reinhold.

Popejoy, D. I. (1967). *The effects of a physical fitness program on selected psychological and physiological measures of anxiety.* Unpublished doctoral dissertation. University of Illinois.

Posner, M. I. (1993). Seeing the mind. *Science, 262,* 673–674.

Posner, M. I., & McCandliss, B. D. (1993). Converging methods for investigating lexical access. *Science, 4,* 305–309.

Posner, M. I., & Raichle, M. E. (1994). *Images of mind.* New York: W. H. Freeman.

Powell, L. H., Shaker, L. A., & Jones, B. A. (1993). Psychosocial predictors of mortality in 83 women with premature acute myocardial infarction. *Psychosomatic Medicine, 55,* 426–433.

Premack, D. (1965). Reinforcement theory. In D. Levine (Ed.), *Nebraska Symposium on Motivation* (pp. 128–180). Lincoln: University of Nebraska Press.

Prentice, D. A., & Miller, D. T. (1993). Pluralistic ignorance and alcohol use on campus: Some consequences on misperceiving the social norm. *Journal of Personality and Social Psychology, 64,* 243–256.

Price, D. D. (2000). Psychological and neural mechanisms of the affective dimension of pain. *Science, 288,* 1769–1772.

Price, D. D., Rafii, A., Watkins, L. R., & Buckingham, B. (1984). A psychophysical analysis of acupuncture analgesia. *Pain, 19,* 27–42.

Priest, R. F., & Sawyer, J. (1967). Proximity and peership: Bases of balance in interpersonal attraction. *American Journal of Sociology, 72,* 633–649.

Primavera, L. H., & Herron, W. G. (1996). The effect of viewing television violence on aggression. *International Journal of Instructional Media, 23,* 91–104.

Prinzmetal, W. (1995). Visual feature integration in a world of objects. *Current Directions in Psychological Science, 5,* 90–94.

Putnam, F. W., Guroff, J. J., Silberman, E. K., Barban, L., & Post, R. M. (1986). The clinical phenomenology of multiple personality disorder: Review of 100 recent cases. *Journal of Clinical Psychiatry, 47,* 285–293.

Qualls, S. H., & Abeles, N. (2000). *Psychology and the aging revolution: How we adapt to longer life.* Washington, DC: American Psychological Association.

Rabasca, L. (1999, September). High marks for psychologists who prescribe. *APA Monitor, 30*(8), 21.

Rabkin, J. G., & Struening, E. L. (1976). Life events, stress, and illness. *Science, 194,* 1013–1020.

Rachman, S. (1966). Sexual fetishism: An experimental analogue. *Psychological Record, 6,* 293–296.

Ragland, D. R., & Brand, R. J. (1988). Type A behavior and mortality from coronary heart disease. *New England Journal of Medicine, 318,* 65–69.

Rahe, R. H., & Arthur, R. J. (1978, March). Life change and illness studies: Past history and future directions. *Journal of Human Stress,* pp. 3–15.

Raichle, M. E. (1994). Visualizing the mind. *Scientific American, 270* (4), 58–64.

Rakic, P. (1985). Limits of neurogenesis in primates. *Science, 227,* 1054–1057.

Ramachandran, V. S. (1992). Filling in gaps in perception: Part 1. *Current Directions in Psychological Science, 1,* 199–205.

Ramey, C. T., & Ramey, S. L. (1998a). Early intervention and early experience. *American Psychologist, 53,* 109–120.

Ramey, C. T,. & Ramey, S. L. (1998b). In defense of special education. *American Psychologist, 53,* 1159–1160.

Rand, C. S., & Kuldau, J. M. (1992). Epidemiology of bulimia and symptoms in a general population: Sex, age, race, and socioeconomic status. *International Journal of Eating Disorders, 11,* 37–44.

Rapoport, J. L. (1989, March). The biology of obsessions and compulsions. *Scientific American, 263,* 83–89.

Rathus, S. A., Nevid, J. S., & Fichner-Rathus, L. (2000). *Human sexuality in a world of diversity* (4th ed.). Boston: Allyn & Bacon.

Ravussin, E., & Danforth, E., Jr. (1999, January 8). Beyond sloth—physical activity and weight gain. *Science, 283,* 184–185.

Raymond, C. (1989, September 20). Scientists examining behavior of a man who lost his memory gain new insights into the workings of the human mind. *The Chronicle of Higher Education,* pp. A4, A6.

Raymond, J. L., Lisberger, S. G., & Mauk, M. D. (1996, May 24). The cerebellum: A neuronal learning machine? *Science, 272,* 1126–1131.

Raynor, J. O. (1970). Relationships between achievement-related motives, future orientation, and academic performance. *Journal of Personality and Social Psychology, 15,* 28–33.

Raz, S., & Raz, N. (1990). Structural brain abnormalities in the major psychoses: A quantitative review of the evidence from computerized imaging. *Psychological Bulletin, 16,* 491–402.

Reber, A. S. (1993). *Implicit learning and tacit knowledge: An essay on the cognitive unconscious.* (Oxford Psychology Series No. 19). Oxford, U.K.: Oxford University Press.

Rechtschaffen, A. (1998). Current perspectives on the function of sleep. *Perspectives in Biology and Medicine, 41,* 359–390.

Regier, D. A., Boyd, J. H., Burke, J. D., Rae, D. S., Myers, J. K., Kramer, M., Robins, L. N., George, L. K., Karno, M., & Locke, B. Z. (1988). One-month prevalence of mental disorders in the United States. *Archives of General Psychiatry, 45,* 977–986.

Regier, D. A., Narrow, W. E., Rae, D. S., Manderscheid, R. W., Locke, B. Z., & Goodwin, F. K. (1993). The de facto US mental and addictive disorders service system: Epidemiologic Catchment Area prospective 1-year prevalence rates of disorders and services. *Archives of General Psychiatry, 50,* 85–94.

Reinisch, J. M. (1990). *The Kinsey Institute new report on sex: What you must know to be sexually literate.* New York: St. Martin's Press.

Rescorla, R. A. (1972). Information variables in Pavlovian conditioning. In G. Bower (Ed.), *The psychology of learning and motivation* (Vol. 6). New York: Academic Press.

Rescorla, R. A., & Wagner, A. R. (1972). A theory of Pavlovian conditioning: Variations in the effectiveness of reinforcement and non-reinforcement. In A. H. Black & W. F. Prokasy (Eds.), *Classical conditioning, II: Current research and theory* (pp. 64–94). New York: Appleton-Century-Crofts.

Resnick, S. M. (1992). Positron emission tomography in psychiatric illness. *Current Directions in Psychological Science, 1,* 92–98.

Rest, J. R., & Thoma, S. J. (1976). Relation of moral judgment development to formal education. *Developmental Psychology, 21,* 709–714.

Reuter-Lorenz, P. A., & Miller, A. C. (1998). The cognitive neuroscience of human laterality: Lessons from the bisected brain. *Current Directions in Psychological Science, 7,* 15–20.

Rhodes, G., Sumich, A., & Byatt, G. (1999). Are average facial configurations attractive only because of their symmetry? *Psychological Science, 10,* 52–58.

Richards, J. M., & Gross, J. J. (2000). Emotion regulation and memory: The cognitive costs of keeping one's cool. *Journal of Personality & Social Psychology, 79,* 410–424.

Riddle, D., & Morin, S. (1977). Removing the stigma from individuals. *American Psychological Association Monitor, 16,* 28.

Ripple, C. H., Gilliam, W. S., Chanana, N., & Zigler. (1999). Will fifty cooks spoil the broth? The debate over entrusting Head Start to the states. *American Psychologist, 54,* 327–343.

Robbins, D. (1971). Partial reinforcement: A selective review of the alleyway literature since 1960. *Psychological Bulletin, 76,* 415–431.

Robbins, J. (2000, April). Wired for sadness. *Discover, 21*(4), 77–81.

Roberts, A. H. (1985). Biofeedback: Research, training, and clinical roles. *American Psychologist, 40,* 938–941.

Robins, C. J. (1988). Attributions and depression: Why is the literature so inconsistent? *Journal of Personality and Social Psychology, 54,* 880–889.

Robins, L. N., Locke, B. Z., & Regier, D. A. (1991). An overview of psychiatric disorders in America. In L. N. Robins & D. A. Regier (Eds.), *Psychiatric disorders in America: The epidemiologic catchment area study.* New York: Free Press.

Robinson, N. M., Zigler, E., & Gallagher, J. J. (2000). Two tails of the normal curve: Similarities and differences in the study of mental retardation and giftedness. *American Psychologist, 55,* 1413–1424.

Rock, I., & Palmer, S. (1990, December). The legacy of Gestalt psychology. *Scientific American, 263,* 84–90.

Rodin, J. (1986). Aging and health: Effects of the sense of control. *Science, 233,* 1271–1276.

Rodin, J., & Salovey, P. (1989). Health psychology. *Annual Review of Psychology, 40,* 533–579.

Rodin, J., Striegel-Moore, R. H., & Silberstein, L. R. (1985, July). *A prospective study of bulimia among college students on three U. S. campuses.* Unpublished manuscript. New Haven: Yale University.

Roediger, H. L., III. (1990). Implicit memory: Retention without remembering. *American Psychologist, 45,* 1043–1056.

Roediger, H. L., III, & McDermott, K. B. (1995). Creating false memories: Remembering words not presented in lists. *Journal of Experimental Psychology: Learning, Memory, and Cognition, 21,* 803–814.

Roediger, H. L., III, & McDermott, K. B. (2000, January/February). *Psychological Science Agenda,* 8–9.

Rogers, C. R. (1951). *Client-centered therapy: Its current practice, implications and theory.* Boston: Houghton Mifflin.

Rogers, C. R. (1957). The necessary and sufficient conditions of therapeutic personality change. *Journal of Consulting Psychology, 21,* 95–103.

Rogers, C. R. (1961). *On becoming a person: A therapist's view of psychotherapy.* Boston: Houghton Mifflin.

Rogers, C. R. (1977). *On personal power: Inner strength and its revolutionary impact.* New York: Delacorte.

Rogers, C. R. (1980). *A way of being.* Boston: Houghton Mifflin.

Rogers, C. R. (1982, July/August) Roots of madness. In T. H. Carr & H. E. Fitzgerald (Eds.), *Psychology 83/84* (pp. 263–267). Guilford, CT: Dushkin. (Originally published in *Science 82,* July/August, 1982).

Rogoff, B. (1990). *Apprenticeship in thinking: Cognitive development in social context.* New York: Oxford University Press.

Roll, S., Hinton, R., & Glazer, M. (1974). Dreams and death: Mexican Americans vs. Anglo-American. *Interamerican Journal of Psychology, 8,* 111–115.

Rollman, G. B., & Harris, G. (1987). The detectability, discriminability, and perceived magnitude of painful electrical shock. *Perception & Psychophysics, 42,* 257–268.

Rolls, B. J., Federoff, I. C., & Guthrie, J. F. (1991). Gender differences in eating behavior and body weight regulation. *Health Psychology, 10,* 133–142.

Rolnick, J. (1998, December 4). Treating mental disorders: A neuroscientist says no to drugs. *The Chronicle of Higher Education,* A10.

Rorschach, H. (1942). *Psychodiagnostics: A diagnostic test based on perception.* New York: Grune & Stratton.

Rosa, L., Rosa, E., Sarner, L., & Barrett, S. (1998). A close look at therapeutic touch. *Journal of the American Medical Association, 279,* 1005–1010.

Rosch, E. (1999). Is wisdom in the brain? *Psychological Science, 10,* 222–224.

Rosch, E., & Mervis, C. B. (1975). Family resemblances: Studies in the internal structure of categories. *Cognitive Psychology, 7,* 573–605.

Rosch, E. H., Mervis, C. B., Gray, W. D., Johnson, D. M., & Boyes-Braem, P. (1976). Basic objects in natural categories. *Cognitive Psychology, 8,* 382–439.

Rosen, J. B., & Schulkin, J. (1998). From normal fear to pathological anxiety. *Psychological Review, 105,* 325–350.

Rosenblatt, P. C. (1966). A cross-cultural study of child-rearing and romantic love. *Journal of Personality and Social Psychology, 4,* 336–338.

Rosenhan, D. L. (1969). Some origins of concern for others. In P. Mussen, J. Langer, & M. Covington (Eds.), *Trends and issues in developmental psychology.* New York: Holt, Rinehart & Winston.

Rosenhan, D. L. (1973). On being sane in insane places. *Science, 179,* 250–258.

Rosenhan, D. L. (1983). Psychological abnormality and law. In C. J. Scheirer & B. C. Hammonds (Eds.)., *The master lecture series: Vol. 2. Psychology and the law.* Washington, DC: American Psychological Association.

Rosenhan, D. L., & Seligman, M. E. P. (1995). *Abnormal psychology* (3rd ed.) New York: Norton.

Rosenthal, R. (1994). Science and ethics in conducting, analyzing, and reporting psychological research. *Psychological Science, 5,* 127–134.

Rosenthal, R. & Jacobson, L. F. (1968a). *Pygmalion in the classroom: Teacher expectations and intellectual development.* New York: Holt.

Rosenthal, R., & Jacobson, L. F. (1968b). Teacher expectations for the disadvantaged. *Scientific American, 218*(4), 19–23.

Rosenzweig, M. R. (1992). Psychological science around the world. *American Psychologist, 47,* 718–722.

Rosenzweig, M. R. (1999). Continuity and change in the development of psychology around the world. *American Psychologist, 54,* 252–259.

Ross, C. A., Miller, S. D., Reagor, P., Bjornson, L., Fraser, G. A., & Anderson, G. (1990). Structured interview data on 102 cases of multiple personality disorder from four centers. *American Journal of Psychiatry, 147,* 596–601.

Ross, C. A., Norton, G. R., & Wozney, K. (1989). Multiple personality disorder: An analysis of 236 cases. *Canadian Journal of Psychiatry, 34,* 413–418.

Ross, L., & Nisbett, R. E. (1991). *The person and the situation: Perspectives of social psychology.* New York: McGraw-Hill.

Ross, P. E. (1992, July). Compulsive canines. *Scientific American, 266* (5), 24–25.

Rothbaum, B. O., & Hodges, L. F. (1999). The use of virtual reality exposure in the treatment of anxiety disorders. *Behavior Modification, 23,* 507–525.

Rothbaum, B. O., Smith, S., Hodges, & Jeong, H. L. (2001). A controlled study of virtual reality exposure therapy for the fear of flying. *Journal of Consulting & Clinical Psychology, 69,* 1020–1026.

Rotter, J. B. (1954). *Social learning and clinical psychology.* Englewood Cliffs, NJ: Prentice-Hall.

Rotter, J. B. (1966). Generalized expectancies for internal versus external control of reinforcement. *Psychological Monographs, 80* (Whole no. 609).

Rotter, J. B. (1971, June). External control and internal control. *Psychology Today, 4,* 37–42, 58–59.

Rotter, J. B. (1990). Internal versus external control of reinforcement: A case history of a variable. *American Psychologist, 45,* 489–493.

Rouhana, N. N., & Kelman, H. C. (1994). Promoting joint thinking in international conflicts: An Israeli-Palestinian continuing workshop. *Journal of Social Issues, 50,* 157–168.

Roush, W. (1996, July 5). Live long and prosper? *Science, 273,* 42–46.

Roush, W. (1997, April 18). Herbert Benson: Mind–body maverick pushes the envelope. *American Psychologist, 276,* 357–359.

Rozin, P. (1976). The evolution of intelligence and access to the cognitive unconscious. In J. M. Sprague & A. A. Epstein (Eds.), *Progress in psychobiology and physiological psychology* (pp. 245–280). New York: Academic Press.

Rozin, P. (1996). Towards a psychology of food and eating: From motivation to module to model to marker, morality, meaning, and metaphor. *Current Directions in Psychological Science, 5,* 18–24.

Rusting, C. L., & Nolen-Hoeksema, S. (1998). Regulating responses to anger: Effects of rumination and distraction on angry mood. *Journal of Personality and Social Psychology, 74,* 790–803.

Rutter, M., Macdonald, H., Le Courteur, A., Harrington, R., Bolton, P., & Bailey, A. (1990). Genetic factors in child psychiatric disorders–II. Empirical findings. *Journal of Child Psychology and Psychiatry, 31,* 39–83.

Ryan, R. M., & Deci, E. L. (2000). Self-determination theory and the facilitation of intrinsic motivation, social development, and well-being. *American Psychologist, 55,* 68–78.

Ryff, C. D. (1989). In the eye of the beholder: Views of psychological well-being among middle-aged and older adults. *Psychology and Aging, 4,* 195–210.

Sackheim, H. A., Prudic, J., Devanand, D. P., Nobler, M. S., Lisanby, S. H., Peyser, S., Fitzsimons, L., Moody, B. J., & Clark, J. (2000). A prospective, randomized, double-blind comparison of bilateral and right unilateral electroconvulsive therapy at different stimulus intensities. *Archives of General Psychiatry, 57,* 425–434.

Sacks, O. (1995). *An anthropologist on Mars.* New York: Random House.

St. George-Hyslop, P. H. (2000). Piecing together Alzheimer's. *Scientific American, 283*(6), 76–83.

Salovey, P., & Mayer, J. D. (1990). Emotional intelligence. *Imagination, Cognition, and Personality, 9,* 185–211.

Salovey, P., Rothman, A. J., Detweiler, J. B., & Steward, W. T. (2000). Emotional states and physical health. *American Psychologist, 55,* 110–121.

Salter, S. (1993). "Buried Memories/Broken Families," *San Francisco Examiner,* April 4, pp. A1,ff.

Saltzstein, H. D., & Sandberg, L. (1979). Indirect social influence: Change in judgmental processor anticipatory conformity. *Journal of Experimental Social Psychology, 15,* 209–216.

Sanger, M. (1971). *Margaret Sanger: An autobiography.* New York: W. W. Norton/Dover Publications, Inc. (Original work published in 1938).

Sapolsky, R. (1997, October). A gene for nothing. *Discover, 40,* 42–44, 46.

Sapolsky, R. M. (1990). Adrenocortical function, social rank, and personality among wild baboons. *Biological Psychiatry, 28,* pp. 1–17.

Sapolsky, R. M. (1992). *Stress: The aging brain and the mechanisms of neuron death.* Cambridge, MA: MIT Press.

Sapolsky, R. M. (1996, August 9). Why stress is bad for your brain. *Science, 273,* 749–750.

Satir, V. (1983). *Conjoint family therapy* (3rd ed.). Palo Alto, CA: Science & Behavior Books.

Satir, V., Banmen, J., Gerber, J., & Gomori, M. (1991). *Satir model: Family therapy and beyond.* Palo Alto, CA: Science & Behavior Books.

Sattler, J. M. (1970). Racial "experimenter effects" in experimentation, testing, interviewing, and psychotherapy. *Psychological Bulletin, 73,* 137–160.

Saudino, K. J. (1997, August). Moving beyond the heritability question: New directions in behavioral genetic studies of personality. *Current Directions in Psychological Science, 6,* 86–90.

Saufley, W. H., Otaka, S. R., & Bavaresco, J. L. (1985). Context independence. *Memory and Cognition, 13,* 522–528.

Savitsky, J. C., & Lindblom, W. D. (1986). The impact of the guilty but mentally ill verdict on juror decisions: An empirical analysis. *Journal of Applied Social Psychology.*

Saxe, L. (1991). Lying: Thoughts of an applied social psychologist. *American Psychologist, 46,* 409–415.

Saxe, L. (1994). Detection of deception: Polygraph and integrity tests. *Current Directions in Psychological Science, 3,* 69–73.

Saxe, L. Dougherty, D., & Cross, T. (1985). The validity of polygraph testing: Scientific analysis and public controversy. *American Psychologist, 40,* 355–366.

Scarr, S. (1997). Why child care has little impact on most children's development. *Current Directions in Psychological Science, 6,* 143–148.

Scarr, S. (1998). American child care today. *American Psychologist, 53,* 95–108.

Scarr, S., & Weinberg, R. (1976). IQ test performance of black children adopted by white families. *American Psychologist, 31,* 726–739.

Scarr, S., & Weinberg, R. A. (1978, April). Attitudes, interests, and IQ. *Human Nature,* pp. 29–36.

Schacter, D. L. (1996). *Searching for memory: The brain, the mind, and the past.* New York: Basic Books.

Schacter, D. L. (1999). The seven sins of memory: Insights from psychology and cognitive neuroscience. *American Psychologist, 54,* 182–203.

Schacter, D. L. (2001). The Seven Sins of Memory: How the Mind Forgets and Remembers. Boston: Houghton Mifflin.

Schachter, S. (1977). Nicotine regulation in heavy and light smokers. *Journal of Experimental Psychology: General, 106,* 5–12.

Schaefer, H. H., & Martin, P. L. (1966). Behavioral therapy for "apathy" of hospitalized patients. *Psychological Reports, 19,* 1147–1158.

Schank, R. C., & Abelson, R. (1977). *Scripts, plans, goals and understanding: An inquiry into human knowledge and structures.* Hillsdale, NJ: Erlbaum.

Scharfe, E., & Bartholomew, K. (1998). Do you remember? Recollections of adult attachment patterns. *Personal Relationships, 5,* 219–234.

Schatzberg, A. F. (1991). Overview of anxiety disorders: Prevalence, biology, course, and treatment. *Journal of Clinical Psychiatry, 42,* 5–9.

Schaufeli, W. B., Maslach, C., & Marek, T. (Ed.) (1993). Professional burnout: Recent developments in theory and research. Washington, DC: Taylor & Francis.

Schechter, B. (1996, October 18). How the brain gets rhythm. *Science, 274,* 339–340.

Schiff, M., & Bargal, D. (2000). Helping characteristics of self-help and support groups: Their contribution to participants' subjective well-being. *Small Group Research, 31,* 275–304.

Schleifer, S. J., Keller, S. E., Camerino, M., Thornton, J. C., & Stein, M. (1983). Suppression of lymphocyte stimulation following bereavement. *Journal of the American Medical Association, 250,* 374–377.

Schlenker, B. R., Weingold, M. F., Hallam, J. R. (1990). Self-serving attributions in social context: Effects of self-esteem and social pressure. *Journal of Personality and Social Psychology, 58,* 855–863.

Schmidt, R. A., & Bjork, R. A. (1992). New conceptualizations of practice: Common principles in three paradigms suggest new concepts for training. *Psychological Science, 3,* 207–217.

Schmidt, W. E. (1987, June 7). Paddling in school: A tradition is under fire. *The New York Times,* pp. A1, A22.

Schmolck, H., Buffalo, E. A., & Squire, L. R. (2000). Memory distortions develop over time: Recollections of the O. J. Simpson trial verdict after 15 and 32 months. *Psychological Science, 11,* 39–45.

Schneider, K., & May, R. (1995). *The psychology of existence: An integrative, clinical perspective.* New York: McGraw-Hill.

Schou, M. (1997). Forty years of lithium treatment. *Archives of General Psychiatry, 54,* 9–13.

Schreiber, F. R. (1973). *Sybil.* New York: Warner Books.

Schroeder, D. A., Penner, L. A., Dovidio, J. F., & Piliavin, J. A. (1995). *The psychology of helping and altruism.* New York: McGraw-Hill.

Schroeder, D. A., & Prentice, D. A. (1995). *Pluralistic ignorance and alcohol use on campus II: Correcting misperceptions of the social norm.* Unpublished manuscript, Princeton University.

Schroeder, S. R., Schroeder, C. S., & Landesman, S. (1987). Psychological services in educational settings to persons with mental retardation. *American Psychologist, 42,* 805–808.

Schulkin, J. (1994). Melancholic depression and the hormones of adversity: A role for the amygdala. *Current Directions in Psychological Science, 3,* 41–44.

Schulz, R., & Heckhausen, J. (1996). A life span model of successful aging. *American Psychologist, 51,* 702–714.

Schwartz, B. (1997). Psychology, idea technology, and ideology. *Psychological Science, 8,* 21–27.

Schwartz, J. M., Stoessel, P. W., Baxter, L. R., Martin, K. M., & Phelps, M. E. (1996). Systematic changes in cerebral glucose metabolic rate after successful behavior modification treatment of obsessive–compulsive disorder. *Archives of General Psychiatry, 53,* 109–116.

Schwartz, P. (1994). *Peer marriage: How love between equals really works.* New York: The Free Press.

Schwarz, N. (1999). Self-reports: How the questions shape the answers. *American Psychologist, 54,* 93–105.

Schwarzer, R. (Ed.). (1992). *Self-efficacy: Thought control of action.* Washington, DC: Hemisphere.

Schwebel, A. I., & Fine, M. A. (1994). *Understanding and helping families: A cognitive behavioral approach.* Hillsdale, NJ: Erlbaum.

Schweinhart, L. J., & Weikart, D. P. (1986, January). What do we know so far? A review of the Head Start Synthesis Project. *Young Children, 41*(2), 49–55.

Scott, K. G., & Carran, D. T. (1987). The epidemiology and prevention of mental retardation. *American Psychologist, 42,* 801–804.

Scovern, A. W., & Kilmann, P. R. (1980). Status of electro-convulsive therapy: Review of outcome literature. *Psychological Bulletin, 87,* 260–303.

Segal, M. W. (1974). Alphabet and attraction: An unobtrusive measure of the effect of propinquity in a field setting. *Journal of Personality and Social Psychology, 30,* 654–657.

Segall, M. H. (1994). A cross-cultural research contribution to unraveling the nativist/empiricist controversy. In W. J. Lonner & R.

Malpass, *Psychology and culture* (pp. 135–138). Boston: Allyn & Bacon.

Segall, M. H., Dasen, P. R., Berry, J. W., & Poortinga, Y. H. (1990). *Human behavior in global perspective: An introduction to cross-cultural psychology.* Boston: Allyn & Bacon.

Segall, M. H., Dasen, P. R., Berry, J. W., & Poortinga, Y. H. (1999). *Human behavior in global perspective: An introduction to cross-cultural psychology* (2nd ed.). Boston: Allyn and Bacon.

Segall, M. H., Lonner, W. J., & Berry, J. W. (1998). Cross-cultural psychology as a scholarly discipline: On the flowering of culture in behavioral research. *American Psychologist, 53,* 1101–1110.

Segall, M. N., Campbell, D. T., & Herskovits, M. J. (1966). *The influence of culture on visual perception.* Indianapolis: Bobbs-Merrill.

Seger, C. A. (1994). Implicit learning. *Psychological Bulletin, 115* (2), 163–196.

Selfridge, O. G. (1955). Pattern recognition and modern computers. *Proceedings of the Western Joint Computer Conference.* New York: Institute of Electrical and Electronics Engineers.

Seligman, M. E. P. (1971). Preparedness and phobias. *Behavior Therapy, 2,* 307–320.

Seligman, M. E. P. (1973, June). Fall into helplessness. *Psychology Today, 7,* 43–48

Seligman, M. E. P. (1975). *Helplessness: On depression, development and death.* San Francisco: Freeman.

Seligman, M. E. P. (1991). *Learned optimism.* New York: Knopf.

Seligman, M. E. P. (1995). The effectiveness of psychotherapy: The *Consumer Reports* study. *American Psychologist, 50,* 965–974.

Seligman, M. E. P., Abramson, L. Y., Semmel, A., & von Baeyer, C. (1979). Depressive attributional style. *Journal of Abnormal Psychology, 88,* 242–247.

Seligman, M. E. P., & Csikszentmihalyi, M. (2000). Positive psychology: An introduction. *American Psychologist, 55,* 5–14.

Seligman, M. E. P., & Maier, S. F. (1967). Failure to escape traumatic shock. *Journal of Experimental Psychology, 74,* 1–9.

Seligson, S. V. (1994, November/December). Say good night to snoring. *Health, 8*(7), 89–93.

Selye, H. (1956). The *stress of life.* New York: McGraw-Hill.

Selye, H. (1974). *Stress without distress.* New York: New American Library.

Selye, H. (1980). The stress concept today. In I. L. Kutash et al. (Eds.), *Handbook on stress and anxiety.* San Francisco: Jossey-Bass.

Serpell, R. (1994). The cultural construction of intelligence. In Lonner, W. J. & Malpass, R. *Psychology and culture* (pp. 157–163). Boston: Allyn & Bacon.

Service, R. F. (1999, April 23). Bypassing nervous system damage with electronics. *Science, 284,* 579.

Sexton, V. S., & Misiak, H. (1984). American psychologists and psychology abroad. *American Psychologist, 39,* 1026–1031.

Seybold, K. S., & Hill, P. C. (2001). The role of religion and spirituality in mental and physical health. *Current Directions in Psychological Science, 10,* 21–24.

Shadish, W. R., Matt, G. E., Navarro, A. M., &

Phillips, G. (2000). The effects of psychological therapies under clinically representative conditions: A meta-analysis. *Psychological Bulletin, 126,* 512–529.

Shapiro, D. H. (1985). Clinical use of meditation as a self-regulation strategy: Comments on Holmes's conclusions and implications. *American Psychologist, 40,* 719–722.

Shapiro, F. (1995). *Desensitization and reprocessing: Basic principles, protocols, and procedures.* New York: Guilford.

Shatz, M., Wellman, H. M., & Silber, S. (1983). The acquisition of mental verbs: A systematic investigation of the first reference to mental state. *Cognition, 14,* 301–321.

Shaver, P., & Hazan, C. (1987). Romantic love conceptualized as an attachment process. *Journal of Personality and Social Psychology, 52,* 511–524.

Shaver, P. R., & Hazan, C. (1993). Adult attachment: Theory and research. In W. Jones & D. Perlman (Eds.), *Advances in personal relationships,* Vol. 4, 29–70. London, England: Jessica Kingsley.

Shaver, P. R., & Hazan, C. (1994). Attachment. In A. L. Weber & J. H. Harvey (Eds.), *Perspectives on close relationships* (Chapter 6, 110–130). Boston: Allyn & Bacon.

Shea, C. (1998, January 30). Why depression strikes more women than men: "Ruminative coping" may provide answers. *The Chronicle of Higher Education,* p. 14.

Sherif, C. W. (1981, August). *Social and psychological bases of social psychology.* The G. Stanley Hall Lecture on social psychology, presented at the annual convention of the American Psychological Association, Los Angeles, CA.

Sherif, M., Harvey, O. J., White, B. J., Hood, W., & Sherif, C. (1961). *Intergroup conflict and cooperation: The Robbers Cave experiment.* Norman, OK: University of Oklahoma Institute of Intergroup Relations.

Shields, S. A. (1991). Gender in the psychology of emotion: A selective research review. In K. T. Strongman (Ed.), *International review of studies on emotion* (Vol 1). New York: Wiley.

Shiffrin, R. M. (1993). Short-term memory: A brief commentary. *Memory and Cognition, 21* (2), 193–197.

Shimamura, A. P. (1996, September/October). Unraveling the mystery of the frontal lobes: Explorations in cognitive neuroscience. *Psychological Science Agenda,* 8–9.

Shiraev, E., & Levy, D. (2001). *Introduction cross-cultural: Critical thinking and contemporary applications.* Boston: Allyn and Bacon.

Shobe, K. K., & Kihlstrom, J. F. (1997). Is traumatic memory special? *Current Directions in Psychological Science, 6,* 70–74.

Siegel, B. (1988). *Love, medicine & miracles.* New York: Harper & Row.

Siegel, J. M. (1990). Stressful life events and use of physician services among the elderly: The moderating role of pet ownership. *Journal of Personality and Social Psychology, 58,* 1081–1086.

Siegel, R. K. (1980). The psychology of life after death. *American Psychologist, 35,* 911–931.

Siegler, R. S. (1994). Cognitive variability: A key to understanding cognitive development. *Current Directions in Psychological Science, 3,* 1–5.

Sigelman, C. K., Thomas, D. B., Sigelman, L., & Robich, F. D. (1986). Gender, physical attractiveness, and electability: An experimental investigation of voter biases. *Journal of Applied Social Psychology, 16,* 229–248.

Silbersweig, D. A., Stern, E., Frith, C., Cahill, C., Holmes, A., Grootoonk, S., Seaward, J., McKenna, P., Chua, S. E., Schnorr, L., Jones, T., & Frackowiak, R. S. J. (1995). A functional neuroanatomy of hallucinations in schizophrenia. *Nature, 378* (November 9), 176–179.

Silver, R. L. (1983). Coping with an undesirable life event: A study of early reactions to physical disability. *Dissertation Abstracts International, 43,* 3415.

Silver, R. L., Boon, C., & Stones, M. L. (1983). Searching for meaning in misfortune: Making sense of incest. *Journal of Social Issues, 39,* 81–101.

Silver, R. L., & Wortman, C. B. (1980). Coping with undesirable life events. In J. Garber & M. E. P. Seligman (Eds.), *Human helplessness: Theory and application.* New York: Academic Press.

Simon, H. A. (1992). What is an "explanation" of behavior? *Psychological Science, 3,* 150–161.

Simpson, J. A. (1990). The influence of attachment styles on romantic relationships. *Journal of Personality and Social Psychology, 59,* 971–980.

Simpson, J. A., & Harris, B. A. (1994). Interpersonal attraction. In A. L. Weber & J. H. Harvey (Eds.), *Perspectives on close relationships* (pp. 45–66). Boston: Allyn & Bacon.

Sinclair, R. C., Hoffman, C., Mark, M. M., Martin L. L., & Pickering, T. L. (1994). Construct accessibility and the misattribution of arousal: Schacter and Singer revisited. *Psychological Sciences, 5,* 15–18.

Singer, J. L. (1966). *Daydreaming: An introduction to the experimental study of inner experience.* New York: Random House.

Singer, J. L. (1975). Navigating the stream of consciousness: Research in daydreaming and related inner experience. *American Psychologist, 30,* 727–739.

Singer, J. L., & McCraven, V. J. (1961). Some characteristics of adult daydreaming. *Journal of Psychology, 51,* 151–164.

Singer, J. L., Singer, D. G., & Rapaczynski, W. S. (1984). Family patterns and television viewing as predictors of children's beliefs and aggression. *Journal of Communication, 34,* 73–89.

Singer, W. (1995, November 3). Development and plasticity of cortical processing architectures. *Science, 270,* 758–763.

Skinner, B. F. (1953). *Science and human behavior.* New York: Macmillan.

Skinner, B. F. (1956). A case history in scientific method. *American Psychologist, 11,* 221–233. (Reprinted in S. Koch [Ed.]. *Psychology: A study of a science* [Vol 2, 359–379]. New York: McGraw-Hill.)

Skinner, B. F. (1987). Whatever happened to psychology as the science of behavior? *American Psychologist, 42,* 780–786.

Skinner, B. F. (1989). The origins of cognitive thought. *American Psychologist, 44,* 13–18.

Skinner, B. F. (1990). Can psychology be a science of mind? *American Psychologist, 45,* 1206–1210.

Skoog, I., Nilsson, L., Palmertz, B., Andreasson, L. A., & Svanborg, A. (1993). A population-based study of dementia in 85-year-olds. *New England Journal of Medicine, 328,* 153.

Sleek, S. (1994, April). Could Prozac replace demand for therapy? *APA Monitor,* p. 28.

Sleek, S. (1996, May). Shifting the paradigm for prescribing drugs. *APA Monitor,* pp. 1, 29.

Slobin, D. I. (1985a). Introduction: Why study acquisition crosslinguistically? In D.I. Slobin (Ed.), *The crosslinguistic study of language acquisition. Vol. 1: The data* (pp. 3–24). Hillsdale, NJ: Erlbaum.

Slobin, D. I. (1985b). Cross-linguistic evidence of the language making capacity. In D. I. Slobin (Ed.), *The crosslinguistic study of language acquisition. Vol. 2: Theoretical issues* (pp. 1157–1256). Hillsdale, NJ: Erlbaum.

Smith, C. A., & Ellsworth, P. C. (1987). Patterns of appraisal and emotion related to taking an exam. *Journal of Personality and Social Psychology, 52,* 475–488.

Smith, E. E. (2000). Neural bases of human working memory. *Current Directions in Psychological Science, 9,* 45–49.

Smith, E. E., & Jonides, J. (1999, March 12). Storage and executive processes in the frontal lobes. *Science, 283,* 1657–1661.

Smith, E. E., & Medin, D. L. (1981). *Cognitive Science Series: 4. Categories and concepts.* Cambridge, MA: Harvard University Press.

Smith, G. B., Schwebel, A. I., Dunn, R. L., & McIver, S. D. (1993). The role of psychologists in the treatment, management, and prevention of chronic mental illness. *American Psychologist, 48,* 966–971.

Smith, M. L., & Glass, G. V. (1977). Meta-analysis of psychotherapy outcome studies. *American Psychologist, 32,* 752–760.

Smith, R. E., Haroutunian, V., Davis, K. L., & Meador-Woodruff, J. H. (2001). Expression of excitatory amino acid transporter transcripts in the thalamus of subjects with schizophrenia. *American Journal of Psychiatry, 158,* 1393–1399.

Smith, S. (1991, Spring). Two-generation program models: A new intervention strategy. *Social Policy Report of the Society for Research in Child Development, 5* (No. 1).

Smith, T., Eikeseth, S., Klevstrand, M., & Lovaas, O. I. (1997). Intensive behavioral treatment for preschoolers with severe mental retardation and pervasive developmental disorder. *American Journal of Mental Retardation, 102,* 238–249.

Snyder, D. K., Wills, R. M., & Grady-Fletcher, A. (1991). Long-term effectiveness of behavioral versus insight-oriented marital therapy: A 4-year follow-up study. *Journal of Consulting and Clinical Psychology, 59,* 138-141.

Snyder, S. H. (1986). *Drugs and the brain.* New York: Scientific American Books.

Sokol, M. M. (Ed.). (1987). *Psychological testing and American society, 1890–1930.* New Brunswick, NJ: Rutgers University Press.

Solanto, M. V., & Connors, C. K. (1982). A dose-response and time-action analysis of autonomic and behavioral effects of methylphenidate in attention deficit disorder with hyperactivity. *Psychophysiology, 19,* 658–667.

Solso, R. L. (1991). *Cognitive psychology* (3rd ed.). Boston: Allyn and Bacon.

Solvason, H. B., Ghanta, V. K., & Hiramoto, R. N. (1988). Conditioned augmentation of natural killer cell activity: Independence from nociceptive effects and dependence on interferon-beta. *Journal of Immunology, 140,* 661–665.

Sorenson, R. C. (1973). *Adolescent sexuality in contemporary America.* Cleveland: World.

Sow, I. (1977). *Psychiatrie dynamique africaine.* Paris: Payot.

Spear, L. P. (2000). Neurobehavioral changes in adolescence. *Current Directions in Psychological Science, 9,* 111–114.

Spearman, C. (1927). *The abilities of man.* New York: Macmillan.

Spelke, E. S. (2000). Core knowledge. *American Psychologist, 55,* 1233–1243.

Spelke, E. S., and Owsley, C. J. (1979). Intermodal exploration and knowledge in infancy. *Infant Behavior and Development, 2,* 13–27.

Sperling, G. (1960). The information available in brief visual presentations. *Psychological Monographs, 74,* 1–29.

Sperling, G. (1963). A model for visual memory tasks. *Human Factors, 5,* 19–31.

Sperry, R. W. (1968). Mental unity following surgical disconnection of the cerebral hemispheres. *The Harvey Lectures,* Series 62. New York: Academic Press.

Sperry, R. W. (1982). Some effects of disconnecting the cerebral hemispheres. *Science, 217,* 1223–1226.

Sperry, R. W. (1988). Psychology's mentalist paradigm and the religion/science tension. *American Psychologist, 43,* 607–613.

Spiegel, D., & Cardeña, E. (1991). Disintegrated experience: The dissociate disorders revisited. *Psychological Bulletin, 100,* 366–378.

Spiegel, D. A., Wiegel, M., Baker, S. L., & Greene, K. A. I. (2000). Pharmacological management of anxiety disorders. In D. I. Mostofsky & D. H. Barlow (Eds.), *The management of stress and anxiety in medical disorders* (pp. 36–65). Boston: Allyn and Bacon.

Spinweber, C. (1990). *Insomnias and parasomnias in young adults.* Paper presented to the annual meeting of the Western Psychological Association, Los Angeles, CA.

Spitzer, R. L., Gibbon, M., Skodol, A. E., Williams, J. B. W., & First, M. B. (1989). *DSM-III-R casebook.* Washington, DC: American Psychiatric Press.

Sprecher, S., & McKinney, K. (1994). Sexuality in close relationships. In A. L. Weber & J. H. Harvey (Eds.), *Perspectives on close relationships* (pp. 193–216). Boston: Allyn & Bacon.

Springer, S. P., & Deutsch, G. (1993). *Left brain, right brain* (4th ed.). New York: W. H. Freeman.

Sprock, J., & Blashfield, R. K. (1991). Classification and nosology. In M. Hersen, A. E. Kazdin, & A. S. Bellack (Eds.), *The clinical psychology handbook* (2nd ed., pp. 329–344). New York: Pergamon Press.

Squier, L. H., & Domhoff, G. W. (1998). The presentation of dreaming and dreams in introductory psychology textbooks: A critical examination with suggestions for textbook authors and course instructors. *Dreaming: Journal of the Association for the Study of Dreams, 8,* 149–168.

Squire, L. R. (1992). Memory and the hippocampus: A synthesis from findings with rats, monkeys, and humans. *Psychological Review, 99,* 195–231.

Squire, S. (1983). *The slender balance: Causes and cures for bulimia, anorexia, and the weight loss/weight gain seesaw.* New York: Putnam.

Stapley, J. C., & Haviland, J. M. (1989). Beyond depression: Gender differences in normal adolescents' emotional experiences. *Sex Roles, 20,* 295–308.

Stapp, J., Tucker, A. M., & VandenBos, G. R. (1985). Census of psychological personnel: 1983. *American Psychologist, 40,* 1317–1351.

Stavish, S. (1994a, May/June). On the biology of temperament. *APS Observer, 7,* 35.

Stavish, S. (1994b, Fall). Breathing room. *Stanford Medicine, 12*(1), 18–23.

Steele, C. M. (1997). A threat in the air: How stereotypes shape intellectual identity and performance. *American Psychologist, 52,* 613–629.

Stein, M. B., Walker, J. R., & Forde, D. R. (1996). Public-speaking fears in a community sample: Prevalence, impact on functioning, and diagnostic classification. *Archives of General Psychiatry, 53,* 169–174.

Stern, J. A., Brown, M., Ulett, G. A., & Sletten, I. (1977). A comparison of hypnosis, acupuncture, morphine, valium, aspirin, and placebo in the management of experimentally induced pain. *Annals of the New York Academy of Sciences, 296,* 175–193.

Stern, W. C., & Morgane, P. S. (1974). Theoretical view of REM sleep function: Maintenance of catecholamine systems in the central nervous system. *Behavioral Biology, 11,* 1–32.

Sternberg, R. J. (1994). A triarchic model for teaching and assessing students in general psychology. *The General Psychologist, 30,* 42–48.

Sternberg, R. J. (1998). *Cupid's arrow: The course of love through time.* New York: Cambridge University Press.

Sternberg, R. J. (1999). The theory of successful intelligence. *Review of General Psychology, 3,* 292–316.

Sternberg, R. J. (2000, July 21). The holy grail of general intelligence. *Science, 289,* 399, 401.

Sternberg, R. J., & Grigorenko, E. L. (1997). Are cognitive styles still in style? *American Psychologist, 52,* 700–712.

Sternberg, R. J., & Lubart, T. I. (1991). An investment theory of creativity and its development. *Human Development, 34,* 1–31.

Sternberg, R. J., & Lubart, T. I. (1992). Buy low and sell high: An investment approach to creativity. *Current Directions in Psychological Science, 1,* 1–5.

Sternberg, R. J., Wagner, R. K., Williams, W. M., & Horvath, J. A. (1995). Testing common sense. *American Psychologist, 50,* 912–927.

Stevenson, H. W. (1992, December). Learning from Asian schools. *Scientific American, 267,* 70–76.

Stevenson, H. W., Chen, C., & Lee, S-Y. (1993). Mathematics achievement of Chinese,

Japanese, and American children: Ten years later. *Science, 259,* 53–58.

Stevenson, J., Graham, P., Fredman, G., & McLoughlin, V. A. (1987). Twin study of genetic influences on reading and spelling ability and disability. *Journal of Child Psychiatry, 28,* 229–247.

Stock, M. B., & Smythe, P. M. (1963). Does undernutrition during infancy inhibit brain growth and subsequent intellectual development? *Archives of Disorders in Childhood, 38,* 546–552.

Storms, M. D. (1980). Theories of sexual orientation. *Journal of Personality and Social Psychology, 38,* 783–792.

Storms, M. D. (1981). A theory of erotic orientation development. *Psychological Review, 88,* 340–353.

Strauss, E. (1998). Writing, speech separated in split brain. *Science, 280,* 827.

Strauss, M. A., & Gelles, R. J. (1980). *Behind closed doors: Violence in the American family.* New York: Anchor/Doubleday.

Strickland, B. R. (1992). Women and depression. *Current Directions in Psychological Science, 1,* 132–135.

Strickland, B. R. (2000). Misassumptions, misadventures, and the misuse of psychology. *American Psychologist, 55,* 331–338.

Striegel-Moore, R. H., Silberstein, L. R., & Rodin, J. (1986). Toward an understanding of risk factors for bulimia. *American Psychologist, 41,* 246–263.

Stromeyer, C. F., & Psotka, J. (1970). The detailed texture of eidetic images. *Nature, 225,* 346–349.

Strupp, H. H. (1996). The tripartite model and the *Consumer Reports* study. *American Psychologist, 51,* 1017–1024.

Styron, W. (1990). *Darkness visible: A memoir of madness.* New York: Random House.

Suchman, A. L., & Ader, R. (1989). Placebo response in humans can be shaped by prior pharmacologic experience. *Psychosomatic Medicine, 51,* 251.

Suddath, R. L., Christison, G. W., Torrey, E. F., Casanova, M. F., & Weinberger, D. R. (1990). Anatomical abnormalities in the brains of nonpsychotic twins discordant for schizophrenia. *New England Journal of Medicine, 322,* 789–794.

Sue, S. (1991). Ethnicity and culture in psychological research and practice. In J. D. Goodchilds (Ed.), *Psychological perspectives on human diversity in America* (pp. 47–86). Washington, DC: American Psychological Association.

Sulloway, F. J. (1996). *Born to rebel: Birth order, family dynamics, and creative lives.* New York: Pantheon.

Suls, J., & Marco, C. A. (1990). Relationship between JAS- and FTAS-Type A behavior and non-CHD illness: A prospective study controlling for negative affectivity. *Health Psychology, 9,* 479–492.

Suls, J., & Sanders, G. S. (1988). Type A behavior as a general risk factor for physical disorder. *Journal of Behavioral Medicine, 11,* 201–226.

Swann, W. B., Jr., Hixon, J. G., & De La Ronde, C. (1992). Embracing the bitter "truth": Negative self-concepts and marital commitment. *Psychological Science, 3,* 118–121.

Swazey, J. P. (1974). *Chlorpromazine in psychiatry: A study of therapeutic innovation.* Cambridge, MA: MIT Press.

Sweeney, P. D., Anderson, K., & Bailey, S. (1986). Attributional style in depression: A meta-analytic review. *Journal of Personality and Social Psychology, 50,* 974–991.

Swets, J. A., & Bjork, R. A. (1990). Enhancing human performance: An evaluation of "new age" techniques considered by the U.S. Army. *Psychological Science, 1,* 85–96.

Szasz, T. S. (1961). *The myth of mental illness.* New York: Harper & Row.

Szasz, T. S. (1977). *The manufacture of models.* New York: Dell.

Task Force on Promotion and Dissemination of Psychological Procedures. (1993). *A report adopted by the Division 12 Board—October 1993.* Washington, D C: American Psychological Association, Division 12.

Taubes, G. (1998, May 29). As obesity rates rise, experts struggle to explain why. *Science, 280,* 1367–1368.

Tavris, C. (1983). *Anger: The misunderstood emotion.* New York: Simon & Schuster.

Tavris, C. (1991). The mismeasure of woman: Paradoxes and perspectives in the study of gender. In J. D. Goodchilds (Ed.), *Psychological perspectives on human diversity in America* (pp. 87–136). Washington, DC: American Psychological Association.

Tavris, C. (1995). From excessive rage to useful anger. *Contemporary Psychology, 40* (11), 1101–1102.

Tavris, C. (2000). *Psychobabble and biobunk: Using psychology to think critically about Issues in the news.* Upper Saddle River, NJ: Prentice Hall.

Taylor, S. E. (1986). *Health psychology.* New York: Random House.

Taylor, S. E. (1990). Health psychology: The science and the field. *American Psychologist, 45,* 40–50.

Taylor, S. E. (1992). *Health psychology* (3rd ed.). New York: Random House.

Taylor, S. E. (1995). *Health psychology* (3rd ed). New York: McGraw Hill.

Taylor, S. E., Kemeny, M. E., Reed, G. M., Bower, J. E., & Gruenewald, T. L. (2000). Psychological resources, positive illusions, and health. *American Psychologist, 55,* 99–109.

Taylor, S. E., Klein, L., Lewis, B. P., Gruenewald, T. L., Gurung, R. A. R., & Updegraff, J. A. (2000). Biobehavioral responses to stress in females: Tend-and-befriend, not fight-or-flight. *Psychological Review, 107,* 411–429.

Tellegen, A., Lykken, D. T., Bouchard, T. J., Wilcox, K. J., Segal, N. L., & Rich, S. (1988). Personality similarity in twins reared apart and together. *Journal of Personality and Social Psychology, 54,* 1031–1039.

Templin, M. (1957). Certain language skills in children: Their development and interrelationships. *Institute of Child Welfare Monograph,* Series No. 26. Minneapolis: University of Minnesota Press.

Terman, L., & Oden, M. H. (1959). *Genetic studies of genius: Vol 4. The gifted group at midlife.* Stanford, CA: Stanford University Press.

Terman, L. M. (1916). *The measurement of intelligence.* Boston: Houghton Mifflin.

Terry, W. S. (2000). *Learning and memory: Basic*

principles, processes, and procedures. Boston: Allyn and Bacon.

Tesser, A., & Brodie, M. (1971). A note on the evaluation of a "computer date." *Psychonomic Science, 23,* 300.

Thackwray, D. E., Smith, M. C., Bodfish, J. W., & Myers, A. W. (1993). A comparison of behavioral and cognitive–behavioral interventions for bulimia nervosa. *Journal of Consulting and Clinical Psychology, 61,* 639–645.

Thigpen, C. H., & Cleckley, H. A. (1957). *Three faces of Eve.* New York: McGraw-Hill.

Thio, A. (1995). *Deviant behavior.* New York: HarperCollins.

Thomas, F. F. (1991). *Impact on teaching: Research with culturally diverse populations.* Symposium conducted at the Western Psychological Association Convention, San Francisco.

Thompson, D. M. (1988). Context and false recognition. In G. M. Davies & D. M. Thompson (Eds.), *Memory in context: Context in memory* (pp. 285–304). New York: Wiley.

Thompson, J. K. (1986, April). Larger than life. *Psychology Today,* pp. 38–44.

Thoresen, C. E. (1990). *Recurrent coronary prevention project: Results after 8¹/₂ years.* Symposium presented at the First International Congress of Behavioral Medicine, Uppsala, Sweden.

Thorndike, E. L. (1998). Animal intelligence: An experimental study of the associate processes in animals. *American Psychologist, 53,* 1125–1127. (Originally published by E. L. Thorndike, 1898, *Psychological Review Monograph Supplement, 2(4),* 1–8.)

Thorndyke, P. W., & Hayes-Roth, B. (1979). *Spatial knowledge acquisition from maps and navigation.* Paper presented at the Psychonomic Society Meeting, San Antonio, TX.

Thorpe, S. J., & Fabre-Thorpe, M. (2001, January 12). Seeking categories in the brain. *Science, 291,* 260–263.

Tienari, P., Sorri, A., Lahti, I., Naarala, M., Wahlberg, K.-E., Moring, J., Pohjola, J., & Wynne, L. C. (1987). Genetic and psychosocial factors in schizophrenia: The Finnish adoptive family study. *Schizophrenia Bulletin, 13,* 476–483.

Tilson, R. L., & Seal, U. S. (Eds.). (1988). *Tigers of the world: The biology, biopolitics, management, and conservation of an endangered species.* Park Ridge, NJ: Noyes Publications.

Todes, D. P. (1997). From the machine to the ghost within: Pavlov's transition from digestive physiology to conditional reflexes. *American Psychologist, 52,* 947–955.

Tolman, E. C. (1932). *Purposive behavior in animals and men.* New York: Appleton.

Tolman, E. C. (1948). Cognitive maps in rats and men. *Psychological Review, 55,* 189–208.

Tolman, E. C., & Honzik, C. H. (1930). "Insight" in rats. *University of California Publications in Psychology, 4,* 215–232.

Tolman, E. C., Ritchie, B. G., & Kalish, D. (1946). Studies in spatial learning: I. Orientation and the short-cut. *Journal of Experimental Psychology, 36,* 13–24.

Tomasello, M. (2000). Culture and cognitive development. *Current Directions in Psychological Science, 9,* 37–40.

Tononi, G., & Edelman, G. M. (1998, December 4). Consciousness and complexity. *Science, 282,* 1846–1850.

Torrey, E. F. (1996). *Out of the shadows: Confronting America's mental illness crisis.* New York: Wiley.

Torrey, E. F. (1997). The release of the mentally ill from institutions: A well-intentioned disaster. *The Chronicle of Higher Education,* B4–B5.

Totterdell, P. (2000). Catching moods and hitting runs: Mood linkage and subjective performance in professional sport. *Journal of Applied Psychology, 85,* 848–859.

Totterdell, P., Kellett, S., Briner, R. B., & Teuchmann, K. (1998). Evidence of mood linkage in work groups. *Journal of Personality and Social Psychology, 74,* 1504–1515.

Travis, J. (1998, October 31). Adult human brains add new cells. *Science News, 154,* 276.

Travis, J. (2000, September 23). Snap, crackle, and feel good? Magnetic fields that map the brain may also treat its disorders. *Science News, 158,* 204–206.

Travis, J. (2000, October 14). Pioneers of brain-cell signaling earn Nobel. *Science News, 158,* 247.

Triandis, H. (1989). The self and social behavior in differing cultural contexts. *Psychological Review, 96,* 506–520.

Triandis, H. (1990). Cross-cultural studies of individualism and collectivism. In J. Berman (Ed.), *Nebraska Symposium on Motivation, 1989* (pp. 42–133). Lincoln: University of Nebraska Press.

Triandis, H. C. (1994). *Culture and social behavior.* New York: McGraw-Hill.

Triandis, H. C. (1995). *Individualism & collectivism.* Boulder, CO: Westview Press.

Triandis, H. C. (1996). The psychological measurement of cultural syndromes. *American Psychologist, 51,* 407–415.

Tronick, E., Als, H., & Brazelton, T. B. (1980). Moradic phases: A structural description analysis of infant-mother face to face interaction. *Merrill-Palmer Quarterly, 26,* 3–24.

Trope, I., Rozin, P., Nelson, D. K., & Gur, R. C. (1992). Information processing in separated hemispheres of the callosotomy patients: Does the analytic–holistic dichotomy hold? *Brain and Cognition, 19,* 123–147.

Tsai, M., & Uemura, A. (1988). Asian Americans: The struggles, the conflicts, and the successes. In P. Bronstein & K. Quina (Eds.), *Teaching a psychology of people: Resources for gender and sociocultural awareness.* Washington, DC: American Psychological Association.

Tsuang, M. T., & Faraone, S. V. (1990). *The genetics of mood disorders.* Baltimore, MD: Johns Hopkins University Press.

Tulving, E. (1983). *Elements of episodic memory.* Oxford, U.K.: Clarendon Press.

Turk, D. C. (1994). Perspectives on chronic pain: The role of psychological factors. *Current Directions in Psychological Science, 3,* 45–48.

Turkington, C. (1992, February). Depression? It's in the eye of the beholder. *APA Monitor,* pp. 14–15.

Turner, J. C., & Oakes, P. J. (1989). Self-categorization theory and social influence. In P. B. Paulus (Ed.), *Psychology of group influence* (2nd ed.). Hillsdale, NJ: Erlbaum.

Turvey, M. T. (1996). Dynamic touch. *American Psychologist, 51,* 1134–1152.

Tversky, A., & Kahneman, D. (1973). Availability: A heuristic for judging frequency and probability. *Cognitive Psychology, 5,* 207–232.

Tversky, A., & Kahneman, D. (1974). Judgment under uncertainty: Heuristics and biases. *Science, 185,* 1124–1131.

Tyler, L. (1988). Mental testing. In E. R. Hilgard (Ed.), *Fifty years of psychology* (pp. 127–138). Glenview, IL: Scott, Foresman.

Uleman, J. S., & Bargh, J. A. (1989). *Unintended thought.* New York: Guilford Press.

Ulrich, R. E., & Azrin, N. H. (1962). Reflexive fighting in response to aversive stimulation. *Journal of the Experimental Analysis of Behavior, 5,* 511–520.

U. S. Department of Health and Human Services (2000). *Reducing tobacco use: A report of the Surgeon General.* Atlanta, GA: U. S. Department of Health and Human Services.

U.S. Merit Systems Protection Board (1995). *Sexual harassment in the federal workplace: Trends, progress, continuing challenges.* Washington, DC: U.S. Government Printing Office.

Valenstein, E. S. (Ed.). (1980). *The psychosurgery debate.* New York: Freeman.

Valenstein, E. S. (1998). *Blaming the brain: The truth about drugs and mental health.* New York: The Free Press.

Vallee, B. L. (1998, June). Alcohol in the western world. *Scientific American, 278(6),* 80–85.

van Dam, L. (1996, October 1). Mindful healing: An interview with Herbert Benson. *Technology Review, 99(7),* 31–38.

Van de Castle, R. L. (1983). Animal figures in fantasy and dreams. In A. Katcher & A. Beck (Eds.), New perspectives on our lives with companion animals. Philadelphia: University of Pennsylvania Press.

Van de Castle, R. L. (1994). *Our dreaming mind.* New York: Ballantine Books.

VandenBos, G. R. (1986). Psychotherapy research: A special issue. *American Psychologist, 41,* 111–112.

Vernon, P. E. (1969). *Intelligence and cultural environment.* London: Methuen.

Vernon, P. E. (1987). The demise of the Stanford-Binet Scale. *Canadian Psychology, 28,* 251–258.

Viken, R. J., & McFall, R. M. (1994). Paradox lost: Implications of contemporary reinforcement theory for behavior therapy. *Current Directions in Psychological Science, 3,* 121–125.

Vincent, K. R. (1991). Black/white IQ differences: Does age make a difference? *Journal of Clinical Psychology, 47,* 266–270.

Vincent, M., & Pickering, M. R. (1988). Multiple personality disorder in childhood. *Canadian Journal of Psychiatry, 33,* 524–529.

Vitaliano, P. P., Russo, J., Young, H. M., Becker, J., & Maiuro, R. D. (1991). The screen for caregiver burden. *The Gerontologist, 31,* 76–83.

Vogel, G. (1996, November 22). Illusion reveals pain locus in brain. *Science, 274,* 1301.

Vogel, G. (1997a, February 28). Scientists probe feelings behind decision-making. *Science, 275,* 1269.

Vogel, G. (1997b, October 3). Cocaine wreaks subtle damage on developing brains. *Science, 278,* 38–39.

Volz, J. (2000, February). In search of the good life. *Monitor on Psychology, 31*(2), 68–69.

von Hofsten, C., & Lindhagen, K. (1979). Observations on the development of reaching for moving objects. *Journal of Child Psychology, 28,* 158–173.

Wade, T. J. (1991). Race and sex differences in adolescent self-perceptions of physical attractiveness and level of self-esteem during early and late adolescence. *Journal of Personality and Individual Differences, 12,* 1319–1324.

Walden, J., Normann, C., Langosch, J., Berger, M., & Grunze, H. (1998). Differential treatment of bipolar disorder with old and new antiepileptic drugs. *Neuropsychobiology, 38,* 181–184.

Walker, E. F., & Diforio, D. (1997). Schizophrenia: A neural diathesis-stress model. *Psychological Review, 104,* 667–685.

Walker, L. J. (1989). A longitudinal study of moral reasoning. *Child Development, 60,* 157–166.

Walker, L. J. (1991). Sex differences in moral reasoning. In W. M. Kurtines & J. L. Gewirtz (Eds.), *Handbook of moral behavior and development: Research* (Vol. 2, pp. 333–364). Hillsdale, NJ: Erlbaum.

Walker, L. J., & de Vries, B. (1985). Moral stages/moral orientations: Do the sexes really differ? Paper presented at the annual meeting of the American Psychological Association, Los Angeles.

Walker, L. J., de Vries, B., & Trevethan, S. D. (1987). Moral stages and moral orientations in real-life and hypothetical dilemmas. *Child Development, 58,* 842–858.

Wallace, A. F. C. (1959). Cultural determinants of response to hallucinatory experience. *Archives of General Psychiatry, 1,* 58–69.

Wallbott, H. G., Ricci-Bitti, P., & Baenninger-Huber, E. (1986). Non-verbal reactions to emotional experiences. In K. R. Scherer, H. G. Wallbott, & A. B. Summerfield (Eds.), *Experiencing emotion: A cross-cultural study* (pp. 98–116). Cambridge, England: Cambridge University Press.

Wallis, C. (1984, June 11). Unlocking pain's secrets. *Time,* pp. 58–66.

Walsh, R. (1984). Asian psychologies. In R. Corsini (Ed.), *Encyclopedia of psychology* (pp. 90–94). New York: Wiley.

Walster (Hatfield), E., Aronson, V., Abrahams, D., & Rottman, L. (1966). Importance of physical attractiveness in dating behavior. *Journal of Personality and Social Psychology, 5,* 508–516.

Walters, C. C., & Grusec, J. E. (1977). *Punishment.* San Francisco: Freeman.

Walters, E. E., Neale, M. C., Eaves, L. J., Heath, A. C., Kessler, R. C., & Kendler, K. S. (1992). Bulimia nervosa and major depression: A study of common genetic and environmental factors. *Psychological Medicine, 22* (3), 617–622.

Wardle, J., Steptoe, A., Bellisle, F., Davou, B., Reschke, K., & Lappalainen, M. (1997). Healthy dietary practices among European students. *Health Psychology, 16,* 443–450.

Wassermann, E. M., & Lisanby, S. H. (2001). Therapeutic application of repetitive transcranial magnetic stimulation: A review. *Clinical Neurophysiology, 112,* 1367–1377.

Watkins, L. R., & Mayer, D. J. (1982). Organization of the endogenous opiate and nonopiate pain control systems. *Science, 216,* 1185–1193.

Watson, J. B., & Rayner, R. (2000). Conditioned emotional reactions. *American Psychologist, 55,* 313–317. (Original work published by J. B. Watson and R. Rayner, 1920, *Journal of Experimental Psychology, 3,* pp. 1–14.)

Weber, A. L., & Harvey, J. H. (Eds.) (1994a). *Perspectives on close relationships.* Boston, MA: Allyn & Bacon.

Weber, A. L., & Harvey, J. H. (1994b). Accounts in coping with relationship loss. In A. L. Weber & J. H. Harvey (Eds.), *Perspectives on close relationships,* pp. 285–306. Boston: Allyn & Bacon.

Wegner, D. M. (1989). *White bears and other unwanted thoughts.* New York: Guilford.

Wegner, D. M., Schneider, D. J., Carter, S., III, & White, T. (1987). Paradoxical effects of thought suppression. *Journal of Personality and Social Psychology, 53,* 5–13.

Wehr, T. A., & Rosenthal, N. E. (1989). Seasonality and affective illness. *American Journal of Psychiatry, 146,* 829–839.

Weil, A. T. (1977). The marriage of the sun and the moon. In N. E. Zinberg (Ed.), *Alternate states of consciousness* (pp. 37–52). New York: Free Press.

Weinberger, M., Hiner, S. L, & Tierney, W. M. (1987). In support of hassles as a measure of stress in predicting health outcomes. *Journal of Behavioral Medicine, 10,* 19–31.

Weiner, J. (1994). *The beak of the finch.* New York: Vintage Books.

Weingardt, K. R., Loftus, E. F., & Lindsay, D. S. (1995). Misinformation revisited: New evidence on the suggestibility of memory. *Memory and Cognition, 23,* 72–82.

Weisberg, R. (1986). *Creativity, genius, and other myths.* New York: Freeman.

Weissman, M. M., Bland, R. C., Canino, G. J., Faravelli, C., Greenwald, S., Hwu, H. G., Joyce, P. R., Karam, E. G., Lee, C. K., Lellouch, J., Lepine, J. P., Newman, S. C., Rubio-Stipec, M., Wells, J. E., Wickramaratne, P. J., Wittchen, H., Yeh, E. K. (1996, July 24–31). Cross-national epidemiology of major depression and bipolar disorder. *Journal of the American Medical Association, 276,* 293–299.

Weissman, M. M., Merikangas, K. R., Wickramaratne, P., Kidd, K. K., Prusoff, B. A., Leckman, J. F., & Pauls, D. L. (1986). Understanding the clinical heterogeneity of major depression using family data. *Archives of General Psychiatry, 43,* 430–434.

Wellman, H. M., & Estes, D. (1986). Early understanding of mental entities: A reexamination of childhood realism. *Child Development, 57,* 910–923.

Welsh, E. J., Gullotta, C., & Rapoport, J. (1993). Classroom academic performance: Improvement with both methylphenidate and dextroamphetamine in ADHD boys. *Journal of Child Psychology and Psychiatry and Allied Disciplines, 34,* 785–804.

Wertheimer, M. (1923). Untersuchungen zur Lehre von der Gestalt, II. *Psychologische Forschung, 4,* 301–350.

Wesson, D. R., Smith, D. E., & Seymour, R. B. (1992). Sedative-hypnotics and tricyclics. In J. H. Lowinson, P. Ruiz, R. B. Millman, & J. G. Langrod (Eds.), *Substance abuse: A comprehensive textbook* (2nd ed.) (pp. 271–279). Baltimore: Williams & Wilkins.

Whalen, C. K., & Henker, B. (1991). Therapies for hyperactive children: Comparisons, combinations, and compromises. *Journal of Consulting and Clinical Psychology, 59,* 126–137.

Whalen, P. J. (1998a). *Current Directions in Psychological Science, 7,* 177–188.

Whalen, P. J. (1998b). Fear, vigilance, and ambiguity: Initial neuroimaging studies of the human amygdala. *Current Directions in Psychological Science, 7,* 177–188.

Wheeler, D. L. (1999, January 22). Prospect of fetal-gene therapy stimulates high hopes and deep fears. *The Chronicle of Higher Education,* A13.

Whiteman, M. C., & Fowkes, F. G. R. (1997, August 16). Hostility and the heart. *British Medical Journal,* Issue 7105, 379–380.

Whitley, B. E., Jr. (1999). Right-wing authoritarianism, social dominance orientation, and prejudice. *Journal of Personality and Social Psychology, 7,* 126–134.

Who wants to be a genius? (2001, January 13). *The Economist, 358*(8204), 77–78.

Whyte, W. F. (1972, April). Skinnerian theory in organizations. *Psychology Today,* pp. 67–68, 96, 98, 100.

Wickelgren, I. (1997, June 27). Marijuana: Harder than thought? *Science, 276,* 1967–1968.

Wickelgren, I. (1998a, June 26). Teaching the brain to take drugs. *Science, 280,* 2045–2047.

Wickelgren, I. (1998b, August 28). A new route to treating schizophrenia? *Science, 281,* 1264–1265.

Wickelgren, I. (1998c, September 11). The cerebellum: The brain's engine of agility. *Science, 281,* 1588–1590.

Wickelgren, I. (1998d, May 29). Obesity: How big a problem? *Science, 280,* 1364–1367.

Wickelgren, I. (1999, March 19). Nurture helps mold able minds. *Science, 283,* 1832–1834.

Wickelgren, I. (2001, March 2). Working memory helps the mind focus. *Science, 291,* 1684–1685.

Wickelgren, W. (1974). *How to solve problems: Elements of a theory of problems and problem solving.* San Francisco: W. H. Freeman.

Wiggins, J. S. (1973). *Personality and prediction: Principles of personality assessment.* Reading, MA: Addison-Wesley.

Williams, T. M. (Ed.). (1986). *The impact of television: A natural experiment in three communities.* Orlando, FL: Academic Press.

Wills, T. A., & DePaulo, B. M. (1991). Interpersonal analysis of the help-seeking process. In C. R. Snyder & D. R. Forsyth (Eds.), *Handbook of social and clinical psychology: The health perspective* (pp. 350–375). New York: Pergamon Press.

Wilner, D., Walkley, R., & Cook, S. (1955). *Human relations in interracial housing.* Minneapolis: University of Minnesota Press.

Wilson, E. D., Reeves, A., & Culver, C. (1977).

Cerebral commissurotomy for control of intractable seizures. *Neurology, 27,* 708–715.

Wilson, S. M., & Medora, N. P. (1990). Gender comparisons of college students' attitudes toward sexual behavior. *Adolescence, 25,* 615–627.

Windholz, G. (1997). Ivan P. Pavlov: An overview of his life and psychological work. *American Psychologist, 52,* 941–946.

Winograd, E., & Neisser, U. (Eds.). (1992). *Affect and accuracy in recall: Studies of "flashbulb" memories.* New York: Cambridge University Press.

Winson, J. (1990, November). The meaning of dreams. *Scientific American, 263,* 86–96.

Wolpe, J. (1958). *Psychotherapy by reciprocal inhibition.* Stanford, CA: Stanford University Press.

Wolpe, J. (1973). *The practice of behavior therapy* (2nd ed.). New York: Pergamon.

Wolpe, J. (1985). Existential problems and behavior therapy. *The Behavior Therapist, 8,* 126–127.

Wolpe, J., & Plaud, J. J. (1997). Pavlov's contributions to behavior therapy: The obvious and the not so obvious. *American Psychologist, 52,* 966–972.

Wong, M. M., & Csikszentmihalyi, M. (1991). Motivation and academic achievement: The effects of personality traits and the quality of experience. *Journal of Personality, 59,* 539–574.

Wood, J. M., Nezworski, M. T., & Stejskal, W. J. (1996). The comprehensive system for the Rorschach: A critical examination. *Psychological Science, 7,* 3–10.

Wood, J. V., Saltzberg, J. A., & Goldsamt, L. A. (1990a). Does affect induce self-focused attention? *Journal of Personality and Social Psychology, 58,* 899–908.

Wood, J. V., Saltzberg, J. A., Neale, J. M., Stone, A. A., & Rachmiel, T. B. (1990b). Self-focused attention, coping responses, and distressed mood in everyday life. *Journal of Personality and Social Psychology, 58,* 1027–1036.

Woods, S. C., Seeley, R. J., Porte, Jr., D., Schwartz, M. W. (1998, May 29). Signals that regulate food intake and energy homeostasis. *Science, 280,* 1378–1383.

Woodworth, R. S. (1918). *Dynamic psychology.* New York: Columbia University Press.

Wooten, P. (1994). *Heart, humor and healing.* Salt Lake City, UT: Commune A Key Publishing.

Wooten, P. (1996). Humor: An antidote for stress. *Holistic Nursing Practice, 10,* 49–55.

World Health Organization (1973). *Report of the International Pilot Study of Schizophrenia* (Vol. 1). Geneva: Author.

World Health Organization (1979). *Schizophrenia: An international follow-up study.* New York: Wiley.

Wright, E. R., Gronfein, W. P., & Owens, T. J. (2000). Deinstitutionalization, social rejection, and self-esteem of former mental patients. *Journal of Health and Social Behavior, 41,* 68–90.

Wright, K., & Mahurin, M. (1997, October). Babies, bonds, and brains. *Discover,* 74–78.

Wright, L. (1988). The Type A behavior pattern and coronary artery disease: Quest for the active ingredients and the elusive mechanism. *American Psychologist, 43,* 2–14.

Wu, C. (1998, April 4). Ritalin may work better as a purer compound. *Science News, 153,* 213.

Wurtman, R. J. (1982, April). Nutrients that modify brain functions. *Scientific American, 242,* 50–59.

Wyatt, G. E., Peters, S. D., & Guthrie, D. (1988). Kinsey revisited, Part I: Comparisons of the sexual socialization and sexual behavior of white women over 33 years. *Archives of Sexual Behavior, 17,* 201–239.

Wynn, K. (1992). Addition and subtraction by human infants. *Nature, 358,* 749–759.

Wynn, K. (1995). Infants possess a system of numerical knowledge. *Current Directions in Psychological Science, 4,* 172–177.

Yalom, I. D., & Greaves, C. (1977). Group therapy with the terminally ill. *American Journal of Psychiatry, 134,* 396–400.

Yerkes, R. M. (1921). Psychological examining in the United States Army. In R. M. Yerkes (Ed.), *Memoirs of the National Academy of Sciences: Vol. 15.* Washington, DC: U.S. Government Printing Office.

Zajonc, R. B. (1968). Attitudinal effects of mere exposure. *Journal of Personality and Social Psychology. Monograph Supplement, 9* (2 Part 2), 1–27.

Zajonc, R. B. (1980). Feeling and thinking: Preferences need no inferences. *American Psychologist, 35,* 151–175.

Zajonc, R. B. (1984). On the primacy of affect. *American Psychologist, 39,* 117–123.

Zajonc, R. B. (2001). *Mere exposure effects explained . . . finally!* Address given to the Western Psychological Association annual convention in Lahaina (Maui), Hawaii.

Zeki, S. (1992, September). The visual image in mind and brain. *Scientific American, 267,* 68–76.

Zeman, N. (1990, Summer/Fall). The new rules of courtship (Special Edition). *Newsweek,* 24–27.

Zigler, E., & Muenchow, S. (1992). *Head Start: The inside story of America's most successful educational experiment.* New York: Basic Books.

Zigler, E., & Styfco, S. J. (1994). Head Start: Criticisms in a constructive context. *American Psychologist, 49,* 127–132.

Zilbergeld, B. (1986, June). Psychabuse. *Science 86, 7,* 48.

Zimbardo, P. G. (1973). On the ethics of investigation in human psychological research: With special reference to the Stanford Prison Experiment. *Cognition, 2,* 243–256.

Zimbardo, P. G. (1975). On transforming experimental research into advocacy for social change. In M. Deutsch & H. Hornstein (Eds.), *Applying social psychology: Implications for research, practice, and training* (pp. 33–66). Hillsdale, NJ: Erlbaum.

Zimbardo, P. G. (1990). *Shyness: What it is, what to do about it* (Rev. ed.). Reading, MA: Perseus Books. (Original work published 1977).

Zimbardo, P. G. (1995). *The psychology of time perspective:* Selected readings. Stanford, CA: Stanford University Custom Publishing.

Zimbardo, P. G. (2001). Opposing terrorism by understanding the human capacity for evil. *Monitor on Psychology, 32*(10), 48–50.

Zimbardo, P. G., Andersen, S. M., & Kabat, L. (1981). Induced hearing deficit generates experimental paranoia. *Science, 212,* 1529–1531.

Zimbardo, P. G., & Leippe, M. (1991). *The psychology of attitude change and social influence.* New York: McGraw-Hill.

Zimbardo, P. G., Maslach, C., & Haney, C. (1999). Reflections on the Stanford prison Experiment: Genesis, transformations, consequences. In T. Blass (Ed.), *Obedience to authority: Current perspectives on the Milgram paradigm* (pp. 193-237). Mahwah, NJ: Erlbaum.

Zimbardo, P. G., & Montgomery, K. D. (1957). The relative strengths of consummatory responses in hunger, thirst, and exploratory drive. *Journal of Comparative and Physiological Psychology, 50,* 504–508.

Zucker, G. S., & Weiner, B. (1993). Conservatism and perceptions of poverty: An attributional analysis. *Journal of Applied Social Psychology, 23,* 925–943.

Zuckerman, M. (1971). Dimensions of sensation seeking. *Journal of Consulting and Clinical Psychology, 36,* 45–52.

Zuckerman, M. (1974). The sensation-seeking motive. In B. Maher (Ed.), *Progress in experimental personality research* (Vol. 7). New York: Academic Press.

Zuckerman, M. (1978, February). The search for high sensation. *Psychology Today, 12,* 38–46.

Zuckerman, M. (1979). *Sensation seeking: Beyond the optimal level of arousal.* Hillsdale, NJ: Erlbaum.

Zuckerman, M. (1990). Some dubious premises in research and theory on racial differences: Scientific, social, and ethical issues. *American Psychologist, 45,* 1297–1303.

Zuckerman, M. (1995). Good and bad humors: Biochemical bases of personality and its disorders. *Psychological Science, 6,* 325–332.

Zuckerman, M., Buchsbaum, M. S., & Murphy, D. L. (1980). Sensation seeking and its biological correlates. *Psychological Bulletin, 88,* 187–214.

Zuckerman, M., Depaulo, B. M., & Rosenthal, R. (1981). Verbal and nonverbal communication of deception. *Advances in Experimental Social Psychology, 14,* 1–59.

Zuckerman, M., Eysenck, S., & Eysenck, H. J. (1978). Sensation seeking in England and America: Cross-cultural, age and sex comparisons. *Journal of Consulting and Clinical Psychology, 46,* 139–149.

CREDITS

Chapter 1: page 2, top, © Dion Ogust/The Image Works; page 2, middle, © Matthew McVay/Stock Boston; page 2, bottom middle, © Bettmann /CORBIS; page 2, bottom, Courtesy of the author; page 5, © Davis Barber/PhotoEdit; page 6, Archives of the History of American Psychology, University of Akron; page 8, © Dion Ogust/The Image Works; page 10, © Larry Mulvehill/Photo Researchers, Inc.; page 12, AP/Wide World Photos; page 13, © R. Lord/The Image Works; page 15, © Matthew McVay/Stock Boston; page 19, © Bettmann/CORBIS; page 22, V. Richard Haro/Fort Collins Coloradoan; page 23, from "The Cartoon Guide to Statistics" by Larry Gonick & Wollcott Smith; page 25, © The New Yorker Collection 1993. Donald Reilly from cartoonbank.com. All Rights Reserved; page 27, © Hugo Van Lawick/National Geographic Image Collection; page 29, © P. Gontier/Explorer/Photo Researchers, Inc.; page 30, Courtesy of the author.

Chapter 2: page 38, AP/Wide World Photos; page 40, Courtesy of Robert Lee Johnson; page 42, © Tim Davis/Getty Images/Stone; page 46, AP/Wide World Photos; page 54, © AFP/CORBIS; page 60, Damasio H, Grabowski T, Frank R, Galaburda A M, Damasio A R: The return of Phineas Gage: Clues about the brain from a famous patient. *Science,* 264:1102–1105, 1994. Department of Neurology and Image Analysis Facility, University of Iowa; page 61 top, bottom, Courtesy of Monte S. Buchsbaum, M.D., Mt. Sinai School of Medicine, New York, NY; page 61 middle, © Roger Tully/Getty Images/Stone; page 63, © Myrleen F. Cate/PhotoEdit; page 64 left, © Dana White/PhotoEdit; page 64 right, © Jeff Greenberg/PhotoEdit; page 64 bottom, © Esbin-Anderson/The Image Works.

Chapter 3: page 80 top, © Ogust/The Image Works; page 80 bottom, © David Young-Wolff/Getty Images/Stone; page 83, Chagall, Marc (1887–1986) *Priere ,* 1976 Coll. Privata St. Paul de Vence Scala/Art Resource, NY; page 84, Volker Steger/Peter Arnold, Inc.; page 88, © Rhoda Sidney/The Image Works; page 94 , Norman Kelly Tjampiginpa, *Flying Ant Dreaming.* Jennifer Steele/Art Resource, NY; page 96, © Ogust/The Image Works; page 99, © Chad Slattery/Getty Images/Stone; page 100, © Amy Etra/PhotoEdit; page 101, PhotoDisc, Inc.; page 102 left, © Richard Heinzen/Superstock, Inc.; page 102 right, © Michael Newman/PhotoEdit; page 104, © Jeff Greenberg/PhotoEdit; page 105, Images in Neuroscience, Carol

A. Tamminga, M.D., Editor, Neuroimaging, XIII, SPECT Imaging of Synaptic Dopamine, Photographs courtesy of Dr. Innis, *Am J Psychiatry 153:*10, October 1996; page 107 top, © David Young-Wolff/ Getty Images/Stone; page 107 bottom, © Mark M. Lawrence/CORBIS Stock Market.

Chapter 4: page 114 top, © Chemical Design Ltd/Science Photo Library/Photo Researchers, Inc.; page 114 middle top, © Getty Images; page 114 middle bottom, © 1996 Thomas Hoepker/Magnum Photos; page 114 bottom, © Bob Daemmrich/The Image Works; page 118, © T.K. Wanstal/The Image Works; page 119 left, © CNP/Arnie Sachs/Hulton Archive/Getty Images; page 119 middle and right, AP/Wide World Photos; page 120, © Chemical Design Ltd/Science Photo Library/Photo Researchers, Inc.; page 122, © Lennart Nilsson, *A Child Is Born*/Bonnier-Forlagen AB; page 128, © Getty Images; page 132, © George Goodwin Photography; page 135, © Lew Merrim/Photo Researchers, Inc.; page 136 , © Marcia Weinstein; page 139, © 1996 Thomas Hoepker/Magnum Photos; page 141, © Martin Roger/Stock Boston; page 146, © Bob Daemmrich/ Stock Boston; page 148, © Grantpix/Stock Boston; page 149, Genaro Moline from *A Day in California*; page 151, © Bob Daemmrich/The Image Works.

Chapter 5: page 160 top, © Chuck Fishman/Woodfin Camp & Associates; page 160 middle, © Superstock, Inc.; page 160 bottom, © Cary Wolinksy/Stock Boston; page 162, © Stephen Dalton/Animals, Animals; page 166, © Tony Freeman/PhotoEdit; page 167, © Chuck Fishman/Woodfin Camp & Associates; page 175, © Fitz Goro/TimePix; page 184, © Superstock, Inc.; page 187 left, AP/Wide World Photos; page 187 middle, © John Neubauer/PhotoEdit; page 187 right, © John Neubauer/PhotoEdit; page 188, Public Domain; page 190, © 2002 Artists Rights Society (ARS) New York/ADAGP, Paris; page 191, Cordon Art-Bam-Holland, M. C. Escher Heirs, collection of C. V. S. Roosevelt, Washington D.C.; page 191 left, © CORBIS Sygma; page 191 right, © CORBIS Sygma; page 192, "The Moment Before Death, " Russell Sorgi, from *Life: The First Fifty Years, 19361986* (Little Brown); page 195, Tate Gallery, London/Art Resource, NY 1999 © Artist Rights Society, New York; page 197, © Bob Daemmrich/Stock Boston; page 198, © Cary Wolinksy/Stock Boston.

NAME INDEX

Batista, A. P., 172
Batson, C. D., 559, 561
Baum, A., 381–382
Baum, W. M., 223
Baumeister, A. A., 314
Baumeister, R. F., 350, 360, 434, 572
Baumrind, D., 29
Baynes, K., 73
Beach, F. A., 370
Beall, A. E., 570
Beaman, A. L., 558
Beardsley, T., 89, 250, 258, 263, 291
Bechara, A., 292, 345
Beck, A. T., 521
Becker, M. H., 407
Bédard, J., 331
Bee, H., 130, 139
Beeman, M. J., 69
Begley, S., 347, 522
Behrmann, M., 291, 292
Bell, A. P., 147, 371
Bem, D. J., 371, 446
Benassi, V. A., 437
Benedict, R., 451
Benjamin, L. T., Jr., 18, 218
Bennet, A. B., 443–444
Bennett, P. J., 124
Benson, H., 101
Berenbaum, H., 401
Berk, L. E., 142, 407
Berkman, L. F., 404, 405
Berlyne, D. E., 358
Berman, J. S., 527
Berndt, T. J., 148
Bernstein, I. L., 123, 215
Berridge, K. C., 101
Berry, J., 320–321
Berry, J. W., 451
Berscheid, E., 570
Betz, N. E., 484
Beutler, L. E., 524
Biddle, N., 522
Biederman, I., 192
Biehl, M., 341
Billings, A. G., 404
Binet, A., 307
Binitie, A., 480
Bink, M. L., 304
Birenbaum, M., 443
Bishop, A. C., 532
Bjork, R., 101
Bjork, R. A., 169, 268, 280, 406, 447, 448
Bjorklund, D. F., 371
Blashfield, R. K., 463
Blass, E. M., 124
Blass, T., 553
Blatt, S. J., 450, 525
Blum, D., 29
Bodmer, W. F., 328
Bolger, N., 386
Bond, M. H., 443
Bongiovanni, A., 225
Boomsma, D., 45, 466
Booth-Kewley, S., 393
Bootzin, R. R., 97
Bornstein, R. F., 562

Borod, C., 347
Bostwick, J. M., 472
Bouchard, T. J., Jr., 45, 118, 120, 442
Bourguignon, E., 451
Bowden, C. L., 530
Bower, B., 29, 130, 136, 140, 141, 186, 255, 290, 372, 426, 473, 505, 565
Bower, G. H., 276, 278
Bowers, K. S., 100
Bowlby, J., 139
Boyatzis, R. E., 149
Bradbury, J., 472
Bradley, G. W., 566
Bradshaw, G., 298
Bradshaw, J. L., 69
Braine, M. D. S., 131
Brand, R. J., 399
Bransford, J., 32, 331
Bransford, J. D., 261
Breakey, W. R., 536
Breggin, G. R., 530
Breggin, P. R., 530, 534
Brehm, S. S., 360, 561, 562, 570
Brewer, M. B., 152
Brigham, J. C., 563
Brislin, R., 195, 294, 451
Brodie, M., 563
Broman, S. H., 330
Bronfenbrenner, U., 117
Bronte, L., 151
Brookhart, S., 577
Brooks-Gunn, J., 148
Brown, A. L., 32
Brown, A. M., 324
Brown, B., 121
Brown, D. E., 531
Brown, J. D., 268, 434
Brown, J. L., 327
Brown, R., 264, 269
Brown, S. A., 108
Brown, W. A., 185
Bruch, H., 483
Bruck, M., 275, 276
Brucker, B. S., 405
Brumberg, J. J., 483
Bruner, J. S., 135, 357
Brunner, H. G., 45
Bryden, M. P., 69
Buck, L., 181
Buie, J., 400
Buss, D. M., 42, 142, 339, 362, 370, 436
Butcher, J. N., 444, 445
Butterfield, E. C., 315
Byne, W., 372
Byrne, D., 562

Cahill, L., 265
Caldwell, M., 68, 346, 402
Calev, A., 534
Callahan, J., 100
Callaway, C. W., 366
Calvert, J. D., 563
Cameron, J., 361
Campbell, L., 276
Campbell, S. S., 473
Campfield, L. A., 367

Campione, J. C., 32
Campos, J. J., 139
Cann, A., 402
Caplow, T., 150
Caporeal, L. R., 463
Caprara, G. V., 444
Cardeña, E., 481
Carducci, B. J., 490
Carey, S., 130
Carlson, N. R., 52, 102, 236, 393
Carlsson, A., 486
Carmichael, L., 122
Carpenter, G. C., 123
Carpenter, S., 186, 226, 353
Carran, D. T., 314
Carskadon, T. G., 447
Carson, R. C., 461, 471, 480, 482, 485
Carstensen, L. L., 152
Cartwright, R. D., 94, 95, 96
Carver, C. S., 431, 443
Casey, J. F., 482
Cash, T. F., 562, 563
Cassileth, B. R., 407
Cattell, R. B., 317
Cavalli-Sforza, L. L., 328
Ceci, S., 275
Ceci, S. J., 117, 276, 319, 325
Cervone, D., 422
Chalmers, D. J., 83
Chamberlain, K., 386
Chambless, D. L., 525, 526
Chapman, P. D., 309
Charcot, J.-M., 464
Charness, N., 331
Chartrand, T. L., 550
Chaudhari, N., 182
Chi, M., 331
Chi, M. T. H., 331
Chiarello, C., 69
Chilman, C. S., 147
Chittajallu, R., 53
Chomsky, N., 129
Chorney, M. J., 324
Christensen, A., 509, 519, 525, 527
Churchland, P. M., 83
Cialdini, R., 577
Clark, E. V., 130
Clark, H. H., 130
Clark, M. S., 561
Clark, R. E., 237
Clarke-Stewart, K. A., 141
Clay, R. A., 398, 399, 506, 532
Cleckley, H. A., 482
Cleek, M. B., 150
Cloud, J., 379
Cobb, S., 405
Coe, W.C., 100
Cohen, A., 494
Cohen, N., 391
Cohen, R. E., 383
Cohen, S., 188, 395, 404, 405
Cole, M., 12
Coles, R., 147
Collins, A. W., 149
Collins, G. P., 61
Collins, M. E., 569

Fowers, B. J., 12
Fowkes, F. G. R., 398
Fowler, H., 358
Frager, R., 432
Frank, J., 523, 525
Frank, J. B., 523
Frank, J. D., 523
Franks, J. J., 261
Fraser, S., 329
Frasure-Smith, N., 399
Freedman, D. J., 291
Freedman, J. L., 235
French, E. G., 364
Freud, S., 86
Freund, A. M., 152
Fridlund, A. J., 138
Friedman, H. S., 388, 393, 399
Friedman, M., 398, 399
Friend, R., 552
Friesen, W. V., 341
Frith, C. D., 137
Frith, U., 137, 514
Fromm, E., 100
Fujita, F., 413
Funder, D. C., 446
Furnham, A., 566
Furumoto, L., 13, 15

Gabbay, F. H., 339
Gadsby, P., 182
Gage, F. H., 50
Gainetdinov, R. R., 532
Galambos, N. L., 149
Galef, B. G., 217
Gallagher, W., 138
Gallo, P. S., 450
Gallo, V., 53
Galluscio, E. H., 65
Ganchrow, J. R., 341
Garcia, J., 214, 215, 328
Gardiner, H. W., 450
Gardner, C. O., Jr., 473
Gardner, H., 11, 305, 319, 331
Gardyn, R., 106
Garland, A., 148
Garnets, L., 15
Garnsey, S. M., 291
Gazzaniga, M., 70, 71, 72
Gazzaniga, M. S., 11, 101, 107, 138
Gelernter, J., 45
Gelles, R. J., 225
Gelman, S. A., 135
Gentner, D., 331
George, M. S., 535
Gerard, H. B., 552
Gergen, K. J., 12
Gerrig, R.J., 217, 221
Getzels, J. W., 305
Gibbons, A., 42
Gibbs, W. W., 120, 189, 366
Gilbert, E. H., 483
Gilbert, R. M., 438
Gill, J. J., 399
Gilligan, C., 137
Gilligan, S. G., 276
Girgus, J. S., 188

Gitlin, M. J., 529
Givens, D. B., 184
Glanz, J., 255
Glaser, R., 32, 331, 395
Glass, G. V., 512
Glenberg, A. M., 268
Glutting, J. J., 323
Goddard, C. R., 401
Goldberg, L. R., 443
Goldenberg, J., 304
Goldin-Meadow, S., 130
Goldman-Rakic, P. S., 250, 288
Goldstein, A., 100
Goleman, D., 315, 352
Golombok, S., 371
Gonzalvo, P., 331
Goodchilds, J. D., 15
Goodman, G., 519
Goodwin, F. K., 472–473
Gordon, L., 286
Gorman, J., 3
Gottesman, I. I., 117, 486, 487
Gottlib, I. H., 474
Gottlieb, B. H., 404, 405, 410
Gottman, J., 350, 520, 571
Gottman, J. M., 150, 350
Gould, E., 394
Gould, S. J., 330, 445
Graham, J. R., 445
Gray, C. R., 251
Gray, P., 430
Graziano, M. S. A., 67
Greaves, C., 520
Greeley, S., 568
Green, D. M., 167
Greenberg, B. S., 568
Greenberg, L. S., 520
Greenberg, R. P., 430
Greene, B., 285, 286
Greene, R. L., 444, 445
Greeno, J. G., 331
Greenspan, S., 314
Greenwald, A. G., 87, 169, 357
Gregory, R., 186
Grevert, P., 100
Grigorenko, E. L., 238
Grinspoon, L., 102
Gross, J. J., 339, 353
Grove, W. M., 487
Grusec, J. E., 225
Guilford, J. P., 304, 317–318
Guisinger, S., 450
Gulya, M., 135
Gummerman, K., 251
Gur, R. E., 466, 530
Gura, T., 365, 366
Gustafson, S. B., 149
Guthrie, G. M., 443–444
Guthrie, R., 27

Haber, R. N., 251, 252
Haberlandt, K., 247, 280
Hacker, A., 286
Haimov, I., 92
Hall, C., 94, 95
Hall, C. S., 95

Haller, E., 366
Halpern, D. F., 286
Hamer, D., 45, 118, 120, 372
Hamer, D. H., 120
Hampson, R. E., 53
Haney, C., 546
Harber, K. D., 382
Haring, M. J., 413
Harlow, H. F., 141, 184
Harlow, M. K., 141
Harrington, D. M., 304, 305
Harris, B., 213, 561
Harris, G., 123, 184
Harris, J. R., 148
Hart, R. A., 290
Hartmann, E. L., 92
Hartup, W. W., 148
Harvey, J. H., 360, 384, 563, 570, 571
Harvey, S. M., 147
Hass, A., 147
Hassebrauck, M., 563
Hastie, R., 302
Hatfield, E., 146, 360, 562, 563, 570
Haviland, J. M., 350
Hawkins, R. D., 236
Hawkins, S. A., 302
Hayes, S. C., 529
Hayes-Roth, B., 290
Haynes, S. G., 398
Hazan, C., 140, 350
Headey, B., 413
Hecht, A., 531
Heckhausen, J., 152
Heeger, D. J., 186
Heiby, E., 529
Heine, S. L., 436, 565
Heinrichs, R. W., 486
Heller, W., 70, 346
Helmes, E., 444
Helms, J., 328
Helms, J. E., 328
Helmuth, L., 67
Hendrick, C., 562
Hendrick, S. S., 562
Henker, B., 532
Henley, N., 184
Herek, G. M., 372
Herman, C., 483
Herman, J. L., 276
Heron, W. G., 235
Heston, L. L., 486
Hetherington, E. M., 138
Hetherington, M. M., 484
Hilgard, E. R., 100
Hill, J. O., 366
Hill, P. C., 413
Hilts, P. J., 65, 261
Hinton, G. F., 73
Hirai, T., 101
Hiroto, D. S., 400
Hirsch, J., 330
Hirschfeld, R. M. A., 472–473, 530
Hobson, J. A., 96
Hochwalder, J., 449
Hodges, L. F., 512
Hogan, R., 385, 441

SUBJECT INDEX

Appearance, self-esteem and, 146–147
Appetitive conditioning, 212
Applied psychology, 13
Aptitudes, 305, 306
Archetypes, 431
Arousal
    performance and, 342
    sexual, 368
    in stressful situation, 390–391
Artificial concepts, 289
Asch studies, 550–552, 551f
Assimilation, 132–133, 293
Association cortex, 68
Asylums, 464
Attachment
    infant, 138–139
    needs, 359, 360f
    socialization and, 138–142
    styles, 140
Attention deficit/hyperactivity disorder
    (ADHD), 105, 532
Attitudes, health effects of, 407
Attraction, self-justification and, 564–565
Attributions. See also Misattribution
    cultural differences in, 451
    making, 565–566
Auditory cortex, 68, 178
Auditory nerve, 178
Auditory system
    sensations
        physiology of, 177–178
        vs. visual sensations, 180
    stimulation, 179f
Aura, 74
Authoritarian personality, 552–553
Authority
    classroom persuasion and, 577
    obeying, 555
Autohypnosis, 99
Automatic action, 383
Automation, diminished social contact and,
    490
Autonomic nervous system
    divisions of, 49, 50f
    responses, emotions and, 347, 347t
    stress response and, 392
Autonomy
    happiness/well-being and, 412
    vs. self-doubt, 142, 143, 145t
Availability bias, 303
Aversion therapy, 512–513, 512f
Aversive conditioning, 212–213
Avoidant attachment, 140
Axon, 52

Babbling stage, 130
Backwards knowledge, 321
Bandura, Albert, 436–437
Barbiturates, 103t, 104, 531
Basic anxiety, 432
Basilar membrane, 177, 178f, 179
Behavior
    abnormal
        indicators of, 466–467
        normal circumstances for, 468
    brain damage and, 74, 74f

genetic basis for, 41–47, 76
    social situation and, 547–560, 578
    social standards of, 548–550
    unacceptable/undesirable
        continuum of, 493f
        in mental abnormalities, 467
    uniformities, 549–550
    unusual, 439–440
    variability, motivation and, 356–357
Behavioral learning, 207, 235–236. See also
    Classical conditioning; Operant
    conditioning
Behavioral medicine, 409–412, 411f
Behavioral perspective, 465
Behavioral therapy
    compared with other therapies, 523–525,
        524f, 526f
    used by psychologists, 511–516
Behavioral view. See Behaviorism
Behavior genetics, 45
Behaviorism (behavioral view)
    human nature and, 12, 14t, 33
    radical, 217–218
Behavior modification therapy, 315, 511
Behavior self-modification, 513
Behavior therapy, efficacy of, 525, 526f
The Bell Curve: Intelligence and Class Structure
    in American Life (Herrnstein), 329
Benzodiazepines, 103t, 104
Bias
    cultural, 12
    in decision making, 302–303
    in intelligence tests, 328
    sources of, 27–28
Big five, 443
"Binge-and-purge" syndrome, 483–484
Biofeedback, 405
Biological drives, 367
Biological needs, 359, 360f
Biological perspective, of terrorism, 574
Biological view, 10, 10f, 14t, 33
Biomedical therapies
    community mental health movement, 536
    definition of, 508
    deinstitutionalization, 535–536
    drugs, 529–533
    electroconvulsive therapy, 534
    hospitalization and alternatives, 535–536
    for mental disorders, 528–536, 540
    psychosurgery, 533–534
    therapeutic community, 535
    transcranial magnetic stimulation, 535
    vs. other therapies, 523–525, 524f, 526f
Biopsychology
    definition of, 41
    of mental disorders, 465–466
Bipolar cells, 171, 172f
Bipolar disorder, 471–472
Birth order differences, 115–116
Blind, 27–28
Blinding problem, 186
Blind spot, 171, 173
Blocking
    avoiding, 280
    memory failure and, 271–273, 272f
Bodily-kinesthetic intelligence, 319

Body image, female, 483, 484f
Body-mind connection, 59–60
Bottom-up processing, 186–187
Brain
    body-mind connection and, 59–60
    damage, behavior and, 74, 74f
    endocrine system and, 56
    evolutionary shaping of, 40–41
    hemispheres, 66f, 69–70, 70f
    layers of, 61–65, 62f
    lesions, 60
    mechanisms, in learning, 236–237
    as nerve center, 47–48
    organization of, 77
    prenatal development, 123
    random activity of, 96
    responsive, cortical cooperation and,
        68–69
    sensation and, 163
    serotonin pathways in, 58, 58f
    visual sensation processing in, 171–172
Brain-imaging methods, 60–61
Brain scans, 60–61, 466
Brain stem, 62–63, 62f, 63f
Brainstorming, 304
Brain tumor, 337–338
Brain waves, 60, 90, 91f
Brightness, 175
Broca, Paul, 69
Bulimia, 483–484
Burnout, 384–385
Bystander problem, 555–558, 557f

Caffeine, 103t, 105–106
Cannabis (marijuana), 102–103, 103t
Cannon, Walter, 348
Cardiovascular disease
    prevention, behavioral medicine for,
        411–412, 411f
    type A behavior and, 398–399
Case study, 26–27, 118
Cataplexy, 97
Catastrophe, 381–384
Catatonic type of schizophrenia, 485
Cell body (soma), 52
Central fissure, 66
Central nervous system (CNS), 48–49
Centration, 134
Cerebellum, 63, 63f
Cerebral achromatopsia, 161–162
Cerebral cortex
    anatomy, 62f, 65, 66f
    emotions and, 346–347
    lobes of, 66, 67f, 68
Cerebral dominance, 69–70, 70f
Cerebral hemispheres
    anatomy, 65, 69–70, 70f
    damage, effects of, 74, 74f
Cerebrum, 65
Chameleon effect, 550
Change, health aspects of, 387–388
Charcot, Jean-Martin, 464
Chemotherapy, taste aversions and, 215
Childhood
    developmental tasks, 155
        cognitive. See Cognitive development

language acquisition, 129–132, 130*f*
 moral thinking, 136–137, 137*t*
 social/emotional, 137–142
 social/emotional development, 137–142
early experiences, personality and, 425
influence on personality, 142–143
Child's play, observations from, 136
Chlorpromazine (Thorazine), 529
Choleric temperament, 441
Chromosomes, 44, 45*f*
Chronic stress, 391
Chronological age, 308
 intelligence quotient and, 309–310
Chunking, 257
Circadian clock, *vs.* sleep debt, 92–93
Circadian rhythms, 89
Classical conditioning
 applications of, 212–215, 214*f*
 cerebellum and, 63
 features of, 209–212, 210*f*
 inborn tendencies and, 214, 214*f*
 of infants, 124
 learning and, 124, 208, 240
 taste-aversion learning and, 213–215
 techniques, 511
 vs. operant conditioning, 227–230, 228*f*,
  229*f*
Clinical method, 27. *See also* Case study
Clinical psychologists, 17, 507*t*
Clinical psychology, 18
Clinical social worker, 507*t*
Cloning, 46
Closure, 195–196
Clozapine (Clozaril), 529
CNS (central nervous system), 48–49
Cocaine, 103*t*, 105
Cochlea, 177, 178*f*
Codeine, 103–104, 103*t*
Codependence, 438–439
Cognition. *See also* Thought
 definition of, 11, 287
 emotion and, 348–350
Cognitive-behavioral approach, 465
Cognitive-behavioral therapy, 522–525, 526*f*
Cognitive development
 assimilation and accommodation,
  132–133
 in college students, 154
 contemporary perspectives, 135–136
 definition of, 132
 Piaget's stages of, 133–135, 155
 schemes, 132
Cognitive dissonance theory, 564–565
Cognitive learning, "higher," 237
Cognitive maps
 cultural influences on, 290–291, 291*f*,
  292*f*
 imagery and, 290–293
 in maze learning, 232–233, 233*f*
Cognitive neuroscience, 83
Cognitive perspective, 465
Cognitive psychology, learning and,
  231–237, 241
Cognitive restructuring, 406
Cognitive theory
 of intelligence, 318–320

locus of control and, 359
 of personality, 436–440, 437*f*
Cognitive therapy
 definition of, 520–521
 for depression, 521–522
 vs. other therapies, 523–525, 524*f*, 526*f*
Cognitive view, 10–11, 14*t*, 33
Cohesiveness, 572
Collective unconscious, 431–432
Collectivism, 364
Collectivistic cultures
 fundamental attribution error and, 449
 personality and, 450
College students, cognitive development in,
  154
Color
 sensation of, 170–171
 visual system creation of, 172–173, 175
Color blindness, 175
Color blindness test, 176*f*
Common fate, law of, 198
Common sense, 292
Communal effort, 383
Communication
 by emotional expression, 339–341
 internal systems of, 47–48, 76–77
Community mental health movement, 536
Competence
 happiness/well-being and, 412
 needs, 149
 vs. inferiority, 143, 145*t*
Complete love (consumate), 570
Complexity, preference for, 305
Componential intelligence, 319
Compulsions, 478
Computed tomography scanning, 61
Computerized tomography, 61
Computers, diminished social contact and,
  490
Concept hierarchies, 289, 289*f*
Concepts
 artificial, 289
 culture and, 290
 definition of, 287–288
 formation of, 288
 memory for, 295
 natural, 288
Conceptually driven processing, 187
Concordance rate, 486–487
Concrete operational stage, 134–135
Conditioned reinforcers, 219
Conditioned taste aversions, 213–214
Cones, 170, 172*f*
Confirmation bias, 302
Conformity
 Asch studies and, 550–552, 551*f*
 group characteristics of, 552
 to social norms, 568
Confounding variables, 28
Conscience, 427
Conscientiousness, 443
Conscious motivation, 357
Consciousness
 altered states of, 98–99, 110
  hypnosis, 99–101, 100*f*
  meditation, 101, 101*f*

from psychoactive drugs, 101–106
cycles of, 88–98, 110
 daydreaming, 88–89
 sleep. *See* Sleep
expansion of, 109
functions of, 84–85
levels of, 86
nature of, 82–83, 83*f*, 84*f*, 110
structures of, 84–85, 85*f*
studying, tools for, 83–84
Conservation, 134
Contact comfort, 141
Context
 learning-based inference and, 192–193
 retrieval of explicit memories and,
  267–268
Contextual intelligence, 319
Contingency management, 513–514
Continuity, law of, 197
Continuity view, 119, 120
Continuous reinforcement, 219–220
Contraception, 422
Contrived emergencies, 556–558
Control condition, 25
Control group, 25
Controlled tests
 performing, 22–23, 22*f*
 results
  analysis of, 23
  publishing, criticizing and replicating,
   23–24
Convergent thinking, 304, 306
Conversion disorder, 479–480
Coping
 strategies, 385
 with stress, psychological resources for,
  404–409
 with test anxiety, 415
Core knowledge, 124
Corpus callosum
 anatomy, 65, 71*f*
 severing, for epilepsy treatment, 70–72,
  71*f*–73*f*
Correlation, negative, 26
Correlational study, 25–26, 118
Correlation coefficient, 26
Counseling psychologists, 17, 507*t*
Counterconditioning, 511
Couples counseling, 520
Creativity, 304–306
Crime, diminished social contact and, 490
Cross-cultural psychologists, 12, 13*f*, 15
Cross-cultural psychology, 18
Crystallized intelligence, 317
CT scanning, 61
Culture
 concepts and, 290
 context
  for mental disorders, 493–494
  for therapy, 508–509
 definition of, 12
 differences
  in adolescence, 145–146
  in personality, 439
 influences
  on cognitive maps, 290–291, 291*f*, 292*f*

Culture (Cont.)
    on drug-taking behavior, 102
    on perception, 194–195
    on scripts, 294
    morality and, 137
    reinforcement and, 222
    terrorism perspective, 573–575
    thought and, 290
Current Directions in Psychological Science,
    30
Cycles per second, 177

Darwin, Charles, 10, 42
Data
    definition of, 23
    gathering of, 23
Day care
    developmental effects from, 141–142
    quality of, 142
Daydreaming, 88–89
Death, causes of, 405t
Debriefing, 29
Deception
    detecting, 353–354
    in psychological research, 28–29
Decision making, 302–303
Declarative memory, 260, 280
Deinstitutionalization, 535–536
Déjà vu experience, 287–288
Demographic, 150, 151
Dendrites, 52
Denial, 402
Depakote (divalproex), 530
Dependent variable, 23
Depersonalization disorder, 481
Depressants, 103t, 104–105
Depression
    in bipolar disorder, 471
    causes of, 472–474
    cognitive-behavioral cycle of, 474–475,
        474f
    cognitive therapy, 521–522
    drug therapy for, 532–533
    incidence, 472
    risk of, 472, 473t
    seasonal, 473, 473f
    tendencies, self-check of, 475
Descartes, René, 5–6
Desensitization therapy, 514–515
Despair, vs. ego-integrity, 145t, 150,
        151
Development
    adolescent, 144–149
    adulthood, 149–152
    childhood tasks of. See Childhood,
        developmental tasks
    continuity vs. discontinuity view of, 119,
        120
    heredity-environment interaction and,
        117–119
    milestones in, 126f–127f, 128
    prenatal, 122–123
    psychosexual stages of, 426, 427t
Developmental psychology, 116–117, 155
Developmental stages, 119
Dewey, John, 7

Diagnostic and Statistical Manual of Mental
        Disorders -IV (DSM-IV), 467,
        469–471, 470t, 496
Diagnostic labeling, consequences of,
        492–494, 497
Diathesis-stress hypothesis, 487
Diet, stress reduction and, 408, 409t
Difference threshold, 166
Differentiation, 122
Diffusion of responsibility, 558
Discontinuity view, 119, 120
Discontinuous stage model of development,
        132
Discover, 30
Discrimination, 567
Discrimination learning, 212
Disorganized type of schizophrenia, 485
Displacement, 402, 403
Display rules, 350, 351
Dispositional variables, 558
Dissociative disorders, 470t, 480–482
Dissociative fugue, 480–481
Dissociative identity disorder, 481–482
Distress, 380, 394, 466
Distributed learning, 279, 280
Divalproex (Depakote), 530
Divergent thinking, 304, 306
DNA, 44, 45f, 46
Dopamine, 56t
Double-blind control, 28
Down syndrome, 45, 46, 314
Dreams, 80–81
    cross-cultural perspective, 94
    Freudian analysis of, 94–95
    as meaningful events, 94–96
    as random brain activity, 96
    recent events and, 95–96
Drive, 357
Drives, 362–363, 424–425
Drive theory, 358–359
Drugs. See also specific drugs
    psychoactive. See Psychoactive drugs
    as stress relievers, 408–409
Drug-taking behavior, culture and, 102
Drug therapy
    avoiding, 537
    evaluation of, 532–533
    for mental disorders, 529–533
DSM-IV (Diagnostic and Statistical Manual of
        Mental Disorders -IV), 467, 469–471,
        470t, 496
Duality of consciousness, 72

Ear, anatomy of, 178
Eating disorders, 470t, 483–484, 484f
Eclectic, 451, 452
Ecological model, 494
Economic competition, 567–568
ECT (electroconvulsive therapy), 534
Education, therapy and, 539
EEG. See Electroencephalogram
        (electroencephalograph)
Ego, 83, 428
Egocentricism, 134
Ego defense mechanisms, 402, 428
Ego ideal, 427–428

Ego-integrity, vs. despair, 145t, 150, 151
Eidetic imagery, 250–252
Elaboration, 249
Elaborative rehearsal, 258, 261, 280
Elderly, cultural differences in status of,
        450–451
Electroconvulsive therapy (ECT), 534
Electroencephalogram
        (electroencephalograph)
    definition of, 60
    during hypnosis, 99
    during sleep, 89–90, 91f
Electromagnetic spectrum, 173, 174f
Electronic resources, in psychology, 30–31
Embryo, 122
Emotion
    cognition and, 348–350
    as communication, 339–341
    controlling, 351–355, 374
    counting, 341, 341f
    definition of, 338
    evolution of, 339
    facial expression of, 340
    functions of, 338–342, 373
    gender differences in, 350
    hormones and, 348
    neuroscience of, 345–346, 345f
    personality and, 437
    responses to
        autonomic nervous system and, 347,
            347t
        James-Lange theory of emotion and,
            348
    sources of, 344–348, 345f, 347t, 373–374
    subjective well-being and, 412–413
Emotional intelligence
    development of, 351, 352–353
    environment and, 353
    heredity and, 353
    predictive power of, 352–353
Emotion-processing pathways, 344–346,
        345f
Emotion wheel, 341, 341f
Empathetic listening, 527
Empirical, 86, 87
Empirical investigation, 21
Encoding, 249, 261
Encoding specificity, 267–268, 281
Endocrine glands, hormone functions of, 57t
Endocrine system, 41, 47, 55–56, 55f,
        76–77
Endorphins, 56t
Engineering psychologists, 17
Engram, 261
Environment
    emotional intelligence and, 353
    intelligence and, 323, 325
    interaction with heredity, 117–119,
        120–121
Epilepsy
    definition of, 60
    treatment, 70–72, 71f–73f
Episodic memory, 260
Equal status contact, 569
Equilibrium, sense of, 165t
Eros, 424

Esteem needs, 359, 360f
Ethical issues, in psychological research, 28–29
Ethical Principles of Psychologists and Code of Conduct, 28, 29
Etiology, 466
Eugenics, 330
Eustress, 396
Event-related potentials, 292
Evolution, 41
   natural selection and, 42–43
   sexuality and, 370–371
   terrorism and, 574
Evolutionary view, 10, 14t, 33
Excitement phase, 368
Exercise, stress reduction and, 407–408
"Exotic becomes erotic" theory, 371
Expectancy bias, 27
Expectancy-value theory, 563–564
Expectations
   learning-based inference and, 192–193
   negative, 322
   schemas and, 293
   student performance and, 322
Experience, learning and, 205–207
Experiential intelligence, 319
Experimental condition, 25
Experimental group, 25
Experimental neurosis, 212
Experimental psychology, 16
Experiments, 24–25
Expert, 305
Expertise, as organized knowledge, 331–332
Experts, 330, 331–332
Explicit memory, 266, 267
Exposure therapy, 511, 512
External locus of control, 359
Extinction
   as alternative to punishment, 226
   classical conditioning and, 210–211, 211f
   reinforcement and, 220–221, 230
Extraversion, 443
Extrinsic motivation, 357
Extroversion, 432
Eye, anatomy of, 170–171, 171f
Eye-hand coordination, of split-brain patients, 72, 73f
Eyewitnesses, accuracy of, 275

Faces scale, 413
Family structure, diminished social contact and, 490
Family systems theory, 438
Feature detectors, 186
Feedback, 527
Feeling *vs.* thinking, cultural differences in, 451
Feminist viewpoint, of psychodynamic psychology, 432–433
Fetal alcohol syndrome, 314
Fetus, 122
"Fight-or-flight" response, 56, 391–392, 392f
Figure, ground and, 195, 196
Five-factor theory, 443–444
Fixation, 426

Fixed-action patterns, 358
Fixed interval schedules, 221–222
Fixed ratio schedules, 221
Flashbulb memory, 264–265
Flow, 372, 373, 412
Fluid intelligence, 317
Forced choice test, 437
Forgetting curve, 270, 271f
Formal operational stage, 135
Fovea, 171
Fox, Michael J., 54f
Frequency, 177, 179
Frequency theory, 179
Freud, Sigmund
   dream interpretation, 94
   ego concept, 83
   psychoanalytic theory of. *See* Psychoanalytic theory
   psychodynamic view and, 11, 18, 19f
Freudian slip, 425
Friendship, 570
Frontal lobes
   anatomy of, 66
   injury, 59
Fugue, dissociative, 480–481
Fully functioning person, 434–435
Functional fixedness, 299–300, 300f
Functionalism, 7
Fundamental attribution error, 449, 566

GABA, 56t
Gage, Phineas, 59
Ganglion cells, 171, 172f
Gender
   differences
     in emotion, 350
     in socialization, 142
   happiness and, 413
   morality and, 137
General adaptation syndrome, 393–395, 393f, 394f
Generalization, stimulus, 211–212
Generativity, *vs.* stagnation, 145t, 150
Genes
   behavior and, 76
   definition of, 44, 45f
   inheritance and, 43–46
   psychological traits in, 120–121
Genetic code, 120
Genetic factors
   in bipolar disorder, 472
   intelligence and, 323, 324–325, 324f
   in panic disorder, 476
   in psychological processes, 44–45
   in schizophrenia, 45–46, 486–487, 487f, 488f
Genital stage, 427t
Genius, 304–305
Genotype, 44
Gestalt Bleue (Vasarely), 189–190, 190f
Gestalt psychology, 195–198, 197f
G factor, 317
Giftedness, 313, 314, 315
Glial cells, 53
Glove anesthesia, 479, 480f
Glutamate, 56t

Good Samaritan, 558–559
Grammar, 130–131
Grasping reflex, 123
Greek psychological views, 5
Ground, figure and, 195, 196
Group differences
   heritability and, 325–326
   in IQ scores, 329–330
Group therapy
   description of, 519–522
   vs. other therapies, 523–525, 524f, 526f
Growth spurt, pubescent, 146
Guilford's structure-of-intellect, 317–318, 318f
Guilt, *vs.* initiative, 143, 145t
Gustation, 182

Habituation, 207
Hall, G. Stanley, 13
Hallucinations, from stimulants, 105
Hallucinogens, 102–103, 103t
Haloperidol (Haldol), 529
Hand-eye coordination, of split-brain patients, 72, 73f
Happiness, well-being and, 412–413
Hardiness, 399–400
Hashish, 102–103
Hassles, 385–386, 386t
Head Start, 327–328
Health, attitudes and, 407
Health promotion
   psychological resources for, 404–409
   strategies, 416
   stress reduction for, 404–413
Health psychology, 409–412, 410t, 411f
Hearing, sense of
   age-related changes in, 152
   features of, 165t
   function of, 176–177
Heart disease prevention, 411–412, 411f
Hedonistic capacity, 401
Helping
   Good Samaritan, 558–559
   situational power and, 559–560
Heredity. *See also* Genetic factors
   emotional intelligence and, 353
   intelligence and, 323, 324–325, 324f
   interaction with environment, 117–121, 125
Heritability, 325–326
Hermann grid, 189f
Heroin, 103–104, 103t
Hertz, 177
Heuristics, 296–298, 297f
Hierarchy
   of concepts, 289, 289f
   for systematic desensitization, 511–512, 512t
Hindsight bias, 302
Hippocampus
   anatomy, 64f, 65
   removal, anterograde amnesia and, 261–263, 263f
Hippocrates, 463
Historical perspective, of terrorism, 574
Homeostasis, 65, 358

Hormones. *See also specific hormones*
    circadian rhythms and, 89
    emotions and, 348
    function of, 47, 55
Horney, Karen, 432–433
Human Genome Project, 46
Humanistic psychologists, 12*f*
Humanistic theory
    needs hierarchy and, 359–360, 360*f*
    of personality, 433–436, 440
Humanistic therapy
    description of, 517–519
    vs. other therapies, 523–525, 524*f*, 526*f*
Humanistic view, 11–12, 14*t*, 33
Humor, 406–407
"Humors," 441, 463
Hunger
    motivation, 364–367, 374
    multiple systems approach to, 364–366, 365*f*
    weight control and, 366–367
Hypnosis, 99–101, 100*f*
Hypnotic analgesia, 100, 100*f*
Hypnotizability, 99–100, 100*f*
Hypochondriasis, 480
Hypothalamus, 55*f*, 62*f*, 64*f*, 65, 365
Hypothesis
    acceptance of, 23
    development of, 21–22
    rejection of, 23
Hypothetical construct, 307

Id, 427
Identity crisis, 147
Illusion, 188–189, 189*f*–191*f*
Imagery, cognitive maps and, 290–293
Imitation, learning by, 234–235
Immigration Restriction Act, 323
Immune system, stress and, 395–396
Immunosuppression, 395–396
Implicit memory, 266–267
Implicit personality theory, 449
Imprinting, 139
Inborn tendencies, classical conditioning
    and, 214, 214*f*
Incongruence, 434
Indentity, *vs.* role confusion, 145*t*
Independence, 305
Independent variable, 22
Individualism, 364
Individualistic cultures, 439, 450
Industrial psychologists, 17
Infancy, 124. *See also* Newborns
Infant attachment, socialization and,
    138–142
Infatuation, 570
Inferences, 293–294
Inferiority, *vs.* competence, 143, 145*t*
In-group, 567
Inheritance, genes and, 43–46
Initiative, *vs.* guilt, 143, 145*t*
Innate, 41, 124
Innateness theory of language, 129
Insanity plea, 491, 494–495
Insecure attachment, 140
Insight learning, 231–232

Insight therapy
    description of, 516–519
    efficacy of, 526*f*, 5225
Insomnia, 96–97
Instincts, 424–425
Instinct theory, 358
Intelligence
    age-related changes in, 152
    components of, 316–321, 318*f*, 334
    creativity and, 305
    cultural definitions of, 320–321
    definition of, 287
    environment and, 323, 325
    genetic contribution to, 120
    heredity and, 323, 324–325, 324*f*
    heritability, 325–326
    measurement of, 306–313, 333–334
    politics of immigration and, 323–324
    theories
        cognitive, 318–320
        psychometric, 317–318, 318*f*
Intelligence quotient (IQ). *See also*
        Intelligence tests
    "Bell Curve" argument and, 329
    definition of, 309–310
    formula
        calculating "on the curve," 312–313,
            313*f*
        problems with, 312
    giftedness and, 313, 314, 315
    group differences, 323–330, 334
    mental retardation and, 314
    race and, 326–327, 328
    social class and, 327, 328
Intelligence tests
    appeal of, in America, 308–309
    biases in, 328
    Binet-Simon approach for, 307–308, 308*f*
    civilian consequences of, 309
    current usage of, 310, 312
    gold standard for, 310
    sample questions, 311
    Stanford-Binet intelligence scale, 309–310
    during World War I, 309
Interaction
    behavior and, 446
    definition of, 117
    personality and, 438
    of personality and culture, 451
Interactionist view, of mental disorder, 466
Intermittent reinforcement, 220
Internal locus of control, 359
Internet, diminished social contact and, 490
Interneurons, 51
Interpersonal ability, 320
Interpersonal attraction, 561–565
Interpersonal intelligence, 320
Interpretation, behavior and, 446
Interval schedule, 221
Intimacy, *vs.* isolation, 145*t*, 149–150
Intrapersonal intelligence, 320
Intrinsic motivation, 357
Introspection, 6–7, 83
Introversion, 432
Inverted U function, 342
Ions, 53

IQ. *See* Intelligence quotient
Irrationality, in mental abnormalities, 466
Ishihani color blindness test, 176*f*
Isolation, *vs.* intimacy, 145*t*, 149–150

James, William, 7, 348
James-Lange theory of emotion, 348
Jensen controversy, 326
Jet lag, 89
JND (just noticeable difference), 166
Jones, Reverend Jim, 553
Journals, psychology-related, 30
Judgment
    biases in, 302–303
    influences on, 578
        interpersonal attraction, 561–565
        making attributions, 565–566
        prejudice/discrimination, 566–570
    social reality and, 560–561
Jung, Carl, 431–433, 4477
Just noticeable difference (JND), 166

Kinesthetic sense, 165*t*, 181
King, Martin Luther, 12*f*

LAD (language acquisition device), 129–130
Lange, Carl, 348
Language acquisition, 129–132, 130*f*
Language acquisition device (LAD), 129–130
Latency stage, 427*t*
Lateral fissure, 66
Lateralization of emotion, 346–347
Law of common fate, 198
Law of continuity, 197
Law of Prägnanz, 198
Law of proximity, 197
Law of similarity, 196–197
Laws of perceptual grouping, 195–198, 197*f*
LCUs (life-change units), 387
Learned helplessness, 400–401, 474
Learning
    brain mechanisms in, 236–237
    classical conditioning and, 208–215, 240
    cognitive psychology and, 231–237, 241
    discrimination, 212
    experience and, 205–207
    in neonatal development, 124
    styles, 238
    trial-and-error, 217
    without reinforcement, 233–234
Learning-based inference, 190, 192–193
Left-brain individuals, 238
Legislation, in combating prejudice,
    569–570
Lesions, 60
Letdown, 383
Levels-of-processing theory, 258, 259
Libido, 424, 430
Lie detectors, 354
Life-change units (LCUs), 387
Light
    detection threshold, 167*t*
    nervous system processing of. *See* Vision
    wavelengths of, 175
Liking, 570
Limbic system

anatomy, 55f, 62–65, 62f, 64f
emotions and, 346
Linguistic intelligence, 319
Lithium carbonate, 530
Little Albert, 213
Locomotion, maturational timetable for, 126f–127f
Locus of control
academic, 454
cultural differences in, 451
definition of, 359, 437, 438
Logical-mathmatical intelligence, 319
Logical reasoning, 319
Loneliness, in adolescence, 148
Long-term memory
biological basis of, 261–264
capacity of, 259
definition of, 249, 250–251
encoding, 261
model of, 260f
neuroscience and, 263
partitions of, 259
processing, 259–261
Long-term potentiation, 236, 264
Loudness, 179–180, 180f
Love, work and, 149
LSD, 103t
Lunacy, 463

Madness, biopsychology of, 465–466
Magicians, perception and, 198
Magnetic resonance imaging (MRI), 61, 61f
Maintenance rehearsal, 257
Major tranquilizers, 486
Maladaptiveness, in mental abnormalities, 466
Malingering, 489
Mania, 471
MAOIs (monoamine oxidase inhibitors), 530
Marijuana, 102–103, 103t
Marital therapy, 520
Marriage, 150
"Marshmallow test," 352
Maslow, Abraham, 11, 434
Matching hypothesis, 563
Maturation, 125
Maze learning, cognitive maps for, 232–233, 233f
MBTI (Myers-Briggs type indicator), 446, 447–448
Media stereotypes, 568
Media violence, effects of, 234–235
Medical model, 463–464
Meditation, 101, 101f
Medulla, 62, 63f
Melancholic temperament, 441
Melatonin, 92
Memory
accuracy, of eyewitnesses, 275
age-related changes in, 152
bias, 276–277
for concepts, 295
connection with wrong context, 273
creation, 274–275
definition of, 247, 281
distortion, 274
fading, 270, 271f

failure, 269–277, 282
formation, 281
function of, 249
improving, 76, 278–279, 280–281
metaphors for, 247–249, 248f
model of, 250f
mood and, 276–277
neurons and, 263–264
persistence, 277
photographic, 250–252
plasticity and, 54
recovered, erroneous, 245–247
retrieval, 266–269, 281
"seven sins" of, 269–270, 277
stages of, 249–250
synapses and, 263–264
Menarche, 146
Mental age, intelligence quotient and, 308, 309–310
Mental disorders. See also specific mental disorders
abnormality indicators, 466–467
biopsychology of, 465–466
classification of, 469, 496–497
adjustment disorders, 489
anxiety disorders, 475–479, 478f
dissociative disorders, 480–482
DSM-IV system for, 469–471, 470t
mood disorders, 471–475, 473f, 474f
other conditions that may be a focus of clinical attention, 489
personality disorders, 487–489
schizophrenia, 484–487
somatoform disorders, 479–480
cultural context of, 493–494
definition of, 496
diagnosing, in friends/family, 496
diagnostic labeling, consequences of, 492–494, 493f
evolving concepts of, 463–466
interactionist view of, 466
medical model of, 463–464
pseudopatients, experience of, 459–461
psychological models of, 464–466
spectrum of, 461–462, 462t
therapies, 501–502
biomedical. See Biomedical therapies
description of, 503–504
entering, 504–505
Mental health professionals. See also specific mental health professionals
paraprofessionals, 509
types of, 507t
Mental operations, 134–135
Mental representations, 133
Mental retardation, 313–315
Mental set, 298–299, 299f
Mentor, 305
Mere exposure effect, 207
Mescaline, 103t
Mesmer, Franz Anton, 464
Mesmerism, 464
Message systems, internal, 47–48
Method of loci, 278, 279
Miligram's obedience experiment, 553–555, 556f

Mind, Freudian model of, 424–425, 425f
Minnesota Multiphasic Personality Inventory (MMPI-2), 444–445, 444t
Minorities, in psychology, 13
Minor tranquilizers, 104, 408–409, 531
Misattribution, 273, 349
Mistrust, vs. trust, 143, 145t
MMPI-2 (Minnesota Multiphasic Personality Inventory), 444–445, 444t
Mneumonics, 278, 279
Money, happiness and, 413
Monitor on Psychology, 30
Monkeys/chimpanzees, as human ancestors, 42, 42f
Monoamine oxidase inhibitors (MAOIs), 530
Monosodium glutamate (MSG), 182
Mood, memory and, 276–277
Mood-congruent memory, 276–277
Mood disorders, 471–475, 473f, 474f
Morality
culture and, 137
gender and, 137
Moral thinking, 136–137
Morphemes, 131
Morphine, 103–104, 103t
Mothers, surrogate, 141
Motivation
achievement, 363–364, 363f
flow experience and, 373
hunger, 364–367
psychologists utilization of, 356–357
rewards and, 361
theories of, 357–360, 374
types of, 357
Motive, 357
Motor cortex, 66
Motor memory, 76
Motor neurons, 51, 52f
Motor speech area, 67
Movement, position and, 180–181
MRI (magnetic resonance imaging), 61, 61f
MSG (monosodium glutamate), 182
Multiculturalism, 15
Multiple intelligences, 319–320
Multiple systems approach, to hunger, 364–366, 365f
Musical intelligence, 319
Mutations, 44
Mutual interdependence, 573
Myelin sheath, 53
Myers-Briggs type indicator (MBTI), 446, 447–448

Names, remembering, 278–279
Naming explosion, 130
Narcissistic personality, 488
Narcolepsy, 97, 109
Native Americans, intelligence concepts of, 320–321
Natural concepts, 288
Naturalistic observation, 26–27, 27f
Natural language mediators, 278
Natural selection, 10, 42–43, 43f
Nature-nurture controversy, 44, 117–119
Necker cube, 7
Need, 358

PET (positron emission tomography), 61, 61*f*
Phallic stage, 427*t*
Phenomenal field, 434–435
Phenotype, 44
Pheromones, 182
Phlegmatic temperament, 441
Phobia or phobic disorders, 476–477, 478*t*
Phosphenes, 180, 181
Photoreceptors, 170
Physical abilities, of newborns, 125–127
Physical appearance, self-esteem and, 146–147
Physical attractiveness, interpersonal attraction and, 562–563
Physical maturation, in adolescence, 146–147
Physiological dependence, 107
Piaget, Jean, cognitive development stages of, 132–135
Pitch, 179
Pituitary gland, 55*f*, 56, 57*t*
PKU, 314
Placebo effect, 184, 185
Placebos, 184, 185, 523
Placenta, 122
Place theory, 179
Plasticity, 54–55
Plateau phase, 368
Play, child's, 136
Poison parasite argument, 577
Political perspective, of terrorism, 574
Polygraph, 354
Pons, 62, 63*f*
Ponzo illusion, 194
Position, movement and, 180–181
Positive afterimages, 176
Positive psychology, 436
Positive punishment, 222
Positive reinforcement, 218, 224*f*, 230
Positive schizophrenia, 486
Positron emission tomography (PET), 61, 61*f*
Posterior pituitary, hormone functions of, 57*t*
Post-Freudian psychodynamic therapies, 432–433, 517
Posttraumatic stress disorder (PTSD), 401–402
Postural reflex, 123
Poverty
  intelligence quotient and, 327, 328
  terrorism and, 574
Practical intelligence, 319
Prägnanz, law of, 198
Preconscious memories, 86
Prefrontal lobotomy, 533–534
Pregnancy, prevention of, 421–422
Prejudice
  causes of, 567–568
  combating, 569–570
  definition of, 567
Premack principle, 227
Prenatal development, 122–123
Preoperational stage, 134
Preparedness hypothesis, 477
Prevention, of heart disease, 411–412, 411*f*

Primary reinforcers, 219
Priming, 84, 266–267
Principle of opposites, 432
Principle of proximity, 562
Proactive interference, 271–272, 272*f*
Problem
  breaking into smaller problems, 297–298
  identification, 296
  intense interest in, 305
  restructuring, willingness for, 305
Problem solving, 296–301, 297*f*, 299*f*–301*f*
  obstacles to, 298–301, 299*f*–301*f*
  strategies
    algorithms, 296
    heuristics, 296–298, 297*f*
Procedural memory, 260
Professional organizations, 30
Projection, 363, 402, 403, 428, 516
Projective tests, 428–430
Prompting, 227
Prototype, 288
Proximity
  interpersonal attraction and, 561–562
  law of, 197
Prozac, 58, 530–531
Pseudoscience, 20
Psilocybin, 103*t*
Psychedelics, 102–103
Psychiatric nurse practitioner, 507*t*
Psychiatrists, 18, 507*t*
Psychic determinism, 425–426
Psychic numbing, 235
Psychic numbness, 383
PsychInfo, 31
PsychLit, 31
Psychoactive drugs. *See also specific psychoactive drugs*
  definition of, 58
  depressants, 103*t*, 104–105
  hallucinogens, 102–103
  mechanism of action, 48, 101
  for mental disorders, 529–533
  opiates, 103–104, 103*t*
  side effects of, 58
  stimulants, 103*t*, 105–106, 105*f*, 532
Psychoanalysis ("talking cure"), 424, 508, 516
Psychoanalysts, 18, 507*t*
Psychoanalytic theory
  basic concepts in, 424–430, 425*f*, 427*t*
  criticisms of, 430–431
  dreams and, 94–95
"Psychobabble," 8–9
Psychodynamic psychology, feminist viewpoint of, 432–433
Psychodynamic theory of personality, 424–433, 440
Psychodynamic therapy
  description of, 516
  post-Freudian, 517
  vs. other therapies, 523–525, 524*f,* 526*f*
Psychodynamic view, 11, 14*t,* 33
Psychogenic symptoms, 464, 479
Psychological dependence, 107
Psychological models, of mental disorders, 464–466

Psychological processes, genetic explanations for, 44–45
Psychological research
  ethical issues in, 28–29
  types of, 24–28
Psychological response, to stress, 397–403
Psychological Science, 30
Psychological therapies
  description of, 506–508
  evaluation of, 523–525, 524, 526*f*
Psychologists
  applied, 13
  characteristics of, 4–5
  clinical, 17
  counseling, 17
  development of new knowledge, 20–31, 33–34
  education/training for, 19
  engineering, 17
  industrial, 17
  organizational, 17
  perspectives, current, 9–13, 14*t,* 33
  rehabilitation, 18
  school, 18
  scientific method and, 20–21, 21*t*
  therapies of, 510
    behavioral, 511–516
    cognitive, 520–522
    cognitive-behavioral, 522–523
    group, 519–522
    insight, 516–519
  treatment of mental disorders, 540
  utilization of motivation, 356–357
  work settings for, 16, 17*f,* 33
Psychology
  applied, 16–17
  changing face of, 13
  definition of, 5, 33
  experimental, 16
  history of, 5–6, 9, 33
  as major, 19
  minorities in, 13
  perspectives, current, 16
  relation to other disciplines, 18–19
  scientific basis for, 8
  using, to learn psychology, 32
  women in, 13, 15*t*
Psychometrics, 317
Psychometric theories of intelligence, 317–318, 318*f*
Psychoneuroimmunology, 395
Psychopathology. *See* Mental disorders
Psychopaths, 488
Psychosexual stages, 426, 427*t*
Psychosocial crises, 142, 143, 145*t*
Psychosocial development, across life span, 143
Psychosocial dwarfism, 141
Psychosurgery, 533–534
Psychotherapy, 501–502, 505, 527
Psychotic disorder (psychosis), 470*t,* 471
PTSD (posttraumatic stress disorder), 401–402
Puberty, 145
Pubescent growth spurt, 146

Situational variables, 558
Situationism, 548
Skeptical Inquirer, The, 30
Skinner, B.F., 12
Skinner box, 218–219
Skin senses, 165t, 182
Sky and Winter (Escher), 189–190, 191f
Sleep
   circadian rhythms and, 89
   cycle, 90–91, 91f
   function of, 91–92
   main events of, 89–90
   need for, 92
   patterns, over lifetime, 92, 92f
   stages of, 90–91, 91f
Sleep apnea, 12, 97
Sleep cycle, 109
Sleep debt, *vs.* circadian clock, 92–93
Sleep disorders, 96–97
"Sleeping pills," 104
Sleep paralysis, 90
Sleep spindles, 90, 91f
Smell, sense of, 181–182
   detection threshold, 167t
   features of, 165t
   receptors for, 183f
Smiling, 138
Smoking, stress relief and, 409
Smoking cessation, aversion therapy for, 512–513, 512f
Social abilities, neonatal, 124–125
Social acceptance, 149
Social class, intelligence quotient and, 327, 328
Social contact, diminished, 490
Social development, 155
Social distance, 567
Social interaction, age-related changes in, 152
Socialization, attachment and, 138–142
Social learning
   imitation and, 234–235
   personality and, 436–437
Social learning therapy, 514–515, 514f, 515f
Social norms, 549–550, 568
Social psychology, 547
   of aggression/violence, 572–573
Social readjustment rating scale (SRRS), 386, 387–389
Social reality, 560–561
Social role, 548
Social sciences, *vs.* psychology, 18–20
Social situation, behavioral effects, 547–560, 578
Social support, 404–405
Social validation, 577
Societal stressors, 284
Sociocultural view, 12–13, 14t, 15, 33
Socioemotional support, 404–405
Sociology, 18
Sociopaths, 488
Somatic nervous system, 49
Somatoform disorders, 470t, 479–480, 480f
Somatosensory cortex, 67–68, 67f
Sound
   becoming auditory sensation, 177–178

detection threshold, 167t
   loudness of, 179–180, 180f
   physics of, 177
   psychological qualities of, 178–180
   waveforms, 182f
Spatial intelligence, 319
Spatial orientation, 69
Spearman's g factor, 317
Spinal cord, 62f
Spirituality, happiness and, 413
Split-brain patients, 70–72, 71f–73f
Split personality, 481–482
Spontaneous recovery, 210–211, 211f
SRRS (social readjustment rating scale), 386, 387–389
Stage of exhaustion, in general adaptation syndrome, 393f, 395
Stage of resistance, in general adaptation syndrome, 393f, 394–395
Stagnation, *vs.* generativity, 145t, 150
Stanford-Binet intelligence scale, 309–310
Stanford prison experiment, 545–546, 548–549
Stereotypes, media, 568
Stimulants, 103t, 105–106, 105f, 532
Stimulation
   becoming perception, 163–164, 164f
   sensation and, 200
Stimulus-driven processing, 187
Stimulus generalization, 211–212
Stockholm syndrome, 401
Stoicism, cultural differences in, 451
Storage, 249
Strange Situation, 139–140
Stress
   acute, 390–391
   catastrophe, 381–384
   chronic, 391
   coping with
      biofeedback for, 405
      biophysical resources for, 407–409
      optimistic thinking for, 406
      relaxation training for, 405
      social support for, 404–405
   definition of, 380–381, 415
   destructive, 380
   immune system and, 395–396
   intensity of, 381
   model of, 382f
   physical effects of, 390–396, 392f–394f, 416
   positive aspects of, 396
   psychological effects of, 416
   response
      biological and behavioral, 390–396, 392f–394f
      psychological, 397–403
   traumatic, 379–380
Stressors
   ancient *vs.* modern, 381–384
   definition of, 381, 415
   psychological, 392
Stroke, 54, 74
Structuralism, 6–7
Structure-of-intellect, 317–318, 318f
Subconscious, 86, 87

Subjective contours, 195
Subjective well-being (SWB), 412–413
Subliminal persuasion, 168–169
Success, emotional intelligence and, 352–353
Suggestibility, 273–274
Superego, 427
Supertasters, 182
Surrogate mothers, 141
Survey, 26
SWB (subjective well-being), 412–413
Symbolic modeling, 514–515
Sympathetic division, 49, 50f
Sympathetic nervous system, stress response and, 394, 394f
Synapses
   definition of, 53
   memory and, 263–264
Synaptic gap or cleft, 53
Synaptic transmission, 53, 54f
Synchronicity, 124
Systematic desensitization, 511–512, 512t

Tardive dyskinesia, 530
Taste, sense of
   detection threshold, 167t
   features of, 165t
Taste-aversion learning, 213–215
Taste buds, 182
Taste receptors, 183f
TAT (Thematic Apperception Test), 363, 429–430, 430f
Telegraphic speech, 130, 131
Temperament
   definition of, 138, 441
   personality and, 441–442
   theories, 445
Temporal lobes, 68
Teratogen, 122
Terminal buttons, 52
Terrorism
   combating, 574–575
   multiple perspectives on, 573–575
   poverty and, 574
   roots of, 572–575, 578
Test anxiety, 348–349
Test biases, 328
Testes, hormone functions of, 57t
Test scores, self-fulfilling prophecy and, 321–322
Thalamus, 62f, 63
Thantos, 425
Thematic Apperception Test (TAT), 363, 429–430, 430f
Theory, 21. *See also specific theories*
Theory of mind, 137–138
Therapeutic community, 535
Therapeutic relationship, 505–506
Therapeutic touch, 3–4
Therapy. *See also specific therapies*
   checklist for, 537
   comparison of, 523–525, 524, 526f
   contemporary approaches, 506–508
   cultural context, 508–509
   description of, 503–504, 539
   education and, 539